# Financial Derivatives

# Financial Derivatives
## (Theory, Concepts and Problems)
### Second Edition

**S.L. GUPTA**

Former Professor and Dean
University School of Management
Kurukshetra University

**PHI Learning Private Limited**

Delhi-110092
2018

₹ 695.00

**FINANCIAL DERIVATIVES (Theory, Concepts and Problems), Second Edition**
S.L. Gupta

**ISBN-978-81-203-5348-0**

The export rights of this book are vested solely with the publisher.

**Sixteenth Printing (Second Edition)**      ...     ...     **February, 2018**

Published by Asoke K. Ghosh, PHI Learning Private Limited, Rimjhim House, 111, Patparganj Industrial Estate, Delhi-110092 and Printed by Rajkamal Electric Press, Plot No. 2, Phase IV, HSIDC, Kundli-131028, Sonepat, Haryana.

# Dedicated to

Almighty Goddess Vedmata Gayatri Ji,
Guru Ji and Parents

# Contents

## 3.  FORWARD MARKET: PRICING AND TRADING MECHANISM.....................73–98

## 4.  FUTURES PRICING: THEORIES AND CHARACTERISTICS .........................99–132

## Section II:  FINANCIAL DERIVATIVES—INDIAN SCENARIO

## Section III:   SPECIFIC FINANCIAL FUTURES AND FORWARDS

## Section IV:  FINANCIAL SWAPS

## Section V:   OPTIONS DERIVATIVES

## Section VI:   OTHER DERIVATIVES

**Section VII:  FINANCIAL DERIVATIVES—MISCELLANEOUS ISSUES**

# Preface

The first edition of this book was published in 2005. Since then the pace of globalisation all over the world has accelerated the growth of financial markets. Various developments in this field have earmarked which are related to trading in stocks, foreign currencies, commodities, real assets and other financial instruments in cash as well as future markets. Besides, a lot of changes have emerged in regulatory field both at domestic and international level. Further, the situation has changed altogether in recent years due to liberalisation of exchange control regimes, much flexibility in various exposures, foreign institutional investors, etc. In the light of these, the main objective of revision of this book is to update it thoroughly by incorporating the latest data and information available by replacing the old data, as well as by adding new instruments which have been recently introduced for trading in the derivatives markets.

**Important features in this edition include:**

1. The book has been reorganised from five sections to seven sections by adding four more chapters. Two separate sections on 'Swaps' and 'Other Financial Instruments' have been incorporated in this edition.
2. The effort has been made to incorporate latest data, information, developments, regulatory measures, etc. in the text so that recent view can be presented on this subject.
3. The major focus is made to present latest data on domestic derivatives market specifically from NSE, RBI, SEBI, etc.
4. In Chapter 5 and Chapter 6, the developments in Indian derivatives market have been updated upto year 2015.
5. In Section III, a new chapter entitled 'Forward Rate Agreements' is added since this topic is gaining much popularity in the financial markets.
6. Chapter 10 'Short-Term Interest Rate Futures' is further extended by introducing trading mechanism, specifications and guidelines of RBI in this respect.

7. In Chapter 11, the trading mechanism of long-term interest rate futures (IRF) in India at NSE is added. Further recent developments of IRF in India and latest data of CME are also placed.

8. Chapter 12 'Foreign Currency Futures' is updated with the recent data of CME as well as of India. The chapter is further supplemented with trading of foreign currency futures in India alongwith recent guidelines of RBI on this topic.

9. Chapter 13 'Foreign Currency Forwards' is supplemented with Non-deliverable forwards (NDF) contracts explaining their features, developments, operations, implications and arbitrage. Further, hedging and speculating with forward contracts are also added in this edition.

10. 'Swap' is an important financial derivative instrument which is popular all over the world. So, material on this topic has been expanded in two chapters instead of one as given in the first edition. Chapter 14 on 'Swap Markets' is further extended with Swap Arrangements in India. Chapter 15 on 'Pricing and Hedging of Swaps' is added explaining in detail the approaches of interest rate swap pricing and various aspects of hedging with swaps

11. In Chapter 17 on 'Option Pricing Models' various concepts like volatility, implied volatility (IV), volatility index (VIX), bounds of option prices, risk neutrality etc. are added in this edition.

12. In Chapter 19—'Hedging With Option'—the concept of position derivatives like position delta, position gamma, dynamic hedging, position risk etc. have been added.

13. In Chapter 20—'Currency Options'—the currency option contracts in India alongwith trading mechanism of currency options at NSE have been included with examples in this edition.

14. Chapter 22 on 'Credit Derivatives' is further expanded by adding the Models on measurement of credit risk, credit events by ISDA, and credit risk management in India.

15. 'Real option' is an upcoming new financial derivative instrument, frequently used in corporate world, further widening and deepening the financial markets. The same has been added in this edition by presenting important aspects of it in Chapter 23.

16. In India, an important amendment in the Finance Act, 2015 came into force. As a result, Securities and Exchange Board of India (SEBI) commenced the regulating of commodity derivatives markets. So, Chapter 24 on 'Commodity Derivatives Market' has been incorporated in this edition, explaining all important aspects of commodity derivatives trading in India.

17. Chapter 26 on 'Risk Management in Derivatives' has been substantially revised to place specific emphasis on Value at Risk (VaR). Important approaches of computing VaR have been discussed with suitable examples along with risk management value chain.

18. This edition continues to focus on conceptual understanding with practical examples along with solved and unsolved problems in most of the chapters.

19. A list of selected websites is provided in the Appendix 'C' at the end of this book so that the readers can visit these sites for further information more on various topics of financial derivatives.

20. **Glossary of some commonly used terms** in financial derivatives, appended at the end, has been further extended.

**S.L. GUPTA**

# Preface to the First Edition

Most of financial derivatives trading activities began extensively during nineteen seventies with the introduction of futures trading in foreign exchange in 1973 which was followed by the interest rate futures in 1975, stock index futures in 1982 and so on. Derivatives, today, have become an integral part of the financial system of a country as well as at the international level. They have influenced almost every aspect of capital and money markets all over the world ranging from investing, raising of funds and managing the risk.

Due to globalization and liberalization process initiated by the states all over the world, the international trade and financial activities have grown multifold resulting into rising level of all types of risks for market participants such as market risk, interest rate risk, foreign exchange risk, inflation risk and price risk. Managing all these risks is essential and significant to be successful in financial and trading activities. Financial derivatives like options, futures, forwards and swaps have emerged in the financial markets to handle and manage such risks. New products and strategies are being developed at the fast rate in order to cope with the changing environment.

Financial markets in India continue to evolve towards growth and efficiency resulting into a manifold rise in financial activities in depth and width. Market participants, financial institutions and investors are looking in a different way to play efficiently in the market. During the mid 1990s, with Indian government initiated the process of liberalizing of the financial market in all sectors specifically opening the market for foreign investment. As a result, the infrastructure of the financial markets geared to international norms in all respects. The stock market's structure and trading in India have gone under a sea change. Institutionalization of broking activities, modernization, automation of stock exchanges and entry of foreign institutional investors have opened a multiple options to various participants in the financial markets.

Options and futures trading in India commenced from June, 2000 on National Stock Exchange and Bombay Stock Exchange in stock index futures, stock futures, stock index option and stock option. It was a welcome step on the part of the government since it was important in the present environment. This was significant development in the history of Indian stock markets. A lot of trading in futures and options segment in Indian stock market was seen and the number of market participants increased phenominal in a short period. As a result, awareness about the financial derivatives instruments and their application has increased among the investing people at large. On the other side of this development was that element of risk and volatility in the stock market have risen.

Since Trading volume in Indian financial derivatives market has increased at fast rate ranging from ₹ **35 crore in June 2000 to ₹ 2,60,470 crore in March 2004**, so it is evident that a large number of investors (both institutional and individuals) have shown overwhelming interest in this market. To be successful investor and trader in this market, it is essential to understand the basics of the various instruments operating in this market along with their trading mechanism and regulations. So the objective at the outset was to write a book, which should be simple in theoretical description with suitable examples so that the readers can acquire a general conceptual understanding of these instruments and then can apply them to specific markets.

## Organization

This book can be viewed as being organized into 5 sections with 26 chapters in total. The first section consisting of Chapters 1 to 4, covers the basics of financial derivatives; their contracting, trading mechanism and pricing of specific financial instruments, i.e., futures and forwards in general. The second section of this book comprises of Chapter 5 and 6 which exhibit a brief view of financial derivatives market in India comprising its regulatory aspects, so that before entering into financial derivatives market in India, the reader should be aware of its structure and regulation.

The third section of this book includes Chapters 7 to 13, focusing on specific financial derivatives instruments such as stock index futures, short-term interest rate futures, long-term interest rate futures, foreign currency futures, foreign currency forwards and hedging strategy using futures. Each chapter concentrates on conceptual description, trading mechanism, pricing and hedging of the financial futures.

Fourth section of the book (Chapters 14 to 24) comprises other financial derivative instruments, i.e., options and swaps. Chapter 14 describes about the swap market covering both interest rate swap and currency swap. Chapters 14 to 18 cover all the important aspects of option instrument like its basics, various pricing models, trading with options, hedging with option and options on foreign currencies. Fifth and last section, which covers Chapters 19 to 22, emphasizes with other important issues of financial derivatives like their accounting and tax treatment, management of derivative exposures, introduction to other important advanced instruments available in financial derivatives markets such as caps and floors, and credit derivatives at the end.

## Key Features

This textbook is written with the objective that a reader should be acquainted with both theory and practice of various financial derivatives functioning. Therefore, each chapter of this book is designed with a brief theoretical description followed with the relevant examples. To make more clarity about the text, various diagrams, charts and tables have been incorporated at the appropriate places. Short numerical examples and problems followed by working solutions are presented wherever they are required, allowing the readers to self-check their level of understanding. The text of each chapter begins with the learning objectives and ends with the review questions, solved problems and summary. A comprehensive glossary, a list of important stock exchanges all over the world where derivatives are traded and solutions of the unsolved problems are incorporated at the end of the text.

## Intended Audiences

This book will be accessible to a wide range of readers who seek to know about the functioning of financial derivatives market in general. It is an introductory book aimed primarily to the following audiences:

- Teachers and students of finance, commerce and management like MBA, PGDBM, M.Com, MFC, MBE, MFM
- Derivatives practitioners like equity researchers, portfolio managers, financial executives, members of stock exchanges, chartered financial analyst, chartered accountants
- Investors, policy makers, risk managers and regulators

**S.L. GUPTA**

# Acknowledgements

In writing a textbook on such a theme, one naturally depends on a large set of one's learned colleagues. I am grateful to all my friends and experts who made excellent and fruitful suggestions while was writing this book. I wish to acknowledge the materials referred from various publications of Securities and Exchange Board of India, Reserve Bank of India, National Stock Exchange (NSE), Bombay Stock Exchange (BSE) and the other related publications.

I would like to thank PHI Learning for publishing this book.

I wish to express my appreciation to all the members of my family, especially my wife Shashi Gupta, for her encouragement and support.

I eagerly look forward to the constructive comments, criticism and suggestions from the learned readers to assist me in improving the quality of the book.

**S.L. GUPTA**

# Abbreviations Used in This Book

| | |
|---|---|
| ABS | Asset Backed Security |
| AD | Authorized Dealers |
| ADP | Alternative Delivery Procedure |
| ALM | Asset Liability Management |
| ARCH | Autoregressive Conditional Heterosedacity Model |
| AS | Accounting Standard |
| ATM | At-the-Money |
| BBA | British Bankers Association |
| BIS | Bank International Subtenant |
| B-S Model | Block-Scholes Model |
| BSE | Bombay Stock Exchange |
| CAPM | Capital Assets Pricing Model |
| CBOT | Chicago Board of Trade |
| CFTC | Commodity Futures Trading Commission |
| CIR Model | Cox, Fingerstalls and Ross Model |
| CME | Chicago Mercantile Exchange |
| COMEX | Commodity Exchange |
| CTD | Cheapest-to-Delivery |
| CY | Convenience Yield |
| DFIs | Derivatives Financial Instruments |
| DJIA | Dow Jones Industrial Average |
| DTM | Days Untill Maturity |

| | |
|---|---|
| ECP | Euro Commercial Paper |
| EEFC | Exchange Earners Foreign Currency Accounts |
| EFP | Exchange for Physicals |
| EMS | European Monetary System |
| ERA | Exchange Rate Agreement |
| ERM | External Risk Management |
| EWMA | Exponentially Weighted Moving Average |
| FASB | Financial Accounting Standard Board |
| FC/INR Option | Foreign Currency-Indian Rupee Option |
| FCM | Futures Commission Merchants |
| FCNR | Foreign Currency Non-Resident Account |
| FEDAI | Foreign Exchange Dealers Association of India |
| FEMA | Foreign Exchange Management Act |
| FIMDA | Fixed Income Money Market and Derivatives Association of India |
| FMC | Forward Market Commission |
| FRA | Forward Rate Agreement |
| FSA | Forward Spread Agreement |
| GAAP | Generally Accepted Accounting Principles |
| GARCH | Generalized Autoregressive Conditional Heteroskedasticity Model |
| G-SEC | Government Securities |
| HR | Hedge Ratio |
| IRS | Interest Rate Swaps |
| IAS | International Accounting Standard |
| ICOM | International Currency Options Market |
| IMM | International Monetary Market |
| IRR | Implied Rate of Return |
| ISDA | International Swap Dealers Association |
| ISMA | International Securities Markets Association |
| ITM | In-the-Money |
| IV | Implied Volatility |
| KC BOT | Kansas City Board of Trade |
| LIBID | London Inter Bank Bid Rate |
| LIBOR | London Inter Bank Offer Rate |
| MBO | Market By Order |
| MIBOR | Mumbai Inter Bank Offer Rate |
| MIT | Market-if-Touched |
| MOC | Market-on-Close |
| MD | MaCauley's Duration |
| NASDAQ | National Association of Securities Dealers Automated Quotation System |

| | |
|---|---|
| NDF | Non-deliverable Forward |
| NFA | National Futures Association |
| NRE | Non-Resident External Rupee Account |
| NSE | National Stock Exchange |
| NYSE | New York Stock Exchange |
| OECD | Organization of Economic Co-operation and Development |
| OI | Open Interest |
| OTC | Over-the-Counter |
| OTM | Out-of-Money |
| P-C Ratio | Put-Call Ratio |
| PHLX | Philadelphia Stock Exchange |
| PPP | Purchasing Power Parity |
| REER | Real Effective Exchange Rate |
| Repo | Repurchase Agreement |
| RFC | Regulated Futures Contracts |
| S & P | Standard and Poor's |
| SCRA | Securities Contract and Regulation |
| SEBI | Securities and Exchange Board of India |
| SEC | Securities Exchange Commission |
| SENSEX | Sensitive Index |
| SIMEX | Singapore International Mercantile Exchange |
| SPAN | Standard Portfolio Analysis of Risk |
| SWIFT | Society for Worldwide Inter-bank Financial Telecommunication |
| T-Bill | Treasury Bill |
| TED Spread | T-Bill/Eurodollar Spread |
| VAR | Value at Risk |
| VLI | Value Line Index |
| YTM | Yield-to-Maturity |
| ZCYC | Zero Coupon Yield Curve |

# SECTION I

# Financial Derivatives— The Background

# Chapter 1

# Financial Derivatives
## An Introduction

---

### LEARNING OBJECTIVES

*After reading this chapter, students will be able to*

➤ Understand the meaning of financial derivatives.
➤ Know about the various features of financial derivatives.
➤ Understand the various types of financial derivatives like forward, futures, options, swaps, convertible, securities, warrants, commodities, credits, weather, idea, etc.
➤ Know about the exchange traded derivatives and OTC derivatives.
➤ Know about the historical background of financial derivatives.
➤ Know about various uses of financial derivatives.
➤ Understand about the myths of financial derivatives.

---

## 1.1 INTRODUCTION

The past decade has witnessed the multiple growth in the volume of international trade and business due to the wave of globalization and liberalization all over the world. As a result, the demand for the international money and financial instruments increased significantly at the global level. In this respect, changes in the interest rates, exchange rates and stock market prices at the different financial markets have increased the financial risks of the corporate world. Adverse changes have even threatened the very survival of the business world. It is, therefore, to manage such risks, the new financial instruments have been developed in the financial markets, which are also popularly known as *financial derivatives*.

The basic purpose of these instruments is to provide commitments to prices for future dates for giving protection against adverse movements in future prices, in order to reduce the extent of financial risks. Not only this, they also provide opportunities to earn profit for those people who are ready to go for higher risks. In other words, these instruments, indeed, facilitate to transfer the risk from those who wish to avoid it to those who are willing to accept the same.

Today, the financial derivatives have become increasingly popular and most commonly used in the world of finance. This has grown with so phenomenal speed all over the world that now it is called the derivatives revolution. In an estimate, the present annual trading volume of derivative markets has crossed US $30,000 billion, representing more than 100 times gross domestic product of India.

## 1.2 DEFINITION OF FINANCIAL DERIVATIVE

Before explaining the term financial derivative, let us see the dictionary meaning of 'derivative'. Webster's Ninth New Collegiate Dictionary (1987) states **derivatives** as:

1. A word formed by derivation. It means, this word has been arisen by derivation.
2. Something derived; it means that some things have to be derived or arisen out of the underlying variables. For example, financial derivative is an instrument indeed derived from the financial market.
3. The limit of the ratio of the change is a function to the corresponding change in its independent variable. This explains that the value of financial derivative will change as per the change in the value of the underlying financial instrument.
4. A chemical substance is related structurally to another substance, and theoretically derivable from it. In other words, derivatives are structurally related to other substances.
5. A substance that can be made from another substance in one or more steps. In case of financial derivatives, they are derived from a combination of cash market instruments or other derivative instruments.

**EXAMPLE:** You have purchased a gold futures on June 10, 2015 for delivery in Sept. 2015. Assume that the price of gold in June 2015 in the spot market is ₹25,000 per 10 grams and for futures delivery in September 2015 is ₹28,000 per 10 grams. Suppose in August 2015 the spot price of the gold changed and increased to ₹28,000 per 10 grams. As a result, value of financial derivatives or gold futures would also be changed.

From the above, the term derivative may be termed as follows:

The term "Derivative" indicates that it has no independent value, i.e., its value is entirely *derived* from the value of the underlying asset. The underlying asset can be securities, commodities, bullion, currency, livestock or anything else. In other words, derivative means forwards, futures, options or any other hybrid contract of predetermined fixed duration, linked for the purpose of contract fulfilment to the value of a specified real or financial asset or to an index of securities.

*The Securities Contracts (Regulation) Act, 1956 defines "derivative" as under:*

"Derivative" includes

1. Security derived from a debt instrument, share, loan whether secured or unsecured, risk instrument or contract for differences or any other form of security.
2. A contract which derives its value from the prices, or index of prices of underlying securities.

The above definition conveys that:

1. The derivatives are financial products.
2. Derivative is derived from another financial instrument/contract called the underlying. In the case of Nifty futures, Nifty index is the underlying. A derivative derives its value from the underlying assets.

**Accounting Standard SFAS133 defines a derivative as,** 'a derivative instrument is a financial derivative or other contract with all three of the following characteristics:

(i) It has (1) one or more underlyings, and (2) one or more notional amount or payments provisions or both. Those terms determine the amount of the settlement or settlements.

(ii) It requires no initial net investment or an initial net investment that is smaller than would be required for other types of contract that would be expected to have a similar response to changes in market factors.

(iii) Its terms require or permit net settlement. It can be readily settled net by a means outside the contract or it provides for delivery of an asset that puts the recipients in a position not substantially different from net settlement.

*In the RBI Act-1934 as amended vide RBI (Amendment) Act, 2006, derivatives have been defined in Section 45(u)(a) as:*

"*Derivative* means an instrument, to be settled in a future date, whose value is derived from all interest rates, foreign exchange rate, credit rating or credit index, price of securities (also called 'underlying'), or a combination of more than one of them and includes interest rate swaps, forward rate agreements, foreign currency swaps, foreign currency rupee-swaps, foreign currency options, foreign currency-rupee options or such other instruments as may be specified by the Bank from time to time".

*Repurchase agreement or 'repo' a quasi-derivative instrument comprising a simultaneous spot and forward transaction has been separately defined in section 45(u)(c) as:*

"*Repo* means an instrument for borrowing funds by selling securities with an agreement to repurchase the securities on a mutually agreed future date at an agreed price which includes interest for the funds borrowed.

*Exception of RBI*–the RBI Act, 1934, however makes an exception in sofar as its regulatory ambit is concerned with regard to instruments falling under its jurisdiction when they are tracked and settled on an exchange (section 45W) "provided that the direction issued under this sub-section shall not relate to the procedure for execution or settlement of the trades in respect of the transactions mentioned therein, on the stock exchanges recognised under Section 4 of the Securities Contracts (Regulation) Act, 1952 (42 of 1956)".

According to Mr. Warren Buffett, the derivatives are just like time bombs both for the parties that deal with them and the economic system. They are financial weapons of mass destruction, carrying dangers that, while now latent, are potentially lethal.

*The derivative is also defined as:*

• The derivatives are the financial product which are derived from more basic instruments which are called *underlying assets/instruments*.

- Derivatives are financial instruments whose payoffs are derived from other, more important financial variables, for example, a stock price, a commodity price, an exchange rate, an interest rate, an index level, etc.
- Derivative instruments are referred to those contracts/instruments whose values are linked to the future value of an underlying instrument to which they represent.

In general, from the aforementioned, derivatives refer to securities or to contracts that derive from another—whose value depends on another contract or assets. As such the financial derivatives are financial instruments whose prices or values are derived from the prices of other underlying financial instruments or financial assets. The underlying instruments may be an equity share, a stock, a bond, a debenture, a treasury bill, a foreign currency or even another derivative asset. For example, a stock option's value depends upon the value of a stock on which the option is written. Similarly, the value of a treasury bill of futures contracts or foreign currency forward contract will depend upon the price or value of the underlying assets, such as treasury bill or foreign currency. In other words, the price of the derivative is not arbitrary rather it is linked or affected to the price of the underlying asset that will automatically affect the price of the financial derivative. Due to this reason, transactions in derivative markets are used to offset the risk of price changes in the underlying assets. In fact, the derivatives can be formed on almost any variable, for example, from the price of hogs to the amount of snow falling at a certain ski resort.

Futures contracts are the most important form of derivatives, which are in existence long before the term 'derivative' was coined. Financial derivatives can also be derived from a combination of cash market instruments or other financial derivative instruments. In fact, most of the financial derivatives are not revolutionary new instruments rather they are merely combinations of older generation derivatives and/or standard cash market instruments.

In the 1980s, the financial derivatives were also known as off-balance sheet instruments because no asset or liability underlying the contract was put on the balance sheet as such. Since the value of such derivatives depend upon the movement of market prices of the underlying assets, they were treated as contingent asset or liabilities, and such transactions and positions in derivatives were not recorded on the balance sheet. However, it is a matter of considerable debate whether off-balance sheet instruments should be included in the definition of derivatives. Which item or product given in the balance sheet should be considered for derivative is a debatable issue.

In brief, the term financial market derivative can be defined as a treasury or capital market instrument which is derived from, or bears a close relation to a cash instrument or another derivative instrument. Hence, financial derivatives are financial instruments whose prices are derived from the prices of other financial instruments.

## 1.3   FEATURES OF A FINANCIAL DERIVATIVE

As observed earlier, a financial derivative is a financial instrument whose value is derived from the value of an underlying asset, hence, the name 'derivative' came into existence. There are a variety of such instruments which are extensively traded in the financial markets all over the world, such as forward contracts, futures contracts, call and put options, swaps, etc. Since each financial derivative has its own unique features, in this section, we will discuss some of the general features of a simple financial derivative instrument.

The basic features of the derivative instrument can be drawn from the general definition of a derivative irrespective of its type. Derivatives or derivative securities are future contracts which are written between two parties (counter parties) and whose value are derived from the value of underlying widely held and easily marketable assets such as agricultural and other physical (tangible) commodities, or short-term and long-term financial instruments, or intangible things like weather, commodities price index (inflation rate), equity price index, bond price index, stock market index, etc. Usually, the counter parties to such contracts are those other than the original issuer (holder) of the underlying asset. In the light of this, the basic features of a derivative may be stated as follows:

1. A derivative instrument relates to the future contract between two parties. It means there must be a contract-binding on the underlying parties and the same to be fulfilled in future. The future period may be short or long depending upon the nature of contract, for example, short-term interest rate futures and long term interest rate futures contract.

2. The derivative instruments have the value which is derived from the values of other underlying assets, such as agricultural commodities, metals, financial assets, intangible assets, etc. Value of derivatives depends upon the value of underlying instrument and which changes as per the changes in the underlying assets, and sometimes, it may be nil or zero. Hence, they are closely related.

3. The counter parties have specified obligation under the derivative contract. Obviously, the nature of the obligation would be different as per the type of the instrument of a derivative. For example, the obligation of the counter parties, under the different derivatives, such as forward contract, future contract, option contract and swap contract would be different.

4. The derivatives contracts can be undertaken directly between the two parties or through the particular exchange like financial futures contracts. The exchange-traded derivatives are quite liquid and have low transaction costs in comparison to tailor-made contracts. Example of exchange traded derivatives are Dow Jons, S&P 500, Nikki 225, NIFTY option, S&P Junior that are traded on New York Stock Exchange, Tokyo Stock Exchange, National Stock Exchange, Bombay Stock Exchange and so on.

5. In general, the financial derivatives are carried off-balance sheet. The size of the derivative contract depends upon its notional amount. The notional amount is the amount used to calculate the pay off. For instance, in the option contract, the potential loss and potential payoff, both may be different from the value of underlying shares, because the payoff of derivative products differ from the payoff that their notional amount might suggest.

6. In derivatives trading, usually the delivery of underlying assets is not involved, rather underlying transactions are mostly settled by taking offsetting positions in the derivatives themselves. There is, therefore, no effective limit on the quantity of claims, which can be traded in respect of underlying assets.

7. Derivatives are also known as deferred delivery or deferred payment instrument. It means that it is easier to take short or long position in derivatives in comparison to other assets or securities. Further, it is possible to combine them to match specific, i.e.,, they are more easily amenable to financial engineering.

8. Derivatives are mostly secondary market instruments and have little usefulness in mobilizing fresh capital by the corporate world, however, warrants and convertibles are exception in this respect.

9. Although in the market, the standardized, general and exchange-traded derivatives are being increasingly evolved, still so many privately negotiated customized, over-the-counter (OTC) traded derivatives exist. They expose the trading parties to operational risk, counter-party risk and legal risk. Further, there may also be uncertainty about the regulatory status of such derivatives.

10. Finally, the derivative instruments, sometimes, because of their off-balance sheet nature, can be used to clear up the balance sheet. For example, a fund manager who is restricted from taking particular currency can buy a structured note whose coupon is tied to the performance of a particular currency pair.

## 1.4  CLASSIFICATION OF FINANCIAL DERIVATIVES

In the past section, it is observed that financial derivatives are those assets whose values are determined by the value of some other assets, known as the underlying assets. Presently, there are bewilderingly complex varieties of derivatives already in existence, and the markets are innovating newer and newer ones continuously. For example, various types of financial derivatives based on their different properties such as, plain, simple or straightforward, composite, joint or hybrid, synthetic, leveraged, mildly leveraged, customized or OTC traded, standardized or organized exchange traded, etc. are available in the market.

Due to complexity in nature, it is difficult to classify the financial derivatives. So, in the present context, the basic financial derivatives which are popular in the market have been described in brief. The details of their operations, mechanism and trading are discussed in the respective chapters of this book. In this section, two important classifications of the derivative instruments have been explained; firstly according to their basic nature of the instrument, and secondly as per the nature of the market. The derivatives can be classified into different categories as per their nature (Figure. 1.1).

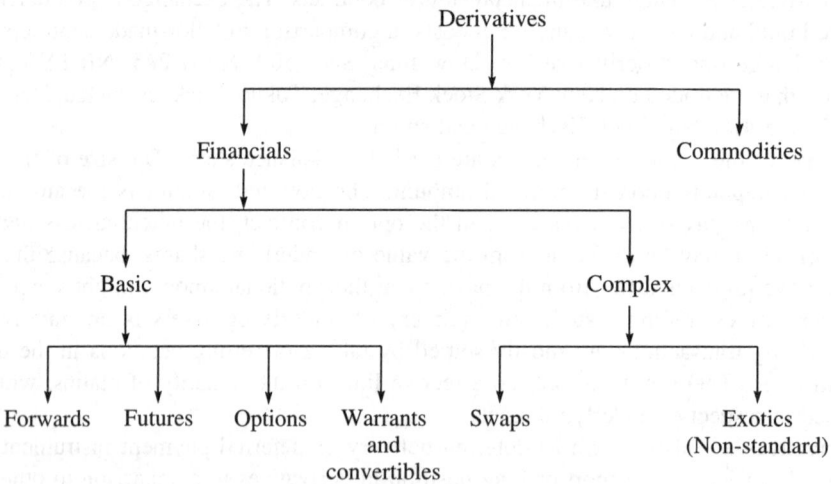

**FIGURE 1.1**   Classification of derivatives on the basis of their nature.

## 1.4.1  Classification of the Derivatives on the Basis of their Nature

One form of classification of derivative instruments is between commodity derivatives and financial derivatives. The basic difference between these is the nature of the underlying instrument or asset. In a commodity derivatives, the underlying instrument is a commodity which may be wheat, cotton, pepper, sugar, jute, turmeric, corn, soyabeans, crude oil, natural gas, gold, silver, copper and so on. In a financial derivative, the underlying instrument may be treasury bills, stocks, bonds, foreign exchange, stock index, gilt-edged securities, cost of living index, etc. It is to be noted that financial derivative is fairly standard and there is no quality issue, whereas in commodity derivative, the quality may be the underlying matters. However, the distinction between these two from structure and functioning point of view, both are almost similar in nature.

Another way of classifying the financial derivatives is into basic and complex derivatives. In this, forward contracts, futures contracts and option contracts are included in the basic derivatives, whereas swaps and other complex derivatives are included in the complex category because they are built up from either forwards/futures or options contracts, or both. In fact, such derivatives are effectively derivatives of derivatives.

## 1.4.2 Classification of the Derivatives on the Basis of Market Trading

On the basis of market trading, the financial derivatives can be classified in to two categories, i.e., Exchange-traded derivatives (ETD) and over-the-counter (OTC) derivatives. Derivative contracts that are traded (and privately negotiated) directly between the two parties without going through an exchange or other intermediary are called *OTC derivatives*. Whereas, the derivatives which are traded on the recognised exchanges are known as *Exchange-traded derivatives* (ETD) or (ETC).These are shown as under in Figure 1.2.

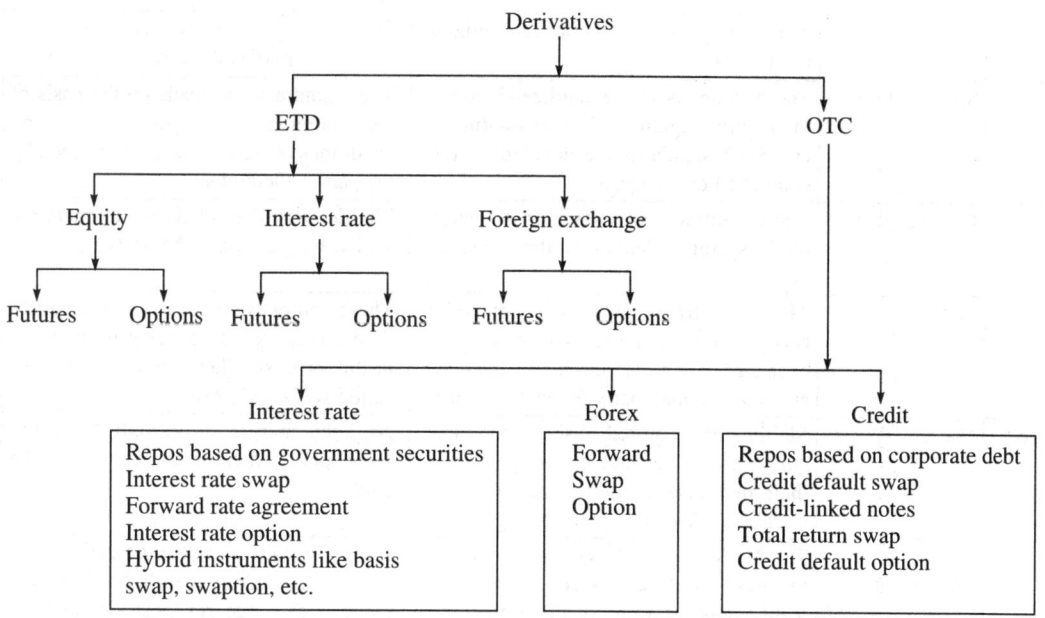

**FIGURE 1.2** Classification of derivatives on the basis of market trading.

The OTC derivate market is the largest market for derivatives and largely unregulated and directly executed by the parties themselves. The information relating to some of these are not disclosed generally. On the other hand, a derivative exchange is a market where individuals trade in standardised contracts which have been specified by the respective exchange. These exchanges act as an intermediary between the members through which transactions are initiated on behalf of their clients. The trading mechanism in both the derivatives markets differ in many respects which are stated below:

### OTC Vs ETD derivatives

*Derivative market structure*:   The structure of derivatives market from trading point of view may be classified into two segments; Exchange Trade Contracts (ETD) and Over The Counter (OTC) contract. The derivatives instruments traded on recognized exchanges (whether they are stock exchanges, commodity exchanges, currency exchanges, etc.) are called *exchange traded derivative instruments*. On other hand, the derivatives which are privately negotiated and traded between the parties directly are known as *OTC derivative instruments*. Trading mechanism in both the markets differ in various aspects which are mentioned as under.

**Distinction between ETD and OTC Derivatives**

| S.No. | Particulars | ETD | OTC |
|---|---|---|---|
| 1. | Parties to the contract | These are done through the recognized exchanges. There are more than two parties in such contracts. | These contracts are privately placed. They are bilateral contracts, which may be routed directly or through broker/agent. |
| 2. | Exchange | These are traded on the recognized exchanges. | These are traded over the counters of the respective parties directly. |
| 3. | Specification | These contracts are standardized in terms of quantity, quality of asset, maturity, etc. Such standards are decided by the concerned exchanges. | These contracts are made on the basis of the requirements of the parties. Terms and conditions of the contracts are decided by the parties themselves. |
| 4. | Delivery date | These contracts are offset or delivered on the specified date as per the exchange notifications. | The delivery date of these contracts are settled by the parties themselves. |
| 5. | Settlement | These contracts are settled through recognized clearing house of the exchange. Such clearing house operates as central counter party for each contract. | These contracts are settled by the parties themselves. No third party is involved in this process. These contracts are also called *self-regulatory contracts*. |
| 6. | Margin | Margins are required in these contracts which are to be paid by the parties to their members of the exchanges. The margin is decided by the exchanges. | No such margin is normally required to be paid either of the parties of the contract. |
| 7. | Daily adjustment | The Mark-to-market system is followed in these contracts. Daily settlement feature sets the value of these contracts at zero at the each trading day. | These contracts are settled on the maturity date and not before that date unless both the parties agree for postponement or preponement of the contract. |
| 8. | Cost of contract | These contracts are done through the members of the exchange, hence, entails brokerage fee for buy and sell orders. | Cost of these is based on the bid-ask spread, i.e., difference of buying and selling price. |
| 9. | Credits risk | These contracts are settled through clearing house. There is no risk of settling the contract at the maturity date. | There is credit risk for each party. These contracts are riskier in nature. Credit limits must be fixed for each party. |

**EXAMPLE:**   Some important examples of these derivatives traded at OTC and the Exchanges are stated below:

| OTC Derivatives | Exchange Traded Derivatives |
|---|---|
| Forward contracts on equity shares, foreign exchange, commodities, forward rate agreements. | Futures contracts on equity shares, stock index, foreign currencies, commodities. |
| Options contracts on stocks, foreign exchange, commodities. | Options contracts on equity shares, stock index, foreign currencies, commodities. |
| Interest rate swaps, currency swaps , caps, floors, swaption, caption, floortion, exotic derivatives. | Interest Rate (both short term and long term), Swap Note Futures, warrants and convertible securities. |

**Global Market-size of OTC and ETD Derivative:**   In this section, a brief view of various derivatives traded both in OTC and ETD markets at international level is presented to understand the size and growth of the world derivatives market. To understand this, it is important to know the terms like notional or nominal amount of outstanding and gross market value. Notional outstanding is a measure of market size and it refers to the potential transfer of risk in the derivative market, usually, it refers to the principal amount of the derivative contracts. For example, if an option gives to the holder a right to buy 10,000 equity shares of State Bank of India at ₹3,00/ share, the notional outstanding in the contract would be ₹(10,000 × 300) = ₹3 million,  Gross market value is a measure of gross transfer of price risks in the derivative market. In other words, it refers to the sum of the absolute replacement value of all outstanding contracts. For example, in the above stated call option, if the market call premium (i.e., price of each call option) is ₹20, then the gross market value of the contract would be ₹(10,000 × 20) = ₹20 lacs. Table 1.1 exhibits the trend of the derivatives market both of OTC and ETC.

**TABLE 1.1**   Global OTC derivatives market[1]
(Amounts outstanding, in billions of US dollars)

| | Notional amounts outstanding | | | | Gross market value | | | |
|---|---|---|---|---|---|---|---|---|
| | H1 2013 | H2 2013 | H1 2014 | H2 2014 | H1 2013 | H2 2013 | H1 2014 | H2 2014 |
| **GRAND TOTAL** | **6,96,408** | **7,10,633** | **6,91,640** | **6,30,150** | **20,245** | **18,825** | **17,438** | **20,880** |
| **A. Foreign exchange contracts** | 73,121 | 70,553 | 74,782 | 75,879 | 2,427 | 2,284 | 1,724 | 2,944 |
| Outright forwards and forex swaps | 34,421 | 33,218 | 35,190 | 37,076 | 957 | 824 | 572 | 1,205 |
| Currency swaps | 24,654 | 25,448 | 26,141 | 24,204 | 1,131 | 1,186 | 939 | 1,351 |
| Options | 14,046 | 11,886 | 13,451 | 14,600 | 339 | 273 | 213 | 389 |
| *Memo: Exchange-traded contracts*[2] | 344 | 386 | 379 | 393 | ... | ... | ... | ... |
| **B. Interest rate contracts**[3] | **5,64,673** | **5,84,799** | **5,63,290** | **5,05,454** | **15,238** | **14,200** | **13,461** | **15,608** |
| FRAs | 86,892 | 78,810 | 92,575 | 80,836 | 168 | 108 | 126 | 145 |
| Swaps | 428,385 | 456,725 | 421,273 | 381,028 | 13,745 | 12,919 | 12,042 | 13,946 |
| Options | 49,396 | 49,264 | 49,442 | 43,591 | 1,325 | 1,174 | 1,292 | 1,517 |
| *Memo: Exchange-traded contracts*[3] | 62,160 | 56,951 | 65,624 | 57,222 | ... | ... | ... | ... |

*(Contd.)*

*(Contd.)*

| | Notional amounts outstanding | | | | Gross market value | | | |
|---|---|---|---|---|---|---|---|---|
| | H1 2013 | H2 2013 | H1 2014 | H2 2014 | H1 2013 | H2 2013 | H1 2014 | H2 2014 |
| **C. Equity-linked contracts** | **6,821** | **6,560** | **7,084** | **7,941** | **692** | **700** | **678** | **615** |
| Forwards and swaps | 2,321 | 2,277 | 2,505 | 2,495 | 206 | 202 | 199 | 178 |
| Options | 4,501 | 4,284 | 4,579 | 5,446 | 486 | 498 | 479 | 437 |
| *Memo: Exchange-traded contracts[2]* | 6,614 | 6,760 | 7,460 | 7,243 | ... | ... | ... | ... |
| **D. Commodity contracts[4]** | **2,458** | **2,204** | **2,206** | **1,868** | **384** | **264** | **269** | **317** |
| Gold | 461 | 341 | 319 | 300 | 80 | 47 | 32 | 32 |
| Other | 1,997 | 1,863 | 1,887 | 1,568 | 304 | 217 | 237 | 285 |
| Forwards and swaps | 1,327 | 1,260 | 1,283 | 1,053 | ... | ... | ... | ... |
| Options | 670 | 603 | 604 | 515 | ... | ... | ... | ... |
| **E. Credit default swaps[5]** | **24,349** | **21,020** | **19,462** | **16,399** | **725** | **653** | **635** | **593** |
| Single-name instruments | 13,135 | 11,324 | 10,845 | 9,041 | 430 | 369 | 368 | 366 |
| Multi-name instruments | 11,214 | 9,696 | 8,617 | 7,358 | 295 | 284 | 266 | 227 |
| Index products | ... | 8,746 | 7,939 | 6,747 | ... | ... | ... | ... |
| **F. Unallocated[6]** | **24,986** | **25,496** | **24,815** | **22,609** | **779** | **724** | **671** | **803** |
| **GROSS CREDIT EXPOSURE[7]** | **...** | **...** | **...** | **...** | **3,784** | **3,033** | **2,826** | **3,358** |
| Memo: Exchange-traded contracts[2,8] | 69,117 | 64,098 | 73,462 | 64,858 | ... | ... | ... | ... |

(*Source:* Bank for International Settlements–Statistical Release-OTC Derivative Statisticsc Dec. 2014)

[1]*Based on the data reported by 11 countries up to H1 2013. Includes data reported by Australia and Spain from H2 2014 onwards. Data on total notional amounts outstanding, gross market value and gross credit exposure are shown on the basis of the information available on the Net, i.e., transactions between reporting dealers are counted only once. The definitions of notional amounts outstanding, gross market value and gross credit exposure are available under Section 3 of the statistical notes.*

[2]*Sources: FOW TRADE data; Futures Industry Association; various futures and options exchanges.*

[3]*Single currency contracts only.*

[4]*Adjustments for double-counting partly estimated.*

[5]*Includes foreign exchange, interest rate, equity, commodity and credit derivatives of non-reporting institutions, based on the latest Triennial Central Bank Survey of Foreign Exchange and Derivatives Market Activity, in 2013.*

[6]*Before 2011, excludes CDS contracts for all countries except the United States.*

[7]*Excludes commodity and single equity contracts.*)

The above stated Table 1.1 reveals the size of various derivatives, traded at the OTC markets at global level. Among the derivatives, as per the survey of BIS at the end of December 2014, interest rate contracts found to be most dominating accounting for over 80 percent of the total notional outstanding. Currency derivatives stood at the second, accounting for 12 percent, whereas commodity derivative contracts remain at the lowest level. Further, currency derivatives and interest rate derivatives also noted from other data rising trend from December 2007 to December 2011, in comparison to equity-linked derivatives, commodity derivatives and credit default swaps which show downward trend in the corresponding period.

## 1.5 BASIC FINANCIAL DERIVATIVES

### 1.5.1 Forward Contracts

A forward contract is a simple customized contract between two parties to buy or sell an asset at a certain time in the future for a certain price. Unlike futures contracts, they are not traded on an exchange, rather traded in the over-the-counter market, usually between two financial institutions or between a financial institution and one of its client. These are bilateral contracts and are negotiated directly between the buyers and sellers, and all the terms of the contract are decided by themselves.

**EXAMPLE:** An Indian company buys Automobile parts from the USA with payment of one million dollar due in 90 days. The importer, thus, is short of dollar, i.e., it owes dollars for future delivery. Suppose present price of dollar is ₹63. Over the next 90 days, however, dollar might rise against ₹63. The importer can hedge this exchange risk by negotiating a 90 days forward contract with a bank at a price ₹65. According to the forward contract, in 90 days the bank will give to the importer one million dollar and the importer will pay the bank ₹65 million hedging a future payment with forward contract. On the due date the importer will make a payment of ₹65 million to bank and the bank will pay one million dollar to importer, whatever rate of the dollar is after 90 days. So, this is a simple example of forward contract in foreign currency.

The basic features of a forward contract are given in brief here as under:

1. Forward contracts are bilateral contracts, and hence, they are exposed to counter-party risk. There is risk of non-performance of obligation either of the parties, so these are riskier than to futures contracts.
2. Each contract is custom designed, and hence, is unique in terms of contract size, expiration date, the asset type, quality, etc.
3. In the forward contract, one of the parties takes a long position by agreeing to buy the asset at a certain specified future date. The other party assumes a short position by agreeing to sell the same asset at the same date for the same specified price. A party with no obligation offsetting the forward contract is said to have an open position. A party with a closed position is, sometimes, called a hedger.
4. The specified price in a forward contract is referred to as the delivery price. The forward price for a particular forward contract at a particular time is the delivery price that would apply if the contract were entered into at that time. It is important to differentiate between the forward price and the delivery price. Both are equal at the time the contract is entered into. However, as time passes, the forward price is likely to change, whereas the delivery price remains the same.
5. In the forward contract, derivative assets can often be contracted from the combination of underlying assets, such assets are oftenly known as *synthetic assets* in the forward market.
6. In the forward market, the contract has to be settled by delivery of the asset on expiration date. In case the party wishes to reverse the contract, it has to compulsory go to the same

counter party, which may dominate and command the price it wants as being in a monopoly situation.

7. In the forward contract, covered parity or cost-of-carry relations are relation between the prices of forward and underlying assets. Such relations further assist in determining the arbitrage-based forward asset prices.

8. Forward contracts are very popular in foreign exchange market as well as interest rate bearing instruments. Most of the large and international banks quote the forward rate through their 'forward desk' lying within their foreign exchange trading room. Forward foreign exchange quotes by these banks are displayed with the spot rates.

9. As per the Indian Forward Contract Act, 1952, different kinds of forward contracts can be done like hedge contracts, transferable specific delivery (TSD) contracts and non-transferable specify delivery (NTSD) contracts. Hedge contracts are freely transferable and do not specify, any particular lot, consignment or variety for delivery. Transferable specific delivery contracts are though freely transferable from one party to another, but are concerned with a specific and predetermined consignment. Delivery is mandatory. Non-transferable specific delivery contracts, as the name indicates, are not transferable at all, and as such, they are highly specific.

In brief, a forward contract is an agreement between the counter parties to buy or sell a specified quantity of an asset at a specified price, with delivery at a specified time (future) and place. These contracts are not standardized, each one is usually being customized to its owner's specifications.

## 1.5.2   Futures Contracts

Like a forward contract, a futures contract is an agreement between two parties to buy or sell a specified quantity of an asset at a specified price and at a specified time and place. Futures contracts are normally traded on an exchange which set the certain standardized norms for trading in the futures contracts. The participants in the futures market, follow the norms set by the respective exchange, and are required to post margin which is essentially collateral against default of the participants.

**EXAMPLE:**   X has purchased a futures contract of State Bank of India on May 11, 2015 for delivery in August, 2015. The price of SBI on May 11, 2015 in the cash market assumes ₹280 and in futures market ₹285. Suppose in July 1, 2015, the spot price of SBI is 290 and futures price is ₹293. It means the buyer of the contract is in profit and futures price of SBI is also changed on the basis of spot price of SBI..

## 1.5.3   Options Contracts

Options are the most important group of derivative securities. *Option* may be defined as a contract, between two parties whereby one party obtains the right, but not the obligation, to buy or sell a particular asset, at a specified price, on or before a specified date. The person who acquires the right is known as the *option buyer* or *option holder*, while the other person (who confers the right) is known as *option seller* or *option writer*. The seller of the option for giving such option to the buyer charges an amount which is known as the *option premium*.

Options can be divided into two types *calls* and *puts*. A call option gives the holder the right to buy an asset at a specified date for a specified price, whereas in a put option, the holder gets the right to sell an asset at the specified price and time. The specified price in such contract is known as the *exercise price* or the *strike price* and the date in the contract is known as the *expiration date* or the *exercise date* or the *maturity date*. The asset or security instrument or commodity covered under the contract is called the *underlying asset*. They include shares, stocks, stock indices, foreign currencies, bonds, commodities, futures contracts, etc. Further options can be American or European. A European option can be exercised on the expiration date only, whereas an American option can be exercised at any time before the maturity date.

**EXAMPLE:** Suppose the current price of CIPLA share is ₹750 per share. X owns 1000 shares of CIPLA Ltd. and apprehends in the decline in price of share. The option (put) contract available at BSE is of ₹800, in next two-month delivery. Premium cost is ₹10 per share. The X will buy a put option at 10 per share at a strike price of ₹800. In this way the X has hedged his risk of price fall of stock. The X will exercise the put option if the price of stock goes down below ₹800 and will not exercise the option if price is more than ₹800, on the exercise date. In case of options, buyer has a limited loss and unlimited profit potential unlike in case of forward and futures.

In April 1973, the options on stocks were first traded on an organized exchange, i.e., Chicago Board Options Exchange. Since then, there has been a dramatic growth in options markets. Options are now traded on various exchanges in various countries all over the world. Options are now traded both on organized exchanges and over-the-counter (OTC). The option trading mechanism on both are quite different and which leads to important differences in market conventions. Recently, options contracts on OTC are getting popular because they are more liquid. Further, most of the banks and other financial institutions now prefer the OTC options market because of the ease and customized nature of contract.

It should be emphasized that the option contract gives the holder the right to do something. The holder may exercise his option or may not. The holder can make a reassessment of the situation and seek either the execution of the contracts or its non-execution as be profitable to him. He is not under obligation to exercise the option. So, this fact distinguishes options from forward contracts and futures contracts, where the holder is under obligation to buy or sell the underlying asset. Recently in India, the banks are allowed to write cross-currency options after obtaining the permission from the Reserve Bank of India.

## 1.5.4 Warrants and Convertibles

Warrants and convertibles are another important categories of financial derivatives, which are frequently traded in the market. Warrant is just like an option contract where the holder has the right to buy shares of a specified company at a certain price during the given time period. In other words, the holder of a warrant instrument has the right to purchase a specific number of shares at a fixed price in a fixed period from an issuing company. If the holder exercised the right, it increases the number of shares of the issuing company, and thus, dilutes the equities of its shareholders. Warrants are usually issued as sweeteners attached to senior securities like bonds and debentures so that they are successful in their equity issues in terms of volume and price. Warrants can be detached and traded separately. Warrants are highly speculative and leverage instruments, so trading in them must be done cautiously.

Convertibles are hybrid securities which combine the basic attributes of fixed interest and variable return securities. Most popular among these are convertible bonds, convertible debentures and convertible preference shares. These are also called equity derivative securities. They can be fully or partially converted into the equity shares of the issuing company at the predetermined specified terms with regards to the conversion period, conversion ratio and conversion price. These terms may be different from company to company, as per nature of the instrument and particular equity issue of the company. The further details of these instruments will be discussed in the respective chapters.

### 1.5.5 Swap Contracts

Swaps have become popular derivative instruments in recent years all over the world. A swap is an agreement between two counter parties to exchange cash flows in the future. Under the swap agreement, various terms like the dates when the cash flows are to be paid, the type of currency to be paid and the mode of payment are determined and finalized by the parties. Usually the calculation of cash flows involves the future values of one or more market variables.

There are two most popular forms of swap contracts, i.e., interest rate swaps and currency swaps. In the interest rate swap one party agrees to pay the other party interest at a fixed rate on a notional principal amount, and in return, it receives interest at a floating rate on the same principal notional amount for a specified period. The currencies of the two sets of cash flows are the same. In case of currency swap, it involves in exchanging of interest flows in one currency for interest flows in other currency. In other words, it requires the exchange of cash flows in two currencies. There are various forms of swaps, based upon these two, but having different features in general.

**EXAMPLE 1:** In an interest rate Swap contract, suppose counterparties 'X' and 'Y' agree to exchange over a period of say, 3 years, two streams of semi-annual payments. The payments made by the counter party X at a fixed rate of 8 percent p.a., while the payments to be made by counter party Y through floating rate of interest on the basis of LIBOR (6-month). The notional principal amount of swap contract is ₹10 million. This is an example of simple 'plain vanilla' interest rate swaps.

The above swap rate contract may be simplified as follows:

| | |
|---|---|
| Counter Parties | : X and Y |
| Maturity | : 03 years |
| Fixed Rate Payment | : Counter party X at 8% p.a. |
| Floating Rate Payment | : Counter party Y at LIBOR (6-month) |
| Payment Terms | : Semi-annual |
| Notional Principal amount | : ₹10 million |

**TABLE**   Cash flows in the Swap Contract (figures in ₹)

| Payment at the end of 6-month | Fixed Rate Payments | Floating Rate Payments LIBOR 6-month* | Net Cash from X to Y |
|---|---|---|---|
| 1 | 4,00,000.00 | 4,20,000.00 | −20,000.00 |
| 2 | 4,00,000.00 | 4,20,000.00 | −20,000.00 |
| 3 | 4,00,000.00 | 4,25,000.00 | −25,000.00 |
| 4 | 4,00,000.00 | 3,90,000.00 | +10,000.00 |
| 5 | 4,00,000.00 | 3,80,000.00 | +20,000.00 |
| 6 | 4,00,000.00 | 4,10,000.00 | −10,000.00 |

*the LIBOR (6-month) rates prevailing at the respective due dates are assumed as 8.4%, 8.4%, 8.5%, 7.8%, 7.6% and 8.2% p.a.

**EXAMPLE 2:** Suppose that two companies A and B both wish to borrow 1 million rupees for five-years and rate of interest is:

| Company | Fixed | Floating |
|---------|-------|----------|
| Company A | 10.00% per annum | 6-month LIBOR + 0.30% |
| Company B | 11.20% per annum | 6-month LIBOR + 1.00% |

A wants to borrow funds at floating interest rate and B wants to borrow at fixed interest rate. B has low credit rating than company A since it pays higher rate of interest than company A in both fixed and floating markets. They will contract to Financial Institution for swapping their assets and liabilities and make a swap contract with bank.

Both companies will initially raise loans, A in fixed and B in floating interest rate and then contract to bank, which in return pays fixed interest rate to A and receive floating interest rate to A and from B. Bank will pay floating interest rate and receive fixed interest rates and also charges commission from both. A and B have the liability in which both were interested.

## 1.5.6 Other Derivatives

As discussed earlier, forwards, futures, options, swaps, etc. are described usually as standard or 'plain vanilla' derivatives. In the early 1980s, some banks and other financial institutions have been very imaginative and designed some new derivatives to meet the specific needs of their clients. These derivatives have been described as 'non-standard' derivatives. The basis of the structure of these derivatives was not unique, for example, some non-standard derivatives were formed by combining two or more 'plain vanilla' call and put options, whereas some others were far more complex. In fact, there is no boundary for designing the non-standard financial derivatives, and hence, they are sometimes termed as 'exotic options' or just 'exotics'. There are various examples of such non-standard derivatives, such as packages, forward start option, compound options, choose options, barrier options, binary options, look back options, shout options, Asian options, basket options, Standard Oil's Bond Issue, Index Currency Option Notes (ICON), range forward contracts or flexible forwards and so on.

Traditionally, it is evident that important variables underlying the financial derivatives have been interest rates, exchange rates, commodity prices, stock prices, stock indices, etc. However, recently, some other underlying variables are also getting popular in the financial derivative markets such as creditworthiness, weather, insurance, electricity and so on. In fact, there is no limit to the innovations in the field of derivatives.

### *Credit derivatives*

The *credit derivatives* refer to the offsetting of credit risk in a firm due to default in the credit assets. It is a contract between the two parties which compensate credit risk by one party to other. In the other words, the credit derivatives relate to hedging of credit risk which arises due to default of non-payment of a loan. For example, a bank can enter into a credit derivatives contract with an investor in which the bank transfers the credit risk in a loan or portfolio of loans to the investor, and against this, the banker will pay premium to the investor. These instruments were first introduced in 1993 and have grown so rapidly since then, being now the third largest segment of the derivatives market as presented in the Table 1.1.

The credit derivatives contracts are of different forms with different features such as credit default swaps, total return swaps, credit options, credit liked notes, etc. Details of which have been discussed in forth coming chapter of credit derivatives. In this book the most popular form of credit derivatives is the credit default swap (CDS), in which the buyer (normally a banker) makes a regular payment, called the *CDS premium*, to the seller (an investor) against the protection of default risk of a loan or portfolio of loan of the seller. The payments of the premium continue until maturity or default on the reference obligation, whichever comes first. In effect the buyer takes the short position while the seller takes the long position in the credit risk of the reference obligation. Total return swaps are bilateral contracts designed to synthetically replicate the economic return arising of underlying asset or a portfolio of assets for a pre-specified time. In other words, in the total return swap contract, one party pays the total returns of (including any interest payments and capital appreciation) of the total returns of a designed asset and in return the other party pays to him a regular floating rate payment such as LIBOR, MIBOR, etc.

Credit options are derivatives instruments with pay-offs linked to the credit characteristics of a particular underlying asset or issuer. The basic underlying the credit spreads is to understand the relative credit value changes in contract to change in interest rates, credit spread expectation and the term structure of credit spread. Credit linked note enables the investor to purchase an asset with a return linked to the credit risk of the asset itself and additional risk transferred by way of credit derivatives between the parties.

### Weather derivatives

Weather derivatives is another important derivative instrument which is being introduced by the different countries. As the name indicates, weather derivatives are used to hedge risk caused due to change of weather on the business in future. Most of the industries are directly or indirectly affected by weather fluctuations. So, *weather risk* may be defined as an uncertainly in the occurrence of normal weather condition in future period, the risk to be termed as the uncertainty in the earnings and cash flows on account of changes in weather conditions. Important industries which are subject to weather conditions are utilities, gas and power, energy, insurance sector, agriculture sector, etc. First weather derivatives contracts appeared in US energy industry in 1996. The markets of such derivatives grew rapidly and soon expanded to other industries and to Europe and Japan. Currently, a large number of energy companies, insurance companies, banks, hedge funds, insurance, etc. have started trading in weather derivatives. In this respect, an association named The Weather Risk Management Association (WRMA) has contributed to represent the weather market.

A standard weather contract must include the important attributes such as contract period, measurement technique, weather variable measurement at the measurement station, an index relating to weather, pay-off detail, etc. A weather derivative is distinct from weather insurance. Weather derivatives have a pay-off that depends on a weather index which is chosen to represent the weather conditions against which protection is given. Insurance policy is given for loss due to an event, thus to be entitled for a claim, the policy holder must have incurred the loss. However a weather derivative is enforceable on the happening of an event whether or not a loss is incurred. The potential for such a difference is known as *basis risk*. Weather risk is unique which is related with the volume and more to do with yield changes/losses rather than price changes. Weather derivatives are very much useful for the industries and the government should take appropriate measures to develop them in right perspective.

### Commodity derivatives

The *commodity derivatives market* is a market where future instruments like forwards, futures, options, swaps, etc. are traded on the commodities. As discussed earlier, a derivatives instrument is that whose value is derived from an underlying asset. In commodity derivatives, the underlying assets are commodities. In business sense, a commodity may be defined as a tangible as well as movable goods used for trading and exchanging purposes. Forward Contacts Regulation Act (FCRA), 1952 defines that goods as every kind of movable property other than actionable claims, money and securities, currently important commodities like food grains, spices, cotton, coco, oilcakes, oil, rubber, metals, coffee, sugar, livestock's, energy, etc. are traded on various exchanges all over the world.

This history of commodity derivatives can be traced back to the Yodoya rice market in Osaka (Japan) in around 1650, after which a lot on ups and downs were noted across the world in this market till 1925. The first futures clearing house came into existence. After that in 1948, the Chicago Board of Trade (CBOT) started derivative trading in commodities, and today it is the largest exchange of futures and options on agricultural commodities. In India, the trading in derivatives market has taken place in 1875 through the establishment of Cotton Trade Association followed by oilseeds, jute, wheat, etc. Forward market Commission initiated the modern commodity exchange that can work electrically and in November 2002, the National Multi-Commodity Exchange of Ahmedabad (NMCE) came into existence. After that in 2003, the Multi-Commodity Exchange (MCX) and the National Multi-Commodity Derivatives Exchange (NCDEX) started their operations. Currently, derivative trading is permitted in all commodities through almost 25 exchanges/associations and six indices are measuring commodities prices. These exchanges offer both cash and delivery-based settlement system in commodities. The commodity derivatives market has taken momentum and the market regulator, FMC is being merged with SEBI.

### Idea futures

Another important development in the derivatives market is the emergence of idea futures which is related with creation to the new ideas, opinions, etc. to be applicable in shape of future events. The basic aim of the idea futures is to predict and develop new ideas by collecting information. These may be designed to different fields ranging from science and technology to public policy. In other words, the basic objective of the idea futures is to predict major events likely to be happened in future and accordingly taking strategic decisions which may have national or international impact.

Like other financial futures contracts, the idea futures also combines two phenomena, i.e., convergence and markets. The price of a futures contract is determined on the basis of demand and supply of that future asset and the traders' beliefs about the future. Similarly, in idea futures, converged beliefs based on the available information determine the price of an idea futures. The factors to determine the price of idea futures reflects on time factor, probability of the issue never being resolved, and the number of interested traders, time and expenditure involved in them. The idea futures markets trades on the probability of the realization of the idea, whether an event will occur and if so, when. There are numerous examples of idea futures. For example, Foresight Exchange deals with idea futures and the place to check the current odds of upcoming events. It is a play money future prediction market. Similarly, Low Electronic Market deals with real money idea, i.e., future economic and political events, such as earning per share (EPS), stock returns, dividends declaration, strategic relationship among companies, growth rate, etc. Another example of idea futures is of Hollywood Stock Exchange which trades in buying and selling idea futures based on movie stocks. The movie stock range includes movies running in theatres and also in production.

## 1.6  HISTORICAL BACKGROUND OF DERIVATIVES MARKETS

It is difficult to trace the main origin of derivative trading since it is not clearly established as to where and when the first forward market came into existence. Historically, it is evident that the development of futures markets followed the development of forward markets. It is believed that the forward trading has been in existence since 12th century in England and France. Forward trading in rice was started in 17th century in Japan, known as Cho-at-Mai a kind (rice trade-on-book) concentrated around Dojima in Osaka. Later on the trade in rice grew with a high degree of standardization. In 1730, this market got official recognition from the Tokugawa Shogurate. As such, the Dojima rice market became the first futures market in the sense that it was registered on organized exchange with the standardized trading norms.

The butter and eggs dealers of Chicago Produce Exchange joined hands in 1898 to form the Chicago Mercantile Exchange for futures trading. The exchange provided a futures market for many commodities including pork bellies (1961), live cattle (1964), live hogs (1966), and feeder cattle (1971). The International Monetary Market was formed as a division of the Chicago Mercantile Exchange in 1972 for futures trading in foreign currencies. In 1982, it introduced a futures contract on the S&P 500 Stock Index. Many other exchanges throughout the world now trade futures contracts. Important among them are the Chicago Rice and Cotton Exchange, the New York Futures Exchange, the London International Financial Futures Exchange, the Toronto Futures Exchange and the Singapore International Monetary Exchange. They grew so rapidly that the number of shares underlying the option contracts sold each day exceeded the daily volume of shares traded on the New York Stock Exchange.

In the 1980's, markets developed for options in foreign exchange, options on stock indices, and options on futures contracts. The Philadelphia Stock Exchange is the premier exchange for trading foreign exchange options. The Chicago Board Options Exchange trades options on the S&P 100 and the S&P 500 stock indices while the American Stock Exchange trades options on the Major Market Stock Index, and the New York Stock Exchange trades options on the NYSE Index. Most exchanges offering futures contracts now also offer options on these futures contracts. Thus, the Chicago Board of Trade's offers options on corn futures, the Chicago Mercantile Exchange offers options on live cattle futures, the International Monetary Market offers options on foreign currency futures, and so on.

The basic cause of forward trading was to cover the price risk. In earlier years, transporting goods from one market to other markets took many months. For example, in the 1800s, food grains produced in England sent through ships to the United States which normally took few months. Sometimes, during this time, the price crashed due to unfavourable events before the goods reached to the destination. In such cases, the producers had to sell their goods at the loss. Therefore, the producers sought to avoid such price risk by selling their goods forward, or on a "to arrive" basis. The basic idea behind this move at that time was simply to cover future price risk. On the other hand, the speculator or other commercial firms seeking to offset their price risk came forward to go for such trading. In this way, the forward trading in commodities came into existence.

In the beginning, these forward trading agreements were formed to buy and sell food grains in the future for actual delivery at the pre-determined price. Later, these agreements became transferable, and during the American Civil War period, i.e., 1860 to 1865, it became a common place to sell and resell such agreements where actual delivery of produce was not necessary. Gradually, the traders realized that the agreements were easier to buy and sell if the same were standardized in terms of quantity, quality and place of delivery relating to food grains. In the nineteenth century this activity was centred in Chicago which was the main food grains marketing centre in the United States. In this way, the modern futures contracts first came into existence with the establishment of the Chicago Board of Trade (CBOT) in the year 1848, and today, it is the largest futures market of the world. In 1865, the CBOT framed the general rules for such trading which later on became a trendsetter for so many other markets.

In 1874, the Chicago Produce Exchange was established which provided the market for butter, eggs, poultry, and other perishable agricultural products. In the year 1877, the London Metal Exchange came into existence, and today, it is leading market in metal trading both in spot as well as forward. In the year 1898, the butter and egg dealers withdrew from the Chicago Produce Exchange to form separately the Chicago Butter and Egg Board, and thus, in 1919 this exchange was renamed as the Chicago Mercantile Exchange (CME) and was reorganized for futures trading. Since then, so many other exchanges came into existence throughout the world which trade in futures contracts.

Although financial derivatives have been in operation since long, but they have become a major force in financial markets in the early 1970s. The basic reason behind this development was the failure of Bretton Woods System and the fixed exchange rate regime was broken down. As a result, new exchange rate regime, i.e., floating rate (flexible) system based upon market forces came into existence. But due to pressure of demand and supply on different currencies, the exchange rates were constantly changing, and often, substantially. As a result, the business firms faced a new risk, known as currency or foreign exchange risk. Accordingly, a new financial instrument was developed to overcome this risk in the new financial environment.

Another important reason for the instability in the financial market was fluctuation in the short-term interests. This was mainly due to the reason that most of the government at that time tried to manage foreign exchange fluctuations through short-term interest rates by maintaining money supply targets, but those were contrary to each other. Further, the increased instability of short-term interest rates created adverse impact on long-term interest rates, and hence, instability in bond prices because they are largely determined by long-term interest rates. The result is that it created another risk, named interest rate risk, for both the issuers and the investors of debt instruments.

Interest rate fluctuations had not only created instability in bond prices, but also in other long-term assets, such as company stocks and shares. Share prices are determined on the basis of expected present values of future dividends payments discounted at the appropriate discount rate. Discount rates are usually based on long-term interest rates in the market. So increased instability in the long-term interest rates caused to enhanced fluctuations in the share prices in the stock markets. Further volatility in stock prices is reflected in the volatility in stock market indices which causes to systematic risk or market risk.

In the early 1970s, it is witnessed that the financial markets were highly instable, as a result, so many financial derivatives have been emerged as the means to manage the different types of risks stated above, and also of taking advantage of it. Hence, the first financial futures market was the International Monetary Market, established in 1972 by the Chicago Mercantile Exchange which was followed by the London International Financial Futures Exchange in 1982. For further details see the 'growth of futures market' in the forthcoming chapter.

## 1.7 USES OF DERIVATIVES

Derivatives are supposed to provide the following services:

   1. One of the most important services provided by the derivatives is to control, avoid, shift and manage efficiently different types of risks through various strategies like hedging,

arbitraging, spreading, etc. Derivatives assist the holders to shift or modify suitably the risk characteristics of their portfolios. These are specifically useful in highly volatile financial market conditions like erratic trading, highly flexible interest rates, volatile exchange rates and monetary chaos.

2. Derivatives serve as barometers of the future trends in prices which result in the discovery of new prices both on the spot and futures markets. Further, they help in disseminating different information regarding the futures markets trading of various commodities and securities to the society which enable to discover or form suitable or correct or true equilibrium prices in the markets. As a result, they assist in appropriate and superior allocation of resources in the society.

3. As we see that in derivatives trading no immediate full amount of the transaction is required since most of them are based on margin trading. As a result, large number of traders, speculators arbitrageurs operate in such markets. So, derivatives trading enhance liquidity and reduce transaction costs in the markets for underlying assets.

4. The derivatives assist the investors, traders and managers of large pools of funds to devise such strategies so that they may make proper asset allocation increase their yields and achieve other investment goals.

5. It has been observed from the derivatives trading in the market that the derivatives have smoothen out price fluctuations, squeeze the price spread, integrate price structure at different points of time and remove gluts and shortages in the markets.

6. The derivatives trading encourage the competitive trading in the markets, different risk taking preference of the market operators like speculators, hedgers, traders, arbitrageurs, etc. resulting in increase in trading volume in the country. They also attract young investors, professionals and other experts who will act as catalysts to the growth of financial markets.

7. Lastly, it is observed that derivatives trading develop the market towards 'complete markets'. Complete market concept refers to that situation where no particular investors is better than others, or patterns of returns of all additional securities are spanned by the already existing securities in it, or there is no further scope of additional security.

## 1.8 CRITIQUES OF DERIVATIVES

Besides the important services provided by the derivatives, some experts have raised doubts and have become critique on the growth of derivatives. They have warned against them and believe that the derivatives will cause to destabilization, volatility, financial excesses and oscillations in financial markets. It is alleged that they assist the speculators in the market to earn lots of money, and hence, these are exotic instruments. In this section, a few important arguments of the critiques against derivatives have been discussed.

### 1.8.1 Speculative and Gambling Motives

One of most important arguments against the derivatives is that they promote speculative activities in the market. It is witnessed from the financial markets throughout the world that the trading volume in derivatives have increased in multiples of the value of the underlying assets and hardly one to two percent derivatives are settled by the actual delivery of the underlying assets. As such speculation has become the primary purpose of the birth, existence and growth of derivatives. Sometimes, these speculative buying and selling by professionals and amateurs adversely affect the genuine producers and distributors.

Some financial experts and economists believe that speculation brings about a better allocation of supplies overtime, reduces the fluctuations in prices, make adjustment between demand and supply, removes periodic gluts and shortages, and thus, brings efficiency to the market. However, in actual practice, such agreements are not visible. Most of the speculative activities are 'professional speculation' or 'movement trading' which lead to destabilization in the market. Sudden and sharp variations in prices have been caused due to common, frequent and widespread consequence of speculation.

## 1.8.2 Increase in Risk

The derivatives are supposed to be efficient tool of risk management in the market. In fact, this is also one-sided argument. It has been observed that the derivatives market—especially OTC markets, as particularly customized, privately managed and negotiated, and thus, they are highly risky. Empirical studies in this respect have shown that derivatives used by the banks have not resulted in the reduction in risk, and rather these have raised new types of risk. They are powerful leveraged mechanism used to create risk. It is further argued that if derivatives are risk management tool, then why 'government securities, a riskless security, are used for trading interest rate futures which is one of the most popular financial derivatives in the world.

## 1.8.3 Instability of the Financial System

It is argued that the derivatives have increased risk not only for their users but also for the whole financial system. The fears of micro and macro financial crisis have caused to the unchecked growth of derivatives which have turned many market players into big losers. The malpractices, desperate behaviour and fraud by the users of derivatives have threatened the stability of the financial markets and the financial system.

## 1.8.4 Price Instability

Some experts argue in favour of the derivatives that their major contribution is towards price stability and price discovery in the market, whereas some others have doubt about this. Rather they argue that derivatives have caused wild fluctuations in asset prices, and moreover, they have widened the range of such fluctuations in the prices. The derivatives may be helpful in price stabilization only if there exist a properly organized, competitive and well-regulated market. Further, the traders behave and function in professional manner and follow standard code of conduct. Unfortunately, all these are not so frequently practiced in the market, and hence, the derivatives sometimes cause to price instability rather than stability.

## 1.8.5 Displacement Effect

There is another doubt about the growth of the derivatives that they will reduce the volume of the business in the primary or new issue market specifically for the new and small corporate units. It is apprehension that most of investors will divert to the derivatives markets, raising fresh capital by such units will be difficult, and hence, this will create displacement effect in the financial market.

However, it is not so strong argument because there is no such rigid segmentation of inventors, and investors behave rationally in the market.

## 1.8.6 Increased Regulatory Burden

As pointed earlier that the derivatives create instability in the financial system as a result, there will be more burden on the government or regulatory authorities to control the activities of the traders in financial derivatives. As we see various financial crises and scams in the market from time to time, most of time and energy of the regulatory authorities just spent on to find out new regulatory, supervisory and monitoring tools so that the derivatives do not lead to the fall of the financial system.

In our fast-changing financial services industry, coercive regulations intended to restrict banks' activities will be unable to keep up with financial innovation. As the lines of demarcation between various types of financial service providers continues to blur, the bureaucratic leviathan responsible for reforming banking regulation must face the fact that fears about derivatives have proved unfounded. New regulations are unnecessary.

Indeed, access to risk-management instruments should not be feared, but with caution, embraced to help the firms to manage the vicissitudes of the market.

In this chapter various misconceptions about financial derivatives are explored. Believing just one or two of the myths could lead one to advocate tighter legislation and regulatory measures designed to restrict derivatives activities and market participants. A careful review of the risks and rewards derivatives offer, however, suggests that regulatory and legislative restrictions are not the answer. To blame organizational failures solely on derivatives is to miss the point. A better answer lies in greater reliance on market forces to control derivative-related risk taking.

Financial derivatives have changed the face of finance by creating new ways to understand, measure and manage risks. Ultimately, financial derivatives should be considered part of any firm's risk-management strategy to ensure that value-enhancing investment opportunities are pursued. The freedom to manage risk effectively must not be taken away.

## 1.9 MYTHS ABOUT DERIVATIVES

There are various myths regarding the derivatives:

### 1.9.1 Myth Number 1

*"Derivatives are new, complex, high-tech financial products created by Wall Street's rocket scientists"*

Financial derivatives are not new; they have been around for years. A description of the first known option contract can be found in Aristotle's writing tells philosopher from Miletus who developed a financial device, which involves a principal of universal application. People reproved Thales, saying that his lack of wealth was proof that philosophy was a useless occupation and of no practical value. But Thales knew what he was doing and made plans to prove to others his wisdom and intellect.

Thales had great skill in forecasting and predicted that the olive harvest would be exceptionally good the next autumn. Confident in his prediction, he made agreements with area olive-press owners to deposit what little money he had with them to guarantee him exclusive use of their olive presses when the harvest was ready. Thales successfully negotiated low prices because the harvest was in the futures and no one knew whether the harvest would be plentiful or pathetic and because the olive-press owners were willing to hedge against the possibility of a poor yield. Aristotle's story about Thales ends as one might guess: "when the harvest-time came, and many [presses] were wanted all at once and all of a sudden, he let them out at any rate which he pleased, and made a quantity of money. Thus, he showed the world that philosophers can easily be rich if they like, but that their ambition is of another sort." So, Thales exercised the first known option contracts about 2,500 years ago. He was not obliged to exercise the option. If the olive harvest had not been good, Thales could have let the option contracts expire unused and limited his loss to the original price paid for the option.

Most financial derivatives traded today are the "plain vanilla" variety—the simplest form of a financial derivatives that are much difficult to measure, manage, and understand. For those instruments, the measurement and control of risk can be far more complicated, creating the increased possibility of unforeseen losses.

Wall Street's "rocket scientist" are continually creating new, complex, sophisticated financial derivative products. However, those products are all built on foundation of the four basis types of derivatives. Most of the newest innovations are designed to hedge complex risks in an effort to reduce future uncertainties and manage risks more effectively. But the newest innovations require a firm understanding of the trade-off of risks and rewards. To that end, derivative users should establish a guiding set of principles to provide a framework for effectively managing and controlling financial derivative activities. Those principles should focus on the role of senior management, valuation and market-risk argument, credit measurement and management, enforceability operating systems and controls and accounting and disclosure of risk-management positions.

## 1.9.2 Myth Number 2

*"Derivatives are purely speculative, highly leveraged instrument"*

Put another way. This myth is that "derivatives" is a fancy name for gambling. Has speculative trading of derivative products fuelled the rapid growth in their use? Are derivatives used only to speculate on the direction of interest rates or currency exchange rates? Of course not. Indeed, the explosive use of financial derivative products in recent years was brought about by three primary forces—more volatile markets, deregulation and new technologies.

The turning point seems to have occurred in the early 1970s with the breakdown of the fixed-rate international currency exchange regime, which was established at the 1944 conference at Bretton Woods and maintained by the International Monetary Fund. Since then currencies have floated freely. Accompanying that development was the gradual removal of government-established interest-rate ceilings when Regulation Q interest-rate restrictions were phased out. Not long afterward came inflationary oil-price shocks and wild interest-rate fluctuations. In sum, financial markets were more volatile than at any time since the Great Depression. Banks and other financial intermediaries responded to the new environment by developing financial risk-management products designed to better control risk. The first were simple foreign exchange forwards that obligated one counterpart to buy, and the other to sell, a fixed amount of currency at an agreed date in the future. By entering into a foreign-exchange forward contract, customers could offset the risk that large movements in foreign exchange rates would destroy the economic viability of their overseas projects. Thus, derivatives were originally intended to be used to effectively hedge certain risks; and, in fact, that was the key that unlocked their explosive development.

Beginning in the early 1980s, a host of new competitors accompanied the deregulation of financial markets, and the arrival of powerful but inexpensive personal computers ushered in new ways to analyze information and break down risk into component parts. To serve customers better, financial intermediaries offered an ever-increasing number of novel products designed to more effectively manage and control financial risks. New technologies quickened the pace of innovation and provided banks with superior methods for tracking and simulating their own derivatives portfolios.

### 1.9.3 Myth Number 3

*"The enormous size of the financial derivatives market dwarfs bank capital, thereby making derivatives trading an unsafe and unsound banking practice"*

The financial derivatives market's worth is regularly reported as more than $20 trillion. That estimate dwarfs not only bank capital but also the nation's $7 trillion annual gross domestic product. Those often-quoted figures are notional amounts. For derivatives, notional principal is the amount on which interest and other payments are based. Notional principal typically does not change hands; it is simply a quantity used to calculate payments.

While notional principal is the most commonly used volume measure in derivatives markets, it is not an accurate measure of credit exposure. A useful proxy for the actual exposure of derivative instruments is replacement-cost credit exposure. That exposure is the cost of replacing the contract at current market values should the counterpart default before the settlement date.

For the 10 largest derivatives players among US bank holding companies, derivative credit exposure averages 15 percent of total assets. The average exposure is 49 percent of assets for those banks' loan portfolios. In other words, if those 10 banks lost 100 percent on their loans, the loss would be more than three times greater than it would be if they had to replace all of their derivative contracts.

Derivatives also help to improve market efficiencies because risks can be isolated and sold to those who are willing to accept them at the least cost. Using derivatives breaks risk into pieces that can be managed independently. Corporations can keep the risks they are most comfortable managing and transfer those they do not want to other companies that are more willing to accept them. From a market-oriented perspective, derivatives offer the free trading of financial risks.

The viability of financial derivatives rests on the principle of comparative advantage, i.e., the relative cost of holding specific risks. Whenever comparative advantages exist, trade can benefit all parties involved. And financial derivatives allow for the free trading of individual risk components.

### 1.9.4 Myth Number 4

*"Only large multinational corporations and large banks have a purpose for using derivatives"*

Very large organizations are the biggest users of derivative instruments. However, firms of all sizes can benefit from using them. For example, consider a small regional bank (SRB) with total assets of $5 million. The SRB has a loan portfolio composed primarily of fixed-rate mortgages, a portfolio of government securities, and interest-bearing deposits that are often repriced. Two illustrations of how SRBs can use derivatives to hedge risks are:

First, rising interest rates will negatively affect prices in the SRB's $1 million securities portfolio. But by selling short a $1 million treasury-bond futures contract, the SRB can effectively hedge against that interest-rate risk and smooth its earnings stream in a volatile market. If interest rates went higher, the SRB would be hurt by a drop in value of its securities portfolio, but that loss would be offset by a gain from its derivative contract. Similarly, if interest rates fell, the bank would gain from the increase in value of its securities portfolio but would record a loss from its derivative contract. By entering into derivatives contracts, the SRB can lock in a guaranteed rate of return on its securities portfolio and not be as concerned about interest-rate volatility.

The second illustration involves a swap contract. As in the first illustration, rising interest rates will harm the SRB because it receives fixed cash flows on its loan portfolio and must pay variable cash flows for its deposits. Once again, the SRB can hedge against interest-rate risk by entering into a swap contract with a dealer to pay fixed and receive floating payments.

## 1.9.5   Myth Number 5

*"Financial derivatives are simply the latest risk-management fad"*

Financial derivatives are important tools that can help organizations to meet their specific risk-management objectives. As is the case with all tools, it is important that the user understand the tool's intended function and that are necessary to undertake various purposes. What kinds of derivative instruments and trading strategies are most appropriate? How will those instruments perform if there is a large increase or decrease in interest rates? How will those instruments perform if there are wild fluctuations in exchange rates? Without a clearly defined risk-management strategy, use of financial derivatives can be dangerous. It can threaten the accomplishment of a firm's long-range objectives and result in unsafe and unsound practices that could lead to the organization's insolvency. But when used wisely, financial derivatives can increase shareholder value by providing a means to better control a firm's risk exposures and cash flows. Clearly, derivatives are here to stay. We are well on our way to truly global financial markets that will continue to develop new financial innovations to improve risk-management practices. Financial derivatives are not the latest risk-management fad. They are important tools for helping organizations to better manage their risk exposures.

## 1.9.6   Myth Number 6

*"Derivatives take money out of productive processes and never put anything back"*

Financial derivatives, by reducing uncertainties, make it possible for corporations to initiate productive activities that might not otherwise be pursued. For example, a company may want to build a manufacturing facility in the United States but is concerned about the project's overall cost because of exchange rate volatility between the dollars. To ensure that the company will have the cash available when it is needed for investment, the manufacturer should devise a prudent risk-management strategy that is in harmony with its broader corporate objective of building a manufacturing facility in the United States. As part of that strategy, the firm should use financial derivatives to hedge against foreign exchange risk. Derivatives used as a hedge can improve the management of cash flows at the individual firm level.

To ensure that productive activities are pursued, corporate finance and treasury groups should transform their operations from mundane bean counting to activist financial risk management. They should integrate a clear set of risk management goals and objectives into the organization's overall corporate strategy. The ultimate goal is to ensure that the organization has the necessary funds at its disposal to pursue investments that maximize shareholder value. Used properly, financial derivatives can help corporations to reduce uncertainties and promote more productive activities.

## 1.9.7   Myth Number 7

*"Only risk-seeking organizations should use derivatives"*

Financial derivatives can be used in two ways—to hedge against unwanted risks or to *speculate* by taking a position in anticipation of a market movement. The olive-press owners, by locking in a guaranteed return no matter how good or bad the harvest, hedged against the risk that the next season's olive harvest might not be plentiful. Thales speculated that the next season's olive harvest would be exceptionally good, and therefore, paid an up-front premium in anticipation of that event. Similarly, organizations today can use financial derivatives to actively seek out specific risks and speculate on the direction of interest-rate or exchange-rate movements, or they can use derivatives to hedge against unwanted risks. Hence, it is not true that only risk-seeking institutions use derivatives. Indeed, organizations should use derivatives as part of their overall risk management strategy for keeping those risks that they are comfortable in managing and selling those, which they do not want, to others who are more willing to accept them. Even conservatively managed institutions can use derivatives to improve their cash flow management to ensure that the necessary funds are available to meet broader corporate objectives. One could argue that organizations that refuse to use financial derivatives are at greater risk than those that use them.

When using financial derivatives, however, organizations should be careful to use only those instruments that they understand and that fit best with their corporate risk-management philosophy. It may be prudent to stay away from the more exotic instruments, unless the risk/reward trade-offs are clearly understood by the firm's senior management and its independent risk-management review team. Exotic contracts should not be used unless there is some obvious reason for doing so.

## 1.9.8 Myth Number 8

*"The risks associated with financial derivatives are new and unknown"*

The kinds of risks associated with derivatives are no different from those associated with traditional financial instruments, although they can be far more complex. There are credit risks, operating risks, markets and so on. Risks from derivatives originate with the customer. With few exceptions, the risks are man-made, i.e., they do not readily appear in nature. For example, when a new homeowner negotiates with a lender to borrow a sum of money, the customer creates risks by the type of mortgage he chooses—risks to himself and the lending company. Financial derivatives allow the lending institution to break up those risks and distribute them around the financial system via secondary markets. Thus, many risks associated with derivatives are actually created by the dealers' customers or by their customers' customers. Those risks have been inherent in our nation's financial system since its inception.

Banks and other financial intermediaries should view themselves as risk managers—blending their knowledge of global financial markets with their clients' needs to help their clients anticipate change and have the flexibility to pursue opportunities that maximize their success. Banking is inherently a risky business. Risk permeates much of what banks do. And, for banks to survive, they must be able to understand, measure and manage financial risks effectively.

The types of risks faced by corporations today have not changed; rather, they are more complex and interrelated. The increased complexity and volatility of the financial markets have paved the way for the growth of numerous financial innovations that can enhance returns relative to risk. But a thorough understanding of the new financial-engineering tools and their proper integration into a firm's overall risk-management strategy and corporate philosophy can help to turn volatility into profitability.

Risk management is not about the elimination of risk; it is about the management of risk: selectively choosing those risks an organization is comfortable with and minimizing those that it does not want. Financial derivatives serve a useful purpose in fulfilling risk-management objectives. Through derivatives, risks from traditional instruments can be efficiently unbundled and managed independently. Used correctly, derivatives can save costs and increase returns.

Today dealers manage portfolios of derivatives and oversee the net, or residual, risk of their overall position. That development has changed the focus of risk management from individual transactions to portfolio exposures and has substantially improved dealers' ability to accommodate a broad spectrum of customer transactions. Because most active derivatives players today trade on portfolio exposures, it appears that financial derivatives do not wind markets together any more tightly than do loans. Derivatives players do not match every trade with an offsetting trade; instead, they continually manage the residual risk of the portfolio. If a counterpart defaults on a swap, the defaulted party does not turn around and default on some other counterpart that offset the original transaction. Instead, a derivatives default is very similar to a loan default. That is why it is important that derivatives players perform with due diligence in determining the financial strength and default risks of potential counter parties.

## 1.9.9   Myth Number 9

*"Because of the risks associated with derivatives, banking regulators should ban their use by any institution covered by federal deposit insurance"*

The problem is not derivatives but the perverse incentive banks have under the current system of federal deposit guarantees. Deposit insurance and other deposit reforms were first introduced to address some of the instabilities associated with systemic risk. Through federally guaranteed deposit insurance, the US government attempted to avoid, by increasing depositors' confidence, the experience of deposit runs that characterized banking crises before the 1930s.

The current deposit guarantee structure has, indeed, reduced the probability of large-scale bank panics, but it has also created some new problems. Deposit insurance effectively eliminates the discipline provided by the market mechanism that encourages banks to maintain appropriate capital levels and restrict unnecessary risk taking. Therefore, banks may wish to pursue higher risk strategies because depositors have a diminished incentive to monitor banks. Further, federal deposit insurance may actually encourage banks to use derivatives as speculative instruments to pursue higher risk strategies, instead of to hedge, or as dealers.

Since federal deposit insurance discourages market discipline, regulators have been put in the position of monitoring banks to ensure that they are managed in a safe and sound manner. Given the present system of federal deposit guarantees, regulatory proposals involving financial derivatives should focus on market-oriented reforms as opposed to laws that might eliminate the economic risk-management benefits of derivatives.

To that end, banking regulators should emphasize more disclosure of derivatives positions in financial statements and be certain that institutions trading huge derivatives portfolios have adequate capital. In addition, because derivatives could have implications for the stability of the financial system, it is important that users maintain sound risk-management practices.

Regulators have issued guidelines that banks with substantial trading or derivatives activity should follow. Those guidelines include:

- active board and senior management oversight of trading activities,
- establishment of an internal risk-management audit function that is independent of the trading function,
- thorough and timely audits to identify internal control weaknesses, and
- risk-measurement and risk-management information systems that include stress tests, simulations, and contingency plans for adverse market movements.

It is the responsibility of a bank's senior management to ensure that risks are effectively controlled and limited to levels that do not pose a serious threat to its capital position. Regulation is an ineffective substitute for sound risk management at the individual form level.

## SUMMARY

In this chapter, first we have taken a look at the basics of derivatives. Derivatives are the instruments which derive their value from the underlying assets. The underlying assets can be commodity, foreign currency, stock, stock index, interest rate bearing securities, etc. Financial derivatives are forward, futures, option, swaps and other exotic derivatives. Forward is a specific contract between two parties who agree to trade at some future date, at a stated price and quantity. No money exchange hands at the time the deal is signed. Futures are the standardized contract traded on the organised exchanges to buy or sell a specified quality of assets at a specified future date and at an agreed price. Options are the right to buy or sell any assets at a rate (strike price) at a specified future date, but no obligation for the buyer. Options are of two types: call option and put option. A swap is an agreement between two counter parties to exchange cash flows in future between the parties at the different time intervals at the agreed terms. There are two important popular forms of swap contracts, i.e., interest rate swaps and currency swaps.

In addition, this chapter also discussed the other derivatives like warrants, convertibles, credit derivatives, commodity derivatives, weather derivatives and idea futures. Warrants are like an options contract where the holder has the right to buy shares of a specified company during the given period. Convertibles are the hybrid securities which combine the basic attributes of fixed interest and variable return securities, popular among them are convertible bonds, debentures, preference shares, etc. Credit derivatives are future instruments in which one party compensates to other party for credit risk arising due to default in payment of credit assets. Weather derivatives are instruments used to hedge risk in change of weather. Weather risk is termed as the uncertainty in earnings and cash flows infirm due to fluctuations of weather in future. Commodity derivatives is a market where future instruments like forwards, futures, swaps, options, etc. are traded on the underlying assets as commodities. In business sense a *commodity* may be defined as a tangible as well as movable goods used for trading purposes. The idea futures are such derivatives which are based on the creation of new ideas, opinions, etc. to be applicable in shape of future events. The price of idea futures contract is determined on the basis of demand and supply of the idea and the traders' beliefs about that idea.

The chapter has described the history and phenomenal growth in financial derivatives and kinds of futures contracts that are traded. In 1848, futures contracts came into existence with the establishment of Chicago Board of trade. Option was traded at Chicago Board options market in 1977. Derivatives are classified as financials and commodities as major categorization. Financials can be further divided into basics and complex derivatives. Basic includes forwards, futures options and warrants and convertible securities, whereas complex involves swaps and exotics derivatives. On the basis of trading the derivatives can be classified as exchange traded derivatives and OTC derivatives. The derivatives which are traded on the recognized exchanges are called *exchange traded derivatives*. The derivatives which are directly traded between the parties without the involvement of third party, exchange, etc., are called *OTC derivatives*. The derivatives have been challenged by the critiques on various grounds. They believe that derivatives keep highly speculative; and gambling motives; increase the risk of the firm; create the instability in prices and financial system; increase the regulatory burden and create the displacement effect for the firm.

The chapter also discussed about the nine myths of financial derivatives because financial derivatives have changed the face of finance by creating new ways to understand measure and manage risks. Ultimately, financial derivatives should be considered part of any firm's risk-management strategy to ensure that value enhancing investment opportunities are pursued. These myths include: 1. Derivatives are new complex, high tech. financial products, 2. Derivatives are purely speculative and highly leveraged instruments, 3. Financial derivatives are simply the latest risk associated with derivatives; banking regulators should ban their use by any institution covered by federal deposit insurance, 4. Only large multinational corporations and large banks have a purpose for using derivatives, 5. Financial derivatives are simply the latest risk-management fad, 6. Derivatives take money out of productive processes and never put anything back, 7. Only risk-seeking organizations should use derivatives, 8. The risks associated with financial derivatives are new and unknown, and 9. Because of the risks associated with derivatives, banking regulators should ban their use by any institution covered by federal deposit insurance.

## SOLVED PROBLEMS

**P.1.** An investor enters into a short gold futures contract when the futures price is 60 cent per pound. One contract is for delivery of 60,000 pounds. How much the investor gain or lose if gold price at the end of the contract is: (a) 58.20 cent per pound (b) 61.30 cent per pound?

*Solution:* (a) In case of price 58.20 cent:

Investor is obligated to sell 60 cent per pound, something that is worth 58.20 cent per pound. So there is a gain to investor per pound. So there is a gain to investor.

$$\text{Gain} = (£0.6000 - £0.5820) \times 60,000 = £1,080$$

(b) In case of price 61.30 cent:

The investor is obligated to sell for 60 cent per pound, something that is worth 61.30 cent per pound. So, there is a net loss to investor.

$$\text{Loss} = (£0.6130 - £0.6000) \times 60,000 = £780$$

**P.2.** Suppose an investor write a put option (selling a put) on stock with a strike price of ₹50 and expiration date in three months. The current price of stock is ₹51. What you committed to yourself? How much could you gain or loss?

*Solution:* You have sold a put option. You have agreed to buy 100 shares for ₹50 per share. If a party on other side charge to exercise. The option will only be exercised by counter party price of share is below ₹50. Suppose party exercise when price is ₹30. You have to buy at ₹50 that are worth only ₹30, so loss to investor or writer will be ₹20 per share or ₹2,000. The worst that can happen is that the price of share decline to zero during the three-month period. The highly unlikely event would cost you ₹5,000. In return for the possible future closed, you receive the premium amount from the buyer of option.

**P.3.** The current stock price is ₹49 and a three-month call with a stock price ₹50, losing ₹3.90 (premium amount). You have ₹15,000 to invest. Identify two alternative strategies. Using option market and cash market:

*Solution:* *Strategy:*

(a) one strategy would be to buy 300 shares in cash market.

(b) second strategy would be to buy 3,000 shares at call price ₹ 3.90 in option market.

If share price goes upward movement, the second (b) strategy will give rise to greater gains. For example, if share price goes up to ₹60, you gain = [3,000 × (₹60 – ₹50)] – ₹11,700 = ₹18,300 (₹11,700 as premium amount), and from first strategy [300 × (₹60 – ₹49)] ₹3,300 from strategy (a).

However, if price of shares goes down to ₹45, the loss on first strategy will be less as compared to strategy second.

$$\text{Strategy (a) Loss} = 300 \times (₹49 – ₹45) = ₹1,200$$

$$\text{Strategy (b) Loss} = 3,000 \times (₹50 – ₹45) = ₹1,500$$

It will be Zero since he will not exercise the option. The loss will be premium paid = ₹11,700.

**P.4.**   An investor owns 10,000 shares worth ₹50 each. How put options can be used to provide insurance against decline in value of investors holding?

*Solution:*   Investor should buy 100 put option contract with an exercise/strike price of ₹50 each and expiration date of four months. If at the end of fourth month, the share price goes less than ₹50, investor should exercise the option and sell the share at ₹50 each. In this way, investor can hedge risk of fall in price of stock.

**P.5.**   A speculator based in USA who in February 2015 thinks that pound sterling will strengthen in next two months. How can be used futures contract for speculating? What can be alternative strategies for speculator? The future price is $1.6420 per pound. Total amount of speculation is £3,75,000.

*Solution*:   *Alternatives:*

(i) Speculator purchase of £3,75,000 in the hope that it can be sold later at a profit. The sterling once purchased will be kept in an interest bearing account, assuming $6,18,000. at the maturity.

(ii) Take a long position in six IMM (International Monetary Market) April futures contract on pound sterling. [value of each contract is £62,500]

*Outcomes:*

(i) Exchange rate $1.7000 in two months. Investor will earn = ($6,37,500 – $6,18,000) = $19,500 by using alternative (i) and ($6,37,500 – $6,15,750) = $21,750.

(ii) Exchange rate $1.6000 in two months. Loss to speculator ($6,00,000 – $6,18,000) = $18,000 by using alternative (i) and ($6,00,000 – $6,15,750) = $15,750 by using alternative (ii).

**P.6.**   Differentiate between

(a) entering in a long futures contract when the future price is ₹500.

(b) taking a long position in call option with a strike price of ₹500.

*Solution:*   In case of (a) investor is obligated to buy at ₹500 [because futures has obligation to buy or sell.

In case of (b) investor has the option to buy at ₹500 [option has right for buyer not obligation to buy or sell.

**P.7.**   Suppose an investor has written 200 futures contract on silver. How can he use call options to provide insurance against a decline in value of net position?

*Solution:*   Investor has written 200 futures contract, means he is obligated to sell at a specified future price. Investor can use call option to provide insurance against a decline in value. He can write a call option and can lock into a predetermined futures price, which he believes to be right. On expiration he can sold his share to option buyer at a price, if price goes below the specified level.

**P.8.** A farmer expects to have ₹50,000 of live hogs to sell in three months. The live hogs futures contract on Multi Commodity Exchange (MCX) is for delivery of ₹25,000 of hogs. How can the farmer use futures for the hedging?

*Solution:* Farmer expects to have ₹50,000 hogs at a future date. He can use futures for hedging in the way that today in MCX. He will take short position on two futures contracts of live hogs. So, he can hedge risk by taking a short position at a specified future price. On the due date he can deliver the live hogs or close out position by offsetting or reverse trading.

## REVIEW QUESTIONS

1. Explain the term 'financial derivative'. What are its important features? Explain with suitable examples.
2. Explain the different types of financial derivatives along with their features in brief.
3. Bring out the historical development of financial derivatives.
4. "The changing nature of financial industry, especially reflected in developments in the financial derivatives market, provides considerable opportunities for risk sharing". What action can be taken to control or plan for these risks? Can value be produced through risk management strategies? Explain.
5. Distinguish between forward contracts and futures contracts with suitable examples.
6. Explain the merits and demerits of financial derivatives.
7. Explain the exchange traded derivatives and OTC derivatives with suitable examples. How are they different to each other?
8. What are warrants and convertible securities? Also explain the critiques of derivatives with suitable examples.
9. Explain the distinction between ETC and OTC derivatives with suitable examples.
10. Compare and contrast between forward, futures, options and swaps.
11. Write note on the commodity derivatives, weather derivatives, idea futures and credit derivatives with suitable examples.
12. "Options and futures are zero-sum games". Critically explain this statement.
13. Critically examine the different myths regarding the financial derivatives with examples.
14. "Last decade has witnessed a tremendous growth of derivatives market worldwide". Discuss the statement in the light of history of derivatives.
15. What advantages futures contract has over forward contract? Explain with suitable example.
16. What do you understand by the terms derivatives and financial derivatives? Discuss types of financial derivatives.
17. Bring out the important features of financial futures contracting.
18. Explain why a futures contract can be used for either speculation or hedging.
19. "Option is a right but not obligation for the buyer of options". Do you agree? Discuss the statement with special reference to types of options.
20. "Derivatives are considered as risk management tools used by organizations/investors/individuals". Comment upon the statement.
21. Write a detailed note on the uses of financial derivatives.
22. "The basic purpose of derivatives instruments is to provide commitments to prices for future dates for giving against adverse movement in future prices". Discuss and critically examine the statement?

# SUGGESTED READINGS

1. Kolb, Robert W., *Financial Derivatives*, John Wiley, New York, 2003.
2. Banks, Erik, *Exchange-Traded Derivatives*, Hoboken, N.J. Wiley, 2003.
3. Overhaus et al., *Equity Derivative: Theory and Applications*, Wiley, New York, 2002.
4. Hunt, P.J., Kennedy, J.E., and Net Library, *Financial Derivatives: Theory and Practice*, J. Wiley and Sons, USA, 2000.
5. Redhead, Keith, *Financial Derivatives: An Introduction to Futures, Forwards, Options and Swaps*, Pearson Education, New Delhi, 1997.
6. Somnathan, T.V., *Derivatives*, Tata McGraw-Hill, New Delhi, 2000.
7. Rene M. Stulz, *Risk Management & Derivatives*, Thomson South-Western, Indian Reprint, 2007.
8. Robert A. Strong *Derivatives* Thomson-South-Western, Indian Reprint, 2006.
9. David A. Dubofsky & Thomas W. Miller, JR., *Derivatives–Valuation & Risk Management*, Oxford University Press, Indian Reprint, 2011.
10. Bank for International Settlements (BIS), *OTC Derivative Statistics*, December 2014, Monetary & Economic Department, April 2015.
11. NSE Website data, Factsheet, 2015.

# Chapter 2

# Futures Market and Contracting

*After reading this chapter, students will be able to*

➤ Understand the concept of financial futures contracts.
➤ Know about the various types of futures contracts like interest rate futures, foreign currency futures, stock index futures, bond index futures, etc.
➤ Understand the various operators in futures markets like hedgers, speculators, spreaders, arbitrageurs, etc.
➤ Know the functions of futures market.
➤ Be aware about the growth of futures markets worldwide as well as in India.
➤ Gain theoretical knowledge of the futures price.
➤ Understand the mechanism of futures market trading.
➤ Know about the role and functions of clearinghouse, stock exchanges, etc.
➤ Be familiar with the concept of margins and their types like initial margin and maintenance margins, how do margins flow from investor or trader to clearinghouse.
➤ Understand how futures contracts are closed.

## 2.1 INTRODUCTION

In the last two decades, the futures markets have experienced a remarkable growth all over the world in size, trading volume and acceptance by the business community. New contracts with new products along with entirely new possibilities in the futures markets have become the reality now. Futures trading was started in the mid-western part of the USA during 1970s, but today it is traded throughout the world, and 24 hours a day. Most common underlying assets used in futures markets today are commodities, agricultural products, metals, energy products, weather, electricity, interest rates, foreign exchange, equities, stock index and so on. In fact, today the futures markets have become an integral part of the financial markets all over the world.

## 2.2  FINANCIAL FUTURES CONTRACTS

A *futures contract* is an agreement between a buyer and a seller where the seller agrees to deliver a specified quantity and grade of a particular asset at a predetermined time in futures at an agreed upon price through a designated market (exchange) under stringent financial safeguards. A futures contract, in other words, is an agreement to buy or sell a particular asset between the two parties in a specified future period at an agreed price through specified exchange. For example, the S&P CNX NIFTY futures are traded on National Stock Exchange (NSE). This provides them transparency, liquidity, anonymity of trades, and also eliminates the counter party risks due to the guarantee provided by National Securities Clearing Corporation Limited (NSCCL).

Bombay Stock Exchange (BSE) website defines futures contract: "Futures are exchange traded contracts to sell or buy financial instruments or physical commodities for future delivery at an agreed price. There is an agreement to buy or sell a specified quantity of financial instrument/commodity in a designated future month at a price agreed upon by the buyer and the seller. The contracts have certain standardized specifications."

The standardized items in any futures contract are:

- Quantity of the underlying asset
- Quality of the underlying asset (not required in financial futures)
- The date and month of delivery
- The units of price quotation (not the price itself) and minimum change in price (tick-size)

From the above, it is evident that a financial futures termed as a notional commitment to buy or sell a standard quantity of a financial instrument at a specified (predetermined) price on a specified future date. In futures contract, the specified or agreed price between the trading parties is called *future price*. Since these contracts are traded on specified exchanges, both the parties of the contract do not know each other. The exchange provides a mechanism (through, its clearing house) which gives confidence to the parties that the contract will be honoured on maturity. In the futures contract one party assumes long position who has agreed to buy the underlying asset on a future specified date for ascertain agreed price, whereas the other party takes the short position who has agreed to sell the same underlying assets on agreed terms. The long futures will be in profit if the current price of the underlying asset on the maturity date is higher than the agreed futures price. On the other hand, if the current price of the asset is less than the futures price on the maturity date, the short futures will be in profit. Important underlying assets in futures markets are found individual equity stock, stock index, foreign currency, commodities, gold, silver, bonds, debentures, etc. This market is rarely used for the exchange of financial instruments. In fact, financial futures markets are independent of the underlying assets. For example, currency futures contracts are different from the currencies themselves. No doubt, currency futures prices normally move in the direction of the related underlying currency prices changes, but sometimes this relationship may not exist.

Currently, all over the world, futures derivatives are traded in different forms at various exchanges. In India, futures contracts in equity stocks were started in 2000 both at NSE and BSE.

In general, financial futures are not different from commodity futures except of the underlying asset, for example, in commodity futures, particular commodity relating to food grains, metals, vegetables, etc. are traded, whereas in financial futures, various particular financial instruments like equity shares, debentures, bond, treasury securities, currencies, etc. are traded. There are now a large variety of financial futures contracts available at the various markets (centres) like Chicago, London, Tokyo and so on.

## 2.3 TYPES OF FINANCIAL FUTURES CONTRACTS

There are different types of contracts in financial futures which are traded in the various futures financial markets of the world. These contracts can be classified into various categories which are as under:

### 2.3.1 Interest Rate Futures

It is one of the important financial futures instruments in the world. Futures trading on interest bearing securities started only in 1975, but the growth in this market has been tremendous. Important interest-bearing securities are like treasury bills, notes, bonds, debentures, eurodollar deposits and municipal bonds. In this market, almost entire range of maturities bearing securities are traded. For example, three-month maturity instruments like treasury bills and eurodollar time deposits, including foreign debt instruments at Chicago Mercantile Exchange (CME), British Government Bonds at London International Financial Futures Exchange (LIFFE), Japanese Government Bonds at CBOT, etc. are traded. This market is also further categorized into short-term and long-term interest bearing instruments. A few important interest rate futures traded on various exchanges are: notional gilt-contracts, short-term deposit futures, Treasury bill futures, eurodollar futures, treasury bond futures and treasury notes futures.

### 2.3.2 Foreign Currencies Futures

These financial futures, as the name indicates, trade in the foreign currencies, is also known as exchange rate futures. Active futures trading in certain foreign currencies started in the early 1970s. Important currencies in which these futures contracts are made are US dollar, Pound Sterling, Yen, French Francs, Marks, Canadian dollar, etc. These contracts have a directly corresponding to spot market, known as interbank foreign exchange market, and also have a parallel interbank forward market. Normally, futures currency contracts are used for hedging purposes by the exporters, importers, bankers, financial institutions and large companies.

### 2.3.3 Stock Index Futures

These are another major group of futures contracts all over the world. These contracts are based on stock market indices. For example, in the US markets, there exist various such futures contracts based on different indices like Dow Jones Industrial Average, Standard and Poor's 500, New York Stock Exchange Index, Value Line Index, etc. Other important futures contracts in different countries are like in London market, based on the Financial Times—Stock Exchange 100 share Index, Japanese Nikkei Index on the Tokyo Futures Exchange and on the Singapore International Monetary Exchange (SIMEX) as well. Similarly, in September, 1990, Chicago Mercantile Exchange began trading based on Nikkei 225 Stock Index and Chicago Board of Trade launched futures contracts based on the TOPIX index of major firms traded on the Tokyo Stock Exchange.

One of the most striking features of these contracts is that they do not insist upon the actual delivery, only trader's obligation must be fulfilled by a reversing trade or settlement by cash payment at the end of trading. Stock Index futures contracts are mainly used for hedging and speculation purposes. These are commonly traded by mutual funds, pension funds, investment trusts, insurance companies, speculators, arbitrageurs and hedgers.

## 2.3.4   Bond Index Futures

Like stock index futures, these futures contracts are also based on particular bond indices, i.e., indices of bond prices. As we know that prices of debt instruments are inversely related to interest rates, so the bond index is also related inversely to them. The important example of such futures contracts based on bond index is the Municipal Bond Index futures based on US Municipal Bonds which is traded on Chicago Board of Trade (CBOT).

## 2.3.5   Cost of Living Index Futures

This is also known as inflation futures. These futures contracts are based on a specified cost of living index, for example, consumer price index, wholesale price index, etc. At International Monetary Market (IMM) in Chicago, such futures contracts based on American Consumer Price Index are traded. Since in the USA, the inflation rates in 1980s and 1990s were very low, hence, such contracts could not be popular in the futures market. Cost of living index futures can be used to hedge against unanticipated inflation which cannot be avoided. Hence, such futures contracts can be very useful to certain investors like provident funds, pension funds, mutual funds, large companies and governments.

## 2.4   EVOLUTION OF FUTURES MARKET

The history of established futures markets goes back to the 1800s, but until the early 1970s, all futures markets were referred to as commodities markets because the products traded were mainly related to agricultural products. However, later on, futures contracts on financial instruments quickly picked up all over the world. They now dominate trading activity, accounting for about 75 percent of all derivatives trading volume in the world.

The CME Group claims credit for the creation of financial futures with the launch of seven foreign currency futures contracts in 1972. According to the CME, these were introduced in response to the breakdown of the Bretton Woods Agreement, instability of the financial markets and large fluctuations in foreign exchange markets at the international level. Also, during the 1970s, the challenges of inflation and volatile interest rate fluctuations spawned the development of futures contracts tied to interest rates.

It was during the forex market turmoil leading up to the initial revision of the US dollar "gold peg" that Leo Melamed, Chairman Emeritus of CME, with the endorsement of Nobel Laureate economist Milton Friedman, championed the idea of foreign exchange futures contracts. On May 16, 1972, International Monetary Market (IMM) was opened for business, which is the first financial futures market launched by the CME.

In 1975, the Chicago Board of Trade (CBDT) launched its first financial futures contract on Government National Mortgage Association mortgage-backed certificates (GNMAs), and further in 1977, it introduced trading in US. Treasury Bonds futures and various other Treasury Futures products.

In 1981, the CME launched Eurodollar futures, which had an innovative feature that paved the way for even more growth in financial contracts to come. Eurodollar futures were the first futures contracts where delivery was not required of an underlying instrument, rather to be settled in cash. The cash-settlement innovation safeguarded their usefulness to hedgers and speculators and other market participants.

Not only this, the cash-delivery feature also helped for the creation of index futures. First came the Kansas City Board of Trade's launch of the Value Line Index in 1982, then the same year the CME launched the Standard & Poor's 500 Index contract. Further, London International Financial Futures Exchange (LIFFE) was established in this year.

In India the futures trading was initiated in the year 2000. The SEBI approved derivatives trading based on future contracts at National State Exchange (NSE) and Bombay Stock Exchange (BSE) in accordance with the rules/bye-laws of the concerned stock exchange. The development of financial derivatives is discussed in the forthcoming chapter on "Financial Derivatives Market in India".

## 2.5  OPERATORS/TRADERS IN FUTURES MARKET

Futures contracts are bought and sold by a large number of individuals, business organizations, governments and others for a variety of purposes. The traders in the futures market can be categorized on the basis of the purposes for which they deal in this market. Usually financial derivatives attract following types of traders which are discussed here as under:

**Hedgers:**  In simple term, a hedge is a position taken in futures or other markets for the purpose of reducing exposure to one or more types of risk. A person who undertakes such position is called *hedger*. In other words, a hedger uses futures markets to reduce risk caused by the movements in prices of securities, commodities, exchange rates, interest rates, indices, etc. As such, a hedger reduces his or her risk by taking an opposite position in the market to which he or she is exposed to. By taking an opposite position to a perceived risk is called *hedging strategy in futures markets*. The essence of hedging strategy is the adoption of a futures position that, on an average, generates profits when the market value of the commitment is higher than the expected value. For example, a treasurer of a company knows the foreign currency amounts to be received at certain futures time may hedge the foreign exchange risk by taking a short position (selling the foreign currency at a particular rate) in the futures markets. Similarly, he can take a long position (buying the foreign currency at a particular rate) in case of futures foreign exchange payments at a specified futures date.

The hedging strategy can be undertaken in all the markets like futures, forwards, options, swap, etc. but their *modus operandi* will be different. Forward agreements are designed to offset risk by fixing the price that the hedger will pay or receive for the underlying asset. In case of option strategy, it provides insurance and protects the investor against adverse price movements. Similarly, in the futures market, the investors may be benefited from favourable price movements.

### Long hedging using futures

**EXAMPLE:**  Silver is an essential input in the production of most types of photographic films and papers and the price of silver is quite volatile. For a manufacturer XYZ Ltd., there is considerable risk, because profit can be dramatically affected by fluctuations in the price of silver. Suppose XYZ Ltd. need 100 kg of silver in two months and prices of silver on May 10, 2015 are:

| Contract | Price (₹) |
|----------|-----------|
| Spot | 33,000.00 |
| July | 34,000.00 |
| September | 35,000.00 |

Fearing the prices of silver may rise unexpectedly, XYZ Ltd. enters into a futures contract at ₹34,000 in July delivery. He, therefore, locked into futures price today and long hedge in silver will be as shown in Table 2.1.

**TABLE 2.1**   A Long Hedge in Silver Futures

| Date | Cash market | Futures market |
|------|-------------|----------------|
| May 10, 2015 | Anticipates the need for 100 kg of silver in two-month and pay ₹34,000 per kg or total amount to ₹34,00,000. | Buys four 100 kg of silver in July futures contract at ₹34,000.00 per kg |
| July 10, 2015 | The spot price of silver assume now ₹35,000 and XYZ Ltd. have to pay and spot prices are equal and four contracts are ₹35,00,000.00 | Because futures contract, at maturity, the futures sold at ₹35,000.00 per kg. |
| Profit/Loss | Loss ₹1,00,000.00 | Futures profit ₹1,00,000.00 |

**Net wealth change = 0**

Since on expiration date spot price and futures price converge, XYZ Ltd. has hedged its position by entering into futures contract.

**Speculators:**   A *speculator* may be defined as an investor who is willing to take a risk by taking futures position with the expectation to earn profits. The speculator forecasts the future economic conditions and decides which position (long or short) to be taken that will yield a profit if the forecast is realized. For example, suppose a speculator has forecasted that the price of ICICI Bank share is ₹350 per share after one month. If the current price of ICICI Bank share is ₹320 per share, he can take long position in ICICI Bank share and expects a profit of ₹30 per share. The expected profit is associated with risk because the ICICI Bank share after one month may fall to ₹300, and he may lose ₹20 per share.

Speculators usually trade in the futures markets to earn profit on the basis of difference in spot and futures prices of the underlying assets. Hedgers use the futures markets for avoiding exposure to adverse movements in the price of an asset, whereas the speculators wish to take position in the market based upon such movements in the price of that asset. It is pertinent to mention here that there is difference in speculating trading between spot market and forward market. In spot market a speculator has to make an initial cash payment equal to the total value of the asset purchased, whereas no initial cash payment except the margin money, if any, to enter into forward market. Therefore, speculative trading provide the investor with a much higher level of leverage than speculating using spot markets. That is why, futures markets being highly leveraged market, minimums are set to ensure that the speculator can afford any potential losses.

Speculators can be classified into different categories. For example, a speculator who uses fundamental analysis of economic conditions of the market is known as a *fundamental analyst*, whereas the one who uses to predict futures prices on the basis of past movements in the prices of the asset is known as a *technical analyst*. A speculator who owns a seat on a particular exchange and trades in his own name is called a *local speculator*. These, local speculators can further be classified into three categories, namely, scalpers, pit traders and floor traders. *Scalpers* usually try to make profits from holding positions for short period of time. They bridge the gap between outside orders by filling orders that come into the brokers in return for slight price concessions. *Pit speculators* like scalpers take bigger positions and hold them longer. They usually do not move quickly by changing positions overnights. They most likely use outside news. *Floor traders* usually consider inter commodity price relationship. They are full members and often watch outside news carefully and can hold positions both short and long.

**Arbitrageurs:** Arbitrageurs are another important group of participants in futures markets. An *arbitrageur* is a trader who attempts to make profits by locking in a riskless trading by simultaneously entering into transactions in two or more markets. In other words, an arbitrageur tries to earn riskless profits from discrepancies between futures and spot prices and among different futures prices. For example, suppose that for December,2015, the ICICI Bank share is quoted at ₹340 on December 1, 2015 in futures market, Current spot rate on December 1, 2015 of ICICI Bank share is ₹330. In this situation, the arbitrageur could purchase the ICICI Bank share in cash market and go short in futures market that expires on December 31, 2015. He will make profit of ₹10 per share in the absence of transaction costs.

The arbitrage opportunities available in the different markets usually do not last long because of heavy transactions by the arbitrageurs where such opportunity arises. Thus, arbitrage keeps the futures and cash prices in line with one another. This relationship is also expressed by the simple cost of carry pricing which shows that fair futures prices, is the set of buying the cash asset now and financing the same till delivery in futures market. It is generalized that the active trading of arbitrageurs will leave small arbitrage opportunities in the financial markets. In brief, arbitrage trading helps to make market liquid, ensures accurate pricing and enhances price stability. It involves making profits from relative mispricing.

**Spreaders:** Spreading is a specific trading activity in which offsetting futures position is involved by creating almost net position. So, the spreaders believe in lower expected return but at the less risk. For a successful trading in spreading, the spreaders must forecast the relevant factors which affect the changes in the spreads. Interest rate behaviour is an important factor which causes changes in the spreads. In a profitable spread position, normally, there is a large gain on one side of the spread in comparison to the loss on the other side of the spread. In this way, a spread reduces the risk even if the forecast is incorrect. On the other hand, the pure speculators would make money by taking only the profitable side of the market but at very high risk.

## 2.6 FUNCTIONS OF FUTURES MARKET

Apart from the various features of different futures contracts and trading, futures markets play a significant role in managing the financial risk of the corporate business world. Recently, financial executives and treasurers are frequently using the various tools available to control their corporate's risks and exposures. Financial derivatives instruments, in this respect, have been very useful, popular and successful innovations in capital markets all over the world. Recently, it is noted that financial futures markets have been actively functioning in both developed as well as developing countries.

Futures markets like any other market or industry serve some social purposes. In the past section of this chapter, we have seen that futures markets have been recognized as meeting the needs of some important users like hedgers, speculators, arbitrageurs, spreaders, etc. In the light of those, we will discuss the uses of financial futures market in the society as a whole in the context of risk transference, price stabilization, price discovery, price registration, etc.

**Hedging:** The primary function of the futures market is the hedging function which is also known as price insurance, risk shifting or risk transference function. Futures markets provide a vehicle through which the traders or participants can hedge their risks or protect themselves from the adverse price movements in the underlying assets in which they deal. For example, An Indian exporter has to receive 10 million US dollar after two months from today against the sales in the USA. Assume current exchange rate of US dollar is ₹65 in the market. The exporter is expecting that dollar may depreciate against rupee in future. To hedge this, he may use the futures market. Assume that two-month futures rate of US dollar is quoted at ₹64.90. In this way the exporter can sell the 10 million dollar @64.90 in futures market and cover the risk of fall in US dollar for just 10 paisa per dollar.

Not only this, the futures market also serves as a substitute for a cash market sale. In this example, we see that the exporter (trader) sells US Dollar in the futures market which is a temporary substitute of a futures anticipated cash market transaction. In this way, the futures market also serves as a substitute futures anticipated cash market transactions.

Such above-said examples can be quoted for futures financial markets like interest rate futures contracts which protect the financial institutions such as commercial banks, insurance companies, mutual funds, pension funds, etc. from the adverse changes in the values of their assets and liabilities due to interest rates movements. Similarly, currency futures contract protect the exporters, importers and others who deal in the foreign exchange market, against exchange rate fluctuations. Stock index futures contracts protect the other investors from the adverse changes in portfolio value.

In brief, futures markets hedging activities are very much useful for society since they control, shift, avoid, reduce, eliminate and manage efficiently various types of risks. Further, derivatives enable the investors to modify suitably the risk characteristics of their portfolios, or to shift risk on to those who are willing to assume it for higher profits. In the absence of futures markets, the cost of risk to economy could be higher and might be worse off.

**Price discovery:** Another important use of futures market is the price discovery which is the revealing of information about futures cash market prices through the futures market. As we know that in futures market contract, a trader agrees to receive or deliver a given commodity or asset at a certain futures time for a price which is determined now. It means that the futures market creates a relationship between the futures price and the price that people expect to prevail at the delivery date. In the words of M.J. Powers and D. Vogel, as stated in their book entitled "Inside the Financial Futures Market", futures markets provide a mechanism by which diverse and scattered opinions of the futures are coalesced into one readily discernible number which provides a consensus of knowledgeable thinking. It is evident from this statement that futures prices provide an expression consensus of the today's expectations about a specified future time. If these expectations are properly published then they also perform an information or publicity function for the users and the society. By using the information about the futures prices today, the different traders/observers in the market can estimate the expected spot price in the future time of a given asset. In this way, a user of the futures prices can make consumption or investment decisions more wisely.

Further, price discovery function of the futures market also leads to the intertemporal inventory allocation function. According to this, the traders can compare the spot and futures prices and will be able to decide the optimum allocation of their quantity of underlying asset between the immediate sale and futures sale. The uses of price discovery function can be explained by an example, supposing, a mine operator is trying to take a decision whether to reopen a marginally profitable gold mine or not. If, we assume that the gold ore in the mine is not of the best quality and so the yield from the mine will be relatively low, the decision will depend upon the cost incurred on mined and refined of gold and the price of the gold to be obtained in futures. Hence, the crucial element in this decision is the futures price of gold. The miner can analyze the gold prices quoted in the futures market today for determining the estimate of the futures price of the gold at a specified futures period. In this situation, the miner has used the futures market as a vehicle of price discovery.

It is evident from the above that price discovery function of futures market is very much useful for producers, farmers, cattle ranchers, wholesalers, economic agents, etc. who can use futures market estimates information of futures cash prices to guide their production or consumption decisions.

**Financing function:**   Another important function of a futures market is to raise finance against the stock of assets or commodities. Since futures contracts are standardized contracts, they make it easier for the lenders about the assurance of quantity, quality and liquidity of the underlying asset. Though this function is very much familiar in the spot market, but it is also unique to futures markets. The reason being the lenders are often more interested to finance hedged asset stock rather than un-hedged stock because the hedged asset stock are protected against the risk of loss of value.

**Liquidity function:**   As we see that the main function of the futures market deals with such transactions which are matured in the future period, they are operated on the basis of margins which are determined on the basis of rides involved in the contract. Under this, the buyer and the seller have to deposit only a fraction of the contract value, say 5 percent or 10 percent, known as margins. It means that the traders in the futures market can do the business a much larger volume of contracts than in a spot market, and thus, makes market more liquid. That is why the volume of the futures markets is much larger in comparison to the spot markets. This is also known as *gearing* or *leverage factor*. It means that a trader in the futures markets can gear up his capital 10 times and 20 times, if the margin/deposit is 10 percent and 5 percent, respectively, resulting in his profit or loss, as a proportion of his capital is 10 times or 20 times magnified. Gearing is the British term and in American parlance it is known as leverage. This is explained by the following example:

**EXAMPLE:**   A speculator estimates a price increase in the silver futures market from the current futures price of ₹35,000 per kg. The market lot being 10 kg, he buys one lot of futures silver for ₹3,50,000 (35,000 × 10). Assuming the 10 percent margin, the speculator is to deposit only ₹35,000. Now, supposing that a 10 percent increase occurs in the price of silver to ₹3,85,000 per kg. The value of transaction will also increase, i.e., ₹3,85,000 and hence, incurring profit of ₹35,000 (3,85,000 – 3,50,000) on this transaction. In other words, the speculator earns in this transaction ₹35,000 on the investment of ₹35,000, being 100 percent profit on investment, and vice-versa.

From the above example, it is evident that futures markets operations are highly risky due to gearing effect. So, they are more attractive for the speculators.

**Price stabilization function:**   Another important function of a futures market is to keep a stabilizing influence on spot prices by reducing the amplitude of short term of fluctuations. In other words, futures market reduces both the heights of the peaks and the depth of the troughs. The major causative factors responsible for such price stabilizing influence are speculation, price discovery, tendency to panic, etc. A detailed discussion on price stabilization function of futures market will be made in the forthcoming chapters.

**Disseminating information:**   Apart from the aforementioned functions of the futures markets like risk-transference (hedging), price discovery, price stabilization, liquidity, and financing, this market is very much useful to the economy too. Futures markets disseminate information quickly, effectively and inexpensively, and, as a result, reducing the monopolistic tendency in the market. Further, such information disseminating service enables the society to discover or form suitable true/correct/equilibrium prices. They serve as barometers of futures in price resulting in the determination of correct prices on spot markets now and in futures. They provide for centralized trading where information about fundamental supply and demand conditions are efficiently assimilated and acted on.

The financial futures markets have generated employment opportunities by creating a significant number of jobs and attracted a considerable volume of transactions from non-residents. Indirectly, it is another way of generating foreign exchange for the countries. Further the futures markets act as 'starter form of investment resulting in a wider participation in the securities markets. They attract young investors and act as catalysts to the growth of securities markets. They enable individuals and managers of funds to devise or design strategies for proper assets allocation, yield enhancements and reducing risks. For example, futures markets quotations are also useful to other sectors of society, besides speculators and hedgers. Which goods or commodities are to be produced and in which financial assets the investment is to be made, such decisions are assisted by the futures market prices. Further, some individuals may not engage in certain clearly beneficial forms of economic activity if they were forced to bear all of the risks of that activity themselves. Futures markets enable the society to reach the position of *pareto optimality* by developing *complete markets*. It means that in the financial markets, no other set of securities can make some investors better off without making at least one other investor worse off. In other words, the securities market is said to be complete if the patterns of returns of all additional securities are spanned by the already existing securities or if it provides company securities that no additional security can be created whose returns a portfolio of existing securities cannot duplicate. In brief, the futures markets enhance economic activities in the society in general, resulting in growth of economic development of the country.

## 2.7  GROWTH OF THE FUTURES MARKETS

Financial futures markets were originally established in the United States in 1970s, however, the same was not confined to the United States only. During 1980s, seeing the potential in these markets, some other developed countries like Japan, United Kingdom (UK), France, etc. had quickly introduced the trading in such derivatives instruments, and soon the volume of trading in these countries was so large that it has left behind the founder country, i.e., the USA. Evaluating the growth of futures markets at the world level, it is observed that in 1985, futures exchanges accounted for 83 percent of futures trading in the entire world, and rest through over-the-counter (OTC) markets. However, the same decreased to 61 percent in 1990, a loss of in market share of 22 percent.

It is evident from Table 2.2 that the futures derivatives are having approximately 56 percent of the total volume of the trades during this period, whereas approximately 44 percent shows the share of the options derivatives. Further the volume of options has increased by 3.1 percent in 2014 in comparison to the futures which have grown by only 0.3 percent of the total.

Among the categories of global futures and options, Individual Equity and Equity Index combined are possessing around 57 percent of the total trading volume followed by Interest derivatives and Currency derivatives keeping around 15 percent and 10 percent, respectively, in 2014. Rest is occupied by the commodity derivatives which is around 18 percent of the total trades. From Region-wise analysis of futures and options, it is observed that North America is keeping highest share around 38 percent of the total volume, followed by approx. 33 percent of Asia region.

**TABLE 2.2**   Volume of Global Futures and Options

| Category-wise volume of Global Futures and Options combined | | | | | |
|---|---|---|---|---|---|
| **Category** | **Jan.–Dec. 2013** | **Jan.–Dec. 2014** | **Annual % change** | **% of total 2013** | **% of total 2014** |
| Individual Equity | 6390404778 | 6493177097 | 1.60 | 29.65 | 29.69 |
| Equity Index | 5381657190 | 5827913937 | 8.30 | 24.97 | 26.65 |
| Interest | 3330904991 | 3268154625 | –1.90 | 15.46 | 14.95 |
| Currency | 2496423691 | 2119023131 | –15.10 | 11.58 | 9.69 |
| Agriculture | 1209776849 | 1400153550 | 15.70 | 5.61 | 6.40 |
| Energy | 1315276356 | 1160317682 | –11.80 | 6.10 | 5.31 |
| Non-precious Metals | 646349077 | 872601162 | 35.00 | 3.00 | 3.99 |
| Precious Metals | 433546140 | 370872772 | –14.50 | 2.01 | 1.70 |
| Other | 347412764 | 355224591 | 2.20 | 1.61 | 1.62 |
| **Total** | **21551751836** | **21867438547** | **1.50** | **100** | **100** |
| **Volume of Global Futures and Options combined** | | | | | |
| Futures | 12134552693 | 12165484775 | 0.30 | 56.30 | 55.63 |
| Options | 9417199143 | 9707129486 | 3.10 | 43.70 | 44.39 |
| **Total** | **21551751836** | **21867438547** | **1.50** | **100** | **100** |
| **Region volume of Global Futures and Options combined** | | | | | |
| North America | 7830496564 | 8212951665 | 4.90 | 36.33 | 37.56 |
| Asia | 7301581335 | 7252376703 | –0.70 | 33.88 | 33.17 |
| Europe | 4359086394 | 4450348259 | 2.10 | 20.23 | 20.35 |
| Latin America | 1683182520 | 1514203690 | –10.00 | 7.81 | 6.92 |
| Other | 377405023 | 437558230 | 15.90 | 1.75 | 2.00 |
| **Total** | **21551751836** | **21867438547** | **1.50%** | **100** | **100** |

*Note:* Based on the number of contracts traded and/or cleared at 75 exchanges worldwide
(*Source:* www.fia.org)

From the inception of futures trading on various exchanges, the system of open outcry was followed, though this system continues to dominate for many years, but now automated trading system (electronic trading system) is followed which has virtually changed the entire face of the futures trading all over the world. In 1987, the CME developed its GLOBEX system—an electronic order entry and matching system for trading CME futures, and futures from other participating exchanges during hours when the local open-entry pits were closed. In the beginning, a few other exchanges like CBOT, MATIF, etc. also joined with GLOBEX. However, the CBOT dropped out in 1994 and LIFFE, along with some other exchanges have not allowed their contracts to trade on GLOBEX. Currently the system has evolved into the 'GLOBEX Alliance' linking the five exchanges, i.e., CME, SGX-DT, Brazil's BM&F, Paris Bourse, and the Montreal Exchange. This is the system which permits cross exchange trading privileges and cross-margining of positions to the members.

The internationalization of futures markets reflects elements of both competition and cooperation. While the US futures exchanges have dominated trading volume and product innovation for many years, but outside the USA also this market developed rapidly. For example, in 1993, the volume of futures contracts traded on Non-US exchanges surpassed the US exchanges trading volume for the first time. In 1999, the US futures exchanges accounted for only 38.2 percent of the total 1.25 billion futures contracts traded that year. Not only this, the CBOT and CME were the number one and two exchanges in the world overtaken by EUREX. Table 2.4 shows the top 10 futures exchanges in the world ranked on the basis of trading volume.

Table 2.3 presents the world's leading top 20 derivative exchanges based on the number of contracts traded and/or cleared for the year 2014. Among these CME group, incorporating Chicago Mercantile exchange, Chicago Board of Trade and New York Mercantile Exchange found to be the largest derivatives exchanges in 2014 with approx. 3.44 billion of contracts traded, followed by Intercontinental Exchange which is having approx. 2.276 billion contracts. Indian exchanges NSE and BSE are keeping 4 and 11 rank among the top 20 exchanges of the world. The volume of contracts on BSE significantly rises to 184.80 percent, whereas NSE has shown negative growth 11.6 percent in the year 2014. Further out of 20 top exchanges, 12 exchanges has shown positive growth and 8 exchanges with negative growth in 2014.

**TABLE 2.3** Largest Derivatives Exchange worldwide

| Rank | Exchange | Jan.–Dec. 2013 Volume | Jan.–Dec. 2014 Volume | Annual % change | % of total 2013 | % of total 2014 |
|------|----------|----------------------|----------------------|-----------------|-----------------|-----------------|
| 1 | CME Group | 3161476638 | 3442766942 | 8.90 | 14.67 | 15.74 |
| 2 | Intercontinental Exchange | 2558489589 | 2276171019 | −11.00 | 11.87 | 10.41 |
| 3 | Eurex | 2190727275 | 2097974756 | −4.20 | 10.16 | 9.59 |
| 4 | National Stock Exchange of India | 2127151585 | 1880362513 | −11.60 | 9.87 | 8.60 |
| 5 | BM & FBovespa | 1603706918 | 1417925815 | −11.60 | 7.44 | 6.48 |
| 6 | Moscow Exchange | 1134477258 | 1413222196 | 24.60 | 5.26 | 6.46 |
| 7 | CBOE Holdings | 1187642669 | 1325391523 | 11.60 | 5.51 | 6.06 |
| 8 | Nasdaq OMX | 1142955206 | 1127130071 | −1.40 | 5.30 | 5.15 |
| 9 | Shanghai Futures Exchange | 642473980 | 842294223 | 31.10 | 2.98 | 3.85 |
| 10 | Dalian Commodity Exchange | 700500777 | 769637041 | 9.90 | 3.25 | 3.52 |
| 11 | BSE | 254845929 | 725841680 | 184.80 | 1.18 | 3.32 |
| 12 | Korea Exchange | 820664621 | 677789082 | −17.40 | 3.81 | 3.10 |
| 13 | Zhengzhou Commodity Exchange | 525299023 | 676343283 | 28.80 | 2.44 | 3.09 |
| 14 | Hong Kong Exchanges & Clearing | 301128507 | 319577388 | 6.10 | 1.40 | 1.46 |
| 15 | Japan Exchange | 366234062 | 309732384 | −15.40 | 1.70 | 1.42 |
| 16 | JSE Securities Exchange | 254514072 | 304003143 | 19.40 | 1.18 | 1.39 |
| 17 | ASX | 261790908 | 244070858 | −6.80 | 1.21 | 1.12 |
| 18 | China Financial Futures Exchange | 193549311 | 217581145 | 12.40 | 0.90 | 1.00 |
| 19 | Taiwan Futures Exchange | 153225238 | 202227653 | 32.00 | 0.71 | 0.92 |
| 20 | BATS Exchange | 151814889 | 201985667 | 33.00 | 0.70 | 0.92 |
| | **Total of 75 Exchanges all world** | **21551751836** | **21867438547** | | | |

*Note:* Based on the number of contracts traded

(*Source:* www.fia.org, www.statistia.com)

A few exchanges like Shanghai Futures Exchange, Taiwan Futures Exchange, Bats Exchange, Zhengzhou Commodity Exchange, etc. have shown growth of around 30 percent in the year 2014. On evaluating the individual exchange share in % (percent) of total volume (75 future exchanges), CME group is having approx. 15.8 percent followed by 10.41 percent Intercontinental Exchange. NSE and BSE both exchanges are having 8.6 percent and 3.52 percent share of the total volume of the trades. Around 76 percent of the total volume is traded on the top 10 exchanges and around 94 percent of these 20 top exchanges shown in Table 2.3.

Table 2.4. depicts the list of Rank-wise derivatives exchange on the basis of market capitalisation as on January 2016. It is observed that New York Stock Exchange is having Ist rank, being top in the list with 29.35 percent, followed by NASDAQ with 10.43 percent of the total capital market capitalization. Indian Exchanges NSE and BSE are having 11th and 12th rank, respectively, keeping 5.08 percent of total market capitalisation by them. Top exchanges, namely New York Stock Exchange, NASDAQ, London Stock Exchange Group are having about 50 percent total market capitalization and rest by all the exchanges of the world.

**TABLE 2.4**  Rank-wise Global Derivatives Exchange

| Rank | Exchange | Head-quarters | Market cap (USD bn) | Monthly trade volume (USD bn) | % of total | % of total |
|------|----------|---------------|--------------------|-------------------------------|-----------|-----------|
| 1. | New York Stock Exchange | New York | 19,223 | 1,520 | 29.35 | 22.92 |
| 2. | NASDAQ | New York | 6,831 | 1,183 | 10.43 | 17.84 |
| 3. | London Stock Exchange Group | London | 6,187 | 165 | 9.45 | 2.49 |
| 4. | Japan Exchange Group–Tokyo | Tokyo | 4,485 | 402 | 6.85 | 6.06 |
| 5. | Shanghai Stock Exchange | Shanghai | 3,986 | 1,278 | 6.09 | 19.27 |
| 6. | Hong Kong Stock Exchange | Hong Kong | 3,325 | 155 | 5.08 | 2.34 |
| 7. | Euronext | Paris | 3,321 | 184 | 5.07 | 2.77 |
| 8. | Shenzhen Stock Exchange | Shenzhen | 2,285 | 800 | 3.49 | 12.06 |
| 9. | TMX Group | Toronto | 1,939 | 120 | 2.96 | 1.81 |
| 10. | Deutsche Borse | Frankfurt | 1,762 | 142 | 2.69 | 2.14 |
| 11. | Bombay Stock Exchange | Mumbai | 1,682 | 11.8 | 2.57 | 0.18 |
| 12. | National Stock Exchange of India | Mumbai | 1,642 | 62.2 | 2.51 | 0.94 |
| 13. | SIX Swiss Exchange | Zurich | 1,516 | 126 | 2.31 | 1.90 |
| 14. | Australian Securities Exchange | Sydney | 1,272 | 55.8 | 1.94 | 0.84 |
| 15. | Korea Exchange | Seoul | 1,251 | 136 | 1.91 | 2.05 |
| 16. | OMX Nordic Exchange | Stockholm | 1,212 | 63.2 | 1.85 | 0.95 |
| 17. | JSE Limited | Johannesburg | 951 | 27.6 | 1.45 | 0.42 |
| 18. | BME Spanish Exchanges | Madrid | 942 | 94 | 1.44 | 1.42 |
| 19. | Taiwan Stock Exchange | Taipei | 861 | 54.3 | 1.31 | 0.82 |
| 20. | BM & F Bovespa | Sao Paulo | 824 | 51.1 | 1.26 | 0.77 |
|  |  |  | 65,497 | 6,631 | 100 | 100 |

(*Source:* www.fia.org.www.statistia.com

The competition in futures markets in the European exchanges also developed rapidly. LIFFE which had been the number one exchange in Europe for many years was overtaken by the EUREX in the year 1999. The basic reason for this success was the introduction of the Euro-Bond contract in 1997 with electronic trading, rather than the open cry system used at the LIFFE. In 1999, more than 121 million Euro-Bond futures contracts were traded on EUREX. Further this exchange introduced very successful contracts on short-term and medium-term German securities.

It has been noted later that, in some cases, competition among the exchanges led to the cooperation between them. For example, Non-US futures exchanges have started trading on Eurodollar futures contract like CME, LIFFE and SGX-DT (Singapore Derivatives Trading Ltd.; formerly known as SIMEX). In the year 1984, the CME and SIMEX established their so-called Mutual Offset System (MOS) for the CME's Eurodollar futures contracts. In March 1996, they extended their MOS agreement with new specification. This time the CME adopted the trading of the SIMEX Euro-yen contract. In April 1996, the CME entered into another agreement to permit trading in LIFFE and MATIF interest rate futures contracts on the CME. In this way, the trading volume of the futures markets has grown in multiples.

Presently, there are two important ways of trading in futures contracts like recognized exchanges and Over-The-Counter (OTC) markets. OTC market plays a significant role in derivative trading. Table 2.5 depicts the volume of trades in OTC segment of derivatives market in US dollar billions for the years December 2012 to December 2014. There is downward trend in total contracts volume which decreased from \$7,10,633 billion of 2013 to \$630149 billion in 2014, falling by 11.33 percent. On Product-wise distribution of the total volume of trade, it is observed that interest rate derivative contracts occupy a significant portion, i.e., \$5,05,454 billion of the total trade \$6,30,149 billion, being 80.21 percent, further, interest rate swap is having 75.38 percent of the total interest rate derivative segment, and 60.47 percent of total volume of trade of derivatives. It means that the interest rate swaps contracts are dominating this OTC trades. The total interest rate contracts have decreased in the year 2014 from \$5,84,799 to \$5,05,584 billion, however, the foreign exchange derivative contracts in OTC segment has shown rising trend in the year 2014. It has increased from \$70,533 billion in 2013 to \$75,879 billion in 2014, a rise of 7.58 percent approx.

Equity-linked derivative contracts have shown a rising trend continuously from December 2012 to December 2014, i.e., \$6,251 billion to \$7,940 billion, an increase of 27 percent in two years. However, there is significant fall in credit derivative instrument (CDS) which was \$25,068 billion in 2012 and declined to \$16,399 billion in 2014 being 34.60 percent, highest fall among all the instruments of the OTC derivatives.

The data are derived from the BIS regular OTC derivatives statistics and cover the notional amounts and gross market values outstanding of the worldwide consolidated OTC derivatives exposure of major banks and dealers in the G10 countries plus Australia and Spain. Figures are adjusted for double-counting and cover foreign exchange, interest rate (single currency contracts only), equity, commodity and credit derivatives (CDS). The notional amount, which is generally used as a reference to calculate cash flows under individual contracts, provides a comparison of market size between related cash and derivatives markets. Gross market value is defined as the sum (in absolute terms) of the positive market value of all reporters' contracts and the negative market value of their contracts with non-reporting counterparties. It also measures the replacement cost of all outstanding contracts had they been settled in the reporting period.

**TABLE 2.5** Global OTC Derivatives Amount and Gross Market Value of Outstanding Contracts

| Risk category/ Instrument | Amounts outstanding of over-the-counter (OTC) derivatives By risk category and instrument (In billions of US Dollars) | | | | | | | | | |
|---|---|---|---|---|---|---|---|---|---|---|
| | Notional amounts outstanding 2.5 | | | | | Gross market values | | | | |
| | Dec. 2012 | Jun. 2013 | Dec. 2013 | Jun. 2014 | Dec. 2014 | Dec. 2012 | Jun. 2013 | Dec. 2013 | Jun. 2014 | Dec. 2014 |
| Total contracts | 6,35,685 | 6,96,408 | 7,10,633 | 6,91,640 | 6,30,149 | 24,953 | 20,245 | 18,825 | 17,438 | 20,878 |
| Foreign exchange contracts | 67,358 | 73,121 | 70,553 | 74,782 | 75,879 | 2,313 | 2,427 | 2,284 | 1,724 | 2,944 |
| Forwards and forex swaps | 31,718 | 34,421 | 33,218 | 35,190 | 37,076 | 806 | 957 | 824 | 572 | 1,205 |
| Currency swaps | 25,420 | 24,654 | 25,448 | 26,141 | 24,204 | 1,259 | 1,131 | 1,186 | 939 | 1,351 |
| Options | 10,220 | 14,046 | 11,886 | 13,451 | 14,600 | 249 | 339 | 273 | 213 | 389 |
| Interest rate contracts | 4,92,605 | 5,64,673 | 5,84,799 | 5,63,290 | 5,05,454 | 19,038 | 15,238 | 14,200 | 13,461 | 15,608 |
| Forward rate agreements | 71,960 | 86,892 | 78,810 | 92,575 | 80,836 | 48 | 168 | 108 | 126 | 145 |
| Interest rate swaps | 3,72,293 | 4,28,385 | 4,56,725 | 4,21,273 | 3,81,028 | 17,285 | 13,745 | 12,919 | 12,042 | 13,946 |
| Options | 48,351 | 49,396 | 49,264 | 49,442 | 43,591 | 1,706 | 1,325 | 1,174 | 1,292 | 1,517 |
| Equity-linked contracts | 6,251 | 6,821 | 6,560 | 7,084 | 7,940 | 600 | 692 | 700 | 678 | 612 |
| Forwards and swaps | 2,045 | 2,321 | 2,277 | 2,505 | 2,495 | 157 | 206 | 202 | 199 | 177 |
| Options | 4,207 | 4,501 | 4,284 | 4,579 | 5,445 | 443 | 486 | 498 | 479 | 435 |
| Commodity contracts | 2,587 | 2,458 | 2,204 | 2,206 | 1,868 | 347 | 384 | 264 | 269 | 317 |
| Gold | 486 | 461 | 341 | 319 | 300 | 42 | 80 | 47 | 32 | 32 |
| Other commodities | 2,101 | 1,997 | 1,863 | 1,887 | 1,568 | 304 | 304 | 217 | 237 | 285 |
| Forwards and swaps | 1,363 | 1,327 | 1,260 | 1,283 | 1,053 | | | | | |
| Options | 739 | 670 | 603 | 604 | 515 | | | | | |
| Credit default swaps | 25,068 | 24,349 | 21,020 | 19,462 | 16,399 | 848 | 725 | 653 | 635 | 593 |
| Single-name instruments | 14,309 | 13,135 | 11,324 | 10,845 | 9,041 | 527 | 430 | 369 | 368 | 366 |
| Multi-name instruments | 10,760 | 11,214 | 9,696 | 8,617 | 7,358 | 321 | 295 | 284 | 266 | 227 |
| of which index products | 9,656 | 10,163 | 8,746 | 7,939 | 6,747 | | | | | |
| Unallocated | 41,815 | 24,986 | 25,496 | 24,815 | 22,609 | 1,808 | 779 | 724 | 671 | 803 |
| Memorandum item: Gross Credit Exposure | | | | | | 3,612 | 3,784 | 3,033 | 2,826 | 3,356 |

*Source: Bank for International Settlements, OTC Derivatives Statistics, April, 2015*

## 2.8 THEORETICAL DESCRIPTION OF FUTURE PRICE

The futures price is the agreed price of the asset between the contracting parties at the specified maturity date. Normally, there exists a deterministic relationship between the spot price and futures price of the underlying asset. Since futures prices are related with the spot price, a theoretical spot futures relationship can be developed to determine the futures prices. Certain factors like risk-free rate, dividend yield, time to maturity, future expectation, risk factor, etc. are usually considered in this respect.

In a future contract, the buyer (long position) believes that the price of the asset in future will increase, and hence he will cash profit. Similarly, the seller (short position) thinks that the future price of the asset will decline, and will be in profit. Theoretically, this position in the futures market can be mentioned as follows:

Profit in the long futures contract = $S_T - F_t$

Profit in the Short futures contract = $F_t - ST$

Where,   $S_t$:  Spot or current price of the underlying asset.

$\quad\quad$ $F_T$:  Future price of the underlying asset at the maturity, also called delivery price.

$\quad\quad$ t:  Time at the making of a futures contract (present)

$\quad\quad$ T:  Time at the executing of a futures contract (maturity)

$\quad\quad$ $S_T$:  The spot market price of the asset at the maturity/execution.

$\quad\quad$ $F_t$:  Futures market price of the asset at the beginning.

In the beginning the $F_T$ and $F_t$ will be equal. However, as the time passes, the futures price ($F_t$) may be changing as per market conditions. However, $F_t$ will remain constant till maturity.

**EXAMPLE**:   Suppose the spot price of SBI share in the stock market on August 5, 2015 is ₹260 and futures price quoted for August, 2015 maturing on August 27, 2015 is ₹270. Further, assume if the current market price of the SBI on maturity is ₹280, then the buyer of the futures contract will earn profit of ₹10 = (₹280 – ₹270).

## 2.9   FUTURES MARKET TRADING MECHANISM

Futures contract, as stated in past, is an agreement between the two parties to buy or sell an asset at a certain futures time for a certain price. Futures contracts are traded on recognized stock exchanges. Since the value of a futures contract is derived from the value of the underlying asset, they are called *derivative instruments*. If the underlying assets are financial instruments, then these are called financial derivatives or financial futures contracts.

Futures trading refers to entering into contracts to buy or sell financial asset or commodities for futures delivery as settlement on standardized terms. In this section, we will discuss the general mechanism in which the exchanges organize the trading of futures contracts. The important issues relating to such trading mechanism like specification of contracts, the operation of margin accounts, delivery/settlement of the contract, the organization of exchanges, the regulation of the markets, the way in which quotes are made, etc. will be discussed. We will be following here the mechanism of futures trading in general and popular all over the world rather of a particular exchange, because there can be some variations in the terms of the futures contract on different exchanges.

Prior to the discussion on the mechanism of futures trading, it is to be noted that the vast majority of the futures contracts which are initiated do not lead to delivery because most of the investors or traders choose to close out their positions prior to the delivery period specified in the contract. The execution of the futures contracts through delivery is often inconvenient and, in some instances even quite expensive. This has been observed even in case of hedgers. However, a detail of this will be discussed in the section on delivery arrangements of the futures contracts.

For understanding trading mechanism of futures contract, one must be aware about the mechanism of quoting the futures prices as well as the specifications about the assets. Table 2.6 presents the daily future prices of Axis Bank Ltd. quoted at the NSE of India. From this table, the trader can know about the opening price, highest price of the day, lowest price of the day, day's closing and settlement price, total number of contracts executed along with total amount of turnover of the Axis Bank for the month of December 2015. Further, daily change in prices, volatility, open interest, volume of trading, etc. give another important indication about the position of stock in the market.

TABLE 2.6 Futures Prices of AXIS BANK Ltd. At NSE (India)
(all figures in ₹)

| Date | Open | High | Low | Close | Settle price | Change | Number of contracts | Turnover (in lacs) | OI |
|------|------|------|-----|-------|--------------|--------|---------------------|--------------------|----|
| 01 Dec. 15 | 475.00 | 475.45 | 463.60 | 467.55 | 467.55 | – | 230 | 1,077.1 | 2,64,000 |
| 02 Dec. 15 | 466.60 | 467.80 | 462.55 | 465.00 | 465.00 | –2.55 | 134 | 623.31 | 3,17,000 |
| 03 Dec. 15 | 466.30 | 470.55 | 463.05 | 467.30 | 467.30 | 2.3 | 110 | 513.63 | 3,15,000 |
| 04 Dec. 15 | 465.00 | 467.45 | 461.00 | 465.55 | 465.55 | –1.75 | 140 | 649.66 | 3,35,000 |
| 07 Dec. 15 | 469.10 | 469.95 | 465.50 | 467.40 | 467.40 | 1.85 | 53 | 247.64 | 3,44,000 |
| 08 Dec. 15 | 465.00 | 467.80 | 461.90 | 462.90 | 462.90 | –4.5 | 114 | 529.85 | 3,72,000 |
| 09 Dec. 15 | 462.60 | 465.95 | 452.00 | 454.65 | 454.65 | –8.25 | 430 | 1,964.12 | 4,97,000 |
| 10 Dec. 15 | 458.40 | 458.95 | 450.00 | 455.05 | 455.05 | 0.4 | 390 | 1,769.3 | 5,98,000 |
| 11 Dec. 15 | 455.15 | 455.15 | 441.55 | 444.00 | 444.00 | –11.05 | 596 | 2,662.53 | 8,26,000 |
| 14 Dec. 15 | 440.35 | 445.90 | 434.50 | 436.25 | 436.25 | –7.75 | 674 | 2,960.95 | 10,17,000 |
| 15 Dec. 15 | 436.95 | 440.80 | 433.50 | 439.35 | 439.35 | 3.1 | 486 | 2,130.36 | 11,64,000 |
| 16 Dec. 15 | 439.95 | 445.65 | 438.00 | 441.25 | 441.25 | 1.9 | 644 | 2,851.24 | 13,74,000 |
| 17 Dec. 15 | 446.30 | 447.50 | 435.00 | 439.95 | 439.95 | –1.3 | 1,274 | 5,602.2 | 18,70,000 |
| 18 Dec. 15 | 439.00 | 444.75 | 435.30 | 436.60 | 436.60 | –3.35 | 1,494 | 6,564.96 | 24,53,000 |
| 21 Dec. 15 | 436.00 | 446.20 | 436.00 | 445.25 | 445.25 | 8.65 | 1,214 | 5,374.39 | 27,93,000 |
| 22 Dec. 15 | 445.00 | 454.00 | 444.50 | 449.00 | 449.00 | 3.75 | 4,889 | 21,996.19 | 64,59,000 |
| 23 Dec. 15 | 452.00 | 454.90 | 450.60 | 453.90 | 453.90 | 4.9 | 1,426 | 6,461.13 | 68,68,000 |
| 24 Dec. 15 | 455.60 | 456.95 | 451.00 | 453.25 | 453.25 | –0.65 | 1,839 | 8,342.47 | 75,16,000 |
| 28 Dec. 15 | 453.50 | 457.50 | 451.30 | 456.45 | 456.45 | 3.2 | 8,144 | 3,6949.3 | 1,31,11,000 |
| 29 Dec. 15 | 457.90 | 460.85 | 453.90 | 460.05 | 460.05 | 3.6 | 10,062 | 4,6002.14 | 1,80,61,000 |
| 30 Dec. 15 | 459.15 | 461.65 | 455.20 | 456.35 | 456.35 | –3.7 | 15,426 | 70,709.06 | 2,83,98,000 |
| 31 Dec. 15 | 457.05 | 458.70 | 450.60 | 451.45 | 451.45 | –4.9 | 15,928 | 72,215.39 | 3,69,24,000 |

(*Source:* www.nseindia.com)

## 2.10 SPECIFICATION OF THE FUTURES CONTRACT

The specifications of the futures contract are discussed below:

### 2.10.1 Exchanges

All the futures contracts are initiated through a particular exchange. When a new futures contract is developed, an exchange must specify in some detail the exact nature of the contract of the agreement between the two parties. Further, it must specify the underlying asset, size of the contract, how price will be quoted, where and when delivery will be made, and how the price will be determined.

Before a futures contract registered at the exchange, first of all, the trader or investor willing to buy or sell futures will have to contract a 'broker' who is authorized to trade on the floor of an exchange on behalf of their clients or customers. Customers open their account with the broker member, who in turn sees that the order is executed on the floor of an exchange. He collects margin money from the customers, maintains customer money balances, records all the financial details and report all trading activities of the customers. Normally, the brokers provide monthly statements to their clients reporting all the details of their trading activity and end-of-month account balances.

Stock exchanges normally perform three functions:

(i) They provide and maintain a physical market place known as *The Floor* where futures transactions are sold and purchased by the members of the exchange.

(ii) They maintain and enforce ethical and financial norms applicable to the futures trading undertaken on the exchange.

(iii) They make efforts to promote business interests of the members because the exchange's main objective is to extend the facilities for such trading to its members.

Each exchange has usually membership organization whose members can be individuals or business organizations. Membership is limited to a specified number of seats. The members of the exchange have the right to trade on the floor of exchange, in turn, they agree to follow and abide by the rules of the exchange. Only a limited number of seats exist, but at any given time there is an active market in the seats.

There are two basic objectives to buy a seat on the exchange: to engage in floor trading activities, and to get the right, as per the exchange's norms, to execute futures, trades without paying the commission to the broker. For example, a large business organization may purchase the seat of an exchange only to make hedging activities through futures trading which may find it cost effective than to commission fee paid to a floor member of that exchange. Sometimes, a person buys the seat on an exchange for the investment purpose because the value of the exchange membership seat generally depends upon the volume of trading on that exchange. If the trading business increases, the price of the seat will also rise and, hence, vice-versa.

Futures contracts are traded in trading pits on the floors of the exchanges only during official trading hours. The classical/traditional style of trading in futures contracts is called the *open outcry system*. In this system, a trader, for instance, who wants to enter into a futures contract will declare the proposed trade to the entire pit using both voice and hand signals. The other trader in the trading pit can agree to the trade or offer alternative terms.

There are two types of traders (brokers) on the floor of the exchanges, i.e., commission brokers charge a fee for executing contracts/trades on behalf of their customer, whereas local traders trade for their own account. There are different types of trades which can be passed to a commission broker. Further, there can be different types of order which can be placed by a customer to the broker, such as market order, limit order, stop order, stop limit order, scale order, contingent order and spread order. *Market order* means that the investor is prepared to trade at the current market price. This means that they place a market order with their broker and then these are passed on to the commission broker representing the two sides. In case of a *limit order*, the customer specifies a certain price and requests that the transaction be executed only at a specified price or a better one is obtained, otherwise not.

In this way, a trade is finalized when two traders agree to take opposite sides of the contract, for example given price for a specified quantity at a futures period specified. However, now most of the exchanges in the world have online trading (computerized trading system), for example, Chicago Mercantile Exchange has developed a system known as GLOBEX, Swiss Options and Futures Exchange (SOFEX) is a fully computerized exchange.

In the *stop order*, the investor informs the member/broker to trade at any price once the market price has reached at a certain level. At that point the broker will execute the order regardless of whether the price is above, below or equal to the stop price. So, stop order is sure to be executed once the stop price has been reached. Stop orders are often used to protect losses, preserve profits, and take new positions. In usual stock market terms, buy stop orders mean stop prices above the current market price, and sell stop orders usually specify stop prices below current price. For example, an investor who has gone long SBI share may limit his potential loss on the position with a stop order into an offsetting short position of the futures prices drops to.

A *stop limit order* is just like a stop order where the investor instructs the broker to enter into a position after the market price has reached at a certain level. However, in this order, instead of allowing the order to be executed at any price once the stop level is reached, it places a limit on the price of transaction. The limit price may or may not be equal to the stop price. For example, an investor who took the long position of SBI share at ₹350 may instruct his broker to sell if the futures price falls to ₹340 but to accept no less than ₹330.

Another type of the order named *market-if-touched* (MIT) order instructs the broker to trade at whatever price can be obtained once the market has reached at a certain level. This type of orders are normally used by the technical analysts who believe that the market will reach on extreme before turning and wish to trade as soon as that price is reached. By using MIT order, the investors can be sure for their orders to be filled up.

Another type of order which the investor can place to the broker is called *alternative order*. On this, the investor puts two orders but wants only one to be filled up, which limits the potential profit orders. For example, the customer who entered a long position for SBI share at ₹350 may instruct the broker to sell if the price either increase to ₹360 or falls to ₹340. Similarly, in a scale order, the investor who wishes to offset the position on the market follows (rise or fall), he may specify successive positions to be taken if the market price moves up or down by certain increments. For example, the investor may instruct the broker to go long of 100 SBI shares if price rises by ₹360 and then go again long if the price falls another ₹340 and so on.

In a *contingent order*, the broker is asked to take a certain position if the price of another contract reaches a given level. For example, the investor may place an order to go long September SBI share futures, if the November SBI share futures price reaches to ₹370.

A *spread order* specifies the broker to take a spread position composed of opposite positions in similar contracts. Spread orders normally require a certain difference between the prices of the opposing contracts, rather than specific prices for them.

## 2.10.2   Standardization

Futures contracts have standardized terms set by the exchanges on which these futures contracts are to be traded. Normally each futures exchange specifies the number of futures contracts, however, they are usually limited. The benefit of the standardized specification is that the trading is concentrated in just a few contracts resulting in more liquidity of these contracts. Further, if the delivery dates were not standardized then there could be a futures contract which expires every day of the year. Further, standardization also makes it easier to compare futures prices. For the understanding of the contract specification of the futures contract, the examples of Gold Futures Contract traded on Chicago Board of Trade (CBOT) is shown in Table 2.7 and example of Axis Bank an equity futures contract traded at NSE is shown in Table 2.8. A futures contract specifies about every aspects of the deal regarding the asset, size, price limits futures period, trading hours, delivery, settlement, etc. These have been discussed in brief here as under:

**The asset:**    The first important term of the futures contract is the underlying 'asset'. As we know that on commodity futures market, the assets are commodities like food grains, metals, oils, gas, and so on, whereas on financial futures markets, financial assets like equities, debts, currencies, etc. are the specified assets. When the asset is commodity, there may be wide variations in the quality of what is available in the market place. Therefore, it is important that while specifying the asset, the exchange must stipulate the grade or grades of the commodity which are acceptable. For example, the specification of the deliverable grade of gold is given as "Refined gold in the form of one 100-ounce bar on three 1-kilo gold bars arraying not less than 995 fineness. The total pack cannot vary from a 100-troy-ounce weight by more than 5 percent". It means that the gold must be at least 995 fineness and cannot deviate 100 troy ounces by more than 5 percent.

In case of financial assets, the problem of quality do not arise. These assets are generally well defined and unambiguous. For example, there is no need to specify the grade of US Dollar, UK Pound Sterling, etc. However, there can be variations in features of the assets like treasury bonds, treasury notes, etc. These have been discussed in detail in the chapters of interest rate futures contracts.

**Contract size:**    A futures contract must specify the amount of the asset that has to be delivered under one contract. For example, the contract size or (trading unit) of the CBOT 100-ounce gold futures shown in Table 2.8 is 100 troy ounces. It is a very important decision for the exchange for the smooth functioning of the futures contract. For example, if the contract size is too large, then the traders will be hesitating and there will be small speculative positions. On the other hand, if the contract size is very small, then the trading may be expensive because there is a cost associated with each contract traded. Therefore, the correct size of the contract is a very important decision and it depends on the likely users. It very much depends on the value of the assets underlying in the contract.

**TABLE 2.7**    Contract Specifications of Futures Market

|  | *CBOT 100-ounce gold futures* |
|---|---|
| *Trading unit* | 100 troy ounces. |
| *Tick size* | 10 cents per troy ounce ($10 per contract). |
| *Daily price limit* | $50 per troy ounce ($5,000 per contract) above or below the previous day's settlement price. |
| *Contract months* | Current month and the next two calendar months and February, April, June, August, October, December. |
| *Trading hours* | 7:20 a.m. to 1:40 p.m. (Chicago time), Monday through Friday. Evening trading hours are from 5:00 to 8:30 p.m. (Chicago time), or from 6:00 to 9:30 p.m. (Central daylight savings time), Sunday through Thursday. |
| *Last trading day* | The fourth to last business day of the delivery month. |
| *Deliverable grades* | Refined gold in the form of one 100 ounce bar or three 1-kilo gold bars assaying not less than 995 fineness. The total pack cannot vary from a 100 troy ounce weight by more than 5 percent. |
| *Delivery* | By vault receipt issued by a CBOT-approved vault in Chicago or New York. |

*Source: Derivative Securities*, Jarrow & Turnbull, p. 7.

**Delivery months:** A futures contract is referred to be its delivery months. In other words, the contract months identify the expiry cycle of delivery dates. The exchange must specify the certain period during the month when delivery can be made. The delivery months vary from contract to contract and are chosen by the exchange to meet the requirements of market traders. For example, Table 2.7 shows the contract months for gold futures are the current months and the next two calendar months and February, April, June, August, October and December. In case of currency futures on the Chicago Mercantile Exchange, the delivery months are March, June, September and December. Further, the exchange also specifies when trading in a particular month's contract will begin, and also the last day on which the trading can take place for a given contract.

**Delivery arrangement:** Another important term in a futures contract is a delivery arrangement. The place where the delivery will be made must be specified by the exchange. It is more important in commodities than the financial instruments due to transportation costs to be incurred on delivery of the goods. For example, the place of delivery is also described in the CBOT-100-ounce gold futures, i.e., for gold futures, this is either Chicago or New York City in a vault-specified by the CBOT.

As already pointed out that the vast majority of the futures contracts (97 to 99 percent) do not lead to delivery of the underlying assets. Normally, they are closed out with an offsetting transactions prior to their maturities. Therefore, it is observed that in futures trading the delivery arrangement is not very much important in understanding the relationship between the futures and spot prices of the asset. It is the obligation of the seller or writer of a futures contract to deliver the underlying asset, sometime, during contract's expiration period. Buyer of the futures contract is under obligation to accept the delivery of the asset unless there is an offsetting transaction, called a closing transaction which can be done at any time during a contracts' expiration month. In this process, the clearing house specify the mechanism under which the sellers make delivery of the asset to the qualified buyer. In general, the actual delivery process is similar in structure but may vary from exchange to exchange. A futures contract generally specifies a First notice day, Last notice day and Last trading day. The *First notice day* specifies the first day on which a notice of intention for making the delivery of the asset by the seller (short) is submitted to the exchange. The *Last notice day* is referred to the last such day. The Last trading day occurs generally a few days before the Last notice day.

A typical example of delivery process of a futures contract is given below. Suppose that a seller decides to make delivery. The three-day delivery process as required by the rules of the Chicago Board of Trade is as follows:

*Day 1 (Position day or presentation day):* On this day, the broker (trader) representing the seller notifies the clearing house of the CBOT-Board of Trade Clearing Corporation that its customer wants to deliver the asset on a futures contract.

*Day 2 (Notice day):* Prior to the opening of the market on Day 2, the Board of Trade Clearing Corporation matches the seller with the buyer holding oldest reported long position (usually the longest outstanding long position) and then notifies both parties.

*Day 3 (Delivery day):* After receiving a cheque (amount due on the sold underlying asset) from the buyer's broker, the seller's broker gives the appropriate ownership receipts to the buyer's broker.

**Daily price movement limits:** The exchange can set a daily price movement limits of the underlying asset, which puts bounds on the maximum price change permitted per day. For example, in case of CBOT 100-ounce gold futures, it is $50 per troy ounce ($5,000 per contract) above or below the previous days' settlement price.

If the price moves down by an amount equal to the daily price limit, the contract is said to 'limit down', if it moves up by the limit, it is said to be 'limit-up'. So a limit move means a move in either direction equal to the daily price limit. The exchange can cease the trading on a futures contract for the day, if the contract is limit up or limit down. However, in certain cases, the exchange can also change the limits, if it so desires.

Why set price limit? It is a debatable issue. However, it is argued that it is an attempt to reduce 'hysteria' trading and price volatility by forcing the market traders to 'cool off'. If the price limits is reached on a number of successive day, the exchange can remove the price limit altogether. It should also be noted that not all the futures contracts have price limits. Whether the price limits are good for futures markets is still controversial.

**Position limits:**   Some futures exchanges also restrict the members to the number of futures contracts. Position limit means that the maximum number of contracts that a speculator may hold. For example, Chicago Mercantile Exchange has put the position limit of 1000 for the speculator with not more than 300 in any one delivery month. However, this limit is not for bonafide hedgers. The basic objective of this limit is to protect the market from excessive trading from the speculators.

**TABLE 2.8**   NSE Futures Contract Specification–Axis Bank Ltd.

| AXIS BANK LTD. Futures Contract Specifications | |
|---|---|
| Ticker Symbol | AXIS BANK |
| Contract Size | 1000 units |
| Notional value | Contract size multiplied by the stock level (For example: if the current stock value is 450 then the notional value would be 450 × 1000 = ₹4,50,000) |
| Tick Size | ₹0.05 |
| Expiry Date | 9.15 a.m. to 3.30 p.m. |
| Contract months | 3 serial monthly contracts (1, 2, 3 Month) |
| Daily Settlement Price | Last half hour's weighted average price |
| Initial Margin | SPAM-based Margin |
| Daily Settlement | Daily MTM settlement on T+1 in cash based on daily settlement price |
| Final Settlement Price | Final settlement price of AXIS BANK on expiry day |
| Final Settlement Procedure | Final settlement will be Cash settled in INR based on final settlement price |
| Final Settlement day | All open positions on expiry date shall be settled on the next working day of the expiry date |
| Last Trading/Expiration Day | Last Thursday of each contract maturity month. *Note:* A. Business day is a day during which the underlying stock market is open for trading. B. If expiry day is a holiday, then the immediately preceding business day. |

(*Source:* www.nseindia.com)

## 2.11   CLEARING HOUSE

For the smooth functioning of the futures trading in the futures market, each futures exchange has an associated clearing house. The clearing house acts as an intermediary or middleman in futures contracts. It may be constituted as a separate body as corporation or it may be a part of the futures exchange, but each exchange is closely associated with a particular clear house, which clears all transactions of that exchange. Each clearing house has a number of members, all of which have their offices near to the clearing house. Brokers who are not clearing house member themselves, then they have to channel their business through a member of the clearing house.

Thus, clearing house is a financial institution associated with the futures and options exchanges that guarantees the financial integrity of the market and the performance on futures and options contracts. It can be considered a third party between the buyer and seller of futures and options contracts, taking no active position in the market but assuring that for every short position there is a long position.

### Settlement basis at NSE

1. S&P CNX NIFTY futures/Mark-to-Market and final settlement
2. Futures on individual securities settlement be settled in cash on T+1 basis
3. S&P CNX NIFTY options cash settlement on T+1 basis
4. Options on individual securities premium settlement on T+1 basis
5. Option exercise settlement on T+3 basis

### Settlement price

1. S&P CNX NIFTY futures/Futures daily settlement price will be on individual securities. The closing price of the futures contracts for the trading day and the final settlement price shall be the closing value of the underlying index/security on the last trading day.
2. S&P CNX NIFTY options settlement price shall be on individual security, closing price of the underlying security.

The trading volumes on NSE's derivatives market has seen a steady increase since the launch of the first derivative contract. The average turnover now exceeds ₹2,000 crores on daily basis.

The clearing house performs several functions. First, the members of an exchange provide daily reports to the clearing house containing the details of all futures trades. In other words, clearing house keeps track records of all the transactions taken place during a day so that it can calculate the net position of each of its members. Once this is done, the clearing house accepts the trade and is legally substituted as both buyer and seller on the contract trades. If we add all the outstanding long and short futures market positions, the total will be always zero. Second, the clearing house guarantees that all the traders in the futures market will honour their obligations. It means it serves the role by having the position of buyer to the every seller and seller to every buyer. So, it plays the role of middleman in all the futures contracts. Thirdly, all the buying and selling futures contracts require daily collections and payments of funds to parties of futures transactions. The clearing house computes daily, for each clearing member, the net gain or loss on the member's futures positions (both its customers and its proprietary account) due to changes in the prices during the day. After that it collects the amount of the net losses and pays the net gains for the day to the respective member. The details of this has been discussed in the following section of this chapter. A brief view of the functioning of the clearing house has been shown in Figure. 2.1.

In the futures markets functioning, the role of the clearing house is very much significant. The two trading parties may not need to trust each other or even to know each other's identity. Instead, they should have to be concerned about the reliability and credit worthiness of the clearing house. In actual practice it has been observed that the clearing houses are wholly well established, large, financially sound institutions, and the risk of futures default by the clearing house is very small.

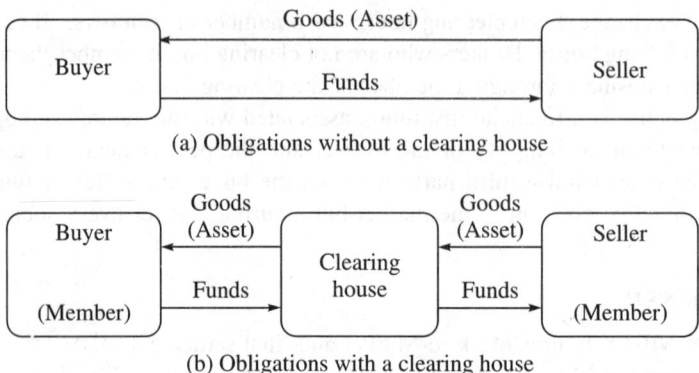

(a) Obligations without a clearing house

(b) Obligations with a clearing house

**FIGURE 2.1** The functions of the clearing house in futures market.

## 2.12 OPERATION OF MARGIN

In addition to the clearing house, there are some other safeguards for futures contracts, important among these are requirements for margin and daily settlement. In this section, we will discuss the margin requirement applicable in case of investor and as a trader of the clearing house. As we know that two parties are directly trading an asset in the futures market for a certain price there are obvious risks for backing out of any of the parties to the contract. It is also possible that one of them may not have the financial resources to honour the contract. That is why one of the important role of the exchange is to organize the futures trading in such a way that the default risk will be minimum. This is why margins come into picture.

### 2.12.1 Concept of Margin

Before entering into a futures contract, the prospective trader (investor) must deposit some funds with his broker which serve as a good faith deposit. In other words, an investor who enters into a futures contract is required to deposit funds with the broker called a margin. The basic objective of margin is to provide a financial safeguard for ensuring that the investors will perform their contract obligations. The exchanges set minimum margins but the brokers may require larger margins if they are concerned about an investor's financial situation because they are ultimately responsible for their clients' losses. The amount of margins may vary from contract to contract and even from broker to broker. The margin may be deposited in different forms like cash, bank's letter of credit and treasury securities. Normally the investor who posts this margin retains the title of the securities deposited as margin. The margin account may or may not earn interest. Some brokers may simply pay them money market interest rates on their margin account. However, most of the brokers usually do not pay interest on margin in money. This loss of interest is the cost of margin requirement.

### 2.12.2 Types of Margin

There are three types of margin such as initial margin, maintenance margin and variation margin. The *initial margin* is the original amount that must be deposited into account to establish futures position. It varies from stock to stock. To determine the initial margin, the exchange usually considers the degree of volatility of price movements in the past of the underlying asset. After that, the exchange sets the initial margin so that the clearing house covers losses on the position even in most adverse situation. The initial margin approximately equals the maximum daily price fluctuation permitted by the exchange for that underlying asset.

The exchange has the right to increase or decrease the quantum of initial marginal depending upon the likely anticipated changes in the futures price. For most of the futures contracts, the initial margin may be 5 percent or less of the underlying asset's value. After proper completion of all the obligations associated with an investor's futures position, the initial margin is returned to trader.

### 2.12.3  Maintenance Margin

The maintenance margin is the minimum amount which must be remained (kept) in a margin account. In other words, so much minimum balance in the margin account must be maintained by the investor. This is normally about 75 percent of the initial margin. If the futures prices move against the investor resulting in falling the margin account below the maintenance margin, the broker will make a call, i.e., asking the client to replenish the margin account by paying the variation. Hence, the demand for additional fund is known as *a margin call*. For example, assume that the initial margin on a futures contract is ₹5,000 and the maintenance margin ₹3,750 (75% of the initial margin). The next day assume that the party has sustained a loss of ₹1,000, reducing the balance in margin to ₹4,000. Further assume that on the next day the price decreased and sustained loss is ₹500. Thus, the balance remained in the margin account to ₹3,500, below the maintenance margin. In this situation, the broker will make a call (margin call) to replenish the margin account to ₹5,000, the level of initial margin.

### 2.12.4  Variation Margin

It refers to that additional amount which has to be deposited by the trader with the broker to bring the balance of the margin account to the initial margin level. For instance, in the above mentioned example, the variation margin would be ₹1,500 (₹5,000 – ₹3,500), i.e., the difference of initial margin and the balance in the margin account, the same has been shown in Figure. 2.2. If the investor does not pay the initial margin immediately, the broker may proceed to unilaterally close out the account by entering into an offsetting futures position.

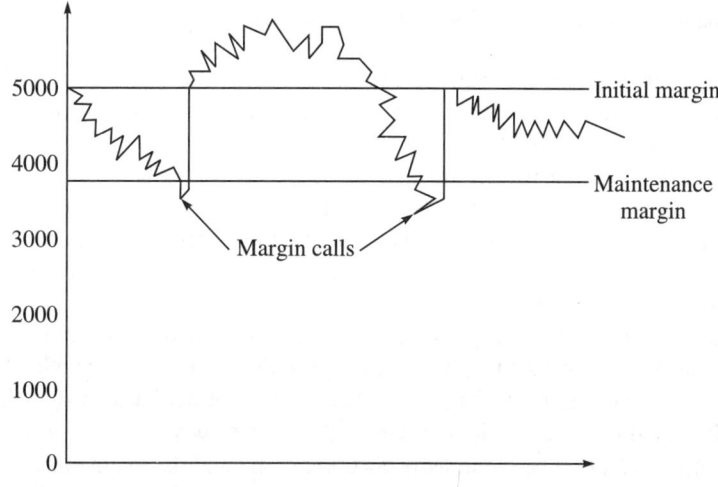

**FIGURE 2.2**  Account equity and margin requirements.

## 2.12.5  Margins and Marking-to-market (Daily Settlement)

It has been observed that the initial margin, sometimes, is even less than 5 percent which seems to be very small considering the total value of the futures contract. This smallness is reasonable because there is another safeguard built in the system, known as daily settlement marking-to-market. In the futures market, all the transactions are settled on daily basis. Thus, the system of daily settlement in the futures market is called *marking-to-market*. The traders realize their gains or losses on the daily basis to understand this process of daily settlement, let us see Table 2.9.

**TABLE 2.9**   Operation of Margins for a Long Position in Two Gold Futures Contracts

| Day | Futures price ($) | Daily gain (Loss) ($) | Cumulative gain (Loss) ($) | Margin account balance ($) | Margin call ($) |
|---|---|---|---|---|---|
| June 3 | 400.00 | | | 4,000 | |
| June 3 | 397.00 | (600) | (600) | 3,400 | |
| June 4 | 396.10 | (180) | (780) | 3,220 | |
| June 7 | 398.20 | 420 | (360) | 3,640 | |
| June 8 | 397.10 | (220) | (580) | 3,420 | |
| June 9 | 396.70 | (80) | (660) | 3,340 | |
| June 10 | 395.40 | (260) | (920) | 3,080 | |
| June 11 | 393.30 | (420) | (1,340) | 2,660 | 1,340 |
| June 14 | 393.60 | 60 | (1,280) | 4,060 | |
| June 15 | 391.80 | (360) | (1,640) | 3,700 | |
| June 16 | 392.70 | 180 | (1,460) | 3,880 | |
| June 17 | 387.00 | (1,140) | (2,600) | 2,740 | 1,260 |
| June 18 | 387.00 | 0 | (2,600) | 4,000 | |
| June 21 | 388.10 | 220 | (2,380) | 4,220 | |
| June 22 | 388.70 | 120 | (2,260) | 4,340 | |
| June 23 | 391.00 | 460 | (1,800) | 4,800 | |
| June 24 | 392.30 | 260 | (1,540) | 5,060 | |

*Source:* Introduction to Futures and Options Markets, John C. Hull, p. 24.

If we examine Table 2.9, it is observed that on June 11, the balance in the margin account falls $340 below the maintenance margin level. This requires a margin call to the participant for depositing an additional margin of $1,340.

The table assumes that the trader, in fact, provides this margin by close of the trading on June 12. It is also noted that on June 12, 19, 20 and 21, trader has excess margin. The table also assumes that excess margin is not withdrawn. On June 24, the trader decides to close out the position by shorting the two contracts, being futures price on that day $392.30, and the trader has suffered accumulative loss of $1,540 in this contract.

The basic purpose of the mark-to-marking is that the futures contracts should be daily marked or settled and not at the end of its life. Every day, the trader's gain (loss) is added or (subtracted), the margin on the case may be. This brings the value of the contract back to zero. In other words, a futures contract is closed out and rewritten at a new price every day.

The initial margin is $2,000 per contract or $4,000 in total and the maintenance margin is $1,500 per contract or $3,000 in total. The contract is entered into on June 3 at $400 and closed out on June

24 at $392.30. The numbers in column 2, except the first and the last, are the futures price at the close of trading.

**TABLE 2.10** Operation of Margins for a Long Position in AXIS Bank Stock Futures Contracts (all figures in ₹)

| Date | Open price | Close price | Settle price | Change | Gain/Loss | Margin account balances | Margin Call/ withdrawl |
|---|---|---|---|---|---|---|---|
| 01 Dec. 15 | 475.00 | 467.55 | 467.55 | – | | 45,000 | |
| 02 Dec. 15 | 466.60 | 465.00 | 465.00 | −2.55 | −2,550 | 42,450 | |
| 03 Dec. 15 | 466.30 | 467.30 | 467.30 | 2.30 | 2,300 | 44,750 | |
| 04 Dec. 15 | 465.00 | 465.55 | 465.55 | −1.75 | −1,750 | 43,000 | |
| 07 Dec. 15 | 469.10 | 467.40 | 467.40 | 1.85 | 1,850 | 44,850 | |
| 08 Dec. 15 | 465.00 | 462.90 | 462.90 | −4.50 | −4,500 | 40,350 | |
| 09 Dec. 15 | 462.60 | 454.65 | 454.65 | −8.25 | −8,250 | 32,100 | −12,900 |
| 10 Dec. 15 | 458.40 | 455.05 | 455.05 | 0.40 | 400 | 45,400 | |
| 11 Dec. 15 | 455.15 | 444.00 | 444.00 | −11.05 | −11,050 | 33,950 | |
| 14 Dec. 15 | 440.35 | 436.25 | 436.25 | −7.75 | −7,750 | 26,600 | −18,400 |
| 15 Dec. 15 | 436.95 | 439.35 | 439.35 | 3.10 | 3,100 | 48,100 | |
| 16 Dec. 15 | 439.95 | 441.25 | 441.25 | 1.90 | 1,900 | 46,900 | |
| 17 Dec. 15 | 446.30 | 439.95 | 439.95 | −1.30 | −1,300 | 43,700 | |
| 18 Dec. 15 | 439.00 | 436.60 | 436.60 | −3.35 | −3,350 | 41,650 | |
| 21 Dec. 15 | 436.00 | 445.25 | 445.25 | 8.65 | 8,650 | 53,650 | |
| 22 Dec. 15 | 445.00 | 449.00 | 449.00 | 3.75 | 3,750 | 57,750 | 12,750 |
| 23 Dec. 15 | 452.00 | 453.90 | 453.90 | 4.90 | 4,900 | 49,900 | |
| 24 Dec. 15 | 455.60 | 453.25 | 453.25 | −0.65 | −650 | 44,350 | |
| 28 Dec. 15 | 453.50 | 456.45 | 456.45 | 3.20 | 3,200 | 48,200 | |
| 29 Dec. 15 | 457.90 | 460.05 | 460.05 | 3.60 | 3,600 | 56,050 | 11,050 |
| 30 Dec. 15 | 459.15 | 456.35 | 456.35 | −3.70 | −3,700 | 41,300 | |
| 31 Dec. 15 | 457.05 | 451.45 | 451.45 | −4.90 | −4,900 | 40,100 | |

(*Source:* www.nseindia.com)

In case of Axis Bank, let us assume that approx. 10 percent initial margin is required for trading in futures contracts in the month of December, 2015. Further, assume that the investor deposits ₹45,000 as initial margin on one transaction of 1,000 shares with his member/broker subject to withdraw and deposit in the balance of margin account to this initial amount, above and less than 75 percent of ₹45,000. It is noted that on 9th December and 14th December, the balance is less than 75 percent, i.e., ₹33,750, the broker will give margin call for depositing the money in the margin account so that the initial margin is maintained. Further, on 22nd December and 29th December, the balance exceeds to ₹45,000. In this situation, the investor can withdraw the surplus amount from the margin account. The initial margin is subject to change by the regulatory authority as per change in the volatility of the stock.

## 2.13   MARGIN CASH FLOWS (CLEARING MARGIN AND CLEARING HOUSE)

In this section, we will discuss the flow of margin funds from the investors (trader) to the clearing house through the members of the clearing house. Just as a trader is required to maintain a margin account with a broker, a member of the clearing house is also required to maintain a margin account with the clearing house. This is known as *clearing margin*. Brokers who are not clearing house members must maintain a margin account with a member of clearing house. The margin account of the clearing house members are adjusted for gains or losses at the end of each trading day as in the case of an investor/trader keeps with the broker. However, in case of clearing margin, there is no maintenance margin, and they are maintained at original margin daily. Thus, depending upon the transactions during the day and price movements, the members may have to add or remove the funds to its margin account, as the case may be.

There are two basis of calculating the clearing margins; the gross basis and the net basis. In the gross basis, all the long positions and short positions of all the clients are added and then entered in the records. Whereas in case of 'Net basis', it allows these to be offset against each other. For example, a clearing house member has two traders, one with a long position in 20 contracts and other one with a short position in 15 contracts. In gross system, clearing margin will be calculated on the basis of 35 contracts, wherein net system, margin on the basis of 5 (20 – 15) contracts. Most of the exchanges currently are using net margin system.

Figure 2.3 shows the margin cash flows from a trader to clearing house. Trader X trades through clearing member where trader Y through non-clearing member. In this case, Y trader deposits margin with his broker where he (broker) deposits with the clearing house through clearing member. However, it is not very important whether the trading is done directly through clearing member or non-clearing member. Most of the large brokers also normally function as clearing members.

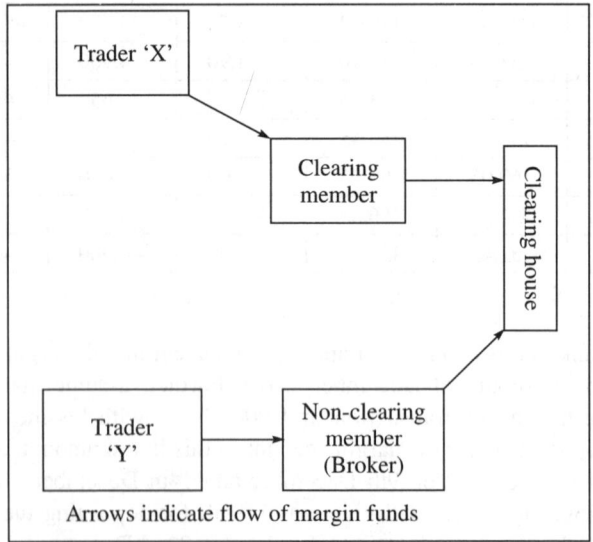

**FIGURE 2.3**   Margin cash flows.
*Source: Understanding futures markets* by Robert W. Kolb, p.14.

## 2.14   CLOSING A FUTURES POSITION (SETTLEMENT)

There are four ways to close the futures position, namely, physical delivery, cash settlement, offsetting and exchange of future for physicals (EFP).

**Physical delivery:**   One way of liquidating of futures position is by making or taking physical delivery of the goods/asset. The exchange has provided alternatives as to when, where and what will be delivered. It is the choice of the party with a short position. When the party is ready to deliver, it will send a notice of intention to deliver to the exchange. The price is settled which normally most recent with a possible adjustment for the quality of the asset and chosen delivery location. After that, the exchange selects a party with an outstanding long position to accept delivery. Let us see how physical delivery works.

Let us take an example of particular futures contract: Silver traded on COMEX where a short-trader is required to make delivery of 5000 troy ounce (6 percent more or less) of refined silver bar cost in heights of 1000 to 1100 ounces each and at 0.999 fineness. Which should bear the serial number and identifying stamp of a refiner approved by the COMEX exchange. At the beginning of the delivery month on the exchange-designated notice days, say, December 99 contract, exchange rules requires that all traders having open positions in December 1999 contract notify their member brokers to take or make delivery for this. In turn, the brokers will inform to the clearing house of their customer's intention. After this notification, the clearing house matches longs and shorts usually by matching the oldest short to the oldest long position, until all short quantities are matched. Delivery notices are then to all the traders through their brokers indicating to whom their delivery obligations runs and when, where and in what quantities is to be made. Some exchanges impose heavy penalty in case of default by any party. When delivery is satisfactorily made then the clearing house notify and accord the same. In case of financial futures, delivery is usually made by wire transfer.

**Cash settlement/delivery:**   This is relatively new procedure followed for setting futures obligations is through cash delivery. This procedure is a substitute of physical delivery and hence, do not require physical delivery. The exchange notifies about this where cash delivery as the settlement procedure. There are certain financial futures like stock indices futures, certain treasury securities, Eurodollar, time deposits, municipal bonds, etc. When a cash settlement contract expires, the exchange sets its final settlement price equal to the spot price of the underlying asset on that day. In other words, it is simply marked-to-market at the end of the last trading day to handover the underlying assets. Since cash settlement contracts are settled at the spot price, their futures prices are converged to the underlying spot prices. Therefore, the prices of cash settlement contracts behave just like the prices of delivery contracts at their expiration period.

**Offsetting:**   The most common and popular method of liquidating the open futures position is to effect an offsetting futures transaction or via a reversing trade which reverses the existing open position. For example, the initial buyer (long) liquidates his position by selling (going short) an identical futures contract (which means same delivery month and same underlying asset). Similarly, the initial seller (short) goes for buying (long) an identical futures contract. After executing these trades, these are reported to the clearing house then both trade obligations are extinguished on the books of the brokers and the clearing house. No doubt, the clearing house plays a significant role in facilitating settlement by offset. In comparison to the physical delivery, this method is relatively simple which requires good liquidity in the market, and entails only, the usual brokerage costs.

For example, there are two parties X and Y. X has an obligation to the clearing house to accept 10,000 bushels of cotton in September and to pay ₹180 per bushels. For them at that time, X does not wish to actually receive the oats and want to exit the futures market earlier.

Similarly, Y has an obligation to the clearing house to deliver 10,000 bushels of cotton in September and to receive ₹180 per bushel. Both party can reverse or offset their position in that way whereby buyer becomes seller and seller becomes the buyer. Before the due date, i.e., September, X will sell September contract for cotton at ₹190 per bushels Y will buy at ₹190 per bushels.

**Exchange of futures for physicals (EFP):**   This is another method of liquidating the futures contract in a form of physical delivery, called exchange of futures for physicals. In this method, a party who holds a futures contract may like to liquidate his position that is different from those the exchange offers. For example, a party may like to deliver the assets before the specified futures period, or may deliver the asset at different place, or deliver outside the normal trading hours, etc. In simple terms, the contracts fulfilled by the parties on non-contract terms under this technique. For example, a party with a long gold futures position may wish to take delivery in Los Angeles rather than in New York, as the contract specifies. Further, the EFP system permits to exchange a futures position for a cash position that meets both the parties' preferences, of course, for EFP, the party must find another party willing to make the trade.

The exchanges allow the parties to deliver under non-contract terms, and without going through the trading pits. However, both the short and the long in an EFP transaction must notify the exchange and the clearing house of the said EFP agreement so that the clearing house can make proper book entries to extinguish the respective short and long positions on its books.

The Exchange of Futures for Physicals (EFP) differs in certain respects from the offsetting method. First, the trader actually exchange the asset in physical form. Second, such agreements are not performed/closed by a transaction on the floor of the exchange. Third, the two trade negotiate privately the price and other terms of the contract which are usually different from the specifications. Since these agreements are negotiated outside the trading pit, so they are also called ex-pit transaction. Further, regulatory authorities and exchange rules require that all the futures trading be liquidated in the pit, hence, the EFP is the one recognized exception to this general rule. These contracts are also known as against actual or versus cash transactions.

**EXAMPLE:**   Delivery using an Exchange of Futures for physicals, A is holding long January Comex Metal futures contract and B is holding short January Comex Metal futures. Both A and B live in Chicago and prefer to close out their positions with delivery in Chicago rather than New York as specified in Comex metal contract. Under EFP A will transfer his long futures position to B at a price $400 per ounce. Broker of both parties submit an EFP order with information to Comex. At the same time B agrees to sell 100 ounces of metal in Chicago at a price $400 per ounce. B delivers the 100 ounces of gold at 2.00 a.m., if A and B wish, transaction will be recorded in Exchange next morning.

## 2.15   TRADING MECHANISM OF A FUTURES CONTRACT (IN BRIEF)

Futures trading in brief can be divided into pre-trading, trading, execution, clearing and closing.

**Pre-trading:**   Pre-trading relates to the origination and channelizing of futures orders to market places for the execution of transaction. Futures brokers/dealers initiate and collect orders from their customers, for buying and selling stocks.

**Trading:**   Usually consists of matching buyers to sellers in futures contracts. Exchanges are central market places where all such orders are collected and matched.

**Execution:**   Execution refers to that the buyers and the sellers enter into the derivative contract. Trading parties usually remain anonymous. Matched orders are then adjusted into open interest of the asset which is maintained by the concerned exchanges. It means these may add to open contracts, or offset existing open contracts balance.

**Clearing:** After matching the orders by the exchange, then these are referred for clearing. The clearing function is performed by a clearing house which is linked with the exchange. They provide clearing for all trades and make position management of all open contracts throughout the maturity duration of the contract.

**Closing:** The clearing house, besides managing the position, it also involves in the settlement and closing of the futures contracts. The termination of the futures and other derivatives can be done in any of the following four actions on behalf of the traders.

1. Termination through offsetting
2. Termination through transferring
3. Termination through expiry of the contract
4. Termination through exercise.

**EXAMPLE:** Let us explain this with an example, An investor who enters into a futures contract on AXIS Bank by taking a long position on December 2, 2015, expiring on December, 31 2015, and creates an open position in the exchange. The closing price on December 2, 2015 of AXIS Bank is ₹465 and trading lot is of 1,000 shares.

In the above example, the termination of the contract can be triggered as follows:

1. **Through offsetting:** The above long position in AXIS Bank can be terminated by the trader through offsetting, in which opposite position is taken. So, he may take short position, say, on December 7, 2015, the AXIS Bank stock price is ₹467.40. He may cancel the original contract by selling futures of an equal quantity of stock.
2. **Through transferring:** In this method, the trader can terminate the contract by trading in the market. He may, after certain days, closeout his position by trading in the futures to another trader, say at a price of ₹440 on December 17, 2015. In this method, while the open position of the stock is existed in the market, but for the trader, the futures position remains cancelled.
3. **Through at the expiring of the contract:** In this method, the trader will retain the contract up to maturity of the contract, the expiry of the said long contract is on December 31, 2015. He will exercise and pay the amount at settlement on expiry of the contract. For example, in this, the trader will pay (451.45 × 1000) = ₹4,51,450 in case for taking the delivery of the stock. However, most of the futures position do not require the delivery of stock, and settle through price differentials, i.e., difference of purchase price and settlement price of stock.
4. **Through exercise:** In this method, the trader can terminate the contract by exercising before the expiration of date. Though futures contract cannot be exercised before the expiry date, however, other derivatives like American type option contracts, the trader can terminate the contact by exercising before the expiry date of the contract.

## SUMMARY

This chapter has introduced futures markets and trading by describing the concept, nature and features of futures contracts. Futures contracts are exchange traded contracts between two parties to buy or sell a specified quantity of an asset for future delivery at an agreed price at a specified time in future.

It includes various types of financial futures contracts like interest rate futures, foreign currencies futures, stock index futures, bond index futures, etc. This chapter has further described the various types of traders in the futures markets which includes hedgers, speculators, and arbitrageurs with their different motives to trade in futures markets. Hedgers are traders who enter into futures markets to reduce their exposures. If hedgers are the persons who wish to avoid risk, speculators are the persons who wish to take risk to book the profits. Arbitrageurs are the traders who attempt to make profits by locking in a riskless trading by simultaneously entering into transactions in two or more markets. The chapter then describes the functions of futures market which includes hedging, price discovery, liquidity, financing and price stabilization. The chapter also highlights the growth of futures markets worldwide, trading mechanism of futures markets with various specifications of the futures contract like standardization asset, contract size, delivery month, arrangement, etc. Clearing house are the key institution in futures trading through facilitating settlement of futures contracts among its members.

Margins are important aspects of futures markets. There are three types of margins that operate in futures market: initial margin, maintenance margin and variation margin. Initial margin is the original amount that must be deposited into account to establish futures positions.

Maintenance margin is the minimum amount which must be retained in margin account. In other words, minimum balance in the margin account must be maintained by the investor. Maintenance margin is kept normally 75 percent of the initial margin.

Variation margin refers to that additional amount which has to be deposited by the trader with the broker to bring the balance of the margin account to the initial margin level. Margins flow from trader to clearing house member and then to clearing house.

At the end, the chapter describes how a futures position can be closed out by a trader. There are various ways in which a futures position can be closed out. First by physical delivery, in which the party will deliver or receive the assets from the clearing house on the due date. Second, cash settlement in which the positions are settled in cash by the concerned parties. Third, offsetting, in which the parties reverse their initial positions. It means buyer becomes seller and seller becomes buyer for the same underlying asset. Fourth, exchange of futures for physicals (EFP) which include private agreement by the parties at a specified route and then reporting back their EFP transactions to the exchanges so that exchange can settle their positions and accounts. These contracts are also known as against actual or cash transactions.

## SOLVED PROBLEMS

**P.1.** An investor enter into futures (short) contract to sell January cotton for ₹50 per kg on the commodity exchange. The size of contract is 5000 kg. Initial margin is ₹40,000 and maintenance margin is ₹30,000. What price change will lead to margin call to investor? If investor does not deposit margin call what will happen?

*Solution:* Margin call to investor will occur when ₹10,000 lost from margin account. It will happen when price of cotton increased by ₹2 per kg. So price of cotton must rise to ₹52 per bundle for margin call. And in case investor does not make a payment of margin call, broker will close out investor's position.

**P.2.** On December 15, ABC Ltd. establish a long position in 200 shares of TISCO on January 1 at a futures price ₹600 per share. Initial margin for contract is ₹30,000 and maintenance margin is ₹20,000. Draw a table showing margin and marking-to-market for ABC on Ist January with the following information:

| Date: | December | | | | | | | | | | | | January |
|-------|----|----|----|----|----|----|----|----|----|----|----|----|----|
|       | 15 | 16 | 17 | 18 | 19 | 21 | 22 | 23 | 24 | 25 | 27 | 31 | 1 |
| *Futures prices:* | 600 | 550 | 650 | 600 | 605 | 590 | 580 | 600 | 620 | 630 | 640 | 660 | 690 |

*Solution:*  Margins and marking-to-market for ABC Ltd.

Initial margin: ₹30,000
Maintenance margin: ₹20,000

| Date | Futures price | Daily gains/ losses | Withdrawn/ Deposit | Initial margin | Balance at end |
|------|-------|-------|-------|-------|-------|
| December 15 | 600 | — | — | 30,000 | 30,000 |
| December 16 | 550 | – 10,000 | 0 | 20,000 | 20,000 |
| December 17 | 650 | +20,000 | – 10,000(w) | 40,000 | 30,000 |
| December 18 | 600 | – 10,000 | +10,000 | 20,000 | 30,000 |
| December 19 | 605 | +1,000 | – 1,000(w) | 31,000 | 30,000 |
| December 21 | 590 | – 3,000 | 2,000 | 28,000 | 30,000 |
| December 22 | 580 | (–) 2,000 | +2,000 | 28,000 | 30,000 |
| December 23 | 600 | (+) 4,000 | – 4,000(w) | 34,000 | 30,000 |
| December 24 | 620 | ·+4,000 | – 4,000(w) | 34,000 | 30,000 |
| December 25 | 630 | +2,000 | – 2,000(w) | 32,000 | 30,000 |
| December 27 | 640 | +2,000 | – 4,000(w) | 32,000 | 30,000 |
| December 31 | 660 | (+) 4,000 | – 4,000(w) | 34,000 | 30,000 |
| January 1 | 690 | +6,000 | – 6,000(w) | 36,000 | 30,000 |

**P.3.**   An investor has purchased S & PCNX NIFTY futures on National Stock Exchange. How will the final settlement be done of the transaction.

*Solution:*   The delivery transaction will be settled on the basis of marking-to-market and on the basis of final settlement on the S & PCNX NIFTY futures.

**P.4.**   Assume on Bombay Stock Exchange (BSE), Stock Index Contract is traded. One stock index consists of 30 shares of 30 companies. One tick size is ₹1/4 per share. What is the amount of tick size per contract?

*Solution:*   Since one contract consists of 30 shares of different companies and tick size is 1/4 per share. So total amount of tick size per contract will be 30 × 1/4 = ₹7.5 per contract of BSE Stock Index.

**P.5.**   A speculator predicts a price increase in the gold futures market from current futures price of ₹25,000 per 10 g. The market lot is 100 g. Speculator buys one lot of futures gold of (₹25,000 × 10) = ₹2,50,000. Assume that margin is 10%. What amount of margin money, is required, if prices of gold increase by 20%? What will be profit to speculator?

*Solution:*

Margin money = contract value of the futures contract, ₹2,50,000.

Margin amount =  2,50,000 × 10% = ₹25,000.

If price of gold increased by 20%, price of gold futures contract will be

$$= 2,50,000 \times 20\% = ₹2,50,000 + ₹50,000 = ₹3,00,000$$

Profit to speculator = ₹3,00,000 – ₹2,50,000 = ₹50,000

**P.6.** Suppose, current price of Bank of Baroda share at NSE is ₹200 per share and futures price for delivery in next 3 months is ₹250 per share. An arbitrageur can borrow at 10% per annum. What should arbitrageur do?

*Solution:* Arbitrageur can borrow at 10% per annum, so cost of borrowing will be. $200 \times 10\% = 20$

Total amount to be paid on maturity = ₹220

Bank of Baroda's futures price = ₹250

So arbitrageur will buy shares and sell at futures date for delivery in next 3 months at ₹250 and can earn a profit of ₹250 – ₹220 = ₹30 per share.

**P.7.** XYZ Ltd. expects to receive a payment of 10,00,000 pound after 3 months. The pound (£) is currently worth $1.60 but the three months futures price is $1.56. XYZ expects the price of the pound (£) to decline (value of dollar will rise). If this expectation is fulfilled, XYZ will suffer a loss when pounds (£) are converted in dollars when you receive them three months in futures.

(a) Given a current price, what is expected payment in dollars?

(b) Given the futures price, how much XYZ Ltd. will receive in dollars?

(c) If after three months, pound is worth $1.38 what is amount of loss to XYZ Ltd.?

*Solution*:

(a) Given the current price expected payment in dollars is

$$= \$1.60 \times 10,00,000 = \$16,00,000$$

(b) Given the futures price amount to be received in dollars is

$$= 1.56 \times 10,00,000 = \$15,60,000$$

(c) If after three months = $1.38/£

Then loss = $13,80,000 – $16,00,000 = $2,20,000

**P.8.** Suppose Amit enters into a short futures contract to sell July silver for ₹35,200 per kg on the Multi Commodity Exchange. The size of contract is 10 kg. Assume the initial margin is ₹50,000 and maintenance margin is ₹40,000. What changes in futures price will lead to margin call?

*Solution:* There will be a margin call when ₹10,000 has been lost from the margin account. This will occur if the silver price is increased to more than ₹36,200 per kg.

**P.9.** An investor predicts a price increase in the silver futures market from current futures price of ₹38,000 per kg. The market lot is being 10 kg. He buys one lot of futures silver of ₹(38,000 × 10) = ₹3,80,000. Assume that margin is 20%. What is amount of margin money? Suppose, if the price of silver increases by 20%, what will be profit/loss to investor?

*Solution:*

Margin money = 20% of the contract value

₹3,80,000 × 20% = ₹76,000.

If price of silver increased by 20%, price of silver futures contract will be

$$3,80,000 \times 20 = 76,000 = ₹3,80,000 + ₹76,000 = ₹4,56,000$$

Profit to investor = ₹4,56,000 – ₹3,80,000 = ₹76,000.

**P.10.** Assume price of Infosys spot on NSE on November 30, 2015 is ₹1,280. December futures price close on of November 30 is ₹1,300. Days left for expiration are 28. Riskless rate of return for 28 days @ market rate of 11.5% p.a. is 0.88%. How arbitrageur can earn profit from the above transaction?

*Solution:* Implied futures interest rate = ₹1,300 – ₹1,280

$$= ₹20 \times 100/1,280 = 1.56\%.$$

The futures price locked in expiration is equal to the value of an investment in spot Infosys at the implied rate of return of 1.56% while market interest rate is 0.88%. This implies that futures are quoting at a premium. To take advantage of this mispricing, an arbitrageur can borrow (200 × 1,280) = ₹2,56,000 over same period at lower rate of 0.88% to finance his purchase of the Infosys shares. Simultaneously, an arbitrageur lends forward at an implied rate of 1.56% by selling of contract of December futures at ₹1,300 and can earn profit through a difference of (1.56% – 0.88%) = 0.68% return on the investment.

**P.11.** Assume on January 15, pepper prices at Kochi are as under:

| | |
|---|---|
| Spot futures April | ₹ 9,500 per quintal |
| Matures on 15/4 | ₹9,700 per quintal |

Storage cost is estimated at ₹100 per monsem. On March 15, prices are as follows:

| | |
|---|---|
| Spot | ₹9,200 per quintal |
| Futures (April) | ₹9,250 per quintal |

Mr. X undertakes the following transactions:

Jan. 15 Sell one quintal pepper for actual delivery in March at ₹9,600.

Jan. 15 Buy one quintal April pepper futures at ₹9,700.

March 15 Sell one quintal April futures at ₹9,250.

March 15 Buy one quintal spot pepper at ₹9,200.

Show the profit/loss of Mr. X on April 15.

*Solution:*

| Transaction | Mr. X's position | | | |
|---|---|---|---|---|
| | Spot market | | Futures market | |
| | Date | Price (₹) | Date | Price (₹) |
| Sell | March 15 | 9,600 | April 15 | 9,250 |
| Buy | April 15 | 9,200 | March 15 | 9,700 |
| Gain/loss | | +400 | | (–)(450) |
| | | 400 Profit | | –450 Loss |

**Net return = ₹50 (Loss)**

## REVIEW QUESTIONS

1. What is a financial futures contract? Discuss the growth of financial futures with examples.
2. Explain the importance of futures markets in context to economic growth of a country.
3. What is futures contracting? Explain with examples. Also discuss the types of financial futures contracts.

4. How do commodity and financial futures differ from each other? Explain with the help of suitable examples.
5. Discuss the types of traders in futures markets with suitable examples.
6. What is futures market? Discuss the functions of futures market.
7. Explain the difference between a long futures position and short futures position with the help of examples.
8. "Hedging is the basic function of futures market". Discuss the statement in the light of uses of futures contract.
9. Write a detailed note on growth of futures markets worldwide.
10. Writes short notes on:
    (a) Hedging v/s speculating
    (b) Arbitraging v/s spreading
    (c) Hedging v/s insurance
11. What is the legal difference between forward and futures contract?
12. What are the main functions of a clearing house? Do clearing associations guarantee all futures contract in the event of customer default?
13. Write a note on futures market trading mechanism.
14. What are different types of orders in the futures market? Explain with the help of suitable examples.
15. What are various specifications of the futures contract?
16. Discuss the role of exchanges in futures market.
17. Write detailed notes on delivery process in futures market with the help of suitable examples.
18. What do you understand by the term 'margin'? Discuss various types of margins with the help of suitable examples.
19. Write notes on:
    (a) Linkage between margins and making to marking system
    (b) Process of flow of margins
20. How a futures position can be closed? Discuss with the help of suitable examples.
21. Write a note on role of clearing house with special emphasis upon 'delivery mechanism' in futures market.
22. "Do hedgers need speculators in futures market"? Critically evaluate the statement.
23. Explain the concept of futures contract. What are its important specifications. Explain with suitable examples.
24. Define the term 'margin' in context to futures contract. What are its different types?
25. Explain the marking-to-market term used in futures trading and its mechanism with suitable examples.
26. Explain how a trader closes its futures market position. Explain with suitable examples.
27. Explain the 'delivery' mechanism under the futures trading along with the role of the clearing house in this respect.
28. Explain the role of the exchange in futures trading mechanism with suitable examples.
29. What are the most important aspects of the design of new futures contract?
30. From two types of contracts available to you forward and futures contracts, examine critically which contract has less counter party risk and why?

31. What are possible advantages by owning a seat of an exchange?

32. Explain the important futures exchange available globally and also explain their role in economic growth.

33. What are the various types of traders on the floor of the exchange? Discuss them briefly with their functions?

34. What do you understand by the term standardization in the context of financial futures? Discuss various standardized features of futures contract.

35. "Options and futures are zero sum games". Critically examine the statement.

36. "For effecting hedging, market needs speculators". Discuss the statement in the light of functions of speculators and hedger.

## UNSOLVED PROBLEMS

**P.1.** An investor enters into futures (short) contract to sell August cotton for ₹50 per bundle on the commodity exchange. The size of contract is 5,000 bundle. Initial margin is ₹4,000 and maintenance margin is ₹3,000. What price change will lead to margin call to investor? If investor does not deposit margin call what will happen?

**P.2.** On January 14 XYZ Ltd. establishes a long position in 100 shares of February 1 HLL at a futures price ₹450 per share. Initial margin for contract is ₹2,000 and Maintenance margin is ₹1,500. Draw a table showing margin X marking-to-market for XYZ on 1 February.

**P.3.** Amit, an investor, holds stock in BPL Ltd. He feels that stock market will decline in coming days. He has two options: selling equity short, or sell the stock index futures based on NIFTY junior exchange composite index. Index is currently trading at ₹150 and a contract have a value 100 times from the amount of the index. Margin requirement for the index is ₹4,000 and maintenance margin is ₹1,500. Amit goes for second one option, i.e., sell the stock index futures based on NIFTY Junior.
Solve the following:
(a) How much investor has to pay while selling the contract?
(b) How much is the value of contract based on index?
(c) If 15 days later index is at ₹155, how much profit or loss Amit has?
(d) If index falls by 1%, what is percentage loss to Amit?
(e) If Amit instead of selling buy the contract, how much he has to put up, while buying?

**P.4.** The cotton contract is traded at commodity exchange. Each contract is for 3,000 bushels and prices are quoted as per bushel. Party A on 1st May buys (long) in futures contract of (after) at ₹170 per bushel. How can party A on 25 May reverse the trade? Draw a table showing reverse trading mechanism.

**P.5.** An exporter will receive a payment of $30,00,000 after one year. Current rate is ₹48 for one dollar and one year futures rate of dollar is ₹46. Exports expect a decline in price of dollar value of rupee. On the basis of above statement, answer the following:
(a) At futures prices, how much exporter will get in rupee?
(b) In terms of current prices what will be payment in rupee?
(c) If after one year Dollar is worth ₹40, what is exporter loss in terms of dollar?

**P.6.** An investor takes a long position in a pound futures, which will mature on three days later (Wednesday). The day on which investor takes a position is Monday. The price is $1.70 for £62,500. At the close of day 1st futures, price rises to $1.71 on day 2nd price further rises to $1.72. At

Wednesday close, price falls to $1.702. Contract is market-to-market on daily settlement process. What will be profit or loss to investor on Wednesday?

**P.7.** The current price of silver is ₹10,000 per kg. The forward price for delivery in one year is ₹12,000. What an arbitrageur will do? Assume the cost of storing is zero.

**P.8.** On June 1 pepper price at Mumbai are quoted as follows:

Spot                        ₹9,600 (per quintal)
Futures (July)              ₹9,750 (per quintal)
Price on July 15 is ₹9100 per quintal
Mr. Sachin has following transactions:

| | |
|---|---|
| June | Sell one quintal pepper for actual delivery in July at ₹9,750. |
| June | Buy one quintal July pepper futures at ₹9,750. |
| July 15 | Sell one quintal only pepper futures at ₹9,100. |
| July 15 | Buy one pepper at ₹9,100. |

Show the actual position of Sachin on July 15.

# SUGGESTED READINGS

1. Campbell, T.S. and Kracaw, W.A., *Financial Risk Management*, Harper Collins, New York, 1993.
2. Carleton, Dennis, *Futures Markets: Their Purpose, Their History, Their Growth, Their Successes and Failures: Center for The Study of The Futures Market*, 1984.
3. Hull, John C., *Introduction to Futures and Options Markets*, Prentice-Hall of India, New Delhi, 1985.
4. Kolb, Robert W., *Understanding Futures Markets*, Prentice-Hall of India, New Delhi, 1991.
5. Siegel, Danniel R. and Siegel, Diane F., *The Futures Market*, McGraw Hill, USA, 1990.
6. Wasendorf, Russell R., *All About Futures: The Easy Way To Get Started*, McGraw Hill, New York, 2001.
7. www.statistia.com
8. Bank for International Settlements, OTC Derivatives Statistics, April, 2015
9. www.nseindia.com

# Chapter 3

# Forward Market
## Pricing and Trading Mechanism

### LEARNING OBJECTIVES

*After reading this chapter, students will be able to*

➢ Understand the concept of forward contract.
➢ Explain the various features of a forward contract.
➢ Know that forward markets as fore-runner of futures markets, and also know about the historically growth of forward market.
➢ Understand the various differences between futures and forward contracts.
➢ Know about the classification of forward contracts like hedge contracts, transferable specific delivery, non-transferable specific delivery (NTSD) and other forward contracts.
➢ Understand the trading mechanism of forward market.
➢ Understand the pay-off from the forward contracts.
➢ Know about how to closeout a forward position.
➢ Know about the various assumptions for determination of forward prices.
➢ Understand the distinction between investment assets and consumption assets, compounding, short selling, repo rate, etc.

## 3.1 INTRODUCTION

Financial derivatives like futures, forwards options and swaps are important tools to manage assets, portfolios and financial risks. Thus, it is essential to know the terminology and conceptual framework of all these financial derivatives in order to analyze and manage the financial risks. The prices of these financial derivatives contracts depend upon the spot prices of the underlying assets, costs of carrying assets into the future and relationship with spot prices. For example, forward and futures contracts are similar in nature, but their prices in future may differ. Therefore, before using any financial derivative instruments for hedging, speculating, or arbitraging purpose, the trader or investor must carefully examine all the important aspects relating to them.

The derivative is a financial instrument whose value is derived from or depend on the price of underlying asset. These assets are of varied nature which represent as equity, stock indices, commodities like gold, silver, metals, food grains, crude oil, interest rate products like Treasury bills and bonds, corporate bonds, foreign currencies, etc. Important derivatives instruments which are popular in the market are futures, forwards, options and swaps. Corporates, all over the world, transact in forward markets. There are well developed forward markets in many products like energy products, foreign currencies, government securities, precious metals, such as gold and silver, other metals, agricultural products, etc. Forward contracts are not traded on the exchanges rather the firms usually trade with financial institutions which constitute forward markets. This is often called the *over-the-counter* or the (OTC) market. Forward contracts are specialized contracts which are entered by the counter parties directly. There exists a significant credit risk, caused due to defaulting by either of the counter-parties. So, in this market, mostly large institutional firms having high credit-worthiness participate.

**EXAMPLE:** Party X is a farmer who produces agricultural produce like wheat, paddy, etc. in different seasons. Party Y is a manufacture who produces the wheat-flour and rice after processing the wheat and paddy, respectively. X has planned to crop wheat that is expected to yield 500 quintal of wheat to meet an order of 500 quintal wheat flour after four months. Assume current price of wheat is ₹500 per quintal. The farmer is expecting the decline in wheat price before the harvest, and on the other hand, the miller is expecting the rise in wheat price in future. In this situation, both the parties may agree to make a forward contract in which 'X' agrees to deliver 500 quintal of wheat to Y at forward price of ₹1,600 per quintal after four months. Y agrees to pay ₹8 lacs to X after four months for the value of produce, i.e., $1,600 \times 500 = ₹8,00,000$. However, no money changes hands now for entering into this forward contract.

## 3.2 FORWARD CONTRACTS—CONCEPT

Forward contract is a simple form of financial derivative instruments. It is an agreement to buy or sell a specified quantity of an asset at a certain future date for a certain price agreed upon now. In a forward contract, two parties agree to do a trade at some future date at a stated price and quantity. No money changes at the time the deal is signed. However, unlike futures contracts, they are not traded on an exchange. They are private contracts between two parties which may be between financial institutions, between a financial institution and one of its corporate client, etc. Further, these contracts differ from 'cash' or 'spot' contracts where delivery is made immediate within a short settlement period. Most of the forward contracts are traded on the over-the-counter (OTC) market or by telephones. Honouring the contract is made generally by taking and giving delivery and counter parties risk depends on the counter party only.

At the time the forward contract is written, a specified price is fixed at which the asset is purchased or sold. This specified price is referred to as the delivery price. This delivery price is set such that the value of the forward contract is zero at the time of its formation. This means that it costs nothing to take either a long (buyer) or a short (seller) position. This is done by convention so that no cash is exchanged between the parties entering into the contracts. In this way, the delivery price yields a 'fair' price for the future delivery of the underlying asset. One of the parties to a forward contract agrees to buy the underlying asset is said to have a 'long' position. On the other hand, the party that agrees to sell the same underlying asset is said to have a 'short' position.

**EXAMPLE:** Here is an example of forward contract relating to foreign exchange market. A forward contract entered into a rate quoted in the foreign exchange market at the time is a normally 'zero-cost-contract', i.e., neither party pays anything to the other party up-front. They simply exchange two promises to pay in the future just like exchange of two promissory notes. For example, a firm purchases, say, one million US dollar six-month forward at a market rate (forward) of ₹65.40 when the spot rate is ₹64.40 from a bank, say, State Bank of India. Thus, in such contract, there are exchanges of two promises, i.e., the State Bank of India promises to pay one million US Dollar to the firm at the rate of ₹65.40, whereas the other firm promises to pay ₹65.40 million to the SBI. Both payments are to be made after six months. Thus, both parties agree that at the present value of US Dollar one million to be paid 6 months later equals the present value of ₹65.40 million to be paid after six months.

Forward contracts do not have to conform to the standards as followed in the futures contracts. All the terms are mutually agreed by the counter parties at the time of making the contract. A forward contract is settled at the maturity date which is also called delivery date or expiration date. The holder of the short position (seller) will deliver the specified quantity of the underlying asset at the delivery date and at the specified place to the other party (buyer or long), and in return, the holder of long position pays the cash amount equal to the delivery price to the holder of the short position. In simple terms, at the maturity date one party (short) delivers the asset, to other party (long) who in turn pays the amount in cash for the asset purchased.

## 3.3 FEATURES OF FORWARD CONTRACT

Forward contracts are negotiated contracts which are entered by the two counter-parties. The exact terms can be customized to the needs of individuals.. Both the parties must spell out, the quantity and quality of the delivered product, and the date and location of delivery. Being self-regulatory in nature, the consequences in case of default by either party should also be spelled out in the forward contract. Since each party may default, hence, the credit-worthiness of the counter-party is an important issue. Further, the forward contract is a unique contract customized to fit the needs of the counter-parties. So, it is difficult to determine fair market value, if any one of the party wants to terminate the contract prior to the maturity date. The important features of a general forward contract are discussed below in brief:

1. It is an agreement between the two counter-parties in which one is buyer and other is seller. All the terms are mutually agreed upon by the counter-parties at the time of the formation of the forward contract. In forward contract, one of the parties takes a long position by agreeing to buy the asset at a certain specified future date. The other party assumes a short position by agreeing to sell the same asset at the same date for the same specified price. A party with no obligation offsetting the forward contract is said to have an open position. A party with a closed position is, sometimes, called a *hedger*.
2. It specifies a quantity and type of the asset (commodity or security) to be sold and purchased. Each contract is custom designed, and hence, is unique in terms of contract size, expiration date, the asset type, quality, etc.
3. It specifies the future date at which the delivery and payment are to be made.
4. It specifies a price at which the payment is to be made by the seller to the buyer. The price is determined presently to be paid in future. The specified price in a forward contract is referred to as the delivery price. The forward price for a particular forward contract at a particular

time is the delivery price that would apply if the contract were entered into at that time. It is important to differentiate between the forward price and the delivery price. Both the prices are equal at the time the contract is entered into. However, as time passes, the forward price is likely to change, whereas the delivery price remains the same.

5. It obligates the seller to deliver the asset and also obligates the buyer to buy the asset. In the forward market, the contract has to be settled by delivery of the asset on expiration date. In case the party wishes to reverse the contract, it has to compulsorily go to the same counterparty, which may dominate and command the price it wants as being in a monopoly situation.

6. No money changes hands until the delivery date reaches, except for a small service fee, if there is. At the time of making forward contract, neither party has to pay any amount to other party. It means no cash is required to enter into forward contract.

7. In the forward contract, covered parity or cost-of-carry relations are relations between the prices of forward and underlying assets. Such relations further assist in determining the arbitrage-based forward asset prices.

8. Forward contracts are very popular in foreign exchange market as well as interest rate bearing instruments. Most of the large and international banks quoted the forward rate through their 'forward desk' lying within their foreign exchange trading room. Forward foreign exchange quotes by these banks are displayed with the spot rates.

## 3.4 FORWARD MARKETS AS FORE-RUNNERS OF FUTURES MARKETS

Historically, the growth of futures markets followed the growth of forward market. In early years, transport facility was not so good, and hence, a lot of time was taken to deliver the goods at their destination. Sometimes, it took so much time that the prices drastically changed, and even the producers of the goods had to sell at loss. Producers, therefore, thought avoid this price risk and they started selling their goods forward even at the prices somewhat lower than their expectations. For example, the producers thought they could get ₹600 per quintal price for wheat after six months from now when the grain arrived at market, they might still be willing to sell it forward for ₹570 per quintal in order to lock in a certain selling price. The 5 percent price difference might be taken as simply the cost of insurance fee, i.e., insurance fee against the guarantee a fixed selling price. If the producer voluntarily ready to pay this price difference (fee), he obviously thinks selling forward as a superior alternative to bearing the price risk himself.

Another important point arises, in above said forward arrangements, who would be willing to take the other side of the contract. Who would be the purchaser (or long)? One such possibility is that the speculator or arbitrageur may come forward and take the short position. Second, a miller, for example, might need to purchase grain in six months to fulfil a future commitment of delivering flour at an already agreed upon price. So, to protect his profit margin, the miller could purchase grain forward, booking both the fixed price at ₹ 570 per quintal, as well as a source of supply. In this way, he could achieve by taking the long side of the producer's forward contract.

As we see in the earlier example that on one side there is a producer who wants to sell his goods forward and on the other side there is a miller who wants to buy forward, it means both the parties' needs happened to be coincide. So, if they know of each other's existence then they could quietly reach a forward contract which was mutually beneficial to each other. Both would get what they wanted, i.e., price certainty. Further, both of them would not have to pay a fee for this uncertainty if the contract made directly by them. But this ideal state of affairs seldom exists and more likely both buyers and sellers do not know each other's existence. Hence, in most markets a middleman is required to bring together both the parties. The middleman or dealer matches buyers and sellers and against this service he receives a fee, also known as commission.

Further, in the case of forward markets, a dealer (middleman) simultaneously enters into forward contracts with both the parties, i.e., buyer and seller. The dealer will be long with the seller (short) and short with the buyer (long). If the two contracts are identical, the dealer will have no price risk. But sometimes, both the contracts may be different in relation to quantity and quality of the goods, then the dealer will have to bear the risk. In addition, the dealer will have to bear the risk of a default by any of the parties, even if the forward contracts are perfectly matched. It is quite possible that the seller may not be able to supply the goods at the agreed upon price or the buyer may hesitate to take the delivery of the goods at the agreed price. Therefore, the dealer must be compensated for both the risks, i.e., price risk as well as credit risk he bears in the forward contract.

It is further observed that sometimes the dealers also become counter-party to the excess hedging in case of net imbalance of hedgers or they may become speculators. For example, if there is a surplus of short-hedger, the dealer may take long speculative position and vice versa. Thus, the dealers play a significant role in the forward market to make it more active and liquid. It is observed from the above that forward markets throughout the world are faced with several problems like (a) lack of centralization of trading, (b) ill liquidity, and (c) counter-party risk.

## 3.5  MAIN DISTINCTIONS BETWEEN FUTURES AND FORWARD CONTRACTS

Both forward contracts and futures contracts trade in future markets where the underlying assets are sold and purchased at a specified price, specified future time and at a specified place. However, both the contracts differ on certain points which are briefly discussed here as under:

1. Futures contracts are standardized contracts which are traded on organized futures markets. They are done through specified/recognized stock exchanges. The forward contracts on the other hand, are private deal and are traded between the two parties who can sign a forward contract directly or indirectly through a middleman (dealer).

2. The terms of the futures contracts are standardized with respect to the quantity of the asset, future period, future place which are generally common and determined by the exchange, whereas the terms of the forward contracts are decided by both the parties mutually. Hence, forward contracts are individually tailor made and tend to be much larger than the standardized contracts. In other words, futures contracts are traded in a competitive arena whereas forward contracts are traded by telephone, fax, telex, and so on.

3. The futures contracts are regulated through the respective exchanges where they are registered. On the other hand, forward contracts are self-regulatory and need not require any registration. Hence, forward contracts are riskier than the futures contracts.

4. Futures contracts are settled through a clearing house which in effect, takes the guarantee to fulfil the contract. In other words, it reduces the default risk of trading. In case of forward contract, these are private deals between the two parties and are subject to the risk of default on the terms of the agreement.

5. Futures contracts require margin payments and daily settlements. Daily settlement feature sets the value of the futures contract at zero at the each trading day. On the other hand, the

forward contracts are settled on the maturity date and not before that unless both the parties agree for this. However, a middleman (Bank) in a forward contract can ask for a margin. The procedure for maintaining the margin on a forward contract depends upon the bank's relationship with customer.

6. Futures contracts are available for delivery only on a few specified dates in a year, whereas forward contracts can be delivered on any date as agreed by the parties.

7. Most of the futures contracts (around 95 percent) are settled without delivery. It means either they are off settled or settled by the payment of cash. On the other hand, more than 90 percent forward contracts are settled by actual delivery of the assets.

8. Futures contracts entail brokerage fee for purchase and sale orders, whereas the cost of forward contracts is based on bid-ask spread.

In brief, the forward contracts are self-regulated agreements between the two parties to sell or purchase a particular underlying asset at the futures date at an agreed price. On the other hand, the futures contracts are traded on recognized exchanges under the specified rules and guidelines of that exchange.

**TABLE 3.1**  Comparison of Forward and Futures Contracts

| S. No. | Forwards | Futures |
|--------|----------|---------|
| 1. | Private contracts between the two parties; bilateral contracts | Traded on organized exchanges |
| 2. | Not standardized (customized) | Standardized contract |
| 3. | Normally one specified delivery date | Range of delivery dates |
| 4. | Settled at the end of maturity. No cash exchange prior to delivery date | Daily settled. Profit/Loss are paid in cash |
| 5. | More than 90 percent of all forward contracts are settled by actual delivery of assets | Not more than 5 percent of the futures contracts are settled by delivery |
| 6. | Delivery or final cash settlement usually takes place | Contracts normally closed out prior to the delivery |
| 7. | Usually no margin money required | Margins are required of all the participants |
| 8. | Cost of forward contracts based on bid-ask spread | Entail brokerage fee for buy and sell orders |
| 9. | There is credit risk for each party. Hence, credit limits must be set for each customer | The exchange's clearing house becomes the opposite side to each futures contract, thereby reducing credit risk substantially |

## 3.6  CLASSIFICATION OF FORWARD CONTRACTS

As discussed earlier, forward contracts are entered at OTC markets. So, these contracts are very popular in various products like commodities, foreign, currencies and interest rates. Most common forward contracts in currencies and interest rates have been discussed in different chapters of this book. In the section, a brief view of classification of forward contracts in India is described:

1. Forward contracts in commodities
2. Forward contracts in foreign currencies
3. Forward contracts in interest rates

Commodity markets play an important role in the development of an economy, of course, that are dependent to a large extent on the agriculture sector. In India, no formal institutional set up for commodity derivative was exist. After independence, in 1952, the Forward Contracts (Regulation) Act, 1952 was enacted. The Act defines the forward contract as a contract for the delivery of goods that is not a ready delivery contract

The FC(R)Act further describes the ready delivery contract which provides for the delivery of goods and the payment of price, either immediately or within period not exceeding 11 days. The Act has classified the forward contracts in different categories which have been stated below in brief.

**Hedge contracts:** The basic features of such forward contracts are that they are freely transferable and do not specify any particular lot, consignment or variety of delivery of the underlying goods or assets. Delivery in such contracts is necessary except in a residual or optional sense. These contracts are governed under the provisions of the Forward Contracts (Regulation) Act, 1952.

**Transferable specific delivery (TSD) contracts:** These forward contracts are freely transferable from one party to other party. These are concerned with a specific and predetermined consignment or variety of the commodity. There must be delivery of the underlying asset at the expiration time. It is mandatory. Such contracts are subject to the regulatory provisions of the Forward Contracts (Regulation) Act, 1952, but the Central Government has the power to exempt (in specified cases) such forward contracts.

**Non-transferable specific delivery (NTSD) contracts:** These contracts are of such nature which cannot be transferred at all. These may concern with specific variety or consignment of goods or their terms may be highly specific. The delivery in these contracts is mandatory at the time of expiration. Normally, these contracts have been exempted from the regulatory provisions of Forward Act, but the Central Government, whenever feels necessary, may bring them under the regulation of the Act.

It is evident from the above that the definition of hedge contracts corresponds to the definition of futures contracts while the latter two are not futures contracts, and hence, termed as *forward contracts*. Since in both hedge contracts and futures contracts, no specification about the underlying asset/commodity is mentioned because such limits are set by the rules of the exchange on which types can or cannot be delivered. If the variety is superior or inferior to the basis variety for delivery, in that case the prices are adjusted by means of premium or discount as the case may be. Such adjustments are popularly known as *tendering differences*. Thus, on this basis, it may be generalized that every futures contract is a forward contract but every forward contract may not be futures contract.

## 3.6.1 Other Forward Contracts

**Forward rate agreements (FRA):** Forward contracts are commonly arranged on domestic interest-rate bearing instruments as well as on foreign currencies. A forward rate agreement is a contract between the two parties, (usually one being the banker and other a banker's customer or independent party), in which one party (the banker) has given the other party (customer) a guaranteed future rate of interest to cover a specified sum of money over a specified period of time in the future. For example, two parties agree that a 6 percent per annum rate of interest will apply to one year deposit in six months' time. If the actual rate of interest proves to be different from 6 percent then one company will pay and other receives the difference between the two sets of interest cash flows.

In forward rate agreement, no actual lending or borrowing is affected. Only it fixes the rate of interest for a futures transaction. At the time of maturity, when the customer actually needs funds, then he has to borrow the funds at the prevailing rate of interest from the market. If the market rate of interest is higher than the FRA interest then the banker will have to pay to the other party (customer) the difference in the interest rate. However, if market interest is lesser than the FRA rate then the customer will have to pay the difference to the banker. This transaction is known as *purchase of FRA from the bank*.

Sometimes, a customer (depositor) may also make a FRA contract with the bank for his deposits for seeking a guaranteed rate of interest on his deposits. If the market rate on his deposit turns out to be lower than that guaranteed interest rate in the FRA, the bank will compensate him for the difference, i.e., FRA rate minus market interest. Similarly, if the FRA is lower than the deposit rate, then the customer will pay difference to the banker. This transaction is known as *sale of a FRA* to the bank. In this way, purchase of FRA protects the customer against a rise in interest in case of borrowing from the bank. Similarly, sale of FRA will protect the customer from deposits point of view. The bank charges different rates of interest for borrowing and lending, and the spread between these two constitutes bank's profit margin. As a result, no other fee is chargeable for FRA contracts.

**EXAMPLE 1:** Suppose three month forward rupee is at ₹45 per US dollar. A quotation is given in terms of range. The forward rupee would be quoted at "₹48 to ₹50". If the spot rate rises above the maximum, i.e., ₹50 then the maximum level is used. If the spot rate falls below the minimum rate, i.e., ₹48, then the minimum level will be used.

**EXAMPLE 2:** Assume two companies might agree that 8 percent per annum rate of interest will apply to a one-year deposit in fix months' time. If the actual rate proves to be different from 8 percent per annum, one company pays and the other receives the present value of the difference between two sets of interest (cash flows). This is known as a *forward-rate agreement* (FRA).

**Range forwards:** These instruments are very much popular in foreign exchange markets. Under this instrument, instead of quoting a single forward rate, a quotation is given in terms of a range, i.e., a range may be quoted for Indian rupee against US dollar at ₹47 to ₹49. It means there is no single forward rate rather a series of rate ranging from ₹47 to ₹49 has been quoted. This is also known as flexible forward contracts. At the maturity, if the spot exchange rate is between these two levels, then the actual spot rate is used. On the other hand, if the spot rate rises above the maximum of the range, i.e., ₹49 in the present case then the maximum level is used. Further, if the spot rate falls below the minimum level, i.e., ₹47, then the minimum rate will be used. As such we see that these forward range contracts differ from normal forward contracts in two respects, namely (a) they give the customer a range within which he can earn or use from the exchange rate fluctuations, and (b) further they provide protection to the party from the extreme variation in exchange rates.

## 3.7 FORWARD TRADING MECHANISM

Forward contracts are very much popular in foreign exchange markets to hedge the foreign currency risks. Most of the large and international banks have a separate 'Forward Desk' within their foreign exchange trading room which are devoted to the trading of forward contracts. Let us take an example to explain the forward contract.

Suppose on April 10, 2015, the treasurer of an UK Multinational firm (MNC) knows that the corporation will receive one million US dollar after three months, i.e., July 10, 2015 and wants to hedge against the exchange rate movements. In this situation, the treasurer of the MNC will contact a bank and find out that the exchange rate for a three-month forward contract on dollar against pound sterling, i.e., £/$ = 0.8250 and agrees to sell one million dollar. It means that the corporation has short forward contract on US dollar. The MNC has agreed to sell one million dollar on July 10, 2015 to the bank at the future dollar rate at 0.8250. On the other hand, the bank has a long forward contract on dollar. Both sides have made a binding contract/commitment.

Before discussing the forward trading mechanism, let us see some important terminologies frequently used in the forward trading.

**Long position:** The party who agrees to buy in the future is said to hold long position. For example, in the earlier case, the bank has taken a long position agreeing to buy 3-month dollar in futures.

**Short position:** The party who agrees to sell in the future holds a short position in the contract. In the previous example, UK MNC has taken a short position by selling the dollar to the bank for a three-month future.

**The underlying asset:** It means any asset in the form of commodity, security or currency that will be bought and sold when the contract expires, e.g., in the earlier example US dollar is the underlying asset which is sold and purchased in future.

**Spot-price:** This refers to the purchase of the underlying asset for immediate delivery. In other words, it is the quoted price for buying and selling of an asset at the spot or immediate delivery.

**Future spot price:** The spot price of the underlying asset when the contract expires is called *the future spot price*, since it is market price that will prevail at some future date.

**Delivery price:** The specified price in a forward contract will be referred to as the delivery price. This is decided or chosen at the time of entering into forward contract so that the value of the contract to both parties is zero. It means that it costs nothing to take a long or a short position. In other words, at the day on writing of a forward contract, the price which is determined to be paid or received at the maturity or delivery period of the forward contract is called *delivery price*. On the first day of the forward contract, the forward price may be same as to delivery price. This is determined by considering each aspect of forward trading including demand and supply position of the underlying asset. However, a further detail regarding this will be presented in the forthcoming chapter.

**The forward price:** It refers to the agreed upon price at which both the counter parties will transact when the contract expires. In other words, the forward price for a particular forward contract at a particular time is the delivery price that would apply if the contracts were entered into at that time. In the example discussed earlier, on April 10, 2015, 0.8250 is the forward price for a forward contract that involves the delivery of US dollar on July 10, 2015.

## 3.7.1 Concept of Forward Price

As discussed earlier, a forward contract is the contract in which a party agrees to buy or sell an asset at an agreed price at a future date. The buyer takes the long position, whereas the seller takes the short position. The spot price is the price in the open market of the asset at a particular date. The delivery price ($K_T$) is the price agreed in the forward contract for the transaction to be enacted at a time ($T$) when the money is paid and the delivery is taken. $Ft_T$ is the forward price at the initiation of the contract.

When the contract is written, the delivery price is the prevailing forward price. It means $K_T = F_{t,T}$. However, after sometime, the forward price and the delivery price may diverge.

The returns to the party after taking the short position in the forward contract is $K_T - S_T$, and the returns to the party taking long position is $S_T - K_T$. However, the real gain (return) will be only after compensating for the opportunity cost incurred in the forward contract. Opportunity cost is the carrying cost of tying up the capital by holding the asset until Time ($T$). The opportunity cost is ($R$)

determined on the best riskless alternative investment on its capital. Thus, the real gain from the transaction for the short position is only if $K_T - S_T > R$ and gain for long position is if $R > K_T - S_T$. The gain of the short party is the loss for the long party and vice-versa.

The delivery price $(K_T)$ is the sum of two components. The first is the expected spot price which will prevail at time $T$(maturity) $E(S_T)$, expected being formed at the time $(t)$ when the contract is written. The second component is to compensate the party taking the short position, i.e,. for the loss of investment income '$R$' occasioned by holding the asset. It means

$$K_T = E(S_T) + R$$

Now, let us assume that the contract is to mature in one year time, current price of the asset $(St)$, annual riskless rate is $(r)$ then $R = r(St)$ Also, the current price provides the best estimate of the spot price after one year time, so there is $E(S_T) = St$. Substituting these values into the previous equation, we get

$$K_T = (1 + r) St.$$

**EXAMPLE:**  Let us consider that the price of US dollar today is ₹65, and that the annual rate of return of riskless asset is 5 percent. Assume that the one year forward price of US dollar is ₹70. In this, situation, the trader can take short position by borrowing ₹65 to buy the US dollar. By taking short position in US dollar in one year time, then $K_T =$ ₹70, The return would be $K_T - St =$ ₹5. The interest payment for the loan over a price of one year:

$$R = ₹65 \times 0.05 = ₹3.25$$

So, the trader would have a guaranteed overall profit of (₹5 − ₹3.25) = ₹1.75 on one US dollar.

It is unlikely that such an opportunity would persist for long. The demand to exploit it would derive the contract price of US dollar to the level ₹68.25, where there would be no remaining profit from this strategy. This is also known as arbitrage process in the stock market.

Now, let us further assume that the one year forward price of US dollar is quoted in the market at ₹67. In such situation, the return would be $K_T - St =$ ₹2. However, net gain would be ₹2 − ₹3.25 = ₹1.25 on one US dollar. Then the trader will go for long position, i.e., sell the US dollar today at ₹65 and buy the same at ₹67. It means the receipt of ₹65 will be invested at 5 percent for one year, amounting to ₹68.25, delivering the US dollar at ₹67 by purchasing from the market, and net earning of (₹68.25 − ₹67.0) = ₹1.25 per US dollar. Again through the arbitrage process in the market, the super gain of the ₹1.25 per dollar will be over, or till the market reaches to its equilibrium.

## 3.7.2  Determination of Forward Prices

In Section 3.2, we have already discussed about the forward contracts and market. Forward contracts are generally easier to analyse than futures contracts because in forward contracts there is no daily settlement and only a single payment is made at maturity. However, both futures prices and forward prices are closely related, this will be described in the latter part of the chapter.

It is essential to know about certain terms before going to determine the forward prices, such as distinction between investment assets and consumption assets, compounding, short selling, repo rate and so on because these will be frequently used in such computation. We are not discussing these here in detail but the traders must be aware of them thoroughly. A brief view of these terms is explained here as under:

An *investment asset* is an asset that is held for investment purposes, such as stocks, shares, bonds, treasury, securities, etc. The *consumption assets* are those assets which are held primarily for consumption, and not usually for investment purposes. There are commodities like copper, oil, food grains and live hogs.

*Compounding* is a quantitative tool which is used to know the lump-sum value of the proceeds received in a particular period. Consider an amount $A$ invested for $n$ years at an interest rate of $R$ per annum. If the rate is compounded once per annum, the terminal value of that investment will be

$$\text{Terminal value} = A\,(1 + R)^{n},$$

and if it is compounded $m$ times per annum, then the terminal value will be

$$\text{Terminal value} = A\,(1 + R/m)^{mn}$$

Where, $A$ is amount for investment, $R$ is rate of return, $n$ is period for return and $m$ is period of compounding.

Suppose $A$ = ₹100, $R$ = 10% per annum, $n$ = 1 (one year), and if we compound once per annum ($m$ = 1), then as per this formula, terminal value will be

$$100\,(1 + 10)^{1} = 100\,(1.10) = ₹110,$$

if $m$ = 2, then

$$100\,(1 + 0.05)^{2 \times 1} = 100 \times 1.05 \times 1.05 = ₹110.25$$

and so on.

*Short selling* refers to selling securities which are not owned by the investor at the time of sale. It is also called 'shorting', with the intention of buying later. Short selling may not be possible for all investment assets. It yields a profit to the investor when the price of the asset goes down and it is loss when the price goes up. For example, an investor might contract his broker to short 500 State Bank of India shares, then the broker will borrow the shares from another client and sell them in the open market. So, the investor can maintain the short position provided there are shares available for the broker to borrow. However, if the contract is open, the broker has no shares to borrow, then the investor has to close his position immediately, this is known as *short-squeezed*.

The *repo rate* refers to the risk-free rate of interest for many arbitrageurs operating in the future markets. Further, the 'repo' or repurchase agreement refers to that agreement where the owner of the securities agrees to sell them to a financial institution, and buy the same back later (after a particular period). The repurchase price is slightly higher than the price at which they are sold. This difference is usually called *interest earned on the loan*. Repo rate is usually slightly higher than the Treasury bill rate.

## 3.7.3 Assumptions and Notations

Certain **assumptions** considered here for determination of forward or futures prices are:

- There are no transaction costs.
- Same tax rate for all the trading profits.
- Borrowing and lending of money at the risk-free interest rate.
- Traders are ready to take advantage of arbitrage opportunities as and when arise. These assumptions are equally available for all the market participants; large or small.

Further, some **Notations** which have been used here are:
$T$ = Time remained up to delivery date in the contract
$S$ = Price of the underlying asset at present; also called as spot or cash or current

$K$ = Delivery price in the contract at time $T$

$F$ = Forward or future price today

$f$ = Value of a long forward contract today

$r$ = Risk-free rate of interest per annum today

$t$ = Current or today or present period of entering the contract

Now, we will discuss the mechanism of determination of forward prices of different types of assets.

## 3.7.4 Forward Price for Investment Asset (Securities)

Here we will consider three situations in case of investment assets:

1. Investment assets providing no income
2. Investment assets providing a known income
3. Investment assets providing a known dividend income

**Forward price for an asset that provides no income:** This is the easiest forward contract to value because such assets do not give any income to the holder. These are usually non-dividend paying equity shares and discount bonds. Let us consider the relationship between the forward price and spot price with an example.

**EXAMPLE:** Consider a long forward contract to purchase a share (Non-dividend paying) in three-months. Assume that the current stock price is ₹100 and the three-month risk-free rate of interest is 6% per annum. Further, assume that the three months forward price is ₹105.

Arbitrageur can adopt the following strategy:

Borrow ₹100 @6 percent for three months, buy one share at ₹100 and short a forward contract for ₹105. At the end of three months, the arbitrageur delivers the share for ₹105, the sum of money required to pay off the loan is $100e^{0.06 \times 0.25}$ = ₹101.50, and in this way, he will book a profit of ₹3.50, (₹105 – ₹101.50).

Further suppose that the three-month forward price is ₹99. Now, an arbitrageur can short one share, invest the proceeds of the short sale at 6 percent per annum for three months, and a long position in a three-month forward contract. The proceeds of short sales will grow to $100e^{0.06 \times 0.25}$ = ₹101.50, at the end of three months, the arbitrageur will pay ₹99 and takes the delivery of the share under forward contract, and uses it to close its short sale position. His net gain is ₹101.50 – ₹99 = ₹2.5.

*Generalization.* We can generalize from the previous example using the notations mentioned earlier for investment asset providing no income:

$$F = Se^{rT}$$

Where, $F$ is forward price of the stock, $S$ is spot price of the stock, $T$ is maturity period (remained), $r$ is risk-free interest rate.

If $F > Se^{rT}$, then the arbitrageur can buy the asset and will go for short forward contract on the asset.

If $F < Se^{rT}$, then he can short the asset and go for long forward contract on it.

**Forward prices for security that provides a known cash income:** We will consider forward contracts on such assets which provide a known cash income, for example, coupon bearing bonds, treasury securities, known dividend, etc. Let us explain with an example:

**EXAMPLE:** Consider a long forward contract to purchase a coupon bond whose current price is ₹900 maturing after 5 years. We assume that the forward contract matures in one year, so that the forward contract is a contract to purchase a four-year bond in one year. Further, assume that the coupon payment of ₹40 are expected after six months and 12 months, and six-month and one-year risk-free interest rate are 9 percent and 10 percent, respectively.

In the first situation, we assume that the forward price is high at ₹930. In this case, an arbitrageur can borrow ₹900 to buy the bond and short forward contract. Then the first coupon payment has a present value of $40e^{-0.09 \times 0.5} = ₹38.24$. So the balance amount ₹861.76 $(900 - 38.24)$ is borrowed @10 percent for year. The amount owing at the end of the year is $861.76e^{0.1 \times 1} = ₹952.39$. The second coupon provides ₹40 towards this amount, and ₹930 is received for the bond under the terms of the forward contract. The arbitrageur will earn

$$= (₹40 + ₹930) - ₹952.39 = ₹17.61$$

Similarly, in the second situation, we may assume the low forward price at ₹905, then in that case the arbitrageur can short the bond and outer into long forward contract. Likewise above, the arbitrageur will earn:

$$₹952.39 - (₹40 + 905) = ₹7.39$$

*Generalization.* From the above example, it can be generalized that such assets which provide known income (i.e. *I*) during the life of a forward contract, then forward price would be as follows:

$$F = (S - I)e^{rT},$$

In the earlier example, $S = ₹900$, $I = 40$, $r = 0.09$ and $0.1$ and $T = 1$.

*I* is calculated as:

$$I = 40e^{-0.09 \times .05} + 40e^{-0.10 \times 1} = ₹74.433$$

Then $$F = (900 - 74.333)^{0.10 \times 1} = ₹912.39$$

This can be an agreement with our calculation, and it applies to any investment asset that provides a known cash income. So, we can generalize from the above: If $F > (S - I)e^{rT}$, the investor can earn the profit by buying the asset and shorting a forward contract on the asset. If $F < (S - I)e^{rT}$, an arbitrageur can earn the profit by shorting the asset and taking a long position in a forward contract. Further, if there is no short sale, the arbitrageur who owns the asset will find it profitable to sell the asset and go long forward contract.

**Forward price where the income is a known dividend yield:** A known dividend yield means that when income expressed as a percentage of the asset life is known. Let us assume that the dividend yield is paid continuously as a constant annual rate at $q$ then the forward price for an asset would be $F = Se^{(r-q)T}$.

**EXAMPLE:** Let us consider a six-month forward contract on a security where 4 percent per annum continuous dividend is expected. The risk-free rate of interest is 10 percent per annum. The asset's current price is ₹25. Then, we can calculate the forward price as:

$$F = Se^{(r-q)T}$$
$$F = 25e^{(0.10-0.04) \times 0.5} = ₹25.76$$

If $F > Se^{(r-q)T}$, then an investor can buy the asset and enter into a short forward contract to lock in a riskless profit. If $F < Se^{(r-q)T}$, then an investor can enter into a long forward contract and short the stock to earn a riskless profit. Further, if dividend yield varies during the life of a forward contract, the $q$ should be set equal to the average dividend yield during the life of the contract.

## 3.7.5 Valuing Forward Contracts

On the basis of generalization in different situations, we can find out the value of a forward contract. As we know that the value of a forward contract at the time it is first written (entered) into is zero.

However, at later stage, it may prove to have a positive or negative value. In general, the value of a forward contract can be determined as follows:

$$f = (F - K)e^{-rT}$$

where, $f$ is value of a forward contract, $F$ is forward price (current) of the asset, $K$ is delivery price of the asset in the contract, $T$ is time to maturity of contract and $r$ is risk-free rate of interest.

Let us examine the equation:

We compare a long forward contract that has a delivery price of $F$ with an otherwise identical long forward contract with a delivery price of $K$. As we know, the forward price is changing with the passage of time, and that is why later on, $F$ and $K$ may not be equal which were otherwise equal at the time of entrance of the contract. The difference between the two is only in the amount that will be paid for the security at time $T$. Under the first contract, this amount is $F$, and under the second contract, it is $K$. A cash outflow difference of $F - K$ at time $T$ translates to a difference of $(F - K)e^{-rT}$ today. Therefore, the contract with a delivery price $F$ is less valuable than the contract with a delivery price $K$ by an amount $(F - K)e^{-rT}$. The value of contract that has a delivery price of $F$ is by definition, zero.

Similarly, the value of a short forward contract with the delivery price $K$ is $f = (K - F)e^{-rT}$.

**EXAMPLE:**   Consider a six-month long forward contract of a non-income-paying security. The risk-free rate of interest is 6 percent per annum. The stock price is ₹30 and the delivery price is ₹28. Compute the value of forward contract.

$$\text{Forward price } F = 30e^{0.06 \times 0.5} = ₹30.90$$

$$\text{Value of forward contract } f = (F - K)e^{-rT}$$

$$= (30.90 - 28)e^{-0.06 \times 0.5}$$

$$= ₹2.90 - 0.09 = 2.81^* \text{ (app.)}$$

Alternatively, using the other equation:

$$f = 30 - 28^{-0.06 \times 0.5}$$

$$f = 30 - 27.16 = 2.84 \text{ (app.)}$$

*The above difference is due to annual compounding.

Using the earlier equation of value of forward contract, we can show the value of long forward contract in all the three situations, which are as under:

(a) Asset with no income: $f = S - Ke^{-rT}$
(b) Asset with known income (1): $f = S - I - Ke^{-rT}$
(c) Asset with known dividend yield at the rate $q$ : $f = Se^{-qT} - Ke^{-rT}$

Note that in each case the forward price $F$ is the value of $K$ which makes $f$ equal to zero.

## 3.8   FORWARD PRICES VERSUS FUTURES PRICES

Whether the forward prices are equal to futures prices, this is very important and debatable issue. It is argued that if risk-free interest rate is constant and the same for all maturities, in such market situations, the forward price will be same as the futures price for the contract. However, in actual practice, the interest rates do not remain constant and usually vary unpredictably, then forward prices and futures prices no longer remain the same. We can get a sense of the nature of the relationship by considering the situation where the price of the underlying asset is strongly positively correlated with interest rates.

Since in futures contracts, there is daily settlement, so if current price(s) increases, an investor who holds a long future position, makes an immediate profit, which will be reinvested at a higher than average rate of interest. Similarly when current price(s) decreases, the investor will incur immediate loss, and this loss will be financed at a lower than average rate of interest. However, this position does not arise in the forward contract because there is no daily settlement and interest rate movements will not have any affect till maturity.

Whether the futures price and forward price will be equal before the expiration of the contract is studied earlier by various financial experts, like Black (1976), COX. Ingersoll, and Loss (1981), Richard and Sundaresan (1981), Jarrow and Old Field (1981) and so on. It is observed that if future interest rate is perfectly known today, a futures contract can be transformed into a forward contract. It means that in future period, the forward price and future price will be identical or equal, however, ignoring default risk, transaction costs, taxes and other market imperfections. On the other hand, if interest rates are stochastic, the futures prices will exceed forward prices and vice-versa. This relationship indicates that the correlationship between change in futures prices ($\Delta F$) with the change in interest rates ($\Delta r$). In case where Corr ($\Delta F$, $\Delta r$) > o, then if futures prices rise, interest rates also tend to rise. Similarly, if Corr ($\Delta F$, $\Delta r$) < o, then if futures prices rise, interest rates tend to fall.

It is further argued that when spot (current) prices are strongly positively correlated with the interest rates, futures prices will tend to higher than the forward prices. Similarly, if spot prices are strongly negatively correlated with the interest rates, then forward prices tend to be higher than the futures prices. It is further observed that though there may be theoretical difference between forward prices and futures prices due to various factors like taxes, transaction costs, treatment of margin and default risk, this difference is very small which may be ignored. Thus, in our further discussion in various other chapters, both forward contracts and futures contracts are assumed to be the same and the symbol $F$ will be used to represent both futures price and forward price as same at time zero.

## 3.9 FURTHER DISCUSSION ON FORWARD PRICE

In general, concept of the forward price for a forward contract is just like to the future price for a future contract. A contract's current forward price is the delivery price that would apply if the contract were negotiated today. More specifically, the forward price is the delivery price which would make that contract to zero value. In other words, the forward price and the delivery price are equal at the time when the contract is written. However, in practice, as the time passes, the forward price is liable to change, whereas the delivery price, of course, remains the same. It means, the forward price and delivery price may not be equal at any time after the start of the contract, except by chance. In fact, the forward price at any given time varies with the maturity of the contract being considered.

Distinction between forward price and delivery price is explained with our foreign exchange example given above, in which forward price and delivery price is the same, i.e., 0.8250 pound per dollar on April 10, 2015 for a contract with delivery date of July 10, 2015. Let us consider the situation on May 10, 2015 when the forward contract has been in existence for one month. The delivery price will remain the same, i.e., £/$ = 0.8250, but forward price will not remain same, reason being that now price of dollar on May 10, 2015 for a (two-month) forward contract with a delivery date of July 10, 2015 will be different. This may increase or decrease depending upon the market forces. Therefore, if the dollar rate increases between April 10 to May 10, 2015, the forward rate will also increase and vice versa.

The forward price of a contract usually depends upon spot and forward foreign exchange quotations given by the various banks on their desk. Since the forward rates are normally quoted for one year, and available in forward exchange market, the trader/dealer can easily make the adjustments in their forward rates. Table 3.2 shows the spot and forward exchange quotation sterling, January 20, 2012.

**TABLE 3.2** Spot and Forward Foreign Exchange Quotes on Pound Sterling–US Dollar Rate on Jan. 20, 2012

|  | $/£ | £/$ |
|---|---|---|
| Spot | 1.6273 | 0.6145 |
| 1-month forward | 1.6246 | 0.6155 |
| 2-month forward | 1.6196 | 0.6174 |
| 3-month forward | 1.6222 | 0.6164 |
| 6-month forward | 1.6117 | 0.6204 |
| 1-year forward | 1.5973 | 0.6260 |

Table 3.2 indicates that ignoring commission and other transaction costs, sterling pound can be bought and sold in the spot market (immediate delivery) at the rate of $1.6273 per pound; the second quote indicates that the forward price for a contract to buy or sell pound sterling in one month is $1.6246; likewise 2-month rate is 1.6196 and so on. It means that the value of pound sterling against the dollar has fallen in the forward market which will also have impact on the forward price in the forward contracts.

In the discussion of forward contracting, we will use the following notation and time line:

*Time line*:

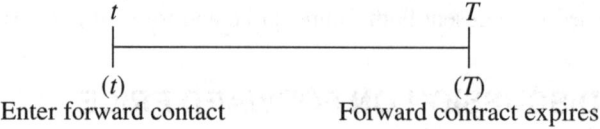

(t)                                 (T)
Enter forward contact          Forward contract expires

*Notation*:

$F_tT$ = Forward price at time $t$ of a contract that expires at time $T$

$S_t$ = Spot price at $t$ (enter period)

$S_T$ = Future spot price at $T$ (at expiration on contract)

$K$ = Delivery price

The profit and loss on a forward contract (position) is determined by the future spot rate $S_T$. Those holding long forward positions, the profit will arise if the futures spot price is higher than the delivery price (here in further discussion, we are assuming that the forward price and delivery price are the same, though both may be different). Since the market price of the asset is higher than the price at which the buyers (long) have contracted to buy.

***Gain on long position per contract:***

= Number of units × (Future spot price – Forward price or delivery price)

= Number of units × $[S_T – K$ (or $F_tT)]$

where, the number of units is per contract.

Those holding short forward positions, the gain will incur to them of the futures spot price falls below the forward price. Then the market price of underlying asset is lower than the price at which the sellers (short) have agreed to sell.

***Gain on short position per contract:***

$$= \text{Number of units} \times (\text{Future price} - \text{Futures spot price or delivery price})$$

$$= \text{Number of units} \times [F_t T \text{ (or } K) - S_T]$$

where, the number of units is per contract.

## 3.9.1   Payoff from the Forward Contracts

To explain the profit and loss incurred (payoff) on a forward contract, let us take a simple example of Gold forward contract. Suppose on January 1, 2015, two parties enter into a forward contract for delivery of 1 kg of gold on April 1, 2015 at a price of ₹25,000 per 10 g of gold. Thus,

$$t = \text{January 1, 2015}$$

$$T = \text{April 1, 2015}$$

$$F_t T = ₹25,000 \text{ per 10 g of gold}$$

Let us assume the future spot price of gold on April 1, 2015, both higher and lower to the forward price, say, ₹24,500 and ₹25,400 per 10 g of gold, respectively.

If the future spot price of gold is ₹25,400, then

***Gain to long position per contract:***

$$= \text{Number of units} \times (\text{Future spot price} - \text{Forward price})$$

$$= 100 \, (25,400 - 25,000) = ₹40,000$$

The long position gains by having purchased gold worth ₹25,400 per 10 g at the forward price of ₹25,000 per 10 g. On the other hand, there will be loss to the person holding short position.

***Loss to short position per contract:***

$$= \text{Number of units} \times (\text{Forward price} - \text{Future spot price})$$

$$= 100 \, (25,000 - 25,400)$$

$$= 100 \times -400 = -₹40,000$$

Similarly, we can assess the position of both long as well as of short by taking the future spot price of gold for ₹24,500 per 10 grams.

$$\text{Loss of long} = 100 \, (24,500 - 25,000)$$

$$= 100 \times (-500) = ₹50,000 \text{ (Loss)}$$

$$\text{Gain to short} = 100 \, (25,000 - 24,500)$$

$$= 100 \times 500 = ₹50,000 \text{ (Profit)}$$

The payoff position from forward contract can be shown through Figure. 3.1.

Assuming no storage cost and transaction cost, etc. in forward contract, the payoff from the forward contracts have been shown in Figure 3.1 for both long position and short position. It is assumed here that the forward price and delivery price are same. The payoff shown in the figure can be positive or negative. For example, in long position, as shown in Figure 3.1(a), if the forward price $F$ is less than the futures spot price $ST$, there will be a profit and vice versa. In case of short position, shown in Figure 3.1(b), if the forward price is higher than the futures spot price, there will be a gain and vice versa.

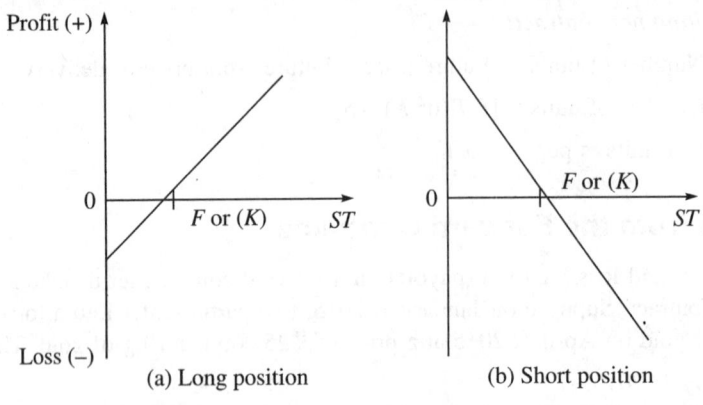

ST = Future spot price;    F = Forward price;    K = Delivery price

**FIGURE 3.1**    Forward price and spot prices.

Now, we can extend this discussion further by assuming that the spot price of gold on January 1, 2015 is ₹24,800 per 10 g and the risk-free interest rate for investment in the market is 8 percent per annum and is easily available in the market. Considering this, what is the reasonable value for one-year forward price of gold?

Suppose that the one-year forward price of gold is ₹27,000 per 10 g. A trader (speculator) may take immediate the following actions:

(a)  Borrow ₹24,80,000 at @8 percent for one year.
(b)  Buy one kg of gold.
(c)  Enter into a short forward contract to sell gold at ₹27,000 per 10 g.

The interest accrued on ₹24,80,000 @8 percent per annum will be ₹1,98,400 (assuming annual compounding), the total amount due to the trader will be after one year ₹26,78,400 (24,80,000 + 1,98,400) which he can get by selling the gold for ₹27,00,000. Hence, the net profit accrued out of this deal will be ₹21,600 (27,00,000 − 26,78,400). In other words, any one-year forward price above than ₹26,784 per 10 g of gold will lead to the arbitrage trading strategy being profitable.

Similarly, we can take opposite position too. Suppose next that the forward price is ₹24,800 per 10 g of gold. An investor who has a portfolio (here gold) can take immediate actions as follows:

(a)  Sell the gold for ₹24,80,000 (₹24,800 per 10 g).
(b)  Invest the proceeds in the market at the rate of 8 percent.
(c)  Enter into a long position (forward contract) to repurchase the gold after one year for ₹24,800 per 10 g.

In the position, the trader will earn interest accrued on amount ₹24,80,000, i.e., ₹1,98,400. Since the spot price and forward price are the same. In simple term, if the forward price is less than ₹26,784, investors holding gold have an incentive to sell the gold and enter into a long forward contract.

In brief, forward trading is important activity in an economy which leads to arbitrage opportunities, assuming that the traders are always willing to take advantage of arbitrage opportunities when they arise in all other assets too.

## 3.10 GETTING OUT OF A FORWARD POSITION

As observed earlier that having any position in forward contract like long or short, the party bears the risk until the contract is expired, because profit to be incurred will depend upon the future spot price of the underlying asset. In other words, the major risk in a forward contract arises due to the degree of volatility of future spot price. So, in this section, we will see whether it is possible to limit this risk be effectively getting out of the position before the expiration date. As we know that one cannot unilaterally back out from the obligation arisen in the forward contract, but he can certainly enter into another forward position exactly opposite the original position. This strategy is popularly known as *offsetting the forward contract*, which can be with the help of following example:

**EXAMPLE:** **Offsetting the forward position:** Let us suppose that on January 1, 2015, a party X enters into a forward contract with another party Y, in which he agrees to buy 10 kg of silver on April 1, 2015 for ₹35,000 per 1 kg of silver. On February 1, 2015, X decides to get out of his position, and hence, enters into another forward contract with Z in which he agrees to sell 10 kg of silver on April 1, 2015 for ₹35,200 per 1 kg of silver.

*Explanation.* Consider the following timeline:

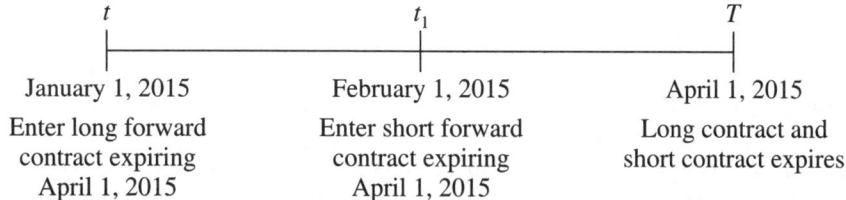

Let us see the position of X party on April 1, 2015.

*Transaction*

| X's account | Cash flow on April 1, 2015 (₹) |
|---|---|
| Take delivery from Y at ₹35,000 per 1 kg of silver | −3,50,000 |
| Deliver to Z at ₹35,200 per 1kg of silver (Total weight of the silver 10 kg) | +3,52,000 |
| Profit | ₹2,000 |

It is to be noted that X's gain is exactly equal to the increase in the forward price of the silver between January 1 and February 1, 2015, multiplied by the number of units. Now, it does not depend upon the futures spot price of the silver as on April, 2015. In other words, after this contract, X is no longer subject to the risk from changing prices in silver. Hence, it can be generalized now that gain or loss of a party be completely determined by forward prices. This can be shown as follows:

*Transaction*

| X's account | Cash flow on April 1, 2015 (₹) |
|---|---|
| Gain from January long position | $(S_T - F_t T)$ (Number of units) |
| Gain from February short position | $(F_{t1} T - S_T)$ (Number of units) |
| Gain | $(F_{t1} T - F_t T)$ (Number of units) |

It is evident from the above that profit or loss from offsetting a forward contract before the expiration date can be expressed in the long position as (Number of units) $(F_{t1}T - F_tT)$. In other words, there will be gain if forward price at time $t$ increases after the contract and before signing offset time $(T - I)$. Similarly, in short position, there will be gain if the transfer price decreases after the forward contract and before the offset time $(t - I)$. Thus, short positions gain if forward prices fall.

In brief, the offsetting the forward contract is an important technique to get out of a forward position. Movements in forward prices generate paper gains and losses for those holding forward positions. By taking the offsetting position, the holder of forward contract locks the difference of transfer price between the two period, i.e., $t$, $(t + 1)$. This gain or loss is not realized until the expiration date $T$. In simple term, once the party has offset the position, there will be no further gain or losses out of the forward position.

Like futures contracts, forward contracts can be used for hedging purposes. For example, An Indian multinational corporation knows that it is due to pay one million US dollar after six months and suppose the six-month forward rate is ₹65 per US dollar. Thus, the corporation can choose at no cost to enter into a long forward contract to buy one million US dollar for six months at ₹65. In this way, it hedges its foreign exchange risk by locking in the exchange rate that will apply to the US dollar.

Similarly, the forward contracts can be used for speculation purposes too. For example, the speculators who think that US dollar will increase against Indian rupee more than ₹65 as given in the above example in futures, they can go by taking a long position in the forward market. Similarly, the speculators who feel that US dollar will decrease against rupee, now he can go by taking a short position in the forward market. The speculators may well be required to pay a margin up-front. However, this is usually a very small proportion of the value of the underlying asset in the forward contract. In brief, like futures market, the forward market is also beneficial to all the market participants, such as investors, traders, speculators, arbitrageurs, etc.

## SUMMARY

The chapter explains the various aspects of forward trading. A forward contract is a simple form of financial derivative instruments. It is an agreement to buy or sell a specified quantity of an asset at a certain futures date for a certain price agreed upon. They are not traded on an exchange. They are private contracts between two parties, which may be between the financial institutions or between a financial institution and one of its corporate client.

This chapter further explained the mechanism of pricing forward in different assets like investments assets and consumption assets. An investment asset is an asset that is held for investment purposes, such as stock, shares, bonds, treasury, securities, etc. Consumption assets are those assets, which are held primarily for consumption, and not usually for investment purposes. These are commodities like copper, oil, food grains, live hogs, etc.

Forward market acts as fore-runners of futures market. Historically, the growth of futures markets followed the growth of forward market. In early years there was not much transporting facilities available and lot of time was taken to reach the goods at their destination. Sometimes, it took so much time that prices change drastically. In case of forward markets, the contract can be done either directly between the counter parties or through a dealer. In case of forward contracts through dealer, a dealer will simultaneously enter into forward contracts with both the parties, i.e., buyer and seller. The dealer will be long with the seller and short with the buyer. If two contracts are identical, dealer will have no price risk. It is further observed that sometimes the dealers also become counter-party to the excess hedging in case of net imbalance of hedgers, or they may become speculators. For example, if there is a surplus of short hedger, the dealer may take long speculative position and vice versa. The dealers play a significant role in the forward market to make it more active and liquid.

Both forward contracts and futures contracts trade in futures markets where the underlying assets are sold and purchased at a specified price at specified future time and at a specified place. There are certain points, which differentiate between forward and futures contract. Futures contracts are standardized contracts but forward contracts are traded directly or indirectly through middlemen. Futures contracts are regulated by an organized exchange as compared to forward, which are self-regulated, settled at the end of maturity as compared to futures, which daily re-settled. There is no margin money required in case of forward contract but futures requires margin money to be deposited by both the parties.

Forward contracts can be classified as: hedge contracts, transferable specific delivery contract (TSD), non-transferable specific delivery contract (NTSD), forward rate agreements (FRA) and range forward. Forward contracts are very much popular in foreign exchange market to hedge the foreign currency risk. Most of the large banks and MNC's have a separate "Forward desk" within their foreign exchange trading room which engage in trading of forward contract.

This chapter further elaborate some terms used in forward trading like long position, short position, the underlying assets, spot price, futures spot price, forward price, and so on. A party can close out its position either by delivery of assets or by offsetting the forward position. Offsetting the forward contract is an important technique to get out of a forward position. Movements in forward prices generate paper gains and losses for those holding forward position. By taking the offsetting position, the holder of forward contract locks the difference of transfer price between the two periods, i.e., of $t$, $(t + 1)$. This gain or loss is to realize until the expiration date $T$.

Last section of the chapter throws light on determination of forward prices. Forward contracts are generally easier to analyze than futures contracts because in forward contract there is no daily settlement and only a single payment is made at maturity.

## SOLVED PROBLEMS

**P.1.** Suppose that on March 1, two parties enter into a forward contract for delivery of 2 kg of gold on August 1 at a price of ₹25,500 per 10 g. What will be profit/loss to the party (long forward price), if the price of gold on August 1 turns out to be ₹27,000 per 10 g.

*Solution:*    In this problem, following notations may be set time line as:

Date of entering forward contract $t$ = March 1

Date of expiration forward contract $T$ = August 1

Forward price at time $T$, $F_t T$ = ₹25,500 per 10 g

Future spot price at time $T$, $P_T$ = ₹27,000 per 10 g

Then,

Gain/Loss to long position (per contract)

$$= \text{Number of units} \times (\text{Future spot price} - \text{Forward price})$$

$$= \text{Number of units} \times (P_T - F_t T)$$

$$= 200 \ (₹27,000 - 25,500) = ₹30,000$$

**P.2.**  Consider the problem 1 and find out the profit/loss of the long forward position, if the price on August 1 turns out to be ₹25,000 per 10 g.

*Solution:*   Given: $t$ = March 1, $T$ = August 1, $F_tT$ = ₹25,500 per 10 g and $P_T$ = ₹25,000 per 10 g

Then,

  Gain/loss to long position (per contract)

$$= \text{Number of units} \times (\text{Future spot price} - \text{Forward price})$$

$$= (\text{Number of units}) \times (P_T - F_tT)$$

$$= 200\ (₹25,000 - ₹25,500)$$

  Loss $= -₹10,000$

**P.3.**  Suppose that on January 1, price of Tata Motors share is ₹450 and two parties enter into a forward contract for delivery of 1,000 shares of Tata Motors on April 15 at a price of ₹460. Find out the profit/loss profile of seller (short position) if the price of Tata Motors share turns out to be: (a) ₹470 (b) ₹400 on April 15.

*Solution:*   In case of short position, the equation will be

  Gain/loss on short position = Number of units × (Forward price − Future spot price)

$$= \text{Number of unit} \times (F_tT - P_T)$$

Now,

Date of entering forward contract $t$ = January 1

Date of expiration forward contract $T$ = August 15

Forward price at time $t$, $F_t\,T$ = ₹460 per share

Futures spot price at time $T$, $P_T$ = ₹470 and ₹400 per share

Then

Gain/Loss to long position (per contract)

$$= (\text{Number of units}) \times (\text{Futures spot price} - \text{Forward price})$$

(a)  In case price of Tata Motors share turns to be ₹470

$$\text{Gain/Loss} = 1,000\ (₹460 - ₹470)$$

$$= 1,000\ (-10) = -₹10,000$$

  Loss $= ₹10,000$

(b)  In case price of Tata Motors share turns to be ₹400

$$\text{Gain/Loss} = 1,000\ (₹460 - ₹400)$$

$$= 1,000\ (60) = ₹60,000$$

  Profit $= ₹60,000$

**P.4.**  Suppose on March 15, 2015, the price of State Bank of India (SBI) share in cash market is ₹250 per share, X enter into an forward agreement with Y to buy 1,500 shares of SBI at agreed price of ₹270 per share on April 15, 2015. Find out the profit profile of X, if price of SBI on April 15, 2015 turns to be 280 in spot market.

*Solution:*   Profit profile of X is given by

  Profit profile of X = Number of units × (Future spot price − Forward price)

Here,

$t$ = March 15, $T$ = April 15, $F_tT$ = ₹270, $P_T$ = ₹280 and Number of units = 1,500

Then

$$\text{Profit} = 1,500 \, (280 - 270)$$

$$= 1,500 \, (10) = ₹15,000$$

**P.5.** Suppose that on March 5, X enters into a forward contract with Y in which he agrees to buy 200 g of gold on August 5 at ₹26,000 per 10 g. On June 1, X decides to get out of his position. He enters into a forward contract with Z in which he agrees to sell 200 g of gold on August 5, for ₹26,250 per 10 g. Show the proficiency of the X on the delivery date, i.e., August 5.

*Solution:* Following is the time line:

| $t$ | $t_1$ | $T$ |
|---|---|---|
| March 1, Enter long forward contract expiring August 5 | June 1, Enter short forward contract expiring August 5 | August 5, Long contract and short contract expires |

X's account

| Transaction | Cash flow on August 5 |
|---|---|
| Take delivery from Y at ₹26,000 per 10 grams | –5,20,000 |
| Deliver to Z at ₹26,250 per 10 grams | +5,25,000 |
| Gain on transaction | ₹5,000 |

**P.6.** Suppose on January 10, Manoj enters into a contract (forward) with Amar in which he agrees to buy 1,000 shares of TVS motor company on July 1 at ₹950 per share on April 1. Manoj decided to get out of his position. He enters into a forward with Chandesh in which he agrees to sell 1000 shares of TVS motor company on July 1 for ₹1,000 per share. Show the position of Manoj on July 1.

*Solution:* Consider the following time line:

| $t$ | $t_1$ | $T$ |
|---|---|---|
| January 10 Enter long forward contract expiring July 1 | April 1 Enter short forward contract expiring July 1 | July 1 Long contract and short contract expire |

Manoj's account

| Transaction | Cash flow payment |
|---|---|
| Take delivery from Amar at ₹950 per share of 1,000 shares | $-(950 \times 1,000) = ₹9,50,000$ |
| Deliver to Chandesh at ₹1,000 per share | $+(1,000 \times 1,000) = ₹10,00,000$ |
| Gain on transaction | ₹50,000 |

**P.7.** Suppose that an investor A has a long 100 shares in a 90 days forward contract at ₹120 per share and an investor B has a long 100 shares at ₹120 per share in 90 days futures contract.

Investor B must purchase 10 contracts. Assume that the spot rate of shares moves to be ₹130 per share. Show the profit profile from futures and forward contracts.

*Solution:*   The payoffs from futures and forward contract:

*From the trader desk*

(a) Investor A takes a long position in a 90-day forward contract on 100 shares. Forward price is 120 per share.

(b) Investor B takes a long position in a 90-day futures contract on 100 shares. Futures price is 120 per share.

*Outcome*

Investor A and B both make a total gain equal to:

$$(130 - 120) \times 100 = ₹1,000$$

Investor A's gain made entirely on the ninetieth day, while investor B's gain is realized day by day over the 90 days period. On some days, investor B may realize a loss while on other days, he or she will realize gains.

**P.8.**   Consider the following:

| Assets | Spot (Cash market) | | Forward market | |
|---|---|---|---|---|
| | Price | Rate (Annual) | Price | Rate (Annual) |
| 3-month T-bill | 99 | 4% | — | — |
| 6-month T-bill | 97 | 6% | — | — |
| Forward price higher than spot price and cost & carry | | | | |
| 3 month T-bill delivery three months | — | — | 99 | 4% |

Show the arbitrage, spot and forward price from the above problem.

*Solution:*

| | | Spot price | Forward rate |
|---|---|---|---|
| Action now | (a)  Sell 3-month T-bill for delivery in 3 months | | 0 |
| | (b)  Borrow to buy 6-month T-bill at T-bill rate | | +9,700 |
| | (c)  Buy 6-month T-bill | | −9,700 |
| Action in 3 months | (a)  Delivery 3-month T-bill to forward contract | | +9,900 |
| | (b)  Pay off loan | | −9,780 |
| | Profit | | +120 |

**P.9.**   Consider the problem 8 and show the profit profile if the forward price is lower than the spot price and cost of carry 3-month T-bill, delivery 3 months ₹98.00 and percent, respectively.

| Assets | Spot price | Market price | Forward market price | Forward rate |
|---|---|---|---|---|
| 3-month T-bill for delivery in 3 months | – | – | 98 | 8% |

*Solution:*

|  | Spot price | Forward rate |
|---|---|---|
| Action now | (a) Buy 3-month T-bill for delivery in 3 months | 0 |
|  | (b) Sell 6-months at T-bill short | +9,850 |
|  | (c) Buy (₹98,50/99) 3-month T-bill | −9,850 |
| Action in 3 months | (a) 3-month T-bill matures | +9,946 |
|  | (b) Take delivery of 3-month T-bill and returned to cover short | −9,800 |
|  | Profit | +146 |

**P.10.** Assume on January, 2015, a commercial bank holds a 10-year, face value of ₹10 million bond priced at 104 with yield-to-maturity of 7 percent. The duration of the bond is 8 years. The bank intends to sell this bond after two months. The bank is predicting that after two months the interest rate may rise to 8 percent. However, most of the other analysts in the market are estimating no change in the interest rate in next two months. Further, assume that 2-month forward contract for 10-year bonds are available at 104 price. The bank wants to hedge against the expected change in the interest rates with an appropriate position in a forward contract. Examine that if the interest rate rises by one percent, how the bank will protect from the loss.

*Solution:* Current yield on the bond is 7 percent, and expected rise in the interest rate is 8 percent. The price of the bond is 104. So, the value of the bonds is ₹10(104/100) ₹10.4 million. The expected change in the spot position is 8 × ₹10.4 m × (1/1.07) = ₹7,77,570. It means that market value of the bond will fall after 2 months if the rate of interest rises to 8 percent. Now, the bank hedges this by making short forward contract of the same value, i.e., ₹10 m at 104 price. As predicted, if the interest rate rises by 1 percent, and the bond value decreased by ₹7,77,570, the bank can close out its forward position by getting 104 for bonds which are now value of ₹96.2243 per ₹100 face value. So, the profit incurred on the forward contract will be offset for the loss in the spot position.

## REVIEW QUESTIONS

1. Define the forward contract. Also, discuss the features of forward contract.
2. 'Forward contracts act as fore-runners of futures market'. Critically evaluate the statement in the light of growth of forward market worldwide.
3. Compare and contrast between forward contracts and futures contracts with suitable examples.
4. Write a detailed note on classification of forward contracts with examples.
5. Define forward contract and discuss the trading mechanism of forward market.
6. What are important terms used in trading forward contract? Explain.
7. What are important factors that help in determination of pricing of financial derivatives? Discuss with examples.
8. Discuss the pricing mechanism of forward contract.
9. Taking a hypothetical examples, discuss the payoff profile from the forward contract.
10. Bring out the ways through which a forward contract can be closed out. Discuss with by giving suitable examples.

11. Write short note on:
    (a) Assumptions and notations in determination of forward prices
    (b) Forward price of an investment asset
12. Discuss the concept of valuation of forward control in details with suitable illustrations.
13. Write a detailed note on the growth pattern of forward contract in Indian stock market.
14. Explain the various uses of forward contract with suitable examples.
15. Bring out the relationship between forward and spot prices. Explain with the help of suitable examples.
16. Compare and contrast the trading mechanism of forward market and futures market.
17. Write short note on:
    (a) Forward rate agreements (FRA)
    (b) Range forward
18. What is the difference between the way in which prices are quoted in the forward market, spot market and futures market? Discuss with suitable illustrations.
19. "A long forward contract is equivalent to a long position in call option and a short position in put option". Explain this statement.
20. What are various risks associated with forward contract? Explain how these can be reduced by using futures contract.
21. Write short note on:
    (a) Consumption assets
    (b) Investment assets
    (c) Terminal value
22. Under what circumstances a firm may choose to use futures rather than forward while hedging its risk?

## SUGGESTED READINGS

1. Margrabe, W., *A Theory of Forward and Futures Price*, The Wharton School, University of Pennsylvania, 1976.
2. Richard, S. and Sundaresan, M., A continuous time model of forward and futures prices in a multigoods economy, *Journal of Financial Economics*, pp. 347–372, December, 1981.
3. Dubofsky, D.A., *Options and Financial Futures*, McGraw Hill, Maidenhead, 1995.
4. Kolb, R.W., *Financial Derivatives*, Kolb Publishing, Miami, 1993.
5. Wistone, D., *Financial Derivatives*, Champon and Hall, London, 1995.
6. Marshall, John F. and Bansal, Vipul K., *Financial Engineering: A Complete Guide to Financial Innovation*, Prentice-Hall of India, New Delhi, 1999.
7. Rene M. Stulz, "*Risk Management & Derivatives*. Thomson South-Western, Indian-Reprint-2007.
8. Robert A. Strong, "*Derivatives*" Thomson-South-Western, Indian-Reprint-2006.

# Chapter 4

# Futures Pricing
## Theories and Characteristics

*After reading this chapter, students will be able to*

➤ Understand the concept of futures pricing.
➤ Understand how futures prices are read.
➤ Know about the patterns and characteristics of futures prices.
➤ Be aware of the assumptions for determination of futures prices.
➤ Explain the mechanism of determining futures prices.
➤ Be aware of the valuation of futures contracts.
➤ Be familiar about how spot prices and futures prices equal at expiration.
➤ Know about the various theories of futures pricing like (a) cost-of-carry approach, (b) the expectation approach and (c) the theory of normal backwardation.
➤ Understand the futures prices and the capital asset pricing (CAPM) model.
➤ Be aware about the integrated approach to futures pricing, which describes the futures prices of those assets which have continuous production and discontinuous production.
➤ Know about the determination of futures prices of specific assets like stock index futures, foreign currencies and commodities.
➤ Understand the concept of basis and spreads and various types of spreads.

## 4.1 INTRODUCTION

Futures trading is an important economic activity for the development of an economy. Being the first form of derivatives trading, it is a specialized field which requires professional expertise and adequate knowledge in this area. To be a successful market operator (as a speculator, arbitrageur, trader, investor or hedger) one must have adequate information and proper understanding of the functioning of the futures markets. These are essential to make evaluation of derivatives products in terms of their prices and values so that the market participants can select them as per their objectives.

Futures are useful to the market participants only if futures prices reflect information about the prices of the underlying assets. That is why it is essential to understand how futures markets work and how the prices of futures contracts relate to the spot prices. In this section, we will examine the factors that affect futures prices in general. The futures prices of different assets like commodities, foreign exchanges and securities are influenced by various factors which are not common for all such assets. For example, futures prices of foreign currencies may be determined by different factors as different for determination of futures prices of foodgrains and vegetables. Further, we will discuss the terms Basis and Spreads used in trading in futures markets along with the different theories of futures pricing with their applications.

## 4.2   READING FUTURES PRICES

Today, futures contracts in various assets are traded all over the world. Futures prices are published in important magazines, dailies and journals, and one such journal is most popular in the world is Wall Street Journal (WSJ), which publishes futures prices daily and other relevant information in context to financial markets. These prices are reported in a standardized format. We are presenting here in Table 4.1, an example of quoted Nifty Index futures prices, as reported in the NSE website in the month of Dec15, just to understand the mechanism of presentation of futures prices.

**TABLE 4.1**   Futures Price of Nifty Index for December, 2015

| Date | Open | High | Low | Settle Price | Daily Change | Contracts | Turnover (in lacs) | Open Interest |
|------|------|------|-----|--------------|--------------|-----------|--------------------|---------------|
| 01 Dec.15 | 8,028.80 | 8,040.95 | 7,999.00 | 8,023.30 | – | 2,328.00 | 14,005.81 | 8,12,550 |
| 02 Dec.15 | 8,037.20 | 8,037.20 | 7,972.55 | 7,999.25 | –24.05 | 2,816.00 | 16,899.14 | 8,15,925 |
| 03 Dec.15 | 7,969.85 | 7,984.60 | 7,917.00 | 7,929.45 | –69.80 | 3,870.00 | 23,083.04 | 8,62,125 |
| 04 Dec.15 | 7,877.20 | 7,893.50 | 7,848.60 | 7,856.25 | –73.20 | 4,296.00 | 25,352.13 | 9,22,050 |
| 07 Dec.15 | 7,892.00 | 7,892.95 | 7,827.45 | 7,847.20 | –9.05 | 3,882.00 | 22,869.81 | 9,74,325 |
| 08 Dec.15 | 7,810.00 | 7,841.00 | 7,749.10 | 7,766.35 | –80.85 | 4,858.00 | 28,402.63 | 10,81,575 |
| 09 Dec.15 | 7,747.05 | 7,764.75 | 7,660.60 | 7,681.65 | –84.70 | 6,445.00 | 37,293.66 | 11,46,300 |
| 10 Dec.15 | 7,703.30 | 7,758.80 | 7,677.95 | 7,747.35 | 65.70 | 5,468.00 | 31,639.15 | 12,08,475 |
| 11 Dec.15 | 7,735.05 | 7,740.35 | 7,625.00 | 7,664.95 | –82.40 | 8,341.00 | 48,046.16 | 13,24,200 |
| 14 Dec.15 | 7,601.00 | 7,730.00 | 7,601.00 | 7,702.05 | 37.10 | 6,182.00 | 35629.90 | 13,98,825 |
| 15 Dec.15 | 7,708.95 | 7,750.00 | 7,672.15 | 7,743.70 | 41.65 | 4,049.00 | 23,425.69 | 14,18,025 |
| 16 Dec.15 | 7,770.35 | 7,823.55 | 7,763.00 | 7,792.65 | 48.95 | 10,762.00 | 62,936.99 | 15,78,675 |
| 17 Dec.15 | 7,828.10 | 7,895.80 | 7,780.00 | 7,886.55 | 93.90 | 15,009.00 | 88,375.68 | 19,58,625 |
| 18 Dec.15 | 7,846.00 | 7,881.00 | 7,814.10 | 7,822.50 | –64.05 | 11,297.00 | 66,522.40 | 17,45,100 |
| 21 Dec.15 | 7849.95 | 7,885.00 | 7,799.60 | 7,871.10 | 48.60 | 7,931.00 | 46,758.17 | 18,89,100 |
| 22 Dec.15 | 7,865.05 | 7,889.00 | 7,805.00 | 7,816.75 | –54.35 | 14,600.00 | 85,919.37 | 22,15,575 |

*(Contd.)*

| Date | Open | High | Low | Settle Price | Daily Change | Contracts | Turnover (in lacs) | Open Interest |
|------|------|------|-----|--------------|--------------|-----------|--------------------|---------------|
| 23 Dec. 15 | 7,849.95 | 7,907.50 | 7,849.90 | 7,894.10 | 77.35 | 32,034.00 | 1,89,558.84 | 34,83,300 |
| 24 Dec. 15 | 7,917.00 | 7,925.00 | 7,871.00 | 7,902.15 | 8.05 | 20,797.00 | 1,23,102.43 | 41,08,500 |
| 28 Dec. 15 | 7,893.05 | 7,947.25 | 7,889.15 | 7,934.65 | 32.50 | 55,283.00 | 3,28,809.04 | 70,81,500 |
| 29 Dec. 15 | 7,940.00 | 7,963.00 | 7,921.35 | 7,955.85 | 21.20 | 90,283.00 | 5,37,836.02 | 1,15,13850 |
| 30 Dec. 15 | 7,960.00 | 7,964.80 | 7,916.50 | 7,925.05 | -30.80 | 70,238.00 | 4,18,456.99 | 1,43,27,550 |
| 31 Dec. 15 | 7,925.00 | 7,958.40 | 7,917.55 | 7,952.05 | 27.00 | 1,21,751.00 | 7,24,817.74 | 1,89,77,400 |

*Source:* www.nseindia.com

The following explains the Quotation relating to the (Nifty Index) contract traded on the National Stock Exchange (NSE) that appears in each column of Table 4.1:

**Open:**   The open column refers to the price at which the first contract of the day was transacted. In other words, the price for the day's first trade which occurs during the designated time period, for example, in Table 4.1 for the December, 2015 contract, the open price was ₹7,925 on December 31.

**High:**   The highest price of the contract recorded during the day, e.g., for the December 31, 2015 contract, the highest price is ₹7,958.40

**Low:**   The lowest price of the contract recorded during the day, e.g., for the December 31, 2015 contract, the lowest price is ₹7,917.55

**Settle:**   The settle column refers to the settlement price. It is the price determined daily to settle and adjust all investors' margin accounts for the daily change in futures prices, for example, for the December 31, 2015 contract, the settle price is ₹7,952.05

The settlement price is usually determined by the formula using the range of prices recorded within the closing period, such as last minute of the trading. This price is determined by the exchange's settlement committee and is intended to reach a fair value of the futures contract at the close of the day.

**Change:**   This column shows the change in previous day's settlement price and today's settlement price. This change can, of course, be either positive or negative. For the December 31, 2015 contract, the change is +₹27 (i.e., ₹7,952.05 – ₹7,925.05).

**Open interest:**   This column refers to the 'open interest' which refers to the total number of contract outstanding at the close of the previous day's trading. For example, for the month December 31, 2015 was 1,89,77,400 and the total number as 1,21,751 contracts.

**Turnover:**   This refers to the estimated volume of trading (in turnover) for Nifty Index on December 31, 2015 is ₹7,24,817.74 lakhs.

### Contract specifications of Nifty Index

### Security descriptor

The security descriptor for the CNX Nifty futures contracts is:

- Market type: N
- Instrument Type: FUTIDX

- Underlying: NIFTY
- Expiry date: Date of contract expiry
- Instrument type represents the instrument, i.e., Futures on Index.
- Underlying symbol denotes the underlying index which is CNX Nifty
- Expiry date identifies the date of expiry of the contract

**Underlying instrument**

The underlying index is CNX NIFTY.

**Trading cycle**

NIFTY futures contracts have a maximum of 3-month trading cycle—the near month (one), the next month (two) and the far month (three). A new contract is introduced on the trading day following the expiry of the near month contract. The new contract will be introduced for a three-month duration. This way, at any point in time, there will be 3 contracts available for trading in the market, i.e., one near month, one mid month and one far month duration, respectively

**Expiry day**

CNX Nifty futures contracts expire on the last Thursday of the expiry month. If the last Thursday is a trading holiday, the contracts expire on the previous trading day.

*Trading parameters*

**Contract size**

The value of the futures contracts on Nifty may not be less than ₹2 lakhs at the time of introduction. The permitted lot size for futures contracts and options contracts shall be the same for a given underlying or such lot size as may be stipulated by the Exchange from time to time.

**Price steps**

The price step in respect of CNX Nifty futures contracts is ₹0.05.

**Base prices**

Base price of CNX Nifty futures contracts on the first day of trading would be theoretical futures price. The base price of the contracts on subsequent trading days would be the daily settlement price of the futures contracts.

**Price bands**

There are no day minimum/maximum price ranges applicable for CNX Nifty futures contracts. However, in order to prevent erroneous order entry by trading members, operating ranges are kept at +/– 10 percent. In respect of orders which have come under price freeze, members would be required to confirm to the Exchange that there is no inadvertent error in the order entry and that the order is genuine. On such confirmation the Exchange may approve such order.

## 4.3  CHARACTERISTICS OF FUTURES PRICES

To understand the relationship between spot, futures and forward prices, it is important to understand the term basis and convergence. Basis is usually defined as the difference of cash price and futures price. If cash price is higher than futures price, the basis is termed as positive, and if cash price is less than futures price, then the basis is called negative. In normal circumstances, or normal market, the basis will be negative because futures prices usually exceed cash prices due to cost and carry pricing model, as explained further in this chapter. In an inverted market', the basis will be positive where futures price exceeds cash prices. The basis will be decreasing as the contract is reaching to maturity. Normally it will be equal to zero on maturity date.

The term 'convergence' is defined as the process of basis moving towards zero. It is observed that regardless of current basis, due to the possibility of arbitrage, the basis will be zero on the maturity of the contract. Further, it is also possible that the basis may fluctuate due to various reasons as time passes, but convergence will still take place at the final day of contract.

A few important characteristics of futures prices are as under:

## 4.3.1 Relationship with Forward Price

We have already seen in the past the differences between futures contracts and forward contracts and also the determination of futures as well as forward prices. Now, we will visualize the relationship of futures prices with the forward prices. Forward prices are indifferent with the changes in the market and spot prices before the maturity because the settlement and delivery of the underlying assets are to be executed at the time of expiration. The chances of default may be higher in a forward contract than futures contract which is cleared through the clearing house and settled on a daily basis. Hence, the main conceptual reason for a possible difference in prices arises from the daily settlement and margin requirement. Let us discuss this with an example.

Consider a gold futures and a gold forward both expire after one year and we assume the current price of the gold is ₹25,000 per 10 g. Further, we also assume that futures spot price after one year is ₹25,000 per 10 g. Thus, there will be no profit or loss on either contract. Also, assume that when the contract will expire, the forward price, the futures price and spot price must all be equal. We further assume 250 trading days in a year. Now, let us consider two possible situations. First, we assume that the futures price rises by ₹20 per day for 125 days and then falls by ₹20 per day till maturity. Similarly, the second situation where the futures price falls by ₹20 per day for 125 days and then rises by ₹20 per day till maturity. At the end, the price will be ₹25,000 and there is no profit or loss on either contract. Let us show these futures price paths in Figure. 4.1.

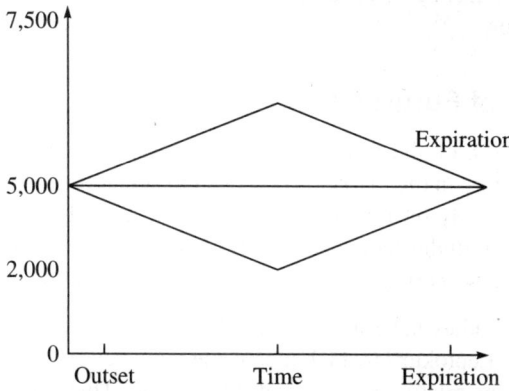

**FIGURE 4.1** Possible futures price paths.

From Figure. 4.1, it is evident that the forward trader is indifferent between the two possible price paths because he has no cash flow at the outset and at the end. However, the futures traders are affected due to daily cash settlement of their futures transactions. For example, a long futures trader would prefer the beginning price rise because there is daily rise of ₹20 per 10 g in gold, and so, he will be getting the difference of the prices and investing the same in the market and vice-versa.

Let us further assume a 10 percent interest rates on the difference in these two price paths is about ₹250 for the futures trader. If the price rises first then the long futures trader received payment which he will invest and earn interest on that amount. Later on he is to pay the amount when the price falls. In brief, it is to be noted that these differences stem strictly from the interest gains or losses on the daily settlement basis and the futures trader can be better or worse off than the forward trader.

We can generalize the above analysis. For example, if the futures price is positively correlated with interest rates then a long trader will prefer a futures position over a forward position. If the futures price and interest rates rise together then the long futures trader will receive settlements that can be invested at the higher interest rate. Further, if futures prices and interest rates both fall then the futures trader must make the payment at the lower interest rate. So, we can conclude as under:

*Theoretical relationship of forward and futures prices.*

| Correlation of spot price and interest rates | Price relationship |
|---|---|
| Positive correlation | Futures price > Forward price |
| Negative correlation | Futures price < Forward price |
| No correlation | Futures price = Forward price |

## 4.3.2   Futures Prices and Expected Future Spot Prices

It is already observed that futures prices and markets serve the society by providing a mechanism for market traders to form expectation about future spot prices. This is also called *price discovery function*. Since the futures prices change continuously, so quite possible that they may not be equal to the future or observed spot price. The futures price could be an estimate of the expected future spot price. This relationship has been discussed in detail in the section of 'normal backwardation' in section 4.5.1 of this chapter.

## 4.3.3   Distribution of Futures Prices

In this section, we will see how the futures prices are distributed in the futures markets. In other words, the trend of these prices in the market is reviewed in actual practice. Most of the statistical tests conducted on futures prices rely on the assumption that the underlying price changes are normally distributed. From the various studies conducted in this respect on different commodities and financial instruments with different time periods show the following observations in general:

(a) Almost all of the studies have noticed that the futures price are not normally distributed in general, rather it is Leptokurtic which means the tendency for a distribution to have too many extreme observations relative to a normal distribution. This is shown in Figure. 4.2.

   In Figure. 4.2, solid line shows the normal distribution, whereas dotted line shows the leptokurtic distribution. The greater frequency of extreme observations makes the tail of a leptokurtic distribution 'fat tails'. Almost all of the studies have rejected the hypothesis, i.e., normal distribution of futures prices on the grounds of leptokurtosis.

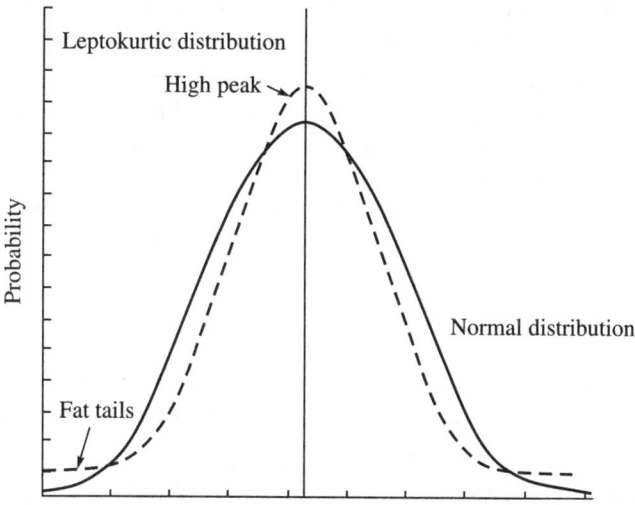

**FIGURE 4.2** Normality and Leptokurtosis.

(b) Some other studies have tried to find out what distribution of futures prices follow if they are not normal. There are two views in this respect: First, the distribution may be stable Paretien. It is symmetrical but it is leptokurtic relative to a normal distribution. Second, some other studies have found that the distribution of futures prices changes seem to be similar to a mixture of two or more normal distributions. Thus, both groups agree that this non-normally requires extra caution in making statistical inferences about futures prices.

(c) Further, some studies have tested whether the time series of futures price changes is auto-correlated which means that value of one observation in the series is statistically related to each other. For example, first order auto correlation states that one observation is related to the immediately preceding observation. So, most of the studies have found that futures prices exhibit statistically significant first-order auto-correlation.

## 4.3.4 Volatility of Futures Prices

In this section, we will discuss two dimensions of futures price volatility: First, relationship between futures trading and the volatility of prices for the underlying asset. Here volatility is measured as the variance of price changes. Second, patterns in the volatility of futures prices themselves would be analyzed.

**Futures trading and cash market volatility:** Some studies have observed that the futures trading makes prices for the underlying asset more volatile, specifically, in equities. Further, some studies had also been conducted to see the volatility in cash market prices due to futures trading. However, in general, it is observed that futures trading does increase the volatility of the cash market. In other words, it does not de-stabilize the cash market.

**Time to expiration and futures price volatility:** Paul Samuelson, a renowned economist, argued that the volatility of futures prices should increase as the contract approaches expiration. In other words, near expiration, there is more volatility than in the beginning. Virtually, all the studies agree that futures prices exhibit seasonal volatility—they are more volatile at some specific periods rather than at others. Finally, there also seems to be a day-of-week effect in price volatility, i.e., volatility defers depending on the day of the week, as seen higher on Monday than the other days.

**Trading volume and futures price volatility:**    In addition to the above mentioned observations, some studies have analyzed that there appears to be a strong positive relationship between the volume of futures trading volumes and the volatility of the futures prices. As observed earlier that when more information are coming to the market, the futures prices turn more volatile. Hence, traders who trade based on information are also more likely to trade when information are received more rapidly. So, the futures prices become more volatile with the increase in the trading volume.

## 4.4  BASIS

The basis is an important term in futures trading. The basis is the difference between the current/cash/spot price and the futures price of a particular asset at a specified location at a particular point of time.

### 4.4.1  Basis: Current Cash Price—Futures Price

Since the futures prices are different from place to place, hence, usually people speaking on the basis are referring to the difference between the cash price and the nearby futures price of a contract. When the futures contract is at expiration, the futures price and spot price of an asset becomes the same. The basis must be zero, but subject to the discrepancy due to transaction costs. As discussed in the preceding section, this behaviour of the basis over time is known as *convergence*.

From Figure. 4.4, it is observed that as the delivery month of a futures contract is approached, the futures price converges to the spot price of the asset, and at the delivery period, futures price equals or is very close to the spot price. Thus, as the time passes, the basis narrows near maturity of the contract. Further, in Figure. 4.5, a significant behaviour pattern between cash prices and futures prices observed that fluctuation in the basis was much less than the range of fluctuation in the futures price itself. The basis is almost much more stable than the futures prices or the cash prices.

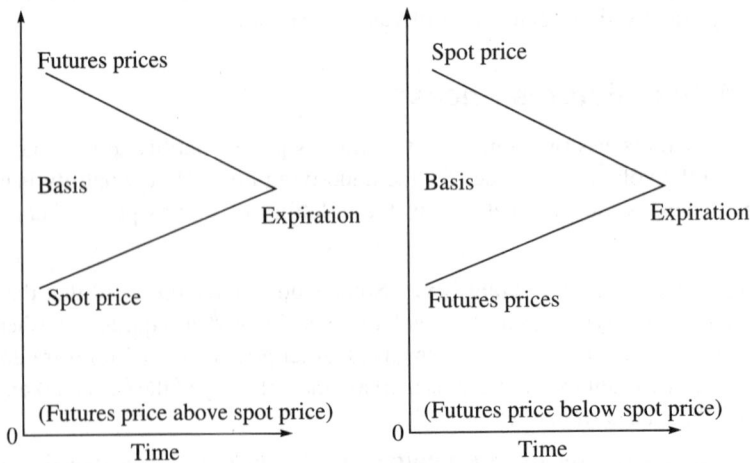

**FIGURE 4.4**  Convergence of futures price to spot price.

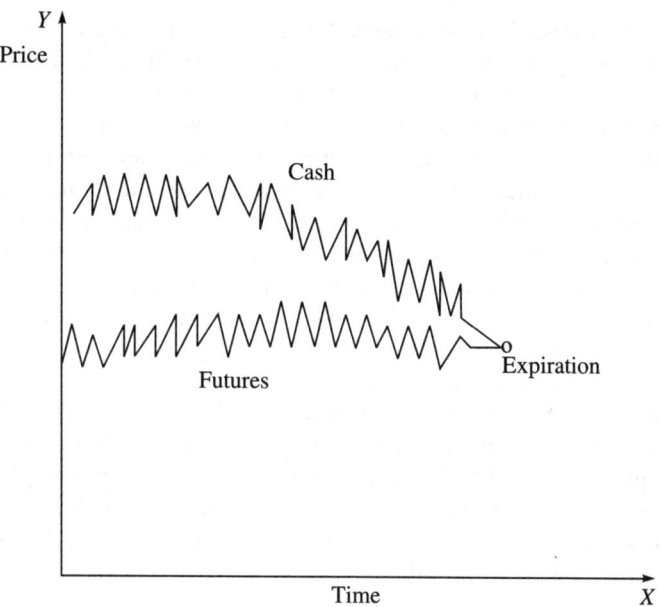

**FIGURE 4.5** Converging cash and futures prices.

***Why this is so? Why spot price and futures price equals at expiration?***

The basic reason is that if the futures price is above the spot price during the delivery period, this will give rise to a clear arbitrage opportunity for the traders in the market which may be followed as:

1. Short a futures contract
2. Buy the underlying asset
3. Make delivery

Due to arbitrage process, the futures price will tend to fall, and suppose that futures price is much below the spot price. Again there will be arbitrage opportunity, resulting in, traders find it attractive in acquiring the asset and there will be more long futures contracts in the market. Due to this, the futures price will tend to arise. In this way, whether the futures price is higher or lower to the spot price, at the maturity, either will be equal or near equal. The market participants, who take advantage of the above said so called cash futures arbitrage opportunities, assure that cash and futures prices will usually have a well-defined relationship to each other. In particular, they differ only due to transaction costs associated with doing such arbitrage transaction. A further discussion on 'Basis' is made in the forthcoming chapter on "hedging strategy".

## 4.5 THEORIES OF FUTURES PRICES

Before discussing the various theories of futures pricing, let us have a look on the nature of futures contract whether it is forward or futures. Futures or forward price of an asset is the price that is agreed or quoted today for delivery of the same in future. It means the futures price is fixed today, but is paid when the asset is delivered in the future. In theory, futures prices are determined by the force of arbitrage process. In other words, the fair price of a futures derivative is the price at which profitable opportunity ceases, or arbitrages opportunity is not available. For example, if futures prices are not fair, or 'wrong' or 'misquoted', market will not be in equilibrium, which will cause to arbitraging in the market. It means supply does not equal whole demand for an asset, so arbitrage process (buying selling of the assets) will be in operation. The traders will quickly act to exploit the opportunity to cash profit. It means price of the asset is not same at all the market places. Then, it will give an opportunity for arbitrate process. For example, assume that US dollar price for Indian rupee quoted in Delhi 64, 3 month future and 65, 3 month futures at Mumbai. There is difference of ₹1 per dollar in both markets, resulting into arbitrate process. The traders will buy the asset at the market where the price is lesser and sell the same where the price is higher. As a result, the price of asset will rise at lower price location because of heavy supply. This process will continue till the market reaches to its equilibrium and price becomes equal at all locations.

Another important point to be noted is the distinction between futures price and price in future period. Futures price is current price fixed today, whereas the price in future period means the cash or spot price prevailing in future period at a particular date. For example: Assume US dollar futures price is quoted today on August 5, 2015 at ₹66 for maturity on September 4, 2015 at Delhi. Assume the spot price quoted on August 25, 2015, is ₹65.80 in the market, then it will be called *price at future period*, however, the futures price will not be changed, rather remains same till September 4, 2015.

Determining the future prices is a very complicated and risky task, estimating the futures prices of assets related with the future which is uncertain and full of many unknown factors and events to be happened in the markets. So, while predicting future prices, we have to consider various experts' studies which have been conducted from time to time in different assets. There is no unanimity among these but important observations have been noted by the analysts. Empirical researches show that while predicting future prices, various aspects like future cost, participants' expectations, inherent risk in future, etc. should be taken into consideration. In the light of these factors, this section will describe important theories, in brief, for estimating the futures prices.

There are several theories which have made efforts to explain the relationship between spot and futures prices. A few important theories are as follows:

## 4.5.1   Cost-of-carry Approach

Cost-of-carry approach is very popular approach in commodity derivatives and is an arbitrage free pricing model. The model will be examined both imperfect market and in perfect market. Under perfect market conditions, this theory determines the one futures price, but markets are imperfect. The degree of imperfection has direct impact on the futures pricing which creates the arbitrate opportunity in the market.

**Cost and carry stock arbitrate transaction:**   Some top economists like Keynes and Hicks, have argued that futures prices essentially reflect the carrying cost of the underlying assets. In other words, the inter-relationship between spot and futures prices reflect the carrying costs, i.e., the amount to be paid to store the asset from the present time to the futures maturity time (date). For example, food grains on hand in June can be carried forward to, or stored until, December.

Carrying costs are of several types, important among these are:

1. Storage costs
2. Insurance costs

3. Transportation costs
4. Financing costs

**Storage costs** refer to those expenses which are done on storing and maintaining the asset in safe custody. It includes rent of the warehouse and others expenses associated with like deterioration, pilferage, normal wastage, etc. In case of financial instruments, the costs incurred on keeping the securities in a bank vault or with custodians.

**Insurance costs** refer to amount incurred on safety of the assets against fire, accidents and others. For example, stored wheat be protected against fire, water damage, weather, natural disaster, etc. So insurance is necessary for protection against such hazards. Thus, premium and other costs incurred on insurance is called *insurance costs*.

In some cases, carrying costs also include the **transportation costs**. When the futures contract matures the delivery of the assets is given at a particular place which may be far away from the warehouse of stored goods. Obviously, transportation costs will be different from location to location and also to the nature of the commodities.

Another important carrying cost is **cost of financing** the underlying asset. For example, if gold costs ₹25,000 per 10 g and the financing rate is one percent per month then the financing charge for carrying the gold forward is ₹250 per month (1 percent of 25,000).

Apart from the carrying cost on an underlying asset, there can be a possibility of earning a yield on storing the asset. Such yield is known as *convenience yield* from holding stocks. For example, in case of wheat, there could arise extra yield due to low production of wheat due to bad weather in futures. Thus, up to a certain level, stock holding has a yield in the event of stock out and unanticipated demand. This may be termed as a *negative carrying cost*. Hence, the *net marginal carrying cost* for any given asset may be expressed as:

$$C_T = C_{gt} - Y_t$$

where, $C_T$ is the net carrying cost of that quantity, $C_{gt}$ is the gross carrying cost of that quantity, $Y_t$ is the convenience yield of that quantity and $t$ is the time period of storage.

**The cost-of-carry model in perfect market:** The following formula describes a general cost-of-carry price relationship between the cash (spot) price and futures price of any asset:

Futures price = Cash (spot) price + Carrying cost

In addition, the formula assumes the conditions of perfect competition which are as under:

1. There are no information or transaction costs associated with the buying and selling the asset.
2. There is unlimited capacity to borrow and lend.
3. Borrowing and lending rates are the same.
4. There is no credit risk. No margin is required on buying and selling the asset.
5. Goods can be stored indefinitely without loss to the quality of the goods.
6. There are no taxes.

Before discussing the various rules of carrying cost, let us see cash-and-carry arbitrage. In this, the trader buys the goods at the cash price and carries it to the expiration of the futures contract. Let us take an example as given in Table 4.2.

**TABLE 4.2 (a)**   Cash-and-Carry Gold Arbitrage Transactions

| Prices for the analysis | (₹) |
|---|---|
| Spot price of gold (per 10 g) | 25,000 |
| Futures price of gold (for delivery after six months) | 28,000 |
| Interest rate 8% per annum | |
| Other carrying cost assumes | − |
| **Transaction** | **Cash flows (₹)** |
| $t = 0$ Borrow ₹25,000 for six months @8% p.a. | +25,000 |
| Buy 10 g of gold at the spot rate | +25,000 |
| Sell a futures contract for ₹28,000 (for delivery after six months) | −28,000 |
| Total cash flows | 0 |
| $T = 1$ Remove the gold from storage | 0 |
| Deliver the gold against the futures contract | +28,000 |
| Repay loan including interest for 6 months (25,000 + 1,000) | −26,000 |
| Total cash flows | 2,000 |

($t = 0$ and $T = 1$ refer to present and future period respectfully)

**TABLE 4.2 (b)**

| Prices for analysis | (₹) |
|---|---|
| Spot price of Tata Motors Company Share | 360 |
| Futures Price of Tata Motors Co. Share (for delivery three months) | 380 |
| Interest rate 8% per annum | − |
| Other carrying charges (assumed) | − |
| Trading lot size | 100 |
| **Transaction** | **Cash flows (₹)** |
| Long futures contract =@₹380 (delivery for three months), being total amount ₹380 × 100 | 38,000 |
| Borrow at (t = 0) ₹3,800, assuming 10% of margin to be paid on the total amount of futures purchase stock (100 × 3,800) = ₹38,000 and 10% of this amount. | 3,800 |
| Cost of transaction (interest on ₹3,800 @8% for three months) | 76 |
| Futures settlement price after at (T = 1) 3 months (on maturity) of Tata Motors Co. Share | 400 |
| Total amount to be received on settlement date (₹400 × 100) by selling the shares in the market | 40,000 |
| Cost of transactions ₹76 and amount to be paid on maturity; 100 × 380 = 38,000 + 76 = ₹38,076 | 38,076 |
| Net Cash flows (Profit) on the transaction | 1,924 |

Some financial experts have suggested certain rules relating to cost-of-carry which have been briefly given as follows:

*Rule I:*   The futures price must be less than or equal to the spot price of the asset plus the carrying charges necessary to carry the spot asset forward to delivery. Mathematically, we can express it as follows:

$$F_{0,t} \leq S_0 (1 + C)$$

where $F_{0,t}$ is the futures price at $t = 0$ for delivery at $t = 1$, $S_0$ is the spot price at $t = 0$ and $C$ is the cost-of-carry, expressed as fraction proportion of the spot price.

*Rule II:*   The futures price must be equal to or greater than the spot price plus the cost-of-carrying the goods to the futures delivery date.

Mathematically,          $$F_{0,t} \geq S_0 (1 + C)$$

If the prices do not obey this rule, there will be arbitrage opportunity. Both the above rules are opposite to each other which are also known as cash and carry arbitrage, and reverse cash and carry arbitrage. The above two rules together implies to Rule III.

*Rule III:*   The futures price must equal the spot price plus the cost-of-carrying the spot commodity forward to the delivery date of the futures contract.

Mathematically,          $$F_{0,t} = S_0 (1 + C)$$

This is applicable under the conditions of the perfect market.

*Rule IV:*   The distant futures price must be less than or equal to the nearby futures price plus the cost-of-carrying the asset from the nearby delivery date to the distant delivery date.

Mathematically,          $$F_{0,d} \leq F_{0,n} (1 + C) \, d > n$$

where $F_{0,d}$ is the futures price at $t = 0$ for the distant delivery contract maturing at $t = d$, $F_{0,n}$ is the futures price at $t = 0$ for the nearby delivery contract maturing at $t = n$ and $C$ is the percentage cost-of-carrying the asset from $t = n$ to $t = d$.

It is observed that if this relationship did not hold then a trader may purchase the nearby futures contract and sell the distant contract. He will then accept the delivery on nearby contract and carry the asset until the delivery of the distant contract, and thereby earning a profit.

*Rule V:*   The nearby futures price plus the cost-of-carrying the asset from the nearby delivery date to the distant delivery date cannot exceed the distant futures price.

Mathematically,          $$F_{0,d} \geq F_{0,n} (1 + C) \, d > n$$

Following the same pattern of argument for spot and futures prices, we may use for the above also.

*Rule VI:*   The distant futures price must equal the nearby futures price plus the cost-of-carrying the asset from the nearby to the distant delivery date.

Mathematically,          $$F_{0,d} = F_{0,n} (1 + C) \, d > n$$

It should be noted that if the above relationships are not fulfilled or violated, the traders would immediately recognize all the arbitrage opportunities until prices are adjusted. However, the basic rules (Rule III and VI) developed above provide a very useful framework for analyzing the relationship between cash and futures prices and spreads between futures prices.

**The cost-of-carry model in imperfect market:**   We have seen the relationship between the spot price and futures price in the conditions of perfect market which is rare in actual practice. There are various imperfections in real markets which disturb the relationship of Rule III and Rule VI. Among the various imperfections, five are important which have been discussed herein after:

**Direct transaction cost:**   In actual practice, when a trader makes the spot or futures transactions he has to pay a fee; known as brokerage fee or commission. In other words, *transaction costs* refer to all such costs which have to be borne by the trader to buy or sell a particular asset for spot or futures. These costs are transaction fees, exchanges charges and fee, fee for arranging funds, etc. It is also called the *round-trip fee*.

**Unequal or differential borrowing and lending rates:**   It refers to that market situation where the rates of interest on borrowing and lending are different and they are not equal. Normally, in real market, borrowing rates are higher than the lending rate. These differential of borrowing and lending rates serve to widen the no-arbitrage boundaries.

**Restriction on short-selling:**   This is another market imperfection. Earlier, we have assumed that traders can sell assets short and use the proceeds from the short sale without any restrictions. Due to inherent risks in short sales, there are restrictions on short selling virtually in all markets.

**Bid-ask spread:**   It is another market imperfection because we see in actual practice that the trader tries to sell the asset at higher price than to purchase the same. The difference between bid price and ask price is called *bid-ask spread*.

**Storage problem:**   It is another market imperfection because except gold and financial securities, most of the commodities cannot be stored very well at all. The storability of a commodity is very important in futures market trading. If a commodity cannot be stored then full arbitrage opportunity will not be available in the market.

Let us see the futures prices after adjusting the above market imperfections.

After transaction cost, equation will be

(a) $F_{0,t} \leq S_0 (1 + T) (1 + C)$
    (where $T$ is transaction cost in cash and carry arbitrage)
(b) $F_{0,t} \geq S_0 (1 - T) (1 + C)$
    (Reverse cash and carry arbitrage)

Combining the above equations, we get

$$S_0 (1 - T) (1 + C) \leq F_{0,t} \leq S_0 (1 + T) (1 + C)$$

There will be **no-arbitrage bounds**, which means within which the futures price must remain to prevent arbitrage. If the futures price goes beyond these boundaries, arbitrage is possible. Hence, the futures price can wonder within the bounds without offering arbitrage opportunities. For example, in our earlier example; if transaction cost is 3 percent and carrying cost is 8 percent then (a) $F_{0,t} = 25,000$ $(1 - 0.03) (1 + 0.08) = ₹26,190$ and (b) $F_{0,t} = 25,000 (1 + 0.03) (1 + 0.08) = ₹27,810$. This is shown in Table 4.3 and in Figure. 4.5.

**TABLE 4.3**   Illustration on No-arbitrage Bounds

| Price for analysis |
| --- |
| Spot Price of Gold (10 g) = 25,000 |
| Interest rate @8% p.a. = 8% |
| Transaction cost ($T$) = 3% |
| *No-arbitrage futures price in perfect markets (one year basis):*<br><br>$$F_{0,t} = S_0 (1 + C)$$<br><br>$$= 25,000 + 2,000 = 27,000$$ |
| *Upper no-arbitrage bound with transaction cost (one year):*<br><br>$$F_{0,t} \leq S_0 (1 + T) (1 + C)$$<br><br>$$= 5,000 (103) (1.08) = ₹27,810$$ |
| *Lower no-arbitrage bound with transaction cost (one year):*<br><br>$$F_{0,t} \geq S_0 (1 - t) (1 + C)$$<br><br>$$= 25,000 (1 - 0.03) (10.08) = ₹26,190$$ |

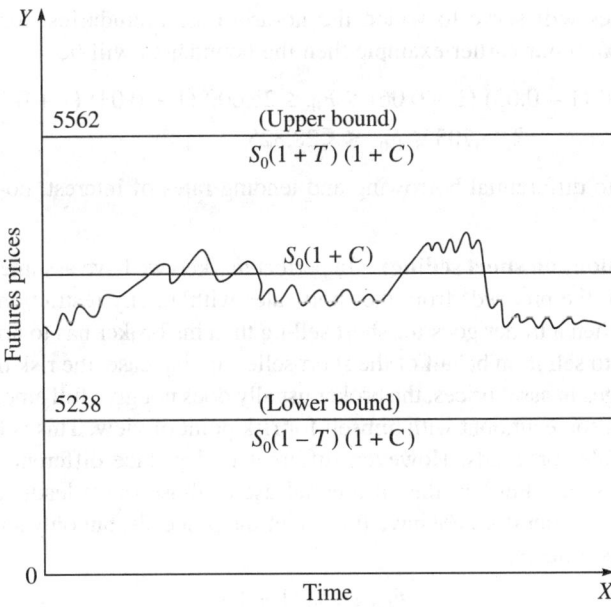

**FIGURE 4.5**   No-arbitrage bounds (with transaction cost).

If the futures price stays between the bounds, no arbitrage is possible. If the futures price crosses the boundaries the traders will immediate act in the market to exploit arbitrage opportunities. For example, if the futures price is too high then the arbitrageurs will buy the spot and sell the futures. This action will raise the price of spot goods relative to futures price, as a result, the futures price will drive back within the no-arbitrage boundaries.

Sometimes, we see in the market that transaction costs are not equal for all the investors. For example, for a retail investor, the transaction cost may be higher, even double than an arbitrageur, floor trader or a member of an exchange. Let us presume that for a retail investor, the transaction cost is double, i.e., $2T$ instead of $T$, then for this trader, the no-arbitrage bounds would be twice and much wider. Differences in transaction costs will give rise to the concept of **quasi-arbitrage**. Those traders which have lower transaction costs than others, are called *quasi-arbitrageurs*. They have relatively lower bounds than the others. Thus, in actual practice, futures prices move within the no-arbitrage bounds of the lowest transaction cost trader. In other words, the traders with higher transaction costs will not be able to exploit any arbitrage opportunities.

**Adjusting the equal borrowing and lending rates:**    As we have seen in the perfect capital market conditions that all the traders can borrow and lend at the risk-free rate, but in real market, this is not possible, and even the borrowing rate and lending rates of interest are also different.

Thus, if these borrowing and lending rates are not same and are different, then they require adjustment to reflect the fact. Normally, we assume that for a trader, the borrowing rate will be higher than lending rate, hence, we assume, lending rate to be $C_L$ and borrowing rate is $C_B$.

Now, the equation will be with different rates of interest:

$$S_0 (1 - T) (1 + C_L) \leq F_{0,t} \leq S_0 (1 + T) (1 + C_B)$$

These differential rates will serve to widen the no-arbitrage boundaries, for example, assuming $C_B = 10\%$ and $C_L = 6\%$ in our earlier example then the boundaries will be

$$25{,}000 (1 - 0.03) (1 + 0.06) \leq F_{0t} \leq 25{,}000 (1 + 0.03) (1 + 0.10)$$

$$₹25{,}705 \leq F_{0,t} \leq ₹28{,}325$$

It is evident that due to differential borrowing and lending rates of interest, no-arbitrage boundaries have been widened.

**Adjusting the restrictions on short selling:**    In perfect market, we have assumed that traders can sell assets short and use all the proceeds from the short sales without any restriction. However, in actual practice, we see that when a trader goes for short selling then his broker has to arrange the assets from the market from other to sell it on behalf of the short seller. In that case, the risk of broker increases. If later on there are changes in asset prices, the broker usually does not give full amount of short selling to the trader, rather keeps some amount with himself for risk point of view. This is known as 'fractional' amount of the short sales proceeds. However, different traders face different restrictions on using proceeds from a short seller. Further, the differential use of those funds leads to quasi-arbitrage. To reflect this fact that short seller does not have full use of the proceeds, but only some fraction $f$, we can readjust the equation as follows:

$$F_{0,t} \geq fS_0 (1 + C)$$

where $f$ is the fraction of usable funds derived from the short sales ranging between $I$ to $O$.

With restrict short sales, our no-arbitrage bounds will be

$$fS_0(1 + C) \leq F_{0,t} \leq S_0 (1 + C)$$

With other market imperfections, our no-arbitrage bounds will be

$$fS_0(1 - T) (1 + C_L) \leq F_{0,t} \leq S_0 (1 + T) (1 + C_B)$$

The above equation seems to be complicated and far from our simple perfect capital market no-arbitrage relationship. However, these two are closely related. For example, if we assume the following:

$T$ = 0      There is no transaction cost.

$CB = CL = C$ Borrowing and lending rates are equal.

$f$ = 1.0      Traders have full use of short sales proceeds.

Then, it reduces the earlier equation to

$$f S_0 (1 - T) (1 + C_L) \le F_{0,t} \le S_0 (1 + T) (1 + C_B)$$
$$= (1.0) S_0 (1 - 0) (1 + C) \le F_{0,t} \le S_0 (1 + 0) (1 + C)$$
$$= S_0 (1 + C) \le F_{0,t} \le S_0 (1 + 0) (1 + C)$$
$$= S_0 (1 + C) \le F_{0,t} \le S_0 (1 + C)$$
$$= F_{0,t} = S_0 (1 + C)$$

This final expression is a simple equation of the perfect capital markets version of our cost-of-carry model.

**The concept of a full-carry-market:** The concept of a full-carry-market refers to the degree of restriction relating to the underlying asset. For example, nature of restriction on short selling, supply of goods, non-seasonal production and consumption, etc. will determine the degree of full-carry-market. So, it varies from asset to asset and market to near-market. There are five main factors that affect market prices and move them towards or away from full-carry-market. These are short selling conditions, supply condition, seasonality of production, seasonality of consumption and ease of storage. In other words, to promote the full-carry-market concept, these restrictions/conditions should be eased. For example, short selling is to be fully eased; there must be large supply of goods, in case of seasonal production, there must be ample stock of goods and subject to large shifting, in case of non-seasonal consumption goods like petroleum products, the supply should be on the pattern of demand, and lastly there must be high storage capacity in case of seasonal goods to make regular supply without any interruption.

## 4.5.2 Expectation Approach

This approach is advocated by distinguished luminaries like J.M. Keynes, J.R. Hicks and N. Kalidor who argued the futures price as the market expectation of the price at the futures date. Many traders/investors, especially those using futures market to hedge, would like to study how today's futures prices are related to market expectations about futures prices. For example, there is a general expectation that the price of the gold next year on April 1 of Tata Motor Co. stock will be ₹400. The futures price today assumed to be ₹380. So, going long futures, the expected yield on the stock would be as:

Expected futures profit = Expected futures price – Initial futures price

₹20 = ₹400 – ₹380

Any major deviation of the futures prices from the expected price will be corrected by speculative activity. Profit seeking speculators will trade as long as the futures price is sufficiently far away from the expected futures spot price. This approach may be expressed as follows:

$$F_{0,t} = E_0 (S_t)$$

where $F_{0,t}$ is Futures price at time $t = 0$ and $E_0 (S_t)$ is the expectation at $t = 0$ of the spot price to prevail at time $t$.

The above equation states that the futures price approximately equals the spot price currently expected to prevail at the delivery date, and if, this relationship did not hold, there would be attractive speculative opportunities. In simple terms, the futures price are influenced to some extent on expectations prevailing at the current time. Under this hypothesis, if markets are operating properly, then

Current futures price = Expected futures spot price

This is also known as *hypothesis of unbiased futures pricing* because it advocates that the futures price is an unbiased predictor of the futures spot price, and on an average, the futures price will forecast the futures spot price correctly.

We have seen above that 'on an average' or 'approximately' words have been used to equalize the current futures price with the expected futures spot price. Why does this relationship hold only approximately? There are two arguments to the question. Firstly, it is due to transaction costs, and secondly due to risk aversion of the traders. Transaction costs can keep the futures price from exactly equalling the expected futures spot price. This has already been discussed in detail in the previous section of this chapter.

## 4.6  FUTURES PRICES AND RISK AVERSION

In this section, we will discuss the 'Risk Aversion' in more detail with its two theories, namely the Theory of Normal Backwardation and Theory of Capital Asset Pricing Model (CAPM). Traders in futures markets can be classified roughly into two categories, i.e., hedgers and speculators. *Hedgers* have a pre-existing risk associated with the asset and enter the market to cover that risk. *Speculators*, on the other hand, trade in the market in the hope to earn profit which is a risky venture. In general, all the investors are risk averse, however, they incur risk willingly only if the expected profit from bearing the risk will compensate them from risk exposure.

### 4.6.1  Theory of Normal Backwardation

Backwardation, in general, refers to a market in which the futures price is less than the cash (spot price). In such case, the basis is positive, i.e., basis is cash price – futures price. This situation can occur only if futures prices are determined by considerations other than, or in addition, to cost-of-carry factors. Further, if the futures prices are higher than the cash prices, this condition is usually referred to as a 'cantongo' market; and the basis is negative. **Normal backwardation** is used to refer to a market where futures prices are below expected futures spot prices.

Another way of describing the cantango and backwardation market is that the former (cantango) is one in which futures prices are reasonably described most of time by cost-of-carry pricing relationship, whereas later (backwardation) is one in which futures prices do not fit into a full cost-of-carry pricing relationship. In other words, futures prices are consistently lower than those predicted by the cost-of-carry pricing formula.

It has been observed in many futures markets that the trading volume of short hedging (sales) exceeds the volume of long hedging (purchases), resulting in net short position. In such situation, Keynes has argued that, in order to induce long speculator to take up the net-short-hedging volume, the hedgers had to pay a risk premium to the speculators. As a result, the futures price would generally be less than the expected futures spot price, by the amount of risk premium which can be stated in equation as:

$$F = E - r$$

where, $F$ is futures price for a futures date, $E$ is expected price at that date and $r$ is risk premium.

In brief, the theory of normal backwardation state that futures prices should rise overtime because hedgers tend to be net-short and pay speculators to assume risk by holding long positions.

Figure 4.6 illustrates the price patterns of futures which is expected under different situations. If the traders correctly assess the futures spot price so that the expected futures spot price turns out to be the actual spot price at the maturity. If the futures price equals the expected futures spot price, then it will lie on the dotted line. However, such situations, sometimes, do not occur, and alternative conceptions exist like normal backwardation and cantango. If speculators are net long, then futures prices must rise over the life of the contract if speculators to be compensated for bearing risk. Futures prices then follow the path as labelled normal backwardation in Figure. 4.6. It is to be noted that this line will terminate at the expected futures spot price.

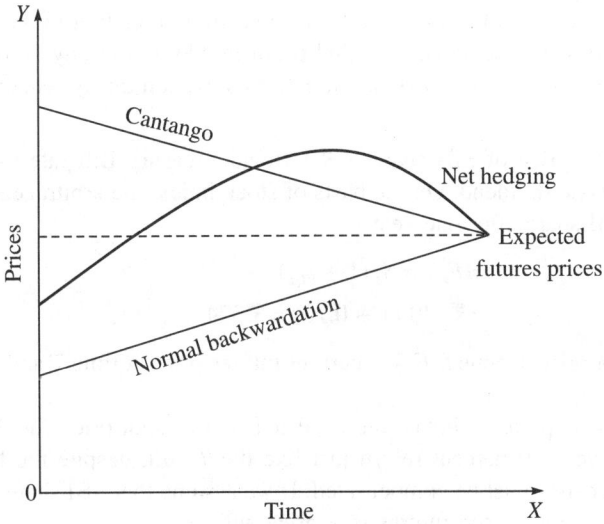

**FIGURE 4.6**   Patterns of futures prices.

If speculators are net short and are compensated for bearing the risk, then the futures prices must follow the path of cantango as shown in Figure. 4.6. The fall in futures prices will give the short speculators the compensation that induced them to enter the market. Final possibility, as shown in Figure 4.6, is known as net hedging hypothesis. According to it, net position of the hedgers might change over the life of the futures contract. In the beginning, the hedgers are net short and the speculators are net long, then the futures price lies below the expected futures spot price. Later on, over time the hedgers gradually change their net position, being net long, and hence, requiring the speculators to be net short. In such situation for having their compensation for risk, by the speculators, the futures price must lie above the expected futures spot-price, as it did in cantango shown in Figure. 4.6.

## 4.6.2    Futures Prices and the Capital Asset Pricing Model (Systematic Risk Explanation)

The Capital Asset Pricing Model (CAPM) has been widely applied to all kinds of financial instruments including futures contracts. In general, the higher the risk of an investment, the higher the expected return demanded by an investor. The expected return demanded by the holders of futures positions is reflected in the difference between futures prices and expected future spot prices. This risk return model can be used for other assets like stocks and bonds. The CAPM leads to the conclusion that there are two types of risk in the economy; systematic and unsystematic. Unsystematic risk is not so important since it can be almost completely eliminated by holding a well-diversified portfolio. Systematic risk or market risk cannot be diversified away. So, as per this model, the investors should be compensated only for systematic risk. In general, an investor requires a higher expected return than the risk-free interest rate for being the systematic risk.

**Systematic risk explanation:**    It is observed that, sometimes, the futures prices differ from expected futures spot prices even after adjusting for systematic risk because of unevenly distributed demand by hedgers for futures positions. For example, if hedgers are dominating in the market through short sales, then long hedgers will receive an expected profit in addition to any systematic risk premium. This theory is called *hedging pressure explanation*. Let us explain the systematic risk explanation by an example.

Suppose the current price of SBI share is ₹340 and Treasury Bill rate is 10 percent per year, assuming that SBI pays no dividend. On the basis of stock index, the arbitrageurs will guarantee that the futures price of SBI share after one year is:

$$= F_{t,T} = S_t\,(1 + r_{t,T})$$
$$= ₹340\,(1 + 0.10) = ₹374$$

where $S_t$ is current spot price at time $t$, $F_{p,T}$ is current futures price at time $T$ and $r_{t,T}$ is rate of return at time $T$.

If the unbiasedness hypothesis holds, the expected futures spot price should be ₹374. It means that SBI share will have a 10 percent return just like the $T$ Bill, despite the fact that the SBI is a riskier stock. So, higher risk must be compensated. If we assume that SBI share should give expected return 15 percent, then the expected futures spot price will be

$$E_t\,(S_T) = S_t(1 + r_{t,T}^*)$$

$$= ₹340\,(1 + 0.15) = ₹391$$

where $E_t\,(S_T)$ is expected futures spot price at time $T$ and $r_{t,T}^*$ is expected rate of return on stock.

Thus, in this example, the futures price is less than the expected futures spot price in equilibrium.

Futures price < Expected futures spot price

or
$$F_{t,T} < E_t\,(S_T)$$

₹374 < ₹391

This result implies that, on an average, a long futures position will provide a profit equal to ₹17 (391 − 374). In other words, ₹17 expected profit on the futures position will compensate the holder for the risk of synthetic stock (Synthetic stock = T-bill + Long futures), that is above the risk of T-Bill.

In brief, it implies that the difference between the futures price and the expected futures spot price is the same as the difference between the expected profit on riskless securities and that on a pure asset with the systematic price risk as the futures contract. Thus, we would expect that

$$\frac{E_t(S_T) - F_{t,T}}{P_t^*} = r_{t,T}^* - r_{t,T}$$

where $P_t$ is price of a pure asset with the same price risk as the underlying asset of the futures contract, $r_{t,T}$ is expected rate return on that asset and $r_{t,T}^* - r_{t,T}$ is premium of pure asset with same risk as futures over the riskless rate.

The price of such a pure asset at $t$, $P_t$ can easily be calculated at the present value of the expected futures price of the underlying asset:

$$P_t = \frac{E_t(S_T)}{1 + r_{t,T}^*}$$

where $S_t$ is price of a pure asset.

If the underlying asset of a futures contract is a pure asset then $P_t^*$ will be equal to $P_t$ and vice-versa. The discount rate $r_{t,T}^*$ can be determined with the CAPM too.

CAPM defines the relationship between risk and return as:

$$r_i^* = r_f + B_i (r_m^* - r_f)$$

$$B_i = \rho_{im} \sigma_i / \sigma_m$$

where $r_i^*$ is expected (required) rate of return on a pure asset $i$, $r_m^*$ is expected rate of return on the market portfolio, $r_f$ is riskless return (essentially equal to $r_{t,T}$), $\rho_{im}$ is correlation between asset return and market return, $\sigma_i$ is standard deviation of rate of return on the asset and $\sigma_m$ is standard deviation of rate of return on market portfolio.

The expected return on each pure asset is earned from the difference between the current spot price and expected futures spot price. The CAPM shows this difference as to be:

$$F_t(S_t) - P_t^* - r_i^* P_t^* \mid b_i(r_m^* - r_f)P_t^*$$

Our earlier principle of futures pricing shown above states that the difference between the futures price and the expected futures spot price must also equal this differential:

$$E_t(S_t) = F_{t,T} = \beta_i(r_m^* - r_f)P_t^*$$

The earlier equation has an important view that futures prices can be unbiased predictor of futures spot price only if the asset has zero systematic risk, i.e., $B_i = 0$. In such situation, the investor can diversify away the risk of the futures position. In general, futures prices will reflect an equilibrium bias. If $B_i > 0$, bearing positive systematic risk, in such case, $F_{t,T} < E_t - (S_T)$, and if $B_i < 0$, a long futures position has negative systematic risk, such a position will yield an expected loss, so $F_{t,T} > E_t - (S_T)$. This situation purely reflects the CAPM. In brief, according to CAPM, the expected return on a long futures position depends on the beta of the futures contract if $B_I > 0$, the futures price should rise overtime; if $B_i = 0$, the futures price should not change, and if $B_i < 0$, the futures price should fall over time and vice-versa in the case of short futures.

## 4.6.3 An Integrated Approach

The various theories presented earlier, sometimes, present controversial view, e.g., one theory states that futures price are based on carrying costs, whereas other one argues purely on expectations or forecast. A number of empirical studies have attempted to verify the reliability of these theories and have resulted in greater clarity and better applicability. In this section, an attempt is made to integrate the various stands of these theories here in brief:

1. Futures prices of those assets which have continuous production or continuous storage capacity broadly follow the carrying cost approach.
2. Those goods or assets which are of discontinuous production or storage nature (perishable nature) should follow expectation approach.
3. It was also observed that the expectations also influence the futures prices of continuous production or storage products. It was seen that the carry cost approach determines the maximum limit of spread but not the minimum limit. Further, fluctuations within the maximum limit are often related to expectation approach.
4. It is also observed that expectations may predominate, sometimes, even in continuous production or storage markets, for such periods indicated in the present by some futures events like ongoing strike, railway disruption, futures labour unrest weather conditions, expected election, etc. which are expected to change the market situation.
5. It is also noticed that the normal backwardation approach tends to exist in those markets which are relatively thin, where speculators are induced to enter in the market.

## 4.7   SPREADS

We have seen the significant relationship between the futures contract and cash price of the asset. Similarly, the trader can view the relationship between futures prices on the same assets themselves. So spread refers to the relationship of two different futures prices of an asset. In other words, a spread position is initiated by the simultaneous purchase and sale of futures contracts on the same asset but with different delivery months, or by the simultaneous purchase and sale of futures on different commodities for delivery in the same or different months. Changes in financial futures spreads depend upon the behaviour of interest rate. A profitable spread creates a gain on one side of the spread which is larger than the loss on the other side of the spread. In this way, a pure speculator would try to make more money by taking only the profitable side of the market.

### 4.7.1   Types of Spreads

The following are the important forms of spreads which are traded in the futures markets:

**Intra-commodity spreads (Time spread):**   An *intra-company commodity* spread is the difference in prices between two futures contracts of different maturity dates on the same commodity. These spreads are important because they indicate the relative price differentials for a commodity to be delivered at two points in time. In other words, a spread between different contract months in the same commodity is called *intra-commodity spread*. It is also called *Time Spread*. For example, the April–July spread in Axis Bank share refers to the difference between April and July futures prices. Suppose, on January 11, 2015, the April 2015, Axis futures price was ₹495 while the July, 2015 Axis futures price was ₹505. Therefore, the April–July, 2015 price spread was ₹10 (₹505–₹495).

**Inter-commodity spreads:**   This refers to a spread between the futures prices of two different but related commodities. Inter-products or commodities are such products which have some economic relationship to each other, for example, soyabeans and its two products, soyabean oil and soyabean meal. So, a special type of inter-commodity spread is the spread between prices of a commodity and its products. For instance, a spread is a long December in petrol and a short December in diesel oil. In this spread, period is same but the commodities are inter-related.

**Inter-market spreads:** Inter-market price spreads are a variant of inter-commodity spreads. It is related with different markets for inter-related commodities. For example, New York heating oil futures price against London gas-oil futures prices. Since this spread is concerned with different markets, so theoretically, regional prices difference in a commodity should be equal to transportation costs between the regions or the markets. Sometimes, variation in regional supply, demand patterns seasonality and the availability of transport also influence the price, resulting in regional price differing by more than transportation costs. However, if the spread between the two regions exceeds the cost of transportations, an arbitrage opportunity may arise for the traders.

## 4.7.2 Why Spreads Trading?

Spread trading has always been popular in futures markets. Commercial users (traders-exporters and importers) are frequently trading spreads as a tool of hedging from one contract month to another. They also, sometimes, trade spreads to recover the costs of storing and financing their stocks. It is also further observed that spread positions are usually less volatile than outright position. So spreads are less risky, and therefore, the exchanges allow less margins on spreads trading.

## 4.7.3 Spread Prices

Spread price is referred to as the difference between the futures prices (indifferent spreads stated earlier) which forms the legs of the spread. What determines the magnitude of a spread at any particular time? Here we will discuss in context to intra-commodity (time-spread) because it is most common and popular spreads traded in the markets.

In general, an $n$-month price spread, on any given time, is measured in amount per unit of the commodity. It is defined as:

$$E_{t,T+n} - F_{t,T} = \text{Spread}_{t,(F^{T+n,T})}$$

where $F_{t,T+n}$ is futures price at $n$-month, say December, 2015, $F_{t,T}$ is futures price at before $n$-month, say August, 2015 and spread$_{t,(T+n,T)}$ is difference of the two periods, i.e., $F_{t,T+n}$, and $F_{t,T}$, i.e., December, 2015 and August, 2015.

Thus, the magnitude of a price spread at a given time depends upon the relevant financing costs, storage costs and the convenience yields which can be expressed as:

$$F_{t,T+n} - F_{t,T} = \text{Difference in financing costs} + \text{Difference in storage costs}$$
$$- \text{Difference in convenience yields}$$

Such commodities which have no convenience yield and no storage cost the inter month price simple will show the relevant forward interest rate, i.e., financing costs during the time period covered by the spreads. These spreads are expressed as annualized percentages which can be determined by dividing the spread by $F_{t,T}$ (futures price at $t$ period) and then annualizing the same. In brief, it is concluded that the spread prices change for a variety of reasons; changes in storage costs, interest rates, convenience yields, and the price levels. While trading in the futures markets, the traders must be aware of normal spread relationship among different periods, commodities and the markets.

## 4.8 DETERMINATION OF FUTURES PRICES OF SPECIFIC ASSETS

In the previous chapter, we have already discussed about the forward contract and markets. The mechanism of determination of futures prices in a few important assets are described here briefly. However, a further detail discussion relating to these will be made in their respective chapters.

### 4.8.1 Stock Index Futures

A stock index is based upon various stocks in a portfolio depending upon the objective of constructing that particular index. The weights of the stocks in portfolio at any given time reflect the stocks total market capitalization (i.e., Stock price × Number of shares outstanding). So, a stock index tracks the changes in the value of a hypothetical portfolio of stocks. In brief, the weight of a stock in the portfolio equals the proportion of the portfolio invested in the stock. For example, the Standard & Poor's 500 (S&P 500) Index is based upon a portfolio of 500 stocks: 400 industrials, 40 utilities, 20 transportation companies and 40 financial institutions. The index accounts for 80 percent of the market capitalization of all the stocks listed on the New York Stock Exchange. Example of NIFTY, SENSEX, etc. be given.

### 4.8.2 Futures Prices of Stock Indices

A stock index can be regarded as an investment asset which pays dividends. The asset is the portfolio of stocks underlying the index. So the dividends paid by the assets are the dividends that would be received by the holder of the portfolio. Since there are many assets which pay dividends at the different times, the index can then be considered as an asset providing a continuous dividend yield. Hence, we can assume $q$ as the dividend yield, then the futures price of an index can be:

$$F = Se^{(r-q)T}$$

*Note:* This has been already discussed in forward pricing section. Let us discuss the above by an example.

**EXAMPLE:** Consider a three-month futures contract on a particular stock index. Further assume that the stock index provides a dividend yield of 3 percent per annum. The current value of the stock index is 900 and the continuously compounded risk-free interest rate is 8 percent per annum. The futures prices of the index can be determined as follows:

$$F = Se^{(r-q)T}$$

In above example, $S = 900$, $r = 0.08$, $q = 0.03$ and $T = 0.25$

So, $$F = 900e^{(0.08 - 0.03) \times 0.25} = 911.32$$

However, in actual practice it has been observed that dividend yield on the portfolio underlying an index varies week by week throughout the year. For example, in general, it has seen that a large proportion of dividends on New York Stock Exchange (NYSE) are paid in the months of February, May, August and November each year. Hence, the value of $q$ should be taken an average annualized dividend yield during the life of the contract. However, if the investor wants to estimate the futures price on the basis of actual dividend paid by the portfolio underlying an index and the timing of the dividends, he can do the same by considering the index such asset providing known income and then using the equation $F = (S - I)e^{rt}$ for calculation of futures price.

## 4.8.3 Index Arbitrage

As seen in the past section, the same can be considered here too. If $F > Se^{(r-q)T}$ then profits can be booked by buying the stocks underlying the index and shorting futures contracts. Further, if $F < Se^{(r-q)T}$ then the profit can be made by selling the stocks underlying the index and taking long position in futures contracts. These strategies are also called *index arbitrage*. Usually, an index arbitrage is implemented using program trading in which computer system is used to generate the trades. A further detail on operation of stock index futures will be made in the forthcoming chapter on stock index futures with suitable examples.

## 4.8.4 Foreign Currencies

In this section, we will discuss the forward and futures contracts on foreign currencies. In such contracts underlying assets are foreign currencies. Let us assume the variable $S$ as the current price (spot) price in home currency (say, Indian rupee) of one unit of the foreign currency (say, like US dollar, UK pound sterling, French franc, etc.), and $F$ as the forward price, measured in Indian rupees, of one unit of the foreign currency. A foreign currency has the property that the holder of the currency can earn interest at the risk-free interest rate prevailing in the foreign currency (e.g., investing in foreign denominated bond). We further assume $rf$ as the value of this foreign risk-free interest rate with continuous compounding for a maturity $T$, and as already assumed $r$ is the domestic risk-free rate.

With the above assumption, the futures price of a foreign currency (relationship between futures price and spot price) can be determined with the following equation:

$$F = Se^{(r-rf)T}$$

where, $F$ is futures price, $S$ is spot price, $r$ is domestic risk-free interest rate, $rf$ is risk-free rate on foreign currency and $T$ is contract or maturity period.

The above equation is a well-known interest rate parity relationship in the field of international finance.

**If $F > Se^{(r-rf)T}$ then the investor trading strategy can be**

1. Borrow $Se(-rf)T$ in the domestic currency at rate $r$ for Time $T$.
2. Use the cash to buy $Se-rfT$ of the foreign currency and invest this at the foreign risk-free rate.
3. Short a forward contract on one unit of the foreign currency.

**Suppose $F < Se^{(r-ft)T}$ then investor can**

1. Borrow $Se^{-rfT}$ in the foreign currency at rate $rf$ for time $T$.
2. Use the cash to buy $Se^{-rfT}$ of the domestic currency and invest this at the domestic risk-free rate.
3. Take a long position in a forward contract on one unit of foreign currency.

It is to be noted that the only difference between the stock index asset and foreign currency is that in stock index asset, we assume a continuous regular dividend income termed as $q$, whereas in foreign currency as an investment asset paying 'dividend yield' in the form of risk-free rate of interest as $rf$.

**EXAMPLE:** Consider that six-month interest rates in United States and India are 1 percent and 5 percent per annum, respectively. The current Indian rupee/US dollar exchange rate is quoted as ₹48. It means that ₹48 is equal to one US dollar. For a six-month forward contract on the Indian rupee $S = 48$, $r = 5\%$, $rf = 1\%$, gives the forward exchange rate as:

$$F = 48e^{(0.05 - 0.01) \times 0.5} = ₹48.97 \text{ app.}$$

The above example, in brief, observes that when the foreign interest rate is lesser than the domestic rate of interest $(rf < r)$, the equation shows that $F$ (forward rate) is always higher than spot (current) rate at the maturity of the contract. Similarly, if the foreign interest rate is greater than the domestic interest rate $(rf > r)$, the forward rate will be lesser than the spot rate $s$ at the maturity.

## 4.9   FUTURES ON COMMODITIES

In this section, we will discuss how the commodity futures contracts are priced. The commodity can be purchased for solely investment purposes like gold and silver, whereas some other commodities may be purchased for consumption purposes.

### 4.9.1   Commodities as Investment Assets (Like Gold and Silver)

Some investors purchase gold and silver for investment purposes. If the storage costs assume to be zero, these can be considered asset paying no income, then in that case the futures price of gold/silver will be

$$F = Se^{rt}$$

If the storage costs are to be incurred, assuming $u$ as present value of all the storage costs that will be incurred during the life of a futures contract, then the futures value $F$ will be

$$F = (S + u)e^{rt}$$

where $u$ is the present value of storage costs.

Further, if we assume that storage costs incurred at any time are proportional to the price of the commodity then it will be treated as negative dividend yield, and in this case the futures price of a commodity:

$$F = Se^{(r+u)T}$$

where $u$ is storage cost per annum as a proportion of the spot price.

**EXAMPLE:**   Suppose a one-year futures contract on gold with a storage costs of ₹20 per 10 g per year to store gold to be paid at the end of the year. Assume that the spot price of ₹24,500 and risk-free interest rate is 7 percent per annum for all maturities. In this case, $S = ₹24,500$, $r = 0.07$ and $T = 1$, then

$$u = 20e^{-0.07} = 18.65$$

Now,
$$F = (S + u)e^{rT}$$

$$= (24,500 + 18.65)^{0.07 \times 1} = ₹26,235$$

If $F > ₹26,235$, an arbitrageur can buy gold and short one-year gold futures contract and in this way he can lock in a profit. Similarly, if $F < ₹26,235$, then he can sell the gold that he owns and can purchase gold futures contracts.

## 4.9.2 Consumption Commodities

The commodities which are not held for investment purposes, the arbitrage arguments used to determine futures prices must be considered and examined carefully. The investors or firms which keep such a commodity in inventory do so because of its consumption value. It means that they are reluctant to sell the commodity and buy futures contracts because futures contracts cannot be consumed. In brief, the futures price for a consumption commodity is:

1.  $F \leq (S + u) \, e^{rT}$, where storage are expressed in present value $u$.
2.  $F \leq Se^{(r+u)T}$, where $u$ is storage cost per annum as a proportion of the spot price.
3.  Sometime there are benefits in holding the commodities which is termed as convenience yield. If the convenience yield is denoted by $y$, then the above equation will be expressed as:

$$F = Se^{(r+u-y)T}$$

where $y$ is convenience yield per annum as a proportion of the spot price.

$$Fe^{yT} = (S + u)e^{rT}$$

where $y$, convenience yield, is expressed in present value.

In brief, while determining the futures prices of a commodity, the consideration of storage costs as well as any return available (convenience yield) on such commodities should be considered and adjusted.

## SUMMARY

This chapter has introduced the mechanism of pricing the futures contracts in different situations. The chapter further explains the relationship between forward prices and futures prices whether the forward prices are equal to futures prices, this is very important issue and debatable. It is argued that if the risk-free interest is constant and the same for all maturities, in such market situations, the forward price will be same as the futures price for the contract. Next section deals with the pricing of stock index futures and futures prices of stock indices. A stock index can be regarded as an investment asset, which pays dividends. Next section deals with the pricing of foreign currencies in situations if $F < Se \, (r - rf) \, T$. Similarly, suppose $F > Se \, (r - ft)T$, what will be the investor trading strategy. The chapter further describes the futures on commodities in cases where (a) commodities as investment assets (like gold, silver) and (b) consumption commodities, etc., as described such commodities which are not held for investment purposes. The arbitrage arguments used to determine futures prices must be considered and examined carefully.

The chapter describes how futures prices and spot prices are converged. The basic reason of convergence is that if the futures prices is above the spot price during the delivery period, this will rise to a clear arbitrage opportunity for the trader in the market which may be followed as (a) short a futures contract, (b) buy the underlying asset and (c) make delivery. And due to arbitrage process futures price will tend to fall.

There are three theories (models) which explain the pricing of futures. The cost-of-carry approach, given by Keynes and Hicks, argued that futures prices essentially reflect the carrying cost of the underlying assets. It means the inter-relationship between spot and futures prices reflect the carrying costs, i.e., the amount to be paid to store the asset from the present time to the futures maturity period. This approach is explained in two ways: cost-of-carry model in perfect markets and the cost-of-carry model in imperfect market. The next approach to futures pricing is the expectation approach, which argues the futures price as the market expectation of the price at the futures date. According to this theory, expected futures profit is equal to expected futures price minus initial futures price. Another theory of futures pricing is normal backwardation. Backwardation, in general, refers to a market in which the futures price is less than the cash or spot price. In such case the basis is positive. Basis is referred to cash price minus futures price. Further, if the futures prices are higher than the cash prices, this situation is usually referred to as a cantango market, and the basis is negative. Normal backwardation is used to refer to a market where futures prices are below expected futures spot prices.

Chapter further throws light on the relationship between futures prices and the capital asset pricing model (CAPM), which is widely applied to all kinds of financial instruments including futures contracts. The expected return on each pure asset is earned from the difference between the current spot price and expected futures spot price. The chapter ends with the discussion on integrated approach which explains that futures prices of those assets which have continuous production or continuous storage capacity broadly follow the carrying cost approach. The assets or goods which are of discontinuous production or storage should follow expectation approach and normal backwardation approach tends to exist in those markets which are relatively thin, where speculator are induced in the market.

## SOLVED PROBLEMS

**P.1.**    Suppose an amount $200 invested for 1 year at an interest rate of 10% per annum. If the rate is compounded once per annum, what will be the terminal value of the investment?

*Solution:*    Investment amount $A = $200, Rate of return $R = 10\%$ and Maturity period $T = 1$ year
So, the terminal value of investment is:

$$TV = A (1 + R)n$$

$$= \$200 (1 + 0.10)1 = \$200 \times 1.1 = \$220$$

**P.2.**    What will be the value of investment if we compound twice a year, with the interest being reinvested as given in Problem 1.

*Solution:*    Investment amount $A = $200, Compounded period/Time $M = 2$ and Rate of return $R = 10\%$ per annum
So, value of investment will be

$$A (1 + R/2)mn$$

$$= \$200 (1 + 10/2)^{2 \times 1} = \$200 (1 + 5\%)^2$$

$$= \$200 \times 1.05 \times 1.05 = \$220.50 = \$220.50$$

**P.3.**    Consider the position of an investor who shorts 1,000 TISCO shares in May when the price per share is ₹100 and closes out the position by buying them back in August when the price per share is ₹80. Suppose that a dividend of ₹2 per share is paid in June, what will be the gain/loss to investor?

*Solution:*    Investor receives = 1,000 × 100 = ₹1,00,000 in May when short position is initiated.

Dividend payment 1,000 × 2 = ₹2,000 in the month of June.

Investor will pay ₹1,000 × 80 = ₹80,000 when position is closed out in August.

So, the net gain to investor:

$$= ₹1,00,000 - ₹2,000 - ₹80,000 = ₹18,000$$

**P.4.** Current price of HLL share is ₹300 and is expected to pay no dividend over the next two years. Assume that after two years, the market price of the HLL will be ₹350. Whether there are any arbitrage opportunity, and, if yes, what will be the profits to the arbitrageurs, if an investment of ₹3,000 is done by taking a loan?

*Solution:* Since current share price of HLL is ₹300 and 5% risk-free interest. So amount to be paid after two years will be ₹3,316 for, taking a loan of ₹3,000 ($3,000e^{0.05×2}$). After two years, price of HLL share is ₹350, so there exists arbitrage opportunities and profit to arbitrageur will be

1. Borrow ₹3,000 at an interest of 5% per annum for 2 years
2. Buy 10 shares of the stock
3. Enter in forward contract to sell 10 share for ₹3,500 in two years.

Profit/gains to arbitrageur: ₹3,500 – ₹3,316 = ₹184

**P.5.** Consider a long forward contract to purchase a coupon-bearing bond where current price is ₹1,000. Forward contract matures in one year and bond matures in five years so that the forward contract is a contract to purchase a four-year bond in one year. Suppose ₹40 are expected after six months as a coupon payment. Assume the six months as a coupon payment. Assume the six-month and one year, risk-free interest rate compounds are 9% per annum and 10% per annum, respectively. Suppose forward price for delivery in one year is ₹1,100.

*Solution:* The forward price is too high.

1. Arbitrageur can borrow ₹1,000 to buy one bond
2. Short a forward contract on one bond
3. ₹1,000 loan is made up of ₹38.23 borrowed at a percent per annum for six-month and ₹961.77 borrowed at 10% per annum for one year. First coupon payment of ₹40 are exactly sufficient to repay interest and principal on ₹38.23. The net profit is, therefore,

$$₹40 + ₹1,030 - ₹1,052.40 = ₹17.60$$

**P.6.** Suppose that Ramesh enters into a six-month forward contract on non-dividend paying stock when stock price is ₹30 and stock (risk-free interest rate) is 12% per annum. Calculate forward price.

*Solution:* Current price of stock = ₹30, Risk-free interest rate = 12% per annum and semi annual (Rft) = 6%

So, Forward price = $30e^{0.12×0.5}$ = ₹31.86

**P.7.** Consider the following:

Spot price of gold (10 g) = ₹26,000

Futures price of gold (for delivery in six months) = ₹28,000

Interest rate = 8% per annum

Carrying cost = Nil

Calculate the gain/loss in above transaction.

**Solution:**

| Transaction | Cash flows (₹) |
|---|---|
| (a)  Borrow ₹6,000 for six months 8% | +26,000 |
| (b)  Buy 10 g of gold at the spot rate | – 26,000 |
| (c)  Sell a futures contract for 28,000 for delivery | – |
|      After six months | 0 |
|      Total cash flow | 0 |
|      Remove gold from storage | 0 |
| (d)  Deliver the gold against futures contract | +28,000 |
|      Repay loan including interest for six months (1,040) | –27,040 |
|      Total cash flow | +960 |
| Net gain to the trader | = ₹960 |

**P.8.**   In May, the price of August pepper is ₹9,000 per quintal, while the spot price is ₹8,000. The carrying cost per quintal for 3 months is ₹500. How a market participant can take advantage of above transaction?

**Solution:**   Market participant will operate the following transactions:

1. Buy spot and store it: one quintal of pepper for ₹8,000
2. Sell futures and deliver in August at ₹9,000

Net gain to trader: ₹9,000 – ₹8,000 – ₹500 = ₹500

**P.9.**   On April 11, 2003 the cash price of gold was ₹5,000 per 10 g. And price of December 2003 futures contract was ₹4,500. On April 11, 2003, the relevant annualized financing rate was 12%, and the storage cost was 0.5% per month. Calculate the carrying cost and implicit annualized convenience yield from the above date.

**Solution:**   Calculation of carrying cost:

$$C^c + T = 5,000 \times 0.12 \times \frac{240}{365} - 0.5 \times 8 = ₹400$$

Implicit convenience yield:

$$\frac{5,000 + 400 - 4,500}{5,000} \times \frac{365}{240}$$

$$\frac{5,000 - 4,500}{5,000} = \frac{900}{5,000} \times \frac{365}{240}$$

$$\frac{900}{5,000} \times \frac{365}{240} = 27.38\%$$

**P.10.**   Suppose, on May 2003, the cash price of Infosys stock was ₹4,500 and price for December 2003 futures contract was ₹4,000. Financing cost was 15% per annum. Calculate the carrying cost for 7 months and also calculate the implied convenience yield.

***Solution:*** Cost-of-carry: $CC_tT = 4{,}500 \times 0.12 \times \dfrac{7}{12}$

$$= 4{,}500 \times 0.12 \times \dfrac{7}{12} = ₹315$$

Convenience yield (Annualized):

$$= \dfrac{4{,}500 + 315 - 4{,}000}{4{,}500} \times \dfrac{12}{7}$$

$$= \dfrac{4{,}815 - 4{,}000}{4{,}500} \times \dfrac{12}{7}$$

$$= 31.05\%$$

**P.11.** From the following table, calculate the basis of Equity share

| Contract | Share (₹) |
|----------|-----------|
| Cash | 4,370 |
| July 2015 | 4,500 |
| August | 4,520 |
| October | 4,600 |
| November | 4,670 |
| December | 4,685 |

***Solution:*** Basis: Current cash price – Futures price

| Contract | Share price | The basis (₹) |
|----------|-------------|---------------|
| Cash | 4,370 | – |
| July | 4,500 | – 130 |
| August | 4,520 | – 150 |
| October | 4,600 | – 230 |
| November | 4,670 | – 300 |
| December | 4,685 | – 315 |

## REVIEW QUESTIONS

1. How will you determine the futures prices of specific futures products? Explain.
2. Explain the relationship between forwards and futures prices with examples.
3. Explain the important characteristics of futures prices with examples.
4. Explain what happens when an investor shorts a certain shares.
5. Explain carefully why the futures price of silver can be calculated from its spot price and other observable variables while the futures price of copper cannot be calculated.

6. Explain the concepts of
   (a) Convenience yield
   (b) Cost-of-carry

7. Discuss in detail the relationship between the futures price, the spot price, convenience yield and cost-of-carry.

8. 'Whether the futures price of a stock index greater than or less than the expected futures value of index'? Critically examine the statement and explain your answer with suitable examples.

9. What are various assumptions and notations for determination of forward prices?

10. Write the notes with suitable examples on
    (a) Forward price for investment assets providing no income.
    (b) Forward price for investment assets providing a known income.
    (c) Forward price for investment assets providing a known dividend income.

11. On the basis of different situations given in Question 9, how will you value a forward contract? Explain with suitable examples.

12. Explain the futures prices of:
    (a) Stock index futures
    (b) Foreign currencies
    (c) Futures on commodities

13. Draw a list of characteristics of futures prices with suitable examples.

14. Explain the relationship between the expected futures spot price and futures prices with the help of suitable examples.

15. With the help of an example, show how will you read the futures prices quoted at the Bombay Stock Exchange.

16. 'Basis and spread are important for the determination of futures prices'. Explain the statement in the light of concepts of basis and spread.

17. Explain the concept of convergence of cash and futures prices with suitable illustrations.

18. 'In the absence of convergence, there will arise arbitrage opportunity for trader in market'. Explain the statement in the light of arbitrage process with suitable examples.

19. Explain the models of futures pricing with illustrations.

20. Write notes with suitable data
    (a) Cost-of-carry approach in perfect markets
    (b) Cost-of-carry approach in imperfect markets

21. Explain the concept of full-carry market with suitable illustrations.

22. Write a short note on futures prices and risk-aversion.

23. 'There is no single theory of explaining the pricing of futures'. Explain the above in the light of integrated approach to futures pricing.

24. Critically examine the expectation approach of futures price determination with examples.

25. Explain the term futures price and how it is related with the spot price. Explain with suitable examples.

26. Explain the term spread and its types with the help of illustrations. Also explain its significance in futures pricing.

27. What is the basis? What factors determine the magnitude of the basis and variation in the basis?

28. What are various assumptions of cost-of-carry formula? Critically evaluate the relevance of these assumptions in determining the futures prices.

**29.** 'Cost-of-carry approach does not apply to the financial assets'. Evaluate the statement in the light of various characteristics of a financial assets.

**30.** What is backwardation? Why do reverse cash and carry arbitrage not eliminate backwardation? Examine critically.

**31.** 'When the convenience yield is high, long hedges are likely to be particularly attractive to a company that knows it will require a certain quantity of commodity on a certain futures date'. Discuss the above statement with examples.

## UNSOLVED PROBLEMS

**P.1.**   An investor invests ₹500 for one year at an interest of 12% per annum. If the rate is compounded once per annum, calculate the terminal value of investment.

**P.2.**   Calculate the terminal value by taking the figures of Problem 1, if we compound twice in a year ($m = 2$).

**P.3.**   Consider the current price of Infosys is ₹1,000 and is expected to pay no dividend over the next two years. Risk-free interest rate is 10% per annum with continuous compounding and assume futures price (two year) of stock is ₹1,500. Calculate if there is any arbitrage opportunity, and if yes, what will be the profits to the trader?

**P.4.**   A stock index currently stands at 350. The risk-free rate is 8% per annum and dividend yield on index is 4% per annum. What should be the futures price for a four-month contract?

**P.5.**   Consider the following:

Spot price of IDFC (one share) = ₹150
Futures price of IDFC stock = ₹180
Interest rate = 12% pa
Carrying cost = Nil
Show the cash flow of the above transaction.

**P.6.**   In the month of September, the price of December pepper is ₹9,500 per quintal. While the spot rate is ₹7,950 per quintal, the carrying cost per quintal for 3 months is ₹1,000. How a market participant can take advantage of above transaction?

**P.7.**   On May 2015, the cash price of product was ₹4,800 and price of December 2015 futures contract was ₹4,600. On May 2015, the relevant annualized financing cost was 12% and storage cost was 1 per rupee per month. Calculate the carrying cost and convenience yield.

**P.8.**   From the following table, calculate the basis of stock:

| Contract | Price (₹) |
|---|---|
| Cash | 200 |
| July 2015 | 210 |
| August 2015 | 230 |
| October 2015 | 240 |
| November 2015 | 290 |
| December 2015 | 305 |
| January 2016 | 310 |

**P.9.**   Consider a six-month long forward contract of a non-income paying security. The risk-free rate interest is 6% per annum. The stock price is ₹30 and the delivery price is ₹28. Compute the value of forward contract.

## SUGGESTED READINGS

1. Chang, C. and Chang, J., Forward and futures prices, Evidence from the foreign exchange markets, *Journal of Futures Market*, 5:3, pp. 385–405, Fall 1985.
2. Houthakkar, Handrik S. and Wiliamson, Peter J., *The Economics of Financial Markets*, Oxford University Press, New York, 1996.
3. Baz, Jamil and Chacko, George, *Financial Derivatives: Pricing, Application and Mathematics*, Cambridge University Press, New York, 2003.
4. Neftci, Salih N., *An Introduction to Mathematics of Financial Derivatives*, Academic Press, San Diego, 2000.
5. Epps, T.W., Pricing derivatives securities, *World Scientific,* River Edge, New Jersey, 2000.
6. Rene M. Stulz, *Risk Management & Derivatives*. Thomson South-Western, India-Reprint-2007.
7. Robert A. Strong, *Derivatives* Thomson-South-Western, Indian-Reprint-2006.
8. www. Nseindia.com. & www.bseindia.com.

# SECTION
# II

# Financial Derivatives— Indian Scenario

# Financial Derivatives Markets in India

*After reading this chapter, students will be able to*

➤ Understand the meaning of financial derivatives.
➤ Understand the need of derivatives.
➤ Know how financial derivatives evolved in India.
➤ Know about major recommendations of Dr. L.C. Gupta Committee on derivatives.
➤ Understand the various concepts involved in the various recommendations made by Dr. L.C. Gupta Committee on derivatives.
➤ Understand trading mechanism at National Stock Exchange (NSE) and Bombay Stock Exchange (BSE).
➤ Be aware of the eligibility of the stocks for derivatives trading in India.
➤ Understand the emerging structure of derivatives market in India.
➤ Know the problems and prospects of financial derivatives in India.
➤ Know the weaknesses of Indian stock market.

## 5.1 INTRODUCTION

The individuals and the corporate sector units are freely using derivatives, also popularly known as future market instruments, in most of the developed countries of the world to manage different risks by the individuals and the corporate sector units. Emerged in 1970s, the derivatives markets have seen exponential growth and trading volumes have nearly doubled in every three years, making it a multi-trillion dollar business market. The future markets in various segments have developed so much that now one cannot think of the existence of financial markets without the derivatives instruments. In other words, the derivatives markets whether belonging to commodities or financials have become, today, an integral part of the financial system of a country.

The Indian financial markets indeed waited for too long for derivatives trading to emerge. The phase of waiting is over. The statutory hurdles have been cleared. Regulatory issues have been sorted out. Stock exchanges are gearing up for derivatives. Mutual funds, foreign institutional investors, financial institutions, banks, insurance companies, investment companies, pension funds and other investors who are deprived of hedging opportunities now find the derivatives market to bank on. They would find very soon all other important derivatives instruments in the Indian financial markets to manage their portfolios and associated risks.

## 5.2 NEED FOR DERIVATIVES

Since 1991, due to liberalization of economic policy, the Indian economy has entered an era in which Indian companies cannot ignore global markets. Before the 1990s, prices of many commodities, metals and other assets were controlled. Others, which were not controlled, were largely based on regulated prices of inputs. As such there was limited uncertainty, and hence, limited volatility of prices. But after 1991, starting the process of deregulation, prices of most commodities are decontrolled. It has also resulted in partly deregulating the exchange rates, removing the trade controls, reducing the interest rates, making major changes for the capital market entry of foreign institutional investors, introducing market-based pricing of government securities, etc. All these measures have increased the volatility of prices of various goods and services in India to producers and consumers alike. Further, market determined exchange rates and interest rates also created volatility and instability in portfolio values and securities prices. Hence, hedging activities through various derivatives emerged to different risks.

Futures trading offers a risk-reduction mechanism to the farmers, producers, exporters, importers, investors, bankers, trader, etc. which are essential for any country. In the words of Alan Greenspan; Chairman of the US Federal Reserve Board, "The array of derivative products that has been developed in recent years has enhanced economic efficiency. The economic function of these contracts is to allow risks that formerly had been combined to be unbundled and transferred to those most willing to assume and manage each risk components." Development of futures markets in many countries has contributed significantly in terms of invisible earnings in the balance of payments, through the fees and other charges paid by the foreigners for using the markets. Further, economic progress of any country, today, much depends upon the service sector as on agriculture or industry. Services are now backbone of the economy of the future. India has already crossed the roads of revolution in industry and agriculture sector and has allowed the same now in services like financial futures. India has all the infrastructure facilities and potential exists for the whole spectrum of financial futures trading in various financial derivatives like stock market indices, treasury bills, gilt-edged securities, foreign currencies, cost of living index, stock market index, etc. For all these reasons, there is a major potential for the growth of financial derivatives markets in India.

## 5.3   EVOLUTION OF DERIVATIVES IN INDIA

Commodities futures trading in India was initiated long back in 1950s, however, the 1960s marked a period of great decline in futures trading. Market after market was closed usually because different commodities' prices increase were attributed to speculation on these markets. Accordingly, the Central Government imposed the ban on trading in derivatives in 1969 under a notification issue. The late 1990s shows this signs of opposite trends—a large scale revival of futures markets in India, and hence, the Central Government revoked the ban on futures trading in October, 1995. The Civil Supplies Ministry agreed in principle for starting of futures trading in Basmati rice. Further, in 1996 the Government granted permission to the Indian Pepper and Spice Trade Association to convert its Pepper Futures Exchange into an International Pepper Exchange. As such, on November 17, 1997, India's first international futures exchange at Kochi, known as the India Pepper and Spice Trade Association—International Commodity Exchange (IPSTA-ICE) was established.

Similarly, the Cochin Oil Millers Association, in June 1996, demanded the introduction of futures trading in coconut oils. The Central Minister for Agriculture announced in June 1996 that he was in favour of introduction of futures trading both domestic and international. Further, a new coffee futures exchange (The Coffee Futures Exchange of India) is being started at Bangalore. In August, 1997, the Central Government proposed that Indian companies with commodity price exposures should be allowed to use foreign futures and option markets. The trend is not confined to the commodity markets alone, it has initiated in financial futures too.

The Reserve Bank of India set up the Sodhani Expert Group which recommended major liberalization of the forward exchange market and had urged the setting up of rupee-based derivatives in financial instruments. The RBI accepted several of its recommendations in August, 1996. A landmark step taken in this regard when the Securities and Exchange Board of India (SEBI) appointed a Committee named the Dr. L.C. Gupta Committee (LCGC) by its resolution, dated November 18, 1996 in order to develop appropriate regulatory framework for derivatives trading in India. While the Committee's focus was on equity derivatives but it had maintained a broad perspective of derivatives in general.

The Board of SEBI, on May 11, 1998, accepted the recommendations of the Dr. L.C. Gupta Committee and approved introduction of derivatives trading in India in the phased manner. The recommendation sequence is stock index futures, index options and options on stocks. The Board also approved the 'Suggestive Bye-Laws' recommended by the Committee for regulation and control of trading and settlement of derivatives contracts in India. Subsequently, the SEBI appointed J.R. Varma Committee to look into the operational aspects of derivatives markets. To remove the road-block of non-recognition of derivatives as securities under Securities Contract Regulation Act, the Securities Law (Amendment) Bill, 1999 was introduced to bring about the much needed changes. Accordingly, in December, 1999, the new framework has been approved and 'Derivatives' have been accorded the status of 'Securities'. However, due to certain completion of formalities, the launch of the Index Futures was delayed by more than two years. In June, 2000, the National Stock Exchange and the Bombay Stock Exchange started stock index based futures trading in India. Further, the growth of this market did not take off as anticipated. This is mainly attributed to the low awareness about the product and mechanism among the market players and investors. The volumes, however, are gradually picking up due to active interest of the institutional investors.

## 5.4  MAJOR RECOMMENDATIONS OF DR. L.C. GUPTA COMMITTEE

Before discussing the emerging structure of derivatives markets in India, let us have a brief view of the important recommendations made by the Dr. L.C. Gupta Committee on the introduction of derivatives markets in India. These are as under:

1. The Committee is strongly of the view that there is urgent need of introducing of financial derivatives to facilitate market development and hedging in a most cost-efficient way against market risk by the participants such as mutual funds and other investment institutions.
2. There is need for equity derivatives, interest rate derivatives and currency derivatives.
3. Futures trading through derivatives should be introduced in phased manner starting with stock index futures, which will be followed by options on index and later options on stocks. It will enhance the efficiency and liquidity of cash markets in equities through arbitrage process.
4. There should be two-level regulation (regulatory framework for derivatives trading), i.e., exchange level and SEBI level. Further, there must be considerable emphasis on self-regulatory competence of derivative exchanges under the overall supervision and guidance of SEBI.
5. The derivative trading should be initiated on a separate segment of existing stock exchanges having an independent governing council. The number of the trading members will be limited to 40 percent of the total number. The Chairman of the governing council will not be permitted to trade on any of the stock exchanges.
6. The settlement of derivatives will be through an independent clearing Corporation/Clearing house, which will become counter-party for all trades or alternatively guarantees the settlement of all trades. The clearing corporation will have adequate risk containment measures and will collect margins through EFT.
7. The derivatives exchange will have on-line-trading and adequate surveillance systems. It will disseminate trade and price information on real time basis through two information vending networks. It should inspect 100 percent of members every year.
8. There will be complete segregation of client money at the level of trading/clearing member and even at the level of clearing corporation.
9. The trading and clearing member will have stringent eligibility conditions. At least two persons should have passed the certification programme approved by the SEBI.
10. The clearing members should deposit minimum ₹50 lakh with clearing corporation and should have a net worth of ₹3 crore.
11. Removal of the regulatory prohibition on the use of derivatives by mutual funds while making the trustees responsible to restrict the use of derivatives by mutual funds only to hedging and portfolio balancing and not for specification.
12. The operations of the cash market on which the derivatives market will be based, needed improvement in many respects.
13. Creation of a Derivation Cell, a Derivative Advisory Committee, and Economic Research Wing by SEBI.
14. Declaration of derivatives as 'securities' under Section 2(h) of the SCRA and suitable amendments in the notification issued by the Central Government in June, 1969 under Section 16 of the SCRA.

The SEBI Board approved the suggested Bye-Laws recommended by the L.C. Gupta Committee for regulation and control of trading and settlement of derivatives contracts.

## 5.4.1 Explanation of Some Important Terms Used in the Committee's Recommendations

**Derivatives concept:** A derivative product, or simply 'derivative', is to be sharply distinguished from the underlying cash asset. Cash asset is the asset which is bought or sold in the cash market on normal delivery terms. Thus, the term 'derivative' indicates that it has no independent value. It means that its value is entirely 'derived' from the value of the cash asset. The main point is that derivatives are forward or futures contracts, i.e., contracts for delivery and payment on a specified future date. They are essentially to facilitate hedging of price risk of the cash asset. In the market term, they are called *Risk Management Tools*.

**Financial derivatives—Types:** Though the Committee was mainly concerned with equity-based derivatives but it has tried to examine the need for derivatives in a broad perspective for creating a better understanding and showing inter-relationship. Broadly, there are three kinds of price risk exposed to a financial transaction, viz.

1. Exchange rate risk, a position arisen in a foreign currency transaction like import, export, foreign loans, foreign investment, rendering foreign services, etc.
2. Interest rate risk, as in the case of fixed-income securities, like Treasury bond holdings whose market price could fall heavily if interest rates shot up.
3. Equities', 'market risk', also called 'systematic risk'—a risk which cannot be diversified away because the stock market as a whole may go up or down from time to time.

The above said classification indicates towards the emergence of three types of financial derivatives, namely currency futures, interest rate futures and equity futures. As both forward contracts and futures contracts can be used for hedging, but the Committee favours the introduction of futures wherever possible.

Forward contracts are presently being used in India to provide forward cover against exchange rate risk. Currency and interest rate futures lie in the sphere of Reserve Bank of India (RBI).

The Dr. L.C. Gupta Committee recognizes that the basic principles underlying the organization, control and regulation of markets of all kinds of financial futures are the more or less same and that the trading infrastructure may be common or separate, partially or wholly. The Committee is of further opinion that there must be a formal mechanism for coordination between SEBI and RBI in respect of financial derivatives markets so that all kinds of overlapping of jurisdiction in respect of trading mechanism, be removed.

Financial derivatives markets in India have been developed so far in three important instruments like equity, interest and currency. First one is regulated by the SEBI, whereas the other two are controlled by the RBI. The markets of these instruments are in their preliminary stage.

## 5.5 EQUITY DERIVATIVES

Dr. L.C. Gupta Committee considered in its study both types of equity like stock index derivatives and individual stocks derivatives. At the international level, stock index derivative is more popular than the individual stock. The Committee found in its survey that index futures are more preferable than individual stock from the respondents. The order of over all preference in India as per the survey of the Committee, was as follows: (i) Stock index futures, (ii) Stock index options, (iii) Individual stock options and (iv) Individual stock futures.

**Basic reasons for the preference of stock index futures:**   Not only in India, in other countries too, stock index futures is most popular financial derivatives due to the following reasons:

1. Institutional investors and other large equity holders prefer the most this instrument in terms of portfolio hedging purpose.

2. Stock index futures are the most cost-efficient hedging device, whereas hedging through individual stock futures is costlier as observed in other countries.

3. Stock index futures cannot be easily manipulated, whereas individual stock price can be exploited more easily. In India it is rather more easy to play this game as witnessed in the past scams.

4. This is in fact that due to a limited supply of an individual stock, supply can easily be cornered even in large companies in India like Reliance Industries, State Bank of India, etc. The Management of these companies have complained many times about their share prices being manipulated by some interested parties. On the other hand, the supply of stock index futures is unlimited, and hence, the possibility of cornering is ruled out. In fact, the manipulation of stock index futures can be possible only if the cash prices of each component securities in the index be influenced, which is rare and not so high.

5. It is observed from the experiences of other countries that stock index futures are more liquid, more popular and favourable than individual stock futures. The same is also witnessed by the L.C. Gupta Committee in its survey from the responses of the respondents.

6. Since the stock index futures consists of many securities, so being an average stock, it is much less volatile than an individual stock price. Further, it implies much lower capital adequacy and margin requirements in comparison of individual stock futures.

7. In case of stock index futures trading, there is always clearing house guarantee, so the chances of the clearing house going to be bankrupt is very rare, and hence, it is less risky.

8. Another important reason is that in case of individual stocks, the outstanding positions are settled normally against physical delivery of the shares. Hence, it is necessary that futures and cash prices remained firmly tied to each other. However, in case of stock index futures, the physical delivery is almost impractical, and they are settled in cash all over the world on the premise that index value, as independently derived from the cash market, is safely accepted as the settlement price.

9. Lastly, it is also seen that regulatory complexity is much less in the case of stock index futures in comparison to other kinds of equity derivatives.

In brief, it is observed that the stock index futures are more safer, popular and attractive derivative instrument than the individuals stock. Even in the US market, the regulatory framework does not allow use of futures on the individual stocks. Further, only very few countries of world, say one or two, have futures trading on individual stock.

## 5.6   STRENGTHENING OF CASH MARKET

The Dr. L.C. Gupta Committee observed that for successful introduction of futures market in any country, there must be a strong cash market because derivatives extract their value from the cash asset. The constant feedback between these two markets through arbitrage will keep these markets in alignment with each other. The Committee noted certain weaknesses of the Indian equities markets which should be taken care for success of the futures trading in India. A few important weaknesses observed are as follow:

## 5.6.1 Mixing of Cash and Forward Transactions

1. There is queer mixture of cash and future transactions in the Indian stock markets. For example, cash transactions (involving delivery), in most active scripts, deliveries are just around 5 percent of the trading volume, whereas in many others, it is just, 20–30 percent. In fact, the dominant cash transactions are the non-delivery which are the equivalent of futures/forward transactions.

2. It is further noted that the above said mixed system (cash-cum-carry forward) is not very sound for futures trading because (i) no transparency in the carry forward system, (ii) the influence of fundamental factors is not so strong due to dominance of short-term speculation and (iii) creating a future market on such basis may have the effect of compounding the existing weaknesses.

3. The Committee is of the view that there must be separation between cash market and futures market. It will promote the markets, economic efficiency. This has led to the adoption of the rolling settlement system because, in this way, cash market will function as genuine cash markets but no carry forward facility. Even futures market does not permit carry forward from one settlement to another in the way it is practised in India.

4. The trading in Indian stock market was shifted to rolling settlement recently where it is emphasized for settlement by delivery. But in India, 'squaring up or closing' business (i.e., offsetting of buying and selling transactions within the settlement) is accounted for in bulk which is not appropriate for futures trading.

## 5.6.2 Differences in Trading Cycles Among Stock Exchanges

1. Indian stock exchanges, now, most of them, have a weekly trading cycle but the cycles are not uniform. For example, NSE has from Wednesday to Tuesday and BSE has from Monday to Friday. Due to difference in trading cycles, the brokers who have membership in both the exchanges can easily go on circulating their trades from one exchange to the other without ever having to deliver. Such situation is a complete travesty of the cash market and an abuse to the stock market system.

2. It seems that in Indian stock markets, the different trading cycles have been kept with a vested interest in order to deliberately generate arbitrage opportunities. It is seen that due to this, the prices for the same securities on two (NSE and BSE) stock exchanges differ from 0.5 to 1.5 percent even it is larger on expiration days. The Committee feels that the different cycles serve the interest of only speculators and not of genuine investors. It is not even good for market development and futures trading.

3. It is also noted that the prices of various securities on both exchanges (NSE and BSE), sometimes, are not the same. As a result, the value of the stock indices on both the exchanges will not be same, if computed separately from the NSE and BSE prices. This will create a problem in valuation of future market stock.

4. The Committee also noted that for a successful future trading, a coordinated but pro-competitive nation-wide market system be achieved. So, it is suggested that before implementing a uniform trading cycle system among all exchanges, till such time the rolling settlement system can be adopted. This system will provide a sound and reliable basis for futures trading in India.

### 5.6.3 Weakness of Stock Exchange Administrative Machinery

The Dr. L.C. Gupta Committee members were of the strong opinion that for successful derivatives trading on the stock exchanges, there must be stringent monitoring norms and much higher standard of discipline, than in the present, be maintained. Though the SEBI has already made a good efforts but much more still is to be done specifically in the controlling of trading members.

### 5.6.4 Inadequate Depository System

The Committee is of the view that all such securities which are composing in stock index and used for stock index futures, should necessarily be in depository mode. As observed earlier, settlement problems of the cash market may weaken the arbitrage process by making it risky and costly. Since, index-based derivatives trading does not itself involve deliveries, it will increase the arbitrage trading between cash and index derivatives markets. The arbitrage process keeps the two markets in alignment. Thus, due to this reason, it is essential for successful futures trading that all the scripts of the particular stock index futures must be in the depository mode. Hence, depository scripts in India should be enhanced.

The Committee has no doubt that the creation of futures markets by introducing the financial derivatives, including equity futures, currency futures and interest rate futures would be a major step towards the further growth and development of the Indian financial markets provided that the trading must be cost-efficient and risk hedging facilities.

## 5.7 BENEFITS OF DERIVATIVES IN INDIA

During December, 1995, the NSE applied to the SEBI for permission to undertake trading in stock index futures. Later, SEBI appointed the Dr. L.C. Gupta Committee, which conducted a survey amongst market participants and observed an overwhelming interest in stock index futures, followed by other derivatives products. The LCGC recommended derivatives trading in the stock exchanges in a phased manner. It is in this context SEBI permitted both NSE and BSE in the year 2000 to commence trading in stock index futures. The question, therefore, becomes relevant—what are the benefits of trading in Derivatives for the country and in particular for choosing stock index futures as the first preferred product? Following are some benefits of derivatives:

1. India's financial market system will strongly benefit from smoothly functioning index derivatives markets.
2. Internationally, the launch of derivatives has been associated with substantial improvements in market quality on the underlying equity market. Liquidity and market efficiency on India's equity market will improve once the derivatives commence trading.
3. Many risks in the financial markets can be eliminated by diversification. Index derivatives are special insofar as they can be used by the investors to protect themselves from the one risk in the equity market that cannot be diversified away, i.e., a fall in the market index. Once the investors use index derivatives, they will suffer less when fluctuations in the market index take place.
4. Foreign investors coming into India would be more comfortable if the hedging vehicles routinely used by them worldwide are available to them.

5. The launch of derivatives is a logical next step in the development of human capital in India. Skills in the financial sector have grown tremendously in the last few years. Thanks to the structural changes in the market, the economy is now ripe for derivatives as the next area for addition of skills.

## 5.8 DERIVATIVES TRADING AT NSE/BSE

The most notable of development in the history of secondary segment of the Indian stock market is the commencement of derivatives trading in June, 2000. The SEBI approved derivatives trading based on futures contracts at National Stock Exchange (NSE) and Bombay Stock Exchange (BSE) in accordance with the rules/bye-laws and regulations of the stock exchanges. To begin with, the SEBI permitted equity derivatives named stock index futures. The BSE introduced on June 9, 2000 stock index futures based on the sensitive Index (also called SENSEX comprising 30 scripts) named BSX, and NSE started on June 12, 2000 stock index future based on its index S&P CNX NIFTY (comprised 50 scripts) in the name of N FUTIDX NIFTY. Further details of these are given in Table 5.1.

**TABLE 5.1**   Salient Features of Index Futures Contracts at BSE and NSE

| S. No. | Items | BSE | NSE |
|--------|-------|-----|-----|
| 1. | Date of introduction | June 9, 2000 | June 12, 2000 |
| 2. | Name of security | BSX | N FUTIDX NIFTY |
| 3. | Underlying asset | BSE Sensitive Index (SENSEX) | S&P CNX NIFTY |
| 4. | Contract size | Sensex value × 50 | 200 or multiples of 200 |
| 5. | Tick size/Price step | 0.1 point of Sensex (equivalent to ₹5) | ₹0.05 |
| 6. | Minimum price fluctuations | ₹5 | Not applicable |
| 7. | Price bands | NA | NA |
| 8. | Expiration months | 3-near months | 3-near months |
| 9. | Trading cycle | A maximum of 3 months; the near month (1), the next month (2) and the a month (3) | As in previous column |
| 10. | Last trading/Expiry day | Last Thursday of the month or the preceding day | As in previous column |
| 11. | Settlement | In cash on *T*+1 bas | As in previous column |
| 12. | Final settlement price | Index closing price on the last trading day (a) | Index closing price on the 1st trading day (s) |
| 13. | Daily settlement price | Closing of futures contract (a) (a) | Closing of future contract |
| 14. | Trading hours | 9.30 a.m. to 3.30 p.m. | – |
| 15. | Margin | Upfront margin on daily basis | As in previous column |

(a)   Computed on the basis of the weighted average of last 15 minutes trading.

(a)(a)  Computed on the basis of weighted average of the last 5 minutes, or if the no, of weighted average of last 5 trades.

(s)   Weighted average price for the last half an hour's trade.

In India, stock index futures are available for one-month, two-month and three-month maturities. All the open positions in these contracts are settled daily. Further, the buyers and sellers are required to deposit margin with the respective stock exchanges determined as per the SEBI guidelines. To facilitate the effective risk management in the derivatives segment, all the important measures like minimum net worth requirement for the broker, determination of margin based on value at risk model, position limit for various participants, mechanism for collection and enforcement of margin, etc. have been put in place. Subsequently, the derivative products range had been increased by including options and futures on the indices and on several highly traded stocks. In an estimate, the product-wise turnover of derivatives on the Indian stock markets as on July 6, 2002 is stock futures (50 percent), index futures (21 percent), stock options (25 percent) and index option (4 percent). It means stock futures are most popular derivative traded at the stock market of India.

During the last decade, to make stock market functioning effective for futures trading, the SEBI has adopted several internationally tested and accepted mechanism for implementation at the Indian stock exchanges. For this, proper surveillance and risk containment like the circuit breaker, price bands, value at risk (VaR) based margin collections, etc. have been introduced.

The SEBI set up a 'Technical Group' headed by Prof. J.R. Varma to prescribe risk containment measures for new derivative products. The group recommended the introduction of exchange traded options on Indices which is also conformity with the sequence of introduction of derivatives products recommended by Dr. L.C. Gupta Committee.

The Technical Group has recommended the risk containment measure for exchange traded options on indices. The following are the important features of the risk containment framework for the trading and settlement of both index futures and index option contracts:

1. European style index options will be permitted initially. These will be settled in cash.
2. Index option contracts will have a minimum contract size of ₹2 lakhs, at the time of its introduction.
3. The risk containment measures described hereunder are only for premium style European option.
4. Index option contract will have a maximum maturity of 12 months and a minimum of three strikes, i.e., in the money, near the money and out of the money.
5. A portfolio-based margining approach, which would take an integrated view of the risk involved in the portfolio of individual client will be adopted. It is for the first time that such an approach is introduced in the Indian stock market. It is inconsistent with the practices followed in the countries. This approach will not only cover the risk but also help in reducing the transaction costs in derivatives.
6. The initial margin requirements will be based on worst case loss of a portfolio of an individual client to cover a 99 percent value at risk (Va) over a one day horizon. The initial margin requirement will be netted at level of individual client and it will be on gross basis at the level of Trading/Clearing member. Further, the initial margin requirement for the proprietary position of Trading/Clearing member will also be on net basis.
7. The short option minimum margin equal to 30 percent of the Notional value of all short index option will be charged if sum of the worst scenario loss and the calendar spread margin is lower than the short option minimum margin.
8. Net option value will be calculated on the current market value of the option times the number of options (positive for long options and negative for short options) in the portfolio. The net option value will be added to the Liquid Net Worth of the clearing member.

9. For option positions, the premium will be paid in by the buyer in cash and paid out to the seller in cash on $T + 1$ day until the buyer pays in the premium due shall be deducted from the available Liquid Net Worth on a real time basis. In case of index futures contracts, the mark-to-market gains losses for index futures position will continue to be settled.

Contrary to international experience, the growth of derivatives market did not take off as anticipated. The value of trading have been low. This is mainly attributed to the low awareness about the products and mechanism of trading among the market players and investors. SEBI's technical group on new derivative products has recently examined this issue and recommended the following measures for the development of derivatives market:

1. The system of sub-brokers be used for increasing the volume of trading in this market.
2. Financial institutions and mutual funds be permitted to sell short in the cash market for facilitating the free arbitrage between cash and derivatives market. However, such short sale may be restricted to the extent of corresponding exposure in the derivative market.
3. Arbitrage between cash and derivatives markets will assist in better price discovery in both the markets.

Countries like USA, UK and Singapore have reaped considerably economic benefit from foreign participation in their futures markets. Foreign participation in futures markets hedge the potential to act as a substantial 'invisible earner' of foreign exchange. Earlier the SEBI and the RBI both were hesitant to allow the foreign institutional investors (FIIs) for trading in the futures markets. However, recently the RBI has allowed FIIs to trade in derivatives market subject to the condition that the overall open position of the FII shall not exceed 100 percent of the market value of the concerned FII's total investment. As per the recent notification of the Central Government, SEBI and RBI will jointly examine the issues concerning trading in financial derivatives by FIs and FII(s).

## 5.9 DEVELOPMENT OF DERIVATIVES TRADING IN INDIA

1. Commodities futures for coffee, oil seeds, oil, gold, silver, pepper, cotton, jute and jute goods are traded in the commodities futures. Forward Markets Commission regulates the trading of commodities futures, which is now merged with the SEBI w.e.f. September, 2015.
2. Index futures based on Sensex and NIFTY index are also traded under the supervision of Securities and Exchange Board of India (SEBI).
3. The RBI has permitted banks, Financial Institutions (FI's) and Primary Dealers (PD's) to enter into forward rate agreement (FRAs)/interest rate swaps in order to facilitate hedging of interest rate risk and ensuring orderly development of the derivatives market.
4. The National Stock Exchange (NSE) became the first exchange to launch trading in options on individual securities. Trading in options on individual securities commenced from July, 2001. Options contracts are American style and cash settled and are available in about 40 securities stipulated by the Securities and Exchange Board of India.
5. The NSE commenced trading in futures on individual securities on November 9, 2001. The futures contracts are available in about 31 securities stipulated by SEBI. The BSE also started trading in stock options and futures (both Index and Stocks) around at the same time as the NSE.

6. The National Stock Exchange commenced trading in interest rate future on June 2003. Interest rate futures contracts are available on 91-day T-bills, 10-year bonds and 10-year zero coupon bonds as specified by the SEBI.

7. The National Stock Exchange launched the futures and options in CNX IT Index on September 13, 2004 and weekly options were started at the Bombay Stock Exchange from June, 2005. It is a unique product unparalleled worldwide in the derivatives market.

8. The NSE launched on December, 2006, futures and options In Bank Nifty Index, which has become a popular index after the NIFTY Index in India

9. The NSE launched derivatives on NIFTY Junior and CNX 100 on futures and options, in October, 2007.

10. On January 1, 2008, NSE launched derivatives of futures and options on NIFTY MIDCAP-50, and on the same date, the BSE started trading on Chhota (Mini) SENSEX.

11. On August 29, 2008 long-term option contracts on S×P CNX NIFTY Index were launched by the NSE. Futures and options on sectorial indices like BSE TECK, BSE FMCG, BSE METAL, BSE BANKERS, and BSE OILS & GAS were launched on BSE.

12. Trading currency futures was started by the NSE in August, 2008 and on October 1, 2008 interest rate futures were launched by the NSE. On December 10, 2008, the BSE launched currency derivatives contracts.

13. The NSE launched trading on Mini Index Futures & Options-(S&P CNX NIFTY Index) on March 3, 2009.

14. On August 7, 2009, NSE launched S&P CNX Nifty Futures & Options Index and interest rate futures for trading purpose

15. On December 18, 2009, BSE-USE form alliance to develop currency and interest rate derivatives markets. The BSE in February, 2010 issued new derivative norms to lower transaction costs for all.

16. The NSE, in April, 2010, started currency futures contracts on additional currency pairs.

17. The NSE introduced in October, 2010, European style stock option contracts and commenced trading of S&P CNX NIFTY futures at CME.

18. In July, 2011, NSE introduced the currency options contracts on USD-INR.

19. In August, 2011, The NSE launched derivative on Global Indices and trading of 91-day Treasury Bills futures contracts. Further, in September, 2011, it launched derivatives on CNX PSE & CNX Infrastructure Indices.

20. The BSE launched trading in BRICS MART Indices derivatives on March 30, 2012, and currency derivatives segment was launched on November 29, 2013.

**TABLE 5.2**   Financial Derivatives in India: A Chronology

| Date | Progress |
| --- | --- |
| December 14, 1995 | NSE asked SEBI for permission to trade futures |
| November 18, 1996 | SEBI setup L.C. Gupta Committee to draft a policy framework for index futures |
| May 11, 1998 | L.C. Gupta Committee submitted report |
| July 7, 1999 | RBI gave permission for OTC forward rate agreement (FRAs) and interest rate swaps |
| May 24, 2000 | SIMES chose NIFTY for trading futures and options on an Indian index |
| May 25, 2000 | SEBI gave permission to NSE and BSE to do index futures trading |

*(Contd.)*

*(Contd.)*

| Date | Progress |
|---|---|
| June 9, 2000 | Trading of BSE Sensex futures commenced at BSE |
| June 12, 2000 | Trading of NIFTY futures commenced at NSE |
| August 31, 2000 | Trading of futures and options on NIFTY to commence at SIMES |
| July, 2001 | Trading on equity futures commenced at NSE on 31 securities |
| June, 2003 | Trading on interest rate futures commenced at NSE |
| July, 2003 | Trading of FC-rupee options started |
| August, 2003 | Launch of futures & options in CNX IT index |
| September 13, 2004 | Weekly options of BSE |
| June, 2005 | Launch of futures & options in Bank Nifty index |
| December, 2006 | Derivative Exchange of the Year by Asia risk magazine |
| June, 2007 | NSE launches derivatives on Nifty Junior & CNX 100 |
| October, 2007 | NSE launches derivatives on Nifty Midcap -50 |
| January 1, 2008 | Trading of Chhota (Mini) Sensex at BSE |
| January 1, 2008 | Trading of mini index futures & options at NSE |
| March 3, 2009 | Long-term options contracts on S&P CNX Nifty index |
| NA | Futures & options on sectoral indices (BSE TECK, BSE FMCG, BSE Metal, BSE Bankex & BSE Oil & Gas) |
| August 29, 2008 | Trading of currency futures at NSE |
| August, 2008 | Launch of interest rate futures |
| October 1, 2008 | Currency derivative introduced at BSE |
| December 10, 2008 | S&P CNX Defty futures & options at NSE |
| August, 2009 | Launch of interest rate futures at NSE |
| August 7, 2009 | BSE-USE form alliance to develop currency & interest rate derivative markets |
| December 18, 2009 | BSE's new derivatives rate to lower transaction costs for all |
| February, 2010 | Launch of currency future on additional currency pairs at NSE |
| April, 2010 | Financial derivatives exchange award of the year by Asian Banker to NSE |
| July, 2010 | Commencement trading of S&P CNX Nifty futures on CME at NSE |
| October, 2010 | Introduction of European style stock option at NSE |
| October, 2010 | Introduction of Currency options on USD INR by NSE |
| July, 2011 | Commencement of 91-day GOI trading bill futures by NSE |
| August, 2011 | Launch of derivative on Global Indices at NSE |
| September, 2011 | Launch of derivative on CNX PSE & CNX infrastructure indices at NSE |
| March 30, 2012 | BSE launched trading in BRICSMART indices derivatives |
| November 29, 2013 | BSE launched currency derivative segment |

## 5.10   GROWTH OF DERIVATIVES MARKET IN INDIA

Derivative instruments were launched in Indian stock market in 2000, and since then a remarkable growth both in terms of volumes and number of traded contracts have been recorded. These instruments have been well received by the stock market participants throughout the country. The trading volume of derivatives exceed many times to the turnover of cash market. NSE alone accounts for about 99 percent of derivatives trading in Indian markets. The position of the NSE at the global level is remarkable as per the survey report of WFE, shown in Table 5.3.

**TABLE 5.3**   NSE's Global Rank

| Parameters | Rank |
|---|---|
| Single Stock Options | 8th |
| Single Stock Futures | 2nd |
| Index Options | 1st |
| Index Futures | 7th |

*Source:* WFE (ranking done for the period Jan–Dec.-2014. ranking for single stock options and futures and index option, and futures is based on number of contracts traded.)

*Data Source:* NSE Newsletter, July, 2015

Growth of derivatives trading in India specifically of NSE is shown in three aspects, namely market segments (F&O) segment contract-wise, FO segment turnover-wise:

**Trading value of different market segments:**   The whole market is bifurcated into various segments like Capital Market (CM), Equity Futures and Options, Wholesale Debt Market (WDM), Currency (F&O) and Interest Rate Futures (IRF). (EF&O). The turnover of these segments is shown in Table 5.4

**TABLE 5.4**   Trading Value of Different Market Segments

(₹ crores)

| Segment/Year | 2010–11 | 2011–12 | 2012–13 | 2013–14 | 2014–15 | % of total 2014–15 |
|---|---|---|---|---|---|---|
| Capital Market | 35,77,410 | 28,10,893 | 27,08,279 | 28,08,488 | 43,29,655 | 6.7 |
| Equity Futures & Options | 2,92,48,221 | 3,13,49,732 | 3,15,33,004 | 3,82,11,408 | 5,56,06,453 | 86.7 |
| Wholesale Debt Market | 5,59,447 | 6,33,179 | 7,92,214 | 8,51,434 | 7,72,369 | 1.2 |
| Currency F&O* | 34,49,788 | 46,74,990 | 52,74,465 | 40,12,513 | 30,23,908 | 4.7 |
| Interest Rate Futures** | 62 | 3,959 | 0.22 | 30,173 | 4,21,558 | 0.7 |
| **Total** | **3,68,34,927** | **3,94,72,753** | **4,03,07,962** | **4,59,14,017** | **6,41,53,943** | **100** |
| | 100 | 107.16 | 109.42 | 124.65 | 174.17 | |

*Trading in Currency Futures commenced on August 28, 2008
**Trading in Interest Rate Futures were Relaunched on January 21, 2010
*Source:* NSE newsletter July, 2015

It is observed from Table 5.4 that Equity Futures and Options segment is most popular and significant in terms of turn-over throughout from 2010–11 to 2014–15. It has more than 85 percent of the total turn-over and traded ₹5,56,06,453 crores in 2014–15. The Capital Market segment trading volume stands at the 2nd place, having about 6.7 percent in the year 2014–15. The Interest Rate Futures segment is at the lowest position just having 0.7 percent and trading volume of ₹4,21,558 crores in 2014–15. Interest rate futures were originally launched in 2003, but could not be successfully taken by the market participants. These were again launched in January, 2010. The trading volume of wholesale Debt Market segment could not also be grown as per the expectation. There is thin trading in this segment just 1.2 percent of the total volume of turnover. The year-wise growth of the total derivative market at NSE from 2010–11 to 2014–015 is just 74.17 percent which is not satisfactory, and moreover, it is just picked up in the year 2014–15, as observed from Table 5.4

**Business Growth of Futures & Options Products:**   To examine business growth of the derivatives, market is classified into four products, Index Futures, Stock Futures, Index Options and Stock Options. Trading volume in rupees and number of contracts entered by these segments have been shown in Table 5.5 for the year 2014–15.

**TABLE 5.5**   Business Growth F&O for the Year 2014–15

| S. No. | Derivatives | Turnover (₹ Crores) | No. of Contracts | % Turnover | % Contracts |
|--------|-------------|---------------------|------------------|------------|-------------|
| 1 | Index Futures | 7,81,940 | 2,18,66,521 | 8.75 | 8.87 |
| 2 | Stock Futures | 17,89,643 | 4,84,15,080 | 20.03 | 19.63 |
| 3 | Index Options (Notional) | 56,96,734 | 1,58,73,4718 | 63.76 | 64.36 |
| 4 | Stock Options (Notional) | 6,66,655 | 1,76,04,910 | 07.46 | 7.14 |
| **Total** | | **89,34,972** | **24,66,21,229** | **100.00** | **100.00** |

*Source:* www. Nseindia.com/content/fo/fo-business growth.htm

Table 5.5 depicts the total trading volume turnover and number of contracts executed of various products of futures & options for the year 2014–15. The volume of option products is of notional amount. Among all the products traded on NSE in F&O segment, Index options are most popular in term of volumes as well as number of contracts traded, having share of 63.76 percent and 64.36 percent, respectively, followed by Stock Futures with turnover share of 20.03 percent and number of contracts by 19.63 percent. Both the Index Futures and Stock Options are having share approximately 8 percent of the total volume. In brief, Index Options are dominating the Indian derivatives market with regards to volume and contracts performed.

**Product-wise Growth:**   Indian derivatives market witnessed a significant growth in different years. This section depicts the year-wise growth of Indian derivatives (Futures & Options) along with various derivative products like Index Futures, Stock Futures, Index Options and Stock Options. The details of number of contracts traded and volume of turnover are presented in Table 5.6 and Table 5.7.

**TABLE 5.6**   Futures and Options Product-wise Growth

| Year | Index Futures | | Stock Futures | | Index Options | | Stock Options | | Average Daily Turnover (₹ Cr.) |
|------|-----------------|---------------------------|-----------------|---------------------------|-----------------|---------------------------|-----------------|---------------------------|---------|
| | No. of Contracts | Notional Turnover (₹ Cr.) | No. of Contracts | Notional Turnover (₹ Cr.) | No. of Contracts | Notional Turnover (₹ Cr.) | No. of Contracts | Notional Turnover (₹ Cr.) | |
| 2014–15 | 2,18,66,521 | 7,81,940.72 | 4,84,15,080 | 17,89,643.7 | 15,87,34,718 | 56,96,734 | 1,76,04,910 | 6,66,655.4 | 1,75,195.6 |
| 2013–14 | 10,52,70,529 | 30,85,296.5 | 17,04,14,186 | 49,49,281.7 | 92,85,65,175 | 2,77,67,341 | 8,01,74,431 | 24,09,489 | 1,52,236.7 |

*(Contd.)*

*(Contd.)*

| Year | Index Futures | | Stock Futures | | Index Options | | Stock Options | | Average Daily Turnover (₹ Cr.) |
|------|---------------|---|---------------|---|---------------|---|---------------|---|---------|
| | No. of Contracts | Notional Turnover (₹ Cr.) | No. of Contracts | Notional Turnover (₹ Cr.) | No. of Contracts | Notional Turnover (₹ Cr.) | No. of Contracts | Notional Turnover (₹ Cr.) | |
| 2012–13 | 9,61,00,385 | 25,27,130.8 | 14,77,11,691 | 42,23,872 | 82,08,77,149 | 2,27,81,574 | 6,67,78,193 | 20,00,427 | 1,26,638.6 |
| 2011–12 | 14,61,88,740 | 35,77,998.4 | 15,83,44,617 | 40,74,670.7 | 86,40,17,736 | 2,27,20,032 | 3,64,94,371 | 9,77,031.1 | 1,25,902.5 |
| 2010–11 | 16,50,23,653 | 43,56,754.5 | 18,60,41,459 | 54,95,756.7 | 65,06,38,557 | 1,83,65,366 | 3,25,08,393 | 10,30,344 | 1,15,150.5 |
| 2009–10 | 17,83,06,889 | 39,34,388.7 | 14,55,91,240 | 51,95,246.6 | 34,13,79,523 | 80,27,964 | 1,40,16,270 | 5,06,065.2 | 72,392.07 |
| 2008–09 | 21,04,28,103 | 35,70,111.4 | 22,15,77,980 | 34,79,642.1 | 21,20,88,444 | 37,31,502 | 1,32,95,970 | 2,29,226.8 | 45,310.63 |
| 2007–08 | 15,65,98,579 | 38,20,667.3 | 20,35,87,952 | 75,48,563.2 | 5,53,66,038 | 13,62,111 | 94,60,631 | 3,59,136.6 | 52,153.3 |
| 2006–07 | 8,14,87,424 | 25,39,574 | 10,49,55,401 | 38,30,967 | 2,51,57,438 | 7,91,906 | 52,83,310 | 1,93,795 | 29,543 |
| 2005–06 | 5,85,37,886 | 15,13,755 | 8,09,05,493 | 27,91,697 | 1,29,35,116 | 3,38,469 | 52,40,776 | 1,80,253 | 19,220 |
| 2004–05 | 2,16,35,449 | 7,72,147 | 4,70,43,066 | 14,84,056 | 32,93,558 | 1,21,943 | 50,45,112 | 1,68,836 | 10,107 |
| 2003–04 | 1,71,91,668 | 5,54,446 | 3,23,68,842 | 13,05,939 | 17,32,414 | 52,816 | 55,83,071 | 2,17,207 | 8,388 |
| 2002–03 | 21,26,763 | 43,952 | 1,06,76,843 | 2,86,533 | 4,42,241 | 9,246 | 35,23,062 | 1,00,131 | 1,752 |
| 2001–02 | 10,25,588 | 21,483 | 19,57,856 | 51,515 | 1,75,900 | 3,765 | 10,37,529 | 25,163 | 410 |
| 2000–01 | 90,580 | 2,365 | – | – | – | – | – | – | 11 |

*(Source:* http://www.nseindia.com/content/fo/fo_businessgrowth.htm)

**TABLE 5.7**  Changes in Derivatives (F&O) Growth Product-wise

| Year | % Change in Turnover Index Future | % Change in Turnover Stock Future | % Change in Turnover Index Option | % Change in Turnover Stock Option |
|------|-----------------------------------|-----------------------------------|-----------------------------------|-----------------------------------|
| 2000–01 | | | | |
| 2001–02 | 808.3721 | | | |
| 2002–03 | 104.5897 | 456.21275 | 145.57769 | 297.9295 |
| 2003–04 | 1161.481 | 355.77263 | 471.2308 | 116.92283 |
| 2004–05 | 39.2646 | 13.638998 | 130.88269 | −22.26954 |
| 2005–06 | 96.04492 | 88.112645 | 177.56329 | 6.7621834 |
| 2006–07 | 67.76651 | 37.227178 | 133.96707 | 7.5127737 |
| 2007–08 | 50.4452 | 97.040674 | 72.004127 | 85.317784 |
| 2008–09 | −6.55791 | −53.903253 | 173.94992 | −36.17281 |
| 2009–10 | 10.20353 | 49.304051 | 115.14028 | 120.77052 |
| 2010–11 | 10.73523 | 5.7843279 | 128.76742 | 103.59906 |
| 2011–12 | −17.8747 | −25.857877 | 23.711294 | −5.1742816 |
| 2012–13 | −29.3703 | 3.6616775 | 0.2708711 | 104.74548 |
| 2013–14 | 22.08693 | 17.174046 | 21.885086 | 20.448734 |

*(Source:* www.nseindia.com, www.iosrjournals.org, Sep.–Oct. 2014)

On the analysis of the data presented in Table 5.6, it is observed that average daily turnover of F&O derivatives have increased from ₹11 crores in 2001–01 to 1,75,195.60 crores in the year 2014–15. But, there is significant growth from 2008–09 and onward where average turnover increased from ₹45,310.63 crores to ₹1,75,195.6 crores. Among the various products of derivative (F&O), it is noted that all the products have shown negative growth except Index Options, in the year 2008–10 and 2011–12. The percentage growth of these products as shown in Table 5.7 presents that Index options derivative product has grown continuously in all years since 2000–01. All the products have shown uneven growth in terms of trades in different years.

Table 5.8 presents the NSE derivatives (F&O) segment and (CD) segment for the year 2008–09 to 2013–14. On evaluating Table 5.8, it is noted that Average daily total turnover of both the segments is showing rising trend ranging from ₹46,478 crores in 2008–09 to 1,71,963.60 crores in 2013–14, with 367 percent growth. On the comparison of Futures & Options (F&O) segment with currency derivatives (CD), it is observed that in the year 2013–14, F&O segment is 88.52 percent, whereas CD segment is 11.48 percent. It means the turnover of F&O segment is almost 8 times of the CD segment. But on analysing the year-wise detail, it is noted that the CD segment has grown from 2.5 percent in 2008–09 to 11.48 percent in 2013–14, whereas F&O segment has declined from 97.50 percent to 88.75 percent in year 2013–14.

**TABLE 5.8**   NSE (F&O) and (CD) Derivatives

| Year | Total Number of Contracts | Total Turnover (₹ Cr.) | Average Daily Turnover (₹ Cr.) | Total Number of Contracts | Total Turnover (₹ Crs.) | Average Daily Turnover (₹ Crs.) | Total Turnover (₹ Crs.) | % of Total | % of Total |
|---|---|---|---|---|---|---|---|---|---|
| | NSE F&O segment | NSE F&O segment | NSE F&O segment | NSE CD segment | NSE CD segment | NSE CD segment | F&O + CD | F&O | CD |
| 2013–2014 | 91,11,18,963 | 3,80,34,680.05 | 1,52,236.60 | 54,88,48,391 | 32,94,408.65 | 19,727.00 | 1,71,963.60 | 88.52 | 11.48 |
| 2012–2013 | 1,13,14,67,418 | 3,15,33,003.96 | 1,26,638.57 | 95,92,43,448 | 52,74,464.65 | 21,705.62 | 1,48,344.19 | 85.37 | 14.63 |
| 2011–2012 | 1,20,50,45,464 | 3,13,49,731.74 | 1,25,902.54 | 97,33,44,132 | 46,74,989.91 | 19,479.12 | 1,45,381.66 | 86.60 | 13.40 |
| 2010–2011 | 1,03,42,12,062 | 2,92,48,221.09 | 1,15,150.48 | 74,96,02,075 | 34,49,787.72 | 13,854.57 | 1,29,005.05 | 89.26 | 10.74 |
| 2009–2010 | 67,92,93,922 | 1,76,63,664.57 | 72,392.07 | 37,86,06,983 | 17,82,608.04 | 7,427.53 | 79,819.60 | 90.69 | 9.31 |
| 2008–2009 | 65,73,90,497 | 1,10,10,482.2 | 45,310.63 | 3,26,72,768 | 1,62,272.43 | 1,167.43 | 46,478.06 | 97.49 | 2.51 |

(Source: www.nseindia.com, www.iosrjournals.org, Sep-Oct.-2014)

Table 5.9 depicts the Total Turnover and Average Turnover per day of NSE and BSE. It is observed that the NSE alone is dominating around 49 percent till the year 2009–10. If compare the turnover volume with BSE, the trading at BSE just picked up in the year 2010–11. After that the share of BSE increased to 11.29 percent and 34.06 percent in the year 2012–13 and 2013–14. The turnover of derivatives trading during the years 2010 and 2011 was almost negligible. Analysts have pointed on that.

**TABLE 5.9**   Total Turnover and Average Turnover per day of NSE and BSE(F&O)

| Year | Total Number of Contracts | Total Turnover (₹ Cr) | Average Daily Turnover (₹ Cr) | Total Number of Contracts | Total Turnover (₹ Cr) | Average Daily Turnover (₹ Cr) | Total | % of Total | % of Total |
|---|---|---|---|---|---|---|---|---|---|
| | NSE | NSE | NSE | BSE | BSE | BSE | NSE + BSE | NSE | BSE |
| 2013–14 | 1,27,92,43,623 | 3,82,11,408.05 | 1,52,236.6 | 75,03,405 | 1,94,21,854.8 | 78,630.99 | 2,30,867.59 | 65.94 | 34.06 |
| 2012–13 | 1,13,14,67,418 | 3,15,33,003.96 | 1,26,638.57 | 15,00,68,157 | 38,84,370.96 | 16,117.72 | 1,42,756.29 | 88.71 | 11.29 |

*(Contd.)*

*(Contd.)*

| Year | Total Number of Contracts | Total Turnover (₹ Cr) | Average Daily Turnover (₹ Cr) | Total Number of Contracts | Total Turnover (₹ Cr) | Average Daily Turnover (₹ Cr) | Total | % of Total | % of Total |
|---|---|---|---|---|---|---|---|---|---|
| | NSE | NSE | NSE | BSE | BSE | BSE | NSE + BSE | NSE | BSE |
| 2011–12 | 1,20,50,45,464 | 3,13,49,731.74 | 1,25,902.54 | 3,22,22,825 | 8,08,475.99 | 3,246.89 | 1,29,149.43 | 97.49 | 2.51 |
| 2010–11 | 1,03,42,12,062 | 2,92,48,221.09 | 1,15,150.48 | 5,623 | 154.33 | 0.61 | 1,15,151.09 | 100.00 | 0.00 |
| 2009–10 | 67,92,93,922 | 1,76,63,664.57 | 72,392.07 | 9,028 | 234.06 | 1.04 | 72,393.11 | 100.00 | 0.00 |
| 2008–09 | 65,73,90,497 | 1,10,10,482.2 | 45,310.63 | 4,96,502 | 11,774.83 | 48.46 | 45,359.09 | 99.89 | 0.11 |
| 2007–08 | 42,50,13,200 | 1,30,90,477.75 | 52,153.3 | 74,53,371 | 2,42,308.41 | 965.37 | 53,118.67 | 98.18 | 1.82 |
| 2006–07 | 21,68,83,573 | 73,56,242 | 29,543 | 17,81,220 | 59,006.62 | 259.94 | 29,802.94 | 99.13 | 0.87 |
| 2005–06 | 15,76,19,271 | 48,24,174 | 19,220 | 203 | 8.78 | 0.14 | 19,220.14 | 100.00 | 0.00 |
| 2004–05 | 7,70,17,185 | 25,46,982 | 10,107 | 5,31,719 | 16,112.32 | 77.09 | 10,184.09 | 99.24 | 0.76 |
| 2003–04 | 5,68,86,776 | 21,30,610 | 8,388 | 1,43,224 | 5,021.81 | 81 | 8,469 | 99.04 | 0.96 |

*(Source:* www.nseindia.com, www.bseindia.com, www.iosrjournals.org, Sep.–Oct.–2014)

A brief view of various products of equity derivatives is shown in Table 5.10 traded at NSE.

**TABLE 5.10**    Equity Derivatives Products at NSE

| Parameter | Index Futures | Index Options | Futures on Individual Securities | Options on Individual Securities | Long-term Index Options |
|---|---|---|---|---|---|
| **Equity Derivatives** | | | | | |
| **Underlying** | 6 indices | 6 indices | 166 securities | 166 securities | Nifty 50 |
| **Security Descriptor** | | | | | |
| **Instrument** | FUTIDX | OPTIDX | FUTSTK | OPTSTK | OPTIDX |
| **Underlying Symbol** | Symbol of Underlying Index | Symbol of Underlying Index | Symbol of Underlying Security | Symbol of Underlying Security | NIFTY |
| **Expiry Date** | DD-MM-YYYY | DD-MM-YYYY | DD-MM-YYYY | DD-MM-YYYY | DD-MM-YYYY |
| **Option Type** | – | CE/PE | – | CE/PE | CE/PE |
| **Strike Price** | – | Strike Price | – | Strike Price | Strike Price |
| **Trading Cycle** | 3-month trading cycle—the near month (one), the next month (two) and the far month (three) | | | | Three quarterly expiries (March, June, September and December cycle) and next half-yearly expiries (June, December cycle) |
| **Expiry Day** | Last Thursday of the expiry month. If the last Thursday is a trading holiday, then the expiry day is the previous trading day. | | | | |
| **Strike Price Intervals** | – | Depending on underlying price | – | Depending on underlying volatility* | Depending on underlying price |

*(Contd.)*

*(Contd.)*

| Equity Derivatives | | | | | |
|---|---|---|---|---|---|
| Parameter | Index Futures | Index Options | Futures on Individual Securities | Options on Individual Securities | Long-term Index Options |
| Permitted Lot Size | Underlying specific | Underlying specific | Underlying specific | Underlying specific | Underlying specific |
| Price Steps | ₹0.05 | ₹0.05 | ₹0.05 | ₹0.05 | ₹0.05 |
| Price Bands | Operating range of 10% of the base price | A contract specific price range based on its delta value is computed and updated on a daily basis | Operating range of 10% of the base price | A contract specific price range based on its delta value is computed and updated on a daily basis | A contract specific price range based on its delta value is computed and updated on a daily basis |

*Source:* www.nseindia.com

## 5.11 EMERGING STRUCTURE OF DERIVATIVES MARKETS IN INDIA

Organisational structure of derivatives market of a country differs across the world. In some countries, all financial markets including those for commodities derivatives and securities derivatives are organised under one regulator. Certain countries keep the entire money market operations and instruments exclusively under the Central Bank regulation, and all other segments of financial markets under a separate regulator. On the other hand, some countries have a fragmented system of organisational structure under separate regulators for each class of product. Further, in some other countries, the market for non-standardised contracts or better known as over the counter markets or negotiated market are not under any specific regulators.

Derivatives instruments in India are regulated by the **Reserve Bank of India (RBI), Securities and Exchange Board of India (SEBI)** and **Forward Markets Commission (FMC)**. After passing of the Finance Act, 2015, FMC was merged with SBI in September, 2015.

The framewok for regulating derivative transactions is provided in the various Acts of Government of India, such as Securities Contracts (Regulation) Act, 1956, Reserve Bank of India Act, 1934, and Forward Contracts (Regulation) Act, 1952 and related Rules, Regulations, Guidelines, Circulars, etc. of these. The Forward Contracts (Regulation) Act or FCRA would be repealed following the merger of FMC with SEBI. The emerging structure of the derivatives market in India based on the regulatory norms is shown in Figure 5.1.

On the basis of regulatory system, the derivatives markets in India can be broadly categorized into two markets, namely Exchange trade derivatives market and over-the-counter (OTC) derivative market. Exchange trade instrument can be further classified into financial derivatives and commodities derivatives. *Financial derivatives markets* deal with the financial futures instruments like stock futures, index futures, stock options, index options, interest rate futures, currency forwards and futures, financial swaps, etc. Whereas, *commodity futures markets* deal with commodity instruments like agricultural products; food grains, cotton and oil; metals like gold, silver, copper and steel and other assets like livestock, vegetables and so on.

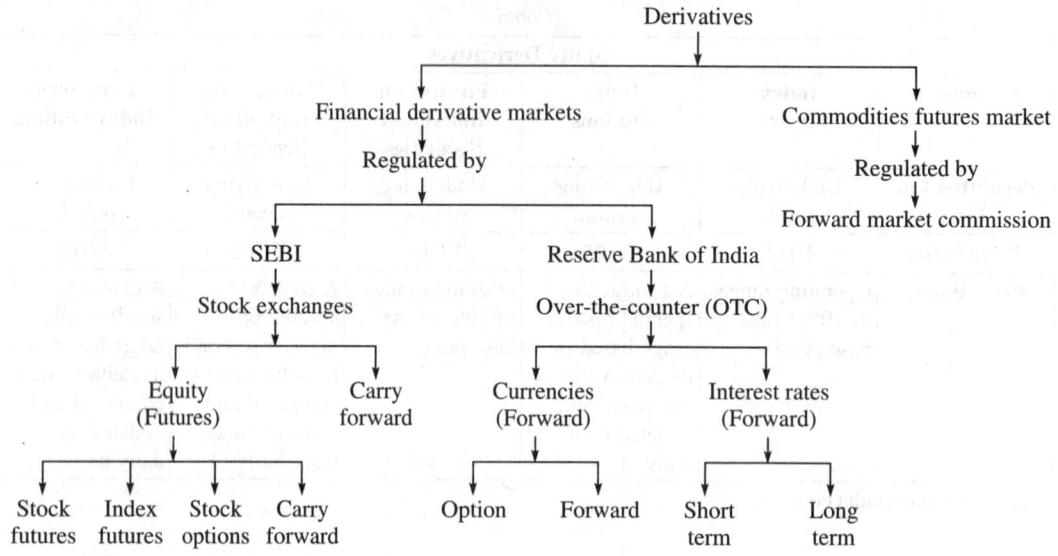

**FIGURE 5.1**    Emerging Structure of Derivative Market in India.

Equity derivatives markets in India are regulated and controlled by the Securities and Exchange Board of India (SEBI). The SEBI is authorized under the SEBI Act to frame rules and regulations for financial futures trading on the stock exchanges with the objective to protect the interest of the investors in the market. Further carry forward trading (Badla trading) is also regulated by the SEBI which is traded on the stock exchanges.

Prior to the merging of FMC with SEBI, the FMC was regulated the exchange traded commodity derivatives market in India. Now, the RBI as well as SEBI jointly regulates the exchange traded foreign currency and interest rate futures. Exchange traded equity and commodity derivatives markets are regulated by the SEBI. The foreign currency, interest rate and credit derivatives traded in the over-the-counter (OTC) market is regulated by the RBI and is permitted as long as at least one of the parties in the transaction is regulated by RBI.

Some of the other financial derivatives like currency options and futures and interest rate futures are controlled by the Reserve Bank of India (RBI) and the SEBI. These are traded on the stock exchanges. Financial futures on interest rate include both short-term interest rate and long-term interest rate forwards. Currencies include options and forwards. Since the RBI is the apex body to regulate currencies and interest rates in India, hence, financial derivatives relating to foreign currencies and interest rates traded in the OTC markets are generally come under the RBI regulation.

Major stock exchanges in India, under the regulation of the SEBI, trade in two kinds of products, namely futures and options. Equity futures include stock futures, index futures, stock options and index options. Currently these are traded on National Stock Exchange and Bombay Stock Exchange. Examples of such companies on which options and futures are available are. ACC, SBI, CIPLA, HPCL, TELCO, GRASIM,

Dr. Reddy, Lab, HLL, HDFC, Hero Honda, etc. A brief view of various products of equity derivatives traded at NSE is shown in Table 5.11.

Commodity futures markets were regulated in India by Forward Market Commission (FMC). The Commission is entrusted with to regulate commodities futures trading in India. Now, FMC is merged with the SEBI from September, 2005. Products like hessian, potatoes, pepper, cotton, etc. are traded on Coimbatore Commodity Exchange and Calcutta Commodity Exchange. Recently the Central Government has allowed futures trading on 54 new commodities of different categories to be eligible for trading on exchanges.

In brief, currently the organisational structure of derivatives markets in India is of mixed nature. Some derivatives instruments traded on exchanges relating to equity and commodities are regulated by the SEBI, whereas some others exchange traded instruments like foreign currencies, interest rates, etc. jointly by the RBI and SEBI, and OTC derivatives such as credit derivatives, currency and interest rates derivatives are under the supervision of RBI.

# SUMMARY

This chapter has introduced financial derivatives markets in India by briefly describing the need of derivatives markets in India. The need of derivatives in India has arisen due to economic liberalization. Since 1991 individuals and corporates were facing exchange risk, interest rate risk and other risks. The management of these risks is very important in the globalized world, and derivatives play an important role in this respect. This chapter also highlighted the various recommendations of the Dr. L.C. Gupta Committee on financial derivatives in India which emphasises the urgent need of introduction of financial derivatives and which should be in phased manner.

In addition, it has discussed the derivatives trading at NSE/BSE. Derivatives trading was started in June, 2001 with the introduction of stock index futures based on Sensex name BSE on BSE and on NSE June 12, 2000 named N FUTIDX NIFTY. In India, Stock index futures are available for one-month, two-month and three-month maturities. Indian derivatives market can be divided into two parts: (a) commodities futures markets and (b) financial derivative market. Financial derivatives market is regulated by the SEBI and RBI. SEBI regulates equity futures and options through various exchanges and RBI regulates currencies and interest rates forward both short-term and long-term mature through OTC. Commodity futures market is regulated by forward market commission (FMC), now merged with SEBI. The chapter ends with a list of showing growth of derivatives markets in India. In terms of Index options trading, NSE is having 1st rank and 2nd rank in single stock futures at the global level. It is also observed that among the exchange traded derivatives, index options trading is highest among all the derivatives. On comparison with BSE, NSE is dominating in the derivatives market in terms of volumes of trading.

# REVIEW QUESTIONS

1. Explain the term financial derivative. What are the different types of financial derivatives as given under SEBI guidelines? Explain them.
2. Clearly bring out the need of derivatives market in India with suitable arguments in favour and disfavour.
3. Discuss the growth of financial derivatives in India, in the light of major recommendations of Dr. L.C. Gupta Committee on derivatives trading.
4. "Derivatives are considered as most important tools used by organization to hedge their risks." Comment on this statement with suggestions.
5. Explain the important recommendations of Dr. L.C. Gupta Committee regarding derivative trading in India with suitable examples.

6. Explain the emerging structure of financial derivatives markets in India with suitable examples.
7. Write a note on evolution of derivative markets in India.
8. Discuss the recent trends of financial derivative in India with special reference to international finance.
9. Explain the risk containment measures for the financial derivatives trading in India.
10. Explain the weakness of the Indian stock market for launching of futures trading. Discuss the measures taken by the SEBI in this regard.
11. Write a detailed note on historical development of financial derivatives in India.
12. "Indian financial system is strong enough to introduce the advance instruments of risk management like financial derivatives." Critically examine the above statement along with your suggestions.
13. What are the needs of financial derivatives market in India? Discuss with suitable examples and precautions in the respect.
14. "The 1970's has witnessed an exponential growth in derivative market." Explain the statement in the light of evaluation of financial derivatives markets in India.
15. "Stock exchange futures are most popular tools used by big investors to hedge their risk." Discuss the statement in the light of advantages of stock index futures.
16. Discuss the salient features of Index futures contracts at the BSE and the NSE.
17. Name the important securities which are using derivatives instruments with their lot size.
18. Explain in general the trading mechanism of stock futures at National Stock Exchange (NSE) with suitable examples.
19. Write an explanatory note on the important terms used in Dr. L.C. Gupta Committee's recommendations.
20. Discuss the various important financial derivatives instruments traded on organized exchanges in world financial markets.
21. Write notes on
    (a) Position of financial derivatives in India
    (b) Evaluation of derivatives in India
    (c) Historical background of financial derivatives in India
22. Differentiate between Exchange traded derivatives and Over-the-Counter traded derivatives with suitable examples.

# SUGGESTED READINGS

1. Susan, Thomas, *Derivatives Markets in India* (edited), Tata McGraw-Hill, New Delhi, 2003.
2. Susan, Thomas, *Derivatives Markets in India*, Tata McGraw-Hill, New Delhi, 1998.
3. *Taxmann's SEBI Manual*, Taxman Allied Services (P) Ltd., New Delhi, 2002.
4. Corporate miscellany–Derivatives market in India: A framework of economic purpose, *Chartered Secretary*, October, 1997.
5. Reforms in Secondary Markets in India, Working paper from National Stock Exchange (NSE), India, 2000.
6. Somanathan, T.V., *Derivatives*, Tata McGraw-Hill, New Delhi, 1999.
7. Rene M. Stulz, *Risk Management & Derivatives*, Thomson South-Western, Indian-Reprint-2007.
8. Robert A. Strong, *Derivatives*, Thomson South-Western, Indian-Reprint-2006.
9. www. Nseindia.com. www.bseindia.com.

**Chapter 6**

# Regulation of Financial Derivatives in India

**LEARNING OBJECTIVES**

*After reading this chapter, students will be able to*

➢ Understand the concept of stock market in India.

➢ Know about the securities listing and grouping mechanism in Indian stock market.

➢ Understand the trading system, badla system, merits and demerits of badla in Indian stock market.

➢ Differentiate between badla and forward trading.

➢ Be aware of the SEBI prudential conditions and precautions on RCFS(1995).

➢ Know the recommendations of various committees like L.C. Gupta, J.R. Varma, on the regulation of forward trading in India on derivative segment.

➢ Understand the various regulatory measures taken by Regulatory Agencies.

➢ Explain the various regulatory instruments like margin, role of margins, daily or weekly limits on price changes.

➢ Understand important eligibility/regulatory conditions specified by SEBI.

## 6.1  INTRODUCTION

Stock market plays a significant role in an economy's growth and development. *Stock markets*, also called secondary markets, refer to those markets where existing issued securities like shares, debentures, mutual funds, and other government securities are traded. The stock markets mostly deal in stock or equity shares but now other securities like bonds, gilt-edged and debts are also becoming popular. Thus, the stock markets enable the investors to sell their stock holdings readily and thereby ensuring liquidity. Further, they can also continuously rearrange their stocks if they so desire. In this way, they can update their stock holdings in the light of changes in the market. The functions of the stock markets are facilitated at the stock exchanges. In brief, stock exchanges provide a market where stock trading are performed.

At present, in India, there are 23 stock exchanges which are operating, however, their organizations vary, for example 15 are public limited companies, 5 are limited by guarantees and 3 are voluntary non-profit making organizations. Presently, 8 exchanges have been granted permanent recognition, whereas the rest others have to renew their recognition every year. The Securities and Exchange Board of India Act, 1992 provides for the establishment of Securities and Exchange Board of India (SEBI) whose main functions are to protect the interest of the investors and to promote, develop and regulate the securities market. Though each exchange has its own bye-laws and regulations for regulation and control of stock trading activities, but the SEBI has also framed certain guidelines in this respect.

The Indian capital markets have metamorphosized over the last few years. A sea changes in the stock markets have seen dematerialized stocks, faster settlements, increased transparency, reduced fraud and competitive costs. The introduction of derivatives in the market required the existence of a clean, efficient and paperless cash market, which was delivered just in time. Introduction of exchange traded derivatives in June, 2000 was proceeded by parleys for over 5 years, involving a lot of serious deliberations for introducing the best practices from around the world. Before discussing the forward trading in Indian stock market, a brief view of functioning of stock exchanges in India is discussed in this section.

## 6.2  STRUCTURE OF THE MARKET

The stock market in India has developed more over the last few years than it has over its history of over hundred years. The introduction of screen-based trading in 1995 by the then newly developed National Stock Exchange of India (NSE) was responsible for a similar development by other stock exchanges in the country. The capital market is essentially consists of the Bombay Stock Exchange (BSE, perhaps the oldest stock exchange in Asia) and the National Stock Exchange. Together they account for over 90 percent of the trades in the secondary markets. Development of a screen-based trading system brought far reaching access and speed, but the market infrastructure still was poorly developed and a typical clearing and settlement cycle took over 14 days. For registering a share after a transaction, postal delays, the mercy of the share registrars, thefts while in postal service and mismatched transfer or signatures were some of the systemic risks a buyer of an Indian stock had to face. Over the last few years more and more stocks have been put on the compulsorily dematerialized list (over 99 percent of all shares traded today are in a paperless form). If someone has a particular desire for a physical stock certificate, he/she would still need to buy a dematerialized stock and then would send it for conversion into physical mode, since trading in physical stocks is prohibited while holding is not.

Competition amongst the two largest exchanges has brought enormous benefits to shareholders in terms of providing better and more cost effective services. As if that were not enough, a competing depository (established by the BSE) has brought down prices in that industry by over 80 percent. The market for exchange traded derivatives started in June 2000 when the two stock exchanges almost simultaneously started trading in futures on indices. The exchanges created separate segments where derivatives trading would take place. These segments would have a separate set of regulations and a separate clearing and settlement mechanism. The guarantee fund is also separate from the stock market (also called the cash segment). The last few months have seen a movement in the cash segment to a $T + 5$ settlement and beginning April 1, 2002 the exchanges have moved to a $T + 3$ settlement, with daily net settlement (i.e., a buy and a sell order of the same person made on a day shall be set off). Reduction of fraud, easing of costs, easing of complications and a virtual elimination of mistakes in clearing and settlement of securities have made the Indian capital markets amongst the best in terms of efficiency, technology and costs. Unfortunately, with the recent downturn in the economy, liquidity has dried up and exchanges are facing larger volatility in stocks. The markets in derivatives, though they took off with a tepid start, have seen double digit growth almost every month over the last year. The exchanges are clamoring for a smaller contract size and, therefore, have access to more investors. With growing evidence that small investors benefit greatly from investing in stock futures rather than from investing in mutual funds, the case of protecting smaller investors by keeping them away from the derivatives market might not sound very noble in the future.

## 6.3   SECURITIES' LISTING AND GROUPINGS

The stock exchanges provide an organized market place for the investors to buy and sell securities freely. Only such securities are traded on stock exchanges which are 'listed' or 'quoted' on them. So, each stock exchange has its own listing requirements and rules which are to be adhered by a company which intends to go for trading on that exchange. For example, any company that wants to be traded on Bombay Stock Exchange (BSE), has to abide by all the rules of BSE for listing purposes.

The listed securities on a stock exchange are classified into various groups. Till recently, they were classified as 'cleared' or 'specified' or 'group A' securities, and other one as 'non-cleared' or 'unspecified' or 'group B' or 'cash securities'. The Governing Board of the Exchange frames the guidelines for inclusion of a security into 'Group A' category. However, recently the BSE has changed the above mentioned classification and adopted a new one which is as under:

- Group 'A' or 'Specified' securities have weekly settlement and carry forward is allowed in their case.
- The non-specified group has been split into group $B_1$ and group $B_2$ securities.
- Group '$B_1$' has weekly settlement and is at par with group 'A' in every respect, but carry forward is not allowed in its case. It includes actively traded securities.
- Group $B_2$ securities are subject to settlement procedure which earlier existed in case of 'group B' securities.
- Group 'C' relates to odd lots securities.
- Recently, from 1996, the BSE has also included another group called 'group F' for trading all the debentures listed on it.
- The BSE has also introduced 'Z' category of scrips for companies not employing with listing requirements and not entertaining the investors' complaints.

## 6.4   TRADING SYSTEMS

Most of the exchanges carry out stock trading transactions on either 'cash basis' or 'carry over' basis, through their own clearing houses. Let us discuss herein brief the system of trading in general which is usually followed on the stock exchanges.

The trading business in 'Group A' securities is settled through clearing houses in addition to other methods of settlements. The year of a stock exchange is divided into periods called *Accounts*, which normally runs into a fortnight; but sometimes, it may be of a longer durations of three to four weeks. Thus, all the transactions performed during that period (one account period) are settled by payment and delivery of securities by the traders on the 'notified days' of the clearing programme of a given stock exchange.

Non-specified securities transactions are settled compulsorily by delivery and payment, there is no further carryover of the transaction. It is allowed only in Group 'A' securities. In this category, the investor has three options at the end of settlement period which are as under:

1. He can terminate the contract by sale or purchase by a cross contract, i.e., by squaring up transaction. For example, if he has an outstanding contract of sale, then he can make purchase of the same security and same quantity.
2. He can fulfill the contract by delivery or payment as the case may be. For purchase of securities, he will make the payment and for the sale he will hand over the delivery of securities to the broker.
3. He can carry over the contract to the next settlement. In other words, if an investor has purchased some shares but has no money to pay for delivery, then he can request to his broker to carry forward his business transaction to the next settlement account. In such situation, the broker of the investor would then find out someone who would pay on due date, (also called as pay-in day) on the behalf of the investor and would take delivery of the shares. The financer who finances in such carry forward transaction will charge interest on such funds, this is also known as *cantango* or *badla*, for the fortnight till the next pay-in-day. Similarly, on the other side, the seller, sometimes, may also have to pay the 'charge' to the buyer when the shares are over sold and the buyer demands the delivery of the shares, this is known as *backwardation charges* or *andha badla*. The badla system or charges play a significant role in forward trading. This system has to be operated with the approval of the concerned stock exchange which may even fix badla charges under exceptional circumstances.

## 6.5   BADLA SYSTEM IN INDIAN STOCK MARKET

In India, *badla system* was allowed for speculation in shares without paying up the full cost of the transaction. The term 'badla' refers to that system whereby the buyer or seller of shares may be allowed to postpone payment of money, or delivery of the shares, as the case may be, in return for paying or receiving a certain amount of money. It is also often known as carry forward trading. Badla can be classified into two types, namely 'Badla' (or Cantango) and 'Ulta' or Undha badla (or backwardation). The following example will explain the system of badla trading:

**Example of 'Badla':**   On March 3, X buys a State Bank of India (SBI) share for ₹300 and he is required to pay ₹30,000 for 100 shares on the settlement day, i.e., 16 March to take the delivery. Assuming that the price of the share is still ₹300 on that day, instead of paying of ₹30,000, he informs his broker that he would like to carry forward the transaction to the next settlement period ending on 30 March. Then the broker locates the other party (seller) who is also willing to carry forward the transaction, i.e., who does not insist the payment of the shares amount on 16 March. In return for agreeing to postpone the receipt of money from 16 March to 30 March, the seller imposes a charge on the buyer, which is popularly known as 'Badla'. It means it is a charge in the form of interest for the postponement of the payment for the period from one settlement to the next settlement. Assuming the price of SBI share ₹300 and a badla rate 4 percent per month, X, therefore, will pay to the seller ₹6 (4 × 300/2 × 100) per share, being the badla charge for 15 days (half a month).

If the market price of the SBI share changes on 16 March, for example, if it is ₹315, then the seller is to adjust and settle this transaction as follows: X has to pay badla charges @4 percent per month for a period of 15 days, i.e., 6.30 (4 × 315/2 × 100) per share being total ₹630 (100 × 6.30). Separately, the seller has to pay to X the appreciation in the share price, i.e., ₹15. The net amount of ₹8.70 (1 – 6.30) per share will be paid by the seller, being total ₹870 to the buyer. In this way, X is allowed to postpone (i.e., carry forward) payment till the next settlement date. Similarly, if the share price has decreased, i.e., from ₹300 to 290, then the buyer has to pay badla charges, i.e., ₹5.80 (290 × 4/2 × 100) and ₹10 (difference of ₹300 – 290), being ₹15.80 per share, totalling ₹1,580 in order to carry forward.

**Ulta or Undha Badla:**  Sometimes, there are certain cases where the sellers of the shares may ask for postponing the delivery of the shares which may occur due to various reasons, for example number of carry forward sellers as a whole significantly exceeds the number of buyers on carry forward basis. In such situation, the brokers would face a situation of lack of floating shares and will persuade to some buyers to postpone the settlement to the next one. Alternatively, they would find scrip lender who lend shares. Thus, the charges paid by the seller in such case to the buyer is known as 'ulta' or 'undha badla' or 'backwardation' charges.

**EXAMPLE:**  Continuing the earlier stated example, let us assume that the party Y is the seller who is expecting the price of the SBI share to fall below ₹300 per share by the settlement date. Assume that the price remains unchanged on settlement date, i.e., March 16. However, Y feels that it will fall later, and hence, wishes to carry forward the transaction to the next settlement date. In such situation, sometimes, the seller has to pay charges to the buyer for such postponement, which is known as *undha badla* or *backwardation charges*.

# 6.6  PARTIAL VOLUME EQUILIBRIUM

It has been observed that the buyers and the sellers in the stock market usually show their intention at the settlement date for settling the transactions or carry forward them to the next settlement date. Sometimes, buyer initially intending to carry forward may decide to pay money instead, if he finds the badla rate too high or vice versa. The position on the settlement day is explained with the help of following example:

*Symbols used:*

$B_d$ = Purchases for delivery
$B_c$ = Purchases for carry forward
$B$ = Total purchases; $B_d + B_c$
$S_d$ = Sales for delivery
$S_c$ = Sales for carry forward
$S$ = Total sales = $S_d + S_c$

**EXAMPLE:**  Assume that on a particular settlement period, the total trading volume of State Bank of India shares is 10,000 lots, i.e., $B = S = 10,000$. Let us further assume that out of this, 8,000 lots want delivery and rest 2,000 lots want to carry forward to next settlement. Further, among the sellers, sellers for 8,500 lots want delivery while the rest others want to carry forward the transaction. Hence, in this situation:

$B_d = 8,000$, $S_d = 8,500$, $B_c = 2,000$ and $S_c = 1,500$

i.e., $$B_c > S_c \text{ and } B_d < S_d$$

It is observed that the total number of buying lots is less than the corresponding total number of selling lots. This is called *partial volume inequality*. How is equilibrium achieved? This can be achieved by two ways/mechanism:

1. Some of the buyers or sellers change their positions/preferences and agreeing to carry forward against the 'badla' charges.
2. Some financiers or money lenders come forward to finance the excess forward purchases in return for receiving badla charges.

Both the mechanisms are discussed as follows:

## 6.6.1 First Mechanism

In this mechanism, the sellers may find this position more attractive, and hence, may agree to carry forward 500 lots (8,500 – 8,000) sales get shifted from delivery to carry forward. This means that
$S'_d = 8,500 - 500 = 8,000$, $B'_d = 8,000$, $B_c = 2,000$ and $S'_c = 1,500 + 500 = 2,000$

i.e., $$S'_d = B_d = 8,000 \text{ lots and } S'_c = B_c = 2,000 \text{ lots}$$

Hence, partial equilibrium is achieved.

## 6.6.2 Second Mechanism

In this mechanism, the third party (financier/money lender) come forward to finance money to the buyers of 500 lots. In such case, they do this simultaneously buying for delivery and selling on carry forward basis. It is also called *vyaj badla*. Hence, the money lender pays the amount to the seller and takes the shares as security, and get badla charges from the buyers. The revised position will be as follows:

$$B'_d = B_d + B_v = 8,000 + 500 = 8,500 \qquad\qquad B_v = \text{Vyaj Badla delivery}$$
$$S'_d = S_d = 8,500$$
$$B'_c = B_c = 2,000 \qquad\qquad S_v = \text{Vyaj Badla Carry Forward}$$
$$S'_c = S_c + S_v = 1,500 + 500 = 2,000 \qquad\qquad \text{Hence, } B_v = S_v$$

Partial volume equilibrium is achieved.

Similarly, the same mechanisms can be shown for such situations where $B_d > S_d$ and $B_c < S_c$. In actual practice, both the mechanisms operate together. In fact, the badla transaction is identical to a spot market transaction in shares financed by lending against the security of shares. It is explained by the following example:

**EXAMPLE:** At time $T$, X buys SBI share for ₹300 from Y. At the time of settlement day, $T_2$, the price of the share has increased to ₹320. Assuming that X does not have the money to pay the seller to take delivery of the shares, so he arranged money from a financier Z to pledge the shares to Z as security. Since the worth of the share is ₹320, Z agrees to give loan to X at ₹320 per share, assuming 100 percent financing without margin. X pays ₹300 per share to Y, and thus, it leaves X with cash in hand of ₹20 per share which he invests in deposits. Further, assuming that at the next settlement day, $T_3$, the price remains ₹320 per share, X raises funds of ₹320 from other sources and repays Z with interest and takes back the pledged shares. It means at the settlement day, $T_3$, the profit to X will be the appreciation in share price i.e., ₹20 (320 – 300), less interest on ₹320 for the prior $T_2$ to $T_3$, plus interest on the deposit of ₹20 for the same period, i.e., $T_2$ to $T_3$. This can be explained mathematically as follows:

$$R = (P_3 - P_1) - iP_2 + I(P_2 - P_1)$$

where $R$ is return on the transaction, $P_1$ is share price at the time $T_1$, $P_2$ is share price at the time $T_2$, $P_3$ is share price at the time $T_3$ and $i$ is interest rate for the period.

From the above example, it is noted that it does not involve any forward trading provided that funds are available in the market at the 100 percent on market price.

Now, let us assume that instead of arranging the funds from the market, the X requests to Y (seller) to carry forward the transaction subject to the payment of 'Badla' charges. Agreeing by Y, he then pays to X the appreciation of ₹20 (320 – 300) in the share value less badla charges. At the next settlement day $T_3$, assuming the price remains ₹320, X pays to Y ₹320 arranging from other source and then Y deliver the shares to X. Thus, the return to X in such situation will be as:

$$R = (P_3 - P_1) - bP_2 + I (P_2 - P_1)$$

where $b$ is interest rate on deposit.

If badla rate $b$ assumes to be equal to interest rate $i$, i.e., $b = i$, then both the equations mentioned above will be identical. In brief, 'badla' is simply a system of lending against shares wherein the loans are provided at the full market value of the shares on the date of each carry forward. This, badla (carry forward) trading is different from forward trading.

## 6.7 BADLA VS FORWARD TRADING

**Similarities:**

1. Both permit/initiate speculation without paying the full amount on the market price of share.
2. Both enhance the liquidity of the stock market.

**Differences:**

1. The price for future delivery is defined in advance in the forward trading, whereas in 'badla' it is known only at the time of final settlement. Badla charges change from time to time.
2. Forward trade is for a specified period, defined in advance in the forward trading, whereas in 'badla' the period of transaction is undefined as the transaction can be carry forward indefinitely from settlement to settlement.
3. In forward trading, there is invariably a deposit or margin payment usually ranging from 5 to 15 percent of the transaction value, whereas in old badla system, no margin was required, and hence that led to high speculation.

It may be concluded that badla has an indeterminate price. So, there is no relationship between spot price and future price and the future price is uncertain. It means the badla trading cannot be used for hedging and price stabling purposes.

In brief, the settlement system in vogue for trading in specified shares is called the *badla system*. It has the facility for carry forward the transactions from one settlement to another. The facility of carry forward extends liquidity and breadth of the stock market. Badla system has three components:

1. Transfer of market position
2. Stock lending
3. Borrowing/lending in money market

Transfer of market position refers here that the purchaser or seller has the facility to carry forward the transaction from one settlement to another. For example, a purchaser on the settlement day either can take the delivery of the shares and pay the amount to the seller, or alternatively carry forward his purchase position to the next settlement by reversing the purchase position by a sale transaction at the 'making up' price fixed by the stock exchange authorities which is normally closing price, of the last trading day. So, he will pay or receive, as the case may be, the difference between his contract price and making up price, and thus, creating a fresh position in the next settlement. Similarly, a seller can also do the same as seen in the case of a purchaser.

Stock lending is a legitimate activity in most of the financial markets all over the world. Badla system facilitates stock lending for short sellers. In general, a customer has to sign a stock loan consent form which allows the broker to lend the clients' securities to others for short sales. Short sellers provide liquidity to the genuine investors. Further, badla operators also provide finance to the members who need to meet their commitment in the current settlement and transfer their position to the later settlement.

## 6.8 BAN ON BADLA SYSTEM

The carry forward system (CFS) or badla system remained a controversial matter, specifically on Bombay Stock Exchange (BSE), and it had a chequered history, for example, it was banned between June 1969 to June 1972. Further, it was officially banned but continued to exist in practice from 1972–1982. It was permitted to function from August 1982 to December 13, 1993. However, in October, 1987, there was some checks put on this system like laying down the 'bands' within which the shares prices could fluctuate and limits on sales and purchases of the stocks. However, all the measures could not control the excessive speculation in the market. Consequently, on December 13, 1993, the Securities and Exchange Board of India (SEBI) issued an order abolishing 'badla system'—a Directive not to permit any further carryover in 'specified shares' and to reduce to zero the outstanding carryover position in two settlements issued to the Bombay, Calcutta, Delhi and Ahmedabad Stock Exchanges. However, this order later on extended by four more settlements. Thus, it came to a halt on March 12, 1994.

## 6.9 REVISED CARRY FORWARD OR REVISED BADLA SYSTEM

After discontinuing the traditional system of carry forward in December, 1993, the SEBI subsequently proposed an alternative system in March 14, 1994 but unanimity (agreement) could be reached on its implementation. Thus, in February, 1995, the SEBI set up the G.S. Patel Committee (GSPC) to review the system of carry forward transaction. In March, 1995, the GSPC submitted its reports and recommended drastic changes in the existing system and the introduction of the 'Revised system'. The SEBI adopted the 'Revised system' with some modifications in its decision on July 27, 1995 and on October 5, 1995.

The 'Revised system', called Revised Carry Forward System (RCFS), was implemented by the BSE in January, 1996, but the other exchanges in which traditional carry forward system had been prevalent before December, 1993 did not adopt this system. In January, 1997, the President of the BSE wrote to the SEBI for making some relaxations in the existing system (RCFS) to make it more practical and efficient. Consequently, on March 27, 1997, the SEBI reviewed the entire system and decided that the implementation of the revised carry forward system would be reviewed periodically by the SEBI, the first review being after three months.

## 6.10 SEBI PRUDENTIAL CONDITIONS AND PRECAUTIONS ON RCFS (1995)

Consequent to the Patel Committee Report and recommendations on the carry forward system, the SEBI introduced a revised carry forward system subject to the following prudential conditions and precautions:

1. Stock exchange would be allowed to introduce carry forward system only with the prior permission of SEBI. For this screen-based trading and systems capability for effective monitoring and surveillance would be essential pre-requisite. There must be full transparency.
2. The Executive Director would be responsible for transparency, monitoring, surveillance and reporting. The exchanges would also ensure for prompt and regular submission of information about the various parameters and their implementation.
3. The transaction can be carried forward for a maximum period of 90 days, and would be allowed to square off up to the 5th settlement (75th day). The transactions remained unsettled until that day, they will have to be settled by delivery or payment, as the case may be.
4. The stock exchange should record and report at the end of trading period, transactions into those for delivery, jobbing, carry forward and own account separately. This is known as *four track trading*. However, the SEBI implemented as a thin trade system in which transaction for delivery were separated from those for carry forward.
5. A daily margin at the flat rate of 15 percent will be recorded from the brokers for carry forward deals and on a marked-to-market basis every week. Margin will depend upon the volatility of share prices.
6. The stock exchanges would be introducing the capital adequacy norm of 3 percent for individual brokers and 6 percent for corporate to begin with. Brokers are allowed self certification, in place of audit, regarding their deals carried forward.
7. The financiers funding the carry forward transactions should not be permitted under buy circumstances to square up their positions till the repayment of the loan.
8. Every member would be required to keep books of record showing the source of the finance with sub-accounts being maintained in the clearing house.
9. There should be overall limits on carry forward transactions of a broker with separate sub-limits for purchases and sales and a limit on the transactions in any one share.
10. Vandhas (or objection memos) would be rectified immediately and the *Kapli* system and *Chalu upla* transactions will not be permitted.

Since the market operators and speculators made a lot of resentment over the implementation of the RCFS, ultimately the SEBI set up another committee J.R. Committee in March, 1997 to review this revised system. The Committee submitted its report in July, 1997 and its main recommendations (popularly known as the Modified Carry Forward System or MCFS), are as follows:

### 6.10.1   Recommendations of J.R. Varma Committee (1997)

1. Abolition of the twin-track system of segregating carry forward and delivery transactions.
2. A uniform margin of 10 percent on gross basis (position), instead of 15 percent as earlier on forward trade and 7.5 percent on delivery trade, with daily marking-to-market prices on both the transactions.
3. Elimination of the limit of 90 days for carry forward transactions.
4. Elimination of settlement only by delivery after 75 days.
5. Removal of the limit of ₹10 crores on the financing funding or on badla financing.
6. Scrapping the overall limit on carry forward of transaction of ₹5 crores.
7. The new system should be introduced only when an exchange has the necessary software for calculating margins on a daily basis.
8. Capital adequacy and other prudential safeguards should be strictly enforced.
9. The scrips chosen for carry forward trade should have sufficient floating stock.
10. The financiers should be allowed to take custody of the shares with safeguards in case of vyaj badla. The shares lent by badla financiers will continue to be deposited with the clearing house.
11. The exchanges should strengthen the regulatory and surveillance system to enforce the rules on the carry forward trading.

Hopefully, the above recommendations should lead to a strong and vibrant forward trading, generating liquidity, reducing volatility and providing medium for hedging.

Undoubtedly the carry forward trading can be misused, particularly in the context of computerized trading where huge positions build up quickly and easily. So both the committees (Varma and Patel) insisted the exchanges should be given adequate powers to regulate the market. In brief, these powers relate to suspending carry forward facility, fixing different rates of making up prices, imposition of price corrective measures, prohibiting short sales and long purchases, imposing limits on forward trading, suspending off the floor trades, fixing minimum and maximum prices, etc. SEBI has accepted most of the recommendations but has stipulated that screen based on line trading has to be provided by the exchange for opting the modified carry forward system.

Further to enhance liquidity and to shorten the carry forward cycle, the SEBI has introduced compulsory rolling settlement on a $T + 5$ basis for 119 scrips from May 8, 2000 and which are subject to compulsory dematerialized trading. The SEBI has also instructed to the stock exchanges to complete their settlement within seven days and to conduct the auction immediately after the completion of relevant trading period in those cases where the members have failed to give the delivery.

It is observed that the above said norms have created a positive impact on carry forward trading as well as functioning of the stock exchanges in the country. The stock exchanges have enforced the disclosures and transparency norms on the listed companies. The surveillance systems have improved and their boards are now broad based. The trading cycle is made uniformly for seven days, and there are almost 8000 electronic trading terminals all over the country. Further, now the stock exchanges have set up trade guarantee funds to ensure smooth trading and reduce counter-party risk.

## 6.11   DERIVATIVES REGULATIONS IN INDIAN STOCK MARKET

June, 2000 saw the introduction of financial derivatives in the country for the first time—even though carry forward of positions and weekly settlement had meant that a quasi-forward market existed for over a century. The first trade in derivatives was a culmination of legislative and legal efforts which had begun as early as 1995. In 1995, SEBI appointed a committee for exploring issues in introduction and creating a regulatory framework for a derivative market.

After the committee report was tabled, the first action taken was to wet nurse the derivatives market by adopting the entire regulatory framework of securities. This was done simply by defining securities to include derivatives and removing certain prohibitions on forward and options trading. Thus, the entire framework of existing securities regulations including anti-fraud and various disclosure obligations have become part of the regulations of derivatives in India. This is in sharp contrast to the introduction of futures on individual stocks in US. Their introduction took 20 years, endless bickering between the two regulators Securities Exchange Commission (SEC) and Commodity Futures Trading Commission (CFTC), a new Act which lays down several requirements for trading which should rightfully be in the bye-laws of the exchange/board of trade. By that standard, India managed to leapfrog as far as not just technology but also regulations. The introduction of new products has seen more of changes in the micro regulations like margining and default which are discussed subsequently.

In this section, the regulatory framework of forwards and futures trading in India will be discussed. Though the details relating to various issues concerning various aspects of futures trading have also been taken in other chapters, however, here some important regulatory issues of financial derivatives will be discussed. A brief structure of financial derivatives market in India has already been shown in Chapter 5, the same will be elaborated further here.

## 6.11.1 Participants and their Role in the Structure of the Exchange

A graphic presentation of an overview of regulatory framework of financial derivatives in India is shown in brief in Figure 6.1. The Indian trading system, as presented in Figure 6.1, comprises the exchange at the top—which is governed by the three governing bodies: Governing Council, Governing Board and Clearing Council. It is further assisted by Clearing House, Clearing Bank, Clearing Member, Trading Member and the Client, and also, part of the risk reduction scheme are the Trade Guarantee Fund and the Investor Protection Fund. Structurally, the exchange performs several functions like order matching, clearance and settlement, risk management including default management and investor protection.

The clearing house of the Bombay Stock Exchange (BSE) is a part of the exchange currently though it may, in the future, be spun off into an independent company. The clearing banks are banks that have agreed to clear the trades through their branches and transfer payments efficiently and often automatically after order execution. The banks work under the terms of an agreement signed with the clearing house of the exchange for terms of automatic withdrawal and payment of funds into the accounts of the members, who must have accounts with the designated clearing banks.

The clearing member is a member of the derivatives segment who is directly responsible for all trades entered by trading members clearing with it. On the other hand, trading members are responsible for being in touch with clients and placing the trade orders through the terminals provided them. A trading member should be a member of the exchange, i.e., of the cash segment of the exchange. A trading member must clear through a clearing member. A clearing member may refuse or restrict the trading rights of any or all its trading members clearing under it (even if legitimate under existing rules) because a clearing member is responsible for any default of trading members clearing under his/her tutelage. A clearing member can also be a trading member, however, no separate membership category exists for such persons because such persons must comply with the rights and obligations of both independently.

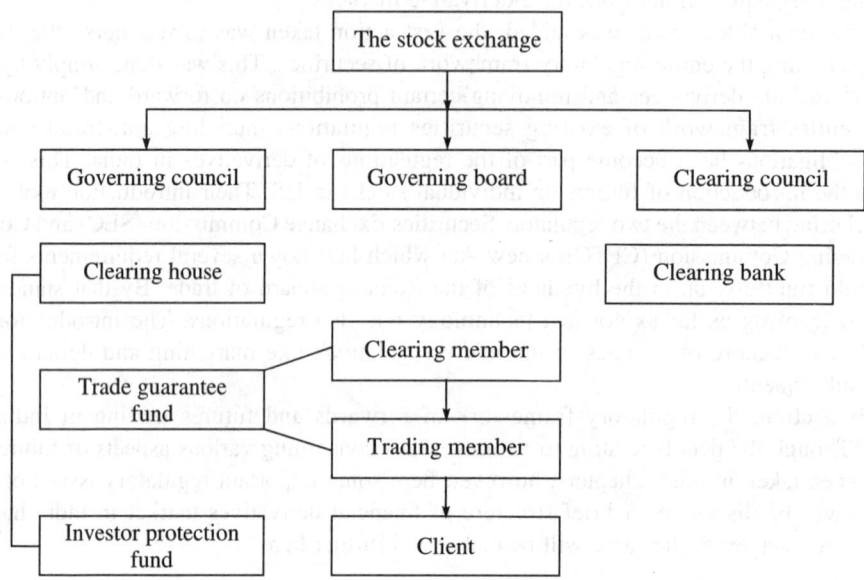

**FIGURE 6.1** An overview of regulation of financial derivatives in India.

Membership of the derivatives segment is a personal privilege and cannot be transferred. In the event of default, the terms of the rules and bye-laws override the insolvency laws of the land and the clearing house has the first right not only over the capital invested in the clearing house but also the right of his membership, which can be auctioned to pay for his market debts before external creditors are satisfied.

## 6.11.2 Products Available

The first derivative product introduced in India was Index Futures. Subsequently, options on index, futures on single stock and option on single stocks were introduced. The 87 stocks have been permitted for individual futures/option trading based on fairly stringent measures of the particular exchange. Till now, all products are cash settled, however, securities settled products are intended to be inducted into the market soon to provide better arbitrage opportunities to market players. In the future, the markets might even play the games at the Over-the-Counter (OTC) derivatives markets— which usually handle currency, interest rates and other products. Currently, the financial derivatives are regulated almost exclusively by SEBI. If currency and interest rates are introduced, the regulatory bodies may have some overlap as to regulations.

The regulatory framework and the existing infrastructure of the markets were suitably modified and most issues around the cash segment were resolved by the time the derivatives contracts were introduced. Further improvements, in the settlement of the cash segment have seen a correlated increased confidence in the markets, resulting into better volumes and reduced arbitrage opportunity. What has worked most in favour of the derivatives market, however, is the checks and balances, the systematic strength of the structure of the markets and the regulations which have translated into volumes.

## 6.11.3   Market Regulations

The primary laws in relation to derivatives are not legislative. They are created by the respective stock exchanges. In fact, the only legislative acts passed are those that define derivatives and remove earlier bans on options and forward trading. The Bombay Stock Exchange and the National Stock Exchange, both these two exchanges authorized by the regulator to start trading have passed extensive regulations for the organized trading of derivatives. Thus, the regulations at the exchange level are discussed in substantial detail. Before that we will briefly introduce the statutory background of the markets.

The relevant acts and statutory provisions are contained in the Securities Contract (Regulations) Act, 1957, Securities and Exchange Board of India, 1992 (SEBI Act) and various rules and regulations passed under them. SEBI has passed guidelines from time to time regulating the role of market intermediaries and Self Regulating Organizations (SROs). Guidelines under the SEBI Act do not pass through the muster of Parliament. In fact, some people have challenged the validity of these guidelines—unsuccessfully. These regulations, in fact, provide the regulatory framework for securities regulations by the Indian regulator (SEBI). Though the guidelines of SEBI do not pass the muster of Parliament, the rules and bye-laws of a stock exchange are tabled in the Indian Parliament. In fact, the rules and regulations of the BSE have been held to bypass certain statutory provisions like insolvency laws and the arbitration statute in limited parts because to do otherwise would be to affect the risk profile of the market.

The extant regulations which regulate securities automatically apply to derivatives because of the definitional change in the term securities. Thus, for instance, Securities and Exchange Board of India (Stock Brokers and Sub-brokers) Regulations, 1992 would automatically apply to all trading members of the derivatives segment.

## 6.11.4   Eligibility for Entering in Derivatives Trading

A person (individual or corporate) must be admitted as a member of the cash segment of the exchange, and therefore, satisfy all capital and other entry requirements of the cash segment before he/she can be considered for membership to trade in the derivatives segment. There appear no restriction as to residence of the individual or the country of registration of a company so long as they abide by all Indian regulations and furnish their annual books as required. The person must further satisfy the net worth requirement of the derivatives segment and pay in a base capital and other amounts which are called its liquid net worth to be used as security not merely for its own default, but partly also that of other members. The member must have at least two individuals who have passed a certification course in its exclusive employment. And most importantly, the trading member needs a clearing member who is willing to clear its trades. It is the clearing member's prerogative to allow his trading members to trade and set exposure limits for them.

A clearing member is not required to be a member of the cash segment of the exchange, but must satisfy net worth and capital requirements set by the exchange and shall have two members in its exclusive employ who are certified in a manner described earlier.

At the time of admission to either membership the clearing/trading member shall provide security for trading—such security can be cash, bank guarantee and securities as approved. The security deposit is utilized not merely in temporary margin shortfalls but also provides a buffer in the event of a default by the member. Part of the contribution goes towards the Trade Guarantee Fund which guarantees the trades in the exchange from default. The exchange has a primary lien over the security deposited—superior to that of external creditors.

Before a trading member starts to trade, it must be associated with a clearing member who is willing to clear its trades. The clearing member in its absolute discretion may allow a particular trading member to trade and set limits for trades for that trading member. A clearing member may ask to be disassociated from a trading member and can ask the exchange to do so. Similarly, a trading member in good standing may apply to be disassociated from a clearing member if it can find another clearing member to clear its trades.

## 6.11.5   Important Eligibility/Regulatory Conditions Specified by SEBI

- Derivative trading to take place through an on-line screen-based trading system.
- The derivatives exchange/segment should have on-line surveillance capability to monitor positions, prices and volumes on a real time basis so as to deter market manipulation.
- The derivatives exchange/segment should have arrangements for dissemination of information about trades, quantities and quotes on a real time basis through at least two information vending networks, which are easily accessible to investors across the country.
- The derivatives exchange/segment should have arbitration and investor grievances redressal mechanism operative from all the four areas/regions of the country.
- The derivatives exchange/segment should have satisfactory system of monitoring investor complaints and preventing irregularities in trading.
- The derivative segment of the exchange would have a separate Investor Protection Fund.
- The clearing corporation/house will perform full novation, i.e., the clearing corporation/house will interpose itself between both legs of every trade, becoming the legal counterparty to both or alternatively should provide an unconditional guarantee for settlement of all trades.
- The clearing corporation/house should have the capacity to monitor the overall position of members across both derivatives market and the underlying securities market for those members who are participating in both.
- The level of initial margin on index futures contracts will be related to the risk of loss on the position. The concept of value-at-risk will be used in calculating the required level of initial margins. The initial margins should be large enough to cover the one-day loss that can be encountered on the position on 99 percent of the days.
- The clearing corporation/house will establish facilities for electronic funds transfer (EFT) for swift movement of margin payments.
- In the event of a member defaulting in meeting its liabilities, the clearing corporation/house shall transfer client positions and assets to another solvent member or close-out all open positions.
- The clearing corporation/house should have capabilities to segregate initial margins deposited by clearing members for trades on their own account and on account of his client. The clearing corporation/house will hold the clients' margin money in trust for the client purposes only and should not allow its diversion for any other purpose.
- The clearing corporation/house should have a separate Trade Guarantee Fund for the trades executed on derivative exchange/segment.

## 6.11.6   Order Execution

Market integrity depends in part upon fair and efficient execution of orders. Order execution in the Indian context is part of the algorithm of the trading system. The system executes orders by price, time and size in that order. Thus, the best price will always have priority and there is no human intervention or margin for error in the market. Thus, rules are clearly defined and applied consistently—ensuring transparency and enhancing confidence in the order execution and the market place. Derivatives orders must be executed through the market and off-exchange trades are not permitted. As far as allocation of securities (or final settlement) upon exercise of an option before its maturity is concerned, the search for a writer of the option is done randomly by the trading system—without any human intervention—and the person so chosen is expected to deliver his/her obligation under the terms of the call/put contract.

## 6.11.7 Surveillance

The surveillance division of the exchange attempts to ensure market integrity. The fact that the derivatives market is inherently connected with the cash segment that means surveillance needs to be unified in its approach—which they are. Ideally, surveillance should be coordinated between all exchanges and to the extent possible between exchanges in different countries for the same contract. Large positions are monitored by the surveillance divisions and they regularly send notices to members to whom they consider might be involved in suspicious activity. Since large transactions are automatically marked for review by the surveillance division, a more cumbersome review of every trade would only be required where small trades are reported to be in violation of some regulation.

## 6.11.8 Risk Structure of the Market

A large part of the risk is delegated by the derivatives segment to the clearing member. If a trading member defaults in its obligations, the clearing member needs to make up for the shortfall and recover the balance from the trading member. Because of this burden, a clearing member is given a lot of powers over the workings of trading members clearing under him/her. A clearing member can restrict the exposure levels or even stop the trading rights of any of its clearing members. Of course, the derivatives segment too maintains collateral power over the trading member.

Clearing guarantees are given by the clearing house (in the case of NSE, the clearing corporation stands as a counterparty to each trade), so that if either side of the trade defaults, the clearing house would make good the shortfall in the settlement. Because of the daily settlement nature of the market, the guarantee needs to be fulfilled before the beginning of the next trading day ($T + 1$). Thus, the guarantee is akin to the counter party obligations of the exchange/clearing corporation in the NSE.

## 6.11.9 Exposure Limits

Further each member has exposure limits circumscribed by its capital/security deposited. If for reasons of adverse price change, a member exceeds its exposure limits beyond that afforded by its deposit, its trading terminal will not permit any further trades which will increase its exposure. The member may be permitted to enter trades which will reduce the exposure limit—since on a portfolio basis adding further exposure can reduce overall exposure obligations. The member is also obliged to immediately furnish further deposit or reduce his/her exposure to be in compliance with margin requirements. Such compliance measures are in very large part taken by the trading system without human intervention. Failure to settle margins within a short span of time would attract further action for compliance by the exchange.

If a trading member defaults, action can be taken by the clearing member and the exchange. The clearing member has an obligation to report the exposure violation to the exchange. Further the clearing member's algorithms added to the trading member's trading terminals would automatically limit that trading member's ability to transact contracts which would increase its exposure liabilities. The clearing member can also close out contracts of its trading members to reduce such excess exposure. Similarly, the clearing house can close out individual contracts of a clearing member, and a trading member can close out contracts of a client who has exceeded exposure limits. In case of any shortfall, the margin and other amounts can be utilized to pay off the dues of such constituents. The exchange has first lien over every property of a member in its possession. The exchange also has right of suspension or declaration of default of the member in case the member is not able to satisfy the shortfall within a specified time.

There are position limits in each contract set by SEBI and/or the exchange for one participant and also market wide limits for one particular contract. Such restrictions are necessary to observe and restrict potential manipulation in the derivatives market. Special limits were also prescribed for Foreign Institutional Investors and Mutual Funds. These limits are constantly reviewed and changed as liquidity demands change.

## 6.11.10　Capital Requirements

To be admitted to trading/clearing a member must make certain deposits besides the admission fee charged. The member will contribute an initial contribution to capital. The initial contribution is non-refundable. It can be in the form of cash, bank guarantee and securities as prescribed. The member will be entitled to interest and corporate benefits like dividend and bonus shares on the deposit so long as they are not dilutive of the contribution.

The member will also be obliged to pay on a continuous basis a capital contribution—such contribution would normally be a small percentage of the member's turnover. The initial contribution to capital, the member's continuous contribution and the contribution of the exchange to the corpus of the Trade Guarantee Fund will form the basis of General Access Funds. General access funds can be utilized towards the default of any member of the exchange. The member may also be required to pay additional capital contribution if so required by the exchange. Specific Access Funds, are those funds which may be used only for the default of the defaulting member and on account of no other person.

## 6.11.11　Clearance and Settlement

The clearing house acts as the common agent of the members for clearing contracts between members and for delivering securities (if required) to and receiving securities (if required) from and for receiving or paying any amounts payable to or payable by such members in connection with any contracts and to do all things necessary or proper for carrying out the foregoing purposes. The clearing house stands as a counterparty in the trade. Therefore, in the event of default of any member, the settlement is completed by pulling money out of the Trade Guarantee Fund and completing the settlement. Subsequently the defaulting party is pursued by the exchange which is holding the members' deposits and margins in lien. The extent of loss is usually limited in the event of default because of the daily settlement and the margin deposited by the member. A second protection is the fact that if a client or a trading member defaults, the clearing member is responsible for its actions. The third line of defence of course is the fact that the clearing house stands as a guarantor/counterparty to each trade.

Payment for the guarantee/counterparty is made out of a Trade Guarantee Fund, described in more detail subsequently in Section 6.11.20 of this chapter. The last line of defence is the insurance cover on the Trade Guarantee Fund if it gets completely depleted. Because of the algorithm fed into the trading system, there is a real time/continuous surveillance of positions of members and there is little systemic risk involved as far as the solvency of the exchange is concerned.

The primary aspects of work of the clearing house are:

(a) monitor the overall positions of members across all segments of the exchange.
(b) establish facilities for electronic funds transfer.
(c) specify the types of margins to be collected, the person by whom margins are to be paid in terms of Bye-law 4.7, in manner of payment of margin, the amount of margin, the method of computation of margin, valuation of collateral, the time of payment of margin and the manner and circumstances in which margin is to be adjusted, appropriated, applied or returned.
(d) monitor and supervise the collection of margin, collect margins and initiate and take action for non-payment of margin.

## 6.11.12 Margining Structure

Margins are collected with only one purpose in mind—as a collateral for due settlement of trades keeping in mind a worst case scenario. They contribute to the amount of leverage a person can use. Thus, lower margins would increase leverage, and therefore, increase the risk of a person defaulting. However, higher margins would suck away liquidity from the market. To determine a safe margin which would balance with the costs associated with higher margin, statisticians calculate the worst case scenario loss—and provide for a reasonable degree of safety.

The computation of worst scenario loss has two components. The first is the valuation of the portfolio under sixteen scenarios. At the second stage, these scenario contract values are applied to the actual portfolio positions to compute the portfolio values and the initial margin (worst scenario loss). For computational ease, exchanges are permitted to update the scenario contract values only at discrete time points each day, and the latest available scenario contract values is applied to member/client portfolios on a real time basis.

Normally, a three sigma standard is used in futures contracts so that the margin levels would cover approximately 99 percent of scenario. So, in case of default, the margin would be sufficient to meet with the shortfall. Options attract a higher standard since only one person, the writer/short, takes up more risk.

## 6.11.13 Margin Collection and Enforcement

The mark-to-market settlement of futures and options is collected before the start of the next day's trading, in cash. The members in turn collect the initial margin from their clients. The members can collect excess margin either for convenience or for extra safety of their position from his client. The margin money, and mark to market margin (daily settlement price) typically moves from the client to the trading member to the clearing member to the clearing bank on account of the clearing house and down the chain on the other side down to the client level. If any part of the chain does not pay its obligations, the chain is made whole by another element. For a client's default the trading member pays, for the trading member's obligation, the clearing member is still obliged to pay (and then take process against the trading member). If the clearing member defaults in paying, the clearing house invokes the trade guarantee fund to pay down the other side of the chain of persons. The collection of margin is done electronically by the trading system and communicated to the clearing house which intimates the clearing bank to debit/credit the accounts of various members.

### 6.11.14   Methodology of Calculating

Margins are collected on a gross basis between persons, however, the position of one person is calculated considering his/her entire portfolio. Thus, some securities may reduce the margin requirements created by other positions.

### 6.11.15   Initial Margin

Initial margin is collected by the clearing house at the time when a contract is entered into. It may be collected in cash, bank guarantees and securities in various percentages as mentioned from time to time. Till the time the long of a contract pays the initial margin or the premium, the amount is deducted from the liquid net worth of the member on a real time basis.

### 6.11.16   Mark-to-Market

The trades are settled on a daily basis, thus, any profit or loss made during the day is passed on to the respective counterparty through the clearing house. Such payments are known as mark-to-market margins. They are not really margins but daily clearance amounts for settlement of a trade. Typically these are collected at the end of the business day but the exchange has the power to collect advance daily settlement amounts on expectations of excess volatility. These settlement margins are always collected in cash. Funds for settlement are automatically debited and credited to the respective accounts of the clearing members. Each clearing member must open an account with one of the clearing banks and sufficient funds must be available for the process of settlements and margins—at the risk of default proceedings.

### 6.11.17   Cross Margining with Cash Segment

Portfolio-based margining approach which takes an integrated view of the risk involved in the portfolio of each individual client comprising positions in all derivatives contracts, i.e., index futures, index options, stock options and single stock futures. However, the cash segment and derivatives segment are not allowed to be treated as a single portfolio and exposure in one does not reduce the liability in another on the basis of a unified portfolio. However, this author strongly recommends cross margining be allowed between the two segments. Doing so will allow easy arbitrage and a more efficient market in both the cash and the derivatives segment. The physical settlement of stock option contracts is proposed to be introduced to provide inter linkages in the prices of the stock in the cash and the derivative markets.

### 6.11.18   Closing Out

On default the exchange may close out open positions of the defaulting member. However, such close out creates a problem for people clearing or trading through such member. Their positions would also normally be closed out. This is a weak part of the regulations because clients or trading members are faced with a close out of their entire portfolio despite the fact that they were in good standing. However, the exchange leaves the possibility of transfer of positions of such member to other clearing/trading member. If the default of the clearing member is due to the default of its trading member or the trading member's client, then the clearing house can exercise lien over such defaulting cause's properties. Closing out is usually effected by auction or placing an order or using a formula to come to a price.

## 6.11.19 Suspension and Default

A member can be declared defaulter if it defaults on any payment obligations or any other obligations imposed according to the regulations or if an arbitration order is not followed or if it is declared defaulter in another segment or another exchange. Suspension of membership entails a temporary bar on trading/clearing rights of the person while expulsion is a permanent exclusion of the persons from membership. Default in one segment will automatically make a person a defaulter in all segments of the exchange. Suspension in one segment will similarly entail suspension from all segments of the exchange.

In the event of declaration of default of a member, all its positions can be either closed out or at the discretion of the clearing house transferred to another member willing to accept the exposure. The shortfall is met by the clearing house by invoking the trade guarantee fund. The Trade Guarantee Fund (TGF) was created with an initial contribution by the exchange and has pooled into it the non-refundable part of its member's capital contribution and continuous contribution by members based on their turnover. Further amounts may be demanded by the exchange to pay the resources of the fund in the event of necessity.

## 6.11.20 Use of the Trade Guarantee Fund

In the event of any default, the Trade Guarantee Fund (TGF) shall pay to the clearing house the amount of money that the member had defaulted in the settlement in which the default was made. Such payments are made before the beginning of the next settlement cycle, which is in the absence of holidays, the next day. Such settlements can be withdrawn after giving notice, if evidence of fraud or collusive behaviour are evident in the claim. The TGF funds can be used for the settlement of the defaulting member in the settlement in which it defaulted and not other. Further all dues of the defaulter are not covered by the fund but only the settlement dues of the member.

## 6.11.21 Investor Protection Fund

The fund was established to protect such investors who suffer not as a result of a member defaulting its settlement dues but for making whole an investor who despite a proper settlement is not paid his/her due by the member.

## 6.11.22 Appropriation of Defaulting Member's Assets

As discussed earlier, the case law is clear that the assets of a defaulter in the custody of the exchange can be utilized by the exchange before any third party creditor can lay a claim to it. The application of a defaulter's assets are specified in Bye-law 15.36. In short, it lays down eight categories of application of defaulter's assets before the assets can be paid back to the defaulter, i.e., his other creditors if they exist.

### 6.11.23   Suspension of Trading in a Contract or Several Contracts

The provision for suspension of a contract or of the market is self-explanatory:

A contract in a particular derivative or the entire market can be suspended for the following reasons:

(a) Suspension of trading in the underlying securities
(b) For protection of the interests of investors
(c) For the purpose of maintaining a fair and orderly market

### 6.11.24   Dispute Settlement

Dispute settlement between trading member(s) and other members are resolved by arbitration as per the terms of the bye-laws of the exchange. It has been held that the terms of the arbitration under the Stock Exchange Bye-laws will overrule to the extent of conflict the terms of arbitration set by the Indian Arbitration and Conciliation Act, 1996. The arbitrators are selected from a panel of arbitrators, most of whom have significant knowledge of the markets. The venue of the arbitration is set in Mumbai and the jurisdiction is that of the Mumbai courts.

In case of dispute between members, the provisions are somewhat different from the case of resolution of dispute between a member and non-member. For instance, the appeal provisions for a member-member dispute is more restrictive than that of a member-non-member dispute.

### 6.11.25   Member Regulations

Each client has a client ID assigned so that clients' assets are segregated from those of the member. The clearing house will segregate upfront and initial margins deposited by clearing members for trades on their own account, on account of trading members and on account of clients of the clearing or trading members. The clearing house will hold the clients' and trading members' margin money in trust for the purpose of meeting the obligations of the clients and the trading members only and shall not allow its diversion for any other purpose.

Not only are the monies of a client not permitted to be pooled with that of a member but the monies of one client are not permitted to be pooled with that of other clients. Similarly, a clearing member cannot pool the assets of trading members clearing under it or mix its own assets with those of the trading member. A similar segregation is ordered in the books of the members who must maintain separate accounts for proprietary trades from those of its clients.

Futures trading like other economic activities is an important and sophisticated economic tool for the development and growth of a country. It can be beneficial as well as detrimental if the same is efficiently framed and effectively regulated. This has been already witnessed by the various financial scams occurring not only in our country rather throughout the world. Before discussing the regulatory framework of futures trading in India, let us see the various tools which are often used in such regulation.

### 6.12   REGULATORY INSTRUMENTS

As we know that the derivatives are of different types and are managed by various bodies like stock exchanges, trade associations, clearing houses, over-the-counter bodies, etc. Thus, the issues relating to their implementation and regulation are also different. A careful balancing of various considerations is necessary in deciding these. We will discuss here the important instruments of regulation used for this purpose by the different regulatory authorities and governing bodies from time to time.

**Margin variation:**   A margin is a proportion of the derivative contract value which has to be paid in cash or securities by the seller or the buyer or both, as the case may be, in the futures market. The basic objective of such margin is to ensure the safety of the contract or preventing from the defaults caused by one of the parties to the contract. The higher the margin ratio the greater the amount of capital which is locked up against a particular transaction. In other words, the higher margin will have more safety for the parties but at the higher cost. Further, increase or decrease in margin will affect the volume of trading in that asset. The regulatory authority frequently use this instrument to check the high speculation and thinness of the market.

**Imposition of special margins:**   The special margins refer to those margins which are imposed by the regulatory authorities over and above the ordinary margin as referred in above paragraph. For example, if the volume of speculative trading in the market has crossed its normal limits, and the market has become explosive, then to check this excessiveness, the special margin in addition to normal margin may be levied. In general, special margins are imposed with 'threshold' prices, so that they are imposed only when prices are higher or lower to specified limits.

**Daily or weekly limits on price changes:**   This is another important tool which is used to control the futures trading. The basic objective of this tool is to keep the prices of the futures instruments in a particular band or limits, for example,. 10 percent upper and lower band of the normal price. The idea is to put limits temporarily on the price fluctuations or blind price movements.

**Limits on open position:**   The term open position relates to the limit on volume of trading for a particular instrument/scrip for the traders in the market. The basic idea of making such restriction on open positions of the market participants is just to avoid manipulation or excessive speculation by the large operators. This limit is normally imposed in case of speculative open positions.

**Temporary suspension of trading:**   According to this measure, the regulatory authority stops the trading in particular asset temporarily for a particular period. The basic objective is to kerb speculation because it has been noticed in the market that, sometimes, over dose of speculative manipulation which rendered the markets completely out of tune with reality. As per this measure, the authority can close out all the existing futures contracts at a fixed rate which does not give the 'offending' parties the speculative gain for which such deals were initiated.

**Changes in number and/or timing of contracts:**   This measure is related to change in number and timings of the futures contracts being traded because, sometimes, it is not well suited to the seasonality of supply or demand of the particular asset or commodity. For example, regulatory authority may change the trading months from February, March to April and May, etc. However, this method is not so popular in the futures market.

**Fixation of price limits:**   In this technique, the regulatory authority fixes the price limits, i.e., maximum and/or minimum, which the futures market is not allowed to move. Once the limits are reached then in that case all the transactions can be undertaken at the price or within the acceptable price range. The basic idea of this technique is to protect the markets at the time of shortage or gluts.

**Indefinite suspension or banning of trading:**   Sometimes, the futures market reached in such position where trading is to be stopped indefinitely or till further order of the authority for restarting of the trading. It has been witnessed many times in Indian futures markets that the SEBI has ordered to stop trading in the market. This is done in rare cases where the authority feels that no other alternative is available except indefinite suspension of trading in the market.

## 6.13   GENESIS OF REGULATION IN FINANCIAL DERIVATIVES

Futures trading in India are currently regulated by the three agencies, namely Securities and Exchange Board of India (SEBI), Forward Markets Commission (FMC) and Reserve Bank of India (RBI). The derivatives can be classified into two categories: *Commodities derivatives* and *Financial derivatives*. In India, the statutory basis for regulating commodities futures, commodities derivatives trading is enacted through the Forward Contracts Regulation Act (FCRA), 1953 which has laid down certain fundamental ground rules. Under this Act, a permanent regulatory body, known as the Forward Markets Commission is also created which carries out its function through the recognized associations, and holds the overall charge of the regulation of all forwards in commodities specifically.

For the smooth functioning of the commodity derivatives in India, the FCR Act makes it mandatory for associations to obtain Central Government's recognition to carry on forward trading. The Act prescribes the procedures by which the associations can seek recognition through the FMC. Under the Act, the legal definitions of various types of forwards and options contracts have been given. Currently, it has banned all options in goods. The Act has laid down in detail the functions and powers of the FMC. Under the Act, a world class regulatory structure has been created for the smooth functioning of forward trading in India.

The SEBI is entrusted to regulate the carry-forward trading on stock market and other financial derivatives like equity stock, stock index, options, etc. through recognized stock exchanges of the country. Over-the-counter (OTC) forward contracts and options on foreign currencies are regulated by the Reserve Bank of India (RBI). A further detail regarding these futures contracts have been given in the concerned chapters.

## 6.14   COMMITTEES ON FORWARD AND FUTURES MARKETS

The Government of India appointed various committees at various time to go into the regulatory framework of futures trading in the country. In this section, we are not going to discuss in details of all the committees, rather a few recent committee's recommendations on certain forward and futures markets have been presented.

In 1950, the Indian Government appointed the A.D. Shroff Committee whose report formed the basis of the Forward Contracts (Regulations) Act, 1952. In 1966, the M.L. Dantwala Committee reviewed the SCR Act and the functioning of the Forward Markets Commission and made certain recommendation. In 1979, the

A.M. Khusro Committee was set up to further review the functioning of forward markets and FMC. Further, in 1993, the Indian Government constituted the committee named K.N. Kabra Committee, which submitted its report in September, 1994 with the following major recommendations:

### 6.14.1   Kabra Committee Recommendations (1994)

(a) The commodity exchanges should enrol more members.
(b) Capital adequacy norms must be ensured for smooth functioning.
(c) The commodity exchanges should be computerized so that online trading be ensured.

(d) Internal vigilance mechanism of the exchanges should be strengthened.

(e) Non-transferable specific delivery forward contracts should be freed from restrictions.

(f) Options and range forward contracts may be introduced. However, this was not agreed by the Chairman of the Committee.

(g) The exchanges should be recognized on permanent basis.

(h) The exchanges should be developed into self-regulatory organizations.

(i) The Forward Markets Commission should be strengthened with more powers.

(j) More commodities should be included in futures trading like basmati rice, cotton seed, ground nut, rapeseed, linseed, copra, Seasame seed, mustard seed, soyabean, etc.

## 6.14.2 Sodhani Expert Group Recommendations (1994)

The forward contracts and options on foreign exchange are conducted through the over-the-counter (OTC) markets and regulated by the Reserve Bank of India. In November, 1994, the RBI constituted a committee under the headship of O.P. Sodhani on foreign exchange markets functioning. The committee's main recommendations were as follows:

(a) The companies should be given permission to book, cancel and rebook options on foreign currencies.

(b) Banks should offer range forward contracts.

(c) There should be no withholding taxes on derivatives transactions.

(d) More liberty should be given to banks to use derivatives.

(e) More derivative instruments like caps, dollars, floors, FRAs, swaps should be allowed to offer by the banks to the traders without the approval of RBI.

(f) Different specific dealers should be allowed to offer derivative instruments.

(g) Proper documentation and market practices should be evolved for better functioning of the markets.

## 6.14.3 R.V. Gupta Committee's Recommendations (1997)

Reserve Bank of India set up a committee under the chairmanship of R.V. Gupta to review 'Hedging' through International Commodity Exchanges and other related issues. The committee's main recommendations were as follows:

(a) All the Indian companies with genuine commodity price risk exposures be allowed to hedge through off shore commodity futures and option markets.

(b) The Central Government should grant permission for such hedging transactions and the RBI should grant the necessary exchange control permission.

(c) Only hedging contracts for genuine price exposure through international markets should be allowed, and not the speculative or profit seeking objectives.

(d) OTC instruments like vanilla swaps would only be permitted where they have only efficient means of hedging.

(e) Use of options would not be allowed.

(f) The committee recommended a phased manner approach.

(g) In Phase-I, the hedging should ordinarily be through exchange traded commodity futures.

(h) Phase-I would be a period of acclimatization. At this stage prior approval would be required (i) to ensure existence of genuine underlying risk, (ii) the appropriateness of the hedging instrument, and (iii) adequateness of risk management procedures.

(i) In Phase-II, no prior approval, as recommended in Phase-I should be needed. Only periodic scrutiny of actual transactions and auditor's certification adequacy of control are sufficient.

(j) The committee further recommends that hedging should be allowed through foreign derivatives markets.

However, the futures markets experts observed that due to lack of experience of the Indian corporate sector regarding the functioning of international commodity derivatives and inadequate experience amongst auditors, a longer 'acclimatization' period of at least three years is desirable instead of one year as recommended by the committee.

## 6.14.4  Dr. L.C. Gupta Committee Report (1998)

In November, 1996, the SEBI set up a committee under the chairmanship of Dr. L.C. Gupta to develop an appropriate regulatory framework for derivatives trading in India. The recommendations of this committee have been discussed in Chapter 5 in detail. Subsequently, the SEBI appointed J.R. Varma Committee to look into the operational aspects of derivative markets. The major recommendations of this committee have also been given in Chapter 5. The students are advised to go through them. As a result in 2000, the SEBI allowed derivatives trading in India with certain regulatory requirements.

## 6.15  RISK CONTAINMENT MEASURES IN THE INDIAN DERIVATIVE MARKET RECOMMENDATIONS OF DR. J.R. VARMA COMMITTEE

The Securities and Exchange Board of India (SEBI) appointed a committee under the chairmanship of Dr. L.C. Gupta in November, 1996 to "develop appropriate regulatory framework for derivatives trading in India". In March, 1998, the L.C. Gupta Committee (LCGC) submitted its report recommending the introduction of derivatives markets in a phased manner beginning with the introduction of index futures. The SEBI Board while approving the introduction of index futures trading mandated the setting up of a group to recommend measures for risk containment in the derivative market in India. Accordingly, SEBI constituted a group in June, 1998, with Prof. J.R. Varma, as Chairman. The group submitted its report in the same year. The group began by enumerating the risk containment issues that assume importance in the Indian context while setting up an index futures market. The recommendations of the group as covered by its report are as under:

### 6.15.1  Estimation of Volatility (Clause 2.1)

Several issues arise in the estimation of volatility:

1. Volatility in Indian market is quite high as compared to developed markets.
2. The volatility in Indian market is not constant and is varying over time.
3. The statistics on the volatility of the index futures markets do not exist (as these markets are yet to be introduced), and therefore, in the initial period, reliance has to be made on the volatility in the underlying securities market. The LCGC has prescribed that no cross margining would be permitted and separate margins would be charged on the position in the futures market and the underlying securities market. In the absence of cross margining, index arbitrage would be costly, and therefore, possibly inefficient.

## 6.15.2   Calendar Spreads (Clause 2.2)

In developed markets, calendar spreads are essentially a play on interest rates with negligible stock market exposure. As such margins for calendar spreads are very low. However, in India, the calendar basis risk could be high because of the absence of efficient index arbitrage and the lack of channels for the flow of funds from the organized money market into the index future market.

## 6.15.3   Trader Net Worth (Clause 2.3)

Even an accurate 99 percent "value at risk" model would give rise to end of day mark to market losses exceeding the margin approximately once every six months. Trader net worth provides an additional level of safety to the market and works as a deterrent to the incidence of defaults. A member with high net worth would try harder to avoid defaults as his own net worth would be at stake. The definition of net worth needs to be made precise having regard to prevailing accounting practices and laws.

## 6.15.4   Margin Collection and Enforcement (Clause 2.4)

Apart from the correct calculation of margin, the actual collection of margin is also of equal importance. Since initial margins can be deposited in the form of bank guarantee and securities, the risk containment issues in regard to these need to be tackled.

## 6.15.5   Clearing Corporation (Clause 2.5)

The clearing corporation provides novation and becomes the counter party for each trade. In the circumstances, the credibility of the clearing corporation assumes importance and issues of governance and transparency need to be addressed.

## 6.15.6   Position Limit (Clause 2.6)

It may be necessary to prescribe position limits for the market as a whole and for the individual clearing member/trading member/client.

## 6.15.7   Margining System (Clause 3.1)

**Mandating a margin methodology not specific margins (Clause 3.1.1):**   The LCGC recommended that margins in the derivatives markets would be based on a 99 percent Value at Risk (VAR) approach. The group discussed ways of operationalizing this recommendation keeping in mind the issues relating to estimation of volatility discussed in clause 2.1. It is decided that the SEBI should authorize the use of a particular VAR estimation methodology but should not mandate a specific minimum margin level. The specific recommendations of the group are as follows:

**Initial methodology (Clause 3.1.2):**   The group has evaluated and approved a particular risk estimation methodology that is described in Clause 3.2 and discussed in further detail in Appendix 1. The derivatives exchange and clearing corporation should be authorized to start index futures trading using this methodology for fixing margins.

**Continuous refining (Clause 3.1.3):** The derivatives exchange and clearing corporation should be encouraged to refine this methodology continuously on the basis of further experience. Any proposal for changes in the methodology should be filed with SEBI and released to the public for comments along with detailed comparative backtesting results of the proposed methodology and the current methodology. The proposal shall specify the date from which the new methodology will become effective and this effective date shall not be less than three months after the date of filing with SEBI. At any time up to two weeks before the effective date, SEBI may instruct the derivatives exchange and clearing corporation not to implement the change, or the derivatives exchange and clearing corporation may on its own decide not to implement the change.

### 6.15.8 Initial Margin Fixation Methodology (Clause 3.2)

The group took on record the estimation and backtesting results provided by Prof. Varma from his ongoing research work on value at risk calculations in Indian financial markets. The group, being satisfied with these backtesting results, recommends the following margin fixation methodology as the initial methodology for the purposes of Clause 3.1.1.

The exponential moving average method would be used to obtain the volatility estimate every day.

### 6.15.9 Daily Changes in Margins (Clause 3.3)

The group recommends that the volatility estimated at the end of the day's trading would be used in calculating margin calls at the end of the same day. This implies that during the course of trading, market participants would not know the exact margin that would apply to their position. It was agreed, therefore, that the volatility estimation and margin fixation methodology would be clearly made known to all market participants so that they can compute what the margin would be for any given closing level of the index. It was also agreed that the trading software would itself provide this information on a real time basis on the trading workstation screen.

### 6.15.10 Margining for Calendar Spreads (Clause 3.4)

The group took note of the international practice of levying very low margins on calendar spreads. A calendar spread is a position at one maturity which is hedged by an offsetting position at a different maturity, for example, a short position in the six-month contract coupled with a long position in the nine-month contract. The justification for low margins is that a calendar spread is not exposed to the market risk in the underlying at all. If the underlying rises, one leg of the spread loses money while the other gains money resulting in a hedged position. Standard futures pricing models state that the futures price is equal to the cash price plus a net cost of carry (interest cost reduced by dividend yield on the underlying). This means that the only risk in a calendar spread is the risk that the cost of carry might change; this is essentially an interest rate risk in a money market position. In fact, a calendar spread can be viewed as a synthetic money market position. The above example of a short position in the six-month contract matched by a long position in the nine-month contract can be regarded as a six-month future on a three-month T-bill. In developed financial markets, the cost of carry is driven by a money market interest rate and the risk in calendar spreads is very low.

In India, however, unless banks and institutions enter the calendar spread in a big way, it is possible that the cost of carry would be driven by an unorganized money market rate as in the case of the badla market. These interest rates could be highly volatile.

Given the evidence that the cost of carry is not an efficient money market rate, prudence demands that the margin on calendar spreads be far higher than the international practice. Moreover, the margin system should operate smoothly when a calendar spread is turned into a naked short or long position on the index either by the expiry of one of the legs or by the closing out of the position in one of the legs. The group, therefore, recommends that:

(a) The margin on calendar spreads be levied at a flat rate of 0.5 percent per month of spread on the far month contract of the spread subject to a minimum margin of 1 percent and a maximum margin of 3 percent on the far side of the spread for spreads with legs up to 1 year apart. A spread with the two legs three months apart would thus attract a margin of 1.5 percent on the far month contract.

(b) The margining of calendar spreads be reviewed at the end of six months of index futures trading.

(c) A calendar spread should be treated as a naked position in the far month contract as the near month contract approaches expiry. This change should be affected in gradual steps over the last few days of trading of the near month contract. Specifically, during the last five days of trading of the near month contract, the following percentages of a calendar spread will be treated as a naked position in the far month contract: 100 percent on day of expiry, 80 percent one day before expiry, 60 percent two days before expiry, 40 percent three days before expiry, 20 percent four days before expiry. The balance of the spread will continue to be treated as a spread. This phasing in will apply both to margining and to the computation of exposure limits.

(d) If the closing out of one leg of a calendar spread causes the members' liquid net worth to fall below the minimum levels specified in Clause 4.2, his terminal will be disabled and the clearing corporation will take steps to liquidate sufficient positions to restore the members' liquid net worth to the levels mandated in Clause 4.2.

(e) The derivatives exchange should explore the possibility that the trading system could incorporate the ability to place a single order to buy or sell spreads without placing two separate orders for the two legs.

(f) For the purposes of the exposure limit in Clause 4.2(b), a calendar spread will be regarded as an open position of one third of the mark to market value of the far month contract. As the near month contract approaches expiry, the spread will be treated as a naked position in the far month contract in the same manner as in Clause 3.4(c).

## 6.15.11   Margin Collection and Enforcement (Clause 3.5)

Apart from the correct calculation of margin, the actual collection of margin is also of equal importance. The group recommends that the clearing corporation should lay down operational guidelines on collection of margin and standard guidelines for back office accounting at the clearing member and trading member level to facilitate the detection of non-compliance at each level.

## 6.15.12   Transparency and Disclosure (Clause 3.6)

The group recommends that the clearing corporation/clearing house will be required to disclose the details of incidences of failures in collection of margin and/or the settlement dues at least on a quarterly basis. Failure for this purpose means a shortfall for three consecutive trading days of 50 percent or more of the liquid net worth of the member.

### 6.15.13 Definition of Liquid Net Worth (Clause 4.1)

Even an accurate 99 percent "value at risk" model would give rise to end of day mark to market losses exceeding the margin approximately once every six months. Obviously, the futures market should not be subject to a payment crisis every six months, and this means that there must be a second level of defence in the form of the broker's net worth. The group is of the view that given the reality of the Indian situation, liquid net worth is a far more meaningful defence against market risk than book net worth.

**Liquid net worth means**

    (a) Total liquid assets deposited with the exchange/clearing corporation towards initial margin and capital adequacy, LESS.

    (b) Initial margin applicable to the total gross open positions at any given point of time of all trades cleared through the clearing member.

### 6.15.14 Minimum Liquid Net Worth Requirement (Clause 4.2)

The group examined the evidence from the backtesting exercise showing that over an eight-year period, a margin shortfall (mark to market losses exceeding the initial margin) of more than 3 percent of the previous day's mark to market value happens only twice in the case of NIFTY and does not happen at all in case of Sensex. The group also took into account the recommendation of the LCGC that the clearing member's liquid net worth must be at least ₹50 lakhs.

The group recommends that the clearing member's liquid net worth must satisfy the following conditions 1 and 2 on a real time basis:

*Condition 1:*   Liquid net worth should not be less than ₹50 lakhs at any point of time.

*Condition 2:*   The mark to market value of gross open positions at any point of time of all trades cleared through the clearing member should not exceed 33-1/3 times the members' liquid net worth.

### 6.15.15 Definition of Liquid Assets (Clause 5)

As recommended by the LCGC, liquid assets for the purposes of initial margins as well as liquid net worth include cash, fixed deposits, bank guarantees, treasury bills, government securities or dematerialized securities (with suitable haircuts) pledged in favour of the exchange/clearing corporation or bank guarantees.

### 6.15.16 Bank Guarantees (Clause 5.1)

The group deliberated on the question of the acceptability of bank guarantees in the futures market where (unlike in the cash market) banks and institutions are themselves subject to margins. The question also arose as to whether a bank could offer its own bank guarantee to meet the margin requirements on its own position. This problem would arise if a bank itself became a member of the futures exchange or if it gave a bank guarantee for a broker through whom it has originated a large open position on its own account.

The group concluded that given the Indian realities, it is necessary to accept bank guarantees as part of the liquid net worth of the broker. It is also of the view that a requirement that a bank cannot give its own bank guarantee on its own behalf would be neither conceptually sound nor easy to enforce (for example, two banks could give guarantees to each other).

The group is also of the view that all banks cannot be treated alike by the clearing corporation without regard to their net worth, capital adequacy, credit rating and other characteristics. Considering all the above, the group decided that the clearing corporation would set an exposure limit for each bank taking into account all relevant factors.

The Board of Directors or other equivalent organ of the clearing corporation will lay down exposure limits either in rupee terms or as percentage of the trade guarantee fund that can be exposed to a single bank directly or indirectly. The total exposure would include guarantees provided by the bank for itself or for others as well as debt or equity securities of the bank which have been deposited by members as liquid assets for margins or net worth requirement.

Not more than 5 percent of the trade guarantee fund or 1 percent of the total liquid assets deposited with the clearing house whichever is lower shall be exposed to any single bank which is not rated $P1$(or $P1+$) or equivalent by a RBI recognized credit rating agency and not more than 50 percent of the trade guarantee fund or 10 percent of the total liquid assets deposited with the clearing house whichever is lower will be exposed to all such banks put together.

The exposure limits and any changes thereto will be promptly communicated to SEBI. The clearing corporation will also periodically disclose to SEBI its actual exposure to various banks.

## 6.15.17 Securities (Clause 5.2)

The group recommends that the Board of Directors or other equivalent organ of the clearing corporation will approve the list of acceptable securities, the haircuts applicable to various classes of securities, and the method of periodic revaluation (marking-to-market). The clearing corporation is free to adopt more stringent conditions than those described as follows. These policies will be promptly disclosed to SEBI.

(a) The marking-to-market of securities will be carried out at least weekly for all securities.

(b) Debt securities will be acceptable only if they are investment grade. Haircuts will be at least 10 percent with weekly mark to market.

(c) The total exposure of the clearing corporation to the debt or equity securities of any company will not exceed 75 percent of the trade guarantee fund or 15 percent of the total liquid assets of the clearing corporation/house whichever is lower. Exposure for this purpose means the mark to market value of the securities less the applicable haircuts.

(d) Equity securities shall be in dematerialized form. The acceptable securities will be the top 100 securities by market capitalization out of the top 200 securities by market capitalization and also by trading value. This list will be updated on the basis of the average market capitalization over the previous six months. When a security is dropped from the list of acceptable securities, existing deposits of that security will continue to be counted for liquid assets for a period of one month. Haircuts on equity will be at least 15 percent with weekly mark to market. The clearing corporation may charge a higher haircut on concentrated portfolios of equity securities deposited by a member.

(e) All securities deposited for liquid assets will be pledged in favour of the clearing corporation.

## 6.15.18 Minimum Cash Requirement (Clause 5.3)

At least 50 percent of the total liquid assets will be in the form of cash equivalents, viz. cash, bank guarantee, fixed deposits, T-bills and dated government securities.

## 6.15.19 Bank Accounts (Clause 5.4)

The SEBI requirement of segregation of client funds could, in the futures market, lead to a situation where a large amount of customer funds lie in a current account which earns no interest. This is ultimately a matter to be negotiated between the broker/exchange and the banks. The group recommends, however, that the segregation rules themselves should not bar the deployment of customer funds in liquid interest earning instruments of equivalent safety.

## 6.15.20 Beginning of Day One

Suppose that the position at the beginning of day one is as follows:

| | |
|---|---|
| Member's liquid assets | Cash equivalent deposits 35,00,000 |
| | Securities deposits (net of haircuts) 40,00,000 |
| Member's open position | 200 contract long in the three-month contract |
| Futures prices | Three-month contract is ₹1,00,000 |
| | one-month contract is ₹98,000 |
| Initial margin | 5% |
| Days to expiry | Fifth days before expiry of one-month contract |

The margin and capital adequacy calculations will be as follows:

- Initial margin = 5% × 200 × 1,00,000 = 10,00,000
- Total open position = 2,00,00,000
- Total liquid assets will be treated as 70,00,000 only since at least 50 percent of total liquid assets must be in cash equivalents (see Clause 5.3).
- Liquid net worth = 70,00,000 – 10,00,000 = 60,00,000

Both conditions in Clause 4.2 are satisfied as follows:
- *Condition 1:* 60,00,000 > 50,00,000
- *Condition 2:* 60,00,000 × $33^{1/3}$ = (20,00,00,000) > 2,00,00,000

## 6.15.21 Initiation of Spread Trade on Day One (Clause 5.5.2)

Suppose that the member does a calendar spread trade by buying 300 contracts of 3 months futures and selling 300 contracts of 1 month futures.

Since the near month contract of the spread is five days to expiry, the member will have the full benefit of spread margining:

- Margin on spread = 1% × 300 × 1,00,000 = 3,00,000
- Spread open position = 300 × 1,00,000 × 1/3 = 1,00,00,000

Adding the figures for the earlier long position, we get

- Total open position = 2,00,00,000 + 1,00,00,000 = 3,00,00,000
- Liquid net worth = 70,00,000 − 10,00,000 − 3,00,000 = 57,00,000

Both conditions in Clause 5.2 are satisfied as follows:

- *Condition 1:* 57,00,000 > 50,00,000
- *Condition 2:* 57,00,000 × $33^{1/3}$ = 19,00,00,000 > 3,00,00,000

## 6.15.22   Margin and Capital Adequacy Calculations on Day Two

Suppose that on day two, the member does not initiate any new trades, but prices move up so that the situation is as follows:

| | |
|---|---|
| Member's liquid assets | Cash equivalent deposits 35,00,000 |
| | Securities deposits (net of haircuts) 40,00,000 |
| Member's open position | 200 contracts long in the three-month contract |
| | 300 contracts spread position (long in three-month contract and short in near month contract) |
| Futures prices | Three-month contracts is ₹1,01,000 |
| | one-month contract is ₹99,000 |
| Initial margin | 5% |
| Days to expiry | Fourth day before expiry of one-month contract |

The margins and exposures for the 200 contract long position would be

- Open position − 200 × 1,01,000 = 2,02,00,000
- Initial margin = 5% × 200 × 1,01,000 = 10,10,000

The spread open position for exposure purposes would be 1,41,4.

- 20% of far month = 20% × 300 × 1,01,000 = 60,60,000 PLUS
- 80% of far month = 80% × 1/3 × 300 × 1,01,000 = 80,80,000

The initial margin on spread would be 5,45,000 as shown below:

- 20% of far month = 20% × 5% × 300 × 1,01,000 = 3,03,000
- 80% of spread = 80% × 1% × 300 × 1,01,000 = 2,42,000

The margin, exposure and liquid net worth of the member would be as follows:

- Total open position = 2,02,00,000 + 1,41,40,000 = 3,43,40,000
- Total initial margin = 10,10,000 + 5,45,400 = 15,55,400
- Liquid net worth = 70,00,000 − 15,55,400 = 54,44,600

Both conditions in Clause 4.2 are satisfied as follows:

- *Condition 1:* 54,44,600 > 50,00,000
- *Condition 2:* 54,44,600 × $33^{1/3}$ = (18,14,86,667) > 3,43,40,000

## 6.15.23   Position Limits (Clause 6)

The group considered the issue of position limits at the customer level, trading member level, clearing member level and market level.

**Customer level:**   The group agreed that though position limits make most sense conceptually when imposed at the customer level, it is not practical to enforce such a requirement unless

- The aggregate position of a customer who operates through several brokers can be determined by the use of a single customer code (for example, the Income Tax permanent account number). Currently, each broker assigns a code to a customer independently so the customer has as many codes as the number of brokers through whom he operates.
- A customer operating under multiple names and through multiple shell companies can be identified as a single customer using an operationalizable definition of "acting in concert".

Instead of recommending position limits at the client level, the group recommends a self-disclosure requirement similar to that in the take-over regulations:

(a) Any person or persons acting in concert who together own 15 percent or more of the open interest will be required to report this fact to the exchange and failure to do so will attract a penalty as laid down by the exchange/clearing corporation/SEBI.
(b) This requirement may not be monitored by the exchange on a real time basis, but if during any investigation or otherwise, any violation is proved, penalties can be levied.
(c) This would not mean a ban on large open positions but only a disclosure requirement.

## 6.15.24   Trading Member Level (Clause 6.2)

The group recommends:

(a) There shall be a position limit at the trading member level of 15 percent of the open interest or ₹100 crores whichever is higher.
(b) This is to be reviewed after six months of index futures trading.

## 6.15.25   Clearing Member Level (Clause 6.3)

No separate position limit should be imposed at this level on aggregate trades cleared by a member. However, the clearing member shall ensure that his own positions and the positions of members clearing through him are within the limits specified in Clause 6.2.

## 6.15.26   Market Level (Clause 6.4)

The group recommends:

(a) No limits should be imposed at this stage on the total market wide open interest (as a percentage of the underlying market capitalization).
(b) This should be reviewed at the end of six months of index futures trading to determine whether position limits are required at this level to guard against situations where a very large open interest leads to attempts to manipulate the underlying market.

## 6.15.27 Customer Level and Trading Member Level Margins and Capital (Clause 7)

The clearing corporation may specify:

(a) The minimum margins to be collected from customers which may be more than the margins charged to members.
(b) The minimum capital requirements for trading members in the form of deposits with the clearing member or the clearing corporation.

## 6.15.28 Review After Six Months (Clause 8)

The group recommends that at the end of six months of futures trading, SEBI should review the risk containment measures with specific reference to the following:

(a) Removal of the transitional provisions in Clause 3.2(g) and (h)
(b) Review of the margins for calendar spreads as mentioned in Clause 3.4(b)
(c) Review of position limits as mentioned in Clause 6.2(b) and 6.4(b)
(d) Cross margining between cash and futures markets (see 6.9 of LCGC report)

## 6.15.29 Risk Containment in Cash Market (Clause 9)

The group recognizes that it is easier to introduce stringent risk containment measures in the derivatives market which are being set up from scratch. However, it does not make sense to have lesser risk containment measures in the cash market than in the derivatives market. The group recommends that the basic ideas enshrined in this report be extended to the cash market. In particular:

(a) The margins in the cash market should be based on the 99 percent VaR. As an interim measure, the margins could be twice that in the index futures market since individual securities are roughly twice as volatile as the index. Exposure limits could also be commensurately lower than in the derivatives market.
(b) The recommendations on the computation of liquid net worth and the upfront margins could be readily applied to the cash market.

## SUMMARY

This chapter has introduced the basic concepts of regulations of futures market in India. It is well known that stock markets play a significant role in an economy's growth and development. Presently in India, there are 23 stock exchanges which are operating, however, their organizations vary. Out of those, 15 are public limited companies, 5 limited by guarantees and 3 are voluntary non-profit making organizations.

The Securities and Exchange Board of India (SEBI), whose main functions are to protect the interest of the investors and to promote, develop and regulate the securities markets in India. The SEBI has framed various guidelines for the exchanges. This chapter further explains the securities listing and grouping, such as group A or specified securities which have weekly settlement and carry forward is allowed. Non-specified group is split into two groups: Group $B_1$ has weekly settlement and carry forward is not allowed. Group $B_2$ securities are subject to settlement procedure which earlier existed in case of 'group B securities'. Group C relates to add lots securities. Most of the exchanges carry out stock trading transactions on either cash basis or carry over basis. Non-specified securities transactions are settled compulsorily by delivery and payment, and no further carryover of the transaction.

The chapter further explains the Badla system in Indian stock market. In India, Badla system allowed for speculation in shares without paying up two full transactions. The term badla refers to that system whereby the buyer or seller of the shares may be allowed to postpone payment of money or delivery of shares.

In partial volume equilibrium, it was been observed that the buyer and the seller in the stock market usually show their intention at the settlement date for setting the transaction or carry forward them to the next settlement date. Badla system was banned due to its certain problems. Consequently, the Patel committee report and recommendations on the carry forward system, SEBI introduced a revised carry forward system subject to various preconditions like stock exchanges would be allowed. to introduce carry forward system only with the prior permission of SEBI. Every member would be required to keep books of record showing the source of finance with sub-accounts being maintained in the clearing house.

Recommendations of J.R. Varma Committee like abolition of twin track system of segregating carry forward and delivery transactions, elimination of limit of 90 days for carry forward transactions, elimination of settlement only by delivery after 75 days, scraping the overall limit on carry forward of transaction of ₹5 crores, exchange should strengthen the regulatory and surveillance system to enforce rules on the carry forward trading, etc. were accepted by the SEBI.

The chapter further explains the regulation of forward and futures market in India. Futures trading like other economic activity is an important and sophisticated economic tool for the development and growth of a country. It can be beneficial as well as detrimental if the same is not efficiently organized and effectively regulated. There are various tools to regulate the futures trading in India like margin variations imposition of special margins, daily or weekly limits on price changes, fixation of price limits, etc. In India, futures trading is regulated by Forward Market Commission and Reserve Bank of India. The derivatives can be classified into two: commodities and financial derivatives. The SEBI to entrust with to regulate the carry forward trading stock market and other financial derivatives like equity stock, stock index, options, etc. Over-the-counter forward contracts and options on foreign currencies are regulated by the RBI. The chapter in the last section discuss about the major recommendations of various committees like Kabra committee, Sodhani expert group, R.V. Gupta committee's recommendation, L.C. Gupta Committee on derivatives and so on.

## REVIEW QUESTIONS

1. Discuss the role of stock market in the development of an economy.
2. Write a note on securities listing and grouping in Indian stock markets.
3. Explain the Badla system in Indian stock market with suitable examples.
4. Differentiate between Badla and Forward Trading in Indian stock market.
5. List out major recommendations of J.R.Varma Committee (1997) on derivatives.
6. Write a detailed note on regulation of forward and futures markets in India.
7. What are important eligibility/regulatory conditions specified by SEBI?
8. Explain the carry forward trading. What are its features? Explain with examples.
9. Explain the regulatory framework of futures trading in India.

10. Discuss various measures specified by SEBI to enhance protection of the rights of investors in the derivative market.
11. Write a detailed note on margining system in the derivatives market.
12. Draw out major recommendations of different committees on derivatives trading in India.
13. Write a note on "Role of SEBI in derivatives market."
14. Compare and contrast between US regulation and Indian regulation in derivatives market.
15. List out major advantages of derivatives like forward, futures from traditional system of Badla in Indian stock market.
16. Discuss the regulatory framework and also objectives in Indian derivatives market with examples.
17. List out recent developments in derivatives segment with special emphasis on regulatory framework.
18. Discuss the impact of globalization of financial market on Indian stock market exchanges in terms of trading, instruments and regulatory point of view.
19. What are the most important aspects of design of new futures contract?
20. Explain the following terms differentiating them with each other:
    (a) Market maker
    (b) Stock broker
    (c) Traders
21. List out various types of derivatives securities traded in Indian stock market with their settlement period.
22. Discuss the position limits as well as market wide limits of a trader in derivatives market.
23. Discuss the various risk containment measures in the Indian derivative market as per the recommendations of Dr. J.R. Varma Committee.
24. Write a detailed note on developmental role of regulator.
25. What are the various shortcomings of regulatory system of Indian stock market with special reference to financial derivatives?
26. Discuss the various recommendations related to policy from the regulatory point of view.
27. "Regulation of derivatives market in India as per the regulation of derivatives market in USA". Critically examine the statement.
28. Discuss the various measures specified by SEBI to enhance protection of rights of investors in the derivative market.

## SUGGESTED READINGS

1. Kalamkar, D.S., Regulation and policy issues for derivatives in India, a research paper, published in *Derivatives Market in India*, Tata McGraw-Hill, New Delhi, 2003.
2. Krishan, Bal and Natra, S.S., *Security Market in India*, Kanishka Publisher, New Delhi, 1998.
3. Kane, E., Regulatory structure in futures markets: Jurisdictional competition between the SEC the CFTC and other agencies, *The Journal of Futures Markets*, Vol. 4, pp. 367–384, Fall 1984.
4. Peitrzak, A.R., Insider trading in futures, *Commodities Law Letters*, Vol. VIII, No. 3, pp. 1–7, May 1987.
5. Narasimhan, M.S. and Ramachandaran, G., "Carry Forward Trading-I: Patel Report should be modified," Business Line, May, 1995.
6. Stein, J.L., *The Economics of Futures Markets*, op. cit., p. 239.
7. Turnbull and Jarrow, *Derivatives Securities*, Thomson Asia Pvt. Ltd., Singapore, 2001.

# SECTION III

# Specific Financial Futures and Forwards

# Hedging Strategy
# Using Futures

*After reading this chapter, students will be able to*

➢ Understand the concept of hedging.
➢ Know about the nature and features of hedging.
➢ Know about the multipurpose concept of hedging.
➢ Understand the basic long and short hedges.
➢ Aware of the concept of cross hedging along with its equation.
➢ Understand the concept of basis risk and hedging and difference between basis risk and price risk.
➢ Explain the mechanism of devising a hedging strategy, which includes
   (a) deciding on the futures contract, (b) which futures contract, and (c) which contract month.
➢ Analyse the hedge ratio and its estimation.
➢ Understand the various steps involved in management of a hedge.

## 7.1 INTRODUCTION

Today, the corporate units operate in a complex business environment. Managers often find that the profitability of their organizations heavily depends upon on such factors which are beyond their control. Important among these are external influences like commodity prices, stock prices, interest

195

rates, exchange rates, etc. As a result, modern business has become more complex, uncertain and risky. So, it is essential for the executives of the firms to control such uncertainty and risk so that the business can be run successfully. An important function of futures market is to permit managers to reduce or control risks by transferring it to others who are willing to bear the risk. In other words, futures markets can provide the managers certain tools to reduce and control their price risks. So the activity of trading futures with the objectives of reducing or controlling risk is called *hedging*.

In this chapter, we will discuss the nature of hedging, fundamentals of hedging and how futures hedges can be tailored to the need of the hedger. In other words, we will consider here different issues associated with the way the hedges are set up. When is a short futures position appropriate? When is a long futures position appropriate? Which futures contract should be used? What is the optimal size of the futures position appropriate?

**EXAMPLE 1:**    Firm A is a manufacturer of automobile cars of different gradation. For this A requires auto parts which he imports from USA. A is of the view that the prices of imported parts will increase in futures, thereby increasing the cost of cars, which can have significant effect on the profit profile of this firm. So there is a considerable risk that prices will rise in future. Consequently the firm wants to avoid such risk which it bears from increasing the price of imported parts. So he wants to hedge this risk in futures by entering into derivative market. In derivative market, he can lock today for futures prices of the imported parts and can hedge the risk which he bears.

**EXAMPLE 2:**    A farmer expects that there will be 5,000 quintals of food grains, which he will harvest in coming month. But he fears that price of grain could fluctuate in coming month. So farmer suspects of heavy losses in coming month. He can enter into derivative/futures market today and sell the grain for delivery in next month at an acceptable price and can hedge the price fluctuation risk. This kind of hedging is known as anticipating hedging.

**EXAMPLE 3:**    A corporate treasurer intends to borrow money in middle of March for a three-month period. The treasurer may fear that interest rates will increase from the date of borrowing. Rise in interest rate would add to the cost of borrowing. A futures position is taken so that there would be an offsetting profit in the event of rise in interest rates. So, in this example, treasurer can do hedging by selling three-month interest rate futures.

## 7.2  HEDGING CONCEPTS

Hedging, in its broadest sense, is the act of protecting oneself against futures loss. More specifically in the context of futures trading, hedging is regarded as the use of futures transactions to avoid or reduce price risk in the spot market. In other words, a hedge is a position that is taken as a temporary substitute for a later position in another asset (or liability) or to protect the value of an existing position in an asset (or liability) until the position is liquidated. According to this concept, the firm seeks hedging whether it is on the asset side or on the liability side of the balance sheet.

**EXAMPLE:**    In the month of March, 2015, a Jute mill anticipates a requirement of 10,000 candies of Jute in the month of July, 2015. Assume current price of jute is ₹1,000 per candy. Based on this price, the company has entered into other financial arrangements. It is of great importance to the mill that, at the time of jute is actually purchased, price is not changed substantially higher than ₹1,000 per candy. To avoid this, it buys 10,000 candies of jute on the jute futures market, where current price of jute is ₹1,050 per candy. In the month of July, the price of jute has risen sharply with the current spot price being ₹1,500 per candy. The corresponding futures price for July jute is found to be ₹1,470 per candy.

At this point of time jute mill has two options:

1. It can sell its futures contract on market at prevailing rate of ₹1,470, and buys its requirement from spot market. Profit/Loss profile of this transaction will be as follows:

$$\text{Jute purchased} = ₹1,000 \text{ per candy}$$

$$\text{Sale proceeds} = ₹1,470 \text{ per candy}$$

Profit from sale = ₹470 per candy and current price of jute ₹1,500 per candy to be paid and net cost of candy to mill is ₹1,030 per candy.

So futures transaction has ensured the minimization of upward price risk a mere for ₹30 per candy.

2. The mill could take delivery of jute directly from futures market. In this case the mill would pay ₹1,000 per candy, but for taking delivery there may be possibilities of not delivery of same variety of jute.

It is observed from the above example that by buying futures the firm has hedged against the upward price risk.

## 7.3 MULTI-PURPOSE CONCEPT OF HEDGING

Earlier hedging was taken to be only one kind (known as routine or naive hedging), whereby the trader always hedged all his transactions purely for covering all the price risks. However, this concept was challenged by Holbrook Working, in his article "New Concepts Concerning Futures Markets and Prices" and propounded the multi-purpose concept of hedging which is widely accepted. According to this concept, the hedging can be used for many other purposes:

**Carrying charge hedging:** According to this approach, the stockist watch the price spread between the spot and futures prices, and if the spread covers even carrying costs, then the stockist buy ready stocks. It means that the traders may go for hedging if the spread is adequate to cover carrying costs, whereas earlier view was that hedges are used to protect against loss on stock held. Thus, according to H. Working, "it is not primarily whether to hedge or not, but whether to store or not".

**Operational hedging:** According to this view, hedgers use the futures market for their operations and use the same as substitute for cash or forward transactions. They think that the futures markets are more liquid and have lower difference between 'bid' and 'ask' prices.

**Selective or discretionary hedging:** As per this concept, the traders do not always (in routine) hedge themselves but only do so on selected occasions when they predict adverse price movements in futures. Here, the objective is to cover the risk of adverse price fluctuation rather to avoid price risk. So they use hedging technique selectively at the time of adverse price movements.

**Anticipatory hedging:** This is done in anticipation of subsequent sales or purchases. For example, a farmer might hedge by selling in anticipation of his crop while a miller might hedge by buying futures in anticipation of subsequent raw material needs.

In brief, it is evident that now hedging is not used only for reducing or controlling the price risk but it also serves other purposes for the market participants. However, largely, the hedging is used to eliminate or reduce the price risk in our further discussion.

## 7.4 PERFECT HEDGING MODEL

The perfect hedge is referred to that position which completely eliminate the risk. In other words, the use of futures or forward position to reduce completely the business risk is called *perfect hedge*, for example, a jewellery manufacturer wants to lock in a price for purchasing silver for the coming June. This he can do by going long June silver futures. If silver prices rise, the risk of increased cost of silver will be offset by the profits earned on the futures position. Similarly, if the silver prices fall, the savings on the silver purchase will be offset by futures losses. In either case, the net silver cost is locked in at the futures price. However, it should be noted that only price risk is covered and not the quantity risk—the uncertainty about the quantity that will be sold or purchased at some futures date. No doubt, availability of quantity of the asset at futures date may also influence the determination of futures prices.

**EXAMPLE:** Suppose a firm has an inventory of 100 kg of silver and it intends to sell in June. The current spot price of silver is ₹35,000 per kg but firm is worried that the price of silver will fall by June. To hedge itself against this possibility, the firm enters into 100 kg of short position in June silver futures at a futures price of ₹36,600 per kg. Firm is now protected against falling silver prices because the futures position will protect the firm and firm will gain if silver prices do fall. To see how the firm is hedged, consider what happens to its revenue under two price scenarios:

1. In first scenario, spot silver price rise to ₹37,700 per kg.
2. In second scenario, silver price falls to ₹34,400 per kg in June.

**TABLE 7.1**   Silver Inventory and Sales Revenue

| Scenario ($P_T$) | Silver revenues ($Q_T \times P_T$) | Profit/loss [$Q_T(F_{tT} - P_T)$] | Net revenue |
|---|---|---|---|
| I.  ₹37,700 | ₹37,70,000 | 100(₹36,600 – ₹37,700) = – ₹1,10,000 (Loss) | ₹36,60,000 |
| II.  ₹34,400 | ₹34,40,000 | 100(36,600 – 34,400) = ₹2,20,000 (Profit) | ₹7,60,000 |

In both the scenarios, firm locks in today's futures price of ₹36,600 per kg. When silver prices rise, there will be an off-setting futures loss; when silver prices fall, an off-setting gain will occur. But it is to be noticed that the firm does not lock in current spot price of ₹35,000 per kg.

Short inventory hedge can also be shown in general terms:

| Scenario | Revenues | Profit/loss | Net revenues |
|---|---|---|---|
| $P_T$ | $Q_TP_T$ | $Q_T(F_{t,T} - F_{T,T})$ $= Q_T(F_{t,T} - P_T)$ | $Q_TF_{t,T}$ |

We assume in this illustration that the firm sells its inventory at silver in the spot market. The firm would get the same result if it delivered its silver into futures market to fulfill its short position; because the futures settlement price at expiration equals to spot price ($P_T$) due to convergence effect on the prices.

The above examples show the two basic steps in futures hedging:

1. Hedger determines how its profits are affected by change in commodity price, security price, interest rate or exchange rate.
2. Hedger enters into a futures position with the opposite exposure. As a result, risk is eliminated.

Several conditions must be fulfilled before a perfect hedge is possible. In brief, these are as under:

1. The business firm must know exactly the effect of change in price on the profit, and further this relationship must be linear.
2. There must be futures or forward contracts available in the market with the following features.
   (a) It is written on the underlying asset which will affect the firm's profit.
   (b) The expiration date of the contract should be the same on which the firm's profits will be affected by the price of the said asset.
   (c) It specifies a quantity equal to which will affect the firm.

How a perfect hedge works:

Let us denote $t$ is today period (present), $T$ is date in June on which purchase will be effected, $Q_T$ is the quantity of asset to be purchased, $P_T$ is spot price at the time $T$, $F_{T,T}$ is futures price at the time $T$ and $F_{t,T}$ is futures price at time $t$.

The net cost to the manufacturer is the price of the asset less the profit on the futures position:

| Scenario | Asset costs | Silver costs | Time line |
|----------|-------------|--------------|-----------|
|          |             | *Futures profits* | *Net asset cost* |
| $P_T$ | $Q_T P_T$ | $Q_T (F_{T,T} - F_{t,T})$ $Q_T (P_{T,T} - F_{t,T})$ | $Q_T F_{t,T}$ |

Here $P_T = F_{t,T}$ because delivery date convergence, and

$$\text{Net asset cost} = \text{Asset costs} - \text{Futures profit}$$

$$Q_T F_{t,T} = Q_T P_T - Q_T (P_T - F_{t,T})$$

It is observed that the above hedge meets all the requirements of a perfect hedge. The manufacturer know that asset cost at $T$ (June) will be $Q_T P_T$, which is linear function of the asset price because every rupee change in the asset price will change $Q_T P_T$ by $Q_T$. By entering into the long futures at time $t$, the manufacturer establishes that his costs at time $T$ will be $Q_T F_{t,T}$. He, thus, locks in today's futures price for his asset purchase. Note that, here the gains or losses have been computed on the futures position as it were a forward position.

## 7.5 BASIC LONG AND SHORT HEDGES

Basically, the hedging refers to by taking a position in the futures that is opposite to a position taken in cash market or to a future cash obligation that one has or will incur. Thus, the hedges can be classified into two categories: short hedges and long hedges.

### 7.5.1 Short Hedge

A short hedge (or a selling hedge) is a hedge that involves short position in futures contract. In other words, it occurs when a firm/trader plans to purchase or produce a cash commodity sells futures to hedge the cash position. In general sense, it means 'being short' having a net sold position, or a commitment to deliver', etc. Thus, here the main objective is to protect the value of the cash position against a decline in cash prices. A short hedge is appropriate when the hedger already owns an asset and expects to sell it at sometime in the futures. Once the short futures position is established, it is expected that a decrease (increase) in the value of the cash position will be fully or partially compensated by a gain (loss) on the short futures position.

**EXAMPLE:** A US exporter who knows that he will receive German mark in three months from a German company. Exporter will realize gain if the mark increases its value in relation to the US dollar and a loss if the mark decreases its value relative to the US dollar. A short futures position leads to a loss if mark increases in value and a gain if it decreases in value. It has the effect of offsetting the exporter's risk.

**EXAMPLE:** A miner, who is manufacturer of silver and having a mine, wants to take a decision whether to open the mine or not. It is based upon the price of silver in futures because production of silver takes two months. He wants to plan his profitability for his firm. If the silver prices fall, he may suspend production of silver. Assume today is June 10. The price of silver in spot market on June 10 is ₹34,000 per kg and August ₹35,000 per kg will be satisfactory price for him. To establish the price of ₹34,000 per kg, the miner decides to enter in silver futures market. By hedging, he can avoid the risk that silver prices might fall in next two months. Anticipating the sale to be 50,0 kg silver in two months, he sells ten 50 kg futures contracts for August delivery at ₹34,000 per kg.

**TABLE 7.2**    Short Hedge Position of Silver Manufacturer

| Spot market | Futures market |
|---|---|
| **June 10** | **June 10** |
| Anticipate the sale of 500 kg silver in two months and expected to receive ₹34,000 per kg or ₹1,70,00,000 for total contract | Sell ten futures contract for August delivery at ₹34,000 per kg |
| **August 10** | **August 10** |
| Spot price of silver is now ₹35,000 per kg, the miner sells 50,0 kg silver ₹17,50,00,000 for whole contract | Buys futures contract at ₹35,000 amounting to ₹17,50,00,000 |
| Profit = ₹50,00,000 | Futures loss = ₹5,00,000 |

In this example, the miner has hedged his risk perfectly by selling futures in June for delivery in August on the maturity/delivery date he sells in spot market and earn a profit of ₹5,00,0000 and in futures market miner has a loss of same amount thereby offsetting and prices hedging against price fall risk.

## 7.5.2  Long Hedge

On the other hand, a long hedge (or a buying hedge) involves where a long position is taken in a futures contract. The basic objective here is to protect itself against a price increase in the underlying asset prior to purchasing it in either the spot or forward market. A long hedge is appropriate when a firm has to purchase a certain asset in futures and wants to lock in a price now. It is also called 'being long' or having a net bought position or an actual holding of the asset. It is also known as *inventory hedge* because the firm already holds the asset in inventory.

**EXAMPLE:** A fund manager anticipates to receipt of $1 million on January 10 and intends to use it to buy a balanced portfolio of UK equities. He fears that one month later, stock prices will rise before the money is received. He can go in futures market and buy today futures contract at 2,200, current index (FTSE 100) is at 2,200. He can close out his position by selling March 18, FTSE contract.

**TABLE 7.3**  Long Hedge using Futures

| Spot market | Futures market |
|---|---|
| **December 10** | **December 10** |
| Anticipate receipt of $1 million on January 10. Current FTSE 100 index is at 2,200 fears a rise in the index | Buys March 18 FTSE index futures contract at a price of 2200. He thereby commits himself to pay (2,200 × £18 × £25) = £9,90,000. Stock in futures date |
| **January 10** | |
| The new FTSE index at 2,300 Requires additional £45,000 in order to buy the stock that $1 million would have been bought on December 10 | Close out position by selling at a price of 2,300. He notionally receipt of £10,35,000 upon maturity of contract profit from futures £45,000 |
| Loss = £45,000 in spot market | Profit = £45,000 in futures market. |

In the above example, fund managers used stock index futures to hedge his risk of price fluctuation in coming one month.

The terms 'long' and 'short' apply to both spot and futures market and are widely used in the futures trading. A person who hold stocks of an asset is obviously regarded as 'being long' in the spot market but it is not necessary to actually hold stock. Similarly, it is in the case of 'short', where one who has made a forward sale, regarded as 'being short' on the spot market. In brief, the position of long and short hedges are shown in Table 7.4.

**TABLE 7.4**  Long vs Short Hedging

|  | Short hedger | Long hedger |
|---|---|---|
| Position in spot market | Long | Short |
| Protection need against | Price fall | Price rise |
| Position in futures market | Short | Long |

**EXAMPLE:**  A farmer anticipates a bumper crop amounting to 150 quintals, which he expects to harvest in the month of January. It is October and current price of crop is ₹10,000 per quintal. This price is acceptable to the farmer and give him a sufficient return. But he is apprehensive of a fall in price by the time crop will be ready. He, therefore, sells 150 quintals on the commodity futures market at a current price of ₹9,500 per quintal. In the month of January, price of crop has in fact risen. Current spot price is ₹11,000 per quintal. Now, farmer has two alternatives:

1. He can buy back 150 quintals of January crop on the futures market at a present futures price of ₹10,500. He can then deliver his actual crop of pepper in spot market at the ruling rate of ₹11,000 per quintal. As a result farmer will have following profit/loss:
   January contract sale @ ₹9,500 per quintal. January contract buys @ ₹10,500. So, there is a net loss of ₹1,000 per quintal. Further he sells his output @ ₹11,000 in the spot market and by deducting the loss on futures market position of ₹1,000, net price obtained by former is ₹10,000 per quintal.
2. He can deliver in the futures market @ ₹9,500 per quintal.

In this situation, where sale of futures by those hedging against price fall is called *short hedge* and taken guarding against downward price movements.

## 7.6  OTHER CONCEPTS IN HEDGING

### 7.6.1  Strip Hedge and Stacking Hedge (or rolling hedge)

The above distinction is made when there are several hedging horizon data. For example, a foreign exchange dealer might anticipate the purchase of US dollar every three months over the next two years. Strip hedge is referred to the application or use of the contract with different delivery dates. On the other hand, a stacking hedge requires using contracts with only one delivery data, preferably the nearest one.

Decision relating to use of strip hedge or stacking hedge depends upon the preference of the hedger. Various factors like liquidity, transaction costs, riskiness, mispricing of the contract, etc. are considered in this respect. If liquidity is the consideration, a hedge will be more appropriate, whereas transaction costs will usually be lower in strip hedge. Further, the futures contract with more distant period may be mispriced than the nearby contract. Similarly, the basis risk for a stacking hedge usually greater than strip hedge. In brief, the hedge should carefully decide between these hedges.

### 7.6.2  Microhedging and Macrohedging

In deciding a hedging strategy, it is important to understand the difference between micro hedging and macro hedging. A micro hedge uses a derivative contract-to hedge the risk exposure of a single or specific transaction, while a macro hedge is used to cover the firm's overall risk exposure. Macro hedge covers the entire balance sheet, -however, it is excessively costly. Sometimes, instead of macro hedging, the hedges may go for selective hedging which involves an explicit attempt by accepting some risk on the balance sheet. It is an attempt to improve profit performance being selective in terms of risks.

### 7.6.3  Tailing the Hedge

The tailing, in general, refers to the act of buying the present value of the number of the futures contracts. The difference between 1.0 and the present value of 1.0 is called the *tail*. It is noticed in the hedging activity, the impact of marking-to-market cash flows for the futures contract is ignored. It is obvious that a long hedger will experience daily resettlement cash outflows if futures prices fall, and vice versa. These cash flows should be recouped at the termination of hedge contract. These gains can be reinvested to generate interest income cash flows, resulting into the number of futures contracts needed to hedge an original cash position. To tail the hedge, we multiply the forward hedge on each hedging day with the present value of the next day (when settlement takes place) of a rupee to be paid at maturity of the hedge. As a result, the tailed hedge ratio will be lesser in comparison to the hedge ratio without tailing the hedge.

Two important consequences arise due to such interim Cash outflows due to mark-to-market process:

1. Daily resettlement cash outflows will invite an opportunity cost. These cash flows would be financed through borrowing. On the other hand, if futures price rises, the long header will receive mark-to-market-cash inflows, then these can be reinvested to earn additional interest. So, both cash inflows and outflows will be considered and handled by tailing the hedge. If future interest rates are known, then tailing effectively transforms the futures contract in to a forward contract.

2. Another's consequence of interim cash outflows is that, they could be accumulated to such a limit that the assets of the hedger could be depleted to large extent. As a result, they will be unable to obtain additional funding, and hence, such hedges be liquidated prematurely.

In brief, tailing requires to trade only the present value of the number of futures contracts which found to be optimal. Hedges should be tailed when interest rates are high and the hedging horizon is long. However, it is observed in practice that tailing is oftenly neglected, but ignoring tailing lead to a big hedging error.

For a hedge with a short maturity, the present value of rupee cash flow to be paid at maturity of the hedge with be very close to one rupee, so tailing will not affect the hedge much. But, in long maturity hedge, say 10 years, the present value of rupee to be matured will be very less on would be without tailing. So without tailing the hedging ratio would be larger. It is known as *over hedging*.

## 7.6.4  Cross Hedging

All the hedged positions discussed earlier used futures contracts which are undertaken on the assets whose price is to be hedged and that expires exactly when the hedge is to be lifted. Sometimes, it is seen that the firms wish to hedge against in particular asset but no futures contract available. This situation is called an *asset mismatch*. Further, in many cases, same futures period (maturity) on a particular asset is not available, it is called a *maturity mismatch*.

Referring to the different situations referred earlier, there is still possibility to hedge against price risk in related assets (commodities or securities) or by using futures contracts that expire on dates other than those on which the hedges are lifted. Such hedges are called *cross hedges*. In actual practice and in real business world, it will be rare for all factors to match so well. Thus, *across hedge* is a hedge in which the characteristics of the spot and futures positions do not match perfectly.

Mismatch situations which make the hedge a cross hedge:

- The hedging horizon (maturity) may not match the futures expiration date.
- The quantity to be hedged may not match with the quantity of the futures contract.
- The physical features of the asset to be hedged may differ from the futures contract asset.

In general, one cannot expect a cross-hedge to be as effective in reducing risk as a direct hedge. However, cross hedges are commonly used to reduce the price risk. Now, the question is which futures contracts are good candidates for a cross hedge. For example, if we want to hedge a portfolio of silver coins, then a silver futures contract will be more effective cross-hedge rather than a gold futures contract. Thus, comparing the price of the underlying asset and the price of correlated asset, one can analyze the nature of hedging. If perfectly correlated, it is perfect, in closely correlated, it is cross hedge, and in negatively correlated, there will be no hedging, rather more risk will be added by taking a position in the futures.

### *Cross-hedging silver coins with silver futures*

**EXAMPLE:**  Suppose a firm has a collection of 100 kg of rare silver coin and the firm is concerned that value of those coins will drop over the next six months. There is no silver coin futures contract but we know the price of silver futures. Therefore, we consider cross-hedging the value of our coin collection with a short position in silver futures expiring in the three months. The current silver futures price is assumed as ₹7,600 per kg. Also, the relationship between the price of silver coins and silver futures is:

$$\text{Silver coin price} = 100 + 1.20 \text{ (Silver futures)} + e$$

Where error term, $e$ take on values of only $-10$, 0 and 10 and both silver coin price and silver futures price are in kg. From the above equation, it is clear that on average the silver coin price is 20 percent more volatile than silver futures price. Because each ₹1 movement in the silver futures price is associated with ₹1.20 movement in silver coins price. So size of futures position:

$$\text{Size of futures position} = \text{Hedge ratio} \times \text{Size of cash position}$$

$$= 1.2 \times 10 \text{ kg} = 12 \text{ kg}$$

To see how this cross hedge might work, we calculate the hedged value of contract. We consider two values for spot silver price in three months, ₹7,500 and ₹7,650 and three levels ($e$) $-10$, 0 and 10.

**Case 1:**

TABLE 7.5(a)    Silver Futures Price ₹7,500

| Basis error | Coin value | Futures profit | Hedged value |
|---|---|---|---|
| $e = -10$ | 10 kg[100 + 1.2(7,500) – 10] = 10(9,090)<br>= 90,900 | = 12(7,600 – 7,500) = + ₹1,200 | ₹92,100 |
| $e = 0$ | 10 kg[100 + 1.2(7,500) + 0] = 10(9,100)<br>= 91,000 | = 12(7,600 – 7,500) = + ₹1,200 | ₹92,200 |
| $e = 10$ | 10 kg[100 + 1.2(7,500) + 10] = 91,100 | = 12(7,600 – 7,500) = + ₹1,200 | ₹92,300 |

**Case 2:**

TABLE 7.5(b)    Silver Futures Price ₹7,650

| Basis error | Silver coin value | Futures profit | Hedged value |
|---|---|---|---|
| $e = -10$ | 10 kg[100 + 1.2(7,650) – 10] = 10(9,270)<br>= 92,700 | = 12(7,600 – 7,650) = – ₹600 | ₹92,100 |
| $e = 0$ | 10 kg[100 + 1.2(7,650) + 0] = 10(9,280)<br>= 92,800 | = 12(7,600–7,650) = – ₹600 | ₹92,200 |
| $e = 10$ | 10 kg[100 + 1.2(7,650) + 10] = 10(9,290)<br>= 92,900 | = 12(7,600–7,650) = – ₹600 | ₹92,300 |

No matter what the spot price of silver in next three months, the hedged value of contract (silver coin) equals ₹92,200 plus or minus 100. The unhedged value of contract can range from ₹91,500 to ₹92,900. Thus a cross hedging reduces the risk of position.

**EXAMPLE:** Consider the problem faced by a film manufacturer that uses silver, a key ingredient in manufacturing photographic film. Film production is process industry, with more or less continuous production. COMEX silver futures trade for delivery in January, March, July, September and December. Suppose the film manufacture needs silver in February, April and June. So hedging horizon and futures expiration date do not match perfectly. Second, consider the difference in quality of silver required by the firm for production of film but at COMEX futures contract available are of 100 percent pure quality. There is also a probability that hedge may not be perfect. Further, if say the manufacturer needs 7,000 ounces of silver, he has a problem to choose one or two contracts of this portion because at Comex one standard contract is of 5,000 ounce. These all are the cases of cross hedges.

### *The cross-hedge equation*

After deciding the most closely correlated contract to the price, we wish to hedge, then the number of contracts are to be determined for minimising risk. One way to estimate the statistical relationship between them, i.e., by a linear equation which is as under:

$$P_T = a + bF_{T,T}^* + e_T^*$$

where $e_T^*$ is a random error with zero mean, $T$ is the expiration date of the futures contracts and $T^*$ is the date the hedge will be closed out.

If $T^* \neq T$, there is maturity mismatch. The following time line will show this situation:

### *Time line:*

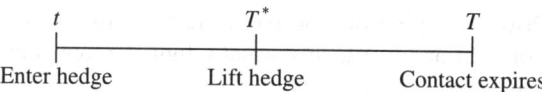

The equation considers that hedges have both asset and maturity mismatch. We can interpret the constant term by assuming $b = I$, $et = 0$, and $T = T^*$.

Suppose a firm holds silver inventory in Mumbai. Also suppose that because of transportation cost, spot price of silver in Mumbai is always ₹50 per kg more than it is in Delhi. Delivery, location etc. are specified in the silver contract. In this case, the equation will be

$$P_T^M = a + P_T$$

where superscript $M$ refers to Mumbai.

**EXAMPLE:** Show the net difference between the inventory scenario in Mumbai and Delhi in the example shown in perfect hedge model by assuming ₹50 difference in silver prices between two cities.

**TABLE 7.6** Silver Inventory Revenue Hedging

| Scenario Delhi/Mumbai | New silver revenue | Futures profits | Net revenue |
|---|---|---|---|
| 7,700/7,750 | 7,75,000 | 100(7,600 – 7,700) = – 10,000 | ₹7,65,000 |
| 7,400/7,450 | 7,45,000 | 100(7,600 – 7,400) = 20,000 | ₹7,65,000 |

The coefficient $b$ in equation indicates that on an average spot will move 'b' rupees for every rupee move in futures price. A cross-hedging strategy must adjust for the relationship between movements in the spot and futures prices. This can be done by choosing the correct hedge ratio.

$$\text{Hedge ratio} = \frac{\text{Quantity of futures position}}{\text{Quantity of cash position}}$$

Hedge ratio has been further explained later on in this chapter.

## 7.7 CONCEPT OF BASIS RISK AND HEDGING

Understanding basis risk is fundamental to hedging. It is noted earlier that basis is the difference between the spot price (cash price) and futures price of an underlying asset. If the spot price is higher than the futures price, then the basis will be called *positive* or *over* and vice-versa. This concept in equation form is as under:

$$\text{Basis}_{t,T} = \text{Cash price}_t - \text{Futures price}_{t,T}$$

If the futures prices and cash prices always change by the same amount, then the basis will not change and it will be zero. It means there could be no change in the basis, if Futures price = Cash price, then

$$\text{Basis}_{t,T} = \text{Futures price} - \text{Cash price} = 0$$

There is basis risk when the changes in futures prices and cash prices are not equal.

Further in this case, if the magnitude (in units) of the cash futures positions are identical, then any loss (gain) in the value of the cash position will be totally offset by the gain (loss) in the value of the futures position. Prior to expiration, the basis may be positive or negative. For example, low-interest rate currency or gold or silver assets, usually futures price is greater than the spot price, which means that basis is negative and vice-versa.

When the change in spot price is more than the change in futures price, the basis will increase which is known as a strengthening of the basis. Similarly, if the change in spot price is less than the change in futures price, the basis will decrease, it is referred to as a weakening of the basis. Let us see the following:

It is observed from Table 7.7 that change in spot price is 60 = (7,560 – 7,500), whereas change in futures price is 10 (₹7,590 – ₹7,580), and change in basis is 50 = (–30 + 80), is a situation of strengthening the basis.

**TABLE 7.7**   Basis Position of Silver (Price in rupees per 100 gm)

| Scenario | Cash price | Futures price | Basis |
|----------|-----------|---------------|-------|
| April 8, 2002 | 7,500 | 7,580 | – 80 |
| May 10, 2002 | 7,560 | 7,590 | – 30 |
| Change | + 60 | + 10 | + 50 |

To examine the basis risk, let us use the following notations:

$S_1$ = Spot price at time $t_1$
$S_2$ = Spot price at time $t_2$
$F_1$ = Futures price at time $t_1$
$F_2$ = Futures price at time $t_2$
$b_1$ = Basis at time $t_1$
$b_2$ = Basis at time $t_2$

From the example given in Table 7.7, the basis will be

$$b_1 = S_1 - F_1 = 7,500 - 7,580 = -80$$
$$b_2 = S_2 - F_2 = 7,560 - 7,590 = -30$$

Let us consider a situation of a hedger who knows that the asset will be sold at time $t_2$ and takes a short futures position at time $t_1$. The price realized for the asset is $S_2$ and the profit on the futures position is $F_1 - F_2$. The effective price that is obtained for the asset with hedging is, therefore,

$$S_2 + (F_1 - F_2) = F_1 + b_2$$

From the example, this will be ₹7,550.

$$₹7,560 + (₹7,580 – ₹7,590) = ₹7,580 + (–30)$$
$$7,560 – 10 = 7,580 – 30$$

Thus, the value of $F_1$ is known at time $t_1$, $b_2$ were also known at this time, a perfect hedge would result. The hedging risk is the uncertainty associated with the $b_2$. This is known as *basis risk.* Similarly, we can consider the next situation where a company knows it will buy the asset at time $t_2$ and initiate a long hedge at time $t_1$. The price paid for the asset is $S_2$ and the loss on the hedge is $F_1 – F_2$. The effective price which will be paid with hedging is, therefore,

$$S_2 + (F_1 – F_2) = F_1 + b_2$$

This is the same expression as we have seen earlier. The value of $F_1$ is known at time $t_1$ and the term $b_2$ represents basis risk.

Basis risk for the investment assets like securities arises mainly from uncertainty as to the level of the risk-free interest rate in the futures, whereas in the case of consumption assets, in balances between supply and demand, difficulties in storing, convenience yield, etc. also provide the additional source of basis risk.

Basis risk = Spot price of asset to be hedged – Futures price of contract used

Suppose spot price of the share of XYZ Ltd. at the time of hedge initiated is ₹2.50 and futures price is ₹2.20, respectively. And at the time of closing at hedge prices are ₹2.00 and ₹1.90, respectively. So basis will be:

$$b_1 = S_1 – F_1 = 2.50 – 2.20 = 0.30$$
$$b_2 = S_2 – F_2 = 2.00 – 1.90 = 0.10$$

Also, consider a hedger who knows that the shares will be sold at time $t_2$ and takes a short futures position at time $t_1$. Effective price that is obtained for the assets with hedging is, therefore,

$$S_2 + (F_1 – F_2) = F_1 + b_2$$
$$= 2.00 + 2.20 – 1.90 = 2.20 + 0.10$$
$$= 4.20 – 1.90 = 2.30$$
$$= 2.30 = 2.30$$

Value is ₹2.30, and where $b_2$ represents the basis risk.

## 7.8 BASIS RISK VERSUS PRICE RISK

We have already seen that the basis $b$ is the difference between the cash or spot price $s$ and the futures price $F$.

$$B_{t,T} = S_t – F_{t,T}$$

A change in the basis, therefore, is:

$$\Delta b_{t,T} = \Delta S_t – \Delta F_{t,T}$$

**EXAMPLE:** Suppose spot and futures price on March 1 in cent per yen is 0.7800 and 0.7850, whereas on July 1, when contract is closed out these are 0.7200 and 0.7250, respectively.

Basis risk $(T) = 0.7800 - 0.7850 = -0.0050$

If the changes in futures and spot prices were assumed to be equal, then there would be no change in the basis.

If $$\Delta S_t = \Delta F_{t,T}$$

Then $$\Delta b_{t,T} = \Delta S_t - \Delta F_{t,t} = 0$$

When changes in futures and cash price are not equal, which is normal in practice, then there will be basis risk. Thus, the *basis risk* is defined as the variance of the basis, i.e., $\sigma^2(b)_{t,T}$ which will be equal to

$$\sigma^2(b_{t,T}) = \sigma^2(S_t - F_{t,T})$$

It can be rewritten as:

$$\sigma^2(b_{t,T}) = \sigma^2(S_t) + \sigma^2(F_{t,T}) - 2\rho\sigma\,(S_t)\,\sigma(F_{t,T})$$

where $\sigma^2$ is the variance, $\sigma$ is the standard deviation and $\rho$ is the correlation coefficient between the futures and spot price series.

From the above, it is revealed that the basis risk is zero when the variances of the futures and cash prices are identical and the correlation coefficient between cash and futures prices equals to one. Let us explain this by an example. If the variance of both futures and cash prices are ₹25 and there is perfect correlation between the spot and futures prices, i.e., $\rho = 1$, then

$$\sigma^2(b_{t,T}) = 25 + 25 - 2 \times 1 \times 5 \times 5 = 50 - 50 = 0$$

Let us further assume that there is perfect correlation between spot and futures prices (i.e., $\rho \neq 1$), and if it equals only 0.50, basis risk will not be zero. In that case the basis risk will be

$$\sigma^2(b_{t,T}) = 25 + 25 - 2 \times (0.5)\,(5)\,(5) = 50 - 25 = 25$$

Similarly, a difference between the variance of the futures and cash prices will result in some basis risk. However, in real world situation, the magnitude of the basis risk depends mainly on the degree of correlation between cash and futures prices, i.e., the higher the correlation, the less the basis risk.

As we see that perfect correlation between the cash and futures prices is very rare, the hedgers, then, always assume some basis risk. So to reduce their exposure to price risk (or to the variance of spot prices), they must accept in return an exposure to basis risk. In brief, it is evident that for a hedge to be attractive, the basis risk should be significantly less than the hedger's price risk.

## 7.9  HEDGING EFFECTIVENESS

As noted earlier that the objective of the hedging is to reduce the exposure to price risk, and so the hedgers trade price risk for basis risk. Thus, one measure of anticipated hedging effectiveness (H.E.) is to compare the basis risk with the price risk. The smaller the anticipated basis risk in comparison to the anticipated price risk, the more effective is the hedge. This can be stated as follows:

$$\text{H.E.} = 1 - \frac{\sigma^2(b_{t,T})}{\sigma^2(S_t)}$$

i.e., 1 minus the ratio of the expected variance of the basis to the expected variance of cash prices.

This means that the closer the H.E., the more effective is the hedge. However, H.E. is only a way of judging how good a particular hedge is likely to be a priori. It should not be confused with the concept of an optimal hedge.

## 7.10  DEVISING A HEDGING STRATEGY

In this section, we will discuss the concepts and principles involved in designing a specific hedging strategy. So, different issues concerning to it like how to select a futures contract for hedging, how to determine and calculate the optimal hedge ratio, how to design and manage a hedging strategy and so on will be discussed.

**Deciding on the futures contract:**   The basic objective of a hedging strategy is to minimize risk or to maximize hedging effectiveness. In this respect, the first step towards designing a particular hedging strategy is to decide about the futures contract to be undertaken. For this purpose, two aspects are considered—first, what kind of futures to use, and second, which contract month of that futures to be used.

**Which futures contract:**   While deciding about the futures contract to be undertaken, the hedger must consider that the correlation between the cash and futures prices must be very high. When hedging an asset on which no futures contract is traded, the choice is more difficult. Thus, first starting point to select a futures contract is to select such assets which are inter-related. In other words, evaluating the correlation coefficients of various price risk associated with, for example, with jet fuel, heating oil, gasoline, crude oil, etc. Likewise, with gold we can use gold coins, bullion, silver, silver coins, etc.

**Which contract month:**   The second important consideration in designing a hedging strategy is to select the contract month. We see that futures contracts are available in the market of different months. So the selection of month of a futures contract will depend upon such a period where the futures and spot prices are highly correlated. Obviously, the prices of the near month contract are the most highly correlated with cash price. Thus, using the near month futures contract will reduce basis risk (or variance of the basis) the most. Since it is seen that the variance of the basis increases as the price correlation between cash and futures price decreases. Hence, hedging with the near month futures contract is preferable because it minimizes the basis variation.

It should be noted that the principle of choosing the futures contract should be applied in the context of specific hedging situations. Matching cash and futures obligations in different situations will be another way of dominating or minimizing basis risk. This strategy, of course, will be useful only if the duration of a hedger's cash obligations is fixed and known in advance, and there exist a matching futures contract where the hedger cannot estimate his cash obligation with certainty, then in this situation he will not be able to pursue a matching strategy, but may want to hedge continuously. Thus, while hedging a continuous cash obligation, hedgers have to decide between two alternatives:

  (a) Hedging with a nearby futures and rolling the hedge forward,
  (b) Hedging with a more distant futures contract, and rolling it less frequently.

Both the alternatives have their own mechanism depending upon the hedging objective. For example, using a more distant contract usually increases basis risk because its price will be less correlated with spot market prices. But the brokerage cost and other transaction costs will be more due to frequent sales and purchases in the market. No specific rule can be made to decide between these alternatives. However, the hedgers in most cases, prefer to hedge with a futures contract that has a high price correlation either with the near month or the second month contract.

## 7.11  HEDGE RATIO CONCEPT

The next important decision in devising a hedging strategy is to determine the optimal futures position to follow, popularly known as *optimal hedge ratio*. In other words, in order to minimize the risk, the hedger must take a futures position, i.e., the number of the futures contracts times the quantity represented by each contract, which will result in the maximum reduction in the variability of the value of his total (hedged) position. In simple form, the hedge ratio *HR* is the ratio of size of the position taken in futures contracts to the size of the exposure.

The general definition of a hedge ratio *HR* is:

$$HR = \frac{\text{Futures position}}{\text{Cash market position}} = \frac{Q_F}{Q_S}$$

where *HR* is Hedging ratio, $Q_F$ is quantity (or units) of the asset represented by the futures position and $Q_S$ is quantity (or units) of the spot (cash) asset that is being hedged.

**EXAMPLE:** If, for example, $30,000 short futures position is taken to hedge $40,000 kg silver in spot position, the *HR* equals 0.75,

i.e.,    $\dfrac{\$30,000}{\$40,000}$

The hedge ratio which minimizes risk is defined as:

$$HR^* = \frac{Q_F^*}{Q_C}$$

where $HR^*$ is hedging ratio which minimizes the risk, $Q_F^*$ is the quantity (units) of futures that minimizes the risk and $Q_C$ is the quantity (units) of the spot (cash) that is being hedged.

To know how the value of the ratio is determined, consider the following:

$$\Delta V_H = \Delta S \times QS - \Delta F \times Q_F^*$$

where $\Delta V_H$ is change in value of the total hedged position, $\Delta S$ is change in the spot (cash) price and $\Delta F$ is change in futures price.

Both *QS* and *QF* are assumed to be constant for the life of the hedge. If the change in the value of the hedged position is set equal to zero (making variability equal to zero), then

$$\Delta S \times Q_S = \Delta F \times Q_F^*$$

and

$$\frac{\Delta S}{\Delta F} = \frac{Q_F^*}{Q_s}$$

Thus, since $HR^* = Q_F^*/Q_s$, as given above, the value of $HR^* = \Delta S/\Delta F$, or equal to the ratio of change in the spot price to the change in the futures price. For example, if the cash price change by ₹10, futures price changes by ₹12, then the minimum-variance hedge ratio will be

$$HR = \frac{₹10}{₹12} = 0.8333 \text{ app.}$$

This above ratio can be used to determine the number of futures contracts with which to hedge. In above case

$$Q_F^* = Q_S \times \frac{\Delta S}{\Delta F}$$

As

$$Q_F^* = Q_S \times HR$$

But

$$Q_F^* = N_{FC} \times Q_{FC}$$

where $N_{FC}$ is Number of futures contracts which minimizes risk and $Q_{FC}$ is the quantity (or units) of the asset represented by each futures contract.

From the above

$$N_{FC}^* \times Q_{FC} = Q_S \times HR^*$$

$$N_{FC}^* = \frac{Q_S}{Q_{FC}} \times HR^*$$

This is most common formula which is used frequently in the futures trading for hedge in order to achieve the minimum-variance hedge.

The hedge determines the optimal futures position to assure or to determine the optimal hedge ratio. If the hedger wishes to minimize risk, he must take a futures position that will result in the maximum possible reduction in the viability of the value of his total hedged position.

$$\text{Hedge ratio} = \frac{Q_F}{Q_C}$$

where $Q_F$ is the quantity of commodity represented by the futures position and $Q_C$ is the quantity of the cash commodity that is being hedged.

**EXAMPLE:** If 2,000 tonnes of wheat short futures position is taken to hedge a 4,000 tonnes of wheat cash position then *HR* is 0.50.

$$HR = \frac{2,000}{4,000} = 0.5$$

**EXAMPLE:** Let us consider an example of hedging a long position of 2,000 kg silver by selling silver coins. Assume that for every ₹100 per kg change in silver coins price, there is of ₹80 per kg change in silver price. To determine the minimum-variance hedge, how many futures contracts should be sold? Applying the formula, we know that

$$HR = \frac{80}{100} = 0.80$$

Therefore,
$$NFC = \frac{2,000}{100} \times 0.80 - 16$$

Thus, the minimum-variance hedge requires selling 16 contracts.

**EXAMPLE:** An MNC has assets denominated is British Pound sterling $250 million and liabilities of $200 million. Comment on the following:

(a) What is the net exposure of the MNC?
The net exposure is $250 million –$200 million $50 million
(b) Is the MNC exposed to a dollar appreciation or depreciation?
The MNC is exposed to dollar appreciation or depreciation in the pound sterling relative to US dollar.
(c) How can the MNC use the futures contracts to hedge its foreign exchange rate risk?
The MVC can hedge its foreign exchange, risk by selling futures contract-in pound (short Futures in pound) assuming direct quote terms is the US, and quoted as $/£.
(d) What is the number of futures contracts to be entered to hedge the foreign exchange exposure in full by the MNC? To hedge $50 million, and assuming the one futures contract size for pound is £62,500, then the MNC must sell 800 futures contracts:

$$NF = \frac{\$50 \text{ million}}{\$62,500} = 800 \text{ pound futures contracts}$$

(e) Assume that the pound sterling falls from $1.40/£ to $1.30/£, then what will be the impact on the MNC cash position and of futures position? If the pound sterling depreciates to US dollar, then the cash position of the MNC would be in loss, which will be equal to the net exposure in US dollar ($) multiplied by change exchange rate, i.e.,

$$50 \text{ million } (\$1.30 - \$1.40) = -\$ 5.0 \text{ million}$$

**Impact on futures position:**

There will be a gain because 800 futures contracts in short have been entered by the MNC in pound sterling.

**The Gain:**

$$\text{NF} \times 62{,}500 \times \Delta \text{Ft} = -800(\$62{,}500) \ (\$1.30 - \$1.40) = +\$5.0 \text{ million}$$

(f) Assume that pound futures price falls from $1.35 to $1.25, then what will be the impact on futures position? Also, comment on the basis risk.

In short futures hedge the MNC will be in profit:

$$\text{Gain} = 800 \times \$62{,}500 \times (\$1.25 - \$1.35) = +\$5.0 \text{ million.}$$

**Basis Risk:**

Since, in the above example, basis risk does not occur, a perfect hedge is possible, i.e., hedge ratio can be in this case = 1.0

(g) Further assume that pound futures price falls from $1.35/£ to $1.23/£, what will be your comment on this situation? How will you fully hedge in this?

Gain on the short-hedge would be:

$$800 \times 62{,}500 \times (\$1.23 - \$1.35) = +\$6.0 \text{ million.}$$

In the said example, there is basis risk because $\Delta \text{St} \neq \text{ft}$ in the foreign exchange market. Futures price is more volatile than cash price.

**Perfect hedge in new situation:**

Since $h = \dfrac{\Delta S_1}{\Delta F_t} = \dfrac{0.10}{0.12} = 0.8333$, the number of futures contract sold to fully hedge is NF = $50 million × (.833)/($62,500)666.4 contracts. The gain in futures hedge will be: $-666.4 \times (\$62.500) \ (\$1.23 - \$1.35) = -\$5.0$ million

**EXAMPLE:** An MNC is planning to hedge its one year 500 million US dollar denominated loan against exchange rate risk. Assume the current spot rate is £0.60/$. A one year $ futures contract is currently trading at £0.58/$. Standard size of US dollar futures contract assume to be 1,00,000 units. How many futures contract the MNC should buy or sell if a regression of past one year spot price on futures price, generates an estimated scope of 1.25. Further, show that if the MNC repatriates its principal amount of ₹500 million, how it will hedge at year-end, assuming the spot rate of £ at year end is £0.55/$, and future rate is £0.545/$.

The MNC should generate futures contract:

Principal amount ₹500 million, contract size 1,00,000 unit of $, Beta Value is 1.25, then, number of futures contract

$$\text{NF} = (\text{Long asset position} \times \text{B}) \ (\text{Futures contract size})$$

$$= (\pounds 500 \text{ million} \times 1.25)/(\$1{,}00{,}000) = 6{,}250 \text{ contracts}$$

The original loan in dollars = $500 × £0.60 = 300 million. And the loan value at the year-end = 500 × $55 = $275 million. The balance sheet has decreased in value by $25 million. The gain from hedge = ($0.58 – $0.545) × 6,250 × 1,00,000 = $2,18,75,000.

## 7.12 ESTIMATING THE HEDGE RATIO

To determine the number of futures contracts to hedge with, it is essential that a prior estimate of hedge ratio be obtained. Various methods are used to estimate the ratio depending upon the nature of futures contracts. Here, in this section, a few important methods frequently used in estimating hedging ratio will be discussed. It is important to note that no one can know with certainty what the relationship will be in the futures between the cash and futures prices of the underlying asset being hedged. One can just rely on the past behaviour and relationship of these prices, and normally it is expected that the same would be happened in futures too. Following are the methods of estimation of hedging ratio:

**The Naive method:** This method is based on the two types of information like knowledge of current market conditions and a forecast of futures market condition; and secondly, knowledge of what the relationship between cash and futures prices has been in the past. Since various hedges are made with nearby futures traded on the same asset that is being hedged, it is common to assume that the minimum-variance hedge ratio will be equal to one. An assumption that the minimum variance hedge ratio is equal to one is called the *Naïve hedging model*. But it is not safe that all the times we can use this method, assuming the minimum-variance ratio equal to one.

**Regression analysis (Statistical method):** Another important method to be used to determine the minimum-variance hedge ratio is regression analysis. This method is specifically constructed to provide the best linear relationship between the two prices, i.e., futures price and the price to be hedged. More specifically, regression analysis can be used to estimate the following linear equation:

$$\Delta S_t = \alpha + \beta \times \Delta F_t + e_t$$

where $\Delta S_t$ is changes in cash (spot) prices (dependent variable), $\Delta F_t$ is changes in futures prices (independent variable), is $e_t$ is random error form with zero mean and $\alpha$ & $\beta$ are estimated coefficients.

In this method, statistical procedure used to estimate the value of $\alpha$ & $\beta$ in such that it guarantees the sum of the squared error terms $(\Sigma e_t^2)$ will be minimum and that can better describe the relationship between the changes in futures and cash prices. ($\Delta S_t$ and $\Delta F_t$). Further, it gives us the value of $\alpha$ and $\beta$ that best depict the historical relationship between these two prices. The estimates of $\beta$ provides good approximations of minimum-variance hedge ratio.

## 7.13 EX-ANTE HEDGE RATIO VS EX-POST HEDGING RESULTS

For managing the futures risk, it is essential to examine the hedge ratio for the life of a hedge (or the ex-ante hedge ratio) with the result if there is no hedging (or ex-post-hedging result). One cannot say exactly that the hedging is full proof mechanism because the market conditions may vary, unusual events may occur, etc. In general, we should expect that the hedge is used to reduce the losses in case we have not gone for hedging.

Various studies conducted from time to time had witnessed that the cash flows of the hedged position are more stable and it succeeds in reducing the variability in cash flows. However, it is also equally clear that it does not eliminate all exposure to price risk even if we assume the hedge ratio equal to one ($\beta = 1$). In brief, one should give careful thought in devising a hedging strategy. The ex-ante minimum-variance hedging ratio should closely approximated with the ex-post minimum-variance hedge ratio. This requires accurately predicting the relationship between cash and futures prices which will prevail during the life of the hedge.

## 7.14 HEDGING OBJECTIVES

In the prior discussion of hedging strategies, we have assumed the only objective of hedging is to minimize the risk. However, sometimes, the hedgers may be willing to assume more risk in order to earn more profit because eliminating all price risk will lead to eliminating the profit of the firm, which may not be good at all the time. Thus, the hedgers may use such hedging ratio other than the minimum-variance hedge ratio, or willingly may go for under hedging.

Undoubtedly the decision relating to hedging ratio or how much to hedge will depend upon the hedger's risk preference. The lesser he hedges, the more risk he assumes. Not only this, the hedger may change his hedging strategy later on due to his strong belief about the futures price movements. So hedging objective is a relative concept and much depends upon the risk and return. In other words, it is the trade off between profits and risk reduction through hedging because it is observed that risk could be reduced but at the cost of lost profits.

Figure 7.1 depicts trade off between risk and profit at the different level of hedge ratios. The hedger may choose the risk and return combination that he most prefers, or that he finds optimal. In this figure, line EE represents the hedging efficiency frontier: the most efficient combinations of risk and return that can be achieved by varying the hedge ratio. The line UU represents the highest level of utility which the hedger can achieve by hedging (being on the efficient frontier EE). The slope of UU represents how the hedger values change in risk relative to changes in profits. The value replaces on changes in risk versus changes in profit will determine his decision. For example, at the point E, the hedge ratio is 0.60 where the expected profit is ₹5,200 at ₹2,000 standard deviation. Further, if he chooses the hedge ratio 0.40, by doing so he will increase risk to ₹2,500 (by standard deviation). Point A where UU and EE touch (or tangent), indicates the hedger's optimal ratio ($\beta = 0.40$). This hedge strategy yields a profit of ₹5,300 and a standard deviation of ₹2,500, which yields a profit utility to the hedger. In brief, the hedge can remain completely unhedged ($\beta = 0$), or can adopt the minimum-variance hedge ($\beta = 0.60$) yielding lower utility than that it would be at a hedge ratio of 0.40.

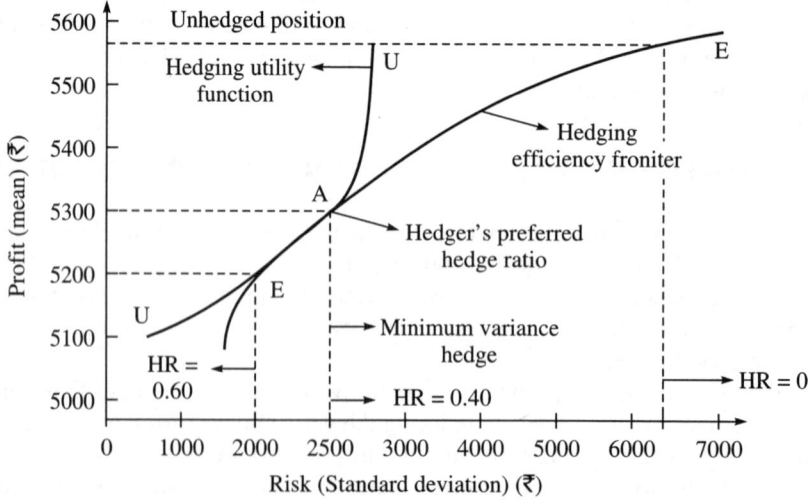

**FIGURE 7.1** Optimal hedge ratio.

## 7.15   MANAGEMENT OF THE HEDGE

After establishing a hedge, it is essential to manage it effectively. So regular monitoring and making adjustments are the key factors in managing of the hedge. There is also need for a systematic evaluation of the effectiveness of the hedge relative to its anticipated (or ex-ante measure). Further, if the desired results are not being achieved from the hedging, then the reasons should be identified and necessary steps be taken to improve hedge effectiveness in the futures. To manage effectively the hedging, following steps are taken:

### 7.15.1   Monitoring the Hedge

Continuous monitoring on the performance of a hedging is essential. For this purpose, the following information should be available regularly on an up-to-date basis:

**Cash position:**   The hedger must get the information of the current size of the cash position being hedged. What are the changes in its magnitude since the inception of hedge? What are the gains or losses on this position to date? What are the reasons of such deviation, if any?

**Futures position:**   Likewise cash position, the information regarding the size of futures position, profits and losses incurred to date on this position, etc. be collected for further consideration.

**Margins:**   All such information concerning the margin like the total amounts of funds dedicated to margin requirements, net financing costs to-date, and further, the availability of funding arrangements to meet futures margin calls, etc. should be available continuously.

**Basis movements:**   All such information regarding the changes in basis should be collected to see whether they are consistent with a priori expectations or there is any major deviations at the particular time intervals.

**New information:**   Sometimes, new events occur in the market or there are new information regarding the underlying assets which cause to change in the prices either of the spot or futures must be noted and analyzed further to evaluate their impact on hedging strategy followed by the firm.

### 7.15.2   Adjustments to the Hedge

After monitoring the hedging performance through the information network, sometimes, there is need to make some adjustments during the life of a hedge. A few important adjustments, in general, have been discussed here as under:

**Changes in risk exposure:**   During the monitoring period, if the size of the cash position being hedge changed, then the size of the hedging futures position should be changed accordingly. Further, changes in risk exposure will also lead to change in cash position.

**Changes in hedge ratio:**   Sometimes there is change in risk preference of the hedger. For example, the hedger may be in position to absorb more risk, then in that situation, the hedge ratio should also be changed accordingly.

**New hedging goals:**   Managing the hedging position effectively much depends upon the information network of the hedger. As the new information becomes available, there may be need to change the goal of the hedger. Based upon such changes, the hedging strategies should be adjusted accordingly.

**Basis management:**   With the changes in the basis, the new opportunities may arise for the hedgers. In order to take the advantages of such developments in the basis movements, futures position may be adjusted from one contract month to another and so forth.

**Rolling the hedge:**   Sometimes, such events and developments occur in the market that it becomes necessary for the hedgers to change their hedging strategies. Then in that situation, futures positions may be lifted periodically from one month to other month. In other words, the futures position may be initiated or to switch them like from less liquid period to more liquid period.

## 7.15.3   Hedge Evaluation

The final step in effective hedge management is to evaluate how prior hedging strategies have worked and to determine whether they can be improved or not. In order to evaluate a hedging strategy, we can use an ex-post measure of effectiveness which is as under:

$$1 - \frac{\text{Variance (Gains or losses in hedged position)}}{\text{Variance (Gains or losses in unhedged cash position)}}$$

If the value of the above is closer or nearer to one, the more successful is the hedge. This concept has been already discussed in this chapter. According to this measure, a comparison is done between the ex-ante (or anticipated) hedging effectiveness and the ex-post hedge effectiveness. If there is significant difference or deviation between these two, then the situation will be analyzed in depth to find out the reasons behind such departure. Further, the overall cost of hedging program should also be evaluated into order to determine the hedger's cost-effectiveness. All such costs like brokerage fees, translation costs, management costs, etc. should also examined from time to time. After considering these, the hedging should be compared with alternative risk management strategies.

## SUMMARY

This chapter has introduced the concept of hedging, tools for hedging and how to devise a hedging strategy. Hedging, in broadest sense, is the act of protecting oneself against futures loss. More specifically hedging is regarded as the use of futures transactions to avoid or reduce price risks in the spot market. Hedging is used in multipurpose concept like (a) carrying charge hedging, according to this approach, the stockists watch the price spread between the spot and futures price, and if the spread is such which covers even carrying cost, then the stockist buy ready stocks, (b) operational hedging which says that hedges use the futures market for their operations and see the same as substitute for cash or forward transactions, and (c) anticipatory hedging, which is done in anticipation of subsequent sales or purchases. For example, a farmer might hedge by selling in anticipation of his crop while a miller might hedge by buying futures in anticipation of subsequent raw material needs. Perfect hedging is referred to that position which eliminates the total risk. In other words, the use of futures or forward position to reduce completely the business risk is called *perfect hedge*.

The chapter further elaborates the basics of long and short hedges. A short hedge is a hedge that involves short position in futures contract. In other words, it occurs when a firm/trader plans to purchase or produce a cash commodity sells futures to hedge the cash position. In general sense, it means 'being short' having a net sold position. On the other hand, a long hedge (or a buying hedge) involves where a long position is taken in futures contract. The basic objective here is to protect itself against a price increase in the underlying asset prior to purchasing it in either the spot or forward market. Another concept, 'cross hedging' arises when hedging horizon (maturity) may not match with the futures expiration date, quantity to be hedged may not match with the quantity of futures contract, physical features of the asset to be hedged may differ from the futures contract itself.

The chapter in next section explains the basis risk and price risk. Basis is the difference between the cash price and the futures price. When changes in the futures and cash price are not equal, which is normal in practice, then there will be basis risk. Basis risk is defined as the variance of the basis. The chapter further explains how to devise a hedging strategy and how to manage the hedging strategy. Devising a hedging strategy involves deciding on the futures contract, hedge ratio concept, estimating the hedge ratio and deciding about the hedging objectives.

The last section of the chapter discusses the management of hedge position which includes (a) monitoring the hedge, (b) adjustments to the hedge and hedge evaluation and monitoring the hedge which includes, information of the current size of the cash position being hedged, changes in its magnitude since the inception of hedge, the information regarding the size of futures position and so on.

## SOLVED PROBLEMS

**P.1.** On January 15, a copper fabricator requires 20,000 kg of copper on May 20 to meet a certain contract. The spot price of copper is ₹120 per kg and May 20 futures price is ₹150 per kg. Each contract is traded on Comex is of 5000 kg. What type of position copper fabricator should take in the futures market? Show the statement of result from the above transaction.

*Solution:* As copper fabricator is exposed to price risk in upward movement, he should take a long position in futures market. The strategy has the effect of locking in the price of copper, which is required at close ₹150 per kg.

| *Long Hedge with Futures* | |
|---|---|
| *Cash market* | *Futures market* |
| **January 15** | **January 15** |
| Anticipate the need of 20,000 kg of copper on May 20. Spot price is ₹120 per kg | Take a long position in futures market and buy four May 20 contract on copper at a price ₹150 per kg |
| **May 20** | **May 20** |
| Price of copper is ₹150 per kg have to pay 30,00,000 | Close out position by selling at ₹150 per kg |
| Loss in cash market ₹6,00,000 | Futures profit = ₹6,00,000 |
| **Net change in wealth = 0** | |

So trader has hedged the risk of price fluctuation by buying in the futures market at ₹120 per kg. On May 20, spot price turns to be ₹150 per kg, so there is a loss in the spot market of ₹6,00,000, and in futures market, close out position by selling at ₹150 per kg and earning a profit of ₹6,00,000. So net position is hedged by trader by entering into long futures market.

**P.2.** On March 20, a company X has just negotiated a contract to sell two million barrels of oil. It has been agreed that the price that will apply in the contract is the market price on August 20.

Suppose the spot price on March 20 is ₹30 per barrel and August oil futures price on the commodity exchange is ₹29 per barrel. Since contract on (commodity market) is for the delivery of two million barrel. How company can hedge the risk of prices of oil fall down. Explain the hedging strategy with a table, assuming that actual price on August 20 is ₹26 per barrel.

*Solution:*

| Short Hedge Using Futures | |
|---|---|
| **March 20** | **Cash market** |
| Company has negotiated a contract to sell 2 million barrels of oil. The price in sale contract is spot price on August 20 quotes.<br>Spot price of oil = ₹30 per barrel<br>August futures price = ₹29 per barrel | |
| | **Futures market** |
| March 20—Sells or short August 2000 futures contract on crude oil.<br>August 20—Close out position at ₹26 per barrels.<br>Company receives ₹26 per barrel under sale contract. Company's loss is about ₹3 per barrel from futures contract.<br>Loss in cash market = (₹29 – ₹26) = ₹3 per barrel, total loss – 2m × R3 = ₹6m | |

**P.3.**    A company knows that it will buy two million gallon fuel of jet in six months. The standard deviation of the change in price per gallon of fuel over a six months period is calculated as 0.020. The company chooses to hedge by buying futures contract on heating oil. The standard deviation of the change in the futures price over a three months period is 0.025 and the coefficient of correlation between the three months change in the price of jet fuel and the three months change in futures price is 0.5. Calculate the optimal hedge ratio and number of contracts company should buy to hedge the risk.

*Solution:*    Standard deviation = 0.020 (over six months)
   Coefficient of correlation = 0.50
   Standard deviation of change in jet fuel = 0.025 (over three months)
   Then optimal hedge ratio

$$= \text{Coefficient of correlation} \times \frac{\text{Standard deviation}}{\text{Standard deviation of future price change}}$$

$$= 0.5 \times \frac{0.020}{0.025} = 0.40$$

On heating oil futures contract is one 42,000 gallons, so number of contract the company should buy

$$= \frac{0.40 \times 20,00,000}{42,000} = 19.04$$

No. of contract required = 19 to hedge the risk

**P.4.**   On May 1 pepper prices at Kochi are as follows:

| Market | ₹ (per quintal) |
|---|---|
| Spot | 9,000 |
| Futures (July) | 9,200 |

Storage cost of one quintal from May 1 up to delivery date (July 15) are estimated at ₹250 (i.e., 100 per month). On July 15 both spot and futures are trading at ₹9,100. Mr. X entered in following transactions:

    May 1   Buy one quintal July pepper futures at ₹9,200.

    July 15  Buy one quintal spot pepper at ₹9,100.

    July 15  Sell one quintal July pepper futures at ₹9,100.

Show the final outcome of the above transactions:

*Solution:*   Mr. X position from holding hedged commitment

| Transaction | Spot market | | Futures market | |
|---|---|---|---|---|
| | Date | Price (₹) | Date | Price (₹) |
| Sell | 1/5 | 9,400 | 15/7 | 9,100 |
| Buy | 15/7 | 9,100 | 1/5 | 9,200 |
| Gain/Loss | | (300) | | 100 |

**Net loss = 200**

**P.5.**   On August 15 pepper prices at Kochi are as follows:

    Market                ₹ per quintal

    Spot                  ₹9,500 per quintal

    Futures (Matures on 15/11)   ₹9,791 per quintal

Storage cost is estimated at ₹100 per month. On October 15, prices are as follows:

    Spot (November)         ₹9,200 per quintal

    Futures (November)      ₹9,260 per quintal

Mr. Long takes the following transactions:

    1.  August 15: Sell one quintal grain for October delivery at ₹9,700.

    2.  August 15: Buy one quintal November grain futures at ₹9,791.

    3.  October: Sell one quintal November grain futures at ₹9,260.

    4.  Buy one quintal spot grain at ₹9,200.

Show the transaction profile of Mr. Long.

*Solution:*   Mr. Long's return from hedging commitment

| Transaction | Spot market | | Futures market | |
|---|---|---|---|---|
| | Date | Price (₹) | Date | Price (₹) |
| Sell | 15/8 | 9,700 | 15/10 | 9,260 |
| Buy | 15/10 | 9,200 | 15/8 | 9,791 |
| Gain/Loss | | 500 | | (531) |

**Net return = ₹31**

**P.6.**   On June 30, wheat prices at Kochi are as follows:

| Market | ₹ per quintal |
|---|---|
| Spot | 9,600 |
| Futures (Maturities on September 15) | 9,830 |

Carrying cost is estimated at ₹ 100 per month. On August 30, prices are as follows:

| Market | ₹ per quintal |
|---|---|
| Spot | 9,250 |
| Futures (September) | 9,300 |

Mr. Long's transactions are as follows:

June 30:       Sell one quintal pepper for actual August delivery at (fixed price) ₹9,800.
June 30:       Buy one quintal September pepper futures at ₹9,830.
August 30:    Sell one quintal September pepper futures at ₹9,300.
August 30:    Buy one quintal spot pepper at ₹9,250.

*Solution:*   Mr. Long's return from holding commitment

| Transaction | Spot market | | Futures market | |
|---|---|---|---|---|
| | Date | Price (₹) | Date | Price (₹) |
| Sell | 30/6 | 9,800 | 30/8 | 9,300 |
| Buy | 30/8 | 9,250 | 30/6 | 9,830 |
| Gain/Loss | | 550 | | (530) |

**Net return = ₹ 20**

**P.7.**   On January 15, a company plans to borrow ₹ 20 crores for 3 months on February 15. The spot three months interest rate is 12% p.a., April three months rupee futures price is 88, the coefficient of correlation between three months interest rate changes and changes in the price of futures maturing two months later is 0.95, the standard deviation of spot three months interest rate change is 2, whereas the standard deviation of three months interest rate futures price is 2.5 (for futures maturity in two months time) design a hedge.

*Solution:*   Basic hedge would involve dividing the exposure by size of the futures contract and selling the resulting number of futures contracts:

$$\frac{₹\,20 \text{ crores}}{₹\,0.5 \text{ crore}} = 40 \text{ contracts}$$

This number need to be adjusted for relative volatility:

$$= 40 \times \text{Correlation coefficient} \times \frac{\text{S.D. of spot}}{\text{S.D. of futures prices}}$$

$$= 40 \times 0.95 \times \frac{2}{2.5} = 30.4$$

So, no. of contracts needed to hedge risk are 30.

**P.8.** A paper company anticipates a large inflow of funds at the end of February when retail outlets pay for stock of paper sold during the holiday season in January. Management intend to put ₹one crore of these funds into a long-term bond because of high yields on these bonds. Current date is December 1 and the financial manager of paper company project that and long-term interest rate will fall significantly by the time the firm receives the funds on March 1. Which type of hedge is suitable for paper company? Also show the position of the company with futures.

*Solution:* Long hedge is suitable for company. Objective is to benefit from the high long-term interest rates, even though funds are not currently available for investment.

*Long Hedge*

| Date | Cash market | Futures market |
|---|---|---|
| December 1 | Bonds at 86–20/32 to yield 9.95%, 8% coupon, 12 years to maturity; ₹1 crore to invest March 1 | Buy 100 April T-Bond futures at 87–16/32 as a long hedge (9.4% projected yield) |
| March 1 | Receive ₹1 crore; buy ₹1 crore of T-bond at 100 to yield 8%. | Sell futures at 100–2/32 to cover long position. |
| Change | Opportunity loss ₹13,37,500 (₹1 crore × 13 – 12/32) | Gain ₹12,56,250 (₹1,00,000 × 100 × 12 – 18/32) |

Net change = ₹12,56,250 – ₹13,37,500 = ₹81,250

**Net yield with futures: 9.83%**

**P.9.** XYZ mutual fund holds ₹10 crore in stocks, with the portfolio configured to match ABC 100 index. The fund's money manager forecasts an increase in volatility in the market, which increases the probability of a major market decline. To reduce risk the money manager sells ABC 500 futures. But it does not match with ABC 100 price movement exactly. Which type of hedge the XYZ are using? Also show the position of XYZ in cash and futures market.

*Solution:* XYZ mutual fund's money manager is using ABC 500 futures, this is an example of cross hedge; the hedging strategy in which all the conditions do not match with the original position.

| Date | Cash market | Futures market |
|---|---|---|
| December 15 | Stock portfolio of ₹10 crores, with ABC 100 = 325.09 | Sell 574 May ABC 500 futures, with ABC 500 futures = 348.20 for a value of 9,99,33,400 |
| March 25 | The ABC 100 declines to 315.82 for a portfolio value of ₹97,14,848.19 = (10 crores × 315.82/325.09) | Buy Back ABC 500 futures at 335.25 for a value of ₹9,62,16,750. (335.25 × 500 × 574) |

Change loss of ₹2,85,151.81
Gain in futures market ₹37,16,650

$$= [574 \times 500 \times (348.20 - 335.25)]$$

Net gain = ₹34,31,498.19

**P.10.**   A treasury manager needs to borrow ₹10 crores for three months. It is January 25 and money is to be borrowed on April 1. How can the treasury manager hedge against a rise in interest rate using futures? It is also assumed that futures index is ₹25 per index point.

*Solution:*   Treasury manager is of view that interest rate may rise in futures. So he wants to hedge the interest rate risk. Treasure manager can reduce the interest rate risk by entering into futures market and activity in values selling 10 interest rate futures contracts.

**P.11.**   A portfolio manager has the following assets in his portfolio:

| Company | No. of shares | Share price (₹) | Share beta |
|---|---|---|---|
| Andira auto | 5,000 | 30 | 0.8 |
| Bombay cement | 10,000 | 15 | 1.2 |
| Calcutta cotton | 10,000 | 30 | 1.5 |
| Delhi textile mill | 20,000 | 50 | 0.5 |

On September 25 and the December XYZ 100 futures prices is ₹200.

(a) How portfolio manager can hedge the portfolio, with futures (assume ₹30 per index point).

(b) What are the various factors which might reduce the effectiveness of measures taken by portfolio manager?

*Solution:*   Calculate the market exposure as follows:

$5,000 \times 30 \times 0.8$      = ₹1,20,000

$10,000 \times 15 \times 1.2$      = ₹1,80,000

$10,000 \times 30 \times 1.5$      = ₹4,50,000

$20,000 \times 50 \times 0.5$      = ₹5,00,000

Total market exposure    = ₹12,50,000

The market exposure provided by one futures contract is:

$$= 200 \times 30 = ₹6,000$$

(a) Hedging the portfolio with futures would in value selling:

$$= \frac{12,50,000}{6,000} = 20.83$$

So, the number of contracts required to sell will be 20.

(b) Factors that could reduce hedge effectiveness include:

    (i) Basis risk

    (ii) Indivisibility risk

    (iii) Unsystematic risk

    (iv) Beta (Systematic risk)

**P.12.**   Hedging of a long cash position of 10,000 tonnes of wheat by selling rice futures. Assume that for every ₹50 change in rice futures prices, there is ₹35 change in wheat cash prices. To establish a minimum-variance hedge, how many futures contractor should be sold?

***Solution:*** Given $HR = Q_F = 35$, $Q_C = 50$

So
$$HR = \frac{Q_E}{Q_C} = \frac{35}{50} = 0.70$$

The number of futures contract NFC that minimize risk is given by

$$NFC = \frac{Q_C \times HR}{Q_{FC}}$$

$$= \frac{10,000 \times 0.7}{1,000} = \frac{7,000}{1,000} = 7$$

**P.13.**  A short cash position of 1,000 shares of BPL Ltd. is hedged by buying shares of ACC Ltd. Assume every ₹30 change in ACC futures prices, there is ₹20 change in BPL cash prices. Determine how much number of contracts are required to minimize risk.

***Solution:***  $HR = \dfrac{Q_F}{Q_C} = \dfrac{20}{30} = 0.67$

Then  $NFC = \dfrac{1,000 \times 0.67}{100} = 6.7$ contracts

Thus, the minimum variance hedge requires buying 7 contracts.

## REVIEW QUESTIONS

1. Under what circumstances are a short hedge and a long hedge appropriate? Explain with examples.
2. Explain what is meant by basis risk and price risk when futures contracts are used for hedging.
3. What do you understand by hedging? Discuss with suitable examples.
4. Discuss various concepts of hedging, with suitable examples.
5. What do you understand by perfect hedging model? Discuss various conditions that must be fulfilled before a perfect hedge is possible. Also explain how a perfect hedge works.
6. What do you understand by long hedge? Discuss with suitable examples.
7. "Seller's takes short position in the futures market." Explain the statement with suitable examples.
8. What is cross hedging? Discuss with suitable examples. Also discuss the situations which make a hedge to cross hedge.
9. "Hedging is to provide insurance against adverse fluctuations in the price monuments." Do you agree. Discuss the statement with the help of suitable examples.
10. Write a detailed note on devising a hedging strategy.
11. Taking a hypothetical example, define how a long hedge is used by an importer.
12. Explain the use of optimal hedging ratio in hedging a position in futures market.
13. Write note on the following with the help of suitable data:
    (a) Basis risk
    (b) Price risk
14. What rationale is there for hedging specific assets and liabilities risk with futures or forward contracts?
15. What is asset-liability hedge? Explain with suitable example.

16. Explain the difference between hedging and speculation. Give an example of a short hedger and a long hedger.

17. "The hedging effectiveness improves when the cash instrument to be more volatile." Discuss.

18. Explain the various steps taken in devising a hedging strategy. Also explain the effect of hedging objectives in this respect.

19. Explain how would you determine the exposure of cash position to potential losses.

20. Differentiate ex-ante hedge ratio vs ex-post hedging ratio with suitable examples.

21. What do you understand by optimal hedge ratio? What are various methods of determining the hedge ratio? Explain with examples.

22. Does a perfect hedge always lead to a better outcome than an imperfect hedge? Explain your answer with suitable illustrations.

23. Does a perfect hedge always succeed in locking in the current spot price of an asset for a futures transaction? Explain your answer.

24. A transport executive has argued "there is no point in our using oil futures. There is just as much chance that the price of oil in the futures will be less than the futures price as it will be greater than this price." Discuss this viewpoint in the light of advantages and disadvantages of hedging.

25. Consider that you are the treasurer of an Indian company exporting textile to USA. Discuss what points you would keep in mind while designing a foreign exchange hedging strategy.

26. Write short notes on:
    (a) Hedging objectives
    (b) Management of hedging
    (c) Hedging effectiveness

27. Critically examine the relationship between basis risk and hedging.

28. What is basis risk and why it is fundamental to evaluating a hedging strategy?

29. Differentiate between an optimal hedge ratio and a minimum variance hedge ratio. Explain with suitable examples.

30. "An important function of futures market is to permit commercial traders to reduce or control risk by transferring into others more able or more willing to bear the risk." Do you agree with this statement? Explain with suitable illustrations.

## UNSOLVED PROBLEMS

**P.1.** Cash price of XYZ share on 31-12-2014 at Delhi Stock Exchange is ₹400 and futures price of XYZ share is ₹440. Calculate the basis of XYZ share on 31-12-2014 at Delhi Stock Exchange.

**P.2.** A company wants to hedge a long cash position of 5,00,000 gallons of jet fuel by selling heating oil futures. Assume that every 50% change in heating oil futures price, there is 30% change in the jet fuel cash price to establish minimum-variance hedge, how many futures contracts should be sold?

**P.3.** Suppose the standard deviation of quarterly changes in the prices of a stock is $0.65, the standard deviation of quarterly changes in a futures price on the stock is $0.81, and coefficient of correlation between the two changes is 0.8. What is optimal hedge ratio for a three-month contract?

**P.4.** A company has a $1 million portfolio with a beta of 1.2. It would like to use futures contracts on the major market index to hedge its risk. The index is currently at 250 and each contract for delivery of $500 times the index. Calculate the number of contracts need to hedge the value. What should the company do if it wants to reduce the beta of the portfolio to 0.6?

**P.5.** On December 1 an investor holds 5,000 shares of certain stock. The stock is ₹2,000. Investor interested in hedging against movements in the market over the next two months and decides to use the July NSE Index futures contract. Futures price is currently ₹150 and one contract is for delivery of ₹500 times the index. Beta of stock is 1.3. What strategy should the investor follow?

**P.6.** A is an importer of textile firm in USA. He expects that the price of textile to be volatile in the coming future and will increase, and thereby affecting the profitability of A. Current price of textile is ₹2,000 per 100 m and in futures market price of textile is ₹2,500 for 100 m, for delivery in next three months. A needs 20,000 m textile in next three months. So he enters into futures market. Show the profit profile of cash and spot/cash market if price of textile is ₹2,800 per 100 m.

**P.7.** On January a company knows that it will need to purchase 10,000 barrels of crude oil at some time in October or November. Oil futures contractors are currently traded for delivery every month on NYMEX and the contract size is 1000 barrels. The company, therefore, decides to use the December contract for hedging and takes a long position in December 10 contracts. Futures price on January 8 is $18.00 per barrel. The company finds that it is ready to purchase the crude oil on November 20. It is, therefore, close out futures position on that date. Spot price and futures price on November 20 are $20 per barrel and $19.10 per barrel, respectively. Show how much company gain/loss from the above long position.

**P.8.** A corporate treasurer intends to borrow money in the middle of May for a three months period. The treasurer may fear that interest rates might rise from the date of borrowing. Since a rise in interest rates would add to the cost of borrowing, a futures position is taken so that there would be on offsetting profit in the event of rise in interest rates. Three months interest rate futures are quoted on index basis. Index is 100 minus the futures interest rate. So futures interest rate of 6.5% p.a. would entail a quote of $100 - 6.5 = 93.5\%$. The amount of borrowing is £5,00,000. Show the position of treasurer from futures contract. Suppose the interest rate stands at 6.5% and on May interest rate rises to 8%.

## SUGGESTED READINGS

1. Meyers, Thomas A., *The Technical Analysis Course*, McGraw Hill Book Company, London, 1989.
2. Nielsen, Lars Tyge, *Pricing and Hedging of Derivatives Securities*, Oxford University Press, 1999.
3. Collins, Bruce M., *Derivatives and Equity Portfolio Management*, New Hope, Frank J. Fabozzi, 1999.
4. Working, H., Hedging reconsidered, *Journal of Farm Economics*, pp. 544–561, November, 1953.
5. Ederington, L.H., The hedging performance of the new futures market, *Journal of Finance*, pp. 157–170, March, 1979.
6. Chicago Board of Trade, *Introduction to Hedging*, Chicago, 1984.
7. Rene M. Stulz, *Risk Management & Derivatives*, Thomson-South-Western, Indian-Reprint-2007.
8. Robert A. Strong *Derivatives* Thomson-South-Western, Indian-Reprint-2006.
9. www. Nseindia.com. www.bseindia.com.

# Chapter 8

# Stock Index Futures

## LEARNING OBJECTIVES

*After reading this chapter, students will be able to*

➤ Understand the concept of stock index and stock index futures.
➤ Be aware of the common features of a stock index.
➤ Know about the specifications of stock index futures contract.
➤ Know about the settlement procedure or delivery mechanism of stock index futures.
➤ Understand how stock index futures are priced and traded in the futures market.
➤ Be aware of the relationship between actual and theoretical futures prices of stock index futures.
➤ Know how stock index futures can be used as a portfolio management tool.
➤ Explain the types of risks like systematic and unsystematic risk and their measurement.
➤ Be aware of the concept of minimum-variance hedge ratio.
➤ Know the stock index futures trading in Indian Stock Market, contract specifications, market size and major market index on which index futures are traded.

## 8.1  INTRODUCTION

Stock index futures today have become most popular financial derivative instruments and widely traded all over the world. In the early 1980s, several futures contracts written on various stock indices were introduced. The first of these was introduced in 1982 by the Kansas City Board of Trade in USA. These instruments have become very useful to both individual and institutional investors due to their low cost and efficient instrument for trading on expectations of futures general movements in the stock markets.

Before the introduction of these derivative futures, the investors who wanted to trade in stock market movements had to buy and sell large proportion of the various stocks in which transaction costs were extremely high and the execution was very slow. However, now those who are interested to trade in such markets can deal with one simple transaction—choosing a particular stock index futures instrument. Institutional investors are also finding these instruments most favourable for their asset allocations. In this chapter, we will discuss about the concepts and features of stock index futures.

## 8.2  CONCEPT OF STOCK INDEX

Before discussing the concept of stock index futures, we should know about the term stock index. An *index* may be defined as a number which is computed to allow measurement of the value of a portfolio of assets. An index number measures how much available changes overtime the current movement or change in a variable is compared to the previous day's value price and then overall trend is observed. The general movement of the stock market is usually measured by a stock market index consisting of a group of securities that is supposed to reflect the whole market.

A *stock index* or *stock market index* is a portfolio consisting of a collection of different stocks. In others words, a stock index is just like a portfolio of different securities' proportions traded on a particular stock exchange like NIFTY S&P CNX traded on National Stock Exchange of India, the S&P 500 Index is composed of 500 common stocks, etc. Table 8.1 shows the major thirty-eight different stock market indexes. Stock market indexes are computed by using different methods like price-weighted indexes, value-weighted indexes, value-line indexes, etc. The selection of the method depends upon the objective underlying the construction of that index. However, it is not important here to discuss the detail of these methods.

These indices provide summary measure of changes in the value of particular segments of the stock markets which is covered by the specific index. This means that a change in a particular index reflects the change in the average value of the stocks included in that index. The number of stocks included in a particular index may depend on its objective, and thus, the size varies index to index. For example, the number of stocks included in SENSEX is 30, whereas 500 stocks are covered in Standard and Poor's 500. There are, however, some common features of these stock indices which are as under:

### 8.2.1  Common Features

1. A stock index contains a specific number of stocks, i.e., specification of certain sector number of stocks like 30, 50, 100, 200, 500 and so on.
2. Selection of a base period on which index is based. Starting value of base of index is set to large round like 100, 1,000, etc.
3. The method or rule of selection of a stock for inclusion in the index to determine the value of the index.
4. There are several methods commonly used to combine the prices of individual stock like arithmetic average, weighted average, etc.
5. There are three types of index construction like price weighted index, return equally weighted index and market capitalization weighted index.
6. A stock index represents the change in the value of a set of stocks which constitute the index. Hence, it is a relative value expressed as weighted average of prices at a specific date.

**TABLE 8.1**   Stock Index Futures at NSE

| Instrument Type | Underlying | Expiry Date | Prev. Close | Open Price | High Price | Low Price | Last Price |
|---|---|---|---|---|---|---|---|
| **Nifty 50 Futures** | | | | | | | |
| Index Futures | NIFTY | 28-Jan-16 | 7,433.40 | 7,431.00 | 7,465.00 | 7,411.00 | 7,424.90 |
| Index Futures | NIFTY | 25-Feb-16 | 7,443.30 | 7,436.00 | 7,480.00 | 7,432.70 | 7,452.00 |
| Index Futures | NIFTY | 31-Mar-16 | 7,455.75 | 7,449.45 | 7,492.85 | 7,447.90 | 7,467.40 |
| **Nifty Midcap 50 Futures** | | | | | | | |
| Index Futures | NIFTYMID50 | 28-Jan-16 | 3,389.20 | 3,210.00 | 3,210.00 | 3,100.00 | 3,100.00 |
| Index Futures | NIFTYMID50 | 25-Feb-16 | 3,418.80 | – | – | – | – |
| Index Futures | NIFTYMID50 | 31-Mar-16 | 3,479.00 | – | – | – | – |
| **Nifty Bank Futures** | | | | | | | |
| Index Futures | BANKNIFTY | 28-Jan-16 | 15,518.30 | 15,549.70 | 15,564.90 | 15,355.00 | 15,380.85 |
| Index Futures | BANKNIFTY | 25-Feb-16 | 15,518.10 | 15,519.95 | 15,577.95 | 15,405.00 | 15,470.00 |
| Index Futures | BANKNIFTY | 31-Mar-16 | 15,557.50 | 15,550.70 | 15,609.75 | 15,451.00 | 15,509.00 |
| **Nifty Infra Futures** | | | | | | | |
| Index Futures | NIFTYINFRA | 31-Mar-16 | 2,820.75 | – | – | – | – |
| Index Futures | NIFTYINFRA | 28-Jan-16 | 2,934.60 | – | – | – | – |
| Index Futures | NIFTYINFRA | 25-Feb-16 | 2,799.25 | – | – | – | – |
| **Nifty IT Futures** | | | | | | | |
| Index Futures | NIFTYIT | 28-Jan-16 | 11,018.50 | 11,049.95 | 11,057.90 | 10,976.00 | 10,999.00 |
| Index Futures | NIFTYIT | 25-Feb-16 | 11,070.15 | 11,050.00 | 11,119.95 | 11,024.55 | 11,065.20 |
| Index Futures | NIFTYIT | 31-Mar-16 | 11,421.90 | – | – | – | – |
| **Nifty PSE Futures** | | | | | | | |
| Index Futures | NIFTYPSE | 25-Feb-16 | 3,127.20 | – | – | – | – |
| Index Futures | NIFTYPSE | 28-Jan-16 | 3,114.10 | – | – | – | – |
| Index Futures | NIFTYPSE | 31-Mar-16 | 3,190.05 | – | – | – | – |
| **Global Indices listed at NSE** | | | | | | | |
| **S&P 500 Futures** | | | | | | | |
| Index Futures | S&P500 | 19-Feb-16 | 1,887.00 | 1,885.00 | 1,897.00 | 1,882.25 | 1,892.00 |
| Index Futures | S&P500 | 18-Mar-16 | 1,870.25 | 1,899.75 | 1,899.75 | 1,895.00 | 1,895.00 |
| Index Futures | S&P500 | 13-Apr-16 | 1,957.00 | – | – | – | – |
| **FTSE 100 Futures** | | | | | | | |
| Index Futures | FTSE100 | 19-Feb-16 | 5,735.00 | – | – | – | 5,735.00 |
| Index Futures | FTSE100 | 18-Mar-16 | 7,571.00 | – | – | – | – |
| **DJIA Futures** | | | | | | | |
| Index Futures | DJIA | 19-Feb-16 | 16,022.50 | 15,920.00 | 16,035.00 | 15,895.00 | 15,970.00 |
| Index Futures | DJIA | 18-Mar-16 | 16,077.50 | 16,000.00 | 16,000.00 | 16,000.00 | 16,000.00 |
| Index Futures | DJIA | 17-Jun-16 | 16,385.00 | – | – | – | 16,385.00 |
| Index Futures | DJIA | 16-Sep-16 | 16,702.50 | – | – | – | 16,702.50 |
| Index Futures | DJIA | 13-Apr-16 | 16,677.50 | – | – | – | – |

*Source : www.nseindia.com, figures as on 28jan2016.*

7. The index should represent the market and be able to represent the returns obtained by a typical portfolio of that market.
8. A stock index acts as a barometer for market behaviour, a benchmark for portfolio performance. Further, it also reflects the changing expectations about the market.
9. The index components should be highly liquid, professionally maintained and accurately calculated. In the present section, we will not discuss the mechanism of construction of a stock index. However, it is beneficial to understand thoroughly the details of construction of a stock index, particularly in which the investor is interested to trade. When the differences and inter-relationships among the indexes are understood, it becomes easier to understand the differences among the futures contracts that are based on those indexes.

## 8.3  STOCK INDEX FUTURES

Table 8.1 depicts certain important Stock Index futures, both national and international, traded at NSE of India, for example, Nifty 50 Futures, Nifty MIDCAP 50 Futures, Nifty Bank Futures, Nifty Infra Futures, Nifty IT Futures, Nifty PSE Futures, S&P 500 Futures, FTSE-100 Futures, DJIA Futures, etc. Table further shows, the underlying assets, expiry dates, previous close price, open price, highest price, lowest price, last price relating to these futures. Contract specifications of NSE and BSE have been shown at the end of the chapter.

### 8.3.1  Specification of Stock Index Futures Contracts

All the stock index futures contracts are traded on the specified stock exchanges. For example, Standard and Poor's 500 Futures contract has the following specifications:
Standard and Poor's 500 futures contract specifications:

1. Contract        : Standard and Poor's 500 index
2. Exchange        : Chicago Mercantile Exchange
3. Quantity         : $500 times the S&P 500 index
4. Delivery months     : March, June, September, December
5. Delivery specifications   : Cash settlement according to the value of the index at the opening on the Friday after the last day of trading
6. Minimum price movements : 0.05 index points, or $25 per contract

In India, both the BSE and the NSE have introduced one month contracts on the Sensex and NIFTY, respectively. At any point of time, index futures of different maturities would trade simultaneously on the exchanges. Both BSE and NSE have introduced three contracts on BSE sensitive index for one, two and three months, maturities. Tick size on BSE has proposed of 0.1 index point for trading in Sensex futures. Every index point for trading of Sensex contract is priced at ₹50, 0.1 point would be equivalent to ₹5.00.

The salient features of these contracts have been shown in Table 3.1 of this book. It is being reproduced to further elaborate on stock index futures.

### 8.3.2  Settlement Procedures or Delivery

Stock index futures are nearly always settled for cash delivery, in contrast to most futures contracts where physical delivery of an underlying asset is called for. Thus, in the stock index futures contract, no physical delivery (shares or securities certificates) are delivered by the seller (short). This means that all the futures positions which are open at the close of the final trading day of the futures contract are settled by a cash transfer. This amount is determined by reference to the cash price at the close of trading in the cash market in the last trading day in the futures contract.

Probably the stock index futures were the first to employ cash settlement as a substitute for physical delivery. The reason being that it is very difficult to deliver (for example, the 500 proportions of various stocks in S&P Index 500) all the stocks which is more cumbersome and costly than the cash settlement. Further, if any investor is interested in actual delivery of a stock, he can easily purchase the same from the cash market. Hence, the settlement in futures index contracts is convenient and less costly. Further, the effect of the cash settlement forces the futures prices of stock index futures to be identical to the cash stock index at the settlement.

## 8.3.3    Stock Index Futures Prices

Stock index futures, like most other financial futures, are also traded in a full carry market. It means that cost-of-carry model provides (which we have been already discussed in detail in Chapter 4) a virtually complete understanding of the stock index futures pricing. As per this, futures price must be equal to the spot price plus other cost of carrying charges, and if the conditions of this model are not fulfilled or violated, then arbitrage opportunities will arise. A trader (or investor) would buy the stocks that underlie the futures contract and sell the futures and will carry the same until the futures expiration. When the stocks are priced very low relative to the futures, the cash-and-carry strategy is attractive.

We have already seen in Chapter 4 that the basic cost-of-carry model for a perfect market with unrestricted short selling is as follows:

$$F_{t,T} = S_t(1 + C) \tag{8.1}$$

where $F_{t,T}$ is futures price at $t$ for delivery at futures time $T$, $S_t$ is spot price at time $t$ (today or current) and $C$ is the percentage cost of carrying the asset from $t$ (current) to $T$ (futures).

This model can be applied to the stock index futures contracts with some little modifications.

## 8.3.4    Cost-of-Carry Model for Stock Index

The cost-of-carry model as described in Eq. (8.1) can be easily applied to the commodities and such assets where no futures cash income is available. As we know that nothing is earned on a stock investment unless it appreciates (rise in market value) or gets dividends from the company. In fact, we incur an opportunity cost because we could have earned elsewhere by investing the same amount, say, bank deposits, government securities, etc. In this way, satisfying the margin requirement, the futures trader supposes to earn interest, which is termed as an *opportunity cost*. In case of stock index futures, holding of the stocks gives dividends to the owner, because the companies usually declare the dividends out of their usual profits to the shareholders. However, each of the indexes is simply a price index. The value of any index at any time depends solely on the price of the stocks, not the dividends that the underlying stocks might pay. Since the futures prices are tied or influenced directly to the index values, the futures prices do not include dividends.

Since Eq. (8.1) of futures price does not include dividends, thus, it must be adjusted to include the dividends that would be received between the present and the futures expiration date of the futures contract. The trader will receive dividends from the stock which will reduce the value of the stocks. A major difference lies in the fact that stocks pay dividends, whereas futures contracts do not pay. As per the basic investment principle, on ex-dividend dates, stock prices tend to fall by almost equivalent to the amount of the dividend earned. It means holding stocks, one gets dividends while holding futures, one does not get dividends. This phenomenon shows us a price difference in the futures price and underlying stock price. Thus, the cost of carrying is the financing costs for stocks, less the dividends to be received while the stock is being carried.

**EXAMPLE:**  Let us explain the above concept with an example. Assume that the present time is zero and an investor decides to purchase one share of State Bank of India (SBI) for ₹300, as currently trading in the market. For this he borrows from the market ₹300 to buy this stock. We assume that the SBI will declare after six months 6 percent dividend which will be further invested the proceeds for another six months at the rate of 10 percent. In this transaction, the investor's cash flows is given in Table 8.2.

$$\text{Total profit} = P_1 + 19.80 - 330$$

where $P_1$ is current value of the stock at the expiration.

**TABLE 8.2**  Cash Flows from Carrying Stock

| (i) | Present period (t) | Borrow ₹300 for one year at 10% | +300 |
| | | Buy one share of SBI | −300 |
| (ii) | Between the period (six month) | Received dividends at 6% | +18 |
| | | Invest ₹18 for six month at 10% | −18 |
| (iii) | Expiration period (T) (after one year) | Collect proceeds from dividends | +19.80 |
| | | Sell SBI share for loan payment | +$P_1$ |
| | | Repayment of debt (principle + interest) | −330 |

If the current value of the SBI at expiration is ₹320, then the profit from this transaction to the investor will be ₹9.80 (320 + 19.80 − 330). From the aforementioned example, we can generalize to understand the total cash inflows from a cash-and-carry strategy. The *futures prices* must be equal to the price of the shares underlying stock index plus the cost of carrying the stock minus the futures value of the received dividends. So, in the stock index futures valuation, two considerations are important: *carrying cost* and *dividend* income to be earned on the underlying stocks. Then Eq. (8.1) will be modified as under:

$$F_{t,T} = S_t(1+C) - \sum_{i=1}^{n} D_i(1+r_i) \tag{8.2}$$

or

$$F_{t,T} = S_t\, e^{(r-d)T-t}$$

where $F_{t,T}$ is stock index futures price at time $t$ for a futures contract which expires at time $T$, $S_t$ is the value of the stocks underlying the stock index at time $t$, $C$ is the percentage cost of carrying the stocks from time $t$ to the expiration at time $T$, $D_i$ is the $i$th dividend and $r_i$ is the interest earned on carrying the $i$th dividend from the time of receipt until the futures expiration at time $T$.

From Eq. (8.2), we can observe that the cash-and-carry trading opportunity requires that the futures price must be less than or equal to the cash inflows at the futures expiration. Similarly, on the other hand, in the reverse cash-and-carry trading opportunity requires that the futures price must be equal or more than futures cash inflows at the expiration. Thus, it can be concluded that the futures price of a stock index futures contract must be equal to price of the shares underlying the stock index plus the cost of carrying the stock to the futures expiration, minus the futures value of the dividends the stock will pay before expiration. Equation (8.2) is also known at no-arbitrage equation and such trading strategies are also called *index arbitrage*.

## 8.3.5   Theoretical Value or Fair Value for Stock Index Futures

A stock index futures price has its fair value when the entire cost of buying the stock and carrying them to expiration is covered, i.e., the purchase price of the stocks plus interest, less the futures value of the dividends. Thus, in the cost-of-carry model the futures price must equal this entire cost-of-carry.

**EXAMPLE:**   Calculation of fair or theoretical (or no arbitrage) price. Assume on August 1, 2015, BSE Sensex Index is 27,000. What is theoretical price on that date for December, 2015 Sensex Index futures contract, which matures on December, 2015? Further assume, the borrowing cost for short period is 10 percent and expected dividend (return) available annualized is 4 percent based on historical yields.

Carrying period = 44 days from November 1, 2015 to December 15, 2015

$$\text{Fair value} = F_{t,T} = S_t(1+C) - \sum_{i=1}^{n} D_i(1+r_i)$$

OR

$$F_{t,T} = S_t + S_t(C_i - D_t)\frac{T-t}{365}$$

$$= 27,000 + 27,000(0.10 - 0.04)\frac{44}{365}$$

$$= 27,000 + 195.28 = 27,195.28$$

The example observed how to calculate the futures theoretical value BSE index (sensitive) using actual cash index actual and the actual borrowing and dividend rates. In this case, the theoretical BSE index value is 27,195.28, which is greater than the cash index value of 27,000 by 195.98 points because the borrowing (financing cost) rate is higher than the dividend yield. The theoretical value of the futures contract, therefore, is (₹200 × 27,195.28) = ₹5,43,905.60, assuming lot size of 200 of Sensex Index.

Further, if index futures for the above period from now are trading at a level above 27,195.28, the investor can buy index and simultaneously sell index futures to lock in the gain equivalent to the futures price-fair price. However, it should be noted that the cost of transportation, taxes, margins, etc. are not taken into consideration while calculating the fair value. Similarly, if index is at a level below the fair value, it will trigger severe arbitrage. This arbitrage between the cash and the futures market will continue till the prices between both markets get aligned.

It should also be further noted that the cost-and-carry model gives an approximate index about the true futures price (theoretical value). But in the market, the observed price is an outcome of price discovery mechanism through the forces of demand supply and others. These forces may change from time to time resulting in the difference between the fair price and actual price of the index futures, and thus, leads to arbitrage opportunities in the market. However, market forces of arbitrageurs will quickly restore parity when the variation becomes wide.

Earlier we have observed the calculation of the theoretical value of stock index futures contract, and then, the arbitrage opportunities available on such contracts. Stock arbitrage, in reality, may not be as easy and cost-less as explained earlier. There are several reasons observed for the difference between the actual and theoretical futures prices. A few important explanations for the observed differences are stated below in brief.

1. We may make an error in estimating theoretical futures values due to assumed variables like dividend yield, interest rate, etc. Further, the cash index value may have been either wrong or not up-to-date.
2. Trading in the stock markets incurs transaction costs. This involves commission to the brokers, execution costs and others. These costs result in the different valuation of futures prices, whereas cash prices do not usually based on these.
3. The asset underlying a stock index futures contract is in reality more concept than an asset. In other words, it is difficult to buy the large number of securities needed in the proportions required to duplicate exactly a stock index futures.

4. The reported value of the cash stock index may almost be correct due to 'sale' price quotations. Index quotations are based on the last sale prices of the shares included in that index, which sometimes may not be the current quotes.

5. All proceeds from the short sales are usually not available to potential arbitrageurs, as normally, observed in the case of small or retail investors.

6. Sometimes, it is also difficult to borrow the required stock to short an entire cash portfolio.

7. Finally, it is evident that the theoretical values are calculated on the assumption of constant dividend yield over the holding period, which sometimes in reality may not be true. The actual dividend yield usually vary, and further, there is a seasonality in dividends too.

Besides the observed relationship of differences between the actual and theoretical values of stock index futures, there are also consistency found between these, but within the transaction costs bounds. The difference exceeds two index points on only three days. However, it has been noted that the stock index arbitrage has been highly successful in maintaining the theoretical relationship between cash and futures stock index prices.

**EXAMPLE:**  Let us consider a value weighted index of three stock X,Y,Z. Assume, today October 19, 2015, at time '0', their prices, share outstanding and market value are as follows:

| Stock | Price | (₹) | No. of shares (outstanding) | Market Value (₹) | Composition of Market Share |
|-------|-------|-----|------------------------------|-------------------|------------------------------|
| 1. | X | 80 | 2,500 | 2,00,000 | .20 |
| 2. | Y | 60 | 5,000 | 3,00,000 | .30 |
| 3. | Z | 50 | 10,000 | 5,00,000 | .50 |
| | | | 17,500 | 10,00,000 | |

Further Assume that the present price of spot index is 1,000 and the multiplier of the index is 200. The total value of the (St) Spot index is $200 \times 1,000 = ₹2,00,000$. Considering it, the contribution of the number of shares of each stock would be as follows:

| Value of Stock in the Index (₹) | Price (₹) | No. of shares (in the Index) | Value (₹) |
|----------------------------------|-----------|-------------------------------|-----------|
| (.20) (2,00,000) | 80 | 500 | 40,000 |
| (.30) (2,00,000) | 60 | 1,000 | 60,000 |
| (.50) (2,00,000) | 50 | 2,000 | 1,00,000 |
| | | | 2,00,000 |

In addition, suppose that stock 'X' is trading ex-dividend in the market and the rate of dividend is ₹1.0 per share 20 days from today. Stock 'Y' will trade ex-dividend in the amount of ₹0.80 per share 30 days from today. Assume that stock Z pays no dividend and dividend will be paid on the ex-dates. Risk-free return is 6 percent per year. Calculate the theoretical futures value of the contract expires on December 31, 2015.

*Solution:*  No. of days in futures contract from October 19, 2015 to December 31, 2015 = 73 days

Return on the Index = $F_{t,T}(0,73) = \dfrac{rt}{365} = \dfrac{(0.06)\,(73)}{365} = 1.20\%$

Dividend on stock X is received 20 days, and can be invested

for 53 days, the return will be: $r(20,73) = \dfrac{(0.06)\,(53)}{365} = 0.0087 = 0.87\%$

Dividend from stock 'Y' can be invested

for 43 days, and the return will be: $r(30,43) = \dfrac{(0.06)\,(43)}{365} = 0.0071 = 0.71\%$

Ignoring transaction cost the theoretical futures price for the index is:

Theoretical Futures Price of the Index:

$$F_{t,T} = [S_t\,(1 + C) - \sum_{t=1}^{n} D_t\,(1 + ri)] / \text{multiplier of Index}$$

Dividend on Stock X = ₹1 per share will be $500 \times 1 = ₹500$

Dividend on Stock Y = ₹0.80 per share will be $1,000 \times 0.80 = ₹800$

$$= 2,00,000\,(1 + .0120) - \sum_{t=1}^{2} (500)\,(1.0087) + (800)\,(1.0071) / 200$$

$$= 2,02,400 - [504 - 35 + 805.68] / 200$$

$$= 2,02,400 - [1,310.03] / 200$$

$$= 2,01,089.97 / 200$$

$$= 1,005.4499$$

$$= 1,005.45$$

It is concluded from the above that the Index theoretical futures price on December 31, 2015 would be 1,005.45. So, if in the market observed or prevailing futures price of the Index exceeds 1,005.45, then the traders will buy the stock and short the futures contract. Similarly, if the observed futures price of the index is less than the theoretical price i.e., 1,005.45, then they will buy the futures contract and short the stocks in the market. In other words, in this situation, they will sell the stock and invest the sale proceeds, for purchasing the futures contract.

## 8.3.6   Fair Futures Prices and No-arbitrage Bands

As already observed, the fair futures price is based upon arbitrage, and in case of stock index futures, it would be cash-and-carry arbitrage. It means that the futures price should be such that there is no arbitrage profit from buying stock (with borrowed money) and simultaneously selling futures. However, an arbitrageur's net gain will occur only if it covers the transaction costs too. The actual futures price can deviate from the fair arbitrage pressure that tends to prevent deviations of actual futures prices within a range (the no-arbitrage band) rather than equality with the theoretical prices. In other words, transaction costs may lead to fair prices to be in band and arbitrage occurs only when the actual futures price moves outside the no-arbitrage band. This we will see in the following example:

**EXAMPLE 1:**   Assume that the current price of a stock Index is ₹3,000. The three-month interest rate is 10 percent per annum, and the expected rate of dividend yield over the next three months is 6 percent per annum. Calculate the theoretical future price, for a futures contract maturing in three months' time. Further, determine an arbitrage profit be made if the actual futures price were (a) ₹3,050, (b) ₹3,000 and there were no transactions costs. Also, examine if the total transactions costs (Commissions, bid-offer spreads, stamp duty, etc.) amounted to ₹1,000 per ₹1,50,000 (₹50 × 3,000) of one futures contract of stock, would arbitrage profits still be available?

*Solution:*   Fair value $F_{t,T} = S_t + S_t(C_t - D_t)\dfrac{T - t}{365}$

The fair futures price will be $= ₹3,000 + ₹3,000\,(0.10 - 0.06)3/12$

$$= ₹3,000 + ₹30 = ₹3,030$$

(a) If the actual futures price were ₹3,050, then the futures would be over-valued in the absence of transactions costs. Thus, a profit is available from a long cash-and-carry arbitrage which provides buying stock and selling futures. It means there will be guaranteed profit from the stock and futures of 50 index points (amounting to ₹50 × 50 = ₹2,500 per ₹1,50,000 of stock and one futures contract). The corresponding cost-of-carry is 30 index points (30 × ₹50 = ₹1,500). So there is a net profit of 20 index points, i.e., ₹1,000 (20 × ₹50) in this contract.

(b) If the actual futures price were ₹3,000, the futures would be undervalued, so the stock should be sold and futures be purchased (short cash and carry). In this contract, there is neither profit nor loss from the stock and futures position because net cost-of-carry accrues (30 × ₹50 = ₹1,500) as profit and is 30 index points (30 × ₹50 = ₹1,500).

If the total transactions costs were ₹1,000, there would be no net profit remaining in case (a) and only (₹1,500 – ₹1,000) = ₹500 in case of (b).

The futures price has to be divided by 20 index points from its fair value before any arbitrage profits become available. Thus, in the present case, there will be a no-arbitrage band of 20 points either side of the fair futures price, i.e., ₹3,010 – ₹3,050. Futures prices within this band do not induce arbitrage since they offer no arbitrage profit.

It should be noted that in the absence of transactions costs, cash-and-carry arbitrage would keep the actual futures price equals to the fair price because undervalued futures would be bought and overvalued futures would be sold by the arbitrageurs, hence, pushing the price up and downs. Further, in the absence of the transaction costs, the cash-and-carry arbitrage merely keeps the futures price within the no-arbitrage band, and there will be no further buying or selling by the arbitrageurs. But if the futures price falls below the bottom of the no-arbitrage band, arbitrageurs would purchase futures until the futures price reaches the bottom of the band, at which point arbitrage would stop, and vice versa. Once the futures price is within the band, arbitrage opportunities would cease.

As noted above, the arbitrage process will continue until the actual futures prices reach the theoretical futures price lend. But in the stock market, this opportunity may not last long. It may vanish in a few seconds because prices are changing randomly in the market. However, there are certain prerequisites for ideal arbitrage opportunity for futures contracts in the market, such as high liquidity equity in the futures market, low transaction cost, low interest rate, minimum margin requirement, mispricing of stocks, etc. However, in actual practice, these are rare and different from market to market. A few important limitations in the risk-free arbitrage opportunity are discussed.

### Limitations of stock index futures arbitrage

- The transaction cost in stock market operations, as assumed to be nil or minimum, is not practically correct. Further, these costs vary from market to market and as per status of investors.
- The interests rates both borrowing and lending, in the financial markets are not same, and vary in the different markets.
- Annual dividends as assumed to be constant is not feasible. As observed, dividends tend to vary quarter after quarter. Further, there is increased risk of unexpected changes in dividends yields because stable dividend policy is followed by a few companies.
- Market inefficiency is another important limitation of this mechanism. Inefficiency leads to super or lower profits and too much variations in the stock prices.
- Arbitrage opportunity, as observed, usually lasts for a few second, thus, the arbitrageur requires a latest telecommunication network system so that this opportunity can be exploited. However, it is difficult for retail investors in comparison to institutional investors.
- Another limitation of this opportunity is a tracking error. Sometimes, the arbitrageur cannot match composition of his portfolio with the stock index underlying the futures, then there can be potential tracking error.

Besides the limitations stated in the arbitrage opportunity, some experts are of the view that instead of fair or theoretical price, fair range of prices that lie in a window about the value of underlying stock index be considered.

## 8.4  STOCK INDEX FUTURES AS A PORTFOLIO MANAGEMENT TOOL

Funds managers or money managers use stock index futures basically for three purposes; hedging, asset allocation and yield enhancement. These are discussed here in this section.

### 8.4.1   Stock Index Futures as a Hedging Tool

First of all, we should know who need the stock index futures for using them as a hedging tool. All such investors, specifically managing a huge pool of funds or public funds like pension funds, mutual funds, life insurance companies, investment and finance companies, banks, endowment funds, public provident funds, etc. would like to reduce their fund's exposure to a fall in stock values caused due to uncertainties about futures market developments. This can be done by selling the shares and repurchasing them at a later time, but this strategy is not so appropriate because it would incur substantial transaction costs. As a result, the funds managers prefer to hedge with stock index futures instead of altering their portfolio structure, directly and repeatedly. Hedging is also done through stock index options but this will be discussed in other chapter concerning to the 'options'.

Before proceeding to the discussion regarding hedging, one needs to understand some background on risks relating to stock investments and portfolio management. There are two types of risks associated with holding a security:

1. Systematic risk
2. Unsystematic risk

All the stocks are exposed to such factors which are not controlled by the firm itself, these are called *market risk factors* like changes in the interest rates, inflation rates, government trade policies, economic activities, political factors, changes in tax laws and so on. Such risk is termed as *market risk* or *systematic risk*. On the other hand, unsystematic or firm specific risk is related to the particular firm or an industry. This risk can be diversified by having diversified portfolio of many shares. Market risk cannot be eliminated by diversification since each of the stock moves with the market to some degree. Thus, stock index futures can be used to hedge or manage this risk.

**Measuring market risk:**    Beta is a measure of the systematic risk. It measures the sensitivity of the scrip (asset) vis-à-vis index movements. Beta ($\beta$) is defined as the *Covariance* (Cov.) between a stock's return and the return on the overall market divided by the variance (var) of return on the market. The formula of a beta ($\beta$) of a security ($i$) is as under:

$$\beta_i = \frac{\text{Cov}(R_i, R_m)}{\text{Var}(R_m)} \qquad (8.3)$$

where $R_m$ is the return on market portfolio (or market return) and $R_i$ is the return on the security ($i$).

Stock betas can be estimated with the regression equation (also called linear regression line) as follows:

$$R_{i,t} = a + b \times R_{m,t} + -e_{i,t}$$

where $R_{i,t}$ is the observed returns over a period $t$ for stock $i$, $a$ is the constant return, $b$ is the estimate of the beta of stocks, $e_{i,t}$ is the usual error term and $R_m$ is the return on market portfolio (or market return).

In brief, from Eq. (8.3), it is observed that the estimate of a stock's beta shows the value of that stock is likely to change relative to change in the value of the market portfolio (or a particular stock index). It also shows the stock's relative volatility. A portfolio of stocks has its own beta. Individual betas are used to calculate the portfolio beta. It is weighted average of the betas of the individual scrips in the portfolio where weights are based on the proportion of investment of scrips in the portfolio. If the value of a beta is more than one, the stock is more volatile than the market, and if beta is less than one, then stock will be less volatile than the market. Further detail on this model can be studied from the CAPM and Sharpe Single Index Model.

**The minimum-variance hedge ratio:**     As discussed in the preceding chapter, hedging that the hedger is to determine the appropriate hedge ratio (HR)—which is the ratio of the futures position to the cash position being hedged. We have seen that a benchmark ratio is the minimum-variance hedge ratio (HR) or the value of HR that can be expected to reduce the fluctuations in the total portfolio to the minimum possible. In this section, we will discuss the determination of HR in the context of the 'stock index futures contracts'.

$$HR = \frac{\text{Value of hedged portfolio}}{\text{Price of the futures contract}} \times B_i \qquad (8.4)$$

or
$$HR = \frac{\text{\% change in weighted average portfolio price}}{\text{\% change of future index}}$$

**EXAMPLE:**

Value of a stock Index = 3,000
Value of portfolio = 6,08,000
Risk-free interest rate = 10 percent per annum
Dividend yield on index = 6 percent per annum
Beta of the portfolio = 1.5

We assume that a futures contract on the stock Index with four months to maturity is used to hedge the value of the portfolio over the next three months. Our futures contract is for delivery of ₹50 times the index. Calculate the HR from the above information also calculate the gain on short futures position if index turns out to be 2,700 in three months.

*Solution:*   Current futures price of the index:

$$F_{t,T} = S_t + S_t (C_t - d_t) \frac{T-t}{365}$$

$$= 3{,}000 + ₹3{,}000 \ (0.10 - 0.06) \ 4/12$$

$$= ₹3{,}000 + ₹40 = ₹3{,}040$$

Price of the futures contract = ₹50 × 3,040 = ₹1,52,000

Using Eq. (8.4) the HR or number of the futures contracts that should be shorted to hedge the portfolio is:

$$HR = \frac{6{,}08{,}000}{1{,}52{,}000} \times 1.5 = 6$$

Suppose the index turns out to be 2,700 in three months. The futures price will be

$$= 2{,}700 + 2{,}700 \ (0.10 - 0.06) \ 1/3$$

$$= 2{,}700 + 36 = 2{,}736$$

The gain from the short futures position is, therefore,

$$6 \times (3{,}040 - 2{,}736) \times 50 = ₹91{,}200$$

In the example, the loss on index is 10 percent. The index pays a dividend of 6 percent per annum or 1.5 percent per three months. When dividend are taken into account, an investor in the index would cash. Therefore, earn 9 percent in the three-month period. The risk free interest is approximately 2.5 percent per three months. Since the portfolio has a $\beta$ of 1.5, expected return of portfolio will be equal to:

$$= \beta \times (\text{Return on portfolio} - \text{Risk-free interest rate})$$

$$= 1.5 \times (\text{Return on index} - \text{Risk-free interest rate})$$

Using the formula, the expected return on the portfolio is:

$$= 2.5 + [1.5 \times (9.0 - 2.5)]$$

$$= 2.5 + (-17.25) = 14.75\%$$

The expected value of the portfolio (inclusive of dividends) at the end of the three months is, therefore,

$$₹ \ 6,08,000 \times (1 - 0.1475) = ₹5,18,320$$

It follows that the expected value of the hedger's position including the gain on the hedge is:

$$₹5,18,320 + ₹91,200 = ₹6,09,520$$

**Changing beta:** Sometimes, the stock index futures contracts are used to change the beta of a portfolio to some value other than zero. For example, we want to reduce to beta of the portfolio from 1.5 to 0.75, then in that situation, the number of the contracts would be changed, and now they will be 3 instead of 6. In general, to change the beta of the portfolio from $\beta$ to $\beta^*$ where $\beta > \beta^*$, a short position is

$$(\beta - \beta^*) \left[ \frac{\text{Value of hedged portfolio}}{\text{Price of the futures contract}} \right]$$

**Rolling the hedged forward:** Sometimes, it happens that the expiration date of the hedge is later than the delivery dates of all the futures contracts that can be used. In this situation, the hedger must then roll the hedge forward. In other words, it means that closing out one futures contract and taking the same position in a futures contract with a later delivery date. Hence, the hedge can be rolled forward many times. Consider a company which intends to use a short hedge to reduce the risk associated with the price to be received for an asset at time $T$. Assume, if there are futures contracts 1, 2, 3, ..., $n$ (not all necessary in existence at the present time), the company can use the following strategy:

Time $t_1$ = Short futures contract 1

Time $t_2$ = Close out futures contract 1

= Short futures contract 2

Time $t_3$ = Close out futures contract 2

= Short futures contract 3

Time $T_n$ = Close out futures contract $(n - 1)$

= Short futures contract $n$

Time $T$ = Close out futures contract $n$

Let us explain this by a hypothetical example:

**EXAMPLE:** Suppose in April 2015 a company realize that it will have 1,00,000 barrels of oil to sell in June 2015 and it decides to hedge its risk with a hedge ratio of 1.0. The current spot price is $19. Futures contracts are traded for every month of the year up to one year in future, we suppose that only the first six delivery months have sufficient liquidity to meet the company's needs. Company, therefore, shorts 100 October 2015 contracts. In September, it rolls the hedge forward into March 2015 contract. In February 2015, it rolls the hedge forward again into the July 2015 contract. The contract size is 1,000 barrels.

Company uses the following strategy to hedge the risk:

| April 2015 | : | The company shorts 100 October 2015 contracts. |
|---|---|---|
| September 2015 | : | The company closes out the 100 October 2015 contracts. |
| | | The company shorts 100 March 2016 contracts. |
| February 2016 | : | The company closes out 100 March 2016 contracts. |
| | | The company shorts 100 July 2016 contracts. |
| July 2016 | : | The company closes out the 100 July 2016 contracts. |
| | | The company sells 1,00,000 barrels of oil. |

It is evident from the above that when there is no liquid and futures contract which matures later than the expiration of the hedge, a strategy known as *rolling the hedge forward* may be followed. This involves entering into a sequence of futures contracts as shown above. Rolling the hedge will be appropriate if there is a close correlation between changes in the futures prices and the changes in the spot prices.

## 8.4.2 Asset Allocation by the Funds Managers

The term asset allocation refers to the distribution of portfolio assets among equity shares, bonds, debentures and other money market instruments. It means that how to divide funds among broad asset classes like 60 percent in equities and 40 percent in treasury bills is an asset allocation decision. Usually it does include changing of the assets from one equity to other equity asset rather concentrates on asset allocation from equity to debt or treasury bills and vice versa. Further, asset allocation focuses on the macro level commitment of funds to various asset classes and the shifting of funds among these major asset classes.

It is often preferable to use stock index futures to change the portfolio mix, even though portfolio managers structure and restructure their portfolio by buying and selling the different assets using futures because it is cheaper. It has been noted that equity stock index and interest rate futures trading cost are less in comparison to the direct trading in stocks.

Let us see this with an example given in Table 8.3.

**TABLE 8.3** Transaction Costs Associated with Stock Versus Stock Futures Index

| Particulars | Stocks | Stock index futures |
|---|---|---|
| Average price per share/contract | $60 | $35 |
| Number of shares/units | 2,933* | 500 |
| Market value of portfolio/contract | $1,76,000 | $1,76,000 |
| Round-trip commission per share/contract | $0.07** | $15 |
| Commission cost | $205.31 | $15 |
| Bid/ask spread costs | 0.125 index points/share $2,933 \times 0.125 = 366.33$ | 0.05 index point or I tick per contract $500 \times 0.05 = \$25$ |
| Total transaction cost commission plus bid/ask spread | $571.94 | $40 |

\* The precise number of shares that would equal in portfolio of stock with the average stock price to the value of one futures contract is 2,933.333 ($1,76,000/$60).
\*\* Commission that would be paid by large investment investors.

### 8.4.3 Yield Enhancement

Yield enhancement refers to the portfolio strategies of holding a 'synthetic' stock index fund that is capable of earning higher return than a cash stock index fund. A portfolio consisting of a long position in stock index futures and treasury bills will produce the same return (with the same risk) structured as stock portfolio to mirror the stock index underlying the futures. However, a portfolio of stock index futures and treasury bills (synthetic stock) can be constructed to outperform the corresponding stock portfolio (higher return with the similar risk), if stock index futures are correctly priced or their actual value is higher or lower than their theoretical (fair) value. In this way, with the use of stock index futures, a yield enhancement strategy be followed to enhance the return on a portfolio.

## 8.5 SPECULATION AND STOCK INDEX FUTURES

After discussing the case of arbitrage and hedging, let us now consider the speculating with stock index futures. As we know that basic objective of the speculators is to earn super profit by going either bullish or bearish in the market. Index futures permits them an ideal instrument where the vagaries of individual stocks, settlement cycles, etc. do not have so much of an impact as they do on specific stock. The speculators can select a strategy where they can have a bullish view and go long on futures. Similarly, they can have a bearish view and go short in futures.

Earlier, before the stock index futures came into existence, the speculators had two alternatives. Firstly, they can select the liquid stocks which would move with the index so that they can take a position in them for the expected move. But this move would be too risky. Secondly, they can select the entire stocks as in the index and trade in all of them. The basic of liquid stocks may mimic the index to some extent but still individual stock variations will affect the returns, and moreover, it is too costly with high amount of commission, etc. But now with the introduction of stock index futures, such limitations mentioned are taken care of. Now, the speculators can take up either long position on the contract, paying a small margin, and seek to ride the expected trend and vice-versa for the bearish view-sell short index contract and cover when the index falls lower.

## 8.6 STOCK INDEX FUTURES TRADING IN INDIAN STOCK MARKET

As discussed in Chapter 5, SEBI Board accepted the recommendations of Dr. L.C. Gupta Committee on May 11, 1998 and approved introduction of derivatives trading in India in the phased manner. The recommendation sequence was stock index futures, index options and options on stocks. The Board also approved the suggestive bye-laws recommended by the Committee for regulation and control of derivatives trading in India. As a result, both the stock exchanges, National Stock Exchange of India (NSE) and Bombay Stock Exchange of India (BSE) took the initiative to introduce futures trading in India. The brief particulars of their products are given here as under.

### 8.6.1 Concept of Synthetic Index Portfolio

The concept of synthetic index portfolio is very much important specifically for institutional investors like mutual funds, insurance companies, pension funds, financial institutions, etc. They can replicate their diversified portfolio of equity shares by simply buying a long position in the stock index futures and simultaneously creating long position with treasury bills, it is also called margining. This is also frequently termed as a long synthetic stock position. This will be cheaper than actual buying the shares from the market.

For example, consider that an investor owns ₹19,20,000 (One year) Treasury bills which will be worth ₹20,00,000 after one year. Assume that he has two options, firstly he can liquidate his T-bills and invest the whole amount into stocks. Second, since he already owns the T-bills, he has the opportunity to buy synthetic stock position, just by taking a long position in stock index futures with an equal amount of T-bills investment, i.e., ₹19,20,000, based on spot index. Assume that spot index price at present is ₹1,000, futures prices is ₹1,100 and the multiplier is 200. So, total futures contracts, i.e., [₹19,20,000/(1,000 × 200)] = 9.6 could be purchased from this investment. Of course, the transaction costs would be much lesser in second option in comparison to first option.

After one year, let us assume that ST = Ft = ₹1200 price of the index. The value of the portfolio would be (a) ₹20,00,000 in maturing of treasury bills and (b) profit from the stock index futures contract, i.e., (100 × 200 × 96) would be ₹1,92,000. Thus, total value of synthetic stock portfolio (or index portfolio), i.e., long treasury bills and long stock index futures contracts is (₹20,00,000 + ₹1,92,000) = ₹21,92,000 incurring 14.17 percent gain excluding the transaction costs.

Similarly, an investor can create a position of synthetic Treasury bill in which he buys the stocks and simultaneously selling a futures contract (ignoring the effects of daily settlement on futures contracts). It is just like the purchase of spot treasury bills, a riskless lending position. It is known as *synthetic T-bill*. In other words, it is created by buying the spot assets and selling futures contracts on that asset. It is to be noted that when observed prices are higher than the theoretical futures prices the investor can borrow at a rate lower than the synthetic lending rate. The investor should be very cautious while using the said synthetic positions.

**Synthetic Index Portfolio**

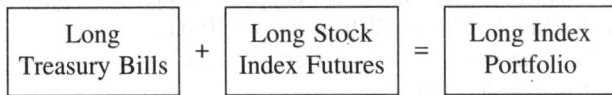

| Long Treasury Bills | + | Long Stock Index Futures | = | Long Index Portfolio |

## 8.7  PROGRAM TRADING

This is a new technique of trading in stock market launched after the crash of the stock market in 1987. The first stock exchange 'NYSE' started it. According to it, the program trading is defined as "a wide range of portfolio trading strategies involving the purchase or sale of a basket of 15 stocks or more, and valued at more than $1 million". Various strategies like stock index arbitrage, option replication strategy, asset allocation shifts, etc. are involved in this. The brokers are very active in this program who often offer to their institutional clients who can trade large portfolio stocks at low cost and low price impact.

Program trading is the computerized submission of multiple trades at the NYSE via the Super Dot System which was launched in 1984. Under this, any market order less than 2,100 shares of a stock will be executed within 3 minutes at the prevailing market price at the time the order entered. Currently this time is taken just 22 seconds to execute orders. In the practice, the programs like "buy programs" and "sell programs" are popular. When the futures contracts are cheap (F < S + CC – CR), the "sell programs" are used. Similarly, if the futures contracts are costlier (F > S + CC – CR), then the "buy programs" are practiced in the market.

## 8.8 NSE'S N FUTIDX NIFTY (NIFTY)

The National Stock Exchange of India introduced futures named 'NIFTY' on June 12, 2000. The salient features of this instrument are:

1. Name of the instrument is N FUTIDX NIFTY.
2. The underlying index S&P CNX NIFTY (NSE 500).
3. *Contract size.* The index futures will be quoted as per the underlying asset which means that it will quote just like the Nifty in points. The value of the contract (contract size), a multiplier of 200 is applied to the index. It means that the value of a contract will be (₹200 × index value) on that particular date. The multiplier can be thought of as the market lot for the futures contract. This can be changed from time to time.
4. NSE has introduced three contracts for one month, two months and three months maturities. These contracts of different maturities may be called near month (one month), middle month (two months) and far month (three months) contracts. The month in which the contract will expire is called *the contract month*, for example, contract month of April 2003 contract will be April, 2003.
5. *Expiry.* Each contract would have a specific code for representation purpose on the system. All these contracts will expire on a specific day of the month and currently they are fixed for the last Thursday of the month. As soon as the near month contract expires, middle contract will become near and so on.
6. *Tick size/price step.* Tick size is the minimum difference between two quotes of similar nature. Since the index futures would be traded in terms of index points, the tick size is to be defined in points only. The Nifty tick size is ₹0.05 which will be converted into points.
7. *Position limits.* Present, both types of contracts as for speculation and hedging purposes are allowed to be traded. However, these are subject to change from time to time.
8. *Trading hours.* Trading hours are 10.30 a.m. to 3.30 p.m.
9. *Margins.* NSE fixes the minimum margin requirements and price limits on daily basis which are subject to change periodically.
10. *Settlement.* Position remaining open at the close of business on the last day of trading are marked-to-market according to the official opening level of the NSE-NIFTY on the following day. There is daily settlement also on the closing of futures contract.
11. *Volumes and open interest.* Futures contracts have a unique way of reporting volumes which is called *open interest*. It provides the information about the number of outstanding/unsettled positions in the market as a whole at a specific point of time. In the futures market, total long positions would be equal to the total short positions, hence, only one side of the contracts are counted for determining the open interest position. Major stock exchanges of the world publish the open interest position regularly.

## 8.9 BSE'S BSX

The Bombay Stock Exchange introduced stock index futures trading on June 9, 2000 with the name of the instrument as BSX with the underlying BSE Sensitive Index (SENSEX). The features regarding its trading are more or less same with the NSE's NIFTY index futures. A few important features are given in brief here follows:

1. Date of start          June 9, 2000
2. Security name          BSX
3. Underlying security    BSE Sensitive Index (SENSEX)
4. Contract size          Sensex value × 50
5. Tick size              0.1 point of Sensex (equivalent to ₹5)
6. Minimum price fluctuation ₹5
7. Price band             Not applicable
8. Expiration months      Three months
9. Trading cycle          A maximum of three months, the near month, next month and far month.
10. Last trading day/Expiry day   Last Thursday of the month or the preceding trading day.
11. Settlement            In cash on $T + 1$ basis.
12. Final settlement      Index closing price on the last trading days
13. Daily settlement price   Closing of futures contract price
14. Trading hours         9.30 a.m. to 3.30 p.m.
15. Margin                Up front margin on daily basis

## SUMMARY

This chapter on stock index futures has highlighted in general the concept of stock index futures. A stock index or stock market index is a portfolio consisting of a collection of different stocks. In other words, a stock index is just like a portfolio of different securities proportion traded on a particular stock exchange like NIFTY S&P CNX traded on NSE. The S&P 500 index traded on NYSE, New York, etc. A stock index represents the change in the value of set of stocks which constitutes the index.

A stock index futures contract in simple terms is futures contract to buy or sell the face value of a stock index. The most actively traded index is the American Standard & Poor's 500 index, FTSE100, Dow & Jones 30 Index. Further, various specifications of stock index futures contracts which includes contract specification, exchange, quantity, delivery months, delivery specifications and minimum price movements have been stated.

In Section 8.3.2, the chapter explains the settlement procedure or delivery mechanism of stock index futures. Stock index futures are normally settled for cash delivery in contrast to most futures contracts where physical delivery of an underlying asset is called for. Then, in stock index futures contract, no physical delivery (shares or securities certificates) are delivered by the seller.

The chapter also explains the pricing of stock index futures which also like other most financial futures trade in full carry market. It means that cost-of-carry model provides virtually complete understanding of the stock index futures pricing. As per this, futures price must be equal to the spot price plus other of carrying charges, and if the conditions of this model are not fulfilled, then arbitrage opportunities will arise. A trader or investor would buy the stocks that underlie the futures contract and sell the futures and will carry the same until the futures expiration. When the stocks are priced very low relative to the futures, the cash- and carry-strategy is attractive. Theoretical value or fair price/value for stock index futures is where the entire cost of buying the stock and carrying them to expiration is covered. It means fair value will be price of the stock plus interest less the futures value of the dividends.

There are various observations between actual and theoretical futures prices of stock index futures which may be due to error in estimating theoretical futures valued with assumed variables, like dividend yield, interest rate, etc. Further cash index value may have been either wrong or not up-to-date. Second is that trading in the stock markets incurs transaction cost. This involves commission to the brokers, execution costs and others.

The chapter further discusses the fair or theoretical price and no-arbitrage bands. The futures price should be such that there is no arbitrage profit from buying stock and simultaneously selling futures. However, an arbitrager's net gain will occur only if it covers the transaction costs too. The actual futures price can deviate from the fair arbitrage pressure that tends to prevent deviations of actual futures prices within a range, rather than ensuring equality with the theoretical price.

Stock index futures can be used as a portfolio management tool by the funds managers or the money managers basically for three purposes: (i) hedging (ii) asset allocation, and (iii) for yield enhancement. Stock index as hedging tool can be used by fund managers, who has a pool of public funds, such as pension funds, mutual funds, insurance companies, investment and finance companies to reduce their funds exposure to a fall in stock values caused due to uncertainties about future market developments. This can be done by selling the shares and repurchasing them at a later time. Before taking a position, one needs to understand the types of risk associated with holding a security, namely, systematic risk and unsystematic risk.

The chapter further discusses about the speculation and stock index futures. The basic objective of speculators is to earn super profit by going bullish or bearish in the market. Index futures permit them an ideal instrument where the vagaries of individual stocks and settlement as they do on specific stock. The speculators select a strategy where they can have a bullish view and go long on futures. Similarly, they can have a bearish view and go short on futures.

Stock index futures trading in Indian stock market started on BSE (Index) at Bombay Stock Exchange and NSE (National Stock Exchange) with their various specifications like expiry date, price stop, position limits, trading hours and so on.

## SOLVED PROBLEMS

**P.1.**   An investor has a portfolio consisting of shares given as follows:

|  | No. of shares | Share price (£) | Share beta (β) |
|---|---|---|---|
| Bank of conventry | 20,000 | 350 | 0.9 |
| Conventry motors | 30,000 | 100 | 1.5 |
| Numeration manufacturing | 10,000 | 500 | 1.3 |
| Cheylesmore stores | 20,000 | 300 | 0.8 |

On 15 March and April FTSE futures price is 3,000.
   (a) How can an investor hedge the portfolio with futures?
   (b) What factors might reduce the effectiveness of the measures taken in (a)?

***Solution:***    (a) Calculation of market exposure of portfolio:

| No. of shares | Share price (£) | Share beta (β) Market exposure (£) |
|---|---|---|
| 20,000 × 350 P × | 0.9 = | 6.3 million |
| 30,000 × 100 P × | 1.5 = | 4.5 million |
| 10,000 × 500 P × | 1.3 = | 6.5 million |
| 20,000 × 300 P × | 0.8 = | 4.8 million |
| Total market exposure | = | £22.1 million |

The market exposure provided by one contract (futures) is:

$$3,000 \times £25 = £75,000$$

Hedging the portfolio with futures would be value selling:

$$\frac{£22,10,000}{£75,000} = 2.946 \text{ contracts}$$

Since futures contracts are indivisible, this would indicate three contracts.

(b) Factors that could reduce hedge effectiveness include basis risk, the indivisibility of beta and presence of firm or sector, specific risk (i.e., non-systematic risk).

**P.2.**   A fund manager anticipates the receipt of $1 million on January 10 and intends to use it to buy a balanced portfolio of UK equities. He fears, one month earlier that stock price will rise before the money is received. Current FTSE-100 futures contract is at a price of 2,200. The new FTSE 100 index is at 2,300, show how index futures can be used to hedge the price increase risk?

***Solution:***

| Cash (Spot market) | Futures market |
|---|---|
| **December 10** | **December 10** |
| Anticipates receipt of $1 million on January 10. Current FTSE 100 index is 2,200, fears a rise in the index. | Buy March 18 FTSE futures contract at a price of 2,200. He thereby notionally commits himself to paying $ 9,90,000. (18 × 2,200 × $25) |
| **March 18** | **March 18** |
| The new FTSE 100 index is 2,300. | Close out by selling March 18 FTSE futures contracts at a price of 2,300. He notionally guarantees a receipt of 10,35,000 (18 × 2,300 × $25) upon maturity of the contracts. |
| Requires an additional $45,000 in order to buy the quantity of stock that $1 million would have bought on December 10. | Profit from futures by $45,000 |

**P.3.**   Value of S&P 500 index = 200
        Value of portfolio = $20,40,000
        Risk-free interest rate = 10% p.a.

Dividend yield on S&P 500 = 4% p.a.

Calculate the number of contract (futures) that should be shorted to hedge the portfolio.

**Solution:**    Current futures price of the index is given by.

$$F_{t,T} = S_t + S_t(C_t - d_t)\frac{ft}{365}$$

$$= 200 + 200(0.10 - 0.04) \times \frac{4}{12}$$

$$= 200 + \frac{12}{3} = 200 + 4 = \$204$$

Price of futures contract = 204 × 500 = $1,02,000

$$\text{Hedge ratio} = \frac{\$20,40,000}{\$1,02,000} = 20$$

Thus, the number of contracts to be shorted is 20.

**P.4.**    The FTSE 100 is 3,000. Three-month interest rate is 8% p.a. and expected rate of dividend yield over the next three months is 4% p.a. What is fair futures price for a futures contract maturing in three-month's time?

**Solution:**    Fair futures premium FTSE 100 = 3,000 + 3,000 (0.08 – 0.04) $\frac{3}{12}$ = 3,000 + 30
So, the fair price is 3,000 + 30= 3,030.

**P.5.**    From the following information, calculate the value of a price equally weighted index.

| Stocks | Base period price | Current period price |
|--------|------------------|---------------------|
| HLL | 50 | 70 |
| SBI | 100 | 90 |
| HDFC | 80 | 90 |
| | ₹230 | ₹250 |

The current divisor for these three stocks is 5.

**Solution:** (1) Base period index value = $\frac{230}{5}$ = ₹46

(2) Current period index value = $\frac{250}{5}$ = ₹50

**P.6.**    Determine the value of weighted index for three stocks with following prices and capitalization. The current index divisor is 0.10.

| Stock | Share out standing | Price base period | Current price |
|-------|-------------------|-------------------|---------------|
| HLL | 1,000 | 50 | 70 |
| SBI | 800 | 100 | 90 |
| HDFC | 500 | 80 | 90 |

**Solution:**

| Stock | Share outstanding | Price base period | Capitalization (₹) | Current | Current price |
|-------|-------------------|-------------------|--------------------|---------|----------------|
| HLL | 1,000 | 50 | 50,000 | 70 | 70,000 |
| SBI | 800 | 100 | 80,000 | 90 | 72,000 |
| HDFC | 500 | 80 | 40,000 | 90 | 45,000 |
| | | | 1,70,000 | | 2,17,000 |

Current divisor = 0.10

$$\text{Index} = \left(\frac{1}{\text{Divisor}}\right)\left[\frac{\sum_{i=1}^{N} n_i P_i}{\sum_{i=1}^{N} n_i^b P_i^b}\right]$$

$$= \left(\frac{1}{0.10}\right)\left(\frac{₹2,17,000}{₹1,70,000}\right) = 10 \times 1.276 = 12.76$$

**P.7.** Suppose a return equally-weighted index contains the three stocks and have a previous day value of 270. Compute the index's value today.

| Stock | Previous day's price | Current price |
|-------|----------------------|---------------|
| HLL | 70 | 77 |
| SBI | 90 | 108 |
| HDFC | 90 | 95 |

**Solution:** To calculate the index's value, we have to calculate 1 plus rate of change.

| Stock | Previous day's price | Current price | 1 plus rate of change |
|-------|----------------------|---------------|------------------------|
| HLL | 70 | 77 | 1.10 |
| SBI | 90 | 108 | 1.20 |
| HDFC | 90 | 95 | 1.05 |

$$\text{Average of 1 plus rate of change} = \frac{1.10 + 1.2 + 1.05}{3}$$

$$= \frac{3.35}{3} = 1.1166$$

So,

$$\text{Index} = \text{Index}(-1)\left(\frac{1}{N}\right)\left(\sum_{i=1}^{N}\left[\frac{P_i}{P_i - 1}\right]\right)$$

(−1 refers to the previous day's value.)

$$= 270(1.1166) = 301.50$$

Current index value = 301.50

**P.8.** From the following figure, calculate the hedge ratio, using individual stock betas.

| Stock | Shares price (₹) | Shares outstanding | Value (₹) | Beta | Proportion of portfolio |
|---|---|---|---|---|---|
| Bank of Baroda | 115 | 1,000 | 1,15,000 | 0.95 | 40% |
| ACC | 160 | 2,000 | 3,20,000 | 1.20 | 40% |
| Bata | 40 | 4,000 | 1,60,000 | 1.40 | 10% |
| Ballarpur Industry | 50 | 6,000 | 3,00,000 | 1.30 | 10% |
| Total Value | | | 8,95,000 | | |

**Solution:** Beta of entire portfolio is:

$$= (0.40)(0.95) + (0.40)(1.20) + (0.10)(1.40) + (0.10)(1.3)$$

$$= 0.38 + 0.48 + 0.14 + 0.13 = 1.13$$

Assume, Value of NIFTY 50 index = 5,00,000

So, 
$$\text{Hedge ratio} = \left(\frac{P_c}{P_t}\right)\beta_p$$

where $P_c$ is market value of portfolio (firm), $P_t$ is spot value of index and $B_p$ is beta of portfolio

Then 
$$\text{Hedge ratio} = \left(\frac{8,95,000}{5,00,000}\right)1.13$$

$$= 2.0227 \text{ contract on NSE NIFTY 50 index}$$

So 
$$\text{Hedge ratio} = 2 \text{ Contracts of NIFTY 50.}$$

**P.9.** An investor is holding 10,000 shares of portfolio valued at ₹ 10,00,000. Investor is of fear that prices of the shares will fall in next two months and thereby value of his portfolio will also fall, leading to loss to investor. Suppose current NIFTY 50 index is at ₹950. And one futures contract is for delivery of 1,000 shares. So value of one contract is (950 × 50 = ₹47,500). Show how stock index futures can protect the investor from falling value of his holding. Assume that the index price after two months would be 900.

**Solution:** Short hedge using index futures

| Spot/Cash market | Futures market |
|---|---|
| Current index is at 950, investor fears the value of index may fall in next two months. | Sell 20 futures index contract at 950, thereby be notionally commit himself to deliver 1,000 shares valued (950 × 50 × 20 = 9,50,000) |
| Two months later, the current index is at 900 and thereby value of index portfolio falls by ₹50,000. | Because contract is at expiry. Close out position by buying at 900 and thereby enjoying profit of ₹50,000 on each contract. |

Net futures position change = 0

So, we can see that the investor can protect the value of his portfolio by entering in futures market.

**P.10.** Suppose an investor goes long in a July futures contract on the NSE NIFTY. The current index value is 8,100.70. Suppose that often the contract is mark-to-market, futures price has increased by the minimum trading price change (one tick) to 8,100.75. Calculate the minimum price change in value.

*Solution:*   Current NSE 500 index = 8,100.70

   Minimum price change = 1,000(8,100.75 – 8,100.70)

   Contract size in rupee = 1,000 × 0.05 = ₹50

We multiply by 1,000 because contract size in rupee is 1,000 times the NIFTY 50 price index.

**P.11.** From the following figures, calculate the futures price of the index.

Value of the index = 4,000

Value of portfolio = ₹10,00,000

Risk-free interest rate = 8%

Dividend yield on index = 6% per annum

Beta of the portfolio ($\beta$) = 1.5

Also, assume that futures contract on the index with five months to maturity is used to hedge the value of portfolio over the next three months. One futures contract is for delivery of ₹50 times the index.

*Solution:*

$$F_{t,T} = S_t + S_t(C_t - d_t)\,\frac{T-t}{365}$$

$$= 4,000 + 4,000(0.08 - 0.06)\,\frac{5}{12}$$

$$= 4,000 + 80 \times \frac{5}{12}$$

$$= 4,000 + 33.33 = 4,033.33 = 4,034$$

   Price of futures contract – ₹50 × 4,034 = ₹2,01,700

**P.12.** Using the equations and figures of problem 11, calculate the hedge ratio that should be shorted to hedge the portfolio. What happens if index turns to be 3,500 in three months?

*Solution:*   Price of futures contract = 50 × 4,034 = 2,01,700

$$\text{Hedge ratio} = \frac{\text{Value of hedge portfolio}}{\text{Price of the futures contract}} \times \beta_I$$

Here      Value of hedged portfolio = 10,00,000

   Price of futures contract = 2,01,700

   $\beta_I$ (Beta) of portfolio = 1.5

$$\text{Hedge ratio} = \frac{10,00,000}{2,01,700} \times 1.5$$

$$= 7.43 = 8 \text{ contract}$$

Suppose index after three months falls to 3,500. Futures price will be

$$= 3,500 + 3,500(0.08 - 0.06) \times \frac{5}{12}$$

$$= 3,500 + 29.16 = 3,530$$

The gain/loss from the short futures position is:

$$= 8 \times (4,034 - 3,530) \times 50$$

$$= 8 \times (504) \times 50 = 2,01,600$$

Gain on short position = ₹2,01,600

**P.13.**    Suppose that the current level of NIFTY INDEX is 8,200. The dividend yield on the index is 1.50%, and risk-free rate of interest is 5.60%. What is the theoretical price of a NIFTY INDEX futures contracts with delivery in 73 days? Further, assume that if interest rate falls to 4.80%, what will be impact on theoretical value of futures contract.

*Solution:*    Theoretical Futures Price of NIFTY INDEX:

(a)

$$F_{t,T} = St + St\,(C_t - D_t)\,\frac{T-t}{365}$$

$$F_{t,73} = 8,200 + 8,200\,(5.6\% - 1.5\%)\,\frac{73}{365}$$

$$F_{t,73} = 8,200 + 67.24$$

$$= ₹8,267.24$$

| Cash Price of NIFTY INDEX | −8,200 |
| Risk-Free Interest | −5.6% |
| Dividend Yield | −1.5% |
| Days to deliver futures Contract | −73 days |

(b)  If interest rate fall to 4.80%, then theoretical value:

$$\text{Fo, 73} = 8,200 + 8,200\,(4.8\% - 1.5\%)$$

$$= 8,200 + 54.12 = ₹8,254.12$$

**P.14.**    The NIFTY INDEX stands at current level is ₹8,000. A NIFTY INDEX futures contracts with delivery in 146 days sells for 8,200. If the dividend yield on the index is 2.4%, What T-bill rate is implied in these prices?

*Solution*:    NIFTY INDEX current price = 8,000

NIFTY INDEX futures price = 8,200

Delivery of futures contract = 146 days

Dividend Yields on Index = 2.4%

Carrying Cost (Risk-free rate of interest) = ? assume 'X'

Theoretical Futures Price equation is:

$$F_{t,T} = St + St\,(C_t - D_t)\,\frac{T-t}{365}$$

$$8,200 = 8,000 + 8,000(X - 2.4\%)$$

$$8,200 - 8,000 = 8,000(X - 2.4\%)\,.40$$

$$200 = 3,200(X - 2.4\%)$$

$$200 = 3,200X - 76.80$$

$$200 - 76.80 = 3,200X$$

$$X = \frac{200 + 76.80}{3,200}$$

$$X = \frac{276.80}{3,200}$$

$X = 8.65\%$, Hence, Risk-free rate of interest is 8.65%

**P.15.** Consider the NIFTY Stock INDEX futures information:
Spot Index = 7,800
T-bill Yield = 6.4%
Index Dividend Yield = 2.2%
Days until futures delivery = 120
How could an arbitrageur take advantages of this information?

*Solution*: Theoretical Futures price of NIFTY INDEX Futures:

$$F_{t,T} = St + St(C_t - D_t)\frac{T-t}{365}$$

$$Fo, 120 = 7,800 + 7,800(6.4\% - 2.2\%)$$

$$= 7,800 + 107.70$$

$$= 7,907.70$$

If the futures price of NIFTY Index is currently prevailing in the market delivery for 120 days below 7,907.70, then the arbitrageur will enter long the NIFTY Futures and short the NIFTY cash, and vice-versa.

## REVIEW QUESTIONS

1. What do you understand by stock index futures? Discuss with suitable examples.
2. What is the difference between stock index futures and stock futures? Explain with examples.
3. Write notes on:
   (a) Hedging strategies using futures
   (b) Hedging strategies using stock index futures
4. Can stock index futures contracts be used to hedge both systematic and unsystematic risk? What is systematic risk and how it is measured?
5. "Stock index futures are the derivative instruments which are used by large portfolio managers for hedging their risks." Explain the statement in the light of features of stock index futures.
6. Explain the various uses of stock index futures with suitable examples.
7. Explain the various types of weighted stock index with examples.
8. How might a fund manager use stock index futures? Explain with the help of examples.
9. Compare and contrast between stock futures and stock index futures with suitable examples?
10. How pricing of stock index futures is different from other futures? Explain with suitable illustrations.
11. What are various types of stock index futures traded in Indian stock market? Discuss with specifications of each contract.

12. "Stock index futures as the powerful tool of risk management used by mutual funds and pensions funds and investment companies". Explain the statement.

13. Considering a hypothetical situation, explain short hedging and long hedging with stock index futures.

14. "Basic purpose of stock index futures is hedging". Critically evaluate the statement.

15. What is a stock index? How a stock index can be constructed? Explain with examples.

16. What are various features and significance of stock index futures? Explain with examples.

17. List out various stock index traded on various stock exchanges worldwide with their specifications.

18. What rational is there for hedging specific asset and liability risk with stock index futures?

19. Why does an equity portfolio using stock index futures work best if the portfolio being hedged is very similar to the underlying stock index of the futures contracts? Comment.

20. What are various uses and limitations of stock index futures? Discuss with examples.

# UNSOLVED PROBLEMS

**P.1.** A is long Reliance worth 3,85,000. He wants to hedge the position with short NIFTY futures so as to completely remove the market risk and make it a pure stock play. Calculate the position of A on entering into short index futures on NIFTY. Suppose beta of Reliance is 0.8.

**P.2.** A mutual fund which held a large portfolio of stock is facing with the possibility that market may decline. The value of his portfolio is ₹1 crore, and beta of the portfolio is 1.25. Current NIFTY is 1,250, and, say, two months later index be valued at 1,300. Which position will be appropriate? Show profit/loss profile with position after two months.

**P.3.** Consider a manager of well diversified portfolio with a value of $4,00,00,000 and assume that portfolio beta is 1.2 measured relative to S&P 500. This implies that a movement of 1% in S&P 500 index would be expected to induce a change of 1.22% in the value of stock portfolio. The portfolio manager fear's that a bear market is imminent and wishes to hedge his portfolio value against that possibility. Current S&P is at 212.00 and it is May 15. Show the short hedge position and also calculate the hedge ratio.

**P.4.** A portfolio manager wants to hedge a ₹10 million cash portfolio with Standard and Portfolio July 2003 futures contract. On March, the S&P closed at 354.75. The futures contract value is for the index comes ₹500. Compute the hedge ratio or risk minimizing position of portfolio manager. Suppose beta of portfolio is 0.8801.

**P.5.** Suppose a company has a portfolio with a beta of 1.2. It would like to use futures contracts on NSE futures (index) NIFTY to hedge its risk. Value of portfolio is ₹20 lakhs. NIFTY index is standing at 1,200 and each contract is for delivery of ₹200 times to index. What hedge will minimize the risk? What should company do if it wants to reduce the beta to 0.5?

**P.6.** Consider the following figures:
1. Amount to be invested = ₹20 lakhs
2. Current value of NIFTY = 1,000
3. Futures value of near month NIFTY = 1,020
4. Expected annualized dividend = 4%
5. Annualized bond equivalent yield on T-bill = 8%
6. Theoretical futures price = 1,025

What can be the alternative investment strategies for an investor? Also evaluate the strategies by considering the fact that, if market increases by 10%, no change and market decreases by 10%.

**P.7.** A treasurer intends to borrow ₹50,00,000 on June 20. Current interest rate is 8%. p.a. Three-month interest rate futures are quoted on an index basis. The index is 100 minus futures interest rate. Treasurer fears that interest rate will rise in futures and thereby increasing the borrowing cost. After three months, interest rate increases to 10%.

How stock index futures will be helpful for treasurer in hedging the risk? Suppose today it is April 15.

**P.8.** Calculate the market exposure from the following data:

| Stock | Share price (₹) | No. of shares | Share beta |
|---|---|---|---|
| Bank of Baroda | 140 | 1,000 | 0.9 |
| HLL | 120 | 3,000 | 1.5 |
| BHEL | 50 | 5,000 | 1.3 |
| ACC | 140 | 10,000 | 0.8 |
| Reliance Petroleum | 470 | 12,000 | 0.8 |

**P.9.** Assume that in December an investor has ₹10,00,000 to invest, but he wants to keep that investment fairly liquid. Investor is also of the belief that blue chip stocks will appreciate. Current (February) NSE S&P CNX NIFTY futures is at 1,500. What strategy will be appropriate for investor? Also, calculate the profit/loss on expiration from index. Futures price in December is 1,600.

**P.10.** Suppose you have a portfolio of primarily blue chip stock valued at ₹8,00,000. You believe the market has peaked and expected a near term correction. Today's price of NSE S&P NIFTY is 1,400. It is December 2002. February 2003 NSE S&P NIFTY futures is at 1,450 and contract size of NIFTY futures is 200. What strategy you like to take in futures market if futures contract is settled at 1,250.

**P.11.** XYZ sold a February NIFTY futures contract for ₹2,69,000. Each NIFTY futures contract is for delivery of 200 shares. On expiry, index closed at 1,260. What is profit/loss amount to XYZ?

**P.12.** In July, A bought an August NIFTY futures contract which costs him ₹3,00,000. Initial margin paid by him was 20,000. Each NIFTY futures contract is for delivery of 200 shares. On expiry, index closed at 1,530. How much profit did A make?

**P.13.** A long position of 20 market lots of NIFTY September futures is purchased at 1,000 and held till expiry when the NIFTY closes at expiry in September at 1,025. Calculate profit/loss on this position.

## SUGGESTED READINGS

1. Edwards, F.R. and Ma, C.W., *Futures and Options*, McGraw Hill, Maidon Head, 1992.
2. Sutcliffe, C.M.S., *Stock Index Futures*, Chapman and Hall, London, 1992.
3. Vohra, N.D. and Bagri, B.R., *Futures and Options*, Tata McGraw-Hill, New Delhi, 2003.
4. Hull, Johan, *Option Futures and Other Derivatives*, Pearson Higher Education, USA, 2000.

5. Battley, Nick and EFFAS, *The World's Futures and Options Markets*, Wiley, New York, 2000.

6. Fabozzi, Frank H. and Kipens, Gregory M. (Eds), *The Handbook of Stock Index Futures and Options*, Homewood, IL: Dow Jones-Irwin; 1989.

7. Rene M. Stulz, *Risk Management & Derivatives*; Thomson-South-Western, Indian-Reprint-2007.

8. Robert A. Strong, *Derivatives*, Thomson-South-Western, Indian-Reprint-2006.

9. www. Nseindia.com. www.bseindia.com.

# Chapter 9

# Forward Rate Agreements

**LEARNING OBJECTIVES**

*After reading this chapter, students will be able to*

➢ Know about the types of interest rates like treasury rates, LIBOR rate, repo rate, zero coupon rate, etc.
➢ Understand the term structure of interest rates and its various theories.
➢ Distinguish between spot v/s forward yields and the forward yield curve.
➢ Explain the concept of forward rate agreements and hedging the same.
➢ Know about the types of interest rates like treasury rate, repo rate, zero coupon rate, etc.
➢ Explain the concept of the forward rate agreements (FRA)
➢ Understand the trading mechanism of the FRA
➢ Know the features and uses of the FRA
➢ Explain the mechanism of pricing of FRA
➢ Know how to hedge with FRA
➢ Know the guidelines of the FRAs in India.

## 9.1 INTRODUCTION

Globalization of the economy and adoption of the liberalized policies by the states all over the world, the business houses have exposed to various risks such as exchange rate risk, interest rate risk, political risk, operational risk, economic risk, etc. Further, deregulation of interest rate structure is continuously exposing the market players to risk arising from unanticipated movement in interest rates. In the present time, the change in the interest rates in any country has direct impact on the economic variables like stock prices, interest rates, inflation, foreign exchange rates, forex reserve, commodity prices, etc. of other countries. In a nutshell, liberalization has increased the overall risks of the corporate sector, as a result, it has become indispensable to hedge the risk. Derivatives market witnessed a mammoth change in the recent past. Equity derivatives, credit derivatives, foreign exchange derivatives, interest rate derivatives, etc. are the various derivative products available all over the world.

## 9.2  SOME PRELIMINARIES

Interest rates futures are such financial derivatives which are written on fixed income (return) securities or instruments. A fixed income security needs the payment of interest in the form of fixed amount (in particular currency) at predetermined point of time along with the payment of principal amount at predetermined maturity period. In the financial markets, these debt obligations are often arbitrarily separated into short-term (money market) and long-term (capital market) instruments. *Money market instruments* are the financial assets having initial maturity of one year or less, whereas the *capital market instruments* are those having initial obligation longer than a year, for instance, US treasury bills are the examples of money market instruments and US treasury bonds are the examples of capital market instruments.

An *interest rate futures contract* is a futures contract on an asset whose price is dependent solely on the level of interest rates. Interest rate futures contracts are more complicated than other types of futures contracts because interest rate futures requires not only the full description of the level of interest rates but also the maturity of interest rate to which it is exposed. It must then find a way of using available interest rate futures contracts so that an appropriate strategy is followed. Before discussing the nature of interest rate futures contracts, it is essential to know some basic concepts about the interest rate structure.

## 9.3  TYPES OF INTEREST RATES

There are different types of interest rates which are regularly quoted like mortgage rates, deposit rates, borrowing rates and so on. However, here we will discuss the interest rates which are relevant in the analysis of such financial derivatives.

### 9.3.1  Treasury Rates

The treasury rate is the rate of interest applicable to borrowing by a government in its own currency. For example, the US treasury rate is the rate at which the US government can borrow in US dollars. Similarly, Indian government can borrow in Indian rupees on treasury rates prescribed. It is generally assumed that there is less possibility that government defaults in making interest payment and repaying the loans. Hence, the treasury rates are regarded as risk-free rates.

### 9.3.2  LIBOR Rate

It is the short form of the London Inter Bank Offer Rate at which large international banks are willing to lend money to another large international bank. LIBOR rates are normally changing as per the changes in economic conditions, quantum of international financial flows, market position of funds requirements, etc. LIBOR rates are generally higher than the treasury rates because they are not risk free.

### 9.3.3  Repo Rate

Sometimes, the investment dealers operate funds trading activities with a 'repo' or 'repurchase agreement'. It is a contract where the owner of the funds (securities) agrees to sell them to a counter-party now and buy them back later at a slightly higher rate. So the counter-party is giving a loan to other party. The difference between selling price and repurchase price of the security is called interest earned by the counter-party. This interest rate is referred to as the *repo rate*. The repo rate is slightly higher than the corresponding treasury rate. *Repo rate* is popularly used by the governments in raising funds from the markets.

### 9.3.4  Zero Rate/Spot Rate

It is also known as *n*-year zero rate or *n*-year zero or *n*-spot rate. It is the rate of interest earned on an investment that starts today and lasts for *n*-years. All the amounts of accrued interest and principal are realized at the end of *n*-years. There are no intermediate payments. For example, if the 5-year treasury zero rate with annual compounding is quoted at 5 percent per annum, it means that ₹100 would grow to $100 \times 1.05^5 = ₹127.63$, at the end of five years. Thus, the *n*-year spot interest rate or *n*-year zero coupon rate is the interest rate on an investment that is made for a period of time starting today and lasting for *n*-years. Hence, the 5-year spot rate is the rate of interest on an investment lasting five years.

### 9.3.5  Forward Rates

Forward interest rates are the rates of interest implied by current spot rates for periods of time in the futures.

## 9.4  UNDERLYING MARKETS

There are a number of money markets operating in different segments, and sometimes, collectively known as the *parallel markets*. The parallel markets comprise the following main markets:

1. The interbank market
2. Certificate of deposits (CD) market
3. The Commercial papers (CP) market
4. The local government securities market

For the understanding of interest rate futures, a brief description of these markets have been given below. The first three of these markets have equivalent parallel euro currency markets which are much bigger in size.

The **interbank market** involves the borrowing and lending among banks and other large entities, such as corporations, government bodies, central banks, International Monetary Fund, government bodies, etc.. The interbank market, whether in the domestic currency or in euro currencies, is a whole-sale market where one single transaction is usually in millions. Often money passes through many banks between the original lender and the ultimate borrower. Money brokers operate to bring borrowers and lenders together. The interbank interest rates have become the most common benchmarks for other interest rates. Usually both the interest rate offer and bid on different currencies are available in this market. There may be some variations in these rates at the different financial centres. For example, LIBOR (London Interbank Offer Rate) may differ from the corresponding rates in, say, Paris (PIBOR), Madrid (MIBOR), Hongkong (HIBOR), etc. Similarly, their corresponding bid rates at which the major banks will take deposits, known as LIBID, PIBID, MIBID, HIBID, etc. may also differ. The difference between offer rate and bid rate known as spread is usually around 1/8 percent, and the average of offer and bid rates is known as LIMEAN, PIMEAN, MIMEAN, HIMEAN and so forth.

The other segment of the money market is **CDs market**. The certificates of deposits are bearer certificates acknowledging a deposit for a period, such as 3 or 6 months. It is negotiable instrument which can be bought and sold between dates of issue and maturity. This market is dominated by the banks and usually the discount houses operate market makers in this market. **Commercial Papers (CP)** is similar to certificate of deposits but is issued by corporate borrowers rather than banks. Corporate firms directly approach the investors and can borrow at rates equal to, or even perhaps lower than the interest rates charged by the banks from them.

Another important segment of the money market is **government borrowing**. Most of the governments issue the different instruments like treasury notes, treasury bills, treasury bonds, etc. for financing their spending and budget deficits (expenditures greater than revenues). The local government authorities may find it cheaper to take deposits directly rather than borrowing from the banks and other financial institutions.

## 9.5   RISKS IN DEALING THE SECURITIES

Basically there are two types of risks involved in holding or dealing in interest rate bearing securities: interest rate risk and default risk. The default risk is concerned with losing or some of the principal amount of the loan due to bankruptcy of the borrower. In general, credit-worthiness of the borrowers will determine the rate of interest. Since the government securities are generally viewed as being default free, so these deposits/securities carry the lowest rate of interest for a given maturity in the market.

Interest rate risk is the risk which is arisen due to macro-economic factors resulting in changes in the price (or market values) of a security. These are such factors which are not in the control of a firm, like inflation rates, money supply growth rates, economic growth rates, government policy, etc. These factors influence the interest rates in the market both way (increase and decrease), and thus, resulting in change of the prices of the securities. Further, a change in expectations about futures interest rate levels causes changes in the yield demanded by the investors, which in turn causes the market value of outstanding fixed return securities' to change. The more volatile are the expectations of the investors, the more flexible the prices of these instruments.

## 9.6   TERM STRUCTURE OF INTEREST RATES

Before discussing the interest rate futures, it is important to understand the yield relationship implicit in the term structure of interest rates. The volatility of a debt instrument price is dependent on its maturity, i.e., longer the maturity, the greater the price volatility. Since the maturity of a bond is referred as its term to maturity or simply 'term', the relationship between yield and maturity is referred to as the term structure of interest rates. It is also popularly called *yield-maturity relationship* or '*yield-curve*'. These curves can be of three hypothetical types which have been shown in Figure. 9.1(a), (b) and (c).

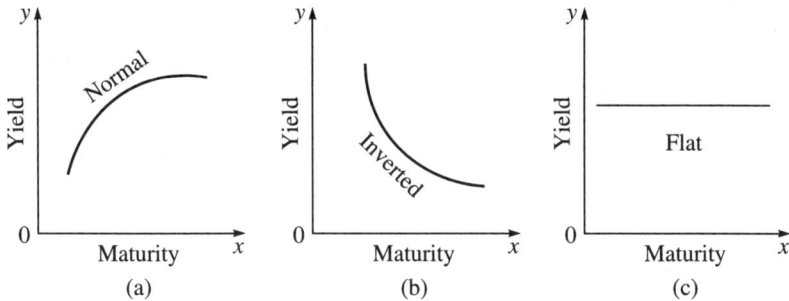

**FIGURE 9.1**   Yield curves.

These figures show three shapes of yield curves that have appeared with some degree of frequency over time. Figure 9.1(a) shows an upward-sloping yield curve, i.e., yield rises steadily as maturity increases. This is normally referred as *normal* or *positive yield curve*. Figure 9.1(b) shows a downward sloping or *inverted yield curve* where yields decrease as maturity increases, and Figure 9.1(c) shows flat yield curve where yields remain same irrespective of the changes in maturities.

## 9.7   THEORIES OF THE TERM STRUCTURE

Several theories have been evolved on the determination of the term structure of interest rates which have been discussed here in brief. The simplest is the **Expectations Theory** which states that the entire term structure at a given time reflects the market's current expectations. It states that spot interest rate on a long-term bond will equal an average of the short-term spot interest rates that are expected to occur over the life of the long-term bond. In other words, long-term interest rates should reflect expected future short-term interest rates. For example, if short-term interest rate during the next 5 years (or say, successive I-year securities) are expected to average 10 percent, the interest rate on a 5-year bond will also be 10 percent. And if today's rate is decreased, then long-term interest will also be decreased. More precisely, it emphasises that a forward interest rate corresponding to a certain period is equal to the expected futures spot interest rate for that period.

Another theory, known as **Market Segmentation Theory**, according to which the market is segmented into three sections, namely short-term, medium-term and long-term, and there is no relationship among these. Each maturity is a separate market and the interest rate in every such market is determined by the demand and supply. Thus, interest rate at any maturity is totally unrelated to expectations of future rates. However, this theory is of doubtful use. Another important and most appealing theory is **Liquidity Preference Theory** or **Liquidity Premium Theory**. This theory argues that the forward rate should always be higher than the expected future spot interest rate. The basic assumption is that the investors prefer liquidity, and thus, invest in the short-term funds. On the other hand, the borrowers prefer to borrow for longer period at fixed rate. The theory states that the investors are not indifferent between investments of all maturities, but have preference of short-term funds due to their superior liquidity. Further, short-term interest rates are less risky and have lower volatility, and thus, price changes are also less. Further, they will be ready to lend at the lower interest rate. Alternatively, for long-term investment, the investors must be paid something extra, and this extra is called *liquidity premium*.

The liquidity preference theory also implies that the total return on successive short-term investments (say, ten successive six-month securities) will be less than the return available on 5-year security, by the amount of the liquidity premium embedded in the 5-year security. This theory is widely accepted as an explanation of the term structure of interest rates. It leads to a situation in which the forward rates are greater than the expected futures spot rates. It is also consistent with the empirical result that yield curves tend to be upward sloping more often than they are downward sloping. However, the theory makes it more difficult to infer forward rates from existing term structure due to existing complex economic conditions and investors psychology.

## 9.8  FORWARD INTEREST RATES

To trade in interest rate futures market, the investors must understand the concept of forward interest rate and the mechanism of calculating it. Forward interest rates are the rates of interest implied by current spot rates for periods of time in the futures. To understand how they are calculated, let us take an example as shown in Table 9.1.

**TABLE 9.1**   Comparison of Spot and Forward Interest Rate

| Year (n) | Spot rate for an n-year investment (% per annum) | Forward rate for n-th year (% per annum) |
|---|---|---|
| 1 | 10.0 | 10.0 |
| 2 | 10.5 | 11.0 |
| 3 | 10.8 | 11.4 |
| 4 | 11.0 | 11.6 |
| 5 | 11.1 | 11.5 |

From Table 9.1, the second column shows the spot rates and assume that the rates are continuously compounded. Assuming 10 percent rate of interest for one year means that for an investment of ₹ 100, the investor will receive ₹ 110.52 ($100e^{0.1} = 110.52$), and at the rate of 10.5 percent per annum, he will get ₹ 123.37 ($100e^{0.105 \times 2} = 123.37$) in two years and so on.

The forward interest rate as shown in Table 9.1 for year-2 is 11 percent per annum. As stated earlier, the forward rate is implied to the spot rate, it can be calculated from the one-year spot interest rate of 10 percent per annum and the two-year spot interest rate of 10.5 percent per annum. To show the exact forward rate of interest of 11 percent per annum, let us assume that ₹ 100 is invested. A rate of 10 percent for the first year and 11 percent for the second year yields will be

$$100e^{0.1}e^{0.11} = ₹123.37$$

We have already seen that a rate of 10.5 percent per annum for two years yields: $100e^{0.105 \times 2}$ = ₹ 123.37. Similarly, the forward rate for the third year is the rate of interest that is implied by 10.5 percent per annum spot rate and 10.8 percent per annum three-year spot rate. It is 11.4 percent per annum.

This is because an investment for two years at 10.5 percent per annum averaged with the investment for one year at 11.4 percent per annum gives an overall return for the three years at

10.8 percent per annum. The other forward rates can be calculated similarly which are shown in the third column of Table 9.1.

**EXAMPLE:** Assume the six-month interest is 10% per annum on a security. The three-month rate of interest is 8 percent per annum. Calculate the forward rate for the three months commencing three months from the present.

*Solution:*

$$(1 + 0.08/4)(1 + x/4) = (1 + 0.10/2)$$

$$(1.02)(1 + x/4) = 1.05$$

$$x/4 = 1.0294 - 1$$

$$x = 0.1176 = 11.76\% \text{ per annum}$$

So, the three-month forward rate available from the present is 11.76 percent per annum.

**Formula for calculating forward interest rate**: A popular formula for calculating forward rates is as follows:

Formula:

$$\left(1 + SR_1 \times \frac{t_1}{365 \text{ days}}\right) = \left(1 + SR_2 \times \frac{t_2}{365 \text{ days}}\right) \times \left(1 + FR_2 \times \frac{t_1 - t_2}{365 \text{ days}}\right) \tag{9.1}$$

$$FR_2 = \left(\frac{1 + SR_1 \times \dfrac{t_1}{365}}{1 + SR_2 \times \dfrac{t_2}{365}} - 1\right) \times \frac{365}{t_1 - t_2} \tag{9.1a}$$

where, $SR_1$ = Spot interest rate to the far end of the forward period

$SR_2$ = Spot interest rate to the near end of the forward period

$t_1$ = Number of days for the far end

$t_2$ = Number of days for near end

$FR_2$ = Implicit forward rate for the near end period

From the example given above the forward rate will be:

$$FR_2 = \left[\frac{1 + SR_1 \times \dfrac{t_1}{365}}{1 + SR_2 \times \dfrac{t_2}{365}} - 1\right] \times \frac{365}{t_1 - t_2}$$

$$= \left(\frac{1 + 0.10 \times \dfrac{6}{12}}{1 + 0.08 \times \dfrac{1}{4}} - 1\right) \times \frac{12}{6 - 3}$$

$$= \left(\frac{1 + 0.05}{1 + 0.02} - 1\right) \times \frac{12}{3}$$

$$= (1.0294 - 1) \times 4$$

$$= (0.0294) \times 4 = 0.1176$$

$$= 11.76 \text{ percent per annum}$$

**EXAMPLE:**   Supposing that a bank assesses and quotes the following rates to a company, based on the annual spot yield curve for that company's risk class:

One years: 3.50%
Two years: 4.60%
Three years: 5.40%
Four years: 6.10%
Five years: 6.30%

This indicates that the company would have to: pay interest at 3.50% if it wants to borrow a sum of money for one year; pay interest at 4.60% per year if it wants to borrow a sum of money for two years; pay interest at 5.40% per year if it wants to borrow a sum of money for three years; and so on.

Alternatively, for a two-year loan, the company could opt to borrow a sum of money for only one year, at an interest rate of 3.50%, and then again for another year, commencing in one year's time, instead of borrowing the money for a total of two years.

A forward rate commencing in one year for a borrowed sum lasting a year can be calculated as follows:

The compound factor for the total interest rate for two years = $1.046^2$

The compound factor for the one year interest rate = 1.035

The one year forward interest rate can be calculated as follows:

$$\frac{1.0460^2}{1.0350} = 1.0571 \text{ or } 5.71\%$$

The interest rate forward commencing in one year for a borrowed sum lasting a year would be 5.71%. The 12v24 FRA = 5.71%.

Similarly, annual interest rate forward rates for future years can be calculated as follows:

The interest rate forward starting in year 3, for a year (24v36 FRA)

$$= \frac{1.0540^3}{1.0460^2} = 1.0702 \text{ or } 7.02\% \quad \text{or} \quad \left[\frac{1.0540^3}{(1.0350 \times 1.0571)}\right]$$

The interest rate forward starting in year 4, for a year (36v48 FRA)

$$= \frac{1.0610^4}{1.0540^3} = 1.0823 \text{ or } 8.23\% \quad \text{or} \quad \left[\frac{1.0610^4}{(1.0350 \times 1.0571 \times 1.0702)}\right]$$

The interest rate forward starting in year 5, for a year (48v60 FRA)

$$= \frac{1.0630^5}{1.0610^4} = 1.0710 \text{ or } 7.10\% \quad \text{or} \quad \left[\frac{1.0630^5}{(1.0350 \times 1.0571 \times 1.0702 \times 1.0823)}\right]$$

In summary:

| Year | Annual spot yield curve | Annual forward rates |
|---|---|---|
| 1 | 3.50% | |
| 2 | 4.60% | 5.71% |
| 3 | 5.40% | 7.02% |
| 4 | 6.10% | 8.23% |
| 5 | 6.30% | 7.10% |

Suppose the company wants to borrow a sum of money for three years on the basis of the above rates:

    (i) it could pay annual interest at a rate of 5.40% in each of the three years, or

   (ii) it could pay interest at a rate of 3.50% in the first year, 5.71% in the second year and 7.02% in the third year, or

  (iii) it could pay annual interest at a rate of 4.60% in each of the first two years and 7.02% in the third year.

## 9.9  SPOT VS FORWARD YIELDS

The spot yield on an interest rate instrument is the cash market yield on that instrument at a particular moment in time. A forward yield is a term used to describe the market's expectation about what the spot yield will be at some point of time in the futures on a particular maturity instrument. According to the expectation theory, the forward interest rates is unbiased estimator of futures spot interest rates.

As discussed earlier, the current yield on 90 day T-bill futures contract is the spot yield on (cash) 90 day. T-bill that is currently expected to prevail on the expiration date on the futures contract. Therefore, the yields available on interest rate futures contracts can be directly compared with the forward yield in the term structure of interest rates. If these two yields, i.e., futures and forward yields, are not identicals then arbitrage opportunity will arise. This will be further elaborated later on in this lesson.

## 9.10  FORWARD YIELD CURVE

Forward yield curve is very much useful yield curve to understand and to ascertain the market expectations of interest rates. It relates futures short-term interest rates implied by long spot rates (forward rates) to the point of time to which these implied rates relate, for example, return on 5-year bonds and on 4-year bonds imply rate one-year instruments to be entered into 4 years from the present. Thus, the implied forward rate can also be calculated by the following formula:

$$(1 + {}_4FR_1)\frac{(1 + SR_5)^5}{(1 + SR_4)^4}$$

where $SR_5$ is the 5-year interest rate, $SR_4$ is the 4-year interest rate and ${}_4FR_1$ is the one-year rate expected in 4 years' time. The formula arises from the relation:

$$(1 + SR_5)^5 = (1 + SR_4)^4 + (1 + {}_4FR_1)$$

This describes that a 5-year instrument at the 5-year interest should yield the same amount as a 4-year instrument at the 4-year rate with the proceeds reinvested for one-year at the one-year expected to be available 4-year hence.

In brief, forward interest rates might be seen from marginal interest rate point of view. If the average rate (spot yield) curve slopes upward, then the marginal interest rate (forward rate) must exceed the average rate. Similarly, if the average rate (spot yield) curve slopes downward, then the marginal rate (forward rates) will be below the average rate (spot rate). Thus, the forward yield curve would be above upward sloping spot yield curve and below a downward sloping spot curve as shown in Figure 9.2.

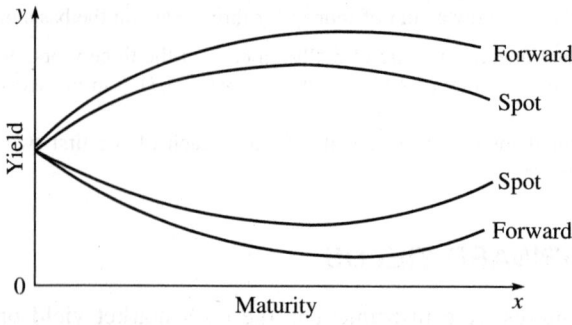

**FIGURE 9.2** Spot and forward yields curves.

## 9.11 CONCEPT OF FORWARD RATE AGREEMENT

A Forward Rate Agreement (FRA), in simple terms, is an agreement between two parties who intend to protect themselves against future movements in interest rates. It is a forward contract in which the buyer effectively promises today to borrow an amount of money in the future at an agreed upon interest rate. Just like other derivatives, the FRA is an off-balance sheet contract between the two parties conducted in the OTC markets. It is equivalent of exchange-traded-short-interest rate futures, customized to meet the specific requirements of the counterparties. Both the parties in the FRA determine the forward interest rate which will apply to an agreed notional principal amount for a specified period. In such an agreement, loan amount is not extended, even though a notional amount is mentioned in the agreement. Instead, the counterparties, i.e., the borrower (buyer) and the tender (seller), who have agreed to pay each the interest difference between the agreed rate (the forward rate) and the actual interest rate (reference rate) on the specified future date.

For example, a financial institution needs ₹50 million in the month of March which it can pay back in May. Assume the current month is January and the institution is expecting rise of the interest rate in March. So, in order to hedge against the risk that interest may be higher in March, the institution enters into an FRA with a bank at 7 percent FRA rate with a notional principal of ₹50 million. Suppose, in March, the rate of interest rises to 9 percent, then the bank would pay to the institution the difference (i.e., increased interest and FRA (9 – 7 percent) = 2 percent. If the actual interest decreased to 5 percent in March, then the institution will pay the difference (7 – 5 percent) = 2 percent to the bank.

## 9.12 TERMINOLOGY OF FRA

As discussed earlier, the FRAs are the technique for a firm to lock in an interest rate today, for the amount of money which the company wants to borrow or lend in the specified future period. The fixed rate (also known as the FRA), is negotiated and agreed upon by the counterparties before they enter into contract. The *floating rate* (also called the reference rate) is an interest rate that will fluctuate between the period of contract, i.e., from beginning to end of the contract.

In the present section, though today FRAs are frequently used in most of the countries, here we are describing the important standard terms of FRA which are recommended by the British Banker's Association, also known as *BBAFRA terms*.

| *FRA Terminology* | *Meaning/Definition* |
|---|---|
| FRA | FRA Forward Rate Agreement |
| Forward/Contract Rate | The forward rate of interest for the Contract Period as agreed between the parties. |
| BBA Designated Banks | Means the panel of not less than 12 banks designated from time to time by the BBA for the purpose of establishing the BBA Interest Settlement Rate. |
| BBA Interest Settlement Rate | The rate quoted by specified reference banks for the relevant period and currency. Most currencies LIBOR can be taken as shown on LIBO or LIBOR01 on Reuters or page 3750 on Telerate. For AUD the corresponding Reuter page is BBSW. |
| Buyer (Borrower) | Party seeking to protect itself against a future rise in interest rate. |
| Seller (Lender) | Party seeking to protect itself against a future fall in interest rate. |
| Settlement Date | The date the contract period commences, being the date on which the Settlement Sum is paid. |
| Maturity Date | The date on which the contract period ends. |
| Settlement Sum | As calculated by the BBA formula. |
| Fixing Date | The day that is two business days prior to the Settlement Date except for pound sterling for which the Fixing Date and Settlement Date are the same. |
| Contract Amount | The notional principal on which the FRA is based. |
| Contract Currency | The currency on which the FRA is based. |
| Contract Period | The period from the Settlement Date to the Maturity Date. |
| Broken Date | Contract Period of a different duration from that used in the fixing of the BBA Interest Settlement Rate and any period exceeding 1 year |

FRA's are quoted in the format of money market rate, i.e., an annualized percentage. They are quoted or written as AXB, A.B, A–B, AVsB, etc. The first figure 'A' denotes the number of months until the loan is set to begin, and second figure 'B' represents the number of months until the loan ends. It means, 'A' represents the period remains from entering into contract to start of the contract and 'B' represents the period of the contract, i.e., from start to end period of the contract. For example, 1 × 4 would mean that the agreement set to begin 1 month in the future and the period of agreement is 3 months, i.e., 4 − 1 = 3. However, the common formats of these quotes are: 1 × 4, 1 × 7, 3 × 6, 3 × 9, 6 × 9 and 6 × 12.

## 9.13 BASIC FEATURES OF FRA

The important features of a FRA are as follows:

1. FRAs are traded at the over-the-counter (OTC) markets. It means the parties to the FRA are dealing directly with each other. The term and conditions of the FRA are negotiated by the parties as per their requirements. So, the FRAs are tailor-made customized agreements.

The British Banker Association (BBA) has set certain standards of FRA which are normally followed in the market.

2. FRAs are off-balance sheet contracts because the principal among the counterparties amount decided in the FRA is notional and it is not exchanged. It is fixed just to calculate the interest amount of compensation.

3. There are normally two parties in a FRA. One is the borrower (buyer) and another is called lender (seller) of the FRA. The buyer is usually called customer or client, whereas seller is referred to FRA dealer or banker, etc.

4. FRA is a future derivative and serves the same purpose as a forward-to-forward agreement.

5. FRAs are negotiated and entered directly between the counterparties, hence, no transaction is normally incurred in these agreements, except for any fee or commission of the broker, if conducted through the broker.

6. FRAs are sometimes quoted as "offer-bid" rates, as usually followed in the money markets. Buyer of the FRA, being borrower, gets the higher rate whereas the seller, being the lender or depositor, gets the lower rate.

7. The popular periods in the FRAs are normally 3 months and 6 months, however, recently 12 months are also gaining popularity. Broken dates have also been noted in the certain FRAs. Contracts periods of FRAs less than 3 months are rare since slim prompt margin makes them uneconomical.

8. The FRA markets are concentrated in a few currencies like US dollars, pound sterling, euro, Japanese Yen, Swiss francs, etc. However, they are available in such currencies where there are no financial futures.

9. FRAs are credit instruments. So, same conditions apply to them as levied on the non-performing loan, however, the credit risk is limited to the compensation amount only.

10. FRAs are OTC driven contracts, so no initial or variation margins are required by either of the party. Nothing is paid at the entering of the FRA, by the counterparty.

11. FRA transaction can be closed at any stage with the consent of the counterparty by entering into a new or opposing FRA at a new price.

12. FRAs are used more frequently by the banks, which use them for hedging their interest rate exposures arisen due to mis-matches of their money market transactions.

13. Value dates for FRAs usually follow the dates applicable to money markets called *straight dates*. Normally trading lots of FRAs are good for 5 million units of currency except Yen.

14. FRAs are cash settled contracts. It means that money is not actually borrowed or lent at settlement date, rather winning party pays the compensation amount (calculated as per compensation formula) the losing party.

15. FRA is effectively a one-period swap. The buyer receives the floating interest rate and pays a fixed interest rate. The seller of the FRA pays floating rate of interest and receives the fixed rate of interest. The fixed interest rate in a swap is analogous to the forward rate which is specified in the FRAs.

16. FRA market is very liquid and rates are readily quoted on screens by both banks and brokers. Dealing is over the telephone or over a dealing system such as Reuters.

## 9.14  MECHANISM OF FRA

The mechanism of FRA is explained with a simple example of FRA. Suppose 'X' Ltd. Company on March 1, 2015 estimated the requirement of ₹10 lakhs for its current expenditure to occur on

June 1, 2015. The company expects to generate the revenue from its operations and able to repay this amount on September 1, 2015. Assume that from the various options available to meet this requirement, the company decides to go for a FRA arrangement.

The company has currently made its short-term funds arrangements with the Bank 'Y' at LIBOR plus 150 basis points (bps), a flexible interest rate mechanism, since LIBOR is not fixed over the period. If the company goes for this option, then after three months, i.e., on September 1, 2015, the due date of settlement, the prevailing LIBOR rate plus 150 (bps) would be paid by the company to its banker 'Y'. Let us assume that the company selects the FRA option and contacts to a FRA dealer on March 1, 2015 who quotes for 8 percent FRA.

After three months on June 1, 2015 there can be three scenarios. First, the LIBOR can be higher than 8 percent, second less than 8 percent and third equal to 8 percent. If LIBOR on June 1, 2015 is lower than 8 percent, then the FRA dealer will earn the difference between 8 percent and actual LIBOR rate, say, 7.5 percent. It means 0.5 percent (8.0 − 7.5%) on 10 lakhs will be paid by the company to the FRA dealer. Similarly, if the LIBOR is higher than 8 percent, then the company will be in profit, and difference amount of loan will be paid by the FRA dealer to the company. Similarly, the FRA dealer would also incur profit or loss in future on such FRA contract.

The exact amount of difference, popularly known as *Compensation* in FRA terminology is calculated here as under:

## Impact of Change in Interest Rates on the FRA

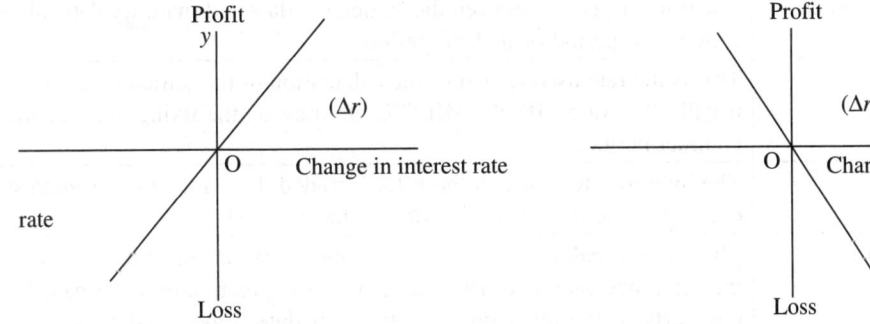

(a) The party that is long will be in profit if interest rate rise (i.e., if ($\Delta r$) positive)

(b) The party that has sold a FRA will be in profit if interest rates decrease is (i.e. if ($\Delta r$) is negative)

**FIGURE 9.3**

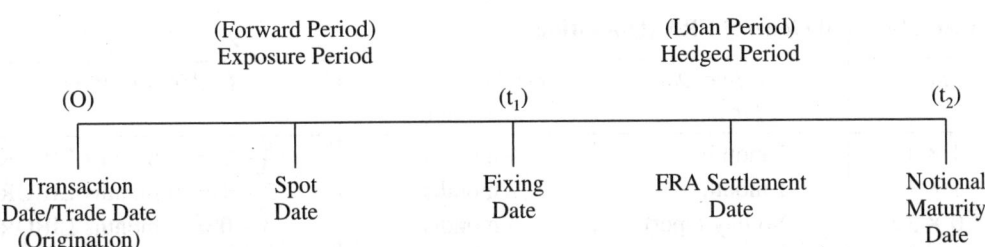

**FIGURE 9.4** Time line for an FRA.

$t_0$ (Time O)    Origination date of (FRA)

$t_1$ (Time $t_1$)    Delivery date of the FRA (end of forward period/start of loan period)

$t_2$ (Time $t_2$)    The end of the loan period

$(t_2 - t_1)$    Length of the loan period

$(t_0 - t_1)$    Length of the forward (exposure) period

## FRA Notations

| 1. | Trade Date | The date which a FRA is traded/transacted by the counterparties. |
|---|---|---|
| 2. | Spot Date | The spot date is usually two business days after the trade date. However, it can, by agreement, be sooner or later than this, to complete the contract's formalities. |
| 3. | Fixing Date | Fixing date is usually 2 business days before the settlement date. This is date on which the reference rate is determined, that is, the rate to which the FRA dealing rate is compared. |
| 4. | Settlement Date | Settlement date will be the time period after the spot date referred to by the FRA terms. On this date, the FRA is to be settled by paying/receiving the compensation amount by the counterparties. |
| 5. | Maturity Date | The date on which the notional loan or deposit expires. |
| 6. | Contract Period | The time or period between the settlement date and maturity date, also called load period or hedged period. |
| 7. | Reference | This is the rate used as part of the calculation of the settlement amount usually the Rate LIBOR, MIBOR, etc. rate on the fixing date for the contract period. |
| 8. | FRA Rate | The interest rate at which the FRA is traded. It is fixed rate of interest decided at the time of origination of the contract. |
| 9. | Settlement Sum | The amount calculated as the difference between the FRA rate and the reference rate as a percentage of the notional sum to be paid by one party to the other on the settlement date. Calculated sum is the discounted present value. It is also called compensation amount. |
| 10. | Contract Currency | The currency on which the FRA is based. |
| 11. | Broken Date | Contract period of a different duration from that used in the fixing of the interest settlement rate and any period exceeding one year. |

## FRA Notation and General FRA (Quotation)

| Notation | Effective Date for now | Termination Date from now | Underlying Rate |
|---|---|---|---|
| 1 × 4 | 1 month | 4 months | 4 – 1 = 3 months LIBOR |
| 1 × 7 | 1 month | 7 months | 7 – 1 = 6 months LIBOR |
| 0 × 3 | No day (spot) | 3 months | 3 – 0 = 3 months LIBOR |
| 3 × 6 | 3 months | 6 months | 6 – 3 = 3 months LIBOR |
| –3 × 9 | 3 months | 9 months | 9 – 3 = 6 months LIBOR |
| 12 × 18 | 12 months | 18 months | 18 – 12 = 6 months LIBOR |

**How to interpret a quote for FRA?**

Assume that a FRA quote is: US $ 3 × 9 = 3.25/3.50 percent p.a. It means deposit interest starting 3 months from now for 6 months is 3.50 percent. Entering as a payer FRA means paying the fixed rate 3.50 percent p.a. and receiving a floating 6 months rate, while entering as a "receiver FRA" means paying the same floating and receiving a fixed rate (3.25 percent p.a.)

## 9.15　SETTLEMENT OF FRAs

The FRAs are settled at the delivery date for cash. The compensating amount reflects the difference between the actual (settlement) rate for the period and the contract rate. There is specified technique to calculate the settlement rate. For example, as per British Bankers' Association (BBA) guidelines, the settlement is calculated by taking the rates quoted by eight BBA Designated Banks offered rate on deposits for such contract period in the London interbank market at 11.00 a.m. on the relevant fixing date for settlement date value. Further, two highest and two lowest are eliminated, and thus, remaining of the four rates are averaged and then rounded upward to five decimal places.

After deciding the settlement rate, then difference of the settlement rate and contract rate is determined. If the settlement rate is higher than the contract rate, then the borrower (buyer) of the FRA would receive from the seller and vice-versa. It is to be noted that settlement of the compensation amount will take place at the beginning of the FRA.

Since the amount is to be paid at the beginning of the FRA, then the compensation amount is to be discounted at a particular rate to calculate the net amount. Normally the LIBOR or the offer rates of money market quote.

## 9.16　COMPENSATION FORMULA

How much amount would be paid by the counterparty on maturity of a FRA is given by the under-mentioned formula:

$$\frac{(R_s - R_f) \times (N/Y) \times A}{1 + R_s(N/Y)}$$

where $R_s$ is settlement (reference) interest rate when the FRA matures, $R_f$ is FRA guaranteed interest rate when the FRA is agreed, $N$ is period in days of borrowing/lending to which the FRA relates, $Y$ is number of days in a year (365) and $A$ is sum of money to which the FRA relates. FRAs are money market instruments, it is not required to calculate rates for periods in excess of one year, hence no compounding of interest is normally needed. However, if FRAs are used for maturing more than one year, then compounding may be used.

**EXAMPLE:**　A firm X has a seasonal need of funds for the period July–October for its business. On January 15, it uses an FRA to guarantee the interest payable on a $2 million three-month loan to be taken out on July 15. On January 15, the rate for three-month LIBOR six months forward is 10 percent. Anticipating a borrowing at LIBOR + 1¼ percent, thus, the firm locks an interest rate of 11¼ percent p.a.

On July 15, LIBOR rises at 12 percent p.a. The firm could borrow $2 million at 13¼ percent p.a. which involves a payment of $20,66,250 on October 15. However, the bank providing the FRA compensates for the deviation of LIBOR on July 15 from 10 percent. The compensation payment is 2 percent for three months on $2 million discounted at LIBOR to reflect the fact that the compensation paid at the beginning of period, whereas the interest is payable at the end of the period. The amount paid by the bank to the firm X on July 15 will $9,786 calculated by the compensation formula:

$$= \frac{(0.12 - 0.10) \times (92/365) \times \$20,00,000}{1 + 0.12(92/365)} - \$9,786$$

The firm, thus, borrows $19,90,214 instead of $2 million at 13¼ p.a. The sum to be repaid on October 15 is $20,56,682. This is equivalent to paying 11.244 percent p.a. on $2 million for three-month period. By using the FRA, the firm has locked in an interest rate of about 11¼ percent and has, thus, avoided the 2 percent p.a. rise in interest rates.

**As per Forward Rate Agreement,** British Banks Association Rules, the cash settlement of the profit & loss is computed as follows:

$$\frac{\text{Profit/Loss} = \text{NotionalAmount} \times (\text{Rfx} - \text{R})/100 \times \text{Gap/Basic}}{1 + \text{Rfx}/100 \times \text{Gap/Basic}}$$

Where,
- R is the dealt rate
- Rfx is the fixing rate
- Gap is the number of days applying to the FRA period.
- 'Basis' is the relevant money market rate basis (360/365 days).
- The fixing rate is usually the officially fixing of a money market period and internationally the most commonly used benchmark is the LIBOR.

**EXAMPLE:**   Consider An Indian Company Y on March 1, 2015, which due to unforeseen circumstances must now find ₹10 million for an expenditure to occur on June 1, 2015. Company Y expects to generate revenue, and the company expects to be able to repay this amount on September 1, 2015. Company Y has a number of ways to meet this expenditure; in this example we only compare a traditional loan to an FRA.

Let us assume Company Y can normally borrow funds for 3 months from its local bank at a rate of 3 month Libor plus 100 basis points (bps). If the company takes the first alternative, the effective interest rate, it would be able to borrow at would remain unknown until June 1, when it borrows the actual ₹10 million at 3 month LIBOR plus 100 bps. Note that this represents a variable interest rate, as the interest rate in 3 months remain unknown until the actual day arrives. What if the company wishes to know on March 1, 2015 the interest they must pay on the loan, which will not occur for another 3 months?

Company Y can also get a quote from a FRA dealer (normally a bank). In this example, the company needs a 3 × 6 FRA quote (with 3 × 6 meaning a 3 month loan, to begin in 3 months). Let us assume the FRA dealer offers a quote of 7.0 percent. This means, if the 3 month Libor on June 1 is lower than 7.0 percent, the FRA dealer will earn the difference between 7.0 percent and the actual interest rate. Intuitively this makes sense, as the FRA dealer is earning 7.0 percent on this loan, but it can borrow at the lower 3 month LIBOR rate. However, if on June 1 the rate is higher than 7.0 percent, it will lose the difference.

If Company Y accepts the FRA rate of 7.0 percent on March 1, then 3 months later (June 1), it will settle in cash the difference between the previously agreed upon 7.0 percent and 3 month LIBOR on June 1, 2015. If the 3 month LIBOR on June 1 is lower than 7.0 percent, the company must pay the FRA dealer. However, if it is higher, the company receives payment from the FRA dealer. Since the company is effectively borrowing at a lower interest rate than otherwise possible, if the 3 month LIBOR is higher than 7.0 percent, and as such receives payment, to calculate the amount of the payment, refer to the formula below.

It may seem confusing how giving or receiving cash payment helps the company to lock in an interest rate. To understand the compensation payment in context, this example will be extended.

On June 1, only 3 possibilities can occur:

1. the 3 month LIBOR is exactly 7.0 percent, no settlement is needed,
2. the 3 month LIBOR is higher than 7.0 percent, Company Y receives payment,
3. the 3 month LIBOR is lower than 7.0 percent, Company Y makes payment.

Suppose if the 3 month LIBOR on June 1 increased to 7.5 percent, then the FRA dealer must make payment to Company Y. Continuing with this example, the FRA dealer will pay Company Y ₹10 millions* {[(7.0 – 7.5%)*(90/360)]/[1+ (7.5%)*(90/360)]}, which amounts to ₹12,269.94. If the 3 month LIBOR fell to 6.5 percent, the company would make an equal payment to the FRA dealer. But how does this help Company Y achieve the previously agreed upon 7.0 percent rate?

If the 3 month LIBOR increased to 7.5 percent, then Company Y receives payment of ₹12,269.94. It then goes to its local bank (from the start of the example), and borrows ₹10 million less ₹12,269.94, or ₹9,987,730.06. Assuming its local bank's mark-up rate has not changed, it would need to repay ₹9,987,730.06 * [1+ ((7.5%+ 100 bps) * 90/360)], or ₹1,01,99,969.32. This implies a quarterly rate of interest of 2.0 percent (₹1,01,99,969.32/₹1,00,00,000 – 1), which annually comes out to exactly 8.0 percent. This 8.0 percent rate is precisely the 7.0 percent locked in rate, plus the 100 bps mark-up rate.

If the 3 month LIBOR decreased to 6.5 percent, Company Y makes payment of ₹12,269.94 to the FRA dealer. It would again go to its local bank, but borrow ₹10 million plus ₹12,269.94, or ₹1,00,12,269.94. In 3 months' time, it would need to repay ₹1,00,12,269.94 * [1+ ((6.5%+ 100 bps) * 90/360) ], or ₹1,02,00,000. This implies a quarterly rate of interest of 2.0 percent, which annually comes out to 8.0 percent. Once again, the variable 3 month LIBOR has been replaced by the previously agreed upon FRA rate of 7.0 percent. As evidenced by this example, Company Y, as of March 1, knows its cost of borrowing ₹10 million, and this amount is independent of fluctuations in the 3 month LIBOR. When the 3 month LIBOR increases, it must borrow at a higher rate, but receives cash compensation from the FRA dealer. If the 3 month LIBOR decreases, it benefits from borrowing at a lower rate, but must pay the FRA dealer compensation.

## 9.17 PRICING OF FRA

A market maker (usually a banker) in FRAs is trading short-term interest rates. The settlement sum or compensation amount is the value of the FRA. It is exactly as short-term interest rate futures. FRAs are priced using forward rate principles. Since, the market makers are usually quoting two-way prices (bid-ask rate) in FRA market, so it is important to value the FRAs for trading purpose. If we view a FRA rate as the break even forward rate between the two periods, then we can simply solve for this forward rate and that is the approximate FRA rate. This rate is sometimes referred to as the interest rate "gap" in the money markets. In pricing of the FRAs, we can use the standard forward rate break even formula to solve for the required FRA rate. The mechanism of calculating the arbitrage-free forward rate is already discussed in the preceding section of this chapter.

### *Cost pricing*

There are different risks associated in the FRAs such as credit risk and market risk. Banks are exposed to credit risk if the counterparty fails before settlement date for the replacement cost of the FRA. There is also risk of the counterparty failing to deliver on settlement date of the FRA. It means the potential loss in this case will affect the ultimate profit of the FRA. As for credit risk, bank can mitigate this by charging margin from the counterparty. Hence, while pricing of the FRA, such risks must be incorporated. Further, the principal sum is not at risk, however, it is subject to interest rate movements. So, the bank is usually exposed to market risk if the instrument is not fully matched. This market risk can generally be managed by including the interest rate positions within a financial institutions overall system.

The pricing of FRAs reflects the costs of alternative ways of constructing a similar hedge. For example, the price of 6 × 9 month FRA will depend on interest rate on six-month and nine-month deposits. They are usually priced from the interbank yield curve, i.e., usually from a zero coupon yield curve. From this zero curve, the bank can determine the zero coupon rate at settlement of the

FRA. The seller of FRA notionally can place deposit or give loan at a certain rate of interest, whereas the buyer of FRA notionally accepts deposits or borrows at a rate of interest to protect against upward movement in interest rates.

Let us explain the FRA valuation through an example. For a 1 × 4 FRA contract, i.e., 3 months loan after one month. Assume that current market interest rate, i.e., 5 percent for one month and 6 percent for 4 months. Then the FRA rate will be based on arbitrage pricing. It means if we invest for one month period and 1 × 4 FRA, then our investment's total worth will be same, if we invest directly for 4 months. Thus, the FRA should be such that if you invest, say, ₹100 millions in one month security, it will become 100 × $(1 + SR_1)$ in one month and then 100 × (1 + 1 × 4 FRA) after the end of 4 months. And, by directly investing in 4 months instrument we will get 100 × $(1 + SR_1)$. So, both of these values should be equal. It can be shown as:

$$100 \times (1 + SR_1) \times (1 + 1 \times 4 \text{ FRA}) = 100 \times (1 + SR_4)$$

$$= 1 \times 4 \text{ FRA} = [(1 + R_4)/(1 + R_1)] - 1$$

Similarly, we can calculate any FRA rate at any time. Now, the value of FRA contract will be zero for both the parties (long and short) at the time of contract initiation. At the expiration, its value will depend on the interest rate for the loan period and that can be calculated simply as explained earlier.

Let us explain this with an example. For calculating the FRA contract value between the contract initiation and contract expiry, following the same approach, let us assume that in 1 × 4 FRA contract, we initiated the contract at 6.5 percent and after 10 days, the interest rates for 20 days and 110 days are 5.5 percent and 6.5 percent, respectively. In such situation, the new FRA rate, after 10 days, will be equal to $[(1 + R110)/(1 + R20) - 1]$. The new FRA rate will be (1.0065 × 110/360)/(1 + 0.055 × 20/360) $-1 = 0.016754$ which is equal to $0.016754 \times \dfrac{360}{90} = 0.67017$ p.a., i.e., 6.70 percent. It means if this rate is more than the FRA rate at the beginning, the FRA contract will be in profit, and thus, we can take long position. The long position holder will gain the interest rate differential multiplied by the notional principal as interest savings. However, this gain will accrue after 110 days, hence, it is to be discounted to get present value. So, for a notional principal of ₹1 million, the interest rate saving will be ₹1 million × (0.067 − 0.065) × 90/360 = ₹500, and the present value of these savings (i.e., the FRA contract value) will be ₹500 (1 + 0.065 × 110/360) = ₹490.27

In practice, FRAs are priced off the exchange traded short-term interest rate futures for that currency. Traders normally use a spread sheet pricing model that has futures prices directly fed into it. Further, FRA positions are also usually hedged with other FRAs or short-term interest rate futures contracts in the market.

## 9.18  HEDGING WITH FRAs

FRAs can also be used to manage the risk by entering a notional agreement to lend or borrow in the futures at a rate of interest determined in the present. A set of bid-offer spreads is published showing rates of interest for different futures time periods. The customer and the bank may agree that compensation will pass between them in respect of any deviation of interest rates, on the date that the loan was due to be made, from the rates published at the time of the agreement.

For example, a firm X has a floating rate loan of $1 million and would like to be certain that rate of interest to be charged on published three-month period commencing three months from the present, which is 10.625 − 10.500 (spread). The firm X could attempt to guarantee what its interest rate will be by entering an FRA, thereby notionally committing itself to borrow $1 million at 10.625 percent in three months' time. In this, further, a settlement interest rate is decided for determination of compensation to be passed between the counterparties. Assume that at the maturity, the spread is increased to 10.625 to 11.500, this increase of 1 percent per annum for three months, would require the bank to pay the customer, amount being totalling $2,500 (10 percent p.a. on 1 million dollars for three months). This money will compensate the firm for a rise in the rate of interest on its floating rate loan and vice versa. It means, if the interest rate decreases, then the firm will compensate bank but it has gained interest accrued on loan. Similarly, if the interest rate increases, the firm will loose on higher payment of interest accrued on loan. Thus, the firm will be compensated through FRA on both the situations, i.e., increase or decrease in interest rate. Hence, the firm would have achieved its aim of removing uncertainty about the interest payable.

FRAs are cash settled forward contracts on interest rates. It means if interest rates rise in future, above the forward rate, then the buyer of the FRA will be in profit and vice-versa. Thus, the FRAs can be used to hedge against higher or lower than expected interest rate in future. It is important to note here that the FRAs are used to hedge just one period of interest.

### Hedging against increase in interest rate

A firm which borrows funds from the lenders to run its business operations at the floating rate, if the rate of interest rises, then the firms interest expense will increase and resulting into lowering of profit, all else equal. Similarly, the investors who own fixed rate debt will experience a decrease in their assets value in case of increase in market interest rate. Thus, in such cases, buying of the FRAs serve to hedge the impact of higher interest rates. Figures 9.5 and 9.6 show the impact of rise in interest on firm's value and profits.

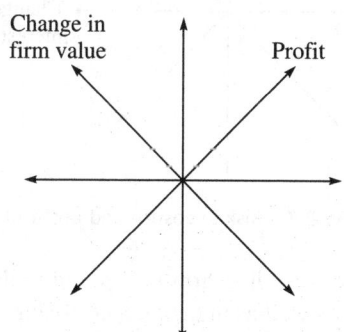

**FIGURE 9.5**   Risk exposure of a firm.

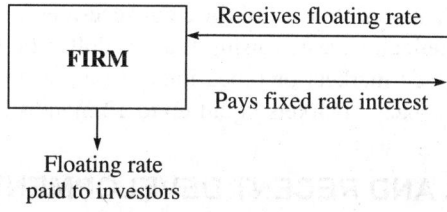

**FIGURE 9.6**   FRA long position.

Figure 9.5 presents the risk exposure of the firm which is expecting a rise in interest rate in future by showing the combine position of value and profits of the firm. If the interest rate increases, the firm's risk is increased and so the profit is also decreased. To hedge this risk, the firm may opt for long position in FRA of equal amount of the debts. The loss incurred on debt due to higher interest will be compensated by earning on FRA. Figure 9.6 shows the impact of long FRA on the interest risk management. Since, a FRA converts a floating rate expense into a fixed rate expense for a firm, so by taking long position in FRA the firm will pay fixed rate interest rate and receive floating rate. In this case, if the floating rates are same, then the firm is left with a locked in fixed rate a future expense.

### Hedging against a decline in interest rates

If the firm is a financial institution, a banker or a lender which is lending the money to the borrowers on a floating rate, then decline in interest rate will decrease the interest income of the firm. In such situation, if the firm has sold a FRA (short position in FRA), then the firm will have hedged, because the lower interest rates also result in a profit on the FRA. The investor who has invested in the short term floating rate bonds is also exposed to decline in future interest rate, he will also be hedged by taking short position in FRA. Figure 9.7 illustrates the risk exposure and profit position through decline in interest rate.

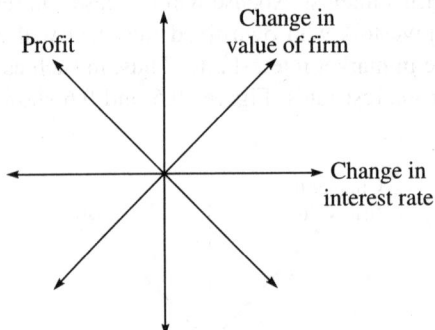

**FIGURE 9.7**    Risk exposure and profit of firm.

It is observed from Figure 9.7, a lending firm is exposed to decrease of interest rate which will result into decrease in firm's value as well as in the income arising due to interest. This can be hedged by selling a FRA which will be profitable if interest rates fall below the contracted floating rate of interest. The decline of firm's value to decrease in interest income will be compensated from the amount of compensation to be received from the selling of the FRA.

Foreign Banks have recently started trading in FRAs in Indian currency by quoting their prices of FRAs. Forward rates are being constructed of different securities with different maturities: FRAs in Indian rupee can be synthetically created using the US dollar FRA in conjunction with rupee forwards in the foreign currency markets or rupee interest rate swaps against MIBOR. However, forward rates in the foreign exchange markets liquid up to 12 months only.

## 9.19   FRA's IN INDIA AND RECENT DEVELOPMENTS

The Reserve Bank of India (RBI) vide its circular (RBI circular MPD.BC. 187 (07.01.279/1999–2000 dated July 7, 1999) issued guidelines and permitted to issue Forward Rate Agreements (FRA) in the rupee in India. According to this circular, the RBI permits corporate entities to hedge interest rate risk on both the asset and liability side, using rupee (IRD) interest rate derivatives. Corporate customers need to identify and earmark genuine exposures against each IRD, ensuring that the tenor and the notional of the hedge do not exceed that of the underlying. Further, Banks dealing with customers must also satisfy themselves that the customer has genuine underlying exposures. Rupee IRD undertaken by the customers can be freely cancelled and rebooked.

Important benchmarks in IRD in India are dominating the market:

- Those based on the overnight call rate benchmark (Mumbai Interbank offer rate or MIBOR published by the NSE).
- Those based on the rupee rates implied in the US $/INR foreign exchange market (Mumbai Interbank Forward Offer Rate or MIFOR & Mumbai Interbank form offer rate or MITOR).
- Those based on the Government of India bond market. Other benchmarks such as 3 months commercial papers (CP) rate have also been used in a few swaps.
- To provide more flexibility for pricing of interest rate derivatives and to facilitate some integration between money and foreign exchange markets, the use of interest rates implied in the foreign exchange forward market as a benchmark were permitted in addition to existing domestic money and debt market rates.

Foreign Banks have recently started trading in FRAs in Indian currency by quoting their prices of FRAs. Forward rates are being constructed of different securities with different maturities: FRAs in Indian rupee can be synthetically created using the US dollar FRA in conjunction with rupee forwards in the foreign currency markets or rupee interest rate swaps against MIBOR. However, forward rates in the foreign exchange markets liquid up to 12 months only.

**EXAMPLE:**   Let us assume that an Indian company wants to issue a 6-month commercial paper. The current market interest rates of 3-month CP and 6-month CP are 9.50 percent and 10.5 percent, respectively. The company is of the view that the 6-month rates are high and is expecting that rates will fall in future. The company could then sell a 3 × 6 FRA with a bank. If the market rates do fall, the corporate would receive the compensation from the bank, and thus, reducing its borrowing cost.

Another option with the company is to issue 3-month CP at 9.5 percent, lock in the 3 × 6 FRA, and issue another 3-month CP after 3 months, assuming that no issuing cost of CP. Similarly, the bank in turn, can hedge its exposure in the forward markets by paying (borrowing) 6-month forward and receiving (lending) 3-month forward.

### Recent developments in FRA's

Certain variations over the traditional FRAs have been noted and gaining in the market which include:

- "Strip" FRAs or a combination of FRAs to lock a series of interest rates reset periods. So instead of single period FRA, different interest rates of different periods of FRA's are also becoming popular in the market.
- A synthetic FRA in foreign currency—that is by combining FRAs in one currency and foreign currency forward in the other is also available in the market.
- Forward Spread Agreements (FSAs) are essentially used to lock the interest rate differentials between two currencies. In such type of agreements, transactions are entered between two parties who wish to hedge themselves against future changes in the LIBOR for two currencies, one of which being the USD.
- FRA can be now priced off forward-to-forward interest rates. These forward-to-forward rates can be obtained from the cash market yield curve or by the implied forward rate available from the interest rate futures market in the relevant currency.

## SUMMARY

The chapter describes the different types of interest rates which include treasury rates, LIBOR rate, repo rate, zero rate/spot rate and forward rates. There exist two risks in dealing the securities, i.e., interest rate risk and default risk. The default risk is concerned with losing of the principal amount of loan due to bankruptcy of the borrower. Interest rate risk is the risk which is arisen due to macro-economic factors resulting in changes in the price (or market value) of a security. There are such factors which are not in the control of a firm like inflation rate, money supply, growth rate, economic growth rates, policy, social unrest, etc.

The chapter further describes term structure of interest rate. The volatility of a debt instrument price is dependent on its maturity, i.e., longer the maturity, the greater the price volatility. The yield curve can be normal, inverted and flat. There are various theories of term structure like market segmentation theory, liquidity preference theory and expectation theory.

Forward yield curve is very much useful to understand and to ascertain the market expectations of interest rates. It related futures short-term interest rates implied by long spot rates to the point of time to which these implied rates relate. Forward rate agreements refer to a technique for locking futures short-term interest rate contract, sometimes, also called *over-the-counter futures*.

The short-term interest rate derivatives like forward rate agreements, 91-day Treasury bill futures, Eurodollars futures, etc. are popular instruments in the financial markets. Forward rate agreements (FRA) is an agreement between the counterparties who intend to protect against interest rate risk in short term. FRA is an off-balance sheet contract traded on OTC markets and is a forward contract on an interest rate. The parties in the FRA determine the forward interest rate which will to an agreed notional principal amount for a specified period.

The FRAs are quoted in the format of money market rates, quoted in the form of A × B, A – B, A vs B, etc. The first figure 'A' denotes the number of months until the loan is set to begin, and second figure 'B' represents the number of month until the loan ends. FRAs are short-term instruments and FRA of 3 months and 6 months are very popular in this market. These are concentrated in a few currencies like US dollars, pound sterling, Euro Japanese Yen, etc. FRAs are used mostly by the banks and financial institutions to hedge their interest rate exposures. FRAs are settled at the delivery date for cash.

The RBI permitted to issue FRAs in India on July 7, 1999 and issued guidelines in this respect. As per these guidelines, now corporate entities can go for FRAs to hedge interest rate risks on both the assets and liabilities. Corporate customers need to identify and earmark genuine exposure against each IRD, ensuring that the tenor and the notional of the hedge do not exceed that of the underlying. Banks dealing with the customers must ensure themselves that the customer has genuine underlying exposures.

## SOLVED PROBLEMS

**P.1.** ABC company has raised a loan of $10 million at floating rate with rollovers to be fixed by reference to the 6-month USD LIBOR rate. The company expects increase of interest rate in short-term market. The company's next rollover is due in next 2 months. The company intends to hedge this through FRA arrangements, and thus, contracts to a banker to quote FRA for a 2 × 8 USD FRA. Suppose the banker quotes the rate as (bid-offer) 6.68% and 6.71%. The company locks the offered rate 6.71 to be borrowed at the higher rate. Calculate the compensation to be arisen if the 6-month

LIBOR, 2 months from now increased by 100 basis points, i.e., 7.71%, or decreased by 100 basis points to 5.71%.

*Solution:* The facts of the above example are as follows.

Settlement rate (LIBOR) = 7.71%

Reference rate = 6.71%

Days in contract period = 181 days

Notional principal amount = $10 millions

Day basis (360 or 365) = 360 days

Since, the LIBOR increased by 100 bps to 7.71%, hence, the company will be in loss. So, the banker will have to compensate to the company. Calculation of compensation amount would be as:

$$= \frac{(Rs - Rf) \times \left(\dfrac{N}{4}\right) \times A}{1 + Rs\left(\dfrac{N}{Y}\right)}$$

Compensation Formula and Calculation:

$$= (7.71 - 6.71) \times \left(\frac{181}{360}\right) \times \$10 \text{ millions} = 1 + 7.71\left(\frac{181}{360}\right)$$

(b) If the interest rate is decreased by 100 bps, then the banker will be in loss, then the company has to compensate the banker. The amount is calculated as:

$$= \frac{(5.71 - 6.71) \times \left(\dfrac{181}{360}\right) \times \$10 \text{ millions}}{1 + 5.71\left(\dfrac{181}{360}\right)}$$

$$= \frac{5,02,777.777}{1.0287086} = \$48,875$$

**P.2.** A company has to borrow $1 million in three months' time for a 12 months period. It can borrow funds today at LIBOR + 50 bps. LIBOR rates today are at 5.0%, but the company is expecting increase in interest rate in future after three months to 6%. The company decides to hedge this situation by an FRA arrangement. A bank quotes (3 × 15) 5½% for the FRA, which the company accepted the quote of the bank. After three months, assuming that the rate has increased indeed to 6%, i.e., (12 months LIBOR rate 6%), the company will be in loss of 1% (LIBOR 5% rises to LIBOR 6%). The banker will compensate the company which will be as follows:

*Solution:* Compensation formula

$$\frac{Rs - Rf \times \left(\dfrac{N}{y}\right) \times A}{H(Rs)\left(\dfrac{N}{4}\right)}$$

Rs = 6%

Rf = 5.5%

N = 360 (one year)
A = $10 millions

$$\frac{(6\% - 5.5\%) \times \left(\dfrac{360}{360}\right) \$10 \text{ millions}}{1 + (6\%)\left(\dfrac{360}{360}\right)} = \frac{50,000}{1.06} = \$47,170$$

**P.3.**   Suppose that a company has purchased $1 million notional of a 1 × 4 FRA, dealt at 6.75%, and that the market rate in 75% on the fixing date. The contract period is 90 days. What will be the compensation amount in this case?

**Solution:**

Settlement Rate = 7.50%
Reference Rate = 6.75%
Days in Contract = 90 days
Days basis = 360 days
Notional Amount = $10 millions
Compensation amount

$$= \frac{Rs - Rf \times \left(\dfrac{N}{Y}\right) \times A}{1 + Rs\left(\dfrac{N}{4}\right)}$$

$$= \frac{7.5\% - 6.75\% \times \left(\dfrac{90}{360}\right) \times 10,00,000}{1 + 7.5\%\left(\dfrac{90}{360}\right)} = \frac{1875}{1.01875} = 1840.50$$

**P.4.**   An FRA market maker sells a $10 millions 3 × 6 FRA that is an agreement to make a notional deposit for three months' time at a rate of 6.52%. He is exposed to the risk that interest rates will have risen by the FRA settlement date in 3 months time. Current spot rate assumes to be 6.85%.

**Solution:**

Compensation amount

$$= \frac{Rs - Rf \times \left(\dfrac{N}{4}\right) \times A}{1 + Rs\left(\dfrac{N}{4}\right)}$$

$$= \frac{6.85\% - 6.52\% \times \left(\dfrac{90}{360}\right)(10 \text{ millions})}{1 + (6.85\%)\left(\dfrac{90}{360}\right)}$$

$$= \frac{.0033 \times \dfrac{1}{4}(10,00,0000)}{1 + (.685)\left(\dfrac{1}{4}\right)} = \frac{8250}{1.02125} = \$8078.33$$

**P.5.** Assume LIBOR for the floating rate, for a 3 × 5 FRA with a notional amount of $1,00,000 a fixed rate of 4.4% and a 5 months floating rate, as of 3 months from inception is 5.2%. Calculate the compensation amount in this

*Solution:*    Compensation formula:

$$= \frac{Rs - Rf \times \left(\dfrac{N}{y}\right)(A)}{1 + (Rs)\left(\dfrac{N}{y}\right)}$$

$$= \frac{(5.2\% - 4.4\%) \times \left(\dfrac{150}{360}\right)(\$1,00,000)}{1 + (5.2\%)\left(\dfrac{150}{360}\right)} = \frac{333.33}{1.0217} = 326.25$$

**P.6.**    Assume in a 1 × 4 FRA contract, 'X' initiated the contract at 6.5% and after 10 days the interest rates for 20 days and 110 days are 5.5% and 6.5% respectively. Calculate the new FRA rate.

*Solution:*    The new FRA will be:

$$= \frac{\left(1 + 0.065 \times \left(\dfrac{110}{360}\right)\right)}{\left(1 + 0.055 \times \left(\dfrac{20}{360}\right)\right)} - 1$$

$$= \frac{1.01986}{1.00355} = 1.01675 - 1 = 0.16754$$

$$= 0.16754 \times \frac{360}{90} = 0.067017 = 6.70\% \text{ p.a}$$

## REVIEW QUESTIONS

1. What do you understand by the term interest rates? Discuss the various types of interest rates along with different yields curve.
2. Explain the term forward interest rate. How is it determined? Also explain forward rate agreement with suitable illustrations.
3. Explain the concept of term structure of interest rates. Also explain its relevance in determining level of interest rates.
4. Discuss the various theories of term-structure of interest rates along with their significance.
5. Differentiate between spot vs forward yields with suitable examples.
6. Define forward rate agreements (FRA). Discuss hedging mechanism with FRAs with suitable examples.
7. What is implied repo rate? How is it calculated? If the implied repo rate is lower than the borrowing rate then futures contracts would be over or under priced? What arbitrage transaction would you engage in?
8. Explain the term forward interest rate. How is it determined? Explain with suitable examples.

9. Explain the terms spot and forward yield. How are they different to each other? Explain with examples.

10. Explain the forward yield curve. Explain the relationship of forward yield with spot yield curve. Explain with imaginary data and diagram.

11. Differentiate between spot–forward yields with suitable examples.

12. Explain the mechanism of calculating the forward interest rate with a hypothetical example and its relevance in financial futures market.

13. Explain the term Forward Rate Agreements (FRA). What are their features and uses for an investor? Explain with examples.

14. Explain the trading mechanism of forward rate agreement with suitable illustration. Also explain its application in risk management.

15. Explain the important terms used in the forward rate agreement. Also, explain the mechanism of settlement of FRA with example.

16. Write notes on the following:
    (a) FRA Pricing mechanism.
    (b) Risks of FRA

17. How will you value a forward rate agreement? What are major considerations in this respect? Explain with suitable data.

18. Write a detailed note on Forward Rate Agreements in India.

19. Distinguish between forward rate agreement and short-term interest rate futures with imaginary data.

20. Explain the mechanism of hedging with FRA with the help of a hypothetical example.

21. Write note on the following:
    (a) Compensation Formula in FRA
    (b) Risks in dealing the securities.

22. Explain the nature, features and uses of forward rate agreements.

# SUGGESTED READINGS

1. Batten, Jonathan and Featherstone, Thomas, *Asia Pacific Fixed Income Market: An Analysis of The Regime Money, Bond and Interest Rate Derivative Markets*, Wiley, New York, Chichester, 2002.

2. Questa, Grorgro, *Fixed Income Analysis for The Global Financial Market, Money Market and Derivatives*, Wiley, New York, 1999.

3. Sunderesan, Suresh M., *Fixed Income Markets and Their Derivatives*, 2nd ed., Southwestern College Publication, Cincinnati, Ohio, 2002.

4. Stephens, John J., *Managing Interest Risk: Using Financial Derivatives*, John Wiley, Chichester, West Sussex, England, New York, 2002.

5. Fabozzi, Frank J., *Valuation of Fixed Income Securities and Derivatives*, 3rd ed., McGraw Hill, New York, 1998.

6. Rene M. Stulz, *Risk Management & Derivatives*, Thomson-South-Western, Indian-Reprint-2007.

7. Robert A. Strong *Derivatives,* Thomson-South-western, Indian-Reprint-2006.

8. www. Nseindia.com. & www.bseindia.com.

Chapter **10**

# Short-Term Interest Rate Futures

**LEARNING OBJECTIVES**

*After reading this chapter, students will be able to*

➤ Understand the concept of interest rate futures.
➤ Learn the functioning of short-term interest rate futures market and how prices are quoted in this market.
➤ Know the types of interest rate futures like Treasury bill, treasury bonds, municipal bonds, Eurodollar deposit and so on.
➤ Explain Treasury bill futures, cash price quotations on T-bill futures and markets for T-bill futures.
➤ Understand about how T-bill futures are priced.
➤ Explain the trading mechanism of treasury bills futures in India.
➤ Know the historical background of short-term interest futures trading in India.
➤ Know specifications of 91-day Treasury bills futures in India.
➤ Know how to hedge with short-term interest rate futures.
➤ Understand what are Eurodollar futures contract, its various specifications and how Eurodollars futures are priced.
➤ Understand the TED spread and how corporates can hedge their risks by using short-term interest rate futures.

## 10.1 INTRODUCTION

Interest rate futures contracts are most popular and successful financial derivatives instruments today in the global financial markets. Both borrowers and lenders face interest rate risk. For example, the borrowers will suffer losses when the interest rate increases while the lenders suffer loss in decreasing trend of interest rate. If borrowers and lenders both dislike risk and uncertainty then they will seek such instruments through which they can reduce such risk. Thus, interest rate futures are such financial derivatives which assist in reducing the interest rate risk of such persons.

The first such contracts on interest rates futures were traded on October 20, 1975 on Eurodollar time deposits and US treasury bills. The market later on expanded rapidly in the volatile interest rate environment of the 1970s and 1980s. Besides a number of unsuccessful contracts introduced in the beginning like commercial papers and Certificate Delivery GNMA contracts, the market has been a huge success. They are useful to those market participants who wish to protect themselves against movements in short-term interest rates. Since inception, the interest rate futures market has come to represent about one-half of the entire futures market. The most of the industry observers and financial experts expect the same growth in futures too.

In this section, we will discuss some preliminaries about the interest rates, and then we will describe the mechanics of how interest rate futures market works and how prices are quoted. After that, three-month interest rate futures in their most basic hedging use will be explained. It will be visualized how the basic hedge establishes a futures position opposite to the cash market position. Then, determination of the futures prices and see how the futures contracts are used in risk management and arbitrage.

## 10.2   HISTORICAL BACKGROUND

Interest rate derivatives are the most traded and widely used derivative instrument in the global market, specifically in developed countries. Two types of interest rate futures (IRFs), i.e., (long-term and short-term) are traded globally. The long-term futures (above one year) period are also known as *bond futures*, whereas short-term futures (up to one year period) are called *Treasury bills futures* or *reference rate futures*. Interest rate future markets are settled by delivery as well as cash at worldwide. For example, long-term futures on the 10 year municipal bond index of Chicago Board of Trade are settled in cash. Similarly, short-term futures like T-bills futures are settled by delivery. Further, the futures on reference rates like LIBOR are cash settled.

The first interest rate futures (IRF) contract was initiated in 1975 by Chicago Board of Trade (CBOT) based on Ginnie Mae (Government National Mortgage Association-GNMA). This instrument continued up to December 1984 and later on failed. After that in 1977, CBOT introduced the 30-year Treasury bond futures. It is highly successful instrument in the market today. Currently, 2-year, 5-year, 10-year Treasury notes and 30-year ultra Treasury bond futures instrument are being traded at the Chicago Mercantile Exchange (CME). They are mostly settled through since 1981, Eurodollar futures, a short-term futures instrument was launched by CME. Important major international exchanges which are involved in the IRFs trading are Australian Securities Exchange, CME, Eurex, NYSE group, Nasdaq, OMX, Singapore Exchange, Tokyo Stock Exchange, etc.

## 10.3   TREASURY BILLS FUTURES

*Treasury Bills* (TB) are major short-term interest rate securities and normally issued for 90 days and 180 days, respectively. However, 90-day T-bills are most popular instrument. The Treasury bill futures contract was introduced in 1976 and is traded on the International Monetary Market (IMM)—a Division of the Chicago Mercantile Exchange. T-bill futures market is most liquid and contracts are widely traded. To understand the trading in T-bill futures market, let us see first how the T-bill cash market operates.

## 10.3.1  Cash Price Quotations on T-bills

As discussed earlier, T-bills are short-term debt instrument of the US government. They are issued on discount and have maturity less than one year. The difference between the purchase price of a treasury bill and its face value determines the interest earned by a buyer. Thus, T-bills yields are typically quoted on a discount basis; as a percentage of face value rather than actual funds invested.

The purchase price of T-bills = Face value − Discount

= Face value − (Face value) × (Annualized discount asked yield) × Days to maturity/360

or          Face value − (Face value) (Yield) (No. of days to maturity)/360

For example, suppose we have a 180-day T-bill with a 10 percent quoted yield. The T-bill price must be

$$P_t = \$10,00,000 - \$10,00,000 \times 0.10 \times \frac{180}{360}$$

$$= \$10,00,000 - \$50,000$$

$$= \$9,50,000$$

The price of the bill is less than the face value by $50,000 or 5 percent, which is 10 percent annual discount over 180 days. However, the actual interest rate, called the *bond yield*, on this bill will be

$$\text{Bond yield} = \frac{\text{Face value} - \text{Price}}{\text{Price}}$$

$$= \frac{\$10,00,000 - \$9,50,000}{\$9,50,000}$$

$$= 5.26\% \text{ for 180 days}$$

$$= 10.52\% \text{ for a year (annualized)}$$

Discount Yield

$$\text{Discount yield} = \frac{\text{Par value} - \text{Market value}}{\text{Par value}} \times \frac{360}{\text{days}}$$

However, financial press usually reports T-bill prices based on the Ask Discount, which is the discount rate associated with paying the ask price for the security. To fix that, we can calculate the bond equivalent yield

$$\text{BEY} = \frac{\text{Discount amount}}{\text{Discount price}} \times \frac{360}{\text{Days to maturity}} \times 100$$

It is to be noted that the rate published in the wall street Journal on the internet is an annual rate. We need to convert in the paper to our actual cost in dollars. The formula is given as:

**EXAMPLE:** $\dfrac{10,000 - X}{10,000} \times \dfrac{360}{91} = (\text{Discount Rate})$

If discount rate is 6%, then actual cost will be $\dfrac{10,000 - X}{10,000} \times \dfrac{360}{91} = (6\%)$ = Solving X = App. \$9,850 app.

$$(10,000 - X)\, 91 = 360(10,000) = 6\%$$

$$91,00,000 - 91X = 3,60,00,000 = 6\%$$

$$91X = \dfrac{3,60,00,00,000}{91}$$

## 10.3.2 T-bill Futures Quotations, Futures Prices and Futures Market

The futures contract on T-bill is a delivery contract that has a 13-week T-bill on the deliverable grade. Either a newly issued 13-week T-bill or old issued T-bill with longer maturity which has now 13-week remaining until expiration may be delivered. Table 10.1 shows the specification of US Treasury bill

**TABLE 10.1** Summary of Contract Specification of US T-bill

| Contract | US treasury bills |
|---|---|
| Exchange | Chicago mercantile exchange |
| Quantity | $1 million face value |
| Delivery months | March, June, September, December |
| Delivery specification | Delivery of a 90, 91, 92 days T-bills on three successive days, beginning the day after the last day of trading |
| Minimum price/Movements | $25 per contract (1 basis point) |
| Yields | Discount |
| Hours | 7.20 a.m. to 2.00 p.m. |
| Ticker symbol | TB |
| Cash day of trading | The day before the first delivery day |

Price quotation for T-bill futures are on an index basis. The index is 100 minus the annualized discount rate (in percent). For example, annualized discount rate is 8 percent, implies an index price of 92. Treasury securities are sold by the respective government on auction basis. There is also large secondary market for T-bills operated by the government securities dealers through a telephone network. Hence, in transaction with dealer, the customers pay the asked yield when they are buying the security and receive the bid yield when they sell. The bid-asked spread represents the compensation received by the dealer for making the market. Thus, bid yield is higher than the asked yield. The customer's sales price is lower than his purchase price.

The index price is simply a way of quoting the T-bill yield the market set for delivery. It is not the price at which T-bill futures contracts are actually traded. The quoted futures price is related to the actual transaction futures price ($F_{t,T}$) which can be calculated as follows:

$$F_{t,T} = \text{Face value} - \dfrac{(\text{Face value})\,(100 - \text{Quoted futures price})\,(M)}{360 \times 100}$$

where $M$ can be 90, 91, 92 days to maturity.

The relationship between the quoted and transaction futures prices, assuming $M$ is 90, quoted futures price is 92. This quoted price represents a T-bill yield of 8 percent per annum or 2 percent for 90 days Transaction futures price (of the contract) is, therefore, $F_{t,T} = ₹9,80,000$. It is the ₹9,80,000 transaction price and not the 92, quoted price.

Now, suppose the quoted futures price increases from 100 to 92.5. The implied T-bill yield falls from 8 to 7.5 percent and the transaction futures price associated with the new yield increases by ₹11,250 to ₹9,81,250, i.e.,

$$F_{t,T} = 10,00,000 - \frac{10,00,000\ (0.75)\ (90)}{360} ₹9,81,250$$

## 10.3.3 Delivery Requirements and Determination of the Delivery Price

Depending upon the issuing cycle for T-bill and the calendar, a T-bill may be delivered in fulfillment of T-bill futures contract. To ensure the adequate supply of deliverable bills, the particular exchange (IMM) scheduled T-bill futures delivery dates for three successive dates (as discussed in Futures Market Lesson in detail). In general, T-bill futures contracts can be satisfied by delivering either a newly issued 13-week bill or an original issue 52-week bill with 13 weeks left to maturity.

If an investor trader chooses to keep the futures contract until delivery, the contract is marked-to-market at the close of the last trading day. All longs with open positions at that time must be delivered at a purchase price determined by the closing futures price. This price is fixed by the same procedure. Assume that the final futures price were 92.80 (implied yield 7.20 percent), the invoice price for a 90 days T-bill would be:

$$\text{Invoice price} = \$10,00,000 - \frac{\$10,00,000\ (0.072)\ (90)}{360} = \$9,82,000$$

## 10.3.4 Pricing of T-bills Futures

The concept of cost-of-carry pricing relationship has been discussed in the preceding chapter, however, in case of T-bill futures contract, the convention of financial markets is to apply the term not carrying cost (i.e., difference between the interest earned and the cost of borrowing to finance to purchase the security). In general, the theoretical (cost-of-carry) price of a short-term interest rate futures contract is:

$$F_{t,T} = S_{t,T} + S_{t,T}\ (R_{t,T} - D_{t,T}) \times \frac{T-t}{360} \tag{10.1}$$

where $F_{t,T}$ is T-bill futures price at time $t$ with settlement date $T$, $S_{t,T}$ is T-bill spot (cash price) at time $t$ deliverable at $T$, $R_{t,T}$ is the annualized financing cost for period $T - t$ and $D_{t,T}$ is the annualized yield on the T-bill for period $T - t$.

Since T-bills are discount instruments, no explicit interest is paid on these bills. Hence, the cost-of-carry is simply the cost associated with financing to purchase the T-bills over the period during which they are held. Then the Eq. (10.1) may be expressed as $F_{t,T} = S_{t,T}(1 + R_{t,T})$. Further detail will be given in Eurodollar section (Section 10.4). Finally, it is observed that the carrying costs fall as the futures settlement date approaches because the time period for which a cash position must be hold becomes shorter which causes futures prices to converge to the underlying spot T-bills. In brief, we can conclude that the more deferred is the delivery date of a futures contract, the higher the carrying cost resulting in more futures price and lower the futures yield.

## 10.3.5    Repurchase Agreements (Repo)

A repurchase agreement is a transaction involving the sale of a security usually a treasury security, where the seller repurchase the security after a stated period. In other words, one party sells a security to another party at one price and agrees to repurchase the same at another price at a futures date. In other words, this is a contract in which one party sells a security and promises to buy in return at a predetermined price on some future date. In fact, with futures this is rate of return that should prevail in the absence of arbitrage. Thus, the buyer of the security has entered into a reverse repurchase agreement (or reverse repo). The difference between the initial sale price and the subsequent repurchase price of the security is called the *interest rate*, popularly known as *'repo rate'* in RP markets. The borrowing rate is called as *repo rate*, whereas the buyer of the reverse repo receives a lending rate called the *reverse repo rate*. The repo rate is most competitive and liquid market with quotations available on both borrowing and lending.

## 10.3.6    Implied Repo Rate

The implied repo-rate is the riskless return the trader gets from buying the underlying asset and simultaneously selling futures contracts against it.

Since repurchase agreements are a primary financing source for dealers in government securities, so the repo rate is typically used to determine the net carrying cost for T-bills.

The implied repo rate is a measure of the carrying cost that are implicit in the futures spot price relationship. It refers to the difference between the actual price of the futures contract and the price of the cash bill, converted into an annualized rate of return, or

$$IRR = \frac{F_{t,T} - S_{t,T}}{S_{t,T}} \times \frac{360}{T - t} \qquad (10.2)$$

where *IRR* is implied repo rate, $F_{t,T}$ is actual futures price of the security and $S_{t,T}$ is actual cash price of the security.

**EXAMPLE:**  Suppose a finance company X Ltd. owns ₹10 lakhs in T-bills with current market value of ₹9,80,000. Due to cash shortage in the market, the company investigates a repurchase agreement with another finance company 'Y'. The other company 'Y' proposes to advance ₹9,80,000 to the finance company 'X' and the finance company 'X' promising to pay ₹9,84,000 to buy the T-bills back in 30 days. The repo (IRR) rates:

$$\text{Repo Rate} = \frac{₹9,84,000 - ₹9,80,000}{₹9,80,000} \times \frac{360}{30}$$

$$= 0.04898$$

$$= 4.9\%$$

The *IRR* reveals the annualized gross rate of return that can be earned by buying a cash T-bill and simultaneously selling a T-bill futures contract with a delivery date $(T - t)$ days away. In other words, it also reveals the annualized borrowing rate or the no-arbitrage borrowing rate. If we compare the implied repo rate and actual borrowing rate, it will be just like comparing the theoretical and actual futures prices. For example, if the implied repo rate is higher than the actual borrowing rate (repo), it indicates that futures contracts are overpriced; actual futures prices are higher than theoretical futures prices. In such situation, it will be profitable for an arbitrageur to borrow funds to finance the purchase of a cash T-bill and simultaneously to sell futures.

## 10.4   EURODOLLAR FUTURES

Eurodollar is another most popular short-term instrument in the money markets. Eurodollar deposits are US dollar deposits held in a commercial bank outside the USA. These banks may be either foreign banks or foreign branches of US-based banks. The deposits are non-transferable and they cannot be used as collateral security for a loan. Since the amount deposited in a bank is for three months, hence, it is called *Eurodollar Time Deposits (TD)*. London dominates the Eurodollar deposit markets, so LIBOR has become the benchmark short-term interest rate for the traders. The LIBOR is quoted as an 'add-on yield' basis which means that it is a percentage of the TD purchase amount. It is an annualized rate based on a 360-day a year. For example, if the three-month (90 day) LIBOR is 10 percent, the interest on $1 million will be

$$\text{Interest} = (0.10) \left( \frac{90}{360} \right) (\$1 \text{ million}) = \$25,000$$

**Comparison of Treasury Bills and Eurodollars Futures**

|   | *Treasury Bills* | *Eurodollars* |
|---|---|---|
| 1. | Deliverable underlying product | Undeliverable underlying product |
| 2. | Settled through cash after 1997 | Settled through cash |
| 3. | Transferable | Non transferable |
| 4. | Yield quoted on discount basis | Yield quoted on add on basis |
| 5. | Maturities out to one year | Maturities out to 10 years |
| 6. | Onc tick is $25 | One tick is $25 |

Yields on Eurodollars are usually greater than those on T-bills and also other US money market instruments. T-bills instruments' yields are the lowest as they have no default risk. The reason for Eurodollar higher yield are: foreign banks can offer higher return because they operate under less regulation; investors clear and higher yields because they are moving their investment abroad, finally, although US Government rescues domestic banks, it is not clear that foreign governments will do the same.

A Eurodollar futures contract was introduced in December 1981 by the IMM in Chicago. The major specifications of Eurodollar futures contract are given in Table 10.2.

When a Eurodollar futures contract expires, the final settlement price (the expiration futures price) is constructed from an index of the three-month LIBOR at selected banks. The formula for the expiration futures price is:

Expiration futures price (TB) = 100 – LIBOR

Before the expiration, the quoted futures price implies an interest rate will be as under:

Interest rate = 100 – Quoted futures price

This is interest rate which can be locked upon by the futures contract. In other words, Eurodollar futures can be used to hedge (or to lock-in) the borrowing cost of the corporations/banks.

**TABLE 10.2**   Eurodollar Futures Contract Specifications

| Contract | Eurodollar time deposits |
|---|---|
| Exchange | Chicago mercantile exchange |
| Quantity | $1 million |
| Contract grade | Cash settlement |
| Delivery months | March, June, September, December |
| Delivery specifications | Cash settlement based on three-month LIBOR, expiration on third Monday on delivery month |
| Minimum price/Movements | $25 per contract (1 basis point) |
| Yields | Add-on-yield |
| Ticker symbol | TB |
| Delivery date | Last day of trading |

*Source:* Futures and options by Edwards and Ma, p. 284.

## 10.4.1   Futures Quotations and Futures Prices of Eurodollar

Similar to the T-bill futures, Eurodollars are also quoted on index basis, i.e., 100 – LIBOR on the relevant Eurodollar futures contract. For example, if the closing rate is 91.52, the quoting futures rate will be 8.48 percent (100 – 91.52). A change of one basis point in the futures index is worth $25. The yield on Eurodollar is also calculated like T-bill, making the assessment of spot interest rate in futures. For example, if Eurodollar futures rate is 8.48 percent indicates that the market expects three-month rate at 8.48 percent..

## 10.4.2   The Pricing of Eurodollars Futures

While calculating the price of Eurodollar, the futures price should reflect the forward interest rate that is implied by the existing term structure of interest rates. Theoretical futures price of a Eurodollar will be calculated in the same manner as seen in the case of T-bills.

## 10.4.3   Delivery and Settlement Prices of Eurodollars

The Eurodollar futures contracts are settled through cash instead of requiring physical delivery. Eurodollar futures are marked to the cash price at the closing day. Any payments due on longs and shorts at that time are done through clearing house as standard variation margin payments. The settlement price is determined by the IMM clearing house by taking sample of LIBOR at the two different periods, i.e., at the time of termination of trading and at randomly selected time within 90 minutes of trading. The final settlement price is fixed as followed.

On the last day of trading, the clearing house will determine the LIBOR for three-month Eurodollar time deposits funds both at the time of termination of trading and at a randomly selected time within the last 90 minutes of trading to determine the LIBOR at either time, the clearing house will select at random 12 reference banks from the list of not less than 20 participating banks which deal in London Eurodollar market. Each reference bank will quote to the clearing house its perception about the rate. These rates must be confirmed in writing by the Telex before they are accepted as official. The two highest and the two lowest quotes will be eliminated. The arithmetic mean of the remaining eight quotes will be the LIBOR at that time. If for any reason the bank has not given its quote within reasonable time then the bank will be dropped from the sample and another bank will be randomly selected. The final settlement price will be 100 minus the arithmetic mean rounded to the nearest 1/100th of a percentage point of the LIBOR of these two times. The daily settlement price depends upon the quotations in the futures market which may vary the spot rates except for the final day of trading. If the variation between futures settlement price and spot price of LIBOR is significant, the trader may book his profits. Let us explain this by an example. Assume that the discount yield is 10 percent, the spot price is $9,75,000 then discount will be $25,000 and 90 days remain until the bill will mature. The contract size is for $10,00,000 with yield being quoted on an add-on basis.

$$\text{Add-on yield} = \frac{\text{Discount}}{\text{Price}} \times \frac{360}{\text{DTM}} \quad \text{(where DTM is maturity period of TD)}$$

$$\text{Add-on yield} = \frac{\$25,000}{\$9,75,000} \times \frac{360}{90} = 0.103 \text{ or } 10.3\%$$

The discount yield is 10%, whereas add-on yield is 10.3%, it means add-on yield has exceeded the discount yield resulting in arbitrage opportunities.

Theoretical price of Eurodollar futures contract can be calculated with the following formula:

$$\left(1 + R_1 \times \frac{t_1}{360}\right) = \left(1 + R_2 \times \frac{t_2}{360}\right) \times \left(1 + R_3 \times \frac{t_3}{360}\right) \tag{10.3}$$

where $t_1$ is longer period of the investment, $R_1$ is annualized Eurodollar deposit rate, $t_2$ is shorter period of the investment, and $R_2$ is annualized Eurodollar deposit rate, $t_3$ is 90-day investment period and $R_3$ is annualized Eurodollar rate on the $t_3$ period.

**EXAMPLE:** Assume that on January 22, 2003, a trader wishes to put his money into Eurodollar deposits until June 17, 2003 (a period of 146 days for investment). Let us assume that he has two options: First he may invest by obtaining a 146-days Eurodollar time deposit, and second he may obtain 56-day Eurodollar futures contract. This futures contract expires on March 19, 2003, in 56 days. In both the cases, the investor will lock-in a Eurodollar rate for the next 146 days (until June 17, 2003). On January 22, 2003, the two-month rate was 8 × 7/16 to 8 × 5/16 percent. The theoretical price for the March, 2003 Eurodollar futures contract on January 22, 2003 can be calculated as follows:

where, $t_1$ is 146 days, i.e., from January 23 to June 17, 2003, $t_2$ is 56 days, i.e., from January 23 to March 20, 2003, $R_1$ is annualized Eurodollar deposit rate $t_1 = 8.3125\%$, $R_2$ is annualized Eurodollar deposit rate $t_2 = 8.1875\%$, $t_3$ is 90-day investment period, March 20 to January 17, 2003 and $R_3$ is annualized Eurodollar rate on the March 90 futures.

Making the substitutions yields

$$\left(1 + 0.083125 \times \frac{146}{360}\right) = \left(1 + 0.081875 \times \frac{56}{360}\right) \times \left(1 + R_3 \times \frac{90}{360}\right)$$

$$R_3 = 0.08285 \text{ or } 8.29 \text{ percent}$$

Thus, the theoretical futures price is 91.71 (100 − 8 − 0.29).

If the actual futures price were less or more than the theoretical (fair) price, i.e., 91.71, the arbitrage opportunities will arise. For example, if the actual futures price is less than the theoretical price (91.71) or futures rates were higher than 8.29 percent, arbitrageurs would borrow for 146 days and invest the proceeds in a 56-day Eurodollar deposit and simultaneously purchase a March, 2003 Eurodollar contract and vice versa. Thus, to determine the profitable arbitrage opportunity, the forward rate/yield can be calculated and compared with the quoted futures yield. If they are not equal, an arbitrage opportunity may exist.

## 10.5    TED SPREAD

The TED spread refers to the difference between the prices of futures contracts between three-month US treasury bills and three-month Eurodollar time deposits both with the same expiration month. [T stands for T-Bill and ED for the Eurodollar futures contract]. The spread is quoted as the T-bill futures price minus the Eurodollar futures price, i.e., TED Spread = $F_{t,T}$ (T-bill) − $F_{t,T}$ (TD). Alternatively, the TED spread is the expected yield on a futures three-month Eurodollar deposit minus the expected yield on a futures three-month T-bill. The TED spread varies significantly over time. Investors take T-bills as less risky than Eurodollar because T-bills are sold by the US treasury while the Eurodollars deposits are obligations of major commercial banks. Further, they are not guaranteed by any government. Hence, T-bills are risk-free, whereas Eurodollars are not risk-free, rather having low risk, because a bank may default on its obligations. Therefore, T-bills carry a lower rate of return than the Eurodollars. Consequently, the T-bills futures prices are higher than the Eurodollar deposits futures prices, and the TED spread is always a positive number.

The TED spread is taken in the financial market as a quality spread. If the magnitude of spread is changed then it will be taken in the market a significant change because it will change the perception of safety of the Eurodollars. For example, if TED spread is widened, the banks are forced to pay higher Eurodollar rates relative to T-bill yields. In brief, the TED spread is away to speculate on general economic conditions and on the soundness of banks in particular without incurring interest rate risk.

## 10.6    HEDGING USING SHORT-TERM INTEREST RATE FUTURES

Short-term interest rate futures can be used to hedge against interest rate risk and to lock in future investment yield or future cost of borrowing. Further, these can be used by the banks and other corporations to structure their fixed income securities in accordance with the changed economic conditions from time to time. The investor can use both short as well as long hedge in this respect. For example, a short hedge position in interest rate futures can be used to lock in a futures borrowing rate. The firm may estimate that the LIBOR may rise, then to protect itself again rising borrowing costs can hedge through T-bills futures or Eurodollars futures contract. Similarly, a long hedge position in interest rate futures may be used to lock in an investment yield. If the investor is expecting large sum of cash to invest for a short period of time, he can wait until the funds arise and invest them at the rate which prevails at that time, or he can buy short-term instruments like T-bills or Eurodollars futures to look the desired yield.

In the above said long or short hedging techniques, it may be necessary for the trader to do a strip or a stack hedge. A strip hedge engages futures positions in a number of different futures contracts, each with a different delivery date which coincide with the hedger's risk exposures. In case of stack hedge, the investor utilizes only futures positions which are concentrated in nearby delivery months. Though stack hedging has superior liquidity attributes, but it usually entails greater risk than a strip hedge. Thus, the hedger must decide whether the greater liquidity is worth with additional basis risk.

A brief description on hedging strategy with T-Bills Futures and Eurodollars Futures is stated below:

## 10.6.1  Short Hedge Situations

A trader can follow the short hedge position in the following situations:

1. The trader is expecting a rise in short-term interest rates in future which will result in decline in value of his short-term investment, then he can choose for short hedge position.
2. A fund manager or banker has raised loan for one year on floating interest rate basis. This deposit has been invested in advances to corporate entities. The manager fears that interest rate will rise in future, resulting into losses to pay more interest or loan. So, he can take a short hedge position and rolling the same in future.
3. A commercial bank plans to issue Certificate of Deposits (CDs) or to sell Commercial Papers (CPs) or to raise short-term loan in the near future. If short-term future rate of interest is increased or on rising trend, then the banker will have to pay a higher interest. In such situation, he may opt for short hedge position.
4. A person deals in government securities and carrying an inventory of T-bills. He is expecting a rise in interest rate in near future, as a result the value of investment in T-Bills will decline. In such situation, he may opt for short hedge position.
5. A person who is planning to buy a house through taking a loan from the finance company. If his borrowing rate is tied with a short-term treasury security index, then he may go for position of short hedge of T-bills and roll the same in future.
6. A financial institution which is in need of cash in near future plans to sell its short-term investment. The rise in short-term interest rate will cause to decrease return on short-term investment. Thus, it can plan to take position of short hedge.
7. A finance company has raised loan at floating rate in the near future, its interest rate of loan will be reset. In such situation, it can go for short hedge position.

## 10.6.2  Long Hedge Situations

As the various situations of short hedge are discussed in the preceding section, the situations of long hedge can also be described. A trader or investor or portfolio manager may take the position of short hedge in T-bills or Eurodollars if he is expecting decline of interest rate in future for a short period. All such situations will be opposite to short hedges as described earlier. A few among these are stated below:

1. A financial company plans to purchase short-term debt instruments like CDs, postal saving certificates, etc. The company is expecting a fall in interest rate for short period. As a result, the value of short-term investment may decline. In this situation, the company may take the position of long hedge in T-bills/Eurodollars.
2. A portfolio manager knows that a particular investment is going to be matured in future. Currently yields are very attractive. However, the manager is expecting the fall in interest rate, resulting into decrease in value of the investment. In such situation, the manager can take a position of long hedge in T-bills, etc.
3. A banker has invested in variable rate securities. The securities are financed through longer term (CD). Fall in interest rate will decrease the earning on securities. In such position, the banker may plan to take long hedge position.

4. An institution plans to buying of money market instruments through raising short-term loan on fixed rate. Decline in interest rate in future will cause to decline in value of money market instruments. In this situation, the institution can go for long hedge position.

**EXAMPLE:** Suppose on June 23, 2015, 'X' Ltd Company decides to borrow ₹10 Lakhs on July 31, 2015 for a period of 3 months (90 days) and pays of the loan at the end of the period. Further assume that Central Bank of India agrees to provide these funds at 50 basis points above the MIBOR rate as on the borrowing date. The company fears that the interest may increase during this period. Hence, the company wants to protect itself from rising borrow cost of funds. The Company sells 5, July futures contracts of size ₹2 each at ₹95.30 and square off its position in futures by going long at the expiry of the futures, i.e., July 31, 2015. Further, assume that if the MIBOR falls to 4.5%.

**Solution:**    3 months MIBOR increase to 5.00% on July 31, 2015 (September futures are quoted at ₹95.00 as on July 31, 2015).

$$\text{Interest expenses} = (₹10,00,000) \times (0.055) \times \frac{3}{12} = ₹13,750$$

*Less:* Futures gain = (price change) × ₹5 bp) × 10 = (95.30 – 95.00) × 100 × 5 × 5 =    ₹750

Net Borrowing Cost = ₹13,000

Now suppose if 3 = month MIBOR falls to 4.5% by July 31, 2015 (September futures are quoting at ₹95.50 as on July 31, 2015.

$$\text{Interest expense} = (₹10,00,000) \times (0.05) \times \frac{3}{12} = ₹12,500$$

Add futures loss = (price change) × (₹5 bp) × 10 = (95.30 – 95.50) × 100 × 5 × 5 =    ₹500

Net Borrowing Cost = ₹13,000

## 10.7   ESTIMATING HEDGE RATIO

The short-term trader or investor may opt for longer short hedge position depending upon the situations. What will be the hedge ratio? A good hedge ratio is one in which amount of losses in the spot market in future may be made up with the gains in the futures market. So, hedge ratio is the ratio of the number of futures contracts required to hedge cash position.

To determine the hedge ratio, let us explain the following terms:

$\Delta Vs$ = Change in the value of spot position, or estimated spot position assuming interest rates change by one point basis.

$\Delta V_F$ = Change in the value of cash flow generated by the change in the futures price of one futures contract if interest rate change by one basis point.

The HR ratio ($h$.) will be = $\Delta Vs = h\Delta V_F$    (10.4)

$$= h = \frac{\Delta V_S}{\Delta V_F}$$

The above formula assumes that there is a perfect positive correlation between the spot rate and futures interest rate. However, this assumption of perfect correlation may not exist in actual practice. Then the hedger might use the regression equation for determining HR ratio ($h$). The regression equation is as follows:

Where  $\Delta rs = 9 + bDrf$

$\Delta rs$ = Historical changes in interest rates of the cash market.

$\Delta r_F$ = Historical changes in the futures interest rates.

$a,b$ = Regression coefficients: '$a$' is intercept, and '$b$' is estimated slope coefficient

Assume that '$b$' is 0.75, which indicates that the changes in interest rate of the cash security average only 75% of the change in the futures interest rate. It means that spot interest is not as volatile as futures interest rate, since it is less than I, i.e., $b > 1.0$ and vice versa.

The above equation (10.4) be redefined in term as:

$\Delta Vs$ = Change in value of spot position if interest rates change by '$b$' basis point.

$\Delta V_F$ = Change in value of cash flow generated by the change in futures price of one futures contract if the interest rates change by one point basis.

The HR ratio ($h$) in the above said situation will be equivalent to '$b$'. Thus, ($h$) = '$b$'. For example, if '$b$' is 0.9 or 90% then '$h$' will be 90% means fewer futures than spot required. If '$b$' is higher than I, assume 1.2 then 120% higher futures than spot required to hedge the situation.

**EXAMPLE:**   Assume that a portfolio manager, an investment company, has invested one million in short-term T-bills with a maturity of six months. Currently, the discount yield is 5.50% on 6-month T-bills. The manager is expecting rise in short-term rates in near future. Assume that futures discount yield rises by 50 basis point, and six months spot discount yield will rise by 40 basis points. The value of '$b$' is 0.8.

## 10.8   SHORT-TERM INTEREST RATE FUTURES IN INDIA

Interest rate derivatives are very popular and widely used in developed markets. Considering it, the RBI introduced OTC interest rates derivatives (as discussed in preceding chapter of this book) in 1999, such as interest rate swaps (IRS)_and forward rate agreements (FRAs). After that, first time in India, exchange trade interest rate futures (IRF) were introduced in 2003, allowing only two instruments, i.e., 10-year notional bond futures and futures on notional Treasury bills with 91-day duration. The trading of IRF started on the NSE from June 23, 2003. Later on certain amendments were made in the year 2009 and 2014. A brief view of the RBI guidelines relating to short-term interest rate futures has been presented in this section. A detail of long-term interest rate futures contracts has been presented in the next chapter of this book.

**EXAMPLE:**   Assume that on January 1, 2015 the price of a 91-day Treasury bill at issue is ₹98.50. What will be the yield on the said T-bill? Further, assume that after 31 days, if the same Treasury bill is quoting at a price of ₹99, what will be the change in yield of T-bill?

*Solution:*   Yield on T-bill on January 1, 2015

$$\text{Yield} = \left(\frac{100-P}{P}\right) \times \left(\frac{365}{D}\right) \times 100$$

$$= \frac{100-98.50}{98.50} \times \frac{365}{91} \times 100 = 6.11\%$$

After 31 days, the yield on Treasury bill will be:

$$\text{Yield} = \frac{100-99}{99} \times \frac{365}{60} \times 100 = 6.15\%$$

**EXAMPLE:**   Assume on May 1, 2011 market price of T-bill maturing on June 15, 2011 is ₹99.1015. Calculate the yield on T-Bill.

$$\text{YTM} = \frac{\text{Par value} - \text{Market price}}{\text{Market price}} \times \frac{365}{\text{Actual days}}$$

$$\text{YTM} = \left[\frac{(100 - 99.1015)}{99.1015}\right] \times \frac{365}{46}$$

$$\text{YTM} = \frac{7.1940\%}{\text{Discount yield} = \left[\frac{(100 - 99.1015)}{100}\right]} \times \frac{360}{45}$$

$$= 7.1880\%$$

## 10.8.1   Definitions of IRF

According to the RBI (as per Direction 2009), the definition of the IRF are as follows:

(i) Interest rate future means a standardized interest rate derivatives contract traded on a recognized stock exchange to buy or sell a notional security or any other interest bearing instrument or an index of such instruments of interest rates at a specified future date, at a price determined at the time of the contract.

(ii) Interest rate futures market means the market in which interest rate futures are traded.

(iii) The words and expressions used but not defined in these directions shall have the meaning assigned to them in the RBI Act1934.

As per guidelines of 2003, the short-term interest rate futures were allowed on notional Treasury bills with 91-days tenor. After that, the RBI vide its notification IDMD.PCD.27/ED (HRK)-2010 dated March 7, 2011 permitted the interest rate futures on 91 day Treasury bills also.

## 10.8.2   Specifications of the 91-day T-Bill Futures

(a) The contract shall be on 91 day Treasury Bills issued by the Government of India.

(b) The contract shall be cash settled in Indian rupees.

(c) The final settlement price of the contract shall be based on the weighted average price/yield obtained in the weekly auction of the 91-day Treasury Bills on the date of expiry of the contract.

Other important specifications as per RBI guidelines are stated in brief:

| 1. | Underlying Security | 91-Day Government of India Treasury Bills. |
|---|---|---|
| 2. | Quotation | Quotation is similar to the quoted price of GOI T-bill, i.e., 100 minus futures discount yield. For example, for a yield of 5% the quote would be (100 – 5 = 95). The value of 1 basis point change in the futures discount yield would be R 5. |
| 3. | Contract Value | Quoted Price X = 2,000, i.e. ₹2,000 × (100 – 0.25 X Y) Y = Future discount yield. For example, for a futures discount yield of 5% the contract value would be 2,000 × (100 – (0.25 × 5)) = 1,97,500? |

*(Contd.)*

*(Contd.)*

| | | |
|---|---|---|
| 4. | Unit of Trading | ₹2,00,000 face value of T-bills, i.e., 2,000 units (order in lots) |
| 5. | Trading Hours | Monday to Friday: 9.00 a.m. to 5.00 p.m. |
| 6. | Contract Trading Cycle | It consists of three serial monthly contracts followed by three quarterly contracts expiring in March, June, September and December. |
| 7. | Settlement Mechanism | Settled in Cash in Indian Rupees. |
| 8. | Maximum Maturity | The maximum maturity of the contract is for 12 months. |
| 9. | Expiry Day | Last Thursday of the month. In case the last Thursday is a trading holiday, the previous trading day shall be the expiry/last trading day. |
| 10. | Daily Settlement Value/Price | Volume weighted average futures price of last half an hour or theoretical price. $₹2,000 \times (100 - (0.25 \times Yw))$ (here $Yw$ is weighted average futures yield of last half an hour) In absence of last half an hour trading, theoretical futures price would be considered. |
| 11. | Daily Settlement | Daily MTM settlement on T + 1 in cash based on final settlement price. |
| 12. | Final Settlement | Final settlement on T + 1 in cash based on final settlement price. |
| 13. | Final Contract Settlement Value | $₹2,000 \times (100 - [0.25 \times Yf])$ ($Yf$ is weighted average discount yield obtained from weekly auction of 91-day T-bills on the day of expiry). Methodology would be publicly disclosed by RBI. |
| 14. | Price-Operating Range (Extreme Loss Margin) | +1–3% of the base price. Extreme loss margin of 0.03% of the value of the gross open position of the future contract is deducted from the liquid assets of the clearing member on an on time, real time basis. |

Other Important specifications of T-Bills Futures Contract:

**Position Limits:**   Position limits of various member in T-Bills Futures will be as under:

(a) **Client Level:**   The gross open positions of the client across all contracts not to exceed 6 percent of the total open interest or ₹300 crores whichever is higher. The Exchange will alert whenever the gross open position of the client exceed 3 percent of the total open interest at the end of the previous day's trade.

(b) **Trading Member Level:**   The gross open positions of the trading member across all contracts not to exceed 15 percent of the total open interest or ₹1,000 crores whichever is higher.

(c) **Clearing Member Level:**   No separate position is prescribed at the level of clearing member.

(d) **Foreign Institutional Investors (FIIs):**    In case the FII is registered with the SEBI, the total gross long position in cash and IRF markets taken together should not exceed their individual permissible limit for investment in government securities and the total gross short position, for the purpose of hedging only should not exceed their long position in the government securities and in IRFs, at any point in time.

(e) **Calendar Spread Margin in T-Bills Futures:**    A calendar spread is also known as *an inter-delivery spread*. When, the trader purchases a futures contract in one delivery month and simultaneously sell off in another month of same underlying on the same exchange. Such spread is known as *a calendar spread* since it is based on different calendar months. For example, buying (long) a futures contract a July 2015 and simultaneously selling (short) a September, 2015 contract. It means a trader can earn or lose out as the price difference between the two contracts widens or narrows.

As stated above, interest rate futures position at one maturity hedged by an affecting position at different maturity would be referred to a calendar spread. In T-Bill futures, the calendar spread margin shall be at a value of ₹100 for spread of 1 month, ₹150 for 2 months, ₹200 for 3 months and ₹250 for spread of 4 month and beyond. The extreme loss margin shall be 0.01 percent, for a calendar spread position, of the notional value of the four-month contract.

(f) **Margins Requirement**

1. Initial margin—NSCCL shall adopt SPAN® (Standard Portfolio Analysis of Risk) system for the purpose of real time initial margin computation. The initial margin requirement shall be based on a worst case loss of a portfolio of an individual client across various scenarios of price changes. The various scenarios of price changes would be so computed so as to cover a 99 percent VaR over a one day horizon.

2. Initial margin would be subject to a minimum of 0.1 percent of the notional value of the contract on the first day of trading in 91-day T-bill futures and 0.05 percent of the notional value of the contract thereafter. The notional value of the contract shall be 2,00,000.

3. Extreme loss margin—Extreme loss margin shall be calculated at 0.03 percent of the notional value of the contract for all gross open positions.

(g) **Estimation of Volatility in Interest Rate Futures**

Type from FAQ on 91-day Government of India Treasury Bill (T-Bill) Futures:

The EWMA method is used to obtain the volatility estimate every day fixing the price scan range at 3.5 standard deviation. The estimate at the end of time period $t$ ($\sigma_{ydt}$) is arrived at using the volatility estimate at the end of the previous time period, i.e., as at the end of $(t - 1)$ time period ($\sigma_{ydt-1}$), and the return ($r_{ydt}$) observed in the futures market during the time period $t$. The formula is as under:

$$\lambda(\sigma_{ydt})2 = \lambda(\sigma_{ydt} - 1)2 + (1 - \lambda) (r_{ydt})2$$

where, $\lambda$ (lambda) is a parameter which determines how rapidly volatility estimates changes. The value of $\lambda$ is fixed at 0.94.

(i) $\sigma_{ydt}$ (sigma) is the standard deviation of daily logarithmic returns of discount yield of 91-day T-Bill futures at time $t$.

(ii) The "return" is defined as the logarithmic return: $r_{ydt} = \ln(Y_{dt}/Y_{dt-1})$ where $Y_{dt}$ is the discount yield of 91-day T-Bill futures at time $t$. The plus/minus 3.5 sigma limits for a

99 percent VAR based on logarithmic returns on discount yield of 91-day T-Bill futures would have to be converted into price changes through the following formula:

$$\sigma_{pt} = D \times \sigma_{ydt} \times Y_{dt}$$

where, $\sigma_{pt}$ means the standard deviation of percentage change in price at time $t$

$D$ means Modified Duration

$Y_{dt}$ = Discount Yield for 91-day T-Bill futures at time $t$

$\sigma_{ydt}$ (sigma) means the standard deviation of daily logarithmic returns of discount yield at time $t$

The margin on long position would be equal to $100 \times (D \times 3.5\sigma_{ydt} \times Y_{dt})$ percentage of the notional value of the futures contract and the margin on short position would be equal to $100 \, (D \times -3.5\sigma_{ydt} \times Y_{dt})$ percentage of the notional value of the futures contract. The Modified Duration for 91-day T-bill Futures shall be $-0.25$.

(iii) The volatility estimation and margin fixation methodology is to be clearly made known to all market participants so that they can compute the margin for any given closing level of the interest rate futures price. Further, the trading software itself should provide this information on a real time basis on the trading workstation screen.

(iv) During the first time-period on the first day of trading in 91-day T-bill futures, the sigma would be equal to 2.7 percent.

## SUMMARY

This chapter describes the various concepts of short-term interest rate futures. Interest rate futures contracts are most popular and successful financial derivative instruments today in global financial markets. Both borrowers and lenders face interest rate risk. Borrowers will face losses when the interest rate increases while lenders lose when interest rate decreases. The first short-term interest rate futures were traded on October 20, 1975 on Eurodollar time deposit and US treasury bills.

Interest rates futures are such financial derivatives which are written on fixed income securities or instruments. A fixed income security needs the payment of interest in the form of fixed amount at predetermined point of time along with the payment of principal payment at predetermined maturity period. An interest rate futures contract is a futures contract on an asset in which price is dependent mainly on the level of interest rates.

Treasury bills futures are major short-term interest rate futures normally issued for 90 days and 180 days, respectively. 90 days T-bills futures are most popular instruments. These were introduced in 1976 and is traded on the International Monetary Market (IMM)—a division of the Chicago Mercantile Exchange. T-bills are short-term debt instrument of the US government. They are issued on discount and have maturity less than one year. The concept of cost-of-carry pricing relationship may not play an important role in pricing the T-bill futures.

Since short-term interest rates are not carryable, they are priced on the basis of interest rate expectations as embodied in the term structure of interrelates (the yield curve). Eurodollar deposit is another type and most popular short-term instrument in the money markets. Eurodollar deposits are US dollar deposits—held by a commercial bank outside the USA. These banks may be either foreign banks or foreign branches of US base banks. The deposits are non-transferable and they cannot be used as collaterals security for a loan. Since the amount deposited in a bank is for three months, hence it is called Eurodollar Time Deposits (TD). The Eurodollar futures contracts are settled through cash instead of requiring physical delivery. Eurodollar futures are marked to the cash price at the closing day. Any payments due on long and short at that time are done through clearing house as standard variation margin payments.

These financial futures share the characteristics that arbitrage in the process that maintains the pricing relationship. Arbitrate process ensures a close relationship between futures interest rates and the forward interest rates implied by spot rates for differing maturities. Chapter in the end, discusses the TED spread which refers to the difference between the prices of futures contracts between three-month US treasury bills and three-month Eurodollar time deposits both with the same expiration month. Alternatively, the TED spread is the expected yield on a futures three-month T-bill. Short-term interest rate can be used to hedge against interest rate risk and to lock in futures investment yield or futures cost of borrowing. These can be used by banks and other corporations to structure their fixed income securities in accordance with the changed economic conditions from time to time. In this respect hedging strategy has been explained with short hedge and long hedge situations.

Interest Rate Derivatives in India were introduced in 1999 by the RBI in the OTC market. After that in 2003, interest rate futures with two instruments, i.e., 10 years notional bond futures and 91-day Treasury bill futures were launched. Later on certain amendments were made in the years 2009 and 2014. The RBI and NSE have issued guidelines relating to their trading mechanism and regulatory norms in this regard. However, short-term interest rate futures market could not picked up yet in India.

## SOLVED PROBLEMS

**P.1.** If the futures price of a 91-day T-bill were 92.81 and implied yield of 7.19%. What will be the invoice price of a bill with a face value of $1,00,00,000?

*Solution:* Because the face value of T-bill is $10,00,000.

So
$$\text{Invoice price} = 10,00,000 - \left(10,00,000 \times 0.0719 \times \frac{91}{360}\right)$$
$$= \$9,81,825.28$$

**P.2.** Suppose that on July 25, a firm knew that it will have to borrow $10 million on September 22 for three months. A bank agrees to provide these funds at 1% above whatever the three-month LIBOR is on September 22. By chance, September 22 is also the last trading of the September, 2002 Eurodollar futures contract. Firm is concerned about that by that time the LIBOR may rise. How company can hedge its risk by using Eurodollar futures if on July 25, Eurodollar price is 91.72 and implied three-month Eurodollar rate is 8.28%. The three-month LIBOR on July 25 is 8.375%.

*Solution:* Firm can use Eurodollar futures as a hedge against an increase in interest rates between July 25 and September 22. 10 contracts company will buy of Eurodollar deposits.

*Case I.* If Eurodollar does not (LIBOR) between July 25 and September 22, firm's borrowing cost for its three-month loan will be

$$\$1,00,00,000 \times (8.375 + 1\%) \times \frac{3}{12} = \$2,34,375$$

*Case II.* If LIBOR goes up firm can lock-in the three-month Eurodollar futures rate of 8.28% on July 25. If it does borrowing, cost will be

$$1,00,00,000 \times (8.28 + 1\%) \times \frac{3}{12} = \$2,32,000$$

If LIBOR rises to 9% by September 25 (futures are 91)

$$\text{Interest exp.} = 1,00,00,000 \times (9\% + 1\%) \times \frac{3}{12} = \$2,50,000$$

$$\text{Less futures gain} = 91.72 - 91.00 \times 100 \times 25 \times 10 = \$18,000$$

$$\text{Net borrowing cost} = \$2,32,000.$$

**P.3.** Assume that on January 25, a corporate treasurer expects to receive ₹10 millions from an overseas subsidiary on March 2003. He intends to invest the money in three-month T-bills. On three-month T-bill discount yield is 7.66% and current discount (implied) yield on March 90, T-bill is 7.35%. However, a treasurer infers from the futures yield that the market expects that interest rate will decline in futures. How can treasurer use T-bill futures to protect such risk?

*Solution:* He will buy long March 10, 2003 T-bill futures on January 25 at a price of 92.65, locking a discount yield of 7.35% on ₹10 millions and expects to invest in March.

Suppose on March, the three-month cash T-bill has a discount yield by 6.70% (March futures are 93.30)

$$\text{Price of T-bill} = ₹1,00,00,000 \times \left(100 - 6.7 \times \frac{3}{12}\right) = ₹98,32,500$$

$$\text{Less futures gain} = (93.30 - 92.65) \times 100 \times 25 \times 10 = (-)\,₹16,250$$

$$\text{Effective purchase price} = ₹98,16,250$$

Annualized discount yield,

$$= \frac{1,00,00,000 - 98,16,250}{1,00,00,000} \times \frac{12}{3} \times 100$$

$$= 7.35\% \text{ p.a.}$$

**P.4.** Suppose in problem 3 if on March 10 the three-month cash T-bill has a discount yield of 8%. What will be the annualized discount yield?

*Solution:*

$$\text{Price of cash T-bill} = ₹1,00,00,000 \times \left(1 - 8\% \times \frac{3}{12}\right) = ₹98,00,000$$

$$\text{Add futures gain} = (92.00 - 92.65) \times 100 \times 25 \times 10 = (+)\,₹16,250$$

$$\text{Net effective purchase price} = ₹98,16,250$$

Annualized discount yield

$$= \frac{₹1,00,00,000 - ₹98,16,250}{1,00,00,000} \times \frac{12}{3} \times 100$$

$$= 7.35\% \text{ p.a.}$$

**P.5.** A corporate treasure has just learned that ₹3.3 millions will be received on July 5. Treasurer plans to invest the money in six-month treasury bills and would like to hedge against a reduction in interest rates. Six-month T-bill yield is 11.20% per annum. Quoted price for August T-bill futures contract is 89.44. This corresponds to a contract price of ₹9,73,600. Discuss how T-bill futures can be used to hedge against interest rate risk.

*Solution:*

(a) Take a long position in seven August treasury-bill futures contracts on May 20.

(b) Close out position on July 5.

Yield on six-month bills, expressed with semi-annual compounding declined from 11.20% to 9.80% between May and July cost to treasurer, ₹33,00,000 × 0.014 × 0.5 = ₹23,100 in interest.

On July price for August T-bill futures contract was 90.56. This corresponds to contract price of ₹9,76,400. Gain on futures = (9,76,400 – 9,73,600) = ₹19,600 and net loss on position will be 23,100 – 20,560 (invest for six-month @ 9.80%) ₹2,540.

**P.6.** (a) A corporate treasurer needs to borrow ₹20,00,000 for three months. It is May 20, 2003 and money to be borrowed on August 1, 2003. How can treasurer hedge against a rise in interest rates using futures?

(b) If Eurodollar interest rises from 6% to 7% between May 20 and August 1 what is loss? If the prices fell from 93.80 to 92.90 during the same period, how much profit would there be from hedging strategy?

*Solution:* (a) Sell September 20 Eurodollar interest rate futures contracts.

(b) 1% on 2,00,00,000 over three months,

$$= 0.01 \times 2,00,00,000 \times 0.25 = ₹50,000$$

Profit on each 20 futures contract at ₹25 per tick

$$= 90 \times 20 \times 25 = ₹45,000$$

**P.7.** If interest rate in first year is 5% p.a. and second year is 6% p.a. What will be average compounded rate by return over 2 years?

*Solution:* Average compound return over 2 years $= \sqrt{(1.05)\,(1.06)} - 1$

$$= \sqrt{1.113} - 1 = 0.549 = 5.5\%$$

**P.8.** The six-month interest rate is 10% p.a. and the three-month interest rate is 8% p.a. Calculate the forward interest rate for the three months commencing three months from the present.

*Solution:* $(1 + 0.08/4)\,(1 + X/4) = (1 + 0.1/2)$

$$(1.02)(1 + X/4) = (1.05)$$

$$1 + X/4 = (1.05)/(1.02)$$

$$X/4 = 1.0294 - 1$$

$$X = 0.0294 \times 4 = 0.1176$$

$$X = 0.1176$$

So three-month rate available three months from the present is 11.76% p.a.

# SUGGESTED READINGS

1. Batten, Jonathan and Featherstone, Thomas, *Asia Pacific Fixed Income Market: An Analysis of The Regime Money, Bond and Interest Rate Derivative Markets*, Wiley, New York, Chichester, 2002.

2. Questa, Grorgro, *Fixed Income Analysis for The Global Financial Market, Money Market and Derivatives*, Wiley, New York, 1999.

3. Sunderesan, Suresh M., *Fixed Income Markets and Their Derivatives*, 2nd ed., South-Western College Publication, Cincinnati, Ohio, 2002.

4. Stephens, John J., *Managing Interest Risk: Using Financial Derivatives*, John Wiley, Chichester, West Sussex, England, New York, 2002.

5. Fabozzi, Frank J., *Valuation of Fixed Income Securities and Derivatives*, 3rd ed., McGraw Hill, New York, 1998.

6. Rene M. Stulz, *Risk Management & Derivatives*, Thomson South-Western, Indian –Reprint-2007.

7. Robert A. Strong, *Derivatives*, Thomson-South-Western, Indian-Reprint-2006.

8. www. Nseindia.com and www.rbi.org.in.

# REVIEW QUESTIONS

1. "Interest rate futures contracts are most popular and successful financial derivatives instruments today in global financial markets." In the light of above statement, discuss nature, features and growth of interest rate futures contracts worldwide.

2. What are short interest rate futures? Discuss the various features and types of short-term interest rate futures contracts with suitable examples.

3. Explain the short-term interest rate structure and its features with suitable examples.

4. What is Treasury bills futures? What are its main specifications? Explain with suitable examples.

5. Explain the mechanism of Treasury bills futures trading with suitable examples.

6. What are Eurodollar deposits? Explain the distinguish features of Eurodollar deposits with suitable examples.

7. Explain the trading mechanism of Eurodollar futures trading with suitable examples.

8. Explain the applications of short-term interest rate futures.

9. Write notes on:
   (a) The underlying spot interest rate markets
   (b) Risks in dealing the securities

10. Discuss the various specifications of T-bill futures traded on National Stock Exchange (NSE).

11. Write notes on:
    (a) Repurchase agreement (Repo rate)
    (b) The implied repo rate
    (c) Pricing of Eurodollar futures

12. What do you understand by the term TED Spread? Discuss with suitable examples.

13. "Short-term interest rate futures are the same as other futures contract except the change in underlying asset." Discuss the statement in light of the various features of term interest rate futures.

14. Write a detailed note on development of interest rate futures market in India.

15. Discuss the various recommendation by working group on introducing interest rate futures in India.

16. What are the sources of basis risk when using short-term interest rate futures?

17. Why is it necessary to make adjustments for interest on variation margin? Why such adjustments have been particularly important in case of short-term interest rate futures?

18. "If the market is efficient, the yield on Eurodollar futures contract for a given three-month time period in the futures will be equal to the forward yield for the same time period". Comment on the above statement.

19. What is implied repo rate? How it is calculated? If the implied repo rate is lower than the borrowing rate then futures contracts would be over or under priced? What arbitrage transaction would you engage in?

20. Explain the trading mechanism of short-term interest rate futures in India along with recent developments.

21. Explain the term 91-Day Treasury Bills Futures. What are important features of this? Explain with examples.

22. How will you hedge with short-term interest rate futures contracts? Explain in Indian context.

23. Critically examine the recent developments in short-term interest rate futures trading in India. Also, give your suggestions in this respect.

## UNSOLVED PROBLEMS

**P.1.** Company plans to deposit $10 millions on April 10. Current rate of interest on three-month Eurodollar deposit is 10% p.a. Show how company can hedge against the fall in deposit rate. Suppose the price of Eurodollar remains same on the closing date.

**P.2.** A treasurer intends to borrow £20 millions on February 1, fears that interest rate will rise above the current level borrow of 10%. Suppose on February 1 interest rate increase to 12% p.a. Show how treasurer can use interest rate futures to avoid the risk?

**P.3.** Suppose it is May 5, 2002 and the bond under consideration is an 11% coupon bond on September 2003 with a quoted price of $95 - \dfrac{16}{32}$ or $95.50. What will be the cash price of $1,00,000 bond.

**P.4.** Suppose that spot interest with continuous compounding are as follows:

| Maturity | Rate (% per annum) |
|----------|--------------------|
| 1 | 8% |
| 2 | 7.5% |
| 3 | 7.2% |
| 4 | 7% |
| 5 | 6.9% |

Calculate forward interest rate for level third, fourth and fifth years.

**P.5.** The price of a 90-day treasury bill is quoted as 10.00. What continuously compounded return does an investor earn on T-bill for the 90 days period?

**P.6.** Consider a trader who anticipates rising interest rates on September 20, 2002 following the American attacks on Iraq. If a particular trader believes that short-term rates will rise, current rate of Eurodollar is 90.30. How trader will make profit from the situation?

# Long-term Interest Rate Futures

*After reading this chapter, students will be able to*

➤ Understand the concept of long-term interest rate futures contract and their markets.
➤ Know the common features of government bonds, T-bonds, etc.
➤ Explain the concept of bond yield, calculation of bonds' transaction cost and price.
➤ Explain the concept of duration, modified duration and Treasury bond futures contracts.
➤ Understand the specifications of US and Indian long-term interest rate futures contracts.
➤ Explain the concept of conversion factor specified by T-bond futures contracts for bonds of different grades.
➤ Know how to determine the pricing of interest rate futures specifically T-bond futures.
➤ Understand how hedging is possible using T-bond futures which includes calculation of minimum variance hedge ratio.

## 11.1 INTRODUCTION

The long-term government bond futures contracts are the most actively traded contracts on derivative exchanges all over the world. One of the most widely traded long-term interest futures contracts is US government treasury bonds (popularly known as T-bonds) was introduced on the Chicago Board of Trade (CBOT) in 1977. Later on US government treasury notes (T-notes), and municipal bonds were introduced in 1982 and 1985 respectively. The T-bonds and T-notes are most popular due to their large size and being default free investments. Further, their yields are used as benchmark for long-term interest rates at the international level. Since bond price movements reflect the changes in long-term interest rates, government bond futures can alternatively be regarded as long-term interest rate futures.

In this section, we will discuss the long-term government bonds specifically of USA because first such trading in futures was started in the US markets. Though, there are also some successful bonds futures in other countries like Japan, France, London, etc. but in this chapter, major focus will be on the US long-term interest rate futures markets covering important aspects like futures pricing, arbitrage opportunities, hedging, etc. There are almost similarity in the functioning and pricing mechanism of long-term interest rate futures all over the world. In India, trading on interest rate futures contracts was started from 2003, however, these futures could not be as successful as expected. The guidelines of the RBI & SEBI relating to these have been discussed later on in this chapter.

Since, CME is the biggest exchange of futures trading, hence, major focus in this chapter will be on CME.

## 11.2 TREASURY BONDS AND TREASURY NOTES

The long-term Treasury bond market consists of both treasury bonds and treasury notes. Treasury bonds have maturities greater than ten years and as long as 30 years. Treasury notes have original maturities of 10 years or less. Both T-bonds and T-notes are usually identical except for the difference in maturity. Our discussion will be focused primarily on the T-bond markets, but unless specifically stated otherwise, all the explanation of T-bonds will also apply to T-notes. Exchange Traded Interest Rate Futures Contracts at CME Chicago Mercantile Exchange: Contracts expire in March, June, September or December. Contracts on various Assets include: 5 and 10-year Treasury Notes, 30-year Treasury Bonds and Ultra-T-bonds, $1,00,000 par, CBOT. 2 and 3-year Treasury Notes, $2,00,000 par, CBOT. 5, 7, 10 and 30 year interest rate swaps, $1,00,000 Notional CBOT. 13-week Treasury bills, $1,00,000, CHE Euro-dollar futures (LIBOR), $1,00,000, per CHF.

## 11.3 COMMON FEATURES OF THE GOVERNMENT BONDS

Bonds are used for long-term borrowing by the issuer. Central Governments are the major issuers of bonds (also known as *gilt-edged securities* or *gilts*). Bonds are issued in a wide variety of forms. There are some common features of such bonds, which are mentioned here as under:

1. Pay a fixed rate of interest (coupon) per period (usually six months).
2. They have definite redemption date like 5, 10, 20 years and so on.
3. They have a market price expressed as a sum per $100 nominal.

## 11.4 QUOTED BOND PRICE (CASH)

As stated earlier, these bonds are issued by the Central Government for a definite period at a particular coupon rate. At maturity, the holder of bond will receive the principal amount and the last coupon payment. Thus, a bond is like a combination of two securities, one an annuity and other a discount bond. These bonds are also actively traded in the secondary market. The authorized government dealers buy and sell securities. They are large commercial banks, large security firms, institutions, etc. Dealers hold an inventory of these securities and stand ready to buy and sell at announced bid and ask prices. The market is an over-the-counter market, and operated through telephone network.

### Treasury auction cycle

In the US market, Treasury securities are auctioned on a regular basis by the US Treasury, which accepts bid on a yield basis from security dealers. Prior to actual issuance of specific Treasury securities, these may be bought and sold on a "WI" or "When Issued" basis. When traded on the 'WI basis, 'bids' and 'offers' are quoted on yield rather than as a price. After a security is auctioned and the results announced, then the Treasury affixes a particular 'Coupon' to bonds and notes which is near prevailing yields. At that time, the coupon bearing bonds and notes may be quoted on a price rather than a yield basis.

The most recently issued securities of a particular maturity are referred to as "on-the-run" securities. These are such securities which are most liquid and actively traded in the market and oftenly marked as referenced on pricing benchmark. "Off-the-run" securities are less recently issued securities and tend to be less liquid in the market. In the US, the Treasury currently issues 4-week, 13-week, 26-week and 52-week bills, 2-year, 3-year, 5-year, 7-year, 10-year notes and 30-year bonds on a regular schedule. The prices on Treasury notes and bonds are conventionally quoted as a percentage of par value. Fraction of a percentage points are quoted in thirty-two seconds (32nd). For example, 92.16 means 92 percent and 16/32 = 0.5 percent, being net 92.5 percent.

Representative over-the-counter quotations are based on transactions of $1 million or more. Quotes are as of mid-afternoon and are in 32nds: 101–01 means 101 × 1/32. Net changes are in 32nds. All yields are to maturity and are based on the asked quotes. For bonds callable prior to maturity, yields are computed to the earliest call date for issues quoted above par (face) and to the maturity date for issues below par. Let us explain the position of bond prices quoted in the US market to understand the trading mechanism. For this, the prices quoted at the Chicago Mercantile Exchange (CME) have been taken into consideration as presented in Table 11.1.

Table 11.1 presents the information relating to 10-year Treasury Notes which shows the coupon rates, maturity dates, price and yield on January 10, 2013 of different notes. For example, first column states about the category of security like on-the-run, old, old-old, old-old-old which refers to the newly issued or old issued securities. The most recently issued security of any tenor may be referred to as the on-the-run security. The second most recently issued of a particular original tenor may be referred to as the 'old' security and so on. Second column States 1-5/8 percent coupon rate maturing on November 15, 2022, at the price of 97.18¾ and yielding 1.895 percent on the specified security.

## 11.4.1  Bond Yield and Prices

Last column in Table 11.1 shows the yield on each bond at its current market price. This is the yield-to-maturity. It is also called an *internal rate of return*. For example, if the bond is purchased at 97.18¾ then its yield to maturity (its effective annual yield) will be 1.895 percent. However, it is much higher than its coupon, i.e., 1.5/8 percent, because the current price of the bond is 97.18314 which is of far lower face value. It means when the bond matures, the holder will receive principal amount equal only to the bond's par value, i.e., 100 percent of face value. The difference of quoted price and face value will result in loss to the holder which will be subtracted from the interest earning on the bond over its life.

**TABLE 11.1** 10-Year Treasury Notes at CME

(As of January 10, 2013)

| | Coupon | Maturity | Price | Yield |
|---|---|---|---|---|
| WI | | | | |
| On-the-Run | 1-5/8% | 11/15/22 | 97-18 3/4 | 1.895% |
| Old Note | 1-5/8% | 08/15/22 | 98-01 3/4 | 1.847% |
| Old-Old | 1-3/4% | 05/15/22 | 99-18 3/4 | 1.798% |
| Old-Old-Old | 2% | 02/15/22 | 102-04 3/4 | 1.743% |
| | 2% | 11/15/21 | 102-17 3/4 | 1.688% |
| | 2-1/8% | 08/15/21 | 103-28 3/4 | 1.637% |
| | 3-1/8% | 05/15/21 | 112-05 3/4 | 1.562% |
| | 3-5/8% | 02/15/21 | 116-04 1/4 | 1.501% |
| | 2-5/8% | 11/15/20 | 108-18 | 1.465% |
| | 2-5/8% | 08/15/20 | 108-22 | 1.414% |
| | 3-1/2% | 05/15/20 | 115-01+ | 1.341% |
| | 3-5/8% | 02/15/20 | 115-25+ | 1.288% |
| | 1-1/8% | 12/31/19 | 98-27 3/4 | 1.295% |
| | 1% | 11/30/19 | 98-05 3/4 | 1.277% |
| | 3-3/8% | 11/15/19 | 114-00 3/4 | 1.232% |
| | 1-1/4% | 10/31/19 | 99-31 3/4 | 1.251% |
| | 1% | 03/30/19 | 98-16 1/4 | 1.232% |

*Source:* CME Group Understanding Treasury Futures

The general formula for determining the price of a bond assuming the interest is paid semi-annually:

Current price of bond = Present value of coupon annuity + Present value of face value

$$P_0 = \sum_{t=1}^{24} \left( \frac{C/2}{(1 + R/2)^{(t-1)+(t_c/B)}} \right) + \left( \frac{P_t}{(1 + R/2)^{(2N-1)+(t_c/B)}} \right) \quad (11.1)$$

where $P_0$ is current quoted price of the bond, $P_t$ is price of the bond at the end of the period (which is 100), $R$ is annual yield to maturity, $C$ is annual coupon interest in amount, $N$ is number of years to maturity, $t_c$ is number of days remain until the next coupon payment and $B$ is total number of days in a coupon period (if time $t$ is right after a coupon payment, then $t_c = B$).

*Note:* If $P_0$ is known, this formula can be used to calculate the yield-to-maturity $R$.

## 11.4.2 Calculating the Bond's Transaction Price

The quoted bond price is not the actual price at which the bond is sold or purchased. The reason being that, sometimes, the purchase/sold date falls between the two coupon dates. In that case, the buyer has to pay accrued interest to the seller due on that date. Thus, accrued interest on T-bond is calculated as:

$$\text{Accrued interest on T-bond} = \left(\frac{B - t_c}{B}\right) \times \text{Semi-annual coupon payment}$$

where $B$ and $t_c$ have been explained earlier. Then the transaction price of the bond will be calculated as follows:

$$P = \text{Quoted price} + \text{Accrued interest on bond}$$

where $P$ is the transaction price of the bond at period $t$.

**EXAMPLE:** Assume that the bond (May 2031) had a quoted price (asked price) of 92.16 and pays 7.25 percent coupon on May 15 and November 15. If the bond is purchased on December 13, then the cash settlement date will be December 14 and the bond will be 29 days into its May 15 coupon period (there will be 152 days). Thus, transaction price of $1,00,000 of May 2031 bond on December 13, 2014 will be calculated as follows:

$$= (\$1,00,000 \times 0.9250) + (\$1,00,000 \times 0.0725 \times 1/2 \times 29 \text{ days}/181 \text{ days})$$

$$= \$92500 + \$580.80 = \$93080.80$$

**EXAMPLE:** Suppose today January 10, 2015, the trader purchases $1 million face value of the 1-5/8 percent Treasury Bond maturing in November 2024 (a Ten-year note) for a price 97-18, i.e., ($975781) to yield 1.894 percent for settlement of next day, January 11, 2015. The original issue date of the bond is November 15, 2014. So, the transaction price of the bond will be:

$$P = (\$1,00,000 \times .975781) \times (57/181 \times \$16250/2)$$

$$= \$975781 + 2258.70 = \$978339.70$$

## 11.4.3 Duration of the Bond

A bond's duration is an important measure of its price sensitivity to interest rate changes. It is noted that a high duration bond's price is more sensitive to interest rate changes than the low duration bond. The change in interest rate will influence the bond's price, and it will be greater on those bonds which have lower coupon rate and longer maturity. The duration of a bond is generally defined as the weighted average of the maturities of the bond's coupon and the principal repayment cash flows, where the weights are the fractions of the bond's price that the cash flows in each time period represent. This is also known as *Macaulay duration*.

$$D = \frac{1}{P} \times \sum_{t=1}^{m} \frac{t \times X_t}{(1+r)^t} \qquad (11.2)$$

where $D$ is duration of a bond (Macaulay), $X_t$ is rupee payment on the bond in period (either coupon or principal repayment), $r$ is current annual yield to maturity on the bond divided by the number of payment period in a year, $m$ is number of payment periods and $P$ is transaction price of the bond.

**EXAMPLE:** Assume that the market price of a bond is 98. Coupon rate is 8 percent and semi-annual. Yield to maturity is 10 percent and time to maturity is 2 years.

$$D = \frac{1}{98} \times \left(\frac{1 \times 4}{(1+0.05)^1} + \frac{2 \times 4}{(1+0.05)^2} + \frac{3 \times 4}{(1+0.05)^3} + \frac{4 \times 4}{(1+0.05)^4} + \frac{4 \times 100}{(1+0.05)^4}\right)$$

$$= 3.7109$$

Since the coupon payment period is semi-annual, the duration measure is expressed in terms of six months periods. On an annual basis, the bond's duration will be 1.8555 (3.7109 × 1/2) years.

## 11.4.4 Modified Duration

Another usual measure of bond price sensitivity is modified duration which provides a percentage measure of price volatility. The formula is:

$$D_{mod} = \frac{D}{1 + \frac{R}{f}}$$

where $f$ is frequency of the coupon payment.

In above example:

$$D_{mod} = \frac{1.855}{1 + \frac{0.10}{2}} = 1.7671$$

A bond's modified duration measures the percentage change in a price relative to a given percentage change in the bond's yield to maturity.

$$-D_{mod} = \frac{\%\Delta P}{\%\Delta(1 + R)}$$

$$= \%\Delta P = -D_{mod} \times \%\Delta (1 + R)$$

For example, if the yield-to-maturity is increased by 0.50 percentage points, the percentage change in the price will be

$$\%\Delta R = -1.7671 \times \frac{0.005}{1 + 0.10} \times 100$$

$$= -1.7671 \times 0.4545\% = -0.8031\%$$

The price of the two-year notes, therefore, will decrease by

$$98.00 \times 0.008031 = 0.79 \quad \text{or} \quad \frac{25}{32}$$

## 11.4.5 Duration of a Portfolio

Duration of a portfolio can be measured by the weighted average of the duration of each security in the portfolio. The weights are taken the market value of each security in the portfolio divided by the total market value of the entire portfolio.

## 11.5 TREASURY BOND FUTURES CONTRACTS

In this section, we will discuss about the mechanism of trading of futures contracts of the government bonds, specifically focusing on Indian and US treasury bonds. Government bonds are commitments to buy or sell government bonds during specified futures months. Contracts are normally held until maturity but can be closed out by means of taking out position opposite contract. Table 11.2 shows some bond futures prices at the close on September 08, 2015. In this section, the trading mechanism of long-term interest rate futures traded at NSE will be discussed. After that guidelines of NSE relating to interest futures contract in India will be discussed in brief.

**TABLE 11.2**   NSE Bond Futures as on September 8, 2015
as on September 8, 2015 17:00:48 IST

| NSE NBF II NSE Bond Futures II | Underlying symbol | 772GS2025 | 788GS2030 | 827GS2020 | 840GS2024 |
|---|---|---|---|---|---|
| | Price | 99.6400 | 99.8300 | 101.4150 | 102.8575 |
| | Yield | 7.7708 | 7.8994 | 7.9018 | 7.9433 |

| Contract | Best Bid | | Best Ask | | Spread | LTP* | Yield | OI | Volume (Contracts) | Value in Crore |
|---|---|---|---|---|---|---|---|---|---|---|
| | Qty | Price* | Price* | Qty | | | | | | |
| **840GS2024** | | | | | | | | | | |
| 840GS2024 240915 | 10 | 102.8550 | 102.8600 | 10 | 0.0050 | 102.8500 | 7.942 | 59,757 | 10,787 | 221.80 |
| 840GS2024 291015 | 25 | 102.8475 | 102.9550 | 25 | 0.1075 | 102.9000 | 7.9306 | – | 2,040 | 41.98 |
| 840GS2024 261115 | 100 | 100.0150 | – | – | –100.0150 | – | – | – | – | – |
| 840GS2024 311215 | 100 | 100.0150 | – | – | –100.0150 | – | – | – | – | – |
| 840GS2024 310316 | 100 | 100.0150 | – | – | –100.0150 | – | – | – | – | – |
| 840GS2024 300616 | 100 | 100.0150 | – | – | –100.0150 | – | – | – | – | – |
| **827GS2020** | | | | | | | | | | |
| 827GS2020 240915 | 5 | 101.3175 | 101.4825 | 4 | 0.1650 | 101.3150 | 7.9242 | 1,480 | 549 | 11.12 |
| 827GS2020 291015 | 10 | 101.1550 | 101.6750 | 25 | 0.5200 | 101.4500 | 7.885 | 520 | 514 | 10.43 |
| 827GS2020 261115 | 100 | 98.3150 | – | – | –98.3150 | – | – | | | |
| 827GS2020 311215 | 100 | 98.2150 | – | – | –98.2150 | – | – | | | |
| 827GS2020310316 | 100 | 98.0150 | – | – | –98.0150 | – | – | | | |
| **788GS2030** | | | | | | | | | | |
| 788GS2030 240915 | 15 | 99.7575 | 99.7850 | 15 | 0.0275 | 99.7500 | 7.9097 | 14,733 | 1,990 | 39.68 |
| 788GS2030 291015 | 50 | 99.6550 | 99.9650 | 50 | 0.3100 | 99.6300 | 7.9261 | – | – | – |
| 788GS2030 261115 | 100 | 96.5150 | – | – | –96.5150 | – | – | – | – | – |
| 788GS2030 311215 | 100 | 96.5150 | – | – | –96.5150 | – | – | – | – | – |
| 788GS2030 310316 | 100 | 96.5150 | – | – | –96.5150 | – | – | – | – | – |
| 788GS2030 300616 | 100 | 96.5150 | – | – | –96.5150 | – | – | – | – | – |
| **772GS2025** | | | | | | | | | | |
| 772GS2025 240915 | 10 | 99.6475 | 99.6500 | 305 | 0.0025 | 99.6425 | 7.7709 | 132966 | 47,682 | 949.80 |
| 772GS2025 291015 | 10 | 99.6950 | 99.7650 | 10 | 0.0700 | 99.7100 | 7.7621 | 3,831 | 4,644 | 92.58 |
| 772GS2025 261115 | 100 | 97.0150 | – | – | –97.0150 | – | – | – | – | – |
| 772GS2025 311215 | 100 | 97.0150 | – | – | –97.0150 | – | – | – | – | – |
| 772GS2025 310316 | 100 | 97.0150 | – | – | –97.0150 | – | – | – | – | – |
| 772GS2025 300616 | 100 | 97.0150 | – | – | –97.0150 | – | – | – | – | – |

### Trade & Turnover Statistics

| Online Trade Statistics | | | | | | Trade Date | Total Contracts | Total Value (₹Crores) | Open Interest |
|---|---|---|---|---|---|---|---|---|---|
| Instrument Type | Symbol | Volume (Contracts) | Value (₹Crores) | Open Interest | No. of Trades | 08-Sep-2015 | 68,206 | 1,367.40 | 2,13,287 |
| FUTIRC | 840GS2024 | 12,827 | 263.78 | 59,757 | 737 | 07-Sep-2015 | 74,372 | 1,488.21 | 2,09,939 |
| FUTIRC | 827GS2020 | 1,063 | 21.55 | 2,000 | 19 | 04-Sep-2015 | 46,949 | 939.20 | 2,04,450 |
| FUTIRC | 788GS2030 | 1,990 | 39.68 | 14,733 | 148 | 03-Sep-2015 | 63,317 | 1,267.27 | 2,03,362 |
| FUTIRC | 772GS2025 | 52,326 | 1,042.38 | 1,36,797 | 5,439 | 02-Sep-2015 | 47,259 | 945.80 | 2,02459 |
| FUTIRC | 91DTB | 0 | 0.00 | 0 | 0 | | | | |
| **Total** | | 68,206 | 1,367.39 | 2,13,287 | 6,343 | | | | |

*Sources:* NSE Website (http://www.nse-india.com/live_market)

*NSE Bond Futures Prices:*

Table 11.2 shows the Treasury Bond Futures Prices quoted at the NSE as on September 08, 2015 at 17.00 p.m. The Treasury bonds with different maturities and coupon rates are listed on the NSE for futures trading. Table depicts the bid and ask prices along with spread, yield, open interest, volume of contracts, total turnover, etc. It is observed that maximum contracts were done on instrument symbol 772GS2025 in comparison to others. Turnover amount in value of this instrument was ₹ 1042.38 crore whereas total volume was ₹ Crore 1367.39 on September 8, 2015. Similarly, number of contracts were 52,326 as against the total contracts of 68,206. Further the cash price of this instrument was 99.6400 and futures price was September, 2015 was 99.6500. The daily turnover of all futures instruments at NSE was around ₹ 1,400 crore which was not encouraging. This reflects the poor response of the market participants in this respect.

A brief particulars of the bond like size of a contract, country, tick size and exchange have been shown in Table 11.3 for reference. It is observed from Table 11.3 that CBOT's T-bond and T-note contracts are identical except for the maturity of the securities that are acceptable for delivery. CBOT allows delivery of U.S. T-bonds with remaining maturities of at least 15 years whereas in case second two T-note futures contract allow delivery of US. Treasury notes with the remaining maturities of 4 to 5 years and 6 to 10 years respectively.

**TABLE 11.3**    Contract Specifications of CME Group Treasury Bonds Futures Products

| | 2-Year T-Note Futures | 3-Year T-Note Futures | 5-Year T-Note Futures | 10-Year T-Note Futures | Classic T-Bond Futures | Ultra T-Bond Futures |
|---|---|---|---|---|---|---|
| **Contract Size** | $200,000 face-value US Treasury notes | | $100,000 face-value US Treasury notes | | $100,000 face-value US Treasury bonds | |
| **Delivery Grade** | T-notes with original maturity of not more than 5 years and 3 months and remaining maturity of not less than 1 year and 9 months from 1st day of delivery month but not more than 2 years from last day of delivery month | T-notes with original maturity of not more than 5-¼ years and a remaining maturity of not more than 3 years but not less than 2 years, 9 months from last day of delivery month | T-notes with original maturity of not more than 5 years and 3 months and remaining maturity of not less than 4 years and 2 months as of 1st day of delivery month. | T-notes maturing at least 6-½ years but not more than 10 years, from 1st day of delivery month. | T-bonds with remaining maturity of at least 15 years but not more than 25 years. | T-bonds with remaining maturity of at least 25 years but not more than 30 years |
| **Invoice Price** | Invoice price = settlement price × conversion factor (CF) + accrued interest, CF = price to yield 6% | | | | | |
| **Delivery Method** | Via Federal Reserve book-entry wire-transfer | | | | | |

*(Contd.)*

*(Contd.)*

| Contract Months | March quarterly cycle – March, June, September, December | | | |
|---|---|---|---|---|
| **Trading Hours** | Open Auction: 7:20 a.m.–2:00 p.m., Monday–Friday; Electronic: 6:00 p.m.–4:00 p.m., Sunday–Friday (Central Times) | | | |
| **Last Trading and Delivery Day** | Last business day of contract month; delivery may occur on any day of contract month up to and including last business day of month | | Day prior to last seven (7) business days of contract month; delivery may occur on any day of contract month up to and including last business day of month | |
| **Price Quote** | In percent of par to one-quarter of 1/32nd of 1% of par ($15.625 rounded up to nearest cent) | In percent of par to one-quarter of 1/32nd of 1% of par ($7.8125 rounded up to nearest cent) | In percent of par to one-half of 1/32nd of 1% of par ($15.625 rounded up to nearest cent) | In percent of par to 1/32nd of 1% of par ($31.25) |

*Source:* CME Group Understanding Treasury Futures

## 11.5.1 Delivery Process and Deliverable Bonds

The short (seller) initiates, as in all the futures contracts, the delivery process by choosing which bond to deliver and when to deliver it during the delivery month. It is a three-day process. The day on which short declares intention to deliver is called *the position day*. Then the short can notify the exchange for his/her intention to deliver until 8.00 p.m. on the position day. On the next day (the notice day) the clearing house matches the short with the long having the oldest outstanding position and notifies the long that delivery will occur on the next day. The short has to decide on the notice day up to 5.00 p.m. which bond will be delivered. On the delivery day, the short delivers the T-bonds by wire transfer to the long and the long makes the payment to the short's bank by funds wire.

## 11.5.2 Multiple Deliverable Grades of the Bonds

The T-bond futures allows the short to deliver any bonds with a range of coupons and maturities dates, and consequently vary with different market values. To adjust for these differences, the T-bond futures contract specifies conversion factors which are used to adjust invoice prices. The conversion factors ensure that the short receives a higher price for delivering a more valuable bond and vice versa. Table 11.4 gives a list of T-Notes which were eligible for delivery into the March, 2013, T-Notes Futures along with their conversion factors.

**TABLE 11.4**   March 2013 Ten-Year T-Note Futures Basis
(As of January 10, 2013)

| Coupon | Maturity | Price | Yield | CF | Basis | IRR | Duration |
|---|---|---|---|---|---|---|---|
| 1-5/8% | 11/15/22 | 97-18¾ | 1.895% | 0.6867 | 227.966 | −32.838% | 9.016 |
| 1-5/8% | 08/15/22 | 98-01¾ | 1.847% | 0.6928 | 217.252 | −31.092% | 8.775 |
| 1-3/4% | 05/15/22 | 99-18¾ | 1.798% | 0.7077 | 203.441 | −28.414% | 8.558 |

*(Contd.)*

*(Contd.)*

| Coupon | Maturity | Price | Yield | CF | Basis | IRR | Duration |
|--------|----------|-------|-------|-----|-------|-----|----------|
| 2% | 02/15/22 | 102-04¾ | 1.743% | 0.7307 | 118.484 | −25.314% | 8.234 |
| 2% | 11/15/21 | 102-17¾ | 1.688% | 0.7367 | 176.191 | −23.420% | 8.067 |
| 2-1/8% | 08/15/21 | 103-28¾ | 1.637% | 0.7507 | 160.174 | −20.744% | 7.789 |
| 3-1/8% | 05/15/21 | 112-05¾ | 1.562% | 0.8194 | 135.569 | −15.053% | 7.382 |
| 3-5/8% | 02/15/21 | 116-04¼ | 1.501% | 0.8544 | 14.527 | −11.469% | 7.034 |
| 2-5/8% | 11/15/20 | 108-18 | 1.465% | 0.7985 | 107.923 | −12.264% | 7.095 |
| 2-5/8% | 08/15/20 | 108-22 | 1.414% | 0.8039 | 89.160 | −9.727% | 6.853 |
| 3-1/2% | 05/15/20 | 115-01+ | 1.341% | 0.8588 | 61.229 | −4.829% | 6.530 |
| 3-5/8% | 02/15/20 | 115-25+ | 1.288% | 0.8697 | 39.280 | −1.923% | 6.266 |
| 1-1/8% | 12/31/19 | 98-27¾ | 1.295% | 0.7326 | 75.475 | −10.165% | 6.676 |
| 1% | 11/30/19 | 98-05¾ | 1.277% | 0.7341 | 47.151 | −6.095% | 6.585 |
| 3-3/8% | 11/15/19 | 114-00¾ | 1.232% | 0.8604 | 21.734 | 0.121% | 6.153 |
| 1-1/4% | 10/31/19 | 99-31¾ | 1.251% | 0.7474 | 49.085 | −6.008% | 6.485 |
| 1% | 03/30/19 | 98-16¼ | 1.232% | 0.7341 | 57.651 | −7.637% | 6.453 |

*Source:* CME Group Understanding Treasury Futures

## 11.5.3 Delivery Options to the Short in the T-bond Futures

As discussed earlier, the short has several options under T-bond futures delivery rules which are referred here in brief:

**Quality option:** The right to choose which of the many eligible bonds to deliver to the long (purchaser). The short can maximize the return by delivering the 'cheapest-to-deliver' bond. It means that long of a T-Bond futures does not know which particular Treasury security he will receive. Since, the short has the option to choose the security to deliver, by choosing (TI). It has value because the seller can at any time sell the T-Bond and purchase another one (T-Bond), thus, increasing his profits. So, the quality option is also called the switching option.

**Timing option:** The seller of the IRF has the right to choose which day of the month to make delivery. In other words, the short can initiate the delivery process any time the exchange is open during the delivery month. The final invoice price for delivery is set at the final trading day of the contract, which is eight business days before the end of the month. Another consideration in this is relationship between the accrued interest on the bond and the cost of financing the position. If financing rate is higher than the interest accrued on bond, then it might make sense to deliver the bond as soon as feasible and vice versa.

**Wild card options:** In the T-bond futures delivery rule, the short has two wild card options. First, the short does not have to notify the clearing house of his intention up to 8.00 p.m. on the position day. The period of six hours after 2.00 p.m. (2.00 p.m. to 8.00 p.m.), the short may be able to earn profit from changes in cash bond prices. Second, the short can wait up to 5.00 p.m. on notice day to choose which bond is to deliver.

### 11.5.4 Determining the Invoice Price for a T-bond

As discussed earlier in this section that the short will receive an invoice price from the long against the delivery of T-bonds. It is calculated by the following formula:

$$= \text{(Decimal futures settlement price)} \times \text{(Conversion factor)} \times (\$1,00,000)$$
$$+ \text{ Accrued interest on the delivered bond}$$

where

- Decimal futures settlement price is the quoted futures price expressed in decimal terms, for example, a quoted price of 89.16 becomes a decimal futures to settlement price of 0.8950 (16/32 is expressed as 0.50 of a percentage point).
- Conversion factor is taken from the table provided by CBOT.

**EXAMPLE:** Suppose that in March 2015, an investor is holding a short T-bond futures contract that expires in March, 2015. Assume that he decides to deliver into the contract on March 9. He declares his intention to deliver on March 7 when the futures settlement price is $88.10. He selects a 7¼ percent T-bond that expires on May 15, 2031, for the delivery. Table 10.4 shows that the conversion factor for the bond is 0.9175. Calculate the invoice price of bond.

*Solution:* To determine the invoice price, let us first calculate the accrued interest on the bond by a time line.

**Time Line**

| Coupon | 114 days | t | 67 days | Coupon | 184 days | Coupon |
|--------|----------|---|---------|--------|----------|--------|
| 11/15  |          | 3/9 |       | 5/15   |          | 11/15  |

The time line shows that this bond has earned accrued interest over 114 days since most recent coupon on November, 15, 2014. The 7.25 percent coupon rate implies an annual payment of $7250 per $1,00,000 face value, and therefore, a $3625 semi-annual coupon. Thus accrued interest is:

$$\text{Accrued interest} = \left(\frac{114}{181}\right)(\$3,625) = \$2,283$$

Decimal futures settlement price will be $88 + \left(\dfrac{10}{32}\right) = 0.883125$

$$\text{Invoice price} = \text{(Decimal futures settlement price)} \times \text{(Conversion factor )}$$
$$\times (\$1,00,000) + \text{Accrued interest}$$
$$= (0.883125) \times (0.9175) (\$1,00,000) + \$2283$$
$$= \$81,027 + \$2283 = \$83,310$$

Why should the short receive less than the bond's face value where the short is obligated to pay $1,00,000 principal amount that will earn 8 percent a year for at least 15 years? It is simply due to choosing a less coupon bond (7.25 percent) and its conversion factor is 0.9175 which will generate less cash flows in futures than would be the hypothetical 8 percent bond as set in conversion factor, hence, they are less valuable. Now, conversion factor has been changed from 8 to 6 percent.

### 11.5.5 Concept of Conversion Factor

Conversion factors are used to 'standardized' bonds for futures contracts.

The conversion factors specified by the T-bond contract for bonds of different grades are simply the prices, per $1 face value computed by discounting the bond's futures cash flows by the hypothetical 6 percent annual yield. As such, the conversion factor for a bond is a function of (i) the bond's time to maturity from the first day of delivery month and (ii) the actual coupon rate on the bond.

***Conversion Factor Equation:***

$$CF = \frac{1}{(1.03)^{x/6}} \left[ \frac{c}{2} + \frac{c}{0.06} \left( 1 - \frac{1}{(1.03)^{2N}} \right) + \frac{1}{(1.03)^{2N}} \right] - \frac{C}{2} \left( \frac{6-X}{6} \right)$$

Where  $CF$ = Conversion Factor
$\quad\quad\quad C$ = Annual Coupon in Decimal Form
$\quad\quad\quad N$ = Number of whole years to maturity
$\quad\quad\quad X$ = Number of months in excess of the whole $N$ (rounded down to complete quarters).
For example, if maturity is 25 years, 5 months, $N = 25$ and $X = 3$.

Also if $X = 9$, then let $2N = 2N + 1$, and set '$X$' = 3.

Normally, the conversion factor booklets are published by the exchanges which shows the conversion factors differ by coupon rate and maturity. The CBOT publishes these conversion factors on their website (http://www.cbot.com) and in pamphlet form. In addition, the conversion factor is closer to one. Therefore, bonds with coupons higher than 6 percent have conversion factor greater than one; bonds with coupons lower than 6 percent have conversion factor of less than one. Thus, the basic function of the conversion factor is to adjust the invoice price of the bond with its coupon in accordance with 6 percent return on its maturity.

## 11.5.6  Determining the Cheapest-to-Deliver (CTD) T-bond at Expiration

The short (seller) should choose which bond to deliver in fulfilment of the contract. It is in the interest of the short to deliver such bond whose invoice amount exceeds the market price by the largest margin for whose invoice amount falls short of the market price by the smallest margin. It depends on how accurately the conversion factors reflect existing relationship among the market value of different bonds with different maturities. With a flat yield curve, the rule of thumb commonly used by the market participants to determine the cheapest-to-deliver bond by using duration is:

1. If market yields are greater than 6 percent, eligible bond will be with the highest duration.
2. If market yields are less than 6 percent, the eligible bond will be with the lowest duration.

**EXAMPLE:**   Let us consider the conversion factor for delivery of the 3-3/8 percent T-Note of 2019 vs March 2013 10-year T. Note futures is 0.8600. This suggests that a 3.3/8 percent security is valued at 86 percent as much as a 6 percent security. Assuming a futures price 131.24 (or 131.75 in decimal format), the principal invoice amount would be:

Principal Invoice amount = 131.75 × .8600 × $1,13,305.

Similarly, assume the conversion factor for delivery of the 1-¾ percent T-Note of 2022 vs March 2013, 10-year. T-Note futures is .7075. This suggests that a 1-¾ percent security is approximately valued at 71 percent as much as a 6 percent security. Assuming a futures price of 131.24 (or 131.75 in decimal format), the principal invoice amount would be:

Principal Invoice Amount = 131.75 × .7075 × $1000 = $93213

However, to arrive at the total invoice amount, the amount of accrued interest be further added.

In order to choose Cheapest-to-Deliver (CTD), Let us compare the two T-Notes. On January 10, 2014, the trader might have been able to purchase the 3-3/8 percent-2019 at 114.00 ($1,14,000 per $1,00,000 face value unit). The 1-3/4 percent-2022 T-Note was valued at 99-16 ($99,500 per $1,00,000 face value unit). On comparing these cash values to the principal invoice amount one observed as under:

| | 3-3/8%-2019 (T-Note) | 1-3/4%-2022 (T-Note) |
|---|---|---|
| Futures Price | 131–24 + | 131–24 + |
| XCF | 0.8600 | 0.7075 |
| X $1000 | $1000 | $1,000 |
| Principal Invoice | $1,13,305 | $93,213 |
| Cash Price | $1,14,000 | $99,500 |
| Delivery gain/loss | –($695) | –($6,287) |

From the above it is observed that a loss of $695 may be associated with the delivery of the 3-3/8%-2019 T-Note while an even higher loss of $6,287 with the delivery of the 1-3/4%-2022 T. Note. Thus, it is concluded that First Note is cheaper to deliver than the second one.

It should be noted that the above mentioned rule of thumb will work as long as the yield curve is flat. If the yield curves are above or below the 6 percent, the prices of long maturity bonds will fall faster or slower than is implicit in the determination of the conversion factor. Thus, it will be optimal to deliver bond with high duration if the yields are above 6 percent and vice versa.

Identifying the cheapest-to-deliver bond in case where the yield curve is not flat, one method is to calculate the theoretical futures price using, alternatively each of the eligible cash bonds. The bond which has lowest theoretical value will be considered as the cheapest-to-deliver bond. The second method used for this is the using implied repo rate. Under this method, the bond with highest implied repo rate will be the cheapest-to-deliver bond. These methods are time consuming, however, recently various computer software available which are used to find out the CTD in short time.

## 11.6 INTEREST RATE FUTURES IN INDIA

The RBI introduced OTC interest rate derivatives with two instruments; Interest Rate Swaps (IRS) and Forward Rate Agreements (FRAs) in 1999. After that the RBI constituted a committee under the chairmanship of Jaspal Bindra, CEO, Standard Chartered Bank to examine the possibility of trading of the IRFs India. The committee recommended the idea of introducing the exchange traded derivatives in India. Based on this report RBI, SEBI and Fixed Income Money Market and Derivative Association of India (FIMMDA) jointly introduced exchange traded IRFs first time in India on 2003. They are also termed as *Treasury Bond Futures Contract* where the maturity of the bonds is more than one year.

Under the guidelines of the RBI, National Stock Exchange (NSE) and Bombay Stock Exchange (BSE) launched trading in interest rate futures in June, 2003. To begin with the RBI permitted to start trading only in two types of IRF contracts, such as Notional Treasury Bills and Notional 10-year bonds (Coupon bearing and non-coupon bearing). The Scheduled Commercial Banks (SCBs) (excluding Regional Rural Banks (RRBs) and Local Area Banks), Primary Dealers (PDs), specified All India Financial Institution, etc. were allowed to trade in IRFs and to hedge their interest rate risk in their underlying government securities portfolio by booking futures transactions. We will be discussing the basic features if these IRFs issued in 2003, 2009 and 2014 in brief.

## 11.6.1   Basic Features of IRFs Introduced in 2003

1. Derivative is an instrument which derives its value from the underlying asset. So, two types of securities were permitted as underlying asset, i.e., Notional Treasury bills and notional 10-year Treasury bonds. There can be spot and futures contracts on these underlying securities.
2. The delivery of the contract shall be on cash settlement.
3. The contract has to be priced on the basis of the average (YTM) yield to maturity of a basket comprising at least three most liquid bonds with maturity between 9 and 11 years.
4. The quotation and trading price of the IRF contract has to be as 100 minus the YTM of the basket.
5. If there is no trading on a particular trading day, and basket has become illiquid during the life of the contract, then the basket shall be reconstituted, failing which the YTM of the basket shall be determined from the YTMs of the remaining bonds.
6. The daily settlement price for unexpired futures contracts shall be the futures prices using the (price of notional bond) spot price arrived at from the applicable ZCYC (zero coupon yield curve).

The contract value of IRF can be minimum lot size of 2000 @ ₹100 (base price) leading to minimum value of ₹2,00,000. So, value of the contract would be Quoted Price * 2000.

The IRF contract is for a period of one year with 3 months continuous contracts for the first three months and fixed quarterly contracts for the entire year. The contract would be expired on last Thursday of the month. In case the last Thursday is a trading holiday, the previous trading day shall be the expiry or last trading day.

Daily Mark-to-Market (MTM) settlement and final settlement in case of IRF would be in cash based on daily settlement which will be in respect of admitted deals in IRFs.

The important feature of 2003 guideline was the settlement price to be determined from the zero coupon yield curve (ZCYC). This is computed from the prices of government securities traded on the exchange or reported on the negotiated dealing system (NDS) of RBI or both taking trades on same day settlement, i.e., t = 0 . In respect of zero coupon national bonds, the price of the bond is the present value of the principal amount discounted at the respective zero coupon yields.

The RBI allowed first time trading on exchange traded rate futures on 10-year notional Treasury bonds in 2003 on the National Stock Exchange (NSE). But this new product could not become much popular among the traders. It was observed that the system of ZCYC could not be understood by the common traders. The calculation of the settlement price of ZCYC was much complicated. Further, the banks were restricted to trade in such products. As a result the IRF of 2003 failed in the Indian market.

## 11.6.2   Exchange Traded IRFs 2009

The RBI and SEBI constituted a committee in the Chairmanship of Mr. V.K. Sharma to look into the trading of IRF in India. On the recommendations of the Committee, certain new guidelines were added in the present norms of IRFs 2003. On the August, 2009, BSE and NSE again introduced IRFs. Important additional features of this IRFs are as follows.

1. The IRF contract shall be on 10-year notional coupon bearing Government of India security.
2. The notional coupon shall be 7 percent per annum with semi-annual compounding.
3. The IRF contracts shall be settled by physical delivery of deliverable grade securities. The

contracts would be cleared by the National Security Depositories Ltd. Central Depository Services (India) and Public Debit Office of the Reserve Bank using electronic both entry system.

4. The securities which could be delivered in the IRF will be as: deliverable grade securities shall comprise Government of India securities maturing at least 7.5 years but not more than 15 years from the first day of the delivery month with a minimum total outstanding stock of ₹10,000 crore.
5. The banks were allowed to participate in trading positions in the IRFs market.
6. The short selling was allowed in the IRFs trading.

On the evaluation of the performance of the product in the market, it was not very much encouraging. The important reasons for this failure were observed as follows:

(i) Short selling was allowed only up to 5 days not beyond this.
(ii) Settlement of these IRFs by physical delivery only, illiquidity in the market and the participation of the banks was very poor.
(iii) Banks found IRF traded at OTC markets more attractive than the exchange traded IRFs.

## 11.6.3  Exchange Traded Interest Rate Futures-2011

Interest Rate Futures on 10-year notional coupon bearing Government of India (GoI) security and 91-Day Treasury Bills were introduced on August 28, 2009 and March 7, 2011, respectively. It has now been decided to introduce Interest Rate Futures (IRF) on 2-year and 5-year notional coupon bearing GoI securities in terms of Amendment Direction IDMD. PCD.15/ED(RG)-2011 dated December 30, 2011 issued by the Reserve Bank of India. 2. The final settlement price of the cash-settled 2-year and 5-year IRF contracts at the expiry of the contract period would be derived from the yields of the GoI securities in the underlying basket of securities identified by the stock exchanges. In this regard, the yields of the GoI securities in the underlying basket would be determined through a polling process as indicated below:

(a) Polling shall be carried out by the Fixed Income, Money Market and Derivatives Association, i.e., FIMMDA;
(b) The yields of the GoI securities shall be polled from Primary Dealers (PDs) registered with the Reserve Bank of India;
(c) Polling would be conducted at three instances, i.e., 11.00 a.m., 11.30 a.m. and 12.00 p.m. on the date of polling;
(d) Each poll shall involve ten PDs who would be selected at random from the universe of PDs;
(e) At each instance of polling, for each bond, out of the ten buy yields, two highest and two lowest yields would be treated as outliers and would be ignored. Similarly, outliers from ten sell yields would be identified and ignored;
(f) After rejecting the outliers as indicated at (e) above, there will be (6 * 2 * 3 * Number of Bonds in Basket) number of remaining yields at the end of 3 polling;
(g) Average settlement yield (Ys) is the simple average of the remaining yields. Ys will be rounded off to 4 decimal digits;
(h) The Average settlement yield (Ys) of each GoI security and the yields polled by each participant would be disseminated by FIMMDA (at its website) immediately after the polling process is completed;

(i) The basket of GoI securities underlying the 2-year and 5-year IRF contracts shall be announced by the stock exchanges and the same shall be based on the following:

1. The basket of GoI securities for the 2-year IRF contract shall comprise GoI securities with residual maturity ranging between 1.5 years and 2.5 years;

2. The basket of GoI securities for the 5-year IRF contract shall comprise GoI securities with residual maturity ranging between 4.5 years and 5.5 years;

3. The residual maturity of the securities for the purpose [indicated at (ii) and (iii) above] shall be the time period between the date of expiry of the IRF contract and the maturity date of the security.

4. The final settlement price of the underlying GoI securities as well as the IRF contracts shall be determined by the stock exchanges based on the guidelines issued by the Securities Exchange Board of India (SEBI) from time to time.

The detailed guidelines of RBI is shown in the Annexure-A.

## 11.6.4 Exchange Traded IRFs-2014

The RBI guidelines issued for the IRF-August 2009 were amended on March 7, 2011 and further amended vide its Amendment Direction IDMD.PCD.15|ED|RG-2011 dated December 30, 2011, vide which certain GoI securities of 2 years and 5 years with a coupon of 7 percent were also included for trading in the IRFs. However, in January 2014, RBI Governor Raghuram Rajan introduced 3rd time exchange traded IRFs in India with certain new changes and on cash settlement basis. On October 29, 2013, RBI mentioned in its 2nd quarter review of monetary policy 2013–14, to allow IRFs in Indian market. On December 5, 2013, RBI and SEBI released circular for introducing this product. This product is launched on three stock exchanges; NSE, BSE and MCX-SX. As per SEBI, the IRF will be launched on a pilot basis and the features of the products will be reviewed on the basis of experience gain from time to time. The guidelines of this vide Notification of January 2014 of RBI.

There was an encouraging response from the market of the cash settled IRF on 10-year Government of India (GoI) security launched on the stock exchanges in January, 2014. To provide market participants with flexibility to hedge their interest rate risk, it was announced in the Sixth Bi-monthly Monetary Policy Statement 2014–15 to introduce cash settled IRF contracts on 5–7 year and 13–15 year Government of India securities. The product specifications for the new 6-year and 13-year contract as well as the existing 10-year contract have been finalized in consultation with the SEBI and other state holders.

In this section, all the details of the guidelines of RBI's IRF-2014 products could not be presented, rather a few important features were discussed. As per this new SEBI circular, there will be two different design options 10-year GoI security which are allowed for trading in IRFs as underlying asset.

Option-A coupon bearing Government of India security as underlying, and

Option-B coupon bearing notional 10-year Government of India security with settlement price based on the basket of securities as underlying.

Exchanges are allowed to launch either one or two of these options.

## 11.6.5 Features of the Product (IRFs-2014)

As stated above, two options of the underlying security of GoI, have been permitted to the exchanges as per SEBI circular. A brief view of their features is discussed here as follows:

**Option A:** The underlying Government of India security in option A of face value ₹100 with semi-annual coupon and residual maturity between 9 and 10 years on the day of expiry of IRF contract, as decided by the stock exchanges (NSE & BSE) in consultation with FIMMDA.

**Option B:** In case of option 'B' the notional coupon bearing 10-year GoI security with a notional coupon paid semi-annually and face value of ₹100 for each contract. There shall be a basket of GoI securities with residual maturity between 9 and 11 years on the day of the expiry of IRF contract along with appropriate weight assigned to each security in the basket.

The exchange offer 10-year GoI bond in two maturity dates comprising two products as:

First-symbol-716GS2023-futures contracts based on 7.16 percent Government of India securities having maturity on May 20, 2023.

Second-symbol-883GS2023-futures contracts based on 8.83 percent Government of India securities having maturity on November 25, 2023.

Contract size shall represent 2000 underlying bonds of total face value of ₹2 lakhs. Contract value shall be Quoted Price × 2000. Quotation shall be similar to the quoted price of the GoI security. The daily settlement value shall be (PW)*2000 where (PW) is volume weighted average futures price of the last half an hour. Final contract settlement value shall be 2000 * (Pf) where (pf) is final settlement price of the underlying/notional bond which shall be determined as:
Formula of (Pf)

$$Pf = \left[\frac{100}{\left(1+\frac{Ys}{2}\right)^{20}}\right] + \left[\sum_{k=1}^{20} \frac{100 \times \frac{c}{2}}{\left(1+\frac{Ys}{2}\right)^{K}}\right]$$

Where   Pf = the final settlement price of the underlying or national bond
    Ys = settlement yield
    C = the notional coupon of underlying bond
    K = the time period

**Note:** A Product Specification of NSE NFB-II (NSE Bond Futures) on 10-year Government of India securities is presented below to know about the specifications of trading mechanism of long-term interest futures contracts in India.

**Product Specifications (NSE)**

NSE now launches NSE NBF II (NSE Bond Futures) on 10-year Government of India Securities.

**Product Specification**

| Instrument Type Symbol | *FUTIRC* |
|---|---|
| | 883GS2023–Futures contracts based on 8.83% Government of India Securities having maturity on November 25, 2023. |
| | 716GS2023–Futures contracts based on 7.16% Government of India Securities having maturity on May 20, 2023. |
| Market Type | N |

*(Contd.)*

*(Contd.)*

| Instrument Type Symbol | FUTIRC |
|---|---|
| Unit of Trading | ₹2 lakhs face value of GoI securities, i.e., 2000 units. (orders in lots). |
| Quotation | Similar to the quoted price of GoI security. |
| Contract Value | Quoted price * 2000 |
| Tick Size | ₹0.0025 |
| Trading Hours | Monday to Friday: 9.00 a.m. to 5.00 p.m. |
| Contract Trading Cycle | Three serial monthly contracts. |
| Spread Contract | Near-Mid, Near-Far and Mid-Far |
|  | All spread orders shall be placed in terms of price difference only |
| Order Type/Order | Regular lot order |
| Book/Order Attribute | Stop loss order |
|  | Immediate or cancel |
|  | Day order |
|  | Spread order |
| Expiry Day | Last Thursday of the month. In case the last Thursday is a trading holiday, the previous trading day shall be the expiry/last trading day. |
| Base Price | Theoretical price of the 1st day of the contract. On all other days. Daily Settlement Price of the contract. |
| Price Operating Range | +/–3% of the base price. (Whenever a trade in any contract is executed at the hightest/lowest price of the band, Exchange may expand the price band for that contract by 0.5% in that direction after 30 minutes after taking into account market trend. Price band may be relaxed only 2 times during the day). |
| Qunatity Freeze | 15,251 lots or greater, i.e., orders having quantity up to 1250 lots shall be allowed. |
| Daily Settlement | Daily MTM settlement on T + 1 in cash based on daily settlement price. |
| Final Settlement | Final settlement on T + 1 day in cash based on final settlement price. |
| Daily Settlement Price | Volume Weighted Average Futures Price of last half an hour or Theoretical Price. |
| Final Settlement Price | Weighted average price of the underlying bond based on the prices during the last two hours of the trading on NDS-OM. If less than 5 trades are executed in the underlying bond during the last two hours of trading, then FIMMDA price shall be used for final settlement. |

*Source:* NSE NBF-II India

## 11.7  MARK-TO-MARK MECHANISM

**EXAMPLE:**   Let us assume:

Trade date: July 6, 2015
Underlying security: 8.83 percent GoI 2023
Expiry date: July 30, 2015
Current futures price: ₹94.50
Strategy: Trader sells 250 contracts on July 6, 2015 at a price ₹94.50
Daily MTM due to change in futures price is tabulated as:

| Mark-To-Mark Mechanism (short position) | | | |
|---|---|---|---|
| *Date* | *Daily Settlement Price* ₹ | *Calculations* | *MTM* ₹ |
| July 6, 2015 | 94.6925 | 250 * 2000 * (94500 – 94.6925) | –96,250 |
| July 7, 2015 | 94.4625 | 250 * 2000 * (94.6925 – 94.4625) | 1,15,000 |
| July 8, 2015 | 94.4575 | 250 * 2000 * (94.4625 – 94.4575) | 2,500 |
| July 9, 2015 | 94.1275 | 250 * 2000 * (94.4575 – 94.1275) | 1,65,000 |

Net MTM gain as on July 9, 2015 is ₹1,86,250

### 11.7.1  Closing Out Position

Assume on July 10, 2015, futures market price ₹94.1125 trader buys 250 contracts at ₹94.1125 and squares off position, so profit to the trader = 250 * 2000 (94.1275 – 94.1125) is ₹7,500

Total profit = Net MTM gain + profit on the trade:

₹1,86,250 + 7,500 = ₹1,93,750

### 11.7.2  Calendar Spread with IRF

As discussed in the proceeding chapter that calendar spread is referred to the simultaneous purchase of a futures contract of one delivery month, say, July, 2015 and sale of the same contract of the another month say, September, 2015 on the same underlying exchange. A trader can earn profit or incur loss at the price difference between the two contracts. So, a long and short position in different contracts on the same underlying asset/security is known as *calendar spread*. Since a calendar spread entails only the basis risk, the trader has little risk on the positions.

**EXAMPLE:**   Let us consider:

Trade date: July 6, 2015
July 2015 futures (₹94.3600 – 94.3800)
August 2015 futures (₹92.9700 – 93.0200)
The difference between the July 2015 and August 2015 futures contracts is currents ₹1.41 (after considering bid ask).

    Let us assume that the trader believes this spread is very high, then he may execute a calendar spread by:
    Buying the July 2015 futures at 94.3800
    Selling the August 2015 futures at 92.9700
    Trade date: July 16, 2015

July 2015 future (₹) 94.0050 – 94.0050
August 2015 future (₹) 92.5000 – 92.3700
The difference between July 2015 and August 2015 is now ₹1.6350 (after considering bid ask).

Consider the trader decided to liquidate his calendar spread trade by selling the July 2015 futures at ₹94.0050 (loss 0.375) and buying the August 2015 futures at ₹92.3700 (profit 0.600 net profit of ₹0.225 without incurring any interest rate risk.)

## 11.8   DETERMINING THE T-BOND FUTURES PRICES

Interest rate futures trade in the stock markets which are at full carry. In other words, the cost-of-carry model provides a complete understanding of the price structure of interest rate futures contracts because they meet the requirements of this model. Futures price should be such that no profit is available from cash and carry arbitrage. It means, in case of long, for no arbitrage profit, the financing cost of holding bonds should be matched by the returns from holding the bonds in the form of coupon receipts, plus capital gain (or loss) guaranteed by the futures premium (or discount) relative to the spot price of the bonds. It should be further noted that if the financing cost (based on short-term interest rates) exceeds the coupon yield, there will be a futures premium over spot to yield a capital gain, whereas if the financing cost is less than coupon receipts, there will be a futures discount, leading to capital loss, should exist.

In case of short, for no arbitrage profit, the interest receipts from short selling are precisely offset by losses in the form of coupon amounts payable to the entity from which the bonds were borrowed plus capital losses (minus capital gains).

In simpler form, the pricing relationship with no coupon before the futures delivery date, the equation 11.3 will be

$$F = S (1 + r_t) \tag{11.3}$$

where $F$ is fair futures price of the bond, $S$ is spot price of the bond and $r_t$ is financing cost.

If, coupon is due before the delivery date, then the equation 11.4 will be

$$F = S (1 + r_t) - D \tag{11.4}$$

where $-D$ is the futures value of the coupon.

### 11.8.1   Fundamental No-arbitrage for T-bond Futures

We can elaborate the equation 11.3 further in context to invoice and market price bond.

$$F_{t,T} = P_t (1 + r_{t,T}) - FV_T \text{ (coupon from } t \text{ to } T) \tag{11.5}$$

where $F_{t,T}$ is total invoice price of the bond, $P_t$ is total market price of the bond, $FV_T$ is futures value of coupon on the bond and $r_t$ is financing cost.

It means that the cost of buying the bond; plus the financing cost $r_t$ and minus, coupon is due before the delivery date should be equal the sum receivable from selling against the futures $F$. Suppose there is just one coupon between dates $t$ and $T$, as shown in the following time line.

**Time Line**

| $T_0$ | $t$ | $t_1$ | $T$ | $t_2$ |
|-------|-----|-------|-----|-------|
| $C/2$ | Enter contract | $C/2$ | Contract expires | $C/2$ |

Since interest is accrued on the bond as of date $t$, the equation 11.5 will be rewritten as follows to determine a no-arbitrage (fair) quoted futures price, $QF_{t,T}$:

$$QF_{t,T} = \frac{P_t\,(1 + r_{t,T}) - FV_T\,(\text{coupon from } t \text{ to } T) - AI_{t,T}}{\text{Conversion factor}} \tag{11.6}$$

where $AI_{t,T}$ is the accrued interest on the bond as of date $T$.

We have seen in the previous section that there are multiple deliverable grades and each deliverable bond will have a different no-arbitrage quoted futures prices. Further, we have seen that the cheapest-to-deliver bond at expiration is the one that minimizes the delivery adjusted spot prices. In this section, we will see CTD bond at time $t$, before expiration, is the one that minimizes the no-arbitrage quoted futures price in equation 11.6.

**EXAMPLE:**  Suppose that on March 31, 2014, the investor wishes to determine which of the T-bonds that are deliverable into a June 2014 futures contract is the cheapest-to-deliver. The current 30-day repo rate is 10 percent. It will be used as the short-term interest rate. We will use here a bond with 7.25 percent coupon and May 2031 as maturity with quoted price $81.125 per $100 face value. Since March 31, 2014 is a Friday, the bond is actually received and paid for on Monday, April 3, as date $t$.

*Solution:*

**Time Line**

| Coupon | $t$ | 42 days coupon | 46 days | $T$ 138 days | Coupon |
|---|---|---|---|---|---|
| 11/15 | 4/3 | | 5/15 | 6/30 | 11/15 |

*First step:*  Calculate the total market price of 7¼ percent May 15, 2031 on April 3 for quoted price $81.125. The bond has earned accrued Interest over the 139 days since November 15, 2013 because there are 181 days in the full coupon period from November 11, 2013 to May 15, 2014.

$$\text{Accrued interest on April 3} = \left(\frac{139}{181}\right)\left(\frac{\$7.25}{2}\right) = 2.784 \text{ per } \$100 \text{ face}$$

Thus, total market price of the bond on April 3 is:

$$\text{Total market price} = \$81.125 + 2.784 = \$83.909 \text{ per } \$100 \text{ face value}$$

*Second step:*  Calculate the future value of the coupons.

Now, we will calculate the futures value at the futures expiration date of the coupon received by holding the T-bond. In this example, the investor will receive a coupon of $7.25/2 = $3.625 per $100 face par on May 15. Thus, the futures value of coupon as on June 30 is given by

$$\text{Futures value of coupons} = FV_T\,(\text{Coupon from } t \text{ to } T)\,(\text{on June 30})$$

$$= (\$3625)\left[1 + \left(\frac{46}{360}\right)(0.10)\right]$$

$$= \$3.691 \text{ per } \$100 \text{ face}$$

*Third step:*  Third step is to compute the interest the bond will accrue over 46 days between the coupon payment on May 15 and the futures expiration on June 30.

$$\text{Futures accrued interest} = \left(\frac{46}{184}\right)\left(\frac{\$7.25}{2}\right)$$

$$= \$0.906 \text{ per } \$100 \text{ face}$$

*Fourth step:*   Calculate the fair total futures price, $(F_{t,T})$

$$\text{Fair total futures price} = P_t(1 + r_{t,T} - FV_T) \text{ (Coupon } t \text{ to } T)$$

$$= (\$83,909)(1 + 0.10)\left(\frac{88}{360}\right) - \$3,671$$

$$= (\$83,909)(1.02444) - \$3,671$$

$$= \$85.960 - 3.671 = \$82.289 \text{ per } \$100 \text{ face}$$

*Fifth step:*   Calculate the quoted futures price $QF_{t,T}$

$$QF_{t,T} = \text{Fair total futures price} - \text{Futures accrued interest}$$

$$= \$82.289 - \$0.906 = \$81.383 \text{ per } \$100 \text{ face}$$

*Sixth step:*   The conversion factor of 7.25 percent bond is 0.9176. The delivery-adjusted fair quoted futures price for 7¼ percent bond is, therefore,

$$\text{Delivery-adjusted fair quoted futures price} = \frac{\$81.383}{0.9176}$$

$$= \$88.69$$

$$= \$88.22 \text{ per } \$100 \text{ face}$$

## 11.9   HEDGING WITH T-BOND FUTURES

An investor or a portfolio manager or a bank manager may fear an increase or decrease in interest rate in futures resulting in occurrence of losses in futures. In other words, anyone who with a position (short or long) in fixed income assets is expected to potential capital losses due to adverse impact of interest rate changes. In this respect, interest rate futures provides a mechanism for managing this interest rate risk. He could take such a position in futures that would provide an offsetting gain from a fall in bond prices. For example, in case of portfolio manager, fear of an increase in long-term interest rates which will reduce the prices of bonds in futures, he would sell futures contracts to offset that risk. A fall in bond prices should be accompanied by fall in the prices of bonds futures. If a loss were made from a decline in the value of the bonds, the portfolio manager would be compensated by profits from the futures position since he would be able to buy bond futures at a price lower than that at which he sold.

### 11.9.1   Hedging a Bond Portfolio

Suppose on August 5, a fund manager has ₹20 lakhs invested in government bonds and is concerned that interest rate is expected to be volatile over the next six months. The fund manager decides to use December Treasury bond futures contract to hedge the value of the portfolio. Current price (futures) is 93.02 or 93.0625. Each contract is for delivery of ₹1,00,000 face value of bonds, futures contract price is ₹93062.50. The average duration of the bond portfolio in three months will be 6.80 years. The cheapest to deliver bond contract is expected to be 20 years 12 percent per annum coupon bond. The yield on this bond is currently 5.80 percent per annum, and the duration will be 9.20 year at maturity of futures.

**Position:**   The fund manager requires a short position in treasury-bond futures to hedge the bond portfolio. The number of bond futures that should be shorted will be

$$\frac{20,00,000}{93062.50} \times \frac{6.80}{9.20} = \frac{1,36,00,000}{8,56,175} = 15.88$$

$$= 16 \text{ contracts will be needed to hedge the position.}$$

## 11.9.2   Hedging the Value of a Portfolio

**EXAMPLE:**   A portfolio manager may fear an increase in long-term interest rate, an occurrence that would reduce the prices of bonds held in a portfolio. The Indian Government futures contract has a nominal value of ₹2,50,000 and price of contract expressed of Indian rupees is ₹100 nominal value. The price of notional bond (upon which the futures are based) would be 100 when the long-term interest rate is 6 percent p.a., but would rise above 100 when interest rate is lower, the tick size, the minimum price movement is ₹0.01 for these bond futures.

**TABLE 11.5**   Hedging with Interest Rate Futures

| Cash market | Futures market |
|---|---|
| **February 5**<br>The long-term interest rate is 6% p.a. The ₹1 million bond portfolio is vulnerable to an increase in long term interest rates. | **February 5**<br>Sell May 14, Indian Government., T–Bond futures contract. Futures price is 1,000, reflecting a 6% p.a. interest rate. |
| **April 2**<br>Long-term interest rate has risen to 7½%.<br>Correspondingly the value of the bond portfolio has fallen to ₹8,65,000.<br>There is a loss of ₹1,35,000 in the value of bond portfolio. | **April 2**<br>Close out by buying May 14 Indian Government Futures contracts the price of contract fallen to 82.22 reflecting 7½% p.a. futures interest rate.<br>There is a profit of ₹1,77,800 from the futures contract. |
| **Net gain from futures position = ₹42,800 = (₹1,77,800 – ₹1,35,000)** ||

## 11.9.3   Determining the Hedge Ratio (*HR*)

Determining the appropriate hedge ratio is a crucial decision. It specifies the magnitude of the futures position that is used in a hedge and usually determined by comparing the relative price sensitive of the futures and cash instruments. We have already seen in the preceding chapter that the ***minimum-variance hedge ratio HR*** is the one that minimizes the variance of gains and losses on the hedged portfolio.

The variance will be zero on a portfolio consisting of cash bonds and T-bonds futures if

$$Q_c \times \Delta CP_t = Q_f \times \$1,00,000 \times \Delta FP_{t,T} \qquad (11.7)$$

where $Q_c$ is the face value of the cash T-bonds, $\Delta CP_t$ is the change in the price of the cash T-bonds at time $t$, $Q_f$ is the number of T-bond futures contracts (each T-bond) futures contract has a face value of $\$1,00,000$ and $\Delta FP_{t,T}$ is the change in the price of the T-bond futures contract being used to hedge during period $t$.

The minimum-variance hedge ratio *HR*, from the equation 11.7, can be expressed as the ratio of change in the price of the cash bond to change in the price of the T-bond futures contract:

$$HR = \frac{Q_f \times \$1,00,000}{Q_c} = \frac{\Delta CP_t}{\Delta FP_{t,T}} \qquad (11.8)$$

Since T-bond futures prices track the adjusted spot prices of the cheapest-to-deliver bond, which can change over the life of futures contract, the ratio must be modified to obtain an accurate measure of the hedge ratio applicable to T-bond futures. To find out hedge ratio, two methods are used which are as under:

1. Duration method
2. Regression methodology

## 11.9.4  Using Duration to Determine Hedge Ratio

We have already observed a close relationship between T-bond futures prices and the adjusted cash prices of the cheapest-to-deliver T-bond. Therefore, any change in the T-bond futures prices can be precisely termed as:

$$\Delta FP_t = \frac{\Delta CP_t}{CF} \tag{11.9}$$

where $\Delta CP_t$ is changes in the price of cheapest-to-deliver bond and $CF$ is an applicable conversion factor.

If we substitute the equation 11.9 for $\Delta FP_t$ in the equation 11.8 hedge ratio $HR$, then the minimum-variance hedge ratio will be written as:

$$HR = \frac{\Delta CP_t}{\Delta CP_t^*} \times CF \tag{11.10}$$

To calculate this hedge ratio, we have to identify the cheapest-to-deliver bond and for a given change in yield, determine by how much both the price of the bond being hedged $(CP_t)$ and the price of the cheapest-to-deliver bond $(CP_t^*)$ will change.

We have already seen that respective bond durations can be expressed as follows:

$$-D_{CP} = \frac{\Delta CP_t}{\%\Delta(1 + R_{CP})^t}$$

After making the appropriate substitutions into the previously defined hedge ratio, the equation yields

$$HR = \frac{-D_{CP} \times CP_t \times (1 + R_{CP_t}^*) \times \Delta R_{CP_t}}{-D_{CP}^* \times CP_t^* \times (1 + R_{CP_t}) \times \Delta R_{CP_t}} \times CF \tag{11.11}$$

where $D_{CP}$ and $D_{CP}^*$ are respective bond durations and $\Delta RCP$ and $\Delta RCP_t$ are changes in the yields on the two bonds.

All the variables, except changes in yields in respective bonds, can be easily obtained. If the changes in the yields of these two bonds are equal, i.e., $\dfrac{\Delta R_{CP_t}}{\Delta CP_t^*} = 1$, then these variables can be easily deleted from the above equation. However, usually, the yields are not identical, then the relationship between these yields, i.e., $\Delta R_{CP_t}$ and $\Delta R*_{CP_t}$ must be determined and be included in the equation 11.11.

Let us explain the above HR with an **example**:

Assume that on December 13, 2014, an investor purchases $10 million of 12 percent, August 2031 bond. To hedge against adverse movements in interest rates, he establishes a short position in the March, 2015 T-bond futures contract. The above said has an average cash price of 137.6875, a yield to maturity of 8.05 percent, and a duration of 8.926. It is assumed that cheapest-to-bond on the March, 2015 T-bond contract is the 10.375 percent, November 2030 bond, which has an average cash price of 121.8125, a yield to maturity of 8.04, and a duration of 9.2888. The applicable conversion factor is 1.2216.

After substituting these values into the equation 11.11 and further assuming that the changes in the yields on the two bonds are the same, the hedge ratio is:

$$HR = \frac{-8.926 \times 137.6875 \times (1 + 0.0804)}{-9.288 \times 121.8125 \times 1\,(1 + 0.0805)} \times 1.2216 = 1.33$$

It is noted that the HR is 1.33. Hence, to hedge $10 million face value of the 12 percent bond, he will have to short 133 T-bond futures contracts:

$$133 = \left(1.33 \times \frac{\$1,00,00,000}{\$1,00,000}\right)$$

## 11.9.5 Using Regression Analysis to Determine Hedge Ratio

The use of regression analysis has also been discussed in the chapter of hedging. This approach takes into account that two yield changes may not be the same. Under this technique, *HR* can be determined by estimating the following regression equation:

$$\Delta CP_t = \alpha + \beta \times \Delta FP_{t,T} + e_t \qquad (11.12)$$

Where:
$CP_t$ = Current price of the security
$FP_{t,T}$ = Futures price of the security at 'T'
$\alpha$ = Intercept of the equation
$\beta$ = Estimate of the beta, i.e., hedge ratio (HR)
$C_t$ = error term.

Hence,
$$HR = \beta = \frac{\Delta CP_t}{\Delta FP_{t,T}}$$

We can explain the above regression analysis by a hypothetical example to structure a hedge ratio.

**EXAMPLE:** **Hedging a corporate bond**–Let us assume that at the beginning of July 2015, our objective is to minimize the interest risk on a $10 million face value position of X Ltd. Company (an MNC) 8 × 5/8 percent of 2032 bond. Being a corporate bond, its yield will behave differently to T-bonds. In particular, the price of the corporate bond may change because of changes in the markets perception of its default risk. However, this does not exist for T-bonds. Table 11.6 provides the monthly price data from January, 2013 to June, 2015 to estimate the hedge ratio. Regressing the monthly price changes of this corporate bond on the monthly price change of the near month T-bond futures over the 30-month sample period given in Table 11.6, value of $\alpha$: 0.0255, $\beta$: 0.899 and $R^2 = 0.86$.

The regression equation is constructed as:

$$\Delta CP_t = 0.0255 + 0.899 \times \Delta FP_{t,T}$$

$$R^2 = 0.86$$

**TABLE 11.6**    Prices of X Ltd. Company 8 5/8% of 2032 Bonds Compared to T-bond Futures Prices

| Month | Corporate bond prices | Cash price changes | Near month futures T-bond prices | Futures price changes |
|---|---|---|---|---|
| Jan 2013 | 98.25 | | 99.90 | |
| Feb 2013 | 99.25 | 1.00 | 99.34 | −0.56 |
| Mar 2013 | 99.75 | 0.50 | 100.78 | 1.44 |
| Apr 2013 | 96.75 | −3.00 | 97.71 | −3.07 |
| May 2013 | 90.78 | −5.97 | 91.81 | −5.90 |
| June 2013 | 89.13 | −1.65 | 90.78 | −1.03 |
| July 2013 | 90.00 | 0.87 | 91.59 | 0.81 |
| Aug 2013 | 86.33 | −3.67 | 88.18 | −3.41 |
| Sep 2013 | 85.50 | −0.83 | 86.03 | −2.15 |
| Oct 2013 | 80.63 | −4.87 | 81.75 | −4.28 |
| Nov 2013 | 85.50 | 4.87 | 87.12 | 5.37 |
| Dec 2013 | 86.25 | 0.75 | 86.43 | −0.69 |
| Jan 2014 | 88.50 | 2.25 | 88.31 | 1.88 |
| Feb 2014 | 92.75 | 4.25 | 93.84 | 5.53 |
| Mar 2014 | 92.87 | 0.12 | 93.68 | −0.16 |
| Apr 2014 | 88.25 | −4.62 | 89.28 | −4.40 |
| May 2014 | 86.50 | −1.75 | 87.34 | −1.94 |
| June 2014 | 87.00 | 0.50 | 88.65 | 1.31 |
| July 2014 | 89.00 | 2.00 | 90.62 | 1.97 |
| Aug 2014 | 86.75 | −2.25 | 88.06 | −2.56 |
| Sep 2014 | 86.19 | −0.56 | 86.28 | −1.78 |
| Oct 2014 | 89.38 | 3.19 | 90.75 | 4.47 |
| Nov 2014 | 92.50 | 3.12 | 91.18 | 0.43 |
| Dec 2014 | 88.88 | −3.62 | 90.53 | −0.65 |
| Jan 2015 | 88.50 | −0.38 | 88.28 | −2.25 |
| Feb 2015 | 90.75 | 2.25 | 90.90 | 2.62 |
| Mar 2015 | 87.88 | −2.87 | 87.59 | −3.31 |
| Apr 2015 | 87.88 | 0.00 | 88.68 | 1.09 |
| May 2015 | 89.25 | 1.37 | 89.34 | 0.66 |
| June 2015 | 92.81 | 3.56 | 93.03 | 3.69 |

The value of the $R^2$ is 0.86 which indicates that T-bond futures price does not trade the market value of the corporate bond, however, $R^2$ of 0.86 is still high which indicates a good linear relationship between the two price series. The estimate 0.899 shows that about 90 T-bonds futures contracts are needed to establish a minimum variance *HR*.

$$Q_f = \frac{\$10,00,000}{\$1,00,000} \times 0.899 = 90$$

### Comparison of performance hedged and unhedged position

Let us discuss now the impact of hedging on the performance of a portfolio. It is explained by a hypothetical example. The respective performances of the hedged and unhedged portfolios are shown in Table 11.7 which shows that the monthly average return on the unhedged portfolio is 1.85 percent with a standard deviation of 4.57 percent. Hedging reduces the standard deviation of returns by about half, i.e., from 4.57 percent to 2.07 percent. But at the same time, it also indicates towards decreasing average monthly return from 1.85 percent to 0.81 percent. Thus, this hedging strategy clearly succeeds in reducing the portfolio's exposure to interest rate risk but at the cost of lowering profits.

**TABLE 11.7**   Performance of Hedged Corporate Bond Portfolio
(X Ltd. Company bonds)
June 1 to December 31, 2015

| Beginning of month | Average portfolio price (1) $ | Accrued coupon interest (1) $ | Change in market value (2) $ | Dollar profit (3) = (1) + (2) $ | % return | Near month futures price | Profit on futures position (4) $ | Net profit (5) = (3) + (4) $ | Net return |
|---|---|---|---|---|---|---|---|---|---|
| | **Unhedged cash position** | | | | | **Futures position** | | **Hedged portfolio (cash +futures)** | |
| June | 92.81 | | | | | 93.03 | | | |
| July | 96.75 | 71,875.00 | 7,88,000.00 | 8,59,875.00 | 9.26 | 97.72 | (4,22,100.00) | 4,37,775.00 | 4.73 |
| August | 97.83 | 71,875.00 | 2,16,000.00 | 2,87,875.00 | 2.98 | 100.38 | (2,39,400.00) | 48,475.00 | 0.51 |
| September | 95.25 | 71,875.00 | (5,16,000.00) | (4,44,125.00) | (4.54) | 97.06 | 2,98,800.00 | (1,45,325.00) | (1.48) |
| October | 94.35 | 71,875.00 | (1,80,000.00) | (1,08,125.00) | (1.14) | 95.84 | 1,09,800.00 | 1,675.00 | 0.02 |
| November | 96.50 | 71,875.00 | 4,30,000.00 | 5,01,875.00 | 5.32 | 99.34 | (3,15,000.00) | 1,86,875.00 | 2.00 |
| December | 95.75 | 71,875.00 | (1,50,000.00) | (78,125.00) | (0.81) | 99.47 | (11,700.00) | (89,825.00) | (0.94) |
| Mean | | | | 1,69,875.00 | 1.85 | | (96,600.00) | 73,275.00 | 0.81 |
| Standard deviation | | | | 4,31,283.36 | 4.57 | | 2,51,724.31 | 1,94,033.67 | 2.07 |

## 11.9.6   Comparison of Duration and Regression Methods

In the preceding section, we have observed both the methods to estimate the hedge ratio. Which technique is superior between these two? As we see that in the duration method it explicitly considers the known information like the maturity, coupon and prices of the relevant bonds. The main thing in this method is reliable estimation of relationship between the changes in the returns of both the bonds. In regression analysis method, historical data and statistical tools are used to find out the hedge ratio. So, it depends upon the implicit assumption that estimated historical credit market relationships will be suitable and will continue in futures too.

Both the methods have their own limitations. An advisable procedure is to estimate hedge ratio using both the methods, i.e., duration and regression, to see whether they give similar results or shot. And if they do not, then the investor should make proper evaluation regarding the underlying assumptions used in finding out a particular hedge ratio.

## 11.10   ARBITRAGING WITH IRFS

In simple term arbitraging is the process of buying and selling an asset simultaneously at different markets and thus earning without any side. In futures trading, the arbitrage is the price difference between the bond prices and IRF contract with a view that the two will converge.

Sometimes the trader can earn the risk less profit from realizing arbitrage opportunity by entering into IRF contract for example, if the futures are expensive then the arbitrager can make profit by taking short position in the futures market and long position in underlying asset by borrowing funds.

**EXAMPLE:**  Assume on July 10, 2015 a trader buys 8.83 percent GoI 2023 bond in the underlying market at the price of ₹90.68. Then he sells the futures contract at ₹90.95 and holds on to the position till expiry on July 30, 2015 (expiry day). The futures contract settled at the price from the underlying market ₹91.59. At this price the trader sells the underlying bond. The pay-off from this arbitrage process would be as follows.

Profit in underlying bond (A) ₹91.59 – ₹90.68 = ₹0.91

Accrued interest on holding period (B) = ₹0.49

Cost of carry (C) = ₹0.42

Profit from underlying bond (A + B – C) = (0.91 + 0.49 – 0.42) = ₹0.98

Loss on IRf contract (₹91.59 – ₹90.95 ) = ₹0.64

Net profit = ₹0.98 – ₹0.64 = ₹0.34

Through arbitraging, the trader earnes ₹0.34 at the expiry day.

## SUMMARY

This chapter has introduced the concept of long-term interest rate futures. The long-term government bond futures are the most actively traded contracts on derivative exchanges all over the world. One of the most widely traded long-term interest rate futures contracts are the US government treasury bonds (popularly known as T-bonds). These were introduced on the Chicago Board of Trade (CBOT) in 1977. Later, T-bills and municipal bonds were introduced in 1982 and 1985, respectively. These interest rate futures instruments are most popular due to their large size and being default-free investments.

Treasury bonds have maturities ten years and more to 30 years. Treasury notes have original maturities of 10 years or less. Both of these instruments are similar except for the difference in maturity. Treasury bonds also known as government bonds have some common features like a fixed rate of interest (coupon) per period (usually six months), definite redemption date like 5, 10, 20 years and so on, market price expressed as a sum per $100 nominal. Bond's price is calculated by adding up the present value of coupon annuity and present value of face value. Transaction price of bond is calculated by adding up quoted price and accrued interest on bond.

A bond duration is a useful summary of its price sensitivity to interest rate changes. A high duration bond's price is more sensitive to interest rate changes than the low duration bond. Duration of a bond is commonly defined as the weighted average of the maturities of the bond's coupon and the principal repayment cash flows, where the weights are the fractions of the bond's price that the cash flows in time period represent. Next section of this chapter deals with the Treasury bond futures contracts relating to mechanism of trading of futures contracts of the government bonds, specifically focusing on US treasury bonds. It further describes the delivery process and deliverable grades of bonds in which short initiates delivery. As in all the futures contracts, the delivery process involves choosing which bond to deliver when to deliver, and during which month to deliver.

The invoicing prices for T-bond can be calculated by taking into consideration the decimal futures settlement price X conversion factor X $1,00,000 and adding up the accrued interest on the delivered bond. The conversion factors specified by the T-bond contract for bonds of different grades are simply discounting the bond's futures cash flow by the hypothetical percentage annual yield. The chapter in next part discusses the T-bond futures prices. Interest rate futures trade in the stock markets which are at full carry. In other words, cost-of-carry model provides a complete understanding of the price structure of interest rate futures contract because they meet the requirements of this model.

In the last section, the chapter states about the hedging with the T-bond futures contracts. Investors or portfolio managers or bank managers may fear increase or decrease in interest rate in future, resulting in occurrence of losses in futures. They can take such a position in futures that would provide an offsetting gain from a fall in bond prices. In other words, interest rate futures proves a mechanism for managing the interest rate risk. Before deciding the types and nature of contract, portfolio managers need to calculate hedge ratio. It specifies the magnitude of the futures position that is used to be in a hedge and usually determined by comparing the relative price sensitivities of the futures and cash instruments. Minimum variance hedge ratio is the one that determine and minimize the variance of gains and losses on the hedged portfolio. Two methods can be used to determine hedge ratio; first is duration method and another one is regression method. Interest rate futures in India was started on June, 2003 with the recommendations of RBI committee and working group on rupees derivatives. Interest rate futures were started on two products 10-year T-bond and 91-days Treasury bill. After that the guidelines relating to them have been changed in the year 2009, 2011 and 2014.

## SOLVED PROBLEMS

**P.1.**    Consider an 8½% treasury bond with a maturity of 22 years and 2 months. For calculating conversion factor, assume that bond has a life of 22 years. First coupon payment of 4.25 is assumed to be paid after six months. Calculate conversion factor of the Treasury bond?

*Solution*:    First of all we have to calculate the value of bond for calculating conversion factor.

$$\text{Value of bond} = \sum_{t-1}^{44} \frac{4.25}{(1+0.04)^t} + \frac{100}{(1+0.04)^{44}} = 105.1372$$

Value of bond is 105.1372, assuming semi-annual coupon payment and a face of 100, so conversion factor = 105.1372 ÷ 100 = 1.0514.

**P.2.**    Calculate the duration for a two-year note:

Market price = 96.00
Coupon rate = 8% p.a.
Coupon payment = Semi-annual
Y TM = 10% p.a.
Time to maturity = 2 years

*Solution*:

| Periods (t = 1 – N ) | Cash flow per 100 face value | 1 × 2 | Discount $(1 + r)^t$ | P.V. cash flows | Duration weight 5/100 |
|---|---|---|---|---|---|
| 1 | ₹4 | 4 | 1.0500 | 3.8095 | 0.0389 |
| 2 | ₹4 | 8 | 1.1025 | 7.2562 | 0.0745 |
| 3 | ₹4 | 12 | 1.1576 | 10.3663 | 0.1058 |
| 4 | ₹4 | 16 | 1.2155 | 13.1633 | 0.1343 |
| 5 | ₹100 | 400 | 1.2155 | 329.0826 | 3.3574 |
| | | | | | 3.7109 |

It can also be calculated by the following formula of duration:

$$D = \frac{1}{P} \times \sum_{t=1}^{m} \frac{t \times X_t}{(1+r)^t}$$

$$= \frac{1}{98} \times \left( \frac{1 \times 4}{(1+0.05)^t} + \frac{2 \times 4}{(1+0.05)^2} + \frac{3 \times 4}{(1+0.05)^3} + \frac{4 \times 4}{(1+0.05)^4} + \frac{4 \times 100}{(1+0.05)^4} \right)$$

Duration = 3.7109

On annual, duration will be

$$\frac{3.7109}{2} = 1.85545 \text{ years}$$

**P.3.** Calculate the price of a T-bill that is traded on IMM, which is having face value of $1,00,000, on a basis point movement in interest rate generates a price change of $2,500. Discount yield is 8.32% on futures contract and date to maturity is 90 days.

**Solution:**

$$\text{T-bill price} = \text{Face value} - \frac{\text{DY (Face value) DTM}}{360}$$

$$= 1,00,000 - \frac{0.0832\,(\$1,00,000) \times 90}{360}$$

Treasury bill price = $1,00,000 – $2,080 = $97,920

**P.4.** Suppose it is January 9, 2016. The price of Treasury bond with a 12% coupon that matures on October 12, 2015 is quoted as 102–07. Calculate invoice price of Treasury bond.

**Solution:** For calculating invoice price, we will calculate number of days between October 12 and January 9.

$$\text{Number of days} = 89 \text{ days}$$

$$\text{Invoice price of a bond} = (\text{Quoted price} + \text{Accrued Interest})$$

$$\text{Invoice price of bond} = 102.21875 \times \frac{89}{182} \times 6$$

$$= 102.21875 + 2.934$$

$$= 105.1528$$

**P.5.** German government bond futures contract has a nominal value of DM 2,50,000 and prices of contract are expressed as Dutch marks per DM 100 nominal value. Price of national bond (upon which futures based) would be 100 when long-term interest rate is 6% p.a. A portfolio manager fears an increase in long-term interest rates, which will reduce the prices of bond held in portfolio. Show how interest rate futures contract will hedge the risk of high interest rate. Also suppose that on expiration interest rate has risen to 7½% p.a.

*Solution*:

| Cash market | Futures market |
|---|---|
| **January 2** | **January 2** |
| Long-term interest rate is 6% p.a., The DM 1 million bond portfolio is vulnerable to an increase in long-term interest rate. | Sell 4, March German government bond futures contracts. Futures price is 100, reflecting a 6% p.a. interest rate. |
| **February 15** | **February 15** |
| The long-term interest rate has risen to 7½% p.a. correspondingly, the value of the bond portfolio has fallen to DM 6,500. | Close out by buying 4 March German futures (bond) contract. The price of contract has fallen to 82.22 reflecting a 7½% p.a. futures interest rate. |
| There is a loss of DM 1,35,000 (10,00,000 – 8,65,000) in the value of bond portfolio. | There is a profit of DM 1,77,800 from the futures position. |

**P.6.** Calculate the number of contract a hedger needs to buy of interest rate futures to hedge his position. Suppose for December 2014 contract month the cheapest-to-deliver gilt was the Exchange 12½% 2010, whose price factor was 1.2. If hedger wishes to hedge ₹10,00,000 nominal of this gilt. Each contract has a nominal value of ₹50,000. How much number of contracts are required by hedger?

*Solution*:  No. of contracts $= \dfrac{\text{Nominal value of position}}{\text{Nominal value of contract}} \times \text{Price factor}$

Here

$$\text{Nominal value of position} = ₹10,00,000$$

$$\text{Nominal value of contract} = ₹50,000$$

$$\text{Total no. of contracts} = \frac{10,00,000}{50,000} \times 1.2 = 24$$

Hedger would have to use 24 gilts futures contracts to hedge the position.

**P.7.** A bond with a final maturity of 2 years pays a coupon of ₹10 monthly. Yield curve is flat at an interest rate of 10% p.a. Calculate price of bond and also calculate the duration of the bond.

*Solution*:  Price of bond is:

$$= \frac{10}{(1.05)^1} + \frac{10}{(1.05)^2} + \frac{10}{(1.05)^3} + \frac{110}{(1.05)^4}$$

$$= \frac{10}{1.05} + \frac{10}{1.1025} + \frac{10}{1.1576} + \frac{110}{1.2155}$$

$$= 9.52 + 9.07 + 8.638 + 90.49$$

$$\text{Price} = ₹117.718$$

Duration of bond equals

$$= \left(\frac{9.52}{117.718}\right)0.5 + \left(\frac{9.07}{117.71}\right) + \left(\frac{8.63}{117.71}\right)1.5 + \left(\frac{90.49}{117.71}\right)2$$

$$= 0.0404 + 0.077 + 0.109 + 1.537$$

$$\text{Duration} = 1.7639 \text{ or } 1.763 \text{ years}$$

**P.8.** A government securities dealer agrees to sell to another firm $2,00,000 face value of 90 days T-bill in four months for $19,34,000, a price that implies a yield of 14.37%. The forward rate (for 90 days T-bill, beginning in four months) from the yield curve also equals to 14.37%, and the yield on the futures contract is also 14.37%. Also assume that 90 days T-bill spot rate is 13%. Show the position of dealer in coming four months in the spot as well as in futures market.

*Solution:*    Short hedge using T-bill futures

| Cash market | Futures market |
|---|---|
| **Time = 0** | Security dealer buys T-bill |
| The security dealer commits to sell in $2,00,000 face value of 90 days T-bill in 4 months for $19,34,000. | Futures contracts that matures in 4 months |
| | Futures price = $19,34,000 |
| | Futures yield = 14.37% |
| Implied yield = 14.37% | |
| Spot yield = 13.00% | |
| **Time 4 months** | |
| Spot yield is 14.37%. The security dealer delivers $2,00,000 of T-bill and receives $19,34,000 as expected. | The security dealer sells T-bill futures contract with yield at 14.37%, futures price is $19,34,000 |
| Profit = 0 | Loss = 0 |

**Net wealth change = 0**

**P.9.** In 2011, the prevailing market interest rate on long dated gilt edged securities is 10%. The government issues a new security with a coupon rate of 14%. By 2014, the market interest rate for long dated gilts is 14%. New issue of gilts bear 9 coupon rate of 14%. Investor in gilt edged market can now have two options: (a) either to buy the new gilt edged stock (producing a return of 14%) or (b) to buy the old stock. Which options should investor choose? Under what price he should exercise or choose the option (a)?

*Solution:*    Investor will not buy old (10% stock) at its issue price when he can get 14% on the latest issue. If, however, price falls to level such that the yield is 14% he will be willing to buy it. If this level is $x$ then

$$\frac{10}{x} = \frac{14}{100}$$

$$x = \frac{1000}{14} = 71.42 \text{ per } ₹100 \text{ of nominal or par value.}$$

For every ₹100 of nominal value, holder gets interest of ₹10 (since this a 10% coupon security). But since he only pays ₹71.42, his yield is = 14 percent.

So for choosing an option (a) price should fall to ₹71.42, which is equal to a yield of 14% on the new issue.

**P.10.** A fund manager has $20 million investment in A–Sec. On August 5 and uses December futures to hedge his risk. Current futures price is 95–00. Since each contract delivery of $2,00,000 face value of bonds. Futures price is $1,90,000. Duration is 6.80 years of the bond portfolio in three months. Yield on bond is currently 8.80% and cheapest-to-deliver bond in T-bond contract is expected to be a 20-year, 12% per annum. Calculate the number of contracts needed to hedge the position.

*Solution*:    Value of funds = \$20 million

Value of futures contract = \$1,90,000

Duration = 6.80 years

Duration at maturity = 9.20 years

So    Number of contracts = $\dfrac{20,00,000}{1,10,000} \times \dfrac{6.80}{9.20} = 77.80$

Since contracts are not divisible, so number of contracts needed will be 78.

# REVIEW QUESTIONS

1. What is interest rate futures contract? Discuss various types of interest rate futures contracts with suitable examples.
2. What is the need of interest rate futures contract? Discuss the various uses of interest rate futures?
3. Explain the terms yield-to-maturity on a bond and bond's current yield. Also explain difference between these.
4. How does the transaction price of a bond differ from the quoted price of the bond?
5. What is Treasury bond futures? Discuss how Treasury bond futures contracts are priced.
6. Discuss the concept of duration in respect to bonds, and also discuss the importance of duration in interest rate risk management.
7. Write short notes on
   (a) Treasury bond
   (b) Treasury notes
8. How the delivery process of Treasury bond futures is different from other derivatives futures? Discuss in context delivery process of Treasury bond futures.
9. Discuss the concept of conversion factors in invoicing of Treasury bond.
10. How prices of T-bond futures are different from other futures contracts prices? Discuss with suitable examples.
11. Discuss the process of futures price determination of Treasury bond futures with suitable example.
12. How will you identify the cheapest-to-deliver bond in interest rate futures market? Is it necessary? Comment.
13. Discuss various features of Treasury bond and Treasury notes futures. Also discuss various specifications of these interest rate futures contracts.
14. Explain the hedging mechanism with T-bond futures with suitable examples.
15. Explain the duration-based hedging strategies with suitable examples.
16. Discuss the importance of yield-to-maturity and duration with special reference to interest rate futures.
17. How does a potential buyer of corporate bonds hedge? Explain with government bond futures. How the hedge ratio is calculated?
18. How a potential issuer of corporate bonds hedge with government bond futures? Discuss with suitable examples.

19. How a portfolio manager can use interest rate futures to reduce his risk? Explain with suitable examples.

20. Discuss the recent developments in the long-term interest risk management in India. Also give your suggestions in this respect.

21. "Interest rate risk is one of the most important risk faced by the corporate sector." Discuss the statement in the light of interest rate futures contracts available to manage this risk.

22. Write a note on interest rate futures contracts in India. Are they successful? Comment.

## UNSOLVED PROBLEMS

**P.1.**   On May 5, 1994, quoted price of government bond with a 12% coupon that matures on July 27, 2001 is 110–17. What is the cash price of government bond?

**P.2.**   A two-year T-Note with a yield-to-maturity of 9% p.a. Coupon rate is 6% p.a. of the T-Note. Suppose it has just paid a coupon and time remaining next coupon, to is six months. Transaction price of the Note is ₹94.619 per ₹100 face value. Calculate duration of the two years Treasury note.

**P.3.**   A corporate treasurer intending to raise money by the sale of securities with a fixed coupon yield. His anxiety is that interest rate might rise before sale is made and intends to raise DM 2 million on February 15 by sale of bonds. Interest rate on bond is 6% p.a. How treasurer can use interest rate futures to hedge position? Also show the position of treasurer in both spot and futures market with imaginary data.

**P.4.**   A hedger wants to hedge ₹3,75,000 in the long gilt market. Contract size of the NSE for long gilts is ₹50,000. The equivalency ratio has already been determined as 1.3. How many futures contracts should hedger trade to hedge his position?

**P.5.**   The party with a short position has decided to deliver and is trying to choose between the three bonds:

| Bond | Quoted price | Conversion factor |
|------|------|------|
| 1 | 99.50 | 1.0382 |
| 2 | 143.50 | 1.5188 |
| 3 | 119.75 | 1.2615 |

Assume that current quoted futures price is ₹93.25. Calculate the cost of delivery of each bond.

**P.6.**   The price of 90-day treasury bill is quoted as 10% p.a. What will be the rate of continuous compounding does an investor earns on Treasury bill for 90-day period?

**P.7.**   A fund manager is managing a bond portfolio of worth ₹50 lakh. Today is February 5. The October Treasury bond futures price is currently 100 and cheapest-to-deliver bond has a duration of 6.2 years. What will be the number of contract needed to hedge the position? Suppose average duration of portfolio is 8.4 years.

**P.8.**   On February 3, the cheapest-to-deliver treasury bond for July has a 12% coupon and a price factor of 1.5. Coupons are paid at the end of March and September. The bond price is ₹110 and rate of interest is 8% per annum. Calculate the fair price of the July Treasury bond futures contract implied by this date.

# SUGGESTED READINGS

1. Robonato, Riccardo, *Modern Pricing of Interest Rate Derivatives*: *The LIBOR Market Model and Beyond*, Princeton University Press, Princeton, 2002.

2. Koh, Annie and Levich, Richard M., Synthetic euro currency interest rate futures contracts: Theory and evidence, *Japan and International Financial Markets: Analytical and Empirical Perspectives*, ed., Cambridge University Press, 1994.

3. Black, F., Derman, E., and Toy, W., One factor model of interest rates and its applications to Treasury bond options, *Financial Analyst Journal*, 11, 1990.

4. Hull, J. and White, A., Pricing interest rate derivatives securities, *Review of Financial Studies*, New York, 1992.

5. Jarrow, Heath D. and Morton, A., *Bond Pricing and Term Structure of Interest Rates: A New Methodology for Contingent Claims Evaluation*, Cornell University, 1989.

6. Arak, M. and Goodman, Treasury bond futures: Valuing the delivery options, *The Journal of Futures Markets*, Vol. 7, pp. 269–286, June, 1987.

7. Maloney, K. and Yawtiz, J., Interest rate risk immunization and duration, *Journal of Portfolio Management*, Vol. 13, pp. 41–49, Spring, 1980.

8. Gay, G. and Kolb, R., *Interest Rate Futures: Concepts and Issues, Richmod*, UA, Robert F. Dame, Inc., 1982.

9. CME group understanding treasury futures.

10. NSE NBF-II India.

# Annexure-A

**RESERVE BANK OF INDIA**
**INTERNAL DEBT MANAGEMENT DEPARTMENT**
**23rd FLOOR, CENTRAL OFFICE FORT**
**MUMBAI 400 001**

**Interest Rate Futures (Reserve Bank) Directions, 2009**
**(as amended till December 30, 2011)**

The Reserve Bank of India having considered it necessary in public interest and to regulate the financial system of the country to its advantage, in exercise of the powers conferred by section 45W of the Reserve Bank of India Act, 1934 and of all the powers enabling it in this behalf, hereby gives the following directions to all the persons dealing in Interest Rate Futures.

## 1. Short Title and Commencement of the Directions

These directions may be called the Interest Rate Futures (Reserve Bank) Directions, 2009 and they shall come into force with immediate effect.

## 2. Definitions

1. Interest Rate Futures means a standardized interest rate derivative contract traded on a recognized stock exchange to buy or sell a notional security or any other interest bearing instrument or an index of such instruments or interest rates at a specified future date, at a price determined at the time of the contract.
2. Interest Rate Futures market means the market in which Interest Rate Futures are traded.
3. The words and expressions used but not defined in these directions shall have the meaning assigned to them in the Reserve Bank of India Act, 1934.

## 3. Permitted Instruments

(i) Interest Rate Futures are permitted on [*91-Day Treasury Bills*][1], [*2-year, 5-year and*][2] 10-year notional coupon bearing Government of India security or any other product, as may be approved by the Reserve Bank from time to time.

(ii) Persons resident in India may purchase or sell Interest Rate Futures referred to in sub-paragraph (i) to hedge an exposure to interest rate risk or otherwise. Foreign Institutional Investors, registered with Securities and Exchange Board of India, may purchase or sell Interest Rate Futures referred to in sub-paragraph (i) subject to the condition that the total gross long (bought) position in cash and Interest Rate Futures markets taken together does not exceed their individual permissible limit for investment in government securities and the total gross short (sold) position, for the purpose of hedging only, does not exceed their long position in the government securities and in Interest Rate Futures at any point in time.

(iii) Notwithstanding anything contained in sub-paragraph (i), no scheduled bank or such other agency falling under the regulatory purview of the Reserve Bank under the Reserve Bank of India Act, 1934, the Banking Regulation Act, 1949 or any other Act or instrument having the force of law shall participate in the Interest Rate Futures market without the permission from the respective regulatory department of the Reserve Bank.

*Explanation*: - The expression 'Person resident in India' shall have the meaning assigned to it in sub-section (v) of section 2 of the Foreign Exchange Management Act, 1999.

(iv) Agencies falling under the regulatory purview of any other regulator established by law shall not participate in Interest Rate Futures market except with the permission of their respective regulators and participation of such agencies as members or clients shall be in accordance with the guidelines issued by the regulator concerned.

## 4. Features of Interest Rate Futures

4.1 The 10-year Interest Rate Futures contract shall have the following features:

(a) The contract shall be on 10-year notional coupon bearing Government of India security.

(b) The notional coupon shall be 7% per annum with semi-annual compounding.

(c) The contract shall be settled by physical delivery of deliverable grade securities using the electronic book entry system of the existing Depositories, namely, National Securities Depositories Ltd. and Central Depository Services (India) Ltd. and Public Debt Office of the Reserve Bank.

(d) Deliverable grade securities' shall comprise GoI securities maturing at least 7.5 years but not more than 15 years from the first day of the delivery month with a minimum total outstanding stock of ₹10,000 crore. {*Exchanges may fix their own basket of securities for delivery from the deliverable grade securities in accordance with guidelines issued by the Securities Exchange Board of India from time to time}*[3].

4.2 {The 91-Day T-Bill Futures shall have the following features:

(a) The contract shall be on 91-Day Treasury Bills issued by the Government of India.

(b) The contract shall be cash settled in Indian Rupees.

(c) The final settlement price of the contract shall be based on the weighted average price/yield obtained in the weekly auction of the 91-Day Treasury Bills on the date of expiry of the contract}[4].

4.3 {The 2-year and 5-year Interest Rate Futures contract shall have the following features:

(a) The 2-year and 5-year Interest Rate Futures contracts shall be on 2-year and 5-year notional coupon bearing Government of India security respectively.

(b) The notional coupon for the 2-year bond shall be 7% per annum and that of the 5-year bond shall be 7% with semi-annual compounding.

(c) The contracts shall be cash-settled by the stock exchanges offering the contracts.

(d) The final settlement price of the 2-year and 5-year Interest Rate Futures contracts shall be based on the yields on basket of securities for each Interest Rate Futures contract specified by the respective stock exchange in accordance with guidelines issued by the Securities Exchange Board of India from time to time.

(e) The yields of the Government of India securities [indicated at para 4.3 (d) above] shall be polled and the same shall be as per the guidelines issued by the Reserve Bank of India from time to time}[5].

## 5. Membership

Interest Rate Futures contracts on instruments referred to in sub-paragraph (i) of paragraph 3 shall be traded on the Currency Derivative Segment of a recognized Stock Exchange. The members registered with Securities and Exchange Board of India for trading in Currency/Equity Derivative Segment shall also be eligible to trade in Interest Rate Futures referred to in sub-paragraph (i) of paragraph 3. Membership for both trading and clearing, in the Interest Rate Futures segment shall be subject to the guidelines issued by the Securities and Exchange Board of India.

## 6. Position Limits

1. The position limits for various classes of participants in the Interest Rate Futures market shall be subject to the guidelines issued by the Securities and Exchange Board of India.
2. All regulated entities shall operate within the prudential limits set by the regulator concerned.

## 7. Risk Management Measures

The trading of Interest Rate Futures contracts referred to in sub-paragraph (i) of paragraph 3 shall be subject to maintaining initial, extreme loss and calendar spread margins and the Clearing Corporations/ Clearing Houses of the exchanges should ensure maintenance of such margins by the participants on the basis of the guidelines issued by the Securities and Exchange Board of India from time to time.

## 8. Surveillance and Disclosures

The surveillance and disclosures of transactions in the Interest Rate Futures market shall be carried out in accordance with the guidelines issued by the Securities and Exchange Board of India.

## 9. Powers of Reserve Bank

The Reserve Bank may from time to time modify the eligibility criteria for the participants, modify participant-wise position limits, prescribe margins and/or impose specific margins for identified participants, fix or modify any other prudential limits, or take such other actions as deemed necessary in public interest, in the interest of financial stability and orderly development and maintenance of interest rate market in India.

# Chapter 12

# Foreign Currency Futures

*After reading this chapter, students will be able to*

➢ Understand the basics of foreign currency spot market functioning.

➢ Explain the foreign exchange quotations like direct, indirect and cross rates.

➢ Know the currency futures and specifications of foreign exchange futures contracts.

➢ Understand the major features of currency futures contracts like organized exchanges, standardization, tick size, etc.

➢ Understand the trading mechanism and settlement procedure of a currency futures contract.

➢ **Know the futures currency trading in India.**

➢ Explain the pricing of currency futures contract.

➢ Understand the covered interest rate parity and currency arbitrage and identification of currency arbitrage.

➢ Know the hedging with currency futures.

## 12.1 INTRODUCTION

Each country has its own currency through which both national and international transactions are performed. All the international business transactions involve an exchange of one currency for another. For example, if any Indian firm borrows funds from international financial market in US dollars for short- or long-term then at maturity the same would be refunded in particular agreed currency along with accrued interest on borrowed money. It means that the borrowed foreign currency brought in the country will be converted into Indian currency, and when borrowed funds are paid to the lender then the home currency will be converted into foreign lender's currency. Thus, the currency unit of a country involves an exchange of one currency for another. The price of one currency in terms of another currency is known as *exchange rate*. The foreign exchange markets of a country provide the mechanism of exchanging different currencies with one and another, and thus, facilitating transfer of purchasing power from one country to another.

With the multiple growth of international trade and finance all over the world, trading in foreign currencies has grown tremendously over the past several decades. Since the exchange rates are continuously changing, so the firms are exposed to the risk of exchange rate movements. As a result the assets or liabilities or cash flows of a firm which are denominated in foreign currencies undergo a change in value over a period of time due to variation in exchange rates. This variability in the value of assets or liabilities or cash flows is referred to exchange rate risk. Since the fixed exchange rate system has been fallen in the early 1970s, specifically in developed countries, the currency risk has become substantial for many business firms. As a result, these firms are increasingly turning to various risk hedging products like foreign currency futures, foreign currency forwards, foreign currency options, and foreign currency swaps.

In this section, we will focus on foreign currency futures covering their nature, pricing, hedging, trading mechanism and so on. To understand the functioning of the currency futures market, it is essential to know the working of the foreign exchange cash (spot) market. A detailed discussion on foreign exchange spot market is outside the purview of this chapter, however, a brief view of it is given in the chapter so that one can understand the mechanism of futures markets in foreign currencies. Further, Chicago Mercantile Exchange (CME) is a biggest exchange of all types of futures trading, so the discussion in this chapter is focused around CME.

## 12.2   FOREIGN EXCHANGE SPOT (CASH) MARKET

The foreign exchange spot market trades in different currencies for both spot and forward delivery. Generally they do not have a specific location, and mostly take place primarily by means of telecommunications both within and between countries. It consists of a network of forex dealers which are often banks, financial institutions, large concerns, etc. The large banks usually make markets in different currencies. There are a number of major financial centres in which the markets that are particularly active are New York, London, Tokyo, Frankfurt, Singapore, Hong Kong, Bahrain, etc.

In the spot exchange market, the business is transacted throughout the world on a continual basis. So, it is possible to make transactions in foreign exchange markets 24 hours a day. The standard settlement period in this market is 48 hours, i.e., two days after the execution of the transaction. There are also no requirement for participation, other than the informal acceptance of other participants. The spot foreign exchange market is similar to the over-the-counter (OTC) market for securities. There is no centralized meeting place and no fixed opening and closing time. Since most of the business in this market is done by the banks, hence, transactions usually do not involve a physical transfer of currency, rather simply a book keeping transfer entry among banks. Important active currencies traded in this market are: Japanese yen, British pound, German Deutsche marks, Canadian dollars, US dollars, French francs, etc. In addition to the spot transactions, banks and other foreign exchange dealers regularly buy and sell currencies for forward delivery, i.e., delivery at specified time in future. This we will discuss in Chapter 13 on forward foreign exchange market.

Exchange rates are generally determined by demand and supply forces (market forces) in this market. The purchase and sale of currencies stem partly from the need to finance trade in goods and services. Further, substantial need for foreign currencies arise from short-term money investment by the banks and other institutions. Another important source of demand and supply arises from the participation of the central banks which would emanate from a desire to influence the direction, extent or speed of exchange rate movements.

## 12.3   FOREIGN EXCHANGE QUOTATIONS

Foreign exchange quotations can be confusing because currencies are quoted in terms of (or relative to) other currencies. It means exchange rate is a relative price. For example, if one US dollar is worth of ₹65 in Indian rupees, then it implies that 65 Indian rupees will buy one dollar of USA, or that one rupee is worth of 0.1538 US dollar which is simply reciprocal of the former dollar exchange rate.

There are two ways of quoting exchange rates: the direct and indirect. Most countries use the direct method in which the number of units of domestic currency stated against one unit of foreign currency, for example, in India the units of Indian rupee against one unit of US dollar may be termed as:

$$₹/\$ = 65.7250 \quad \text{or} \quad \$1 = ₹65.7250$$

The indirect method of quotation takes the form of stating the number of units of foreign currency per unit of domestic currency. In the above example, quotation will be shown as follows:

$$₹1 = \$0.01521$$

In global foreign exchange market, two rates are quoted by the dealer: one rate for buying (bid rate), and another for selling (ask or offered rate) for a currency. This is a unique feature of this market. It should be noted that where the bank sells dollars against rupees, one can say that it buys rupees against dollar. In order to separate buying and selling rate, a small dash or oblique line is drawn after the dash. For example, if US dollar is quoted in the market as ₹66.3500/3580, it means that the forex dealer is ready to purchase the dollar at ₹66.3500 and ready to sell at ₹66.3580. The difference between buying and selling rates is called *spread*. It is important to note that selling rate is always higher than the buying rate. Traders, usually large banks, deal in two-way prices, both buying and selling, are called *market makers*. They create the market by quoting bid and ask prices.

Various financial newspapers daily publish the rates of different currencies as quoted at a certain point of time during the day. The Wall Street Journal gives quotations for selling rates on the interbank market for a minimum sum of one million dollars at 3.00 p.m. In India, Economic Times, Financial Express, Business Line, Business Standard, etc. show US dollar equivalent of foreign currency and the amount of foreign currency per US dollar. Each set of quotations show the rates for the current and the preceding business day.

## 12.4   CROSS RATE

The exchange rate which is obtained by the cross product of two exchange rates is called *cross rate*. These can be easily calculated from direct quotations and are provided daily by various financial publications. Let us explain this with an example. Suppose the exchange rates between Singapore dollar and US dollar, rupee and US dollar are as follows:

| | |
|---|---|
| SGD/USD | = 1.3500/60 |
| INR/USD | = 65.6500/90 |
| INR/SGD | = $\dfrac{65.6500}{1.3500}$ |
| Cross rate (ask) | = 48.6296 |
| INR/SGD | = $\dfrac{65.6590}{1.3560}$ |
| Cross rate (bid) | = 48.4211 |
| INR/SGD | = 48.4211/6296 |

The cross rate can be defined as a rate between a third pair of currencies by using the rates of two pairs, in which one currency is common. It is basically a derived rate. In general, following equations can be used to find out the cross rates between two currencies 'B' and 'C', if the rates between 'A' and 'B' and between 'A' and 'C' are given.

$$(B/C) \text{ bid} = (B/A) \text{ bid} \times (A/C) \text{ ask}$$

$$(B/C) \text{ ask} = (B/A) \text{ ask} \times (A/C) \text{ bid}$$

Here

$$(B/A) \text{ bid} = (A/B) \text{ ask}$$

and

$$(B/A) \text{ ask} = (A/B) \text{ bid}$$

The exchange rate, thus, obtained will be expected spot rate between the two currencies. Once we are able to find out the expected rates at various markets and are able to know the cost of transactions then comparing these rates plus the cost of transactions with the prevailing rates at other markets, we can decide about the arbitrage opportunities existing at a particular point of time. However, if the markets are efficient then these opportunities would not be available.

## 12.5  CURRENCY FUTURES

A currency futures contract provides a simultaneous right and obligation to buy and sell a particular currency at a specified future date, a specified price and a standard quantity. In other words, in currency futures market, the different currencies are sold and purchased at the specified future date, at predetermined price and of specified quantity on a particular recognized exchange. It is similar to other futures contracts like commodities, interest, rates, metals, etc. The foreign currency futures were started in the year 1972 at the International Money Market (IMM)—a division of Chicago Mercantile Exchange at Chicago. The major currencies which at this exchange were launched were British pound, Canadian dollar, Deutsche marks, French francs, Japanese yen, Swiss francs, Australian dollars. The amount of each foreign currency that must be delivered for a contract varies by currency. Before discussing the trading mechanism of currency futures in actual practice in the market, let us review first the specifications of currency futures listed on the CME as shown in Tables 12.1 and 12.2:

**TABLE 12.1**  Specifications of Popular CME FX Futures

| | EUR/USD Futures | JPY/USD Futures | GBP/USD Futures | CHF/USD Futures | EUR/USD Futures | JPY/USD Futures | GBP/USD Futures | CHF/USD Futures |
|---|---|---|---|---|---|---|---|---|
| **Trade Unit** | 1,25,000 EUR | 1,25,00,000 JPY | 62,500 GBP | 125,000 CHF | 1,25,000 EUR | 1,25,00,000 JPY | 62,500 GBP | 1,25,000 CHF |
| **Minimum Price Fluctuation (Tick)** | $0.0001 per EUR ($12.50) | $0.000001 per JPY ($12.50) | $0.0001 per GBP ($6.25) | $0.0001 per CHF ($12.50) | $0.0001 per EUR ($12.50) | $0.000001 per JPY ($12.50) | $0.0001 per GBP ($6.25) | $0.0001 per CHF ($12.50) |
| **Price Limits** | No Limits | | | | | | | |
| **Contract Months** | 1st to 6 months in March quarterly cycle (March, June, Sep. & Dec.) | | | | | | | |
| **CME Globex® Hours** | Sundays thru Thursdays: 5.00 p.m. to 4.00 p.m. the following day (Chicago time) | | | | | | | |
| **Trading Ends** | On 2nd business day before 3rd Wednesday of contract month | | | | | | | |
| **Delivery** | Thru Continuous Linked Settlement (CLS) Facilities | | | | | | | |
| **Position Limits** | No Limits | | | | | | | |
| **Ticker** | "6E" | | "6J" | | "6B" | | "6S" | |

*Source:* CME Group, Currencies Understanding FX Futures April 22, 2013.

**TABLE 12.2**  Selected FX Futures Pricing
(as on April 12, 2013)

| | Settlement | Reciprocal | RTH Volume | Globex Volume | Open Interest |
|---|---|---|---|---|---|
| **EUR/USD Futures (1,25,000 EUR)** | | | | | |
| **June-13** | 1.3085 | 0.7642 | 3,177 | 2,39,944 | 2,14,401 |
| **Sep-13** | 1.3094 | 0.7637 | | 241 | 1,609 |
| **Dec-13** | 1.3106 | 0.7632 | | 21 | 235 |
| **Mar-14** | 1.3116 | 0.7624 | | | 13 |
| **June-14** | 1.3129 | 0.7617 | | | 12 |
| **JPY/USD Futures (12,500,000 JPY)** | | | | | |
| **June-13** | 0.010118 | 98.8338 | 2,164 | 2,04,326 | 2,09,005 |
| **Sep-13** | 0.010125 | 98.7654 | | 325 | 1,863 |
| **Dec-13** | 0.010136 | 98.6582 | | 14 | 130 |
| **Mar-14** | 0.010149 | 98.5319 | | | 22 |
| **June-14** | 0.010163 | 98.3961 | | 2 | 2 |
| **Sep-14** | 0.010179 | 98.2415 | | 1 | 1 |

*Source:* CME Group, Currencies Understanding FX Futures April 22,2013

Over the years, many currency contracts have been added, and important currencies which are traded on the CME are as follows:

Euro vs. USD (EUR/USD)
Jap Yen vs. USD (JPY/USD)
Swiss Francs vs. USD (CHF/USD)
British Pound vs. USD (GBP/USD)
Canadian Dollar vs. USD (CDN/USD)
Australian Dollar vs. USD (AUD/USD)
Mexican Pesos vs. USD (MXN/USD)
New Zealand Dollar vs. USD (NZD/USD)
Russian Rouble vs. USD (RUB/USD)
South Africa Rand vs. USD (ZAR/USD)
Brazilian Real vs. USD (BR/USD)
Chinese Renminbi vs. USD (RMB/USD)
Korean Won vs. USD (KRW/USD)
And many more others.

Further, CME lists smaller sized or "E-mini" version of several other more popular FX futures contracts, which are quoted in American terms (in terms of dollar) for foreign currencies' unit. One may easily convert these quotes foreign currency unit per dollar by simply taking the reciprocal, as presented in Table 12.3

**TABLE 12.3**   American vs. European Term Quotes
(as on April 12, 2013)

| CME Quotes | American Terms | European Terms |
| --- | --- | --- |
| USD per EUR | 1.3085 | 0.7642 |
| USD per JPY | 0.010118 | 98.8338 |
| USD per GBP | 1.5338 | 0.6520 |
| USD per CIIF | 1.0763 | 0.9291 |

## 12.6   SALIENT FEATURES OF CURRENCY FUTURES CONTRACTS

As mentioned, a currency futures contract is a commitment to deliver a specified quantity of a specified currency at a specified future date and at a specified price. The principal features, in general, of the contract are as follows:

### 12.6.1   Organized Exchanges

The currency futures contracts are negotiated only on recognized/organized exchanges with a designated physical location where such tradings take place. These exchanges provide a ready, liquid market in which futures can be bought and sold at any time. Following are a few important organized exchanges where futures currencies transactions are done:

1. Chicago Board of Trade, Chicago
2. Philadelphia Board of Trade, Philadelphia

3. New York Financial Futures Exchange, New York
4. International Monetary Market, Chicago
5. London International Financial Futures Exchange, London
6. Tokyo International Financial Futures Exchange, Tokyo
7. Sydney Futures Exchange, Sydney
8. Singapore International Monetary Exchange, Singapore
9. Le Marche à terme Instruments & Financiers, Paris
10. Deutsche Terminbörse, Frankfurt (DTB)
11. Hong Kong Futures Exchange (HKFE)

## 12.6.2 Standardization

Like other futures contracts, the currency futures contracts are also standardized by the respective organized exchanges on which trading are initiated. The different terms of standardization like quantity, tick size, delivery, margin, etc. have been shown in Table 12.2 at Chicago Mercantile Exchange. Further. FX Futures Prices trading at CME as on February 13, 2016 are given in Table 12.4

**TABLE 12.4**   CME Group FX (Forex) Futures Prices
Dated: February 13, 2016

| MAJOR | | | | | | | |
|---|---|---|---|---|---|---|---|
| **Product** | **Code** | **Contract** | **Last** | **Change** | **Open** | **High** | **Low** |
| Euro FX Futures | 6EH6 | Mar-16 | 1.12635 | **–0.00005** | 1.1324 | 1.1342 | 1.1222 |
| E-mini Euro FX Futures | E7H6 | Mar-16 | 1.1273 | **0.0009** | 1.1323 | 1.1337 | 1.1222 |
| Japanese Yen Futures | 6JH6 | Mar-16 | 0.00884 | **1.5 E-06** | 0.00889 | 0.008964 | 0.008814 |
| E-mini Japanese Yen Futures | J7H6 | Mar-16 | 0.00884 | **0.000007** | 0.0089 | 0.008959 | 0.008813 |
| Australian Dollar Futures | 6AH6 | Mar-16 | 0.7099 | **0.0007** | 0.7115 | 0.7119 | 0.7053 |
| British Pound Futures | 6BH6 | Mar-16 | 1.4498 | **–0.0021** | 1.4482 | 1.4571 | 1.4443 |
| Canadian Dollar Futures | 6CH6 | Mar-16 | 0.7216 | **–0.0007** | 0.7187 | 0.724 | 0.7161 |
| Swiss Franc Futures | 6SH6 | Mar-16 | 1.0252 | **–0.0009** | 1.0294 | 1.0305 | 1.0226 |
| New Zealand Dollar Futures | 6NH6 | Mar-16 | 0.6619 | **0.0015** | 0.672 | 0.6726 | 0.6601 |
| Swedish Krona Futures | SEKH6 | Mar-16 | 0.11884 | 0 | 0.1192 | 0.11938 | 0.11873 |
| Norwegian Krone Futures | NOKH6 | Mar-16 | 0.11666 | 0 | 0.11666 | 0.11666 | 0.11666 |
| FX$ Index Futures | FXDH6 | Mar-16 | – | – | – | – | – |

| EMERGING MARKETS | | | | | | | | |
|---|---|---|---|---|---|---|---|---|
| **Product** | **Code** | **Contract** | **Last** | **Change** | **Open** | **High** | **Low** | **Globex Vol** |
| Mexican Peso Futures | 6MH6 | Mar-16 | 0.05278 | **0.00002** | 0.0522 | 0.0528 | 0.0519 | 93,806 |
| Brazilian Real Futures | 6LH6 | Mar-16 | 0.2489 | **–0.0007** | 0.2506 | 0.2508 | 0.2486 | 707 |
| South African Rand Futures | 6ZH6 | Mar-16 | 0.06268 | 0 | 0.0626 | 0.0632 | 0.0624 | 438 |
| Indian Rupee/USD Futures | SIRG6 | Feb-16 | 146.36 | **0.02** | 145.78 | 146.42 | 145.64 | 464 |
| Chinese Renminbi/USD Futures | RMBH6 | Mar-16 | 0.1531 | **–5 E-05** | 0.153 | 0.1537 | 0.153 | 9 |

*(Contd.)*

(Contd.)

| Product | Code | Contract | Last | Change | Open | High | Low | Globex Vol |
|---|---|---|---|---|---|---|---|---|
| Czech Koruna/Euro (CZK/EUR) Cross Rate Futures | ECKH6 | Mar-16 | – | – | – | – | – | 0 |
| Czech Koruna Futures | CZKH6 | Mar-16 | – | – | – | – | – | 0 |
| Euro/Turkish Lira (EUR/TRY) Physically Deliverable Future | ELIG6 | Feb-16 | – | – | – | – | – | 0 |
| Hungarian Forint/Euro (HUF/EUR) Cross Rate Futures | EHFH6 | Mar-16 | – | – | – | – | – | 0 |
| Hungarian Forint Futures | HUFH6 | Mar-16 | – | – | – | – | – | 0 |
| Israeli Shekel Futures | ILSH6 | Mar-16 | – | – | – | – | – | 0 |
| Korean Won Futures | KRWH6 | Mar-16 | – | – | – | – | – | 0 |
| Polish Zloty Futures | PLNH6 | Mar-16 | 0.25506 | −0.0009 | 0.2549 | 0.2554 | 0.2548 | 7 |
| Polish Zloty/Euro (PLN/EUR) Cross Rate Futures | EPZH6 | Mar-16 | 0.2264 | −0.0009 | 0.2267 | 0.2267 | 0.2264 | 4 |
| Chinese Renminbi/Euro Futures | RMEH6 | Mar-16 | – | – | – | – | – | 0 |
| USD/Chinese Renminbi Futures | CNYH6 | Mar-16 | – | – | – | – | – | 0 |
| Turkish Lira Futures | TRYH6 | Mar-16 | – | – | – | – | – | 0 |

*Source:* CME Group (http://www.cmegroup.com/market-data/delayed-quotes/fx.html)

## 12.6.3 Minimum Variation (Tick Size)

In each futures market, there is minimum price variation, also called *as tick*, which is standardized for every contract. It may vary from exchange to exchange. Generally it is 0.01 percent or 0.0001 dollar per unit of currency. For example, at the CME, the tick size is 0.002 percent or 0.00002 dollar per unit of French franc. Thus, if a futures of French franc passes from US $0.2040 to US $0.2080, the variation is the value of a futures contract and is worked out as follows:

Price variation = US $(0.2080 − 2040) = US $0.0040

So, number of ticks = 0.0040/200 = 0.00002

Value of one fluctuation (tick) = 5,00,000 × 0.00002 = US $10

So, variation in the price of the contract is 200 × 10 = US $2000

The other method of calculating the variation is:

5,00,000 × 0.2040 = US $1,02,000

5,00,000 × 0.2080 = US $1,04,000

The difference is = 1,04,000 − 1,02,000 = US $2,000

## 12.6.4 Marking-to-market (MTM)

At the end of the trading session, all the outstanding contracts are repriced at the settlement price of that session. It means that all the futures contracts are daily settled, and profit and loss is determined on each transaction. This procedure, called marking-to-market, requires that funds change every day.

The funds are added or subtracted from a mandatory margin (initial margin) that traders are required to maintain the balance in the account. Due to this adjustment, futures contract is also called *daily reconnected forwards.*

## 12.6.5  Margins

As discussed in detail regarding maintenance of margins by the members of the clearing house in the chapter on 'future trading', here in brief, we will discuss about the margin requirements regarding futures currency contracts.

As we know that only the members of an exchange can trade in futures contracts on the exchange, so the general public can use the services of the members as broker to trade on their behalf for a commission. A subset of exchange members are 'clearing' members. Every transaction is, thus, between an exchange member and the exchange clearing house.

For the smooth functioning and execution of futures contracts at the exchanges, the exchange requires a performance bond in the form of a margin which must be deposited with the clearing house. It will be treated as security against each party's market position. The margin payment is a good faith deposit which provides evidence of party's ability to settle the contract. The margin account is designed to be sufficient to meet the largest possible day's loss. So, the size of this initial deposit varies with the volatility of the currency. Normally, it varies between 2.5 to 10 percent of the value of the contract. The deposit in the margin account by the member can be in the form of cash or securities, such as treasury bills, and in some cases, even bank's letter of credit. If treasury securities are used, or applied, i.e., the securities will count as something less than 100 percent of their face value. A member acting on behalf of a client in turn requires the client to post a margin with the member.

### Types of margins

Different types of margin terms are used in futures trading mechanism which are described here as under:

*Initial margin:*   When a position is opened, the member (both long and short) has to deposit the margin with the clearing house as per the rate fixed by the exchange which may vary from asset to asset.

*Maintenance margin:*   Member's accounts are debited or credited on a daily basis. In turn customers' accounts are also required to be maintained at a certain level, usually about 75 percent of the initial margin, is called *the maintenance margin.* The customer is required to deposit cash so as to bring the account back to its initial margin.

*Variation margin:*   If the initial margin falls to a pre-set level, the trader is asked to replenish his margin account to its previous (initial) level. This additional margin is called *variation margin.*

*Margin call:*   When the balance in a trader's account falls below a certain level (maintenance margin), the trader receives a margin call to deposit the amount in a specified time usually 24 hours. This is called *paying the variation margin.* If the trader fails to do so then his position is liquidated immediately.

It should be noted that the clearing house imposes margin on the clearing members who, in turn, collect margin from their customers/clients. These may be the public or exchange members who are clearing their transactions through the clearing members.

Let us explain the marking to mark with a small example. X buys a March delivery pound sterling futures on, say, January 15 at the price of $1.65 per British Pound (BP) per contract being

$1,03,125 (62,500 × 1.65). Next day, January 16, the price increases and is settled at 1.68. In other words, X has made profit of 3 cent pound or $1,875 per contract (62500 × 3 percent). Obviously, the other party will incur loss of $1,875. An amount of $1875 will be credited in X margin account and Xs account will be repriced at 1.68 or $1,05,000. X will immediately withdraw a cash of $1,875. On the other hand, if the price has gone down, then X margin account will be debited, and if the balance falls below the maintenance margin, then margin call will be made to deposit the amount by X to maintain the balance of margin account to initial margin level.

## 12.6.6  Clearing House

After a futures contract is agreed between the two parties at the trading floor, the agreement between A and B is immediately replaced by two contracts one between A and clearing house, and the other, between B and the clearing house. The clearing house is responsible for keeping the accounts margin payments, settlement of deliveries and others like information and data collection. The clearing house plays a vital role between the two parties and eliminates the need for A and B to investigate each other's creditworthiness and guarantees the financial integrity of the market. Further, the clearing house gives the guarantee for execution and delivery of the contracts held till their maturity.

## 12.6.7  Deliverable vs. Non-Deliverable Futures

The four major currencies mentioned above call for the actual delivery of the currencies on settlement of future contracts. The currencies are deposited at the designated foreign financial institution through the continuous linked settlement (CLS) system. There are some other currencies future contracts which are based on non-deliverable basis and settled in cash on expiration.

## 12.6.8  Trading Process

Like other futures trading, the futures currency are also traded at the organised exchanges. Figure 12.1 exhibits the common flow diagram of how operations take place on currency futures market.

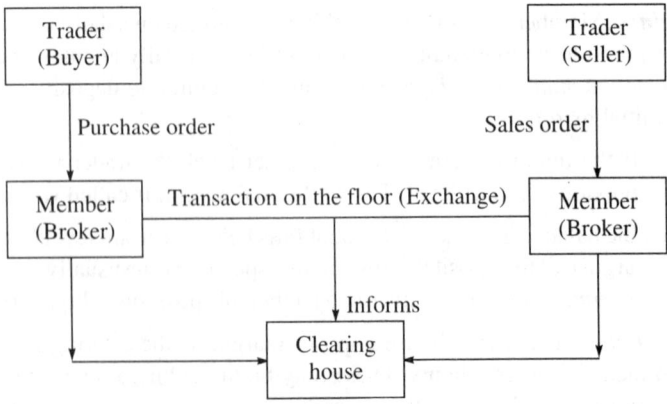

**FIGURE 12.1**  Currency futures contract trading process (Flow of transaction).

Figure 12.1 describes the mechanism of the flow of transactions which are taken place at the recognized exchanges. When the market is open, the transactions take place at the floor of the exchange. Beyond the opening hours, negotiations may take place through an electronic system, called GLOBEX which connects the markets of Chicago, Paris, London and others from 2:30 p.m. until 7:05 a.m. the following morning. The GLOBEX system matches purchase and sale orders for each type of currency futures contract. Orders are confirmed electronically and the traders are informed about the quantity and price of the negotiations. This information is then sent to the clearing house which further make the adjustments in the buyers and sellers margin accounts.

## 12.6.9   Settlement Process and Delivery

It has been observed that in most futures markets, actual physical delivery of the underlying assets is very rare and hardly it ranges from 1 percent to 5 percent. Most often, buyers and sellers offset their original position prior to delivery date by taking an opposite position. This is because most of the futures contracts in different products are predominantly speculative instruments. For example, X purchases British pound futures and Y sells it. It leads to two contracts, first, X party and clearing house and second Y party and clearing house. Assume next day X sells same contract to Z, then X is out of the picture and the clearing house is seller to Z and buyer from Y, and hence, this process goes on.

The settlement process in currency futures contract can be described below with an example. Table 12.5 presents the settlement process of British pound currency with an initial margin of $2,000 and maintenance margin being $1,500. In Table 12.5, we observe that the trader has to deposit and withdraw the money from his margin account depending upon the settlement price each day. For example, he deposits $875.00 on the fifth settlement day due to falling balance below maintenance margin amount of $1,500. He also withdraws the money when he gains on 6th to 8th settlement dates. Assuming that on 8th day, the contract is closed through a reverse operation, then the gain to the trader would be as:

$$(\$1.6105 - 1.6000) \times 62,500 = \$656.25$$

In brief, the futures price is misleading because when you buy or sell a futures contract, you do not have to pay anything. You deposit the initial margin but that is just a performance bond on your behalf. Thus, your commitment in futures contract is:

1. To pay or receive the daily variation margin because the price of the contract keeps on changing and your position is open. When you close out your position, then you can take the balance in the margin account at the end of that day and exit from the contract.
2. You can keep your position open till the maturity of contract, then you must accept delivery (in case of purchase of contract) or take specified amount (in case of sale of contract) of the underlying currency at the settlement price of the last day. However, it is seen that the actual delivery is very rare in futures contracts.

## 12.7   FOREIGN CURRENCY FUTURES IN INDIA

Globalization and liberalization of financial markets alongwith multiple rise of cross border flow of capital have transformed the structure of the Indian financial markets into wider prospective. Further, rising volume of foreign trade and liberalizing foreign exchange norms have also resulted to larger volume of inflow and outflow of foreign currencies in India. International experiences have also witnessed that the future currencies activities facilitate efficient price discovery, better credit risk management, more transparency, reduced transaction cost, etc. Accordingly, as a part of further developing the derivatives market in India, it was decided to introduce currency futures trading in India under the direction of the Reserve Bank of India and Securities Exchange Board of India.

**TABLE 12.5**   Settlement Process of a Futures Currency Contract (BP) at the Opening Price

| Day | | Opening or settlement price ($>£) | Contract price ($) | Margin adjustment ($) | Margin contribution (+) or withdraw (–) ($) | Margin account ($) |
|---|---|---|---|---|---|---|
| Opening | | 1.6000 | 1,00,000 | 0.00 | +2,000.00 | 2,000.00 |
| 1. | Settle | 1.6002 | 1,00,125 | +125.00 | –0.00 | 2125.00 |
| 2. | Settle | 1.6004 | 1,00,250 | +125.00 | –250.00 | 2000.00 |
| 3. | Settle | 1.6003 | 1,00,087.50 | –62.50 | 0.00 | 1937.50 |
| 4. | Settle | 1.5995 | 99,968.75 | –218.75 | 0.00 | 1718.75 |
| 5. | Settle | 1.5900 | 99,375.00 | –593.75 | +875.00 | 2000.00 |
| 6. | Settle | 1.5960 | 99,750.00 | +375.00 | –375.00 | 2000.00 |
| 7. | Settle | 1.5990 | 99,937.50 | +187.50 | –187.50 | 2000.00 |
| 8. | Settle | 1.6105 | 1,00,656.25 | +718.75 | –718.75 | 2000.00 |

The Reserve Bank of India, in its directions contained in the Currency Futures (Reserve Bank) Directions, 2008 (Notification no. FED.1/DG/SG)-2008, dated August 6, 2008, issued the guidelines for trading of currency futures in India which are as under:

Important guidelines of RBI Notification 2008:

1. Currency futures means a standardized foreign exchange derivative contract traded on a recognized stock exchange to buy or sell one currency against another on a specified future date, at a price specified on the date of contract, but does not include a forward contract. Currency futures market means the market in which currency futures are traded.
2. Currency futures are permitted in US dollar-Indian rupee or any other currency pairs as may be approved by RBI from time to time. So, later on three currency pairs: Euro and Rupees (EURINR), Pound sterling (GBPINR) and Japanese Yen (JPYINR) were also permitted for futures trading.
3. Only a person resident in India may purchase or sell currency futures to hedge an exposure to foreign exchange rate risk or otherwise.
4. Standardized currency futures shall have the futures size of each contract 1,000 unit of USD, Euro, Pound and 10,000 of Japanese Yen. These contracts shall be quoted and settled in Indian Rupees. The maturity of the contracts shall not exceed 12 months. Settlement price shall be in RBI's reference rate on the last trading day.
5. Position limits of currency futures shall be subject to maintaining initial extreme loss and calendar spread margin and clearing corporation. Those exchanges should ensure maintenance of such margins by the participants on the basis of the guidelines issued by the SEBI from time to time.

6. The surveillance and disclosures of transactions in the currency futures market shall be carried out in accordance with the guidelines issued by the SEBI.

7. The RBI has the power to modify time to time the norms relating to these futures as demand necessary in public interest.

Trading in currency futures was first started by the NSE on August 29, 2008 and, later on, within a couple of months, started by the BSE and MCX-SX stock exchanges.

Major participants in this market are bankers, importers, exporters, Multinational Corporation, speculators, hedgers, traders, etc. However, at present foreign institutional investors (FIIs) and non-resident Indians are also permitted to trade in currency futures market. The trading member of the exchange will be subject to a balance sheet net worth requirement of ₹1 crore. while the clearing member would be subject to a balance sheet net worth requirement of ₹10 crores.

In India the trading of currency future is subject to maintenance of initial margin, extreme loss and calendar spread margins with clearing house/corporation the details of the margin levied are mentioned in the respective product specification as given in the Annexure. Main trades done at the recognized exchange are guaranteed by the clearing corporation, National Securities Clearing Corporation Ltd. (NSCCL) and hence it eliminates the risk of counterparty defaults.

In July, 2013, a set of measures ever taken by RBI and SEBI which sharply rusticated the exchange traded market are:

1. Banks were disallowed from taking proprietary position by RBI (risk management and interbank dealing).

2. Position limits on exchange traded currency derivatives (ETCD) were brought down to USD 10 millions for client and USD 50 million for member, by the SEBI. Further, in addition, initial and extreme loss margin were increased by 100 percent.

There was reverse effect of the above measures on the volume of the trades of future currencies in India.

On June 20, 2014, the RBI issued two majored notifications with respect to participants rule in currencies future trading. One is related to foreign portfolio investor (FPI) and the other to Indian residents and banks.

Important change in these two notifications are as follows:

1. Foreign Portfolio Investors (FPIs) are permitted to trade in ETCD; for the first time now foreign portfolio investors can also trade in this market.

2. Now ETCD rules have been aligned with OTC currency market rules. As such all position beyond 10 million USD can be taken only after demonstrating underlying rupee exposure.

3. For any participant exposure, the sum of its ETCD + OTC positions cannot exceed its underlying exposure.

4. AD category-I and Banks are allowed back in ETCD subject to open position limit (NDPL). Now the banker AD category-I cannot off their ETCD and OTC positions.

The currency futures contracts specification of MCX-SX is placed in Table 12.6 for understanding the trading mechanism of these products in India.

**TABLE 12.6**    Currency Futures Specifications at MCX-SX

| Symbol | USDINR ($) | EURINR (£) | GBPINR (€) | JPYINR (¥) |
|---|---|---|---|---|
| **Units of trading** | 1(1 unit denotes 1,000 USD) | 1(1 unit denotes 1,000 EURO) | 1(1 unit denotes 1,000 POUND STERLING) | 1(1 unit denotes 1,00,000 YEN) |
| **Underlying** | USD The exchange rate in Indian Rupees for a US Dollar | EURO The exchange rate in Indian Rupees for a EURO | Pound Sterling The exchange rate in Indian Rupees for a Pound Sterling | JPY The exchange rate in Indian Rupees for a 100 JPY |
| **Tick size** | 0.25 paise or INR 0.0025 | | | |
| **Trading hours** | Monday to Friday 9.00 a.m. to 5.00 a.m. | | | |
| **Contract trading cycle** | 12-month trading cycle | | | |
| **Last trading day** | Two working days prior to the last business day of the expiry month at 12.15 noon | | | |
| **Final settlement day** | Last working day (excluding Saturdays) of the expiry month The last working day will be the same as that for Inter bank settlements in Mumbai | | | |
| **Position limitsd** | | | | |
| **Client** | Higher of 6% of total open interest or USD 10 millions | Higher of 6% of total open interest or EUR 5 millions | Higher of 6% of total open interest or GBP 5 million | Higher of 6% of total open interest or JPY 200 millions |
| **Trading Member (other than banks)** | Higher of 15% of the total open interest or USD 50 millions | Higher of 15% of the total open interest or EUR 25 millions | Higher of 15% of the total open interest or GBP 25 millions | Higher of 15% of the total open interest or JPY 100 millions |
| **Banks** | 15% of the total open interest or USD 100 million whichever is lower | Higher of 15% of the total open interest or EUR 50 millions | Higher of 15% of the total open interest or GBP 50 millions | Higher of 15% of the total open interest or JPY 2000 millions |
| **Minimum initial margin** | 1.75% on the first day and 1% thereafter | 2.8% on the first day and 2% thereafter | 3.2% on the first day and 2% thereafter | 4.50% on the first day and 2.30% thereafter |
| **Calender spreads** | ₹400 for a spread of 1 month, ₹500 for a spread of 2 months. ₹800 for a spread of 3 months and ₹1,000 for a spread of 4 months or more | ₹700 for a spread of 1 month. ₹1,000 for a spread of 2 months. ₹1,500 for a spread of 3 months or more | ₹1,500 for a spread of 1 month. ₹1,800 for a spread of 2 months. ₹2,000 for a spread of 3 months or more | ₹600 for a spread of 1 months. ₹1,000 for a spread of 2 months and ₹1,500 for a spread of 3 months or more |
| **Settlement** | Daily settlement: T + 1, Final settlement: T + 2 | | | |
| **Mode of settlement** | Cash settled in Indian Rupees | | | |
| **Daily settlement price (DSP)** | DSP shall be calculated on the basis of the last half an hour weighted average price of such contract or such other price as may be decided by the relevant authority from time to time | | | |
| **Final settlement price (FSP)** | RBI reference rate | | Exchange rate published by the Reserve Bank in its press release captioned RBI Reference Rate for USS and Euro. | |

*Source: MCX (www.mcx-sx.com)*

## 12.8    IMPORTANT USES OF THE CURRENCY FUTURES

1. The currency futures provide protection against exchange rate fluctuations for the investors, traders, bankers, etc.
2. They facilitate the importers and exporters to fix prices for foreign currencies and hedge the risk accordingly.
3. They initiate the investors to take advantages of fluctuations in the foreign exchange rates and take position in the markets in future.
4. They assist the individual investors to trade over and above their foreign allocation.
5. They are safe and secured in comparison to OTC foreign currency contracts as they are granted by the exchanges.
6. They eliminate the counterparty risk.
7. They are highly liquid instruments because they can be easily transferred and sold any time before the maturity.
8. These contracts are subject to margin limits. Investors have to make adjustment of their margin daily, which keeps check on movements in the exchange rates.
9. They are more transparent, efficient and accessible to OTC currency future contracts.
10. They are anonymous and are executed on a price time priority ensuring that the best price is available on each underlying currency.
11. On the futures contracts, the profits or losses are also paid, collected on a daily basis. Hence, the scope of accumulation of losses gets limited for the traders.
12. The main risk associated with these is only from the effect of gearing leverage. With a small amount of margin, one trades for the full nominal value of the contract, resulting in increasing more profits/losses even on initial margin which may lead to more volatile in the underlying currency.

## 12.9    FUNDAMENTAL NO-ARBITRAGE EQUATION (THEORETICAL FUTURES PRICE)

Like other futures contracts, the fundamental no-arbitrage equation for foreign exchange futures can be determined. Since currencies can be carried, futures prices can be determined by cash-and-carry arbitrage. As seen in the cases of bonds and stock index portfolios, the underlying assets provide returns in the form of interest and dividends, respectively. Similarly, in the case of currencies, the return takes the form of interest on the foreign currency. So, cash and carry arbitrage with currencies is also known as *covered interest arbitrage*. This can be further interpreted as an arbitrage of an actual futures contract against a synthetic futures position. This highlights the point that if the derivatives are not available, they could be synthetically constructed.

As observed earlier, the theoretical futures price is the price at which a profitable cash-and-carry (or reverse cash-and-carry) in underlying asset arbitrage does not exist. Therefore, in the similar manner, the cash-and-carry arbitrage foreign currency, one purchases foreign currency at current time $t$, carries it from $t$ to $T$ and then sells it at future time $T$ at a specified price. The following steps are taken in cash-and-carry arbitrage, assuming relationship between two currencies, i.e., home currency Indian rupee (₹) and US dollar ($) as foreign currency.

1. At the current time $t$, convert $Q$ amount of Indian rupee into foreign currency (US \$), $S_t$ using the current exchange rate, $S_t$ $\left(\dfrac{₹}{\$}\right)$ obtaining the following quantity of US \$ at time $t$.

$$Q_t^\$ = Q_t^{Re}\left(\frac{1}{S_t(\$/Re)}\right) \tag{12.1}$$

where $Q_t^\$$ is quantity of foreign currency (US \$) at current time, $Q_t^{Re}$ is quantity of home currency ₹ (Indian Rupee) at current time $t$ and $S_t$ is current spot rate between rupee and dollar.

2. Invest the foreign currency amount $Q_T^\$$ in a riskless security for the period $t$ to $T$, at annual interest rate $R$ of foreign currency. At the maturity $T$, this investment will yield $Q_T^\$$ as:

$$Q_T^\$ = Q_t^\$ \times \left(1 + R^\$ \times \frac{T-t}{360}\right) \tag{12.1a}$$

where $R^\$$ is the annual return on foreign currency, i.e., \$.

3. At time $t$, when short futures contract on foreign currency (\$) expires at time $T$, this will allow conversion of (\$) into home currency (₹) at the locked in rate of $F_{t,T}$ (₹/\$). This will yield the following quantity of home currency (₹) at the time $T$:

$Q_T^{Re} = Q_t^\$\left[F_{t,T}\left(\dfrac{Re}{\$}\right)\right]$ making the appropriate substitutions in the equation 12.1.a:

$$Q_t^\$ = Q_t^\$ \times \left(1 + R^\$ \times \frac{T-t}{360}\right) \times F_{t,T}\left(\frac{Re}{\$}\right)$$

$$= Q_T^{Re}\left(\frac{1}{S_t(\$/Re)}\right) \times \left(1 + R^\$ \times \frac{T-t}{360}\right) \times F_{t,T}\left(\frac{Re}{\$}\right)$$

$$= Q_t^{Re}\frac{F_{t,T}\left(\dfrac{Re}{\$}\right)}{S_t\left(\dfrac{\$}{Re}\right)} \times \left(1 + R^\$ \times \frac{T-t}{360}\right)$$

Thus, the Rupee return on the foreign investment can be stated as:

$$\frac{Q_T^{Re}}{Q_t^{Re}} = \frac{F_{t,T}\left(\dfrac{Re}{\$}\right)}{S_t\left(\dfrac{\$}{Re}\right)} \times \left(1 + R^\$ \times \frac{T-t}{360}\right) \tag{12.2}$$

4. In equilibrium, at which no profitable arbitrage opportunity exists, the return on a riskless rupee investment for the same period or $\left(1 + R^\$ \times \dfrac{T-t}{360}\right)$ must be the same as the rupee return on the riskless foreign currency investment, or

$$1 + R^\$ \times \frac{T-t}{360} = \frac{F_{t,T}\left(\dfrac{\text{Re}}{\$}\right)}{S_t\left(\dfrac{\$}{\text{Re}}\right)} \times \left(1 + R^\$ \times \frac{T-t}{360}\right)$$

This, in turn, implies a no-arbitrage equilibrium condition of

$$F_{t,T}\left(\frac{\text{Re}}{\$}\right) = S_t\left(\frac{\text{Re}}{\$}\right) \times \frac{\left(1 + R^{\text{Re}} \times \dfrac{T-t}{360}\right)}{\left(1 + R^\$ \times \dfrac{T-t}{360}\right)} \tag{12.3}$$

The equation 12.3, therefore, defines the theoretical currency futures price. It shows that the theoretical price is a function of the prevailing spot exchange rate and relative home currency and foreign currency interest rates.

If we further simplify the equation 12.3, we find that

$St$ (Re/$) = Current spot rate of foreign currency in home currency, i.e., Rupee and US dollar

$1 + R^{\text{Re}} \times \left(\dfrac{T-t}{360}\right)$ = Return (interest rate) available on home currency (Indian rupee)

$1 + R^\$ \times \left(\dfrac{T-t}{360}\right)$ = Return (interest rate) available on foreign currency (US dollar)

Thus, in brief, we can explain as:

$$\text{Futures rate} = \text{Spot rate} \left(\frac{1 + \text{Interest rate on home currency} \times \text{Period}}{1 + \text{Interest rate on foreign currency} \times \text{Period}}\right)$$

**EXAMPLE:** Assume that on January 10, 2015, six-month annual interest rate is 7 percent p.a. on Indian rupee and US dollar six-month rate is 6 percent p.a. and spot (Re/$) exchange rate was 62.3500. Using the equation 12.3, the theoretical futures price on January 10, 2015, expiring on June 9, 2015 is:

$$F_{t,T}\left(\frac{\text{Re}}{\$}\right) = 62.3500 \times \frac{1 + 0.07 \times \dfrac{150}{360}}{1 + 0.06 \times \dfrac{150}{360}}$$

$$= 62.3500 \times \frac{1.02916}{1.025} = 62.6030$$

So, theoretical futures price is ₹62.6030 per dollar. Then, this theoretical price is compared with the quoted futures price on January 10, 2015 and the relationship is observed.

## 12.10 COVERED INTEREST RATE PARITY AND CURRENCY ARBITRAGE

The above stated theoretical futures price of foreign currency is often called the *interest rate parity formula* or, alternatively, the *covered interest arbitrage formula* or relationship. It implies that portfolio managers investing abroad cannot simply compare interest rates across countries and invest where the rates are highest. They should also consider the returns they can lock in the currencies in the futures market as well as interest rate differentials among countries. In other words, it describes the equilibrium relationship of four interrelated markets; the domestic and foreign deposit markets and the spot and futures currencies markets. The word 'covered' here signifies that arbitrage strategies can be used to book a riskless return on foreign currency investment.

If the equilibrium condition prevails, then all the currencies will provide same riskless rate of return, and if this does not hold, arbitrage will occur that will re-establish the equilibrium relationships. For example, if the US interest rates are lower than Indian interest rates, then the investors would like to hold Indian rupees deposits. It means they will purchase spot Indian rupees and sell futures/ forward rupees raising the spot exchange rate of rupee and depressing the futures rate for rupee. This process will continue until the rupees sell at a forward discount to US dollars that reflects exactly the Rupee-US interest rate differential.

From the above, it is observed that if the actual exchange rates and interest rates do not correspond to the no-arbitrage equilibrium conditions then cross-border arbitrage will occur. The currencies will be purchased and sold till the changes in spot and futures exchange rates are equal to the current international interest rate differentials. However, it should be noted that to hold interest rate parity relationship, the market must be efficient in terms of freely buying and selling of currencies, unimpeded access to investments in foreign currencies, no cross-border capital controls, no foreign exchange control, no discriminatory taxes, no restriction on international capital flows, etc. If these conditions are not prevailing then the arbitrage opportunities will arise in foreign currencies markets.

## 12.11   IDENTIFYING A FOREIGN CURRENCY ARBITRAGE

The market participants may find various arbitrage opportunities in different currencies in foreign exchange markets. This can be calculated by determining the implied repo rate (IRR) on a foreign currency investment and compare the same with actual borrowing or lending rate. Let us explain this by an example stated in the previous section of this chapter.

**EXAMPLE:**   Assume on January 10, 2015, the following yields and prices existed:

Spot exchange rate (Re/$) = 62.3500
Futures exchange rate ($F_{t,T}$) (Re/$) = 62.6030
                              (quoted on June 9, 2015)
Six-month Indian interest rate = 7 percent per annum
Six-month US interest rate = 6 percent per annum
Thus, the IRR on a six-month US $ investment is 7 percent.

$$\left[\left(\frac{62.6030}{62.3500}\right) \times \left(1 + 0.06 \times \frac{150}{360} - 1\right)\right] \times \frac{360}{150} = 7\%$$

*Note:*   The formula for annualized implied repo rate *IRR* has already been given in previous chapter, however, it is again described here.

$$IRR = \left\{ \frac{F_{t,T}\left(\dfrac{HC}{FC}\right)}{S_t\left(\dfrac{HC}{FC}\right)} \times \left(1 + R^{FR} \times \frac{T-t}{360}\right) - 1 \right\} \times \frac{360}{T-t} \qquad (12.4)$$

where *HC* is home currency and *FC* is foreign currency. From the above, it is observed that there is arbitrage opportunity available if the dollar future rate on June 9, 2015 is 62.6030 because return available on dollar is 7.00 percent where six-month US interest rate (annual) is 6.00 percent. It has been further shown in Tables 12.7 and 12.5.

**TABLE 12.7**   Cash-and-Carry Foreign Currency Arbitrage: (IRR > Indian Rupee Interest Rate = 7%)

|     |                                                                                                                                                  | Cash flows   |
| --- | ------------------------------------------------------------------------------------------------------------------------------------------------ | ------------ |
|     | **January 10, 2015**                                                                                                                             |              |
| 1.  | Borrow ₹10,00,000 @ 7% p.a. for 150 days                                                                                                          | ₹10,00,000   |
| 2.  | Convert the rupee proceeds at the current spot exchange rate (Re/$) 62.35                                                                         | $1,60,385    |
| 3.  | Invest the dollar proceeds in US securities at an interest rate 6% p.a. for 150 days                                                              | $1,60,385    |
| 4.  | Sell dollar futures contract (mature on June 9, 2015) for an amount of $1,60,385 at a futures exchange rate of 62.6030 (Re/$)                     | 0            |
|     | **June 9, 2015**                                                                                                                                 |              |
| 5.  | Received matured US$ investment principal: $1,60,385. Interest accrued [$1,60,385 × 0.06 × (150/360)] = $4,010                                     | $1,64,395    |
| 6.  | Deliver proceeds the short US dollar futures position and obtain rupees proceeds 1,64,395 × 62.6030                                               | ₹10,29,162   |
| 7.  | Return the borrowed rupees amount principal ₹10,00,000. Interest accrued [10,00,000 × 0.07 × (150/360)]= 29,166                                    | ₹10,29,166   |
| 8.  | Net arbitrage profit ₹4 (or NIL) (Difference is due to calculation)                                                                               | ₹4           |

**TABLE 12.8**   Reverse Cash-and-Carry Foreign Currency Arbitrage: (IRR < Indian Rupee Interest Rate Assuming 6%)

|     |                                                                                                                                           | Cash flows   |
| --- | ----------------------------------------------------------------------------------------------------------------------------------------- | ------------ |
|     | **January 10, 2015**                                                                                                                      |              |
| 1.  | Borrow $1,00,000 @ 6% p.a. for 150 days                                                                                                    | $1,00,000    |
| 2.  | Convert the $ proceeds at the current spot rate as given ₹62.35 per dollar and obtain the proceeds (1,00,000 × 62.35)                       | ₹62,35,000   |
| 3.  | Invest the rupee proceeds in government securities at an interest rate 7% p.a. for 150 days                                                 | ₹62,35,000   |
| 4.  | Buy US$ futures contract on June 9, 2015 for an amount of US $1,02,500 at a future exchange rate of 62.6030 (₹/$)                           | 0            |
|     | **June 9, 2015**                                                                                                                          |              |
| 5.  | Received matured rupee investment principal plus interest being ₹as follows: ₹62,35,000 × 1.07 × (150/360)                                  | ₹64,16,854   |
| 6.  | Deliver the rupee against forward position and receive ₹64,16,854/62.6030                                                                  | $1,02,500.7  |
| 7.  | Return the borrowed US $ principal $1,00,000 add interest accrued 1,00,000 × 0.06 × (150/360) = $2,500                                       | $1,02,500    |
| 8.  | Net arbitrage profit (NIL)                                                                                                                 | NIL          |

**EXAMPLE:** The currency futures contract in US dollar is traded on NSE. Assume today September 12, 2015, spot rate of US dollar quoted in the market in ₹65,30 and futures price ₹65.60 October 2015. Futures would expire on October 29, 2015. Short term interest yields of US dollar and Indian rupees are 3% and 5% respectively. Calculate the fair futures price of US dollar in October, 2015 and what would be the price of November, 2015 futures if the expiry is on November 26, 2015.

Spot rate of US dollar on September 12, 2015: ₹65.30
Short-term interest rate on US dollar p.a. 3%
Short-term interest rate on Indian rupees p.a. 5%
Period (T.t) = from September 12, 2015 to October 29, 2015 = 47 days
Futures price formula of US dollar in term of rupee

$$F_T, T = S_t \times \frac{[1 + (r_h)\, 47 \div 365]}{[1 + (r_h)\, 47 \div 365]}$$

$$= 65.30 \times \frac{[1 + (05)\, 47 \div 365]}{[1 + (03)\, 47 \div 365]}$$

$$= 65.30\, [1.0064 \div 1.0039]$$

$$= 65.4626$$

Since the fair futures price is lower than the current futures price, so the trader can short the future price.
Future price for November, 2015 would be:

$$(T - t) = \text{from September 12, 2015 to November 26, 2015} = 73 \text{ days}$$

So
$$F_t T = S_t \times \frac{[1 + (.05)\, 73 \div 365]}{[1 + (0.3)\, 73 \div 365]}$$

$$= 65.30 \times [1.01 \div 1.006]$$

$$= ₹65.56$$

So, in November 2015, fair futures price of dollar should be ₹65.56.

In the above discussion one must also consider the cost incurred to arbitrage like commission, taxes, slippage, etc. As such futures should be traded within a 'band' above and below its theoretical value and width of the band is a reflection of the amount of such cost. It has already been discussed in Chapter 4 of the book.

## 12.12 HEDGING WITH CURRENCY FUTURES

Exchange rates are quite volatile and unpredictable, it is possible that anticipated profit in foreign investment may be eliminated, rather even may incur loss. Thus, in order to hedge this foreign currency risk, the traders often use the currency futures. For example, a long hedge (i.e., buying currency futures contracts) will protect against a rise in a foreign currency value, whereas a short hedge (i.e., selling currency futures contracts) will protect against a decline in a foreign currency's value.

It is noted that corporate profits are exposed to exchange rate risk in many situations. For example, if a trader is exporting or importing any particular product from other countries, then he is exposed to the foreign exchange risk. Similarly, if the firm is borrowing or lending or investing for short or long period from foreign countries, in all these situations, the firm's profit will be affected by change in foreign exchange rates. In all these situations, the firm can take long or short position in futures currency market as per requirement.

The general rule for determining whether a long or short futures position will hedge a potential foreign exchange loss is:

Loss from appreciating in Indian rupee → Short hedge

Loss from depreciating in Indian rupee → Long hedge

The following decisions involve regarding the hedging with currency futures:

## 12.12.1 Choice of Underlying Currency

The first important decision in this respect is deciding the currency in which futures contracts are to be initiated. For example, an Indian manufacturer wants to purchase some raw materials from Germany then he would like futures in German Mark since his exposure in straight forward in Mark against home currency (Indian Rupee). Assume that there is no such futures (between Rupee and Mark) are available in the market, then the trader would choose among other currencies for the hedging in futures. This choice is not that simple. Which contract should he choose? Probably he may choose Rupee with Dollar or Rupee with Pound and so on. This is called *cross hedge*. In brief, the trader must choose the currency in which he decides to go futures.

## 12.12.2 Choice of the Maturity of the Contract

The second important decision in hedging through currency futures is selecting the currency which matures nearest to the need of that currency. For example, an Indian firm contracts a three-month USD payable on February 28, 2015. This would mature on June 1, 2015, and assume that there is no INR/USD futures contract maturing on that date; traded contracts mature on 3rd Wednesday of June, September etc. The immediate concern to the firm is to "sell Rupee (INR) June contract" nearest to the maturity of the payable. In such situation, which maturity of the particular contracts would be considered and finally selected are important considerations. As we know that futures prices converge with spot prices on or near maturity of the contract. The hedging firm must determine whether convergence works in its favour or against it. Two factors should be considered in selecting the maturity of the contracts, first is the liquidity because liquidity in near contract tends to be higher and bid-ask spreads lower as compared to distant contracts. So this avoids against choosing too distant contracts. Second factor is volatility of basis—a difference of spot price and futures price. It is noted that longer the gap between lifting the hedge and delivery date of the futures contract, greater is the basis risk. A thumb rule in this respect is that the expiry month of the futures contract should be as close as possible but later than the expiration of the hedge.

## 12.12.3 Choice of the Number of Contracts (Hedging Ratio)

Another important decision in this respect is to decide hedging ratio *HR*. The value of the futures position should be taken to match as closely as possible the value of the cash market position. As we know that in the futures markets due to their standardization, exact match will generally not be possible but hedge ratio should be as close to unity as possible. We may define the hedge ratio *HR* as follows:

$$HR = \frac{V_F}{V_C}$$

where $V_F$ is the value of the futures position and $V_C$ is the value of the cash position.

Both values are measured in common currency. For example, a British firm has a USD payable of $10,00,000 and it decides to sell June contracts at $1.6/BP. At this price, the BP equivalent of $10,00,000 is BP 6,25,000. Since one BP contract is for BP 62,500 at International Monetary Market (IMM), it should sell

$$\left(\frac{6,25,000}{62,500}\right) = 10 \text{ contracts}$$

**EXAMPLE:** Let us consider that a US company has raised a loan of € 50 millions on January 1, 2015 and the spot rate of the USD/EURO is at $1.3150. The company wishes to protect the anticipated cash flow to be matured on July 1, 2015 by selling the futures. The company sells 400 August 12, 2015 EURO/USD futures at 1.3170. The basis quoted at this time 15 pips (1.3170 less 1.3155).

On July 1, 2015, the spot value of the EURO had fallen to US dollar to 1.2230. As a result, the value of €50 million, had declined. Show the impact of decline of Euro in terms of Dollar:

| | Spot rate | € 50 m in USD | August 12, 2015 Futures | Basis |
|---|---|---|---|---|
| Jan 1,2015 | 1.3150 | $65.75 m | Sell 400 @1.3165 | 15 pips |
| July 1,2015 | 1.2230 | $61.15 m | Buy 400 @1.2236 | 6 pips |
| –$4.60 m +$4.645 m + 9 pips | | | | |
| Net gains of $4.645 – 4.600 million = 45,000 | | | | |

But by selling the 400 futures contract the company would have generated a profit that offset spot market loss. August 2015 futures declined from 1.3165 to 1.2236. The translated into a futures market profit of $4.645 million for the company. The profit offset the spot market losses plus added another $ 45,000 or 9 pips to the bottom line.

## 12.13 'GUARANTEED' EXCHANGE RATE

As seen earlier that the basic objective of hedging is to reduce or eliminate the exchange risk. By hedging with futures, the trader seeks to guarantee the rate of exchange at which he will buy or sell the foreign exchange. He wants to know how much he will receive in terms of foreign currency. Thus, guaranteed exchange rate might be less favourable than the current rate, but at least he is free from the risk due to unfavourable conditions.

Now, the question arises how a firm will get such guaranteed exchange rate. The exchange rate that a hedger obtains will lie between the spot rate and the futures rate, and further depends upon the timing of closing out. For example, if the hedger closes out his position immediate after the contract, then the exchange rate obtained will be spot rate. On the other hand, if he goes up to maturity, then the obtained exchange rate will be the futures rate. Thus, closing out the position on an intermediate date (i.e., between the beginning and end), it would be between these two extremes as indicated in Figure 12.2.

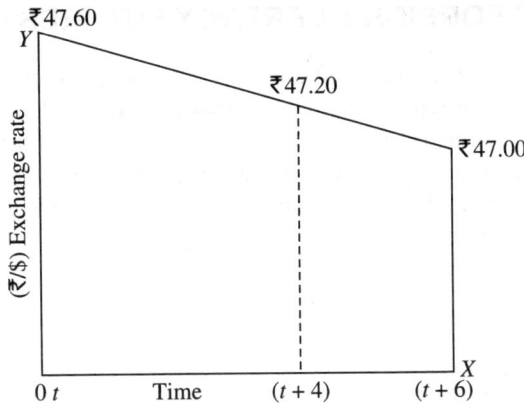

**FIGURE 12.2**   Variation of the effective exchange rate with time.

From Figure 12.2, it is observed that difference of exchange rate of Indian rupee with US dollar between the two extremes is 0.60 (₹47.60 – ₹47.00). This is the difference of beginning exchange rate (spot rate) and end rate at maturity (futures rate). So, if the futures currency contract is agreed at time *t* and closed out after 4 months, then the exchange rate obtained might be ₹47.20 per dollar.

The variation of the realized exchange rate which may be described in terms of changes in basis. Basis, as discussed in Chapter 7, is the difference between spot price and futures price. So, initially basis in the above case is 0.60 (₹47.60 – ₹47.00), but after six months it will be eliminated to zero because, at the maturity of the contract, the futures and spot prices (exchange rates) would be identical. The basis is also taken as the rate of depreciation/appreciation as the case may be. Figure 12.3 shows that basis changes over time beginning from 0.60 to zero.

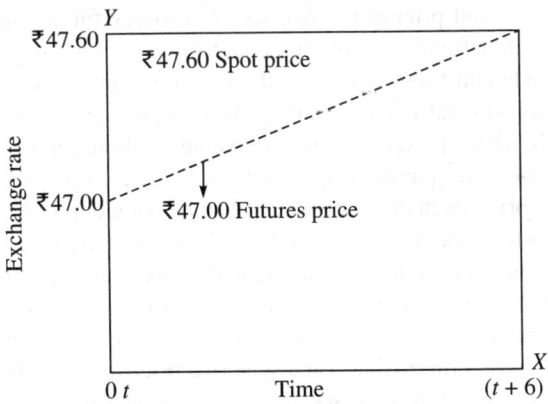

**FIGURE 12.3**   Convergence of the futures price and spot price.

The basic observation from Figure 12.3 is that the change in basis renders hedging imperfect, and the greater the period of time that elapses, the more imperfect is the hedge. For example, if a contract is closed out earlier, then the basis will be very little, as a result, hedge would be nearly perfect and the exchange rate guaranteed would be very close to the spot rate when the contract was agreed. In brief, the 'guaranteed' exchange rate does not depend upon the constancy of the spot rate. The changes in the spot rate should be compensated by the parallel changes in the futures exchange rate.

## 12.14   SYNTHETIC FOREIGN CURRENCY FUTURES CONTRACTS

Synthetic futures currency contracts simply means that instead of going futures in the same currency, the trader may look for other currencies too. For example, US dollar denominated futures contracts can be hedged by buying or selling in another currency futures or to establish a cross-currency futures spread. Suppose a treasurer expects the British pound to appreciate relative to the Japanese yen. For this, he can buy pound futures and sell yen futures, looking in a futures exchange rate between the yen and the pound sterling:

$$F_{t,T}\left(\frac{*\$}{£}\right) = \frac{F_{t,T}\left(\dfrac{\$}{£}\right)}{F_{t,T}\left(\dfrac{\$}{£*}\right)}$$

The above position will be profitable in the following conditions:

1. Both the currencies British pound and Japanese yen appreciate with respect to dollar but the BP appreciate more.
2. Both the BP and the yen depreciate with respect to dollar but the mark depreciate less.
3. The BP appreciates relative to the dollar, and the yen depreciates relative to the dollar.

It should be noted that good results will occur only if the futures positions are established in the correct proportions, i.e., equal dollar value futures positions on both legs of the spread.

## SUMMARY

This chapter on foreign currency futures introduced about the basics of currency futures, markets for foreign exchange futures and pricing mechanism of currency futures. Each country has its own currency through which both national and international transactions are performed. With the multiple growth of international trade and finance all over the world, trading in foreign currencies has grown tremendously over the past several decades. Since the exchange are continuously changing so the trading are exposed to the risk of exchange rate movements. Foreign exchange quotations can be confusing because currencies are quoted in terms of (or relative to) other currencies. It means that exchange rate is a relative price-exchange rate which may be quoted as direct and indirect rate. Direct method is the method in which the number of units of domestic currency are stated against one unit of foreign currency. The indirect method is the method using how many units of foreign currency can be exchanged from the domestic currency. The chapter further explains the concept of currency futures. A currency futures contract provide a simultaneous right and obligations to buy and sell a particular currency at a specified future date, on a specified price and at a standard quantity. Different currencies are traded in currency futures markets. Major features of futures contracts are organized exchanges like Chicago Board of Trade, New York Financial Futures Exchange, Tokyo International Financial Futures Exchange, London International Financial Futures Exchange and Hong Kong Futures Exchange. Another feature is that the futures are standardized in terms of quantity, size, delivery and margin. Futures contracts are mark-to-market in which at the end of trading session all the outstanding contracts are repriced at the settlement price of that session. Like other futures contract trading, the futures currency contracts are also traded at the organized exchange. Settlement process and delivery includes the taking opposite positions, what we know as reverse trading.

Foreign currency futures trading in India started after the approval of the RBI on August, 2008. In the beginning, only one foreign currency US dollar was allowed for trading. Later on, three more currency pairs in Euro, Pound Sterling, and Japanese Yen were also permitted. The trading of these four currencies were allowed on NSE, BSE and MCX-SX stock exchanges. A detailed guidelines relating to the trading of futures currency in India have been issued by the RBI and SEBI jointly.

Chapter further discusses the pricing mechanism of currency futures contract. Since currencies can be carried, futures prices can be determined by cash-and-carry arbitrage. As in case of bonds and stock index portfolio, the underlying assets provide return in the form of interest and dividends, respectively. Similarly, in the case of currencies, the return takes the form of interest on foreign currency. So cash-and-carry arbitrage with currencies is also known as covered interest arbitrage. Theoretical future price is the price at which a profitable cash-and-carry (or reverse cash-and-carry) in underlying asset arbitrage does not exist. In the similar manner, the cash-and-carry arbitrage foreign currency, one purchases foreign currency at current time $t$ carries it from $t$ to $T$, and then sells it at future time $T$ at a specified price. Cash-and-carry arbitrage process is a four-step process.

Covered interest rate parity and currency arbitrage implies that portfolio managers investing abroad cannot simply compare interest rate across countries and invest where the rates are highest. They should also consider the returns they can lock in the currencies in the futures market as well as interest rate differentials among countries. In other words, it describes the equilibrium relationship of four inter-related markets; domestic and foreign deposit markets and the spot and futures currencies markets. The covered signifies that the arbitrage strategies can be used to book a riskless return on foreign currency investment. Market participants may find various arbitrage opportunity in different currencies in foreign exchange markets. This can be calculated by determining the implied repo rate on a foreign currency investment and compare the same with actual borrowing on lending rate.

The last section of the chapter explains the hedging mechanism with currency futures. Exchange rates are quite volatile and predictable. It is possible that anticipated profit in foreign investment may be eliminated, rather even may incur loss. So, trader uses currency futures. A long hedge will protect against a rise in foreign currency value, whereas short hedge will protect against a decline in a foreign currency's value. Hedging with foreign currency futures involves various decisions like choice of underlying currency, which is the first important decision in this respect is deciding the currency in which futures contract are to be initiated. The next decision involves choice of the maturity of the contract, choice of number of contracts (hedge ratio), etc., which are the other decisions involved in hedging. Synthetic futures in some currencies, the trader may look for other currencies too. For example, the US denominated futures contracts can be hedged by buying or selling in other currency futures or to establish a cross-currency futures spread.

## SOLVED PROBLEMS

**P.1.** Suppose if a futures of French franc passes from US $0.2060 to US $0.2090, calculate the variation on the futures position assuming the contract size is 5,00,000.

*Solution:*　Calculation of variation:

$$5,00,000 \times 0.2060 = US\ \$1,03,000$$

$$5,00,000 \times 0.2090 = US\ \$1,04,500$$

$$\text{Difference} = \$1,04,500 - \$\ 1,03,000 = US\ \$1,500$$

**P.2.** On August 9, 2015, the following yields and price existed:

Spot exchange rate £/$ = 0.6262

December 17, 2015 futures price £/$ = 0.6249

Four months dollar interest rate $R^{FC}$ = 8.5% p.a.

Time to maturity $(T - t)$ = 130 days

From the above data, show an arbitrage opportunity.

*Solution:*   IRR (130 days)

$$\left[\left(\frac{0.6249}{0.6262}\right) \times \left(1 + 0.85 \times \frac{130}{360}\right) - 1\right] \times \frac{360}{120} = 0.0792 = 7.92\%$$

### Cash-and-Carry in Foreign Currency Arbitrage

|  | Cash flow |
|---|---|
| **August 9, 2015** |  |
| Borrow US $ 1,00,000 at 7% for 130 days | $1,00,000 |
| Convert the dollar proceeds at the prevailing spot exchange rate of | $1,00,000 |
| 0.6262 (£/$) and obtain of $(1,00,000/0.6262) | £1,59,693.4 |
| Invest the proceeds in £ at 8.5% p.a. | £1,59,693.4 |
| **December 17, 2015** |  |
| Received matured principal + interest accrued in £ | £16,46,009 |
| Deliver the £ proceeds against the short £ forward position and obtain dollar proceed of £, 16,46,009 × 0.6249 | US $10,28,591 |
| Return the borrowed dollar – US $ | $10,25,278 |
| Net arbitrage profit | US $3313 |

**P.3.** Assume on March 10, 2015, six-month annual interest rate was 5% p.a. on Indian rupees and US dollar six-month rate was 6% per annum. The spot ₹/$ exchange rate was 60.3500 using the above futures, calculate the theoretical futures price on March 10, 2015, expiring August 9, 2015.

*Solution:*   Futures rate = Spot rate $\left[\dfrac{1 + \text{Interest rate on home currency} \times \text{Period}}{1 + \text{Interest rate on foreign currency} \times \text{Period}}\right]$

$$F_{t,T} \ (₹/\$) = 60.3500 \times \left[\frac{1 + 0.05 \times \dfrac{150}{360}}{1 + 0.06 \times \dfrac{150}{360}}\right]$$

$$= 60.3500 \times \left[\frac{1.0208}{1.0250}\right]$$

Theoretical futures price = 60.3500 × (0.9959) = 60.1027

$$F_{t,T} \ (₹/\$) = 60.35 \ (0.9959) = 60.1027$$

**P.4.** Suppose on January 10, 2015, three-month annual interest rate was 4% p.a. on Indian rupees and UK pound six-month rate was 6% p.a. Spot (₹/£) exchange rate was 84.2500. Using the figures, calculate the theoretical futures price on January 2015, expiring March 9, 2015.

*Solution:*   Futures rate = Spot rate $\left[ \dfrac{1 + \text{Interest rate on home currency} \times \text{Period}}{1 + \text{Interest rate on foreign currency} \times \text{Period}} \right]$

$$F_{t,T} \, (₹/\$) = 84.2500 \times \left[ \frac{1 + 0.04 \times \dfrac{60}{360}}{1 + 0.05 \times \dfrac{60}{360}} \right] = 84.2500 \times \left[ \frac{1.0066}{1.0083} \right]$$

Theoretical futures price $F_{t,T} \, (₹/£) = 84.2500 \, (0.9983) = 84.1080$

**P.5.** Suppose on March 10, 2003, the following yields and prices existed:
  Spot exchange rate (Re/$) = 47.3500
  Futures exchange rate ($F_{t,T}$ (Re/$)) = 47.7800
  Six-month Indian interest rate = 5% p.a.
  Six-month US interest rate = 6% p.a.

Show that if there is any arbitrage opportunity and also show the profit profile of arbitrage position.

*Solution*:   IRR on six-month US/$ investment is

$$= \left[ \frac{47.7800}{47.3500} \right] \times \left( 1 + 0.5 \times \frac{150}{360} - 1 \right) \times \frac{360}{150}$$

$$= (1.0208 - 1) \times \frac{360}{150}$$

$$= 1.00908 \, (0.0499) = 0.05035$$

$$= 5.035\%$$

Cash-and-Carry Foreign Currency Arbitrage
(Indian rupee interest rate is 5%)

| | **March 10, 2002** | *Cash flow* |
|---|---|---|
| 1. | Borrow ₹10,00,000 @ 5% p.a. for 150 days | = 10,00,000 |
| 2. | Convert the rupee proceeds US dollar ($) at the current spot exchange rate (₹/$) = 47.35 | = 21,119.32($) |
| 3. | Invest the dollar proceeds in US security at an interest rate 6% p.a. for 150 days | = 21,119.32($) |
| 4. | Sell dollar futures contract (Mature on August 9, 2002) for an amount of $21,647.30 at a future exchange rate (₹/$) = 47.78 | = 0 |
| | **August 9, 2002** | |
| 5. | Received in maturity US$ investment principal | = 21,119.32 |
| | Interest income $\left[ 21,119.32 \times 6\% \times \dfrac{150}{360} \right] = \$ 527.98$ | = 21,64,730 |

(Contd.)

*(Contd.)*

| | | |
|---|---|---|
| 6. | Deliver proceeds the short US dollar futures position and obtain rupees proceeds of [21,647.30 × 47.78] | = 10,34,307.994 |
| 7. | Return the borrowed rupees amount principal ₹10,00,000 interest accrued $= \left[ 10,00,000 \times 0.05 \times \dfrac{150}{360} \right]$ ₹= 20,833, being | = 10,20,833.33 |
| 8. | Net arbitrage profit ₹13474.66 | |

**P.6.** Using the information given in Problem 5, show the position in reverse cash-and-carry foreign currency arbitrage if interest on Indian rupee is 9% p.a.

*Solution:*

| | | *Cash flow* |
|---|---|---|
| | **March 10, 2002** | |
| 1. | Borrow US 10,0000 @ 5% p.a. for 150 days | = $1,00,000 |
| 2. | Convert the $ proceeds at the current Spot exchange rate (Re/$) = 47.35 and obtain Indian rupees: = (10,0000 × 47.35) | = ₹47,35,000 |
| 3. | Invest the rupee proceeds in government security at an interest rate of 9% for 150 days | = 47,35,000 |
| 4. | Buy US $ futures contract August for an amount of (US $10,20,833 at a futures exchange rate of ₹47.78) | = 0 |
| | **August 9, 2002** | |
| 5. | Received matured rupee investment principal and interest income: $= \left[ 47.35 \times 0.09 \times \dfrac{150}{360} \right] \times 1,00,000 = 1,77,562 + 47,35,000$ | = 49,12,562 |
| 6. | Deliver proceeds the rupee against long forward position and receive US$ [US$ 1,02,083 × 47.78] | = ₹48,77,540 |
| 7. | Return the borrowed US$ principal | = $1,00,000 |
| | Add interest accrued $= \left[ 1,00,000 \times \dfrac{150}{360} \right] = 2083, \text{ total } \$$ | = 1,02,083 |
| 8. | Net arbitrary profit = ₹4,91,25,62 – 4877540 | = ₹35,022 |

**P.7.** An investor intimated a need of Japanese yen 42,75,000 in November 2015. On April 15, 2015. Importer bears the exchange risk. Spot price of $/yen is 0.04173 and December futures are traded on 0.04265. Show importer can use foreign currency futures to hedge exchange risk.

*Solution:*

| Cash market | Futures market |
|---|---|
| **April 15, 2015** | |
| The importer anticipates need of yen 4,27,50,000 in November. Current value being $1,78,396 and expected value in November be $1,82,329. | The importer buy December yen futures contract at 0.04265 for total commitment of $1,59,938. |
| **November 2015** | |
| Buy yen 42,75,000 and spot rate of 0.04273 for a total of $182671. | Sell December 3 yen futures contract at 0.04265 for total value of $1,60,125 |
| Spot market loss = –$342 | Profit = $187 |
| **Net loss to importer = –$155** | |

**P.8.** On May 10, a US importer signs a contract to buy German machinery for a total cost of DM 12,50,000. The payment date is December 15, 2002. The importer is facing the risk that mark may appreciate between May and December. On May 10, the spot DM exchange rate ($/DM) is 0.6262, while the December 2002 DM futures price is 0.6400. In order to protect from adverse movement, the importer enters into a futures contract at a price of ($/DM)0.6249 (contract calls for delivery of DM 1,25,000). Show how hedging will protect the importer.

*Solution:*

| Cash market | Futures market |
|---|---|
| Importer fears to appreciate in the price of DM spot price is 0.6262 | Buy 10 futures contracts of DM at 0.6249 cash contract calls for delivery of 1,25,000 DM |
| DM appreciates to 0.6400 and importer incur losses and cost of buying DM will be $8,00,000 | Sell futures contract of DM at 0.6400 and earn profit |
| | Futures profits = (0.6400 – 0.6249) × 1,25,000 × 10 = – 18875($) |
| **Net cost of buying = $8,00,000 – $18,875 = US $7,81,125** | |

**P.9.** On September 5, a US exporting firm signs a contract to sell goods to an Indian firm. It will receive ₹10,00,000 for payment on October 15, which coincides with the last trading day of the dollar between now and October 15, The US firm decides to protect itself by going that October 15, 2002 futures contract (each contract calls for delivery of ₹1,00,000). The October 2002 Rupee futures price on September 5 is 49 (Re/$). The spot exchange rate of September 5 is ₹48. The US firm will offset its futures position on October 15 and sells ₹10,00,000 it receives from the Indian firm in the spot market. How US exporter can hedge his risk by using currency futures?

*Solution:*

| Cash market | Futures market |
|---|---|
| **September 5** | |
| US exporter will receive ₹ 10,00,000 in the month of October and is go year that Indian Rupee appreciates. | Sell 10 futures contract (each contract for delivery of ₹ 1,00,000) at ₹ 47. |
| ₹ appreciates to 49 on October 15, 2002 | Buy 10 futures at ₹ 49 and closes out position. |
| Sale revenue = 49 × 10,00,000 = 4,90,00,000 | Futures loss = 2 × 10,00,000 = 20,00,000 |
| **Net sale revenue = 4,90,00,000 – 20,00,000 = 4,70,00,000** | |

**P.10.** From the following information, show the position of a speculator in foreign currency futures.

| Exchange rate | Speculator anticipates the fall in value of DM over the next two months. |
|---|---|
| ($/DM)Spot 0.4140 | |
| June futures = 0.4183 | |
| September futures = 0.4211 | |
| December futures = 0.4286 | |

*Solution:*    Speculation in foreign exchange futures

| Spot market | Futures market |
|---|---|
| **April** | |
| Anticipates a fall in value of DM over next eight months (suppose it is April now) December spot price | Sell December DM futures contract at 0.4286. |
| $/DM = 0.4211 | Buy December 1 DM futures contract at 0.4218 |
| Profit = $(0.4286 – 0.4218) = (DM/$) = 0.0068 | |
| Profit on contract = 0.0068 × 1,25,000 = $850 | |

# REVIEW QUESTIONS

1. What is foreign currency exchange rate? Discuss various types of foreign exchange quotations with suitable examples.
2. Define the concept of foreign currency futures with suitable examples. Also explain various specifications of currency futures contact.
3. Explain the features of a currency futures contract with suitable illustrations.
4. Explain the term margin and its different types with suitable examples in context to currency futures contract.
5. Write a detailed note on trading and settlement procedure of currency futures contract.
6. "The pricing of currency futures is not so different from other futures contract". Discuss the statement in the light of theoretical futures price determination in foreign currency market.

7. "Cash-and-carry" arbitrage opportunity exists in the currency futures markets. Critically examine the statement with suitable illustrations.

8. Write short notes on
   (a) Tick size in currency futures contract
   (b) Organization of a futures exchange
   (c) Margin call
   (d) Mark-to-market

9. Write a detailed note on covered interest rate parity and currency arbitrage with suitable illustrations.

10. How could an investor find a foreign currency arbitrage opportunity? Explain with examples.

11. What do you understand by the term hedging? What are various types of hedging? Explain with suitable illustrations.

12. Explain how hedging is done by an importer who is of fear that price of foreign currency will increase in future.

13. What are various decisions involved regarding the hedging with currency futures? Explain.

14. What is guaranteed exchange rate? Explain with suitable examples.

15. Explain the concept of synthetic foreign currency futures contract. Also explain the various profitable positions in various conditions.

16. Discuss the role of hedge ratio in hedging with currency futures contracts. What factors you will consider in determining the hedge ratio?

17. What do you mean by currency futures market? How it is different from spot currency market? Explain.

18. "Exchange rate theorems affect the pricing of foreign currency futures." Critically evaluate the statement.

19. List out various organized exchanges where currency futures are traded with their specifications in brief.

20. How does the flow of transaction take place in foreign exchange currency futures contract? Explain with the help of diagram.

21. What are various ways through which a currency futures can be closed? Explain with examples.

22. "Currency futures contracts are like forward contractors, recontracted daily". Examine critically.

23. List the ways in which currency futures contracts differ from currency forward contracts.

24. What are the three ways in which futures contract reduce credit risk?

25. Explain the important guidelines on foreign currency futures trading in India.

## UNSOLVED PROBLEMS

**P.1.**   Suppose that the interbank forward bid for January 28 on pounds sterling is $1.2927 at the same time the price at IMM sterling futures for delivery in January is $1.2915. How could the foreign exchange dealer use the arbitrage to earn profit from this situation?

**P.2.**   Suppose a trader buys a futures contract on Indian stock market at National Stock Exchange at a price of ₹48 (against dollar). The contract will mature within three days and also suppose that in three days fluctuations in the price are: on day close futures price rise to ₹49, second day close futures price drops to ₹47.50 and on last day price drops to ₹46. Show the daily settlement.

**P.3.** Suppose on Monday a trader buys on DEM futures contract. The futures price is $0.6246 per DEM and $78,075 per contract. Also assume that he has to deposit a margin of $3,905. The contract calls for delivery on Wednesday of the following week and the last trading day is the Monday before, i.e., a week from the date of the contract. Assume that forward USD/DEM rate for delivery on the same day is also $0.6246. Show what will be cash flow of all the transaction.

**P.4.** Suppose on April 25, 2002 an American Company (Software solution) contracts a six-month, 30 million Belgian franc receivables. The settlement date is September 25. There are no futures contracts on BEF in terms of US dollars. The exporter believes that the BEF is closely tied with DEM so that their movement against US dollar will be closely correlated. Spot and futures prices are as follows:

Spot DEM/USD  = 1.5560
Spot BEF/DEM  = 19.2502
These rates imply
    Spot DEM/USD  = 0.6427
    Spot BEF/DEM  = 0.3333
DEM futures
    November      = 0.6525
    February      = 0.6650
    May           = 0.6525

What this case show and how company can reduce the exchange risk?

**P.5.** Suppose today is March 28. Spot and futures prices by USD/DEM are: Spot 0.5865, March futures 0.5895, June futures 0.5925 and September futures 0.6975. Also these prices imply that the market is expecting the DEM to appreciate against the dollar over next light months. How speculator can earn profit? (Suppose on September, the following rate spot = 0.5940 and September futures 0.5948).

**P.6.** On April 12, you took a long position in Swiss franc (Sfr) on first May IMMs per contract at an opening price of $0.6350. The initial margin was $1,500 and the maintenance margin was $1,200. The settlement price for April, 12,13,14 were $0.6280, $0.6355, $0.6365. On April 14, you close out the position at $0.6365. Compute the cash flow on your account.

**P.7.** Assume a British exporter anticipates receipt of $½ million on June 1. The sale of goods is agreed upon on March 3 and the exporter wants to hedge against the risk that the dollar will depreciate against the pound before June, thus reducing the sterling value of the dollar receipts. Suppose current June 1 exchange rate is 1£ = $1.50 and [1/2 million = £3,33,333] and futures rate = 1.58/£ and assume that on June 1 dollar has fallen 1.60/£. Show how UK exporter can use currency futures to hedge his risk assuming.

**P.8.** Suppose a US investor who owned 1600 shares of a French stock worth 2500 FF per share wanted to hedge the dollar value of his stock. Suppose the $/FF spot and three-month futures exchange rate are both $0.15/FF (or 6.6667 FF/$), making current value of dollar = ($0.15/FF) (1000) (2500 FF) = $3,75,000. How many contracts are needed by the investor to hedge $h$ is risk?

**P.9.** A UK based fund manager decides to increase expense to the US stock market at the expense of UK equity investment. It is desired that £1 million of expense to be reallocated immediately with stock selection. (for both sales and purchase) to take place during the following 2 weeks. It is April 12 and current price are:

July FTSE 100  = 2500

$/£ exchange rate = $2.00/£1

June S&P 500 futures = 200

Design a strategy that might be followed to calculate the numbers of futures contracts involved.

**P.10.**   On September 25, 2002, an Indian importer signs a contract to buy US machinery for a total cost of US $25,000. The payment date is December 25, 2002. The importer is facing the risk that US $ may appreciate between September and December. On September 25, the spot US $ exchange rate (Re/$) is 46.5 while December 90 days US $ futures price is 45.5600. The importer decides to go for long December 2002 US $ futures contract with a view to protect against an adverse movement in exchange. Show the hedging position of importer using above data. What will be the net purchasing cost to importer to import the machinery?

**P.11.**   An Indian exporting company, on August 25, 2001, signs a contract to sell Indian clothes to a US company. It will receive $1,00,000 for payment on November 25, which coincides to the last trading of the November 2001 US$ futures contract. The Indian company decides to protect itself by going short in futures market. The spot price on August 25, 2001 is ₹39.8600 and futures price of November futures is 39.8600. Demonstrate the outcomes of the hedging strategy under two alternatives: (a) when US$ appreciates to 39.8900 and (b) when US$ depreciates to 39.2500.

## SUGGESTED READINGS

1. Chang, Jack S.K., Hsing Fang, and Wong Kie Ann, Hedging with currency futures and forward contracts: An intertemporal generalization, *Review of Futures Markets*, Vol. 12(3), 601–624, 1993.

2. Coyle and Brain, *Currency Futures*, Glenlake Publication Company, Chicago 111, New York.

3. Shoup, Gray and Net Library Inc., *Currency Risk Management: A Handbook for Financial Managers*, Glenlake Publication Company, Chicago 111, New York.

4. Gotthelf, Philip and Net Library Inc., *Currency Trading: How to Access and Trade World's Biggest Market*, Wiley, Hoboken, New Jersey, 2003.

5. Stephens, Johan J. and Institute of International Auditors, Managing Currency Risk Using Financial Derivatives, Wiley, Chichester, 2001.

6. Kodres, L., Tests of unbiaseness in foreign exchange futures markets: The effects of price limits, *The Review of Futures Market*, Vol. 7, No. 1, pp. 138–166, 1988.

7. CME Group Currency understanding Fx Futures April 22, 2013, Feb 2016.

8. CME Group (http://www.cmegroup.com) market data.

9. MCX (www.mcx.sx.com)

# Chapter 13

# Foreign Currency Forwards

*After reading this chapter, students will be able to*

➢ Understand the concept of foreign exchange forward market.

➢ Be aware of the features of a forward contract like nature of contract, terms of the contract, currencies to be traded, cash flows, settlement, etc.

➢ Be aware of the various methods of dealing in forward exchange market.

➢ Understand the various guidelines in determining the forward dates.

➢ Know the distinction between forward and futures currency contracts.

➢ Be aware of the pricing mechanism of currency forward contracts.

➢ Understand the concept of fixed vs option forward contracts.

➢ Be aware of the hedging through the forward contracts.

## 13.1 INTRODUCTION

In most of the financial markets, the traders and market participants, who wish to establish prices for future period, usually use the futures markets as we have seen in the preceding chapters. However, in case of foreign currency markets, futures trading is not so dominating form of contracting on the established futures exchanges. Instead, it is more popular and applicable among the participants in the forward markets. The foreign exchange forward markets operate simultaneously with the foreign exchange futures and options markets. In fact, it has a higher trading volume than the other markets. These markets exist harmoniously due to their clientele's differentiation. The forward foreign exchange markets are generally used by large commercial traders, commercial banks, speculators, arbitrageurs and institutional investors who hedge future commitments through forward markets.

The foreign exchange forward market also co-exists simultaneously with the foreign exchange spot market. Most of the traders, dealers and other participants who deal in the spot foreign exchange markets also operate and make markets in foreign exchange forward contracts. In other words, the foreign exchange markets operate simultaneously in spot, forward, futures and options, and mostly used by the participants in common enjoying the benefits fully from the liquidity of the other markets.

In this section, we will discuss the functioning, structure and mechanism of forward market in foreign exchange all over the world. How the foreign exchange rates are quoted and determined in forward currency market will also be included in this chapter.

## 13.2 FORWARD FOREIGN EXCHANGE MARKET

The basic objective of a forward market in any underlying asset is to fix a price for a contract to be carried through on the future agreed date and is intended to free both the purchaser and the seller from any risk of loss which might incur due to fluctuations in the price of the underlying asset. Likewise, the forward exchange may be defined:

The market in which such forward transactions in foreign currencies are traded is called the *forward exchange market*. Presently active forward markets exist in a few currencies like Deutsche mark, US dollar, Canadian dollar, Japanese yen, and major continental currencies like Swiss franc, Belgian franc, Italian lira, Dutch guilder, French franc, British pound, etc. However, forward markets for the currencies of less developed countries are not very much active rather limited or non-existent.

## 13.3 FEATURES OF A FORWARD EXCHANGE CONTRACT

The forward exchange contract is a device which can be used to protect from the eventual loss due to fluctuation in the foreign exchange rates in future. So, in brief, the following are the main features of a forward contract in the foreign currency:

*Nature of contract:*   The forward foreign exchange contract occurs between two parties, say, a banker and a customer, a banker with another banker, a dealer and a customer and so on. So, it is just like a private contract between the two parties.

*Terms of the contract:*   The various terms of the contract like forward rate, future date, mode of payment, payment in particular currency, etc. are negotiated and settled in advance at the time of formation of forward contract by the contracting parties.

*Currencies:*   Forward contracts are available in all the major strong currencies, including several of developing countries' currencies as well like India, China, Indonesia, etc.

*Cash flows:*   The cash flows in the forward exchange agreements occur only at the time of maturity when the foreign currencies are to be delivered. As observed, a majority (more than 90 percent) of the forward contracts are settled by delivery of currencies.

*Quotations:*   The dealer in the forward exchange markets usually quote the two-way prices, known as bid-ask rates. The rates are locked in for the entire period of contract up to maturity date.

*Risk:*   Since the forward contracts are done between the two parties, hence, the risk of the contract relates with the commitment of the parties. So, a loss can occur in case of default by the either party in the contract.

***Commission:*** The commission of the dealer is inbuilt in the bid-ask quotation of the contract. No separate commission is paid by the either party. This forward market is, by and large, self-regulated.

A typical example of a forward exchange contract can be described whereby an Indian multinational company buys fertilizer from the US firm, with a payment of 10 million US dollars in 90 days. The importer (Indian firm), thus, is short US dollar, i.e., it owes dollars for future delivery. Suppose, the current price of the US dollar in term of Indian rupee is 45.90. It is uncertain how much will be change in the exchange rate between US dollar and Indian rupee. Let us assume that US dollar might rise against the rupee, and thus, raising the rupee cost of the fertilizer. In this respect, the importer can guard against this exchange risk by immediately dealing a 90-day forward contract with a foreign exchange dealer (the banker) at a price, say, ₹46.10. According to the forward contract, in 90 days the dealer will give the importer 10 million dollar (which it will use to pay for its fertilizer order), and the importer will pay the banker ₹46.10 million, which is rupee equivalent of the 10 million dollar at the forward rate of ₹46.10/$. In technical terms, the Indian firm (importer) is offsetting a short position in US dollar by going long in the forward market, i.e., by buying US dollar for future delivery.

The gains and losses arising out of the forward contracts are related to the difference between the contracted forward price and the spot price of the underlying currency at the time of the maturity of the contract. For example, in the abovementioned case, the importer will incur loss in the forward contract if the spot rate of rupee in terms of dollar falls below ₹46.10. But, if the spot rate in 90 days exceeds ₹46.10, the importer will be in gains because the contract obliges the dealer to sell the US dollar at a price less than the current value. Likewise, the position in the forward exchange market can be taken by the other parties like exporters, borrowers, lenders, arbitrageurs, speculators, dealers, etc. as per their needs and objectives.

## 13.4   METHODS OF DEALING IN FORWARD EXCHANGE

A forward exchange contract is a fixed price contract made today for a delivery of a specified amount of a currency at a specified future date. The specified date is also known as *settlement date*. The simplest of the derivative securities, forward contracts are not traded on exchanges, so it is just like private contract between the two parties. Like spot market operations, the bank will buy and sell forward currencies in the same way. A customer or another bank or any other of the exchange market's dealer can offer to buy from or sell to that bank 'forward' currency for future delivery, and within limits will be quoted a rate as easily as for a 'spot' transactions. A simple forward contract is illustrated in Figure 13.1.

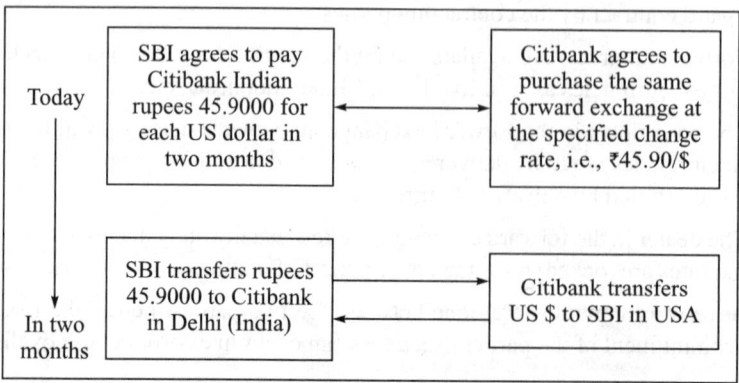

**FIGURE 13.1**   Forward transaction illustrated.

Typically, in forward exchange contract, no money changes hands in present (today) period. The exchange takes place at a future date. On the settlement date, either the full amounts are exchanged or the net value is paid. Normally, forward contract stipulates that the full amount need not be exchanged at the maturity date rather only the difference between the forward rate and the spot rate prevailing on the settlement date (called net value) may be paid. This is shown in Figure 13.2.

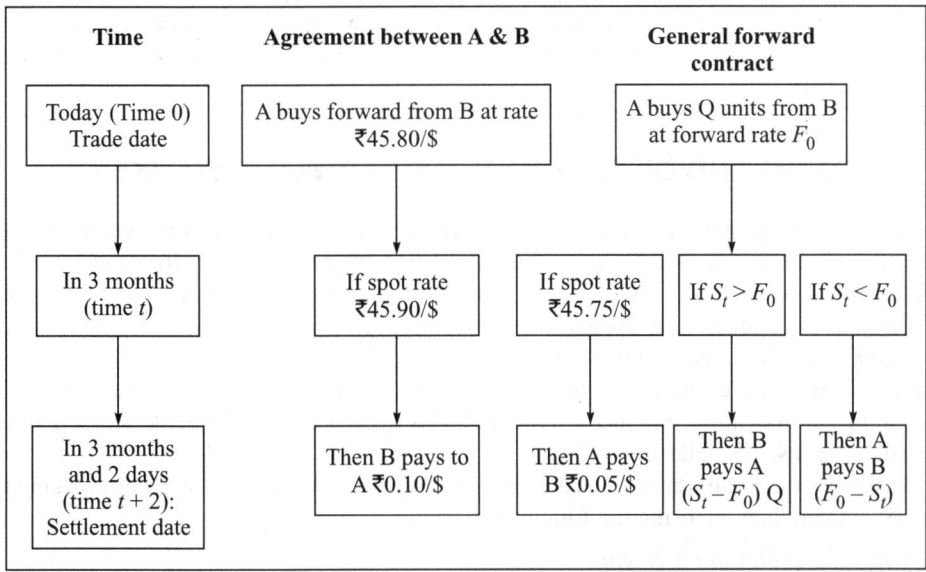

**FIGURE 13.2**   Forward contract mechanism.

It is observed from Figure 12.2 that in a general forward contract, the buyer of the contract will pay to the seller when the future spot rate $S_t$ is lower than the forward rate $F_0$, and the seller of the contract will pay to the buyer when the future spot rate is higher than the forward rate. The net amount payable is determined by multiplying the difference of forward rate and future spot rate with the total units of the underlying currency in the contract $Q$. So, everyone does not qualify to enter into this market. Hence, only well established and large banks, institutions, corporate units and other dealer normally deal in this market.

Forward exchange contracts are amazingly versatile. They are available in two dozen or more currencies, and for maturities ranging from one week to several years. Most of them have a maturity of less than two years. Longer-dated forward contracts have relatively large bid-ask spreads. Yet many traders shun them due to default risk which arises due to non-performance by either of the parties. What would either party have to gain/loss from non-performance? The answer is that on the maturity (settlement) date, one party in effect owes the other party a net amount. This net amount cannot be determined in advance, which depends upon the movement of the future spot currency rate in the market.

## 13.5   FORWARD EXCHANGE QUOTATIONS

The exchange rate for delivery and payment at specified future dates are called *forward exchange rates* or *forward rate*, and are usually denoted by $F(₹/\$)$, which specifies a relationship between domestic and foreign currency. For example, quote denoted as $F(₹/\$)$ is the rate at which the dealer can arrange a forward contract between the rupee and dollar. The forward rates are quoted for different maturities, such as one month, two months, three months, six months, one year, etc. Normally, the maturity dates are fixed as per the needs of the clients in the market.

Forward rates of currencies are quoted as a 'margin' or 'difference' against the spot rate of the underlying currency, or a 'premium' or 'discount' on the spot rate. Further, they may also be quoted, 'outright' by allowing the 'margin' over or under the current 'spot' rate. Forward rates are quoted like spot rates, in the form of 'bid' and 'ask' rates. The difference between the 'bid' and 'ask' rate is known as *spread*.

## 13.6   PREMIUM AND DISCOUNT IN THE FORWARD MARKET

The forex dealers may quote currencies in terms of premium or discount on them in the forward markets. 'Premium' which means that the forward margin is dearer than the spot rate. In other words, if the forward rate of a currency exceeds the spot rate, the currency is said to be at premium. For example, if the spot rate of domestic currency 'Re' is quoted in terms of US dollar ($₹/\$$) = 45.7000/9,000, and the three-month forward rate is 45.6000/7000, the rupee will be at premium. Conversely, if the forward rate is less than the spot rate, the currency is said to be at discount. For example, in the earlier case, if the forward rate $F(₹/\$)$ is quoted as 45.9000/9,500 then the rupee will be at discount against US dollar.

Alternatively, the premium and discount may be expressed in terms of percent per annum. This percentage is ascertained by using the following formula:

1. *When the quotes are in months:*

$$\text{Forward premium} = \frac{\text{Forward rate} - \text{Spot rate}}{\text{Spot rate}} \times 100 \times \frac{12}{\text{Forward contract (length in months)}}$$

(13.1)

   (or discount in percentage)

2. *When the quotes are given in days:*

$$\text{Forward premium} = \frac{\text{Forward rate} - \text{Spot rate}}{\text{Spot rate}} \times 100 \times \frac{365}{\text{No. of days to maturity}}$$

   (or discount in percentage)

The first component of the Equation 13.1 expresses the premium or discount as a proportion of the spot rate. The second component annualizes the figure by calculating either with the total months (12 months) or the total days in a year (i.e., 365 or 360 as the case may be), so in the case of three-month forwards, this adjustment would multiply by the first ratio by 4 while, in case of one-month forwards, it would multiply by 12. Finally, the resulting figure is multiplied by 100 for converting the decimal figure into a percentage.

Following are the examples explaining the calculation of premium, discount and corresponding outright forward rates:

**EXAMPLE:**   Calculate the premium for the three-month forward rate when spot rate is $S$ ($₹/\$$) = 45.7000/8,000 and three-month forward rate is $F$ ($₹/\$$) = 45.5000/6,000, three-month premium on rupee against dollar is:

$$\text{(For buyer or dollar): } \frac{45.5000 - 45.7000}{45.5000} \times \frac{12}{3} \times 100 = -1.76\%$$

$$\text{(For seller or dollar): } \frac{45.6000 - 45.8000}{45.8000} \times \frac{12}{3} \times 100 = -1.74\%$$

Sometimes, the foreign exchange brokers/dealers may quote currencies in terms of premium and discount on them in the forward market, e.g., the broker says that the US dollar is running at 4 percent premium in the three-month market, and assume that the spot rate of is $S$ (₹/\$) = 45.8000 then the outright forward rate can be determined as:

$$\text{Premium (\%)} = \frac{\text{Forward rate} - \text{Spot rate}}{\text{Spot rate}}$$

or

$$F \text{ (₹/\$)} = 1 + \text{Premium (\%)} \times \text{Spot rate}$$

$$= (1 + 0.04) \times 45.800 = 47.6320$$

So the forward outright rate of ₹/\$ = 47.6320.

## 13.7  OUTRIGHT VS SWAP RATE OF FORWARD CONTRACT

Forward rate can be expressed in two ways:

### 13.7.1  Outright Rate

When the forward rate is calculated by using the premium/discount, it is called *outright method* or *outright rate*. Commercial customers are usually quoted the actual rate, otherwise known as *the outright rate*. A currency is said to be at a forward discount when it is found cheaper in the forward market and vice versa. Forward premium or discount is closely related to the difference in interest rates of the underlying currencies.

### 13.7.2  Swap Rate (In Terms of Basis Points)

In inter-bank market, usually the forex dealers quote the forward rate only as a discount or premium in points on the spot rate. So, swap rate is not an exchange rate. It is an exchange rate differentials. The swap rate is the link between the spot rate and forward rate or the link between two forward rates of two different maturities.

A swap rate is used to convert the spot rate into an outright rate by adding the premium (in points) to, or subtracting the discount (in points) from the spot rate. Swap rates usually do not carry plus (+) or minus (−) points but one can easily determine whether the forward rate is at premium or discount by using the swap rule which is stated as follows:

*Swap rule.*   When the forward bid in swap points is smaller than the offer rate in points, the forward rate is at premium and the points should be added in the quoted spot rate for calculating the outright forward rate. On the other hand, if the forward bid points is higher than the offer in points, the forward rate is at discount, and then, the swap points must be subtracted from the spot rate to get the forward outright rate.

To explain the rule, let us assume that the swap rate is 140/150. It implies that buying forward at 140 points above the spot buying rate and selling forward at 150 points above the spot selling (offer) rate. If, in this case, the swap rate is quoted as 150/140, then it indicates that the buying forward at 150 points below spot rate and selling provided 140 points below the spot rate. Thus, in swap transaction, the most important factor is the swap rate and not the spot exchange rate. The above swap rate (140/150) and (150/140) may also be termed as *negative terms* and *positive terms*, respectively. The *negative terms* indicate the discount on the foreign currency in points, whereas *positive terms* indicate premium on the foreign currency in points.

**EXAMPLE:** Assume that the following quotes are received from a forex dealer for spot, one-month, three-month and six-month US dollar and pound sterling:

| | | | | |
|---|---|---|---|---|
| ₹/$ | = 45.5500/9,500 | 200/150 | 500/300 | 900/600 |
| ₹/£ | = 70.2500/8,000 | 300/400 | 700/900 | 1,200/1,500 |

The outright rates are determined as follows in Table 13.1.

**TABLE 13.1**   Comparative Quotation of US Dollar ($) and Pound Sterling (£)

| | US dollar ($) | | | Pound sterling (£) | | |
|---|---|---|---|---|---|---|
| **Maturity** | **Bid** | **Ask** | **Spread (%)** | **Bid** | **Ask** | **Spread (%)** |
| Spot | 45.5500 | 45.9500 | 0.878 | 70.2500 | 70.8000 | 0.783 |
| One-month | 45.5300 | 45.9350 | 0.889 | 70.2800 | 70.8400 | 0.799 |
| Three-month | 45.5000 | 45.9200 | 0.923 | 70.3200 | 70.8900 | 0.811 |
| Four-month | 45.4600 | 45.8900 | 0.946 | 70.3700 | 70.9500 | 0.824 |

It is evident from the example that US dollar is at forward discount and pound sterling is at forward premium against the Indian rupee.

In brief, the following general rules should be followed while computing the outright forward implied by a swap quotation:

1. The bank must always make profit.
2. The bid-ask spread widens as we go into the future.
3. If the swap points are from low to high, they should be added to the spot exchange rate. For example, for a spot rate ₹/$, if the swap points are to be added then rupee is at a discount and dollar is at a premium.
4. If the swap points are from high to low, they should be subtracted from the spot exchange rate. For example, for a spot ₹/$, if the spot points are to be subtracted, the rupee is at premium and the dollar is at discount.

## 13.8   VALUE DATES AND CASH FLOWS

Identification of foreign cash flows in any business organization requires the determination of location and dates on which cash in particular currencies are to be delivered. The treasurer or fund manager of the organization must verify each transaction in context to the points like (1) the name of other party to the transaction, (2) the specific currency is being purchased or sold, (3) the amount involved, (4) the location or place where money is to be delivered, (5) the exchange rate to be used for the transaction, and (6) the value date.

When there are several cash flows in different currencies (as in case of banks) then value dates of interest are to be observed. There are two ways of measuring the cash flows which are as: (1) net cash flow and (2) the net exchange position. The net cash flow in a currency for a given value date is calculated as the net of inflows and outflows. The net cash flow is either net inflows or net outflows of a particular currency. In case of net exchange position, the difference between all cash inflows and outflows in the particular currency aggregated for all the value dates of interest. If inflows are larger than outflows for that period of time then it shows net long or net overbought position. Similarly, if we have more outflows than inflows, then it indicates *net short* or *oversold position*. However, if inflows are equal to outflows, then it is called *square position*.

## 13.9 VALUE DATES (GENERAL GUIDELINES IN DETERMINING THE FORWARD DATES)

Due to technicalities it is involved in forward contracts regarding date, place and cash flow. Following are certain rules (guidelines) stated for determining the value date in forward contracts:

1. Spot-transactions for a value date, two business days following the day when transaction is closed, whereas in forward transactions are values dates in future, usually computed as a number of months from the value date of the spot transaction.

2. Standard forward dates will be the same calendar date as the spot date. However, the value dates for the forward contracts are calculated by adding the forward period (usually number of months) to the spot maturity date. For example, if a three-month forward contract is done on January 5, the settlement date is arrived at by adding three calendar months to spot settlement date (January 7) of the transaction, i.e., April 7 forward settlement date.

3. Each subsequent calendar month will have a standard forward date.

4. If the forward value dates are bank holidays in either of the party's country then the settlement date is shifted to the next eligible business day.

5. A standard forward date would be the same for more than one dealing date. For example, if the spot value date for the next two days is August 6 and 7, respectively, and the standard one-month forward date can be September 9 for all two spot days.

6. One-month forward date is not a standard 30 days term. It is to be taken in month irrespective of days in month. A standard forward date must occur in each successive month.

7. If the current spot value date falls on the last spot date for that month then the standard forward dates will also be the last common business date in each month in the concerned countries. For example, if the spot value date is February 27 and is the last spot date then successive standard forward dates will be the last common business date in each month such as March 30, April 30, May 30 and so on.

## 13.10 COMPARISON OF FORWARD AND FUTURES CURRENCY CONTRACTS

As we have seen in the chapter of futures exchange market that currency futures contract provides a simultaneous right and obligation to buy or sell on a specific future date, a specified amount of a particular currency at an agreed price. The given definition is also almost similar to the concept of forward currency contract. But both are different from various aspects which have been stated in brief in Table 13.2.

**TABLE 13.2** Comparison of Forward and Futures Currency Contracts

| Basis | Forward | Futures |
|---|---|---|
| Size | Structured as per requirement of the party | Standardized |
| Delivery dates | Tailored to individuals needs | Standardized |
| Method of transaction | Established by the bank or broker through electronic media | Open auction among buyers and sellers on the floor of recognized exchange |
| Participants | Banks, brokers, forex dealers, multinational companies, institutional investors, arbitrageurs, traders, etc. | Banks, brokers, multinational companies, institutional investors, small traders, speculators, arbitrageurs, etc. |
| Range of currencies | Approximately 50 currencies including most European and pacific Basin currencies. In principle, any such currency where money market exists | Only major liquid currencies like US$, Canadian dollar, Yen, Mark, Pound sterling, French franc, Swiss franc, Australian dollar, Euro, etc. |
| Commission | Set by spread between dealer's quoted buy and sell price (bid-ask price) of the currency | Published brokerage fee by the Margin deposit required |
| Margins | None as such, but compensating bank balances may be required | |
| Maturity | Tailored to needs; from one week to 10 years | Standardized; typically four settlement dates per year |
| Settlement | Actual delivery or offset with cash settlement. No separate clearing house | Daily settlements to the market and variation margin requirements |
| Market place | Over the telephone worldwide and computer networks | At recognized exchange floor with worldwide communications |
| Accessibility | Limited to large customers banks, institutions, etc. | Open to anyone who is in need of hedging facilities or has risk capital to speculate |
| Regulation | Self regulating | Regulation through exchanges |
| Frequency of delivery | More than 90 percent settled by actual delivery | Actual delivery has very less even below one percent |
| Price fluctuation | No daily limit | Daily limit |
| Secured | Risk is high being less secured | Highly secured through margin deposit, and so low or no risk |

## 13.11 DECIDING ON FUTURES VS FORWARDS

It is observed, in general, that both futures and forward contracts lead to the same value at maturity. The basic distinction, as mentioned in Table 12.2, between futures and forwards are the intermediate cash flows associated with marking-to-market. Thus, the decision to use futures or forward currency contracts depends on the objective and scale of the transaction. Let us see this in two important market activities, i.e., hedging and speculation. The objective under the hedging activities is to offset an underlying business transaction at a particular date, so there is no need for liquidity. Further, the hedgers who match the maturity of their hedge contracts to their underlying exposure do not want to liquidate their contract prior to maturity. So, for them, the marking-to-market will create undesired cash flow risk. Therefore, where the prices are similar and expecting not much fluctuations, the hedger will prefer forward contracts provided they have access to this market.

It is also argued that the hedgers may not be able to construct a perfect hedge since in the futures market standard quantity and delivery date are specified. Thus, futures market may not be so suitable as inter-bank forward market. In contrast to a hedger, the speculators depend heavily on market liquidity which means the ability to buy and sell quickly with transactions having little impact on market prices. Since the forward contracts are relatively illiquid, the short-term speculators usually do not prefer them, and hence, like to go futures contracts through exchanges. However, the long-term speculators may prefer the interbank forward market but they would like to trade in spot market rather than in forwards because the spot transactions are most liquid.

## 13.12 NON-DELIVERABLE FORWARD (NDF) CONTRACTS

Foreign exchange market in the largest almost innovative market among the various financial markets all over the world. Foreign exchange crisis has been arisen from time to time in different countries. Currencies which are not freely traded and are subject to internal capital controls but whose movements are significant and are aligned to international rate movements trading in such currencies becomes essential for international liquidity. As a result, a new product in foreign exchange market developed known as Non-deliverable forward (NDF).

As the name indicates, a non-deliverable contracts is a forward contract where the delivery for the underlying asset whether it is currency or commodity, is not required. In other words, an NDF is forward contracts normally on a thinly traded or non-convertible foreign currency where the contracts is settled not by delivering the underlying pair of currencies, rather by making a net payment. This net payment is paid in any agreed convertible currency, proportional to the difference of the amount at the settlement date. Net payment is calculated to difference between the agreed forward exchange rate and subsequently realized amount at the spot fixing rate.

In most NDF contracts convertible currency is normally used as US Dollar. For example, an exporter based in Hong Kong has RMB 10 million receivable after two months. He is expecting depreciation of RMB in near future. In such case, he may book an NDF in Singapore where foreign exchange NDFs are quoted in RMB for settlement in US Dollar. NDFs are distinct from the normal forward contracts since these are usually traded outside the control of the nation's Central Bank and pricing may not be linked to the domestic currency rates.

### 13.12.1 Development of NDFs

NDFs are, as discussed above, foreign exchange derivative products traded at OTC markets. Their origin was evolved in 1970s when the Australian currency was kept under capital restriction by the central bank. In 1995, when Mexico devalued in currency Peso, then to trigger this market US Banks offered a new product VB, a financial contracts to insure against currency risk, standard in US Dollars and settled outside Latin America, and hence NDFs became popular.

Earlier, Asian currencies were deliverable and highly liquid before the Asian crisis in 1992/98 and no need was felt of the NDFs. But later on, due to heavy exchange restriction and capital control in these countries led to the NDF contracts. Important Asian currencies which become popular in this market are Chinese renminbi (RMB), Indian rupee, Korean won, Indonesian rupiah, Philippine Peso, new Taiwan dollars. Gradually, every currency of the world with some form of capital controls is keeping a parallel NDF market.

As per Triennial Central Bank survey (Bank of England), daily turnover of NDFs on April 2013 are $127 billion. It represented 19 percent of all forward trading globally and 2.4 percent of all currency turnover. Almost two third of these took place in six currencies against the dollar which BRL, CNY, INR, KRW, RUB and TWD. NDF turnover grew rapidly in the five years from 2008 to 2013. London surveys show that the NDF market grew faster than the forward market. Table 13.3 depicts the average daily turnover from 2008 to 2013.

**TABLE 13.3**   NDF Trading in London. Average Daily Volume

*US dollars in billions*

|  | **NDFs** | **All forwards** | **NDFs as % of all forwards** | **All FX** | **NDFs as % of all FX** | **Memo: Tokyo NDF** |
|---|---|---|---|---|---|---|
| **Apr-08** | 23 | 200 | 11.5 | 1,832 | 1.3 | 2.4 |
| **Oct-08** | 19 | 230 | 8.3 | 1,699 | 1.1 | ... |
| **Apr-09** | 16 | 162 | 9.9 | 1,356 | 1.2 | 0.3 |
| **Oct-09** | 26 | 191 | 13.6 | 1,522 | 1.7 | ... |
| **Apr-10** | 25 | 186 | 13.4 | 1,687 | 1.5 | 0.3 |
| **Oct-10** | 37 | 188 | 19.7 | 1,787 | 2.1 | ... |
| **Apr-11** | 42 | 192 | 21.9 | 2,042 | 2.1 | 1.6 |
| **Apr-12** | 36 | 192 | 18.8 | 2,014 | 1.8 | 1.4 |
| **Oct-12** | 45 | 211 | 21.3 | 2,017 | 2.2 | 1.9 |
| **Apr-13** | 60 | 265 | 22.6 | 2,547 | 2.4 | 2.4 |
| **Oct-13** | 43 | 205 | 21 | 2,234 | 1.9 | 1.9 |

*Source:* London Foreign Exchange Joint Standing Committee; Tokyo Foreign Exchange Market Committee
*Source:* BIS Quarterly Review, March 2014.

1. Adjusted for local and cross-border inter-dealer double-counting.
2. Non-deliverable forwards and outright forwards.
3. Transactions in Asian and other emerging market currencies.

It is observed that in these five years the NDF turnover doubled in share to 2.4 percent of overall turnover all is around 20 percent of the all foreign exchange market turnover. Further, as per Table 13.4, it is noted that daily turnover in April 2013, in India, is 5,019 million dollar of Deliverable Forwards (DFs) and 17,204 million dollar of NDFs. It means NDFs volume is 77.41 percent of the total volume per day.

**TABLE 13.4**  Trade Location and Deliverability of Forwards (DFs and NDFs)

*Daily Turnover in Millions of US dollars, April 2013*

| Six currencies | DFs | NDFs | Total | Memo % | DFs | NDFs | Total |
|---|---|---|---|---|---|---|---|
| Onshore | 10,138 | 4,550 | 14,688 | Onshore | 8.90% | 4.00% | 12.80% |
| Offshore | 21,543 | 78,170 | 99,713 | Offshore | 18.80% | 68.30% | 87.20% |
| Total | 31,680 | 82,720 | 1,14,401 | Total | 27.70% | 72.30% | 100.00% |
| Brazilian real | DFs | NDFs | Total | Chinese renminbi | DFs | NDFs | Total |
| Onshore | 2,709 | 559 | 3,268 | Onshore | 2,441 | – | 2,441 |
| Offshore | 6,908 | 15,335 | 22,243 | Offshore | 7,102 | 17,083 | 24,185 |
| Total | 9,617 | 15,894 | 25,511 | Total | 9,543 | 17,083 | 26,626 |
| Indian rupee | DFs | NDFs | Total | Korean won | DFs | NDFs | Total |
| Onshore | 3,140 | – | 3,140 | Onshore | 1,118 | 3,538 | 4,656 |
| Offshore | 1,879 | 17,204 | 19,083 | Offshore | 1,410 | 16,027 | 17,437 |
| Total | 5,019 | 17,204 | 22,223 | Total | 2,528 | 19,565 | 22,094 |
| Russian rouble | DFs | NDFs | Total | New Taiwan dollar | DFs | NDFs | Total |
| Onshore | 512 | 231 | 743 | Onshore | 218 | 222 | 440 |
| Offshore | 3,187 | 3,887 | 7,074 | Offshore | 1,057 | 8,634 | 9,691 |
| Total | 3,699 | 4,118 | 7,817 | Total | 1,274 | 8,856 | 10,130 |

DFs = deliverable forwards; NDFs = non-deliverable forwards. Data are reported on a net-net basis, i.e., adjusted for local and cross-border inter-dealer double-counting. Chi-squared statistics strongly reject the null hypothesis of no relationship between location and deliverability: 14,375 for all six currencies; 3,260 for BRL; 4,811 for CNY; 12,534 for INR; 920 for KRW; 154 for RUB; 572 for TWD. The critical value for $p = .0005$ is 12, so all are highly statistically significant. Sources: Triennial Central Bank Survey; authors' calculations.

*Source: BIS Quarterly Review* March, 2014.

## 13.12.2  Features of NDFs

Important features of NDFs contracts are as under:

1. NDFs are forward currency derivative contents and traded at the OTC markets. It a customized contract to meet the needs of counterparties.
2. An NDF contract is a forward contract in foreign currency where the delivery of underlying pair of currencies is not required at the settlement date.
3. This contract is usually entered into outside of the national boundaries of the respective currencies.
4. The NDF contracts are settled in such currency which is freely acceptable and liquid. They are settled in cash only and mostly in US dollar. Such contracts have a national principle amount.
5. NDFs have a fixing date and settlement date. Fixing date is that date at which the fixing sport rate is determined, which is normally based on the specific rate as indicated on a reference page of the Reuters services.

6. NDFs are commonly traded and quoted for time period of one month to one year, although some would quote up to two years upon request.

7. NDF contracts are popular among the hedgers and speculators where the currency trading is restricted by the central bank. Transaction for hedging were allowed and conducted in the NDF market and so they are also called the *hedge markets*.

8. The NDF enable hedging for the non-resident and foreign participant who are not allowed access to on store markets for these currencies.

9. In brief, an NDF contract is a forward contract wherein delivery of the currencies is not required. It is settled in cash only in such currencies which is freely acceptable in the international market. The most commonly traded NDFs are IMM date, but banks also offered odd-dated NDFs.

## 13.12.3   Operation of the NDF Contracts

The trading mechanism of the NDFs are similar to the other deliverable forward contracts, specifically for hedging purpose. However, their trading mechanism in slightly different to general forward currency contracts. The settlement of an NDF is done in agreed foreign currency in cash (usually US Dollar) with the difference between the forward price and the settlement price over a national principal amount of the contract.

This is calculated as under:

$$\text{Settlement amount} = (1 - \text{forward rate/settlement rate}) \times \text{national amount} \qquad (13.2)$$

Or

$$\text{Settlement amount} = (\text{forward rate} - \text{settlement rate}) \times \text{national amount}$$

**EXAMPLE:**   Let us consider that an exporter of Indonesia who has exported the goods to an Indian firm worth ₹ 10 lakh and has agreed to receive the payment in Indian rupee after 3 months. The exporter fears that Indian rupee might be depreciated in near future. Assume that a 3-month NDF is quoted at US Dollar 0.016 per rupee. The exporter decides to hedge by selling a 3-month NDF at 0.016 by locking his receivable of ₹ 10 lakh in US Dollar at US Dollars at $16,000. The position of the exporters in such case would be as follows:

1. Assume that rupee depreciates to US $ to $0.0156 at the settlement rate:
   Settlement amount (Receivable) = $(0.016 - 0.0156) \times 10$ lakh = +$400
   Realized US Dollar from the receivables = $10,00,000 \times 0.0156 = $15,600
   Total realization = $16,000

2. Assume that rupee appreciates to US Dollar to $0.0165
   Settlement amount (payable) = $(0.016 - 0.0165) \times 10$ lakh = –$500
   Realized US Dollar from the receivables = $10,00,000 \times 0.0165 = $16,500
   Total realization = $16000

## 13.12.4   NDF and Its Implication

NDFs play significant role in the financial markets. Some banks offer deposits in a complete adaptable currency. The return on these deposits indicates the implied local interest rates resulting from the NDF markets which are normally higher than the deposits on the same currency deposits. These deposits may be connected only to principal or both principal and interest. None only this, NDFs also facilitate their deposits to pressure a low credit risk quite often.

As already discussed in the preceding section that forward markets and the spot markets are linked with the interest rate parity (IRP) which means that interest rate differential will be equal to the difference in spot rate and forward rate in a freely accessible or efficient financial market. However, the capital control restrictions imposed by the central banks, sometimes, create distortions in the IRP. Since NDFs are not subjects to capitals controls of the central bank, so there will be interest rate differential on off share and on share deposits in the underlying currencies of the NDFs. Let us explain this with an example.

Let us consider that a 6-month NDF contracts in Indian rupee is quoted in the market at ₹62.80 per US Dollar as against the spot rate of ₹62.2.0 with an 80 percent interest rate is in US Dollars. So, the implied rate of return in Indian rupee would be 5 percent, calculated as $(1+r_{ndf})$ = $1.04 \times 62.80/62.20 = 1.0500 = 5$ percent.

The differential between the off share and the on share rate as implied in the NDFs and the forward rate would give rise to the arbitrage opportunity. Due to this arbitrage process, there would be close proximity between these rates, with a nominal difference which may be just equal to transaction cost to be incurred in the two markets. Hence, the NDF would be regarded as a truer reflector of free market conditions than the prevailing local control or conditions prevailing in the off share markets.

## 13.12.5 Synthetic Foreign Currency Loans with NDF

NDFs can be used to create a foreign currency loan in a currency that may not be of interest to the lender. For example, a company intends to borrow funds in US Dollar but wants to make repayment of loan in pound. So the company (borrower) receives a dollar sum and repayments will still be calculated in Dollars. However, the payment of this sum will be made in pound, using the current exchange rate of time of repayment. Similarly, the banker (the lender) wants to lend dollars and receive repayments in dollars so, at the same time as disbursing the dollar sum to the borrower company, the banker (lender) enters into an NDF agreement with a counterparty (for example, on the Chicago market) that matches the cash flows from the foreign currency repayments. Effectively, the borrower has a synthetic dollar loan and the counterparty has an NDF contract with lender.

## 13.12.6 NDF and Arbitrage

It has been observed in certain cases that the rates achievable using synthetic foreign currency lending may be lesser than borrowing in this foreign currency directly, which may result to a possible arbitrage opportunity. Although, this is theoretical identical to a second currency loan (with settlement in dollars as in the above said example) the borrowing may face basis risk. There is a possibility that a difference arises between the swap markets exchange rate and the home market exchange rate. The lender also bears counterparty risk. Similarly, the borrower could, in theory, enters into contracts directly and borrow in dollars separately and achieve the same result. NDF counterparties however, may prefer to work with a limited range of firms.

## 13.13 FIXED FORWARD CONTRACT

The forward contracts can be classified into two categories: fixed and option. Fixed forward contract, a forward contract under which the delivery of foreign exchange should take place on a specified future date is known as *fixed forward contract* or *outright forward contract*. In other words, it calls for delivery on a specific day, the settlement date for the contract. For example, if on January 10, a trader enters into a two-month forward contract with a bank to purchase 10,000 US dollar, it means the trader would be presenting a bill or any other instrument on February 12, to the bank for 10,000 Dollar. He cannot offer to deliver foreign exchange prior to or later than the determined (fixed) date, i.e., in the above case February 12.

## 13.14   OPTION FORWARD CONTRACT

In the option forward contract no specific date is fixed, rather a period is mentioned during which the contract can be completed. So a forward contract wherein one of the parties has an option to make or take delivery of any day within a specified interval is called *option forward contract*. Therefore, in an option forward contract, the contracting cannot state definitely at the time of entering into the forward contract on what exact date the contract would be completed. The rate at which the deal takes place is called the *option forward rate*. For example, a trader enters into a three-month forward contract with a bank on March 15, with option over June. It means that the trader can sell the foreign exchange to the bank on any day between June 1 and June 30. The period from June 1 to June 30, is known as the *option period*. Further detail regarding option trading has been given in chapter concerning options.

## 13.15   BROKEN DATES FORWARD CONTRACTS

Normally, the standard forward contracts are fixed value dates for standard months. In other words, forward rates quoted in forward markets relate to certain standard maturities, viz. 1, 2, 3, 6, 9, 12 months. However, the dealer (bank) can offer deals other than standard months, with any maturity, e.g., 35 days, 85 days, 245 days, etc. which is not a whole month. Such contracts are called *broken date* or *odd date deals*. The forward rates, thus, are also calculated by interpolating between the two standard period dates. For example, a forex dealer has given a forward quotation as (₹/$) spot 46.2000/4000 on September 7, being the spot date on September 9. The premium on US Dollar over 2-month and 3-month period are 4/35, 120/110, respectively. Suppose we want the bid rate for $ for November 24. This is 2 months and 16 days from the spot date. The premium on rupee over the third month is (120 – 40) = 80 points, and there are 30 days between November 9 and December 9. This is distributed pro-rate to get points for 15 days, (15/30) = 40. This is added to the two-month premium to give total premium of 81 (42 + 39) points and an outright bid rate of (46.2000 – 0.0040) = 46.1960. However, this interpolating has drawbacks which should be carefully handled.

## 13.16   PRICING CURRENCY FORWARD CONTRACTS

It is observed in the preceding section of this chapter that a forward contract is entered into by two parties, at a rate quoted in the market only two promises are exchanged, viz. one party will deliver a certain amount of currency, say, US Dollar, and the other party will deliver a certain amount of currency, say, Indian Rupee. No money is paid by either party to the other at the time of formation of forward contract. It is just like exchanging two promissory notes which promise to pay the bearer the specified amount of currency $X$ and currency $Y$, respectively, at a specified future date. Since no payment is involved in the beginning, the present value of these two promises must be equal. Further, if the forward contracts entered into at market rates, then they will have a zero value at the time they are entered into.

In this section, we will discuss how the forward currency contracts are priced in the market. In other words, what is the fair or theoretical or no arbitrage price of a forward contract which provides no opportunity for arbitrage profits? The arbitrageurs play an important role in the determination of prices of forward or futures contract in foreign exchange markets. The arbitrage involves buying the cheaper of the two currencies, and simultaneously selling the more expensive. So, the arbitrage may be looked upon as a cash-and-carry arbitrage but it is more usually referred to as covered interest arbitrage.

In order to know the price of forward buying and selling, it is essential to know the interest rates available on the two currencies. Forward price/rate is based upon spot rate and differential of interest rates of two currencies underlying the forward contract. If currency $X$ has a rate of interest higher than currency $Y$ then currency $X$ will be quoted at forward discount and currency $Y$ will be at forward premium with respect to each other.

Let us explain with an example how the forward rate is formed by using the spot rate of the currency. Consider an Indian institutional investor with one-year investment horizon who has two alternatives:

*Alternative I:*   Deposit ₹ 10,00,000 in an Indian bank, say, State Bank of India that pays 6 percent rate of interest compounded annually for one year.

*Alternative II:*   Deposit pound sterling in UK country's bank, say, Bank of England, that pays 4 percent rate of interest compounded annually Indian rupees equivalent of ₹ 10,00,000 for one year.

The two alternatives and their outcomes of one year from the deposits are shown in Figure 13.3. Now the question is which alternative is better. We may say that the alternative which gives more Indian rupees after one year will be better. To decide it, other things remaining constant, we may consider two things:

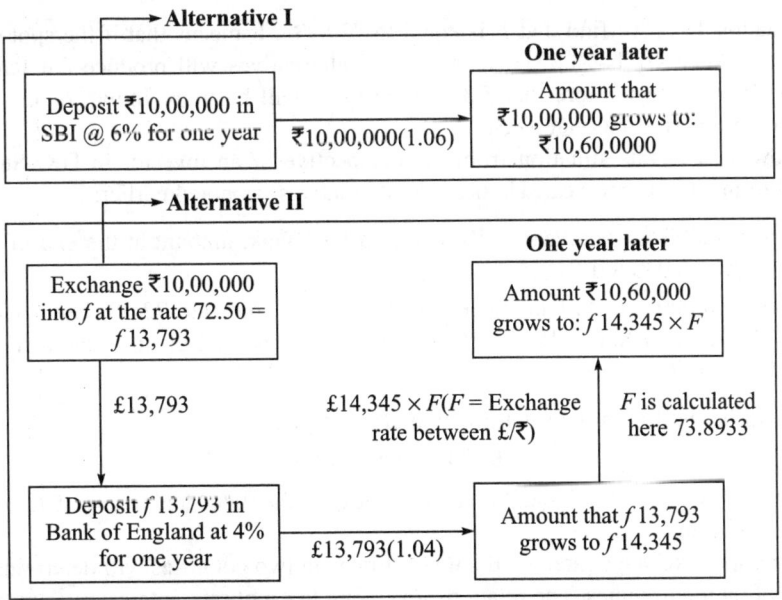

**FIGURE 13.3**  Outcome of two alternatives: Determination of theoretical forward rate.

1. The spot rate between the two countries' currencies, i.e., Indian rupee and British pound, assume to it, ₹/£: 72.5000.
2. The spot exchange rate after one year between Indian rupee and British pound.

The former is known to us, whereas the latter is not. However, we can determine the spot rate after one year that will make the investor indifferent between the two alternatives.

*Alternative I:* The amount of Indian rupees available for one year would be ₹10,60,000 [10,00,000 (1.06)].

*Alternative II:* Assume that spot rate between ₹/£ is 72.5000 at this time. We will convert these into British Pound (£) at the spot rate, i.e., 13,793, then it will be available for one year @4%, being £14,345, [13,793(1.04)].

The amount of Indian rupees for which the £14,345 can be exchanged will depend on the exchange rate available after one year. Let $F$ denote the exchange rate between these currencies after one year. Thus, the amount of Indian rupee available after one year through the second alternative would be

Amount of Indian rupees after one year = £14,345 × $F$

The investor will be indifferent between the two alternatives if the number of Indian rupees is 10,60,000, i.e.,

$$₹10,60,000 = £14345 × F$$

$$F = \frac{₹10,60,000}{£14,345}$$

$$F\,(₹/\$) = 73.89$$

From Equation 12.2, we find that $F$ is equal to 73.8933. It means that if the spot exchange rate after one year between ₹/£ is 73.8933, then the two alternatives will produce the same number of Indian rupees. If this rate is more than 73.89 then there will be more Indian rupees (₹10,60,000) available with the investor and vice versa.

Let us now look at this situation from the perspective of an investor in UK. Suppose he has 10,000 pound to invest for one year. He has two alternatives, as noted earlier:

1. Deposit £10,000 for one year @4% p.a. in a UK Bank, amount at the end of one year will be £10,400 (10,000 × 1.04).
2. Convert £10,000 into Indian rupees, at the current spot rate 72.50, being ₹7,25,000, and invest the same in Indian Bank @6 p.a., amount at the end of one year will be ₹7,68,500, (7,25,000 × 1.06).

The investor will be indifferent between the two alternatives:

$$£10,400 = ₹7,68,500 × F$$

The value of $F$ is 73.89 ($F = 7,68,500/10,400$) between the rupee and pound. The equation yields the same exchange rate.

In brief, the spot exchange rate and the interest rates in two countries will determine the forward exchange rate of their currencies. The relationship among the spot rate, interest rates in two countries, and the forward rate is called *interest rate party*. It means that an investor, by hedging in the forward exchange market, will realize the same return whether investing domestically or in a foreign country. The arbitrage process that forces interest rate parity is called *covered interest arbitrage*.

Interest rate parity can be expressed mathematically as:

$$X (I + i_A) = (X/S) (1 + i_B)F \tag{13.3}$$

where $X$ is amount of A's currency to be invested for period, $S$ is spot exchange rate between currencies A and B, $F$ is $T$-period forward rate (theoretical), $i_A$ is interest rate on an investment in currency A and $i_B$ is interest rate on an investment in currency B.

In our previous preceding example between India and England:

$$₹10,00,000 (I + 0.06) = \left(\frac{10,00,000}{72.50}\right) (1 + 0.04)\ 73.89$$

$$₹10,60,000 = 10,59,939$$

The above slight difference is due rounding of forward spot rate.

Interest rate parity can also be expressed as:

$$(I + i_A) = (F/S) (1 + i_B) \tag{13.4}$$

Rewriting the equation 13.4, we can calculate the fair (theoretical) forward exchange rate that is implied by the two interest rates and spot exchange rate:

$$F = S\left(\frac{1 + i_A}{1 + i_B}\right) \tag{13.5}$$

It should be noted that the theoretical forward rate is derived after making certain assumptions. If these assumptions are violated then actual forward rate may deviate from the theoretical forward rate. A few important assumptions are like commission to the forex dealer, borrowing and lending rates in each currency are same in both the countries. The taxes are ignored. Restrictions on borrowing and lending in another country are also not taken into consideration.

## 13.17 CALCULATION OF FORWARD BUYING AND SELLING RATES

In the preceding section we have determined the forward rate where only one interest rate is mentioned without differentiating between the borrowing rate and lending rate. If these two interest rates are different, the mechanism of calculation of forward buying and selling rates are stated as follows:

**EXAMPLE:** Following are the interest rates on a particular date:

| | Borrowing rate | Lending rate |
|---|---|---|
| British £ (1 year) | 4.00% p.a. | 4.25% p.a. |
| Indian ₹(1 year) | 5.50% p.a. | 6.00% p.a. |
| Spot rate (₹/£) | 72.5000/8,000 | |

Calculate the forward buying and selling rates.

*Solution:* Let us assume that a bank manager itself to buy £10,000 against Indian rupee after one year. In this respect how much rupees will have to pay out? It is explained in the following steps:

(i) Borrow a certain amount of £ BP from the money market—the sum being such that it would become £10,000 after one year (principal plus interest). Thus, the amount borrowed is the present value of £10,000 after one year.

$$\text{Borrowed money (BP £)} = \frac{10,000}{(1 + 4.25\%)} = \frac{10,000}{(1.0425)} = £9,592$$

(ii) Transform this amount in Indian rupees at market buying rate to get and invest.

$$£9,592 \times 72.5 = ₹6,95,420$$

(iii) Invest these rupees in Indian money market at borrowing one year rate for

$$₹6,95,420 \, (1.0550) = ₹7,33,668$$

(iv) Give these rupees to buy £10,000, thus, forward buying rate becomes

$$\frac{1}{£10,000} \, (₹\,7,33,668) \; = F(₹/£)(\text{buying}) = 7,33,668$$

or

$$F_b(₹/£) = \; 72.50 \left( \frac{1+5.5\%}{1+4.25\%} \right) = 73.3693$$

where $F_b$ is forward buying (Bid) rate. Thus, difference is due to rounding up the figure.

Let us now calculate the forward selling rate:

Suppose the bank engages itself to sell £10,000 against Indian rupees. The bank borrows a sum of rupees such that their conversion in £ and subsequent placement of these pounds in the money market which will result into £10,000 after one year. The following steps are taken:

(i) Borrowing of a sum, say $X$, of Indian rupees.

(ii) Conversion of $X$ rupees into British £ at the market spot selling rate to get British pound.

$$\frac{X}{72.8000} \; \text{British pound}$$

(iii) Invest these pounds in money market. After one year this will give

$$\frac{X}{72.8000} \, (1 + 0.04) \; \text{pound which should be equal to 10,000 pound.}$$

(iv) Reimbursing the Indian rupees along with interest which would be $X \, (1 + 0.06) = 10,000$ pounds.

or

$$f \frac{X}{72.8000} (1 + 1.04) \; = ₹X(1 + 0.06)$$

or

$$£1 = ₹ \, 72.8000 \times \frac{1 + 0.06}{1 + 0.04}$$

$F$ ask $(₹/£) = 74.2000$, this is forward selling rate.

Thus, one year forward ₹/£ quotation would be

$F \, (₹/£)$ one year $= 73.3693/74.2000$

## 13.18    EQUILIBRIUM IN THE FORWARD CURRENCY MARKET

As observed earlier that forward rates and currency rates are linked through interest rates. Usually forward rates do not fully incorporate with the interest rates. As a result, the forward exchange rate may be either overstated or understated what it should be as per the prevailing interest rates. It will create a position of disequilibrium in the market. In that case, arbitrage would take the benefit from the disequilibrium. Let us explain this by an example.

**EXAMPLE:**    Find the possible arbitrage gain from the following information:

Spot exchange rate $(₹/\$) = 46.1000$

Three-month forward rate $(₹/\$) = 46.5000$

Interest rates (Three-month) = ₹ 8.00% p.a.

Interest rates (Three-month) = $ 6.00% p.a.

*Solution:* Since rate of interest in US$ is lesser than Indian rupee, hence, there will be forward premium on US Dollar. Interest rate differential is 8% – 6% = 2%. Here US$ is at forward premium.

$$\frac{₹\,46.5000 - ₹\,46.1000}{₹\,46.1000} \times \frac{12}{3} \times 100 = 3.47\%$$

Interest rate differential:

$$8\% - 6\% = 2\% \text{ p.a.}$$

$$F(₹/\$) = S\left(\frac{1 + i_₹ \times t/12}{1 + i_\$ \times t/12}\right)$$

$$= ₹\,46.1000\left(\frac{1 + 0.08 \times 3/12}{1 + 0.06 \times 3/12}\right)$$

$$= ₹\,46.1000\left(\frac{1.020}{1.015}\right)$$

$$(₹/\$) = 46.3271 = \text{Theoretical forward rate}$$

Indian rupee is undervalued by ₹0.1729 (₹46.5000 – ₹46.3271) against US dollar. So there is arbitrage gain for selling the Indian rupee in forward market or taking short position against US dollar is beneficial. Let us explain this by the following examples:

If we borrow, say, ₹50,000 from Indian bank and exchange the same in US Dollar at current spot rate of 46.1000 and then invest the same in US money market @6 percent p.a. for three months. We will get $1100.87 (50,000/₹46.1000 × 1.015), and then exchange the same at the forward rate with Indian rupees to pay the loan taken from Indian bank @ 8 percent p.a., being ₹51,000 (50,000 × 1.02). We will get ₹51,190, ($1100.87 × 46.5000), and thus incurring gain of ₹190 (51,190 – 51,000) on this transaction. In other words, we will pay lesser amount in rupees if we borrow from Indian bank and investing the same in USA, since there is forward premium on US Dollar against Indian rupee.

On the other hand, if we borrow $1000 from US bank and exchange it in Indian rupee at the current spot rate of ₹46.1000 and then investing the same amount in Indian market, we will get after three months Indian rupee 47,022 (46,100 × 1.02). After that exchange this amount into US dollar at the forward rate (46.5000) in order to pay the loan taken from US bank being $1015 (1000 × 1.015 for three months @6 percent p.a.) which would be 1011.2, (₹47,022/46.5000), so there is loss of $3.8 (1,015 – 1,011.2).

## 13.19 HEDGING THROUGH FORWARD CONTRACTS

Forward rate is the unbiased predictor of future spot exchange rate. It is a well-known theory of foreign exchange rate determination. It means a forward exchange rate can be used to remove uncertainly over future exchange rates by trading in the future market. This market participants in the foreign exchange markets like exporters, importers, bankers, speculators, corporate houses borrowers, lender etc. can use this market to protect themselves from the foreign exchange risk. In other words, they can safeguard themselves against any reduction in the value of their payables and loans increasing due to change in exchange rates in future.

The importers who have to make a specified amount in foreign currency at a future date would be subject to loss due to increase in the price of the foreign currency. Similarly, the exporters who have to receive a definite amount of foreign currency at a future date may increase loss due to decrease in price of foreign currency in future period. For example, assume an exporter has sold goods worth $1,00,000 to a customer in USA on January 1, 2015 the spot rate of US Dollar on that date in the market was ₹63 per dollars. The exporters will receive the amount of sale proceeds after six months, i.e., June 30, 2015. The exporter is expecting to depreciate the dollar to ₹62.30 in the next six months.

On the enquiry from his bankers the exporter came to know that six months forward contract on US Dollar quotation was ₹62.50/80 per dollar. It means the banker is ready to purchase dollar at ₹62.50 (per dollar rate) after six months. Since the dollar will not depreciate as much as estimated, so the exporter decides to sell the said sale amount of $1,00,000 by booking forward contract of short with the banker. At maturity after six months, the position of the exporter on the settlement of the forward contract would be as:

The exporter will deliver to the banker: $1,00,000

The bank will pay to the exporters: ₹62,50,000

The impact of forward contract is to hedge against the future losses arise due to change in foreign exchange rates. Here the exporter by booking the forward contract of selling one lakh dollar at ₹62.50 per dollar after six months has mitigated any anticipated loss and has assured itself a specified cash flow in local currency in future. Consider, if the forward contract was not booked, then the exporter would have to sell its 1 lakh dollar at the spot market rate on June 30, 2015. If the rate falls to ₹62.30 per dollar as expected then he would have realized only ₹62,30,000. However, if the actual spot rate of dollar on June 30, 2015, might be higher or lower to the ₹62.50. So it should be noted that a forward contract just fixed cash flows in the domestic currency. They are used to protect future cash flows and not to maximize value on those cash flows, rather providing protection from any downside in return.

## 13.20 SPECULATING WITH FORWARD CONTRACTS

The basic objective of any speculator is to make profit in future, simply on the difference of prices and intending for delivery of the underlying asset. For example, if a speculator finds forward rates attractive bets on them with the making a super profit. Let us assume that spot rate of US Dollar is ₹63.60 and 3 months forward price is 63.80 at an annualized premium of 1.258 percent. The speculator feels that the dollar is undervalued and should command better premium the speculator decides to buy US Dollar 3 months at ₹63.80. The speculator keeps a continuous watch on the exchange rate movements and act as per market developments. Let us assume that after 3 months, actual spot rate of US Dollar is ₹64 and he can earn a profit of ₹0.20 per dollar. Alternatively, if the spot rate moves below ₹63.80 per US Dollar, then he can wait till the contract matures or can exercise the contract as per market development.

**EXAMPLE:** From the following data, calculate the lower and upper bound to forward rates for three months.

| Spot rate (rupee per dollar) | Bid Rate/64.00 | Ask Rate/65.00 |
|---|---|---|
| Interest rate on | Borrowing rate | Lending rate |
| Rupee (₹) | 8% p.a. | 10.00% p.a. |
| US Dollar ($) | 4% p.a. | 6.00% p.a. |

***Solution***:   To determine lower bound of the Ask rate:

- Borrow dollars at the lending rate at 6% p.a. for three months. Borrow 1$ @1.5% (for three months) amount to repay = $1.015
- Convert spot into local currency (rupee ) at the bid rate: ₹64.00
- Invest the local currency at the lending rate for period of forward = Invest for 3 months at 8% p.a. and get ₹1.02 × 64 = ₹65.28
- Sell at the forward ask rate the matured amount to convert into foreign currency

$$= 65.28/FA < 1.015$$
$$FA = 65.28/1.015 = ₹64.3153$$

For no arbitrage, we must have FA > ₹64.3153

To determine the upper bound on the bid rate:

Borrow  rupee at lending rate 10 % p.a. for three months

- Borrow 1.00 @10 % p.a. (3 months). Amount to pay = 1.025
- Convert spot into local currency (dollar) at the ask rate convert dollar at the spot ask rate and get $1/65.00 = 0.0154
- Invest the foreign currency at the lending rate for the period of forward.
- Invest for 3 months at 4% p.a. = 1.00 × 0.0154 = 0.01555
- Sell at the forward rate $F_b$ to get = $F_b$ × 0.01555

$$= F_b × 0.01555 \leq 1.025 = 65.9164$$

For no arbitrage, we must have ≤ ₹65.9164

# SUMMARY

This chapter has introduced the basic concepts of foreign exchange forward market. In most financial markets, the traders and market participants who wish to establish prices for futures period usually use the futures markets. The foreign exchange forward market also co-exists simultaneously with the foreign exchange spot market, foreign exchange option market and foreign future market.

The basic objective of a forward market in any underlying asset is to fix at once a price for a contract to be carried through on the futures agreed date, and intend to free both the purchaser and seller from any risk of loss which might incur due to fluctuations in the price of the underlying asset. Forward exchange contract may be defined as an operation of foreign exchange whereby a rate is fixed at once for a purchase and sale of one currency for another which is to be executed in future on a specified date.

There are various features of forward contract like nature of contract, terms of contract, future date, mode of payment, payment in particular currency, commission, etc. Trading mechanism in forward exchange market is very simple because forward contracts are not traded on the particular exchange. They are just like private contracts between the two parties. Forward exchange contracts are amazingly versatile. They are available in two dozen or more currencies, and for maturities ranging from one week to several years. Most of them have a maturity of less than two years. Long dated contracts have relatively large bid-ask asked spreads.

The forex dealers may quote currencies in terms of premium and discount on them in the forward markets. Premium which means that forward rate is dearer than the spot rate. Discount means that the forward rate is less than the spot rate. Forward rate can be expressed in two ways: (a) outright rate (b) swap rate. When the forward rate is calculated by using the premium/discount, it is called outright rate. A swap rate is used to convert the spot rate into outright rate by adding or subtracting swap points.

A non-deliverable forward contract refers to that forward contract where the delivery for the underlying asset whether it is currency, commodity, financial security, etc. is not required. The NDF contract is settled by making a net payment. The net payment is paid in any agreed convertible underlying pair of currencies. Net payment is calculated to difference between the agreed forward exchange rate and subsequently realized amount at the spot fixing rate.

On comparison of forward and futures currency contracts, it is observed that both the contracts offer the sale and purchase of a particular currency in future period at a specified rate. However, both are different in many respects like that the futures contracts are performed through the recognized exchanges which have their own bye-laws to regulate the future trading. Hence future currency contracts are standardized in all respects like specified size, maturity dates, settlement, delivery, pricing, etc. In case of forward contracts, these are basically arisen to fulfil the specific needs of one of the contracting party. In other words, they are tailor-made contracts and thus they are just like personal contract between the two parties.

The no-arbitrage or theoretical or fair price of a forward contract is that which provides no opportunity for arbitrage profits. It is related with the interest rates differential of the concerned currencies in the forward contract, which is also referred to as covered interest-arbitrage. Forward rate is based upon spot rate and differential of interest rates of two currencies underlying the forward contract. A currency will be at premium/in future if its rate of interest is lower in comparison to other currency in the forward contract.

Chapter discusses the fixed vs option forward contracts. Fixed forward contract under which the delivery of foreign exchange should take place on a specified futures date, it is known as outright forward contract. On the other hand, in option forward contract no specific date is fixed, rather a period is mentioned during which the contract can be completed. So a forward contract wherein one of the parties has an option to make or take delivery of any day within a specified interval is called option forward contract.

In the last, chapter discusses the hedging, arbitraging and speculating with the forward contracts. How the trader will use the forward contract for hedging the risk, earning through speculation and arbitrage process is discussed with examples.

## SOLVED PROBLEMS

**P.1.**   Calculate the premium for the three-month forward rate, if spot $S(₹/\$) = 45.6500/7,000$ and three-month forward rate is $F(₹/\$) = 45.5000/5,500$.

*Solution:*                     Buying spot rate (₹/$) = 45.65
                                Buying forward rate (₹/$) = 45.50

$$\text{For the buyer of dollar} = \frac{₹\,45.5000 - ₹\,45.6500}{₹\,45.50000} \times \frac{12}{3} \times 100$$

$$= 1.318\%$$

$$\text{For the seller of dollar} = \frac{₹\,45.5500 - ₹\,45.7000}{₹\,45.5500} \times \frac{12}{3} \times 100$$

$$= ₹1.317\%$$

**P.2.** From the following figures calculate the forward discount/premium:

Dollars spot price of pound = 1.5386

Dollars three-month forward rate = 1.5530

*Solution:*
$$\text{Forward premium} = \frac{1.5530 - 1.5386}{1.5386} \times \frac{12}{3} \times 100$$

Pound on premium = 3.74% per annum

**P.3.** Assume a Hong Kong based firm, XYZ Company, wishes to pay its Singaporean supplier $1 million. An officer of the treasury department of XYZ has his exchange trading at his bank. Hong Kong Bank wants to sell him $1 million. Bank quoted rate, say HK$21.00 per Singapore dollar. How transaction will take place of the above problem?

*Solution:*

(a) Hong Kong Bank will debit XYZ's current account in Hong Kong for HK$2,10,00,000 (and credit that amount to its correspondent bank's account).

(b) It will instruct its correspondent bank in Singapore (one in which it keeps a current account balance) to debit Hong Kong's Bank account and credit the amount to the account of the Singaporean firm with banking system of Singapore.

**P.4.** From the US$ based quotations for the New Zealand dollar (NZ$) and the Indonesian rupiah (IR), calculate the cross rate for the NZ$ in terms of the rupiah. Quotations are as follows:

New Zealand dollar = NZ$/US$1.9552

Indonesia rupiah = IR/US$2054

*Solution:* Calculation of cross rate by dividing the rate for rupiah by the rate for the New Zealand

$$\frac{NZ\$}{US\$} = \frac{1.955}{1}$$

$$\frac{IR}{US\$} = \frac{2054}{1}$$

$$\text{Cross rate (IR/NZ\$)} = \frac{IR/US\$2054}{NZ\$/US\$1.9552} = IR/NZ\$1050.5$$

$$\frac{IR}{US\$} = \frac{2054}{1.955} = 1050.5$$

**P.5.** A company based in US buys spare parts from UK with payment of £2 million due in 90 days. The importer, thus, is short pounds, i.e., he owes pounds for future delivery. Present price of pound is $1.72. But importer is of fear that value of pound will rise in coming 90 days. How US based company can use the forward contract to reduce this risk. Suppose three-month forward rate is $1.75/£.

*Solution:* Importer will buy a forward contract at $1.75 from American Express bank and can hedge the position. American Express will deliver $2 million whatsoever is the rate of the pound after three months in the market. The position can be shown as follows:

Spot rate ($/£) = 1.72

Three-month forward rate ($/£) = 1.75

Buy a forward contract at $1.75/£

**P.6.** Following are the interest rate on a particular date:

|  | Borrowing rate | Lending rate |
|---|---|---|
| British £ (1 year) | 5% p.a. | 5.25% p.a. |
| Indian ₹(1 year) | 6% p.a. | 6.50% p.a. |
| Spot rate (₹/$) | 72.5000/8,000 |  |

Calculate the forward buying and selling rates. Let us assume that the bank manager itself has to buy £10,000 against Indian rupees after one year. In this respect how much rupees he will have to pay out?

*Solution:*

(i) Borrow a certain amount of (£) BP from money market and sum would become £10,000 after one year (principal plus interest).

So amount borrowed:

$$BP(£) = \frac{10,000}{1 + 5.25\%} = \frac{10,000}{1.0525} = £9501$$

(ii) Transform this amount in Indian rupees at market buying rate to get and invest:

$$£9501 \times 72.5 = ₹6,88,822$$

(iii) Invest these rupees in Indian money market at borrowing rate for one year:

$$₹6,88,822(1.060) = ₹7,30,15,132$$

(iv) Give these rupees to buy £10,000, thus forward buying rate:

$$\frac{1}{£10,000}(₹\,7,30,151) \ = F(₹/£)\text{buying rate}$$

$$= 73.151$$

or

$$F(₹/£) = 72.50 \, \frac{1 + 6\%}{1 + 5.25\%}$$

$$= 72.50 \, \frac{1.06}{1.0525}$$

$$= 72.50 \, (1.0071)$$

$$\text{Buying} = 73.01$$

*Selling rate:* Suppose bank engage itself to sell £10,000 against Indian rupees. Following steps are taken:

(i) Borrowing of a sum, say, $X$ of Indian rupees.

(ii) Conversion of $X$ rupees into British £ at the spot selling rate to sell BP.

$$\frac{X}{72.5000}\text{BP}$$

(iii) Invest these pounds in money market. After one year this will give

$$\frac{X}{72.5000}\text{BP} \,(1.05) \text{ pound which should be equal to } 10,000 \text{ pound.}$$

(iv) Reimbursing the Indian rupees along with interest which would be $X(1 + 0.065) = X(1.065)$ ₹ = 10,000 pounds.

or $\qquad \pounds \dfrac{X}{72.5000}(1 + 0.05) = X(1 + 0.065)$ ₹

or $\qquad\qquad \pounds 1 = 72.500 \times \dfrac{1 + 0.065}{1 + 0.05}$ ₹

$$= 72.500 \times \dfrac{1.065}{1.05} \text{ ₹} = 73.537$$

Selling rate $= 73.54$ and $F(\text{₹}/\pounds) = 73.01/73.54$

## SUGGESTED READINGS

1. Winbtone, David, *Financial Derivatives*, Chapman and Hall, London, 1995.
2. Adrian, Buckley, *The Essence of International Money*, 2nd ed., Prentice-Hall, Hemel Hempstead, 1996.
3. Stonban, Paul, and Redhead Keith, *European Casebook on Finance*, Prentice-Hall, Hamel Hempstead, 1995.
4. Apte, P.G., *Global Business Finance*, Tata McGraw-Hill, New Delhi, 1998.
5. Cavanaugh, K., Price dynamics in foreign currency markets, *Journal of International Money and Finance*, pp. 295–314, 1987.
6. Chang, C. and Chang, J., Forward and futures prices: Evidence from the foreign exchange markets, *Journal of Finance*, 45:4, pp. 1333–1336, September 1990.
7. French, K., Detecting spot price forecasts in futures prices, *Journal of Business,* 59, pp. 539–554, 1986.
8. BIS Quarterly Review, March 2014.

## REVIEW QUESTIONS

1. Explain the forward foreign exchange market. What are its important features? Explain with examples.
2. Explain the mechanism of dealing at the forward exchange market with suitable examples.
3. Explain the term forward exchange rate quotation. How forward rates are quoted? Explain.
4. Differentiate between foreign exchange forward and foreign exchange futures contracts with suitable example.
5. "Currency futures are safer as compared to currency forward contracts." Explain the statement with suitable examples.
6. List out actively traded currencies on which foreign exchange forward contracts are available, and their mechanism of trading.
7. Write a note on methods of dealing in forward exchange.
8. Write short notes on
   (a) Forward exchange quotations
   (b) Premium and discount in the forward exchange markets
9. What are various ways in which currency forward rate can be expressed? Explain with suitable examples.

10. What are various general guidelines in determining the value dates in forward contract? Explain with suitable examples.

11. Compare and contrast between currency forward and futures contracts. Which one is better for a trader, and why? Examine critically?

12. "Pricing of currency forward contract is no different from the other financial derivatives." Do you agree? Examine and explain the statement.

13. Write a detailed note on currency forward buying and selling rates.

14. "Usually forward rates do not fully incorporate with the interest rates." Explain the statement in the light of equilibrium in the forward currency markets.

15. Write short notes on the following with suitable examples:
    (a) Fixed v/s option forward contracts
    (b) Broken dates forward contracts

16. Discuss the structure of forward currency market in India.

17. Explain with suitable examples how a trader can hedge his risk in forward exchange market.

18. Discuss the relationship between spot and forward prices in context to foreign exchange markets.

19. What are various steps in booking of forward contracts? Explain.

20. Discuss the role of bid-ask in pricing the foreign forward exchange contracts.

21. Write a detailed note on importance of forward exchange market in managing the corporate financial risk with suitable examples.

22. What are various factors that determine the price of a foreign currency?

23. Explain the nature, features and trading mechanism of non-deliverable forward contracts in foreign exchange.

24. Explain the role of NDF in foreign exchange markets with suitable examples.

# Annexure

## Forward Foreign Exchange Market in India Eligibility for Entering in Forward Contract in India

### As per the website of the RBI

**A. Forward contract**

1. A person resident in India may enter into a forward contract with an authorized dealer in India to hedge an exposure to exchange risk in respect of a transaction for which sale and/or purchase of foreign exchange is permitted under the act or rules or regulations or directions or orders made or issued thereunder, subject to the following terms and conditions:

   (a) The authorized dealer through verification of documentary evidence is satisfied about the genuineness of the underlying exposure.

   (b) The maturity of the hedge does not exceed the maturity of the underlying transaction.

   (c) The currency of hedge and tenor are left to the choice of the customer.

   (d) Where the exact amount of the underlying transaction is not ascertainable, the contract is booked on the basis of a reasonable estimate.

   (e) Foreign currency loans/bonds will be eligible for hedge only after final approval is accorded by the Reserve Bank where such approval is necessary.

   (f) In case of Global Depository Receipts (GDRs) the issue price has been finalized.

   (g) Balances in the Exchange Earner's Foreign Currency (EEFC) accounts sold forward by the account holders will remain earmarked for delivery and such contracts will not be cancelled. They may however, be rolled over.

   (h) Contracts involving rupee as one of the currencies, once cancelled will not be rebooked although they can be rolled over at ongoing rates on or before maturity. This restriction will not apply to contracts covering export transactions which may be cancelled, rebooked or rolled over at ongoing rates.

   (i) Substitution of contracts for hedging trade transactions may be permitted by an authorized dealer on being satisfied with the circumstances under which such substitution has become necessary.

**B. Contract other than forward contract**

2(1) A person resident in India who has borrowed foreign exchange in accordance with the provisions of Foreign Exchange Management (Borrowing and Lending in Foreign Exchange) Regulations, 2000, may enter into an interest rate swap or currency swap or coupon swap or foreign currency option or interest rate cap or collar (purchases) or Forward Rate Agreement (FRA) contract with an authorized dealer in India or with a branch outside India of an authorized dealer for hedging his loan exposure and unwinding from such hedges, provided that

   (a) the contract does not involve rupee

   (b) the Reserve Bank has accorded final approval for borrowing in foreign currency

   (c) the maturity of the hedge does not exceed the un-expired maturity of the underlying loan

(2) A person resident in India, who owes a foreign exchange or rupee liability, may enter into a contract for foreign currency-rupee swap with an authorized dealer in India to hedge long-term exposure.

(3) The contract entered into under sub-paragraph 2, if cancelled, will not be rebooked or re-entered, by whatever name called.

3(1) A person resident in India may enter into a foreign currency option contract with an authorized dealer in India to hedge foreign exchange exposure of such person arising out of his trade. Provided that in respect of cost effective risk reduction strategies like range forwards, ratio-range forwards or any other variable, by whatever name called, there will not be any net inflow of premium.

*Explanation:*   The contingent foreign exchange exposure arising out of submission of a tender bid in foreign exchange is also eligible for hedging under this sub-paragraph.

(2) The transactions undertaken under sub-paragraph (1) may be freely booked and/or cancelled.

## SCHEDULE II

Foreign exchange derivative contracts permissible for a person resident outside India

1. A registered Foreign Institutional Investor (FII) may enter into a forward contract with rupee as one of the currencies with an authorized dealer in India to hedge its exposure in India, provided that

   (a) the value of the hedge does not exceed the current market value in respect of investments in debt instruments

   (b) the value of the hedge does not exceed 15 percent of the market value of the equity as at the close of business on March 31, 1999, converted at the rate of US$1 = ₹42.43 plus the increase in market value/inflows after March 31, 1999 provided that the forward cover once taken shall be allowed to continue as long as it does not exceed the value of the underlying investment

   (c) forward contracts once cancelled shall not be rebooked but may be rolled over on or before the maturity

   (d) the cost of hedge is met out of repatriable funds and/or inward remittance through normal banking channel

   (e) all outward remittances incidental to hedge are net of applicable Indian taxes

2. A non-resident Indian or Overseas Corporate Body may enter into forward contract with rupee as one of the currencies, with an authorized dealer in India to hedge;

   (a) the amount of dividend due to him/it on shares held in an Indian company

   (b) the balances held in Foreign Currency Non-Resident (FCNR) account or Non-Resident External Rupee (NRE) account

3. Reserve Bank may, on application, allow a person resident outside India to purchase a forward contract to hedge his investment made since January 1, 1993.

## SCHEDULE III

Procedure for application for approval for hedging of commodity price risk

1. A person resident in India, engaged in export–import trade, who seeks to hedge price risk in respect of any commodity including gold, but excluding oil and petroleum products, may

submit an application to the International Banking Division of an authorized dealer giving the following details.

(i) A brief description of the hedging strategy proposed, namely,

    (a) description of business activity and nature of risk

    (b) instruments proposed to be used for hedging

    (c) names of commodity exchange and brokers through whom the risk is proposed to be hedged and credit lines proposed to be availed. The name and address of the regulatory authority in the country concerned may also be given

    (d) size/average tenure of exposure and/or total turnover in a year, together with expected peak positions thereof and the basis of calculation

(ii) Copy of the Risk Management Policy approved by the management covering:

    (a) risk identification

    (b) risk measurements

    (c) guidelines and procedures to be followed with respect to revaluation and/or monitoring of positions

    (d) names and designations of the officials authorized to undertake transactions and limits

(iii) Any other relevant information

2. Authorized dealer after ensuring that the application is supported by documents indicated in Paragraph 1, may forward the application with its recommendations to Reserve Bank for consideration.

# SECTION IV

# Financial Swaps

# Swaps Markets

After reading this chapter, students will be able to

➢ Understand the basic concept of swap, its nature and features.
➢ Be aware of the evolution of swap market.
➢ Know the major types of financial swaps like interest rate swaps, currency swaps and equity swaps, along with their features.
➢ Be aware of the different types of interest rate swaps available in swap markets.
➢ Know risks related to swap trading.
➢ Understand the structure and of trading mechanism of swaps.
➢ Know the valuation of interest rate swaps.
➢ Explain the concept of debt-equity swap.
➢ Know the motivation underlying swap transactions.
➢ Know the swap arrangement in India.
➢ Understand the basis swap, leveraged swap, commodity swap, differential swap, etc.
➢ Know about the amortizing swap, At-market and off-market swap, etc.
➢ Understand applications of swap.

## 14.1 INTRODUCTION

The swap market, today, makes the most significant development in the global financial market. It has fundamentally transformed the way in which corporate business world and the bankers look at funding choices. Swaps are frequently used by them to arrange complex and innovative financing which decrease borrowing costs and increase control over other financial variables. This market has gained popularity specifically after the end of Bretton Woods System which caused to the instability in international funds movements.

Recently, the volume and size of swaps markets has grown multifold as a result of liberalization, globalization, deregulation and integration of national capital markets. They have created a major impact on the corporate's treasury functions, permitting them to tap new capital markets and to take further use of new financial instruments without increasing risk thereon. In fact, swaps have led to refinement of the risk management technique, which in turn facilitate corporate involvement in functioning of international financial markets.

In this section, we will discuss the concept of the 'swap', evolution of swap markets, features of swap markets, different types of swap instruments, valuation of swap, and then finally, mechanism of hedging with the swaps.

## 14.2  SWAP: CONCEPT AND NATURE

The meanings of word 'Swap' or 'Swop' as per the Chambers Dictionary are to barter or to give in exchange or to exchange one for another. So, in the business world, swaps have been defined as *private agreements between the two parties to exchange cash flows in the future according to a prearranged formula.* In simple words, a swap is an agreement to exchange payments of two different kinds in the future. Since it involves exchange of cash flows or payments, it is also called *financial swap* in global financial markets.

In the context of financial markets, the term 'swap' has two meanings. First, it is a purchase and simultaneous forward sale or vice versa. Second, it is defined as the agreed exchange of future cash flows, possibly, but not necessarily with a spot exchange of cash flows. The second definition of swap is most commonly used stating as an agreement to the future exchange of cash flows. These can be regarded as series or portfolios of forward contracts. Such a currency swap is similar to a succession of forward foreign exchange contracts with relatively more distant maturity basis. The study of swap is, thus, a natural extension of the study of forward and futures contracts.

Financial swap is a specific funding technique which permits a borrower to access one market and then exchange the liability for another type of liability. In other words, swaps can be helpful to change the nature of liability accrued on a particular instrument with the others. It means that swaps are not a funding instrument, rather just like a device to obtain the desired form of financing indirectly which otherwise might be inaccessible or too expensive.

Since, the swaps involve the exchange of cash flows, there is a wide variety of basis of cash flows in a business firm. For example, in case of interest payments, the typical exchange may be of cash flows arising from a fixed rate of interest to cash flows arising from floating rate of interest. Foreign currency transactions can be exchanged with the different cash flows arising out in different currencies. Equity swaps tend to involve cash flows based on the returns from a stock index portfolio being exchanged for the cash flows based on an interest rate. Basically, swaps involve the exchange of interest or currency exposures or a combination of both by two or more borrowers. They may not necessarily involve the legal swapping of actual debts but an agreement is executed to meet certain cash flows under loan or lease agreements.

Swaps market exists because different companies and institutions have specific access to various financial markets, and further they have different needs. For example, some of the firms may have better access in Japanese market than others, whereas some others may have good reputation in the

US market. Further, some firms need floating rate payments. It is often a more advantageous to 'swap' payments with another party, thus, transforming one's liability, rather than borrowing directly in the desired markets.

In brief, it is noted that the 'swap' is OTC agreement between the two parties to exchange predetermined amount of cash flows in future as per desired predetermined formula along with others terms and conditions. Only the net payment changes hands, known as *difference check*.

**EXAMPLE:** January 1, 2015, Company X and Company Y enters into a 5-year interest rate swap with the following terms:

- Company X pays Company Y an amount equal to 10 percent at fixed interest rate per annum on a notional principal of ₹5,00,000.
- Company Y pays Company X an amount equal to one-year MIBOR + 4 percent per annum on a notional principal of ₹5,00,000.

The payoff for both the parties will be assuming the MIBOR as 8 percent on January 1, 2016.

As per swap agreement, the Company X will pay to Company Y ₹5,00,000 @10 percent p.a. and the Company Y will pay to Company X ₹5,00,000 @ MIBOR + 4 percent p.a. The settlement will take place at the differential amount on January 1, 2016. Since MIBOR is 8 percent on January 1, 2016, so Company 'Y' will be in loss by 2 percent because he will be paying (8 + 4 = 12%) to 'X' Company and receiving 10 percent only. So, compensation amount, also called differential check, of 2 percent on ₹5,00,000, i.e., ₹10,000 will be paid by Company Y to Company X.

## 14.3 EVOLUTION OF SWAP MARKET

Like most other new products/instruments in the international finance, 'swaps' are not executed in a physical market. Participants and dealers in the swap markets are many and varied in their location, character and motives in existing swaps. Most of the financial experts agree that the origin of the swap markets can be traced back to 1970s when many countries imposed foreign exchange regulations and restrictions in order to control cross-border capital flows. Some experts are of the opinion that swap markets owe their origin to the exchange rate instability that followed the end of Bretton Wood System during the years 1971 to 1973. As a result, most of the borrowers and investors at the international level wishing to diversify their assets and liabilities compositions in varied currencies in order to control losses arising due to fluctuations in exchange rates.

In 1980s, a few countries liberalized their exchange regulatory measures, as a result, some of the MNCs' treasurers structured their portfolios and brought out a new financial product, known as *swaps*. They replaced their existing contracts like parallel and back-to-back loans with the swap deals which found them more flexible and suitable due to simpler documentation and single jurisdiction. Further, swaps were found to lower financing cost and tax differences in comparison to above stated contracts. Not only this, the disintermediation process of 1980s, most of the MNCs and other corporate borrowers were approaching to the investors directly rather than through banks, also encourage them to make financial arrangements through swaps.

The first swap contract was negotiated in 1981 between Deutsche Bank and an undisclosed counter party. Since then, the swaps market has grown very rapidly. In the early years, the bankers were only acting as brokers in the swap markets to match the complimentary requirements of the counter parties. The major dramatic change in the swap market has been the emergence of the large banks and performed as aggressive market makers specifically in dollar interest rate swaps. As market makers, they provide bid/offer quotes for both interest rate and currency swaps. Subsequently, the banks started to find out a counter party with exactly or nearly matching requirements to hedge the original swap by entering into a matching swap. Such swap warehousing or running mismatches offered two immediate benefits; for the customer it was possible to cover an exposure almost as soon as the decision to do so, and for the swap bank to quote the most competitive price to their clients in order to get maximum business from the clients.

The formation of the International Swap Dealers Association (ISDA) in 1984 was a significant development to speed up the growth in the swaps market by standardizing swap documentation. In 1985, the ISDA published the first standardized swap code. This code was revised in 1986, and in 1987 published its Standard Form Agreements. These contracts are structured as master agreements. As such, all subsequent swaps entered by the same parties are treated as supplements to the original agreement.

As observed above, a swap is essentially a way of changing risk in future, and the range of risks hedged through swap transactions is expanding day-by-day. For instance, currency swaps were first introduced in late 1970s, and then interest rate swaps in 1981, equity and commodity swaps in mid-1980s and credit derivatives in 1990, were floated. Climatic derivatives have also been introduced recently, and further, a few new products are also being examined to include in this market.

## 14.4 FEATURES OF SWAPS

Important features of a swap agreement, in general, are stated as follows:

**A. Counterparties:** All swaps involve the exchange of a series of periodic payments between at least two parties. For example, a firm having a loan of ten million dollar payable at ten percent fixed coupon rate for five years, wants to exchange for a floating interest rate with that party who is also interested to exchange its liability from floating to fixed. It means, for a swap agreement, there must be two parties who are ready to exchange their liabilities with each other. The firm paying the floating rate is the swap seller, and the firm paying the fixed rate is swap buyer.

**B. Facilitators:** Swap agreements are arranged mostly, (known as swap facilitators), through an intermediary which is usually a large international financial institution/bank having network of its operations in major countries. This institution is normally having contracts with major international business firms who have direct link with other firms. These intermediaries play a significant role in bringing closer the various parties for such deals. They will note down the requirements of the parties and try to match and fulfill these with other parties. Swap facilitators can be classified into two categories:

*Brokers.* They function as agents that identify and bring the counterparties on the table for the swap deal. The broker's basic objective is to initiate the counterparties to finalize the swap deal according to their respective requirements.

*Swap dealers.* They themselves become counterparties and takeover the risk. They are also called *Swap Bank.* Since the swap dealers are the part of the swap deals, therefore, they face two important problems. First, how to price swap to provide for his service. Second, the swap dealer creates a portfolio, therefore, the second problem is to manage this portfolio, known as *Swap book.*

**C. Cash flows:** In the swap deal, two different payment streams in terms of cash flows are estimated to have identical present values at the outset when discounted at the respective cost of funds in the relevant primary markets. As described earlier, swap deal is an exchange of two financial obligations in future, obviously, both the parties would desire to have same financial liabilities as before the swap deal. So, in swap deal, the present value of future cash streams are examined, and then appropriate decision is taken.

**D. Documentations:** Swap transactions may be set up with great speed since their documentations and formalities are generally much less in comparable to loan deals. Basically, in swap deals, it is an evaluation of various futures cash streams arose out in various contracts done in past. If the terms of different contracts suit the interested firm's requirements, the deal will be enacted. Thus, such deals are less complicated, less time consuming and simpler in terms of documentations and other formalities.

**E. Transaction costs:** It has been also observed that transaction costs are relatively low in swap transactions in comparison to loan agreements. They are unlikely to exceed half percent of the total sum involved in the swap agreement.

**F. Benefit to parties:** Swap deals are needed as long as it is profitable to transform them. In other words, swap agreements will be done only when the parties will be benefited by such agreement, otherwise such deals will not be accepted. This will be discussed further in the economics of swaps.

**G. Termination:** Since swap is an agreement between two parties, therefore, it cannot be terminated at one's instance. The termination also requires to be accepted by counter parties.

**H. Default risk:** Since most of the swap deals are bilateral agreements, therefore, the problems of potential default by either of the counter party exist, hence, making them more risky products in comparison to futures and options.

## 14.5 MAJOR TYPES OF FINANCIAL SWAPS

As observed earlier, the basic objective of a swap deal is to hedge the risk as desired by the counter parties. The major risks, which can be changed with the swap transactions, are relating to interest rate, currency, commodity, equity, credit, climate and so on. Hence, in this section only important financial swaps, which are popular in financial markets, have been discussed.

1. Interest Rate Swaps
2. Currency Swaps
3. Equity Swaps
4. Miscellaneous Swaps

## 14.6 INTEREST RATE SWAPS

An interest rate swap is a financial agreement between the two parties who wish to change the interest payments or receipts in the same currency on assets or liabilities to a different basis. There is no exchange of principal amount in this swap. In other words, it is an exchange of interest payment for a specific maturity on an agreed upon notional amount. The term 'notional' refers to the theoretical principal underlying the swap. The principal amount applies only for the purpose of calculating the interest to be exchanged under an interest rate swap. Maturities range from a year to over 15 years, however, most transactions fall within two years to ten years period.

The simplest example of interest rate swap is to exchange of fixed for floating rate interest payments between two parties in the same currency. This is also known as *plain vanilla swap* in the market, exchange of borrowings, or coupon swap. It involves credit differentials between two borrowers in the fixed and floating debt markets which generate substantial cost savings for both the counter parties. The party who pays the fixed rate, is called *the buyer of the swap*. It means he has long the swap. Similarly, the party who pays the floating rate, is called *the seller of the swap*, which means he has short the swap. Only, the net payment changes hands, so the firm obliged to pay the higher rate remits cash to the other, popularly known as *difference check*.

**EXAMPLE:**   December, 2013, Company X and Company Y enters into a five-year swap with the following terms:

- Company X pays Company Y an amount equal to 8.50% (fixed interest rate) as per annum on a notional principal of ₹5,00,000
- Company Y pays Company X an amount equal to one-year MIBOR + 2% per annum on a notional principal of ₹5,00,000

Decide the payoff for both the parties.

*Solution:*   As on December 31, 2014:

- Company X will pay to Company Y ₹5,00,000 × 8.5% = ₹4,25,000
- Let us assume as on December 31, 2014, one-year MIBOR is 7%. Therefore, Company B will pay Company X ₹5,00,000 × (7.00 + 2.1%) = ₹4,50,000. Hence, Company X would be profitable.
- The settlement takes place through the net payment that is Company Y would pay ₹25,000 to Company X. At no point does the principal change hands, which is why it is referred to as a "notional" amount.
- Assume if MIBOR in December, 2015 becomes 6%, then Company Y would pay to Company X at the rate 8% (6% + 2%) and Company X would pay Company Y at the rate of 8.5%. In this case Company Y would be profitable. Here Company X will pay ₹25,000 to Company Y.
- Diagram below indicates the cash flows between the parties, which occur annually.

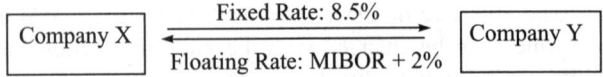

Company rating generally plays vital role in case of market borrowing. A good rating reduced the cost of borrowing significantly. It may also happen that a company may be good in getting funds at lower floating rate and another company may be getting fund at lower fixed rate. Hence, there are many possibilities for arrangement of interest rate swaps.

## 14.6.1   Features of Interest Rate Swaps

The key features of interest rate swaps are stated as follows:

- (i) **Notional principal:**   In the interest rate swap agreement, the interest amount whether fixed or floating is calculated on a specified amount borrowed or lent. It is notional because the parties do not exchange this amount at any time. Normally, it remains constant throughout the life of the swap. It is used to compute the sequence of the payment of cash flows.
- (ii) **Fixed rate:**   This is the rate, which is used to calculate the size of the fixed payment. Banks or the other financial institutions who make market in interest rate swaps quote the fixed rate, they are willing to pay if they are fixed rate payers in a swap (bid swap rates),

they are willing to receive if they are floating rate payers in a swap (ask swap rate). For example, a bank might quote a US dollar floating to fixed 5-year swap rate:

Treasuries + 20 bp/Treasuries + 40 bp. vs. six-month LIBOR

This quote indicates the following:

1. The said bank is willing to make fixed payment at a rate equal to the current yield on 5-year treasury notes plus 20 basis points (0.20%) in return for receiving floating payments, say at six-month LIBOR.

2. The bank has offered to accept at a rate equal to 5-year treasury notes plus 40 basis points in return for payment of six-month LIBOR.

(iii) **Floating rate:** Floating rate may be defined as one of the market indexes like LIBOR, SIBOR, and MIBOR. The floating interest rate in the swap agreement is determined on the basis of Treasury Bill rate, primary rate, etc. The maturity of the underlying index equals the interval between payment dates. Floating rate payment is set one period before the payment date. It means that the net payment to be made on any date is actually known one period earlier. On the fixed payment side, a year is assumed to be 365 days, whereas on floating payment side a year is assumed to be 360 days.

(iv) **Swap quotation:** A dealer can quote a swap into two different ways. First way is the all in quote. Swap rate is the interest rate paid on the fixed interest rate leg of the swap, also called swap price. For example, if a dealer quotes a swap rate of 7.75–7.25. The quote would mean that the dealer receives 7.75 percent fixed and pays LIBOR, or pays 7.25 percent fixed and receives LIBOR. The second way to quote the swap is called as *swap spread*. Swap spread is the difference between the fixed rate paid on the swap and the fixed rate on a par risk-free bond of same maturity. For example, a quote on a 5-year bond at a spread rate: 40–50. It means that the dealer would pay the rate on 5-year bond plus 40 basis points and received LIBOR. Further, he will receive the rate on 5-year bond plus 50 basis points and will pay LIBOR. In both the cases, the swap dealer makes a market and is willing to pay either the fixed rate or floating rate.

(v) **Trade date, effective date, reset date and payment date:** All the above stated dates are important terms in the swap deal. Therefore, the concept of these dates must be clear to the swap dealers. The fixed rate payments are normally paid semi-annually or annually. For example, it may be March 1, September 1, etc. The *trade date* may be defined as the date on which the swap deal is concluded. Effective date is that date from which the first fixed and floating payment start to accrue. Normally after two days of the trade date. For example, a 5-year swap is traded on August 30, 2002, the effective date may be September 1, 2002, and ten payment dates from March 1, 2003 to September 1, 2007. It should be noted that the floating rate payments in a standard swap are set in advance paid in arrears.

Each floating rate payment in a standard swap deal has three dates associated with it, which is shown as follows:

*Relevant dates for the floating payment.*

(1) $D(S)$,      (2) $D(1)$, and      (3) $D(2)$

where $D(S)$ is the setting date on which the floating rate applicable for the next payment is set, $D(1)$ is that date from which the next floating payment starts to accrue and $D(2)$ is such date on which the payment is due.

*Fixed and floating payments:* In a standard swap deal the fixed and floating payments are calculated as follows:

$$\text{Fixed payment} = (P) \times (Rfx) \times (Ffx)$$
$$\text{Floating payment} = (P) \times (Rfe) \times (Ffe)$$

where $P$ is the notional payment, $Rfx$ is the fixed price, $Rfe$ is the floating rate set on the reset date, $Ffx$ is the fixed rate day count fraction and $Ffe$ is the floating rate day count fraction.

The last two are time periods over which the interest is to be calculated.

## 14.6.2 Example of Interest Rate Swap

Assume there are two firms A and B. Firm A is an institution that invests $100 million in fixed rate mortgages yielding 8.5 percent. Assume Firm A is not the high rated firm and funding its assets through a floating rate loan for the banks, i.e., charging six month London Inter Bank Offer Rate (LIBOR) plus 50 basis point (a basis equals 0.01 percent). It means that Firm A's profitability depends upon the actual level of the floating interest rate in future that is to be paid over the long run. Therefore, if fluctuation in interest rates will be high then Firm A's debt service expenses will increase, consequently the profit will also decline. In other words, Firm A will lose money whenever LIBOR exceeds 8 percent (8.50 – 0.50) on any reset date.

Suppose, another Firm B, has also borrowed $100 million for five years but at a fixed rate. Assuming that this firm is high graded firm and is funding its loan portfolio at 6.25 percent coupon. Firm B's portfolio is yielding LIBOR plus 75 basis points. It means Firm B's profitability depends upon the actual floating interest rate that is received on its portfolio. Whenever, LIBOR is less than 5.50 percent (6.25 – 0.75) on any reset date, Firm B is losing money. This situation is shown in Figure 14.1.

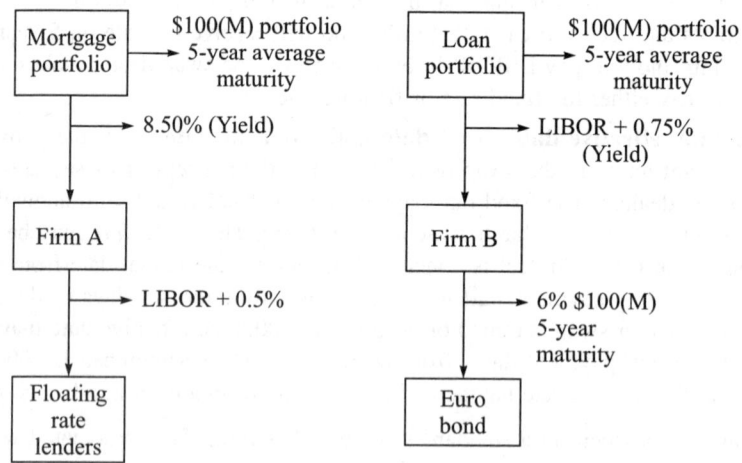

**FIGURE 14.1**   Situation of A and B firms before the swap.

In order to eliminate interest rate risk, Firm A may enter into interest rate swap deal with any Big Bank. Assume that 6.50 percent will be paid by Firm A to Big Bank for five years with payments calculated by multiplying that rate by $100 (M) notional principal amount. In return for this payment, Big Bank agrees to pay the Firm A six-month LIBOR over five years, with reset dates matching the reset on its floating rate loan. This is shown in Figure 14.2 relating to Firm A.

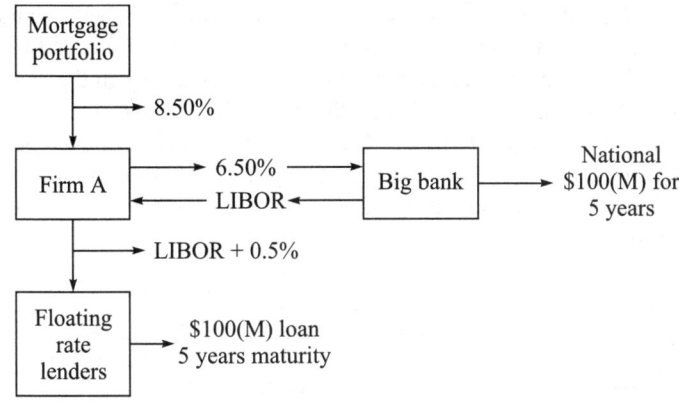

**FIGURE 14.2**    Firm A interest rate swap agreement with big bank.

| Receipt on portfolio | 8.50 percent |
| --- | --- |
| Pay big bank | 6.50 percent |
| Receive from big bank | LIBOR |
| Pay on loan | (LIBOR + 50 bp) |
| Cost of fund | (6.50 + 50) = 7.00 percent |
| Locked in spread | 1.50 percent |

Similarly, Firm B enters into portfolio with Big Bank where it agrees to pay six-month LIBOR to Big Bank on a notional principal amount of $100 (M) for five years in exchange for receiving payments of 6.40 percent. The net result to B and swap are shown in Figure 14.3.

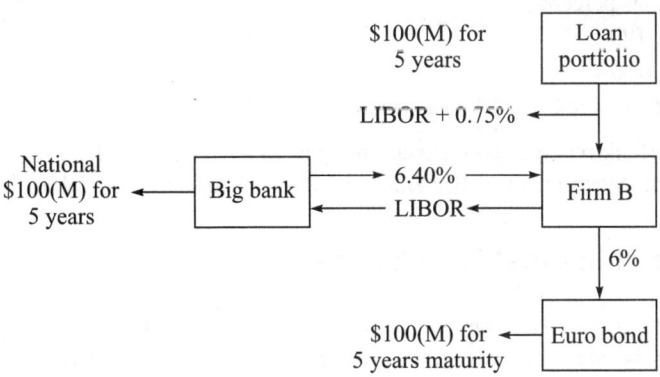

**FIGURE 14.3**    Firm B interest rate swap with big bank.

The net result to B is as follows:

| Receipt on portfolio | LIBOR + 0.75 bp |
| --- | --- |
| Pay big bank | LIBOR |
| Received from big bank | 6.40 percent |
| Pay on euro bond | 6.00 percent |
| Cost of funds | (LIBOR − 0.40 percent) |
| Locked in spread | 0.75 + 0.40 = 1.15 percent |

It is evident from the example that the cost of funds of Firm B has been reduced to LIBOR less 40 basis points resulting Firm B has been locked in spread on its portfolio of 115 basis points.

In this swap deal, the interest of Big Bank (a financial intermediary in the deal) is to be assessed. The net result in each of these transactions is that the risk of loss due to interest rate fluctuations has been transferred from the counter party to Big Bank. The Big Bank will only be interested to enter into such deals with Firm A and B if it will also be in beneficial position. As a financial intermediary, the Big Bank puts together both transactions, the risks net out is left with a speed of 10 basis points. This is shown in Figure 14.4.

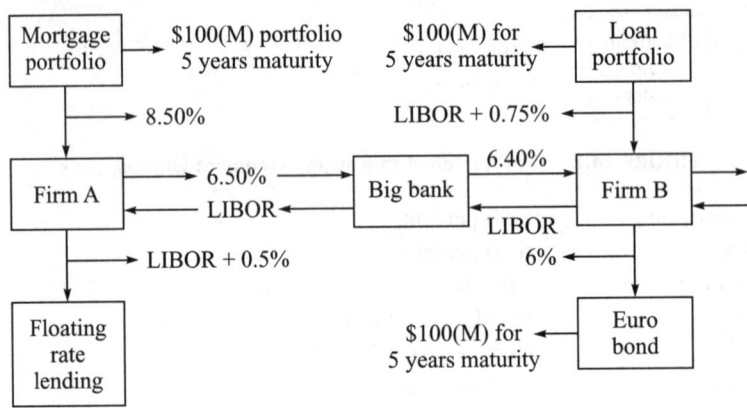

**FIGURE 14.4**    Swap structure.

| | |
|---|---|
| Receive | 6.50 percent |
| Pay | 6.40 percent |
| Receive | LIBOR |
| Pay | LIBOR |
| Net | (6.50 – 6.40) = 10 basis points |

Thus, the Big Bank receives compensation equal to $1 lakh annually for the next five years on $100 (M) swap deal. Swap profit to Big Bank = 0.001 × 1 million = $1 lakh.

### 14.6.3    Types of Interest Rate Swaps

**Plain vanilla swap:**    It is also known as *fixed-for-floating swap*. In this swap, one party with a floating interest rate liability is exchanged with fixed rate liability. Usually swap period ranges from 2 years to over 15 years for a pre-determined notional principal amount. Most of deals occur within four years period.

**Zero coupon to floating:**    The holders of zero-coupon bonds get the full amount of loan and interest accrued at the maturity of the bond. Hence, in this swap, the fixed rate player makes a bullet payment at the end and floating rate player makes the periodic payment throughout the swap period.

**Alternative floating rate:**    In this type of swap, the floating reference can be switched to other alternatives as per the requirement of the counter party. These alternatives include three-month LIBOR, one-month commercial paper (which refers to the Federal Reserve release), T-Bill rate, etc. In other words, alternative floating interest rates are charged in order to meet the exposure of other party.

**Floating-to-floating:** In this swap, one counter party pays one floating rate, say, LIBOR while the other counter party pays another basis, say, prime for a specified time period. These swap deals are mainly used by the non-US banks to manage their dollar exposure. It is also called *basis swap*. Basis swap is an interest rate swap in which both the interest rates are based on floating system based on particular indexes. For example, one party may be interested to receive interest payment based on particular index, 6-month LIBOR, and ready to pay interest based on other index, say, MIBOR. It is also called *floating-to- floating* swap. If one or both of the floating rates in a long-term rate, then the basis swap may be called a *yield-curve-swap*.

In basis swap, at each settlement date, both the floating rates are observed, and then multiplied by the notional principal amount of swap so that both the cash flows are determined. Since floating rates are changing over time, hence, both the interest rates change at each settlement date in basis swap. The basis swap is useful to those firms which have floating rate liability, because these swaps allow to change the index rates from one to another as per their needs.

**Forward swap:** This swap involves an exchange of interest rate payment that does not begin until a specified future point in time. It is also kind of swap involving fixed for floating interest rate.

**Rate capped swap:** In this type of swap, there is exchange of fixed rate payments for floating rate payments, whereby the floating rate payments are capped. An upfront fee is paid by floating rate party to fixed rate party for the cap.

**Swaptions:** Swaptions are combination of the features of two derivative instruments, i.e., *option* and *swap*. Option interest rate swaps are referred as *swaptions*. The buyer of the swaption has the right to enter into an interest rate swap agreement by some specified date in the future. The swaption agreement will specify whether the buyer of the swaption will be a fixed rate receiver or a fixed rate payer. If the buyer exercises the option then the writer of the option will become the counter party.

*Swaption can be of two types:* Call swaption or callable swap and put swaption or putable swap. A callable swap provides the party making the fixed payments with the right to terminate the swap to its maturity. The writer, therefore, becomes the fixed rate receiver and floating rate payer. On the other hand, a putable swap provides the party making the floating rate payments with a right to terminate the swap. The writer of the put swaption, therefore, becomes the floating rate receiver and fixed rate payer.

**Extendable swap:** Extendable swap contains an extendable feature, which allows fixed for floating counter party to extend the swap period. It means, at the maturity of the swap agreement, if the counter parties desire to extend the agreement period, they may do so if there exists extendable feature in the agreement of swap.

**Equity swap:** The equity swap involves the exchange of interest payment linked to the change in the stock index. For example, an equity swap agreement may allow a company to swap a fixed interest rate of 6 percent in exchange for the rate of appreciation on a particular index, say, BSE or NSE Index, each year over the next various years.

Equity index swap, or equity swap, is an interest rate swap in which the counterparties pay and receive cash flows based on the returns calculated on particular stock market index against either a fixed rate payment or floating rate payment. For example, one party may be interested to receive payment in terms of return to be incurred on an equity index, say, NSE NIFTY, BSE SENSEX, and so on, and pay the interest on LIBOR or MIBOR and vice versa. Sometimes, a party wants to pay the return on its stock portfolio and receives return in shape of interest based on any index. The objective of the party here is to protect from the risk of falling return on its equity portfolio.

Sometimes, it is possible that the return on a stock index of a swap deal could be negative. In such case, if the party is a receiver of stock index return, it means the party will receive a negative return, i.e., the party will have to pay interest amount as well as negative return based on stock index to the counter party. The security dealers also use equity index swaps who finance their equity portfolios with the borrowed funds at LIBOR/MIBOR to hedge against unexpected changes in the value of their portfolios.

**Amortizing swap:**   We have discussed earlier various types of swaps whose interest payments are computed using a constant notional amount for the swap over its life. However, sometimes, a firm might be interested to hedge a position which is equivalent to a bond with the principal that changes over time. In such situation, the amount under swap is required to be changed. So, there can be many situations where the firm would like to change their notional principals of the swap contracts. For example, an investment banker puts together a portfolio of mortgages which it buys from various mortgages issues. The total balance amount of loans under a portfolio of mortgages is changing overtime due to prepayments or postponement of the mortgages. Similarly, a firm has issued debt whose principal amount changes over time. Further, in an index amortizing swap, the rate is based on the notional principal is based on some interest rate index which changes randomly over time. For example, if an index, say, LIBOR declines to some level, the notional principal may drop to 80 percent of its original level, as per swap agreement, and so on. In brief, where the principal amount of swap does not remain constant, or the party wants to change the principal amount such a swap is known as *an amortizing swap*.

## At Market and off-Market Swaps

In a simple interest rate swap, fixed rate, or swap price, is such that swap has no value initially, ignoring the bid-asked spread. It means the swap price is equal to market interest rate. It will be called *at market swap*. If interest rates subsequently change in the market, or we can say that market rate of interest is not at par with the swap fixed rate (swap price), then the one party will be in profit and other will be in loss. The swap will have a value in the market. The swap value reflects the difference between the swap price and market interest rate. It is called *off-market swap*. It means when the fixed rate of swap is away from the market, and swap does have value to one of the counterparties of the swap. For example, swap price (fixed rate) in a swap deal is 5.6 percent, but in the market, current rate of interest is quoted at 6 percent, which means swap has the value, then such swap is called *an off-market swap*. It is clearly a good situation for the fixed rate receiver. The value of the swap can be calculated by multiplying the difference of the swap fixed rate and market fixed rate with the notional principal of the swap.

In another example, a swap may be quoting a price of 40 basis points above the five-year Treasury Note of 8.00 percent for a swap with a tenor of 5 years. The firm, however, is not interested to pay 8.40 percent fixed. It may want to pay only 7.80 percent and still receive LIBOR. In such situation, there may be off-market swap arrangement in which an initial payment from the firm to the swap dealer will have to be negotiated. The payment reflects the value only paying 7.80 percent fixed, when the current market price is 8.40 percent. In another case, if the firm might desire to pay 9.00 percent fixed, then the swap dealer will make an initial payment to the firm.

It should be noted that by entering into the off-market swap, the firm will effectively offset its old swap, the tenor of the off-market swap should be equal to the remaining time to maturity of its old swap. By doing this, the floating rate should not be changed.

### *Leveraged Swap*

Leverage swap is a highly risky and exotic interest rate derivative instrument in which the counter parties agree to exchange the difference between short-term and long-term interest rates. The counter parties will be in profit if the interest rate moves as expected. However, if it moves in reverse direction, then the parties will incur heavy losses. For example, a party has raised a 10-year foreign currency loan of $ 100 million on which the company pays 8 percent fixed rate of interest. The company is expecting a fall in the US dollar interest in future, thus decides to switch over to floating interest rate. Assume that the company has enter a swap deal with a swap dealer (bank) in which it will receive fixed rate 8 percent and pays floating rate based on say LIBOR (six months) US dollar. Assume that current LIBOR is quoted at 5 percent which means that the company will earn 3 percent on this deal.

Suppose now that we change the plain vanilla swap so that the size of the short bond position is increased by $100 million to maintain the value of swap equal to zero at inception, we invest the proceeds, from the increase in short position and invest then in the risk-free securities at 7 percent. The resulting swap is called "levered" or "leveraged" swap, because its cash flows are those of the plain vanilla swaps with additional borrowing. The net interest payments of the swap are the interest payments (5 percent on 200 million) on the short position minus interest earned on the investment in the risk-free securities. In the above example, total receipts in swaps of interest—(100 + 100 = 200 m × 8%, $16 m) and payments of interest—(100 + 100 = 200 × 5 percent, $10 m) benefit of $6 m Net benefit will be $6 m—(8–7 percent) × 100 m)] = $5 m. When the floating rate (index) is low, the company will be in profit, however, if the index starts rising, swap may turn to negative. Therefore, it is highly speculative derivatives which should be used after a proper evaluation.

One interest payment is calculated using one floating rate index and other may be based on fixed rate or another floating rate index denominated in other currency.

## 14.6.4  An Example of Plain Vanilla Swap

Let us consider a simple example of plain vanilla swap (Figure 14.5) to show the net cash flows arising in the swap. Let us assume Party X on a semi-annual basis, pays 7 percent rate of interest on the notional amount and receives from the Party Y LIBOR + 30 basis points as per details given below. The current six-month LIBOR rate is 6.30 percent per annum. The notional principal is $35 million.

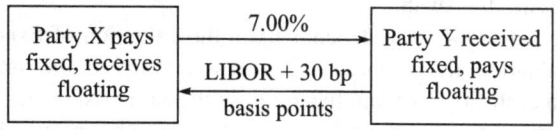

**FIGURE 14.5**  Structure of plain vanilla swap.

**Amount to be paid as per fixed rate:**  The fixed rate in a swap is usually quoted on a semi-annual bond equivalent yield basis. Therefore, the interest is paid every six months is:

Notional principal (Days in period/365) (Interest rate/100)

$$= \$ 35,00,00,000 \ (182/365) \ (7.00/100) = \$12,21,643.83 \qquad (14.1)$$

(Where it is assumed that there are 182 days in the particular period)

**Amount to be paid as per floating rate:**   The floating side is quoted on a money market yield basis. The difference between the two-rate computation is the number of days in a year conversion employed. Therefore, the payment is:

(Notional principal) (Days in period/360) (Interest rate/100)

$$= \$35,00,00,000 \times (182/360) \times (6.30 + 0.30/100) = \$11,67,833.33$$

In a swap, the payments are netted. In this case, Party X pays Party Y the net difference.

$$\$12,21,643.83 - \$11,67,833.33 = \$53,810$$

*Important observations from the above examples.*

1. Payments are netted in interest rate swaps. In this example, Party X sent Party Y a payment for the net amount.
2. Principal is not exchanged. That is why the notional principal is sued.
3. One party (i.e., paying party—Party X) is exposed to the risk that Party Y might default and conversely, Party Y is exposed to the risk of Party X defaulting. If one party makes defaults, then the swap normally terminates.
4. On the fixed amount side a 365-day year is assumed while on the floating side a 360-day year is used. The number of days in the year is one of the issues specified in the swap contract.

## 14.6.5   Valuation of Interest Rate Swap

Assuming no default risk, an interest rate swap can be valued either as a long position in one bond combined with short in another bond or as a portfolio of forward contracts. In other words, interest rate swap (fixed or floating) can be valued by treating the fixed rate payments as being equivalent to the cash flows on a conventional bond and the floating rate payments as being equivalent to a floating rate note (FRN). In interest rate swap, the principal amount is not exchanged, and further amount is paid in the same currency. Thus, the value of swap could be expressed as the value of fixed rate bond and value of the floating rate underlying the swap. It may be expressed as:

$$V = B_1 - B_2 \tag{14.2}$$

where $V$ is value of swap, $B_1$ is value of fixed rate bond underlying the swap and $B_2$ is value of floating rate bond underlying the swap.

In Equation 14.2, valuation of swap depends upon the valuation of fixed rate bond and floating rate bond. To find out valuation, the discount rate used should reflect the riskiness of the cash flows. In practice, the fixed rate cash flows stream has roughly the same risk as the floating rate cash flows stream because if one party commits default in payments, then other party will terminate the contract and will stop the payment as well. Therefore, it is appropriate to use the same discount rate for both the bonds $B_1$ and $B_2$.

$$\text{Value of the bond } B_1 = \sum_{i=1}^{n} Ke^{-r_i t_i} + Qe^{-r_n t_n} \tag{14.3}$$

where $K$ is periodic fixed payment in the swap, $r_i$ is discount rate corresponding to maturity $t$, $Q$ is the principal sum and $t_i$ is length of the time to corresponding maturity.

Now, Value of the bond

$$B_2 = K^* e^{-r_1 t_1} + Q e^{-r_1 t_1}$$

where $K^*$ is floating rate payment, $Q$ is the principal sum, $r_1$ is discount rate and $t_1$ is length of the time to the next interest payment.

It should be noted that usually the value of the swap is zero when it is first negotiated and zero at the end of its life. However, during its life, the value may be positive or negative.

**EXAMPLE:** Let us explain the value of swap by an example. Consider a bank has agreed to pay six-month LIBOR and receive 8 percent per annum (with semi-annual compounding) on a notional principal of $100 million. The swap has a remaining life of 1.25 years. The relevant fixed rate of interest with continuous compounding for 3-month, 9-month and 15-month maturities are 10 percent, 10.5 percent and 11.0 percent, respectively. The six-month LIBOR rate at the last payment date was 10.2 percent (with semi-annual compounding). Assuming in this example, $K = \$4$ million and $k^0 = \$5.1$ million:

$$B_1 = 4e^{-0.25 \times 0.1} + 4e^{-0.75 \times 0.105} + 100e^{-1.25 \times 0.11}$$
$$= \$98.24 \text{ million}$$
$$B_2 = 5.1e^{-0.25 \times 0.1} + 100e^{-0.25 \times 0.1}$$
$$= \$102.51 \text{ million}$$

Hence, the value of swap is $98 - 102.51 = -\$4.27$ million. If the bank takes the opposite position of paying fixed and receiving floating, the value of the swap then would be $+\$4.27$ million.

## 14.7 CURRENCY SWAP

A swap deal can also be arranged across currencies. It is an oldest technique in swap market. In this swap, the two payment streams being exchanged are denominated in two different currencies. For example, a firm which has borrowed Japanese yen at a fixed interest rate can 'swap away' the exchange rate risk by setting up a contract whereby it receives yen at a fixed rate in return for dollars at either a fixed or a floating interest rate.

The currency swap is, like interest rate swap, also two party transaction, involving two counter parties with different but complimentary needs being bought by a bank. In this swap, normally three basic steps are involved which are as under:

1. Initial exchange of principal amount
2. Ongoing exchange of interest
3. Re-exchange of principal amounts on maturity

The first step in this swap is the initial exchange of the principal amounts at an agreed rate of exchange. This rate is usually based on the spot exchange rate. This initial exchange can be on a notional basis, i.e., no physical exchange of principal amounts. The counter parties simply convert principal amounts into the required currency-via-the spot market.

The second step is related with ongoing exchange of interest. After establishing the principal amounts, the counter parties exchange interest payment on agreed date based on the outstanding principal amounts at the fixed interest rates agreed at the outset of the transaction.

The third step is the re-exchange of principal to principal amounts. Agreement on this enables the counter parties to re-exchange the principal sums at the maturity date. These three steps have been shown through an example.

**Example of currency swap:**    Assume that Firm *A* has a Swiss franc 100 million liability but interested to have a dollar loan instead. Also assume that another Firm B has a $100 million liability but prefers to have a Swiss franc liability instead. There can be a good solution through the currency swap deal and which can be arranged through a financial intermediary (an experienced bank) for a fee. A currency swap in this case can be seen from the following flowchart in three steps: [Refer Figures 14.5(a), 14.6 and 14.7].

*Step I    Spot transaction.*    This spot transaction is carried out at the prevailing spot rate in the market.

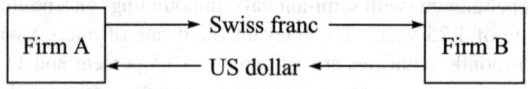

**FIGURE 14.5(a)**    Transaction under currency swap.

*Step II    Settlement of notional annual interest.*

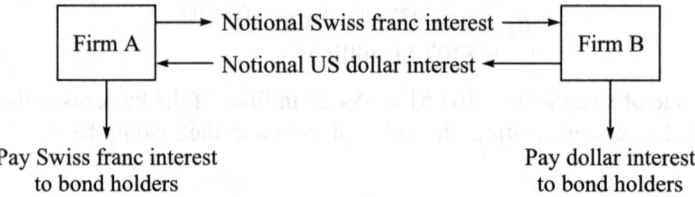

**FIGURE 14.6**    Transaction under currency swap.

*Step III    Exchange of final contract.*

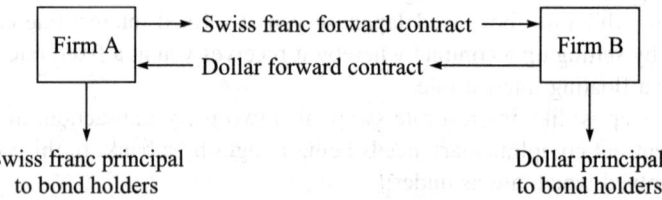

**FIGURE 14.7**    Transaction under currency swap.

From the above example, it is noted that exchange of principal amounts, both at the beginning and at the end of swap contract is notional and not real. However, then cash flows resulting from interest rates are real. The benefits arising out of such swap to the counterparties depend upon the movements in underlying currency exchange rates and interest rates thereon.

## 14.7.1   Types of Currency Swaps

The structure of currency swaps differs from interest rate swaps in a variety of ways. The major difference is that in a currency swap, there is always an exchange of principal amounts at maturity at a predetermined exchange rate. Thus, the swap contract behaves like a long dated forward. Foreign exchange contract, where the forward is the current spot rate. The currency swaps can be of different types based on their term structure such as fixed-to-fixed currency swap, floating-to-floating currency swap, fixed-to-floating currency swap and so on. These have been discussed in brief.

**Fixed-to-fixed currency swap:** In this category, the currencies are exchanged at fixed rate. This swap works like this. One firm raises a fixed rate liability in currency X, say US dollar ($) while the other firm raises fixed rate funding in currency Y, say, Pound (£). The principal amounts are equivalent at the current market rate of exchange. In swap deal, first party will get pound, whereas the second party gets dollars. Subsequently, the first party will make periodic get (pound) payments to the second, in turn gets dollars computed at interest at a fixed rate on the respective principal amount of both currencies. At maturity, the dollar and pound principal are re-exchanged.

**Floating -to-floating swap:** In this category, the counter parties will have payments at floating rate in different currencies. It means, the currencies are exchanged between the parties at a specified floating rates such as from MIBOR to LIBOR, etc.

**Fixed-to-floating currency swap:** This swap is a combination of a fixed-to-fixed currency swap and floating swap. In this, one party makes the payment at a fixed rate in currency, say, X while the other party makes the payment at a floating rate in currency, say, Y. Contracts without the exchange and re-exchange of principals do exist. In most cases, a financial intermediary (a swap bank) structures the swaps deal and routes the payments from one party to other party.

The most important currencies in the currency swap market are the US dollar, the Swiss franc. The Deutsche mark, the ECU, the Sterling pound, the Canadian dollar and the Japanese yen. The currency swap is an important tool to manage currency exposures and cost benefits at the same time. These are often used to provide long-term financing in foreign currencies. This function is important because in many foreign countries, long-term capital and forward foreign exchange markets are notably absent or not well developed. However, if the international financial markets were fully developed from all the angles then the incentive to swap would not be so much due to availability of arbitrage opportunities.

### *Differential Swaps*

Differential swaps are popularly known as *diff swaps*. It is a floating-to-floating currency swap, in which both floating rates are applied to the notional principal of just one of the currencies, and the swapped payments are only in that single currency. Since one currency is involved, therefore, notional principal of the swap is not exchanged. The exchanged cash flows are netted. It means only the difference 'check' is paid by the one party to the other. The differential swaps allow the firms to eliminate currency risk exposure instead of changing over the principal amounts. For example, a firm may wish to make six monthly payments based on six-month MIBOR and receive six-month US dollar LIBOR. In such case, suppose the firms want to have both the payments and receipts denominated in single currency, say, US dollar, then the firm will have to pay spread in such case, i.e., the difference of amount of interest calculated six monthly as per the indexes rates.

### *Cross Currency Swap*

Like all other swaps, cross-currency swap is an OTC derivative instrument where each leg of the swap is denominated in a different currency. It has two principal amount one for each currency. Normally the exchange rate used to determine the two principal is the prevailing spot rate, although for delayed start transaction, the other rate may be agreed. Cross-currency swaps are also known as (CIRCA) *Currency and Interest Rate Conversion Agreement.*

Cross-currency swaps involve the exchange of principal in different currencies and the payment of interest in one currency and the receipt of interest in another currency at a fixed exchange rate determined at the contract's initiation. These interest payments at specified intervals over the term of the swap as agreed between them. Another definition of cross-currency swap is "it is an agreement between two parties to exchange interest payments denominated is two different currencies for a specified term. One interest payment is calculated using one floating rate index and other may be based on fixed rate by other another floating rate index denominated in other currency".

Cross-currency swaps come in different forms, but popular among them is cross-currency basis swap, where counterparties exchange floating interest rate payment, tied to a benchmark of money market at set intervals of the swap. Normally these swaps can be replicated using on-balance sheet instrument like loans and deposits in different currencies. The counterparty can or cannot elect to exchange principal at the start of the contract. Most of the banks manage long-term foreign exchange forwards as part of the cross-currency swap business given the similarities.

Let us explain the cross-currency swap with an example. Consider that a firm has raised loan in US dollar 5 years ago and currently on a floating rate basis. In the 5 years since then, the firm's business has grown in multiple and is now exporting to European countries. As a result, the firm in facing difficulty in managing its foreign exchange. Now, the firm is considering cross-currency interest rate swap to solve the problem. The new swap contract allows the firm to switch its loan and interest payments from one currency into another. Further, it also allows the firm to switch loan from floating to fixed rate of interest. The cross-currency swaps can solve the problem of the firm in a single contract.

In the above example, the firm decides to do a cross-currency swap arrangement with a bank. Assume that the US dollar exchange rate against the European currency Euro is $/€ 1.2. The bank will do a foreign exchange deal so that the firm sells to the bank the amount of loan in US dollar at the current rate and the bank sells to the firm euro (€). The bank will pay the firm a floating interest rate on the dollar and the principal amount after 5 years. In return, the bank will receive a fixed (or floating) interest rate on the euro currency amount. The firm will pay to the bank euro at the end of the contract period. In doing this, the firm creates a loan in euro and it can use the euro from its exports to pay off the loan. Not only this, if the firm chooses a fixed interest rate on the euro loan, it can also avoid of any possible interest rate risk.

In brief, cross-currency swaps allow the firm to switch its loan from one currency to another, along with to choose interest payments between fixed or floating. The firm can also switch the loan back into any currency it chose. These are highly flexible in terms of interest and principal payments in different currencies.

**Example (Currency Swap):** A currency swap can be motivated by comparative advantage. Let us assume that Firm X and Firm Y are offered the following fixed rates of interest in German mark (DEM) and French franc (FRF) as shown in Table 14.1.

**TABLE 14.1**   Comparative Interest Rates for Firm X and Firm Y

| Firm | DEM | FRF |
|---|---|---|
| Firm X | 6.00% | 9.60% |
| Firm Y | 8.0% | 10.0% |

Table 14.1 shows that FRF interest rates are generally higher than DEM, and Firm X is more creditworthy than Firm Y, since it can raise the funds at the lower interest rates. However, the differences between the rates offered to X and Y in the two markets are not the same since firm Y pays 2 percent more in DEM and 0.04 in FRF. Firm X has a comparative advantage in the DEM market while Firm Y has a comparative advantage in the FRF, reason being that Firm X is German

firm and Firm Y is a French firm, both are better known in their countries and raise the funds in their respective country's currencies.

Let us assume that both the firms want to change their currency liabilities. Firm X wants to exchange with FRF and Firm Y with DEM. The difference between the DEM interest and FRF interest are 2 percent (0.08 – 0.06), 0.4 percent (0.10 – 0.096), respectively. By analogy with the interest rate swap, expected total gain will be 2 percent – 0.4% = 1.6 percent to all parties. There are many ways of arranging of such swap. Figure 14.8 shows one possible arrangement.

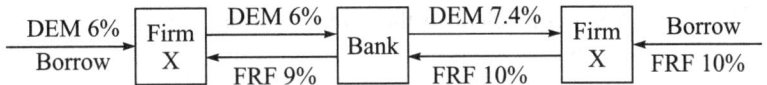

**FIGURE 14.8**   Currency swap arrangement.

The strategy of currency swap in the above case is designed in such a way that Firm X borrows DEM at 6 percent, while Firm Y borrows FRF at 10 percent to provide FRF to Firm X at 9 percent and DEM to Firm Y at 7.4 percent per annum. This makes each firm 0.06 percent better off that it would be. The financial intermediary swap dealer (a bank) gains 1.4 percent on DEM and losses 1.0 percent on FRF, and makes a net gain of 0.4 percent per annum. Thus, as predicted, the total gain to all parties (i.e., 0.6 + 0.6 + 0.4) 1.6 percent per annum.

## 14.7.2   Alternative Strategy for Currency Swap

There can be different alternative arrangements depending upon the firm's considerations. An alternative arrangement in the above said example is shown in Figure 14.9.

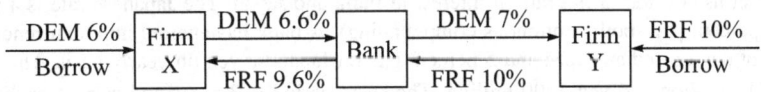

**FIGURE 14.9**   Alternative strategy for currency swap.

In the above strategy Firm 'X' borrows DEM at 6 percent and lends to Bank at 6.6 percent who in turn transfers the same to the Firm 'Y' at 7 percent. On the other hand, Firm 'Y' borrows FRF at 10 percent and lends to Bank at 9.6 percent, who transfers the same to the firm 'X' at 9.6 percent. In this way, Firm 'X' saves (6.6 – 6.0 %) = 0.6 percent in DEM, Firm Y earns in DEM (8 – 7 %) = 1 percent but incur loss of (10 – 9.6 %) = 0.4 percent in FRF, net gain of 0.06 percent, and Bank earns (7 – 6.6 %) = 0.04 in DEM, being total gains of 0.06% + 0.06% + 0.04% = 1.6%.

In the same manner, there can be some other possibilities, depending upon the credit-worthiness of the parties, bargaining power of the parties, exchange risk loss bearing of swap dealer, etc.

## 14.7.3   Valuation of Currency Swap

Considering the example of a currency swap in the preceding section that entails fixed rate payments in the other currency, the swap can be valued as the difference between the current values of two conventional bonds. The technique used for valuation of currency swap is just synonymous to valuation of interest rate swap. Here, the value of a foreign currency bond, and the corresponding value of a domestic currency bond would be taken into considered which are as under:

$$V = SB_F - B_D$$

where $V$ is value of the swap, $S$ is current exchange rate (expressed as number of units of domestic currency per unit of foreign currency), $B_F$ is value in (foreign currency) of the foreign currency bond and $B_D$ is the value of local currency bond underlying the swap.

In simple term, the value of currency swap can be determined from the term structure of interest rates in domestic currency, the term structure of interests in the foreign currency and the spot exchange rate.

**Calculation of $B_F$:**    The bond equivalent to the foreign currency interest flows has the value as shown in the following equation:

$$B_F = \sum_{i=1}^{n} K_F e^{-r_i^F t_i} + Q e^{-r_n^F t_n}$$

where $K_F$ is constant foreign currency interest payment, $r_i^F$ is the foreign currency discount rate, $t_i$ is corresponding periods to the interest payments and $Q$ and the principal sum in foreign currency.

**Calculation of $B_D$:**    The bond equivalent to the domestic currency cash flow is determined as shown in the following equation:

$$B_D = \sum_{i=1}^{n} K_D e^{-r_i^D t_i} + S' Q e^{-r_n^D t_n}$$

where $K_D$ is the constant foreign currency interest payment, $r_i^D$ is discount rates for the various periods to cash flows, $t_i$ is length of those periods to cash flows, $S'$ is exchange rate at the time that the swap was agreed and $Q$ is foreign currency principal sum converted into the equivalent domestic currency principal sum.

**EXAMPLE:**    Let us consider a flat rate of interest in India and Japan. The Japanese rate is 4 percent p.a. and Indian rate is 9 percent p.a. (both continuous compounding). A bank has entered into a currency swap where it receives 8 percent p.a. on Indian rupee and 5 percent p.a. on Japanese yen on yearly basis. The principal in two currencies are ₹10 million and yen 1200 million. The swap period is 3 years and current exchange rate is 100 yen = ₹1 in this case.

The value of swap is given by,

$$V = SB_F - B_D$$
$$B_D = 0.8e^{-0.09} + 0.8e^{-0.09 \times 2} + 10.8e^{-0.09 \times 3} = ₹9.64 \text{ million}$$
$$B_F = 60e^{-0.04} + 60e^{-0.04 \times 2} + 1260e^{-0.04 \times 3} = ¥1230.55 \text{ million}$$

$$\frac{1230.55}{110} - 9.64 = ₹1.55 \text{ million}$$

If the bank had been paying yen and receiving the rupee, the value of the swap would have been ₹1.55 million.

## 14.8    DEBT-EQUITY SWAP

There can be different structure of swap contracts but the basics are fairly simple. In debt-equity swap, a firm buy's a country's debt on the secondary loan market at a discount and swaps it into local equity. In other words, the debts are exchanged for equity by one firm with the other.

Recently, a market for less-developed countries (LDC) debt-equity swap has developed that enable the investors to purchase the external debts of such underdeveloped countries to acquire equity or domestic currency in those same countries. Earlier, six major debt notions—Chile, Brazil, Mexico, Venezuela, Argentina and the Philippines have initiated such debt-equity swap programmes. This market was developed in 1985, and by the 1988, the same was reached to $15 billion in size, and further it is on the rising trend.

In this typical swap deal, for example, a multinational firm wants to invest in, say, Brazil, hires an intermediary (normally a bank) to buy Brazil loans in the secondary market. The MNC (again through a middleman) presents the loans, denominated in dollar as, to the Brazil Central Bank, which redeems them for Brazil currency. The Central Bank, which redeems them at face value but more than the loans trade in the secondary markets. For example, Mexico pays 88 percent and Chile 92 percent for such swaps.

Further, in such deal, if an MNC wants to develop in Chile can pick up $100 million of loans in the secondary market for $70 million and swap them for $92 million in pesos. Chile gets $100 million of debt off its books and does not have to part with precious currency dollars. The MNC gets $92 million of investment for $70 million, which amounts to a 24 percent approx. (22/92) as subsidy.

## 14.8.1 Debt-Equity Swap Examples

One such deal was done in 1986 in which Citi-corp. Bank structured a debt swap for Nissan Motors. Citi-corp. learned that Nissan Motors to get them $54 million in pesos for much less than $54 million through debt-equity swap, which Nissan gave green signal to go ahead. After that, Citi-corp. went to the Mexico Government and got their approval for the swap. The Mexico Government agreed to pay $54 million in pesos for approximately $60 million of their external debt, a 10 percent discount. Consequently, Citi-corp. went out and bought the $60 million in Mexican Bank debt for about $38 million. Nissan would paid-up with the peso equivalent of $54 million at a price of only $40 million. Mexico retired about $60 million in bank debt and Citi-corp. was paid about $2 million as a fee for structuring the deal.

In such debt-equity swap, the residents of the debtor countries may enable to purchase their country's foreign debt at a discount and convert this debt into domestic currency. To finance these purchases, the residents normally use funds held abroad or hard currency acquired from international market. For example, a resident of a debtor country may exchange 100 percent in domestic currency in the official exchange market to acquire a dollar. Then the resident may use this dollar to purchase via the debt swap market, 125 pesos in domestic currency, and thus, gain a 25-peso profit. Exchange controls will not necessarily be effective in prevailing this. For several years, European and regional US commercial banks have been selling troubled LDC loans in the secondary market.

## 14.9 MISCELLANEOUS SWAPS

### Commodity Swaps

Commodity swaps are very popular swap contracts in the commodity markets. These are contracts in which the counter parties agree to exchange cash flows that are determined on the basis of commodity prices. They are just like a series of forward contracts on a commodity, each of which has different maturity date, but at the same forward price. The commodity swaps are very much popular in crude oil, energy-related products, precious metals like gold and silver, etc.

Most of the commodity swaps are done in the market for fixed-floating swaps based on normally one commodity product. In this swap, one party agrees to pay a fixed price for a notional principal of the commodity at agreed future settlement dates. The counterparty will pay the floating price, the prevailing market price of the commodity. It has been observed in the markets that in some commodity swaps, two commodities serve as the notional principals. In such swaps, the fixed price applied to the notional principal of one commodity is exchanged for the floating price applied to the notional principal of different commodity.

Each commodity swap agreement requires that the quantity and quality (grades, brands, trade market) of the commodity be defined, along with at which price to be charged at a specific location.

**EXAMPLE:**    Let us consider a commodity swap contract involving a notional principal of 1,00,000 barrels of crude oil. Assume that one party has agreed to pay fixed semi-annual payments at a fixed price of $20/bbl and receives floating payments. The payments are to be paid in one currency, suppose in US dollar. Assume that on the settlement date, if the spot price of the crude oil is $21/bbl, then pay-fixed party will receive [($21 − $20) × 1,00,000] = $1,00,000 from the counterparty.

The commodity swap markets also witness the floating-floating commodity swap in which two different commodities exist. They are called *basis swaps*. Further, in such contracts, it is also noted that some commodity swaps compute the average floating price during the period as the floating price of the swap. The commodity swaps allow the producers and users of different commodities to fix the prices of commodities on each of several dates in the future.

## 14.10   MOTIVATIONS UNDERLYING SWAPS

What is the economic rationale for swaps? And under what circumstances it is beneficial for a company to employ other features of an asset or liability?

Swaps are important technique or technology for transforming the characteristics of financial claims. Several explanations have been given for the existence of a large and growing volume of activity in the swap markets. Most of them are relying on various assumptions like capital market imperfection, differences in investors attitudes, informational asymmetries, differing financial norms, special features of national regulatory and tax structures and so forth. Brief views of these factors have been discussed here.

As we observe earlier that swaps are needed as long as it is profitable to transform them. In other words, if the world had a complete set of claims with all possible combinations of characteristics or if all the firms could issue securities in all markets at identical terms, then swaps and other hedging techniques may not be needed as long as such conditions are fulfilled. However, in actual practice such conditions are not always fulfilled. Thus, incomplete markets and market inefficiencies provide the economic rationale for swaps.

Second, there is a different risk perception between markets. For example, bond market and bank credit market evaluate the companies differently because their credit assessment is subjective. Sometimes, a company can raise the fund in particular market at lower cost where it receives better evaluation, which it can swap into the desired type of instrument. In this way, this will give the BBB rated borrower the comparative advantage in the floating rate credit market over the AAA rated borrower because it pays a smaller risk premium. The net interest rate differential can then be arbitraged and split between the counterparties.

Third, it relates with regulation of issuers and investors concerning the respective governments. It has been observed that in most markets there is government regulation that seeks to limit the amount of debt issued by the foreign companies to protect domestic investors from increased risks and preventing to borrow from local markets. Thus, government regulation makes certain markets more attractive to particular companies (usually domestic) than others. A bond swap can get around all this by allowing a company to enter directly through such party, which has favourable reputation in the market.

Fourth, sometimes there is subsidized financing available in certain type of business, for example, export financing. In that case, a currency swap may allow a company to take advantage of such situation. The company then can swap the exchange risk out of the subsidized borrowing and can have that currency in which it is interested.

Fifth, sometimes the availability of funds in different markets changes due to temporary supply/demand imbalances. This may be because two countries are in different stages of their development. For example, lowering reserve requirements for bank will result in increase of supply of funds in the bank credit and hence, rates fall down. Further, the borrower will desire to go in such markets where the supply is in excess. Thus, a swap can be used to arbitrage the differing economic conditions between markets and provide the desired traits to the borrowers.

Sixth, it is related balance-sheet position of the counter parties. Sometimes, swapping provides better opportunities to determine the types of assets and liabilities it wants to carry. For example, a banking company's assets are the loans issued to the customers. Normally, these loans are for short term and on a floating rate basis. So, the bank would like the liabilities to match with the nature of assets it has. Hence, the swap can be useful to tap the resources as per the firm's requirement.

Lastly, it is observed that changes overtime may affect the differences between markets and the prevailing rates may be changed. These relative changes can create arbitrage opportunities between debt issued before and after the changes occur. Therefore, currency swaps can be much helpful in such conditions.

## 14.11   SWAP ARRANGEMENT IN INDIA

The swaps were initiated in India since 1999, with a view to deepening the money market activities both spot and future. The Reserve Bank of India has allowed to scheduled commercial banks, primary dealers and all India financial institutions to make market in interest rate swaps (IRS) from July, 1999. However, the markets which have become popular in India so far is the one based on Overnight Index Swaps (OIS). The swaps of different tenors, viz. overnight, 14 days, 1 month, 3 months, 6 months, 1 year, etc. were allowed. However, only (OIS) overnight swap index could get vibrant recognition in comparison to others due to the absence of a larger inter-bank term money market in India. In India interest rate swaps are commonly traded on two benchmarks, viz. Mumbai Interbank Offered Rate (MIFOR) and Mumbai Interbank Forward Offered Rate (MIFOR)

### 14.11.1   Overnight Index Swaps (OIS)—Concept

OIS is an INR interest rate swap where the floating rate is linked to an overnight inter-bank call money index. Under this swap contract, the investor is allowed to swap floating interest rate in exchange for a fixed rate and to swap fixed interest rate in exchange for floating interest rate. Important features of this derivative are mentioned as under:

*Features OIS*

1. It is an interest rate swap contract in Indian rupee.

2. Floating rate (MIBOR) linked to an overnight inter-bank call money index, based on weighted average of interest rates contracted on unsecured Overnight loans in the interbank market.
3. Currently NSE Overnight MIBOR is the most widely used floating rate index in India.
4. The term for OIS varies between one week to one year. There is flexibility tenor which means that there is no restriction on the tenor of the swap.
5. The interest would be computed on a notional principal amount and settled on a net basis at maturity.
6. On the floating rate side, the interest amount is compounded on a daily basis based on the index. The **Reuters** O/N MIBOR is widely used on this respect.

**EXAMPLE:**   Let us consider a swap contract in which State Bank of India is a fixed rate receiver for ₹50 crore for a period of one week at 10 percent and Punjab National Bank is a receiver of floating rate linked to the overnight index (NSEO/N MIBOR). The NSE MIBOR rates for the seven days are taken and settled at the end of the swap period. At the end of the period of one week, i.e., the 8th day, the transaction is settled by paying the difference amount to other. How much amount is paid? It is calculated as under:

**Fixed Rate Receiver** (State Bank of India)

Fixed rate payment in this swap Contract is calculated as under:

| | | |
|---|---|---|
| Notional amount | : | ₹50 crore |
| Fixed rate of interest | : | 10% p.a. |
| Term of Swap | : | 07 days |
| Amount of fixed interest | : | (₹50 crore × 10 × 365) = ₹9,58,900 |

**Floating Rate Payer** (Punjab National Bank)

This is calculated as under and floating rates are assumed.

**TABLE 14.2**   Calculation of Floating Rate Payments

| Day | NSE (MIBOR) Index (%) | Notional Principal Amount | Interest for one day |
|---|---|---|---|
| 1st day | 10.25 | 50,00,00,000 | 1,40,411 |
| 2nd day | 10.00 | 50,01,40,411 | 1,37,025 |
| 3rd day | 9.75 | 50,02,77,436 | 1,33,636 |
| 4th day | 10.125 | 50,04,11,072 | 1,38,813 |
| 5th day | 10.25 | 5,00,54,98,850 | 1,40,565 |
| 6th day | 10.25 | 50,06,90,450 | 1,40,605 |
| 7th day | 10.50 | 50,08,31,055 | 1,44,075 |
| | | ₹50,09,75,130 | ₹9,75,130 |

**Settlement Amount** (Netting)

| | | |
|---|---|---|
| Fixed rate payment of interest | : | ₹9,58,900 |
| Floating rate payment of interest | : | ₹975130 |
| Difference ₹9,75130 – ₹958,900 | : | ₹16230 |

Since floating rate payments is higher by ₹16230 to fixed rate payment hence, State Bank of India will pay only ₹16230 to the Punjab National Bank.

### *Operation of OIS in Indian banking system*

Overnight Index Swaps are most popular among banks in India. The market witnesses average daily volumes of ₹6000 to ₹8000 crore. In this section, we will discuss the operation of OIS by an Indian bank with a hypothetical example let us assume that a bank has received ₹5 crore as one year deposit at the rate of 6 percent per annum. To hedge the interest rate risk, the bank can enter into a one year OIS as a fixed rate receiver, say, at the 6.25 percent p.a. and floating rate payer. In this position, the bank has created a liability of one year of OIS rate minus (6.25–6.00 percent).25 basis point on ₹5 crore. This is shown as under in Figure 14.10.

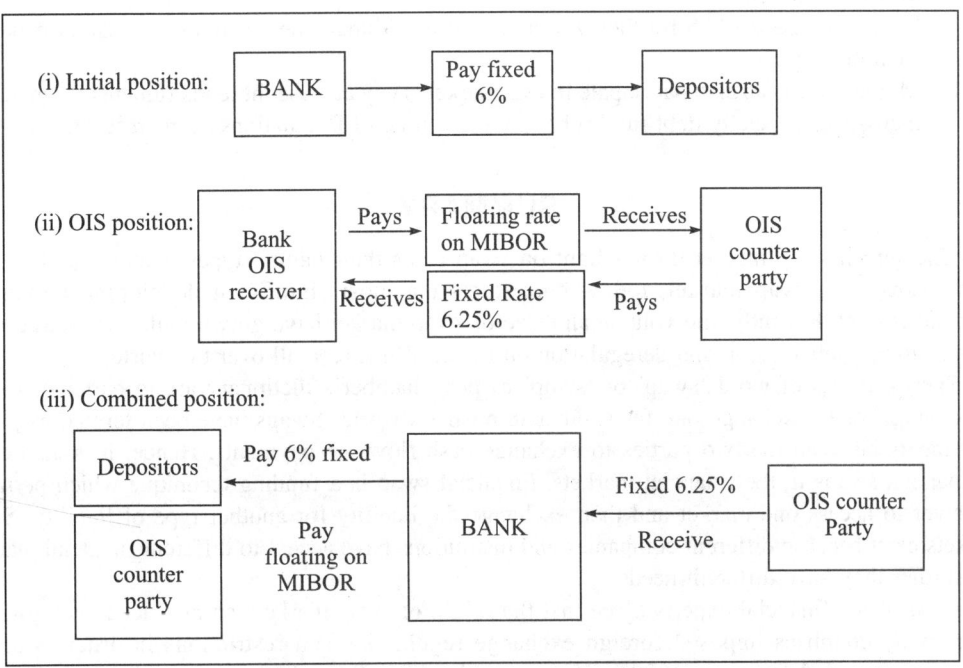

**FIGURE 14.10**    OIS operations in Indian Banking system.

**MIFOR swaps:**    MIFOR is another popular benchmark which has developed into a proxy for the AAA corporate funding in India. This index is derived from USD (LIBOR) and the USD/INR forward Premia and is simply the Indian equivalent of USD (LIBOR) and the USD interest rate Swaps Market. MIFOR behaves like an interest rate benchmark and not a forex benchmark. Currently, large number of Indian companies are using this benchmark regularly in managing their interest rate risk on debt portfolios.

## 14.12  APPLICATIONS OF INTEREST RATE SWAPS

1. The borrowers who anticipate interest rates to increase in future, can swap their floating rate loan into a fixed rate loan.
2. The borrowers who anticipate interest rate to fall can swap their fixed rate loan into a floating rate loan.

3. Borrowers who have taken loans benchmarked to one floating rate can swap into another floating rate to reduce their risk or obtaining benefits of the expected different movements in one benchmark to another one, for example, changing from MIBOR to MIFOR and so on.

4. In an highly risky call money market rates, the dealers in this market can use the IRS by taking fixed position for 90 days in lieu of funding government securities.

5. Interest rate swaps also assist in reducing the cost of financing and improving liquidity for the participants.

6. IRS also assists in creating synthetic instruments by combining other instruments and enter into new markets.

7. Banks can use the IRS for their Assets Liabilities Management and also as market makers in such instruments.

8. Mutual funds can also participate in IRS market. They can use these instruments for managing their funds specially debt fund schemes at the time of fluctuations in interest rates.

## SUMMARY

This chapter on swap market throws light on swap deals their nature, types, features and hedging with swaps. The swap market, today, constitutes the most significant development in global financial market. Recently, the volume and size of swap market have grown multifold as a result of liberalization, globalization and deregulation on financial markets, all over the world.

The meanings of word 'swap' or 'swop' as per Chamber's dictionary are to barter or to give in exchange, or to exchange one for another in business world. Swaps have been termed as private agreements between the two parties to exchange cash flows or payments. Hence, it is also called as financial swaps in the financial markets. Financial swap is a funding technique which permits a borrower to access one market and then exchange the liability for another type of liability. Swaps markets exist because different companies and institutions have access to different financial markets, and further they have different needs.

Most of the financial experts agree that the origin of swap market can be traced back to 1980s when many countries imposed foreign exchange regulations and restrictions in order to control cross-border capital flows. In 1980s, a few countries liberalized their exchange regulatory norms, as a result, some of the MNCs treasurers structured their portfolios and brought out a new financial products, known as Swaps. The first swap contract was negotiated in 1981 between World Bank and an undisclosed counter party. Since then swaps market has grown very rapidly. The major dramatic change in the swap market has been the emergence of large banks and performing as aggressive market makers specifically in dollar interest rate swaps.

The chapter further explains the important features of a swap agreement which includes (a) all swaps involve the exchange of a series of periodic payment between at least two parties, (b) swap agreement are arranged mostly through an intermediary, known as bank, (c) transaction costs are low in case of swap and termination of swap cannot be one's instance. The termination also requires to be accepted by counter parties. Major types of financial swaps are interest rate swaps, currency swaps and equity swaps. An interest rate swap is a financial agreement between two parties who wish to change the interest payments or receipts in same currency on assets or liabilities to a different basis. There is no exchange of principal amount in this swap. Interest rate swaps have various features like the notional principal, the fixed rate, floating rate, trade date, effective date, reset date and payment date. The chapter further explains interest rate swaps with examples. Interest rate swaps are of various types like plain vanilla swap in which one party with a floating interest rate liability is exchanged with fixed rate liability.

Zero coupon to floating holders bond get the full amount of loan and interest accrued at the maturity of the bond. Another type of interest rate swap is floating-to-floating, where one counter party pays one floating rate, say, LIBOR or while the other party pays another, say prime for a specified time period. Rate capped swaps, swaption extendable swap and equity swaps are other types of interest rate swaps. The chapter further discusses the valuation of interest rate swap. Assuming no default risk, an interest rate swap can be valued either as a long position in one bond combined with short in another bond or as portfolio of forward contracts. In other words, interest rate swap can be valued by treating the fixed rate payment as being equivalent to the cash flows on a conventional bond and floating rate payments as being equivalent to a floating rate note (FRN).

In currency swap, two payment streams being exchanged are dominated in two different currencies. In currency swap, three basic steps are involved: (a) initial exchange of principal amount, (b) ongoing exchange of interest and re-exchange of principal amount on maturity. Currency swap can be fixed-to-fixed, floating-to-floating and fixed-to-floating currency swap. Currency swaps can be valued as the difference between the current values of two conventional bonds.

In debt-equity swap, a firm buys a country's debt on the secondary loan market on a discount and swaps into local equity. In other words, the debts are exchanged for equity by one firm with the other. This market was developed in 1985 and by 1988, the same was reached to $15 billion in size, and further it is on rising trend. Various other types of swaps like amortizing swap, differential swap equity index swap, basis swap, At-market and off-market swap, commodity swap, leveraged swap, cross-currency swap, etc. have been discussed. After that the swap arrangement in India had been described in brief. Rationale underlying this swap is that swaps are important technique or technology for transforming the characteristics of financial claims. Swaps are needed as long as it is portfolio to transform them. Sometimes availability of funds in different markets changes due to temporary supply/demand imbalances.

## SOLVED PROBLEMS

**P.1.** Firm A is a US-based multinational firm, whereas Firm B is a France-based multinational firm. Both companies till now have borrowed exclusively from their base countries. Now, both need to raise capital for their new ventures. Due to scarcity, Firm A can issue five-year US$ bond at 7.5% and five-year French franc (FFc) bond in French market at 11% fixed. Firm B can issue five-year US$ bond in US market at 7% and five-year FFc bond in French market at 12%. Firm A requires US$100 million, whereas Firm B needs FFc 550 million. Current exchange rate is FFc 5.5 = US$1.

   (a) What kind of swap can Firm A and firm B enter into?

   (b) What will be the total cost and saving for each party?

*Solution:* Firm A and Firm B can enter into currency swap. In the US$ market, Firm B has 0.5% interest rate advantage over Firm A while in FFc market, Firm A has 1% interest rate advantage over Firm B. Thus, it is possible for A and B to engage in mutually beneficially trade.

   Firm A borrows 550 million francs at 11%.

   Firm B borrows $100 million at 7%.

   Firm A lends FFc 550 million to Firm B, charging 11.25%.

   Firm B lends US$100 million to Firm A, charging 7%.

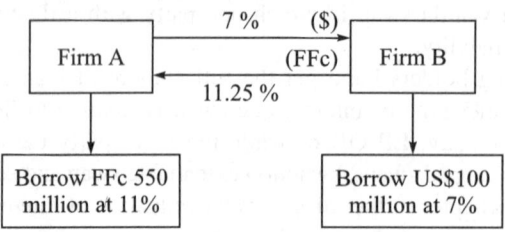

Net cost to Firm A = 11% + 7% – 11.25% = 6.75%

Net cost to Firm B = 7% + 11.25% – 7% = 11.25%

Saving to Firm A = 0.75% (7.50 – 6.75)

Saving to Firm B = 0.75% (12.00 – 11.25)

Total Savings = 1.5%

**P.2.** Companies A and B have been offered the following rate per annum on a $20 million five-year loan:

|  | **Fixed rate** | **Floating rate** |
|---|---|---|
| **Company A** | 12% | LIBOR + 0.1% |
| **Company B** | 13.4% | LIBOR + 0.6% |

Company A requires a floating rate loan, Company B requires a fixed rate loan. Design a swap that will have a bank acting as intermediary 0.1% per annum and be equally attractive to both companies.

*Solution:*   A has a comparative advantages in fixed rate markets but it wants to borrow floating rate loan, B has a comparative advantage in floating rate markets but wants to borrow fixed rate loan. There is a 1.4% per annum differential between the fixed rates offered to the two companies and a 0.5% per annum differential between the floating rate offered to the two companies. Total gain to all parties from the swap is, therefore, 1.4 – 0.5 = 0.9% per annum. Since bank gets 0.1%, the swap should make each of A and B 0.4% per annum better off.

So,            A borrowing cost = LIBOR – 0.3

and            B borrowing cost = 13%

As shown in following diagram:

$$12\% \xleftarrow{} \boxed{\text{Firm A}} \xrightarrow{12.3\%} \boxed{\text{Firm A}} \xrightarrow{12.4\%} \boxed{\text{Firm A}} \xrightarrow{} \text{LIBOR} + 0.4\%$$
$$\text{LIBOR} \qquad \text{LIBOR}$$

**P.3.** Companies X and Y both wish to borrow ₹10 crore for 5 years. Company Y wants to arrange a floating rate loan. The rate of interest is six-month LIBOR. Company Y wants to arrange a fixed rate loan. They have been offered the following terms:

|  | **Fixed rate** | **Floating rate** |
|---|---|---|
| **Company X** | 10.0% | Six-month LIBOR + 0.3% |
| **Company Y** | 11.2% | Six-month LIBOR + 1.0% |

Show the transaction without intermediary and with intermediary.

*Solution:*   Company X borrows fixed rate funds at 10% per annum.

1.  Company Y borrow floating rate funds at LIBOR + 1.0% per annum.
2.  They enter in a swap agreement.

*Swap with no intermediary*

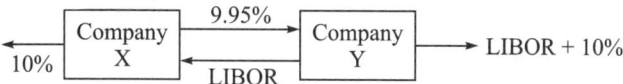

*Swap with intermediary*

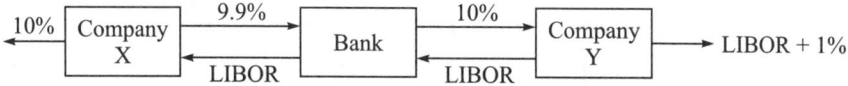

**P.4.**   Company XYZ, a British manufacturer, wished to borrow US dollar at fixed rate of interest. Company ABC, a US MC, wished to borrow sterling at fixed rate of interest. The rates are as follows:

|  | **Sterling** | **US Dollars** |
|---|---|---|
| **Company XYZ** | 11% | 7.50% |
| **Company ABC** | 10.6% | 6.2% |

Design a swap that will have a bank, acting as intermediary, 10 basis points per annum and which will produce a gain of 15 basis point per annum for each of the two companies.

*Solution:*

11% £ → | Company XYZ | —11%→ | Financial institution | —10.85%→ | Company ABC | 6.2% £
         |             | ←7.35% |                       | ←6.2%   |             |

Swap structure with the help of bank

**P.5.**   Sun Pharmaceutical Ltd. wishes to borrow ₹20 crore at a fixed rate for 5 years and has been offered either 11% fixed or six-month LIBOR + 1%. CIPLA Ltd. wishes to borrow ₹20 crore at a floating rate for 5 years and has been offered either six-month LIBOR + 0.5% or 10% fixed. On the basis of above figure:

(a)  How do they enter into swap arrangement in which each is benefited equally?

(b)  What risk may this arrangement generate?

*Solution:* (a) By directly borrowing on the required basis, the total interest paid by Sun Pharma and CIPLA is:

$$₹20 \text{ crore} \times (11 + \text{LIBOR} + 0.5\%)$$

By borrowing according to comparative advantage, total interest paid:

$$₹20 \text{ crore} \times (10 + \text{LIBOR} + 1\%)$$

Borrowing according to comparative advantage provides a total saving of ₹20 crore × ½% to be shared between Sun Pharma and CIPLA Ltd. Both have a ¼% reduction in interest charge.

*Swap transaction*

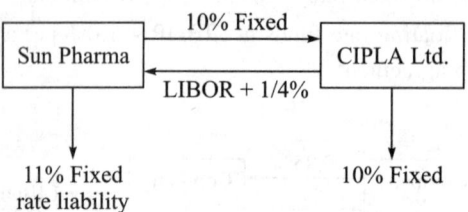

*IInd possibility*

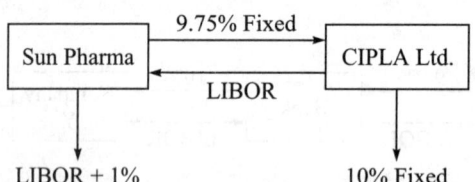

(b) CIPLA Ltd. at risk from LIBOR rising is at risk from an opportunity loss in event Sun Pharma of fall in LIBOR. Both are at risk from default by the other.

**P.6.** A firm issues a 7-year bond callable at par after three years. The issue is priced to yield 9.20 which is 20 bp above what the firm would have paid for a straight, i.e., non-callable bond. The firm then sells a 7-year swap callable after 3 years in which it receives fixed at 9.40% and pays 6-month LIBOR. The counter party to this swap has paid a 40 bp premium for the option to terminate the swap prematurely. The firm has now floating rate debt at LIBOR 20 bp. Then it combines with a plain vanilla coupon swap in which it pays 9% fixed and receives 6-month LIBOR. Show the transaction in a diagram.

***Solution:*** In this swap agreement, one issuing firm makes swap agreement with the two counter parties. The position of swap is shown in the following diagram:

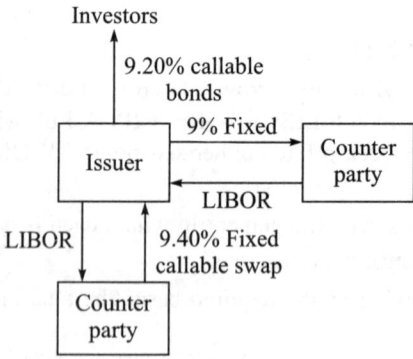

**P.7.** **Suppose** there are two companies X and Y. Company X is rated as 'AAA' and Company Y is rated as 'BBB'. Because of best rating, Company X is able to get funds from market quite lower than Company Y, both in terms of floating rate and fixed rate.

| | Fixed Rate | Floating Rate |
| --- | --- | --- |
| **Company X** | 8% | MIBOR + 25 bps |
| **Company Y** | 8.75% | MIBOR + 50 bps |

With the above information, can it be possible for both the companies go for interest rate swaps?

**Answer:**

|  | Fixed Rate | Floating Rate |
|---|---|---|
| **Company X** | 8% | MIBOR + 25 bps |
| **Company Y** | 8.75% | MIBOR + 50 bps |
| **Differential** | 0.75% | 0.25% |

The above table indicates that Company X is better rated both for fixed and floating rates compared to Company Y. However, Company X has more advantage in fixed rate than in the floating rate if it goes for an interest rate swaps with Company Y.

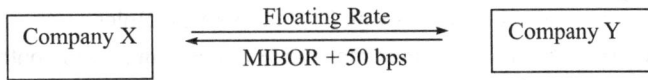

- Company X will be borrowing at fixed rate = 8%
- Company Y will be borrowing at floating rate = MIBOR + 50 bps
- They will be exchanging the interest payment for the notional principal on the settlement date.
- If on the interest payment date, MIBOR is 8.15%, then for Company Y the cost of borrowing would be 8.65% (8.15% + 50 bps) and for Company X it remains fixed at 8%. Hence, company Y would be getting an advantage of 10 bps by fixing its interest cost at 8.65% despite borrowing at a floating rate MIBOR + 50 bps.
- Company X is getting the notional amount at a cost of 8% fixed and same amount it is giving it to Company Y at 8.65% and by that way the Company X is making a profit of 50 bps.

## SUGGESTED READINGS

1. Marshall, J.F. and Kapna, K.R., *Understanding Swap Finance*, Cincinnati, OH, South Western, 1990.
2. Turnbull, S.M., Swaps: A zero sum game, *Financial Management*, 16, No. 1, pp. 15–21, Spring 1981.
3. Richard, Levich M., *International Financial Markets: Prices and Policies*, 2nd ed., McGraw-Hill International Edition, Singapore, 2001.
4. Redhead, Keith, *Introduction to International Money Market*, Woodhead Faulkner, Hamel Hempsted, 1992.
5. Decovny, S., *Swaps*, Woodhead Faulkner, Hamel Hempsted, 1992.
6. Sharpe, W.F. and Alexander, G.J., *Investment*, Prentice-Hall, Englewood Cliffs, 1995.
7. Ian, Giddy, *Global Financial Markets*, A.I.T.B.S. Publication, New Delhi, 1997.

## REVIEW QUESTIONS

1. What is swap and swap contract? Discuss with suitable examples along with risks involved.
2. Write a detailed note on evolution of swap market.
3. What is a financial swap? Discuss the features of a swap contract with example.
4. What are major types of financial swaps? Explain with examples.
5. What is interest rate swap contract? Discuss the various features of an interest rate swaps with suitable examples.

6. Write a note on types of interest rate swaps with examples.

7. "Plain vanilla swap is the simplest form of interest rate swap contract available in interest rates swaps market." Discuss with a suitable example along with its structure and mechanism.

8. How interest rate swaps are valued? Explain with examples.

9. What is currency swap? Explain its features and also show the three steps flow of currency swaps with examples.

10. What are various types of currency swaps? Explain their structure also.

11. Show how a currency swap agreement can be taken place. Explain with examples.

12. Write a note on valuation of currency swap. Explain with examples.

13. What is swap contract? What are various motivations underlying swap contract?

14. Describe debt-equity swaps with its uses with suitable illustrations.

15. Explain the trading mechanism of swap deal with suitable examples.

16. Explain how an investor can hedge his risk by using interest rate swaps. Explain with suitable data.

17. Explain the mechanism of interest rate swaps, and risks inherent therein.

18. "Swaps are private negotiations between the two parties to exchange their future cash flow and liability". Explain the statement in the light of role of financial intermediary in swap market.

19. Compare and contrast between options, futures and swaps contracts.

20. If a bank is a counter party to a large number of interest rate swaps, what risks does it face? How will it manage those risks?

21. Why is the expected loss from a default on a swap less than the expected loss from the default on a loan with the same principal? Examine critically.

22. Write note on the following:
    (a) Amortizing Swap
    (b) Differential Swap
    (c) Basis Swap

23. How can a deferred swap be created from two other swaps?

24. Write a note on Commodity Swap with suitable examples.

25. Distinguish between At-market swap and Off-market swap. Also discuss leveraged swap with suitable examples.

## UNSOLVED PROBLEMS

**P.1.** Suppose Firm A needs fixed rate funds which are available to him at the rate of 10.5% to be computed half yearly but it has access to cheaper floating rate funds available to it at LIBOR + 0.3%. Firm B needs floating-rate funds available to it at six-month LIBOR flat but has access to cheaper fixed rate funds available to it at the rate of 9.50% to be computed half-yearly. Both the principals are identical in size on maturity and are in the same currency. Show how interest rate swap takes place between A and B.

**P.2.** Suppose a car manufacturing firm provides loan to its customer for financing the purchase of car at a fixed rate of 12%. Such loans are financed by medium term notes that firm issues at LIBOR 0.25%. LIBOR is 7.0% and the administrative cost and other costs involved in borrowing/lending came to 2.0%. If LIBOR does not fluctuate, firm will enjoy a margin of 12 – 9.25 = 2.75%. But if LIBOR moves upward, the margin will get squeezed. The firm wants to hedge this risk. How company can use swap to hedge interest rates?

**P.3.** Mr. Ramesh, a pension fund manager, thinks that the stock market is going to move upward sharply in the next three years. In contrast, Mr. Ram, who also runs a pension fund, thinks that the stock market is likely to move downward in the same period of time. Mr. Ramesh is considering selling ₹100 million of bonds and investing the proceeds of common stocks whereas Mr. Ram is thinking of selling ₹100 million of common stocks and using the proceeds to purchase bonds. How can this be used by both parties to exchange their futures cash flow? Also assume that return of standard and poor 500 return during year of swap are equal to 3%, –4%, 1% and 5% and return on bond is 2% of the notional principal.

**P.4.** Company X wants to borrow £20 million at a fixed rate of interest for 10 years. Company Y wants to borrow £25 million at a fixed rate of interest for 10 years. Companies have been offered the following rates:

|                 | **Dollar** | **Sterling** |
|-----------------|------------|--------------|
| **Company X**   | 8%         | 11.6%        |
| **Company Z**   | 10%        | 12%          |

Show how currency swap is possible with effective cost of borrowing.

**P.5.** ICICI Bank wishes to borrow ₹50 crore at a fixed rate for 10 years and has been offered either 10% fixed or raise month LIBOR + 1%. IDBI Bank wishes to borrow ₹50 crore at a floating rate for 10 years and has been offered with six-month LIBOR + 0.5% or 9% fixed. On the basis of above figures:

    (a) How may they enter into swap arrangement in which each benefits equally?

    (b) What risk may this agreement generate?

# Pricing and Hedging of Swaps

After reading this chapter, students will be able to

➤ Understand the basic concept of pricing of swap.
➤ Understand the nature of hedging with swap.
➤ Discuss various methods of pricing of new swap.
➤ Know the method of pricing of old (existing) swap.
➤ Know how to price interest rate swap.
➤ Know how to price currency swap.
➤ Discuss various methods of hedging with swap.
➤ Explain hedging to lower borrowing cost and rising interest rate.
➤ Explain hedging through forward swap and currency swap.
➤ Describe hedging through duration and gap analysis.

## 15.1 INTRODUCTION

Swap derivative market has recently emerged as one of the biggest markets in terms of turnover and volume of trades among all other derivatives markets. For successful trading in this market, one must be aware of all important ingredients of pricing of that product. For determining the fair theoretical price of a swap product, the trader must be having information regarding zero-coupon yield curve structure, default risk concerning the counterparties of swaps, expected floated rate of interest in future, timing of the cash flows and all such other environmental factors which might influence the pricing of a swap product.

In the preceding chapter, we have discussed the conceptual view of swaps like their nature, features, types, trading mechanism, etc. Whereas, in this chapter, we will discuss about the pricing of swaps, various methods of pricing of new swap as well as old one, pricing of interest rate swaps, currency swaps, and then how to hedge with the swaps and finally hedging the swaps.

## 15.2  PRICING OF INTEREST RATE SWAP: THE CONCEPT

Swap, in simple words, is an exchange of cash flows computed on notional amount and corresponding to different underlying. The party who pays the fixed rate is called *the buyer* of the swap. It means he has *long the swap*. Similarly, the party who pays the floating rate is called *the seller* of the swap, which means he has *short the swap*. Only the net payment changes hands. So the firm obliged to pay the higher rate remits cash to the other, popularly known as *difference check*. The swap rate or swap price is the interest rate paid on the fixed interest rate leg of the swap. To understand it, let us first understand the mechanism of a simple swap contract as shown in the example.

**EXAMPLE (Interest Rate Swap):**   Assume that Firm 'A' pays the fixed interest rate and receives the floating rate based on LIBOR (six-month). The counterparty Firm B receives the fixed payment and pays the floating rate. The notional principal is 10 million and fixed rate is 8 percent. The swap contract is done on September 13, 2014, and effective from September 15, 2014. The origination date of the swap is March 15, 2014 and the termination is September 15, 2017. The first payment date is September 15, 2014 and further semi-annual payments will be made on March 15 and September 15. Assume that LIBOR (six-month) rates on subsequent payments are as follow:

| Date | Six-Month LIBOR |
|---|---|
| March 15, 2014 | 7.4% |
| September 15, 2014 | 8.2% |
| March 15, 2015 | 8.0% |
| September 15, 2015 | 7.8% |
| March 15, 2016 | 8.4% |
| September 15, 2016 | 7.6% |
| March 15, 2017 | 7.0% |
| September 15, 2017 | 8.0% |

**TABLE 15.1**   Cash Flows in Swap Contract of Party (Firm A)

| Date | Six month LIBOR | Fixed payment at 8% per 4% (six month) | Floating payment six month (half of LIBOR) | Net cash flows ($) |
|---|---|---|---|---|
| September 15, 2014 | 8.2% | 4,00,000 | 4,10,000 | 10,000 |
| March 15, 2015 | 8.0% | 4,00,000 | 4,00,000 | Zero |
| September 15, 2015 | 7.8% | 4,00,000 | 3,90,000 | –10,000 |
| March 15, 2016 | 8.4% | 4,00,000 | 4,20,000 | 20,000 |
| September 15, 2016 | 7.6% | 4,00,000 | 3,80,000 | –20,000 |
| March 15, 2017 | 7.0% | 4,00,000 | 3,50,000 | –50,000 |
| September 15, 2017 | 8% | 4,00,000 | 4,00,000 | Zero |

Note = Floating rate payment at time '*t*' is determined by the interest rate at time (*t*–1). This net cash flows is the difference between the fixed and floating rate payments.

It is evident from the above example that two cash streams; fixed rate-based payments and floating rate-based payments are arisen in the swap, and the difference of these two, called *net cash flows* are transferred by either of the party to other party at each settlement date. In the said example, the fix rate is 8 percent p.a.

It is also learnt that a swap has zero value when it is originated, also known as *zero sum game*. It means that the present value of cash receipts and cash payments is zero at the time of the origination. Therefore, to determine the fixed rate or fixed price for a swap, a swap trader should estimate the present value of the swap's payments and receipts. The rate which equates these two present values in a zero net value is called *swap price*. After that the swap dealer or market maker in a swap contract can adjust the swap price to quote a bid ask spread in the market. In brief, swap pricing is a mechanism to determine the fixed rate in a swap agreement. The pricing of a swap will be discussed in two forms. First at the time of its origination (as a new swap contract) and then after its origination.

## 15.3   MECHANISM OF SWAP PRICING DETERMINATION

For determining the swap pricing or measuring the current market value of an interest rate swap, it involves four important elements which are as under:

- Constructing a zero-coupon yield curve
- Forecasting of future interest rates for short term
- Driving discount factors to value swap cash flows
- Determining present values of all swap cash flows

### 15.3.1   Constructing a Zero-Coupon Yield Curve

The first important element to determine the price of a swap contract is to build a yield curve based upon the different market instruments or indicators like current cash deposit rates, euro-dollar futures prices, treasury yields, interest rate swap spreads, etc. These known market rates assist us to form today's coupon yield curve. The coupon curve is the basic material from which a zero coupon yield curve is constructed. This is usually done through a method called *boots-trapping*. This is explained later on through a diagram in this chapter. Through this, we can derive each new point on the curve from previously determined zero coupon points.

It is observed that zero rates are higher than coupon rates when the yield curve is positively sloped and lower when the curve is inverted. The gap is widest at the far end of the yield curve. Further, if rates are low and the yield curve flat, the difference between coupon and zero rates will be minimal. But when rates are high and the curve is steep, the difference is significant.

It is also observed that the dates of cash flows of swaps rarely exactly match the dates for which zero curve points developed. So interpolation between data points is needed to solve this issue. For this, some extremely complicated algorithms have been developed to minimize the errors which can arise from interpolation.

### 15.3.2   Forecasting Future Interest Rates for Short Term

The other important element to determine the swap price is to forecast future interest rates because one-half of the cash flows in a simple swap contract are based on floating rates. What makes the floating leg of the swap hard to price is the uncertainty of the forward rates. Only first current floating rate is known certain. Therefore, to find out the future cash flows arising on floating rates, a forward yield curve of short-term interest rates is to be estimated. In fact, the forward curve is just an extension of the zero coupon yield curve. Therefore, once the zero curve has been developed, it is easily transformed into the forward curve needed to generate the swap floating rate cash flows.

## 15.3.3 Driving Discount Factors to Value Swap Cash Flows

After determining the zero yield curve and estimating short-term future interest rate, third important factor is derive the discount factor to get the present values of all the swap cash flows, for both known fixed rate and estimated floating rates. The discount factors will be determined on the basis of creditworthiness of counterparty, market position of interest rate and other economic factors. Like forward interest rate, discount factors are just a transformation of zero coupon rates.

## 15.3.4 Determining Present Value of All Swap Cash Flows

After determining the discount factors, the final step is to apply the discount factors to find the present value of fixed and floating swap cash flows. These values are then netted to determine the swap's current market value and to find out the swap price. The swap value can be positive, negative or zero, depending upon how market interest rates have changed since the inception of the swap. For example, in case of floating to fixed swap, higher market interest rates will create a gain for the hedger and lower rates a loss.

The value of a swap contract measured is shown by a hypothetical example as shown below:

**EXAMPLE:**

| Measuring the Value of an Interest Rate Swap | | | | | |
|---|---|---|---|---|---|
| **Swap Specifications** | | | | | |
| Notional Principal | $50 m | | Original Term | 3 years | |
| Fixed Rate | 5.75% a/360 | | Remaining Term | 2 years | |
| Floating Index | 6 m LIBOR a/360 | | | | |
| Swap Payment Dates | Oct. 14 | Apr. 15 | | Oct. 15 | Apr. 16 |
| Days in Period | 183 | 182 | | 185 | 182 |
| Swap Yield Curve | 6.00% | 6.25% | | 6.50% | 6.75% |
| Zero Coupon Yield Curve | 6.00% | 6.25% | | 6.51% | 6.77% |
| Discount Factors | 97.09% | 94.03% | | 90.84% | 87.53% |
| **Fixed Swap Flows (Hedger Pays Fixed Rate)** | | | | | |
| Undiscounted Cash Flows | (14,61,458) | (14,53,472) | (14,77,430) | (14,53,472) | Fixed total |
| Present Value of Cash Flows | (14,18,930) | (13,66,700) | (13,42,098) | (12,72,224) | (53,99,952) |
| Forward Rates | 6.00% | 6.44% | 6.84% | 7.47% | |
| **Floating Swap Flows (Hedger Receives Floating Rate)** | | | | | |
| Undiscounted Cash Flows | 15,25,000 | 16,27,888 | 17,57,500 | 18,88,250 | Float total |
| Present Value of Cash Flows | 14,80,622 | 15,30,704 | 15,96,514 | 16,52,786 | 6,260,626 |
| Net Present Value of Swap | | | | | 8,60,674 |

## 15.4    PRICING OF A NEW INTEREST RATE SWAP

Determining the fix rate or swap price or theoretical price of a swap is quite simple. It is mechanism of estimating future interest rate in the market. Thus, from valuation or pricing perspective, swaps are not much different from customized bonds or notes. The fixed cash flows in a swap are just like the interest payments on a high quality fixed rate bonds. Similarly, floating cash flows in a swap are akin to the interest payments on a floating rate note. Market variables which affect swap pricing includes changes in the level of interest rates in the market, changes in swap spreads, changes in the yield curve, exchange rate changes, inflation rate, etc. Certain transaction specific variables that affect swap pricing include notional principal amount, amortization, time to maturity (swap tenor), swap payment frequency, floating rate, reference rate (index), creditability of the counterparties (default factor), etc.

## 15.5    APPROACHES OF INTEREST RATE SWAP PRICING

Following are the important approaches of interest rate swap pricing:

   (i)  Bond Equivalent Approach
   (ii) Present Value Approach
   (iii) Forward Rate Agreement Approach
   (iv) Zero Cost Collar Approach

### 15.5.1    Bond Equivalent Approach

Swap contract is just like portfolio of two bonds, in which the party receives interest payment on one bond and pays interest payment on the other bond. It means logically, you can receive as maximum interest as you can, and pay as minimum as you can. So, under bond equivalent approach, the swap rate is determined on the basis of equivalent bond of the same principal amount and maturity to that of the swap. According to this, the swap rate must be equal to the yield of par bond which has face value equal to the notional amount of the swap and upon payments at the same date which the swap payments should be made. For example, for a 5-year swap contract of 100 million rupee notional principal, a particular bond of 5-year maturity with 100 million rupee at 8 percent on the bond can be considered as fixed rate of swap. In an interest rate swap contract, one party simultaneously receives and pays the interest payment over a particular period. For example, for a fixed rate payer, the value of the swap will be equal to as follows:

- **Value of swap for fixed rate payer**

   Present value of floating rate payments – Present value of fixed rate payments $\geq 0$

   PV of floating rate payments – PV of fixed rate payments $\geq 0$ $\hspace{2cm}$ (15.1)

- **Value of swap for floating rate payer**

   Present value of fixed rate payments – Present value of floating rate payments $\geq 0$

   PV of fixed rate payments – PV of floating rate payments $\geq 0$ $\hspace{2cm}$ (15.2)

Because the present value of one is negative of the other, the only way that no present value in negative is that both the present values should be equal to zero. This approach suggests that a swap must be so priced that the present value of the fixed rate payment equals that present value of the floating rate payments.

It is to be ensured that this approach to pricing an interest rate swap requires that we are able to observe the yield on a par bond with the appropriate maturity. If for any reason, later on, the swap rate is not equal to coupon rate of the bond, then an arbitrage opportunity will arise. For example, let us assume that the swap rate is 10 percent and coupon rate is 8 percent, then in such situation, it pays to enter the swap to receive fixed and pay floating rate of interest. Further, we can hedge the swap position by selling fixed rate debt for an 8 percent coupon and invest the proceeds in LIBOR-based bond. In this position, we can earn 2 percent more interest on notional amount of the swap till maturity with no risk. Further, the payment of LIBOR/MIBOR interest on swap will be paid from the receipt of interest on the investment made, and thus, having no risk. So, the difference of 2 percent will create arbitrage opportunity in the swap market. On the other hand, if the swap rate is below the yield of the par bond, we can make money by promising to pay fixed and hedging the position.

In brief, the bond equivalent approach of swap pricing states that the fixed rate or swap price of a swap contract can be determined on the basis of coupon rate on the bond having same maturity in the market.

## 15.5.2 Present Value Approach

Another approach which can be considered for determining the swap price is the present value approach. According to it, the interest rate swap is a combination of two cash streams, i.e., fixed rate payments and floating rate payments over a specified time period in future. This approach advocates that a fixed rate can be determined on the basis of present values of both the streams. The present value approach can be applied where we do not observe a par bond outstanding with same maturity period. The present value of the fixed rate payments can be calculated which is equivalent to the present value of the payments from a fixed rate bond. Similarly, the present value of the floating rate payments is the present value of a bond with floating rate payments. We assume here the floating rate based upon LIBOR, payment semi-annual and 'X' as the principal amount. The value of bond based on the floating rate is calculated as:

$$\text{The value of floating rate bond} = \text{PV [Principal Amount} \times (1 + \text{LIBOR} \times (T - t/360)] \quad (15.3)$$

where,
$$\text{PV} = \text{Present Value}$$
$$\text{LIBOR} = \text{Index interest rate, or any other index}$$
$$T - t = \text{Period of Interest}$$

If interest payment is determined using LIBOR, one expects the risk characteristics of the payment to be thereof LIBOR. Consequently the appropriate discount rate is LIBOR.

The initial terms of an interest rate swap are usually such that they are priced at the market. At market swap is one in which the swap price is set in such way that the present value of the fix rate side of the swap is equal to the present value of the floating rate side. The basic argument behind is that the market uses its best estimate of future cash flows and which come from the spot rate yield and the implied forward rate. There will be one single interest rate which will cause the fixed rate side of the swap, and to make present value equals to the floating rate payments.

The present value of the fixed rate payments including the principal payments should be equal to the amount of floating rate amount. Let 'A' be the fixed rate semi-annual interest payments in the swap. $P(t + i \times 0.5)$ is the price of a zero coupon bond paying ₹1 when the semi-annual interest payment is made at $(t + i + 0.5)$.

In the light of the above, now we have to find out the fixed rate payments. This is to be calculated by finding out the price of the zero coupon bonds paying ₹1 at the different payment dates. This is calculated through the following formula:

Formula for the pricing of a fixed rate payment (bonds) =

$$\sum_{t=1}^{N} P_t(t + 0.5 \times i)A + P_t(t + 0.5 \times N)M \tag{15.4}$$

The above can also be calculated by using the yield-to-maturity (YTM) formula of fixed rate bond which is as under:

$$M = \sum_{i=1}^{N} \frac{A}{(1+k)^i} + \frac{M}{(1+k)^N}$$

where

$M$ = principal amount
$N$ = number of payments period
$A$ = present value of the coupon on principal amount
$K$ = discount rate or (yields-to-maturity)

**EXAMPLE:**    Assume a 10-year swap with semi-annual payment, and notional principal amount of ₹100 m, $K$ is 10% per annum payment. The value of $A$ is calculated as:

$$₹100 \text{ m} = \sum_{i=1}^{20} \frac{A}{(1+0.05)^i} + \frac{₹100 \text{ m}}{(1+0.05)^{20}} = ₹50 \text{ lakhs}$$

So interest pay out on swap will be ₹50 lakhs.

On comparison of the bond equivalent approach and present value approach, both the approaches advocates the same view except that the PV approach can be used for these swaps which do not find equivalent periods of bonds. The discount rate assumed in the PV approach is subject to default risk of the counterparty. Therefore, while fixing the discount rate, the credit rating of the counterparty in the swap is to be taken into consideration. For example, if the fixed rate payer firm has 'A' rating, then it would be appropriate to use the yield of an 'A' grading bond instead of using risk-free interest rates. In other words, the appropriate swap rate for the fixed rate payer would be higher if the fixed rate payers are having low rating but the floating rate payer has no default risk.

## 15.5.3    Forward Rate Agreement (FRA) Approach

Another important approach to find out the swap price, and commonly used, is FRA method. In a plain vanilla interest rate swap (fixed-to-floating), one party pays fixed payment and another party pays the floating payment based on a particular agreed reference index rate, i.e., say LIBOR/ MIBOR. Finding the present value of the fixed payments means finding the present value of an annuity because the fixed payments are known as soon as swap price is fixed. On the other hand, in the floating payments, only the first floating cash flows is known, remaining floating cash flows are unknown, because these are based on the value index rate. One must determine these payments. It means the floating cash flows must either be estimated or set equal to the cash flows be hedged.

Let us explain the above situation with an example. A swap dealer who will receive a series of floating cash flows might use FRAs to pay the same. It means he has hedged floating cash payments. If the market interest rate is declined, then the swap dealer will receive lesser amount from the floating rate swap payments, but simultaneously, he will also pay lesser amount on the FRAs. Since, the swap dealer has hedged the position, so FRA prices can be used to estimate the floating interest rates in the swap agreement.

In brief, for pricing the swap, following steps are taken in FRA approach:

Find the present value of floating rate cash flows by using the forward rates to be exchanged and the spot rates prevailing on zero-coupon bonds (equivalent to swaps in terms of principal and period) as the appropriate discount rate.

Find the fixed rate which makes the present value of the fixed payments equal to the amount calculated for floating payments in the above step. Calculated fixed rate will be fixed amounts to be exchanged, and spot rates are used on zero-coupon bonds as the appropriate discount rates on the swaps.

**EXAMPLE:** To explain the FRA approach to determine the swap price, let us assume the different period payment as spot term structure: $r(0 - 1) = 7$ percent, $r(0 - 2) = 8$ percent, $r(0 - 3) = 9$ percent from these spot rates, the forward rates can be calculated which are as

One-year forward rate $(fr) = (1.08)^2 = (1.07) [1 + fr(1 - 2)] = 0.090093$

$Fr(1 - 2) = 9.01\%$ app

One-year forward rate, two year, hence, is $fr(2 - 3)$

$= (1.09)^3 = (1.08)^2 [1 + fr(2 - 3)] = 0.110278$

$Fr(2 - 3) = 11.03$ percent app

Now consider a 3-year swap with a notional principal ₹100 floating rate is one year LIBOR. Payments are settled annually. Calculate the swap price (fair fixed rate) of the swap by using FRA method.

**Step-1** Expected floating cash flows are as follows:

$CF_1 = 0.07 \times 100 = 7.0000$

$CF_2 = 0.090093 \times 100 = 9.0093$

$CF_3 = 0.110278 \times 100 = 11.0278$

**Step-2** Now calculate the value of above floating cash flows by using appropriate discount rate, i.e., (spot rates on zero-coupon bond);

$$\text{Present value (cash flows)} = \frac{7}{1.07} + \frac{9.0093}{(1.08)^2} + \frac{11.0278}{(1.09)^3} = 22.7816$$

**Step-3** Assuming that value of swap is zero at its origination, then the PV of floating payments should be equal to fixed payments. So,

$$= A\left(\frac{1}{1.07} + \frac{1}{(1.08)^2} + \frac{1}{(1.09)^3}\right) = \left(\frac{A}{(1 + 0.07)} + \frac{A}{(1.08)^2} + \frac{A}{(1.09)^3}\right) = 22.7816$$

$$\text{So } = 22.7816 = A\left[\frac{1}{1.07} + \frac{1}{(1.08)^2} + \frac{1}{(1.09)^3}\right]$$

$$= 22.7816 = A\,(2.5640)$$

$$= A = 22.7816/2.5640 = 8.8851 = 8.89\%$$

It means fixed rate payments in above swap will be 8.8851 percent of the notional principal amount.

## 15.5.4 Zero Cost Collar Approach

The pricing of a fixed rate swap can also be viewed on the basis of a pair of options, i.e., cap option and floor option. In this method, two options are used to estimate the price of a fixed rate payer of swap. An interest rate swap is analogous to a zero cost collar in which cap is purchased and floor is sold. In other words, a collar is a simultaneous purchase of a cap and sale of a floor with the same maturity and strike price. This strategy hedges against an upward movement in interest rates and also simultaneously limits the profits from downward movement in interest payments.

In this approach, suppose a firm purchases a cap option and writes a floor, both with a 10 percent strike price and identical payment schedule. At the next payment dates, on the expiration of options, the firm will receive the amount if the benchmark rate is above 10 percent due to long cap. But, if the benchmark rate is below 10 percent, then the firm has to remit because of the short floor option. If the benchmark rate is same as of strike price, i.e., 10 percent, then both options will expire at-the-money and there is no payout on either side. This strategy is also called *zero cost* since the premium paid on buying of cap is offset by receiving the amount on writing a floor option. Such a strategy that fixes the strike price of the cap and the floor to neutralize the upfront premium is termed as a *zero-cost collar*.

A zero-cost collar would be similar to an interest rate swap. The purchase of cap and sale of a floor converts floating rate bond to fixed rate bond. The cash flows associated with these two options are identical to the cash flows associated with a fixed rate swap. Assume swap fixed rate as the option strike price. If the floating rate is higher than the swap strike price, then the cap will be in-the-money, and the party paying the fixed rate receives the surplus amount. However, if the floating rate is below the fixed rate, then the fixed rate payer will pay the amount to the other party. But, the loss will be minimum, i.e., difference in the market rate and the floor rate. This relationship is known as cap-floor-swap parity. It is shown in Figure 15.1.

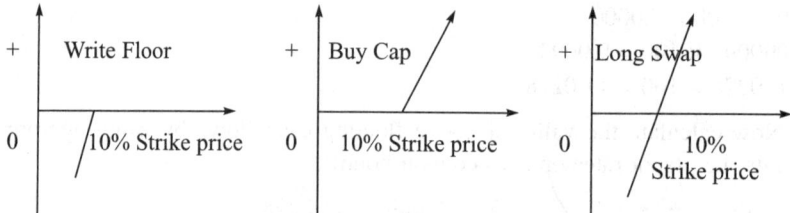

**FIGURE 15.1**   Cap-floor-swap parity.

Figure 15.1 states the position of combining of long cap with short floor for pricing a fixed rate swap, in which the swap fixed rate is priced equivalent to the strike price of cap and floor. If the floating rate of swap increases above the strike price, say in Figure 15.1 to 10 percent, then the strategy results in profits for the trader, compensating for the increase in interest rates. If the floating rate declines below the floor level, the strategy results in loss, and thus, increases the cost to the trader by the difference in the market rate and the floor rate, the payment will be comparatively small.

If interest rate swap are priced in manner different to above said strategy, then the arbitrage opportunity will arise between these instruments. The collar strategy is much popular in the market because participants hedge against the increase and decrease of interest rates in futures.

In brief, zero cost collar strategy assists in determining the price of the interest rate swap in which it gives benefit to the trader by limiting interest cost and at the same time determining the minimum cost to be borne by the firm even in decrease in interest rates in market below the strike price.

## 15.6   SHORT CUT METHOD OF PRICING OF INTEREST RATE SWAP

The basic assumption behind the shortcut method is that the value of a floating rate bond is approximately equal to its face value, because the next cash flow is always reprised as per current interest rates. For example, a two-year floating rate bond assumes as paying annual interest. The floating amount paid one year hence is paid on today one year rate. Similarly, amount paid after two years will be calculated based on the one year rate, which is currently unknown. Conceptually, we assume that one year spot rate that will actually exist one year hence is expected to equal today's one year forward rate, for delivery one year hence.

Based on this theory of expectation, in our previous example, if interest rate changes so that $r$ $(0 - 1) = 8$ percent and $fr$ $(1 - 2) = 9$ percent, the value of the bond is still ₹100 – how:

$$\frac{8}{108} \times \frac{109.0}{(1.08)(1.09)} = ₹100$$

From the above, it can be concluded that the value of a floating rate will always be very close to its per value irrespective of the number of holding years. The same can be applied to finding out the swap price too.

In our previous state example, the value of 'A' (value of fixed coupon amount) will also be equal to principal, i.e., ₹100.

$$100 = \left( \frac{A}{1.07} + \frac{A}{(1.08)^2} + \frac{A}{(1.09)^3} \right) + \frac{100}{(1.09)^3}$$

$$100 = A(2.5640) + 77.2184$$

$$A = \frac{100 - 77.2183}{2.5640} = \frac{22.7816}{2.5640} = 8.89\%$$

From the above, it is concluded that fixed rate which should be quoted for the swap is 7.3674 percent, and same as computed earlier.

After calculating a fixed rate of swap, the swap dealer will quote after adjusting his profit. He may give quotation in bid-ask spread form. For example, in the above example, fixed rate payments is 8.89 percent of the notional principal amount. Then, the swap price may be quoted as 8.86 percent to a firm fixed rate receiver and 8.92 percent to a firm fixed rate payer. If it is to be quoted in swap points, the quoted swap spreads might be 86/92; as bid-ask spread. Assume that current spot rate on a 3 year T-note is 7.05 percent and swap quote is 86/92. Then swap price will be 7.05 + 86 = 7.91 percent as bid, and 7.05 + 92 = 7.97 percent as ask swap price. A firm which wants to pay the fixed rate would be quote higher rate (ask rate) a fix rate of 7.97 percent. A firm which wants to pay floating rate and receive a fixed rate would be quoted the lower rate (bid rate) of 7.91 percent. Thus, 6 basis point differentials is the dealer's gross profit. Further, the swap spread increases with the longer tenor of the swap.

## 15.7   ROLE OF SPOT YIELD CURVE AND FORWARD YIELD CURVE FOR THE SWAP PRICE

As seen earlier that an interest rate swap is analogous to a series of forward contracts. A forward contract is an agreement to exchange of assets at a specified rate in future. As interest rate swap is also an agreement of exchange of assets in future with two rates; fixed and floating interest rate.

For example, a one-year swap with semi-annual payments is just a package or combination of two forward contracts, one with a six-month maturity and another with a twelve-month maturity.

We have also seen that there is a term structure of interest rates. It means the interest rates vary according to the time involved in the agreement. To understand the forward curve, it is important to know the useful notation in the market. If we borrow at LIBOR today for three months, this is noted as SPOT LIBOR. We might also enter into an agreement to borrow for 3 months. This is noted as 3 × 6 forward rate agreement (FRA) with the associated interest shown as $3f6$ and soon. Let us explain this by the diagrams (Figures 15.2 and 15.3).

Let us consider the following LIBOR-based interest rate information as:

**TABLE 15.2**    Interest Rate Information

| Term | Spot (LIBOR) | Implied IRR (LIBOR) (Calculated) |
|------|--------------|----------------------------------|
| Spot $(o, f3)$ | 6.40% | 6.40% |
| Six-month $(o, f6)$ | 6.50% | 6.60156% |
| Nine-month $(o, f9)$ | 6.60% | 6.80464% |
| Twelve-month $(o, f12)$ | 6.70% | 7.0092% |

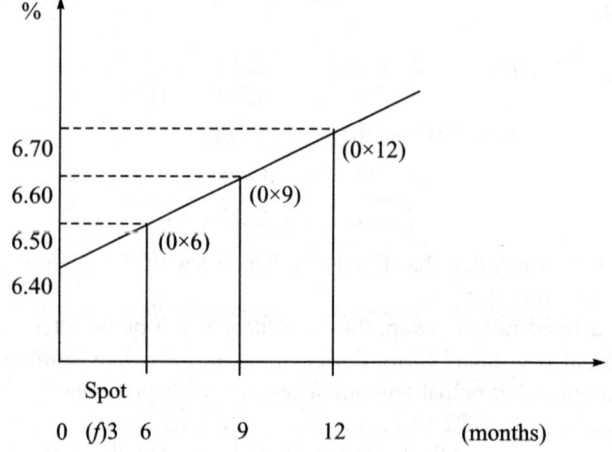

**FIGURE 15.2**    LIBOR spot yield curve.

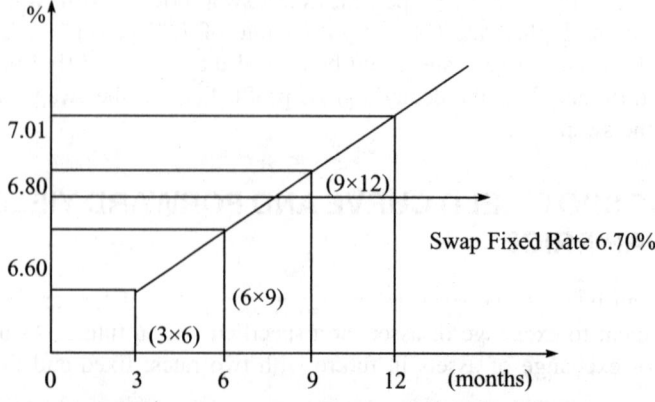

**FIGURE 15.3**    LIBOR implied forward rate curve.

Implied forward rates are such rates which are inbuilt due to spot rates. From the spot rates, one can determine the implied forward rate. From the above data, we can determine the 3-month rate, the market anticipates will prevail in 3-month ($3f6$), six-month ($6f9$), nine-month ($9f12$) and so on. The process is also known as bootstrapping to calculate the IRR values. The mechanism of calculating the FRA has already been discussed in Chapter 10 of this book.

Calculation of fixed rate of swap from the above example:

For this we have to calculate first PV of floating rate payments.

$$\frac{\text{First swap payment}}{\text{(2-month now)}} = 1 + R_3 = 1 + \left[ \frac{91}{360} \times 0.0640 \right] = 1.016177$$

$$\frac{\text{Second swap payment}}{\text{(6-month now)}} = 1 + R_6 = 1 + \left[ \frac{91+90}{360} \times 0.0650 \right] = 1.03268$$

$$\frac{\text{Third swap payment}}{\text{(9-month now)}} = 1 + R_9 = 1 + \left[ \frac{91+90+92}{360} \times 0.0660 \right] = 1.05005$$

$$\frac{\text{Fourth swap payment}}{\text{(12-month now)}} = 1 + R_{12} = 1 + \left[ \frac{91+90+92+92}{360} \times 0.0670 \right] = 0.071065$$

PV of Floating Rate Side is:

$$\text{PV Floating} = \left( \frac{6.40\% \times \dfrac{91}{360}}{1.016177} \right) + \left( \frac{6.50\% \times \dfrac{90}{360}}{1.03260} \right) + \left( \frac{6.60\% \times \dfrac{92}{360}}{1.05005} \right) + \left( \frac{6.70\% \times \dfrac{92}{360}}{1.071065} \right)$$

$$= 0.0159202 + 0.015736 + 0.016063 + 0.015986 = 0.0637052$$

$$\text{PV fixed} = \left( \frac{X\% \dfrac{91}{360}}{1.016177} \right) + \left( \frac{X\% \dfrac{91}{360}}{1.03268} \right) + \left( \frac{X\% \dfrac{92}{360}}{1.05005} \right) + \left( \frac{X\% \dfrac{92}{360}}{1.071065} \right)$$

$$= 0.24875X + 0.244788X + 0.24337X + 0.238599X = 0.975506X$$

Since both the PVs should be equal. The value of $X$ is calculated as

$$0.975506X = 0.0637052$$

$$X = \frac{0.0637052}{0.975506} = 0.06530 = 6.53\%$$

Thus, the equilibrium swap fixed rate or (swap price) is 6.53 percent.

In brief, swap fixed rates is just like bond's yield to maturity (YTM). In some respects, the yield-to-maturity is like an average of the spot rates over the bonds life. In other words, the swap price is the weighted average of the forward rates discounted by when they occur in future.

## 15.8 PRICING AN OUTSTANDING INTEREST RATE SWAP (AFTER ORIGINATION)

Interest rates, exchange rates, inflation rates are such economic variables which are continuously changing in the market. As the interest rates change, the value of the swaps will also change. The value of the swap will be positive for one party while negative for the counterparty. It means one party will be in profit and other will be in loss. The valuation method of the swap for remaining period is same as already discussed in the preceding section of this chapter. Any method can be used for the same.

Sometimes, it is important to make valuation of the swap after its origination due to various reasons. Important among these are stated below:

- The firms want to know the position of their swap contracts and their impact on the current financial position of the firm. Though the swaps are off-balance sheet transactions, they have direct impact on firms' balance sheets.
- Due to change in the market interest rate, the swap's value is adversely affected. If it is timely determined, then the firm can take appropriate position in the market to check the adverse impact of the swap.
- Firms want to know the default risk they face. Sometimes, the counterparty's loss in the swap contract may create chance of default by the other party.
- Many swaps are market-to-market, which require valuing swaps after their origination. Margins are to be adjusted accordingly.

The swap value reflects the difference between the swap price and interest rate that would make the swap to zero value. At origination of the swap, the value of swap is zero for both the parties. As soon as, interest rate changes, the value of the swap also changes. An off-market swap is one in which the fixed rate is such that the value of the swap on both sides; fixed rate side and floating rate side is not same, resulting into value to one of the counterparties.

## 15.8.1 Valuing an Interest Rate Swap (After Origination)

The method of valuing the swap after its origination are same as applied at their initiation. Let us consider our example given the preceding section.

**EXAMPLE:** Spot-term structure: $r\,(0–1) = 7$ percent, $r(0–2) = 8$ percent, $r(0–3) = 9$ percent. Now swap is extended to 4th year, where spot rate $r(0–4)$ is 10 percent. In the example, we computed $fr(1, 2) = 9.0093$ percent and $fr(2–3) = 11.0278$ percent. Now, one year forward rate for delivery three year hence is computed as $fr(3–4) = (1.10)^4 = (1.09)^3\,[1 + fr(3–4)] = 0.130553 = 13.0553$ percent. The swap price for a four-year interest rate swap is calculated as:

$$100 = \left[\frac{A}{(1.07)} + \frac{A}{(1.08)^2} + \frac{A}{(1.09)^3} + \frac{A}{(1.10)^4}\right] + \frac{100}{(1.10)^4}$$

$$100 = \left[\frac{1}{(1.07)} + \frac{1}{(1.08)^2} + \frac{1}{(1.09)^3} + \frac{1}{(1.10)^4}\right] + 68.3013$$

$$100 = (3.2470)\,A + 68.3013$$

$$(3.2470)\,A = \frac{100 - 68.3013}{3.2470} = \frac{31.6987}{3.2470}$$

$A = 9.76245 = 9.76$ percent app.

Swap price would be 9.76 percent in exchange of one year LIBOR. The amount of fixed payment of each fixed, assuming principal amount to ₹30 m would be $(0.0976)\,(\$30\text{ m}) = ₹2.928000$. Further, assume that term structure has also been changed, and now $r(0–1) = 4.5$ percent, $r(0–2) = 5$ percent and $r(0–3) = 5.5$ percent. Calculate value of the swap using the Ist method explained earlier.

First, find the present value of remaining fixed payments and floating payments, and then discount them at current spot rate. The difference of these two values would be value of the swap.

$$\text{PV of fixed payments} = \frac{29,28,000}{1.045} + \frac{29,28,000}{(1.05)^2} + \frac{29,28,000}{(1.055)^3}$$

$$= ₹7,951210$$

Now, calculate the forward rate that will exist one year after the swap's origination:

$Fr\ (1\text{--}2) = 1.045\ [1 + r\ (1\text{--}2)] = 0.055024$
$Fr\ (2\text{--}3) = (1.05)^2\ [1 + r\ (2\text{--}3)] = 0.065072$

Calculation of the floating payments

$$= \frac{(0.045)\,(\$30\,\text{m})}{1.045} + \frac{(0.055024)\,(\$30\,\text{m})}{(1.05)^2} + \frac{(0.065072)\,(\$30\,\text{m})}{(1.055)^3}$$

$$= ₹44,51,604$$

Value of Swap

= Present value of fixed payments = ₹79,51,210
= Present value of floating payments = ₹44,51,604
Difference of these two = ₹34,99,606

The above value of the swap will be negative value for the fixed rate payer party and positive for the fixed rate receiver.

Shortcut Method: According Method, find out first the new price of Swap

$$= 100 = A\left[\frac{1}{1.045} + \frac{1}{(1.05)^2} + \frac{1}{(1.055)^3}\right] + \frac{100}{(1.055)^3}$$

$$= A\ \{2.7156\} + 55.1614$$
$$14.8366 = 2.7156A$$
$$A = 5.46428 = 5.46\%$$

Notional amount is ₹30 m, fixed payments on a new swap would be (0.05464258) (₹30 m) = ₹1.639277. Difference between the old swap and new swap's fixed payments' is ₹29,28,000 − ₹16,39,277 = ₹12,88,723 per year calculate the present value of this difference:

$$\frac{12,88,723}{1.045} + \frac{12,88,723}{(1.05)^2} + \frac{12,88,723}{(1.055)^3} = ₹34,99,630$$

Since the fixed payment payer would be in loss he can approach to the swap dealer (fixed payment receiver) to close the swap early the swap dealer would agree for a payment of ₹34,99,630 by the party.

## 15.9 PRICING OF A CURRENCY SWAP CONTRACT

In the preceding section, we have seen mechanism of pricing of the interest rate swap contract. In the same manner, we will discuss in this section the pricing of a currency swap contract. We have seen that in a currency swap, two different currencies are periodically exchanged. At the origination of swap. The principal amount of one currency is exchanged with the other currency and followed with periodical exchange of accrued interest along with the re-exchange of principal amount at the termination of the swap. Further, we have seen different types of the currency swaps; fixed-to-fixed, floating-to-fixed and floating-to-floating. In brief, a currency swap contract is equivalent to selling or issuing a bond in currency, and buying a bond in other currency. When converted at the current exchange rate, the values of the assets and liabilities are equal.

This section will discuss the mechanism of pricing of a currency swap. Pricing of a swap involves the present value of the payments must be equal to the present value of the receipts, so that the swap has a zero value at its origination. In case of currency swap, the present value of all payments; interest payments occurring and present value of all receipts, interest payments and terminal principal amount should be equal. The present value can be expressed in either currency, and payments either can be based on fixed or floating rate of interest.

The first step in pricing the currency swap is to determine the equilibrium fixed rate on a plain vanilla interest rate swap in each of the two countries. Thus, we need to find the implied forward rates for which relevant spot rates over the tenor of the swap are to be determined, after that present values are matched. Let us explain this with an example.

Consider the data pertaining to a swap contract of two firms, one Indian and other USA. Both are able to borrow in the floating rate market at their respective LIBOR rates or at the fixed rates shown as under:

**Fixed Borrowing Rates**

| Term | Indian Firm | US Firm |
|--------|-------------|---------|
| 1 Year | 5% | 4.5% |
| 2 Year | 6% | 5.0% |

From the above, Indian rates, given one year spot rate is 5%, and to get 2-year spot rate, we can calculate from the following equation.

$$100 = \frac{6}{1.05} + \frac{106}{(1+r)^2} = 6.03\%$$

We can find the implied forward rate $(f_{1-2})$ from this equation as

$$(1.05)\,[1 + f(1\text{--}2)] = (1.0603)^2 = 7.07\%$$

Similarly we can find the US 2-year spot rate and implied forward rate from the following data:

$$100 = \frac{5}{1.045} \times \frac{105}{(1+r)^2} = 5.01\% \text{ (2 years US spot rate)}$$

$(1.045)\,[1 + f(1\text{--}2)] = (1.0501)^2 = 5.52\%$ implied forward rate of US.

Now from the above, we will calculate the equilibrium swap price for a 2-year interest rate swap in both India and US. As discussed earlier, this can be calculated by equating the present values of both sides, i.e., fixed and floating rate. Let us calculate swap fixed rates of these two:

In the Indian Market (Fixed Rate):

$$\frac{0.0500}{1.0500} + \frac{0.0707}{(1.0603)} = \frac{X}{(1.0500)} + \frac{X}{(1.0603)^2} = 6\%$$

In the US Market (Fixed Swap Rate):

$$\frac{0.0450}{1.0450} + \frac{0.0552}{(1.0501)^2} = \frac{X}{(1.0450)} \times \frac{X}{(1.0501)^2} = 5\%$$

It is to be noted that swap fixed rate as calculated above for each country is exactly equal to the 2-year borrowing rate that each firm faces. From the above calculation we can interpret these in terms of swaps. The floating side of the currency swap will be appropriate LIBOR and the fixed rate side will be the equilibrium swap fixed interest rate. For example, if the Indian firm wants to receive floating rate in US dollars and pays a fixed rate in Indian rupee the equilibrium swap would be receiving LIBOR US dollar and paying 6 percent in rupees. On the other hand, of the Indian firm want to receive fixed US rate, then term would be LIBOR of rupee and 5 percent US dollar, and vice versa.

## 15.10 COUNTERPARTY RISK IMPLICATIONS

It is important to understand the relationship between the forward yield curve and the swap price because it has direct impact on the risk of the counterparty. For example, if the yield curve is having upward slope means the floating rate is increasing than the fixed rate in the market. As a result the party who is paying floating rate payments and receiving fixed rate payments will be in loss. The risk factor relating to default on the part of floating rate payer will increase. If he defaults, he would not receive anything and vice versa. This is presented in Figure 15.4.

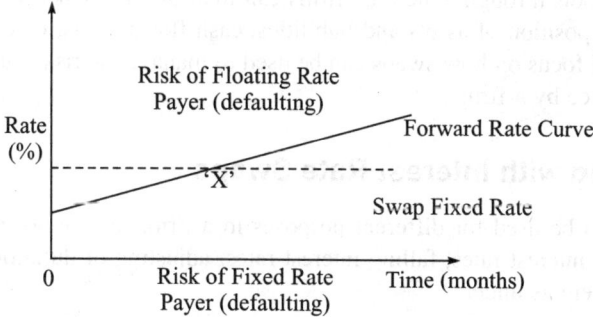

**FIGURE 15.4** Counterparty risk in swap.

From the figure, it is observed that when forward rate curve exceeds the swap fixed rate, the risk of the floating rate payer increases, and when it is lower than the fixed rate, then the risk of the fixed rate payer increases. Besides this, the swap dealers will also consider the credit-worthiness of the counterparty. Dealers will quote wider spreads for less, credit-worthy counterparties and vice versa. The wider spreads serve as risk premiums which will compensate the dealer for bearing credit (default) risk. Further, if the swap dealers are expecting higher default risk on the part of the counterparties, they may also demand for collateral (equivalent to initial margin in case of futures contract) or ask for guaranty from the banker, or may ask for swap insurance, or may demand to go for mark-to-market for swap contract.

**EXAMPLE:** Let us consider that plain vanilla interest swap two counterparties: Company A and Company B enter into a plain vanilla interest rate swap contract. The Company A pays a fixed rate of 8 percent p.a. on a semi-annual basis. He receives from Company B MIBOR + 50 basis points and its current rate is 6 percent p.a. The notional principal is ₹100 million, calculate the net payment to be made by the parties in this respect.

**Solution:**

| Company A | Company B |
|---|---|
| Pays fixed: 8% p.a. receives floating MIBOR + 50 bps notional principal: ₹100 m. Term: Bi-annual | Pays floating: MIBOR + 50 bps, receives: 8% p.a. notional principal ₹100 m. Term: Bi-annual. |

Company 'A' (Receipt)

Notional Principal × (Days period/365) × (Interest Rate/100)

$= ₹100 \text{ m} \times (180/365) \times (6.50\%)$

$= 100 \times \dfrac{180}{365} \times .065 = ₹3.205 \text{ m}$

Company 'B' (Receipt)

$₹100 \text{ m} \times \dfrac{182}{365} \times 08$

$= 3.989 \text{ m}$

Net amount: 3.989 m – 3.205 = 0.784 m = ₹7,84,000 will be paid by the Company A to Company B.

## 15.11   HEDGING WITH SWAPS

Swaps are important tools through which the firms can manage their risks whether it is related with the value of firm, composition of assets and liabilities, cash flows, costs, revenue prices, losses, etc. In this section, we will focus on how swaps can be used to manage the risk caused due to unexpected change in financial price by a firm.

### 15.11.1   Hedging with Interest Rate Swaps

Interest rate swaps can be used for different purposes in a firm, such as lowering borrowing costs, hedging against rising interest rates, falling interest rates, adjusting of duration of bonds, etc. These have been discussed here as under:

### 15.11.2   Hedging to Lower Borrowing Costs

Interest rate swaps in which the cash flows arisen due to interest rates; fixed or floating, are exchanged with the other firm, or swap dealer. It is understood that default risk premium on corporate bonds is greater on the long-term fixed rate bonds in comparison to the floating rate bonds. It means there is a quality differential between fixed and floating on borrow the funds by the firms in the market. The term "quantity difference" here means the difference in credit risk spreads that the two firms face in the two different markets, i.e., fixed and floating rate.

How interest rate swap can be used to exploit comparative advantage occurring due to quality difference is explained with an example. Consider a high credit rated company (AAA firm) can borrow the funds either at a fixed rate of 8 percent or at a floating rate (LIBOR + 25 bps) in the international market. On the other hand, a medium-rated firm (BBB firm) can borrow either at fixed rate of 9.25 percent or floating rate (LIBOR + 75 basis points in the market.

It is observed from the above that the Firm (AAA) has an absolute advantage in both the markets because it can raise funds at a lower rates than the firm (BBB). In fixed rate market it has benefit of 125 basis points, and 50 basis points in floating rate market. If we compare both the markets, then it is visualized that the firm (BBB) has a comparative advantage in the floating rate market because it pays only 50 basis points more than the Firm (AAA) whereas it is 125 basis permits more in fixed rate market.

Let us consider that both with the parties want to exploit comparative advantage by entering into a plain vanilla fixed-for-floating interest rate swap contract. Let us assume the following data to explain the arrangement through swap contract.

| Firm (AAA) | Firm (BBB) |
|---|---|
| Long-term Loan: $100 m | Long-term Loan: $100 m |
| Fixed Coupon Rate: 8% p.a. | Fixed Coupon Rate: 9.25% p.a. |
| Floating Rate: LIBOR + 25 bps (Six month) | Floating Rate: LIBOR + 75 bps (Six month) |

Assume that both the firms have entered a swap contract. As per terms of the swap, the Firm (AAA) will be fixed rate payer at the 8 percent and floating rate receiver at the LIBOR rate. The Firm (BBB) will receive fixed rate at 8 percent and pay floating rate at LIBOR. In such swap arrangements the Firm (AAA) has saved 25 bps by issuing synthetic floating rate debt and Firm (BBB) has benefited by 50 basis points calculated as under:

| Benefits of Firm (AAA) | Benefits of Firm (BBB) |
|---|---|
| Pays 8% to Capital market : –8% | Pays LIBOR + 75 bps : – (LIBOR + 75 bps) |
| Receives 8% in the swap : +8% | Pays 8% fixed : – 8% |
| Pay LIBOR in the swap : –LIBOR | Receives LIBOR : + LIBOR |
| Net Payment : –LIBOR | Net Payment : – 8.75% |
| Net Benefits: (LIBOR + .25 bps – LIBOR) – 25 bps (9.25% – 8.75% fixed) | Net Benefit : 50 bps |

It is noticed that such comparative advantage is still exist in the market. However, it is ensured that such swaps should be done with swap dealers only. Swap is negotiable market, hence, the terms and rates of interests under swaps are fully negotiable among the counterparties. Following is the swap arrangements with swap dealer in above example.

Consider that both the parties make the swap deal through a swap dealer (banker). The banker will also earn something in this swap. Let us assume that now the firm AAA will pay LIBOR and receives fixed rate at 7.95 percent and Firm BBB will pay fixed rate 8.10 percent and receives LIBOR. What will be now net position in the swap agreement? Total benefit between the parties is (9.25 percent – 8 percent) – (75 bps – 25 bps) = and rate differential in the floating rate market. In the new arrangement with swap dealer, the Firm (AAA) will save (25 bps – 05 bps) = 20 bps, Firm (BBB) saves (9.25 – 8.10 percent) = (1.15 bps – 75 bps) = 40 bps, and the swap dealer (Banker) will earn (8.10 percent – 7.95 percent) = 15 bps. Total benefits of all the parties will be 20 bps + 40 bps + 15 bps = 75 bps. However, the above benefits are subject to transaction costs like taxes, fee and other expenses.

It is evident from Figure 15.5 that how interest rate swap can save the borrowing cost of the parties. Further swap deals are having edge on the futures market. Swaps are, sometimes, cheaper in terms of cost to the forward rate agreements (FRA). However, the cost of engaging in these transactions and the prices of the contracts should be carefully analyzed to take final decision in different future derivatives.

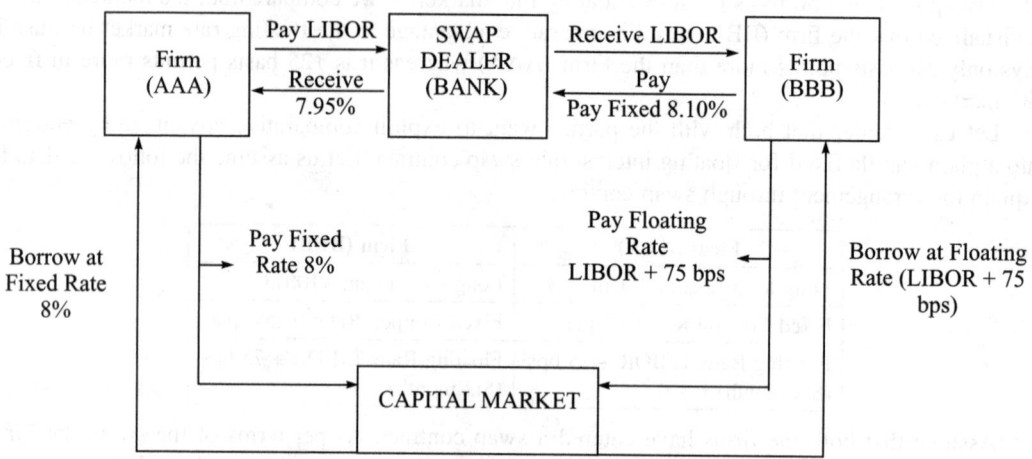

**FIGURE 15.5**   Hedging to lower borrowing cost with swap.

## 15.11.3   Hedge Against the Risk of Rising Interest Rates

Swaps are very valuable hedging tools for the firms to manage their risks in different ways. They assist the corporate firms to hedge their cost of funds in case of rising of interest rates in the market. For example, a firm has raised funds through floating rate (LIBOR). Then the firm will incur high cost of funds if LIBOR increases in future. Thus, the firms with floating rate debt are exposed to the risk of rising interest rates. In this situation, entering into a fixed-for-floating interest rate swap in which the party (fixed rate) permits the other firm (floating rate) to transform existing floating rate debt into synthetic fixed rate debt. In this way, the floating rate party can lock in fixed rate for the remaining life of the debt. This is explained through following example and presented in Figure 15.6.

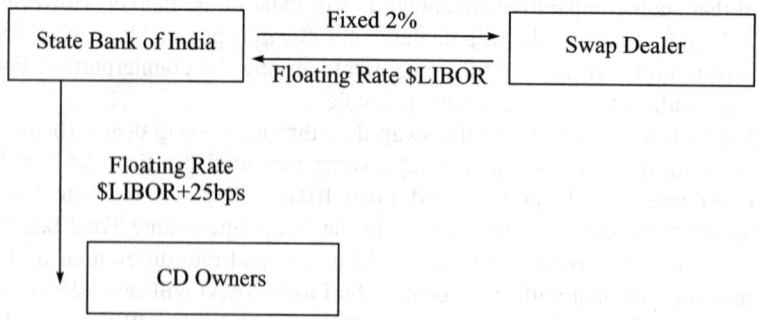

**FIGURE 15.6**   Fixed-for-floating rate swap.

**EXAMPLE:**   Consider that a bank has raised a huge deposits through the 6-month certificate of deposits (CDs) at the floating rate. The bank is expecting rise in the market rate of interest in near future resulting into a heavy payment of amount in terms of interest on CDs. The banker wants to hedge against this expected fear of rise in interest rate. It can enter into a fixed-for-floating interest rate swap in which it is pay fixed party. Assume that

State Bank of India has raised 3-month CDs of $100 m from international market at the LIBOR + 25 bps in dollar. The State Bank of India, to hedge against the risk of rise in interest rate, enters into a swap deal. Under this swap deal, the State Bank of India has locked its floating rate payment for 2 percent fixed rate to be paid to the swap dealer. The swap dealer will pay floating rate ($LIBOR) in future. The total cost of interest incurred to the Bank, now will be 2 percent + 25 bps, being total 2.25 percent.

## 15.12  HEDGING THROUGH FORWARD SWAPS

Forward swap is another tool to hedge the interest rate risk. Forward swap is forward agreement under which it obligates the firm to enter into swap after sometime. In other words, forward swap contracts begin or become effective after a particular period as agreed between the parties. The initial payments in such swap will be exchanged, say six months or one year, after such agreement has been originated.

Suppose a firm plants to raise 100 m funds by issuing a fixed rate bonds after two years and which will mature in seven years from now and the interest is to be paid semi-annually. It enters into a forward swap with a swap dealer (say, Banker A). As per this swap deal, the firm will pay a fixed rate (6 percent) agreed upon receives floating (LIBOR). In two years, the firm enters another swap deal with a swap dealer (say, Banker B) whereby it agrees to pay floating rate (LIBOR) and receives fixed rate of interest prevailing at that time.

Under the above said swap deals with two swap dealers 'A' and 'B', the firm has locked its future rate of occurring after two years from now. In such forward swap arrangement, the firm can use the fixed rate payments it receives from the swap dealer 'B' to pay the debt service on the bonds to be raised after two years. Further, the floating rate payments to be received from swap dealer 'A' will be offset by paying floating payments to the swap dealer 'B'. Now the firm is left with making the fixed rate payments to Swap dealer A. In this way, these forward transactions allow the firm to lock in its fixed rate interest payment on bonds with the swap dealer 'A' at the fixed rate agreed now, i.e., 6 percent and known today. It means the swap enters today, but starting in two years, Swap 'A' is known as forward swap contract.

The forward swaps can be used in different situations to manage the risk exposure:

(i)  To hedge against unanticipated rise in interest rate in future, as discussed above, the firms would enter into a forward swap contract, as a fixed rate payer and floating rate receiver. If the interest rate rises, then the firm will receive higher amount of interest payment on account of floating rate which may be greater than its fixed rate payments to the dealer.

(ii)  If the firm is expecting the fall in the interest rate in future, then the firm can enter forward swap with floating rate payer and fixed rate receiver. In this way, the firm will pay lesser amount than it is expected to pay in future.

(iii)  If the firm has already raised the floating rate loan and anticipates that interest rate will begin to rise in future after a gap of one–two years. Between this period, the rates will be low. In such situation, the firm can enter into a forward swap as the fixed rate payer.

Dealing in forward swaps is highly risky and speculative since these are associated with the foregoing scenarios. Therefore, the firms should use these after a thorough analysis of future scenario.

## 15.13  HEDGING AGAINST THE RISK OF FALLING INTEREST RATES

Another important use of the swaps is to hedge against the falling interest rate in the market specifically for those who are earning from lending funds in the market on floating rate basis, such as the banks, financial institutions, mutual funds, insurance companies, pension funds, investment companies, etc. They can synthetically extend the maturity of investments by engaging in a swap as the fixed rate receiver. Investment firms can enter swap by paying the floating interest rate and receive the fixed interest rate.

Similarly, the swaps can be useful to those borrowers who have taken loans on fixed interest rate basis. If the market rate of interest falls in future, then fixed rate payer will pay more interest in comparison to the current spot rates in the market. Their cost of funds would be higher to those who have raised funds on floating rate basis. In such situation, the fixed rate borrower can enter swap contracts by taking position of floating-for-fixed interest rate in the market. In this way, they will receive fixed rate interest payment from the swap dealer under swap agreement. They can use this amount to pay regular interest payment of their existing loans. Similarly, they will be paying floating rate payment to the swap dealer.

## 15.14  HEDGING THROUGH DURATION AND GAP ANALYSIS

Another important tools like gap analysis and duration which are frequently used by the financial institutions, banks, etc. to manage their exposure to interest rate risks. Gap analysis means the difference between rate sensitive assets minus rate sensitive liabilities. Gap analysis can be sensitive when the issuer of a security has the option to call the security for early prepayment. The question of when the asset or liability will be reprised becomes a random variable on the level of interest rates or other factors. As such, the gap can be calculated as:

$$\text{Gap} = \text{Rate sensitive assets} - \text{Rate sensitive liabilities}$$

The term "rate sensitive" relating to asset or liability refers to that the value of asset or liability is influenced by the change in interest rate. It means an asset or liability is rate sensitive. It will be repriced during a defined period. The defined period is called the *gapping period*. For example, a financial institution has a debt instrument with a maturity of 10 months, similarly, it has also given the funds on interest to a client which is due to be repaid in 10 months. The face value of both the items; security and loan, would be rate sensitive for any gapping period of more than 10 months.

The gap can be positive or negative. Positive gap means that the firm has more rate sensitive assets than rate sensitive liabilities. It indicates that if interest rate is decreased in the market, then the firm will incur more loss since more assets will be repriced at lower rates than the liabilities, and vice versa.

On the other hand if the gap is negative, it means that rate sensitive liabilities are more than the rate sensitive assets. If the market rate of interest is increased, then the interest payment on liabilities will be larger, reducing into reading net income.

"Duration" is another tool which is considered in interest risk management of the firm. The financing companies estimate the duration of their assets and liabilities. Duration can be calculated as:

$$\text{Duration (D)} = -\frac{\% \text{ Change Value}}{\% \Delta (1 + r)} = -\frac{(V_1 - V_0)/V_0}{(r_1 - r_0)/(1 + r_0)}$$

where

$V_0$ = Current value of an (asset or liability) at an initial rate of interest $(r_0)$

$V_1$ = Value of the asset/liability at a new interest rate $(r_1)$

Hence, Duration after solving the above equation

$$\% \Delta \text{ value} = -\text{ duration} \times \% \Delta(1 + r)$$

On the comparison of duration of assets and liabilities, if the assets' duration exceeds the duration of liabilities, an increase in interest rates will result into decline in value of the firm because the value of assets will decline more than the value of its liabilities.

On the other hand, if the duration of the liabilities is higher than the duration of the assets, then the decrease in interest rate will decrease the value of the assets and increase in the value of the liabilities, and finally, resulting into decline in the value of the firm.

It is presented in Table 15.3

**TABLE 15.3**   Impact of Duration on Value of Firm

| Assets | Liabilities |
|---|---|
| Long Duration $\Rightarrow$ If $r$ rises $V$ declines a lot | Short Duration $\Rightarrow$ If $r$ rises, $V$ declines by a smaller amount Owner's Equity $\therefore$ The value of owner equity must decline since equity = Assets – Liabilities |

Impact of duration can be summarised as:

A. Duration of Assets > Duration of Liabilities and/or negative gap = (Risk is that interest will rise).

B. Duration of Assets < Duration of Liabilities and/or positive gap (Risk is that interest rate will fall).

Duration and gap can be helpful to the firm to manage its risk arising due to change in the interest rate. It can use the swap for managing it. If the firm is exposed to the rising interest rate, then it should enter the pay-fixed interest party in the swap deal and receive-floating interest. Similarly, if the firm is exposed to lower interest rate risk, then it should enter the pay floating interest payment and receiver of the fixed rate payments.

## 15.15   HEDGING THROUGH CURRENCY SWAPS

The currency swaps can be useful to the firms in different ways to manage their risks, specifically, arising out of exposure to foreign currencies. For example, a multinational firm operating in many countries is exposed to foreign exchange risk in various currencies. So, how the currency swaps would be helpful in managing such risk is discussed in this section in various respects.

## 15.16   HEDGING TO LOWER BORROWING COSTS IN A FOREIGN CURRENCY

The cost of borrowing funds from different countries varies, depending upon the domestic interest rates and other state regulations. A multinational firm may have a comparative advantage in borrowing funds in some countries in comparison to others. For example, an MNE may be very popular in one country, and may not be well known in other countries. It means it is possible that an MNC can raise funds at lower cost in such countries where it is famous and having good reputation, in comparison to those countries where it is not well known.

In fact, this type of situation can be exploited by the firm to reduce its cost of funds raised in different countries. For example, assume that Firm 'A' has a comparative advantage in raising funds in currency 'X' but it needs funds of different currency, say, currency 'Y'. In such case, the firm can use the currency swap contract. First of all the firm will borrow funds in currency 'X', and then a currency swap contract will be entered with a swap dealer. In such swap contract, the firm will exchange currency X with the currency 'Y' for a particular period at the current exchange rate, and then return the currency 'Y' to the dealer at the maturity. As a result, a lower borrowing cost in currency 'Y' may be realized that if it had directly raised in currency 'Y' by the firm and this can be possible through currency swap deal.

Let us explain this concept of comparative advantage with a hypothetical example. Suppose that a large UK-based company 'A' has never before raised funds through bonds from the US market. But now the company wants to raise funds from USA in dollars to expand its business at the global level. Assuming that this company can easily borrow money at 6 percent in UK and other European countries. However, while issuing bonds in USA, it expects to raise at 8 percent. The company approaches a swap dealer and ask to quote on a fixed-for-fixed swap in which the company will receive US dollars at a fixed rate 8 percent. Assume that the swap dealer quotes a price of 5.8 percent fixed in terms of UK pounds (GBP) for 100 million at and current exchange rate 1.20$/£. In this the company will be able to save of 20 basis points in GBP. This is shown in Figure 15.7.

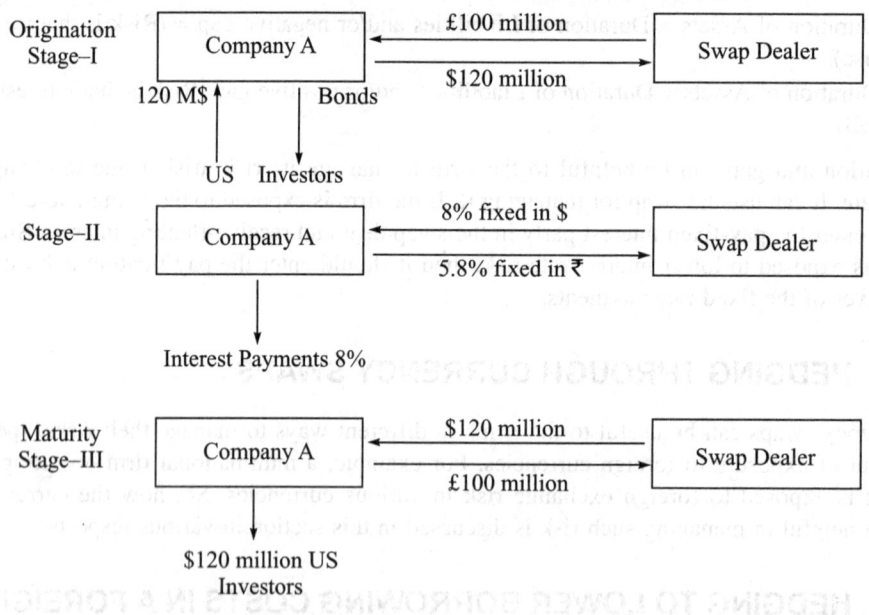

**FIGURE 15.7** Cash flows in currency swap.

## 15.17 HEDGING AGAINST THE RISK OF A DECLINE IN REVENUE

The currency swaps can be used to hedge against the risk in falling of revenue of business operating in other countries. For example, if the US-based multinational company is exporting its products in other countries, then the company's revenue will be affecting by the changes in exchange rates. Suppose, the company is exporting in India and sales proceeds are priced in Indian rupees. Assume that the sale of the company in India is 100 million in rupees and current exchange rate is ₹65 per US dollar. The goal of the company is to maximize its dollar profits, however, it is exposed to the risk of the $/₹ exchange rate. If this rate falls, the profit of the company may decline in future.

In the above situation, the company decides to use a fixed-to-fixed currency swap deal with a swap dealer to hedge its risk exposure in Indian rupees. For example, it can estimate its rupee dominated sales revenue for the future period, and agree to pay fixed rupee and receive fixed dollar in future at the suitable interest rates and exchange rates.

## 15.18   HEDGING AGAINST THE RISK OF AN INCREASE IN COST

As discussed above, the company can hedge against the risk of decline in its revenue in Indian rupees, in the same manner, it can control its costs incurred in terms of Indian rupees if it is importing raw material and other items for its production. If the exchange rate in terms of Indian rupees rises, it means rupee is more expensive against US dollar, then the production of the company will rise in future. In such scenario, the company would like to control its cost in terms of Indian rupee which is likely to be risen. The company can make a fixed-for-fixed currency swap deal with a swap dealer in which it pays US dollar and receive Indian rupees at suitable exchange rates and interest rates.

## 15.19   HEDGING AGAINST THE RISK OF DECLINE OF FIRM'S VALUE

Another important use of currency swaps is to hedge against the risk of decline in the value of the firm. The value of firm may decrease due to decline in the value of its assets or rise in the value of its liabilities which are denominated in foreign currencies. For example, an Indian company has invested $100 million in US bonds which yields 8 percent p.a. in US dollar and current exchange rate is ₹65/$. The company is expecting that the rupee will be strengthened against the US dollar, as a result, the value of US bonds of the company will also decline.

Similarly, assume that the Indian company has a liability in US dollar, say, has borrowed in the dollars at a fixed rate of interest. If the exchange rate of rupee in term of US dollar rises, then the company will have to repay its loan in US dollar at higher rate. As a result, the value of the firm will decline due to higher payments of its liabilities in US dollars.

As observed above, the value of the firm is exposed to the risk arising due to change in exchange rates in the market. The currency swap, in this respect, can be useful to manage such risk. The company can, as per expected changing economic scenario, enter in the swap deals so that the amount of foreign currencies intact in its assets and liabilities be hedged.

## 15.20   HEDGING THE SWAPS

A swap contract is a portfolio long in one bond and short in another bond such that the value at inception is zero. It means that the risk measurement of a simple swap is straight forward or ask in into a bond portfolio. So, in this section, we will discuss the measurement of risk of swap contract and then how the same can be hedged.

### 15.20.1   Measuring the Risk on Swaps

Now the issue is to measure the quantum of risk incurred and a swap position. At the initiation of the swap, the two bonds have exactly the same value, however, subsequently, the value of two bonds differs as per movements in interest rates in the market. If we have the joint distribution of both fixed rate and floating rate, we can compute the volatility of the given from the swap position. As a result, the trader may be either in profit or loss.

To measure the risk on a swap, let us assume various notations as:

| | | |
|---|---|---|
| Origination date of the swap | = | '$t$' |
| Valuation date of the swap | = | '$T$' |
| Return on fixed rate bond | = | $r_B$ |
| Return on floating rate bond | = | $r_L$ |
| Current price of the bond | = | ? |
| Notional principal amount | = | $100 million |

The variance of the floating rate bond will be very small since it corresponds to the variance of the return of a bond with a very short duration. It will be almost zero immediately before a reset date since on that date the floating leg is valued at par.

In general, in swap contract one will be on fixed rate and another will be on floating rate basis. The formula for measuring the risk of the swap will be same as for bond portfolio which is stated below.

**Volatility of change in the value of the Swap (Risk of Swap):**

$$(B_{tT})^2 \times \text{Var}(r_B) + (L_{tT}) \times \text{Var}(r_L) - 2(B_{tT}) \times (L_{tT}) \times \text{Cov}(r_B, r_L)$$

To solve the problem, let us assume further as

| | | |
|---|---|---|
| Notional Principal of the swap | = | $100 million |
| Current price of fixed rate bond [$Bt(T)$] | = | $95 m |
| Current price of the floating rate bond [$Lt,(T)$] | = | $101 m |
| Return on fixed rate bond | = | –5% ($95 m–$100 m/100) |
| Return of floating rate bond | = | +1% ($101 m–$100 m/100) |
| Standard deviation of fixed rate bond | = | 3% |
| Standard deviation of floating rate bond | = | .05% |
| Covariance of fixed return and floating return | = | .0001875 |

*Risk of Swap*

$= (95 \text{ m})^2 \times (0.03)^2 + (101 \text{ m})^2 \times (.05)^2 - 2 \times 95 \times 101 \times (.0001875)$

$= (9025 \text{ m}) \times (.0009) + (10201 \text{ m}) (.000025) - 2 \times 9595 \times (.0001875)$

$= 8.12 \text{ m} + .26 \text{ m} - 3.60 \text{ m}$

$= 4.78 \text{ m or } 4.78\%$

With normally distributed returns, the 5 percent VaR (Value at Risk) of the swap position is 1.65 times its volatility. VaR of the Swap = 1.65 × 4.78 (m) = 7.887 million

## 15.20.2  Hedging of the Risk in Swap Position

Abstracting from the inherent credit risk, the swap dealer can exactly know what will be received overtime, but the size of payments depends upon the reference rate which is to be anticipated. There are certain ways to hedge the swap position like futures, forwards, euro dollars, etc.

The best way to hedge the swap would be to find another firm that also wanted to do precisely the opposite pay floating and receive fixed on the same notional principal for the same time period. The dealer could be the counterparty on both swaps. In this way, the cash flow streams on the two swaps would service each other. For example, a swap dealer enters a swap agreement fixed-for-floating with a party and enters floating-for-fixed with the other party B of the same notional principal amount and time period. The swap dealer will earn a spread on the fixed rate differential; however, he would retain counterparty risk. Further, in such arrangement, interest rate risk would be hedged.

Another important method which is very popular in the swap market is hedging swaps through Eurodollar futures since an interest rate swap is just like a series of LIBOR-based forward rate transactions, the dealer will sell the futures. In such strategy, rising of interest rate will offset the loss in swap deal by the profits in futures contracts. The only matter of concern is to match the quantity and maturity of the futures with the terms of the swap contract.

## 15.21 INTERNATIONAL SWAPS AND DERIVATIVES ASSOCIATION (ISDA)

The International Swap and Derivatives Association (ISDA) is a trade organization of participants in the market for over-the-counter (OTC) derivatives. It was established in 1985 as the International Swap Dealers Association, and subsequently changed its name switching "swap dealers" to Swap and Derivatives. The purpose behind this change was made to focus more attention on their efforts to improve the broader derivative markets and away from strictly interest rate swap contracts.

ISDA has its headquarter in New York and offices in New York, London, Hong Kong, Tokyo, Washington D.C., Brussels and Singapore. Currently, it has more than 820 members in 57 countries. Its membership consists of derivative dealers, service-providers and end-users. ISDA has five Determinations Committees, each having justification over a Specific region of the world (The Americas, Asian excluding Japan, Australia/New Zealand, EMEA and Japan). Each committee consists of ten voting dealers and five voting non-dealers asset managers. The committees make official, binding determinations regarding the existence of "credit events" and "succession events", which may trigger obligations under a credit default swap contracts.

The ISDA has created a standardized contract (known as the ISDA Master Agreement) to enter into the derivative transactions. In addition to legal and policy activities, ISDA also manages FPML (Financial Products Mark-up Language), an XML message standard for the OTC derivative industry. The first Master Agreement of ISDA was published in 1992, and its second edition was published in 2002. The second edition was drafted in response to market difficulties in the late 1990s.

The Master Agreement of ISDA is typically used between a derivatives dealer and its counterparty when discussions begin surrounding a derivative trade. There are two basic forms of Master Agreement—Single jurisdiction/currency and multiple jurisdiction/currency. One of these documents is generally combined with a schedule to set out the basic trading norms between the parties; each subsequent trade is then recorded in a confirmation which references the Master Agreement and Schedule. The terms of the schedule are often negotiated, and many firms have preferred versions of the schedule.

The most important aspect of the ISDA Master Agreement is that the Master Agreement and all the Confirmations entered into it form a single agreement. It allows the parties to an ISDA Agreement to aggregate the amounts owing by each of them under all the transactions outstanding and replace them with a single net amount payable by one party to the other. This 'Netting' allows the parties to net out amounts payable on the same day and in the same currency. ISDA also has produced a model "Netting Act" which can be adopted by jurisdiction where close-out netting does not work effectively at present.

ISDA also produces a Credit Support Annex (CSA) which permits parties of ISDA to mitigate their credit risk by requiring the party which is out-of-the money to post Collateral (usually cash, government securities of highly rated bonds) corresponding to the amount which would be payable by that party were all the outstanding transactions.

From 1998 until August, 2014, ISDA was responsible for releasing a series of interest rate swap reference rates for four currencies (Euro, British pounds, Swiss Franc, US dollars) under the name ISDA fix. Following rate manipulation scandals, these rates are now administrated by the Intercontinental Exchange (ICE) Further, the Swiss Franc rate is no longer reported.

## SUMMARY

This chapter concentrates on pricing and hedging with swaps. Swap is a derivative instrument in which cash flows are exchanged between the two parties as per agreed terms. The swap price is the interest rate paid on the fixed interest rate leg of the swap. It means the rate which equates the present value of both cash inflows and outflows to zero, is called the swap price. Determining the swap price is important to manage the risks arising due to increase or decrease in interest rate, exchange rate, etc. in the firm.

Experts have suggested various approaches for pricing of swaps such as bond equivalent approach, present value approach and forward rate agreement approach. Bond equivalent approach is just like portfolio of two bonds, in which you receive interest payment on one bond and pays interest on the other bond. For example, as a fixed rate payer, the present value of floating rate payment minus present value of fixed rate payments should be more than or equal to zero. Similarly, value for a floating rate payer, the present value of fixed rate payments minus floating rate payments should be equal or more than zero. In this approach, fixed rate or swap price of a swap contract can be determined on the basis of coupon rate on the bond having same maturity in the market.

Present value approach of swap pricing advocates that a fixed rate can be determined on the basis of present value of both the streams, i.e., fixed payments and floating payments in a swap contract. Basic argument behind is that the market uses its best estimate of future cash flows which come from the spot yield and the implied forward rate. Forward rate agreement approach into find out the swap price which is calculated through forward rate applying on the fixed and floating cash flows in swap agreement. There is also shortcut method to calculate the swap price. The basic assumption behind the shortcut method is that the value of a floating rate bond is approximately equal to face value, because the next cash flows is always re-priced as per current interest rates. So, under this method, future cash flows are priced at the appropriate estimated discount rate.

The interest rates, exchange rates, inflation rate, etc. are changing continuously in the market. As a result, the swap price determined earlier may not be an appropriate in present context. So, sometimes we need to price again the swap contract after its origination. The valuation method of the swap for remaining period would be same as already discussed originally. Pricing of a currency swap contract is also similar to the interest rate swap. Pricing of a swap involves the present value of the payments must be equal to the present value of the receipts. In case of currency swap, the present value of all payments occurring and of receipts should be equal. The present value can be expressed in either currency, and payment can be based either on fixed or floating rate of interest.

The chapter further states the hedging through swaps which the firms frequently use to manage their risks. Interest rate swaps can be used for different purposes in the firms, such as lowering borrowing costs, hedging against rising interest rates, falling interest rates, adjusting of duration of bonds, etc. Forward swap is forward agreement under which it obligates the firm to enter into swap after sometime of the original swap agreement. The initial payments in such swap will be exchanged, say six months or one year, after such agreement has been originated.

Another important tools of hedging are gap analysis and duration which are commonly used by the financial institutions, banks, etc. for managing their exposure to interest rate risks. Gap analysis means the difference between rate sensitive assets minus rate sensitive liabilities. This gap can be positive or negative. Positive gap means that the firm has more rate sensitive assets than rate sensitive liabilities. Similarly, negative gap means that rate sensitive liabilities are more than the rate sensitive assets. The firm can manage this gap by taking appropriate measures. Duration is another tool which is considered in managing interest rate risk. If the asset's duration exceeds the duration of liabilities, then increase in interest rates will further decline the value of firm and vice versa.

Currency swaps can be useful to the firms in managing their risks, specifically arising out of exposure to foreign currencies. The currency swaps can be used for hedging to lower borrowing costs in a foreign currency, against the risk of a decline in revenue, against the risk in an increase in cost and decline in firm's value. The management can design appropriate strategy to manage the above said phenomenon through currency swaps.

## SOLVED PROBLEMS

**P.1.**  The spot term structure of interest rate on January 1, 2015 is

| One-year rate | Two-year rate | Three-year rate | Four-year rate |
|:---:|:---:|:---:|:---:|
| 7.5% | 8.0% | 8.5% | 9.00% |

Find the price of a four-year interest rate swap with a notional principal of ₹50 million. The floating rate is one-year MIBOR. Payments are annual.

*Solution:*

Spot term structure of interest as on January 1, 2015:

| Year | Rate | Forward Rate |
|:---:|:---:|:---:|
| 1 | 7.5 | 7.50 |
| 2 | 8.0 | 8.50 |
| 3 | 8.5 | 9.507 |
| 4 | 9.0 | 10.513 |

Find the present value floating cash flows at the appropriate discount rate (the spot zero coupon interest rates):

$$\frac{7.50}{1.0750} + \frac{8.50}{(1.08)^2} + \frac{9.507}{(1.085)^3} + \frac{10.513}{(1.09)^4} = 30.5559$$

$$6.977 + 7.2873 + 7.443 + 8.8486 = 30.5559$$

Since the value of an at-market swap at its origination is zero, the value of the floating payments must be equal to the value of the fixed payments. Therefore, the fixed rate payments must satisfy the following:

$$30.5559 = \frac{A}{1.075} + \frac{A}{(1.08)^2} + \frac{A}{(1.085)^3} + \frac{A}{(1.09)^4} = A\left[\frac{1}{1.075} + \frac{1}{(1.08)^2} + \frac{1}{(1.085)^3} + \frac{1}{(1.09)^4}\right]$$

$$30.5559 = 3.4121\ A$$

$$A = \frac{30.5559}{3.4121} = 8.9551 = 8.955\%$$

This means that four-year fixed rate of swap should be 8.95 percent p.a. and the payments of cash flows on Notional principal of ₹50 m will be:

$$= ₹50\ m \times 8.95\% = ₹4.4775\ m$$

**P.2.**    What is the value of the swap for the receive counterparty if one-year after the swap (in Problem No. 1) the spot term structure is changed to as:

| One-year rate | Two-year rate | Three-year rate | Four-year rate |
|:---:|:---:|:---:|:---:|
| 6% | 7% | 7.5% | 8% |

*Solution:*

Valuing of the swap (one-year after the swap's origination) using short cut method, the new price of the swap is:

$$100 = \frac{A}{1.06} + \frac{A}{(1.07)^2} + \frac{A}{(1.075)^3} + \frac{A}{(1.08)^4} + \frac{100}{(1.08)^4}$$

$$100 = A\left[\frac{1}{1.06} + \frac{1}{(1.07)^2} + \frac{1}{(1.075)^3} + \frac{1}{(1.08)^4}\right] + \frac{100}{(1.08)^4}$$

$$100 = 3.3555A + 73.5023$$

$$3.3555A = 26.4977$$

$$A = 3.3555 = 7.897 = 7.90\%\ app.$$

This means that given the notional principal of ₹50 million, the fixed payments of a new swap would be (₹30 m) (0.07897) = ₹2.369 m. The difference between the old swap's fixed payment and new fixed payments is ₹4.4775 m – ₹2.3690 m = ₹2.1085 million per year. The present value of the difference in fixed cash flows, given the discount rates is:

$$\frac{2.1085\ m}{1.06} + \frac{2.1085\ m}{(1.07)^2} + \frac{2.1085\ m}{(1.075)^3} + \frac{2.1085\ m}{(1.08)^4} =$$

$$₹1.9892\ m + ₹1.8416\ m + ₹1.6945\ m + ₹1.5498\ m = ₹7.0751\ million$$

**P.3.**    Consider the spot term structure in a swap contract as $r$ (0, ½) 5.8%, $r$ (0, 1) 6%, $r$ (0, 1½) 6.6%, $r$ (0, 2) 7%. Compute the price of a plain vanilla fixed-for-floating interest rate swap with a tenure of two years. Payments are semi-annual, beginning six month, hence.

*Solution:*

Spot-term structure of a swap contract when payments are semi-annual:

Floating rates (*fr*)

$r(0, ½) = 5.8\%$ – $= 5.80\%$

$r(0, 1) = 6.0\%$ $(1.06)^2$ $= (1.058)(1+fr\ 0,1) = 6.20\%$

$r(0, 1½) = 6.6\%$ $(1.066)^3 = (1.06)^2(1+fr\ 0, 1½) = 7.81\%$

$r(0, 2) = 7.0\%$ $(1.07)^4 = (1.066)^3(1+fr\ 0,2) = 8.21\%$

Find the present value of floating cash flows using discount rate:

$$\frac{5.80}{1.058} + \frac{6.20}{(1.06)^2} + \frac{7.81}{(1.066)^3} + \frac{8.21}{(1.07)^4} =$$

$$5.482 + 5.5180 + 6.4476 + 6.2633 = 23.7109$$

The fixed rate (price) of swap $= 23.7109 = A\left[\frac{1}{1.058} + \frac{1}{(1.06)^2} + \frac{1}{(1.066)^3} + \frac{1}{(1.07)^4}\right]$

$$23.7109 = 4.5909A$$

$$A = 23.7109/4.5909 = 5.1648 = 5.1648\%$$

**P.4.** An importer enters into a swap contract with a swap dealer for a fixed interest rate on a notional principal of ₹10 million with semi-annual payments for a period of two years on a floating rate of MIBOR + 50 basis points. Assume the MIBOR rate for six months, 1 year, 1.5 year, and 2-year as 3%, 3.20%, 3.40% and 3.6%, respectively. Calculate the fixed rate of swap contract.

*Solution:*

The fixed rate of the swap can be identified as that rate which equates the floating cash out-flows with the cash inflows on the fixed rate cash flows in the contract. This is calculated as:

$$\frac{1.75}{1.015} + \frac{1.85}{(1.016)^2} + \frac{1.95}{(1.017)^3} + \frac{2.05}{(1.018)^4} =$$

$$1.72413 + 1.7922 + 1.8538 + 1.9088 = 7.2789/100 = 7.2789\%$$

$$\text{Fixed Rate} = \frac{072789}{.5 \times 3.8358 \times 1} = 0.03774 = 3.7734\%$$

The present value of cash flows of floating rate and fixed rate obligations are equal with the MIBOR rate as discount rates.

**P.5.** Consider a swap deal for exchange of a floating rate 90-day LIBOR for return on S&P 500 Index. The payments are on the basis of quarters fall in March, June, September and December. The notional principal amount is $100 million. The current S&P Index is assumed as 1150 and current LIBOR (6 months) rate is 5%. The expected rates of S&P Index and respective LIBOR rates are given as follows:

| | **March** | **June** | **September** | **December** |
|---|---|---|---|---|
| S&P Index | 1180 | 1200 | 1130 | 1100 |
| LIBOR rate | 5.2% | 5.4% | 4.6% | 4.4% |

The trader receives S&P returns for the payment of LIBOR rates. Calculate the value of the Swap deal from the above data.

*Solution:*

Swap rate computation:

Notional Principal Amount = $ 100 m

| | S&P Index | Periodic Return (Quarter) | S&P Cash Flows ($) | LIBOR Rate (Six-month) | LIBOR Cash Flows | Net Cash Flows | Present value of Net Cash Flows at LIBOR Rate |
|---|---|---|---|---|---|---|---|
| | 1150 | | | 5% | ($) | ($) | |
| March | 1180 | +2.61% | +2.61 m | 5.2% | +2.5 m | 1,10,000 | 1,12,936 |
| June | 1200 | +1.70% | +1.70 m | 5.4% | +2.6 m | −90,000 | −92,974 |
| September | 1160 | −3.33% | −3.33 m | 4.6% | +2.7 m | −60,30,000 | −61,71,954 |
| December | 1100 | −5.17% | −5.17 m | 4.4% | +2.3 m | −74,70,000 | −76,38,036 |
| | | | | | | | −1,37,90,028 |

The value of the swap deal for the firm receiving S&P index returns and paying the LIBOR rates would be a payment of $1,37,90,028 m.

## SUGGESTED READINGS

1. Marshall, J.F. and Kapna, K.R., *Understanding Swap Finance*, Cincinnati, OH, South Western, 1990.
2. Turnbull, S.M., Swaps: A zero sum game, *Financial Management*, Vol. 16, No. 1, pp. 15–21, Spring 1981.
3. Richard, Levich M., *International Financial Markets: Prices and Policies*: 2nd ed., McGraw-Hill International Edition, Singapore, 2001.
4. Redhead, Keith, *Introduction to International Money Market*, Woodhead Faulkner, Hemel Hempstead, 1992.
5. DeCovny, S., *Swaps*, Woodhead Faulkner, Hemel Hempstead, 1992.
6. Sharpe, W.F. and Alexander, G.J., *Investment*, Prentice-Hall, Englewood Cliffs, 1995.
7. Ian, Giddy, *Global Financial Markets*, A.I.T.B.S. Publication, New Delhi, 1997.

## REVIEW QUESTIONS

1. Explain the term swap. How can you calculate pricing of a swap? Explain with examples.
2. Explain the various methods of pricing of interest rate swap with suitable illustrations.
3. Explain the mechanism of pricing of an outstanding interest rate swap contract with hypothetical illustration.
4. Critically examine the spot and forward yield curves in pricing of a swap with an example.
5. Explain the mechanism of a currency swap contract. Also explain the implication of counter-party risk in this respect.
6. Write note on the following:
   (a) FRA as a method of swap pricing.
   (b) Present value approach of swap pricing.
7. Explain the concept of hedging through swap. What is its significance? Explain with suitable examples.

8. Explain the mechanism of hedging with interest rate swap. Explain the limitations in this respect too.

9. How will you hedge against the rising of interest rate in a firm through swap? Also explain important precautions in this respect.

10. Explain the hedging through forward swap. Also discuss the different situations in which forward swap can be used.

11. Write note on the following:
    (a) Hedging through duration.
    (b) Hedging through gap analysis.

12. Explain the concept of hedging through currency swaps. Explain also its implication in lowering borrowing costs with examples.

13. Write note on the following:
    (a) Hedging against in revenue through currency swap.
    (b) Hedging against the risk of decline in firm's value.

14. How will you measure the risk of swap? Explain with examples.

# SECTION V

# Options Derivatives

# Chapter 16

# The Options—The Basics

## LEARNING OBJECTIVES

*After reading this chapter, students will be able to*

➢ Understand the concept options and option markets.

➢ Be aware of the historical background of option contracts and markets.

➢ Know about the various terminologies used in option trading, such as parties to an option contract, exercise price, expiration date, option premium theoretical and time value of option.

➢ Be aware of the types of option contracts, i.e., call option and put options, American and European options, exchange-traded and OTC options, etc.

➢ Understand the concept of the valuation of an option and its mechanism.

➢ Distinguish between option and futures contracts.

➢ Understand the option positions, viz. four types of position (a) A long position in a call option (b) A long position in a put option (c) A short position in call option (d) A short position in a put option with their payoff profiles.

➢ Explain the naked (uncovered) and covered option, synthetic futures and options.

➢ Know about the exchange-traded options like stock options, foreign currency options, index options, futures options, interest rate option, LEAPS options, FLEX options and Exotic options.

## 16.1 INTRODUCTION

Like futures and forward instruments, the options are also important derivative securities trading all over the world for the last three decades. The *derivative security* is a security or contract or instrument designed in such a way that its price is derived from the price of an underlying asset. For example, the price of dollar currency futures will be derived from the dollar price in relation to other currencies. Similarly, the value of January call option on gold depends on the price of gold. Hence, the price of a derivative security is not arbitrary, rather it is linked to the price of the underlying asset.

A price of a derivative security is affected by its features, rights and obligations arisen out against the underlying parties. That is why, the price of a security would be different as per related derivatives features. For example, the primary difference between an option and a futures or forward contract is that the options confer a right, rather than obligation, to buy or sell the underlying asset. As a result, payoff under options will be different to futures or forward, and hence, the price of underlying security. In this section, we will discuss the nature, features, types and mechanism of options.

## 16.2   CONCEPT OF OPTIONS

An *option* is a particular type of a contract between two parties where one person gives the other person the right to buy or sell a specific asset at a specified price within a specific time period. In other words, the *option* is a specific derivative instrument under which one party gets the right, but no obligation, to buy or sell a specific quantity of an asset at an agreed price, on or before a particular date. For example, one person buys an option contract to purchase 100 shares of State Bank of India at ₹300 per share for a period of 3 months. It means that the said person has the right to purchase the share of State Bank of India at ₹300 per share within 3 months from the date of the contract. If the price of State Bank of India increases, he will exercise the option, and if the price falls below ₹300, then he will not exercise his option.

It is evident from the above that an option is the right, but not the obligation to buy or sell something at a specified date at a stated price. It means the option buyer will exercise the optionally when he is in profit. In case of loss, he will not exercise the option. Today, options are traded on a variety of instruments like commodities, financial assets as diverse as foreign exchange, bank time deposits, treasury securities, stocks, stock indexes, petroleum products, food grains, metals, etc.

**EXAMPLE:**   Assume that a stock is selling in the market the call price $C_T = ₹4.25$ when the market price of stock $S_t = ₹50$ and strike price is ₹46. The arbitrageur can sell the call on 100 shares, and thereby receives ₹425, and buy the stock for ₹5,000. Since the option is in the money, the arbitrager will exercise the option and he will deliver the shares and receives ₹4,600. The arbitrage profit is 425–(5,000 – 4,600) = ₹25.

## 16.3   HISTORICAL BACKGROUND

The history of options are as old as trading in the business world. The idea of options has existed from ancient Roman and Greek times. The references to options have also been found in the famous 'Tulip Bulb Mania' which had gripped Holland in the seventeenth century. It was perhaps one of major cause for the boom as well as its end as many of the option writers refused to take delivery of the tulip bulb when the bubble had burst.

Options on commodities have existed in different forms since 1860 in USA. First such trading was on major grains but the options were met with immediate opposition from the farmers, and as a result, such option trading was eliminated in 1869. Afterwards, by passing the Commodity Exchange Act in 1936, there was ban on option trading in various commodities like wheat, cotton, rice, corn, oats, barley, grain sorghums, milk feeds, butter, eggs, potato, etc. Further, in 1940, more commodities like wool, fats, oils, soya bean, cottonseed meal, etc. were also added in ban. As a result, commodity options disappeared from the listing of US exchanges.

However, in the meanwhile, commodity options were continued to prosper in London, and American brokerage firms started functioning in London options market for their American customers. Options were available in London on cocoa, coffee, copper, silver, sugar, lead, tin, zinc, etc. As a result, by the early 1970s, London options market had become a popular market at the international level.

In 1970s, the option market was rocked due to scandal in USA, and the result was the Commodity Futures Trading Commission Act (CEA) of 1974, and the creation of the Commodity Futures Trading Commission (CFTC). The CFTC responded by proposing regulations governing options traded off-exchange by firms already engaged in such trading. In 1978, the Futures Trading Act reinforced the ban on option trading but also directed the CFTC to develop regulatory structure for option trading. In September 1981, the CFTC initiated an option pilot program for exchange-traded commodity options. Eight futures exchanges subsequently applied to trade options on futures contracts, including options on precious metals, agricultural products, financial instruments, etc.

As observed earlier, the options as stocks have been traded actively for nearly a century in the over-the-counter (OTC) market under the auspices of the Put and Call Dealers Association. The first options were traded as individual stock on an organized exchange in 1973, when the Chicago Board Options Exchange (CBOE) came into existence. The CBOE listed standardized call options on 18 common stocks. Since then, several other exchanges like the American Stock Exchange, the New York Exchange, the Pacific Stock Exchange, and Philadelphia Stock Exchange have introduced trading options on individual stocks.

In 1980s, stock exchanges expanded the scope of option trading by including options on other financial assets. For example, in 1982, the Philadelphia Stock Exchange introduced options on foreign exchange, and the American Stock Exchange on T-bills, T-notes, T-bonds and gold. In 1983, the CBOE began trading options on the Standard and Poor's 100 Index. Several other exchanges also followed such options and futures trading. A list of important options exchanges functioning in the USA is given in Table 16.1.

**TABLE 16.1** Option Exchanges and the Main Items they Trade in USA

| Exchange | Main items |
|---|---|
| American Stock Exchange | Stocks, options on individual stocks and options on stock indexes |
| Chicago Board of Trade | Futures, options on futures for agricultural goods, precious metals, stock, stock indexes and debt instruments |
| Chicago Board Options Exchange | Options on individual stocks, options on stock indexes and options on treasury security |
| Chicago Mercantile Exchange | Futures, options on futures for agricultural goods, stock indexes, debt instruments and currencies. |
| Coffee, Sugar and Cocoa Exchange | Futures and options on agricultural futures |
| Commodity Exchange (COMEX) | Futures and options on futures for metals |
| Kanas City Board of Trade | Futures and options on agricultural futures |
| Mid America Commodity | Futures and options on futures for agricultural goods and precious metals |
| Minneapolis Grain Exchange | Futures and options on agricultural futures |

| Exchange | Main items |
|---|---|
| New York Cotton Exchange | Futures and options on agricultural, currency and debt instrument futures |
| New York Futures Exchange | Futures and options on stock indexes |
| New York Mercantile Exchange | Futures and options on energy futures |
| New York Stock Exchange | Stocks and options on individual stocks and a stock index |
| Pacific Stock Exchange | Options on individual stocks and a stock index |
| Philadelphia Stock Exchange | Stocks, futures and options on individual stocks, currencies and stock indexes. |

In India, options have been traded on the over-the-counter (OTC) markets with names like *Teji*, *Mandi*, *Phatak*, etc. Commodity options trading was banned in India in 1952 and it still continues. Options on securities were banned in 1969. However, it has been allowed in financial markets in 1995. The Reserve Bank of India has allowed certain options to cooperate with high forex exposure and also to all authorized dealers for option trading in rupee dollar exchange markets. The Bombay Stock Exchange and National Stock Exchange have also started options trading in stock from 2001. This has been discussed in other chapters in detail.

## 16.4  OPTIONS TERMINOLOGY

Following are the important terms which are frequently used in option trading:

**Parties of the option contract:**   There are two parties to an option contract: the buyer (the holder) and the writer (the seller). The writer grants the buyer a right to buy or sell a particular asset in exchange for a certain sum of money for the obligation taken by him in the option contract.

**Exercise price:**   The price at which the underlying asset may be sold or purchased by the option buyer from the option writer is called *exercise* or *strike price*. At this price the buyer can exercise his option.

**Expiration date and exercise date:**   The date on which an option contract expires is called *expiration date* or *maturity date*. The option holder has the right to exercise his option on any date before the expiration date. In other words, the date after which an option is void is called *the expiration date*. Exercise date is the date upon which the option is actually exercised, whereas the expiration date is the last day upon which the option may be exercised.

**Option premium:**   The price at which option holder buys the right from the option writer is called *option premium* or *option price*. This is the consideration paid by the buyer to the seller and it remained with the seller whether the option is exercised or not. In other words, the price or premium is paid by the holder to the writer of the option against the obligation undertaken. This is fixed and paid at the time of the formation or writing an option deal.

**Option 'In', 'Out' and At-the-money:**   An option contract at a particular time, can be in-the-money, out-of-the money and at-the-money. When the underlying futures price/stock price is greater than the strike or exercise price, the call option will be in-the-money, and if the futures price is lesser than the strike price, it will be called out-of-the money call option. Further, if the futures price is equal to the strike price, it is said that call option is at-the-money. The reverse is the position in case of put options. This has been shown in Table 16.2.

**TABLE 16.2**   Payoff Profile of Option

| Types of option | Call option | Put option |
|---|---|---|
| In-the-money | Futures > Strike | Futures < Strike |
| At-the-money | Futures = Strike | Futures = Strike |
| Out-of the money | Futures < Strike | Futures > Strike |

It should be noted that some financial experts have considered the market price of the stock options instead of futures price to determine the option as in-the-money or out-of-the money. Since the options are listed with the exchanges and the market price changes as per changes in the price of underlying asset, so it can also be used to see whether the option is profitable or not. As we know that the European option cannot be exercised before maturity, so the futures price will be appropriate to determine the option in money.

**The break-even-price:**   It is that price of the stock where the gain on the option is just equal to the option premium. The break-even-price level is determined by adding the strike price and the premium paid together. In other words, the option is sufficiently deep in-the-money to cover the option premium and yields a potentially unlimited net profit. Since there is zero-sum-game, the profit from selling a call is the mirror image of the profit from buying the call.

**EXAMPLE:**   Suppose that a call with a strike price of $K = ₹150$ is selling for $C_T ₹20$ at expiration, when the stock is selling for $S_t - ₹180$. To arbitrage, an individual trader could buy the call on 100 shares of stock for ₹2,000 (i.e., $100 \times 20$) and acquires the 100 shares of stock for ₹15,000. Finally, he will sell the shares in the spot market for ₹18,000. The arbitrage profit is $(15,000 + 2,000 - 18,000) = ₹1,000$, however subject to present value of option expiration period.

## 16.5   TYPES OF OPTIONS

Options can be classified into different categories:

1. Call and Put options
2. American and European options
3. Exchange-traded and OTC-traded options

## 16.5.1   Call and Put Options

When an option grants the buyer (holder) the right to purchase the underlying asset/stock from the writer (seller) a particular quantity at a specified price within a specified expiration date, it is called *call option* or simply a *call*. It is an option to purchase; its holder has the privilege of purchasing or calling from a second party (i.e., writer) to buy an asset. The call option holder pays the premium to the writer for the right taken in the option.

A put option, on the other hand, is an option contract where the option buyer has the right to sell the underlying asset to the writer, at a specified price at or prior to the option's maturity date. It is also called, simply a *put*. Thus, if you buy a put option on State Bank of India stock, you have gained the right to sell the shares of SBI to the writer at a specified price on or before the expiration date.

**Example of a call option:**   Let us consider that an investor who buys a European call option to purchase 100 shares of State Bank of India (SBI) with a strike price of ₹320 per share. Further assume that the current market price of the share (SBI) is ₹310, the expiration date of the option is 2 months, and the price of the option to purchase one share is ₹20. Initial investment is ₹2,000. Since the option is European, hence, the investor can exercise only on the expiration date. If the SBI share price on that date is less than ₹320 then the investor will not exercise the option. There is no point in buying SBI share for ₹320 if the same is available from the market at the lesser price than ₹320. In this position, the investor will lose the whole of his initial investment of ₹2,000. Let us assume that the share price of SBI is above ₹320 on the expiration date then the option will be exercised. Assume that the SBI share price is 350. By exercising the options, the investor is able to buy 100 shares of SBI for ₹320 per share and if the share is sold immediately, the investor makes a gain of ₹3,000 [(₹350 – ₹320) × 100] ignoring transaction costs. When the initial cost of the option is taken into account, the net profit to the investor is ₹1,000 (i.e., ₹3,000 – ₹2,000). Table 16.3 summarizes the earlier example.

**TABLE 16.3**   Profit from Call Option (European)

| An investor buys a call option to purchase 100 SBI shares | |
|---|---|
| Strike price | ₹320 per share |
| Current stock price | ₹310 per share |
| Price of an option to buy one share | ₹20 |
| The initial investment is | 100 × ₹20 = ₹2,000 |

***The outcome:***   Assume at the expiration of the option, SBI share price is ₹350. At this time, the option is exercised for a gain of (₹350 – ₹320) × 100 = ₹3,000. When the initial cost is taken into account, then the net gain is ₹3,000 – ₹2,000 = ₹1,000.

Figure 16.1 shows the way in which investor's net profit/loss on an option contract to purchase one share of SBI which varies with terminal share price in the earlier example. It is important to note that the investor will incur loss 'till the market price of the share does not increase more than strike

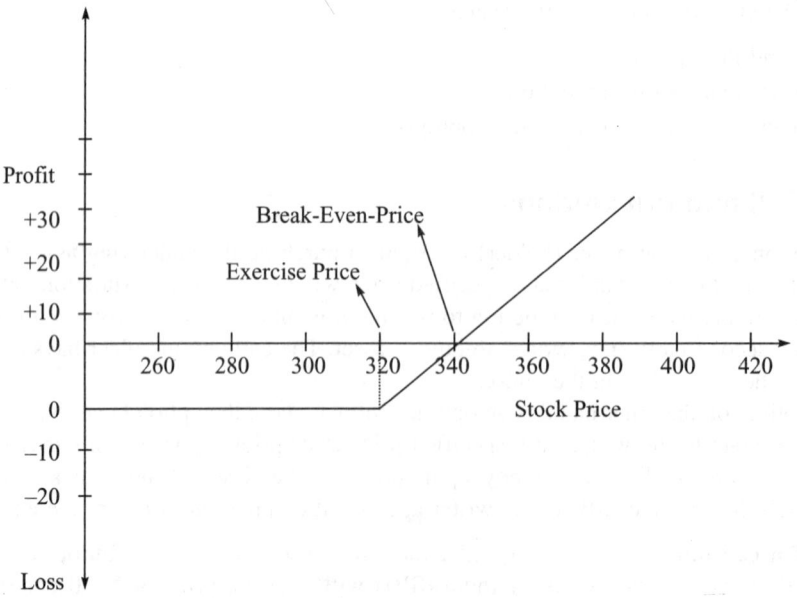

**FIGURE 16.1**   Profit from buying a call option (European).

price, and in the above example, more than ₹340 per share. However, he will exercise the option, if the market price of the share rises above the strike price, i.e., ₹320 per share because some loss will be covered. For example, the market price of the share is ₹330, at the expiration date, then by exercising option, and then by selling the shares in the market, the gain will be ₹1,000 [100 × (330 – 320)]. The net loss to the investor will remain ₹1,000 (₹2,000 – 1,000). In general, the call options should always be exercised at the expiration date if the stock price is above the strike price.

**Example of a put option:** As discussed in earlier section, the buyer of the put option gets the right to sell the underlying asset to the option writer (seller) at the specified price within the particular time. Let us consider the above example of the SBI shares. The investor buys a European put option to sell 100 SBI shares with a strike price of ₹320 per share. Suppose that the current price of the SBI share is ₹310, the expiration date of the option is in three months and the price of a put option to sell one share is ₹15. In this case, the initial investment is ₹1,500 (₹15 × 100). Since the option is European, it will be exercised only if the share price falls below the strike price of ₹320.

Let us assume that the market price on the expiration date is ₹300. In this situation, the investor can purchase 100 shares of SBI from the market at ₹300 and will sell to the option seller (the other party) at ₹320, and hence, making a gain of ₹2,000 [i.e., 100 × (320 – 300)]. After deducting the initial cost of ₹1,500 on the purchase of option, the net gain will be ₹500 (i.e., ₹2,000 – ₹1,500). However, if the market price is ₹320 or more than ₹320, the put option expires worthless and the investor loses ₹1,500. Table 16.4 and Figure 16.2 show the summary of this option transaction and the way in which the investor's profit/loss on an option to sell one share varies with the terminal stock price in this example of SBI share.

**The outcome:** At the expiration of the option, the SBI share price is ₹300. At this time, the investor buy 100 SBI shares at ₹300 and then sells at ₹320 to the option buyer to realize ₹20 per share, being ₹2,000 in total. When the initial cost is taken into account, the net gain ₹2,000 – ₹1,500 = ₹500 in this option.

**TABLE 16.4**  Profit from Put Option (European)

| An investor purchases a put option to sell 100 SBI shares | |
|---|---|
| Strike price | ₹320 per share |
| Current share price | ₹300 |
| Price of put option to sell one share | ₹15 |
| Initial investment on the option | ₹15 × 100 = ₹1,500 |

Figure 16.2 shows the way in which investor's net profit/loss on a put European option contract to sell one share of State Bank of India which varies with terminal stock price, as shown in the example. It should be noted that the investor will incur loss till the market price of the share does not fall below the strike price, i.e., ₹320. The maximum loss to the investor will be ₹1,500, i.e., 100 × 15. However, he will exercise the option if the market price is below ₹320 at the expiration date, i.e., after three months. Assuming the price is ₹300, then the net gain to the investor will be ₹500 (see Table 16.4).

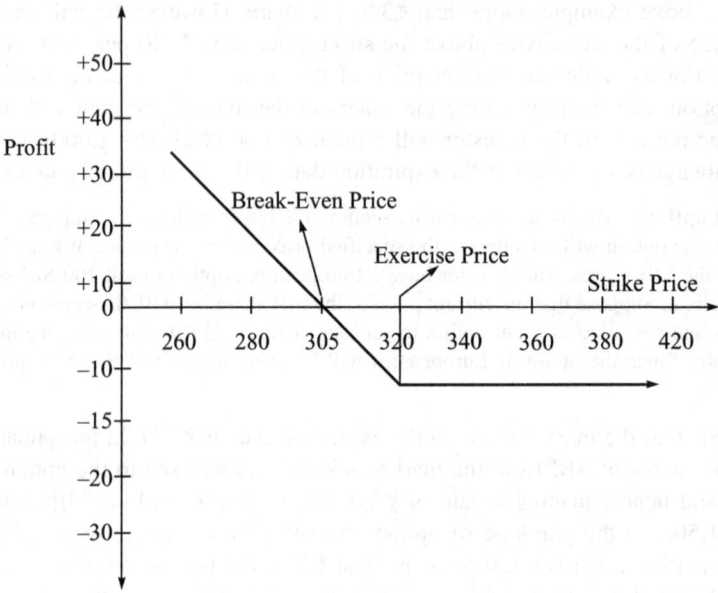

**FIGURE 16.2**   Profit/loss from buying a put option.

## 16.5.2   American and European Options

On the basis of the timing of the possible exercise, the option contracts can also be classified into two categories: American options and European options. A European option can be exercised only at the expiration date, whereas the American option can be exercised at any time up to and including the expiration date. Thus, the definitions given above relating to 'call' and 'put' options apply to the American style options. Most of the options traded in the world today are the American style options. There is nothing particularly geographical about the names, it is just a convention.

## 16.5.3   Exchange-traded and OTC-traded Options

The options can be traded like other financial assets either on an organized exchange or on the over-the-counter (OTC) market. Exchange-traded option contracts, like futures contracts are standardized and are traded on the recognized exchanges. On the other hand, over-the-counter (OTC) options are customer-tailored agreements sold directly by the dealer rather than through an organized exchange. The terms and conditions of these contracts are negotiated by the parties to the contract. Both the options have different mechanism of functioning which is discussed here as under:

1. Exchange-traded options, such as futures contracts, are standardized and are traded on organized (or government designated) exchanges. On the other hand, the OTC options are written on the counters of the large commercial and investment bankers.
2. Exchange-traded options have certain specified norms relating to quantity, maturity dates, underlying assets, etc. which are determined by the exchanges. However, in case of OTC options, all such terms are subject to negotiation and mutually determined by the buyer and the seller of the option contract.

3. Being standardized in nature, an option contract traded through the recognized exchange has uniform underlying asset, limited number of strike prices, limited expiration dates and so on. But in case of options through OTC have not such limitations. They are tailor-made contracts designed normally as per desire of the buyers. So, there are no boundation on strike prices, expiration dates, etc.

4. Exchange-traded options are performed and cleared through a clearing house corporation which interposes itself as a third party to the all options contracts. Since, these options are guaranteed by the exchanges, hence, default risk is almost eliminated. But in case of OTC-traded options, the degree of the default risk is higher because there are only two parties, and if the options writer commits default, there is no guarantee to the buyer.

5. On buying an option contract from a recognized exchange, the obligation can be fulfilled in one of the three ways which are mentioned as follows:

   (a) The option buyer may not exercise the contract, allowing the option to expire. All the premium is retained by the seller and the seller's obligation is discharged.

   (b) In case of American option, the buyer can exercise his right on or before the expiration date, and then, the seller adhere to fulfil all the terms of contract. The writer keeps all of the premium underlying the contract.

   (c) Either of the parties to the option contract can execute an offsetting transaction in the option market to eliminate the future obligations. For example, the buyer sells or the seller buys another option with the identical terms. In such situation, the rights or obligations under the original option contract are transferred to a new option holder. It means the option contracts can be offset even before the expiration.

   In contrast, the OTC-traded options have no such facilities, as mentioned above, like exchange-traded options. Being tailor-made and unstandardized in nature, the OTC-traded option writers may face difficulties in offsetting the options before the maturity.

6. In case of exchange-traded options, the writers are required to deposit the margin funds since they are exposed to considerable risk. However, in case of the OTC options, the writers deposit no such margins.

7. It has been observed that the transaction costs are lower in exchange-traded options in comparison to the OTC-traded options, which depends usually on the creditworthiness of the buyers of the options.

8. In OTC-traded options, market large investment banking firms and commercial banks normally operate as principals as well as brokers, that is why, they are less liquid in comparison to the exchange-traded options. Further, they take them as a part of an asset-liability management in which they intend to hold them to expiration.

## 16.6 DISTINCTION BETWEEN OPTIONS AND FUTURES CONTRACTS

After going through the basic concept of the options and futures contracts, one can visualize the basic difference between these two, and that is to obligation. In the option contracts, one party (the buyer) is not obligated to transact the contract at a later date, only the other party (seller) is under obligation to perform the option contract, and only if the buyer desires so. On the other hand, in case of futures contract, both the parties, the buyers and the sellers, are under obligation to perform the contract.

In case of options contracts, one party (the buyer) has to pay in cash the option price (premium) to the other party (seller) and this is not returned to the buyer whether he insists for actual performance of the contract or not. In case of futures contract, no cash is transferred to either party at the time of the formation of the contract.

The risk and reward characteristics of these two contracts also differ. In the case of futures contract, the buyer of the contract realizes the gains in cash when the price of the futures contract increases and incurs losses in case of fall in the prices. The position is opposite in case of the seller of the futures contract. However, in the case of options contracts, such symmetric risk/reward relationship does not arise. The most that the buyer of an option can lose is the option price against which he possesses all the potential benefits. The maximum profit that the seller of the option contract may realize is the options price. This is. to offset against substantial down side risk.

In case of option contracts, they are brought into existence by being traded; if none is traded, none exists; conversely, there is no limit to the number of option contracts that can be in existence at any time. However, in the case of futures contracts, there is process of closing out position which cause contracts to cease to exist, hence, diminishing the total number in comparison to options.

## 16.7   BASIC PROPERTIES OF OPTIONS

There are certain properties of options whatever the distribution of the underlying the assets, specifically in case of financial assets. A financial asset is an instrument that paysoff in cash or in a form which can be converted into cash. So, stocks and bonds are financial assets. Currency is not a financial asset, since it earns a convenience yield. Before discussing the properties of the option, following are the symbols used which are as under:

$C$ = Call Price of an Option
$P$ = Put Price of an Option
$S$ = Stock Price
$K$ = Strike or Exercise Price
$r$ = Rate of Return
$T$ = Time to Maturity of Option
$t$ = Current Period
$PV$ = Present Value
$K'$ = New Strike Price
$C'$ = New Call Price
$P'$ = New Put Price

In option trading there exists upper and lower bounds on option prices which hold whatever the underlying of the option and its return distribution. As discussed earlier, a call option allows the holder to buy the underlying asset at a fixed price. The upper bound on a call option price is the price of the underlying asset, and in a put option, the upper bound on the price of put option is the exercise price.

A call option cannot have a negative price. To get a higher lower bound for a call option, its value cannot be less than $(S - K)$, where '$S$' is the price of the underlying asset and $K$ is the exercise price. If the price of the option lower than $(S - K)$, one can buy the option, exercise it, and make profit which will be equal to $(S - K)$ minus the call price. However, this result cannot be applied to the European call option since it cannot be exercised before the maturity period.

There will be arbitrage opportunity if the call price plus the present value of the exercise price is lower than the stock price, which is if $C(S, K, T, t) + Pt(T) K < S$, where $Pt(T)$ is the price at $t$'

of zero-coupon bond that pays $I$ at $T$. There is no arbitrage opportunity when $C(S, K, T, t) + Pt(T)$ $K > S$. It means that the call price must exceed the difference between the stock price and the present value of the exercise price:

$$C(S, K, T, t) \geq S_t - P_t(T) \, K$$

### Properties of options

A few important properties of an option contract are as follows:

1. The European call price cannot be less than the current price of the underlying asset minus the present value of the exercise price, the same is applied to the put option in its apposite form, given below in terms of equation as:

   Call option:  $\quad\quad C(S, K, T, t) \geq S_t - PV_t \, (T)K$

2. The European put option price cannot be less than the present value of the exercise price minus the current price of the underlying asset. In terms of equation it is stated as:

   Put option:  $\quad\quad P(S, K, T, t) \geq PV_{t,T} \, K - S_t$

   The above properties (1) and (2) of the options must hold to avoid the existence of arbitrage opportunities. If these do not hold, then the investors can earn through the arbitrage process.

3. Exercise price and option value: This property indicates towards that there is relationship between an option value and its strike price, whatever may be the distribution of the return of the underlying asset. This property can be stated for call option as:

   "All other things remain equal, the price of a European call option is a decreasing function of its exercise price". It is stated in equation as:

   $$C(S, K, T, t) - c'(S, K', T, t) \leq PV_t(T) \, [K' - K]$$

   As per this property, there is relationship between an option value and its exercise price that holds. Consider two calls ($C$ and $C'$) on the same underlying asset that have the same maturity, i.e., one call has exercise price of ₹50, and other call has ₹60 exercise price. Assume that if the asset price is greater than ₹60 on maturity, then the call with lower exercise price pays ₹10 more than the call with the higher exercise price. If the asset price is below ₹50, then neither call is in the money. So, in general, if we have a call with exercise price $K'$ and one with exercise price $K$ where $K' > K$, then it must be that:

   $$C(S, K, T, t) \geq c(S, K', T, t)$$

4. The above call value can be used for put option.

   All other things remain equal, price of the European put option is an increasing function of the exercise price.

   $$P(S, K', T, t) \geq P'(S, K, T, t)$$
   $$P(S, K', T, t) - P'(S, K, T, t) \leq P_t(T) \, (K' - K)$$

5. The absolute value of the difference in price of two otherwise identical European put options or call options cannot exceed the obsolete value of the difference in the present value of the exercise prices.

   Let us explain this with an example. Suppose there are two call options with exercise prices ₹50 and ₹60 and call prices are ₹20 and ₹5, respectively. In such case, the present value of the difference in the exercise prices assumes to be ₹9.50, whereas the difference of call prices is ₹15. It means these option prices violate the above stated property of the option. One can take the advantage of this situation by buying the call with the exercise price at 60 and selling the call with exercise price at ₹50. The difference of call prices ₹15(20 – 5) and invest the present value of the difference in exercise prices. It means the cash flow associated with setting of such portfolio is ₹5 + ₹20 – .95 × ₹10 = ₹5.50. Let us further assume that, at maturity, the price is below ₹50, both the options are unexercised and we have ₹10 which is value of the investment in zero coupon bonds. However, if the stock price at the maturity is ₹55, then we have to pay ₹5 on the option we wrote and get nothing from the option we purchased, and still we have ₹10 and so on. So, it is observed that we make money for sure, and when property does not hold, then there will be an arbitrary opportunity in the market.

6. The value of American option increases with longer time to maturity

The above property of the option relates with the time remain up to maturity in the option contract. The option which has longer maturity in comparison to other option which has shorter maturity, will be having higher option price and vice versa. It means the call with a longer time to maturity cannot be worth less than the one with the lesser time to maturity. The call with longer period has more opportunity to earn for the call buyer, since it has longer period to wait to exercise the call. The same reason applies to the American put options. However, this reasoning does not apply to European option because they cannot be exercised before maturity.

## 16.8 PUT–CALL PARITY THEOREM

Put and call prices are related to each other. This is because if there is a market for the European calls, we can also estimate or produce European puts on our own. In other words, put–call parity establishes a no-arbitrage pricing condition between a call and a put premium. Thus, pricing boundary of a call relatives to a put on the same stock requires that both options have same strike price and same time to expiration.

**Concept:** Let us explain this concept first for European stock option which pays no dividends before the expiration of option. In this, the difference between the price of a call and price of a put on the same stock, with the same strike price and expiration period, equals the price of the underlying asset (stock) minus the present value of the strike price. That is:

Proposition: $C - P = S - K(1 + r)^{-T}$

(Put–Call Theorem) $P(S, K, T, t) = C(S, K, T, t) + PV_{tT} K - S$

The above concept is explained into two parts to prove it

Part A   What if $C - P > S - K(1 + r)^{-T}$

Then: $C - P - S + K(1 + r)^{-T} > 0$

**Position at Expiration of Option**

|  |  | ST < K | ST > K |
|---|---|---|---|
| Sell Call | $+C$ | 0 | $-(S_{T-K})$ |
| Buy Put | $-P$ | $+(K - ST)$ | 0 |
| Buy Stock | $-S$ | $+ST$ | $+S_T$ |
| Borrow | $+K(1 + r)^{-T}$ | $-K$ | $-K$ |
|  | $>0$ | 0 | 0 |

Part 'A' explains the proof of a conversion trade. In a conversion, the arbitrageur exploits by buying the stock, selling the overpriced call, buying the underpriced put and borrowing.

Part B   What if   $C - P < S - K(1 + r)^{-T}$

Then   $C - P - S + K(1 + r)^{-T} < 0$

OR   $-C + P + S - K(1 + r)^{-T} > 0$

### Position at Expiration of Option

|  |  | $S_T < K$ | $S_T > K$ |
|---|---|---|---|
| Buy Call | $-C$ | $0$ | $+(S_T - K)$ |
| Sell Put | $+P$ | $-(K - ST)$ | $0$ |
| Sell Stock | $+S$ | $-ST$ | $-ST$ |
| Lend | $-K(1 + r)^{-T}$ | $+K$ | $+K$ |
|  | $>0$ | $0$ | $0$ |

Part 'B' explains the proof of a reverse conversion or reversal trade. In this we assume that the arbitrageur receives full use of the proceeds of the short sale. However, "quasi-arbitrageurs" already own the stock, and they have the ability to sell the stock and receive the proceeds.

**EXAMPLE:**   Assume that we can buy a call with exercise price of ₹50 that matures in 3 months. Call price is ₹15, and a zero-coupon bond that pays amount in 3 months cost ₹0.95, and stock price is ₹60. Considering this strategy, buying the call investing the present value of the exercise price in bond, then this strategy costs us:

₹15 + (₹50 × .95) – ₹60 = ₹2.5. Let us see now what we have at maturity:

Assume first that the stock price is below ₹50, then the call is worthless. Hence, we have ₹50 from the sale of bond and have to buy the stock to settle the short sale. On net, the value of the portfolio is ₹50–$S_T$. This is the pay-off of a put with an exercise price of ₹50 when it is in the money.

Consider, if the stock price is above ₹50 the call pays $S_T$– ₹50. We use the proceeds of the bond to pay the exercise price, get the stock and deliver it to settle the short sale. On net the value of our portfolio is zero. This is the payoff of a put with an exercise price of ₹50 when it is out of money.

From the above, we would expect ₹2.50 to be the price of the put since the production cost of the put to us is ₹2.50. This result is called *the put-call parity theorem*.

**EXAMPLE:**   Consider stock 'A' call sells for ₹4.800 and put price is at ₹2.800. Stock price is 50. Assume that riskless interest rate is 6 percent p.a. and that there are 90 days to expire. Do these option prices follow put–call parity?

Put–Call Parity:   $C - P = S - K(1 + r)^{-T}$

$= 4.800 - 2.800 = 50 - 48(1.06)^{-.25}$

$= 4.800 - 2.800 = 50 - 47.280$

$= 2 < 2.720$

From the above, it is observed that the call is 'cheap' relative to the put. Thus, the arbitrage traders are to buy the call, write the put, sell the stock, and lead the proceeds. However, it is subject to the conditions that these must be European options and no dividend payment for next 90 days.

**EXAMPLE:**   Consider another example where put and call options mature in 90 days. The underlying asset is worth ₹60, the put is worth ₹10, the exercise price is ₹65 and a zero-coupon bond that matures in 90 days and pays ₹1 is worth ₹0.97. Calculate the call price in this where $S_t$ = ₹60, $K$ = ₹65, $T$, 0.25,

Put–call Parity $C - P = S - K(1 + r)^{-T}$

$\qquad = C - ₹10 = ₹60 - ₹65(1 + r)^{-.25}$

$\qquad = C - 10 = 60 - 63.05$

$\qquad C = 70 - 63.05 = 6.95$

Assume that the call sells for ₹7 or above instead of ₹6.95, then we will sell the call because it is too expensive relative to put and vice-versa. The put-call theorem tells us that the portfolio is long the put, long the underlying asset and purity short the bond that matures at $T$, and have face value ₹65. Buying this hedge portfolio creates a cash outflow of ₹6.95 (₹10 + ₹60 minus the present value of the exercise price. This cash outflow is financed by selling the call for ₹7.50, so that we have ₹0.55 left. The fifty five cents is our arbitrage profit since no cash is needed at maturity.

Further assume that the call is worth ₹6.50, which means that call is cheap. Then we can buy the call and sell the portfolio that has the payoff of the call. In this way we will short the asset write the put and invest in bond with a face value of ₹65 which matures in 3 months. As a result, we have a cash flow of ₹ −6.50 − 63.05 + 60 + 10, or 0.45. Note that with this strategy we never make or lose money at maturity. We gain ₹0.45 today and pay nothing at maturity, and there is an arbitrage opportunity whenever we make money today. Consequently, there is an arbitrage opportunity whenever put-call parity does not hold.

**EXAMPLE:** Consider that the current price of the stock is ₹360 and the-risk free interest rate is 5 percent. If a 90-day call option with a stock price of ₹350 on this stock is trading at ₹25. What will be the put option price of the same maturity?. Further, what will happen if the put option on the same stock is trading at ₹8? Calculate by using the put–call parity relationship.

*Solution:*

Put–call parity relationship equation is: $S + P = C + PV(X)$

The value of $C$ is ₹25, $S$ = ₹360, $X$ = ₹350, $PV(X)$ = ₹345.65

The value of put option would be: $P = C + PV(X) - S$

$P = 25 + 345.65 - 360 = ₹10.65$

If the value of put option is (₹) 8, then portfolio value would be as per portfolio II = ₹8 + ₹360 = ₹368

Comparison of portfolio I and II at the expiration.

Value of portfolio I $\quad = ₹25 + ₹345.65 = ₹370.65$

Value of portfolio II $\; = ₹8 + ₹360 = ₹368.00$

Value of portfolio I is higher by ₹2.65 than portfolio II

It is suggested that trader can realize profit by going short in portfolio I and long in portfolio II through arbitrage.

## 16.9 OPTION VALUATION

Theoretically, the value of an option comprises two components: intrinsic value and time value. Let us explain these separately in order to determine the total value of an option at a particular point of time.

## 16.9.1 Intrinsic Value of the Option

The intrinsic value of an option is the gain to the holder of an option on immediate exercise. Since the investor cannot exercise the option before maturity in European option, intrinsic value will be just notional and not actual. This can be calculated only in American option where the investor can exercise his right at any time before the expiration date. It is also called *fundamental value* or *underlying value*. In other words, this value for a call is nothing more than the difference between the market price and strike price of the underlying asset.

**For a call option:** It is determined as:

$$\text{Max } [(S_t - X), 0]$$

where $S_t$ is current stock price of the underlying asset and $X$ is strike price of the underlying asset.

If $S_t > X$, it is positive intrinsic value and if $S_t = X$, intrinsic value is zero.

But it cannot be negative because the buyer will not exercise the option. So it cannot fall below zero.

**For a put option:** Intrinsic value is:

$$\text{Max } [(X - S_t), 0)]$$

If $X > S_t$, it is positive intrinsic value; if $X = S_t$, intrinsic value is zero; and if $X = S_e$ intrinsic value is zero but it cannot be negative.

## 16.9.2 Time Value of the Option

The value of an American option at any time prior to expiration must be at least to its intrinsic value. In general it will be larger. This is because there is some possibility or probability that the stock price will move further in favour of the option holder. The difference between the value of an option at the particular time $t$ and its intrinsic value at the time is called *the time value of the option*. It should be noted that for the European option, this argument does not hold. The determination of time value is more complex. Major factors which influence the time value are the expected volatility of the stock price, the length of the period remaining to the expiry date, the extent to which the option is in or out of the money. It has been observed that out-of-the-money options have less time value than at-the-money options since the stock price has further to move before intrinsic value is acquired. Similarly, in-the-money options have less time value than at-the-money options, reason being that their prices contain intrinsic value which is vulnerable to a fall in the stock price.

Further, the more time that remains until an option expires, the higher the time value tends to be. For example, if an option with nine months remaining until expiration will have a higher time value than an option with the same strike price but with less expiration time like six months, three months, one month, etc. As the option approaches its maturity, time value will be declining and will reach to zero. The value of a call option prior to maturity is shown in Figure 16.3.

It is evident from Figure 16.3 that the total value of an option is a combination of intrinsic value and time value. In Figure 16.3, three time periods of an option, i.e., one month, three months and six months have been taken. Total value of the option has been shown in dashed line. It is clear from Figure 16.3 that in the beginning of the option, the time value is higher in comparison to the near maturity. Future the time value is higher relatively to the time remained to the expiration. For example, for six months expiration period option, the time value is higher to three months or one month expiration. A further detailed discussion regarding these is given later on in this chapter.

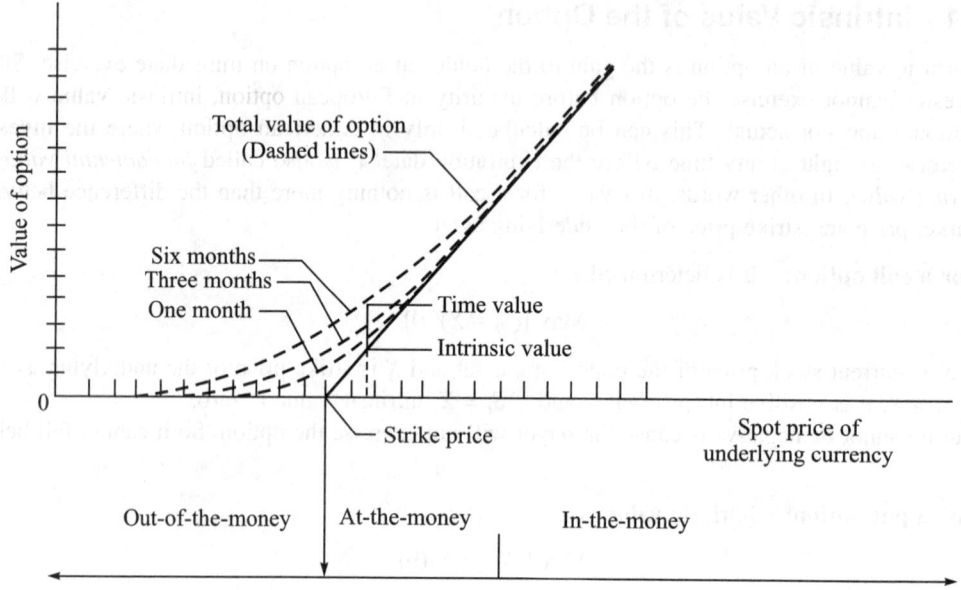

**FIGURE 16.3**  The value of a call option prior to maturity.

## 16.10  OPTION POSITIONS

In every option contract, there are two sides: one is the investor who has taken the long position (i.e., he has purchased the option), second opposite to this is the investor who has taken short position (i.e., he has sold or written the option). Similarly, if one party has taken the short position, then automatically the other party (writer) will be in long position. In this way, there are four types of options positions:

1.  A long position in a call option
2.  A long position in a put option
3.  A short position in a call option
4.  A short position in a put option

Figures 16.4 and 16.5 show profit from writing European call and put option.

Figures 16.4 and 16.5 depict the profit and loss position of options writer in case of writing a European call and a put option. The initial cost is not included in the calculation. If $X$ is the strike price and $S_t$ is the final price of the underlying asset, the difference of strike price and stock price leads to intrinsic value of an option. The intrinsic value of an option is the gain to the holder of the option.

1.  The payoff from a long position in a European call option is:

$$\max(S_t - X, 0)$$

where $S_t$ is stock price and $X$ is strike price.

If $S_t > X$, it is positive intrinsic value and, if $S_t < X$, then intrinsic value is zero.

Intrinsic value can not be zero because the holder will not exercise the option. So it cannot fall below zero. Thus, the option will be exercised if $S_t > X$, and will not be exercised if $S_t < X$.

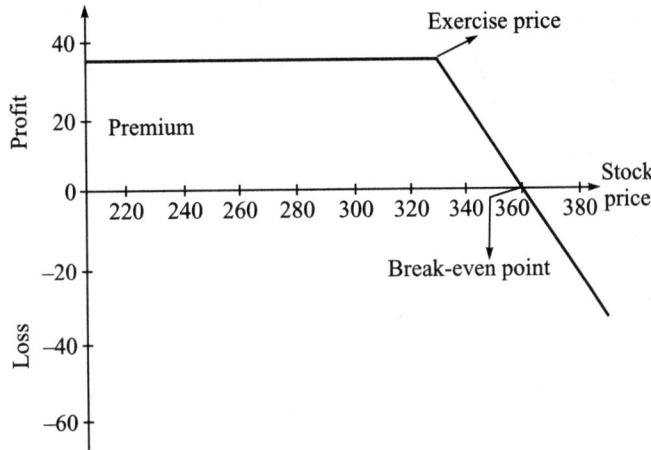

**FIGURE 16.4**    Profit from writing a call option (European).

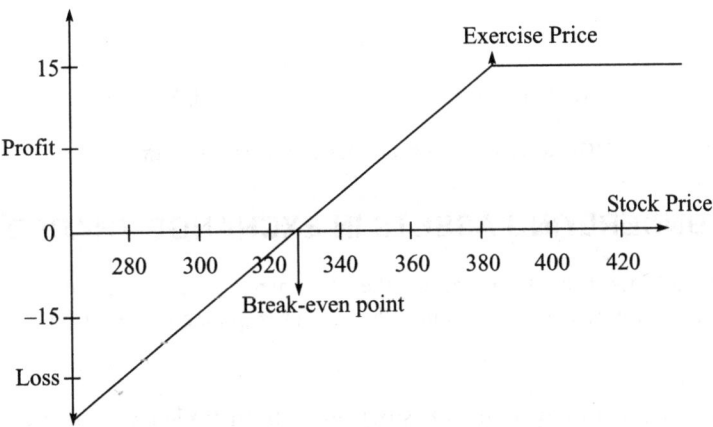

**FIGURE 16.5**    Profit from writing a put option (European).

2.  The payoff to the holder of a short position in the call option:

$$-\max (S_t - X, 0) = \min (X - S_t, 0)$$

3.  The payoff to the holder of a long position in a put option:

$$\max (X - S_t, 0)$$

4.  The payoff from a short position in a put option:

$$-\max (X - S_t, 0) = \min (S_t - X, 0)$$

These payoffs are shown graphically in Figures 16.6 (a), (b), (c) and (d).

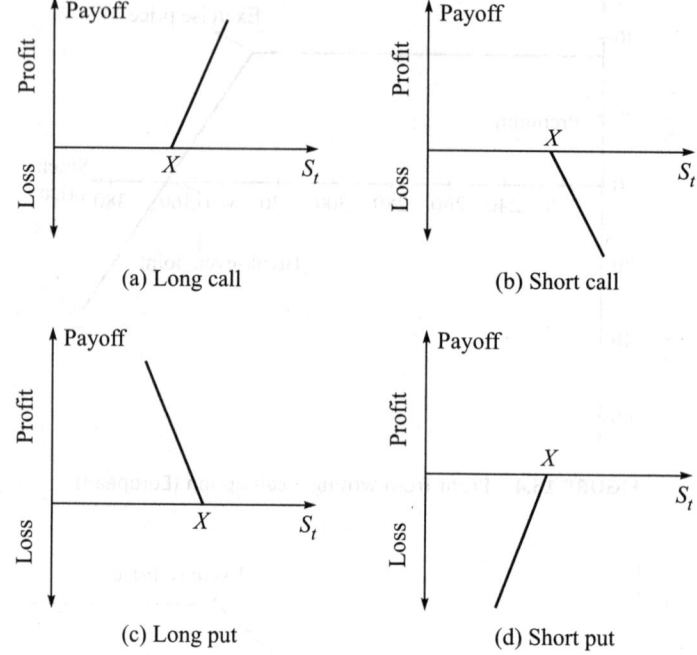

**FIGURE 16.6**   Payoff profiles of call and put options.

# 16.11   THE UNDERLYING ASSETS IN EXCHANGE-TRADED OPTIONS

Various assets, which are actively traded on the recognized exchanges, are stocks, stock indices, foreign currencies and futures contracts. These have been explained in brief here as under:

### Stock options

Options on individual shares of common stock have been traded for many years. Trading on standardized call options on equity shares started in 1973 on CBOE, whereas on put options it began in 1977. Stock options on a number of over-the-counter stocks are also available. While strike prices are not because of cash dividends paid to common stock holders, the strike price is adjusted for stock splits, stock dividends, reorganization, recapitalizations, etc. which affect the value of the underlying stock.

Stock options are most popular assets, which are traded on various exchanges all over the world. For example, more than 500 stocks are traded in United States. One contract gives the holder the right to buy or sell 100 shares at the specified strike price. In India, the National Stock Exchange and Bombay Stock Exchange have started option trading in certain stocks from the year 2001.

### Foreign currency options

Foreign currency is another important asset, which is traded on various exchanges. One among these is the Philadelphia Stock Exchange. It offers both European as well as American option contracts. Major currencies which are traded in the option markets are US dollar, Australian dollar, British pound, Canadian dollar, German mark, French franc, Japanese yen, Swiss franc, etc. The size of the contract differs currency to currency. This has been explained in more detail in the chapter on currency option.

### Index options

Many different index options are currently traded on different exchanges in different countries. For example, the S&P 100 index at CBOE and Major Market Index at AMEX are traded in the US options markets. Similarly, in India, such index options have been started on National Stock Exchange and Bombay Stock Exchange. Like stock option, index option's strike price is the index value at which the buyer of the option can buy or sell the underlying stock index. The strike index is converted into dollar (rupee) value by multiplying the strike index by the multiple for the contract. If the buyer of the stock index option intends to exercise the option then the stock must be delivered. It would be complicated to settle a stock index option by delivering all the stocks that make up that particular index. Hence, instead, stock index options are cash settlement contracts. In other words, if the option is exercised, the exchange assigned option writer pays cash to the option buyer, and there will be no delivery of any share.

The money value of the stock index underlying an index option is equal to the current cash index value multiplied by the contracts multiple. This is calculated as:

Rupee value of the underlying index = Cash index value × Contract multiples

For example, the contract multiple for the S&P 100 is $100. So, assume, the cash index value for the S&P 100 is 750 then the dollar value of the S&P 100 contracts is 750 × 100 = $75,000. Index Options are very much useful in speculating the future direction of the stock market. Some investors have better timing skills than stock selection skills. They may be in better position to predict the stock market when it will rise or fall, and thus, accordingly take the position in stocks or stock options. Further, the index option after a low cost stock trading when a large cash inflow is not currently available. Further they can be used to hedge an existing portfolio against a systematic decease in stock.

### Futures options

In a futures option (or options on futures), the underlying asset is a futures contract. An option contract on futures contract gives the buyer the rights to buy from or sell to the writer a specified future contract at a designated price at a time during the life of the options. If the futures option is a call option, the buyer has the right to acquire a long futures position. Similarly, a put option on a futures contract grants the buyer the right to sell one particular futures contracts to the writer at the exercise price. It is observed that the futures contract normally matures shortly after the expiration of the option. Futures options are now available for most of the assets on which futures contracts are on the Euro dollar at CME and the Treasury bond at the CBOT.

### Interest rate options

They are another important options contract, which are popular in the international financial markets. Interest rate options can be written on cash instruments or futures. There are various debt instruments, which are used as underlying instruments for interest rate options on different exchanges. These contracts are referred to as options on physicals. Recently, these interest rate options have also gained popularity on the over-the-counter markets like on treasury bonds, agency debentures and mortgage-backed-securities. There are governments, large banking firms and mortgage-backed-securities dealers who make a market in such options on specific securities.

### LEAPS options

These options contracts are created for a longer period. The longest time before expiration for a standard exchange traded option is six-months. However, Long Term Equity Anticipated Securities (LEAPS) are option contracts designed to offer with longer period maturities even up to 39 months. These LEAPS options are available on individual stocks and some indexes. Usually, they are designed for a particular purpose.

### FLEX options

It is a specific type of option contract where some terms of the option have been customized. The basic objective of customization of some terms to meet the wide range of portfolio strategy needs of the institutional investors that cannot be satisfied through the standard exchange-traded options. FLEX options can be created for individual stocks, stock indexes, treasury securities, etc. They are traded on an option exchange and cleared and guaranteed by the clearing house of that exchange. The value of FLEX option depends upon the ability to customize the terms on four dimensions, such as underlying asset, strike price, expiration date and settlement style (i.e., American vs European). Moreover, the exchange also provides a secondary market to offset or alter positions and an independent daily marking of prices.

### Exotic options

The option contracts through the OTC market can be customized in any manner desired by an institutional investor. For example, if a dealer can reasonably hedge the risk associated with opposite side of the option sought, it will design an option as desired by the customer. OTC options are not limited to only European or American type of options, rather a particular option can be created with different exercise dates as well as the expiration date of the option. Such options are also referred to as limited exercise options, Bermuda options, Atlantic options, etc. Thus, more complex options created as per the needs of the customers are called *exotic options* which may be with different expiration dates, exercise prices, underlying assets, expiration date and so on.

## 16.12   NAKED (UNCOVERED) AND COVERED OPTION

Naked or uncovered options are those which do not have offsetting positions, and therefore, are more risky. On the other hand, where the writer has corresponding offsetting position in the asset underlying the option is called *covered option*. Writing a simple uncovered (or naked) call option indicates toward exposure of the option writer to unlimited potential losses. The basic aim is to earn the premium. In period of stable or declining prices, call option writing may result in attractive profits by capturing the time value of an option. The strategy of writing uncovered calls reflects an investor's expectations and tolerance for risk.

A covered option position involves the purchase or sale of an option in combination with an offsetting (or opposite) position in the asset which underlies the option. As observed earlier, the writer of the call option incurs losses when stock prices rise, and put writers incur losses when prices fall. In such situation, the writer can cover the short put with a short position and short call with a long position in the underlying asset. This can be stated as:

Covered call sale = Short call + Long futures

Covered put sale = Short put + Short futures

## 16.13 SYNTHETIC FUTURES AND OPTIONS

Synthetic futures positions are created by combining two option positions such that the resulting pay-off remain same or nearly same as that of an outright futures position. It can be both synthetic long and short positions. Synthetic long position is created by combining long call option with short put option having the same strike price. Synthetic short futures is created by combining long put with short call option having the same strike price. In summary, the positions will be

Synthetic long futures = Long call + Short put

Synthetic short futures = Long put + Short call

Similarly, we can explain the synthetic option. Synthetic option positions can be created by combining options and futures positions. Combining a long put option with a long futures position; and whereas, a synthetic long put option is created by combining a long call option with a short futures position creates a synthetic long call option. A more detail of these have been explained in the chapter on trading strategy of the option.

## 16.14 MARGIN REQUIREMENTS IN OPTION CONTRACTS

Some of the option transactions require to maintain a margin. It means investors specifically sellers of the options must post margin to maintain an option position. This is analogous to posting collateral and can be made by depositing of cash or other specified securities into the brokerage account. For example, if one party writes an option, the loss associated with an unfavourable movement in stock price can be too much. So, the margin system is to reduce the likelihood that option writers will be unable to fulfill their obligations under the option terms. Further, when an investor sells an option but does not have a position in the said underlying stock, this practice is known as *selling naked options*.

The writing of naked options is too risky, because losses are theoretically unlimited in both the options—call or put contracts. In such case, the brokers, the exchanges and the regulatory authority want assurance that the writers of naked options will fulfill their obligations. Consequently, a substantial margin requirements are imposed by the exchanges on written naked positions. Further, it is also observed that some brokers do not handle requests to write naked options of the investors/ clients without having substantial equity in their accounts. For example, in 2001 Chicago Board of Exchange (CBOE), the formula for determining the margin required to write a naked call on a common stock was; but subject to change:

$$\text{Max } \{c + 0.1(s), c + 0.2(s) - [\max (o, K - S)]\}$$

where

$C$ : The call premium
$S$ : Price of stock
$K$ : Strike price
Max $\{0, K - S)$ = Out of the money amount

As per this formula, required margin is either (a) the market value of the call options plus 10 percent of the market values of the stock, or (b) the market value of the call plus 20 percent of the market of the stock minus any out-of-the money amount, the required amount is the greater of (a) and (b) Similarly, the initial margin requirements for writing the naked puts of equity share is

$$\text{Max}\{P + 0.1(s)\ P + 0.20 - [\max(0, S - K)]\}$$

where $P$ = Put premium, $S$ = Stock price, $K$ = Exercise price and Max $\{O, S - K\}$ represents the put out-of-the-money.

In practice, although there are guidelines set for brokers as to the amount of margin they should take, it is actually down to the brokers, themselves to decide. Because of this, the funds required to write contract may vary from one broker to another, and also the clients' trading size. It is also possible that the broker may not ask for margin if the client has actually owned the underlying stock in call option and in case of put option, he has taken short position on the relevant underlying security.

Further, there are some other possibilities where you can trade without depositing the margin. For example, writing options by using debit spreads. It means when you create debit, you would usually be purchasing in the money options, and then writing cheaper out-of-the-money options to recover some of the costs of doing so. For example, one could buy call options of stock X with a strike price of ₹100, another write a call option on this stock X with a higher strike price, assuming the same amount of contracts as of written option. In such situation, the losses will be limited, and thus, no need of margin money.

The margins are levied on the contract value and the amount (in percentage terms) as dictated by the concerned exchange. It is largely dependent on the volatility in the price of the option. Higher the volatility, greater is the amount of margin. This amount is typically ranges from 15 percent to as high as 60 percent in times of extreme volatility. So, the seller of the call option of Reliance share at a strike price of ₹970, who receives a premium of ₹10 would have to deposit a margin of ₹1,16,400 assuming a margin of 20 percent of the total value (₹970 × ₹600), even though the value of his outstanding position is ₹5,82,000. Margin requirements differ from exchange to exchange and on the volatility of the underlying stocks. Investors should consult their brokers to learn the rules for margin requirements.

Some brokers classify options trading at different levels. When an investor opens an account with the broker, then he is to request to the broker for option trading authorization. Then the broker will decide his level within different levels ranging usually from 1 to 4. For example, to buy options, one needs the basic level or Level (1) clearance. If he plans on selling naked puts, then he needs Level (2) clearance. Further, if the investor has the necessary experience, then he can try to obtain Level (3) clearance or higher approval.

## 16.15   ROLE OF MARKET MAKERS IN OPTION MARKETS

The market makers play a significant role in the stock option market. If one wants to buy or sell an option in the market, then he/she has to wait for another party to contact you about taking the opposite position. Sometimes, it is difficult to find the opposite party. Generally, the stock exchanges have one more market makers who are ready to create a market for option trading by quoting a bid and ask price. It means the market makers will take opposite position. For example, if one party wish to sell, the market maker will buy the option at the quoted bid price, and vice versa. Normally, the specialist is given the franchise of market making at various exchanges through other competition exists for specialists.

The market makers quote bid and ask prices. The bid is the option price at which the market maker is ready to buy the option and ask the price at which he is ready to sell the option. The ask price always exceeds the bid price. The difference between bid and ask spread varies stock to stock. If the option is thinly traded, i.e. low volume, the bid-ask spread may be wider. However, it is expected that the market makers will maintain fair and orderly markets. Normally, the stock exchanges specify the maximum range of the spreads on the options of the different stocks.

The investors who wish to trade immediately usually place the market orders. The market makers who makes a "market" is always ready to trade and generally earns profit by the difference of the bid and ask prices. Thus, if an investor places a market order to buy an option, he will usually pay ask price, and on the other hand, he wants to sell and option, then he will receive the bid price as quoted by the market maker. The difference between the ask and bid price is the profit of the market maker and the cost for the investor. However, the investors can also quote or place limit order, which are orders to buy or sell at a specified price. In such case, the market makers can change its earlier quoted bid price.

# SUMMARY

This chapter has introduced option markets and contracts by briefly describing what option contracts are, where they are traded, and how they differ from futures and forward contracts. Like futures and forward contracts, the options are also important derivative securities trading all over the world in last three decades.

The history of options are as old as trading in business world. The ideas of options have existed pre-ancient roman and Greek times. Options on commodities have existed in different form since 1860 in USA. Options in stock have been traded actively for nearly a century in over-the-counter (OTC) market under the auspices of the put and call dealers association. The first options were traded on individual stock on an organized exchange in 1973, when the Chicago Board Option Exchange (CBOE) came into existence. In India, SEBI has permitted option trading in Indian capital market securities in the year 2001, both by way of trading in stock options and also index options. Options are currently traded on BSE and NSE and trading on option is regulated by SEBI.

The chapter in next section explains the concept of option contract. An option is particular type of contract between two parties where one person gives the other person the right to buy or sell a specific asset at a specified price within a specific time period. In other words, the option is a specific derivative instrument under which one party gets the right, but no obligation, to buy or sell a specific quantity of an asset at a pre-arranged price. Important terminology used in option contract are parties to a contract, exercise price or strike price, expiration date or maturity date, option premium or option price options can be classification into different categories: (a) call and put options, (b) exchange-traded options and OTC options, (c) American and European options. Call option grants the buyer (holder) the right to purchase the underlying asset/stock from the writer (seller) a particular quantity at a specified price within a specified expiration date. A put option, on the other hand, is an option contract where the option buyer has the right to sell the underlying asset to the writer, at a specified price at or prior to the option's maturity date. American option can be exercised at any time before expiration date whereas European option can be exercised up to only at the expiration date. The options which are traded on a particular recognized exchange are called exchange-traded options, and options which are traded on over-the-counter (OTC) market are called as OTC traded-options.

The chapter further explains the concept of intrinsic value and time value of option which play important role in determining the price (premium) of an option. Intrinsic value of an option is the gain to the holder of an option on immediate exercise. Since the investor cannot exercise the option before maturity in European option, hence, it is also called fundamental value or underlying value. This value for a call option is the difference between the market price and strike price of underlying asset. The value of an American option at any time prior to expiration must be at least to its intrinsic value. In general, it will be higher; because there is some possibility or probability that the stock price may move further in favour of the option holder. The difference between the value of an option at a particular time and its intrinsic value at the time is called time value of the option. It is only in case of American options. Option position can be of four types: a long position in a call option, a long position in a put option, a short position in call option and a short position in put option. Naked (uncovered) options are those which do not have offsetting positions and are, therefore, ore risky whereas covered options are those against which offsetting positions have been taken by the option writers. Many different index options are currently traded on various exchanges such as S&P 100 index at CBOE, Standard and poor's CN × NIFTY junior option on National Stock Exchange, etc. In futures option, the underlying asset is a futures contract. An option contract on futures contract gives right to the buyer to buy from or sell to the writer a specified futures contract at designated price at maturity or during the life of the options. Interest rate options are another important options contract which are popular in the international financial markets. Interest rate options can be written on cash instrument or futures.

LEAPS options contract are created for a longer period. Long-term equity anticipated securities are options contract designed to offer with longer period maturities even up to 39 months. FLEX is a specific type of option contract where some terms of the options have been customized. The basic objective is to meet some terms of wide range of portfolio strategy needs of the institutional investors that cannot be satisfied through the standard exchanged-traded options. Exotic options are more complex options created as per the specific needs of the customers. The options may be with different expiration dates, exercise prices, underlying assets, etc. Various assets, which are actively traded on the recognized exchanges are stock index, foreign currencies futures contracts. Options on individual share of common stock have been traded for many years. Trading on standardized call options on equity shares started in 1973 on CBOE whereas on put options on equity shares started in 1977.

## SOLVED PROBLEMS

**P.1.**    An investor buys a European put option on a share for ₹150. The stock price is ₹2,000 and strike price is ₹1,800. Under what circumstances does the investor make the profit? At what price will the option be exercised? Draw a diagram showing the variations of the investor's profit with the stock price at the maturity of option?

*Solution:*    The investor makes a profit if the price of stock on expiration date is less than ₹1,650. This is because the gain from exercising the option is in these circumstances will be greater than ₹150. Option will be exercised if the stock price is less than ₹1,800 at the maturity of the option. The variation of the investor's profit with the stock price is shown in the following diagram:

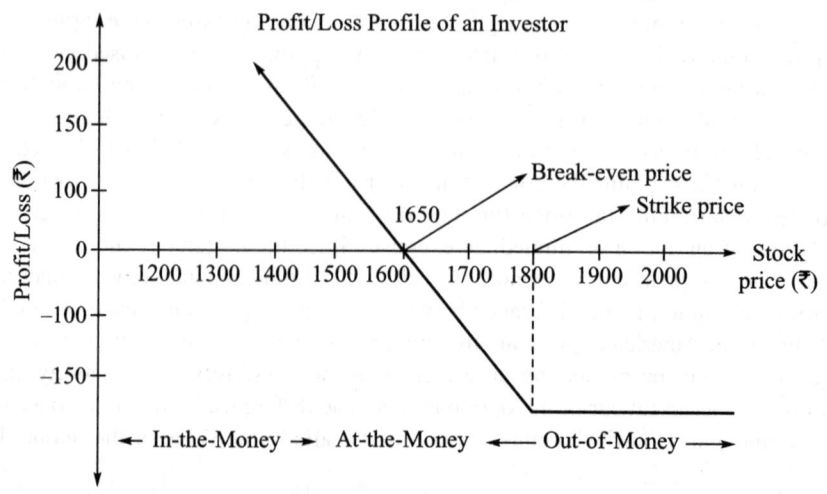

**P.2.** Suppose the stock price of Reliance Industries in spot market is ₹450 and two-month option contract is of ₹450. The price of the option is ₹20 per share. At what price the option will be at-the-money, out-of-money and in-the-money of the option is both call as well as put option?

*Solution:*

Option strike price : ₹450 per share

Premium (price) : ₹20 per share

Call option

   (i) At-the-money : 450 + 20 = ₹470 per share

   (ii) In-the-money : Price greater than ₹470 per share

   (iii) Out-of-money : Price less than ₹470 per share

Put option

   (i) At-the-money : 450 – 20 = ₹430 per share

   (ii) In-the-money : Price less than ₹430 per share

   (iii) Out-of-money : Price above ₹430 per share

**P.3.** Suppose that a European call option to buy a share for ₹3,000 costs ₹120 and it is held until maturity. Under what circumstances the holder of the option will make a profit? Under what circumstances will the option be exercised?

*Solution:* The investor will earn profit if the price of the stock is above (₹3,000 + ₹120) = ₹3,120. The variation of the investor's profit with stock price is shown in the following diagram:

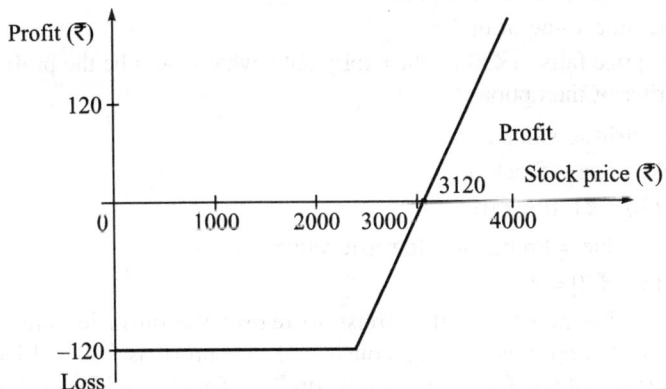

As shown in the figure, investor will exercise the option if the price of stock is above ₹3,120 at the expiration date.

**P.4.** An investor buys a call with a strike price $X$ and writes a put with the same strike price. Describe the investor's position.

*Solution:* Payoff to the investor in various option positions:

Call option : max $(S_t - X, 0)$

Put option : max $(X - S_t, 0)$

So payoff : max $(S_t - X, 0)$ – max $(X - S_t, 0)$

The profit of investor will be $(S_t - X)$ in all circumstances. The investor's position is a forward contract with delivery price $X$.

**P.5.** The FTSE 100 is currently 3800 point. Call options with a strike price of 3,750 point are price at 35 index points. The option contracts are based on £10 per index point and they are both settled.

(a) What is the maximum loss to a buyer of the option?

(b) What is break-even stock index?

(c) Is there a maximum profit?

(d) If the option will be exercised at an index level of 3850, what transaction would occur?

*Solution:*

(a) The maximum loss to the buyer of an option is the premium paid. In this case it is 35 index points, which corresponds to a monetary sum of £350.

(b) If the option were exercised at an index level of 3785, there would be a gross profit (pay off) of 35 index points, amounting to £350. This matches the premium paid. So 3785 is the break-even stock index.

(c) Since there is no upper limit to the stock index, there is no upper limit to the potential profit of a buyer of a call option.

(d) Since stock index are cash settled, no shares change hands upon exercise. Instead there is a cash flow reflecting the intrinsic value of the option. In this case, the intrinsic value is 100 index points. Upon exercise the option holder will receive $1,000.

**P.6.** The share of *X* Ltd. Company stands at ₹120, put options with a strike price of ₹130 are priced at ₹15.

(a) What is the intrinsic value of option?

(b) What is the time value of option?

(c) If the share price falls to ₹50 by the expiry date, what would be the profit/loss for the holder and the writer of the options?

*Solution:* (a) The intrinsic value is:

Strike price – Stock price

= ₹130 – ₹120 = ₹10

(b) Time value = Premium – Intrinsic value

= ₹15 – ₹10 = ₹5

(c) The option holder could exercise to realize the intrinsic value of ₹80. When the payment (premium) of ₹15 considered, net profit is ₹80 – 15 = ₹65. The option writer would pay ₹130 for share worth ₹50. This loss of ₹80 is partially offset by the premium receipt of ₹15. Net loss will be ₹80 – 15 = ₹65. So profit of the buyer is equal to the loss of the writer.

**P.7.** On November 1, 2015 an investor can establish a synthetic long futures by purchasing a December 310 call for ₹11.40 and writing the December 310 put for ₹12.95. If the S&P futures price rise prior to expiration, the gain on the call option will be similar to the gain that would occur on a long futures position. Show the combined position diagrammatically.

*Solution:* Synthetic long futures, using December S&P futures (Long December 310 call and short December 310 put).

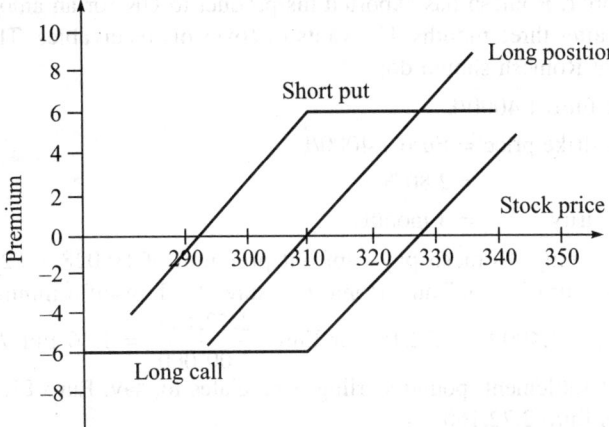

**P.8.** Suppose X holds shares of SBI and is of fear that price of SBI will decrease in futures. He wants to hedge this risk by entering into option market. Suppose a put option of SBI after two-month delivery is ₹450 and current price of SBI is ₹400. The premium (price) of option is ₹20. Show the position of the X if he chooses to exercise and after two months price of SBI declines to ₹390.

*Solution:*

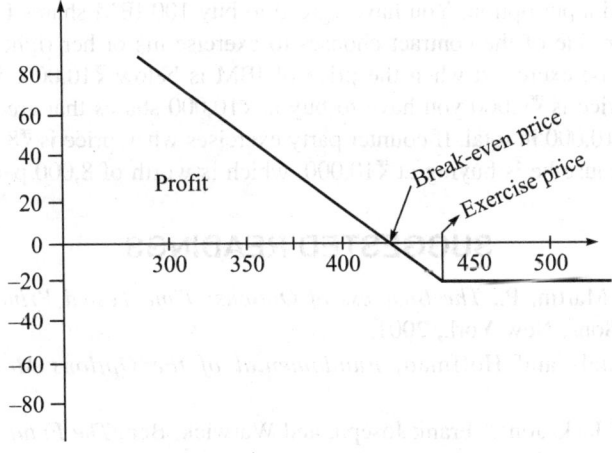

$$\text{Profit to } X = (450 - 20 - 390)$$
$$= 430 - 390 = ₹40 \text{ per share}$$

**P.9.** Suppose a call option enables purchase of a dollar for ₹42 while it is quoted at ₹42.60 in the market and premium paid for call option is ₹1.00. Calculate the time value and intrinsic value of the currency option.

*Solution:* Spot price (₹/\$) = ₹42.60

Strike price (₹/\$) = ₹42.00

Intrinsic value = ₹42.60 – 42.00 = ₹0.60 per dollar

Time value = ₹1.00 – (42.60 – 42.00) = ₹0.40 per dollar

**P.10.**    A French exporter, Romesh has exported his product to UK for an amount of £2,00,000. He is to receive payment after three months. He wants to cover his receivables. The following data are available. Indicate what Romesh should do:

Spot rates: Euro 1.4000/£

Put option strike price = Euro 1.4000/£

Premium          = 2.80%

Option maturity      = 3 months

*Solution:*    At the beginning, Romesh pays upfront premium of £0.028 × £2,00,000 or £0.028 × £2,00,000 × 1.4000 or (Euro 7840). Thus, Romesh ensures for himself a minimum amount of Euro 2,00,000 × (1 – 0.028) × 1.4000 = 2,72,160 or Euro $\dfrac{2,72,160}{2,00,000}$ = 1.36 Euro/£, called break-even point. If on the date of settlement, pound sterling depreciates to, say, Euro £1.37, Romesh exercise his option and receives Euro 2,72,160.

In case pound sterling appreciates to, say, Euro 1.43/£, Romesh does not use his put option and sells pound directly in the market.

**P.11.**    Suppose that *X* writes a put option contract on IBM with a strike price of ₹10,000 and expiration date in three months, the current price of IBM stock is ₹10,500. What (*X*) has committed to yourself? How much could you gain or loss?

*Solution:*    *X* has sold a put option. You have agreed to buy 100 IBM shares for 10,000 per share if the party on the other side of the contract chooses to exercise his or her right to sell for this price. The option will only be exercised when the price of IBM is below ₹10,000. Suppose counterparty exercises when the price is ₹9,000 you have to buy at ₹10,000 shares that are worth ₹9,000. *X* loss ₹1,000 per share or ₹10,000 in total. If counter party exercises when price is ₹8,000 per share *X* loses ₹2,000 per shares because he is buying at ₹10,000, which is worth of 8,000 per share only.

## SUGGESTED READINGS

1.  Connell, O. and Martin, P., *The Business of Options: Time Tested Principles and Practices*, John Wiley and Sons, New York, 2001.
2.  Williams, Michaels and Hoffman, *Fundamental of the Options Market*, McGraw-Hill, New York, 2001.
3.  Teweles, Richard Jack, Jones, Frank Joseph, and Warwick, Ben, *The Futures Game: Who Wins? Who Loss? Why?* 3rd ed., McGraw-Hill, New York, 1998.
4.  Thomsett, Michael, C., *Getting Started in Options*, 4th ed., Wiley, New York, 2001.
5.  James, Peter and Net Library Inc., *Options Theory*, J. Wiley, Chichester, West Sussex, England, Hoboken, New Jersey, 2003.
6.  McMillan, L.G., *Options as a Strategic Investment*, 4th ed., Paramus, New York Institute of Finance, 2001.
7.  Copeland, Tom and Antikarov, Vladimir, *Real Options: A Practitioner Guide*, Texere, 2001.

## REVIEW QUESTIONS

1.  What do you understand by options and option market? Discuss with suitable examples. Also explain its significance in financial markets.

2. Write a detailed note on historical background of options market.
3. What are important terms used in options contract? Explain with examples.
4. What is an option contract? Explain the different classifications of options with suitable illustrations.
5. Explain the concept of option in context to:
   (a) In-the-money
   (b) At-the-money
   (c) Of-the-money
6. Write short notes on
   (a) Intrinsic value of option
   (b) Time value of money
7. Explain the distinction between options and futures contracts with suitable examples.
8. Distinguish between exchange-traded options and OTC-traded options. Which options are popular? And why?
9. "Option position involves two sides, one is the investor who has taken the long position and another is the investor who has taken the short position." Explain the statement in the light of features of options contract.
10. Explain a long position in a call option and a long position in a put option with illustrations.
11. Evaluate a short position in a call option and a short position in a put option with examples.
12. Distinguish between European options and American options in context to valuation of an option contract. Explain with examples.
13. Explain the naked (uncovered) and covered option with suitable examples.
14. Explain various assets which are included for trading purpose on important exchanges.
15. (a) Distinguish between simple option contract and complex option contract.
    (b) Compare and contrast between forward, futures and option contracts.
16. "Options are the safest instrument for the investors for investment purpose." Examine critically the statement.
17. "Options writer has limited profit and unlimited losses whereas option buyer has limited losses and unlimited profits." Critically discuss the statement with example.
18. Write a short note on brief history of options contract in Indian stock market.
19. Write a detailed note on mechanism of option markets.
20. List out major option market along with underlying assets traded on them.
21. "Options provide right and not obligation to the buyer of an option whereas the writer is always under obligation, if the buyer desires so." Explain the statement in the light of features of option contract.
22. What are important positions which can be taken in an option contract by writer in different situations? Explain.
23. What are financial derivatives? Explain the types of financial derivatives with special emphasis on options markets.
24. How does an option on a futures contract differ from an option on physicals? Explain.
25. What is a synthetic futures position? Why should an investor assume a synthetic? Explain with suitable examples.

**26.** Why is an option writer required to post margin while an option buyer normally is not? Comment.

**27.** "It is often said in option contract that the writer has a contingent liability." Do you agree with the statement? If yes, why?

## UNSOLVED PROBLEMS

**P.1.**    Suppose Mr. Manoj owns 5,000 shares worth ₹50 each. How can put options be used to provide Manoj with insurance against a decline in the value of your holding over the next 4 months?

**P.2.**    Consider an investor who in August owns 1,000 shares of IBM corporation. The current share price is $55 per share. The investor is concerned that the share price may decline sharply in the next two months and wishes to protect himself. IBM put options are priced at $4 per share. What could be the investor's strategy and show the position if price of the IBM declined to $50 per share.

**P.3.**    Mr. Romesh wants to buy 1,000 shares of Reliance Industries after a month. He is of fear that price of Reliance may increase in future (after one month). He wants to hedge his risk. Assume the current price of Reliance is ₹400 and call options are priced at ₹10 per share at strike price of ₹450. (a) How could Romesh protect his position by entering into option market? (b) What will be profit/loss to Romesh if Reliance spot after one month is ₹500 per share?

**P.4.**    An investor decides to buy 200 shares of a certain stock in margin and to write two call options contracts on the stock. The stock price is $63, the strike price is $65 and the price of the option is $7. Since the options are out-of-money, margin account allows the investor to borrow 50% of the stock or $6,300. The investor is also able to use the price received for the option, $7 × 200 or £1,400, to finance the purchase of the share. The share cost $63 × 200 = $12,600. What is the total amount/cash initially required from the investor for his or her traders?

**P.5.**    The stock price of Infosys Ltd. in cash market is ₹4,000 and two months call option strike price is of ₹4,500. The price of call option is ₹200 per share. At what price the option will be in-the-money, at-the-money and out-of-the-money?

**P.6.**    An investor buys a put option with a strike price X and writes a call option with the same strike price. Describe the payoff of investor.

**P.7.**    An investor has a short position in put option. Option price is $7, strike price is $70 and stock current price is $65. Draw a position of the investor by writing a European put option on one share.

**P.8.**    Suppose that a European call option to buy a share for ₹2,500 costs ₹125 and is held until maturity. Under what circumstances will the holder of the option make a profit? Under what circumstances will the option be exercised? Draw a diagram illustrating how profit from a long position in the option depends on the stock price at maturity of the option.

**P.9.**    Suppose that a European put option to sell for ₹5,000 costs ₹200 and is held until maturity. Under what circumstances will the seller of the option (that is party with a short position) make a profit? Under what circumstances will the option be exercised?

# Option Pricing Models

*After reading this chapter, students will be able to*

➤ Understand the concept and various determinants of option pricing.

➤ Be aware of the concept of log-normal assumption.

➤ Know the parameters of log-normal distribution.

➤ Estimate the volatility from historical records.

➤ Understand the Black-Scholes Option Pricing Model's assumptions like stock price behaviour corresponds the log-normal distribution, no transaction costs, no taxes, etc.

➤ Know the one-step binomial model for option pricing.

➤ Be aware of the two-step binomial model for option pricing.

➤ Understand the concept of risk-neutral valuation.

➤ Be aware of the concept of generalization of binomial model of option pricing.

➤ Know the Volatility Index in India.

➤ Explain the Upper and Lower Bounds of the options.

## 17.1 INTRODUCTION

It has been observed in preceding chapter that the price of the option is that amount which is paid by the option buyer to the option seller, which is also known as premium. Like any other price mechanism, the premium on a particular option is also to some extent determined by the demand for and supply of that asset underlying the option. Further, it is also pointed out that the option prices can be subdivided into two: intrinsic value and time value. The intrinsic value for a call option is the excess of the stock price over the option strike price if the option is in-the-money. It will be zero if the stock price is less than the strike price. Similarly, in case of put option, the intrinsic value is the strike price minus the stock price, or zero if the stock price exceeds the strike price. Time value of the option is the excess of the option price over the intrinsic value. To deal in option market, it is important to know how the options are priced or valued. There are two reasons for it. First to see whether the existing options premiums quoted in the market are correct, and second, to identify profitable trading and arbitrage opportunities. Further, it is also useful to value non-exchange-traded assets in the market.

In this section first we will discuss the factors which influence the price of the option, and after that two important models of option pricing like Black-Scholes Model and Binomial Model will be explained.

## 17.2   DETERMINANTS OF OPTION PRICES

Before discussing the option pricing models, let us see the factors that influence the option pricing. The six important factors are:

1. Current price of the option
2. Strike price of the option
3. Time to expiration of the option
4. Expected price volatility of the stock
5. Risk-free interest rate
6. Anticipated cash payments on the stock
7. Consideration of dividends

All the above said factors will influence the option pricing depending upon the nature and type of option whether the option is a call or put, or it is American or European. These factors have been discussed as follows:

**Current price of the underlying asset:**   The first important factor which influences the option price is the current price of the asset/stock. The option price will change as the stock price changes. For example, for a call option, the option price increases as the stock price increases and vice versa. The opposite holds in case of put option.

**Strike price of the option:**   Strike or exercise price of the option is fixed for the life of the option. Assuming other factors remain constant, in case of call option, the lower the strike price, the higher will be the option price and vice versa. The same is reverse in case of put option.

**Time to expiration of the option:**   The option is a wasting asset. Since the option has a fixed maturity, so after the expiration of the maturity, there is no value of option. In other words, all other factors remain constant, the longer the time to expiration of the option, the higher will be the option price. This is because as the time to maturity decreases, lesser time remains for stock's price to rise or fall, and therefore, the probability of a favourable price movement decreases.

**Expected stock price volatility:**   Fluctuations in the stock prices in future is a major factor to influence the option price, because greater the expected volatility of the price of the stock, the more an investor would be willing to pay for the option, and more premium an option writer would demand for it due to increased risk in the option contract.

**Risk-free interest rate:** Interest rate is an important factor which creates impact on the option price, since buying an option contract involves investment which bears cost for the investor. Consequently, all other factors remain constant, the higher the interest rate (short-term risk-free), the greater the cost of buying the underlying and carrying it to the expiration date of the call option. Hence, the higher the short-term risk-free interest rate, the greater the price of a call option.

**Anticipated cash payments on the stock:** Anticipated cash payments on the stock tend to decrease the price of a call option because the cash payments make it more attractive to hold stock than to hold the option. On the other hand, for put option, cash payments on the stock tend to increase the price.

## Consideration of Dividends

Another factor which influence the option premium is the extent to which the underlying equity stock pays the dividends. However, speculators often ignore it. There is precise series of events which occur when corporate dividend is to be announced. In practice, Board of directors of the company announces the certain amount of dividends to be paid on a certain date (The date of payment) as of a certain cut-off date (the date of record). To eliminate uncertainty due to processing time and exactly who is on the company's shareholders list on the date of record, the brokerage industry used the ex-dividend date convention. The ex-dividend date is normally two business days before the date of record, and the investor must buy stock before the ex-dividend date to qualify for the dividend receipts. The investors who purchase the stocks on the ex-dividend date do not receive the dividend, and this usually provides downward pressure on the price of the stock.

It is observed in the market that the price of the share to be down by about the amount of the dividend on the ex-dividend date. So, a person who purchases a call option does not like to fall in the price of the underlying stock, yet the payment of dividend will necessarily cause the price to fall. Further, higher the dividend, the more the stock price will fall. Since, the listed stock options are not adjusted for the payment of each dividend, it will certainly influence the option premium. In general, a company which pays a higher amount of dividends will have a smaller option premium than a company which pays smaller dividend.

The influence of these factors on option price is shown in Table 17.1.

**TABLE 17.1** Determinants of Option Price

| Factor | Symbols | Call price | Put price |
|---|---|---|---|
| **Effect on an increase of factor on** | | | |
| Current price of stock | $(S)$ | Increase | Decrease |
| Strike price | $(K)$ | Decrease | Increase |
| Time to expiration of option | $(t)$ | Increase | Increase |
| Price volatility of stock | $(\sigma)$ | Increase | Increase |
| Interest rate (short-term) | $(r)$ | Increase | Decrease |
| Anticipated cash payments | $(c)$ | Decrease | Increase |
| Dividend paid | $(D)$ | Decrease | Increase |

Before discussing the Black-Scholes option pricing model, let us explain certain parameters to understand the model because the same have been used in the construction of the model.

## 17.2.1    Log-Normal Distribution Assumption

A stock option pricing model must make certain assumptions about how stock prices behave over time. For example, if the price of State Bank of India share is ₹300 today in the market, what is the probability distribution for the price in one week or in one month or in one year? The basic assumption in the Black-Scholes option pricing model is that stock prices follow what is termed as random walks. This means that proportional changes in the stock prices in the short period are normally distributed. This in turn implies that the stock price at any future time has a log-normal distribution.

The general shape of a normal and log-normal distribution has been shown in Figure. 17.1 and Figure 17.2, respectively. A variable can take any position; positive or negative in a normal distribution, whereas in a log-normal distribution, it is restricted to being positive. So, a normal distribution is symmetrical, a log-normal distribution is skewed with the mean, median and mode being all different. Further, a random variable is log-normally distributed if the natural logarithm of the variable is normally distributed. One reason for using a log-normal distribution is that the price relative can never be negative. The stock price can rise indefinitely while it can only fall 100 percent which means that the return possibilities is actually skewed to the right, and hence, there are more possible positive outcomes than negative. It is also observed through empirical studies that with stock returns the tail of the distribution are "fatter" than in a truly normal distribution. Hence, the price relatives cannot be normally distributed. The natural logarithm of the price relative can be negative and will be normally distributed.

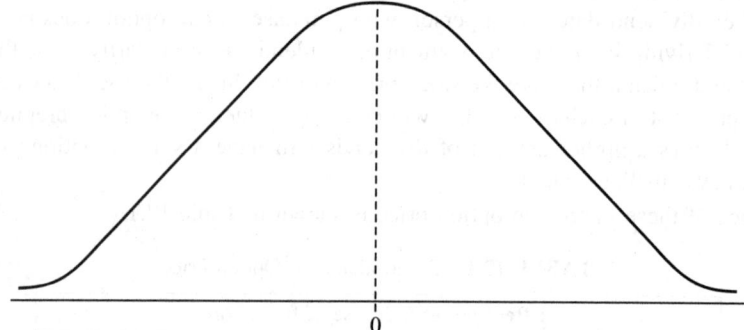

**FIGURE 17.1**   A normal distribution.

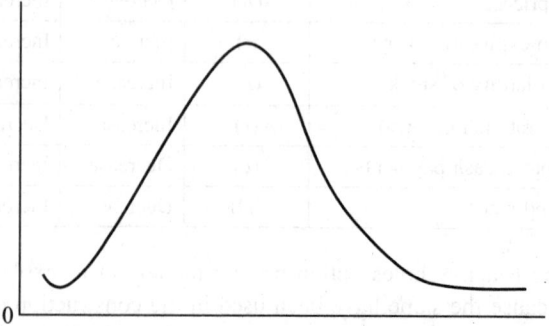

**FIGURE 17.2**   A log-normal distribution.

## 17.2.2 Parameters of Log-Normal Distribution

There are two basic parameters which have described for the behaviour of a stock price under log-normal distribution which are as under:

(a) The expected return from the stock

(b) The volatility of the stock price

**Expected return:** The expected return is the annualized average return earned by investors in a short period of time. Let us denote it by $u$. The expected return desired by investors from a stock depends on the riskiness of the stock. The higher the risk, the higher will be the expected return. It will also depend on the market rate of interest in the economy. For example, if the risk-free interest is higher, then the expected return on a given stock will also be higher. Expected return can be considered with the period of time, and in time limit, we obtain usually two estimates:

(i) The expected return in a very short period

(ii) The expected return (continuously compounded) over a longer period. The expected return in a very short period of time is $u$ and over a longer period is $u - \sigma^2/2$.

Calculation of expected return. In general, the expected return is used in the sense of possible profit outcomes weighted by their probability occurrence. Let us explain with an example shown in Figure 17.3.

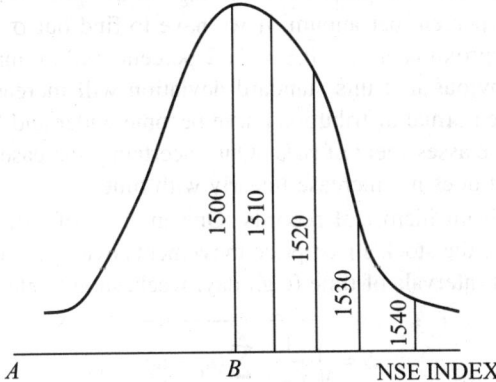

**FIGURE 17.3** Probability distribution of possible futures index levels (with exercise price equals to mean of the distribution).

Figure 17.3 illustrates this with respect to option on the NSE Stock Index. The curve is normal distribution curve and indicates the probabilities of the various possible outcomes. Let us suppose that the area under the normal distribution curve between 1500 and 1510 as a proportion of the total area under the curve is 0.19, which means that there is a 19 percent chance that the index will fall between 1500 to 1510. Further, if the area under the curve between 1510 and 1520 is 0.15 of the total area, it shows that there is a 15 percent probability of the index being between 1510 to 1520. The statistical expectation of the profit is the sum of the possible profits when each possible profit is weighted by its probability of occurrence. The calculation of the expected profit is shown in Table 17.2.

For the simplification, the possible profits are represented by the mid-points of the respective ranges. Note that the probabilities are themselves expectations. In the example shown earlier, the premium expressed in index points is 8.20. At ₹10 per index point this would correspond to a money price of ₹82 per contract.

**TABLE 17.2** Calculation of Expected Profit

| Range of index value | Range of profit possibilities | Probability of occurrences | Contribution to expectation of profit |
|---|---|---|---|
| 1500–10 | 0–10 | 0.19 | 5 × 0.19 = 0.95 |
| 1510–20 | 10–20 | 0.15 | 15 × 0.15 = 2.25 |
| 1520–30 | 20–30 | 0.09 | 25 × 0.09 = 2.25 |
| 1530–40 | 30–40 | 0.05 | 35 × 0.05 = 1.75 |
| 1540–50 | 40–50 | 0.01 | 45 × 0.01 = 0.45 |
| 1550–60 | 50–60 | 0.01 | 55 × 0.01 = 0.55 |
| | | **0.50** | **Expected profit = 8.20** |

**Volatility:**  The volatility of stock, $\sigma$ is a measure of uncertainty about the returns provided by the stock. Oftenly volatilities are expressed in percentages per annum. The volatility may be defined precisely as "the volatility of a stock price is the standard deviation of the return provided by the stock in one year when the return is expressed using continuous compounding." As a rough approximation, $\sigma\sqrt{T}$ is the standard deviation of the proportional change in the stock price in time $T$. For example, assume $\sigma$ on a stock is 30 percent per annum. If we have to find out $\sigma$ of the proportional change in six months, then $\sigma$ is approximately $30\sqrt{0.5} = 21.2$ percent, and on three months, $30\sqrt{0.25} = 15$ percent and so on. It is obvious that this standard deviation will increase as the period lengthens (graphically depicted by the normal distribution curve become wider and flatter). In brief, the square root effect is important in the assessment of risks. Our uncertainty increases as the square root of how far ahead we are looking. It does not increase linearly with time.

Estimating volatility from historical records. One method of estimating the volatility on a particular stock is to analyze the stock's past price movements over a period of time. The stock price is usually observed at fixed intervals of time (e.g., day, week, month, etc.). This is estimated as:

and let

$$S = \sqrt{\frac{1}{n-1}\sum_{i=1}^{n}(u_i - \overline{u})^2} \tag{17.1}$$

$$u_i = \ln\left(\frac{S_i}{S_i - 1}\right) \tag{17.1a}$$

where $S_i$ is stock price at the end of $i$th interval ($i = 0, 1, ..., n$) is the mean of the $u_i$.

An estimate of $S$, of the standard deviation of the $u_i$ is given by:

$$S = \sqrt{\frac{1}{n-1}\sum_{i=1}^{n}u_i^2 - \frac{1}{n(n-1)}\left(\sum_{i=1}^{n}u_i\right)^2} \tag{17.2}$$

From Equation 17.2, the standard deviation of the $u_i$ is $\sigma\sqrt{T}$. The variable '$S$' is therefore an estimate of $\sigma\sqrt{T}$. It follows that $\sigma$ itself can be estimated as $S^*$, where $S^* = \dfrac{S}{\sqrt{T}}$.

The standard error of the estimate can be shown to be approximately $S^*/\sqrt{2n}$.

In brief, the log-normal assumption of stock prices implies that In $(S_T)$ is normal where $S_T$ is the stock price at a future time $T$. The mean and standard deviation of In $S_T$ can be shown as:

$$\text{In } S + \left[u - \frac{\sigma^2}{2}\right]T, \text{ and, } \sigma_{\sqrt{T}} \tag{17.3}$$

where $S$ is the current stock price, $u$ is expected return per annum from a stock and $\sigma$ is the volatility per annum of the stock price. We can write this result as:

$$\text{In } S_T \sim \phi\left(\text{In } S + \left\{u - \frac{\sigma^2}{2}\right\}T, \text{ and, } \sigma_{\sqrt{T}}\right) \tag{17.4}$$

where $\phi$ $(m, s)$ denotes a normal distribution with mean $m$ and standard deviation $s$. The expected value or mean value of $S_T$, $E(S_T)$ is given by $E(S_T) = Se^{uT}$.

The variance of $S_T$ can be given by

$$\text{Var } (S_T) = S^2 e^{2uT} (e^{\sigma 2T} - T) \tag{17.4a}$$

*Note:* It is further explained later in this chapter.

## 17.3  BLACK-SCHOLES OPTION PRICING MODEL

The Black-Scholes (B-S) option pricing model is probably the most commonly used option pricing model in finance. It was initially developed in 1973 by two academicians, Fisher Black and Myron Scholes and was designed to price European options on non-dividend paying stocks. Later on, other academicians further modified the model to make it applicable to American option, option on dividend-paying stock, option on other instruments like futures contracts. In this section, we are not explaining the derivation of the model, rather we simply state the B-S model of pricing formula of option and how to use it to price option.

The reason for popularity of the model is that it allows for an analytical solution. It means that there is a formula into which certain values are input and from which an option price is forthcoming. However, this formula when programmed into a computer, it can produce results (option price) within seconds.

### 17.3.1  Assumptions Underlying Black-Scholes Model

The model is based on certain assumptions which are as under:

1.  Stock price behaviour corresponds to the log-normal distribution which have been explained earlier. It assumes that $u$ and $\sigma$ are constant.
2.  There are no transaction costs or taxes.
3.  All securities/stocks are perfectly divisible.
4.  No dividends payments on stock during the life of the option.
5.  There are no riskless arbitrage opportunities.
6.  Stock trading is continuous.
7.  Investors can borrow or lend at the same risk-free rate of interest.
8.  The short-term risk-free interest rate $r$ is constant.

The foundation of the model is the construction of a hypothetical risk-free portfolio, consisting of long call options and short positions in the underlying stock, on which an investor earns the riskless return. Thus, it is analogous to the no-arbitrage analysis. The reason why a riskless port-folio can be set up is because the stock price and the option price are both affected by the same underlying source of uncertainties and factors. In short period, the stock price is perfectly correlated with the option price, and the price of a put option is perfectly negatively correlated with the price of the underlying stock. In this way, in both cases, when an appropriate portfolio of the stock and option is created, profit and loss from the stock position will offset the profit and gain from option position so that the overall value of the portfolio at the end of the short period of time is known with certainty.

## 17.3.2  (B-S) Pricing Formula

Black and Scholes derived the following equations for pricing European call options on non-dividend paying stocks:

$$C = SN(d_1) - Ke^{-rt} N(d_2) \tag{17.5}$$

$$P = Ke^{-rT} N(-d_2) - SN(-d_1) \tag{17.5a}$$

where

$$d_1 = \frac{\text{In } (S/K) + rT}{\sigma\sqrt{T}} + 0.5\sigma\sqrt{T}$$

$$d_2 = \frac{\text{In } (S/K) + rT}{\sigma\sqrt{T}} - 0.5\sigma\sqrt{T}$$

or

$$d_2 = d_1 - \sigma\sqrt{T}$$

where $C$ is call option price, $P$ is put option price, $S$ is stock price, $K$ is strike price, $e$ is exponential (which has the constant value of 2.7182818), $r$ is risk-free interest rate (annualize), $T$ is time to expiry (in years), $\sigma$ is the annualized standard deviation of stock returns (volatility) as a decimal, $e^{-rt}$ is a discount term similar to $I/(1 + r)^t$ and as such it determines the present value of a future sum of money and its discount on continuous compounding, $I_n$ (.) is the natural logarithm, $N(.)$ is the cumulative probability distribution function for a standardized normal variable, $N(d_1)$ is the area under the distribution to the left of $d_1$ and $N(d_2)$ is the area under the distribution to the left of $d_2$.

Standardized normal distributions have total area as of $I$ so the $N(d_1)$ is the probability of $d$ being $d_1$ or less (likewise for $d_2$). $N(d_1)$ can be interpreted as the probability of the call option being in the money at the expiry.

The above mentioned equations of the model look complicated. The model is based on five inputs (as mentioned in factors, i.e., $S$, $K$, $T$, $\sigma$ and $r$), four of them are easily available but only variable that is not directly observable is the expected volatility of stock return. The best way to understand the model is with an example.

Let us assume values for the five parameters and then we calculate the (B-S) option price:

$$S = ₹100, K = ₹100, T = \text{one year}, r = 12 \text{ percent}, \sigma = 10 \text{ percent}$$

With these values, let us first calculate the value of $d_1$ and $d_2$.

$$d_1 = \frac{\ln{(S/K)} + rT}{\sigma\sqrt{T}} + 0.5\sigma\sqrt{T}$$

$$d_1 = \frac{\ln{(100/100)} + 0.12 \times 1}{0.10\sqrt{1}} + 0.5(0.10)\sqrt{1}$$

$$d_1 = \frac{0 + 0.12}{0.10} + 0.5 = 1.25$$

$$d_2 = d_1 - \sigma\sqrt{T}$$
$$= 1.25 - (0.1(1)) = 1.15$$

After calculating the value of $d_1$ and $d_2$, the next step is to calculate the cumulative normal probability values of these two results. These are simple $Z$ scores from the normal probability function. To determine their values ($d_1$ and $d_2$) we need the proportion of the area under the curve that lies to the left of these as shown in Figure 17.4. These will be determined from the table of Normal Distribution. So values are:

$$N(d_1) = N(1.25) = 0.8944$$
$$N(d_2) = N(1.15) = 0.8749$$

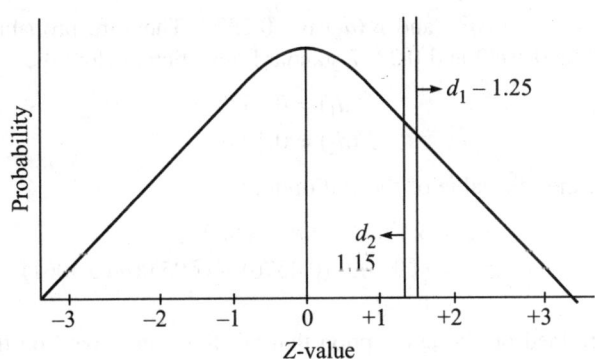

**FIGURE 17.4** Normal probability function.

Returning to the (B-S) model, the final calculations are:

$$C = S.N(d_1) - Ke^{-rt} N(d_2)$$
$$= ₹100 \, (0.8944) - ₹100^{-0.12 \times (1)} \, (0.8749)$$
$$= ₹89.44 - ₹100 \, (0.8869) \, (0.8749)$$
$$= ₹89.44 - ₹77.60$$
$$= ₹11.84$$

In the given example, the option value is ₹11.84. The terms involving the cumulative probability function are the terms that account of risk. Coupled with the rest of the formula, if the stock involves no risk, the calculated value for $d_1$ and $d_2$ would be very large and then the cumulative functions would both approach a value of $I$. In that case, if both $d_1$ and $d_2$ equal to one, the model would be simplified to $C = S -$ Present value $(E)$. This expression simply does not reflect the value of the option as an insurance policy.

**Another example of a call option value:**  Assume that on November 11, 2002, we want to price a December, 2002 European call option on $X$ stock and stock does not pay dividends and further, where:

$S = ₹92.00$, $K = ₹95.00$, $t = 50$ days, or $(50/365$ which is equal to 0.137 of a year as the option expires on December 21, 2002), $r = 7.12$ percent p.a., $\sigma = 3.5$ percent

The call option value is calculated as follows:

1. Compute the present value of the strike price.

$$Ke^{-rt} = ₹95e^{0.0712 \times 0.1370} = ₹94.08$$

2. Compute the values of $d_1$ and $d_2$

$$d_1 = \frac{\text{In } (S/Ke^{-rt})}{\sigma\sqrt{T}} + 0.5\sigma\sqrt{T}$$

$$= \frac{\text{In } (92.00/94.08)}{0.35\sqrt{0.1370}} + (0.5)(0.35)\sqrt{0.1370}$$

$$= -0.1082$$

$$d_2 = -0.1082 - 0.35\sqrt{0.1370} = -0.2377$$

3. Compute $N(d_1)$ and $N(d_2)$.

Value of $N(d_1)$ is $-0.1082$ and $N(d_2)$ is $-0.2377$. They are probabilities that the price at expiration will be 0.1082 and 0.2377 standard deviations below the mean (i.e., 0).

$$N(d_1) = 0.4570$$
$$N(d_2) = 0.4061$$

4. Now, compute the fair value of the call option:

$$C = S.N(d_1) - Ke^{-rt} N(d_2)$$
$$= (₹92.00) (0.4570) - (₹95.00) (0.4061)$$
$$= ₹3.46$$

The value is determined on the assumption that no dividend is paid on the stock and option is not American rather European. It means the investor can not exercise his option before the maturity. Unfortunately no exact analytic formula for the value of an American put on a non-dividend paying stock has been produced so far.

## 17.3.3   Variations on the Basic Black-Scholes Model

Since the Black-Scholes model is strictly applicable only to European options, its use is also made in valuing American style options, European style call option futures and pricing puts and American style options. Following are some of the variants on which Black-Scholes model is applicable for pricing.

**European style call options on dividend paying stock:**  To use the Black-Scholes model to value call options on dividend paying stock, it is necessary to adjust the stock price by remaining the present value of dividends receivable prior to expiry. In other words, the dividends that relate to ex-dividend later which falls before the expiry of the option. After adjusting the dividend for the period, Black Scholes model can be used in the normal way. Discount model is one way to understand the adjustment process. According to this (dividend discount) model, the current stock is the present (discounted) value of all future expected dividends. Only dividends accrued before the expiration date will be included into the current price. So stock price used in Black-Scholes model is the current stock price less than part of the price that arises from dividend that will be received by the expiry day stock. In other words, to ascertain the stock price to be used in the Black-Scholes model, present value of expected dividends prior to expiry need to be subtracted from the current stock price.

**American style call options on dividend paying stock:** One of the basic property of Black-Scholes option pricing model is that it is strictly applicable to European style call options. But later on with the various developments in this model, it was started using for valuing American style call options. This valuation of American Style call option though Black Scholes model is known as Black's approximation. Black's approximation involves calculating the price of two European options:

1. An option that matures at the same time as the American option.
2. An option maturing just before the final ex-dividend date occurring during the life of the option.

Because American style call option can be exercised any time up to the expiry date of the option. So it is very crude procedure to value American style call option by using Black-Scholes model. Black's approximation is based on the principle that the only time that is rational to exercise an American style call option prior to expiry is just before an ex-dividend date, and further, it would be rational to sell an option rather than exercise it because selling would realize both the intrinsic value and tie value also but exercise would realize only the intrinsic value. But if on the ex-dividend date the fall in the share's price would cause a loss in the intrinsic value of the call.

**European style call options on futures:** Futures are the standardized contracted traded through stock exchanges and do not yield an income return as dividends or interest. So margin are involved in the trading of futures and cash related to the futures contract can yield a return. For example, if a futures position is bought, the money which equal to value of the contract can be put on a deposit or into other assets and yield a risk-free interest. So futures contract can be traded as if it yields the risk-free interest rate. The formula for valuation or pricing can be expressed as:

$$C = Fe^{-rt}N(d_1) - Ke^{-rt}N(d_2) \qquad (17.6)$$

$$d_1 = \frac{\ln(F/K)}{\sigma\sqrt{t}} + 0.5\sigma\sqrt{t} \qquad (17.6a)$$

$$d_2 = \frac{\ln(F/K)}{\sigma\sqrt{t}} - 0.5\sigma\sqrt{t} \qquad (17.6b)$$

where $F$ is the current futures price.

Another variant of Black-Scholes model relating to futures options is margined futures option and first equation in the model becomes

$$C = F.\,N(d_1) - K.\,N(d_2) \qquad (17.7)$$

or
$$Ce^{-rt} = Fe^{-rt}\,N(d_1) - K.e^{-rt}\,N(d_2) \qquad (17.7a)$$

European style call option on currencies: Currency call option as we know that is a right to buy a specified number of currencies (US dollar, Pound, Euro, Rupee) at specified rate (strike price) on a specified date, also known as expiration date from the other party known as writer of the option (seller). The pricing of currency option is similar to stock index option pricing. The only difference that will take place is that in place of expected rate of dividend yield foreign currency will be placed. Usually the US dollar is the base currency and the option is treated as being on the other currency whose price is expected in terms units of the US dollar. So Black-Scholes type models are same for the stock indices option and currencies. The option pricing will be:

$$C = Se^{-ft}N(d_1) - Ke^{-rt}N(d_2) \tag{17.8}$$

$$d_1 = \frac{\ln(S/K) + (r - f)t}{\sigma\sqrt{t}} + 0.5\sigma\sqrt{t} \tag{17.8a}$$

$$d_2 = \frac{\ln(S/K) + (r - f)t}{\sigma\sqrt{t}} - 0.5\sigma\sqrt{t} \tag{17.8b}$$

where $S$ is the spot price of currency and $f$ is foreign currency interest rate.

Rest items have same interrelations as in case of European style call options on stock indices. Stock price is used in all the equations for $d_1$ and $d_2$. In case of stock index options, equations for $d_1$ and $d_2$ take the form of subtracting the expected rate of dividend yield from the risk-free interest rate.

So equations for valuation will be

$$C = Se^{-dt}N(d_1) - Ke^{-rt}N(d_2) \tag{17.9}$$

$$d_1 = \frac{\ln(S/K) + (r - d)t}{\sigma\sqrt{t}} + 0.5\sigma\sqrt{t}$$

$$d_2 = \frac{\ln(S/K) + (r - d)t}{\sigma\sqrt{t}} - 0.5\sigma\sqrt{t}$$

where $C$ is call option price, $S$ is spot stock index, $e$ is exponential (natural logarithm), $d$ is expected rate of dividend yield, $t$ is time to expiry, '$N$' is cumulative normal distribution function, $K$ is strike price, $R$ is risk-free interest rate and $\sigma$ is volatility (standard deviations of return).

If this loss exceeds the time value on that date, it would be rational to exercise the option just before the stock as ex-dividend as stated earlier. Using Black's approximation, the stock price is adjusted by deducting the present value dividends expected prior to expiry date. An adjustment would be needed when the actual expiry date is used and expected dividend should be discounted from the date of receipt and not from two ex-dividend date, no adjustment would be required when the day before the ex-dividend date is used as the expiry date.

**European style call options on stock index:**   Stock index portfolio is composed of different stocks from different sectors of the economy. This is also known as well diversified portfolio and standard examples include BSE Sensex, NIFTY, Nikkee 225, CAC 40, S and P NIFTY 50, FTSE 100, etc. Options on stock indices trade in both the over-the-counter and exchange traded markets. Some of the indices are used to track the movement of stock market as a whole, some are based on the performance of a particular sector (computer, FMCG and Technology). Stock index portfolio can be treated as producing a continuous income stream since various component stocks would be paying dividends at different point of time. For the purpose of calculating option price adjustment is required that corresponds to subtracting the present value of expected dividends by discounting the spot index by the expected rate of dividend yield. But in the case of stock paying discrete dividend payment is adjusted.

## 17.4 BINOMIAL OPTION PRICING MODEL

Another important technique of pricing a stock option is through constructing a binomial tree. This is a tree which represents different possible paths that might be followed by the stock price over the life of the option. This model was advocated by Cox, Ross and Rubinstein in 1979 and takes the form of binomial model. This model, like $B$ and $S$ model does not permit an analytical solution rather solves the problem numerically. It means there is no formula that can be programmed into a computer or calculator; instead a computer must be programmed to ascertain solution.

In this section, we will discuss only the introductory aspect of binomial model. Although the explanation of this model will treat the time to expiry of an option as being one period, or divided into 2 periods, and much large number of periods.

### 17.4.1 A One-step Binomial Model

To understand the logic behind this model, we start with a single period (one step) example and then gradually generalize it. Consider a very simple situation where a stock price is currently ₹20, and it is known that after three months, it may be either ₹22 or ₹18. We further assume that we are considering in valuing a European call option to buy the stock for ₹21 in three months. In this option, we are estimating two values, i.e., ₹22 and ₹18, if the value turns up to ₹22, the option value ₹1, and if ₹18, the value will be zero. This situation is shown in Figure 17.5.

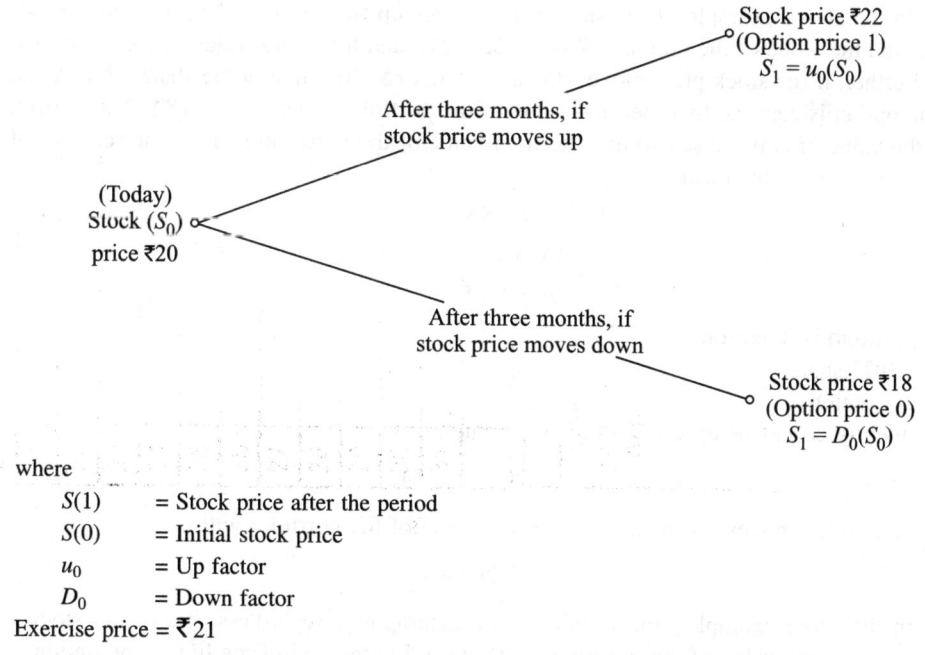

where

| | |
|---|---|
| $S(1)$ | = Stock price after the period |
| $S(0)$ | = Initial stock price |
| $u_0$ | = Up factor |
| $D_0$ | = Down factor |

Exercise price = ₹21

**FIGURE 17.5** Stock price movements in under Binomial Model.

The Binomial Pricing Model is based upon the following standard assumptions:

1. There are no market frictions. It means there are no transaction costs, no bid/ask spreads, no margin requirements, no restriction on short sales, no taxes, etc.

2. Market participants entail no counterparty risk. In other words, there is no risk of default by the other party in the contract.

3. Markets are competitive. It means that market participants act as price takers, and not the makers.

4. There are no arbitrage opportunities. Prices have adjusted in such a way so that there are no arbitrage opportunities in the market.

5. There is no interest rate uncertainty. This is assumed to reduce the complexity of the pricing problems. It is reasonable approximation in case of short dated options or futures contracts, say, less than a year.

Analyzing Figure 17.5, we can represent the stock price at the end of one year or particular period $S(1)$, in the following manner:

$$S_1 = u_0 S_0 \longrightarrow \text{if the stock price moves up} \tag{17.10}$$

$$= D_0 S_0 \longrightarrow \text{if the stock price moves down} \tag{17.10a}$$

In the above examples, $S(0)$ is the initial stock price ₹20, $u_0$ is called the up factor with $u_0 = (22 - 20 = 2/20, 1.10)$ and down factor $D_0$ with $D_0$ $(20 - 18 = 2/20, 0.90)$. These are also called price relatives.

The assumption that the stock price can take only one of the two possible values at the end of each interval is referred as the binomial model. Consider a portfolio consisting of a long position in $\Delta$ shares of the stock and a short position in call option. We can find out the value of a portfolio which is riskless. In the above example, if the stock price moves up from ₹20 to ₹22, the value of shares will be $22\Delta$ and the value of the option will be 1 $(22 - 21)$, and thus, total value of the option will be ₹$22\Delta - 1$. Further, if the stock price moves downward to ₹18, the value of the shares is $18\Delta$ and the value of the option is zero, so that the total value of the portfolio is $18\Delta + 0 = 18\Delta$. The portfolio is riskless if the value of $\Delta$ is chosen so that the final value of the portfolio is the same for both of the alternative stock price. This means

$$22\Delta - 1 = 18\Delta$$

or

$$4\Delta = 1$$

$$\Delta = 0.25$$

A riskless portfolio is, therefore,

   Long : 0.25 share
   Short : 1 option
If the stock price moves upward to ₹22, the value of the portfolio will be

$$₹22 \times 0.25 - 1 = ₹4.5$$

If the stock price moves downward to ₹18, the value of the portfolio will be

$$₹18 \times 0.25 = ₹4.5$$

Thus, in the given example, considering all the assumptions regardless of whether stock price moves up or down, the value of the portfolio is always 4.5 at the end of the life of the option.

Analyzing further, riskless portfolio must earn risk-free rate of interest. Assume risk-free rate 12 percent per annum, the value of portfolio today must be the present value of 4.5 or

$$4.5e^{-0.12 \times 0.25} = 4.367$$

The current price of the stock is ₹20, assuming option price denoted by $f$, the value of the portfolio, today, is:

$$₹20 \times 0.25 - f = 5 - f$$

It follows that $5 - f = 4.367$, or $f = 0.633$

It means that current value of the option must be ₹0.633. If the value of the option were more than 0.633, the portfolio would cost less than ₹4,367 to set up and would earn more than the risk-free rate. On the other hand, if the value of the option were less than ₹0.633, the portfolio would provide a way of borrowing money at less than the risk-free rate for shorting.

**Generalization:** Now, we will generalize the one step Binomial tree. Suppose the stock price is $S$, and stock option price is $f$. Further assuming that in time ($T$), the stock price either moves up to a new level $Su$ or down to new level $S_0$, a proportional increase or decrease, i.e., ($u - 1$), or ($1 - d$), likewise the payoff from option is $fu$ and $fd$.

Imagine a long position in $\Delta$ share and a short position in one option.

$$\text{Value of portfolio} = Su\Delta - fu \text{ (If stock price is up)}$$

$$\text{Value of portfolio} = Sd\Delta - fd \text{ (If stock price is down)}$$

Two are equal, i.e.,

$$Su\Delta - fu = Sd\Delta - fd$$

$$\Delta = \frac{fu - fd}{Su - Sd}$$

$\Delta$ shows the ratio of change in the option price to the change in the stock price.

The present value of the portfolio by denoting the risk-free interest rate to $r$.

$$(Su\Delta - fu)e^{-rt} \tag{17.11}$$

The cost of setting the portfolio is $S\Delta - f$ which follows that

$$S\Delta - f = (Su\Delta - fu)e^{-rT} \tag{17.11a}$$

Substituting the value of $\Delta$ in the equation, we calculate

$$f = e^{-rt}[P\,fu + (1 - P)fd] \quad \text{where } P = \frac{e^{rt} - d}{u - d} \tag{17.11b}$$

In the previous example, if $u = 1.1$, $\sigma = 0.9$, $r = 0.12$, $T = 3$ months (0.25), $fu = 1$ and $f\sigma = 0$, then

$$P = \frac{e^{0.03} - 0.9}{1.1 - 0.9} = 0.6523$$

$$f = e^{-0.03}[0.6523 \times 1 + (1 - 0.6523)\,0.9] = 0.633$$

This agrees with the answer already calculated.

**Risk-neutral valuation:** In the discussion of generalization, we have made assumptions about the probabilities of up and down movements to derive equations $P$ probability of an up movement and then $(1 - P)$ probability of down movements in the stock price so that the expression $P\,fu + (1 - p)fd$ is the expected payoff from the option. Assuming these probabilities, we can calculate the expected stock price at time $T$ as follows:

$$E(ST) = P\,Su + (1 - P)Sd \tag{17.12}$$

or
$$E(ST) = PS\,(u - d) + Sd \tag{17.12a}$$

Substituting the value of $P$, the equation reduces to

$$E(ST) = Se^{rt} \tag{17.12b}$$

which states that the stock price grows on average at the risk-free rate.

The concept of risk neutral refers to a word where all individuals are risk neutral. It means the investors require no compensation for risk and the expected return on all securities is the risk-free interest rate. This is very important principle which states that it is permissible to assume that the world is risk neutral when valuing an option in terms of underlying stock.

The principle of risk-neutral valuation applies to such options too when they are valued using binomial trees. For example, in above stated one-step binomial, we denote the upward probability by $P$, and in such world the expected return on the stock must be the risk-free rate of 12 percent. It means that $P$ must satisfy: $22P + 18(1 - P) = 20e^{0.12 \times 0.25}$ or $4P = 20e^{0.12 \times 0.25} - 18$, that is $P$ must be 0.6523. At the end of three-months, the call option has a probability of 0.6523 being worth of 1 and 0.3477 as zero worth. Its expected value is $0.6523 \times 1 + 0.3477 \times 0 = ₹0.6523$. If we further discount the risk-free rate, the value of the option today is $0.6523^{-0.12 \times 0.25} = ₹0.633$, which is same as calculated earlier. It states that no-arbitrage arguments and risk-neutral valuation give the same results.

## 17.4.2 Two-step Binomial Trees

Similarly, we can extend the above mentioned analysis to a two-step binomial trees which has been shown in Figure 17.6 with the same information.

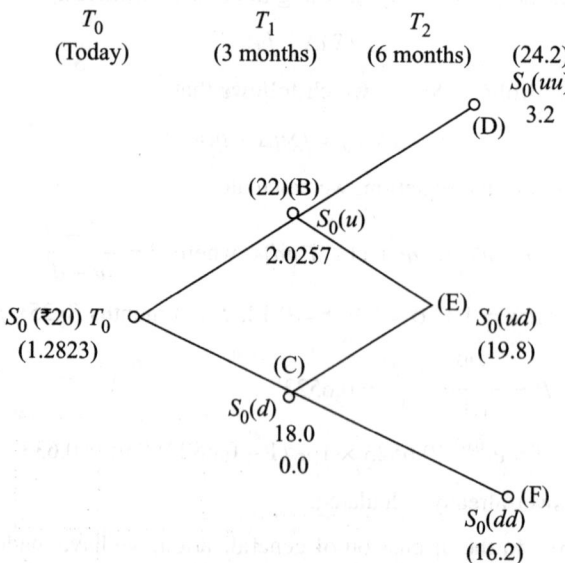

**FIGURE 17.6**   Stock and option price dynamic.

The basic objective of above analysis is to calculate the option price at the initial node of the tree by repeatedly applying the established principles of binomial tree. In Figure 17.6, the stock price is the upper number and option price is the lower number. The option prices at the final nodes of the treasure can be easily calculated, e.g., at B = 2.0257, at D = 3.2 (24.2 − 21) and at nodes E and F, it is zero.

We calculate the option price at node B by focusing our attention on the part of the tree by using the earlier introduced notation: $u = 1.1$, $d = 0.9$, $r = 12$ percent p.a., $T = 0.25$, $P = 0.6523$.

$$f \text{ at Node B} = e^{-0.12 \times 0.25} (0.6523 \times 3.2 + 0.3477 \times 0) = 2.0257$$

$$f \text{ at Node A} = e^{-0.12 \times 0.25} (0.6523 \times 2.0257 + 0.3477 \times 0) = 1.2823$$

It should be noted that in the above example the value of $u$ and $d$ are taken at same proportional up and down movements by assuming risk neutral probability, $p$ being the same at each node.

**Generalization of two-step binomial tree:** As explained in one-step binomial tree, we can generalize the case of two time steps by considering the above example initially, $S_0$ is the stock price. During each time step, either it goes up $u$ or goes down $d$ times of its initial value, for example, after two up movements the value of option is *fuu* and downward value is *fdd*. Assuming further risk-free rate $r$, length of time is $\Delta T$ years. The repeated equation will be

$$fu = e^{-r\Delta T} [p \, fuu + (1 - P) \, fud] \tag{17.13}$$

$$fu = e^{-r\Delta T} [p \, fud + (1 - P) \, fdd] \tag{17.13a}$$

$$f = e^{-r\Delta T} [p \, fu + (1 - P) \, fd] \quad \text{(earlier equation one step)} \tag{17.13b}$$

Substituting from the above equation, we get

$$f = e^{-2r\Delta T} [p^2 \, fuu + 2P(1 - P) \, fud + (1 - P)^2 \, fdd] \tag{17.14}$$

Equation 17.14 holds the value of option in two-step tree where the variables $P^2$, $2P(1 - P)$ and $(1 - P)^2$ are the probabilities of the upper middle and lower final nodes being reached. The option value is equal to its expected payoff in a risk neutral world discounted at the risk-free interest rate. The same generalization can be further extended with three-step or four-step and so on. The option price is always equal to its expected payoff in a risk-neutral world discounted at the risk-free interest rate.

The above said binomial model is just introductory for understanding the basics of binomial concept for using in stock option pricing. It can be used to both call option as well as put option valuation. In brief, when stock price movements are governed by a multistep binomial tree, we can treat each binomial step separately and work back from the end of the life of the option to the starting for determining the current value of the option. In this technique, no-arbitrage arguments are used to find out the value at the each node. In this chapter, we have explained the binomial model applicable in European type option, however, the same can also be extended to American type option.

## 17.5 CONCEPT OF VOLATILITY

Changes in the stock prices in the market refer to volatility. These changes in prices expose the investors to risk, because they may not always be positive for the investors. The whole idea of risk and return is formed to volatility. Investors invest in the market and try to get benefit from these volatile moves.

Some experts say that volatility is nothing but the "fear factor" in the market. If there is a lot of fear, like a war, too much political disturbances and terrorism, recession in the economy, etc. the volatility will usually go up. In other words, if the fear increases, the volatility will reflect the same. If volatility increases, the option prices (calls and put, both) will increase, and vice versa.

Volatility can be divided into two types: historical volatility (HV) and implied volatility (IV). Historical volatility refers to the price fluctuations seen by the underlying in the past. It is the standard deviation of the stock or index over a period of time. Implied volatility, on the over hand, is a forward-looking estimate of the volatility. It is the expected volatility by the market players in the current situation. In the other words, it is the volatility of option prices. The difference between the theoretical price and the actual price is because of the difference in historical and implied volatility.

No one knows with certainly what the volatility will be during the life of the option. So, it must be estimated. One way to estimate future volatility is to use historical price data.

**Following steps are taken in this respect:**

1. Select the length of the interval of historical prices, i.e., daily, weekly, monthly, and quarterly, etc.

2. The number of price observations to be considered. So, it is trade off between too many and too few observations. A good comprise is to use about 100–200 daily prices, 40–60 weekly prices, or 30–50 monthly price observations.

3. Calculate the continuously compounding rate of return for each decided interval through the formula:

$$r_{t2} = \ln \left( \frac{S_{t2}}{S_{t1}} \right)$$

Where $r$ = Rate of return

$S$ = Stock Price

$t$ = Time Interval

Adjustment of ex-dividend day during the interval:

$$r_{t2} = \ln \left( \frac{S_{t2} + \text{div}}{S_{t1}} \right)$$

Adjust also if there is any stock dividends or stock splits during the interval.

4. Calculate the average of the time series of the '$n$' returns:

$$\bar{r} = \left( \frac{1}{n} \right) \sum_{t=1}^{n} rt$$

Where '$n$' is the number of log price relatives.

5. Estimate the variance of the stock's return:

$$\text{Var}(r) = \left( \frac{1}{n-1} \right) \sum_{t=1}^{n} (r_t - \bar{r})^2$$

6. Finally, estimate the variance of the stock's annual return by multiplying the variance of daily return by 365, weekly return by 52, monthly return by 12, and so on.

## 17.5.1   Concept of Implied Volatility

Implied volatility is most popular factor which is used to determine the option price. It is the value of standard deviation ($\sigma$) which causes the pricing model call premium to equal the actual call premium. For example, consider that call option value of a stock at 80 percent standard deviation is estimated ₹ 2 with a stock price. Assume that the market (current) price of the call option ₹ 2.10, which is higher than the estimated value. It means that actual standard deviation is estimated at $\left(\dfrac{2.10 \times 80}{2.0}\right) = 84$ percent. This is known as *implied volatility*.

There is an alternative procedure to determine the implied volatility. Assume that we know that the price of a call price at some date but do not know the volatility of the stock return. We want to calculate theoretical call price of the stock by using B–S option pricing model. For that we have to determine first volatility. For this, we could proceed by making a guess (trial and error method). We can also use the BSOPM file available at the website (http://sw college.stong.com). After computing volatility, then compute the value of the option and compare it with the market call price of the option. The price based on our guess may be either higher or lower than the option market price. We will then make adjustment in our guess until the market price of the option coincides with the B–S model prices. This volatility we estimate is the market's expectation of the volatility assuming that B–S model formula is the correct pricing model for options.

The implied volatility, determined as above, can be used for calculating the option whose price we do not know. There are empirical evidences that the implied volatility is better forecast of the volatility over the life of the option as estimated from the historical data.

**Combining the Implied Volatilities of various Option Prices:**   As we see that there are many options' prices of a single underlying stock at a particular point of time. It means there are different implied volatilities of the same stock. This is due to noise in the data and also that B–S model is not perfect. So, how can we estimate the best implied volatility in this respect? Experts have suggested three approaches which are generally used to combine the different implied volatilities into one for the purpose of pricing options.

- First approach is using equally weighted average of the various implied volatilities. While calculating the weighted average, we can eliminate the deep ATM money option and deep ITM money options, since these are not very sensitive to volatility.
- Second approach suggests such implied volatility which minimizes the absolute deviations of traded options from the B-S formula prices.
- Third and final approach is to use the implied volatility of options whose specifications are closest to the option one is trying to price.

**Computation of Implied Volatility (IV):**   The basic objective of calculating the implied volatility is to use the same for forecasting the future volatility. Despite the wide spread use of implied volatility in option market, yet there is no generally accepted method to calculate the implied volatility. For an exactly at the money call option, the following formula is used:

$$\text{IV } (\sigma \text{ implied}) = \frac{0.5(C+P)\sqrt{2\pi/T}}{K\big/(1+r)^T}$$

where

$C$ = market call price of the asset
$P$ = market put price of the asset

K = strike price
r = risk-free rate of interest
T = life of the option contact
$\pi$ = value: 3.1416

**EXAMPLE:** Suppose at the money call option has 60 days until expiration, a strike price ₹100, the risk-free interest rate is 5 percent, Theoretical B.S. premiums are ₹5 for the call and ₹3 for the put. Calculate the implied volatility of this option.

*Solution:* As per the formula of IV stated above, by substituting the value, we get the value of IV as:

$$\sigma \text{ (implied)} = \frac{0.5(5+3)\sqrt{2 \times 3.1416 / \frac{60}{365}}}{100/(1.05)^{\frac{60}{365}}}$$

$$= \frac{0.5(8)\sqrt{38.22}}{99.20}$$

$$= \frac{24.73}{99.20} = 0.2493 = 24.93 \text{ percent (app. 25 percent)}$$

the computed 25 percent implied volatility indicates that the option prices have been calculated by assuming 25 percent volatility of the asset in the future.

## 17.5.2  Concept of Volatility Index (VIX)

As observed earlier, implied volatility is an important financial information to analyze the option prices quoted in the market. Based upon the fluctuations and fear in the market, an index of volatility is determined which is generally known as volatility index. It is also regarded as a barometer of "fear". It is helpful to know the average level of implied volatility currently prevailing in the market.

VIX is basically the symbol for Chicago Board Options Exchange (CBOE), volatility index of S&P 100 (OEX) and (VXN) is volatility index of the Nasdaq 100 Index. The method of calculating this index varies from exchange to exchange. In India, in February, 2014, NSE introduced volatility index named as 'NVIX' for futures contracts.

**Important Specifications of NVIX of NSE:**

| | | |
|---|---|---|
| Underlying | : | India VIX Index |
| Symbol | : | INDIA VIX |
| Future name | : | NVIX (NOT NIFTY VIX Futures) |
| Instrument Type | : | Fu TIVX |
| Lot size | : | 750 |
| Quotation price | : | India VIX index |
| | : | 100 (means if VIX is 15.56, the quote will be 15.56 × 1 00 = 1556 |
| Contract value | : | Minimum ₹10 lakhs at the time of its introduction |
| Tick size | : | ₹0.25 |
| Expiry Date | : | Every Tuesday of the week |
| Contract cycle | : | Weekly-3 contracts |
| Contracts | : | Near, mid and far |
| Final settlement procedure | : | Cash payment |

### The Volatility Smile and the Term Structure of Volatility

Volatility is a function of the stock price. It is perfectly correlated with the stock prices. It means if the volatility is higher, then the option prices will also be higher. There is contradiction to B–S model, which assumes a constant volatility across all strike prices. However, it is possible that the implied volatility may be changing randomly, then the option prices quoted in the market may not be correct, or market is mispricing the options. This is called the *volatility smile*. In other words, the volatility smile situation arises when the options prices are not being adjusted as per the changes in the market volatility.

There is often a structure to volatilities implied by the B–S models. This volatility structure is divided into two parts—a volatility smile (also called the "skew") and a term structure of volatility. Volatility smile refers where implied volatility varies across strike prices for a stated expiration date. The term structure of volatility describes the relationship among implied volatilities across expiration dates for a given strike price.

In actual practice, the volatility smile looks in different patterns which vary from stock-to-stock.

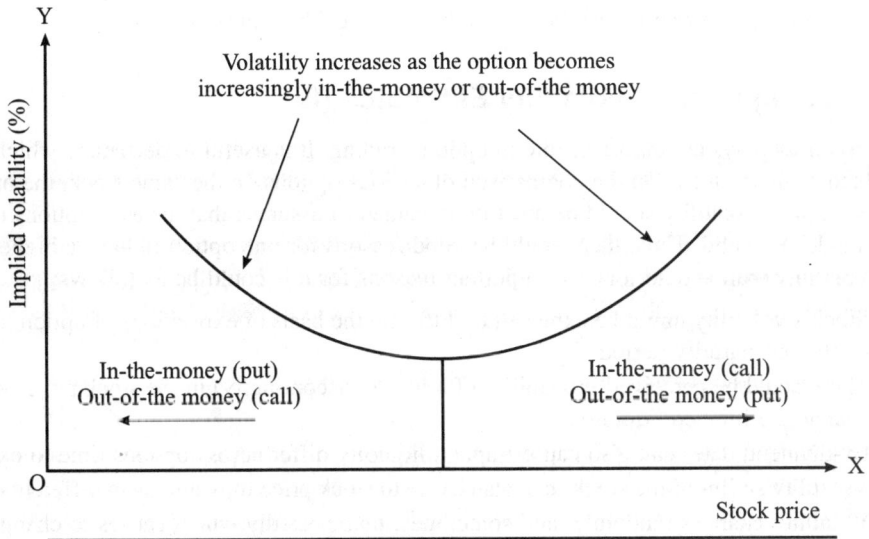

**FIGURE 17.7**  Volatility smile of an hypothetical stock.

Figure 17.7 presents a common graphical shape that results from plotting the strike price and implied volatility of a group of options is with the same expiration date. The volatility smile is so named because, it looks like a person smiling. The IV is derived from the B–S model and the volatility adjusts according to the options maturity and the extent to which it is in-the-money (moneyness). The more an option is in-the-money or out-of-the-money, the greater its implied volatility becomes.

### Important Observations of VIX

VIX is computed by the NSE. It is complex mathematical formula. It is based on the order book of options. All options, and not just NIFTY options, only near and next month's bid and ask quotes are taken. On the basis of post performance, a few important observations of VIX are stated below:

**Important other observations of VIX areas:**

- VIX has a strong relation to NIFTY movements. NIFTY falls, VIX increases and vice versa.
- India VIX has a mean of 26.65 and a median of 23.83. VIX reverts to mean, so option traders can make a note of it. In the year 2014, the India VIX valued in the range of 11.5 to 37.5
- VIX is expressed in percentage term, so range is between 0 and 100.
- It is easier to predict volatility through it.
- Approximate margin requirement for trading of VIX is around (₹) 2 lakhs.
- It indicates the expected market volatility over the next 30 calendar days.

**Benefits of VIX**

- It can be used to hedge equity portfolio.
- The investors can diversify their portfolios by considering India VIX futures.
- Option traders can hedge their volatility risk.
- It gives the directional views on volatility.
- Calendar spread trading can be exposed across weekly contracts.

## 17.5.3  Using Implied Volatility Estimates (IV)

Implied volatility plays an important role in options trading. It is useful to determine which option is undervalued or overvalued. On the comparison of various options on the same stock, the option with the lowest implied volatility should be most undervalued. It assumes that the assumptions underlying the B–S model are valid. Thus, there could be good reasons for one option to have a higher or lower implied volatility than another option. Important reasons for this could be as follows:

- Stock's volatility might be expected to differ on the basis of expirations of option, i.e., longer or shorter maturity period.
- There could be perceived probability of a jump (discontinuity) in the stock price, which may change the implied liquidity.
- Ex-dividend dates can also cause implied liquidity differ across options time to expiration.
- Volatility smiles of the stocks can also cause to stock price movements in different directions.
- Volatility changes randomly, and sometimes, unexpectedly which causes to change in stock prices.

Another important use of computing implied volatility is that the investor can select the mispriced option in the market. For example, if the investor calculates IV for a call to be 20 percent, whereas he believes that the true volatility is 50 percent. It means he believes that the call is undervalued, then he can just buy the call. Believing in the correct prediction, he could earn an above average return for the risk he bears. Through estimating the implied liquidity, one can try to arbitrage by purchasing the undervalued call and selling the equivalent portfolio stock and bonds. Further, you can end up with a profit equal to the difference between the value of call with a volatility of 20 percent and the value of call with a volatility of 50 percent, and so on.

Another important use of the implied liquidity is that changes in the IVs are correlated across stocks. The information about the IV of one stock provides similar information about the IV of another stock. In addition, if a recent IV is considerably different from its past IV or long run average IV, then a "better" volatility could be estimated through weighted average of the recent IV and part IV.

Empirically it is also observed that there appears to be one or more forces which pull IVs back to their long-term average value, which is known as mean reversion. Many traders use this property of IV to improve their trading performance. For example, a trader believes that a particular stock will rise in future if the current IV is below its long-term average value, then the traders may decide to buy calls. In effect, he is buying the underlying stocks and buying volatility. If the price of the stock does not rise substantially, he can still earn profit. If the IV of the option does rise, the trader will be in benefit, since the call price will increase as its IV increases.

The argument "mean reversion" can also be applied in case of when the IV of the stock is above its long-term average value the option prices are high. So, the trader will write the put, rather than buy calls. He is selling volatility here. If the IV of the put option decreases to its long-term average value, the put prices will also decline. As a result, the put writer will earn even if the stock price does not rise.

## 17.6  BOUNDS OF OPTION PRICES

Option contracts are unique in the sense that they have certain peculiar features as compared to other derivative instruments. The option contracts function within rational boundaries, also known as reasonable limits, between which a fair theoretical price of the option will operate. Undoubtedly, these boundaries have been set on the basis of certain assumptions underlying the option contract. Before, we discuss the bounds; let us recall the assumptions which are perfect market scenario, zero transactions costs, unrestricted short sales, risk-free rate of return, identically borrowing and lending rates, infinitely divisible asset, riskless arbitrage opportunities, no tax on profits, etc.

The basic features of an option contract have already been discussed in the proceeding chapter of this book. As we know that the option contract gives the right to the option holder to purchase or sell a particular quantity of the asset at the specified strike price in a specified period at an agreed option premium or price. So, rational boundaries of option contracts can be identified as upper limit and lower limit within which the fair market price of the option will occur. The lower limit for all options contracts are easy to identify, since the option gives the right to the holder and not the obligation to exercise the contract. Since the options can be classified as European and American, call VS put, etc. so the boundaries of option will be discussed separately. Before discussing the bounds, let us explain in brief the payoff in options.

The mathematical formula of payoff in call option can be described as max $(0, S_T - X)$ and in put option:

max $(0, X - S_T)$ where $S_T$ is the price of underlying stock at maturity and '$X$' is the exercise price. As per this formula, in call option, where $S_T > X$ or $S_T - X > 0$, then the option would be exercised and the payoff is $S_T - X$. If $S_T - X$ or $S_T - X < 0$, then the option would not be exercised and the payoff is zero. It means in the former case, max $(0, S_T - X)$ is $S_T - X$ whereas in the latter case, it is 0. The payoff for the call option writer is negative or Table no opposite to the option buyer. It is summarized in Table 17.3.

**TABLE 17.3**  Option Payoff

|  | **Option buyer** | **Option seller** |
|---|---|---|
| Call option | Max $(o, S_T - X)$ | Max $(o, X - S_T)$ |
| Put option | Min $(o, X - S_T)$ | Min $(o, S_T - X)$ |

### 17.6.1   Lower Bound for Call Option Price

As we know that the option holder has only a right and not the obligation to exercise the option, so the option prices whether American or European, are always non-negative which means that an option must be worth at least zero. The lower bound for the price of an American call option is Max $(0, S_T - X)$ the option can be exercised at any time to attain this value. If the market price of the asset $(S)$ is lower than '$X$', then the option holder will not exercise the same. This analysis has two observations:

1. An American call option should not be exercised before its maturity.
2. The value of this option is always greater than or equal to max $(o, S - X)$, it is also known as its intrinsic value.

The above can also be interpreted as a call option is worth at least its intrinsic value.

Further, since the option holder is required to invest money for entering into option contract, so we can get even better lower bound by considering the interest loss on the exercise price. The investment required is the present value of '$X$', i.e., $xe^{-rt}$ where '$r$' is the rate of interest continuously compounded and '$T$' is the time to maturity. Assuming '$C$' is price of the call option, then the total investment required would be $C + Xe^{-rT}$. This gives another lower bound the price of the call option is greater $S - Xe^{-rT}$. Further, the option price cannot be negative, so this gives us a better lower bound than the earlier bound given above:

$$C \geq (0, S - X^{-rt})$$

**EXAMPLE:**   Suppose the exercise price for a 3-month of a stock call option is ₹1,200. The spot price of the stock is ₹1,300, and the risk-free rate of interest is 8 percent p.a. In such case, the lower bound for the option price will be:

$$1,300 - 1,200(1.08)^{-0.25} = \text{approx. } ₹125$$

Suppose the call price is available at a premium of (₹) 110 which is less than theoretical value, then the trader can buy the call and short the stock. This will provide a cash flow of ₹1,300 – 110 = 1,190. If invested this for three months at 8 percent p.a., it will grow to ₹1,190(1.08)$^{25}$ = ₹1,213.8 approx. At the end of three months, the option expires. At this stage, following position could occur:

1. If the index is ₹1,200, in which case the trader will exercise his option and buys back the stock at ₹1,200, making a profit of ₹1,213.8 – ₹1,200 = ₹13.8.
2. If the stock price is below ₹1,200, say ₹1,180, in this case the trader buys back the stock at the market price, and will make a profit of ₹1,213.8 – 1,180 = ₹33.80.

### 17.6.2   Lower Bound for Put Option

In order to arrive at the lower bound of put option, consider that one is currently holding the stock and comparing two alternatives:

1. Sell the stock now for its price '$S$'.
2. Purchase the put option and borrow the money equivalent to the present value of the strike price '$X$' at the risk-free rate '$r$'. Assuming '$P$' is the price of the put option, then the total cash inflow will be $Xe^{-rt} - P$.

In the second strategy, the trader is able to repay the borrowed funds by selling the stock at the maturity of the option without any addition of fund. If the price of the stock is less than strike price (X), then the option to sell the stock at the price 'X', and the amount will be used to repay the borrowed funds. On the other hand, if the market price of stock is greater than 'X' at maturity, then in such situation, the stock will be sold in the market and the proceeds be used to return the loan, and there is possibility of having surplus cash too.

Analyzing the two alternatives, the second alternative is, therefore, better than the first. The immediate cash inflow under the second alternative, i.e., $Xe^{-rt} - P \leq S$ or $P \geq Xe^{-rt} - S$.

European put option can be worthless than its intrinsic value, and is, therefore, less valuable than the American option, because the American put option, sometimes, can be exercised before maturity.

**EXAMPLE:** Consider that the exercise price for a 3-month of a stock put option is ₹1,200. The spot price of the stock is ₹1,130, and risk-free interest rate is 8 percent per annum. In this case, the lower bound for the put option price is:

₹1,200 $(1.08)^{-0.25}$ – ₹1,130, i.e., ₹45. Now assume that the put is available at a premium of ₹30 which is less than its theoretical minimum value ₹45. The trader can borrow ₹1,160 for three months to buy both the put and the stock. At the end of three months, the trader will need to pay ₹1,184 approx; After three months, the following could happen:

1. The stock price is below ₹1,200, the trader will exercise the option, sell, the stock at ₹1200, repay the loan of ₹1,184; and earns the profit of (₹) (1200 – 1184) = ₹16.

2. The stock price is higher to ₹1,200, say, ₹1,250, then the trader will not exercise the option, sells the stock at ₹1,250, repay the loan of ₹1,184, and earns the profit; ₹1,250 – 1,184 = ₹ 66.

## 17.6.3   Upper Bound for Call Option

A call option gives the holder the right to purchase the underlying asset at strike price. It means a call price is always of less value than asset price itself, unless the exercise price is zero. It means the option can never be worth more than the asset price. One, thus, obtains the upper bound $C \leq S$. Combining the earlier discussed lower bounds and similarity of the American and Europe options, the following equation can be obtained as:

$$\max (O, S - X) \leq \max (O, S - Xe^{-rt}) \leq C_E = C_A \leq S$$ where $C_E$ is the European call price and *CA* is the American call option price, and assuming no dividends by the company.

## 17.6.4   Upper Bound for Put Option

A put option gives the holder the right to sell the underlying asset at set strike price. So, it is always of less worth than its strike price, unless the stock price falls to zero. This gives the upper bound $P_A = X$ where $P_A$ is the price of an American put option. If we combine this with the intrinsic value lower bound of American option, we get the bounds as

$$\text{Max } (O, X - S) \leq P_A \leq X.$$

The upper bound for European put option is always less worth than its present value of the exercise price, unless the stock price is zero at maturity:

$$\text{Upper bound of } P_E \leq Xe^{-rt}$$

After combining with the lower bound, the equation would be:

$$\text{Max } (O, Xe^{-rt} - S) \leq P_E \leq Xe^{-rt}$$

## 17.7  CONCEPT OF RISK NEUTRALITY

Risk neutrality is a very important concept in investment world. This concept was introduced by COX and Ross in 1976. Risk neutrality, in simple words, may be defined as an imaginary state of the world where investors are indifferent to risk. It means no premium is required to bear the risk in investment. So, in the risk neutral world, every asset will give risk-free return, and there exists only one rate of return. Further, in this state, expected appreciation is given by the risk-free rate, and same is used for discounting to determine the present value of the asset. In brief, risk neutrality means that all assets are priced in the market to provide the same riskless rate of return.

Risk neutrality, in general, in a state of certainty, where people do not like to take risk and prefer to go for low risk investments. However, when we introduce uncertainty into real practical situation, then we have to adjust for risk. The valuation of uncertain, cash flows must reflect this reality and reduce the value of risky cash flows, for which many ways are suggested.

In the valuation of derivatives, the concept of risk neutral valuation is commonly used. The preferred way of adjusting the risk in derivative valuation to shift from actual probabilities to risk neutral probabilities. By doing this, we can ignore completely and simply discount expected values at the risk-free rate of return. A brief description of calculation of risk neutral valuation through probabilities is stated below. Now the Black-Scholes model assumes that the investors are risk neutral. The model focuses on expected return without regard to the dispersion of outcomes around the mean. The option premium contains an implied probability of the stock price rising. Let us explain this. Following variables are defined as:

$U$   = 1 + percentage increase of the price of stock goes up.

$D$   = 1 + percentage increase of the price of stock goes down.

$P_{up}$ = probability that the stock price goes up.

$P_{Dn}$ = $(1 - P_{up})$ probability that stock price goes down.

$e^{rt}$  = continuously compounded interest rate factor.

From the above variables, the average stock return is determined as the weighted average of the two possible price changes. As explained above, after the average stock return equal to the riskless rate of return in the risk neutral world, we have:

$$P_{up}\, u + P_{Dn}\, D = e^{\gamma t}$$

Substituting $\quad\quad\quad\quad\quad\quad\quad P_{Dn} = (1 - P_{up})$, we have

Rearranging the above

$$P_{up}\, u + (1 - P_{up})D = e^{\gamma t}$$
$$P_{uP}\,(u - D) + D = e^{\gamma t}$$
$$P_{up} = \frac{e^{\gamma t} - D}{u - D}$$

This equation gives us direct method for inferring the probability of the stock price rising. Assuming that if the stock rising by 40 percent and then, down with (1 – 40 percent = 60 percent) and interest rate factor at 10 percent p.a. and continuously compounding is 10.52 percent. By substituting the values in the above equation, we have:

$$P_{up} = \frac{1.1052 - 0.6000}{1.4000 - 0.6000} = \frac{0.5052}{0.8000} = 0.6315 = 63.15 \text{ percent}$$

Thus $P_{Dn} = 1 - P_{up} = 1 - 0.6315 = 0.3685 = 36.85$ percent.

These are the implied probabilities in risk neutral equilibrium. We can use this information to find out the call and put option prices. Let us assume that the stock price today is ₹80. After one year it can rise to either ₹100 or decrease to ₹60. If the stock goes up (with probability 63.15 as calculated above), the call will have its intrinsic value of ₹100 − 80 = ₹20. However, if the stock goes down with (probability 36.85 percent), the call be then worthless, but it will not be less than zero. The expected value of the call option for one-year based on above probabilities would be as:

$$C = (0.6315 \times ₹20) + (0.3685 \times ₹\,0) = ₹12.63.$$

After discounting back to present value today at the discount rate of 10.52 percent p.a., we get ₹12.63/1.1052 = ₹.11.43

## SUMMARY

This chapter on option pricing models is focused on two models for pricing the option, i.e., Black-Scholes Model and Binomial Model. These are just introductory so that the students can understand the basics of options pricing. The chapter starts with discussing the various determinants of option pricing, which include current price of the underlying stock, strike price of the option, time to expiration of the option, expected price volatility, risk-free interest rate, anticipated cash payment of the stock, etc. The first important factor which influences option price is the current price of the asset/stock. The option price will change as the stock price changes. Strike or exercise price of the option is fixed for the life of the option. If other factors remain constant, the lower the strike price, the higher will be the call option price. Risk-free interest rate is another important factor which creates impact on the option price. Since buying an option contract involves investment which incur cost for the investor. Hence, the higher the short-term risk-free interest rate, greater the price of a call option.

The chapter further states the parameters to understand the option pricing model. The log-normal assumption is the first important parameter. A stock option pricing model must make certain assumptions about how stock prices behave overtime. The basic assumption in the Black-Scholes model is that stock prices follow what is termed as random walk. This means that proportional changes in the stock price in the short period are normally distributed. This in turn implies that the stock prices at any future time remain in log-normal distribution. There are two basic parameters which have described for the behaviour of a stock price under log-normal distribution. It includes expected return from a stock and volatility of the stock price. Expected return is the annualized average return earned by investors in a short period of time. Volatility of a stock $\sigma$ is the measure of fluctuations about the returns provided by the stock. Often volatility is expressed in percentage per annum. One method of estimating the volatility of a particular stock is to analyze the stock's past price movements over a period of time. The stock price is usually observed at fixed intervals of time.

In the next section of the chapter, the Black-Scholes option pricing model has been described. Black-Scholes option pricing model is probably most commonly used pricing model in finance. It was initially developed in 1973 by two academicians, Fisher Black and Myron Scholes and designed to price European options for non-dividend paying stocks. The reason for popularity of this model is that it allows for an analytical solution. It means there is one formula into which certain values are input and from which an option price is forthcoming. This model is based on certain assumptions like stock price behaviour corresponds to the log-normal distribution, no transaction cost, stock trading is continuous, all securities are perfectly divisible, funds available at risk-free interest, no dividend on stock, etc.

The chapter in its next section discusses the Binomial Option Pricing Model, which developed by Cox, Ross and Rubinstern in 1979. It can be through contracting a binomial tree—a tree, which represents different possible paths that might be followed by the stock price over the life of the option. There are two types of models—one-step model and two-step model. One-step model has explained with the help of a diagram having two nodes. The standard assumptions of binomial model are: (a) market perfection which means no transaction cost or no bid/ask spread, (b) no interest rate uncertainty, (c) no default risk and (d) markets are competitive.

Chapter further discusses the concept of risk-neutral valuation. In discussion of generalization, there are certain assumptions about the probabilities of up and down movements. The concept of risk neutral refers to world where all individuals are risk neutral. It means that investors require no compensation for risk and the expectation return on all securities is risk-free interest rate. This is very important principle which states that it is permissible to assume that the world is risk neutral when valuing on option in term of underlying stock. The principles of risk-neutral valuation applies to such options too when they are valued using binomial tree as stated in one-step binomial model.

The next section of the chapter describes the generalization of two-step binomial tree. As explained in one-step binomial tree, we can generalize the case of two time steps by considering the examples initially. The binomial model discussed in the chapter is just introductory for understanding the basics of binomial concept for using in stock option pricing. It can be used to both call option as well as put option valuation. When stock price movements are governed by a multi-step binomial tree, we can treat each binomial separately and work back from the ends of the life of the option to determine value of the option.

The chapter further explains the concept of implied volatility, which means expected volatility in the future regarding a stock price. It is a forward-looking estimate of the volatility. Further, the term volatility index (VIX) is discussed. Volatility index is a symbol of volatility determined by NSE named as NVIX. Implied volatility is changing rand only. It is quite possible that the option prices quoted may not be correct as per changed volatility in the market. As a result, the market is mispricing the options. This is known as *volatility simples*. In the last the chapter describes the bounds of option prices. Options contracts function within rational bound arise, also called as *reasonable limits*, between which a fair theoretical price of the option will operate. On the basis of assumptions, these boundaries can be classified into upper and lower bounds of call and put options.

## SOLVED PROBLEMS

**P.1.**   Consider the following data:

|  |  |
|---|---|
| Stock price | = ₹50 |
| Months to expiration | = 3 months |
| Risk-free rate of interest | = 10% p.a. |
| Standard deviation of stock | = 40% |
| Exercise price | = ₹55 |
| Option type | = European call |

Calculate value of call option as per Black-Scholes model.

*Solution:*

$$C = S.N(d_1) - Ke^{-rt}N(d_2)$$

$$d_1 = \frac{\ln(S/K) + rT}{\sigma\sqrt{T}} + 0.5\sigma\sqrt{T}$$

$$d_2 = \frac{\ln(S/K) + rT}{\sigma\sqrt{T}} - 0.5\sigma\sqrt{T}$$

Here,

$$d_1 = \frac{\ln(50/55) + 0.25(0.10)}{0.4\sqrt{0.25}} + 0.5(0.40)\sqrt{0.25}$$

$$d_2 = \frac{\ln(50/55) + 0.25(0.10)}{0.4\sqrt{0.25}} - 0.5(0.40)\sqrt{0.25}$$

$$N(d_1) = 0.5 - 0.0987 = 0.4013$$

$$N(d_2) = 0.5 - 0.1736 = 0.3264$$

$$C = ₹50\,(0.4013) - ₹55^{-0.1\times0.25}\,(0.3264) = ₹2.56$$

**P.2.** Current market price of:

|  |  | X | Y |
|---|---|---|---|
| Option | = | 16.12 | 10.62 |
| Stock | = | ₹80 | ₹80 |
| Exercise price | = | ₹70 | ₹80 |
| Time to expiration | = | 3 months | 3 months |
| Risk-free return | = | 12% p.a. | 12% p.a. |
| Expected dividend | = | 0 | 0 |
| Standard deviation of |  |  |  |
| Stock returns | = | 60% | 60% |

Calculate the option value for X and Y.

***Solution:***  For call option X

$$C = S.N(d_1) - Ke^{-rt}\,N(d_2)$$

Then,

$$d_1 = \frac{\ln(S/K) + rT}{\sigma\sqrt{T}} + 0.5\sigma\sqrt{T}$$

$$= \frac{0.13353 + 0.075}{0.3} = 0.70$$

∴

$$N(d_1) = 0.7580$$

Now,

$$d_2 = \frac{0.13353 - 0.075}{0.3} = 0.40$$

∴

$$N(d_2) = 0.6554$$

$$\text{Value of call option} = ₹\,80(0.7580) - ₹\,70e^{0.12\times0.25}(0.6554)$$

$$= ₹16.62$$

For call option $Y$

$$C = S.N(d_1) - Ke^{-rt}\, N(d_2)$$

Then,

$$d_1 = \frac{\ln(S/K) + rT}{\sigma\sqrt{T}} + 0.5\sigma\sqrt{T}$$

$$= \frac{0.0 + 0.075}{0.03} = 0.25$$

$\therefore$

$$N(d_1) = 0.5987$$

Now,

$$d_2 = \frac{0.0 - 0.015}{0.3} = -0.05$$

$\therefore$

$$N(d_2) = 0.48$$

Value of call option $= ₹80(0.5987) - ₹80e^{0.12 \times 0.25}(0.48)$

$$= ₹10.62$$

**P.3.** Option on ABC 500

| | |
|---|---|
| Stock price | = ₹120 |
| Call exercise price | = ₹100 |
| Exercise date | = 6 months |
| Estimated standard deviation | = 30% |
| Current market price | = ₹28 |
| Risk-free return | = 8% p.a. |

Calculate call option price of the stock as per Black-Scholes model.

*Solution:*   Call option price as per B–S model is

$$C = S.N(d_1) - Ke^{-rt}N(d_2)$$

Then,

$$d_1 = \frac{\ln(120/100) + 180/365(0.08)}{0.3\sqrt{180/365}} + 0.5(0.30)\sqrt{180/365}$$

Thus,        $N(d_1) = 0.8770$

and            $N(d_2) = 0.8289$

Value of call option $= 120 - (0.8770) - 100e^{0.08(180/365)}(0.8289)$

$$= ₹25.56$$

**P.4.** Apply the Black-Scholes model to value a call option under the following circumstances:

| | |
|---|---|
| Stock price | = ₹100 |
| Exercise price | = ₹95 |
| Risk-free interest rate | = 0.10 p.a. |
| Time to expiration | = 3 months |
| Standard deviation | = 0.5 |

*Solution:*   Applying the following Black-Scholes formula of option pricing:

$$C = P_s[N(d_1)] - Pxe^{-rt}[N(d_2)]$$

$$d_1 = \frac{\ln (P_s/P_x) + T\left[RF + \dfrac{\sigma^2}{2}\right]}{\sigma\sqrt{T}}$$

$$d_2 = \frac{\ln (P_s/P_x) + T\left[RF - \dfrac{\sigma^2}{2}\right]}{\sigma\sqrt{T}}$$

Putting values in formula, we get

$$d_1 = \frac{\ln (100/95) + 0.25\left[0.10 + \dfrac{0.5^2}{2}\right]}{0.5\sqrt{0.25}}$$

Then $\quad d_2 = 0.43 - 0.5/0.25 = 0.18$

Thus, $\quad N(d_1) = 0.6664$

$N(d_2) = 0.574$

$C = 100 \times 0.6664 - 95e^{(-0.10\times0.25)} \times 0.5714 = ₹13.70$

**P.5.** Consider a European option on the Standard and Poor's 500, that is two months from maturity. Current value of the index is 930, the exercise price is 900, the risk-free interest rate is 8% per annum and volatility of the index is 20% per annum. Dividend yield of 0.2% and 0.3% per month are expected in the first and second months respectively. Calculate the option value using B–S model.

***Solution:***

$S_0 = 930$ $\qquad T = 2/12,$

$X = 900$ $\qquad Y = 0.25\% \ (3\% \text{ per annum}),$

$r_{ft} = 0.08$ $\qquad Z = 0.03\%,$

$\sigma = 0.2,$

Then

$$d_1 = \frac{\ln (930/900) + (0.08 - 0.3 + 0.2^2)2/12}{0.2\sqrt{2/12}} = 0.5444$$

and

$$d_2 = \frac{\ln (930/900) + (0.08 - 0.3 - 0.2^2)2/12}{0.2\sqrt{2/12}} = 0.4628$$

Thus,

$N(d_1) = 0.7069$

$N(d_2) = 0.6782$

$C = 930 \times 0.7069e^{-0.03 \times 2/12} - 900 \times 0.6782e^{-0.08\times2/12} = ₹51.83$

$C = ₹51.83$

**P.6.** Consider the following:

February 2002 S&P futures $\quad = 308.45$ index points

February 310 call option $\qquad = 11.40$ index points

February 310 put option $\qquad = 12.95$ index points

Show the arbitrage opportunity in above case.

*Solution:*   Suppose February 310 put were at 12.00 index point or that the put option were under priced. So correct arbitrage transaction is to a conversion:

Buy puts, buy futures and sell calls.

Expected arbitrage profit = (12.95 – 12.00) × $500 = $475

January 1, 2002

    (i)  Buy one February 310 put at 12.00 (12 × $500)  = $6,000
          Go long one February 2002 S&P futures at 308.45 = 0
          Sell one call February 310 at 11.40 (11.40 × $500) = $5,700
          Net option premium                   = $300

**P.7.**   Using the data of Problem 6, show the profile of the party if (a) $F > K$ (b) $F < K$.

*Solution:*   (a) $F > K$ [If February 2002, Standard and Poor futures price is at 320]

    (i)  Loss on put (the premium)                          = $6,000

    (ii)  Long futures option is offset by being assigned a short futures
          position at the 310 strike price for a gain of (310 – 308.45) × $500    = $775

    (iii)  Retain call premium                          = $5,700
           Net arbitrage profit                          = $475

    (b)  [If February 2002, Standard and Poor futures price is at 290]

    (i)  Cost of put (premium)                          = $6,000

    (ii)  Long futures option is offset by exercising the put to acquire a short
          futures position at the 310 strike price so gain (310 – 308.45) × $500    = $775

    (iii)  Retain call premium                           = 5700
           Net arbitrage profit                          = $475

## SUGGESTED READINGS

1. Martin, John, *Applied Mathematics for Derivatives*: A *Non-Quant Guide to the Valuation and Modeling of Financial Derivatives*, Wiley, New York, 2001.

2. Ross, Shelon M., *An Elementary Introduction to Mathematical Finance: Options and Other Topics*, Cambridge University Press, New York, 2003.

3. Walker, Beth V., An Employee's Guide to Stock Options, McGraw Hill, New York, 2002.

4. Korn, Rolf and Korn, Elke, *Option Pricing and Portfolio Optimization: Modern Methods of Financial Mathematics*, R.I., American Mathematical Society, 2001.

5. Merton, R.C., The relationship between put and call prices: Comment, *Journal of Finance*, 28, pp. 183–184, March 1973.

6. Stoll, H.R., The relationship between put and call option prices, *Journal of Finance*, 31, pp. 319–332, May 1969.

7. Cox, Ross J.S. and Rubinstein, M., Option pricing: A simplified approach, *Journal of Financial Economics*, pp. 229–264, 7 October 1979.

8. Hull, John C., *Option Futures and Other Derivatives Securities*, Prentice-Hall, Englewood Cliffs, NJ, 1989.

9. Merton, R.C., Theory of rational option pricing, Bell, *Journal of Economics and Management Science*, pp. 141–183, Spring 1973.

10. Whaley, R., On the valuation of American call options on stocks with known dividends, *Journal of Financial Economics*.

# REVIEW QUESTIONS

1. Define the terms option and option contract. What are the features of an option contract? Explain with suitable examples.
2. "Price of an option is that amount which is paid by the option buyer to the option seller." Discuss the statement in the light of types of options with suitable illustrations.
3. "Price of an option depends upon a number of factors". Comment on the statement in the light of various factors which affect the option value.
4. Write notes on:
   (a) Log-normal assumption and the parameters of long-normal distribution
   (b) Volatility and its importance in the option pricing
5. Define the term volatility. What are various methods of measuring volatility? Discuss with examples in context to option pricing.
6. "Black-Scholes option pricing model is one of the important model for pricing the option." Discuss the statement in the light of various models for option pricing.
7. Discuss the Black-Scholes option pricing model with suitable examples.
8. What are various assumptions of Black-Scholes option pricing model? Discuss the various variants of Black-Scholes option pricing model.
9. What is futures options? Discuss the Black-Scholes model for futures option with the help of suitable illustrations.
10. Write short notes on:
    (a) Covered arbitrage with examples
    (b) Reverse conversion arbitrage with examples
11. Write a detailed note on implied price volatility and its implications in option pricing.
12. Discuss the various applications of Block-Scholes option pricing model with examples.
13. What is Binomial pricing model? Differentiate between Binomial pricing model and Black-Scholes pricing model.
14. What are various assumptions of Binomial pricing model? Also discuss one-step binomial pricing model with hypothetical examples.
15. "The one-period case is unrealistic. A stock price can move many times between a given date and the time that the option expires." Evaluate the statement in the light of two-step (multi-period) binomial model.
16. Write notes on:
    (a) Risk-neutral valuation
    (b) Generalization of two-step binomial tree of option pricing
17. If you were a futures commission merchant, what factors would you consider in determining the level of initial margin to secure your option-writing customers? Explain your answer.
18. Explain carefully why B–S option pricing approach for evaluating an American call option on a dividend-paying stock may give an approximate answer even when only one dividend is anticipated. Explain your answer with suitable examples.
19. One of the important function of an option pricing model is to predict the option price that will be established in options markets. If market participants use that model, it seems likely that predictions will be self-fulfilling. Comment upon two statements with basic assumptions of Black-Scholes option pricing model.

**20.** Compare and contrast the various approaches to calculate the option pricing.

**21.** Explain the term implied volatility. How is it calculated? Explain with examples.

**22.** Explain the term volatility Index in India. What are its major features? Also give its major observations in India.

**23.** Explain the term 'Bounds' of option prices. How will you determine upper and lower bounds of call and put options? Explain with suitable examples.

# UNSOLVED PROBLEMS

**P.1.** Assume it is November 1, 2002. What will be the price of a December 2002 European call option on Disney stock?

      Stock price       $S = \$92.00$

      Exercise price    $K = \$95.00$

      Time to expiration $t = 50$ days or 50/365 (which equals to 0.137) of a year (option expires on December 21, 2002)

      Risk-free return     $r = 7.12\%$

      Standard deviation $\sigma = 35\%$

Also assume that stock does not pay dividend.

**P.2.** It is January 24, 2003 and shares of XYZ Ltd. stand at ₹100. The next option expiry date is March 24, 2003 and next dividend is due in May. The two-month interest rate is 6% p.a. and it is estimated that the share price volatility will be 10% p.a. Use Black-Scholes option pricing model to calculate the fair price for the option expiring in March 2003.

**P.3.** Stock price, six months from the expiration of an option, is ₹42. The exercise price of the option is ₹40 and the risk-free interest rate is 10% per annum, and the volatility is 20% per annum. Calculate the option price using Black-Scholes model.

**P.4.** Calculate the price of a three-month European put option on a non-dividend paying stock with a strike price of ₹50 when the current stock price is ₹50. The risk-free interest rate is 10% per annum and also assume that volatility is 30% per annum.

**P.5.** Consider all the data given in Problem 4, and a dividend of ₹1.50 is expected after three months. Calculate the value of European put options.

**P.6.** Consider a European call option on stock when there are ex-dividend dates in two months and four months. The dividend on each dividend date is expected to be 0.50. Current price of share is $40, the exercise price is $40, the stock volatility is 30% per annum, the risk-free rate of interest is 9% per annum, and time to maturity is six months. Calculate the option price using Black-Scholes model.

# Trading with Options

*After reading this chapter, students will be able to*

➢ Understand the basics of trading with options.

➢ Be aware of the basic principles of option trading.

➢ Know the various strategies involving a single option and a stock like short position combined with long position, long position combined with short position in call long position combined with long position in put, etc.

➢ Understand the concept of spreads and types of spreads like vertical spreads, horizontal spreads, bull vertical and bear vertical spreads, etc.

➢ Be aware of the payoff from a bull spread.

➢ Know the various combinations of call and put options like butterfly, bearish call options spread, bullish call options spreads, calendar spread with two put option, etc.

➢ Understand the concept of volatility trading, popularly known as combination which means an option trading strategy that involves taking a position in both call and put on the same asset.

➢ Be aware of the various types of combinations like straddles, short straddle, long straddle.

➢ Understand the concept of strangle strategy and its various forms.

## 18.1  INTRODUCTION

An option is a popular financial derivative in the financial market and traded widely all over the world. It has peculiar quality under which the holder of the option has been given right to buy or sell an underlying asset at a specified price within specified period for a fixed premium. In this section, it will be discussed how the options can be used for the purpose of trading and will see the range of profit patterns obtainable using options. For example, what happens when a position in a stock option is combined with a position created in two or more different options on the same stock?

Like other derivative instruments, options may be used for different purposes like trading, hedging, speculating, etc. In other words, risk management and making speculative profit with options will involve different options strategies with a wide range of payoff. It means option trading may be seen as a mean whereby those intending less risk (hedgers) transfer their unwanted risk to those who may like to go for more risk (speculators). It has seen in the previous chapter, futures provide a mean of transferring risk from hedgers to speculators, where main consideration is the movements in the price of the underlying asset. However, in options, besides this, other different dimensions like volatility and time value of the options are also considered. Since options prices are influenced by market expectations of volatility, time remained to expiration, and the price of the underlying instrument, the participants in the options markets may involve various strategies by combining the above stated dimensions as per their requirements and objectives.

## 18.2    BASIC PRINCIPLES OF OPTION TRADING

The basic idea of option trading is based on views as to whether or not the existing price of an option series is likely to change or not. For example, if a trader believes that the price of an option series will increase, then he may go for buying the option contract. Similarly, if expects that the price may fall, in that situation he may write the option. Further, as an option series moves into the money and becomes deeper in the money, its intrinsic value will rise. So, option trading strategies might be based on options series moving into the money or going deeper in the money.

There are different trading strategies which can be explored in the light of the above said objectives, i.e., increase in intrinsic value. The simplest trading strategies are those which involves buying and selling of a single option series.

## 18.3    STRATEGIES INVOLVING A SINGLE OPTION AND A STOCK

There are a number of different trading strategies involving a single option on a stock and the stock itself. These are shown in Figure 18.1.

In Figures 18.1 (a), (b), (c) and (d) solid lines show the relationship between profit and stock price for the whole portfolio, whereas dotted lines (dashed) show the relationship between profit and stock price for the individual securities constituting the portfolio.

**Covered Call [Figure 18.1(a)]:**    In this figure, the portfolio consists of a long position in a stock plus short position in a call option. This strategy is known as writing a covered call because the long stock positions 'covers' or protects the investors from the possibility of a sharp rise in a stock price.

**EXAMPLE:**    Consider that on November 1, 2015, the investor owns 1,000 shares of one company say (SBI), which is currently trading at ₹260 per share. The investor writes 10 call contracts of SBI with a strike price of ₹280, per share that expires in December, 2015. The call price ₹20 per share which equals ₹2,000 per contract, for a total of ₹20,000. Assume SBI share does not rise above ₹280, then the investor will keep the premium amount of ₹20,000 as well as the stock of the SBI. If SBI share is above ₹280 per share at the maturity date, then he will still keep the option premium of ₹20,000 and also gets ₹280 × 1,000 = ₹2,80,000 for his stock, being total amount ₹20,000 + ₹28,0000 = ₹3,00,000. Further, let us assume that market price of SBI on expiration date ₹290, then the value of this stock of SBI would be ₹290 × 1,000 = ₹2,90,000. Still, he will earn profit of ₹3,00,000 − ₹2,90,000 = ₹10,000, if does not cover through writing of call option on SBI share.

**Protective Call [Figure 18.1(b)]:**    This figure shows that a short position in a stock combined with a long position in a call option. It is opposite to Figure 18.1(a). It protects the investor from the possibility of a sharp decrease in stock price. It is also called *protective call* or *synthetic long put*. The net effect of this strategy is that the investor creates a net credit (receives money on shorting the stock). The strategy hedges the upside in the stock on upside while retaining downside profit potential. Maximum risk is call strike price-stock price + premium. The breakeven is stock price-call premium.

**EXAMPLE:**    Suppose a company's stock is trading in the market at ₹1,250 in June, 2015. The investor buys a call for ₹50 at ₹1,300 strike price while shorting the stock at ₹1,250. The net credit to investor is ₹1,250 – 50 = ₹1,200. Thus, the breakeven price is ₹1,250 – 50 = ₹1,200. The investor will be in profit if the closing stock price is lesser than ₹1,200 and in loss if price goes above ₹1,200.

**Protective Put [Figure 18.1(c)]:**    In this investment strategy, it involves buying a put option on a stock and the stock itself. It is also called protective put strategy.

**EXAMPLE:**    Using the same example given above for the covered call, assume now that the investor instead of writing call, he buys 10 Put contacts at ₹10 per share with a strike, price of stock ₹260, which expires in December, 2015. If the SBI share price drops to ₹255, then the worth of the stock is ₹255 × 1,000 = ₹2,55,000. But exercising the option, he will receive the amount of ₹260 × 1000 = ₹2,60,000. Buying a protective put is very similar to the outright purchase of a call option. It is an example of synthetic call:

$$\text{Long stock} + \text{Long put} = \text{Long call.}$$

**Covered Put [Figure 18.1(d)]:**    In this investment strategy, a short position in a put option is combined with a short position in the stock. This strategy is the reverse of a protective put strategy (called covered put). The investor shorts a stock because he is bearish about it, but does not mind buying it back, if the price decreases to a target price, which the investor shorts the put. Breakeven price is the sale price of the stock + put premium.

**EXAMPLE:**    Assume that a stock of a 'X' Ltd. Company is trading in the market at ₹1,500 in May-2015. An investor shorts a put at a price of ₹50 at a strike price of ₹1,400 for July. The net credit received by the investor is ₹1,500 + 50 = ₹1,550. The investor will make profit if the closing price is below the breakeven point. If the stock price does not change, the investor gets to keep the premium. He can use this strategy as an income in a neutral market.

## 18.4  SPREADS OPTIONS

The trading strategies of options can be further classified into three categories, such as spread, straddle and strangle. A *straddle strategy* involves simultaneous buying or selling of a call and put with the same strike price and expiration date. In *strangle strategy*, the trader buys or sells a call or put with the same expiration date but at different strike prices. A *spread strategy* involves combining two or more options of the same type at different strike prices or expiration dates. These have been further classified into different categories which have been discussed in this section.

Option spreads are the way to trade/speculate on relative price changes. A spread trading strategy can be constructed by taking a position in two or more options of the same type that is combining two or more calls or two or more puts. In other words, the simultaneous purchase of one option contract and sale of another, in the expectation that the price relationship between the two will change so that the subsequent offsetting sale and purchase will yield a net profit.

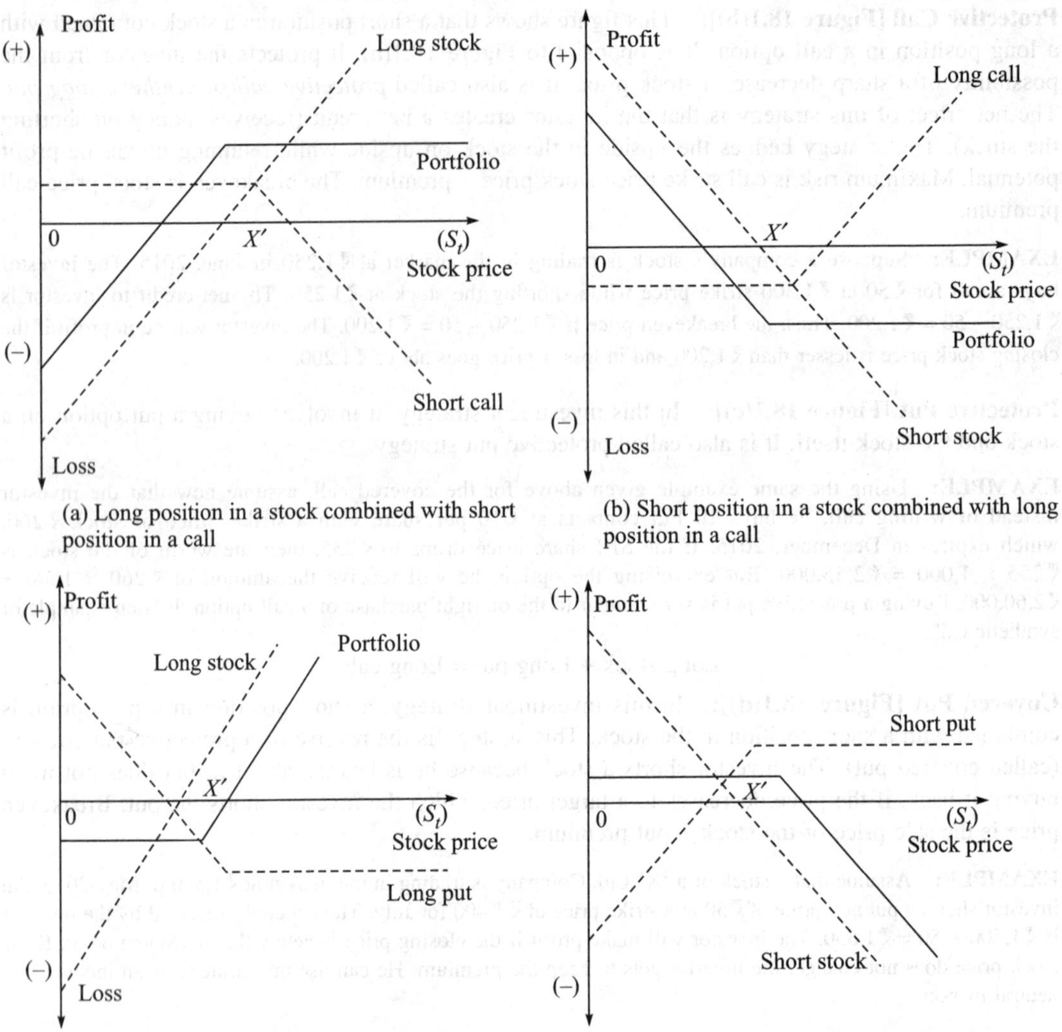

Profit

(+)

Long stock

Portfolio

0     X′     $(S_t)$
Stock price

(−)

Short call

Loss

(a) Long position in a stock combined with short position in a call

Profit

(+)

Long call

X′     $(S_t)$
Stock price

0

Portfolio

(−)

Loss     Short stock

(b) Short position in a stock combined with long position in a call

(+) Profit

Long stock    Portfolio

0    X′     $(S_t)$
Stock price

Long put

(−)

Loss

(c) Long position in a stock combined with long position in a put

(+) Profit

Short put

0    X′     $(S_t)$
Stock price

Short stock

(−)

(d) Short position in a stock combined with short position in a put

**FIGURE 18.1**   Trading strategies.

Option spreads basically can be classified into three categories: (a) Vertical spreads (b) Horizontal spreads (c) Diagonal spreads. Vertical spreads may be divided into two categories. Bullish and bearish spreads. These can be further categorized into two options: call and put.

An option spread in which two legs of the option spread have different strike prices but have the same expiration date is called *vertical spread*. On the other hand, when in option spread two legs have different expiration dates but the same strike price is called *horizontal spread* (also known as calendar or time spread). So the basic difference between the vertical and horizontal spreads is relating to publishing of the option quotation in tables. When changes relate to strike prices, it is *vertical* and when it relates expiration time, it is called *horizontal*. When the two legs of spread option relate to both different strike prices and different expiration dates, such spread is called *diagonal spread*.

In other words, it is hybrid of both different strike prices as well as of different expiration dates. Based upon these, the number and variety of option spreads are almost limitless. One can form different spread options with different features as per his requirements by going long and short. Such classification has been shown in Figure 18.2.

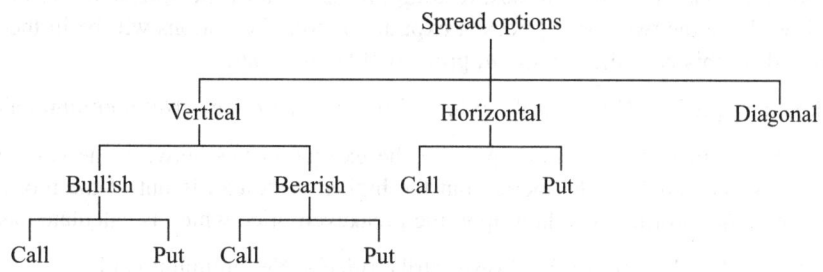

**FIGURE 18.2** Classification of spread option.

The spread options have been further explained in the following sections of this chapter.

## 18.5 VERTICAL SPREADS

Vertical spreads involve the simultaneous buying and selling of options on the same underlying instrument for the same expiry month but with different exercise prices. There are different types of spread which have been explained here as shown in Figure 18.2.

### 18.5.1 Vertical Bull Spread

One of the popular spreads is a vertical bull spread. In this spread, an investor purchases a call option on a stock with certain strike price, and selling a call option on the same stock with a higher strike price. Both the options have the same expiration date. The bull option spread can be further classified into call and put, which have been stated here as under:

- Bullish call option spreads: (Buy call with lower strike and sell call with higher strike price).
- Bearish call option spreads: (Buy call with higher strike price and sell call with lower strike price).

**Bullish call option spreads:** It is created by simultaneously buying and selling call options with the same expiration date. A bullish call option spread is created by purchasing a call option with a low strike price and selling a call option with a higher strike price, both with the same expiration date. So it is constructing by buying an in the money (ITM) call option, and selling another out-of-the-money (OTM) option. The investor will have to pay premium while buying call option and will receive premium on selling the call option. So, the difference of these two premiums will be the cost to the investor on option. It is also commonly known as the net debit among option traders. In other words, the difference of high strike premium and low strike premium will also be net cash investment by the investor in such strategy.

**EXAMPLE:** Assume that an investor buys a Nifty call with a strike price ₹8,100 at a premium of ₹150 and sells a Nifty call option with a strike price ₹8,400 at a premium of ₹50. The difference of premium (Net debit) paid is ₹150 – ₹50 = ₹100 and breakeven point is ₹8,100 + ₹100 = ₹8,200.

From the above strategy, the maximum loss (cost) to the investor will be

Maximum loss = Lower strike premium to be received – Higher strike premium to be paid

If the stock price rises prior to expiration, it means the lower strike call will gain in value faster than the higher strike call will incur losses, resulting in net gain of the spread value. Further, if the stock price rises above the two strike prices at expiration, both the options will be in-the-money and will be exercised. In this case the maximum profit will be as under:

Maximum profit = Higher strike price – Lower strike price – Net premium paid

Let us further assume that the stock price at the expiration lies between the two strike prices, where the lower strike call is in-the-money but the higher strike call is out-of-the money. So there may or may not be net profit, depending upon the breakeven price which is calculated as under:

Break-even price = Lower strike price + Net premium paid

This option spread strategy has been shown in Figure 18.3.

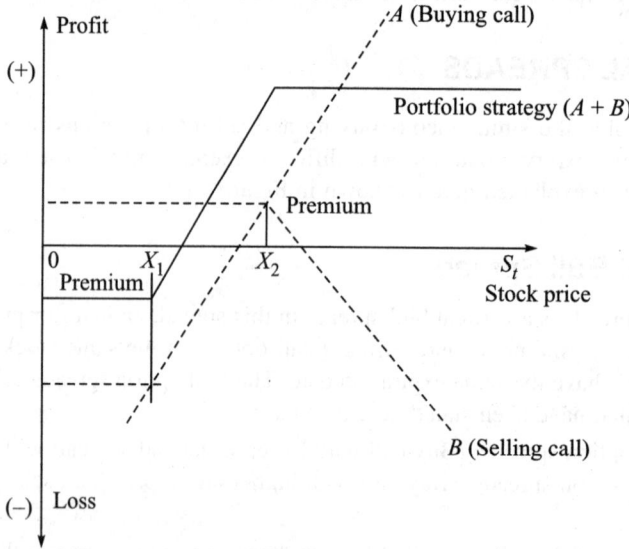

**FIGURE 18.3**   Bullish call vertical option spread.

Figure 18.3 shows the Bull spread strategy using call options with different exercise prices. The dotted (dashed) lines (*A* & *B*) taken separately show the profits from the two option positions, whereas the profit shown by the whole strategy is the sum of the profits given by the dashed lines and is indicated by the solid line. Let us assume that $X_1$ is the strike price of a call option bought and $X_2$ is the strike price of the call option sold, and $S_t$ is the stock price on the expiration date of the options.

**The payoff with different situations:**   (a) If the stock price performs well and increases than the higher strike price (i.e. $S_t \cdot X_2$), the payoff is the difference between the two strike prices, i.e., $X_2 - X_1$ payoff

(b) If the stock price on the expiration date lies between the two, i.e., $(X_1 < S_t < X_2)$ strike prices, the payoff is $(S_t - X_1)$.

(c) If the stock price on the expiration date is below the lower strike price, i.e., $S_t - X_1$, the payoff is zero. This strategy is explained below with an example.

**EXAMPLE:** An investor purchases a call for ₹5 with a strike price of ₹60 and sells for ₹3 a call with a strike price of ₹70. The payoff from this bull strategy is ₹10 (70 – 60) if the stock price is above ₹70 and zero if the stock price is below ₹60. If this is between ₹60 and ₹70, the payoff is the amount by which the stock price exceed ₹60. The cost of strategy is ₹5 – ₹3 = ₹2. The profits, therefore is as follows. The basic argument in favour of a bull spread strategy is that it limits both the investor's upside potential and his downside risk. We can say that the investor has a call option with a strike price to $X_1$ and has chosen to give up some upside potential by selling a call option with strike price $X_2$ $(X_2 > X_1)$. For this hair sacrifice, he gets the price of the option. In the above example, if stock price rise to strike price $X_2$, then the investor will be in gain, i.e., $(X_2 - X_1)$ – cost. On the other hand, if stock price does not increase even to $X_1$ strike price, only the cost (premium) will be the loss to the investor, i.e., (₹5 – ₹3) = ₹2 as he will not exercise the option.

**Bullish put vertical option spread:** An alternative bull call spread is bull vertical put option spread which is created by buying a put option with a low strike price and selling a put option at a higher strike price, both having the same expiration date. In this strategy, the premium paid to purchase the lower strike put option will always be less than the premium received from the sale of the higher strike put so that the net option premium will generate a cash inflow or popularly known as in option markets as net credit.

If the stock price at the expiration is greater than or equal to the higher of the two strike prices, the investor's maximum profit will be the net premium income.

Maximum profit = Maximum premium received – Minimum premium paid

On the other hand, the maximum loss in this strategy will be where the stock price will be less than the lower of the two-strike prices. In this case both puts will be exercised. So maximum loss will be

Maximum loss = Higher strike price – Lower strike price – Net option premium
Break-even price = Higher strike price – Net option premium income

This is shown in Figure 18.4. It is observed that the investor's buying put option is *A* and selling put option is *B*. The maximum profit in this position will be net option premium at $X_1$ and $X_2$ points. Maximum loss will be difference of $X_2$ and $X_1$ and less net option premium income. Some investors prefer this strategy because they receive a net credit rather than incur a net debit. A vertical put spread can be profitable even if the stock prices do not rise, so long as they do not fall. Needless to say, the final payoff from bull spread created using puts are lower than from those created using calls.

**Bearish vertical option spreads:** Bearish option spread will yield profit when there is a decline in the price of the underlying assets. In this option spread, the investor purchases an option with higher strike price and sells the option with a relatively low strike price, and the expiration date is the same. Like bullish vertical option spread, bearish option spread can be divided into two categories:

- Bearish vertical call option spread: (Buy call with higher strike and sell call with lower strike).
- Bearish vertical put option spread: (Buy put with higher strike and sell put with lower strike).

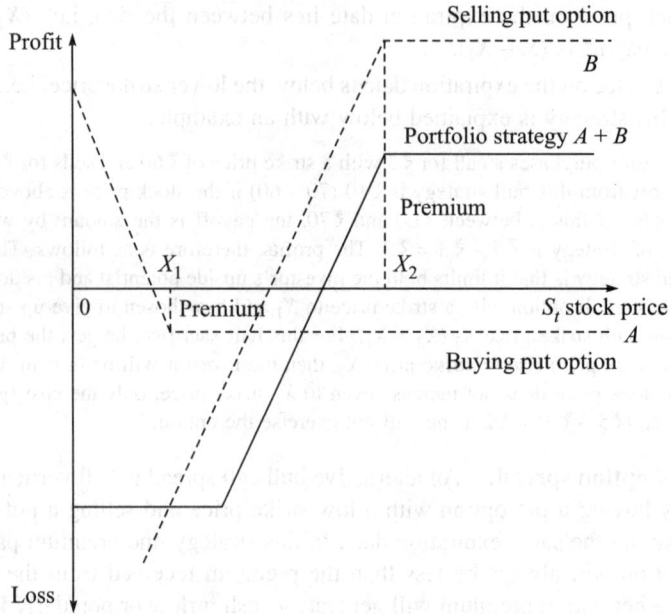

**FIGURE 18.4**    Bullish put vertical option spread.

**Bearish vertical call option spread:**    A bearish vertical call option is created when the investor purchases the option with a high strike price and sells at a lower strike price, both having the same expiration period. If the stock price declines to a level lower than the lower strike price, both the options will be out of the money. The maximum profit in this option position will be the net premium (or the net credit). It is the difference of premium income received on selling and cost of buying the higher strike option.

$$\text{Maximum profit} = \text{Premium on selling option lower strike price}$$
$$- \text{Premium on buying option higher strike price}$$
$$\text{Maximum loss} = \text{Higher strike price} - \text{Lower strike price} - \text{Net premium earned}$$
$$\text{Break-even price} = \text{Higher of the two strike prices} - \text{Net premium per unit}$$

The above option strategy has been shown in Figure 18.5.

Figure 18.5 shows the option position in case of bearish vertical call spread in which $A$ is buying call option with $X_2$ stock price and $B$ selling call option with $X_1$ stock price. The payoff position is shown in Table 18.1.

**TABLE 18.1**    Payoff from a Bearish Vertical Call Spread

| Stock price range | Payoff from long call option | Payoff from short call option | Total range payoff |
|---|---|---|---|
| $S_t \geq X_2$ | $S_t - X_2$ | $X_1 - S_t$ | $-(X_2 - X_1)$ |
| $X_1 < S_t < X_2$ | $S_t, X_1$ | $X_1 - S_t$ | $-(S_t - X_1)$ |
| $S_t \leq X_1$ | 0 | 0 | 0 |

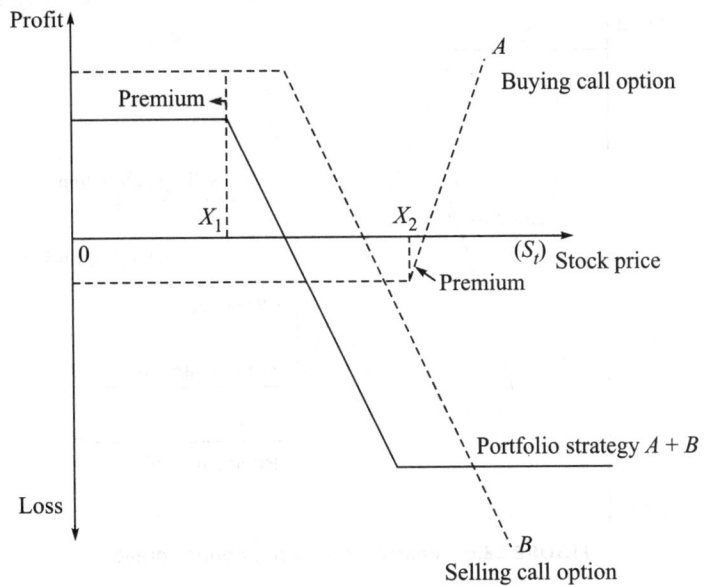

**FIGURE 18.5**   Bearish vertical call option spread.

**EXAMPLE:**   An investor purchases a call option with a strike price of 50 for a ₹2 premium and sells for ₹5 a call with a strike price of ₹40. The payoff with this bear spread strategy is ₹10 (50 – 40) if the stock price is above ₹50 and zero if it is below ₹40. If the stock price is between 50 and 40, the payoff is $-(S_t - 40)$. The investment creates ₹5 – 2 = ₹3 upfront premium. The profit is calculated as follows:

| Stock price range | Profit (₹) |
|---|---|
| $S_t \leq 40$ | +3 |
| $40 < S_t < 50$ | $43 - S_t$ |
| $S_t \geq 50$ | –7 |

It is evident from the above strategy that if the stock price is less than ₹40, then the investor will incur profit from the difference of two premiums, i.e., ₹3 and, if the price goes to ₹50, then there will be loss of ₹7 [50 – (₹40 + ₹3)].

**Bearish vertical put option spread:**   Like bull spread, the bear spread also limits both the upside profit potential and downside risk. In such position the investor creates put spread by purchasing a put with a high strike price and sells a put with a low strike price. This is shown in Figure 18.6.

If the stock price of the underlying asset rises to a level above the higher strike price, both options will expire out-of-the money, and the maximum loss will be the net premium paid. The maximum profit on the option strategy will be the difference between the strike prices less the net premium paid (or the net debit). This will occur if asset prices turn out to be equal to or lower than the lower strike price. In this option position, the break-even price is equal to the higher strike priceless the net premium paid per unit. In brief, the investor intends to go for this strategy by purchasing a put with a certain strike price and chosen to give up some of the profit potential by selling a put with lower strike price. In return, for the profit sacrificed, the investor gets the price of the option sold.

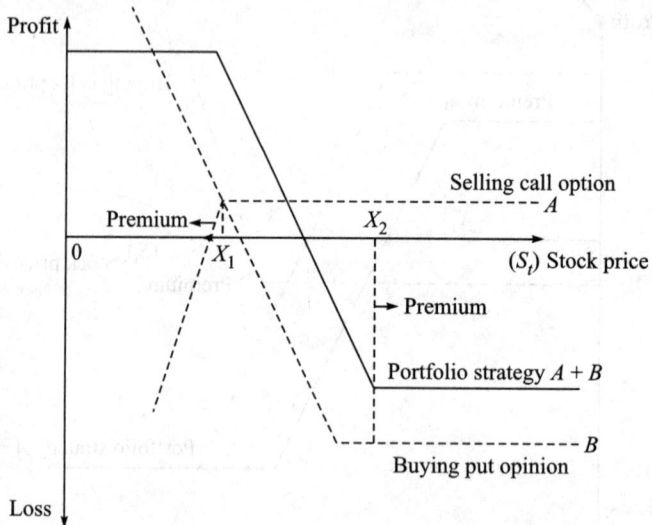

**FIGURE 18.6** Bearish vertical put option spread.

## 18.5.2 Butterfly Spread

A butterfly spread is a particular position in options with three different strike prices. Unlike other spreads, it can be done by using puts and calls, and both options. For example, a butterfly spread can be constructed as:

1. Long call A, short 2 calls B, Long call C
2. Long put A, short 2 puts B, long put C
3. Long call A, short call B, short put B, long put C
4. Long put A, short put B, short call B, long call C

In this strategy, the investor purchases a call option with a relatively low strike price $X_1$ and high strike price $X_3$, and selling two call options with a strike price, $X_2$, halfway between $X_1$ and $X_3$. Usually the $X_2$ is close to the current stock price. This position is shown in Figure 18.7.

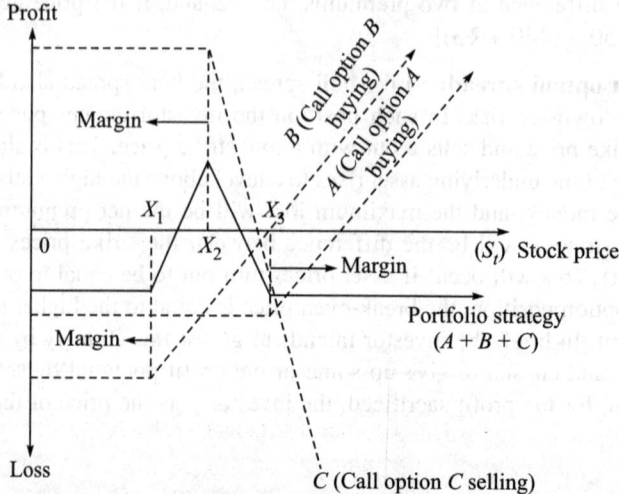

**FIGURE 18.7** Butterfly spread call option.

A butterfly option spread will incur profit if the stock price remains close to $X_2$ but gives rise to a small loss if there is a significant stock price move on either direction. Let us explain this with an example.

**EXAMPLE:**  Suppose that a particular stock is currently selling in the market at ₹91. Consider an investor who feels that the stock price in future (six months) will move randomly. Suppose that the market prices of stock of six-month calls are as follows:

| Strike price (₹) | Call price (₹) |
|---|---|
| 85 | 15 |
| 90 | 10 |
| 95 | 07 |

The investor can create a butterfly spread by purchasing one call with ₹85 strike price and another call at strike price ₹95 and selling two calls with a ₹90 strike price. It costs to the investors ₹15 + 7 − (2 × 10) = ₹2 to create the spread. If the stock price in six months is greater than ₹95 or less than ₹85, there would be no payoff and the investor makes a net loss of ₹2. Further, if the stock price is between ₹86 to 94, then the profit is made. The maximum profit ₹3 will occur when the stock price in six months is ₹90. The payoff from butterfly spread is shown in Table 18.2.

**TABLE 18.2**  Payoff from Butterfly Spread Call Options

| Stock price range | Payoff from first call option | Payoff from second call option | Payoff from short call | Total payoff |
|---|---|---|---|---|
| $S_t < X_1$ | 0 | 0 | 0 | 0 |
| $X_1 < S_t < X_2$ | $S_t - X_1$ | 0 | 0 | $S_t - X_1$ |
| $X_2 < S_t < X_3$ | $S_t - X_1$ | 0 | $-2(S_t - X_2)$ | $X_3 - S_t$ |
| $S_t > X_3$ | $S_t - X_1$ | $S_t - X_3$ | $-2(S_t - X_2)$ | 0 |

Assume that Nifty is trading at ₹8,200. The investor expects very little change in Nifty. He sells 2 ATM call options with a strike price of ₹8,200 at a premium of ₹95 each and buys one ITM NIFTY call option with a strike price at ₹8,100 at a premium of ₹120, and buys one OTM NIFTY call option with a strike price of ₹8,300 at a premium of ₹60. The net debit (premium paid) is (95 × 2 − (120 + 60) = −₹10. The upper break-even point will be strike price of higher strong long call-net premium paid ₹8,290. Lower breakdown point is strike price of lower strike long call + Net premium paid ₹8,110.

**Butterfly spread put option:**  The investor can also create a butterfly-spread position by using put options. In this strategy, he buys a put with a low strike price and high strike price along with selling two puts within an intermediate strike price as shown in Figure 18.8. The butterfly spread can be considered in the example given in the preceding section. Suppose that the market prices of six-month puts are as follows:

| Strike price (₹) | Put price (₹) |
|---|---|
| 85 | 15 |
| 90 | 10 |
| 95 | 7 |

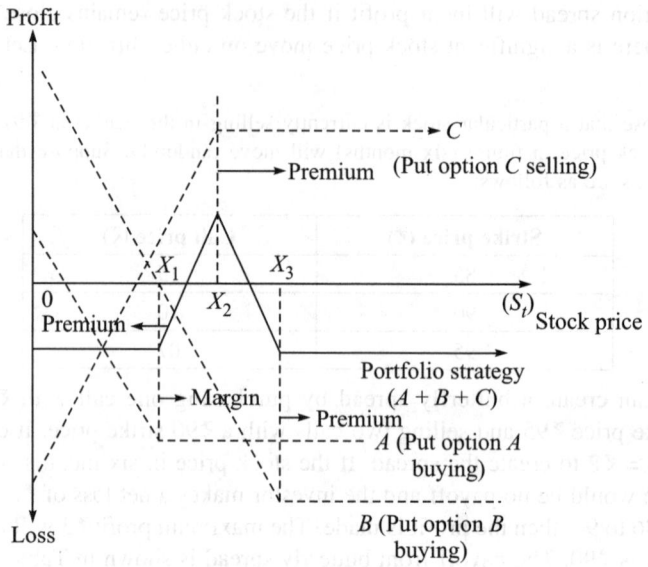

**FIGURE 18.8**   Butterfly spread put option.

The butterfly can be created by purchasing two put options with a strike price ₹85 and ₹95 and selling two put options with ₹90. If all the options are European, the use of put options result will be exactly same as in the case of call butterfly spread seen earlier. Put-call parity can be used to show that the initial investment is the same in both strategies.

Further, a butterfly spread can be created by selling and by following the reverse strategy to that described as earlier. For example, two options are sold with low and high strike price and two options are purchased with the middle strike price. The strategy produced a modest profit if there is a significant movement in the stock price.

## 18.5.3   Horizontal or Time or Calendar Spreads

The expiration period of time is very important specifically in the American options. There is time value in the option strategy, as seen in the proceeding sections of this chapter. Time value decay accelerates as the expiry date is approaching. The time value of the option with the nearby maturity date would decay more rapidly than that of the option with the distant maturity date. The value of the liability declines more rapidly than the value of the asset. In general, calendar spreads, use the same strike price, but with two different expiration dates, can use either calls or puts, and the resulting payoff is earned. This is because one option is still 'alive' at the expiration date of the other.

If the underlying stock prices are believed to be stable in future for a forceable time, one can attempt to make profit from the declining time value of options by setting up a horizontal or time option spread. A horizontal spread is created by using the options with different maturities (expiration dates) but with the same strike price. It is called horizontal spreads because the various expiry months are shown horizontally in the financial press publications.

A horizontal spread is created by selling an option with a relatively short period to expiration and buying an option the same type with a longer period to expiration. The longer the maturity of an option, the more expensive it is. A time or calendar spread requires an initial investment. The option strategy in calendar spread is shown in Figure 18.9 assuming that the long maturity option is sold when the short maturity option expires.

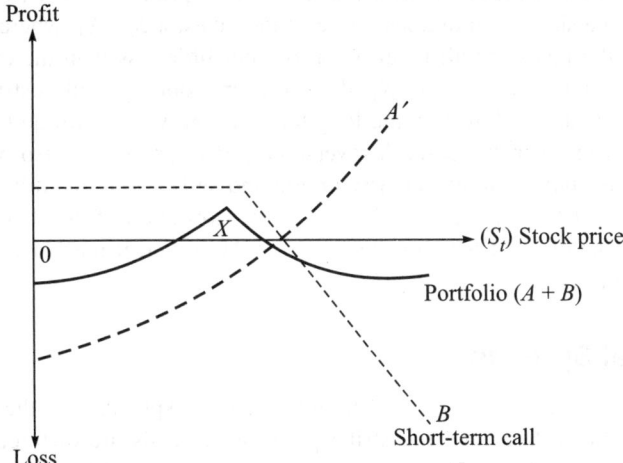

**FIGURE 18.9** Calendar spread with two call options.

Figures 18.9 and 18.10 show the calendar spreads with two call options and two put options, respectively. The profits and losses of the calendar spread (unbroken profiles) are the sums of the profit/losses on the two options (broken line profiles). The rate of decline of an option premium per unit of time elapsing is known as the theta of the option. In other words, theta is a measure of the change in an option premium with respect to a one-day change in time to maturity.

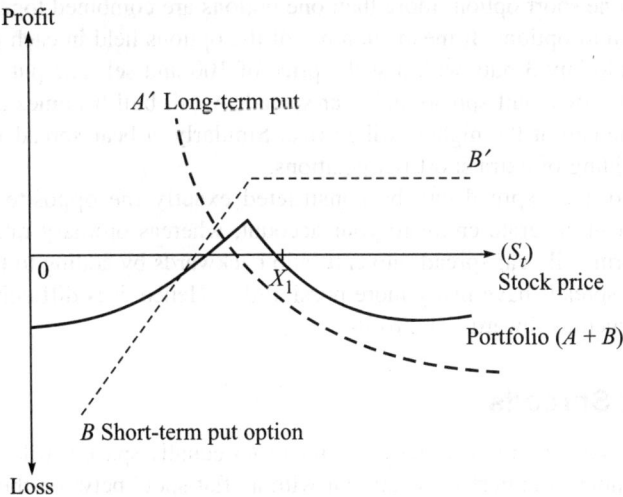

**FIGURE 18.10** Calendar spread with two put options.

The investor makes a profit in a calendar spread if the stock price at the expiration of the short-term option is close to the strike price. However, a loss is incurred when the stock price is significantly above or below the strike price. To understand, let us consider what happens if the stock price is very low when the short-term option expires. The short-term option is worthless and the value of the long-term option is close to zero. So, the investor will incur a loss but less than the cost of setting up the spread initially. Now, suppose the stock price is very high when the short-term options expires. Then the short-term options will cost the investor $S_t - X_1$, where $X$ is the strike price of the options. Again the investor will incur a net loss but little less than the cost of setting up the spread initially. Consider if $S_t$ is close to $X_1$, the short-term options will cost the investor either a small amount or nothing at all. However, the long-term option will be still quite valuable because a significant net profit is made in the case. A reverse calendar spread can also be created, as shown in Figure 18.10. Investor buys a short maturity option and sells a long maturity option. This option strategy will create a small profit, if the stock price at the expiration of the short-term option is well above or below the strike price of the short-term option. However, it may incur a major loss if it is close to the stock price.

## 18.5.4   Diagonal Spreads

Diagonal spreads include both types of vertical and horizontal spreads. In other words, it is spread where both the expirations dates and the strike price of the calls are different. They are chosen diagonally from the option listing. There are several different types of diagonals spreads which can be created. Their profit patterns are generally related with variations on the profit patterns from the corresponding bull or bear spreads. So, diagonal spreads can be bullish or bearish but it is not clear what the investor has in mind with certain diagonal spreads.

## 18.5.5   Ratio Spreads

Ratio spreads involve an unequal number of call and put options. In this spread, instead of having simple one long and one short option, more than one options are combined together, having unequal number of long and short options. It means number of the options held in each position is not same. For example, one could buy 3 puts with a strike price of 100 and sell one put with a strike of 120. It can be classified into two–bull spread and bear spread. A call bull becomes a call ratio spread by writing more than one call at the higher strike price. Similarly, a bear spread with puts becomes a put ratio spread by adding of extra short put positions.

Similarly, a ratio back spread can be constructed exactly the opposite as the ratio spread mentioned above. It can generate credit to your account, whereas ordinary ratio spread result in a debit. We can transform call bear spread into call ratio backwards by adding to the long call position and vice versa. Ratio spreads have many more possibilities. Hence, it is difficult to generalize about their characteristics, such as reward risk profiles.

## 18.5.6   Condor Spreads

It is a specific type of spread option strategy in which four equally spaced strike prices are used. The resulting payoff resembles a butterfly spread, but with a "flat spot" between the middle two strikes. The difference is that the two middle have different strike prices.

A long call Condor involves buying one ITM call (lower strike), selling one ITM call (lower middle), selling one OTM call (higher middle) and buying one OTM call (higher strike). The strategy is to ensure that the risk is capped at both the sides. The resulting position is profitable if the stock remains range bound and shows very little volatility. The maximum profit occurs if the stock remains between the middle strike prices at expiration.

**EXAMPLE:** Assume the Nifty is trading at ₹7,600 in December, 2015. An investor expects low volatility in the Nifty and expects to remain in range bound. He buys one ITM call option with a strike price of ₹7,400 at a premium of 40, sells one ITM Nifty calls option with a strike price of ₹7,500 at a premium of ₹25, sells one OTM Nifty call option with a strike price of ₹7,700 at a premium of ₹10, and buys one OTM Nifty call option with a strike price of ₹7,800 at premium of ₹6. So, net debit is highest (– 40 + 25 + 10 – 6) = ₹11 which is also maximum loss. Upper break-even point in this strategy strike-price-net debit, i.e., ₹7,800 – 11 = ₹7,789. Lowest breakeven point is lowest strike price + Net debit, i.e., ₹7,400 + ₹11 = ₹7,411.

The investor believes that the underlying stock will trade in a range with low volatility until the option expires. So, being limited risk, the return will also be limited. The maximum profit of a long condor will be realized when the stock trading between the two middle strike prices, i.e., ₹7,500 – 7,700. The position of Long Call Condor spread is shown in Figure 18.11.

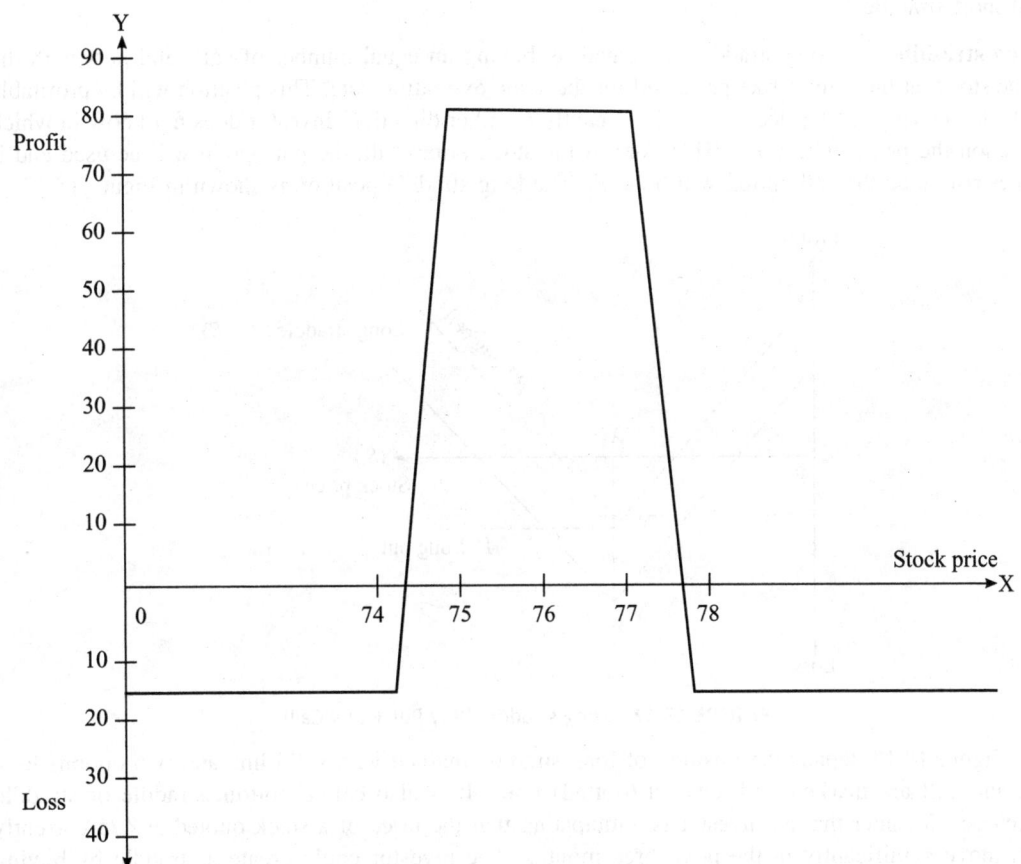

**FIGURE 18.11** Long call condor spread.

From the above example, it is observed that maximum loss is ₹11. Suppose the Nifty is 7,600, the net payoff will be ₹89 (₹160 – ₹75 – 10 – 6). Which will be same for the strike price of ₹7,500 and ₹7,700. The net payoff will be at the strike price of 7,411 and 7,789. The strike price less than 7,411 and above than 7,789, then the maximum loss will be ₹11.

## 18.6   COMBINATIONS (VOLATILITY TRADING)

A combination is an option trading strategy that involves by taking a position in both call and put on the same asset. This is also used as volatility trading which means taking positions on changes in market expectations of price volatility. The main strategies in this respect are as straddles, strangles, strips and straps.

### 18.6.1   Straddles Strategies

One of the popular combinations is known as straddle. It involves simultaneous buying a call and put with the same strike price and expiration date. It can be divided into categories: long straddle and short straddle.

**Long straddle:**   A long straddle is created by buying an equal number of calls and puts with the same stock, at the same strike price and for the same expiration date. This position will be profitable if the underlying stock prices move significantly in either direction. Investor does not know in which direction the prices will move. Therefore, if the stock prices fall, the put option will be used and if prices rise, then the call option will be used. The long straddle position is shown in Figure 18.12.

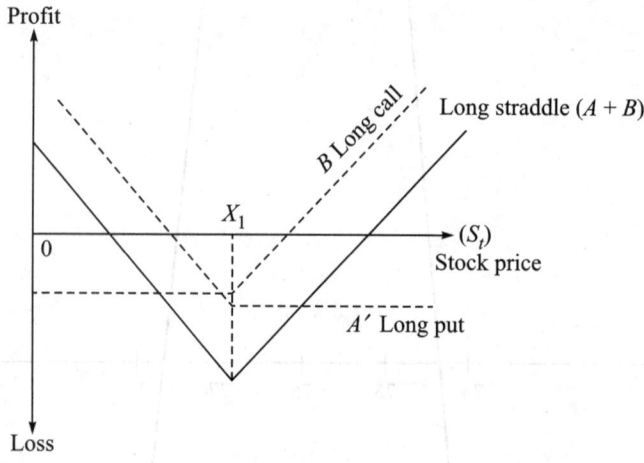

**FIGURE 18.12**   Long straddle (Buy Put + Buy Call).

Figure 18.12 depicts the position of long straddle marked with solid line and two options long put and call are marked with dashed (dotted) lines. It is also called bottom straddle or straddle purchase. Consider that an investor is anticipating that the price of a stock quoted at ₹75 currently will move significantly in the next three months. The investor could create a straddle by buying both a put and a call with a strike price of ₹76 with expiration date in three months. Assume that the option price (premium) is ₹3 for a call and ₹2 for a put, costing ₹3 + ₹2 = ₹5 for a straddle. If the stock price rises to ₹82, then the profit to the investor will be on exercise of call (₹82 – ₹76 – ₹5) = ₹1. And if the stock price decreased to ₹65, then the put option will be used, incurring profit (₹76 – ₹65 – ₹5) = ₹6.

**EXAMPLE:**   Assume that on 14 December 2015, the Nifty is at 7,650. An investor enters a long straddle by buying a January, 2016 at 7,800 Nifty calls for ₹140 and put for ₹80. The net debit taken to enter the straddle option is ₹220, which is also maximum loss to the investor. The break-even price (upper) is strike price of long calls + Net premium paid is 7,800 + 220 = ₹8,020. The lower breakeven point will be strike price of long put – Net premium paid is 7,800 – 220 = ₹7,580. So the risk is limited to ₹220 and reward is unlimited. This strategy is followed in case volatility in the index is expected significant on either side.

This is also called a top straddle or straddle write. It is highly risky strategy because if the price of the stock moves on any direction up and down, the investor may incur loss. It will be beneficial only if the stock prices are stable.

**Short straddle:**   A short straddle is the simultaneous sale of a call and a put on the same stock, at the same exercise price and for the same exercise date. If an investor expects the stock prices to be stable in future, he can sell a straddle. It is just opposite to the long straddle. If the stock price in future remains same to the strike prices both options will expire worthless, and the investor will retain the total premium received from writing the options. This is shown in Figure 18.13.

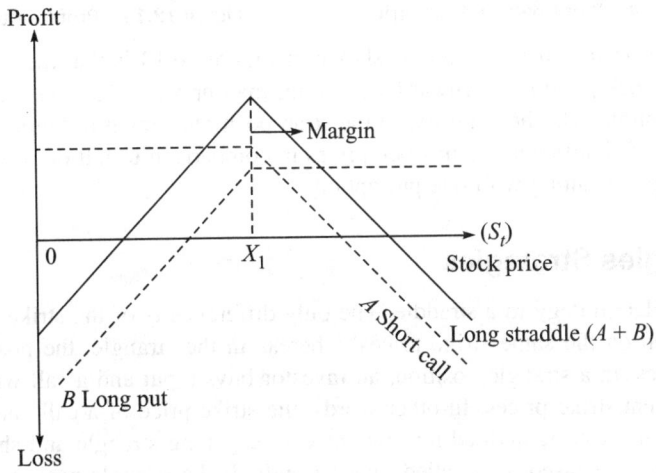

**FIGURE 18.13**   Short straddle (Sell put + Sell call).

This is also called *a top straddle* or *straddle write.* It is highly risky strategy because if the price of the stock moves on any direction; up and down, the investor may incur loss. It will be beneficial only if the stock prices are stable.

**EXAMPLE:**   Assume that the Nifty is at ₹7,450 on October 5, 2015. An investor enters into a short straddle by selling a November, 2015 ₹7,600, put for ₹80 and call for ₹120. The net credit received is ₹200 (₹120 + ₹80), which is also his maximum possible profit. The upper break-even point will be strike price of short call + Net premium received (₹7,600 + 200) = ₹7,800. The lower break-even point is equal to strike price of short put – Net premium received, i.e., 7,600 – 200 = ₹7,400. This strategy is generally used by the investor when the market is expected at very little volatility in the near term. So his reward will be limited to the premium received and the risk is limited on both sides.

## 18.6.2   Strips and Straps

These are specific types of option positions. A strip refers to a long position with one call and two puts options with the same strike price and the expiration date. On the other hand, a strap consists of a long position with two calls and one put options with the same strike price and same expiration date. Since strips and straps are one contract for three options, they are also called *triple options,* and the premiums are less than if each option was purchased individually. The profit position is shown in Figures 18.14 and 18.15.

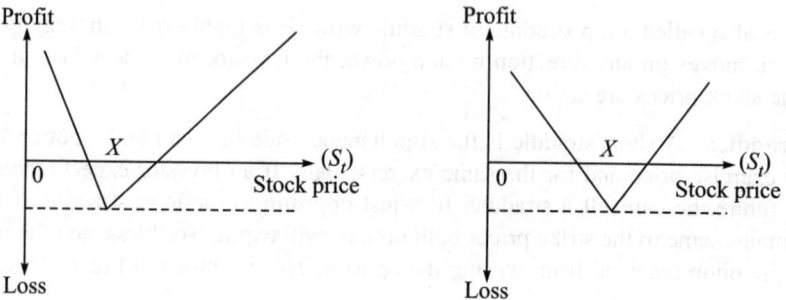

| FIGURE 18.14  Profit pattern from strips. | Figure 18.15  Profit pattern from straps. |

The basic belief in the strip position as shown in Figure 16.13 is that the investor is expecting a big move of the stock price in downward side rather than upward. As a result, he will go for two puts and one call options. On the contrary, in the strap position, shown in Figure 16.14, the investor is betting in favour of significant rise in stock prices in comparison to fall or downward. For this, he goes for two call options along with one put option.

## 18.6.3  Strangles Strategies

A strangle is a similar strategy to a straddle. The only difference is of the strike price. In a straddle the position is taken on the same strike prices, whereas in the strangle, the position is taken with different strike prices. In a strangle position, an investor buys a put and a call with same expiration date but with different strike prices. In other words, the strike price of a call and of a put option is different. The strangles can be divided into two categories—long strangle and short strangle. When a strangle position is purchased, it is called *long strangle*. If the strangle position is sold it is called *short strangle*. They are also known as *bottom vertical combination* and *top vertical combinations*, respectively. Figures 18.16 and 18.17 depict the long and short strangles positions.

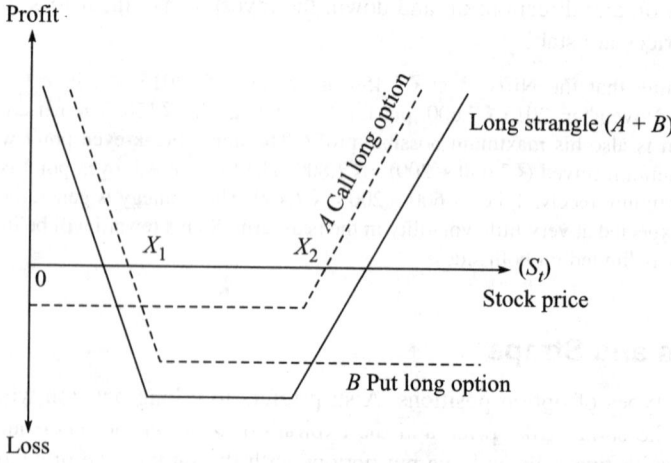

**FIGURE 18.16**  Long strangle (Buy OTM Put + Buy OTM Call).

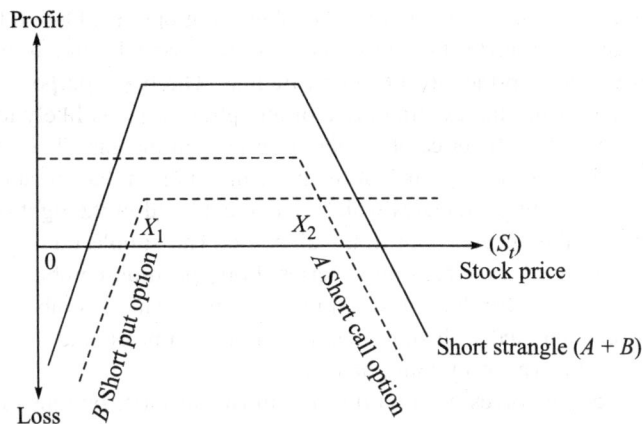

**FIGURE 18.17**　Short strangle (Sell OTM Put + Sell OTM Call).

A strangle would be typically constructed by using an out-of-the-money call and out-of-the money put. It could be constructed with an in-the-money call and an in-the-money put or with one option being in-the-money and the other out-of-the money. The buyer of a strangle takes the view or believes that the volatility is going to be high while the seller believes that the volatility is going to be low. Unlike the simple straddle, the profit of a long strangle is characterized by a broad, flat return between the two strike prices, i.e., $X_2$ and $X_1$. Figure 18.16 shows the long strangle position where the flat zone shows the profit profile and this flat zone will be loss profile for the seller of strangle. Similarly, Figure 18.17 shows the profit profile for the seller of strangle is flat zone, and this zone will be loss profile for the purchaser of the strangle.

**EXAMPLE:**　Assume that the Nifty is traded in October, 2015 at ₹7,500. An investor is a long strangle by buying a ₹7,300 NIFTY put for a premium of ₹25 and ₹7,700 Nifty call for ₹45. The net debit (total premium paid) taken to enter this option is ₹70, which is also a maximum loss for the investor. The upper break-even point is strike price of long call + net premium paid, i.e., ₹7,700 + 70 = ₹7,770, whereas lower break-even point is strike price of long put – Net premium paid, i.e., 7,300 – 70 = ₹7,260. The risk in this strategy is limited to the initial premium paid and reward is unlimited opposite of the long strangle. In the short strangle, the investor gets the premium for selling the call and put both. In the given example, the total premium would be received ₹70, but having unlimited risk.

Although, the long and short strangles are suitable for taking positions on volatility but these are not likely to be used for taking positions on changes in the market expectation of volatility by combining a call and a put as per requirement. It has been observed that short strangles are more popular of the two strategies, i.e., long and short, and are frequently employed to take advantage of the decreasing time value of the options in markets where stock prices are expected to be stable. However, like the sale of straddle, the strangle position is a risky strategy since the investor's potential loss is unlimited.

# SUMMARY

Options are the right given to the buyer to buy or sell an underlying asset at a specified price within the specified period for a fixed premium. Option may be used for different purposes like trading, hedging, speculation, etc. This chapter narrates how options can be used for the purpose of making trading and also see the range of profit pattern obtainable using options. Option trading may be seen a mean for those intending to transfer their unwanted risk to those who like to go for more risk.

Chapter explains the basic principles of option trading. The basic purpose of option trading is based on view as whether or not the existing price of an option series is likely to change or not. For example, if a trader believes that the price of an option series will increase then he may go for buying the option contract. Similarly, if he expects that the price may fall, in that situation, he may write the option. There are different trading strategies which can be explored in the light of various objectives like increase in intrinsic value, decrease in time value, etc. The simple trading strategies are those involving buying and selling of a simple option series. Long position combined with short position in call short position combined with long position in call, long position combined with long position in put and short position combined with short position in put and profit and loss profile of important strategies to be considered in various trading of options.

Spread trading strategy involves where a position in two or more options of the same types are combined. In other words, the simultaneous purchase of one option contract and sale of another, in the expectation that the price relationship between the two will change so that the subsequent offsetting sale and purchase will yield a net profit. Basically options spreads can be classified into vertical spreads, horizontal spreads and diagonal spreads. An option spread in which two legs of the option spread have some strike prices but have the same expiration date is called a *vertical spread*. On the other hand, when in an option spread two legs have same strike prices but different expiration date is called a horizontal spread, and also known as calendar or time spread. Vertical spread option can be classified as bullish vertical on both call and put option and bearish vertical spread on both call and put option. The maximum loss in case of bullish call option spread will be lower strike premium (to be received) higher strike premium (to be paid). In case of bearish vertical call option spread, maximum loss will be the difference of higher strike price and lower strike price by deducting the net premium earned and maximum profit will be difference between the premium on selling option (lower strike price) and premium on buying option (higher strike option). Butterfly spread is a particular position in options with three different strike prices. In this strategy, the investor purchases a call option with a relatively low price, and high strike price and selling two call options with a strike price. Usually $X_1$ selling strike price is close to current stock price. A butterfly option spread will incur profit if the stock price remains close to selling strike price but gives rise to a small loss if there is significant stock price moves over on either direction. Butterfly spread can be on call as well as on put option.

A combination is an option trading strategy that involves taking position in both call and put on the same asset. This is also used as volatility trading, which means taking position on changes in market expectations of price volatility. The main strategies in this respect are straddles, strangles, strips and straps. Straddle involves simultaneous buying a call and put with the same strike price and expiration date. It can be divided into two categories: long straddle and short straddle. A long straddle is created by buying an equal number of calls and puts with same stock at the same strike price and for the same expiration date. Short straddle is the simultaneous sale of a call and put the same stock, at the same exercise price and for the same exercise date. If an investor expects the stock prices to be stable in future, he can sell a straddle it is just opposite to the long straddle.

There are specific types of options position. A strip refers to a long position with one call and two puts options with the same strike price and the expiration date. On the other hand, a strap consists of a long position with two calls and one put options with the same strike price and same expiration date. A strangle is a similar strategy to a straddle. The only difference is of the strike price. In a straddle, the position is taken on the same strike prices, whereas in the strangle, the position is taken with different strike prices. In a strangle position, an investor buys a put and a call with the same expiration date but with different strike prices. In other words, the strike price of call and put is different. Strangle can be long and short. It has observed that short strangles are more popular of two strategies. Long and short strangles are frequently employed to take advantage of decreasing time value of the options in the market where stock prices are expected to be stable. However, like the sale of straddle, the strangle position is risky since the investor's potential loss is unlimited.

## SOLVED PROBLEMS

**P.1.**   Suppose on November 1, 2003 an investor sells a January 2004 S&P CNX NIFTY futures contract at ₹330 anticipating a drop in the stock market. By December S&P CNX NIFTY futures price declines to 310 and the short futures position shows a profit of 20 points ($20 \times 50 = 1{,}000$). Investors buy a January 310 call at 11.40 ($50 \times 11.40 = 570$), locking an unrealised premium of ₹570 from exercisable profit of ₹1,000. Show the payoff profile of synthetic put which is similar to long put option.

*Solution:*

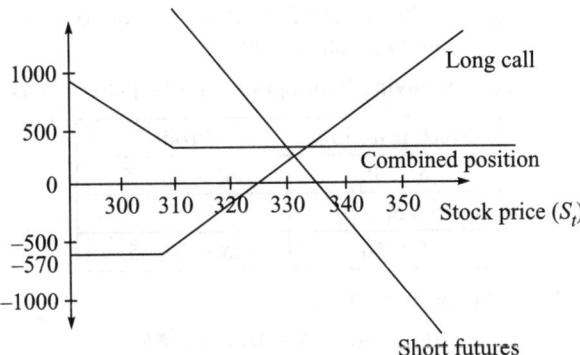

**P.2.**   A stock is currently selling for ₹400. The price of call option expiring six months are as follows:

> Strike price = ₹350, Call price = ₹15
>
> Strike price = ₹390, Call price = ₹11
>
> Strike price = ₹425, Call price = ₹8

Investor feels it is unlikely that stock price will move significantly in next six months. Draw a butterfly spread with the given options.

*Solution:*   Investor set up a butterfly spread by

>   1. Buying one call with ₹350 strike.
>
>   2. Buying one call with ₹425 strike.
>
>   3. Selling two calls with ₹390 strike.

This lost ₹15 + ₹8 − (2 × ₹11) = ₹11. Maximum loss to investor is ₹1 if stock price moves out of the ₹351 and ₹424 range. The maximum profit of ₹5 to the investor, if the stock price is ₹390 on the expiration date.

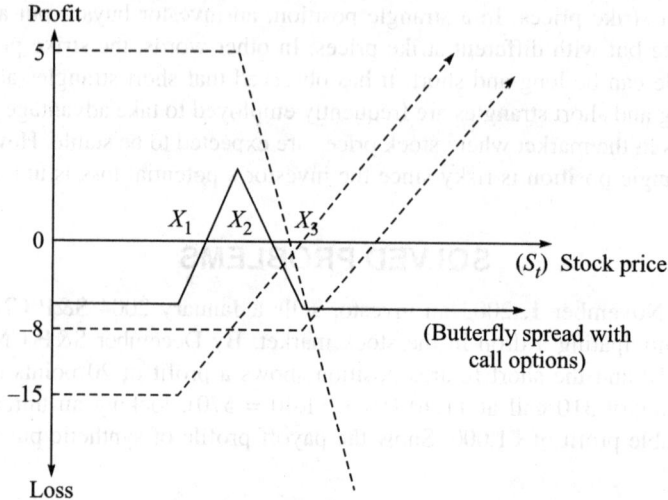

(Butterfly spread with call options)

**P.3.** A call option with an exercise price of ₹50 costs ₹2. A put option with a strike price of ₹45 costs ₹3. Discuss how a strangle can be created from these two options. And show profit profile of strangle, suppose stock price on expiration date is ₹60.

*Solution:* A strangle is created by buying both options. Profit pattern is as follows:

| Stock price ($S_t$) | Profit |
|---|---|
| $S_t < 45$ | $(45 - S_t) - 5$ |
| $45 < S_t < 50$ | $-5$ |
| $S_t > 50$ | $(S_t - 50) - 5$ |

If $S_t$ on expiration is ₹60 then the profit will be

$$(60 - 50) - 5 = 10 - 5 = ₹5$$

**P.4.** A call option on BSES with a strike price of ₹400 costs ₹35. A put option on BSES with a strike price of ₹350 cost ₹40. How strangle can be created from these options? What will be the profit pattern if the price of BSES on expiration is ₹500?

*Solution:* Strangle can be created by buying the two options. The profit will be

| Strike price/stock | Profit |
|---|---|
| $S_t < 350$ | $(350 - S_t) - 75$ |
| $350 < S_t < 400$ | $-75$ |
| $S_t > 400$ | $(S_t - 400) - 75$ |

where $S_t = 500$.

$$\text{Profit} = (500 - 400) - 75 = 100 - 75 = ₹25$$

**P.5.** The call options on Reliance share are available with the strike price of ₹400, ₹500 and ₹600, and expiration date is three months. The call prices are ₹60, ₹40 and ₹30, respectively. Explain how the options can be used to create a butterfly spread? Construct a table showing profit varies with stock price for the butterfly spread.

*Solution:*    An investor can create a butterfly spread by buying a call options with strike price of
₹400 and ₹600 and selling two call options with strike prices of ₹500. Initial investment is ₹60 +
₹30 − 2 × 40 = ₹90 − ₹80 = ₹10.
    Variations in profit with the final stock price:

| Stock price ($S_t$) | Profit (₹) |
|---|---|
| $S_t < 400$ | −10 |
| $400 < S_t < 500$ | $(S_t - 400) - 10$ |
| $500 < S_t < 600$ | $(600 - S_t) - 10$ |
| $S_t > 600$ | −10 |

**P.6.**    Spot exchange rate £1 = $1.30

A $1.35 call is bought at a premium of 2 cent/£

A $1.40 is sold at a premium of 0.5 cent/£

Show the profit and loss profile of call spread prior to expiry and at expiry.

*Solution:*

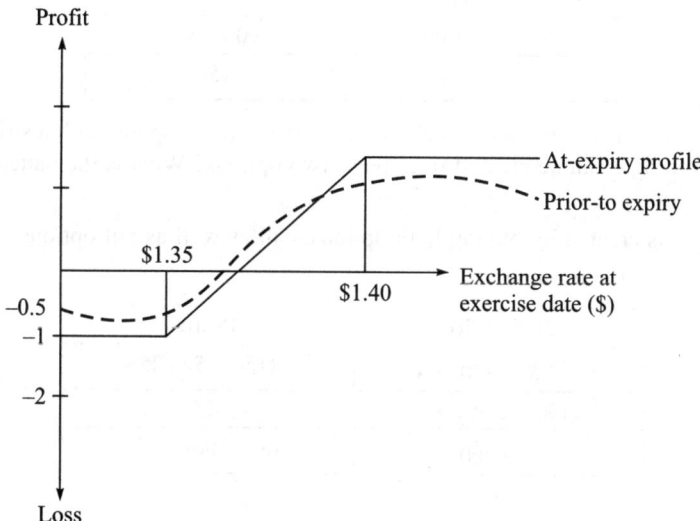

**P.7.**    S&P 500 stock index futures price stands at 200. January 2003 stock index option price are
shown as follows in table:

| Strike price (₹) | Calls (₹) | Puts (₹) |
|---|---|---|
| 195 | 6.80(0.84) | 1.65(−0.16) |
| 200 | 2.79(0.50) | 2.69(−0.50) |
| 205 | 1.75(0.15) | 6.60(−0.85) |

    Describe a strategy using options and futures that will result in a profit from a movement of
futures price, irrespective of direction. In the event of market expectations of volatility remaining
constant, figures given in the brackets are details.

***Solution:***

| | |
|---|---|
| Buy 2 January call | Delta $= 2 \times 0.50$ |
| Sell 1 January futures contract | Delta $= -1$ |
| Net delta | $= 0$ |

A fall in the futures price would cause the options delta to decline. The net delta of the position thus become negative and the trader benefits from the price fall.

A rise in futures price would cause the options delta to rise. The net delta of the position, thus, becomes positive and the trader makes profits from the price rise. Loss could occur if the market expectation of volatility were to decline and thereby reduce option price.

**P.8.** An investor buys for ₹50 a call with a strike price of ₹1,000 and sells for ₹150 a call with a strike price of ₹800. The payoff from this bearish spread strategy is ₹200, if the stock price is above ₹100, and zero if it is below ₹800. If the stock price is between ₹800 and ₹1,000, the payoff is $(S_t - 800)$. Show the profit of the strategy under different stock price range.

***Solution:***

| Stock price $S_t$ (₹) | Profit (₹) |
|---|---|
| $S_t \leq 800$ | 100 |
| $800 < S_t < 1,000$ | $900 - S_t$ |
| $S_t \geq 1,000$ | $-150$ |

**P.9.** A call option with a strike price of ₹200 costs ₹10 and a put option with a strike price of ₹150 costs ₹15. How a strangle can be created from these two options? What is the pattern of profits from the strangle?

***Solution:*** Strangle is created by buying both options, call as well as put options.

*Profit pattern of a strangle:*

| Stock price | Profit |
|---|---|
| $S_t \leq 150$ | $(150 - S_t) - 25$ |
| $150 < S_t < 200$ | $-25$ |
| $S_t \geq 200$ | $(S_t - 200) - 25$ |

## SUGGESTED READINGS

1. Dubofsky, David A., *Options and Financial Futures*, McGraw-Hill, Singapore, 1992.
2. Redhead, Keith, *Introduction to Financial Investment*, Prentice-Hall, Horne, Hempstead, 1995.
3. Eckl, S., Robinson, J.N., and Thomas, D.C., *Financial Engineering*, Blackwell, Oxford, 1990.
4. Arnott, R., Modeling Portfolio with Options: Risks and Returns, *Journal of Portfolio Management*, Vol. 7, pp. 66–73, Fall 1980.
5. Yates, J. and Kopprasch, R., Writing Covered Call Options: Profits and Risks, *Journal of Portfolio Management*, Vol. 7, pp. 74–79, Fall 1980.
6. Slivka, R., Call Options Spreading, *Journal of Portfolio Management*, Vol. 8, pp. 71–76, Spring 1981.
7. Welch, W.H. and Becker, H.P., *Option Strategies and when to Use Them, Futures*, June 1984.

# REVIEW QUESTIONS

1. Define the options contract. How is it different from forward and futures?
2. What are various positions of options? Discuss with suitable examples and diagrams.
3. Write a detailed note on basic objectives and principles of option trading.
4. What do you understand by the term spread in option trading? Discuss the types of spreads with suitable diagrams.
5. What are various types of vertical spreads? Discuss with suitable examples and diagrams in context to option trading.
6. Write notes on:
   (a) Bullish call option spread
   (b) Bearish call option spread
7. What is horizontal spread? Discuss its types with suitable illustrations and diagrams in context to option trading.
8. What is butterfly spread? Discuss the difference between horizontal spread and butterfly spread with suitable examples. Also discuss the different types of butterfly spread option trading.
9. Compare and contrast between vertical, horizontal and diagonal spreads in option trading.
10. What do you understand by volatility-based option trading strategy? Discuss various types of combinations with suitable examples.
11. Write notes on:
    (a) Long straddle
    (b) Short straddle
12. "A strangle is similar strategy to a straddle." Discuss the statement in light of option trading with suitable examples.
13. Compare and contrast between straddle and strangle option strategies.
14. In what ways do speculation with option differ from speculation with future. Which one is better for speculators, and why?
15. A butterfly can be constructed by combining a bull spread with a bear spread. Also, a butterfly can be constructed by combining a straddle with a strangle. Explain these alternative constructions of butterfly.
16. When is it appropriate for a trader to purchase a butterfly spread? Discuss with suitable illustrations.
17. What do you mean by protective put? What position in call options is equivalent to a protective put? Comment.
18. Draw a diagram showing the variation of an option trader's profit or loss with the terminal stock price for a profile consisting of
    (a) One share and a short position in one call option
    (b) Two shares and a short position in one call option
    In each case, assume that the call option has a strike price equal to the current stock price.
19. Explain the following in context to option trading:
    (a) Two ways in which a bearish spread can be created
    (b) Features of diagonal spread

# UNSOLVED PROBLEMS

**P.1.** Call options on shares are available with strike prices of ₹100, ₹120 and ₹125 and expiration dates is six months. Their call prices are ₹20, ₹12 and ₹5, respectively. Explain how the options can be used to create a butterfly spread? Construct a table showing how profit varies with the stock price for the butterfly spread.

**P.2.** A speculator buys for ₹150 a call with a strike price of ₹1,500 and sells for ₹50 a call with a strike price of ₹1,750. Payoff of the bull spread is ₹250 if the stock price is above ₹1,750 and zero if it is below ₹1,500. Show the profit profile of the strategy.

**P.3.** Consider a trader who feels that the price of a certain stock currently value at ₹69 by the market, will now significantly move in next three months. What can be appropriate strategy by using a straddle? Draw a table to show the payoff from a straddle.

**P.4.** A call with a strike price of ₹200 costs ₹80. A put with ₹150 strike price and expiration date costs ₹10. Construct a table to show the profit from a straddle. For what range of stock price would the straddle lead to a loss?

**P.5.** Spot exchange rate 1USD = ₹46

      A ₹47 call is bought at a premium of 2 cent/$

      A ₹48 call is sold at a premium of 0.5 cent/$

      Show the bull spread in a diagram form.

**P.6.** Calculate the profit and loss from the following:

      A $1.85 call is bought for 4 cent/£

      A $1.95 is sold for 1 cent/£

At what price level there will be additional profits? Draw long call and offset from the short call.

# Hedging with Options

*After reading this chapter, students will be able to*

➤ Understand the concept of hedging.

➤ Know about how fixed hedging is done with options.

➤ Be aware of the concept of fixed hedge, naked and covered positions.

➤ Know various hedging strategies such as stoop loss strategy, zero cost options, range forward and so on.

➤ Understand the various sophisticated hedging strategies with options which includes delta hedging, theta hedging, gamma hedging, etc.

➤ Be aware of the variations of Gamma with time to maturity for stock option.

➤ Understand the concept of Vega and variations of Vega with stock price for an option.

➤ Know about Rho and Phi and hedging option portfolio in practice.

➤ Know about the concept of position derivatives and position risk.

## 19.1 INTRODUCTION

Hedging through financial derivatives is an important strategy of financial institutions, traders and other dealers. The ultimate economic function of financial derivatives is to provide means of risk reduction. As seen earlier, hedgers using futures basically attempt to lock in a specific price, whereas in case of options, hedgers seek to set a specific floor or ceiling price. For example, an option hedger can establish a floor price for a long put position, and in case of a long call position, a ceiling price is established. So options can be regarded as means of insurance against adverse price movements.

This section examines the basic option hedging strategies. However, most of these strategies that involve trading strategies have already been discussed in the chapter on Trading with Options. Later, we will show how these strategies can be used by the hedgers to manage their exposure to price risk.

## 19.2    FIXED HEDGING WITH OPTIONS

The basic objective of any financial derivative is to provide means of risk reduction. The same is also true in case of option instrument. Anyone who is at risk from a price change (upward or downward) can use options to offset that risk. For instance, a call option can be used as a means of ensuring a maximum purchase price in which if the market price exceeds the strike price, the option can be exercised in order to buy at the strike price. Similarly, a put option can be used as a means of ensuring a minimum selling price where option is exercised in case the market price falls below the strike price. So it is observed that the options can be used as a means of protection against the adverse changes in the assets' prices.

A hedger needs to compare the use of options with at least two alternatives. One alternative is to leave the exposure unhedged, and second is to cover it with futures or forwards.

## 19.3    CONCEPT OF FIXED HEDGE

When the size of the position being hedged matches the amount of the underlying covered by the options (for example, 10,000 shares with 10 option contracts, each contract to 1,000 shares), the hedge is referred to as a fixed hedge. A fixed hedge with options retains an exposure and entails a cost. While protection is obtained from a stock price movement in one direction, exposure is retained to a movement in other direction. This profit potential is paid for in the form of the option premium. Therefore, it is important, before hedging with the options, to assess whether a hedge is desirable or not. Further, if so, whether options constitute the appropriate hedging instrument. Because, if there is no intention of ever selling a shareholding, then in that case, there is no need to hedge its values. In such situation, other techniques of risk hedging like diversification may be followed.

There is also a choice to be made between options and other derivatives like futures and forwards. Choice depends upon the attitude of the hedger and price movements in the underlying assets. Let us have a look on relative assessment of options and futures.

*Buying options*

- They allow profits on favourable changes in the stock prices
- No obligations on buyers
- Suitable in case of large movements in stock prices
- Entail exposure to volatility
- Payment of premiums are required

*Writing options*

- They incur losses on favourable price movements
- Suitable in case of small change in stock prices
- Entail exposure to volatility
- Receipt of premiums
- Obligation to fulfil the contracts

*Futures/Forwards*

- Outright risk are replaced by basic risk
- Obligation to fulfil the contracts
- Reduces expected portfolio returns towards short term money market rates
- No payment of premiums
- Favourable when future stock price movements are uncertain

It should be noted that buying a put option and writing a call option with the same strike price and expiry date is equivalent to selling a futures contract.

## 19.4 NAKED AND COVERED POSITION

One strategy open to the hedger is to do nothing. This involves what is known as a naked position. A naked call option is also termed as a call option that is not used for hedging an existing exposure. As an alternative to a naked position, the hedger can adopt a covered position. This involves buying the stock as soon as the option has been sold. If the option is exercised, this strategy works well. If the option is not exercised, the covered position could price to be expensive. However, neither a naked position nor a covered position provides a satisfactory hedge.

## 19.5 A STOP-LOSS STRATEGY

This is an interesting hedging strategy where the stocks are purchased and sold against writing a call or put option. For example, an institution which has written a call option with exercise price $X$ to buy one unit of a stock. The hedging strategy will involve purchasing of the stock as soon as the price rises above $X$, and will sell the stock the moment its price falls below $X$. In other words, the objective of this strategy is to hold a naked position whenever the stock price is less than $X$ and covered position if the stock price is higher than $X$. This stop-loss strategy is shown in Figure 19.1.

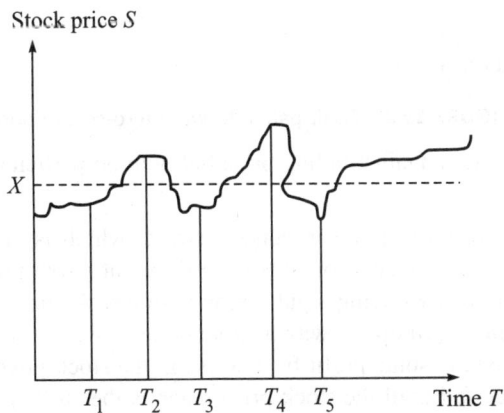

**FIGURE 19.1** A stop-loss hedging strategy.

From Figure 19.1, it is observed that the institution will buy the stock at Time $T_1$, $T_3$ and $T_5$ and will sell at time $T_2$ and $T_4$ and delivering it at time $T$. In other words, the strategy is designed to ensure that the firm owns the stock when the option is in-the-money and does not own it if the option is out-of-the-money, and hence, producing the payoffs that are the same as the payoff on the option.

This strategy has two important considerations. Firstly, the cash flows to the hedger occur at different times and must be discounted, and secondly, the purchases and sales may not be done exactly at the same price X. Besides this, every subsequent purchases and sales involve the transaction cost. So, in brief, a stop-loss strategy, although superficially attractive, but may not work particularly well as a hedging scheme.

## 19.6   ZERO-COST OPTION STRATEGY

This strategy involves when an option is purchased at a particular premium and at the same time, selling an option which gives same size to the receipt of premium. It means paying the premium on one option and receiving the premium on the other option, and thus, bearing zero cost on the options. Zero-cost options are instruments which can be broken down into constituent options—participating forwards and range forwards.

In a participating forward, all the constituent options have the same strike price. For hedging against price fall, a purchase of out-of-the-money puts could be financed by the sale of a smaller number of in-the-money calls (in other words, the stock price is greater than the strike price). In this strategy, put options will fully cover against the price fall, whereas the call option would not fully negate the benefits of a price rise. So, in this situation, net effect is that of a forward contract that allows some participation in the benefits of a price rise. This has been shown in Figure 19.2.

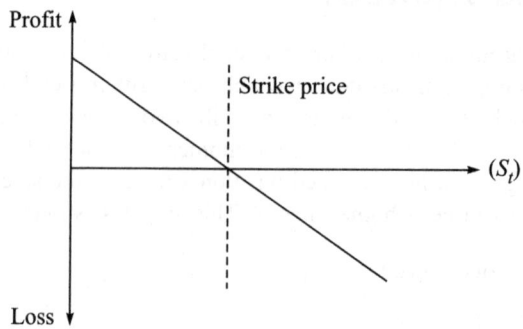

**FIGURE 19.2**   Participating forward zero-cost option.

*Note:* It provides full protection against falling price but with no participation in favourable upward price movements.

The second form of zero-cost option is range forward, which is also called *cylinder or split synthetic*. In this technique, constituents' options have different strike prices. For example, in case of falling price, hedging can be by buying a put option with a strike price below the stock price and financing the same by writing a call option with a strike price above the stock price. As a result, there will be an advantage of allowing some profit from a rise in the stock price, but at the cost of having no protection against a price fall until the stock price reach is the strike price of the put option. The position of short and long range forward are shown in Figures 19.3 and 19.4, respectively.

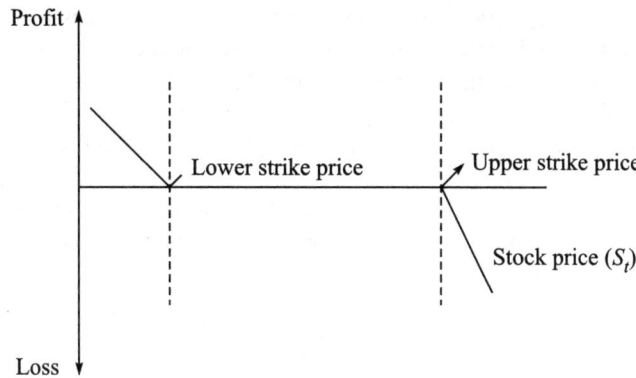

**FIGURE 19.3** Range forward zero-cost option (Cylinders).

*Note:* A long cylinder is used to hedge a short position (i.e., used to hedge against price rises). A high strike price call is bought and low strike price put is written.

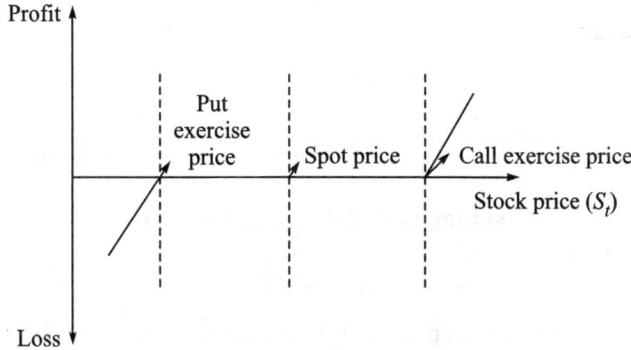

**FIGURE 19.4** Option cylinder (Range forward).

*Note:* The spot price usually lies between the two exercise prices. The cylinder allows price movements within a range between the strike prices but prevents extreme values. The call provides a maximum price and the put a minimum price. If the receipts from selling the put match the costs of buying the call, the cylinder is referred to as a zero-cost option.

## 19.7 OTHER SOPHISTICATED HEDGING STRATEGIES WITH OPTIONS

In this section, we will discuss some more advanced sophisticated hedging techniques with options which are used by the option traders. A few of them are discussed as follows:

### 19.7.1 Delta Hedging ($\Delta$) Hedge Ratio

Delta hedging is a strategy based on an option's delta. It is used to immunize portfolios from small changes in the prices of the underlying asset in the futures small interval of time. The delta of an option is the ratio of the change. If the delta is 0.50, it means that the option premium will change by 50 percent, for the change in the price of the stock. Therefore, if an option with a delta of 0.50

is used as a hedge, then two options must be held for every unit of the asset in order to equate both the option and asset portfolios. In other words, the minimum variance hedge ratio is the reciprocal of the option's delta. If delta is 0.50, then the hedge ratio will be 2. As an option's delta changes, the hedge ratio will be changed.

The delta is the slope of the curve that relates the option price to the price of the asset as shown in Figure 19.5.

Figure 19.5 shows the relationship between an option call price and the underlying asset price. When the asset price corresponds to point A, the option price corresponds to point B, and delta (Δ) is gradient indicated.

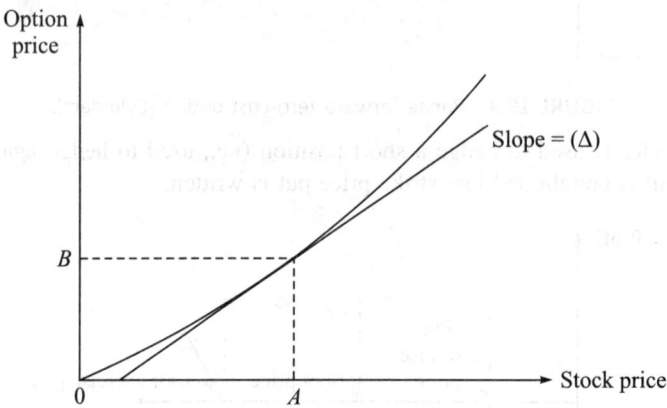

**FIGURE 19.5** Calculation of delta (Δ).

So, as an approximation

$$\Delta = \Delta C/\Delta S$$

where $\Delta$ is delta, $\Delta C$ is change in call price and $\Delta S$ is change in asset (stock) price.

**EXAMPLE (Use of delta hedging):** An investor has sold 20 option contracts, i.e., options to buy 2,000 shares. Suppose the option price is ₹10 and the stock price is ₹100 per share. Assume a call option whose delta is 0.7. The investor wishes to hedge the position.

The investor will immediately buy 0.7 × 2,000 = 1,400 shares. The gain (loss) on the option position would tend to be offset by the loss (gain) on the stock position. For example, if the stock price goes up by ₹1, then the stock will produce a gain of ₹1,400 on the shares purchased, the option price will tend to go up by 0.7 × 1 = ₹0.70, again producing a loss of ₹1,400 on the option written and vice versa.

The value of the delta is subject to change as per the market conditions. If the delta of the asset is 1.0, then the delta of the asset position offsets the delta of the option position. A position with a delta of zero is referred to as being delta neutral. Further, when the delta hedging is implemented in practice, the hedge has to be adjusted periodically. This is known *as rebalancing*. The stock price is increased at the end, then it will also lead to an increase in delta. For example, if delta rises from 0.70 to 0.80, this would mean that an extra 0.10 × 2,000 = 200 shares would have to be bought to maintain the hedge. As the time passes, the delta will change and the position in the stock will have to be adjusted. This hedging schemes which involve frequent adjustments are known as *dynamic hedging schemes*.

**Delta of European calls and puts:** In a European call option on a non-dividend paying stock, it can be shown that

$$\Delta = N(d_1) \text{ where } d_1 = \frac{\ln\left(\dfrac{S}{X}\right) + \left(\dfrac{r+\sigma^2}{2}\right)T}{\sigma\sqrt{T}}$$

Using delta hedging for a short position in a European call options, therefore, involves keeping a long position of $N(d_1)$ shares at any given time. Similarly, using delta hedging for a long position in a European call option involves maintaining a short position of $N(d_1)$ shares at any given time.

For a European put option of a non-dividend paying stock, delta is given by

$$\Delta = N(d_1) - 1$$

This is negative, which means that a long position in a put option should be hedged with a long position in the underlying stock and vice versa. In brief, put option have negative deltas because they become more valuable as the stock price falls. Deep out-of-the-money options have deltas close to zero, at-the-money options have deltas close to –0.05, and deep in-the-money options have deltas that approach-1. The variation of the delta on a call option and a put option with the stock price is shown in Figures 19.6(a) and 19.6(b). Figure 19.7 shows the variation of delta with the time to maturity for an at-the-money and out-of-the money call options.

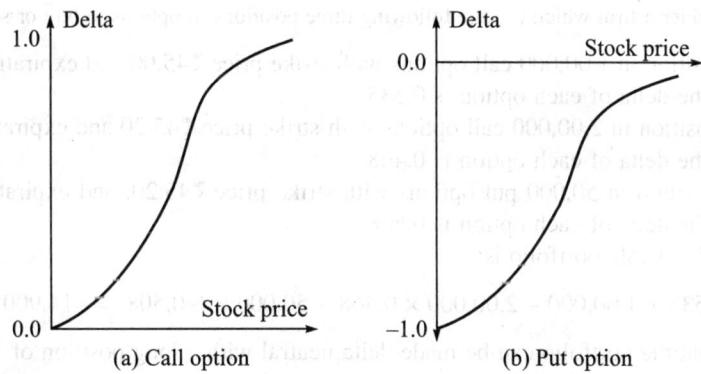

**FIGURE 19.6** Variations of delta with the stock price on a non-dividend paying stock.

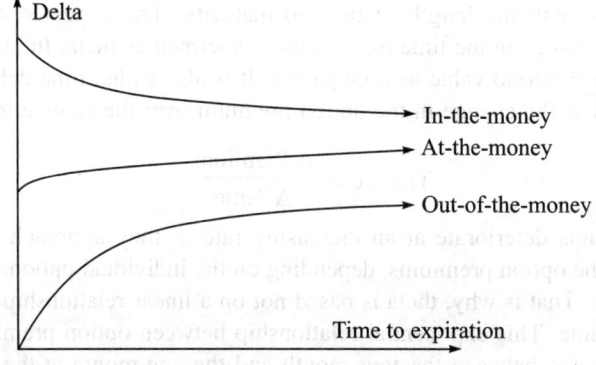

**FIGURE 19.7** Variation of delta with time to maturity for a call option.

**Other considerations in delta hedging:**    While applying the delta hedging, several other factors must be taken into consideration:

*First.*    The movement of the stock price would tend to change the value of the delta, so a delta change must be constantly monitored and the number of options increased and decreased in the light of changed circumstances.

*Second.*    Since adjusting the hedge ratio can entail substantial transaction costs in a volatile market, so it should be properly examined.

*Third.*    There are other factors which cause to change in the option's value like time remaining expiry date, expected volatility of the stock price, etc. These factors are also termed as theta, gamma, lambda, rho, etc. which should also be analysed while determining the hedge ratio.

Therefore, a delta hedging strategy is often used only for short periods of time during which changes in these factors are expected to be small.

**Delta of a portfolio:**    When a number of options on an underlying asset are held, the delta of the portfolio is then the sum of the deltas of the individual options in the portfolio. For example, if a portfolio consists of an amount $WI$ of option $i$ $(I \leq i \leq n)$, the delta of the portfolio will be

$$\Delta = \sum_{i=1}^{n} W_i \Delta_i$$

**EXAMPLE:**    Consider a firm which has the following three positions in options to buy or sell US dollar:

1. A long position in 1,00,000 call options with strike price ₹45.00 and expiration date in three months. The delta of each option is 0.533.
2. A short position in 2,00,000 call options with strike price ₹45.20 and expiration date in five months. The delta of each option is 0.468.
3. A short position in 50,000 put options with strike price ₹45.20, and expiration date in two months. The delta of each option is 0.508.

The delta of the whole portfolio is:

$$0.533 \times 1,00,000 - 2,00,000 \times 0.468 - 50,000 \times (-0.508) = -14,900$$

This means that the portfolio can be made delta neutral with a long position of 14,900 dollars.

## 19.7.2   Theta ($\theta$)

Option values increase with the length of time to maturity. The expected change in the option premium from a small change in the time to expiration is termed as theta. In other words, it is a rate of change in the option portfolio value as time passes. It is also called time delay of the portfolio.

Theta is calculated as the change in the option premium over the change in time.

$$\text{Theta } \theta = \frac{\Delta \text{ Premium}}{\Delta \text{ Time}}$$

The option premiums deteriorate at an increasing rate as they approach expiration. It is also observed that most of the option premiums, depending on the individual option, is lost in the final 30 days prior to expiration. That is why, theta is based not on a linear relationship with time, but rather on the square root of time. This exponential relationship between option premium and time is seen in the ratio of option value between the four-month and the one-month at-the-money maturities. It will be

$$\frac{\text{Premium of four months}}{\text{Premium of one month}} = \frac{\sqrt{4}}{\sqrt{1}} = \frac{2}{1} = 2 \text{ (Times)}$$

Similarly, a six-month option's premium is approximately 2.45 times more expensive than one-month. The implication of time value deterioration for dealers/traders are quite important.

*For a European call option on a non-dividend paying stock.*

$$\text{Theta } \theta = \frac{SN'(d_1)\sigma}{2\sqrt{T}} - r \times e^{-rt} N(d_2)$$

where, $d_1$ and $d_2$ have already been defined, and

$$N'(X) = \frac{I}{\sqrt{2\pi}} e^{-x^2/2}$$

*For a European put option on the stock:*

Theta $\theta$ = Theta is almost always negative for an option. Because, as the time to maturity decreases, the option value also goes down. The variation of theta with the stock price for a call option has shown in Figure 19.8. When the stock price is very low, theta is close to zero. Further, as the stock price goes higher, theta tends to larger in negative. Figure 19.9 shows the variation of $\theta$ with the time to maturity for an in-the-money, at-the-money and out-of-the-money.

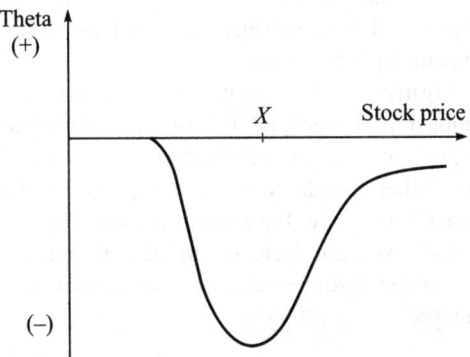

**FIGURE 19.8** Variation of theta of a European call option with the stock price.

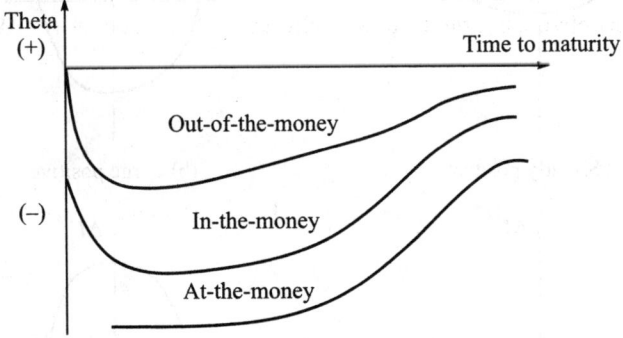

**FIGURE 19.9** Variation of theta of a European call option with time to maturity.

### 19.7.3 Gamma

The gamma $\Gamma$ of a portfolio of options on an underlying asset may be defined as the rate of change of the portfolio's delta with respect to the price of the underlying instrument. In other words, it is change in delta per unit for change in the price of the asset. If the gamma is small and not significant it means that the delta changes only very slowly then adjustments for keeping delta neutral need relatively infrequently. On the other hand, if the gamma is very high which means that delta is highly sensitive to stock price then in that case the adjustment to make delta neutral is immediate needed. Figure 19.10 explains this point.

It is evident from Figure 19.10 that when the stock price moves from $S$ to $S'$, the delta hedging assumes that the option price moves from $C$ to $C'$, whereas in fact it moves to $C''$. The difference between $C'$ and $C''$ leads to hedging error which depends upon the curvature of the relationship between option price and the stock price. Indeed gamma measures the curvature which is, also sometimes, referred to as its curvature by the experts.

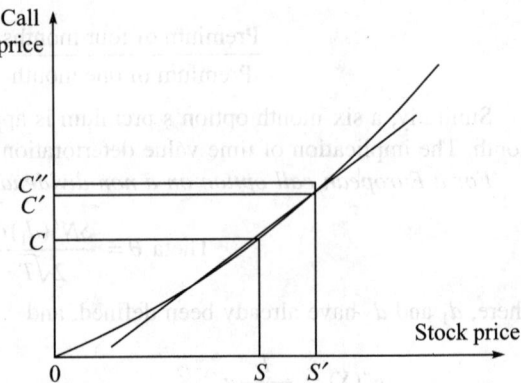

**FIGURE 19.10**    Gamma (Curvature) of the options.

Figure 19.11 shows the nature of relationship between $\Delta\Gamma$ (change in gamma) and $\Delta S$ (change in stock price). It is noted that when gamma is positive, portfolio declines in value if there is no change in stock price $S$, but increase in value if there is a large positive or negative change in stock price $S$. It is further observed that when gamma is negative, the reverse is true. The value of the portfolio increases if there is no change in the stock price but decreases in value if there is a large positive or negative change in the stock price. Thus, as the absolute value of gamma rises, the sensitivity of the value of the portfolio to stock price increases.

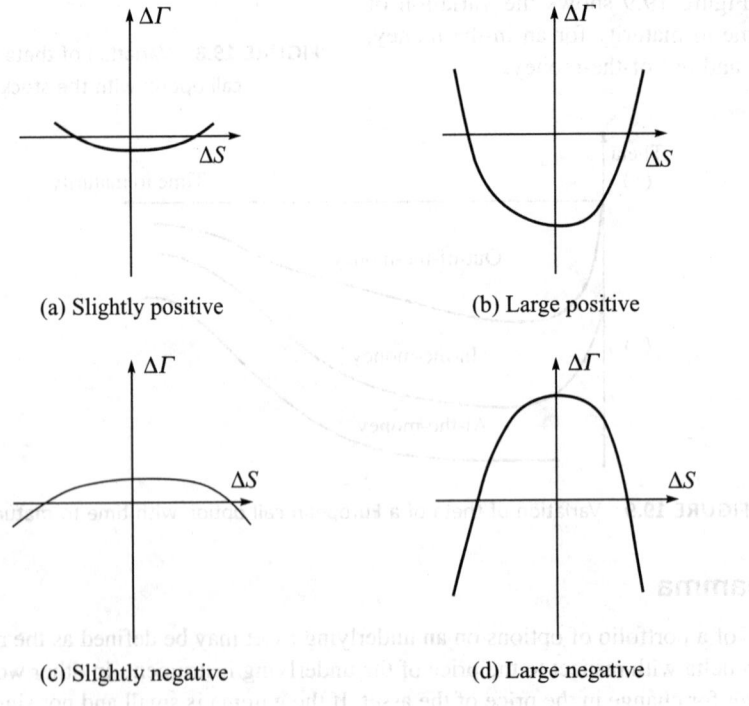

**FIGURE 19.11**    Alternative relationship between $\Delta\Gamma$ for a delta neutral.

**Calculation of gamma:** For European call option on a non-dividend paying asset, the gamma can be calculated by:

$$\Gamma = \frac{N'(d_1)}{S\sigma\sqrt{T}}$$

where $d_1$ is already defined.

This is always positive and varies with stock price $S$ in the way as shown in Figure 19.12. Further the variation of the gamma with the time to maturity has been shown in Figure 19.13.

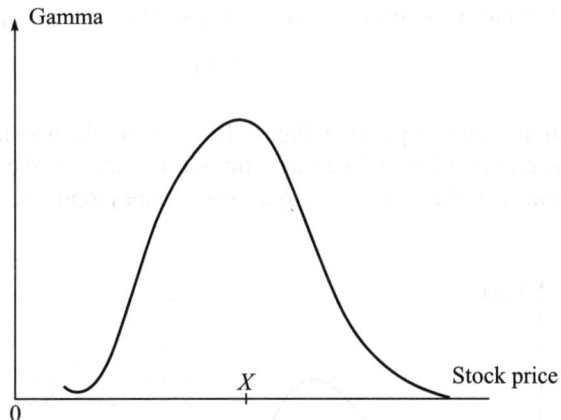

**FIGURE 19.12** Variation of gamma with stock price for an option.

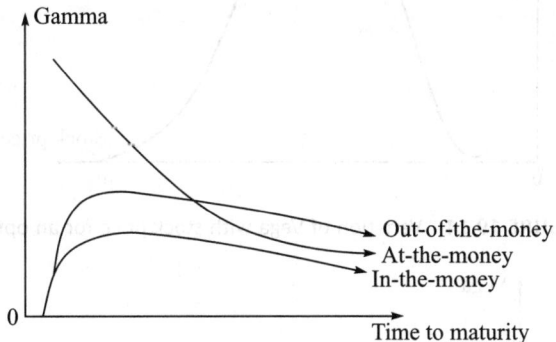

**FIGURE 19.13** Variation of gamma with time to maturity for a stock option.

Figure 19.13 exhibits that for an at-the-money option, gamma increases as the time to maturity decreases. It is further noticed that the short life at-the-money options have very high gammas which shows that the value of the option holder's position is highly sensitive to jumps in the stock price.

## 19.7.4 Vega ($\vee$)

Vega is also referred as lambda, kappa or sigma. *Vega* may be defined as the rate of change of the value of the portfolio of options with respect to change (volatility) of the underlying asset. *Volatility* is defined as the standard deviation of daily percentage changes in the underlying stock price. It is expressed in percentage per annum. In practice, volatility changes over time. This means that the value of an option is liable to change because of movements in stock prices over the passage of time. If Vega is high in absolute terms, the portfolio value is very sensitive to changes in volatility. For example, if the stock's volatility is rising, then the risk of the options being exercised is increasing, and the option premium would also be increasing.

The sensitivity of the option premium to a unit change in volatility is termed as lambda or Vega.

$$\text{Vega} = \frac{\Delta \text{Premium}}{\Delta \text{Volatility}}$$

For a European call or put on a non-dividend paying stock, Vega is expressed as:

$$v = S\sqrt{T}N'(d_1)$$

where $d_1$ is already explained.

The Vega for an option is always positive. Figure 19.14 shows the way how Vega varies with the stock price. Further, general variation of Vega with time to maturity, is the same in all the different situations like at-the-money, in-the-money and out-of-the-money options. This has been shown in Figure 19.15.

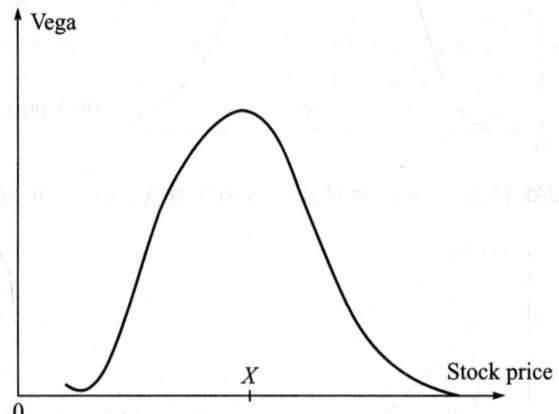

**FIGURE 19.14**    Variation of Vega with stock price for an option.

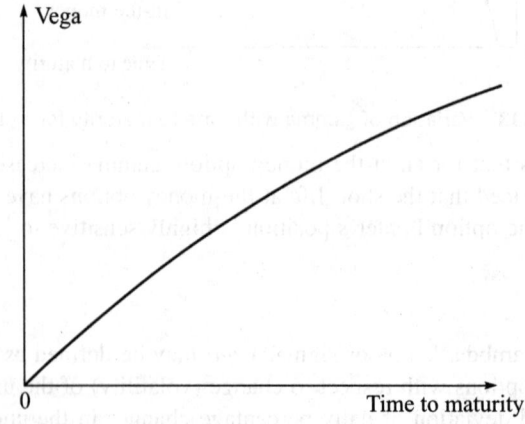

**FIGURE 19.15**    Variation of Vega with time to maturity for an option.

## 19.7.5   Rho and Phi

The Rho of a portfolio of options may be defined as the rate of change in the value of the portfolio option with respect to the interest rate. In other words, the expected change in the option premium from a small change in the domestic interest rate is called *Rho*.

$$\text{Rho} = \frac{\Delta\,\text{Premium}}{\Delta\,\text{Domestic interest rate}}$$

In case of currency options, there are two interest rates—domestic interest rate and foreign interest rate. When the change in the option value is due to change in the foreign interest rate, it is called Phi.

$$\text{Phi} = \frac{\Delta\,\text{Premium}}{\Delta\,\text{Foreign interest rate}}$$

For a European call option on non-dividend stock,

$$\text{Rho} = XTe^{-rt}N(d_2)$$

For a European put option on non-dividend stock,

$$\text{Rho} = -XTe^{-rt}N(-d_2)$$

For the option trader, an expectation on the differential between interest rate obviously help in the evaluation of where the option value is headed.

## 19.8   CONCEPT OF POSITION DERIVATIVES

The portfolio might consist of several calls and puts options on the same asset, with different strikes prices, and expiration dates and also having long and short positions in the asset itself. In other words, the portfolio of the various options has different risk and return. For example, delta of one call option may be positive, whereas another option may have negative value. Not only this, a portfolio may also contains, besides different options, even shares of the underlying stock. So, each portfolio component has its own delta, theta, gamma, etc. The delta, gamma, theta, etc. of a particular security is known as *position delta*, *position gamma*, *position theta*, respectively, and sum of these in a portfolio is called *position derivatives*.

### 19.8.1   Position Deltas ($\Delta$)

The position deltas of the portfolio ($\Delta\pi$) is calculated as a weighted sum of individual

delta i.e. $\Delta\pi$

$$\Delta\pi = \sum_{i=1}^{n} ni\Delta i$$

where ($ni$) is the number of options of one particular type, or the number of the shares of stock. The sign of $ni$ is positive if the options or stock is owned and negative if the options have been written or the stock sold short. ($\Delta i$) is the delta of the option or stock. Example: Let us explain this with an example, given as:

**TABLE 19.1**    Example of Position Deltas Options Portfolio

| Number of options shares | ni | Asset | Delta/unit (Δ) | Total Deltas ni Δi |
|---|---|---|---|---|
| Long 500 shares | +500 | Stock | 1.00 | 500.00 |
| Long 50 contracts | +50 | Puts | −0.40 | −20.00 |
| Short 200 contracts | −200 | Calls | +0.60 | −120.00 |
| Long 100 contracts | +100 | Calls | +0.30 | +30.00 |
| Short 50 contracts | −50 | Puts | +0.20 | −10.00 |
| | | | | Δπ = 380 |

The above example, the position delta of 380 is positive. It means that if the stock were to increase by one ₹ (Rupee), the value of the portfolio would rise by ₹380. If it is decreased by one rupee, then its value will decrease by ₹380. This assumes that the underlying asset of an option is one share of stock.

Position delta of portfolio is very important in option trading as knowing the profit diagrams of the portfolio. Position deltas measure the change in the value of portfolio by given a small change in the value of the underlying stock, as seen in the above example.

Delta neutrality refers to the portfolio's delta that has position of zero. It means combined delta involves net out to zero. Delta neutrality are strategies in which the traders are neutral about the future prospects for the market. Delta neutral position is a portfolio which is immune to changes in the stock prices. It is important for institutional traders who establish large positions using strangles, straddles, ratio spreads, etc. It is a strategy of pure volatility play.

Delta neutral hedging is not totally effective, because there is always a chance that the stock prices may jump unexpectedly. As a result, there is change in the value of a delta-neutral portfolio.

## 19.8.2  Position Gammas ($\Gamma$)

As observed from the above position deltas, position gamma $T_\pi$ can be defined as the weighted sum of the gammas of the components of a portfolio. It is stated as

$$\Gamma_\pi = \sum_{i=1}^{n} n_i \Gamma_i$$

where $n_i$ is the number of options of one particular asset in the portfolio? The sign of $n_i$ is positive if the option is long, and negative if the option has been written (short). $\Gamma_i$ the gamma of the **ith** option. Further, it is to be noted that the gamma of a stock is zero, because the delta of a stock is always to one gamma of a call and put usually cannot be negative, However, a portfolio can have a positive or negative gamma. The value of portfolio with a positive gamma increases if the underlying stock value changes. On the other hand, the value of the portfolio having negative gamma decreases if the value of underlying stock changes. A gamma near zero means that the option position is robust to changes in market factors.

## 19.8.3  Position Theta ($\theta$)

The position theta is the weighted average of thetas in a portfolio. If it is 50, means that if all other variables remain unchanged, the passage of one day will result in an increase of ₹50 in the value of portfolio. It is due to that decrease in value of written options will exceed the decline in time value of the puts purchased. Further, option writer wants time to pass whereas the option buyer wants the time to run slow.

### Example of Position Derivatives

**EXAMPLE:** Let us explain the position derivatives with a hypothetical example. Assume that a portfolio consists of 10,000 shares of stock, 200 calls options written and 100 puts. Their respective deltas, gamma and theta are shown as follows:

**TABLE 19.2** Position Derivatives

| Asset | Number | Delta-$\Delta$ | Gamma-$\Gamma$ | Theta-$\theta$ | Position Delta | Position Gamma | Position Theta |
|-------|--------|---------|---------|--------|----------|----------|----------|
| Stocks | 10,000 | 1.00 | 0.00 | 0.00 | +10,000 | 0.00 | 0.00 |
| Calls(Short) | 200 | .20 | 0.030 | –0.008 | –4,000 | –.600 | +.160 |
| Puts(Long) | 100 | –.10 | 0.015 | –0.004 | –1,000 | +150 | –.40 |
| | | | | | +5,000 | –450 | +120 |

From the above, it is observed that delta of 5,000 suggests that the portfolio in total is equivalent to the market risk to 5,000 shares of stock, or 50 percent of the risk with unopened portfolio. Further, the position theta of 120 means that the passage of one day will increase to +120 in the value of the portfolio. The meaning of a position gamma of –450 is less obvious. It is important to note that position derivatives change continuously in the market. A bullish portfolio can suddenly become bearish if stock prices change adequately. So, there is a regular need of monitoring the portfolio.

It is important to note that a delta-neutral, hedger would like to have a portfolio with a low but positive gamma. The gamma measures the delta which changes on per changes in $S$, $T$, 6, $r$, etc. It means the delta-neutral portfolio may not remain constant in future. A low position gamma will conserve on the transaction costs of readjusting the portfolio delta back to zero if the stock prices changes. Further, a positive gamma will compensate the investor for bearing the risk of fluctuating delta. Such a portfolio is termed as a *delta-gamma neutral portfolio* and the process is known as *delta-gamma hedging*.

**Dynamic hedging:** Dynamic hedging simply states that the portfolio position risk has to be continuously monitored since it changes due to changes in various factors of the market volatility, whether it is change of interest rate, stock prices, volatility expectation change, or portfolio components. Dynamic hedging is a portfolio insurance technique which requires frequent revision of a hedge using stock index futures and options. With a passage of time, the position delta changes and a new position delta exists. Sometimes, overnight has become substantially less bullish because of the changing delta. Therefore, the portfolios need periodic tune-ups. If the portfolio manager wants to maintain the original delta exposure, then, of course, it requires to replace the components of the portfolio like calls, puts, etc.

**EXAMPLE:** Suppose on November 1, 2015, a portfolio consists of 10,000 shares of a company, selling for ₹60 each. Interest rate is 5 percent p.a., volatility is 0.20 and a ₹50 put expires after 90 days. This put has a delta of –0.150. Further, assume that the investor combines 100 of these put contracts with the stock to provide some protection against the decline in the above said stock price.

After the purchase of these put contracts, the position delta of the portfolio will be: $(10,000 \times 1.0) + (10,000 \times -0.150) = 8,500$

Further, assume that on November 2, 2015. The stock price falls to ₹58. The new delta for the put is now –0.220. So, the position of the delta has changed to now:

$$(10,000 \times 1.0) + (10,000 \times -0.220) = 7,800$$

The above decline in stock, the portfolio has become substantially less bullish due to change of delta of the put. To maintain, the investor original delta exposure of about 8,500, for this, the investor would reduce the negative deltas from the portfolio.

For this, some put contracts are to be sold. It will be calculated $(8,500 – 7,800)/0.220 = 3.182$, i.e., selling about –32 put contracts. These put contracts would maintain the original market exposure.

Similarly, another important aspect of dynamic hedging is to minimize the cost of the portfolio through the delta adjustments. As we know that writing options generates income, but involves potentially large losses if prices move adversely. Buying options needs a cash outlay, which involves cost but also results in known maximum loss. It is possible to adjust a portfolio's delta to minimize the cash requirement by using both options, i.e., calls and puts options. Let us explain this by an example as follows:

**EXAMPLE:**   Consider that in October, 2015, a portfolio consists of 10,000 shares of a stock, at a market price of ₹35, risk-free interest rate 5 percent, implied volatility 0.30, premium of December 2015 call at stock price of ₹38 is ₹1.20, delta of December 2015 : 0.380, premium of December 2015 put at strike price of ₹32, ₹0.50 and its delta –0.200. The investor wants to reduce its position delta of 5,000 by reducing its market exposure by 50 percent.

Let us assume C = number of call and P = number of puts.
**Given: Equation I:** Stock delta – Calls delta + Put delta = 5,000

$$10,000 – (0.380)C + (–0.200)P = 5,000$$

**Equation II** Price of puts-Income from calls = 0

$$₹0.50 \times P – 1.20 \times C = 0$$

Solve for 'P' in terms of 'C' as given in Equation II

$$0.50P – 1.20C = 0$$

$$= P = 1.20C/.50$$
$$= P = 2.40C$$

Substitute this in Equation I

**Equation I as given above is:**

| | |
|---|---|
| = 10,000 – (0.380)C + (–0.200P) | = 5,000 |
| = 5,000 – 0.380C + (–0.200) × 2.400C | = 0 |
| = 5,000 – 0.380C – 0.480C | = 0 |
| = 5,000 – 0.860C | = 0 |
| = 0.860C | = 5,000 |
| = C = 5,000/0.860 = 5,813 | = 58 calls contracts of 100 shares. |
| = P = 2.40(5,813) = 13,951 | = 140 put contracts on 100 shares. |

**Round to whole contracts:**

| | |
|---|---|
| P | = 140 contracts. |
| C | = 58 contracts. |

From the above, we can calculate now position delta and position cost.

**Position delta:** Stock delta – Call delta + Put delta
= (10,000 × 1) – (58 × .380)100 + (140 × –0.200)100
= 10,000 – 2,204 + (–2,800)
= 10,000 – 5,004 = 4,996 App 5,000

**Cost of position:**

Cost of puts = 140 contracts × 0.50 = 70 × 100 = –7,000
Income from calls = 58 contracts × 1.20 = 69.6 × 100 = +6,960
Net cost = 7,000 – 6,960 = 40.

## 19.9  POSITION RISK

Position risk is an important phenomenon, however, often overlooked. It is concerned with the riskiness of portfolio management with options. It is defined as the possible loss associated with extreme market conditions. In other words, it is a measure of the consequences of a "dooms day" move, where the market advances or declines sharply. The role of options in managing the position risk is discussed here in context to delta. Delta is a first derivative which became less useful as the magnitude of the change in option variables increases.

Let us explain the position risk when the market moves in extreme situations, i.e., advances and declines. Consider if the market advances very sharply. In such situation, all the put contracts will go to zero because the stock price increases above the strike prices of the puts. All the call options will be exercised. On the other hand, if the market crashes sharply, the all free call option contracts will go to zero, being strike price of the calls higher than the market price of the stock. This relationship of position risk is shown in Figure 19.16.

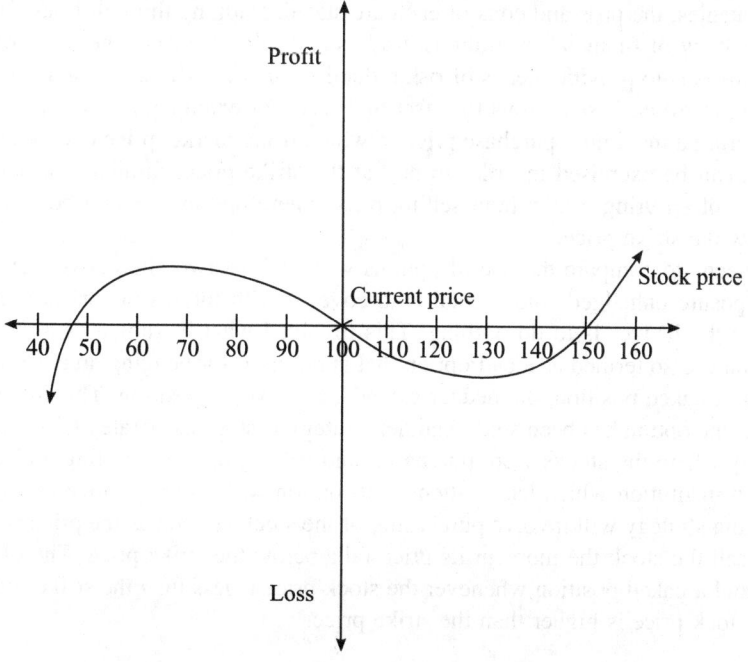

**FIGURE 19.16**  Position risk.

Assuming that all the options are priced exactly in the market, the initial situation has zero profit at market stock price at ₹100. If the market price decline too much, the position delta being negative which means that profits accrue on falling of prices. If the price decreases below 100, then the curve will move in profit zone. If the price further crashes, then the curve will turn down, indicating that large losses are possible. Similarly, on the upper side, if the price rises up to modest amount, the losses will occur. However, if it runs up sharply, then the position delta turns up positive and profits accrue to the position. In brief, it is observed from the position risk that option derivatives are not particularly useful for major movements (up and down) in the price of the underlying asset.

## 19.10   HEDGING OPTION PORTFOLIO IN PRACTICE

We have observed various factors like delta, theta, gamma, Vega, rho, etc. which are considered by the option dealers continually to rebalance their portfolios to maintain a risk neutral portfolio. But one of the important constraint in such rebalancing strategy is the transaction cost which makes it more expensive. Therefore, in this process, an option dealer instead of eliminating all such risks, he usually concentrates on assessing risks and decides whether they are acceptable or not.

The basic purpose of analysing the delta, gamma, theta, Vega, etc. to quantify the different aspects of the risks inherent in the option portfolio so that appropriate different possible futures position may be taken. If the downside risk is acceptable then no adjustment is made in the portfolio, otherwise appropriate adjustment is made in the option portfolio.

## SUMMARY

This chapter has examined the fundamental option hedging strategies used by hedges. In discussing the hedging strategies, the pros and cons of each are stated. Hedging through financial derivatives is an important strategy of financial institutions, traders and other leaders. The basic objective of any financial derivatives is to provide means of risk reduction, anyone who is at risk from a price change (upward or downward) can use options to offset that risk. For example, a call option can be used as a means of ensuring a maximum purchase price in which if the market price exceeds the strike price, then the option can be exercised in order to buy at the strike price. Similarly, a put option can be used as a means of ensuring a minimum selling price where option is exercised in case the market price falls below the strike price.

A hedger needs to compare the use of options with at least two alternatives. One alternative is to leave the exposure unhedged, and second is to cover it with futures or forwards or options. One strategy open to the hedger is to do nothing. This involved what is known as a naked position. A naked call option is also termed as a call option that is not used for hedging an existing exposure. As an alternative to a naked position, the hedger can adopt a covered position. This involves buying the stock as soon as the option has been sold. Another strategy is stop-loss strategy. This is an interesting hedging strategy where the stocks were purchased and sold against the writing a call or put option. For example, an institution which has written a call option with exercise price to buy one unit of a stock, the hedging strategy will involve purchasing of the stock as soon as the price rises above strike price and will sell the stock the moment its price falls below the strike price. The objectives of this strategy is to hold a naked position whenever the stock price is less than the strike price and covered position if the stock price is higher than the strike price.

The chapter further discusses the zero-cost option. This strategy involves when an option is purchased at a particular premium, and at the same time, selling the option which gives same size of the receipt of premium. It means paying the premium on one option and receiving the premium on the other option, and thus, bearing zero cost on the options. It can be further broken into two constituent options—participating forwards and range forwards. Other sophisticated hedging strategies with option is delta hedging—a strategy based on an option's delta. It is used to immunize portfolio from small changes in the price of underlying asset in the small interval of time in future. The delta of an option is the ratio of the change. If the delta is 0.50, it means that the option's premium will change by 50 percent, for the change in the price of the stock. The delta is the slope of the curve that relates the option price to the asset. While applying the delta hedging several factors must be taken into consideration. First, the movement of the stock price would tend to change the value of the delta, so a delta change must be constantly monitored and number of options increased and decreased in the light of changed circumstances. Second, since adjusting the hedge ratio can entail substantial transaction costs in a volatile market, so it should be properly examined.

Options values increase with the length of time to maturity. The expected change in the option premium from a small change in the time to expiration is termed as theta. In other words, it is a rate of change in the option portfolio value as time passes. It is also called time delay of the portfolio. Gamma of a portfolio of options on an underlying asset may be defined as the rate of change of the portfolio's delta with respect to the price of the underlying instrument. In other words, it is change in delta per unit change in price of the asset. If the gamma is small and not significant, it means that the delta changes only very slowly, then adjustments for keeping delta neutral need relatively in frequently.

Vega may be defined as the rate of change of the value of the portfolio of options with respect to the change (volatility) of the underlying asset. It is also referred as lambda, kappa or sigma. Volatility is stated in percentage per annum. The Rho and Phi of a portfolio of options may be defined as the rate of change in the value of option with respect to the interest rate. In other words, the expected change in the option-premium form a small change in the domestic interest rate is called Rho. When the change in the option value is due to change in the foreign interest rate, it is called Phi. The basic purpose of analysing the delta, gamma, theta, Vega, etc. to quantify the different aspects of risks inherent in the option portfolio so that appropriate possible future position may be taken. In the last, the concept of position derivatives is explained which is related with position delta, position gamma, position theta, etc. After that the position risk is defined at the possible loss associated with extreme market conditions. It is a measure of the consequences of a 'dooms day' move, where the market advances or declines sharply.

## SOLVED PROBLEMS

**P.1.** Calculate the delta of an at-the-money six-month European call option for a non-dividend paying stock when the risk-free interest rate is 10% per annum and the stock price volatility is 25% per annum.

*Solution:* In this problem, following information are available:

| | | |
|---|---|---|
| Stock price | $S = X$ | |
| Risk-free return | $R = 0.1$ | |
| Standard deviation | $\sigma = 0.25$ | |

Time to maturity     $T = 0.5$

So     $d_1 = \dfrac{\ln(S/X) + [(0.1 + 0.25^2)/2]\,0.5}{0.25\sqrt{0.5}} = 0.3172$

∴     $N(d_1) = 0.64$

**P.2.**  Calculate the delta of an at-the-money six-month option on a non-dividend paying stock when the risk-free interest rate is 5% per annum and stock price volatility is 12.5% per annum.

*Solution:*  Here, in this problem the following information are given:

Stock price          $S = X$

Risk-free return     $R = 0.05$

Standard deviation   $\sigma = 0.125$

Time to maturity     $T = 0.5$

So     $d_1 = \dfrac{\ln(S/X) + [(0.05 + 0.125^2)/2]\,0.5}{0.125\sqrt{0.5}} = 0.1856$

∴     $N(d_1) = 0.6103$

**P.3.**  An investor has sold 20 option contracts (2000 options) on Infosys shares. The option price is 500, the stock price is 5,000 and option delta is 0.6. If the delta has changed from 0.6 to 0.65, the investor wishes to hedge the position. Show how an investor can hedge his position.

*Solution:*  The investor will immediately buy $0.6 \times 2,000 = 1,200$ shares. Over the next short period of time, the call price will tend to change by 60% of the stock price and the gains (loss) on call option will be offset by the loss (gain) on call stock. As time passes, delta will change and the position in the stock will have to be adjusted. For example, if delta increases to 0.65, a further $0.05 \times 2,000 = 100$ shares will have to be bought.

**P.4.**  Suppose it is April 16. The $/£ spot rate is $1.6080/£. On Philadelphia Stock Exchange, sterling currency May expiry option prices (in cent per pound) are as follows:

| Strike price | Calls | Puts |
|---|---|---|
| 1.55 | 6.28 | 0.65 |
| 0.60 | 2.99 | 2.22 |
| 1.65 | 1.03 | 5.23 |

A UK exporter is due to receive US dollar in early May and intends to convert them to sterling. The exporter would lose from a rise in the price of sterling and loss short position in pound. How exporter can hedge this risk by using option?

*Solution:*  Exporter could hedge by buying call option or writing a put option. Buying a call will be suitable if a large rise is expected, and a put might be written if it was thought that any rise would be modest.

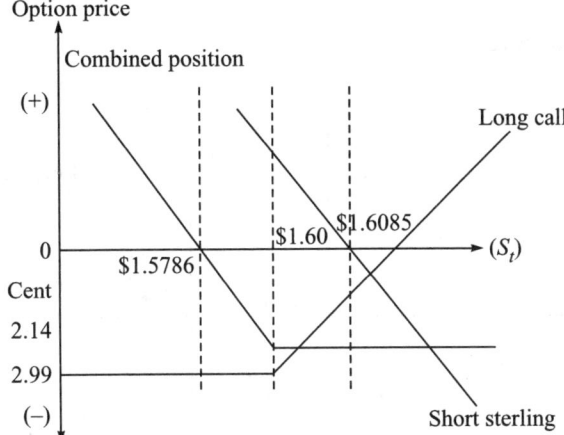

Hedging a short sterling position buying $1.60 call option.

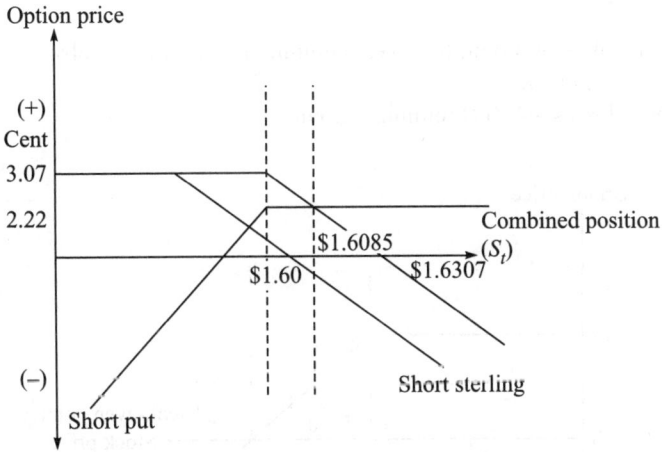

**P.5.** The XYZ option prices are as follows:

| Strike price | Calls | | | Puts | | |
|---|---|---|---|---|---|---|
| | **Oct.** | **Jan.** | **April** | **Oct.** | **Jan.** | **April** |
| 220 | 19 | 30 | 39 | 1.5 | 7 | 12 |
| 240 | 5 | 17 | 27 | 9 | 14 | 22 |
| 260 | 1 | 11 | 18 | 25 | 28 | 32 |

The stock price is ₹236.

1. Draw profit/loss profile for a buyer of January ₹220 call option. What is the break-even price at expiry? Indicate the maximum profit and loss.
2. Draw the profit/loss profile for the writer of an April ₹260 option. What is break-even price at expiry? Indicate the maximum profit and maximum loss.

*Solution:* **(1)**

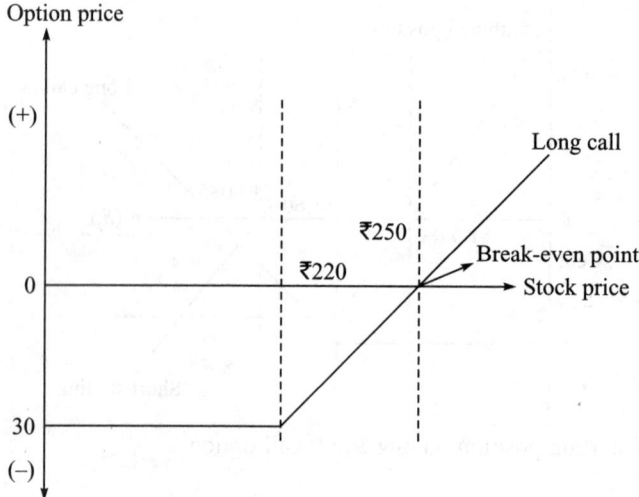

(a) ₹250 is break-even point, to cover premium amount of ₹30 also
(b) No maximum profit
(c) Maximum losses—₹30 (Premium amount)

**(2)**

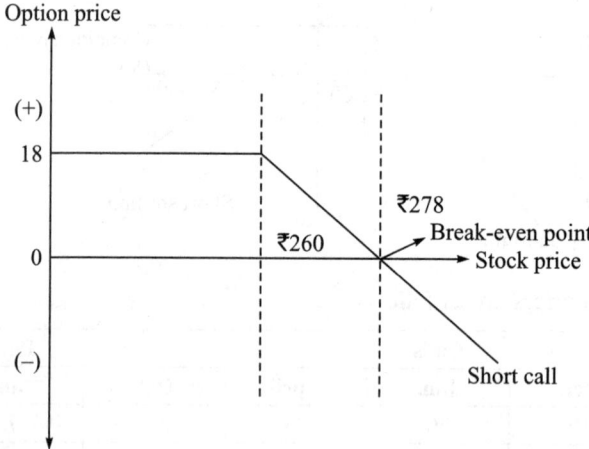

(a) Break-even point = ₹278
(b) Maximum profit = ₹18
(c) No maximum loss

## SUGGESTED READINGS

1. Brain, Eales A., *Financial Risk Management*, McGraw-Hill, Maiden Head, 1995.
2. Winstone, David, *Financial Derivatives*, Chapman and Hall, London, 1995.

3. Lars Tyge, Nielsen, *Pricing and Hedging of Derivatives Securities*, Oxford University Press, 1997.
4. Yates, J., *The Options Strategy Spectrum*, Homewood, IL, Dow Jones Irwin, 1987.
5. Powers, Mark and Voges, David, *Inside the Financial Futures Market*, John Wiley and Sons, 1981.
6. Lyon, Allan, *Winning in the Options Market*, Chicago Probus Publishing Company, 1994.
7. Fontanills, George A., *The Option Course: High Profit and Low Stress Trading Methods*, John Wiley and Sons, New York, 1998.

# REVIEW QUESTIONS

1. Define the term hedging with option. Discuss with suitable examples.
2. Explain the concept of fixed hedging, its mechanism and limitations with suitable examples.
3. Compare and contrast the hedging with options and futures financial derivatives.
4. Compare the implication of writing the options and buying the options with suitable examples.
5. Write a detailed note on a stop-loss strategy in options with hypothetical case?
6. What is zero-cost options? Discuss the types of zero-cost options.
7. Write short notes on (in context to option hedging)
   (a) Range forwards with their payoff profile
   (b) Participating forwards with payoff profile
8. What is delta hedging? How is it used to hedge the risk of a portfolio? Also discuss the variations of delta hedging with suitable examples.
9. Write short notes on
   (a) Delta of an option portfolio
   (b) Other considerations in delta hedging
   (c) Variations of delta with time-to-maturity for a call option
10. Define theta? How it is calculated? Discuss the variations of theta of a European call option with the stock price and time-to-maturity.
11. Write a detailed note on gamma with suitable illustrations in context to hedging with options.
12. Write notes on the following in context to the option hedging:
    (a) Calculation of gamma and variation of gamma
    (b) Vega and variation of Vega with stock price of an option
    (c) Rho and Phi with illustrations
13. Critically evaluate the hedging options portfolio in practice with latest developments in Indian derivatives market.
14. "The ultimate economic functions of financial derivatives is to provide means of risk reduction." Comment upon the statement with comparison of hedging with options with other financial derivatives instruments.
15. Write notes on
    (a) Hedging against a stock price increase with options with examples
    (b) Hedging against a stock price increase/decrease with options with examples
16. If a company is holding an inventory of oil believes that oil prices may fall significantly in the near future, what option hedging strategy would you recommend? Explain your answer with relevant data.

17. If zero-cost-option exists, why should hedgers ever pay for options? Critically examine the statement in the light of zero-cost option with examples.

18. While considering hedging strategies, what are the relative merits of long option positions, short option positions and delta hedging? Explain your answer with suitable illustrations.

19. How a stop-loss hedging scheme can be implemented for the writer of an out-of-the-money call option? Why does it provide a relative poor hedge?

20. "The procedure for creating an option position synthetically is the reverse of procedure for hedging the option position." Explain the statement in the light of concept of synthetic option.

21. A company uses delta hedging to hedge a portfolio of long position in put and call options on a currency. Which of the following would give the most favourable results?
    (a) A virtually constant spot rate
    (b) Wild movements in the spot rate
    Explain you answer.

22. Explain the term of position derivatives. Explain this with suitable example.

23. Write a note on position risk with suitable data and diagram.

# Chapter 20

# Currency Options

*After reading this chapter, students will be able to*

➤ Understand the concept of currency option market.
➤ Know basics of currency options like concept of foreign currency options, types of options, buyer of options, etc.
➤ Be aware of the foreign currency option contracts at over-the-counter and at recognized exchanges.
➤ Understand the currency option quotation and prices and important observations about the price quotations of currency option.
➤ Know the strategies for using options for both buyers and writers.
➤ Be aware of the spread strategies which include bull call spread and bear call spread in currency options.
➤ Know the straddle and strangle strategies in currency options.
➤ Explain the option valuation and components of option valuations like time value and intrinsic value.
➤ Be aware of the various determinants of the currency option value like change in forward rates, change in spot rate, time-to-maturity, impact of changing volatility, alternative option strike price, etc.

## 20.1 INTRODUCTION

Foreign currency options are such financial instruments which have assumed a vital importance in the financial markets all over the world. These are being widely used by the different market participants like importers, exporters, traders, arbitrageurs, speculators, bankers and financial institutions. They protect the holders against the risk of adverse movements in the exchange rates. That is why some commercial banks offer to use currency options to their customers.

The basics of option markets have already been discussed in Chapter 14, which are also applicable in the same manner in currency options markets except that here the underlying assets will be foreign currencies. So, in this section, first we will discuss basic description of currency options and after that important strategies in this respect.

## 20.2   BASICS OF CURRENCY OPTIONS

Before we proceed to describe the functioning of the options and their applications, let us review the basics of options market terminology which are frequently used in this market.

1. Foreign currency option or simply currency option is a financial instrument that gives the option holder a right and not the obligation, to buy or sell a given amount of foreign exchange at a fixed price per unit for a specified time period (until the expiration date). In other words, a foreign currency option is a contract for future delivery of a specific currency in exchange for another in which the holder (buyer) of the option has the right to buy (Call) or sell (Put) a particular currency at an agreed price (the strike or exercise price) for or within specified period. The seller of the option (writer) gets the premium from the buyer of the option for the obligation undertaken in the contract.

2. There are two basic types of options—call option and put option. A call is an option to buy foreign currency and a put is an option to sell the foreign currency.

3. The buyer of an option is termed as *holder*, whereas the seller of an option is called the *writer* or *grantor*. In other words, there are two parties in an option contract buyer and seller. If one party is buyer in a particular currency, the other party will be automatically a seller in that particular currency. It should be further noted that a rupee call option which gives the holder the right to buy rupees against dollar is also a dollar put option, giving the holder the right to sell dollar against rupee.

4. Every currency option contract has three different price elements: (a) the exercise or strike price (rate) at which the foreign currency can be purchased or sold, (b) the premium, which is the cost or price or value of the option itself and (c) the underlying or actual spot exchange rate in the currency market exists on the exercise day.

5. The option contracts can also be classified as American options and European options. In American option, the buyer has the right to exercise the option at any time between the writing date and expiration date, whereas in European option, option can be exercised only at the expiration date, and not before this date. American options are most common but European options are popular in Switzerland and Germany.

6. The fee that the option buyer must pay to the option writer, 'up-front', i.e., at the time the contract is initiated. Thus, it is also called *the option premium*, option price or cost of the option. This is paid in advance and lapses whether the option is exercised or not. Hence, it is price or cost to the option holder for the right conferred, and benefit or premium to the writer of the option contract. Normally, the premiums are quoted as a percentage of the transaction amount in the over-the-counter market (OTC) whereas it is quoted as a domestic currency amount per unit of foreign currency in the exchange traded options.

7. An option is said to be at ITM, OTM and ATM. A currency option whose exercise price is same as the spot price of the underlying currency is said to be at-the-money (ATM). An option that would be profitable if exercised immediately is said to be in-the-money (ITM), and an option which would not be profitable if exercised immediately is referred to as out-of-the-money (OTM).

8. Many market participants describe the above concepts (i.e., ITM, OTM and ATM) with reference to the relevant outright forward rate (Futures rate). A three-month call (put) option on USD against French Franc (FFR) is said to be at-the-money if the strike price equals the three-month FFR/USD forward rate, in-the-money if the strike price is less (or greater) than the forward rate, and out-of-the-money if the strike price is greater (less) than the forward rate. As such the intrinsic value of the option is then defined as the present value of the difference between the forward rate and the strike price.

## 20.3  FOREIGN CURRENCY OPTIONS MARKETS

In the last decade the foreign currency options have been frequently used as a hedging tool and for speculative trading purposes, specifically in the developed countries like USA, UK, Japan, Germany, etc. A number of the commercial banks in the United States (USA) and other capital markets offer flexible foreign currency options on transactions of one million US dollar or more. The bank market or over-the-counter market (OTC), as it is called, offers customer-tailored options on all major trading currencies for any time period up to one year, hence, provide a useful tool or alternative to futures or forward contracts. Options are traded on over-the-counter (OTC) markets as well as on organized markets. The foreign exchange options market, thus, can be divided into two categories-the OTC market and exchange traded market.

### 20.3.1  Over-the-counter Options Market (OTC)

Multinational companies and large commercial international banks have recognized the flexibility of options for many years. In the past, international banks have tailored foreign currencies options for their customers as per their needs. The OTC market today is open only to large firms since it involves amounts in millions of dollars. Options are most frequently written for US dollars against Pound sterling, Deutsche Marks, Swiss francs, Japanese yen, Canadian dollar, Euro, etc.

Average maturity of OTC options ranges from two to six months and very few options are written for more than one year. This market can further be subdivided into two categories—retail market and wholesale market. The retail market is usually concerned with when the clients purchase options from the banks to cover against their exchange risks. The clients in this market are generally traders, financial institutions, portfolio managers, etc. The wholesale market consists of large commercial banks, investment banks and other financial institutions which operate in this market to cover the positions for their clients or for speculative and arbitrage purposes. Branches of foreign banks in the major financial centres are generally willing to write options against the currency of their home country. For example, US Banks in London write options in the US dollars.

The transactions in the OTC option markets are carried out either directly between the counter-parties or through the brokers. These operations are transacted on telephone or by the system of Reuter or Telex and may take place round the clock. Since this market is of customized nature, so the terms and conditions of the contract are negotiated between the holder and the writer of the option. The main advantage of the OTC market is that the clients can make the contracts as per even their specific needs concerning to the period, price and amount. Though this market has grown up in multiples recently, however, it suffers from several limitations, which are as under:

- This market is relatively illiquid because of its tailor-made nature. The contracts are not standardized, due to that there is lack of secondary market operators in this segment.
- The option buyers always face the risk of non-performance by the writers (also termed as counterparty risk). Therefore, the option buyer has to assess thoroughly about the creditworthiness of the writer.
- The small number of writers and buyers for any specific tailor-made arrangement may cause the options to be mispriced due to absence of a competitive market.
- Since the market is of customized nature, so the amount of underlying currency, exercise prices expiration dates and premiums vary widely from contract to contract.

Apart from the above limitations, this market has grown up to such proportions that liquidity is now considered quite favourable. Normally, on the OTC market an option can be resold only to the bank from which it was purchased. In India, the Reserve Bank of India has permitted the banks to write cross-currency options, i.e., options between two foreign currencies since January 1994. Option contracts in Indian Rupee will have to wait for until its full convertibility into capital account.

## 20.3.2 Exchange-traded Currency Options

Apart from the above stated options at the OTC markets, they are also traded today on a number of organized exchanges worldwide. The first such trading was commenced in 1982 by the Philadelphia Stock Exchange (PHLX). Since then the size of this market has grown up very rapidly, and major currencies traded are the Australian dollar, British pound, Canadian dollar, German mark, Japanese yen, French franc, Swiss franc, US dollar, etc. A specification of currency option at Philadelphia Stock Exchange is shown in Table 20.1.

**TABLE 20.1**  Standard Size of Option Contracts on Organized Markets

| **Philadelphia Board of Trade** | |
|---|---|
| 1. Pound sterling | £31,250 |
| 2. Deutsche mark | DM62,500 |
| 3. Swiss franc | SFr62,500 |
| 4. Yen | ¥62,50,000 |
| 5. Canadian dollar | Can $50,000 |
| 6. French franc | FFr250,000 |
| 7. Australian dollar | Aus $50,000 |
| 8. Ecu | Ecu 62,500 |
| **European Options Exchange Amsterdam** | |
| 1. Dutch guilder | DG10,000 |
| 2. Pound sterling | £10,000 |
| **London Market** | |
| 1. Pound sterling | £12,500 |
| 2. Deutsche mark | DM 50,000 |

*(Contd.)*

*(Contd.)*

| | |
|---|---|
| **MATIF of Paris** | |
| 1. US dollar/Mark | US $1,00,000 |
| 2. US dollar/French franc | US $1,00,000 |
| **Chicago Mercantile Exchange** | |
| 1. Australian dollars | Aus $1,00,000 |
| 2. Canadian dollars | Can $1,00,000 |
| 3. Pound sterling | £25,000 |
| 4. Deutsche mark | DM1,25,000 |
| 5. French franc | FFr5,00,000 |
| 6. Swiss franc | SFr1,25,000 |
| 7. Yen | ¥1,25,00,000 |
| **Singapore International Monetary Exchange** | |
| 1. Canadian dollar | Can $50,000 |
| 2. Deutsche mark | DM1,25,000 |
| 3. Yen | ¥1,25,00,000 |

Earlier the currency options were on spot delivery, which required the delivery of the underlying currency contract. However, later on, options on foreign exchange futures at Chicago International Monetary Market, and how most actively traded. In June 1987, a new type of currency option, the Currency Exchange Warrants (CEW) were introduced on the American Stock Exchange (AMEX) with a long maturity exceeding one year. In February 1988, all the twelve CEWs traded in AMEX had foreign currency put options (or alternatively, US dollar call options) with five years to expiration.

The CEW holder has the right to sell a specified amount of foreign currency for US dollar at a predetermined exercise price during a specified period. Unlike the currency option, there is a cash settlement of difference between the issuer and the holder when the warrant is exercised. These puts CEWs are typically issued along with (in conjunction) with a particular note or bond offering so that the total costs of financing be lowered. To hedge the exposed option position, the issuer buys foreign currency put options on the OTC market. Since the option premium in the OTC market is substantially lower than the price of CEW, the issuers can lock in an arbitrage profit, and in this way, reducing their effective borrowing costs.

The Philadelphia Stock Exchange has recently introduced some new features in its option instruments like United Currency Options Market (UCOM). Accordingly, it made options much more flexible and more competitive. For example, some features like cross-rate pairs (non-US dollars), European or American style pricing, settlement via offshore bank arrangements, customized currency options, premium quotation, etc. Further since September 1994 new type of options, called virtual options, have been introduced at this exchange. These virtual options normally have a very short life of one or two weeks. These options are settled by paying of the amount equal to the difference between the established in fixing of the day and the exercise price of the option, and hence, no actual delivery of currencies are taken place.

Exchange-traded options are settled through a clearing house, hence, the buyers do not deal directly with the seller rather through an agency. The clearing house is the counterparty to every option contract and it guarantees the fulfilment of the contracts. For example, in the case of the Philadelphia

Stock Exchange, clearing house services are rendered by the Options Clearing Corporation (OCC). Thus, the option holder is relieved from the onerous task of evaluating the writer's creditworthiness, and what really matters are the resources of the clearing agency. The resources of the clearing agency relate with the margin requirements of the option contracts, which are deposited by the option writers with the clearing house. When a position is opened, the deposit is usually the initial margin plus some amount.

| National Stock Exchange of India (NSE) | |
|---|---|
| 1. USDINR | USD–1000 |
| 2. GBPINR | GBP–1000 |
| 3. EURINR | EUR–1000 |
| 4. JPYINR | JPY– |

## 20.4  CURRENCY OPTION QUOTATIONS AND PRICES

The currency options traded on the organized exchanges are of standardized nature. Call and put options are shown separately. They have standard quantity (size) of different currencies to be traded at the particular exchange. A list of such standard size contracts is shown in Table 20.2, which indicates the size of contracts of different exchanges. On organized exchanges, quotations are given for several exercise prices and several dates of maturity.

To understand the mechanism of option trading at the organized exchange, let us consider a typical quotation given in the Wall Street Journal for options on Swiss francs which are shown in Table 20.2. This quotation refers to transactions completed on the Philadelphia Stock Exchange on the previous day.

**TABLE 20.2**  Foreign Currency Option Quotations (Philadelphia Stock Exchange)

| Options and underlying | Strike price | Calls-last | | | Puts-last | | |
|---|---|---|---|---|---|---|---|
| 62,500 Swiss Francs-cents per unit | | August | September | December | August | September | December |
| 58.51 | 56 | — | — | 2.76 | 0.04 | 0.22 | 1.16 |
| 58.51 | 56½ | — | — | — | 0.06 | 0.30 | — |
| 58.51 | 57 | 1.13 | — | 1.74 | 0.10 | 0.38 | 1.22 |
| 58.51 | 57½ | 0.75 | — | — | 0.17 | 0.55 | — |
| 58.51 | 58 | 0.71 | 1.05 | 1.28 | 0.27 | 0.89 | 1.81 |
| 58.51 | 58½ | 0.50 | — | — | 0.50 | 0.99 | — |
| 58.51 | 59 | 0.30 | 0.66 | 1.21 | 0.90 | 1.36 | — |
| 58.51 | 59½ | 0.15 | 0.40 | — | 2.32 | 2.62 | — |
| 58.51 | 60 | — | 0.31 | — | — | — | 3.30 |

*Source: Adopted from the Wall Street Journal.*

**Important observations from the quotation:**  The figures given in Table 20.2 depict the following observations:

1. The quotation shows different prices, which characterize any foreign currency option, such as spot rate, exercise price and premium.

2. The first column of the table shows the spot rate. 'Options and underlying' means that 58.5 cents or $0.5851, is the spot dollar rate of one Swiss franc at the close of trading on the preceding day. Sometimes, the spot rate is not shown in the Wall Street Journal quotation.

3. The second column shows the 'strike price' or 'exercise price'. It means that the price per franc that must be paid if the option is exercised. The August call option on francs of 58½ means $0.5850 SF. The table lists nine different strike prices ranging from $0.5600 to $0.6000 SF. The exercise prices for Swiss franc are quoted with a difference of 0.5 cents. The figure (–) means that there has been no negotiation of this contract on the day of quotation. Rest columns of the quotation show the calls (last) and puts (last) for the three months August, September and December premium. The premium is the cost or price of the option. The price of the August 58½ call option on Swiss francs is 0.50 US cents per franc or which means $0.0050/SF. The September and December 58½ call did not trade on that day. The indicated price for December to purchase the dollar at the strike price of $0.5600/SF for 2.76 cent preference premium. The price of the call option will be

$$SF\ 62,500 \times \$0.0276/SF = \$1725$$

Similarly, the holder has the right to sell the dollar at the strike price of $0.5600/SF for 1.16 cent per franc premium. In this case, the price of the put option will be

$$SF\ 62,500 \times \$0.0116/SF = \$725$$

## 20.5 CURRENCY OPTION CONTRACTS IN INDIA

In India the derivatives trading in stock started in 2000, which has registered an explosive growth continuously. National Stock Exchange (NSE) alone has accounted more than 90 percent of the total business in derivatives. The NSE added another segment named as Currency Derivatives Segment (CDS) and commenced trading on August 29, 2008 with the launch of currency futures trading in US Dollar with Indian Rupee, and in March, 2010 added three more pairs, namely Euro and Indian Rupee (EURINR), Pound sterling and Indian Rupee (GBP-INR), and Japanese Yen and Indian Rupee (JPYINR). Currency options trading started in India by the NSE on October 29, 2010 in currency pair of US Dollar and Indian Rupee, United Stock Exchange of India has also been permitted for trading in option in US dollar with Indian Rupee.

In December, 2015, the RBI further allowed trading in 3 more currency pairs in futures market, to offer cross-currency futures contracts and exchange traded currency options in three more currency pairs, which are as under:

Cross-currency futures contracts in EUR-USD, GBP-USD, USD-JPY with immediate effect.

Exchange traded currency option contracts in EUR-INR, GBP-INR and JPY-INR pairs. As per the guidelines of the RBI, all the market participants have been allowed to take positions in exchange-traded-currency F&O segments, both rupee and cross-currency, without having an underlying exposure. This would, however, be subject to position limits imposed by the exchanges.

With the starting of currency derivatives in India through the stock exchange, there has been dynamic shift in trading and hedging of currencies. The Indian individuals and entities would be able to take positions on the external value of the rupee without having an underlying foreign currency exposure.

The product specifications of the NSE in option trading in Indian Rupee and US Dollar pair given in Table 20.3 are as follows:

**TABLE 20.3**   Currency Options (Product Specifications of USD-INR at NSE)

| Symbol | USDINR |
|---|---|
| Instrument type | OPTCUR |
| Option type | Premium style European Call & Put Options. |
| Premium | Premium quoted in INR. |
| Unit of trading | 1 contract unit denotes USD 1000. |
| Underlying/Order quotation | The exchange rate in Indian Rupees for US Dollars. |
| Tick size | 0.25 paise i.e. INR 0.0025. |
| Trading hours | Monday to Friday 9:00 a.m. to 5:00 p.m. |
| Contract trading cycle | 3 serial monthly contracts followed by 1 quarterly contracts of the cycle March/June/September/December. |
| Strike price | 12 In-the-money, 12 Out-of-the-money and 1 Near-the-money. (25 CE and 25 PE) |
| Strike price intervals | INR 0.25. |
| Quantity freeze | 10,001 or greater. |
| Expiry/Last trading day | Two working days prior to the last business day of the expiry month at 12.30 noon. |
| Exercise at expiry | All in-the-money open long contracts shall be automatically exercised at the nal settlement price and assigned on a random basis to the open short positions of the same strike and series. |
| Final settlement day | Last working day (excluding Saturdays) of the expiry month. The last working day will be the same as that for Interbank Settlements in Mumbai. |
| Initial margin | SPAN Based Margin. |
| Extreme loss margin | 1.5% of Notional Value of open short position. |
| Settlement of premium | Premium to be paid by the buyer in cash on T+1 day. |
| Settlement | Daily settlement : T + 1<br>Final settlement : T + 2 |
| Mode of settlement | Cash settled in Indian Rupees. |
| Final settlement price | RBI reference rate on the date of the expiry of the contract. |

(Source: nseindia.com)

## 20.5.1   Important Features of Product Specifications of NSE

**1. Currency pairs available for option trading:**   At present, four currency pairs are available which are: (1) USDINR, (2) GBPINR (3) EURINR and (4) JPYINR. The RBI in December, 2015, allows exchanges to offer cross-currency futures and exchange traded currency options in EUR-INR, GBP-INR and JYP-INR. Option contracts would be in European style.

**2. Contract size:** The size of one contract is 1000 Units of USD, and the same size in other pairs. Minimum price fluctuation (tick size) is paise 0.25, or rupee 0.0025.Strike price intervals is INR 0.25.

**3. Trading hours & cycle:** Market time of trading is from IST 9.00 am to 5.00 pm from Monday to Friday in a week. The contract trading cycle is 3 serial-month contracts followed by quarterly contract-March, June, September and December. On expiry, new four month contracts are also introduced. The maturity of the contracts cannot exceed 12 months.

**4. Strike price:** The underlying currency is Indian rupee. The spot rate is mentioned in Indian rupee for US dollar. The strike price will be determined on introduction of new expiry 12 in the money, 12 out of the money and one near the money movements. So, at least 25 call and 25 put option intervals based on underlying price movement, new strike intervals are introduced.

**5. Position limits:** At present, Indian residents, corporate registered in India; involving foreign currency due to their business nature, domestic Indian financial institutions and banks, etc. can participate and use the foreign currency derivatives trading. The position limits for (1) Clients higher 6 percent of total open interest or USD 10 million, (2) Trading members; higher 15 percent of total open interest or USD 50 million, (3) Banks higher 15 percent of total open interest or USD 100 million.

**6. Margin:** For clients, the Risk Management System will work as: The client would need to have adequate margin for any order. The basic margin would be calculated on the basis of Standardized Portfolio Analysis of Risk (SPAN). Initial margin is 1.75 percent of day of trade and thereafter 1 percent. Calendar spread margin defined by exchange will be at ₹ 250. Any additional margin, if and, as notified by the exchange. Finally, Extreme Loss Margin is 1 percent of the value of gross open positions.

**7. Settlement:** The daily clearing and settlement process would be taken into account. Daily trades, position computation, daily settlement price for outstanding contracts, Mark-to-market (MTM), etc. would be followed for each client by the member of the exchange. Last expiry trading day is 2 working days prior to the last business day of the expiry month at 12 noon. Final settlement of the open contracts would be settled in cash in rupees, with the final settlement price being the Reserve Bank Reference Rate. On expiry date, all open long in-the-money contracts would be automatically exercised at the final settlement price.

## 20.5.2 Trading Mechanism of Currency Options at NSE

The traders before making currency options contracts at the exchanges, they should ensure certain considerations which are given as:

- Determination of the amount of foreign exchange exposures along with the respective periods of exposure currency-wise.
- Measurement of hedge ratio of the option contracts for different currencies.
- To decide the degree of foreign exchange risk acceptable to the management.
- Measurement of the expected and historical track record of exchange rate movements.
- Evaluation of the comparative cost benefit analysis of currency option contracts with other derivatives instruments like futures, forwards and swaps in foreign currencies.

After reviewing above said factors, let us understand the trading mechanism of currency option contracts at the NSE. The quotation of such transactions completed on NSE as on December 18, 2015 given in Table 20.4 is presented for such consideration. Following are important observations of the quotation:

1. The quotation shows the different prices which characterize the calls and puts with bid and ask prices, quantities, and strike price, of rupees in terms of US dollar.

2. The quotation shows two important segments—Calls and Puts in which further the open interest, volume, Bid (Qty), Bid price, Ask price, Ask (Qty), Last Trading Price (LTP), Change in open interest, etc. have been shown.

3. As per this quotation, against the strike price of ₹60.50, the call option prices of Bid and Ask are ₹6.3575 and 6.5875, whereas the Ask price of Put option is ₹0.0050. Bid price means purchase price and ask price means sale or offer price of the call or put option. In this way, the strike prices ranging from ₹60.50 to 69.50 have been presented with different bid and ask prices.

4. The RBI Reference Rate as on December 18, 2015 at 13.10 is ₹66.4235.

5. Open Interest (OI) column shows the total number of outstanding contracts which are held by the traders at the end of that particular trading day, e.g., December 18, 2015 in the given quotation. It means such contracts have not yet been exercised (squared off), expired, or fulfilled by delivery.

6. Last Trading Price (LTP) means the previous day's closing price of option against the respective strike price of ₹60.50, the LTP was ₹6.475, against ₹62, it was ₹4.3150 and so on.

7. Quotation shows the final settlement date December 29, 2015 on which all open positions would be settled.

8. Maximum numbers of the option contracts are done against strike price ranging from ₹65 to 68 as per this quotation.

## 20.6 STRATEGIES FOR USING OPTIONS

Options differ from all other type of financial instruments in the patterns of risk they produce. Since the options holder has the right to exercise the options or not to exercise it to expire unused, so he bears no risk at all whether the market foreign exchange rates increase or decrease. Of course, the holder will exercise the option if he incurs the profit. Thus, the options contracts can be designed in accordance with the buyer's needs. In this section, we will discuss a few important such currency option strategies. However, detailed discussion on various options trading, hedging and other strategies have been made in other chapter relating to options which can be consulted to have further view in depth in option markets.

### 20.6.1 Buyer of a Call

This option strategy can be considered in case of anticipating of appreciation of underlying currency. For example, an Indian foreign exchange dealer is expecting that the price of the dollar will appreciate in future then he can buy a call option in US dollar. Let us explain this with an example, as given in Table 20.2, where the August call option has strike price of 58½ ($0.5850/SF) with a premium of $0.005/SF, as shown in Figure 20.1.

**TABLE 20.4** NSE—Option Chain Currency Dated 21.12.2015 (RBI Reference Rate as on 21.12.2015)

| | | | Calls | | | | | | Strike Price | | | | | | | | Puts | |
|---|---|---|---|---|---|---|---|---|---|---|---|---|---|---|---|---|---|---|
| OI | Change in OI | Volume | IV | LTP | Bid Qty | Bid Price | Ask Price | Ask Qty | | Bid Qty | Bid Price | Ask Price | Ask Qty | LTP | IV | Volume | Change in OI | OI |
| 70 | — | — | 18.65 | 6.4725 | 20 | 6.3575 | 6.5875 | 20 | 60.50 | — | — | 0.0050 | 1,200 | — | 0.00 | — | — | — |
| — | — | — | 0.00 | — | — | — | — | — | 60.75 | — | — | 0.0050 | 1,200 | — | 0.00 | — | — | — |
| — | — | — | 0.00 | — | 40 | 5.8025 | 6.0250 | 128 | 61.00 | — | — | 0.0025 | 1 | 0.0150 | 23.38 | — | — | 1 |
| — | — | — | 0.00 | — | — | — | — | — | 61.25 | — | — | 0.0050 | 1,200 | — | 0.00 | — | — | — |
| — | — | — | 0.00 | — | 40 | 5.3025 | 5.5250 | 128 | 61.50 | — | — | 0.0050 | 1,200 | — | 0.00 | — | — | — |
| 1,285 | — | — | 51.14 | 5.4000 | — | — | 4.7225 | 100 | 61.75 | — | — | 0.0050 | 1,200 | — | 0.00 | — | — | — |
| 3,307 | — | 9 | 26.90 | 4.3150 | 413 | 4.3575 | 4.4700 | 50 | 62.00 | — | — | 0.0050 | 1,200 | — | 0.00 | — | — | — |
| — | — | — | 0.00 | — | — | — | — | — | 62.25 | — | — | 0.0050 | 1,200 | — | 0.00 | — | — | — |
| — | — | — | 0.00 | — | — | — | — | — | 62.50 | — | — | 0.0050 | 1,200 | — | 0.00 | — | — | — |
| — | — | — | 0.00 | — | — | — | — | — | 62.75 | — | — | 0.0050 | 1,200 | — | 0.00 | — | — | — |
| 1,142 | — | 10 | 13.34 | 3.5000 | 300 | 3.4075 | 3.4700 | 50 | 63.00 | — | — | 0.0050 | 2,400 | 0.0050 | 13.46 | — | — | 600 |
| — | — | — | 0.00 | — | — | — | — | — | 63.25 | — | — | 0.0050 | 2,400 | — | 0.00 | — | — | — |
| 60 | — | — | 14.89 | 3.0400 | 300 | 2.9075 | 2.9700 | 60 | 63.50 | — | — | 0.0025 | 900 | 0.0025 | 10.78 | — | — | 25 |
| — | — | — | 0.00 | — | — | — | — | — | 63.75 | — | — | 0.0050 | 2,400 | — | 0.00 | — | — | — |
| 1,372 | — | — | 7.76 | 2.5175 | 413 | 2.4375 | 2.4700 | 50 | 64.00 | — | — | 0.0025 | 926 | 0.0025 | 9.16 | 2 | — | 714 |
| 25 | — | — | 16.86 | 2.3775 | — | — | — | — | 64.25 | — | — | 0.0050 | 2,400 | — | 0.00 | — | — | — |
| 145 | — | — | 11.13 | 2.0475 | 1 | 1.9350 | — | — | 64.50 | 1,669 | 0.0025 | 0.0050 | 4,400 | 0.0050 | 8.24 | — | — | 4,467 |
| — | — | — | 0.00 | — | — | — | — | — | 64.75 | 95 | 0.0025 | — | — | 0.0100 | 7.35 | — | — | 3 |
| 6,433 | — | 4,002 | 11.55 | 1.6000 | 300 | 1.4050 | 1.6000 | 1 | 65.00 | 11,669 | 0.0025 | 0.0050 | 488 | 0.0050 | 6.45 | 5,283 | — | 31,589 |
| 80 | — | 10 | 5.47 | 1.2400 | — | — | — | — | 65.25 | — | — | 0.0050 | 1,749 | 0.0025 | 5.00 | 20 | — | 2,294 |
| 12,812 | — | 1,799 | 4.15 | 1.0225 | 500 | 0.9375 | — | — | 65.50 | 8,928 | 0.0075 | 0.0100 | 101 | 0.0075 | 4.93 | 17,605 | — | 62,611 |
| 140 | — | — | 21.83 | 1.4300 | — | — | — | — | 65.75 | 623 | 0.0175 | 0.0225 | 300 | 0.0200 | 4.84 | 14,280 | — | 24,062 |
| 25,723 | — | 9,040 | 2.30 | 0.4875 | 100 | 0.4700 | 0.5200 | 100 | 66.00 | 100 | 0.0325 | 0.0375 | 540 | 0.0350 | 4.28 | 116,354 | — | 119,008 |
| 10,807 | — | 11,582 | 2.96 | 0.3125 | 300 | 0.2875 | 0.3000 | 195 | 66.25 | 710 | 0.0800 | 0.0900 | 150 | 0.0925 | 4.42 | 98,998 | — | 77,493 |

(Contd.)

(Contd.)

| OI | Change in OI | Volume | IV | LTP | Bid Qty | Bid Price | Ask Price | Ask Qty | Strike Price | Bid Qty | Bid Price | Ask Price | Ask Qty | LTP | IV | Volume | Change in OI | OI |
|---|---|---|---|---|---|---|---|---|---|---|---|---|---|---|---|---|---|---|
| | | | | | Calls | | | | | | | | Puts | | | | | |
| 241,540 | — | 182,994 | 3.24 | 0.1600 | 94 | 0.1525 | 0.1600 | 156 | 66.50 | 20 | 0.1900 | 0.2025 | 234 | 0.1900 | 4.47 | 206,402 | — | 166,082 |
| 51,857 | — | 90,229 | 3.76 | 0.0825 | 252 | 0.0775 | 0.0850 | 488 | 66.75 | 100 | 0.3500 | 0.3725 | 100 | 0.3725 | 5.40 | 15,888 | — | 44,145 |
| 344,812 | — | 280,654 | 4.48 | 0.0500 | 25 | 0.0500 | 0.0525 | 3,018 | 67.00 | 100 | 0.5725 | 0.5975 | 100 | 0.6025 | 6.83 | 43,610 | — | 207,375 |
| 44,418 | — | 71,683 | 4.93 | 0.0275 | 1,860 | 0.0250 | 0.0275 | 9 | 67.25 | 20 | 0.8025 | 0.9000 | 1 | 0.7825 | 6.39 | 87 | — | 4,373 |
| 143,579 | — | 104,712 | 5.50 | 0.0155 | 16,601 | 0.0150 | 0.0175 | 4,266 | 67.50 | 4 | 0.9800 | 1.3500 | 1 | 1.0025 | 6.52 | 3,233 | — | 112,038 |
| 32,425 | — | 12,233 | 5.59 | 0.0075 | 5,520 | 0.0075 | 0.0100 | 30 | 67.75 | — | — | — | — | 1.1000 | 4.55 | — | — | 91 |
| 91,039 | — | 17,199 | 6.52 | 0.0075 | 1,576 | 0.0050 | 0.0075 | 17,502 | 68.00 | 25 | 1.4700 | 1.6500 | 1 | 1.6000 | 13.01 | 15 | — | 9,202 |
| 4,625 | — | — | 6.35 | 0.0025 | — | — | 0.0050 | 6,000 | 68.25 | — | — | — | — | — | 0.00 | — | — | — |
| 170,209 | — | 5,165 | 7.13 | 0.0025 | — | — | 0.0025 | 15,925 | 68.50 | 80 | 1.9800 | — | — | 1.6200 | 4.28 | — | — | 1,933 |
| 59,701 | — | 1 | 7.90 | 0.0025 | — | — | 0.0025 | 12,588 | 68.75 | — | — | — | — | — | 0.00 | — | — | — |
| 17,997 | — | 45 | 8.66 | 0.0025 | — | — | 0.0025 | 225 | 69.00 | 80 | 2.4800 | — | — | 1.2500 | 4.57 | — | — | 5 |
| 2 | — | — | 12.69 | 0.0200 | — | — | 0.0050 | 4,800 | 69.25 | — | — | — | — | 2.1050 | 5.94 | — | — | 1 |
| 26.845 | — | — | 10.15 | 0.0025 | — | — | 0.0025 | 15,900 | 69.50 | 80 | 2.9900 | — | — | 2.7350 | 11.64 | — | — | 111 |
| — | — | — | 0.00 | — | — | — | 0.0050 | 4,800 | 69.75 | — | — | — | — | — | 0.00 | — | — | — |
| — | — | — | 0.00 | — | — | — | — | — | 70.00 | — | — | — | — | — | 8.57 | — | — | 8 |
| **1,292,450** | | | | | | | | | | | | | | | | | | **868,231** |

*Source:* www.nseindia.com

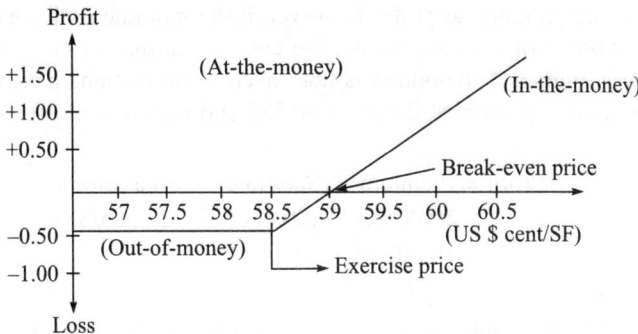

**FIGURE 20.1** Profit and loss for buyer of a call option.

It is evident from Figure 20.1 that if the spot rate ($/SF) is higher than the strike price, i.e., $0.585 SF, then he will exercise the option. If the spot rate remains $0.5850 or below it, then he will not exercise the option. His maximum loss will be the premium, i.e., $0.005/SF. Thus, the buyer will exercise the option only if the spot rate is higher than the strike price. His profit can be determined with the following equation:

$$\text{Profit} = \text{Spot rate} - (\text{Strike price} + \text{Premium})$$
$$= \$6,000/SF - (\$0.5850 + \$0.0050/SF)$$
$$= \$0.0100/SF$$

From Figure 20.1, it is observed that the maximum loss to the option buyer is limited (the premium of the option) but the profit is unlimited because the dollar price of a Swiss franc could rise to an infinite level (of the upper right-hand side of Figure 20.1). The buyer of a call option, thus, possesses an attractive combination of outcomes, i.e., limited loss and unlimited profit potential.

## 20.6.2 Writer of a Call Option

The position of the writer (seller) of the call option is just reverse to that of the buyer of a call option. This is shown in Figure 20.2.

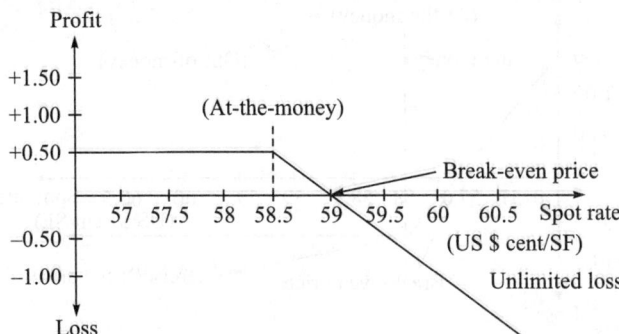

**FIGURE 20.2** Profit and loss for writer of a call option.

From Figure 20.2, it is observed that if the spot rate is below the exercise price, i.e., 0.585, then the option holder does not exercise the option. What the holder losses is the writer gains.

The writer keeps the entire premium as profit. However, if the spot rate is above than the strike price, i.e., $0.585, then the writer would now purchase the currency at the current spot rate and bears the loss. The loss will be unlimited if the option is not covered and remains naked till expiration. The profit to the writer of a call option at strike price $0.585 and premium of $0.005, if the spot rate is $0.6000/SF:

$$Profit = Premium - (Spot\ rate - Strike\ price)$$
$$= \$0.005/SF - (\$0.600/SF - \$0.585/SF)$$
$$= \$0.005/SF - (+ \$0.015/SF)$$
$$= - \$0.010/SF$$

However, if the option goes unexercised (when spot rate remains less than exercise price) then the entire premium will be the profit of the writer. So, the maximum profit to the writer will be limited to premium. In case of unlimited losses there are ways to limit such losses through other option strategies/techniques.

### 20.6.3 Buyer of a Put Option

This option strategy is followed when the exchange rate in future is expected to depreciate or decrease. In such situation, the put option can be purchased. The basic terms of this put option are similar to those of a call. Here, the buyer gets the right to sell the particular currency at the specific exercise price to the writer of the option. If the current spot rate declines to the exercise price, the buyer will exercise the option. For example, in the earlier example, if the spot rate declines to $0.570/SF, then he will deliver francs to the writer and receive $0.585/SF. His profit in this case will be

$$Profit = Strike\ price - (Spot\ rate + Premium)$$
$$= \$0.585/SF - (\$0.570/SF + \$0.005/SF)$$
$$= \$0.585/SF - \$0.575/SF$$
$$= \$0.010/SF$$

It means that the buyer of the put option has unlimited potential to earn and the loss is limited to the extent of the amount of the premium. This option position has been shown in Figure 20.3.

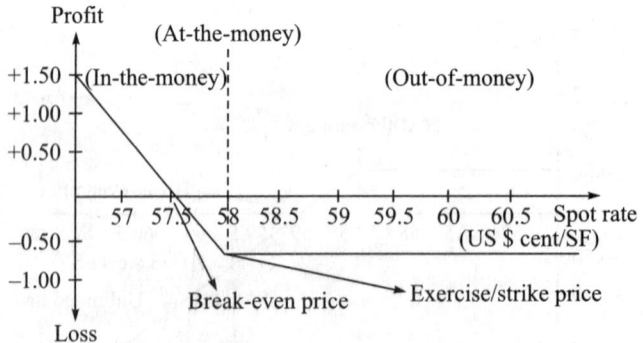

**FIGURE 20.3**  Profit and loss for buyer of a put-option.

From Figure 20.3, it is evident that the break-even price in a put option will be the strike price minus the premium, i.e., $0.5800/SF ($0.585/SF – $0.005/SF). At any spot rate above the strike price, the option will go unexercised and the maximum loss will be the premium to the buyer.

## 20.6.4    Writer of a Put Option

The position of the writer of the option is similar in opposite direction as in the case of the call option. The writer of the put option will incur loss if the option is exercised (the spot price is less than the strike price). In the above said example, the spot rate is less than $0.585/SF, the buyer will exercise the option and the writer has to purchase the currency at the higher rate from the buyer. This option position is shown in Figure 20.4.

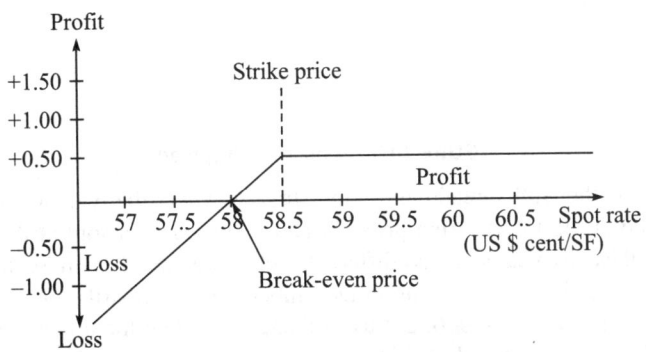

**FIGURE 20.4**    Profit and loss for writer of a call option.

From Figure 20.4, it is noted that the writer will incur loss if the spot rate declines below the exercise rate, i.e., $0.585/SF. Thus, if the spot rate remains constant or rises above the strike price, the option will not be exercised, and the entire premium will be the profit to the writer. Profit will be (by assuming the spot rate to be $0.570/SF).

$$\text{Profit} = \text{Premium} - (\text{Strike rate} - \text{Spot price})$$
$$= \$0.005/SF - (\$0.585/SF - \$0.570/SF)$$
$$= \$0.005/SF - (\$0.015/SF)$$
$$= -\$0.010/SF$$

There is limited profit to the writer of a put option to the extent of premium and the unlimited loss potential.

## 20.6.5    Spread Strategies

A spread trading strategy refers to that position in which two more options of the same type are involved. For example, two or more calls and two or more puts are simultaneously sold or purchased. The basic objective behind the spread is to realize a profit if the underlying price moves in a particular trend while, at the same time, limiting the loss if it does not move in a particular trend. In other words, these are speculative strategies with limited profit potential as well as limited loss. There are a number of spread strategies like bull spreads, bear spreads, butterfly spreads, calendar spreads, diagonal spreads, etc. These all strategies have been explained in detail in Chapter 18, which can be consulted for detailed analysis. However, in this section, we are discussing only a bull spread strategy.

**A bull call spread:**    In this strategy, selling the call with the higher strike price and buying the call with the lower strike price, but with the same expiration date can create the position. This strategy is preferred when the market is bullish. This has been shown in Figure 20.5.

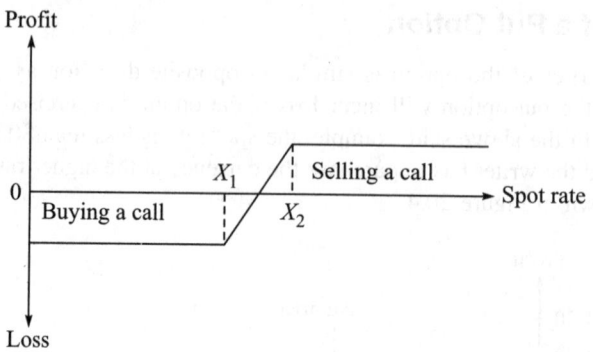

**FIGURE 20.5**    A bullish call spread.

Figure 20.5 depicts the Bull spread call option strategy where the two calls have been involved. First call is purchased at the lower strike price $X_1$ and second call is sold at the higher strike price $X_2$. The premium of these two calls is also different. Let us assume that on September 10, 2003, the USD/DEM spot rate is 0.65. Calls maturing in December 2003 with strike price 0.60 trading at 0.08 and those with strike price 0.76 at 0.006. Let us further assume that the trader is bullish about DEM, hence, he takes the bullish call spread position, i.e., buying the call with less strike price and selling the call with higher strike price.

If the spot rate remains below 0.60 then neither of the calls will be exercised. So, the net loss to the trader will be the premium paid on the lower priced call less the premium received on the higher priced call. In this example, it is 0.074 (0.08 – 0.006). The maximum profit potential will be the difference of the strike prices minus the initial investment (i.e., difference of the premium). So, in this case, it will be 0.076 (0.75 – 0.60 – 0.074).

## 20.6.6   Straddle Strategy

This is another popular option strategy. A straddle consists of buying a call and a put both with identical strike rate and maturity. The basic objective for this strategy is to earn profit in both ways (rising and declining of the spot prices) at the cost of the double premium (premium paid for the buying both a call and a put option). The profit profile for the buyer of a straddle is calculated as:

$$\text{Profit} = X - S_t - (C + P) \text{ for } X > S_t$$
$$\text{Profit} = S_t - X - (C + P) \text{ for } S_t > X$$

where $X$ is the strike price, $S_t$ is the spot price and $C$ and $P$ are the premiums for the call and put options.

The straddle option strategy has been shown in Figure 20.6. It is evident from Figure 20.6 that if the spot rate is close to strike price at the expiration of the options, the straddle leads to a loss. However, if there is a significant move of the spot rate in either direction then straddle will result into profit.

A straddle can be long or short. When the investor buys a call as well as a put it is called *long straddle*. On the other hand, when he sells the call and put options, it is called *short straddle*. The seller of the straddle does not expect the currency to vary too much and hopes to be able to keep his premium. He anticipates a diminishing volatility in spot rates of the currency.

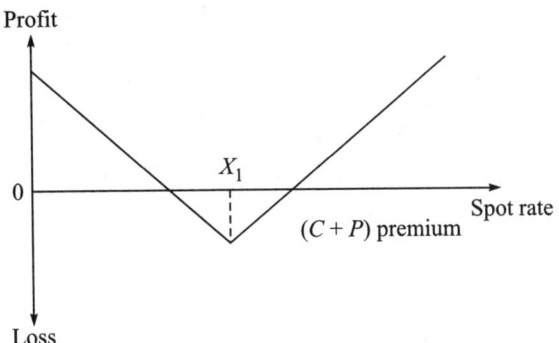

**FIGURE 20.6** Profit/loss profile of a long straddle.

## 20.6.7 Strangle Strategy

A strangle option strategy is similar to straddle except that it involves different strike prices. It is a combination of two options, i.e., call and put with different strike prices but with the same expiration date. In this, one buy a call strike price above the current spot rate and put with strike price lower to the current spot rate. This strategy is followed when a buyer is expecting significant fluctuations of a currency but does not confirm about the direction of the movement. The profit pattern in a strangle strategy depends on how close the strike prices are together. This is shown in Figure 20.7.

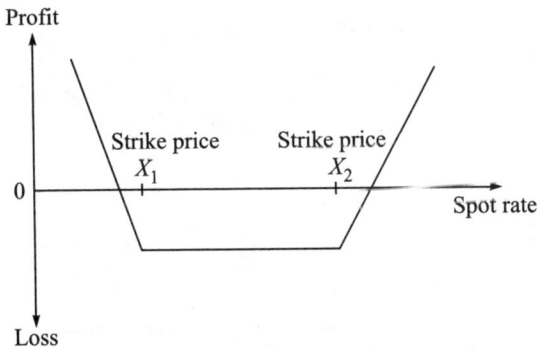

**FIGURE 20.7** Profit profile of a strangle.

## 20.7 OPTION PRICING AND VALUATION

The value of an option or the option price or the option premium is the amount which is paid by the option buyer to the option writer. How much risk is involved in a particular option is a complex and highly technical subject requiring advance quantitative techniques. In this section, we will discuss the components of option valuation and the factors that determine such valuation.

### 20.7.1 Components of Option Pricing

The total value of a call option is actually the sum of two components—Intrinsic value and time value.

**Intrinsic value:**   Intrinsic value is the financial gain if the option is exercised immediately. In other words, it is the amount by which the option is in-the-money, i.e., the current exchange rate is higher than the exercise price. Higher the current price than the exercise price, the more valuable it is. Intrinsic value will be zero when the option is out-of-the-money. It means when the strike price is above the market price and no gain on exercising of the option. For example, the intrinsic value of a call option on Swiss francs with an exercise price of $0.70 and spot rate of $0.74, then profit would be $0.04 per franc.

**Time value:**   Any excess of the option value over its intrinsic value is called *the time value of the contract.* An option will generally sell for at least its intrinsic value. The time value of an option exists because the price of the underlying currency, the spot rate can be expected to move further and further into the money between the current time and the options expiration date. Thus, the time value is just expected value which may be incurred during the life of an option. Since, at the maturity of the option, the intrinsic value will be equal to the difference of the current spot rate and exercise price then the time value will be zero. So, it is always positive prior to the maturity or expiration date of the option. In other words, as the option approaches its maturity, the time value declines to zero. The option value of a call is shown in Figure 20.8.

Figure 20.8 shows the value of a call option on British pound with a strike price of $1.65 per pound. It is observed from the figure that the intrinsic value will be zero at the spot rate of $1.65/£ but time value is positive because there is expectation that the spot rate may move forward. Time value will be zero near maturity. So the total value will be determined by adding the intrinsic value and time value.

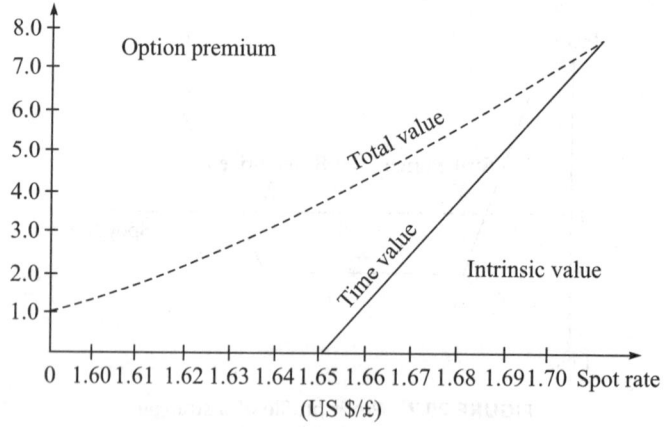

**FIGURE 20.8**   Value of call option.

## 20.7.2   Determinants of the Currency Option Value

Following are the important determinants of the value of a currency option. These are also called *sensitivities* because the currency option value is sensitive to the following factors:

1. Changes in forward rates
2. Changes in spot rate
3. Time to maturity
4. Impact of changing volatility

5. Changes in interest rate differential
6. Alternative option strikes price

**Changes in forward rates (forward rate sensitivity):**    The first important determinant of the option value is forward rate sensitivity because the standard foreign currency options are priced around the forward rate. It gives an important indication how the future exchange rate will move because the forward rate is determined after considering the interest rate differential of both the underlying currencies.

Further, forward rate also provides information for the trader to manage the position. Regardless of the specific strike price chosen, the forward rate is central to valuation. Even the option pricing formula calculates a subjective probability distribution. Hence, it can be observed that forward rate is an important factor to be considered in determining the option price of an underlying currency.

**Spot rate changes (Delta):**    Another important determinant of option pricing is the likely changes in the spot rate. It has direct impact on the time value of the option. For example, if the spot rate is changing in particular direction then besides increase in the intrinsic value, the time value will also increase. As long as the option has time remaining before expiration, the option will possess this time value element. Thus, the trader must analyze the changes in spot rate in the past as well as in the future.

The sensitivity of the option premium to a small change in the spot exchange rate is also called delta. What is the change in spot exchange rate and its impact on the option value is an important consideration. Delta may be calculated as changes in option premium divided by the change in spot rate. It will range between +1 and 0 for a call, and −1 and 0 for a put option. For example, the change in spot rate is from \$1.70/£ to \$1.72/£ and also assume that option premium changes from \$0.038/£ to \$0.032/£. The delta from the above information is:

$$\text{Delta} = \frac{\Delta\,\text{Premium}}{\Delta\,\text{Spot rate}} = \frac{\$0.038/£ - \$0.032/£}{\$1.72/£ - \$1.70/£} = 0.6$$

If we can anticipate the delta appropriately then it will be easy to determine the option premium. For example, if the change in spot rate is by \$0.04/£ and the delta value is 0.5, then premium will change by \$0.02 (0.5 × \$0.04). If the initial premium is \$0.040/£ then new premium will be \$0.040/£ + \$0.02/\$ = \$0.06.

The Rule of Thumb in case of delta is: 'the higher the delta (delta of 0.7 or 0.8 and above are considered high) the greater the probability of the option expiring in the money'.

**Time to maturity (Theta):**    As observed earlier, the option values vary with the length of time to maturity. Longer the period to maturity, the greater will be the option value. This relationship is also referred to theta. The expected change in the option premium from a small change in the time to expiration is called *theta*. It is determined as:

$$\text{Theta} = \frac{\Delta\,\text{Premium}}{\Delta\,\text{Time}}$$

Further, theta is based not on a linear relationship with time, rather by having the square root of time, because it is observed that option premiums deteriorate at an increasing rate as they approach expiration.

Theta analysis is quite significant for traders. A dealer purchasing an option with a shorter period to maturity, say, one or two months, will see that the options value will deteriorate rapidly. So he will not purchase the option at higher premium.

The Rule of Thumb in this regard is: 'a trader will normally find longer maturity options better values, giving the trader the ability to alter an option position without suffering significant time value deterioration.

**Impact of changing volatility (Lambda):**   Another important factor, which is to be considered in option valuation, is volatility of exchange rates or sensitivity to volatility. Volatility in context to option may be defined as the standard deviation of daily percentage changes in the underlying exchange rate. If the exchange rate's volatility is rising then the risk of the option being exercised will also increase. Consequently, it will result into increase in the option premium. Normally, volatility is stated in percent per annum. For example, an option may be stated as having a 10.5 percent annual volatility. The percentage change for a single day will be calculated as follows:

$$\text{Daily volatility (\%)} = \text{Annual volatility}/\sqrt{365} = 10.5/19.105 = 0.55\%$$

The sensitivity of the option premium to a unit change in volatility is termed as lambda. It is calculated as:

$$\text{Lambda} = \frac{\Delta\,\text{Premium}}{\Delta\,\text{Volatility}}$$

For example, an increase in annual volatility of one percentage point, i.e., 10.0 percent will increase the option premium from $0.035/£ to $0.038/£, then the lambda will be

$$\text{Lambda} = \frac{\Delta\,\text{Premium}}{\Delta\,\text{Volatility}} = \frac{\$0.038/£ - \$0.035/£}{0.11 - 0.10} = 0.30$$

Option premiums are highly sensitive to volatility. Volatility may be viewed from three ways—historic, forward looking and implied. Historic volatility is concerned to recent period of time, forward looking volatility is drawn from the expected reflection about future period and implied volatility is backed out of the market price of the option itself.

The Rule of Thumb in respect of volatility is: traders who believe volatility will fall significantly in the near term will sell (write) options now hoping to buy them back for a profit immediately after volatility fall and cause option premium to fall.

**Changes in the interest rate differentials (Rho and Phi):**   As seen earlier in forward rate that change in the interest rate of either currency will alter the forward rate, which in turn will change the option's premium or value. In this respect two terms are referred, i.e., Rho and Phi. The expected change in the option premium from a small change in the domestic interest rate (home currency) is called *Rho*. On the other hand, the expected change in the option premium from a small change in the foreign interest rate (foreign currency) is called *Phi*. Let us assume that local currency (Indian rupee) interest rate increased from 6 percent to 7 percent which in turn increase the option premium on US dollar from ₹0.40/$ to ₹0.042/$. This is called *Rho value* which is positive.

$$\text{Rho} = \frac{\Delta\,\text{Premium}}{\Delta\,\text{Re interest rate}} = \frac{₹\,0.042/\$ - ₹\,0.040/\$}{7\% - 6\%} = 0.2$$

Similarly, we can calculate Phi. An increase of interest rate in foreign currency will decrease the option value. For example, US $ interest rate is increased from 5 percent to 6 percent and the premium is decreased from ₹0.040/$ to ₹0.038/$, is, therefore, a negative 0.2.

$$\text{Phi} = \frac{\Delta\,\text{Premium}}{\Delta\,\text{Foreign interest rate}} = \frac{₹\,0.038/\$ - ₹\,0.040/\$}{7\% - 6\%} = -0.2$$

This is observed from the above terms that difference or change in the interest rates of either of the currencies will have impact on option value. For example, when foreign interest rates are higher than domestic interest rates, the foreign currency sells forward at a discount and vice versa.

The Rule of Thumb in this regard is: 'a trader who is purchasing a call option on foreign currency should do so before the domestic interest rate rises. This will allow the trader to purchase the option before its value increases.'

**Alternative strike prices and option premiums:** Final determinant factor, which is important in option valuation, is availability of the alternative strike prices in the market and finally selecting the same. For example, a firm purchasing an option in the OTC market may choose its own strike price. So important thing is how to choose? This is determined by exercising various strike prices and then respective option premiums at each strike price. Which strike price has more option premium will be examined and then finally a final strike price will be selected. A detail regarding option pricing has been given in Chapter 15 which may be consulted for further study.

## SUMMARY

This chapter on currency option markets introduced the concept of foreign currencies options trading strategies. Foreign currencies are now such instruments which have a vital importance in the financial markets all over the world. These have been widely used by the various market participations like importers, exporters, traders, bankers, financial institutions, etc. Foreign currency or currency option is a financial instrument that gives the option holder a right but not the obligation to buy or sell a given amount of foreign exchange at a fixed price per unit for a specified time period, until the expiration date. There are two basic types of options: call option and put option. A call option refers to buy foreign currency and a put option to sell the foreign currency. Option can also be classified into an American option and a European option. An option is said to be at ITM, OTM and ATM. A currency option whose exercise prices is the same as the spot price of the underlying currency is said to be at-the-money (ATM). An option that would be profitable if exercise immediately is said to be in-the-money (ITM). An option which would not be profitable is exercised immediately is referred to out-of-the-money (OTM).

The chapter further describes the foreign currency option. Market options are traded on over-the-counter (OTC) as well as on organized exchanges. OTC, as it is called, offers customer-oriented options on all major trading currencies for any time period up to one year. Hence, it provides a useful tool or alternative to futures or forward contract. The transaction in the OTC option markets are carried out either directly between the counterparties or through the brokers. These operations are transacted either on telephone or by the system of Reuters or telex and they may take place round the clock. Terms of the contract are negotiated between the holder and the writer of the option. Currency options are also traded on various organized exchanges worldwide. First such trading was commenced in 1982 in the Philadelphia Stock Exchange (PHLX). The first currency options were on spot delivery, which require the delivery of the underlying currency contract. The Philadelphia Stock Exchange has recently introduced all the futures currencies trading its options segment, i.e., United Currency Options Market (UCOM). The currency options traded on the organized exchanges are of standard nature. They have standard quantity (size) of different currencies with specified maturities.

Currency-option contracts were produced in India by the NSE in October, 2010 in currency pair of US dollar and Indian rupee. United Stock Exchange of India was also permitted by the RBI for trading in currency options. RBI further permitted trading in 3 more currency pairs in EUD-INR, GBP-INR and JPY-INR. The NSE has set certain norms for currency options trading in India, ad since then, there has been dynamic shift in trading and hedging of currencies in India.

There are various determinates of currency option value like changes in forward rates, changes in spot rate, time to maturity, impact of changing volatility, changes in interest rate, differential of both the currencies and finally alternative option strike price. Options form all types of financial instruments in the pattern of risk they produce. Since the option holder has the right to exercise the option or not to exercise or it to expire unused, so he bears no risk at all whatever the market foreign exchange rates increase or decrease. The first strategy is for buyer (or call) which can be considered in case of anticipating of appreciation of underlying currency. For example, an Indian forex dealer expecting that the price of the dollar will appreciate in future then he can buy a call option in US dollar. The position of the writer (seller) of a call option is just reverse to that of the buyer of a call option. Buyer (or put) is another strategy used by the trader in the event of expectation of fall in the price of underlying currency. A spread strategy refers to that position in which two or more options of the same types are involved. For example, two or more calls, and two or more puts are simultaneously sold or purchased. The basic objective is to realize a profit if the underlying price moves in a particular trend. Spread can be bull and bearish call as well as put strategy. Another popular strategy is 'straddle' which consists of buying a call and a put with identical strike rate and maturity. Further, another strategy is involving different strike prices but with the same expiration date.

Last section of this chapter discusses the option pricing and valuation. The option premium is the amount which is paid by the option buyer to the option writer. The total value of a call option consists of two components—intrinsic value and time value. Intrinsic value is the financial gain if the option is exercised immediately. In other words, option is in-the-money, i.e., current exchange rate is higher than the exercise price. Any excess of the option value over its intrinsic value is called the time value of the contract. The time value of an option exists because the price of the underlying currency may move further in-the-money between the current time and option expiration date.

## SOLVED PROBLEMS

**P.1.** Consider a four-month European call option on UK pound. Suppose current exchange rate is ($/£) 1.69, strike price is ($/£) 1.6000, the risk-free interest rate in USA is 8% per annum, risk-free interest rate in UK is 11% per annum and option price is 4.3 cents. Calculate the implied volatility.

*Solution:*    In this case

| | |
|---|---|
| Current exchange rate | $S = 1.69$ |
| Strike price | $X = 1.60$ |
| Risk-free return | $r = 0.08$ |
| Risk-free return in foreign currency | $rf = 0.11$ |
| Time to maturity | $T = 4/12$ |
| Call price | $C_P = 0.043$ cent |
| At 20% volatility, an option price is | $= 0.0639$ |
| At 10% volatility, an option price is | $= 0.0285$ |
| Implied volatility | $= 14\%$ |
| Where option price is | $= 0.043$ |

**P.2.** From the following information, prepare a profit profile of a strangle strategy:

| | |
|---|---|
| Current spot price | = $1.7465/£ |
| Call exercise price *Xc* | = $1.7495/£ |
| Put exercise price *Xp* | = $1.7365/£ |
| Price | = 0.0031 cent |

*Solution:*  Profit profile with option strangle strategy

| Spot price | Gain/loss from (Call) | Gain/loss from (put) | Net gain/loss |
|---|---|---|---|
| 1.7065 | –0.0031 | 0.0269 | 0.0238 |
| 1.7145 | –0.0031 | 0.0189 | 0.0158 |
| 1.7895 | +0.0369 | –0.0031 | 0.0338 |
| 1.7925 | +0.0399 | –0.0031 | 0.0368 |

**P.3.** Suppose a call option enables purchase of dollar for ₹45.00 while it is quoted at ₹45.60 in spot market, and the premium paid for call option is ₹1.00. Calculate the intrinsic value of the call option.

*Solution:*  Intrinsic value of call option

| | |
|---|---|
| Spot rate (₹/$) | = 45.60 |
| Exercise (₹/$) | = 45.00 |
| Intrinsic value | = 45.60 – 45.00 = ₹0.60 |
| Time value of the call option | = 1.00 – (45.60 – 45.00) |
| | = 1.00 – 0.60 |
| | = ₹0.40 |

**P.4.** Suppose a call option enables a purchase of dollar for ₹48.00 and it is quoted at ₹50.00 in the market. The premium paid for call option is ₹2.00. Calculate the intrinsic value and time value of call option.

*Solution:*  Calculation of option value

$$\text{Intrinsic value call option} = ₹50 – ₹48.00 = ₹2.00$$
$$\text{Time value of call option} = ₹2.00 \, (₹50 – ₹48) = 0$$

**P.5.** A European style put option enables sale of dollar per ₹50.00 while it is quoted in spot market at ₹48.00. Calculate the intrinsic value of the put option.

*Solution:*  Intrinsic value of put option

| | |
|---|---|
| Spot rate | = (₹/$)48 |
| Exercise rate (₹/$) | = 50 |
| Intrinsic value (₹50 – ₹48) | = ₹2 |

Currency will alter the forward rate, which in turn will change the option's premium or value. The last and another important factor affecting option value is alternative strike prices at option premiums.

**P.6.** From the following information, draw a strategy.

| | |
|---|---|
| Spot price at the time of buying put options | = ₹48/$ |
| Strike price | *X* = ₹50/$ |
| Premium | *P* = ₹2/$ |

The gain/loss profile of put option:

| Spot price ($S_t$) (per dollar) | Gain(+)/Loss(−) |
|---|---|
| ₹45 = (50 − 45) = 5 − 2= | +3 ₹ |
| ₹46 | +2 ₹ |
| ₹47 | +1 ₹ |
| ₹48 | +0 ₹ |
| ₹49 | −2 ₹ |
| ₹50 | −2 ₹ |
| ₹52 | −2.00 |
| ₹54 | −2 ₹ |
| ₹60 | −2 ₹ |
| ₹62 | −2 ₹ |

*Solution:*

1. For $S_t > 50$, the option will not be exercised since dollar has higher price in the market. There will be net loss of ₹2.00.
2. For ₹49 < ($S_t$) < 50, option will be exercised but there will be net loss of ₹1.
3. For $S_t < 48$ the option will be exercised, and there will be net gain.

**P.7.**  A straddle is bought with the following data:

$$X = \$1.7495/£$$
$$C = \$0.0031/£$$
$$P = \$0.0091/£$$

Prepare the profit profile of the option straddle strategy.

*Solution:*    Profit profile with straddle:

| $S_t$ | Gain(+)/loss(−) on call | Gain/loss on put | Net gains/loss |
|---|---|---|---|
| 1.7065 | −0.0031 | +0.6339 | 0.0308 |
| 1.7145 | −0.0031 | +0.0259 | 0.0228 |
| 1.7155 | −0.0031 | +0.0249 | 0.0218 |
| 1.7265 | −0.0031 | +0.0139 | 0.0108 |
| 1.7373 | −0.0031 | +0.0031 | 0.0000 |
| 1.7425 | −0.0031 | −0.0021 | −0.0052 |
| 1.7725 | 0.0199 | −0.0091 | 0.0018 |
| 1.7755 | 0.0229 | −0.0091 | 0.0138 |
| 1.7785 | 0.0259 | −0.0091 | 0.0168 |
| 1.7815 | 0.0289 | −0.0091 | 0.0198 |
| 1.7855 | 0.0329 | −0.0091 | 0.0238 |
| 1.7855 | 0.0359 | −0.0091 | 0.0268 |
| 1.7925 | 0.0399 | −0.0091 | 0.0308 |

**P.8.** A currency is currently worth $0.80£. It is expected to increase or decrease in its value by 2% over the next two months. The domestic and foreign risk-free interest rates are 6% and 8%. Calculate the value of a two-month European call option with strike price 0.80 through Binomial option pricing model.

*Solution:*

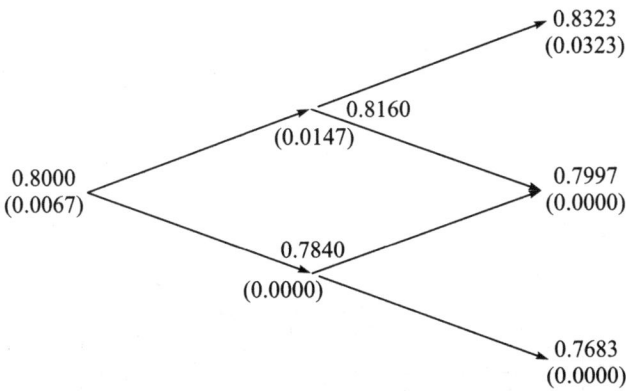

The above tree shows the exchange rate movements. In this case $u = 1.02$ and $d = 0.98$. The probability of upward movement is:

$$P = \frac{e^{(0.06-0.08)\times 0.08333} - 0.98}{1.02 - 0.98} = 0.4584$$

The tree shows that the value of an option to purchase one unit of currency is $0.0067.

**P.9.** Calculate the value of three-month at-the-money European call option on stock index when the index is at 250, risk-free interest rate is 10% per annum, volatility of index is 18% per annum and dividend yield on index is 3% per annum.

*Solution:* In this case $S = 250$, $X = 250$ $r = 0.10$, $s = 0.18$, $T = 0.25$, $q = 0.03$ then

$$d_1 = \frac{\ln(250/250) + (0.010 - 0.03 + 0.18^2/2)\,0.25}{0.18\sqrt{0.23}}$$

$$= 0.2394$$

and

$$d_2 = d_1 - 0.18\sqrt{0.25} = 0.1494$$

The call price is:

$$= 250N(0.2394)e^{-0.03\times 0.25} - 250N(0.1494)e^{-0.10\times 0.25}$$

$$= 250 \times 0.5946e^{-0.03\times 0.25} - 250 \times 0.5594e^{-0.10\times 0.25}$$

So, Price = ₹11.14

**P.10.** Assume that on April 1, an American firm has purchased a mainframe computer from a German firm for 12,50,000 marks. Payment must be made in German marks on August 1. Let us further assume that premium for mark call option with a strike price of $0.5000/DM and premium August expiration date is 0.03 cents. As there are 62,500 units per mark option, US firm will need 20 call option to buy 12,50,000 marks. Current spot rate for marks is $0.4900, the US Company believes that spot rate by August 1 will rise $0.600. Show how American company can use call option to hedge.

***Solution:***    Price of 20 marks call option = $375 (0.030 cent × 20 × 62,500)

Spot price = $0.4900

Strike price = $0.5000

Profit profile of European call option on mark:

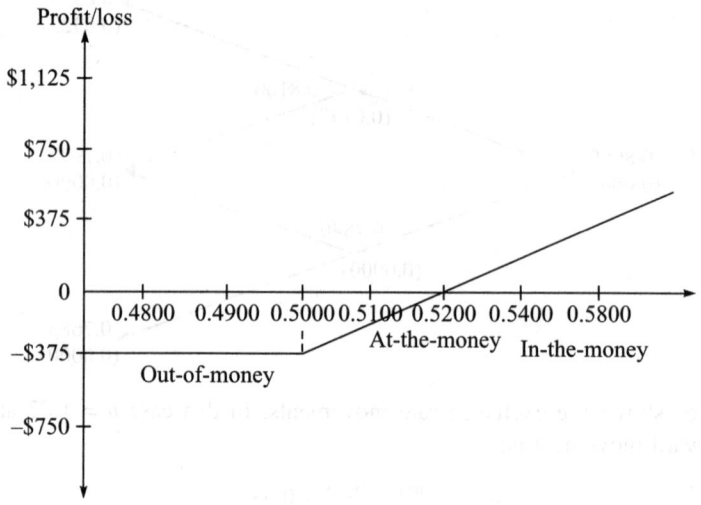

So if on August 1 spot price is $0.6000, the profit to American company by using currency option will be

($0.6000 − $0.5300) = ($0.07 × 62,500 × 20) = $8,75,000

## SUGGESTED READINGS

1. Amin, K. and Jarrow, R.A., Pricing foreign currency options under stochastic interest rates, *Journal of International Money and Finance*, 10, pp. 310–329, 1991.
2. Kodres, R. and Srivastava, Foreign currency futures, *Journal of International Economics*, Vol. 22, pp. 1–24, 1987.
3. Chang, J. and Shankar, L., Hedging effectiveness of currency options and currency futures, *The Journal of Futures Markets*, Vol. 6, No. 3, pp. 295–314, 1987.
4. Garman, M.B. and Kohlhagen, S.W., Foreign currency option values, *Journal of International Money and Finance*, pp. 231–237, December 1983.
5. Westerfield Jaffe, Ross, *Corporate Finance*, Tata MaGraw-Hill, New Delhi, 2005.
6. Biger, N. and Hull, J., The valuation of currency options, *Financial Management*, 12, Spring 1983.
7. Jeff, Madura, *International Financial Management*, International Thomson Publishing, USA, 2000.
8. NSE website

# REVIEW QUESTIONS

1. What is currency option market? What are its features? Explain with examples.
2. Write a detailed note on various terms used in foreign currency options.
3. Explain the foreign currency option contract? What is its mechanism? Explain with suitable examples.
4. Distinguish between the OTC and exchange-traded currency options. Also explain the trading mechanism of options at OTC.
5. Compare and contrast between currency futures and currency options. Which is better for small investors and why?
6. "Pricing of currency is not different from other financial options." Comment on the statement with suitable examples.
7. What are various important observations regarding currency option quotation? Discuss and give your suggestions too in this respect.
8. What are various strategies that a trader can use while trading in currency options?
9. Taking a hypothetical example draw a profit/loss profile of buyer and writer of a call option.
10. Taking a hypothetical example draw a profit/loss profile of buyer and seller (writer) of a currency put option.
11. What is a spread strategy? Discuss its types with examples.
12. Write short notes on
   (a) Bull call spread
   (b) Bull put spread with suitable examples
13. What is straddles strategy? Discuss its types with suitable illustrations.
14. What do you understand by currency straddle strategy? By taking hypothetical examples, draw a profit/loss profile from a straddle strategy.
15. Distinguish between spread, straddle and strangle options strategies and compare them with examples.
16. What are various components of option valuation/option premium? Discuss with suitable examples.
17. Discuss the various determinants of the currency option value with examples.
18. Critically examine the term option valuation with suitable examples.
19. What types of price expectations might cause an investor to assume a long straddle position? Discuss with suitable illustration.
20. Suppose that an investor strategy believes that currency prices will remain stable for at least the next three months. What currency strategy might investor may use to earn profit from this belief?
21. Explain the currency options trading in India along with your suggestions in this respect.

# UNSOLVED PROBLEMS

**P.1.** Assume that call option on British pound on February 1 is $1.60/£ and premium is 1.10 cents, expiration date is June. Raman anticipates that spot rate of the pound will increase to $1.70/£ by May 1. What will be profit to the Raman by exercising the option, if anticipation proves correct?

**P.2.** The put premium per UK pound on August 1 is $0.05, the settlement date is October 25 and the strike price is $1.90. A speculator anticipates that the spot rate for the pound will fall to $1.72 by

October 25. If the speculator's expectation is correct, what would be his profit for speculating two put options (62,500 pounds)?

**P.3.**    A strangle is bought with the following data:

| | |
|---|---|
| Current spot price | = $1.7465/£ |
| Call exercise price | $X_c = $1.7495 |
| Put exercise price | $X_p = $1.7365 |
| | $C = P = 0.0037$ |

Show the profit profile of the strangle.

**P.4.**    An American speculator has purchased a put option on pound sterling with a premium of $0.04/£. Exercise price is $1.65/£. At the time of exercise of option, spot rate is $1.50/£. Standard size of put option is $31,250. What is the profit made on this option?

**P.5.**    Following is the data on a put option on Euro:

| | |
|---|---|
| Premium | = 3% |
| Maturity | = 3 months |
| Strike price | = Euro 0.99/$ |
| Spot rate | = Euro 0.9920/$ |

What is the break-even rate?

**P.6.**    Suppose a call option on a purchase of dollar for ₹46.00 while it is quoted as ₹48.00 in the market, and the premium paid for call action is ₹2.60. Calculate the intrinsic value and time value of the option.

**P.7.**    An exporter knows that he would receive US $5,00,000 in three months. He buys a put option of three-month maturity at the strike price of ₹43/US$. Spot rate is ₹43/US$. Forward rate is also 43.00/US$, premium to be paid is 2.5%. Show the various possibilities of how option is going to be exercised.

**P.8.**    An importer, M/s Sunil & Company is to pay 2 million US dollar in three months. The firm wants to cover his risk with call option. Spot rate, forward rate and strike price are ₹45 per dollar. The premium is 3%. Discuss various possibilities that may occur after two months.

# Annexure

## CURRENCY DERIVATIVES MARKET IN INDIA

### Introduction

Business operations, by their very nature, are exposed to several risks in financial markets. The major financial decision is, of course, the financing mix (Debt vs Equity) but business operations expose the corporate to risks arising from fluctuations in foreign exchange rates, interest rates, commodity prices, equity prices, etc. The risk appetite of the corporate determines the extent of hedging as well as the mechanisms for managing these risks. While market savvy corporates would like to manage their financial exposures actively, the risk-averse corporates would prefer to hedge themselves against them and focus on their core businesses. Irrespective of the risk preferences, understanding the financial risks their businesses are exposed to is critical for the survival of any non-financial corporation.

Financial corporations provide corporates the necessary instruments and solutions to manage their exposures. Further, financial corporations themselves need to cover the risks innate in their balance sheets. Historically, derivatives have emerged as ideal vehicles for transference of risk from one entity to another. Over the decades, financial markets created a variety of derivative products to suit the myriad needs of businesses. Apart from being ideal vehicles for transference of risk, derivatives helped markets by increasing depth and improving transparency. The easy availability, high leverage effect, low credit exposure and flexibility made derivatives popular with the users.

In the pre-liberalization era, Indian business operated in an insular economic environment shielded from global competition. The limited number of financial products and the strict regulatory regime did not lend much scope for a derivative market to develop. Typically an Indian Corporate depended on term lending institutions for their project financing and the commercial banks for working capital finance. Commercial banks were content to keep the asset side of their balance sheet liquid and were hardly alive to the risks arising from the mismatched interest rate re-pricing of assets and liabilities. A simple and much restricted foreign exchange forward contract was the only derivative product in the pre-liberalized era.

The liberalization process initiated in the early nineties brought in momentous change in the economic environment. The need to operate in a rapidly globalizing and progressively deregulating economy forced Indian businesses to take a closer look at all aspects of their operations to remain competitive. In this process, the neglected areas like financial risks have come into sharper focus and treasury has become a hub of action for all major corporates.

The first tentative steps towards developing a derivative market in India started with freeing of the conventional forward contract. Allowing banks to pass on gains upon cancellation to the customers and permitting customers to cancel and re-book were the first significant changes in the long dormant derivatives market in India. Further easing of restrictions came in the form of introduction of Cross Currency Forward Contracts. Prior to this all, structures involving derivatives needed specific approval from the Ministry of Finance and RBI.

## Genesis of Currency Option in India

The Reserve Bank of India has considered introduction of Foreign Currency-Rupee (FC/INR) options as a part of developing derivatives market in India and adding to the spectrum of hedge products available to residents for hedging currency exposures. In this context, it constituted a Technical Committee to lay out the road map and work out the details regarding pricing, risk management, accounting and regulatory issues. Report is outcome of the deliberations the committee had between July 2002 and October 2002.

The committee looked at the evolution of option markets as well as the impact of introduction of currency options in other countries. The current status of derivative markets in India was discussed in detail to make a case for speedy introduction of currency options in India. The committee considered the inputs gained from the above exercise as well as feedback from clients to evolve a roadmap for the introduction of Foreign Currency-Rupee option markets in India. The Committee recommends a phased introduction of the product with further product enhancements in stages as follows:

1. Options may be introduced as OTC contracts with specifications like notional, strike, and maturity tailored to client needs. Initially they may be introduced as vanilla European exercise call and put options and structures thereof.

2. Authorized dealers may provide bid-offer quotes for options of varying maturities and exercise prices to their clients. The clients who would be able to use this product would be within the framework of Schedule I and II of the RBI Notification No. FEMA 25/RB-2000, dated May 3, 2002 (similar to forward contracts). Further, they should also comply with the existing requirements regarding derivative products as per RBI circular A.D. (M.A. Series) circular No.1, dated January 24, 2002. In the initial phase, the clients could be allowed to enter into cost reduction strategies involving selling of options, provided there is no net flow of premium to them.

3. The committee suggests that an interbank market in FC-INR option contracts be allowed to enable Authorized Dealers (ADs) to initiate positions and manage risks on positions arising out of client and interbank transactions within the prescribed limits.

4. Authorized dealers could quote the option premium as absolute amount or as a percentage of notional. The committee does not recommend any particular model/formula for pricing options. However, internationally, implied volatilities on the basis of Black Scholes model (the volatility input in BS formula, which gives the option price) are quoted in the interbank market (by convention). The committee feels that the same convention may be followed in Indian markets for standardization and transparency. The price may be determined independently by any mechanism but can be filtered through BS formulae for quoting. FEDAI could publish on regular basis a matrix of polled implied volatility estimates. Various market participants could then use this matrix and BS valuations for MTM of their portfolios.

5. Regarding hedging of option portfolios the committee suggests that
   - Authorized dealers should be free to access spot market to delta-hedge the option portfolios.
   - Authorized dealers may be allowed to hedge the other "Greeks" through interbank option transactions.

6. With regard to Risk Management Systems, the committee recommends the following in the nature of best practices for authorized dealers:
   - Approval from their Board/Risk Committee/ALCO for dealing in the product with appropriate risk management framework.

- Risk management system, which allows daily computation of the MTM of the portfolio and various Greeks.
- Authorized Dealers (ADs) could also be required to inform their appropriate reporting authority on regular intervals about the activities undertaken on this product.

7. The committee suggests that Authorized Dealers (ADs) report separately the delta equivalent of option positions and total open exchange positions to RBI for the purpose of monitoring the aggregate risk being carried by the system. Authorized dealers may also be required to report to RBI on periodical basis, details of the option transactions undertaken, net option portfolio delta, total open exchange position and portfolio "Greeks" for information.

8. The committee recommends use of International Swap Dealers Association (ISDA) documentation as the basis for recording contracts between authorized dealers and counter-parties.

9. The accounting framework currently applicable for cross-currency options may be followed for FC-INR option transactions.

10. The committee suggests periodic review of the market development by FEDAI and Reserve Bank of India. The committee is of the view that, based on the experience gained, the following may be considered:
    - Introduction of options with exotic features
    - Clients being net receivers of premium

## Derivative Products Available to Indian Players

The Indian derivatives market is continuously evolving; though there have been significant milestones in the development phase, the market has to still traverse a long way to become comparable with developed markets in terms of product variety, market sophistication, liquidity, depth and volumes.

The derivative products can be broadly classified as:

1. Product traded in overseas markets
2. Products involving the Rupee-Rupee derivative markets

RBI allows Indian corporates need based access to a wide range of derivative products available in established international exchanges like LME, Simex, LIFFE, CBOT and the OTC market. Some of these products are:

***Cross currency options:*** All Indian clients are allowed to purchase cross currency options to hedge exposures arising out of trade. They are allowed to use cost reduction strategies and structures as long as they are not net receivers of premium. Authorized dealers in India who offer these products are required to cover these products back to back in international markets and not carry the risk in their own books.

***Foreign currency interest rate swaps/Forward rate agreements/Interest rate options/Swaptions/ Caps/Floors:*** Indian banks are allowed to use the above products to hedge interest rate and currency mismatches on their balance sheets. Clients, resident as well as non-resident, are allowed to use the above products as hedges for liabilities on their balance-sheets.

***Rupee derivatives:*** These include the following:

*Equity derivatives.* Exchange traded derivatives like index swaps, index options, stock futures and stock options are becoming popular with both retail investors and institutions. These are traded on both the major exchanges, Bombay Stock Exchange (BSE) and National Stock Exchange (NSE).

*Commodity futures.* Several commodity futures exchanges have come up in India in places like Mumbai, Kolkata, Bangalore, Cochin, etc. Each of these exchanges specializes in a single commodity. Market action in them is dominated by producers' cartels and public sector units like STC. The modus operandi is similar to major international exchanges. Liquidity is poor with market being dominated by few players.

*Rupee interest rate swaps.* A market in these swaps has evolved quite rapidly over the last year. This is an OTC market wherein the major players are banks (nationalized, private and foreign) as well as corporates. Though the number of players and hence the liquidity is low, daily market turnover has increased from about ₹200 crores last year to current turnover of ₹600 crores with the entry of new players and increased corporate activity. The market has seen deals for maturity up to 10 years and the most popular benchmarks are overnight interest rates (MIBOR rare, overnight forward implied MITOR) and other benchmarks like six-month MIFOR (forward implied rupee rates) as well as Government security benchmark yields (in INBMK swaps).

A major step in the development of OTC rupee derivatives is amendment of Securities Contract and Regulation Act (SCRA) to accord legal sanctity to OTC traded derivatives. SCRA requires a derivative product to be exchange traded and settled to be legally enforceable. Most non-standardized (derivatives other than futures) derivatives world over are OTC traded. Besides, commercial banks are the driving force behind Indian derivatives market and this suggests that OTC market would dominate the derivatives market in times to come. This being the case, unless Securities Contract and Regulation Act accords legal sanctity to OTC traded derivatives, a good many players would perforce continue to stay away from this market. FIMMDA has proposed to RBI an amendment to Securities Contract and Regulation Act. A major fillip to Indian derivative markets would be the evolution of uniform documentation and market practices to fully take care of the complexities of derivative products. The committee feels that the issue would lose criticality as more and more players sign standard International Swap Dealers Association (ISDA) documentation agreements for derivative contracts and the market bodies, FIMMDA and FEDAI, evolve norms for the players in the respective markets.

The establishment of internationally accepted and understood accounting standards and disclosure norms and their recognition by tax authorities in the Indian scenario, is also a required step for a more rapid and orderly development of derivatives market.

## Prospects of Derivatives in India

The rupee derivatives market is characterized by a lower number of active corporates, fewer market makers and the resulting paucity in liquidity and market depth. Only a handful of corporate clients are actively using derivatives for their risk management. As corporate treasuries get sophisticated and new products enter the market, the potential is enormous.

Introduction of derivatives on interest rates (caplets, floorlets, swaptions, etc), credit risk (credit linked corporate notes, credit linked swaps, asset backed securities, etc), currency (rupee options) as well as structures combining these products would be expected to complete the market as well as provide the entire spectrum of investment and hedging products to banks, clients, corporates and retail players to manage their finances. Derivatives should make rapid strides in Indian markets with increasing product familiarity, increasing market participation and development of a supporting regulatory, legal and tax framework to encourage the use of new and innovative products in sophisticated risk management strategies.

## FC-INR Options

The current products available in FX derivative markets to hedge the risks on foreign exchange exposures are rupee forwards, rupee forex swaps, cross currency forwards and long-term swaps and cross currency options. However, for hedging forex risk, corporates are restricted to the use of forwards and long-term currency swaps.

Forwards and swaps do remove the uncertainty by hedging the exposure but they also result in the elimination of potential extraordinary gains from the currency position. Currency options provide a way of availing of the upside from any currency exposure while being protected from the downside for the payment of an upfront premium. Introduction of FC-INR options would enable Indian forex market participants manage their exposures better by hedging the foreign exchange risk.

The advantages of FC-INR currency options are as follows:

1. Hedge for currency exposures to protect the downside while retaining the upside, by paying a premium upfront. This would be a big advantage for importers, exporters (of both goods and services) as well as businesses with exposures to international prices. Currency options would enable Indian industry and businesses to compete better in international markets by hedging currency risk.

2. Non-linear payoff of the product enables its use as hedge for various special cases and possible exposures, e.g., if an Indian company is bidding for an international assignment where the bid quote would be in dollars but the costs would be in rupees then the company runs a risk till the contract is awarded. Using forwards or currency swaps would create the reverse positions if the company is not allotted the contract but the use of an option contract in this case would freeze the liability only to the option premium paid upfront.

3. The nature of the instrument again makes its use possible as a hedge against uncertainty of the cash flows. Option structures can be used to hedge the volatility along with the non-linear nature of payoffs.

4. Attract further forex investment due to the availability of another mechanism for hedging forex risk.

The committee feels a rupee options market would complement the spot and forwards FX market to provide the complete universe of hedging instruments for corporate customers. FC-INR options would be an instrument that also depends on a unique parameter, the volatility of the underlying, and thus help to complete the market.

The committee observes the above compelling reasons for the introduction of an FC-INR options market in India to complete the spectrum of available rupee derivative products to hedge forex exposures.

## Market Framework of Currency Option in India

The committee has considered the experience gained from international examples well as feedback from corporate clients to suggest the following roadmap for the introduction of option markets in India. The committee suggests a phased introduction of the products with further enhancements in stages. This section of the report deals with the following issues:

1. Inception of the FC-INR options market
   (a) Market structure and regulatory framework
   (b) Pricing and quotations

  (c)  Risk management
  (d)  Documentation and regulatory reporting
  (e)  Accounting
2.  Review and further development of the market

## Regulatory Framework and Nature of the Product

The committee makes the following suggestions regarding the regulatory framework at inception:

***Nature of product:***   The committee had an extensive deliberation regarding the product nature at the inception of the market. There were essentially two views:

1.  A stream of thought was that options being a new product, a conservative approach be followed towards the introduction of the product in Indian markets. It was felt that one should introduce the product in its simplest form, and then gradually move to successive levels of complexity. Options being non-linear products require a sophisticated hedging and risk management framework. The opinion was that introduction of vanilla European options and combinations thereof would give all the concerned players familiarity with the product as well as the opportunity to validate their systems and risk management frameworks.

2.  Another point of view was that the introduction of options could be done in a more comprehensive manner by allowing all exotic options to be dealt at the inception of the market itself. This, it was felt, would reduce the cost to the clients as well as create more interest and liquidity in the market. This step, it was opined, would result in increased sophistication and a more rapid development of the market. Players who have extensive experience in overseas markets would have the risk management framework and systems in place, and could start dealing in these at the very inception of the market.

After extensive deliberations on the pros and cons of both approaches, the committee came to the opinion that though development of market in terms of volumes and sophistication is the ultimate aim, the approach to it may be in phases. At inception, the FC-INR options market could start with plain vanilla European call and put options and structures thereof. Variants of the product could then be introduced after a review when players had developed confidence and comfort with their systems and risk management framework to handle products with exotic features (e.g. American exercise, barriers, digital payoffs, Asian payoffs, etc.). Hence, the committee recommends the following product structure at inception:

1.  Options can be introduced as over-the-counter contracts. Initially they may be introduced as plain vanilla European exercise call and put options and structures thereof.
2.  Contract specifications:
    (a)  *Over-the-counter contracts*. It can be tailored to suit the counterparty needs.
    (b)  *Currency pairs*. FC-INR where the foreign currency may be the currency desired by the client.
    (c)  *Exercise style*. European
    (d)  *Notional amount*. No minimum notional amount is suggested. It can be suited to meet counterparties' requirements.
    (e)  *Premium:* Payable, usually on spot basis.
    (f)  *Settlement*. As specified in the contract, either delivery on spot basis or net cash settlement in rupees on spot basis, depending on the FC-INR spot rate on maturity date. (Reference rate could be the RBI reference rate at 12.00 noon or as specified in the contract itself.)

(g) *Strike price.* Tailored to counterparties' needs.

(h) *Maturity.* The maturity of the options could be tailored to the requirements of the transacting parties. The typical maturities observed in international markets in currency options are 1 week, 2 weeks, 1 month, 2 months, 3 months, 6 months, 9 months and 1 year.

*Market participants:* Authorized dealers may be allowed by the RBI to enter into FC-INR option contracts with their clients. Authorized Dealers (ADs) could provide bid-offer quotes for options of varying maturities and exercise prices to their clients.

*Market participants—Clients for option contracts.* A person resident in India could be allowed to use foreign currency—rupee (FC-INR) options to hedge his exposure arising out of trade, foreign currency liabilities, etc. within the framework of Schedule I to the RBI Notification No. FEMA 25/RB-2000, dated May 3, 2002.

Currency options would hedge currency risks similar to forward contracts, and hence the committee suggests that these option contracts may be allowed to all market participants for all exposures on which forward contracts are currently allowed. These would include:

1. Indian residents
   (a) To hedge genuine exchange rate exposures arising out of trade/business (authorized dealer may book transactions on estimated exposure for uncertain amounts or for clients with regular annual transactions)
   (b) FC loans/bonds after approval by the RBI
   (c) In case of Global Depository Receipts (GDRs), after the issue price has been finalized
   (d) Balance in EEFC accounts
2. Foreign institutional investors
   (a) To hedge their exposures in India provided that the value of the hedge does not exceed 15 percent of the market value of the equity at initiation of the hedge.
3. Non-resident Indian or overseas corporate body
   (a) Amount of dividend due on share held in an Indian company
   (b) Balances held in FCNR and NRE accounts
   (c) Amount of investment under portfolio scheme in accordance with FERA or FEMA.

In addition, FC-INR option contracts may be permitted to hedge the following:

1. Special cases and contingent exposures, e.g. if an Indian company is bidding for an international assignment where the bid quote would be in dollars but the costs would be in rupees then the company runs a risk till the contract is awarded. Using forwards or currency swaps would create the reverse positions if the company is not allotted the contract but the use of an option contract in this case would freeze the liability only to the option premium paid upfront.
2. Derived foreign exchange exposure, viz. exposures generated because of swaps and other permitted transactions (An example of a derived exposure is as follows: A corporate XYZ has done a FC/INR swap to move from a rupee liability and take FX exposure, in which it has to pay USD six-month LIBOR semi-annually. In this case, the corporate may be allowed to book rupee options on the next US interest payment due.)

*Principle of one hedge structure transaction for one exposure at any time.* Only one hedge transaction may be booked against a particular exposure for a given time period. At the maturity of the period, the client may decide whether he wants to change the hedge instrument.

**EXAMPLE:**    An exporter has some USD receivables after six months. He might choose to hedge himself in this manner:

- Sell a forward for three months
- At maturity, net settle the contract and buy a put option for three months (or he may do the reverse)

Since options and forwards essentially hedge the same risk, the clients may be allowed to switch between instruments at maturity of the original contract. Participating forwards with embedded optionality may be allowed as long as these are booked/cancelled as a single transaction.

*Market participants—Authorized dealers.* The current regulatory framework allows all authorized dealers to offer all FX derivative products (approval required from RBI Exchange Control Department for offering cross currency options on covered basis). However, making markets in option products requires a certain set of competencies, skills and risk management systems along with strong financials.

To avoid systemic risk that can arise because of failure of authorized dealers to manage their option portfolios, the committee suggests that RBI permission be obtained by the Authorized Dealers (ADs) to make markets in options. Authorized dealers who have the required resources and risk management systems to manage option portfolios may apply to Exchange Control department after getting the necessary internal board approvals.

Other banks may use this product for the purpose of hedging trading books and balance sheet exposures or offering to their clients on covered basis.

*Interbank market.* The committee suggests that an interbank market be allowed in option contracts due to following reasons:

- Allowing interbank market in options will help Authorized Dealers (ADs) to effectively manage their options positions within the limits prescribed.
- Options being non-linear products, the risks of open positions can be completely hedged only by entering into other option contracts.
- It will help in providing liquidity and narrow bid-offer quotes.

The committee suggests that Authorized Dealers (ADs) may be allowed to hedge risks on options positions arising out of contracts with clients as well as initiate positions by entering into contracts with other Authorized Dealers (ADs).

*Clients as net receivers of premium.* The current regulatory framework for cross currency options, as mentioned in RBI circular AP/DIR 19, allows residents to use various cost reduction strategies subject to the provision that there is no net inflow of premium to the client. The committee, in the course of its deliberation, received feedback from various clients who had expressed the opinion that clients should be allowed to write naked options as well as be net receivers of premium in case of structures. The committee feels that the risks arising from a naked option are almost similar to that from a zero cost structure, and in the long run, there is a need for allowing clients to write naked options and be net receivers of premium in case of structures.

However given that rupee options will be a new product in the Indian scenario, the committee felt that it was prudent to take a conservative approach. The rationale proposed was that as long as a client is not a net receiver of premium, he would exercise restraint and caution in using the product. The committee suggests that at the inception of the product, the clients may be allowed to use structures as long as they are not net receivers of premium. However, it recommends that this clause may be reviewed in future based on the developments in the market.

*Cancelling and rebooking of contracts.* The committee suggests that the current rationale regarding cancellations and rebooking for forward contracts may be continued with for the FC-INR options market in India. This may be done with certain modifications intended to increase flexibility to market participants to manage their exposures, as well as generating liquidity and encouraging the development of the market. The modifications are as follows:

1. For exposures having maturity less than a year, as in forwards, clients may cancel and rebook option contracts without any restrictions. The same rationale may be extended for exposures with maturity more than a year keeping in mind the currency reserves and the market scenario at that period of time.

2. In particular market conditions, there could be concerns of volatility arising out of frequent cancellations and rebooking. Under such circumstances, a number of alternatives could be considered. One such alternative is to restrict the minimum maturity of the option contracts to one month in case the underlying exposure has a residual maturity of more than a year. In such cases, the contract once cancelled may not be rebooked till the maturity date of the cancelled contract. Another alternative could be to impose certain limits on the notional amounts for which cancellations and rebooking is permitted.

**EXAMPLE:**   An importer has a USD payable after 1.5 years.

- He books a call options for three months.
- He decides to cancel the option contract after one month. In case he does so, he may not be allowed to reinstate another hedge transaction for the same exposure till the maturity of the original option contract.
- The above measure should remove the possibility of increased volatility because of frequent cancellation/rebooking of contracts.

The same mechanism could be used as regards to use of option contracts, in cases where forward contracts cannot be cancelled and rebooked at will; viz. balances in EEFC accounts, hedge transactions of foreign institutional investors, and so on.

To sum up, cancellation and rebooking may be allowed for option contracts as follows:

| Cancellation/Rebooking allowed | Cancellation/Rebooking permitted conditionally | Cancellation/Rebooking not permitted |
|---|---|---|
| Residents | Exposures of duration greater than 1 year | Cancellation/rebooking of option hedges will not be permitted for the following: |
| • Genuine exposures out of trade/ Business up to 1 year-Cancellation/ rebooking of options booked as hedges allowed for all exporters and importers | Option contracts of minimum maturity of one month; No rebooking until the residual maturity of cancelled contract | 1. Non-resident Indians/Overseas corporate bodies |
| • For exposures more than 1 year— cancellation/rebooking of option hedges allowed for only exporters | Alternatively limits on the amount for which cancellations and rebooking is permitted<br><br>The above conditions to be applicable to | • Dividend<br><br>• FCNR and NRE deposits |

*(Contd.)*

(Contd.)

| GDR receipts-<br>Cancellation/rebooking allowed for all option deals as hedges to above exposures | Residents<br>• Exposures more than 1 year— importers<br>• Balances in EEFC accounts<br>• Option contracts on derived exposures<br><br>FII exposures in India | 2. Investment under portfolio scheme<br>Option contracts in these cases, once cancelled cannot be rebooked for the remaining maturity of the exposure |
|---|---|---|

*Hedging.* Since options involve non-linear payoffs, hedging schemes for options positions tend to be dynamic in nature and hedges are required to be rebalanced frequently. Static-one time hedging of an option position is possible only by entering into an offsetting option transaction. The hedging of an option portfolio entails calculation of various "Greeks" (Details provided in Schedule IV).

The most common form of hedging involves buying/selling of currencies in spot market to hedge the delta of option portfolio. As the spot rate changes, the moneyness of the option portfolio also changes hence the delta needs to be rebalanced frequently. Market makers are required to make their own judgements about the frequency of rebalancing the delta-hedged portfolio. However, if a model is being used to decide about the frequency of rebalancing, such model should be sufficiently back-tested to ensure validity of assumptions. Hedging schemes also involve hedging of gamma and Vega of their portfolios by entering into various option contracts.

The committee suggests that

- Authorized dealers–Market makers should be allowed to hedge the option portfolios by accessing the spot market.
- The extent and frequency of the hedging could be decided by the dealers.
- Authorized dealers could also be allowed to hedge the other "Greeks" of their portfolios by entering into option transactions in the interbank market.

*Pricing and quotation systems.* The premium of FC-INR options is dependent upon the spot rate, interest rates in both currencies and the estimate of future volatility in spot rate. While other parameters are fixed at any point in time, the estimate of future volatility can differ. Internationally, premium is quoted as percentage of the notional amount and can be settled in any of the currencies involved. It is the market practice internationally to use standardized Black-Scholes model (B-S Model) for quoting. The volatility that results in required premium is called implied volatility (implied by the required premium based on standard BS model) and is also quoted in the market.

Implied volatility is, therefore, an estimate of future volatility in B-S context. This estimate can differ significantly from historical observed volatility depending upon the markets expectations about future.

The committee suggests that

- Authorized dealers could quote the option premium in rupees or as a percentage of the Rupee notional amount. The premium could be paid in Rupee terms.
- Authorized dealers could also quote (especially in interbank market) on the basis of the implied volatility as mentioned earlier. Market players will also require pricing estimates for Marking-to-Market of their portfolios at regular intervals. Hence, it is recommended that, FEDAI could publish on regular basis a matrix of Black-Scholes implied volatilities for various maturities and strikes based on market poll. For MTM of a given contract, the price could then be estimated based on the interpolated implied volatility using BS Model. Since

there could be a number of contracts outstanding with different strikes and maturities, the use of B-S implied volatilities is suggested here to ensure standardization of MTM values across various players. The use of Black-Scholes/Garman-Kohlhagen model suggested here does not imply that committee recommends this model as pricing model. The premium of the option could be arrived at using any model as market players deem fit.

## Risk Management Framework

*Authorized dealers:*   The committee has the following recommendations in the nature of best practices:
- Authorized Dealers (ADs) could be required to put in place a risk management system, which allows them to compute daily MTM of the portfolio and various other Greeks.
- Authorized Dealers (ADs) could also be required to obtain product approval from their Board/Risk committee/ALCO. Specifically this approval could include:
  (a) Product structure proposed
  (b) Pricing and hedging
  (c) Segregation of responsibilities between front, middle and back offices with relation to dealing, confirmation and settlement
  (d) Limits for delta and other Greeks
  (e) Stop losses for open positions
- Authorized Dealers (ADs) could also be required to report to their Board/Risk Committees/ ALCO on regular intervals about the activities undertaken on this product.

*Risk management for clients:*   With regard to risk management systems for clients, the committee recommends that clients interested in dealing in options would need to comply with the existing requirements regarding derivative products as per RBI circular A.D. (M.A. Series) circular No.1, dated January 24, 2002.

The Board of Directors of the corporate has to

- Draw up a risk management policy for the corporate
- Lay down clear guidelines for concluding the transactions
- Institutionalize arrangements for a quarterly review of operations and annual audit of transactions to verify compliance with the regulations
- Have in place a board resolution authorizing the corporate to enter into derivative transactions
- Name the authorized signatories who would be allowed to transact on behalf of the corporate

*Documentation:*   The committee considered both the use of ICOM documentation and International Swap Dealers Association (ISDA) documentation for recording contracts between authorized dealers and counterparties. The committee felt that the International Swap Dealers Association (ISDA) documentation was more comprehensive and that market players had familiarity with International Swap Dealers Association (ISDA) documentation, which they had used for other FX derivative transactions.

The committee, therefore, recommends the use of International Swap Dealers Association (ISDA) documentation for recording FC-INR contracts.

*Regulatory reporting:*   The committee suggests that authorized dealers be required to report to RBI on a weekly basis the following information regarding option transactions undertaken and the option portfolio:

Option Transaction Report for the week

| Sr. no. | Trade date | Client/C-party Name* | Notional | Option call/put | Strike | Maturity | Premium |
|---|---|---|---|---|---|---|---|
| | | | | | | | |
| | | | | | | | |

*Mention B/S as the client name along with counterparty, if the transaction has been done for the balance sheet.

Option Positions Report

| USD notional outstanding | | Net portfolio delta | Net portfolio gamma | Net portfolio Vega | Total net open spot position |
|---|---|---|---|---|---|
| Calls | Puts | (USD) | (USD) | (USD) | (USD) |
| | | | | | |

Authorized dealers could also be required to report the change in delta expected for the portfolio if the spot changes by a certain value (0.5%, 1%, etc).

# Other Derivatives

# Chapter 21

# Advanced Financial Derivatives

## LEARNING OBJECTIVES

After reading this chapter, students will be able to

➢ Understand the other advanced derivatives available in the financial derivatives markets.

➢ Be aware of the types of interest rate caps, interest rate floors and collars.

➢ Know the basic of few exotic options.

➢ Know the forward start options, compound options, packages, etc.

➢ Be aware of the concept of shout options, Asian options, exchange options, rainbow options, basket option and barrier options.

➢ Know the pay-off profile of some complex derivatives.

## 21.1 INTRODUCTION

The derivatives securities which are not as standard American or European and have complicated payoff are called *non-standard options* or *derivatives*. Since most of them relate to option, they are also called *exotic options*. A conventional option has a fixed length maturity and the payoff depends upon only on the underlying asset's price at the exercise date in comparison to a fixed strike price. But exotic option include a wide variety of option with some unusual features relating to calculation of underlying asset price, strike price or expiration conditions. In other words, exotic option is contingent claim that obtains value contingent on the occurrence of an event (or events).

Generally most of such derivatives are designed at over-the-counter markets to meet the specific needs of the corporations. In this section, some of the advanced derivatives which are option-based instruments and techniques will be discussed. Afterwards, some of the derivatives relating to interest rate options, and afterward, some more exotic options will be explained.

## 21.2    INTEREST RATE OPTIONS

Interest rate options whose payoff is dependent in some way on the level of interest rates. Recently, they have become very much popular in the derivatives markets. A variety of different types of interest rates are now actively traded in the market. For example, interest rate futures options are traded on exchanges, whereas interest rate caps, floors, collars, etc. are traded on the over-the-counter markets.

## 21.3    INTEREST RATE CAPS (CAPS)

An interest rate cap is an agreement between two parties in which one party, for an up-front premium, agrees to compensate the other party if a designated interest rate, called the reference rate, is different from a predetermined level. In other words, an interest rate cap is an option to fix a ceiling or maximum short-term interest rate payment. The contract is written such that the buyer of the cap will receive a cash payment equal to the difference between the actual market interest rate and the cap strike rate on the notional principal, if the market rate rises above the strike rate. Usually, caps are designed to provide insurance against the rate of interest on a floating-rate loan going above a certain level. This level is known as *the cap rate*.

### 21.3.1    Terms of the Interest Rate Agreement (Caps or Floors)

1. The reference rate
2. The strike rate
3. The length of the agreement
4. The frequency of settlement
5. The notional principal amount

Let us explain the above with an example. Suppose that $X$ buys an interest rate cap from $Y$ with terms as follows: Assume the reference rate—LIBOR six-month rate, strike rate 6 percent, agreement for 5 years, settlement every six months, notional principal amount is $10 million.

As per this contract, every six month for the next 5 years, $Y$ will pay $X$ whenever six-month LIBOR exceeds 6 percent. The payment will be equal to the dollar value of the difference between six-month LIBOR and 6 percent times the notional principal amount divided by two. For example, if six-month from now, six-month LIBOR is 9 percent, then $Y$ will pay $X$ 3 percent (9 percent – 6 percent) times $10 million divided by 2 or $1,50,000. If the six-month LIBOR is 6 percent or less then $Y$ does not have to make any payment to $X$. The operation of an interest rate cap is illustrated in Figure 21.1.

It is observed from Figure 21.1 that first settlement, LIBOR rate is 8 percent, so difference of LIBOR and strike rate (cap rate) 6 percent, i.e., 2 percent will be paid to the buyer, at the second settlement date $T_2$, LIBOR is 4 percent, which is less than cap rate (6 percent), so no payment will be made to the buyer and so on.

No theoretical limit exists to the specification of interest rate caps. They vary in maturities and structures. Majority of trading falls between one and five years. Interest rate caps have further an additional benefit, i.e., reset of interest rate cap after a particular interval. For example, a common interest rate cap would be a three-year cap on the three-month LIBOR. This means that the total cap agreement will last for three years, in which there will be a total of eleven LIBOR interest rate reset dates or fixings. No reset exists for the first three-month period.

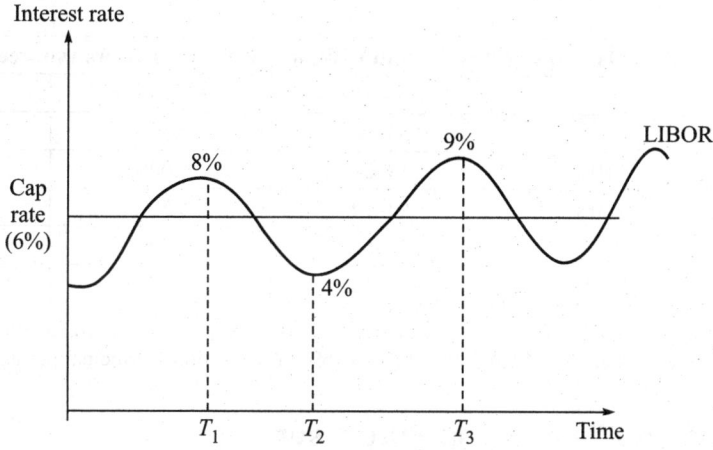

**FIGURE 21.1**    Interest rate cap with LIBOR.

## 21.3.2    Types of Interest Rate Caps

There are two major types of interest rate caps:

**Interest rate guarantee (IRG):**    In this type, the protection to the buyer is provided for a single period only. In other words, the borrower of this option can avail once in the event of a single major variable rate refunding or reinvestment.

**Interest rate cap:**    This protects the borrower for an extended period of time, for example, two to five years, on some interest rate reset. For example, the sub period reset may be the three-month LIBOR or six-month LIBOR. It is also called the cap's tenor.

It is important to note that even though caps are multiperiod options, the full premiums are ordinarily paid upfront.

It is observed that most of the cap dealers are financial institutions, commercial and investment banks. So these dealers, as usual, buy and sell caps and make profit from a spread between the bid price and the ask price. For example, a dealer might bid 1.3 percent and offer 1.35 percent as premium. In other words, the dealer will write a cap for a premium of 1.35 percent and buy a cap for a premium of 1.30 percent. The difference between these two (bid and ask), 0.05 percent (5 basis points), is the dealer's bid-ask spread. Table 21.1 shows interest rate cap and floor quotations.

**TABLE 21.1**    Interest Rate Cap and Floor Quotations

| Maturity | U.S. dollar caps vs three-month LIBOR | | U.S. dollar floors vs three-month LIBOR | |
|---|---|---|---|---|
| | *Cap rate* | *Bid-offer* | *Floor rate* | *Bid-offer* |
| 2 years | 5.00% | 42–46 | 4.00% | 42–47 |
| | 6.00% | 15–19 | 5.00% | 149–154 |
| 3 years | 6.00% | 69–79 | 4.00% | 54–62 |
| | 7.00% | 35–42 | 5.00% | 190–200 |
| 5 years | 7.00% | 147–165 | 5.00% | 245–261 |

*(Contd.)*

*(Contd.)*

| Maturity | U.S. dollar caps vs three-month LIBOR | | U.S. dollar floors vs three-month LIBOR | |
|---|---|---|---|---|
| | *Cap rate* | *Bid-offer* | *Floor rate* | *Bid-offer* |
| 2 years | 6.00% | 35–40 | 5.50% | 57–63 |
| | 6.50% | 19–24 | 6.00% | 101–107 |
| 3 years | 6.00% | 93–99 | 5.50% | 89–96 |
| | 6.50% | 60–65 | 6.00% | 156–161 |
| 5 years | 6.75% | 172–185 | 5.50% | 122–145 |

*Source:* Adapted from *International Financing Review,* July 31, 1993, Issue 990, p. 83. Bid-offer spreads are stated in basis points. For example, "42–46" is 0.42%–0.46% of the notional principal per annum.

## 21.3.3 Payoff Profile of a Cap Purchaser

On the first settlement date, the cap writer will pay the cap holder (buyer) a sum determined as per the following equation:

$$\text{Dealer pays} = D \times \text{MAX [Reference rate} - \text{Cap rate]} \times NP \times LPP$$

where $D$ denotes a dummy variable that takes the values $(+1)$, if the dealer is the cap seller, and $(-1)$, if the dealer is the cap purchaser, MAX is MAX function (as explained in option chapter), $NP$ is notional principal and $LPP$ is length of the payment period. It depends on the reference rate and the frequency of payments.

This is shown in Figure 21.2.

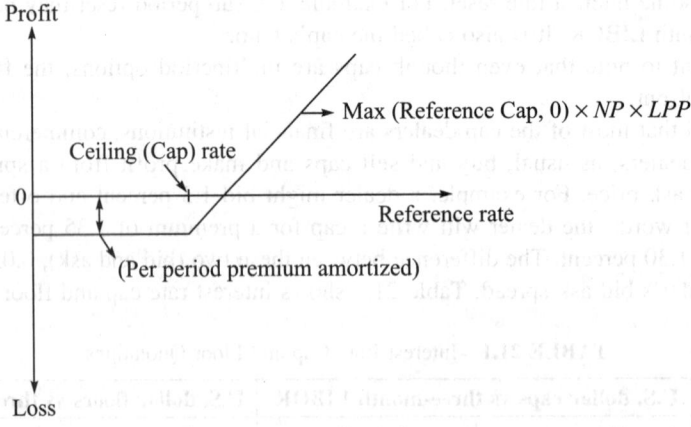

**FIGURE 21.2** Payoff profile for a cap buyer (Per settlement period).

It is observed from Figure 21.2 that the cap's payoff profile looks like long calls but this is not true. A call option usually depicts price rather than rate on the horizontal axis. If the price is substituted for rate on the horizontal axis of the cap's payoff profile then it would like that of long put on a debt instruments. The reason for this is that rates (yields) and prices are inversely related. They are also, sometimes, described as multi-period calls.

## 21.3.4 Per Period Cost on Cap

Normally on a cap option, the premium is paid upfront in a single lump sum, but the cap is a multi-period option, so the payoff profile must amortize the premium to be truly representative. For example, suppose that a four-year semi-annual cap can be purchased for 1.85 percent of the notional principal. Then the premium should be prorated by way of a standard amortization formula in order to find out the true cost of cap per period.

$$\text{Per period cost} = \text{Total premium} + PVAF$$

$$PVAF = \frac{1 - (Y/m)^{-nm}}{Y/m}$$

where $PVAF$ is the present value of annuity factor, $n$ is term of the cap in years, $m$ is number of the payment period and $y$ is annual yield (discount rate).

Suppose that $y$ is 8 percent, then $PVAF$ is 6.7327, and the equation yield 0.2748, which means that the per period value of the premium is 0.2748 percent also called amortized single period premium.

After determining the per period cost ($PPC$), we can find out the effective annual percentage cost as such:

$$\text{Effective annual percentage cost} = (1 + PPC)^m - 1$$

This is significant for the dealer to express the premium paid for the cap as an effective annual percentage cost.

## 21.3.5 A Simple Model of Valuing a Cap

Since caps are multi-period options, the easiest way to value a cap is to decompose it into the actual series of single-period options to which it is equivalent. The series of such single-period option is also called a strip. After that, the fair value of each strip can be determined by using an appropriate single period option pricing model. Hence, the sum of these fair values is the fair value of the cap. The dealer would add or substract a sum to this fair value to obtain the price at which it would ready to buy such a cap.

The factors that usually influence the valuation of a cap are the same as we have seen earlier in the valuation of options. These are like market interest period rate, strike price, volatility and reference rate. Caps are priced as a percentage of the notional principal amount.

Using the Black-Scholes option pricing model, the equation for the cap valuation can be as such:

$$\text{Cap valuation} = \frac{\tau L}{1 + \tau F} e^{-rk_\tau} [FN(d_1) - R_x N(d_2)]$$

where $L$ is the notional principal, $\tau$ is time intervals of payment (tenor), $R_x$ is cap rate, $F$ is forward interest rate, $r$ is risk-free interest rate that matures at time $K_\tau$ and

$$d_1 = \frac{\ln (F/R_x) + \sigma_F^2 K_{\tau/2}}{\sigma_F \sqrt{K_\tau}}, \, d_2 = \frac{\ln (F/R_x) + \sigma_F^2 K_{\tau/2}}{\sigma_F \sqrt{K_\tau}} = d_1 - \sigma \sqrt{K_\tau}$$

Let us explain this with the following example:

Consider an agreement on cap option on ₹10,000 loan at 8 percent per annum (with quarterly compounding) for three-month starting is one year. Further assume that three-month forward interest rate is 7 percent per annum and the current interest rate is 6.5 percent per annum (both quarterly compounding). Assume volatility of forward rate 20 percent per annum.

In this example:    $L = ₹10,000$, $F = 0.07$, $T = 0.25$, $R_x = 0.08$, $r = 0.065$, $\sigma = 0.20$ and $T = 1.0$

Then        Cap price $V_c = \dfrac{TL}{1 + TF} = \dfrac{0.25 \times 10,000}{1 + 0.07 + 0.25} = 2,457$

Since        $d_1 = \dfrac{\text{In } 0.875 + 0.02}{0.20} = -0.5677$

$$d_2 = d_1 - 0.20 = -07677$$

$\therefore$        $V_c = 2457^{-0.065}[0.07N(-0.5677) - 0.08N(-07677)]$

$$= 5.19 \text{ or } ₹5.19$$

## 21.4   INTEREST RATE FLOORS (FLOORS)

Interest rate caps are in fact call options on an interest rate, and equivalently, interest rate floors are put options on an interest rate. An interest rate floor guarantees the buyer of the floor option a minimum interest rate to be received on a specified notional amount for a specified period or series of periods. In other words, the floor writer pays the floor buyer when the reference rate falls below the contract rate, called floor rate. So a floor places a lower limit on the interest rate that will be charged.

If a lending firm fears that interest rates may fall in future, it may wish to purchase a floor so that it can receive a minimum return on invested funds. If the actual market rate of interest falls even below the floor rate, the holder of the floor will receive from the writer of the floor a cash payment equal to the difference between the actual reference rate (if LIBOR) and the floor rate.

Like caps, the cash settlement formula, which is repeated on each settlement date, is given by equation as:

Dealer pays = $D \times$ MAX [Floor rate – Reference rate, 0] $\times NP \times LPP$

This is shown in Figure 21.3.

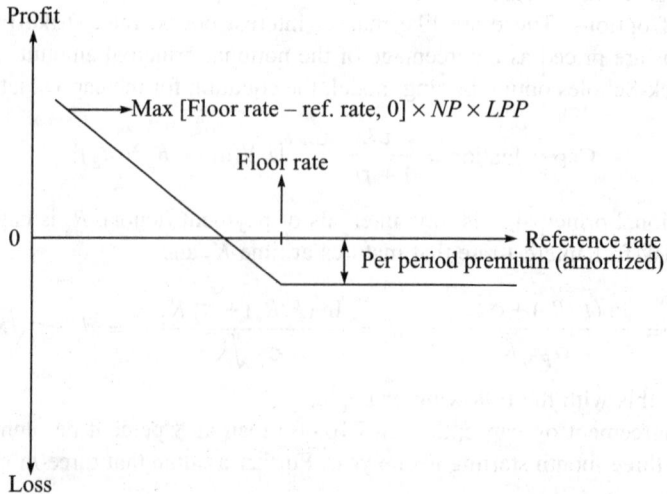

**FIGURE 21.3**   Payoff profile for a floor purchaser (Per settlement period).

It is observed from Figure 21.3 that pay-off profiles in floor position are identical (as seen in caps) except we have reversed the position of the strike price and the reference rate. All other terms are identical. Clearly a floor is a multi-period option. The premium depicted in the single-periodpay-off profile for the floor is an amortized at the time of the floor purchase. Since an interest rate floor is a portfolio of put options on interest rates so its valuation will also be made as we have seen in the case of caps except that here the formula would be used of put option.

## 21.5  INTEREST RATE COLLARS

An interest rate collar is a combination of a cap and a floor in which the buyer buys a cap and simultaneously sells a floor. So collars specify both the upper and lower limits for the rate that will be charged. Collar can be constructed from two separate transactions (one for cap another for floor) or they can be combined into a single transaction. Since the collar has the effect of locking the both high side and the lower side interest rate, it is also called locking into a band or swapping into a band. Further, if the collar is created by two separate contracts, so as a purchaser one will pay the premium, and as a seller the premium will be received. If the two premiums are equal, the position is often referred to as a zero-premium collar.

The basic objective of constructing a collar is to retain some of the benefits of declining rates while paying if the interest rate falls below a particular limit. Let us consider an example. Suppose that a firm holds a fixed rate assets which are yielding 10 percent. These assets are financed through floating rate liabilities tied to the LIBOR, assuming current rate at 8 percent. Suppose that the firm wants to cap the cost at 9.5 percent (buying a cap at 9.5 percent) then it has to pay upfront premium, assuming 0.5 percent p.a. If the firm feels that this premium is too high to pay, but, as it happens, the firm finds that it can sell a prime floor with a floor rate at 7 percent for a premium at 0.5 percent p.a. From the firm's perspective, its annual costs are now bounded between 7 percent to 9.5 percent. It means that when the prime rate rises above 9.5 percent, the dealers pays the firm the difference. If prime rate falls below 7 percent, the firm pays the difference to the dealer. The payoff profile for the interest rate collar is depicted in Figure 21.4.

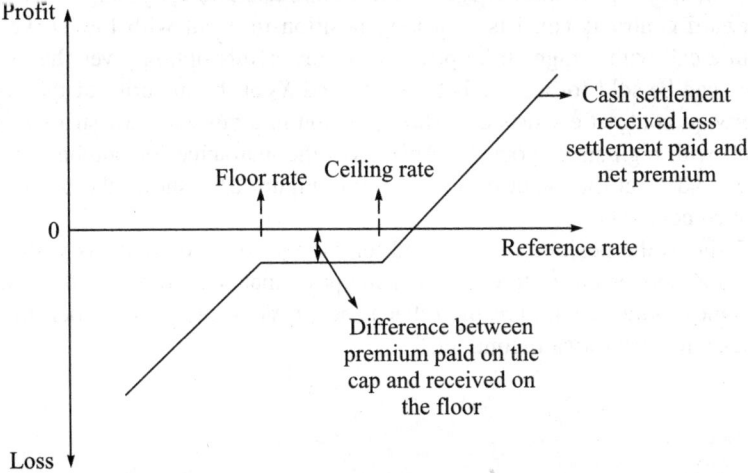

**FIGURE 21.4**  Payoff profile for a collar purchaser (Per settlement period).

Sometimes, in collars, there is no difference between premium received and premium paid, making the collars zero initial costs. However, it is to remember that still there is possibility of payout from the firm to the dealer if the reference rate falls below the floor rate. Because the firm may be called on to make payments to the seller, each party to the transaction has credit exposure to the other like a swap. The valuation formulas for collars are just the sum of the valuation formulas for a cap and floor combined.

## 21.6  SWAPTIONS

A swaption is an option on a swap. It is usually option on interest rate swaps. A swaption gives the right to the holder to enter into a swap on a predetermined notional principal at some defined future date at a specified strike rate. For example, swaption gives the right to enter a swap in which the fixed rate is paid and the floating rate is received. The option would be exercised if the rate had risen above the strike level of the swaption otherwise allows the option to expire.

Swaptions take several forms. One kind is a swap that can be terminated or extended without penalty. For this, one has to pay the writer an upfront fee, in effect, an option premium. A mirror image swaption is one that the fixed receiver has the right to cancel, again, the party who has the right pays the upfront premium to other party.

## 21.7  PACKAGES

Packages are important form of exotic options. It is defined as portfolio consisting of standard European calls, standard European puts, forward contracts and the underlying asset itself. We have already discussed in other chapters a number of different types of packages like spreads, butterfly spreads, bear spreads, calendar spreads, straddle and strangles. The basic objective of a package is usually to have zero cost initially for the holder.

In this respect, another example of package is a range forward contract. It is also termed as zero cost collar, cylinder option, option fence, min-max and forward band. The range forward contract may be of two types: short range forward contracts and long range forward contracts. A short range forward contracts consists of a long position in a put with low strike price $X_1$ and a short position in a call with a high strike price $X_2$. It means this option gives the guarantee that the underlying stock can be sold for a price between $X_1$ and $X_2$ at the maturity of the option. Similarly, a long range forward contract consists of a short position in a put with low strike price $X_1$, and long position in a call with high strike price $X_2$. This gives the guarantee for purchase of the stock for a price between $X_1$ and $X_2$ at the maturity of the option. Figure 21.5 shows the payoff from short and long range forward contracts.

Figure 21.5 shows the position of short and long range forward contracts with $X_1$ and $X_2$ strike prices. As $X_1$ and $X_2$ moves closer to each other the price that will be received or paid for the asset at maturity becomes more certain. On the other hand, if $X_1$ is equal to $X_2$ then the range forward contract becomes a regular forward contract.

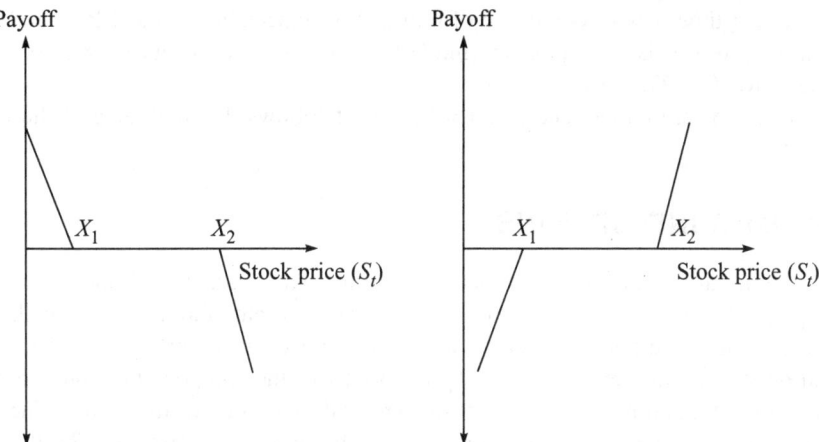

**FIGURE 21.5** Payoff from (a) Short and (b) Long-range forward contracts.

## 21.8  NON-STANDARD AMERICAN OPTIONS

As observed earlier, in a non-standard American option, exercise of the option can be taken place at any time during the life of the option (before the maturity) and the exercise price is always the same. However, in practice, the American options that are traded over the OTC markets do not always have these features.

One of such non-standard American option is known as a 'Bermudan option'. In this option, early exercise is restricted to certain dates during the life of the option. For instance, a bond option (example of Bermudan option) is a option which can be restricted only on coupon payments dated.

Other examples of non-standard American options are sometimes referred to the warrants issued by a company on its own stock. It has observed that a warrant can be exercised during only part of its life, and sometimes, the strike price increases with the passage of time. For example, in a five-year warrant, the exercise might be possible during three to five years with the different strike prices in third, fourth and fifth year. Non-standard American options can usually be valued using a binomial or trinomial tree in the usual way. At the each node the test for early exercise is adjusted to reflect the terms of the option.

## 21.9  FORWARD START OPTIONS

Forward start option is another type of exotic option. They are normally used in employee incentive schemes. Forward start options are options which will start at some specific time in the future. The terms of the options usually at the time of the start will be at-the-time. The value of the start option depends upon the terms inherent, however, for a non-dividend paying stock, it is exactly the same as the value of a regular at-the-money option with the same life as the forward start option. For other type of forward start option, using the risk-neutral valuation, the value at the time zero is:

$$\text{Value of forward start option} = e^{-rT} EC\left(\frac{S_1}{S_0}\right) \text{ (at the time zero)}$$

where $T_1$ is starting time, $r$ is risk-free rate of return, $E$ is expectations in a risk neutral world, $S_0$ is stock price at time zero, $S_1$ is stock price at time $I$ ($T_1$) and $C$ is the value at time zero of at-the-money option that lasts for $T_2 - T_1$.

Because $C$ and $S_0$ are known and $E(S_1) = S_0 e^{(r-q)}$, if follows that the value of the forward start option is $Ce^{-qT}$.

## 21.10   COMPOUND OPTIONS

Compound options are referred to options on options. There are four important categories of compound options; a call on a call, a put on a put, a call on a put, and a put on a call. Further in a compound option, there are two strike prices and two exercise dates. For example, let us consider, a call on a call option, the first exercise date, $T_1$, the holder of the compound option is entitled to pay the first strike price $X_1$, and receive a call option. This call option gives the holder. The right to buy the underlying asset for the second strike price, $X_2$, on the second exercise date, $T_2$. It is to be noted that the compound option will be exercised on the first exercise date only if the value of the option on that date is greater than the first strike price.

## 21.11   CHOOSER OPTIONS

Another exotic option is chooser option which is, also sometimes, referred as an 'As you like it option'. This option has specific feature under which, the holder of the option, after a specified period of time, can choose whether the option is a collar or a put. In other words, the holder can choose any option between call and put which suits to him, or more profitable to him after a specified period. Suppose that the time which the choice is made is $T_1$. At this time the value of the chooser option is max $(C, P)$, where $C$ is the value of the call underlying the option and $P$ is the value of the put underlying the option.

The valuation of such option depends upon the choice of the holder for the option. If both the options are European and have same strike price then put-call parity valuation formula can be used. Put-call parity valuation formula implies that

$$\text{Max } (C, P) = \text{Max } (C, C + Xe^{-r(T_2-T_1)} - S_1\, e^{-q(T_2-T_1)})$$
$$= C + e^{-q(T_2-T_1)} \text{ Max } (0;\, Xe^{-(r-q)(T_2-T_2)} - S_1)$$

It is observed that the chooser option is a package which consists of

1. A call option with strike price $X$ and maturity $T_2$.
2. $e^{-q(T_2-T_1)}$ put option with strike price $Xe^{-(r-q)(T_2-T_1)}$ and maturity $T_1$.

As such, the valuation of the above said option can be readily determined, however, it will be complicated when more complex chooser options are used. For example, where the call and put do not have the same strike price and time to maturity.

## 21.12   BARRIER OPTIONS

These are such options where the payoff depends on whether the underlying asset's price reaches a certain level during a specified period of time. It means the value of a barrier option depends on whether the asset's price crosses the underlying certain level or not. A number of different types of barrier options are regularly traded on the OTC markets. They have been found attractive to some market participants due to their cost as compared to corresponding regular options.

The barrier options can be classified as either knock-out options or knock-in options. A knock-out option ceases to exist when the underlying asset price reaches a certain barrier; and on the other hand, a knock-in option comes into existence only when the underlying asset price reaches a barrier. The barrier options can be further classified into various forms: Down-and-out-option, up-and-out, up-and-in and down-and-in. These have been explained here in brief.

A down-and-out call (one type of knock-out option) is a regular call option that ceases to exist if the asset price reaches a certain level. For this, a lower barrier price is specified. On the other hand, corresponding to this is a down-and-in-call which is a regular call that comes into existence only if the asset price reaches the barrier level. Further, an up-and-out call may be defined as a regular call option that ceases to exist if the asset price reaches a barrier level, which is usually higher than the current asset price. An up-and-in call is a regular call option that comes into existence only if the barrier is reached.

**EXAMPLE:**   Suppose the call option on a share of 'X' Ltd. company with a strike price of ₹500 where the payoff depends on the behaviour of the stock price before maturity. Let us assume that, as per barrier option term, the option holder can exercise it, if the stock price never falls below ₹450 during the life of the option. In such situation, there can be three possibilities (outcomes) of this exotic option which is also shown in Figure 21.6.

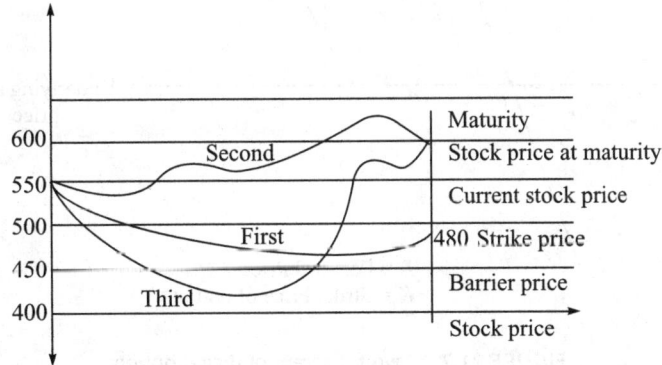

**FIGURE 21.6**   Barrier option (down-and-out barrier call).

1. The option will expire out of the money (OTM) because the stock price is below the strike price of ₹500. Then the option holder will not get anything.
2. The second possibility is that the option expires in the money (ITM) of the stock price never falls below ₹450. In this situation, the holder of the option will get payoff the current stock price minus the strike price.
3. The third possibility is that the option expires in the money (ITM) if the stock price falls below ₹450, then as per the terms of barrier option contract, the option holder receives nothing, whatever the stock price at maturity.

From Figure 21.6 it is observed that in First possibility, since the stock price at maturity is ₹480, above than barrier price, but below the strike price, so the option holder will get nothing. In the second possibility, the holder will get ₹100 (₹600 – ₹500), the difference of strike price and stock price at maturity since the stock price never falls below the barrier price. In third possibility, still he will not get anything because here the stock price has fallen below the barrier price, hence the option expires by paying nothing even the stock price crosses the strike price at the maturity of option.

## 21.13    BINARY OPTIONS (DIGITAL OPTIONS)

Another important exotic option is binary option. Being European type option in nature, it is also called *European digital option*. These options have discontinuous payoff. These are of two types: cash-or-nothing call and cash-or-nothing put. The cash-or-nothing call payoff nothing if the stock price ends up below the strike price at time $T$ and pays a fixed amount $Q$, if it rises above the strike price. In the world of risk neutral, the probability of the stock price being above the strike price at the maturity in general, with our usual notation is $N(d_2)$. Therefore, the value of cash-or-nothing call option is $Qe^{-rt} N(d_2)$. Similarly, a cash-or-nothing put option is that which paysoff $Q$ if the stock price remains below the strike price, and pays nothing if it is above the strike price. The value of a cash-or-nothing put is $Qe^{-rt} N(-d_2)$. Let us compare the payoff a cash or nothing digital call option to a plain vanilla call option and to a forward contract.

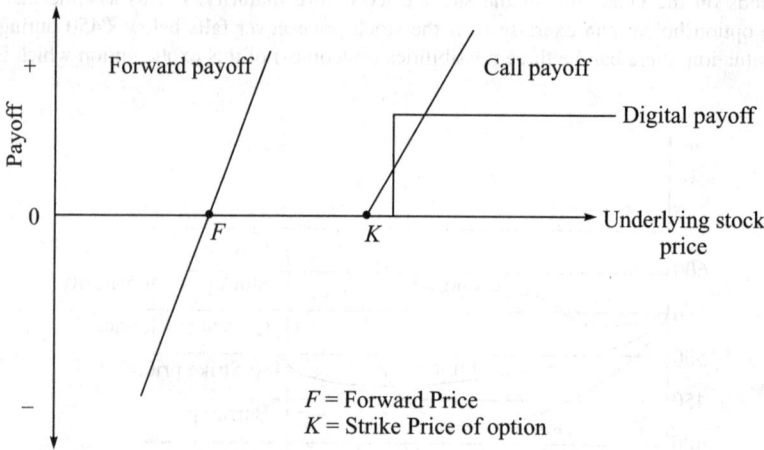

**FIGURE 21.7**    Payoff diagram of digital option.

It is observed from Figure 21.7 that in digital option payoff, a fixed amount is paid if the stock price increases further beyond 'K', whereas in a plain vanilla call option, the payoff will also be increasing. Similarly in forward contract the payoff will also rise on the stock price rises.

Another classification of binary option can be an asset-or-nothing call and asset-or-nothing put. The first pays nothing if the asset price ends up below the strike price and pay an amount equal to the stock price itself if it rises above the strike price. The value of such option is $S_0 e^{-qT} N(d_1)$. Likewise, an asset-or-nothing put option pays off nothing if the stock price ends up below the strike price and pays equal to stock price if it ends up below the strike price. The value of such option is $S_0 e^{-qT} N(-d_1)$.

## 21.14    LOOK BACK OPTIONS

In this option, the payoff on maturity depends upon the maximum or minimum stock price reached during the life of option or upto maturity of the option. It means that one will look back to see the highest or lowest price of the underlying stock to make the payoff. The look back option can be call or put. Thus, the payoff from a European-style look back call option is the amount that final stock price exceeds the minimum stock reached during the life of the option. Similarly, the payoff from the European style look back put is the amount by which the maximum stock price reached during the life of the option exceeds the final stock price.

The basic idea underlying the look back option is that to assess the fluctuations in the price of the underlying asset. For example, under a look back call option, the holder can purchase the underlying asset at the lowest price achieved during the life of that option. In this way, he can earn maximum profit on that option. Similarly, a look back put option is a way under which the holder can sell the underlying stock at the highest price reached during the life of the option.

The valuation formula of European look back option call at time zero is as follows:

$$S_0 e^{-qT} N(a_1) - S_0 e^{-qT} \frac{Q^2}{2(r-q)} N(-a_1) - S_{min} e^{-rt} N\left[(a_2) - \frac{\sigma^2}{2(r-q)} e Y_1 N(-a_3)\right]$$

where

$$a_1 = \frac{\ln(S_0/S_{min}) + (r - q + \sigma^2/2)T}{\sigma\sqrt{T}}$$

$$a_2 = a_1 - \sigma\sqrt{T}$$

$$a_3 = \frac{\ln(S_0/S_{min}) + (-r + q + \sigma^2/2)T}{\sigma\sqrt{T}}$$

$$Y_1 = \frac{-2(r - q - \sigma^2)\ln(S_0/S_{min})}{\sigma^2}$$

and $S_{min}$ is minimum stock price achieved to date.

Let us explain with an example. Consider a newly issued look back put option with the following information. The asset is non-paying dividend, asset price is 50, and asset price volatility is 40 percent per annum. The-risk free rate is 10 percent per annum, and the time to maturity is three months. In this option: $S_{max} = 50$, $S_0 = 50$, $r = 0.1$, $q = 0$, $\sigma = 0.4$ and $T = 0.25$. From the formula, the values of other variables $b_1 = -0.025$ are $b_2 = -0.225$, $b_3 = 0.025$ and $Y_2 = 0$, so that the value of the look back put is 7.79. A newly issued look back call on the same stock is worth 8.04.

## 21.15 SHOUT OPTIONS

This is another type of exotic option of European option nature under which the holder can shout to the writer at one time during its life. At the end of the life of the option, the option holder receives either the usual payoff from a European option or the intrinsic value at the time of the shout, whichever is greater. For example, the strike price is ₹60 and the holder of a call shouts when the price of the underlying asset is ₹70. If the final asset price is less than ₹70 then the holder receives a payoff of ₹10. Further if it is greater than ₹70, the holder receives the excess of the stock price over ₹60.

From the above, it is observed that some features of shout options are similar to the look back options, however, it is less expensive. The valuation of this option is determined by noting that if the option is shouted at a time *t*, when the asset price is $S_t$, then the payoff from the option is:

$$\text{Max}(0, S_T - S_t) + (S_t - X)$$

where $S_t$ is the price of the asset at time $t$ (shout), $S_T$ is the asset price at time $T$ and $X$ is the strike price.

The value of the option at time $t$ (if the option is shouted), is therefore, the present value of $S_t - X$ plus the average strike call pays off max $(0, S_T - S_a)$ value of a European option with strike price $S_T$. Here $S_a$ means average stock price. It can be latter determined by using Black-Scholes formula.

The shout option can also be valued through a binomial or trinomial tree for the underlying stock in the normal way. By rolling back at each node, we can determine the value of the option if we shout and the value if we do not shout. The valuation at the node will be greater between the two. Hence, the procedure for valuing shout option is very similar to a regular American option.

## 21.16 ASIAN OPTIONS

This option is another type of exotic option where the payoff depends upon the average price of the underlying stock during at least some part of the life of the option. The average price of a particular period of the option life is specified and predetermined. The payoff from an average price call is Max $(0, S_a - X)$, and on the put option is Max $(0, X - S_a)$ where $S_a$ means the average value of the underlying stock calculated over a predetermined averaging period.

It has been observed that Asian options are found less expensive in comparison to the regular options. These are suitable for specific purposes. For example, the treasurer of US Multinational Corporation (MNC) expects to receive a cash flow of 100 million Canadian dollar spread evenly over the next year from firm's Canadian subsidiary. In this situation, the treasurer may be interested in such option which can guarantee that the average exchange rate realized during the year is above some level. So, an average price put option may be more appropriate and effective than the regular put options.

There is another type of Asian options which is known as average strike option. The basic objective of this option is to guarantee that the average price received for an asset in frequent trading over a period of time is not less than the final price. Alternatively, the average price paid for an asset is not greater than the final price. An average strike call pays off Max $(0, S_T - S_a)$ and an average strike put pays off Max $(0, S_a - S_T)$. The average price could be based on one observation per week, per day, per hour and so forth.

## 21.17 OPTION ON THE AVERAGE

Another important option which is popular in the option world is 'option on the average'. It is defined as an option where the underlying at exercise is the arithmetic average of a price over a period of time. It means that that option would be in money or not will be decided on the basis of average of stock prices in the life of the option or on at the time of exercise of the option. The payoff in the option would be exercise price minus the average rupee price of the asset.

Let us explain this with an example. Assume that a stock price return follows a binomial distribution where an up move multiples the stock price 1.2 and a down move by 0.80.

The initial stock prices is assumed at ₹20. Further assume that the risk-neutral probability of an up move is 0.60 and down move by 0.40. Take the four dates including the initial date. The exercise price is supposed to be ₹20, and the interest rate 1 percent per period. This is shown in Table 21.2 and Figure 21.8 as under:

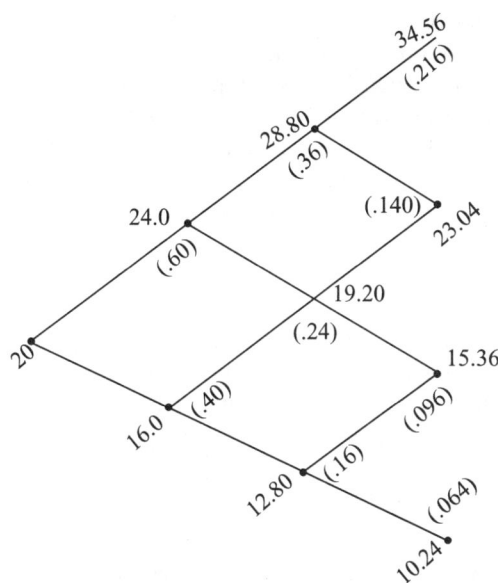

**FIGURE 21.8** Pricing an option on the average (Based on Binomial Distribution).

**TABLE 21.2** Pricing an Option on the Average (Based on Binomial Distribution)

| Strike Price/Risk-neutral Probability | Date-2 | Date-3 | Date-4 | Average of Date 2 & 4 | Option Payoff | Expected Payoff |
|---|---|---|---|---|---|---|
| 20 | 24.00 | 28.80 | 34.56 | 29.28 | 9.28 | 2.005 |
| 1 | 0.60 | 0.36 | 0.216 | 0.216 | | |
| 20 | 24.00 | 28.80 | 23.04 | 23.52 | 3.52 | 0.507 |
| 1 | 0.60 | 0.36 | 0.144 | 0.144 | | |
| 20 | 24.00 | 19.20 | 23.04 | 23.52 | 3.52 | 0.507 |
| 1 | 0.60 | 0.24 | 0.144 | 0.144 | | |
| 20 | 24.00 | 19.20 | 15.36 | 19.68 | 0 | 0 |
| 1 | 0.60 | 0.24 | 0.096 | 0.096 | | |
| 20 | 16.00 | 19.20 | 23.04 | 19.52 | 0 | 0 |
| 1 | 0.40 | 0.24 | 0.144 | 0.144 | | |
| 20 | 16.00 | 19.20 | 15.36 | 15.68 | 0 | 0 |
| 1 | 0.40 | 0.24 | 0.096 | 0.096 | | |
| 20 | 16.00 | 12.80 | 15.36 | 15.68 | 0 | 0 |
| 1 | 0.40 | 0.16 | 0.096 | 0.096 | | |
| 20 | 16.00 | 12.80 | 10.24 | 13.12 | 0 | 0 |
| 1 | 0.40 | 0.16 | 0.064 | 0.064 | | |
| **Total** | | | | | **16.32** | **3.019** |

Table 21.2 states all possible paths of the stock price with the associated risk neutral probabilities. Let us begin with the fourth path, the stock price begins at ₹20. Next the stock has an up move which comes at ₹24. This up moves is then followed by 2 consecutive down moves, and the stock ends at

₹15.36 with a probability of 0.096. The average price as per dates 2 & 4 is ₹19.68 which is less than the strike price of ₹20. Thus, the option is paying nothing.

Now we move to first path, in which the stock price moves upwards and the price at date 4 is ₹34.56. The probability at this path will take place is 0.216 (0.60 × 0.60 × 0.60). The average price is ₹29.28 (24.00 + 34.56)/2 which is higher than strike price by ₹9.28.

This payoff occurs with the probability of 0.216, so that its expected value is 9.28 × 0.216 = 2.005. By adding up the expected payoff for the different paths comes the expected payoff of the option which is ₹3.019. Discounting this expected payoff at the risk-free rate of interest of one percent per period comes the option value of ₹2.93. So, as per average method, the option value is computed as ₹2.93.

The above mentioned example of binomial option method helps us to understand for creating a portfolio strategy which paysoff the average at maturity and is self-financing. It means the current value of the portfolio which paysoff the average at maturity is equal to the present value of the average, and thus, can be further applied to average of the put-call parity formula.

## 21.18   EXCHANGE OPTIONS

Exchange options are also termed as options to exchange one asset for another arise in various contexts. For example, a stock tender offer is an option to exchange shares in one stock for shares in another stock. Similarly, exchange of one currency for another currency. Hence, in such option, consider a European option to give upon an asset worth $U_T$ at time $T$ and receive in return an asset worth $V_T$. Then the payoff from this option would be

Max $(V_T - U_T, 0)$. The valuation formula of such option at time zero is:

$$V_0 e^{-qVT} N(d_1) - U_0 e^{-qUT} N(d_2)$$

where
$$d_1 = \frac{\ln(V_0/U_0) + (q_u - q_v + \sigma^2/2)T}{\sigma\sqrt{T}}$$

$$d_2 = d_1 - \sigma\sqrt{T}$$

$$\sigma = \sqrt{\sigma_u^2 + \sigma_v^2 - 2P\sigma_u\sigma_v}$$

and $V_0$ and $U_0$ are the values of $U$ and $V$ at time zero.

Thus, it is observed that to obtain the better or worse of the two assets can be regarded as a position in one of the assets combined with an option to exchange it for the other asset.

$$\text{Min}(U_T, V_T) = V_T - \text{Max}(V_T - U_T, 0)$$

$$\text{Max}(U_T, V_T) = U_T + \text{Max}(V_T - U_T, 0)$$

## 21.19   RAINBOW OPTIONS

The option in which two or more than two risky assets are involved are referred to as rainbow options. The holder of the option is given the option to choose between a number of different assets. For example, as seen in the bond futures market, the party with the short position is allowed to choose between a large number of different bonds available when making delivery. For such type of option, an other example is a LIBOR contingent FX option. It refers to a foreign currency option whose payoff occurs only if a predetermined interest rate is within a certain range at maturity.

## 21.20 BASKET OPTIONS

Another form of exotic options is basket option under which the payoff is dependent on the value of a portfolio (or basket) of assets. The assets considered for such type of the options are normally individual stocks or stock indices or currencies. The valuation of such basket options are determined through Monte Carlo simulation by assuming that the assets follow correlated geometric Brownian motion processes. Another approach for such valuation is to calculate the first two moments of the basket at the maturity of the option in a risk neutral world, and then assume that the value of the basket is log normally distributed at that time. The basket option should be cheaper than a collection of individual option when the assets selected in the portfolio (basket) are imperfectly correlated.

## SUMMARY

This chapter briefly explains the various advance financial derivatives, which are also traded in the developed markets. The derivatives securities which are not of standard American or European and have complicated payoff are referred as non-standard options or derivatives. Since these are mainly related to options, so these are referred as exotic options. An interest rate cap is an agreement between two parties in which one party, for an upfront premium agrees to compensate the other party if a designated interest rate, called the reference rate, is different from a predetermined level. No theoretical limit exists to the specification of interest rate caps. They vary in maturities and structures. Majority of trading's fall between one and five years. There are two major types of interest rate caps: interest rate guarantee and interest rate cap. Interest rate caps, in fact, are called option on interest rate, and equivalently, interest rate floor guarantees the buyer of the floor option a minimum interest rate to be received on a specified notional amount for a specified period or series of periods.

Interest rate collar is a combination of cap and a floor in which the buyer buys a cap and simultaneously sells a floor. So collars specify both the upper and lower limits for the rate that will be charged. Collars can be constructed from two separate transactions or they can be combined to a single transaction. Further floor rate, collars rate and cap rate are discussed with the help of payoff profile for collar purchaser.

A swaption is an option on a swap. It is usually option on interest rate swaps. A swaption gives the right to the holder to enter into a swap on a predetermined notional principal at some defined future date at a specified strike rate.

Derivatives with more complicated payoff standard European or American call and puts are called exotic or non-standard options. A non-standard American options is one example of such types of exotic options. It can take place at any time during the life of the option. The exercise price is always the same. Other examples of non-standard American options are sometimes referred to the warrants issued by a company on its stock. Compound options are referred to options on options. There are four important categories of compound options: a call on a call, a put on a put, a call on a put and put on a call. In a compound options there are two strike prices and two exercise dates.

American exotic option is chooser option which is, also sometimes referred as 'as you like it option'. This option has specific feature under which the holder on the option, after a specified period of time, can choose whether the option is a collar or a put. Another exotic option 'barrier' depends upon whether the underlying assets price reaches a certain level or not. It means that value of a barrier option depends on whether the assets price crosses the underlying certain level or not. Another important exotic option is binary option. Being European type option in nature, it is also called as European digital option. These options have discontinuous payoff. These are of two types: Cash-or-nothing-call and cash-or-nothing-put. Look-back option is another type of option. In this option, the payoff on maturity depends upon the maximum or minimum stock price reached during the life of option or up to maturity of the option. It means that one will look back to see the highest or lowest price of the underlying stock.

Shout option is another type of exotic option of European option nature under which the holder can shout. Another type of option where the payoff depends upon the average price of the underlying stock during at least same part of the life of the option. The average price of a particular period of the option life is specified and predetermined. Exchange options are also termed as option to exchange one asset for another arise in various contexts. A basket option is the option under which the payoff is dependent on the value of a portfolio (or basket) of assets. The assets considered for such type of the options are normally individual stocks, stock indices or currencies. The valuation of such basket options are determined through Monte Carlo simulation by assuming that the assets follow correlated geometric Brownian motion processor. Packages are also important form of exotic options. It is defined as portfolio consisting of standard European calls, standard European puts, forward contracts and the underlying asset itself. Packages are of different types like spreads, butterfly spreads, bear spreads, calendar spreads, straddle, strangles, etc. The basic objective is to have zero cost initially for the holder of the option.

## SUGGESTED READINGS

1. Amran, M. and Kulatilaka, N., *Real Options*, Harvard Business School Press, Boston, MA, 1999.
2. Boradie, Glarrerman M.P. and Kou, S.G., A continuity correction for discrete barrier options, *Mathematical Finance*, Vol. 7, No. 4, pp. 325–349, October 1997.
3. Goldman, Sosin B.H. and Gatto, M.A., Path dependent options: Buy at low, sell at the higher, *Journal of Finance*, Vol. 34, pp. 1111–1127, December 1979.
4. Ritchken, P., On pricing barrier option, *Journal of Derivatives*, Vol. 3, No. 2, pp. 19–28, Winter 1995.
5. Geske, R., The valuation of compound options, *Journal of Financial Economics*, Vol. 7, pp. 63–81, 1979.
6. Levy, E., Pricing European average rate currency options, *Journal of International Money and Finance*, Vol. 11, pp. 474–491, 1992.
7. Rubinstein, M., Option for the Undecided, *RISK*, pp. 30–32. April 1999.
8. Stephens, Johan J. and Institute of International Auditors, *Managing Currency Risk Using Financial Derivatives*, Wiley, Chichester, 2001.
9. Kodres, L., Tests of unbiasness in foreign exchange futures markets: The effects of price limits, *The Review of Futures Market*, Vol. 7, No. 1, pp. 138–166, 1988.

## REVIEW QUESTIONS

**1.** What do you understand by standard and non-standard derivatives? Explain with suitable examples.

2. What is yield curve? Discuss the various models of yield curves with suitable examples.

3. "European interest rate option always increase in value as the time to maturity increase." Do you agree? Explain your answer.

4. Explain the interest rate caps. What are various types of caps? Also discuss the various terms used in interest rate caps and floors.

5. With the help of hypothetical examples draw out payoff profile of a cap purchaser.

6. What is interest rate floor? Draw out payoff profile for a floor purchaser with the help of suitable illustrations.

7. Write a detailed note on interest rate collars and also discuss the payoff profile of a collar buyer.

8. Write short notes on following:
   (a) Swaptions
   (b) Application of valuing caps with Blacks and Scholes model

9. Can Black-Scholes model of option priding can be used for valuation of bond options? Discuss with suitable illustrations. Also discuss the problems in applying B-S model to bond price.

10. Explain the concept of forward start options and compound options with suitable examples.

11. What are chooser options? Discuss the payoff profile of buyer of chooser options.

12. Write detailed notes on
    (a) Barrier options with examples
    (b) Binary options with examples
    (c) Look back options with examples

13. What is look back option? What are its types? How valuation of European look option is done? Discuss with suitable examples.

14. Write a detailed note on shout options and valuation of shout options.

15. Write short notes on
    (a) Asian option
    (b) Exchange options and their valuation

16. "Rainbow options, basket options and packages are the non-standard derivatives." Critically examine them.

17. With the help of hypothetical example, draw out the payoff from (a) short and (b) long range forward.

18. Compare and contracts between exchange-traded bond options and embedded bond options.

19. Write a detailed note on valuation of interest rate options with suitable illustrations.

20. Consider a chooser option where the holder has the right to choose between a European call and put of any time during one-year period. In both the cases, maturity dates and strike prices for both call and put are same. Is it optimal to make a choice before the end of one-year period? Explain your answer.

21. Show the payoff profile from a portfolio consisting of a look back call and look back put with the same expiration date.

22. "Regular European call option is the sum of a down-and-out European call and a down-and-in European call." Is the same true for American call options? Comment on the statement.

# Chapter 22

# Credit Derivatives

*After reading this chapter, students will be able to*

➤ Understand the concept of credit derivatives.

➤ Know the features of credit derivatives.

➤ Be aware of the concept of credit risk and its importance.

➤ Know the growth of credit derivatives.

➤ Know the components of credit risk.

➤ Explain the various models of measuring the credit risk.

➤ Know the types of credit derivatives like total return swap, credit default swaps, credit linked notes and credit options.

➤ Be aware of the settlement of these derivatives instruments, i.e., cash settlement and physical settlement.

➤ Know the recommendations of RBI Working Group on credit derivatives.

➤ Understand the benefits associated with credit derivatives.

➤ Know the various uses of credit derivatives.

➤ Know the ISDA guidelines on credit derivatives.

## 22.1  INTRODUCTION

Credit derivatives today have become the popular financial instruments all over the world due to increasing debt defaults in the financial markets. It has grown steadily in spite of turbulent economic conditions perplexed with escalating debt burden. Despite the Enron debacle and the Argentine debt default having posed threats to the financial market and specifically the banking industry, the market is efficient enough to absorb the shocks due to credit derivatives.

It was the new international rules of Basel Accord 1988 that brought credit derivatives into existence. These are such instruments designed to protect the lenders against default risk of the borrower by a third party called the reference entity. For example, if a company is exposed to a credit default risk, then it can reduce the same by purchasing credit-derivatives while keeping the original debt on its books. In this way, the firm can protect itself from the inherent credit risk.

## 22.2 CONCEPT OF CREDIT DERIVATIVES

The credit derivatives, as the name indicates, is related to the offsetting of credit risk to be incurred in a firm due to default in the credit asset. The concept of derivative is to create a contract that derives from an original contract or asset. Similarly, a credit derivative is a contract that involves a contract between parties in relation to the return from the credit asset, without transferring the asset as such. It is related to credit asset which may be referred to the extension in some forms: generally a loan, instalment credit or financial lease contract. Every credit risk is required to make certain return on the asset. So, the probability of not getting the expected return is the risk inherent in a credit asset, and hence each credit asset is a bundle of risks and returns.

There are such instruments which transfer either specific or all the inherent risks of a credit-position from one party to the other. In this type of transaction, the risk seller transfers its risk to the risk buyer, against payment of a premium. These contacts are private and confidential which allow the users to manage their exposure to credit risk. They are also termed as off-balance sheet financial instruments which permit one party (beneficiary) to transfer credit risk of a reference asset owned by it to another party (guarantor) without actually selling the asset. For example, if bank 'X' enters into a credit derivative with bank 'Y' relating to the former's portfolio, bank 'Y' bears the risk, of course for a fee, inherent in the portfolio held by bank 'X', while bank 'X' continues to hold the portfolio.

A credit derivative, as noted above, is a specific financial product designed to mitigate or to assume specific forms of credit risk by hedgers and speculators. They deal with credit risk or risk of debtor default as pure debtor risk and not general market risk. They are specifically useful to those institutions which have widespread credit exposures. Thus, credit derivatives increase the breadth of the credit market because they simultaneously deepen the market for hedging and investment.

The credit derivatives generally hedge directly to a particular debtor. The credit risk is typically debtor specific. In this context, the focus is placed on individual solutions specifically designed to fulfill customer specific desires with an eye on their balance sheet. So these solutions in the form of products are hardly standardized, and there is practically no secondary market for such products, even in advanced countries like USA, UK, etc. In brief, credit derivatives provide market participants with efficient, tailor made access to credit sensitive asset market.

## 22.3 FEATURES OF CREDIT DERIVATIVES

In the light of above discussion, the important features of the credit derivatives are as under:

- It is a bilateral contract comprising two parties. One is the credit risk protection buyer or beneficiary and the other is the credit risk protection seller or guarantor.
- Credit derivatives are traded on the Over-the-counter (OTC) markets in developed countries. OTC contracts are such which are taken place outside the regulated exchanges, hence, they permit maximum flexibility in designing the contract as per the needs of the counterparties.

- In credit derivative contract, the beneficiary (protection buyer) pays a fee, called *premium* as in insurance business, to the guarantor (protection seller). In other words, a party that wants to protect itself from the future credit risk will pay fee (premium) to the other party which takes such risk.

- The reference asset for which credit risk protection is purchased and sold is predefined. Examples of such asset can be a bank loan, corporate bonds and debenture, trade receivables, municipal debt, etc. It could also be a portfolio of credit products.

- The protection from credit risk regarding reference asset is arisen due to various causes, which are known as *credit events*. It could be bankruptcy, insolvency, payment-default, delinquency, price decline, rating downgrade of the underlying asset, etc. So the credit event for which protection is bought or sold is also pre-defined.

- Various instruments are being used in the credit-derivatives market like credit-default swaps, total return swaps, credit options, credit-linked notes, etc. These have been explained further in this chapter.

- The settlement between the counterparties in such contract on the credit event can be settled in terms of cash. These could also be settled in terms of the physical financial asset (loan or bond, etc.). For example, if the protection seller (guarantor) is not satisfied with the pricing or valuation of the asset in the credit event, it has the right to ask for physical settlement in the contract.

- In general, credit derivatives guidelines are issued by the International Swaps and Derivatives Association (ISDA), known as *master agreement* and the legal format of a derivative contract.

In brief, credit derivatives are among the most important financial innovations which assist credit managers to realize their credit exposures, and then to act optimally to hedge and replicate such credit risk in their organizations.

## 22.4  NATURE OF CREDIT RISK

As noted in the preceding section, the basic objective of credit-derivative instrument is to protect from the inherent credit risk to the protection seeker. It is important to explain the term credit risk, at first instance, which provides the context within which credit derivatives need to be examined. In broader sense, the credit risk can be categorized into two variables—market risk and firm specific risk. The market risk is the risk that arises due to movements in interest rates, exchange rates, stock prices, commodity prices trade restrictions, economic sanctions, government policies, etc. in adverse direction creating an effect on the firms' value. The firm specific risk refers to the possibility that an individual borrowers circumstances may change for the worse resulting in failing to make obligated payments. The market risk is managed by entering into offsetting or hedging transactions, but in the purview of credit derivatives, we usually consider only firm-specific risk, commonly called *credit risk*. In simple term, a credit risk refers to the possibility that a borrower will fail to service or repay a debt on time. It is also defined as *the possibility of losses associated with diminution in the credit quality of borrowers or counterparties.*

For example, in case of banks or financial institutions, losses stem from the outright default due to inability or unwillingness of a customer to meet commitments regarding lending, trading, settlement, etc. resulting into actual or perceived deterioration in credit quality. In general, the credit risk may take the following forms:

- In case of direct lending, the principal and/or interest amount may not be repaid.

- In the case of guarantee or letter of credit, funds may not be forthcoming from the constituents upon crystallization of the liability.
- In the case of treasury operation, the payment or series of payments due from the counter-parties under the respective contacts may not be forthcoming.
- In the case of securities trading business, funds/securities settlement may not be effected.
- In the case of cross-border exposure, the availability and free transfer of foreign currency funds may either cease or restriction may be imposed by the sovereign.

Another important variant of credit risk is counterparty risk which arises from non-performance of the trading partners. It may arise from counterparty's refusal/inability to perform due to adverse price movements of external constraints which were not anticipated by the principal. This risk is generally viewed as a transient financial risk associated with trading rather than standard risk. In brief, we may observe credit risk or default risk as inability or unwillingness of a customer or counterparty to meet commitments in relation to lending, trading, hedging, settlement and other financial transaction.

## 22.5  COMPONENTS OF CREDIT RISK

Credit risk can be further divided into default risk, downgrade risk and spread risk. These risks are not independent of one another, rather they are linked among themselves. Default risk refers to the probability of default for not repaying the outstanding obligation on the part of the receivers of the loan to the creditors. Default can lead to bad debts, and hence, this quantum of provisions for such bad debts will cause a burden for the issuer. Default not only indicates non-flow of cash back to the suppliers, but also leads to larger problem for the firms in future. Therefore, the firms employ significant resources to analyse and report default instances and patterns. Such understanding is important to manage credit risk.

Downgrade risk refers to the falling of credit rating of a firm from its existing rating. Normally, credit rating agencies publically mention the credit standing of the firms through their evaluation technique after analysing the firm's policies, practices, performance and achievements. It is very much sensitive for the firm whose rating is downgraded. For example, risk-free return is 8 percent and yield on debt is 9 percent, so the credit spread is 1 percent. Not surprisingly the credit spread falls as the value of bond increases. The logarithm of D/F in the given formula is multiplied by $\left[\dfrac{1}{T-t}\right]$. A rise in the value of debt increases D/F, but because the logarithm of D/F is multiplied by a negative number the credit spread will decrease. The firm's credit spread fluctuates as and when the firm's operations, performance and earnings are reviewed by the market players from time to time. Downgrading of credit rating directly affects the firms' existing financial cost to upward side, profitability lower side and adverse impact on financial proposals or projects. Downgrading of credit rating directly affects the firm's existing financial cost to upward side, on profitability lower side and adverse impact on financial proposals or projects. Thus, credit rating agency assigns the rating symbol to the firm after making a thorough investigation.

Credit spread risk refers to the difference between the return on the risky debt and the yield on the risk-free debt of the same maturity. This difference in rates is termed as credit spread in the bond markets. For example, if a corporate bond with 'A' rating grade has a yield of 10 percent while T-bonds (Government securities) of the same maturity have 8 percent yield, then credit spreads would be 2 percent point. The investors can evaluate the credit spreads for different rating grades bonds in the market. An explicit formula can be used for measuring the credit spread as: $\left[\dfrac{I}{T-t}\right] \ln \left[\dfrac{D}{F}\right] - r$

where $r$ is risk-free return, $T$ is maturity period, $D$ is value of debt and $F$ is face value of the debt bond.

## 22.6  CREDIT RISK ASSESSMENT

Banks and other financial institutions are major players in the credit market and are, therefore, exposed to credit risk. Most of these players usually extend loans and have little of bonds in their portfolios. They have competitive advantage in pricing and official capabilities, and therefore, earn comparatively high returns on loans. There are some other institutions like mutual funds, insurance companies, pension funds, hedge funds, etc. which have mostly bonds in their portfolios with little emphasis on loans due to lack of back official capabilities needed for processing, monitoring and supervising loans, and thus, depriving of high returns on loan portfolios.

In the past, the market did not extend necessary credit risk protection to banks and other financial institutions. Even some of them had concentrated portfolios because of location or credit specific business groups. As a result, credit was sub-optimally held across financial institutions and investors. The assessment of credit risk is an ongoing process that requires quantification of the risk, assessment of the desired level of risk and proactive adjustment of a firm's position so that the desired level of credit risk assumed equals its actual level of credit risk assumed. Following are the important three waves of credit risk assessment:

- The first wave had focused on the traditional assessment of credit risk based upon highly judgemental, emphasizing on qualitative factors with a little bit analysis of a financial assessment.
- The second wave has focused on use of discriminant analysis, or credit-scoring models. These assessments include quantitative measures of a borrower's financial position into a statistical model.
- The third wave has focused on advance techniques in risk assessment like option pricing theory, reflecting the fact that default is an option. For example, when a borrower repays its debt, the option expires in the money; when it defaults, the option expires out-of-the money.

## 22.7  MEASUREMENT OF CREDIT RISK

In this section, to measure the credit risk, three important models are discussed:

(i) Merton Model

(ii) Credit Risk$^+$ Model

(iii) Credit Metrics$^{TM}$

### 22.7.1  Merton Model

In 1974, Merton R. provided a detailed analysis of the pricing of risky debts using the Black-Scholes Option Pricing model. To state this model, let us consider a firm which has only one debt and no payment of dividends. Only debt holders and equity holders are having claims against the firm. Now assume the firm has raised debts and the payment of ₹100 million would be paid at the maturity. If the total value of the firm's assets at maturity is ₹125 million, the debt holders will get their promised payment, i.e., ₹100 million and the rest amount of ₹25 million will have equity shareholders. On the other hand, if the value of the assets remains below ₹100 million, assume ₹70 million, then equity holders will get nothing and the whole amount would be given to the debt holders. This can be shown in equation form as: $S_T = \max(V_T - F, 0)$ is the value of equity stock.

Where

$S_T$ : Value of equity stock

$V_T$ : Value of firm

$T$ : Maturity date

$F$ : Face value of the debts.

Since the debt is risky, and when the value of the firm falls below '$F$', then the debt holders will receive the amount less than '$F$', amount equals to $F - V_T$. In put option form, it can be described as $D_T = F - \text{Max}(F - V_T, O)$, where $F$ is assumed as exercise price, $D_T$ is the value of the debt at date $T$. This is shown in Figure 22.1.

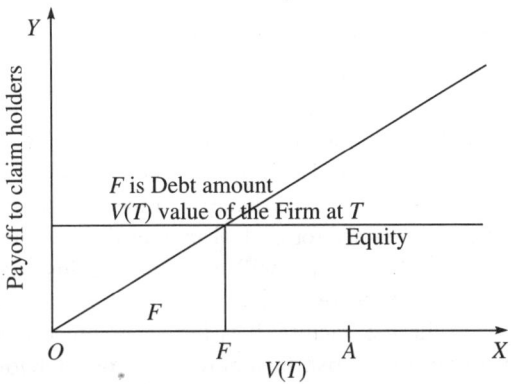

**FIGURE 22.1** Debt & equity payoff in risky debt on firm's value.

It is observed from Figure 22.1 that if the value of the firm is less than point $F$ on the (OX) line, then nothing is given to the equity holders, the debt holders receive less than $F$, by an amount equal to $F - V_T$. If the firm's value is higher than $F$, say, at point '$A$', Merton's Formula for the Value of equity.

Merton has used the B–S option Pricing model to find out the price of debt and of equity by assuming log normal distribution with constant volatility 6, interest rate ($r$) constant, trading take place constantly. The value of equity is as $S(V, F, T, t)$. With the notation, the value of the equity is:

$$S(V, F, T, t) = V_N(d) - P_t(T) F_N (d - \sigma) \sqrt{T - t}$$

$$d = \frac{\text{In} (V/P_t(T)F)}{\sigma\sqrt{T - t}} + \frac{1}{2}\sigma\sqrt{T - t}$$

where $P_t(T)$, the price at $t$ of zero coupon bond that pays at $T$ $N(d)$ the cumulative distribution function evaluated at '$d$'.

**EXAMPLE:** Suppose $V$ is ₹120 million, $F$ is ₹100 million, $T$ is equal to $t + 5$, $P_t(T)$ is 0.6065, $\sigma$ is 20 percent, the value of equity is 60.385, the value of the Debt = $V$ – Value of equity = ₹120 – ₹60.385 = ₹59.615 million.

## 22.7.2 Credit Risk⁺ Model

One of the most popular credit risk models used today is the credit risk$^{+TM}$ model developed by Credit Suisse First Boston (CSFB). The model became popular in 1990s all over the world due to various reasons:

1. It requires few data in comparison to other credit risk models.
2. It is more suitable for illiquid loan portfolios.
3. The model gives only two outcomes for each firm over the risk measurement period: Default or no-default. The default is the main concern for the risk manager. If default occurs. The creditor experiences loss of fixed size amount.
4. The probability default for an obligator (All those who have legal obligation to the firm rather than debtors) depends on its quality of rating, realization of 'K' risk factors, and the sensitivity of the obligor to the risk factors.
5. This model is scalable and computationally efficient, allowing even sensitivity analysis to be performed on a continuous basis.

The model is based on the portfolio approach which considers the credit risk measurement, calculation of economic capital and the application of the same. This model does not make any assumptions about the reasons of default. This approach considers the information relating to the size and maturity of an exposure as well as credit quality of the systematic risk of the firms' obligor.

This model allows only two outcomes for each firm over the risk measurement period—default and no default. If default occurs the creditor will experience a loss of fixed size. However, the probability of default will depend on the firm's credit rating, the realization of 'K' risk factors and the sensibility of the obligor to the risk factors. It is further assumed that risk factors are common across all obligors, but sensitivity to the risk factors differ across obligors. Conditional on the risk factors, defaults are uncorrelated across obligors.

**Components of Credit Risk⁺ Model** The components of credit risk⁺ model and the interrelationships between them are shown in Table 22.1

TABLE 22.1 Components of Credit Risk⁺ Model

| Credit risk measurement | | Economic capital | Applications |
|---|---|---|---|
| Exposure | Default Rates | Credit Default Loss Distribution | Provisioning |
| Recovery Rate | Default Rate Volatilities | Scenario Analysis | Limits |
| | | | Portfolio Management |

This model comprised of three components which are credit risk measurement, economic capital and applications. First element is concerned with measurement of credit risk of each obligor through estimating of credit risk exposure, default rates recovery rate, viability of default rate, etc. Second element is related with the determination of level of economic capital required to cover the risk of unexpected credit default losses. Third element of the model includes several applications like forward looking provisioning methodology, computing the limits and quantitative portfolio management techniques.

### Inputs of Credit Risk⁺ Model

The Credit Risk⁺ Model requires the following inputs:

- **The credit exposures:** In this respect, the exposures of each obligor should be added and netted to reduce the number or exposures in the total calculation.
- **Default rates of the obligors:** Every obligor should be assigned an expected default rate, as no obligor is foolproof. It can be achieved in a number of ways including (a) observed credit spreads from traded instruments to provide market assessed probabilities of default, (b) alternatively, obligors' credit ratings together with a mapping of default rates to credit ratings, provide a easy way of assigning probabilities of default to obligors. Another approach is to calculate default probabilities on a continuous scale, which can be used as a substitute for the combination of credit ratings and assigned default rates.
- **Volatility of default rates of the obligors:** Volatility of default rate of each obligor will be based on the average default rates observed in the past, and calculated by using standard deviation. This can be significantly different from the actual observed default rates.
- **Recovery Rates (RR):** This will be computed considering as whenever a default takes place, the amount of loss incurred to the lending firm will be the amount owed by the obligor, less the amount recovered plus the amount spent on the recovery and other administrative and legal expenses incurred in this respect.

This model does not make any assumptions about the reasons for default nor does it measure the number of defaults. It simply follows the "Poisson" distribution. In this model, first we consider the number of default events in a time period, after that annual probability of default of each obligor is calculated, and then mapping between the default rates and credit rating is done. Once a loss takes place, the following steps are followed:

1. The exposures are adjusted by the anticipated recovery rate to calculate the loss in a given default.
2. The net exposure is divided into bands of exposure with the level of exposure in each band.

The probability of default of the obligors are computed with the following formula:

$$P_i = \Pi_{G(i)} \left[ \sum_{K=1}^{K} X_K W_{iK} \right]$$

$\Pi_{G(i)}$ = Unconditional probability of default for obligor (i) which belongs to grade (G) as per its credit rating.

$K$ = Risk factor and follows a statistical distribution (usually the gamma distribution)

$X$ = Vector of risk factor realization

$W_{ik}$ = Proposition of the obligor's exposure to the risk factor

Often, obligors may not have a rating, or the rating of the company may not reflect the riskiness of the debt. A bank internal grading system could be used to grade obligors. The risk factors can take only positive values and are scaled so that they have a mean of one.

Once the probability of default of each obligor is computed, then we can get the distribution of the total number of defaults in the portfolio, which is also known as *distribution of losses*. The loss upon the default for each loan is termed in standardized units which could be, say, ₹1 million. The exposure of the obligor would be an exposure of $v(i)$ standardized units. A mathematical function gives the unconditional probability of a loss of '$n$' standardized units for each value of $n$, and then getting the volatility of the probability of loss of $n$ standardized units.

## 22.7.3   Credit Metrics™ Model

It is a risk model advocated by J.P. Morgan built on the same principle as those of Risk Metrics™. It is risk model which provides the distribution of the value of a portfolio of debt claims, which further leads to a VaR measure for the portfolio. In other words, it is an approach to evaluate the risk of large portfolio of debt claims with realistic capital structures.

### Features of the Model

- Measurement of the risk of the value of debt claims in one year using VaR for each company or obligor.
- To figure out a rating class for the debt claim. Rating is important to decide the claims. For example, we decide that the claim should have a rating of AA, then later on, the rating could remain at the same level could improve further, or could worsen if default more likely. These can be obtained through historical probability distribution. In this way, the rating transition matrix can be estimated, and usually these are made available by the rating agencies too.

### Credit Metrics™ Methodology

The model methodology assesses individual and portfolio VaR due to credit in three steps:

First step:    It sets up the exposure profile of each obligor in a portfolio.

Second step:    It measures the volatility in value of each instrument caused by possible upgrades, downgrades, and defaults.

Third step:    It takes into account correlation between each of these events. It combines the volatility of the individual instruments to give an aggregate portfolio volatility. It is shown below.

| Diagram Simplified. Roadmap of the Credit Metrics | | |
|---|---|---|
| Exposures | Value-at-Risk (VAR) due to credit | Correlations |
| Compute exposure profile of each assets | Compute the volatility of value caused by up (down) grades and defaults | Compute correlations |

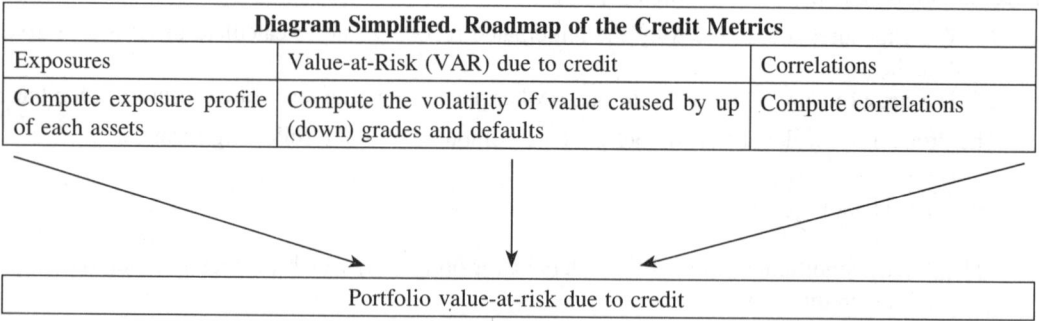

| Portfolio value-at-risk due to credit |
|---|

### (i) Exposure profiles

Credit matrices can easily incorporate the exposures of conventional as well as less straight forward bonds. Exposure deriving from undrawn instruments, such as commitments are captured on the basis of assumptions as to likely changes in drawn amounts upon default or up (down) grade.

### (ii) Volatility of each exposure from up (down) grades and defaults

Likelihoods are attributed to each possible credit event, including upgrades and downgrades, not just defaults. The probability of migration from one rating to other rating of an obligor can be derived from a transition matrix. Further, each migration results in an estimate change in value is derived from the data of credit spread, default recovery rates, etc. Each value outcome is weighted by its likelihood, and then, each asset's expected value, volatility (standard deviation) of value are computed.

### (iii) Correlations

Each expected value distributions for each exposure are then combined to find out the portfolio value. To compute the volatility of portfolio, it requires estimates of correlation in credit quality changes which can be obtained by following various approaches.

The correlations between stock returns can then be used to compute probabilities of various rating outcomes for the credits. With a large number of credits, using stock returns to compute the joint distribution of outcomes is time consuming. To simplify, the model recommends to use factor model in which stock returns depend on country and industry indices and unsystematic risk. However, the Credit Metrics™ technical manual also shows how to implement this model.

## 22.8 DEVELOPMENT OF CREDIT RISK MARKETS

Undoubtedly, today credit risks have substantially increased in global banking over the last few years, as a result the market of credit derivatives has gained momentum at a remarkable pace. The growth of credit derivatives came into existence when the uncertainty in the business world was increasing. In the early 1990s, the banks all over the world were desperately looking for an instrument which can hedge their credit risk retaining to both principal amount and interest rates without transferring the underlying assets. The credit derivative was formally launched by Merrill Lynch in 1991 with USD 368 million. However, the market did not grow much till 1997. The size of the market was USD 40 and 50 billion, respectively in 1996 and 1997. It has reached to USD 130 billions in quarter second, 1998. In 1997, during the Asian financial crisis, several US and European banks who have exposure in Korea, Philippines and Thailand were able to save themselves from losses. The International Swaps and Derivatives Association (ISDA) recently estimated the volume like USD 631.5 billion for the first half of 2001. This information is based upon the survey of 81 members of ISDA who would form 99.99 percent of the market. The average transaction size is between USD 10 to 25 million and the average tenure, which was less than two years, has now gone up to five years. Besides all these, there are only a few active players in the market and the secondary market is still illiquid.

Significant milestones in the developments of credit derivatives:

- 1991    Credit derivatives formally launched by Merrill Lynch with USD 368 million.
- 1992    ISDA first uses the term 'credit derivatives' to describe a new, exotic type of the over-the-counter contract.
- 1993    KMV introduces the first version of the portfolio manager model, the first credit portfolio model.
- 1994    Credit derivative market begins to grow.
- 1996    The first CLO of UK's, National West Minister Bank.
- 1997    J.P. Morgan launches Credit Matrix.
- 1997    Credit Suisse launches Credit Risk$^+$.
- 1997    The first synthetic securitisation introduced.
- 1999    Credit derivatives definitions issued by ISDA.

Today, everyone is optimistic on the growth of credit derivatives. Recently, portfolio derivatives which transfer the credit risk on a portfolio of small loans have come into existence. In such instrument, the protection seller do not even know the composition of the portfolio. It is an effective way of getting a portfolio rated and transferring the risk in the portfolio without transferring the portfolio itself. In the European market, new transactions are becoming popular where credit derivatives have combined with securitization to result into synthetic structures. This is indication of continuous growth in this market in future.

## 22.9   CREDIT DERIVATIVES INSTRUMENTS

The basic feature of credit derivative instruments is that they separate the credit risk from the total risk allowing the trading of credit risk with the purpose of replicating credit risk, transferring credit risk and hedging credit risk. The important instruments of credit derivatives are as under:

1. Credit default swaps
2. Total return swaps
3. Credit options
4. Credit linked notes

## 22.9.1   Credit Default Swaps (CDS)

This is most popular instrument of credit derivatives which has grown rapidly in the credit risk market since its inception in the early 1990s. Credit default products are products that isolate the risk on credit obligations. The instrument can be linked to an individual credit or a basket of credits to create a specified or diversified exposure to default risk.

A credit default swap (CDS) is a bilateral derivative contract where one party agrees to pay another party periodic fixed payments in exchange for receiving "credit event protection", in the form of payment, in the event that a third party or its obligations are subject to one or more pre-agreed adverse credit events over a pre-agreed time period. Typical credit events include bankruptcy, failure to pay, obligation acceleration, restructuring and repudiation/moratorium.

*Important features of CDS*

- It is a bilateral contract between the two parties, i.e., protection buyer and the protection seller. The party which seeks protection from credit event is called *protection buyer* and which provides protection is called *protection seller.*
- The protection buyer pays a fee (periodic fixed payment) to the protection seller for receiving the credit event protection. It is typically expressed in annualized basis points of a transaction's notional amount.
- The third party and the specific obligation, if any, on which event protection is concurrently bought and sold are referred to as the reference entity and reference obligation, respectively.
- Reference credit is the contingent amount/payout which will be paid by the protection seller in case of adverse credit event occurs. The reference credit must be nominated under the default swap contract.
- The reference credit asset issued must be specified under the default swap contract. The price of the asset must be agreed at the commencement of the transaction. It is important where the default payment is based on the post default price of the security.
- The credit event triggers the obligation of the provider of default protection to make the default payment to the buyer. Important examples of events which can be included in credit events can be bankruptcy, insolvency, restructuring, administration, failure to meet a payment obligation, rating down grade below agreed, change in credit spread above agreed level, etc.
- Swap can be settled either in cash or through delivery of underlying asset. The form of compensation will depend upon whether the terms of a particular CDS asks for a physical delivery or cash settlement. In case of physically settled transaction, the protection buyer would deliver the reference obligation (higher or equal payment priority) to the protection seller and receive the face value of the reference obligation. In case of cash settled transaction,

the protection seller makes a cash payment to the protection buyer based on a formula that is agreed by the parties at the inception of the contract. Generally, the formula specifies the difference between par and the then prevailing market value of a reference obligation. It normally depends on the losses actually incurred by the protection buyer in case of default. In some cases, the cash payment is a fixed amount decided at the time of making the agreement.

Figures 22.2 and 22.3 depict the transactions under cash settled and physically settled CDS.

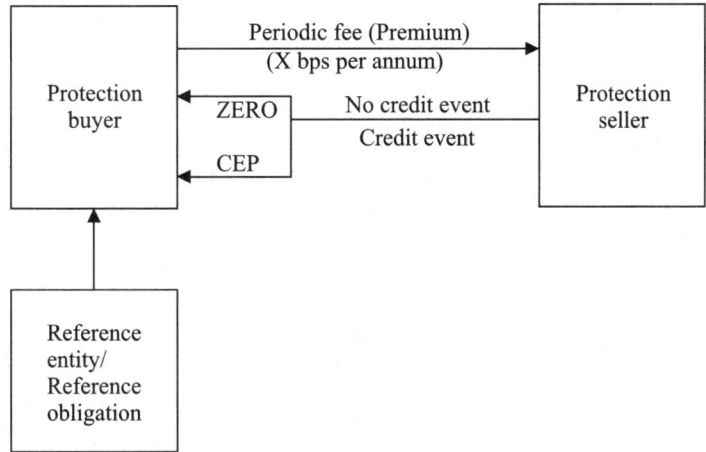

*Note: CEP refers to credit event payment*

**FIGURE 22.2**   Cash settled credit default swap.

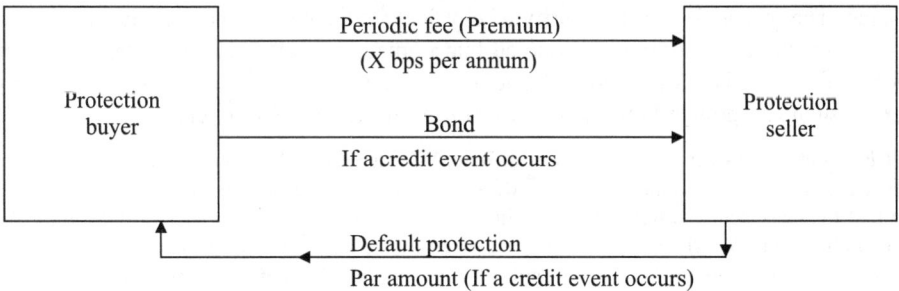

**FIGURE 22.3**   Physically settled credit default swap.

### Mechanism of CDS transaction

- On start date, no payments are made by either party (upon origination).
- On periodic interim dates, the protection buyer pays pre-agreed amount (premium) to the protection seller.
- If a credit event does not occur no payments are made by the protection seller to the protection buyer.
- If a credit event occurs, in case of physically settled contract, the transaction shall accelerate the protection buyer deliver the deliverable obligation (Bond/Loan) to the protection seller against payment of a pre-determined amount (in exchange for par value).

- If a credit event occurs and cash payment applies, then the protection seller shall pay to protection buyer the excess of (a) the par value of the deliverable obligations on start date over (b) the prevailing market value of the deliverable obligation at the time of occurrence of credit event.
- Cash settlement equals to [(Par value – recovery value) × Notional amount]. Cash settlement equals to an agreed percentage of notional, e.g., 50 percent of the notional of the transaction.
- Deliverable obligations define what assets are eligible for delivery as settlement in a physical delivery contract. It may include reference obligation, but will often be broader to include other obligations.
- Obligation defines what assets may trigger a credit event.
- The reference asset takes several forms such as marketable securities, public bond issues by the reference credit, a revolving line of credit, a bank loan, a swap obligation, a trade receivable, and class of assets within the capital structure. In the physical settlement, swap contracts allow for right of substitution of *pari-pasu* obligations. Usually, these above mentioned assets have specific characteristics like bearing simple interest to be paid in specific currency.
- Credit default swap can be terminated like other swaps, prior to its term. The investors can terminate the swap contract with the consent of the counterparty before the maturity at the current market value of the swap. Normally the default swaps are not freely transferable, however, these can be assigned to another acceptable counterparty at the most competitive price.

It is observed from the developments of credit derivatives market that default swap payout structures have evolved with market. Earlier swap contracts were cash settled, whereas today a majority of corporate units and sovereigns prefer swaps by physically settled. Further, the physical settlement has become increasingly standard. Conceptually, the economics of both types of settlements are the same. The reason for the popularity of physical settlement of swap is related to the volatility of market on maturity. Sometimes, it is noted that immediately after a credit event, an asset's price can be volatile the market is illiquid and pricing may not be reliable. In this situation, the physical settlement system can protect both the parties from flaws in price discovery.

**EXAMPLE:**    Let us consider that a development Bank 'X' currently holds a well-diversified portfolio wherein exposures are spread over 20 major industries with a board, imposing ceiling of 10 percent. Hypothetically, assuming that the bank wants to transfer its risk in the pharmaceutical sector, so as a protection buyer, it shifts its risk to another bank 'Y' which, presumably interested in extending loan to pharmaceutical sector, becomes a protection seller for a permission. For example, a company which has pharmaceutical has taken loan from Bank 'A' and has exhausted the total limit of loan to pharmaceutical sector after extending a loan of ₹50 crores to the company. Now, the bank can buy protection on ₹50 crores loan from the bank 'Y' using CDS. The Bank 'Y' can benefit from opportunity to invest synthetically in pharmaceutical sector through balance sheet transaction and also from sector diversification. Bank 'A' reduces credit risk and benefits from reduced exposure to pharmaceutical sector in terms of regulatory norms and thus, in economic form, can deploy the relieved capital in other sector.

### Basket linked credit swaps

In this type of swap contract, credit default is based on a basket of underlying assets with different issuers. For example, a US $100 million transaction may comprise four underlying credit assets—a five-year German bond, a five-year Canadian bond, a five-year French bond and a five-year Swiss bond. In this case, the provider of default protection, since it provides protection on any of the four assets up to a face value of US$ 100 million on a first to default basis, is providing protection of

US$ 400 million of credit assets. The important point in this concept is first to default. It states that the credit event that triggers the default payment or physical settlement with respect to the underlying asset is the first default of any of the credit assets included in the basket of credits.

In basket linked credit swaps, two factors are reflected—the low default correlation in between the credit assets and the element of inherent leverage in the structure. The combination of credit risks in the basket linked credit default swap creates a lower credit quantity in comparison to the individual credit standing of the credit asset. In practice, it is observed that high quality credit assets like European and other sovereigns issuers have been in such basket linked swaps. Protection providers in such swaps are primarily institutional investors seeking higher yields on high quality securities. For Eastern investors, including Japanese banks and institutions, and European and Middle Eastern investors are mainly the major providers of these swaps.

### First Loss and Tranche-Loss Credit Default (FLCDS)

It protects its buyer from losses of a reference pool as a result of credit events. Unlike a first to default credit default swap, in which only the loss from the first credit event is compensated, or an nth-to-default, in which, the losses from nth default are compensated. In FLCDS, it compensates its buyer for any losses from credit events of the reference assets up to a certain portion of the total notional of the assets pool.

### Credit Default Index Swaps (CDS Index)

It is portfolio of single-entity credit default swaps (CDS). It is just as an extension of a CDS on a single entity to a portfolio of entities. The basic difference is that in a CDS the notional is fixed during the life of the CDS and the protection buyer is compensated at most once. Whereas in CDS Index, the premium notional is variable. In case default in the portfolio occurs, the premium notional is reduced by the loss amount of the defaulted entity and at the same time the protection buyer gets compensated by the lost amount. The most popular CDS Indexes are the CDX Index and the ITRAXX Index.

### Credit Default Swap Options

This is also called credit default swaption. It is an option on CDS. A CDS option gives its holder the right but not the obligation to buy (call) or sell (put) protection on a specified reference entity for a specified future time period for a certain spread. The option is knocked out if the reference entity defaults during the life of the option. This knock out feature marks the difference between a CDS option and a plain vanilla option. European style options are most commonly used in the market. The CDS option can be further classified on entity base. CDS option can be on a single entity or on a basket of entities, which can be with a regular payoff for the default leg, or with a binary payoff for the default leg.

### Credit Default Index Swap Options (SDISO)

These are also termed as CD Index swap option or CD Index swaption or CDS Index option. This is an option to buy or sell the underlying CDIS at a specified date. A payer swaption gives the holder of the option the right to buy protection and pays premium for this right. The receiver of swaption gives the holder of the option right to sell protection against the receipt of the premium.

A CD index swaption is significantly different from CDS option, an option on a single entity CDS. In the case of an option on a single entity, if the reference entity defaults before the expiry of the option, the option will be knocked out and becomes worthless. However, an option on a CDIS, when a reference entity default before the expiry of the option, the loss will be paid by the protection seller to the protection buyer on the exercise of the option. It means, a CD Index swaption is always more valuable than a single entity CDS option.

### Synthetic Collateralized Debt Obligations (SCDO)

Synthetic CDOS are credit derivatives on a pool of reference entities that are synthesized through the basic credit derivatives, mostly CDS and CLNs. In other words, CDO is a pool of debit contracts housed within a special purpose of entity (SPE) whose capital structure is sliced and record on difference in credit quality. A common structure of CDOs involves dividing the credit risk of the reference pool into a few different risk levels. The level with a higher credit risk supports the levels with lower credit risks. The risk range of two adjacent risk levels is called a 'tranche.' The lower bound the risk level of a tranche is called an "attachment" point and the upper bound a "detachment" point.

The CDOs, in general, are on CDS and CLN based. The most popular CDOs are so called, standardized CDOs. For a standardized CDO its reference entities are homogenous, i.e., all the reference entities have the same notional and the same recovery rate. Due to the complexity and the large sizes of the reference pools of synthetic CDOS, their valuation is much more complicated and resource intensive than the ordinary single entry CDS or CLNs. Monte Carlo methods have been the most reliable methods in CDO valuation, however, they are not efficient in computation.

## 22.9.2   Total Return Swaps (TRS)

Total return swaps are bilateral contracts designed to synthetically replicate the economic returns arising of underlying asset or a portfolio of assets for a pre-specified time. In other words, in the total return swap contract, one party pays the total return of (including any interest payments and capital appreciation) of a designated asset, and in return the other party pays to him a regular floating rate payments, such as LIBOR + spread. These floating payments represent a funding cost of the TR payer. A TRS contract allows the TRS receiver to obtain the economic returns of an asset without funding thereon its balance sheet. So, TRS is a primarily off-balance sheet financial vehicle.

Total return payers are typically such lenders and other investors who want to reduce their exposure to an asset without removing it from their balance sheet. On the other hand, total return receivers are typically such institutions like insurance companies, hedge funds, corporate treasures and other investors who want to invest or put their funds on a leverage basis or to diversify their portfolios or to intend higher return by taking on risk exposure.

The mechanism functioning of a total return swap is shown in Figure 22.4.

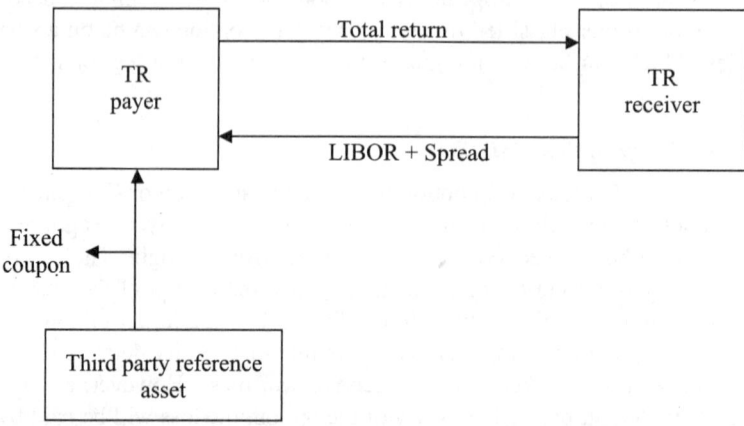

**FIGURE 22.4**   Structure of total return swap.

*Important features of total return swap*

- The counterparties in the TRS contract are two: TR payer and TR receiver. TR payer intends to hedge risk economic, risk of an asset that it holds on balance sheet. The TR receiver is exposed to that risk but does not have the asset on the balance sheet.
- One party (TR payer) pays to the other party (TR receiver) the total return on the specified asset. Total return payment would consist of interest fee (if any) and any change in the reference obligation's value. Change in value (depreciation or appreciation) on the reference obligation is determined on the basis of a poll of dealers. This change in value be made on a periodic interim basis. However, the investors may be given an opportunity to participate in the poll.
- Maturities in total return swaps rarely match the underlying asset. Normally swaps are shorter than the reference asset.
- TRS receiver must pay any negative total return arisen due to decline in value by more than the coupon payments on the underlying assets.
- A TRS reference obligation can be a single asset, e.g., particular bond or loan or basket of assets or an index. The reference baskets are becoming increasingly popular due to cost effective cause they provide to portfolios of credit risk.
- A TRS transfers not only credit risk but also market risk (i.e., any increase or decrease in general market prices).
- The TRS contract normally allows either party to cancel the transaction at the anniversary date of the contract. TRS referencing a single name typically terminates upon default of underlying asset or other such defined credit events. In this situation, the asset can be delivered and the TR receiver will pay the price shortfall.
- To contrast between the CDS and TRS, the payments are exchanged among the counterparties upon changes in market valuation of the underlying, whereas in CDS, it is based upon the occurrence of a credit event.

## 22.9.3 Credit Options (Credit Spread Options)

Credit options are derivatives instruments with payoffs linked to the credit characteristics of a particular underlying asset or issuer. Before discussing the credit option it is essential to understand the term credit spreads. Credit spreads represent the margin between the risk-free rates of return designed to compensate the investor for the risk undertaken on default of the underlying asset. In other words, credit spreads is the difference between return of underlying security and the return on corresponding risk-free security. It is calculated as:

Credit spread = Yield on underlying security loan – Yield on corresponding risk-free security

The basic idea underlying the credit spreads is to understand the relative credit value changes in contract to changes in interest rates, credit spread expectation and the term structure of credit spread. This is required to design credit option derivatives by the participants in the financial market.

As noted in the earlier discussion that credit derivatives represent a natural extension of the financial markets capacity to unbundled risk. They offer to the asset managers to hedge their exposure to credit risk. In this respect, credit option will be discussed in two forms: those triggered by a decline in the value of an asset and others which are triggered by a change in the assets spread over the risk-free rate.

In the credit option mechanism, the option gives the right to the bond (security) holder to sell a bond to the other party (investor) at a certain strike price expressed in terms of a spread over a benchmark. On the expiration, if the actual spread of the underlying bond is lower than the strike price, then the bond holder will not exercise the option, and hence, option expires worthless and the investor pays nothing. On the other hand, if the actual spread is higher than the strike price, then the bond holder will deliver the bond and the investor pays a price whose yield spread over the benchmark equals the strike spread.

Credit options can be primarily categorized into two types—put option and call option. Further, the put option can be divided into two—price options and spread options. In the price put option, the option writer agrees to compensate the option buyer for a decline in value of the underlying asset below the strike price. Upon exercise of the credit option, the payoff is determined by subtracting the market price from the strike price of the asset (bond). Strike price is usually determined by taking the present value of the asset's cash flow discounted at the risk-free rate plus the strike credit spread. The spread put options are based on the spread between the bond yield and the corresponding treasury yield. Second type of credit options are referred as call option which are based on the credit spread. These are structured in such a way that the option is in-the-money when the credit spread exceeds the specified (strike) spread level. The payoff is the difference in the credit spread multiplied with a specified notional value.

Figure 22.4 shows the position of credit put option. The higher the spreads, the higher is the price. The wider the spreads, the lower is the price. In Figure 22.5, the options are assumed in the European style.

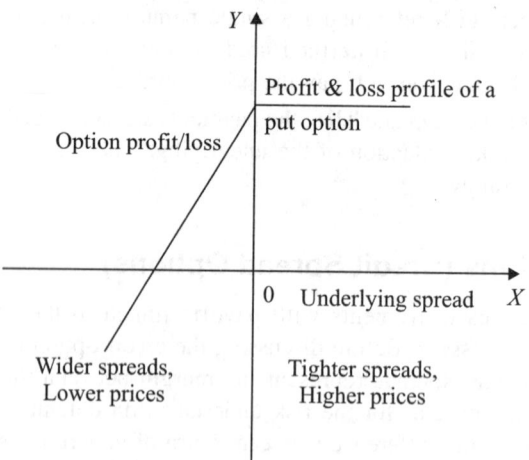

**FIGURE 22.5** Structure of credit put option.

### Important features

- The buyer of the put is entitled to put specific bond to the seller at a pre-determined price or spread.
- The option is not exercised by the option buyer, then the option seller pockets the premium.
- If the option buyer exercises the option, the option writer (seller) purchases the asset at a pre-determined price. He still gets to keep the premium.

- After adjusting the premium received on the option, the seller's break-even purchase price for the asset is generally favourable as compared to market price.
- Credit spread options allow an investor to profit from a spread view. They increase the current yield specifically in case of overweight in cash.
- The investor receives premium income for purchasing bonds (assets) in the future.

## 22.9.4 Credit Linked Notes (CLN)

The credit link note is another important instrument in credit derivatives market. It enables the investor to purchase an asset with a return linked to the credit risk of the asset itself and additional credit risk transferred by way of credit derivative between the parties. So, it is a combination of a regular note (bond or deposit or asset) and a credit option. Being a regular note with coupon, maturity and redemption, it is an on-balance sheet instrument just like credit default swap. Under this arrangement the coupon or price of the note is based on the performance of a reference asset. It means the investor receives a coupon and redemption at par value unless there has been credit event by a reference credit. If there is a credit event, in that case the amount will be redeemed at par value minus a contingent payment to the investor. The issuer receives a premium for taking exposure to the reference credit. The premium forms part of the coupon that is paid to the investor. The structure of the credit link note is shown in Figure 22.6.

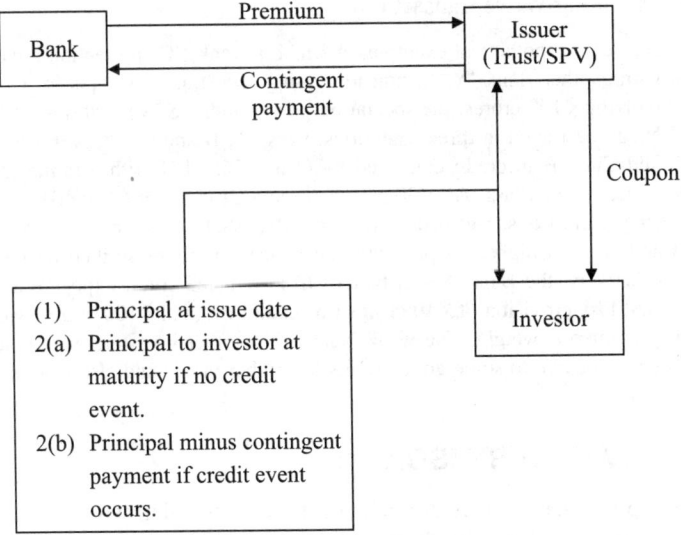

**FIGURE 22.6** Credit linked note structure.

*Mechanism of credit linked note structure*

- Credit Linked Notes (CLNs) are created through a special purpose vehicle (SPV) or trust which is collateralized with usually AAA rated securities. It is credit swap between the bank and the issuer.
- CLNs can also be issued directly by a bank or financial institution or non-banking finance company.

- If the issuer is a trust, it enters into default swap (default protection) with a deal arranger (third counterparty) in return for a premium. In case of default, the trust pays the dealer par amount the recovery rate in exchange for an annual fee. This annual fee is passed on to the investors in the form of higher coupon (yield) on the notes.
- The investors purchase the securities (structure notes) from the issuer (trust) which pays a fixed or floating coupon during the life of the note to the investors. Coupon reflects risk of issuer and credit swap.
- At the time of maturity, the investors receive par amount if no credit event occurs (referenced credit defaults) or declares bankruptcy.
- If credit event occurs, then the principal amount at par minus contingent payment will be paid to the investors. Here the investor is, in fact, selling the credit protection in exchange for higher yield in terms of coupon on the note.

### Types of credit linked notes

The credit linked notes can be classified into following two categories:

**Traditional forms of structured notes:**   This is traditional type of notes where the issuer links the coupon or principal amount to an underlying credit risk component. In turn he hedges out its exposure fully with a back-to-back credit derivative transaction with a dealer.

**Synthetic bonds:**   In this category, the debts are issued where the underlying credit risk exposure is created through a credit derivative transaction.

**EXAMPLE:** Let us consider a hypothetical example, in which a Bank 'X' (protection buyer) wants to go for a credit derivative deal with another Bank 'Y' having low rating. The Bank 'X' opts for CLN. Assume that the Bank 'X' has a loan involving ₹100 crores, the special purpose vehicle (SPV) writes a credit default swap with the Bank X. Then CLN can be issued in three categories: Class A, B and C. Class A gets credit enhancement from Class B and C, and Class B in credit enhanced by Class 'C'. CLN with a rating target of AAA worth ₹60 crores, would be issued under Class 'A', ₹30 crores A rated CLN under Class 'B' and ₹10 crores in class C category. Class C being riskiest is subscribed by the Bank 'A' itself. It means, the first loss risk is borne by the Bank A. Class B and A get a higher coupon rate and hence can be subscribed by the weak Bank 'Y' or any other investors. In this way, the Bank A will benefit from reduced credit exposure and zero counterparty risk. Further, only the first loss provision of ₹10 crores (instead of original ₹100 crores) would attract a capital requirement with 100 percent risk weight. The weak bank 'Y' or other investors experience a dearth of good credit can take a synthetic exposure to some good credits for higher yields and also from sector diversification.

## 22.10   CREDIT EVENTS BY ISDA

The International Swap and Derivatives Association (ISDA) has defined the six events which will trigger a payment by the protection seller in the credit risk market. These are as:

*1. Bankruptcy:*   This refers to the reference entity's insolvency or its inability to pay its debts. This is the most immediately visible event that would trigger payment on a CDS.

*2. Failure to pay:*   It refers to failure on the part of the reference entity to make payment with respect to principal or interest on one or more of its obligations as and when due including the grace period provided for trigger this event.

*3. Obligation default:*   This covers the situation, other than failure to pay as mentioned above, where the relevant obligation becomes capable of being declared due and payable as a result of a default by the reference entity before the time when such obligation would otherwise have been capable of being so declared. The default requirement builds in a minimum threshold, which the relevant sum being defaulted, or capable of being accelerated must exceed before the credit event occurs.

*4. Obligation acceleration:* The scope of this event forms a subset of that of obligation default. Thus, if obligation default is specified on a credit event in the relevant credit derivative transaction, this credit event will only be of relevance if the default requirement is lower than that in respect of default obligation.

*5. Repudiation/Moratorium:* This refers to the situation where the reference entity or a government authority disaffirms, disclaims or otherwise challenges the validity of the relevant obligation, or if the entity or government stops payment on such obligations. This provision now applies only to sovereign reference entities.

*6. Restructuring:* Restructuring covers events as a result of which the terms, as agreed by the reference entity or government authority and the holders of the relevant obligation, governing the relevant obligation have become less favourable to the holders than they would otherwise have been.

## 22.11  BENEFITS OF CREDIT DERIVATIVES

Credit derivatives are important recent innovations in the financial markets across the world. These are used as an alternative to cash market investments as an effective risk management tools and an efficient means to arbitrage different prices among various assets.

The credit derivatives can eliminate the credit risk in a more effective way as compared to traditional techniques like financial guarantees, letter of credits, unfunded sub-participation insurance, etc. In this section, some of the important benefits of credit derivatives to the participants in this market are described here asunder:

1. The major hedging tools available to the banks and other financial institutions to hedge credit risk is to sell their loans assets or debentures which they hold. They require such mechanism which would provide long-term financing without taking credit risk if they so desire. They could also like to assume credit risk in certain sectors.

2. Credit derivatives permit the banks and institutions to transfer credit risk, and hence, free up capital, which can be used in productive opportunities. They enable the banks and institutions to get credit risk off-balance sheet where they might be obstructing higher margin business.

3. Banks/institutions can do the business on existing client relationship in excess of exposure norms and transfer away the risks. For example, a bank which hits its exposure limits with a particular client group may not be able to accept a lucrative guarantee deal under the present circumstances. However, with credit derivatives, the bank can take the said deal and maintain its exposure limits by transferring credit risk on the guarantee or previous exposure. This will allow the banks to maintain client relationship.

4. The banks/financial institutions through various credit derivatives can contract and manage a credit risk portfolio on their own choice and risk appetite constrained by funds, distribution and sales effort.

5. Through credit derivative mechanism, the banks/institutions credit risk would be diversified to other players in the financial markets.

6. Not only the banks/financial institutions can be benefited from the credit derivatives, but also other corporate units in various high-tech field having a large number of customers can also exploit it.

7. The credit derivative investors which are commercial banks, development financial institutions, investment banks, hedge funds, money managers, etc. would also be benefited by the use of credit derivative instruments. Their needs can be summarized as: high yield return potential, efficient access to bank loan markets, off-balance sheet investment, minimum back office administration requirements, low capital requirements and so on could be fulfilled by following various credit derivatives as per the requirements.

8. Apart from the above, the credit derivatives have the following advantages over other credit risk management instruments.

   (a) Other instruments mentioned in the beginning of this section are less efficient.

   (b) Insurance, guarantees and security section are less liquid techniques in the first place.

   (c) Credit insurance scheme would also lead to increase in intermediation since only insurance companies can go for it. So due to this, the banks cannot directly participate in credit risk exposures of other banks for managing their own portfolio exposure.

   (d) Due to prohibition on banks for providing guarantees in favour of other banks or financial institution, guarantees are limited mechanism.

   (e) Transaction costs on classical securitization method are substantial.

   (f) Financial intermediaries like mutual funds and insurance companies also stand to gain through indirect participation in credit linked returns since they are not directly permitted to take certain kinds of direct exposure like lending. However, they can participate in credit protection, and thus, can earn on assets to which they have no access today.

   (g) Non-banking firms can also gain from credit derivatives primarily through hedging of credit exposure.

   (h) Other participants like vendors and suppliers can hedge credit risk without recourse to funding.

   (i) Sovereign risk can also be hedged away through credit derivatives mechanism.

   (j) With credit expenses as being transferred among institutions due to credit derivative mechanism, it will assist in more efficiently use of excess capital of other participants in the capital market and allowing capital-scarce players to generate more business.

   (k) Due to the above mentioned transformation, the financial system of an economy would be benefited and strengthened.

   (l) Since credit risk can be transferred, credit spreads may narrow as illiquidity is no longer a significant risk.

## 22.12   CREDIT RISK MANAGEMENT IN INDIA

The effective management of credit risk is a critical component of comprehensive risk management process. It includes identification, measurement, monitoring and control of credit risk exposures. The rising level of non-performing assets (NPAs) in Indian commercial banks and financial institutions poses a great challenge before the regulators. This brought risk assessment and risk management into focus. Further, the regulatory authorities at the international level (comprising G-7 countries) brought the Basel Committee Accord 1988, as an effective solution for providing risk resistance and protecting banks, which exclusively focuses on credit risk. In this respect, the Reserve Bank of India has recently issued detailed guidelines on credit risk management. These guidelines mainly focus on the perception of risk analysis and the importance given on risk management and the search for hedging tools to minimize the impact of adverse effects of credit failures on the credit institutions.

In the middle of the year 2002, the RBI appointed a Working Group on introduction of Credit Derivatives in India, comprising officers from the Reserve Bank of India and industry. The Working Group was to study the need and scope for allowing banks and financial institutions to use credit derivatives, the regulatory issues involved and to make suitable recommendations in this regard. The Group has submitted its report and is available at the website of RBI.

Reserve Bank of India, based on the findings of the Working Group came out recently with Draft Guidelines to allow banks to use credit derivatives to manage risks relating to lending, including buying protection on loan and investment. Banks would be barred from using these derivatives for trading purposes and only domestic entities would be allowed to enter in credit risk contracts.

The Group recommends that to begin with, the banks, financial institutions, Non-Banking Financial Corporation (NBFCs), mutual funds, insurance companies and corporates may all owed to introduce subject to companies of the following conditions:

## (i) Risk management systems

- The Board of Directors of the bank/financial institutions has approved the policy in this regard.
- The bank/FI/NBFC has adequate Management Information System (MIS) to make Board of Directors and senior management aware of the risks being undertaken.
- Credit risk acquired through a credit derivative is captured within bank's/FIs/NBFC's normal credit approval and monitoring regime.
- The bank/FI/NBFC has systems to assess and account for the possibility of default correlation between reference asset and the protection provider.
- The bank/FI/NBFC has a procedure to determine an appropriate contingency plan against uncertainty in valuation. This is important especially where the reference asset is illiquid like a loan.
- Valuation adjustments are recorded to decrease the asset or increase the liability arising from the initial valuation of a credit derivative transaction by the bank's approved mathematical models.
- Further, it is important to protect the interests of those participants who might be less knowledgeable about credit derivatives. The protection could be asunder:
  - Ensuring that the types of transactions entered into by the counterparty are not inappropriate for their needs.
  - Ensuring that the senior levels of management at the counterparty are involved in transactions.
  - Ensuring that counterparties do not enter into transactions that violate other rules and regulations.
  - Banks, financial institutions and NBFCs that enter into credit derivative transactions should be responsible for ensuring that the transactions are appropriate for the counterparty entering into such transactions.
  - Banks, financial institutions and NBFCs that enter into credit derivative transactions should not be permitted to do so without obtaining from the counterparty, a copy of a resolution passed by their Board of Directors, authorising the counterparty to transact in credit derivatives.
  - Banks, financial institutions and NBFCs that enter into credit derivative transactions should also take necessary steps to ensure that the transaction entered into by the counterparty complies with other regulations in force.

Given that the participation is being restricted to banks and FIs, NBFCs, mutual funds, insurance companies and corporates, each of the counterparty can judge for themselves whether it is in their interest and whether it is within the relevant rules and regulations.

**(ii) Documentation:** The credit derivative transactions should be covered by the ISDA Master Agreement 1992 and the ISDA Credit Derivatives Definitions 1999. The only exception to this should be credit linked notes that are typically issued as bonds and are, therefore, subject to the documentation requirements of bonds. However, the suggested documentation should be agreeable by both the parties.

### (iii) Exposure norms

- In the case of credit derivatives, exposure for a specific credit derivative will be driven mainly by whether the holder of the credit derivative is the protection buyer or the protection seller.

- While determining the overall sectoral/borrower group/individual company exposure, suitable reduction should be given in the level of exposure with respect to the credit protection bought by means of credit derivatives. Conversely, the protection seller's exposure would increase as the protection seller acquires what is equivalent to a credit exposure on the reference asset. Once the exposure is computed to individual/group entities, banks/FIs will have to ensure that they are within the overall ceiling as laid out in the RBI guidelines.

- The benefits available under special category of assets such as priority sector lending/ export finance should be made available to the credit protection seller in the event that the underlying asset is/are such assets.

- Sufficient provisioning (as computed based on what would be the provisioning applicable if the reference assets were on the seller's books) would have to be carried out by the credit protection seller if it is offering credit protection on a non-performing asset.

The protection buyer should not make any provision for a reference asset that has turned to NPA.

**(iv) Capital adequacy:** For capital adequacy purpose, the banks should adopt an approach similar to the guidelines for existing credit transfer products such as financial guarantees. Before being granted capital relief to any form of credit derivative, the banks/FIs must fulfill minimum conditions relating to risk management processes and that the credit derivative is direct, explicit, irrevocable and unconditional.

### (v) Accounting

- The normal accounting entries for credit derivative transactions should be fairly straightforward depending on cash flows that take place at various points in time during the tensor of the transaction, e.g., for a credit default swap, there will be periodic payment of fees by the protection buyer to the protection seller. If there is a credit event then settlement will be appropriately accounted depending on whether cash settled or settled via physical exchange versus par payment.

- However, all derivatives within the scope of the standard must be fair valued at least on a quarterly basis. The changes in fair value must be reported in current earnings unless hedge accounting is allowed in which case some of all of the change in the value of the hedging instrument should be posted directly to the Other Income (OI) account on the balance sheet. This amount would be reversed out of OI and matched in earnings with the impact of the offsetting hedged exposure.

### RBI Guidelines-2011

Reserve Bank of India constituted an internal group to finalize the operational framework for the introduction of plain vanilla OTC single name CDS for corporate bonds in India in the year 2009–2010. Draft guidelines on CDS on the recommendations of this group were placed on the RBI website on February 23, 2011 and were open for comments from all concerned. Comments were received from a wide spectrum of banks, primary dealers (PDs) and other market participants. The guidelines were become effective from October 24, 2011.

The basic objective of these guidelines is to provide market participants a tool to transfer and manage credit risk in an effective manner through redistribution of risk. CDS have benefits such as enhancing investment, borrowing opportunities and reducing transaction costs, etc. Important features of the RBI guidelines on CDS are as follows:

(i) In the CDS market, the participants are classified as either users or market makers. The user concern are permitted to buy credit protection only to hedge their underlying credit risk on corporate bonds. It means the users cannot purchase CDS for amounts higher than the face value of the bonds for which CDS are being created.

(ii) There cannot be naked CDS protection. It means that no users can credit any such CDS where no bonds exist in the firm. In other words, the CDS can be maintained only for eligible underlying bonds. Further, the periods of CDS cannot be longer their tenure of underlying bonds held by the firm.

(iii) The eligible entities under user's category must be permitted by the RBI. These entities can be commercial banks, PDs, non-banking financial corporations (NBFC), mutual funds, insurance companies, housing finance companies, provident funds, foreign institutional investors (FIIs), listed companies, etc.

(iv) CDS will be permitted only on listed corporate bonds as reference obligation. However, the rated bonds but un-listed of the infrastructure companies can also be written. No other corporate bonds have been permitted for written purpose.

(v) The credit events such as bankruptcy, failure to pay, repudiation/moratorium, obligation acceleration, obligation default, restructuring approved under BIFR and corporate debt re-structuring (CDR) mechanism are covered for the CDS contracts.

(vi) The contracting parties in the CDS must agree to the term and conditions of the CDS individually, such as definitions of each events or settlement procedure in order to avoid any dispute later on among the parties. In India, the RBI guidelines specifically states that the Fixed Income Money Market and Derivative Association of India (FIMMDA) shall check-out a Master Agreement for Indian CDS. At the international level and US market, the Master Agreement of International Swap and Derivatives Association (ISDA) would be referred.

(vii) As per the RBI guidelines, the settlement procedure among the parties of CDS shall be determined as per the procedure and method of settlement mentioned in the contract on CDS documentation. However, the guidelines further aid that for transactions involving the users, physical settlement is mandatory. Further, for the market makers, any of the settlement methods, i.e., physical, cash and auction, can be followed provided the CDS documentation envisages such settlement.

(viii) To prevent malpractices like mis-selling and market abuse, the protection sellers of CDS have to ensure that CDS transactions shall be undertaken only on obtaining from the counterparty of CDS, a copy of resolution passed by the Board of Directors wherein the counterparty is authorized to transact in CDS. In other words, counterparty of CDS can only transact in CDS if it is authorized by the Board of Directors to do so.

(ix) With regards to reporting requirement of CDS, the market makers would be required to report their CDS trades with both users and other market makers within 30 minutes from the deal time on the reporting platform of CDS trade repository. On the other hand, the users would be required to affirm or reject their trade already reported by the market makers by the end of the day. Further, the participants of CDS will also report to respective regulators (e.g., IRDA for insurance companies), information as required by them regarding risk position vis-à-vis their network and adherence to risk limit, etc.

## SUMMARY

This chapter has introduced the concept of credit derivatives, their features, growth and types of credit derivatives. Credit derivatives have become the significant financial instruments in the recent past due to default in financial transaction. It has grown steadily in spite of turbulent economic condition prevailed with escalating debt burden.

Credit derivative is a new market segment in the field of financial derivatives. These are such instruments which transfer either specific or all the inherent risks of a credit position from one party to another party. In this type of transactions, risk seller transfers its risk to the risk buyer against payment of a premium. These contracts are private and confidential which allow user to manage their exposure to credit risk. They are also defined as off-balance sheet financial instruments.

The chapter further elaborates the basic features of credit derivatives. Credit derivatives is a bilateral contract comprising two parties. One is the credit risk protection buyer and other is credit risk protection seller or guarantor.

The basic objective of credit derivatives instrument is to protect from the inherent credit risk to the protection seeks. So, credit risk can be categorized into two variables—market risk and firm specific risk. The market risk is risen due to movements in interest rates, exchange rates, stock price, commodity price, trade restrictions, economic sanctions and other market factors. On the other hand, firm specific risk relates to firm's own factors like goodwill, reputation, financial position, credit worthiness, credit policy, management quality, credit rating, etc.

Credit risk can be divided into three components—default risk, downgrade risk and spread risk. Default risk refers to the probability of default for not repaying the loan. Downgrade risk refers to the falling of credit rating of the firm from its existing grade and spread risk refers to the difference between the return on the risky debt and risk-free debt. The chapter further describes the various models of measuring the credit risk. These are Merton Model, Credit Risk$^+$ Model and Credit Metrics$^{TM}$ Model.

Chapter in next section discusses the four types of instruments for managing the credit derivatives such as credit default swaps, total return swaps, credit options and credit linked notes.

Credit default swaps is a bilateral derivative contract where one party agrees to pay another party periodic fixed payments in exchange for receiving "credit event protection", in the form of payment. Such agreements is based on certain conditions and over a free agreed time period. There are other forms of CDS like Basket linked credit swap, First loss and tranche loss credit default, Credit default-index swaps, Credit default-swaptions and Credit default Index swap options.

Total return swaps are bilateral contracts designed to synthetically replicate the economic return arising of underlying asset or a portfolio of assets for a pre-specified time. In other words, in the total return swap contract, one party pays the total returns (including any interest payments and capital appreciation) of the total returns of a designed asset and in return the other party pays to him a regular floating rate payment, such as LIBOR, MIBOR, etc.

Credit options are derivatives instruments with payoffs linked to the credit characteristics of a particular underlying asset or issuer. The basic underlying the credit spreads is to understand the relative credit value changes in contract to change in interest rates, credit spread expectation and the term structure of credit spread. Credit linked note enables the investor to purchase an asset with a return linked to the credit risk of the asset itself and additional risk transferred by way of credit derivatives between the parties.

ISDA has defined six events which will trigger a payment by the protection seller: bankruptcy, failure to pay, obligation default, obligation acceleration, repudiation/moratorium and restructuring. Chapter in the last section explains the benefits associated with credit derivatives. As credit derivatives are important instruments of risk management that evolved during last two decades only, so these are primarily used for the management of credit risk by banks and financial institutions. The RBI issued a detailed guidelines on credit risk management through CDS in 2011 which are to be followed by the banks and other institutions strictly.

# SUGGESTED READINGS

1. Andrew, Kasapi, *Master Financial Derivatives: A Step By Step Guide to Credit Derivatives and Their Application*, Prentice-Hall of India, New Delhi, 2000.

2. Tavakoli, Janet, *Credit Derivatives & Synthetic Structures: A Guide to Instruments and Applications* (2nd edition), John Wiley & Sons, 2001.

3. Tavakoli, Janet, *Credit Derivatives: A Guide to Instruments and Applications* (Ist edition), John Wiley & Sons, USA, 1998.

4. Quemard, Jean-Luc, *Credit Derivatives: Securitization and the New Regulatory Environment*, Eusromoney Books, New York, 2003.

5. Bomfim, *Understanding Credit Derivatives and Related Instruments*, Academic Press, USA, 2002.

6. Bol, Georg, *Credit Risk: Measurement, Evaluation and Management*, Physica-Verlag, New York, 2003.

7. RBI Report of *Working Group on Credit Derivatives in India*, adapted from www.rbi.org.in 2002.

8. Credit Metrics, Technical Document, JP Morgan, 1997.

9. Credit Suisse, Credit Risk[+]: A Credit Risk Management Framework, Credit Suisse Financial Products, 1997.

10. Elton, E.J. and Gruber, M.J., *Modern Portfolio Theory and Investment Analysis,* Wiley, New York, 1995.

11. Fishman, G., *Monte Carlo: Concepts, Algorithms, and Applications*, Springer Series in Operations Research, Springer, Berlin, 1997.

12. Jarrow, R. and Turnbull, S., *Derivatives Securities.* South-Western College Publishing, 1997.

13. Kealhofer, S., *Portfolio Management of Default Risk.* Net Exposure 1 (2), 1998.

14. Lucas, D.J., Default correlation and credit analysis, *Journal of Fixed Income* (March), 76–87, 1995.

15. Merton, R., On the pricing of corporate debt: The risk structure of interest rates. *Journal of Finance* 28, 449–470, 1974.

16. RBI website

17. ISDA website

# REVIEW QUESTIONS

1. What do you understand by the credit derivatives? Explain with suitable examples.
2. Write a detailed note on the history of credit derivatives.
3. Discuss the concept of credit risk. Also discuss the assessment and management of credit risk.
4. Bring out important features of credit derivatives. How will you measure the credit risk?
5. Briefly explain the major recommendations of RBI working group of credit derivatives in India.
6. "Credit risk is one of the crucial risk faced by banks and financial institutions in globalized world economy." Discuss the statement in the light of methods of management of credit risk.
7. Explain the term credit derivatives. Discuss its types and features with suitable illustrations.
8. What is credit default swaps? What are important features of credit default swaps? Also discuss the mechanism of credit default swaps.
9. Write notes on the following:
   (a) Physically settled credit default swaps
   (b) Cash settled credit default swaps
   (c) Structure of credit default swaps
10. What is Total Return Swaps (TRS)? Discuss the important features of TRS. Explain the structure of TRS with suitable examples.
11. Write a detailed note on credit option with suitable illustrations.
12. What is Credit Linked Notes (CLN)? Explain the structure and mechanism of CLN with example.
13. What are different uses of credit derivatives? Explain with examples.
14. "Credit derivatives has changed the mechanism and pattern of risk management in banking and financial institutions." Discuss the statement in the light of historical development of credit derivatives in India.
15. Write a detailed note on growth of credit derivatives market in India. Explain with suitable illustrations. Also explain the recent guidelines of RBI on CDS.
16. What is credit risk? Discuss the other types of risk that affect the business in a significant way. Explain with suitable examples.
17. Explain the components of credit risk. Also explain various models of assessing the credit risk in a firm with suitable examples.
18. Explain the recent measures taken by the RBI to regulate the credit risk management in India with suitable instances.
19. Explain the term credit event. What are its different types? Also explain important guidelines of ISDA relating to credit risk management.
20. Critically examine the various credit risk measurement models alongwith your suggestions in this respect.

# Annexure

## ISDA TERMS

**1.** The undermentioned definitions are samples definitions that merely seek to illustrate possible definitions. These definitions may be different for different trades. The International Swaps and Derivatives Association, Inc. (ISDA) has provided definitions of terms used in such agreements. Some of the important terms are:

**Reference entity:** Reference entity means each entity specified as such in the related confirmation and any successor. A reference entity can be a single name or a basket of names. It can be a corporate, Institution or a sovereign entity. A reference entity may be one as principal or as a guarantor.

**Reference obligation:** Reference obligation means any obligation specified as such or of a type described in the related confirmation (if any are so specified or described) and any substitute reference obligation.

**Credit event:** Credit event means with respect to a credit derivative transaction, one or more of bankruptcy, failure to pay, obligation acceleration, obligation default, inconvertibility, repudiation/ moratorium or restructuring, as specified in the related confirmation. If an occurrence would otherwise constitute a credit event, such occurrence will constitute a credit event whether or not such occurrence arises directly or indirectly from: (a) any lack or alleged lack of authority or capacity of a reference entity to enter into any obligation, (b) any actual or alleged unenforceability, illegality, impossibility or invalidity with respect to any obligation, however described, (c) any applicable law, order, regulation, decree or notice, however described, or the promulgation of, any change in, the interpretation by any court, tribunal, regulatory authority or similar administrative or judicial body with competent or apparent jurisdiction of any applicable law, order, regulation, decree or notice, however described, or (d) the imposition of, or any change in, any exchange controls, capital restrictions or any other similar restrictions imposed by any monetary authority, however described.

**Obligation:** Obligation means each obligation of each reference entity (whether as principal or surety or otherwise) described by the obligation category and the obligation characteristic specific in the related confirmation.

**Deliverable obligation:** Deliverable obligation means any obligation of a reference entity determined pursuant to the method described in the related confirmation that is payable in an amount equal to its outstanding principal balance or due and payable amount, as applicable, and is not subject to any counterclaim, defence or right of setoff by a reference entity; each reference obligation unless specified in the related confirmation as an excluded deliverable obligation and any other obligation of a reference entity specified in the related confirmation. A deliverable obligation may be wider in scope than the reference obligation. The reference obligation determines the rank of each deliverable obligation.

**2. Credit Event Definitions** If an occurrence would otherwise constitute a credit event, such occurrence will constitute a credit event whether or not such occurrence arises directly from:

    (a) any lack or alleged lack of authority or capacity of a reference entity to enter into any obligation.

    (b) any actual or alleged unenforceability, illegality, inconvertibility, impossibility or invalidity with respect to any obligation, however described.

(c) any applicable law, order, regulation, decree or notice, however described, or the imposition of, or any change in, any exchange control, capital restrictions or any other similar restrictions imposed by any monetary or other authority, however described.

**3. Bankruptcy** means a reference entity:

  (i)   is dissolved (other than pursuant to a consolidation, amalgamation or merger).

  (ii)   becomes insolvent or is unable to pay its debts or fails or admits in writing its inability generally to pay its debts as they become due.

  (iii)   makes a general assignment, arrangement or composition with or for the benefit of its creditors.

  (iv)   institutes or has instituted against it a proceeding seeking a judgement of insolvency or bankruptcy or any other relief under any bankruptcy or insolvency law or other similar law affecting creditors' rights, or a petition is presented for its winding-up or liquidation, and, in the case of any such proceeding or petition instituted or presented against it, such proceeding or petition.

      (a) Results in a judgement of insolvency or bankruptcy or the entry of an order for relief of the making of an order for its winding-up or liquidation or

      (b) Is not dismissed, discharged, stayed or restrained in each case within 30 days of the institution or presentation thereof.

  (v)   has a resolution passed for its winding-up, official management or liquidation (other than pursuant to a consolidation, amalgamation or merger).

  (vi)   seeks or becomes subject to the appointment of an administrator, provisional liquidator, conservator, receiver, trustee, custodian or other similar official for it or for all or substantially all its assets.

  (vii)   has a secured party take possession of all or substantially all its assets or has a distress, execution, attachment, sequestration or other legal process levied, enforced or sued on or against all or substantially all its assets and such secured party maintains possession, or any such process is not dismissed, discharged, stayed or restrained, in each case within 30 days thereafter.

  (viii)   cases or is subject to any event with respect to it which, under the applicable laws of any jurisdiction, has an analogous effect to any of the events specified in clauses (i) to (vii) (inclusive), or

  (ix)   takes any action in furtherance of, or indicating its consent to, approval of, or acquiescence in, any of the foregoing acts.

**4. Obligation Acceleration**    "Obligation acceleration" means one or more obligations have become due and payable before they would otherwise have been due and payable as a result of, or on the basis of, the occurrence of a default, event of default or other similar condition or event (however described), other than a failure to make any required payment, in respect of a reference entity under one or more obligations in an aggregate amount of not less than the default requirement.

**5. Obligation Default**    means one or more obligations have become capable or being declared due and payable before they would otherwise become due and payable as a result of, or on the basis of, the occurrence of a default, event of default, or other similar condition or event (however described), other than a failure to make any required payment, in respect of a reference entity under one or more obligations in an aggregate amount of not less than the default requirement.

**6. Failure to Pay**   means, after the expiration of any applicable (or deemed) grace period (after the satisfaction of any conditions precedent to the commencement of such grace period), the failure by a reference entity to make, when and due, any payments in an aggregate amount of not less than the payment requirement under one or more obligation.

**7. Repudiation/Moratorium**   means a reference entity or governmental authority (a) disaffirms, disclaims, repudiates or rejects, in whole or in part, or challenges the validity of, one or more obligations in an aggregate amount not less than the default requirement, or (b) declares or imposes a moratorium, standstill or deferral, whether de facto or de jure, with respect to one or more obligations in an aggregate amount of not less than the default requirement.

**8. Restructuring**   means that, with respect to one or more obligations, including as a result of an obligation exchange, and in relation to an aggregate amount of not less than the default requirement, any one or more of the following events occurs, is agreed between the reference entity or a governmental authority and the holder or holders of such obligation, or is announced (or otherwise decreed) by the reference entity or any governmental authority in a form that is binding upon the reference entity, and such event is not provided for under the terms of such obligation in effect as of the later of the trade date and the date as of which such obligation is issued or incurred:

   (i) a reduction in the rate or amount of interest payable or the amount of scheduled interest accruals
   (ii) a reduction in the amount of principal or premium payable at maturity or at scheduled redemption dates
   (iii) a postponement or other deferral of a date or dates for either (a) the payment or accrual of interest or (b) the payment of principal or premium
   (iv) a change in the ranking in priority of payment of any obligation, causing the subordination of such obligation or
   (v) any change in the currency or composition of any payment of interest or principal

**9.** Notwithstanding the above, none of the following shall constitute a restructuring with respect to any obligation:

   (a) the payment in Euros of interest or principal in relation to an obligation denominated in a currency of a Member State of the European Union that adopts or has adopted the single currency in accordance with the treaty establishing the European Community, as amended by the treaty on European Union.
   (b) the occurrence of, agreement to or announcement of any of the events described in (i) to (v) above due to an administrative adjustment, accounting adjustment or tax adjustment or other technical adjustment.
   (c) the occurrence of, agreement to or announcement of any of the events described in (i) or (v) above in circumstances where such event does not directly or indirectly results from deterioration in the creditworthiness or financial condition of the reference entity.

**10.** If an obligation exchange has occurred, the determination as to whether one of the events described in (i) to (v) above has occurred will be based on a comparison of the terms of the obligation immediately before such obligation exchange and the terms of the resulting obligation immediately following such obligation exchange.

**11. Governmental Authority**   means any de facto or de jure government (or any agency, instrumentally, ministry or department thereof), court, tribunal, administrative or other governmental authority or any other entity (private or public) charged with the regulation of the financial markets (including the Central Bank) of a reference entity or the jurisdiction of organization of a reference entity.

**12. Obligation Currency**    means the currency or currencies in which the obligation is denominated.

**13. Obligation Exchange**    means the mandatory transfer (other than in accordance with the terms in effect as of the later of the trade date or date of issuance of the relevant obligation) of any securities, obligations or assets to holders of obligations in exchange for such obligation. When so transferred, such securities, obligations, or assets will be deemed to be obligations.

**14. Payment Requirement**    means USD 1 million or its equivalent in the currency in which an obligation is denominated.

**15. Default Requirement**    means USD 10 million or its equivalent in the currency in which an obligation is denominated.

Chapter **23**

# Real Options

*After reading this chapter, students will be able to*

➢ Understand the concept of real options or options in projects.
➢ Explain the nature of real options.
➢ Know the features of real options.
➢ Distinguish between real option and financial option.
➢ Discuss the basic types of real options.
➢ Understand the call and put position in real option.
➢ Understand  the portfolio of real option.
➢ Explain the valuation methods of real options.
➢ Know the important applications of real options.
➢ Know about the limitations of the real options.

## 23.1  INTRODUCTION

Options are important financial derivative instruments in which the holder gets the right, but not the obligation to take a specific action at a predetermined date. These are frequently used in corporate world specifically in financial markets. Recently, these have also become popular in other activities like weather, ideas, commodities, real estate, business entities, etc. Most of the companies, today, have changed their business activities in different ways. Others have prioritized those expected to demonstrate at a faster rate. Corporate decisions related to real assets exhibit substantially the option characteristics of financial derivatives.

A corporate entity might be planning a project potentially involving a huge amount of investment. If the project is initially successful, the entity would like to have the option to expand the area of the project. It might also benefit from option to defer to state that project, or option to renew it. Similarly, if the project turns out to be profitable then it would be to abandon the project. All these are the typical examples of real options. In brief, the real options are the derivatives used on the projects, real assets, product mix, investment stages, etc.

## 23.2  CONCEPT OF REAL OPTION

Real options are based on mutual characteristics of investment decisions, and where the investment costs cannot be completely recovered and investment outcomes are not known with certainty. Real option theory refers to the right, but not the obligation, to take different courses of actions (e.g., abandon and expand) with respect to real assets (e.g., an oil well, a new product or acquisition). The notion of the real options is the "idea that one can view firm's discretionary investment opportunities as well as a call option or real asset, in much the same way as a financial call option provides decision rights on financial assets." Real options have been defined as follows:

- Real option is the right but not the obligation to acquire the gross present value of expected cash flows by making an irreversible investment on or before the date the opportunity ceases to exist.
- Real option gives the right to undertake some business decision, typically the option to make a capital expenditure decision. For example, the opportunity to investment in the expansion of a firm's factory, product innovation, customer services, etc.
- Real options are opportunities to respond to changing market conditions and influence the outcomes of a project. The values of the options available are embedded in the opportunities as real options.
- A real option is an option relating to real things that are fixed and permanent, i.e., not unreal. Real options have value when investment involves and irreversible cost in an uncertain environment.
- Real options give the holder of the option the right to an investment project such as project within a stipulated period. They help to hedge against the risk associated with investment in the real assets. Real option is an important tool used in the measurement of investment decisions and for strategic planning under uncertainly. It is used by the corporates for valuing their investment opportunities in various projects. In other words, it is quantitative tool for monitoring, measuring and adjusting decisions as per the changing business environment.

The business firms primarily use techniques for evaluating investment in projects like amounting rate of return, payback period, internal rate of return, net present value (NPV), etc. In NPV technique, we estimate the expected future cash flows at an appropriate discount rate. This is where the problem arises, because the NPV is calculated based on the information available at the time of appraisal. NPV tool loses its significance when there is uncertainty. The real option methodology goes beyond the NPV and tries to measure the uncertainty through option valuation.

The option valuation technique has been much useful for the firms to evaluate their projects. The firms estimate their projects is a realistic context by including various option/possibilities which are presented as the project progresses from one stage to another. In this way, the firms would have the capability of assessing their projects at any time in a better way in terms of desired return at the perceived risk.

## 23.3 CHARACTERISTICS OF REAL OPTIONS

An option derivative is very popular financial instrument and used frequently for managing the risk. The various definitions stated in the preceding section exhibits a few important features of the real options which have been described in brief asunder:

### 23.3.1 Underlying Assets

All the option instruments, irrespective of their nature, have underlying assets which are traded in the market. The spot or current value of these underlying assets is the market value at the time of trading, as we see in the case of financial or commodity products. However, the real options are based on expected cash flows from the underlying investment projects. These projects are not listed on the exchanges for trading purposes. The expected cash flows and discount rates used for estimating the future cash flow on the investment projects also vary overtime due to changes in the environment and the corporate's opportunities. So, the spot prices of the investment projects are not available as market rates. In such situation what should be the spot price of the real assets. The present value of cash inflows from the project, and the value of future opportunities are considered as the spot price of real options.

### 23.3.2 Exercise Price

In an option contract, there is exercise price of the underlying assets on which the option contract is settled at the time of exercise of the option. The underlying asset in real option is an investment project. Firm being the holder in the real option contract is exercised by the firm when the investment activities undertaken. In the real option the exercise price is the cost associated with undertaking of the investment activity. In standard option contract, the exercise price remains till maturity. However, in real option, the exercise price does not remain constant. Escalation in investment cost is an inevitable due to inflationary trend in the economy.

### 23.3.3 Uncertainty in the Underlying Asset Price

The pricing of any option depends upon the degree of volatility in the underlying asset price. The uncertainly of the cash flows from the investment project is similar to that of other standard option assets. The cash flows from the projects in future are uncertain because of market uncertainly or changes in cost estimates. Though it is easy to measure the uncertainty of financial assets because they are traded in the market. However, it is not possible in the real options since they are not having traded prices. Though the investment projects are also evaluated using probability distribution associated with the cash flows projections, however, sometimes, changing economic environment might change the degree of uncertainly of the concerned project in future.

### 23.3.4 Expiration Period of the Option

The duration of the option contract plays important role in determining price of the option. In case of the real option the duration of the project will also decide the price. Longer period projects could be more risky in comparison to short period projects. Mostly real options are of American style rather than European style, in which the holder of the option can be exercised at any time even before the expiry date.

## 23.3.5   Risk-free Rate of Return

In the standard option pricing model, the risk-free rate of return is applied to compute the option prices. However, in case of real option, since the investment projects are evaluated by using the discount rates, while pricing of real options the discount rate is used. This discount rate is often associated with the firm's cost of capital which is based on the riskiness of underlying investment project.

## 23.3.6   Cost of Delay in Projects

One of the important factor for consideration in real option pricing is the expected delay of the implementation of the underlying projects. It is generally observed that the projects are not implemented in the said period which are normally delayed due to one reason or other. As a result, the cost of the project rises which is called *delay cost*. The cost of delay in project execution increases as time to expiration nears. Similarly, the cost of real options can be related to the dividend expected from the underlying investment project or considered in other standard option contracts.

## 23.4   OVERVIEW OF LITERATURE

The business managers have been making capital investment decision for centuries the business activities came into existence. In 1930, **Professor Irving Fisher** has written explicitly on the options. The term 'real option', relatively new, has been coined by **Professor Stewart Myers** in 1977. The description of such opportunities as real option, however, considered on the development of analytical techniques for financial options, such as Black-Scholes option pricing model in 1973 which became so popular that even today it is used all over the world. As such, the term real option is closely tied to these option methods.

The term 'real option' was first used by Professor Myers as stated above, and today it is an active field of academic research in finance. Professor **Lenos Trigeorgis** has been a leading name for many years, publishing several influential books and academic articles in this area. Other pioneer academicians who contributed in this field include Professor Eduardo Schwartz, Gonzalo Cortazar, Michael Brennan, Han Smit, Robert Pindyok, etc.

Important papers on real option were got published by many experts. For example, Mr. Justin Pettit has written an article; "Application in real option and value-based strategy in Trigeorgis in 1996 and, "thinking in real options times" by Joanne Sammer. The idea of treating investment as options was popularized by Timothy Luehrman in his two articles "Investment opportunities as real option-getting started on the numbers", and "Strategy on a portfolio of real options" during 1998.

Another important work done on real option was by Mr. Michael J. Mauboussin, the then chief US investment strategist for Credit Suisse First Boston in 1999, Get real: using real option in security analysis. He uses real options to explain the gap between low the stock market prices of some businesses and the intrinsic value for those businesses.

Mr. Damodaran Aswath in 2005, contributed certain papers on real options as "The promise and peril of real options, and risk adjusted value, strategic risk taking: A framework for risk management etc. Further, Mathews. S. Datar in 2004 contributed "European Real option: An intuitive algorithm, for the Black-Scholes formula, and in 2007, "A practical method for valuing real options: The Boeing Approach. Further. Cortazar, Gangalo, Gravet, Miguel, Urzua, Jorge in 2008 published an article "The Valuation of Multidimensional American real options using the LSM Simulation method," and a paper on "A Fuzzy payoff method for real option valuation" in 2009 by Collan, M., Fuller, R., Mezei, J. Another important contribution in real option is by Zhang, S.X., Babovic, V., in 2011 "An evolutionary real option framework for the design and management of project and system with complex real option and exercising conditions.

Recently real options have been employed in business strategy both for valuation purposes as well as a conceptual framework. A lot of academic research in this field is in the process.

## 23.5 THE METHOD OF REAL OPTION (NPV VS OPTION PRICING MODEL)

To explain the concept of real option, it is essential to understand the nature of investment project which is to be executed in the enterprise. It is enough is use the Net Present Value (NPV) method or Discounted Cash Flow (DCF) analysis for the passive investments, but projects do give the executives enough opportunities to intervene if a change is happened after the implementation of the project. It means it implies a liberty of alternatives and the power of choice subsequent to the knowledge of relevant information. Such opportunities or flexibilities create value for the firm through changes in the old decisions. They are also termed as managerial strategic options, more popularly known as real options. The values of the options available as embedded in the opportunities as real options, which are fixed in nature and not unreal.

As discussed above the real option value, there may be negative NPV of the project in the beginning but may have the potential to provide opportunities, which could be extremely profitable. So, the real options have value and enhance the worth of the project. The project worth, under this method, can be determined as NPV plus the option value estimated. The option value will depend upon the number of the options available. For example, if the number of the option will be larger, the greater is the option value and greater is the worth of underlying investment project.

Real options framework is based on the option pricing model. In a simple financial option contract, in which the holder gets the right to buy or sell a stock at a given (exercise) price within a certain period of time without obligation to do so. If the option is not in profit then the holder will not exercise the option. The only loss to the holder would be price paid to purchase that option contract. The idea is similar to the real option analysis. The manager identified options and their exercise prices for a project, if the future looks favourable, the option is exercised and the project goes ahead. On the other hand, if it looks bad, the only loss is the price paid for the option.

Unlike the tools of capital budgeting for evaluating risk, option pricing is a direct analysis of project specific risk. For example, capital budgeting measures the risk indirectly through discount rate and perceived risk of the cash flows. The measurement of the risk in option pricing technique is through assignment of probabilities. The probabilities distribution of the cost related to the investment underlying suppositions are reflected in the expected future payoff the investment option. After that, the current value of the option is determined by discounting the risk neutral expected payoff by the risk-free rate of return. Practically, the executives point that risk as a distribution of probabilities is more transparent than as a discount premium as considered is NPV method. In brief, real option method yields the better result by considering the flexibilities and diminution of uncertainly through managerial competency.

## 23.6 REAL OPTION VS SPECULATION

As discussed above, real options are embedded in a whole range of management decisions. Options are everywhere, but they are different to speculation. Real options as speculations, no doubt, involve uncertainly. Uncertainly in real options is of two types: First, is related to future period, because developments of future are uncertain. Second is concerned to ability of management to respond the scenario as more information become available. If the management is not capable of responding the new developments appropriately, then the situation will represent as speculation not an option.

Let us explain this with a simple example. Suppose a company is considering to invest ₹500 crores in setting up a plant to enhance production capacity. It faces uncertainty about the future demand for the final product produced with new facility if there is no follow up investment, manager will face speculation, not an option. However, if the management goes first for a pilot project by just investing assuming ₹50 crores and examine the response of the product in the market. If the pilot project proves successful, then the company can go ahead for investing ₹500 crores. This management decision would be called *real option*. If pilot project fails, the management will not go ahead.

## 23.7 REAL OPTION: CALL AND PUT POSITIONS

In a simple real option contract, the holder is required to pay the exercise price and will receive cash flows from the investment opportunities. It is similar to a call option in a simple option deal. On the other hand, if the holder receives the exercise price and pays cash flows in a real option deal, it is called *put option*. Let us explain this with a simple diagrams of Call and Put Options.

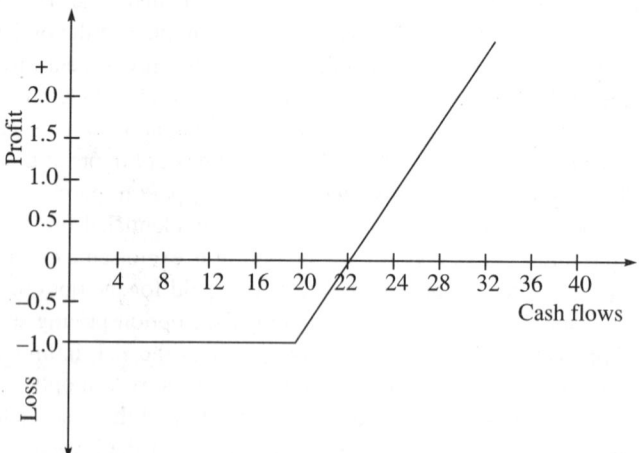

**FIGURE 23.1**   Real option (Call Position).

Figures 23.1 and 23.2 explain the position of call in real option. Here the investor pays the exercise price and receives the cash flows. For example, in Figure 23.1 if the cash flows are less than ₹22 crores, there will be loss and higher than this, the option will be in profit. Similarly, Figure 23.2 exhibits the position of put position of real option where the investor receives the exercise price and pays the cash flows. For example, if the cost estimates of the project is less than ₹110 million, the investor will be in profit and, if the cost estimates of the project is higher than ₹110 million, then he would be in loss. Let us explain these further with the help of examples of call and put positions.

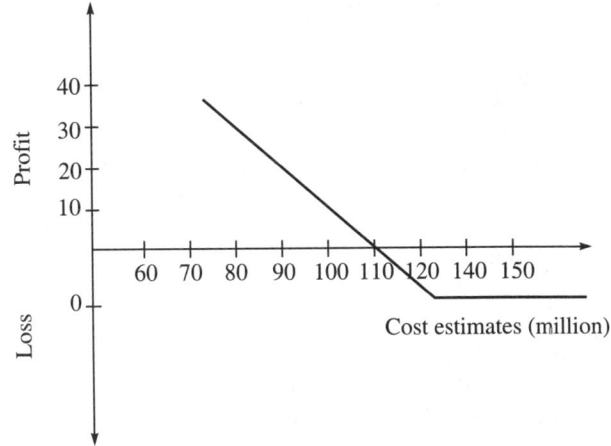

**FIGURE 23.2**   Real option (Put Position).

**EXAMPLE (Call Position):**   Let us assume that a spot garment manufacturing company 'X' Ltd. produces a wide variety of sport wears. The company is exploring the possibility of manufacturing T-shirt with the embossed 'cricket logos' considering the world cup cricket matches in near future. The firm is estimating to yield a benefit of ₹5,00,000. For this, the company is to incur certain expenditure on design and buying of a new knitting machine. For this, there is need of ₹20 lakhs. At this juncture, the company does not justify to go for this project. However, the market can fall and rise daily due to popularity of the game of the cricket.

The company follows the route of real option as such. It prepares the samples for sales promotion and displaying to the distributors at a cost of ₹50,000. The company decides to take risk for preparing the samples. Considering the overwhelming response of the pubic for world cricket matches, the dealer and distributors are ready to take the whole stock for ₹25 lakhs provided they test and approve the sample. Now assume that, all of a sudden, the response is not as expected. As a result, the dealers are now ready to pay only ₹23 lakhs. The company accepts the offer and releases the necessary orders to spend ₹20 lakhs for producing the T shirts. It gives the payoff ₹3 lakhs (₹23 lakhs – ₹20 lakhs), net of sample cost, is 2,50,000 = (₹3,00,000 – ₹50,000).

From the above example, it is observed that the company X Ltd., at the most, stood to lose ₹50,000 spent on making sample, and this gave an option of being able to do business if conditions favour 'X' Ltd. How much to be spent on promotional activates is to be decided by the real option technique. Real option technique decides whether it is worth spending ₹50,000 to buy to the options at outset and is it worth spending the exercise price ₹20 lakhs on expiration day.

**EXAMPLE (Put position):**   A company is considering to change in its production process in one of its plant, which will cost to the firm around ₹100 million. It expects the present value of their operation cost, if the operations continue, to be ₹120 million. The company would be able to implement to shut down its operation five years hence. The estimated cost of shutting down the plant is ₹10 million. There is possibility of 20 percent fluctuation in the cost estimates. The put option's lower value would be zero, since the present value of the future costs (spot price) is higher than the expected operational cost (strike price), i.e., (₹100 million –120 million) at 10 percent risk-free rate of production process of the plant. Assume that the put option value, considering parameter of the option is ₹12 million. The current estimated cost of shutting down operations ₹10 million is less than the value of put option ₹12 million. Therefore, it is beneficial for the company to go for change in production in its plant.

## 23.8 REAL OPTIONS VS FINANCIAL OPTIONS

In strict sense, the real options are not financial options. Real options, in general, represent certain types of management decisions. No doubt, the option methods used to value real options are borrowed from financial option pricing models, but the underlying assumptions on which financial option pricing is based are not strictly applied to real options. Let us elaborate this further by describing the basics of financial option pricing mechanism.

A general financial option is a derivative instrument whose value is derived from the volatility of the underlying securities. Financial options are the right, but not the obligation, to buy or sell the underlying asset at a fixed price over a specified time period. These are traded on recognized option stock exchanges and settled on the basis of market price of the assets.

Unlike financial options, real options are not precisely defined or neatly packaged. But they do exist in almost every business decisions. In general, behind real options are capital budget and resource allocation decisions. These managerial decisions are normally concerned to illiquid assets, such as research and development (R&D), non-financial projects, natural & mineral resources, oil exploration, real estate, tangible and intangible assets, etc.

Since the underlying assets in real options are illiquid in nature, so these are hard to trade on the stock exchanges. However, if they are being traded, they are usually being bought and sold inefficient market, such as in one-to-one negotiated transactions between the trading parties. Consequently, the assumptions of the standard financial option models do not strictly apply to the real options. For example, the Black–Scholes option pricing formula designed to use when there is a single source of uncertainty as measured by the volatility of the underlying asset. Technically, it is the standard deviation squared of the asset returns at a single decision date which means the time of the exercising the option is fixed on a certain date.

Further, the real options are decision choices/possibilities about the real assets that a manager may exercise in future. Hence, many real option are contingent on more than one source of uncertainly and so should be classified as compound real options, also known as options-on-options. In fact, real life investment projects often include a collection of their compound real options whose value may interact, for example many types of R&D projects, investing in an early stage new product development projects, various types of technology licensing agreements, joint ventures, strategic alliances, etc.

As stated above, the real options are concerned with the real or physical assets decisions. By analogy with a financial option, a real option is the right but not the obligation, to take an action affecting a real physical asset at a predetermined cost for a predetermined period of time, i.e., the life of the option. While real and financial options have many similarities, however, the analogy is not exact. Trying to force real option into a standard financial option framework may give into misleading results. The key differences of these options are stated in Table 23.1.

**TABLE 23.1** Comparison of Financial and Real Options

| Sr. No. | Characteristics | Symbol | Financial options | Real options |
|---------|-----------------|--------|-------------------|--------------|
| 1. | Underlying Asset Price | S | Spot price | Net present value of cash flows on investment plus value of other opportunities on investment |
| 2. | Exercise Price | X | Strike price | Present value of cost of investment expenditure to be incurred on project |

*Contd...*

*Contd...*

| 3. | Time to expiration (option period) | T | Time to expiration of the option | Time to implement investment decision |
|----|----|----|----|----|
| 4. | Volatility of asset price | σ | Volatility of stock price (Historical variance of market return) | Volatility of cash flows from investment project/variance associated with firm's value |
| 5. | Risk free rate | r | Risk-free interest rate | Time value of cash flows (risk-free return) |
| 6. | Yield | S | Dividends foregone | Cost of delay opportunity cost (Revenue or profit foregone) |

On the comparison of real options and financial option, following differences are observed:

1. First difference between real option and standard financial option is that the exercise price of a financial option is normally fixed at the initiation of option contract. For real option, this price is associated with development cost or the expenditure to be incurred on the investment activity. This may be volatile, fluctuating with market conditions. So, determining volatility in real options can be relatively difficult.

2. Second difference is related with the uncertainty of the underlying asset in the options. In financial option, the uncertainty is usually external, based upon the external factors mainly. In real options, the uncertainties surround in option underlying asset, based upon the internal factors. Further, in a financial option, the trading parties are outsiders—the option writer and the option purchaser. It means neither of whom can influence the return of the firm. In contrast, a company that owns a real option can affect the underlying asset—by developing technology, actions of the competitors, etc.

3. Third difference is concerned with the discount rate. In financial option, the risk-free rate of return is assumed as risk-free interest rate on government securities. On the other hand, in real option, it is taken as discount rate on which the cash flows are to be discounted considering the risk inherent in the investment project. So, both the rates will not be similar.

4. Finally, in financial option, any dividend declared by the company of the underlying asset is considered and adjusted in option pricing. In case of real option, the cost of delay in implementation of the project, or opportunity cost in this respect, is generally considered as yield in the option pricing.

## 23.9   TYPES OF REAL OPTIONS

In the English language, the word option can be used in two technically different senses. In term of Real Option Valuation (ROV), it is termed as a decision that may be deferred to sometime in the future, and that is accompanied by some uncertainty that can be resolved. On the other hand, in common parlance, an option can simply be an operational alternative, a decision that is to be made today and for which there is future recourse.

Let us explain this with an example. Consider that a company decides to drill a well in a certain location. If the well is dry and no water is available, then the company might lose the money spent on drilling. The well location was an operational alternative, a decision that had to be made there and then. On the other hand, assume that there is another party guaranteeing some minimum return on the well. It means the company drilling the well would have a real option because it could decide in the future whether to call on that guarantee, thereby minimizing any downside risk and maximizing upside potential. Finding options and alternatives is not an easy task. It requires a new way of framing strategic decisions. Uncovering real options can be tough. What will we gain by moving from Point–A to Point–B, especially if we begin down the path from Point A to B? What options will open for us and where will we gain by having these options? Thus first step is to go for reorienting strategic thinking, then, is to identify the real options that exist in investment decisions.

The experts generally classify real options on the basis of the types of flexibility they give to the holders. These include asunder:

1. The option to defer investment
2. Option to abandon
3. The option to expand/contract
4. The option to switch to other plan/project
5. The option to grow
6. The option to stage
7. Option to flexibility

## 23.9.1 Option to Defer Investment

It is also known as the option of waiting to invest. An opportunity to invest at some point of time in future might be more voluble than an opportunity to invest immediately. It is quite possible in the business that the circumstances may not be favourable currently to invest and wait till the conditions become more favourable. For example, a mining company may defer exploration until the resolution of the price uncertainly. The other factors could be the expected revenue adequately to cover the costs of extraction. When the firm remits a license fee for right to explore or extract. It is an example of real option. The company in the status of the option owner, it is entitled to exercise at any time in the future. The company would invest in exploration and development only if oil prices increase and the lease becomes profitable. If the prices decline, the company would allow the lease to lapse or would sell to another company. The exercise price of the option is the money required to develop the acreage.

## 23.9.2 Option to Abandon

This is a put option and intend to hedge against the economic slowdown. If the market conditions change unfavourably, or if the expectations are betrayed, then a right to dispose and recover the salvage value is an option. Considering the example given in the preceding point, let us assume that the prices of the finished products (oil & gas) go into what seems likely to be prolonged decline, then the management may decide to abandon the project. In another example of auto manufacturing company, the option itself will be exercised only when the revenues are not sufficient or the costs committed do not suitable payoff.

## 23.9.3 Option to Expand/Contract a Project

This is the option which recognizes the flexibility to change the capacity in order to react as per the market conditions. It is also termed as the option to change scale once the project is developed. The management may have the option to accelerate the production rate or change the scale of production including downsizing and narrowing of the project. In an oil and gas field, there might be the option to increase the production by investing in an enhanced oil recovery plan or may go for drilling satellite wells. The flexibility obviously will include the option. The expansion of the capacity is termed into call option.

## 23.9.4 Option to Switch to Another Plan/Project

This is the option which recognizes the flexibility of the managers to revise or modify of an investment decision is embedded in this option. A switching option can provide a hedge against the likelihood that another technology or project will be more economic and profitable sometime in the future. The most popular form of switch in the present context is reference technology weighted on cost effectiveness. Further, continuous updation and also adopted with the recent technology will allow the managers to adjust to uncertainties, and thereby catalyzing value creation.

Similarly, another example of switch option may be quoted in the use of assets such as real estate allowing switching between living apartments or space for commercial purpose. Thus, the correlation of the revenues among the various uses with the costs to redevelop is inversely proportional to the value of the flexibility. Lower the said correlation, higher the value of the switch option.

## 23.9.5 Option to Grow

This is the option which fetches a growth option in the long run for the firm. For example, initial investment in a new product, new market or new technology, may be accompanied with huge investment with the expectation to grow in future. In other words, by considering value of growth options, the firm may be able to go ahead with the new project or investment even of that project itself may give lower return even negative for the short period. Hi-Tech firms innovation in biotech firms, IT-based infrastructure, etc. are the examples of growth options, because they create opportunities for expansion in the long run.

A company which is engaged in selling of cosmetics through a network of independent salesmen is exploring to decide whether to enter in the foreign market or not. The initial investment would be huge for creating infrastructure for manufacturing and sales, but it may lead to the opportunity to sell a whole range of products through an established sales network. Thus, the investment would create growth options which have value above and beyond the returns generated by the initial operations.

## 23.9.6 Option to Stage

This is the option which recognizes the investment in the firm in stages. Stage option are quite often in the pharmaceutical, minerals and oil industries. For example, consider that the top management team of an international company in reviewing a proposal from the senior vice-president of the operations to install a new manufacturing system. The proposal calls for huge investment to roll out at all factories over the next two year but the return from the project is uncertain. The company has thus the option to invest in the new system in stages rather all at once. The performance of each stage in turn will provide further options for continuing delaying or abandoning the effort. Such staged options add value to the proposed project. These options are also called as learning options since the firms can test the suitability of the project by developing the initial phase with low costs.

### 23.9.7   Option to Flexibility

This is the option which requires the flexibility relating to product process of manufacturing, input mixing, flexibility, etc. for the management. This flexibility constitutes optionally. This is also known as intensity options. The option to produce different outputs from the same infrastructural facility is known as output mix option or product flexibility. Such types of flexibility are seen in those industries where demand is volatile and varies as per the nature of the product. The management can produce the goods as per the requirement from the market.

Input mix option also called as process flexibility, allows the management to use different inputs to produce the same output an appropriate. For example, an electricity manufacturing concern may have the option to choose between fuel sources to produce electricity, and therefore, a flexible plan may actually be valuable. Similarly, a farmer will have the option to switch between various feeds, preferring to use the cheapest available in the market.

Further, the management may have the option relating to the scales of the production in the plant. It means option to change the output rate per unit of time or change the total length in production process as per response to market conditions.

The options stated above are popular in the business world. However, the list of the options is not exhaustive. Many other types of options are available, such as location, spread options, learning option, abandon for salvage option, etc. In brief, all such opportunities are subject to flexibility in project size, project life and timing, project operations, etc of the business entity which may create real options. More examples of real options may also be found in opportunities to do joint ventures, strategic alliances or mergers and acquisitions with other target technology firms which have promising R&D pipelines.

## 23.10   VALUATION OF REAL OPTIONS

As discussed in the preceding section that the analogies between real and financial options are not exact. Since the real options are more complicated in comparison to financial options, so, their valuation is also complicated. Taking into account the features of the real options, valuation methods such as the discounted cash flow (DCF) techniques are not able to capture the fair value of these options. The DCF calculations ignore the benefits which the managers may get from exercising their judgement and making decisions as future events unfold.

Under the standard DCF/NPV approach, future expected cash flows are present valued under the empirical probability measure at a discount rate which reflects the embedded risk in the project. Only the expected cash flows are considered, however, the flexibility to alter corporate strategy in lieu of actual market scenario is usually ignored. Though some analysts account for this uncertainty by adjusting the discount rate or using the certainty equivalents, or via probability weighting as in NPV, etc. In spite of these, these methods do not properly account for such uncertainties over the project's life, and hence, fail to make fair valuation of the real options.

In contrast to the DCF method, real option valuation (ROV) assumes that management is active and can continually respond to market changes. Every scenario is considered and best corporate action is taken in real option valuation. Management adapts to each negative outcome by decreasing its exposure and to positive scenarios by scaling up. The contingent nature of future profit in real option models is captured by employing of the techniques developed for financial options. The approach, known as risk-neutral-valuation, consists in adjusting the probability distribution for risk consideration, while discounting at the risk-free rate. This method also known as the certainty equivalent martingale approach, uses a risk neutral measure. It is observed generally that the real option value of a project is typically higher than the NPV and the differences are marked in project with major flexibility, contingency and volatility.

## 23.10.1 Inputs in Real Options Valuation

Real option valuation, as discussed in the preceding section, takes into account uncertainty about the future evolution of the parameters which determine the value of the project, coupled with the management's capability respond to such parameter Therefore, it is the combined effect of these which makes ROV more complicated and challenging. While valuing the real options, the analysts should consider the following inputs.

1. First input is options underlying asset. In case of real option, it is project in question. It is modelled in terms of "spot price". Spot price is the starting or current value of the project, and is usually based on the management's best guess. It is calculated as present value of the project's cash flows.

2. Second input is options volatility. It is a measure of uncertainty as to change in project value overtime. Usually, it is derived via Monte Carlo simulation. Some analysts substitute a listed security as a proxy using either its price volatility (historical volatility) or implied volatility.

3. Third input is strike price which corresponds to any (non-recoverable) investment outlays. Usually, it is the present value of the prospective costs of the project. The management would proceed of the option is in-the-money, i.e., present value of expected cash inflows exceeds this amount.

4. Fourth input is option term. The time period or the life of the option. It is the time during which management may decide to act or not to act. For example, time to expiry of a patent, or of the mineral rights for a new mine, etc.

5. Fifth input is option style or option exercise. It is related with the management's ability to respond to changes in value at each decision point as a series of option, these may be comprised of American style call option or other different types of options as stated earlier.

6. Sixth input is the risk-free rate of return which is determined on the basis in of the rate of return available on a risk-free asset, such as government bonds. It is identical for both financial and real options.

7. Finally, profit foregone because of delayed production, etc. are like the lost dividends in the financial option. It means as long as the management holds an unexercised option to invest in a project, it foregoes the money that would have flowed if it had the project been producing revenue.

## 23.10.2 Valuation Methods of Real Options

The valuation methods usually employed are likely adapted from techniques developed for valuing financial options. Mainly three approaches are popular in option pricing which are asunder:

(i) Black-Scholes Approach
(ii) Binomial Lattices Approach
(iii) Monte Carlo Simulation Approach

Though these models have already been discussed in other chapters of this book in detail, however, their applicability in respect to real options would be discussed here instead of going into details of these approaches.

### Black-Scholes approach

The most fundamental and acknowledged European call option valuation model is the Black-Scholes equation which was developed by Fisher Black, Robert Merton and Myron Scholes in the 1973. It is one of the many applications of partial differential approach. It is not only has a significant power in the field of financial options but also in the field of real options. This model states that options could be priced using the arbitrage principle with a portfolio that is constructed to be risk-free, overcoming the need to estimate distributions of returns at all.

The B-S formula states that it is possible to establish the value of an option by constructing a replicating portfolio which consists of a number of shares in the underlying asset and a number of risk-free bonds. The portfolio is constructed in such way that its cash flows exactly replicate those of the option. Since the prices of the underlying stock and bonds are quoted in the market, so the value of the replicating portfolio is also known. If the options were sold for a price which is different from the replicating portfolio, then there would be two identical assets, i.e., the option and the replicating portfolio. The investors would then use the arbitrage strategy buying of the cheaper one and selling the expensive to make profit from the difference of prices.

### Black-Scholes Differential Equation

The most famous equation in European call option valuation of B-S model is as:

$$C_e = SN(d_1) - Xe^{-rt} N(d_2)$$

$$Nd_1 = \text{In}(S/X) + (r + \sigma^{2/2})t/\sigma\sqrt{t}$$

$$Nd_2 = d_1 - \sigma\sqrt{T}$$

or

$$Nd_2 = \text{In } (S/X) + (r - \sigma^{2/2})t/\sigma\sqrt{t}$$

where

$$S = \text{Spot price}$$
$$X = \text{Strike price}$$
$$r = \text{Risk-free rate}$$
$$t = \text{Time to expiry}$$
$$s = \text{Standard derivation}$$
$$C_e = \text{Call (European) price}$$
$$N(d) = \text{Cumulative Probability Function.}$$

B-S model assumes that the distribution for possible stock prices at the end of any finite interval in log normal and that stock price on any day is independent of the price of the previous day. The assumptions of a random walk in stock price is premised on the existence of an efficient market in which the stock is fairly valued on any given day, and all the information available concerning the stock has been taken into account by the market.

Though the B-S equation revolutionized the financial market due to its quickness of the calculation, however, it has fairly limited applicability in real option market. Since the assumptions used in the development are not particularly appropriate in real assets. Real options are different from financial assets because the exercise (in both calls and puts) in not known with certainty, exercise is not instantaneous,) Most real options are not analogies of European options, and the stochastic process for the underlying asset is not the same as it is for the financial option. It is difficult to use this for American option, compound options and options with dividends payments. All these aspects make the calculation of real option value more complicated.

Real option valuation was tried in oil and gas assets by Lohrenj and Sickens by using the Black-Scholes formula in their comparison of option theory and DCF for an actual field in the offshore Gulf of Mexico. They discuss many options which are available during the lifetimes of searchable, developable and producible oil/gas assets. They found that value of the development option (like a call option on a stock) increased dramatically (by a factor greater than 3) as the variance of the oil/gas asset value increased from zero (perfect knowledge) to 1.0/year. However, they and their paper gives warning, we should always temper result from uncertain analysis (both option theory and decision free) and their use with the understanding that the real world and its real uncertainties have not been captured only modelled by necessarily flowed and incomplete practice and practioners ." Hence, in its closed form the B-S model solution, be used in the real option after incorporating all the features of the concerned industries and appropriate boundary conditions.

## Binomial-Lattices Option Valuation Approach

The most commonly applied method in real options is Binomial Lattices model which is developed by Cox, Ross and Rubinstein in 1979. It has gained considerable attention as an example of the dynamic programming approach. It is applicable across a wide range of options. Being lattice-based model, it allows for flexibility to exercise where the relevant and differing, rules may be encoded at each node. Further, it can illustrate the intermediate decision making process between now and the option expiration date.

The binomial option model is generally based on the risk neutral argument, due to this, it does not require risk adjusted discount rates. This model evaluates real options by creating binomial trees, each mode of which represents the actual up or down of values of the underlying asset overtime. This section will state how to construct a lattice for a simple European call option.

A lattice is a way to present how an asset's value changes over a specified time, given that asset has a particular volatility. A binomial lattice has only two possible movements in each time step-up or down. ROV uses two lattices namely underlying asset lattice and valuation lattice. These are discussed as under:

### Lattice of the underlying asset

The underlying asset pricing lattice also known as the lattice of the asset is read from left to right from a binomial model diagram. It indicates how possible future asset values could evolve. At each time interval (AT) the value of the asset increases by a multiplicative factor '$u$'(greater than 1) or decreases by a multiplicative factor '$d$' (between 0 to 1) represented as a step-up or a step-down the lattice as shown in the Figure 23.3. The value of the left most node is the NPV of the underlying asset which is calculated from the DCF model, using normally risk-free rate of interest.

The factors '$u$' and '$d$' which represent the upward and downward movements at each node. These are functions of the volatility of the asset and length of time. Thus, right hand nodes of the lattice represent the distribution of possible future asset value. In the real option valuation, most different issue in constructing the lattice of the underlying asset is estimating volatility. It must reflect the uncertainties, both economic and technical of the asset, and the way in which there uncertainties evolve overtime.

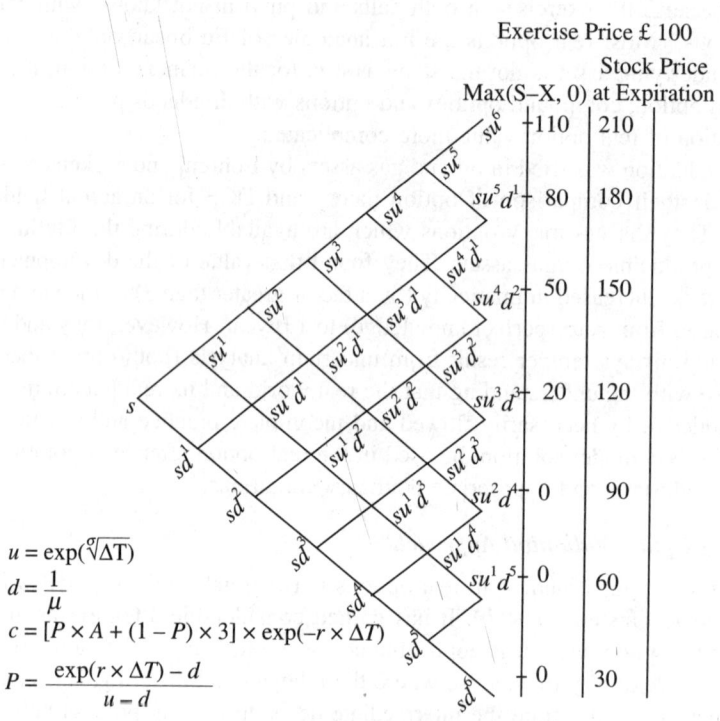

**FIGURE 23.3**   Binomial-lattice.

## Valuation lattice

This is related with the value of the option. The valuation lattice has exactly the same number of nodes and branches as in the case of the underlying asset lattice. It works backward from the values in the terminal nodes at the right side to the side of the lattice. Since, in an option contract, the value cannot be negative. So, value placed in each terminal node is the maximum of zero and the difference of asset price and exercise price, i.e., Max $(S–X, 0)$. After determining those starting values, then to obtain the option value, it is calculated through a process, called *backward induction*. It is possible to work backwards through the lattice. Backward induction depends on a factor '$p$' the risk neutral probability of a movement in a price of the asset. This is the probability in which investors were indifferent to risk. Applying this to each pair of vertically adjacent node in the lattice, we can get the real option value at the farthest left node of the lattice.

## Monte Carlo Simulation Approach

Another major approach which is applied to complex real options valuation is the simulation approach. There are many types of option calculation methods within the simulation approach as well as several specialized software such as Crystal Ball(R), RISK(R) Excel(R) Software, etc. This approach calculates the options values by randomly simulating thousands of possible futures scenarios from the present to the option expiration time for uncertain variables. The most popular approach in this respect is the Monte Carlo Simulation method. This model can also deal with 'path dependent' real option. The analysis methodology of this method is described in four steps. A brief discussion of these theoretically without taking a case is stated below:

### Step-I Creation of initial cash flows proforma

First step in this approach is to calculate the net present value which is used to measure the value and performance of the project. The idea is to represent the decision metric typically used in the current real world practice. The cash flow stream may be discounted at a specified hurdle rate to arrive at NPV amount. Two methods may be used here, such as NPV and IRR for the project. These approaches are mathematically equivalent in the present context, however, the analysts actually prefer to consider the NPV technique of the proposed project. The key point is that this benchmark "static case" which represents the current project analysis, and decision making practice is based on a single cash flow projection for the proposed investment project.

### Step-II Incorporate uncertain variables into the initial model

The second step is to identify the uncertain variables which should be incorporated in the initial model. The uncertain variables are different project to project. For example, in case of real estate development project, the uncertain variables could be future rents, market demand, value of built property, degree of completion, etc. After that random movement of uncertain variables most can be drawn. This random simulation of uncertain variables can be conducted by the Monte Carlo simulation in Excel(R) Software.

After that the analyst can examine how much the uncertainty affects the value and performance of the project.

### Step-III Determination of flexibility and incorporate into model

This third step in this approach is to determine the main sources of flexibility in the projects which can be incorporated in the model. Though all the sources of such flexibility cannot be incorporated in the model, however, a few can be tried without making the model so complex as to lose its value. The introduction of such flexibility into the previous inflexible Monte Carlo model not only help to quantify the value of such flexibility, but it also serves to raise consciousness about the existence of both the uncertainty and the flexibility that actual do exist here.

In the case of real estate development reject, the various examples of flexibility can be phasing a big project, waiting to develop, enabling future expansion abandoning the development, etc. The possible benefit of incorporating flexibility into the project can be graphically illustrated by the value at risk and gain (VARG).

### Step-IV Search for the combination of decision rules to maximize value

The last step is to find out the best result which can maximize the value of the project. The role of flexibility is to adopt efficiently to the uncertain variable scenarios and to create the best results. So this step is critical in determining the value of flexibility. Decision value hererefer to the criteria for determining how to manage flexibility. In case of real estate development project if the future rent is uncertain, a decision rule might begin the construction when the rent keep rising for more than three years continuously. In this way, the analysts can make combination of the sources of these are more than two sources of the flexibility in the project. Then they can find best carbonization of decision rules which enables them to acquire the best result on the entire set of the uncertain variable scenarios. However, it is not so easy practically become many Monte Carlo simulations are required in order to have best result. So, to obtain this it oftenly depends on the ability of the analysts.

In brief, the process discussed above is summarized here as: first the categorization of uncertain variables scenarios into limited set of standardized scenarios. For example, supposing among two thousand scenarios, which can be categorized into four scenarios, says A, B, C, and D. Then, to search for best combination of decision rule, the analysts only need to determine four combinations of decision rules capture two thousand scenarios approximately. These four combinations of the decision rule are called the *catalogue of operating plans*. After that, the analysts examine how much value can be added by incorporating flexibility and using the catalogue of operating plans. Then the ENPV is calculated based on all NPVS computed in each of the two thousand simulations. If there is the value of inflexibility, the ENPV of the flexibility case must be higher than of the inflexibility case. The difference of these two cases can be referred to as "the value of flexibility, and this is known as "the value of real options". The whole exercise can easily be done by using Monte Carlo Simulation is Excel(R) software.

**EXAMPLE:**  A company knows its discounted cash flows if it invests in current year, i.e., ₹5 million. If it invests next year, the discounted cash flows are ₹6 million, a 66.7 percent probability and ₹3 million discounted with 33.3 percent probability. Assuming a risk neutral rate of 10 percent, future discounted cash flows are in its present terms ₹5.45 million and ₹2.73 million. The investment cost is ₹4 million. If the firm invests next year, the present value of the investment cost is ₹3.63 million. Following the net present value rule for investment the firm should invest this year because the discounted cash flows ₹5 million is greater than the investment cost ₹4 million, by ₹One million. Yet if the firm waits for next year, it only invests if discounted cash flows do not decrease. If discounted cash flows decrease to ₹3 million, the investment is no longer profitable. If they grow to ₹6 million, then the firm invests. This implies that the firm invests next year with a 66.7 percent probability, and earns ₹5.45 million – ₹3.63 million if it does invest. Thus, the value to invest next year is ₹1.21 million. Given that the value to invest next year exceeds the value to invest this year, the firm should wait for further information to prevent losses. This simple example shows how the next present value may lead the firm to take unnecessary risk, which could be prevented by real option valuation.

## 23.11  LIMITATIONS OF THE REAL OPTIONS

The relevance of the real options may be limited in practice due to various considerations. When the framework of ROV is to be employed in any projector organization, the following considerations must be ensured by the analysts.

**1. Market Characteristics:**  It is important to note that change is most evident. The market and environment underlying the project are not static. These are continuously changing. The sources, trends and evolution in product demand and supply create the flexibility contingency and volatility in the project underlying. These contingencies are to be an appropriately evaluated and must be incorporated optionally.

**2. Organizational Characteristics:**  The success of real option valuation depends upon the characteristics of on organization. Real options are framed with particular features on which they are dependent. It is important to note whether the organizations are ready to follow real options. These are asunder:

   (i) Corporate strategy must be adaptive to contingent events. Some firms face certain organizational rigidities and are unable to react to market changes.
   (ii) The business must be positioned such that it has appropriate flow of information and opportunities to act. To implement ROV in the organization, it should be ensured that information system or networking is efficient to adapt the same practically.

(iii) Management must understand options, be able to identify and create them, and appropriately exercise them. In other words, the management is generally reluctant to go for new option rather prefer to go traditionally or maintaining the status quo. It means the management is passive and not dynamic. So, it must be considered optionally.

(iv) The financial position of the business must be sufficient or there must be so much funds in the organization, so that the project could be implemented without any problem. In other words, the management must have the appropriate access to the required funds for the proposed project.

(v) Some real options are proprietary owned or exercisable by a single person or a company, whereas some others are shared or exercised through many persons in the organization. It means a good team work is required in the organization to implement such options.

**3. Technical Considerations:** The real options are more complicated than standard financial options, for which there were originally developed. The main difference is that the underlying assets of the real option is often not tradable. For example, the factory owner cannot easily sell the factory upon which he has the option. However, if there is vacant land on which the real option is created to develop that land in the future, this can be bold. Similarity, technology is changing at the fast rate, the life of the physical assets has shortened. They become obsolete in short period. So, the liquidity of these assets has decreased more in comparison to the financial assets. Even if the company can actively adapt to market changes, it remains to determine the right paradigm to discount future claims.

No doubt, the above mentioned limitations are very important, but it does not mean that these complications dissuade the firm to use the real options. Valuation experts can determine when ROV should be used and which method be applied at a particular time. In fact, the firms must be having a real options mind set which is as important as using he mathematics. Real option thinking clearly emphasizes and values management flexibility at the appropriate time. It understands that in a world characterized by change, uncertainly and highly competitive environment, the management has to be active. The management can alter and modify plans and strategies as new information becomes available or as new possibilities arise. Working with managers and experts in other fields, the valuation experts can help and place a value on the options inherent in various projects.

## SUMMARY

The corporate management often has flexibility in carrying out projects capitalizing on new possibilities and new market conditions to improve project performance. Real options analysis or real option evaluation provides a means to determine the value of flexibility in future activities. Real option valuation (ROV) applies option valuation techniques to capital budgeting decisions.

Real option valuation (ROV) is the right but not the obligation, to undertake certain business activities such as, expanding deferring, abandoning, staging, contracting, etc. of a capital investment project. The opportunities to investment in the firm's factory to expand the capacity or alternatively to sell the factory are the examples of a real call option and real put option, respectively. The real options are distinguished from the standard financial options in various respects. Real options are not traded in the open markets as securities. Option holders are here management themselves which can directly influence the value of the option's underlying project. The management cannot lock up for a volatility rather their perceived uncertainty matters in the real option valuation. Moreover, the expected costs to be incurred on the project is considered as strike price in real option valuation.

While making real option valuation, certain basic inputs are required such as spot price, exercise price, time to expiration of the project, volatility factor, risk-free rate of return, expected yield, etc. Spot price for the real option is computed by the present value of the cash flows plus value of the other opportunities on investment project. Exercise price is determined by estimating present value of the cost of the investment or expenditure to be incurred on the project.

There are various opportunities available in the business firm time to time which can be explored as real options. So these can be classified as the option to grow, option to defer or postpone, option to contract, option to shutdown, option to switch, option stages, option to flexibility, etc. After exploring there opportunities, these are to be analysed as real options. Whether these can be implemented in the business or not. Real options often are valued using financial option pricing methods. Since the real options are extremely complex in nature, so any financial option method can provide only a rough valuation. For valuation of real options, various methods have been applied by the analysts. Important methods are Black-Scholes approach, Binomial Lattices approach, Monte Carlo approach, etc. By using the NPVs of the project as a criterion, "the expected net present value (ENPV) can be calculated based on all possible scenarios, and should be compared to the static case NPV. The possible outcome of the NPV can be shown in a histogram distribution. Thus, this model with uncertainty but without flexibility is called the *inflexible case*. The expected net present value (ENPV) of the Monte Carlo representation of uncertainties for the project is determined by the exogenously specified discount rate-same discount rate, i.e. opportunity's cost of capital.

## SUGGESTED READINGS

1. Black, F. and Scholes, M., "The Pricing of Options and Corporate Liabilities," *J. of Political Economy* (May 1973) 637.

2. Merton, R.C., "The Theory of Rational Option Pricing," *Bell J. of Economics & Management Science* (Spring 1973) 4, 441.

3. Copeland, T., Koller, T., and Murrin, J., *Valuation: Measuring and Managing the Value of Companies*, 3rd ed., John Wiley & Sons, Inc., New York City (2000) 395.

4. Trigeorgis, L., *Real Options: Managerial Flexibility and Strategy in Resource Allocation*, The MIT Press, Cambridge, Massachusetts (1996) 9–14.

5. Winston, W., *Financial Models Using Simulation and Optimization*, 2nd ed., Palisade Corporation, Newfield, New York (2000) 505.

6. Winston, W., Financial Models Using Simulation and Optimization II, Palisade Corporation, Newfield, New York (2001) 382.

7. Paddock, J.L., Siegel, D.R., and Smith, J.L.: "Option Valuation of Claims on Real Assets: The Case of Offshore Petroleum Leases," *Quarterly J. of Economics* (August 1988) 103, No. 3, 479.

8. Kemna, A. (1993), "Case Studies on Real Options," *Financial Management 22,3* (Autumn), pp. 259–270.

9. Kester, W.C. (1984). "Today's Options for Tomorrow's Growth," Harvard Business Review 62, 2 (March–April), pp. 153–160.

10. Kulatilaka, N. and E. PEROTTI (1998). "Strategic Growth Options," Management Science 44, 8, pp. 1021–1031.

11. Luehrman, T. (1998), "Strategy as a Portfolio of Real Options." Harvard Business Review (Sept.–Oct.), pp. 89–99.

12. Myers, S.C. (1987). "Finance Theory and Financial Strategy, *Midland Corporate Finance Journal* 5,1 (Spring), pp. 6–13.

13. Paddock, J., Siegel, D. and Smith, J. (1988). "Option Valuation of Claims on Physical Assets: The Case of Offshore Petroleum Leases," *Quarterly Journal of Economics* 103, (August), pp. 479–508.

14. Sick, G. (1989). Capital Budgeting with Real Options, Salomon Brothers Centre, New York University.

## REVIEW QUESTIONS

1. Explain the term "real options'. What are their types? Explain.
2. Distinguish between standard financial option and real option with suitable examples.
3. Explain the real options in context to real estate industry with suitable illustrations.
4. Explain the method of real option with suitable examples.
5. Explain the various categories of real option with suitable illustrations.
6. Explain the call and put real options with suitable diagrams and examples.
7. Critically examine the real option valuation with suitable examples and illustrations.
8. Explain the valuation inputs of real option with illustrations.
9. Explain the various techniques of real option valuation. Which method is reliable? And why?
10. Explain the limitations of real option's valuation with examples.
11. Discuss the various applications of real option along with constraints in this respect.
12. Contrast the various methods of real options valuation with examples.
13. In which respect, the valuation of financial options differs to real options. Explain with suitable illustrations.
14. Write note on the following:
    (i) Partial Differential Equation Approach in real option.
    (ii) Dynamic Programming Approach in real option.

# Chapter 24

# Commodity Derivatives Market

*After reading this chapter, students will be able to*

➢ Understand the concept of commodity derivatives.
➢ Know the segments of commodity derivative markets.
➢ Understand the historical background of the commodity derivatives.
➢ Understand the trading mechanism of commodity futures contracts in India.
➢ Know the trading mechanism of commodity forwards contracts, commodity swaps and commodity option contracts.
➢ Understand the opportunities available from commodity markets for investments.
➢ Understand the structure of commodity derivatives market in India.
➢ Understand the hedging of commodity risk.
➢ Understand the other considerations in commodity derivatives trading.

## 24.1 INTRODUCTION

Global economic recovery, trade liberalization and growing awareness about derivatives and their potential to mitigate the risk have brought the revolution in the commodity markets all over the world. Commodity markets play a significant role in the economic development of a country. Since a major part of GDP generally comes from the agricultural productions, competitive trading in commodities will not only benefit to the farmers but also to the other sectors which depend on it.

Commodity derivatives provide risk management strategies to funds managers and corporate investors to enhance the portfolio risk-return payoff. In the stock markets, the volatility has increased too much. The investors are now interested to diversify their risk by diversifying their investments in other venues like real estate's commodities, etc. Commodities hold out vast perspective to become a separate assets group of market savvy investors because being less volatile as compared to equity portfolios. Besides helping economy with improved resource allocation, it is helpful to all other sectors of the economy. As a result, the commodity derivatives market in India has witnessed a substantial growth and development in terms of transparency, technology and trading activities.

## 24.2 COMMODITY DERIVATIVES: THE CONCEPT

The commodity derivatives market is a market where future instruments like forwards, futures, options, swap, etc. are traded in commodities. A derivatives instrument is that whose value is derived from its underlying asset. So, in commodity derivatives, the underlying assets are commodities. In business sense, a commodity can be defined as a tangible as well as moveable goods used for trading and exchange purposes. Forward Contract Regulations Act (FCRA)-1952 defines the goods as "every kind of moveable property other than actionable claims, money and securities". Currently, important commodities like foodgrains, spices, cotton, oilcakes, oil, rubber, metals, coffee, coco, sugar, livestock, energy, etc., are traded in commodity markets.

In general, the commodity derivatives markets are the markets where buyers and sellers are contracting for the purchase and sale of the specified commodities at the agreed prices for a delivery at the specified future dates. In this respect, a broker member is primarily attached to organized exchanges made under the terms and conditions of standardized future contracts commodity derivatives.

## 24.3 HISTORICAL BACKGROUND

The history of commodity derivatives can be traced back to Yodoya rice market in Osaka (Japan) around 1650. After that, a lot of ups and downs were noted across the world in this market till 1925. The first futures clearing house came into existence. The first organized exchange, the Chicago Board of Trade (CBOT) with standardized contracts on various commodities came into existence in 1848. In 1874, the Chicago Produce Exchange which is now known as Chicago Mercantile Exchange (CME) was formed. Today, CBOT and CME are two of the largest commodity derivatives exchange in the world. Coffee, Sugar and Coco Exchange (CSCE) in New York is also one of the popular exchange. In Latin America, Bolsa de Mercadories and Furniture's (BMF) of Brazil established in 2001. In 2002, South Africa Futures (SAFEX) was set up. In 1990, China established its first commodity exchange. By 2000, China established three more exchanges, namely Dalian Commodity Exchange (DCE), Zhengzhou Commodity Exchange and Shanghai Futures Exchange. In Japan, Tokyo Grain Exchange was established in 1952. By 1999 other countries like Taiwan, Malaysia, Singapore, etc., also set up commodity exchanges. A list of important commodity exchanges all over the world is given in Annexure-I.

Commodity derivatives market has been functioning in India since the nineteenth century with organized trading in cotton through the establishment of Cotton Trade Association in 1875, followed by oil seeds, jute, wheat, etc. In 1900, *Gujarat Vyapari Mandali* was set up to carry put futures trading in ground nut, castor seeds and cotton. In 1919, forward trading in Raw Jute and Jute Goods began in Calcutta with the establishment of the Calcutta Hessian Exchange Ltd. East India Jute Association Ltd. was set up in 1927. For organizing futures trading in Raw Jute. However, later on, these two associations amalgamated in 1945 and formed the present East India Jute Hessian Ltd. to conduct organized trading in both raw jute goods. In 1913, Chamber of Commerce at Hapur was established for future trading in wheat and jute. In 1920, futures markets in Bullions began at Mumbai, and later, similar markets came up at Rajkot, Jam Nagar Kanpur, Delhi and Calcutta. During Second World War, futures trading was banned. However, after independence, Constitution of India brought the subject of "stock exchanges and futures markets" in the Union List. As a result, the responsibility of regulation of commodity futures markets devolved on Govt. of India. Over the years, there have been various bans, suspensions and regulatory dogmas on various contracts. Various futures markets existed in India are localized to specific commodities. For example, Kerala has an exchange for peppers, Ahmedabad for castor seeds, Mumbai as a major centre for gold, etc. These exchanges, however, have only regional presence and are dominated by people who are involved mainly with the physical trade of that commodity.

For this, in December 1952, Forward Contract (Regulation) Act, 1952 (FCRA), was enacted. This Act gives powers to the Central Government to control production, supply, distribution, etc. of essential commodities, for maintaining or increasing supplies and their equitable distribution. In 1980, The Khusro Committee recommended reintroduction of futures trading in most of the major commodities. In 1993, Government of India appointed one more committee under the chairmanship of Prof. K.N. Kabra on forward market, and committee submitted its report in September, 1994.

In 2002, the Forward Market Commission (FMC) decided to encourage the modern commodity exchange, which can work electronically. At the end of 2002, the National Multi-Commodity Exchange, Ahmedabad (NMCE) was established. After that, in 2003, The Multi-Commodity Exchange (MCX), National Commodity Derivatives Exchange (NCDEX), National Board of Trade (NBOT) and National Commodity Exchange of India (NMCE) were set up. After that, India Commodity Exchange Ltd. (ICEX) in 2009 and Ace Derivatives and Commodity Exchange Ltd. in 2010 were established. Currently in India almost 25 exchanges and associations are in operation, and six indices are measuring commodities prices. Recently, an amendment in the Finance Act, 2015, came into force w.e.f. September 28, 2015. As a result, Securities and Exchanges Board of India (SEBI), commenced regulating the commodity derivatives markets under Securities Contract Regulations Act (SCRA), 1956, and the Forward Contract Regulation Act (FCRA), 1952 got replaced w.e.f. September 29, 2015. This is presented in Annexure-II.

By the setting up above mentioned commodity exchanges and introduction of futures trading commodities by the FMC have triggered significant levels of trade. Now, the commodities futures trading business volume is all set to match the volume of the capital markets.

Commodity derivatives market can be classified into four categories: futures, forwards, swaps and options. These will be discussed separately in context to Indian market

## 24.4  SEGMENTS OF COMMODITY DERIVATIVE MARKET

The commodities markets generally exist in two forms, namely the over-the-counter (OTC) market, and Exchange traded contracts (ETC) market. Like equities, there exists the spot and the derivatives segments commodity markets. Spot markets are essentially over-the-counter markets and the participation is usually restricted to the people who are involved with that commodity, say, the farmers,  processors, wholesalers, commission agents, brokers, etc. Majority of the derivatives trading in commodities take place through the recognized exchange all over the world.

### 24.4.1 OTC Commodity Market

OTC markets are generally spot markets and are localized for specific commodities. Transactions are entered almost on delivery based. The buyers and sellers have their set of brokers and commission agents who negotiate the prices for them. The trading mechanism in the OTC markets differ from commodity to commodity. For example, trading mechanism in metals, gold, oils, food grains, vegetables, etc., are slightly different to each other. In general, in an agricultural commodity, a farmer who produces food grains wishing to sell his produce would go to the local food grains market, where he will contract to the broker who would in turn contracts the other brokers representing the buyers. In the event of final deal, the money would be exchanged directly between the buyers and the seller.

### 24.4.2 ETC Commodity Market

When the commodities are purchased and sold through the recognized exchanges, these are called exchange-traded-contracts (ETC). They are essentially derivatives markets and normally are similar to equity derivatives in their functioning. These contracts are standardized and a person can purchase a contract by paying only margin money. Also, even though, there is provision for delivery, most of the contracts are squared off before expiry and are settled in cash. As a result, one can see an active participation by the investing people who are not associated with the commodities.

## 24.5 TRADING MECHANISM OF COMMODITY FUTURES

The commodity futures, most similar to financial futures, are standardized futures contracts where buyers and sellers buy and sell of a commodity at an agreed price for a delivery at a specified future date. They are done on the recognized commodity exchanges. In this section, the trading mechanism of futures contract in commodities will be discussed in context to Indian market. At present, about 113 commodities are listed on five national and 16 regional commodity exchanges for futures trading. The trading in futures contract are governed as per the norms laid by the specified exchange on which that commodity is listed.

The exchanged offer several product classes. Their trade structure is similar, however, minor difference in terms of product quality specification, lot size, etc., may occur. It is difficult to discuss contract specifications of all the commodities, however, a brief view of general norms are described here.

### 24.5.1 Listed Commodities

Various exchanges in India are engaged in for futures trading. The important categories of commodities listed on these exchanges are as follows.

| | | |
|---|---|---|
| Bullion | : | Gold, Silver, Platinum |
| Basic Metal | : | Copper, Nickel. Lead, Tin, Aluminium |
| Energy Production | : | Crude oil, Heating oil, Gasoline, Natural Gas, etc. |
| Agricultural Products | : | Fibre, Pulses, Vegetables, Foods grains, Edible oils, Oils seeds, and oil cakes. |
| Soft commodities | : | Coffee, Cocoa, Sugar |
| Live Stock | : | Live Cattle, Pork, Bellies, etc. |

## 24.5.2 Tick Size

Each exchange sets the tick size of each commodity for trading. Tick size refers to the minimum increment or decrement in the price of listed commodity acceptable to the exchange. For example the tick size of the aluminium is ₹0.05 or five paise. Assume that quoted price is ₹140.50 per kg. Then, minimum change in the quoted price can be 5 paise not below that. Tick size varies according to the prices of the commodities. It has direct impact on the bid ask spread quotation of the derivatives. On the NCDEX, tick size is ₹1 in case of Gold ₹10 in Guar gum, 10 paise in Kalyan Kapas, 10 paise in Natural Gas and so on.

## 24.5.3 Trading Lot Size

Trading lot or size refers to the minimum quantity of one contract of the said commodity for delivery purpose. For example, in gold, unit of trading is 1 kg and delivery unit (Lot size) 1 kg with maximum order size is 50 kg. Similarly, NCDEX has specified trading limit, delivery unit and maximum order size for each of its other listed commodity. It means that the minimum quantity for which an order is placed by the members on the exchange and this is decided by the exchange. Such trading lots may differ from exchange to exchange.

## 24.5.4 Quality Specification of the Commodity

The commodities traded on the exchanges are subject to mark with quality specification. The quality of goods is specified which will be checked before accepting the goods for delivery to the buyer. In other words, the commodity must fulfil the quality standard as specified by the exchange. For example, in case of gold, Gold bars of 995 fineness bearing a serial number and identifying stamp of a refiner approved by the exchange. In case of raw cotton Kalyan Kapas (v – 79) commodity, the quality specifications are Turnout-cotton basis (40 percent +/– 2 percent), cotton seeds –60 percent (+/–20 percent), Trash –1.25 percent and moisture max 8.5 percent. In this way, all the commodity exchanges have specified a detailed quality standard for each commodity.

## 24.5.5 Delivery Specification

Each exchange has mentioned the delivery specification in case of each commodity. It means the mode of delivery of the goods to be delivered at the particular centre and intention for delivery. For example, in case of gold, the buyer and seller shall give intention of taking/giving delivery through the delivery request window at least three trading days prior to the expiry of the contracts and such intention can be given during 3 days which would be notified separately. After that the same will be matched by the Exchange for physical delivery as per the process put in place by the Exchange. The delivery specifications differ exchange to exchange.

## 24.5.6 Price Limits

Price limits refer to the fluctuations in daily base price of the commodity. The exchange has fixed the limits in which the price of goods can fluctuate, and has the right to relax as lighten as per the market conditions. For example in case of gold, the NCDEX has specified daily price fluctuation limit (+/–) 3 percent. If the market trade hits the prescribed base daily price limit, then the limit will be relaxed up to (+/–) 6 percent with any break/cooling off period in the trade. If the limit of 6% is breached, then after 15 minutes the daily price limit will be further relaxed up to (+/–) 9 percent. In case of price movement in international price, limit (currently 9 percent), the same may be further relaxed in steps of 3 percent. In this way the price limits are changed as per the market conditions by the respective exchange.

### 24.5.7   Margin (Initial, Special, Additional)

Each exchange fixes the minimum initial margin to be deposited by the clients with their exchange members for the trading in the future contract. The percentage of margin depends upon the volatility in the commodity's market price as well as other factors, like demand and supply, market conditions, etc. For example, in case of gold, the NCDEX has fixed 5 percent minimum initial margin of the current market price of the gold. In case of unidirectional price movement/increased volatility, an additional/special margin at such other percentage deemed fit by the Regulator/Exchange may be imposed on the buy and the sell side on either of the buy or sell sides in respect of all outstanding positions. Further, reduction/removal of such additional/special margin will be at the discretion of the Regulator/Exchange.

### 24.5.8   Clearing Arrangement

Each exchange has tied with a particular clearing agency for settlement of the futures contracts. The NCDEX has made arrangements with National Security Clearing Corporation Ltd. (NSCCL). It undertakes clearing of all trades executed on the NCDEX. The settlement guarantee fund is maintained and managed by NCEDX. Only clearing members including professional clearing members (PCMS) only are entitled to clear and settle contracts through the clearing house.

After the trading hours on the expiry date, based on the available information, the matching for deliveries takes place, firstly on the basis of locations and then randomly, keeping in view the factors such as available capacity of the vault ware house, commodities, already deposited and dematerialized and offered for delivery, etc. Matching is done by this process is binding on the clearing members. After completion of the matching process, clearing members are informed of the deliverable/receivable position and unmatched position. The unmatched positions have to be settled in cash, based on the incremental gain/loss as determined on the basis of final settlement price.

### 24.5.9   Settlement Arrangement

Futures contracts have two types of settlements. Mark-to-Market (MTM) and Final Settlement. MTM happens on a continuous basis at the end of each day. On the NCDEX, Final Settlement of MTM in respect of admitted deals in futures contracts are cash settled by debiting/crediting the clearing accounts of the clearing members (CMs) with the respective clearing bank. All positions of a CM, brought forward, created during the day or closed out during the day are mark-to-market at the daily settlement prices or the final settlement price at the close of the trading hours on a day.

On the day of expiry, the final settlement price is the spot price on the expiry day. The responsibility of settlement is on a trading-cum-clearing member for all trades done on his own account and his client's trades. A professional clearing member is responsible for settling all the participants' trades, which he has confirmed to the exchange. On the expiry date of a futures contracts, members submit delivery information through delivery request window on the trader work stations provided by NCDEX for all open positions for a commodity for all constituents individually. The NCDEX on receipt of such information matches the information and arrives at delivery positions for a commodity. The seller intending to make delivery takes the commodity from the designated warehouse.

These commodities have to be assayed by the exchange specified assayer. The commodity have to meet the contract specifications with allowed variances. If the commodity meets the specifications the warehouse accepts them. Warehouse then ensures that the receipts get updated in the depository system giving a credit in the depositor's electronic account. The seller then gives invoice to his clearing member, who would send the same to the buyer's clearing members on an appointed date, the buyer goes to the warehouse and takes physical possession of the commodities.

## 24.5.10 Contract Expiry

At the NCDEX exchange, normally all the futures contracts are expired on 20th day of the delivery month. Thus, a January expiration contract would expire on the 20th January, and February expiry contract would cease on the 20th February. If the 20th happens to be a holiday, a Saturday or a Sunday, then the due date shall be the immediately preceding trading day of the NCDEX exchange, which is other than a Saturday. At MCX exchange, the expiry day is the fifteenth of every month. The expiry day also differs for different commodities on different exchanges.

## 24.5.11 National Commodity of Derivatives Exchange (NCDEX)

NCDEX is an online commodity exchange based in India. It provides a commodity exchange platform for market participants to trade in commodity derivatives. It is a public limited company, incorporated on April 23, 2003, under the Companies Act, 1956. It started its operations on December 15, 2003. NCDEX is registered by the Forward Market Commission (FMC) and now by the Security Exchange Board of India (SEBI). It has impendent Board of Directors and professional management to manage commodity markets. The important institutions which have subscribed it are: Canara Bank, Punjab National Bank, CRISIL Ltd., Credit Rating Information Services India Ltd., Indian Farmers Fertilizers Cooperatives Limited (IFFCO), Infrastructure Development Finance Company (IDFC), Intercontinental Exchange (ICE), Day Fee Capital, Life Insurance Corporation of India (LIC), National Bank for Agricultural Rural Development (NABARD), National Stock Exchange of India (NSE), Goldman Sachs, etc.

NCDEX has around 848 registered members and client base of approximate 20 lakhs, offers more than 49000 terminals across 1000 centres in India, as on July 31, 2013. It facilitates delivery of commodities through a network of over 594 accredited warehouses through eight warehouse service providers, with holding capacity of around 1.5 million tonnes. It offers average delivery of 1 lakh MT at every contract expiry.

NCDEX offers futures trading in 31 agricultural and non-agricultural commodities. It also offers an agricultural commodity Index 'DHANYA' which is computed in real time using the prices of the ten most liquid commodity futures traded on the NCDEX platform. It has also introduced N. Charts—a free based charting tool provided to users for technical analysis. It launched COMPTRACK a proprietary electronic warehouse accounting system. It is stared forward market trading on September 25, 2014.

## 24.6   COMMODITY FORWARD CONTRACTS

A general forward contract is a bilateral over-the-counter (OTC) contract in which one party buys or sells assets at agreed price on a future specified date from the other party. The terms of the contract are decided by the parties themselves. As such commodity forwards are forward contracts done in the commodities. To regulate the forward trading in commodities in India, Forward Contract Regulation Act, 1952 was enacted. Further Forward Contract Regulation Rules were notified by the Central Government in July 1954. The Act divides the commodities into 3 categories with reference to extent of regulation:

(a) The commodities in which futures trading can be organized under the auspices of recognized association.

(b) The commodities in which futures trading is prohibited.

(c) Those commodities, which have neither been regulated for being traded under the recognized association nor prohibited, are referred as free commodities, and the associations organized in such free commodities is required to obtain the Certificate of Registration from the Forward Markets Commission.

The FC(R) Act, 1955 gives powers to control production, supply, distribution, etc., of essential commodities for maintaining or increasing supplies and for securing their equitable distribution and availability at fair prices. In the seventies, most of the registered associations became inactive, as futures as well as forward trading in the commodities for which they were registered came to be either suspended or prohibited altogether. However, on April 1, 2003, Central Government issued Notification permitting futures trading in commodities.

### 24.6.1   Forward Contract Specification

Forward Contracts in India have been broadly classified into two categories, i.e., specific delivery contracts, and other than specific delivery contracts.

### 24.6.2   Specific Delivery Contracts

These are essentially merchandising contracts which enable producers and consumers of commodities to market their produce and cover their requirements respectively. These contracts are generally negotiated directly between the parties depending upon availability and requirement of produce. During negotiation, terms of quality, quantity, price, period of delivery, place of delivery, payment terms, etc., are incorporated in the contract. Specific delivery contracts are of two types: (i) Transferable specific delivery contracts (TSD) and non-transferable specific delivery contracts (NSTD). In the TSD contracts, transfer of the right or obligation under the contract is permitted while in NTSD contracts it is not permitted.

### 24.6.3   Other than Specific Delivery Contracts

This contract has not been specifically defined under the Act. These are also called as futures contracts. Futures contracts are forward contracts other than specific delivery contracts. These contracts usually entered into under the auspices of an Exchange or Association. In the futures contract, the quality and quantity of the commodity, time of maturity of contract, place of delivery, etc. are all standardized and contracting parties have to negotiate only the rate at which contract to be entered into.

Forward trading in TSD and NTSD contracts is regulated by the Government. As per Section 15 of the FC(R) Act, 1952, every forward contract in notified goods that entered into except those between members of a recognized associations or through or with any such member is treated as illegal or void. However, later on, the regulatory provision of Act was applied to the NTSD and 79 commodity items are currently prohibited for NTSD contracts. Further, another 15 commodity items are brought under the regulatory provisions of the Act, out of which in the NTSD contract has been suspended in 12 items. At present, the NTSD contracts in cotton, raw jute, and jute goods are permitted only between through or with the members of the associations specifically recognized for the purpose.

### 24.6.4    Exchange Traded Forward Contracts on NCDEX

These are specific types of forward contracts which are launched by NCDEX exchange. In December, 2014 the Forward Markets Commission (FMC) has permitted forward trading in 17 commodities including 29 MM cotton, barley, castor seeds, chilli coriander, crude, palm oil, chana, guar gum, guar seed, jeera, mustard seed, refined, soya oil, Shankar Kapas, soya bean, turmeric, cotton seed, oil cake and wheat.

There are two types of contracts initiated by the NCDEX in such category, Reference Price Contract and Fixed Price Contract. A reference price contract anchored to a particular futures contract traded on the exchange. The contract would be priced at a premium/discount to the NCDEX contract based on the inherent parameters of the forward contract. Fixed price contracts are contracts which are entered at a flat rate. TSD contracts would be netted at the end of the fixed parameters and bid and offer parameters are identical for buy and sell trade for the same client. Any open position at the end shall result in delivery. NSTD contracts would not be given Intraday Square off facility. Every trade shall result in delivery.

These contracts shall carry specific specifications like minimum bid quantity 10 MT and multiple of 10 MT thereafter, mutually agreed between buyers and seller quality of the product, delivery location mutually agreed on any exchange approved warehouse (within 100 km of agreed location) buyer pay-in second day from pricing date, delivery of goods in 10 working days from pay-in, settlement penalty under the provision of contract, etc. In such NCDEX forward contracts, the parties can enjoy reduced counter party risks by executing bilateral trade under the regulatory framework without giving up on the comfort of trading customized (tailor-made) contracts. In brief, the major benefits of such exchange trade forward contracts, as initiated by the NCDEX, will be larger market, increased liquidity, risk management services, compensation guarantee of counterparty default risk, easy and reliable trade, better inventory management and multiple options for delivery.

### 24.7    COMMODITY SWAPS

Buying, selling and trading in commodity is a risky business. For example, a diesel oil burning electric plant might suddenly face a problem of unexpected rise in crude oil price resulting into disturbing on its financial projections. Swaps are a way to shift risk among the parties involved with a particular commodity. Commodity swaps are not contracts to buy or sell the commodity, rather they are fixed length contracts to exchange the commodities' current value for something else. Hence, they play a crucial role in pricing of the commodities in the markets. Commodity swaps are similar to interest rate swap but the parties exchange a fixed price of a commodity with a floating or variable price for the commodity.

A simple description of a swap is that it is bilateral agreement between the counterparties who agree to exchange a series of cash flows at specified future dates. A commodity swap is an agreement involving the exchange of commodity price payments (fixed amount) against variable price payments (market price) resulting exclusively in a cash settlement amount. In other words, the buyer of commodity swap acquires the right to be paid a settlement amount if the market price falls below the fixed amount. Both streams of payments (fixed and variable) are in the same currency and based on the same nominal amount. Various examples of commodity swaps are: a gold producer may hedge his losses related to a fall in the price of gold for his current inventory, while a cattle farmer may seek to hedge his exposure to change in the price of livestock, a company might want to lock in the price at which it purchases electricity to supply its air conditioning units for the upcoming summer month, and an airline may need to look in the price of the jet fuel it needs to purchase in order to satisfy the peak in seasonal demand.

Many types of commodity swap are possible. However, the most common types of commodity swap are classified into two types: **fixed-for-floating and commodity-for-interest swaps.**

**Fixed-for-Floating Swap:** A consumer seeks to nail down the price for a commodity by paying a fixed amount and receiving a floating amount based upon the commodity price. On the other hand, a producer would be interested in paying a floating amount and receiving a fixed amount. For example, an energy company pays a fixed amount to a counterparty every month in return for receiving a variable amount based on the current price of crude oil. In this way, through commodity swap the energy company will receive higher amount if the market price of oil rises in futures, covering the risk of rising of future price of crude oil. It is just like a form of price insurance. Similarly, the oil producing company can look in revenue by swapping the current oil price for the fixed amount, and thus having protection against decline in crude oil prices.

**Commodity-for-Interest Swap:** A commodity-for-interest swap is also known as floating-to-floating swap. In this, one party shells out an amount based on a commodity price and receives an amount equal to short-term interest rate plus or minus a fixed quantity, called a *spread*. On the other hand, the counterparty fork over the adjusted short-term rate and receives the commodity price. The interest rate is based on the specified index like LIBOR, Central Banks rate, etc. Usually the counter-parties exchange only the net difference between the off-setting cash flows.

**EXAMPLE:** A company has agreed a fixed price for 1000 kg of a commodity at ₹45 per kg, Company B has agreed the floating price. This swap has an agreed settlement date 6 months from now. The market data in the commodity's curve shows that on the settlement date, the price of the commodity will be ₹50 per kg. The risk-free interest rate is 4 percent and the risk-free expected value due for company A is, therefore, ₹45,900. The risk free expected value for company is ₹51,000. The total swap NPV is approximately ₹4,902.

It is observed from the above that two main considerations are involved in commodity swap. First is the future price of the commodity at the time of settlement, and second is the reference interest rate. The future price can be determined on the basis of current market price, tied to an index or to a futures contract. The interest rate can be tied to an index like LIBOR, MIBOR, reference interest of the Central Bank, money market rate, etc. Similarly general market indexes in the commodities market like the Goldman Such Commodities Index (GSCI), and the Commodities Research Board Index (CRBI) are also used for creating the commodity swaps.

Besides above, the commodity swaps can also be classified as 'Single Swap' and 'Swap Strip'. In case of single swap, the parties enter into swap agreement with only one settlement date. The flexibility is relating to the settlement date. For example, if the party enters 3-month swap, it means it is entered as a single 3-month swap. On the other hand, the swap strip instrument contains a series of settlement dates. For each settlement date, there are a series of fixing dates on which the underlying asset price is sampled.

The commodity swaps help the producers to manage their exposure to fluctuations in their products' prices, and although, these can be risky. In the commodity markets, swaps are popular among energy, chemical and agricultural companies. The speculators are also very active in these markets since they buy and sell such commodities through various types of swaps which play a key role in pricing these commodities.

**EXAMPLE (commodity swap):**   An industrial producer X. Ltd. Co. needs to buy 1,00,000 barrels of oil one year and 2 years from today. Assume the forward prices for deliveries in 1 year and 2 years are $40 and $42 per barrel, respectively. The 1-year and 2-year zero coupon bond yields are 7 percent and 8 percent. 'X' Ltd. Co. can guarantee the cost of buying oil for the next 2 years by entering into long forward contracts for 1,00,000 barrels in each of the next 2 years. The PV of this cost per barrel and total cost are:

$$\frac{\$40}{1.07} + \frac{\$42}{(1.08)^2} = \$73.391 \times 1,00,000 = \$73.391 \text{ lakhs}$$

Thus, the X Ltd. Co. could pay oil supplier $73.391 lakhs and the supplier would committed to delivers one lakh barrel in each of the next two years. A prepaid swap is a single payment today for multiple deliveries of oil in the future.

With a prepaid swap, the buyer might worry about the resulting credit risk. Therefore, a better solution is to defer payments until the oil is delivered, while still fixing the total price. Any payment stream with a PV of $73.391 is acceptable. Typically, a swap will call for equal payments in each year. For example, the payment per year barrel X will have to be $40.956 to satisfy the following equation:

$$\frac{X}{1.07} + \frac{X}{1.08} = \$73.391 = \$40.956 \text{ per year}$$

We then say that 2-year swap price is $40.956 per barrel Physical settlement of swap is shown in Figure 24.1.

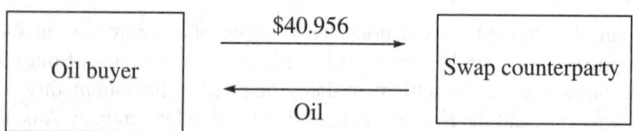

**FIGURE 24.1**   Physical settlement of swap.

**Financial settlement of the swap:**   The oil buyer X. Ltd. Co. pays the swap counterparty the difference between $40.956 and the spot price, and the oil buyer then buys oil at the spot price. If the difference between $40.956 and spot price is negative, then the swap counterparty pays the buyer.

Whatever the market price of oil, the net cost to the buyer is the swap price, $40.956.

Note that 1,00,000 is the national amount of the swap meaning that the 1,00,000 barrels is used to determine the magnitude of payment when the swap is settlement financially.

The result for the buyer are same whether the swap is settled physically or financially. In both cases the net cost to the oil buyer is $40.956.

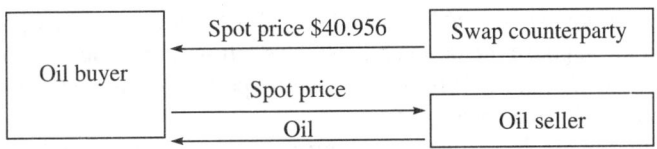

**FIGURE 24.2**  Financial settlement of commodity swap.

Swaps are nothing more than forward contracts couples with borrowing and lending money.

## 24.8  COMMODITY OPTIONS

The option is a derivative instrument in which one party gets the right but no obligation to buy or sell a specific quantity of an asset at an agreed price on or before a particular date. The buyer of the option will pay premium to the seller of the option for the right purchased. There are two types of option—Call and Put. Call option gives the right-to-purchase and put option extends right-to-sell the underlying asset to the counterparty.

When the options are entered on the commodities, these are called *commodity options*. In other words, underlying assets are the commodities in community options. The commodity options market is a market in which producers may purchase the opportunity to sell or buy a commodity future contract at a specified price. The buyer of a commodity put option pays a premium for the right to receive the difference between the stock price and the market price in relation to the nominal amount of the market price follows below the fixed amount. While in call option, the buyer pays a premium for the right to receive the difference between the strike price and the market price if the market price rises above the fixed price. For example, a party purchased a December crude oil $60 call option. It means the buyer of call option has purchased the right, but not the obligation, to purchase 1000 barrels of crude oil @ dollar 60 per barrel of crude oil, in December. If the price of crude oil rises above $60 per barrel, then the buyer will be in profit and will exercise the option. However, if the price of crude oil falls below dollar 60 per barrel, then he will not exercise the option, since he would be in loss. Hence, option will go un-exercised.

Trading norms are almost same in the commodity option as of other standard options. The details of the options trading have been extensively discussed in Chapter 16. Hence, there is no need to explain again these in this section.

Trading in commodity option is currently prohibited in India. The regulators are considering to introduce these contracts in the Indian commodity market in order to provide the investors with more choice and to provide the farmers and traders with more tools to hedge their risk. Currently almost 110 commodity exchanges are operating all over the world. A list of important exchanges trading in futures and options instrument is given in Appendix

### 24.8.1  Intrinsic and Extrinsic Value of the Commodity Options

The option premium of any asset is made up of two values. Intrinsic value and extrinsic value. Intrinsic value is the value of the option if the holder exercised it to the futures contract and then offset it. For example, if the holder of the option has December ₹10 soya bean, Call and the futures price for that contract is ₹10.50, hence there is ₹0.50 intrinsic value for that option. Assume that soya beans are a 5000 bush contract, so intrinsic value of the option will be 5,000 × ₹50 = ₹2,500 on that date. Further, assume that in the market the same call option (December ₹10 soya beans) is in premium of ₹3,500. Then extrinsic value is made up of time value, volatility premium and demand for that specific option. Suppose the option has 60 days left until expiration, it has more time value than it would be with 40 days left. It means longer the period remains in the option's expiration, higher will be the value and vice versa.

As observed, options are by nature a wasting asset because each and every day the option premium is being eroded by time. Time decay is the best friend of option sellers and worst enemy of option buyer. The value of out-of-the money options is composed almost entirely of time value.

Figure 24.3 depicts the time value of an option of a commodity. Time value is highest when it has six months to expiration. It decreases as the time is passing. It will be zero at the maturity. Thus, it shows acceleration of the time decay of an option with a 6-month life span from its inception to its expiration.

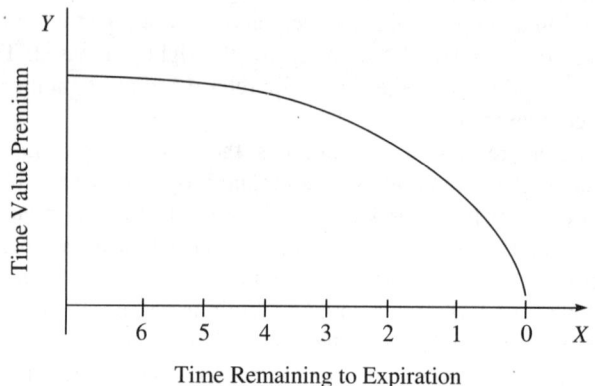

**FIGURE 24.3** Extrinsic value of commodity option.

## 24.8.2 Delta Factor in Commodity Options Premium

The movement of option premium is a function of delta factor of the option. The delta of the option means the change in premium due to change in the market price of the underlying asset. For example, it is expected that December gold will go up by ₹50 per 10 gram, ₹5,000 per contract over a short period of time. Assume that delta factor of gold option is 20, means 20 percent. This option should gain approximately ₹1,000 in premium value of the ₹5,000 expected gold futures price movement if it occurs in a timely factor.

In other words, when we trade in option, basically we are trading volatility. Volatility is the measure of nervousness that is in the markets, based on a sense of uncertainty as far as what the future prices might do, and where these might go. In fact, volatility is basically reflected in this sharp ups and downs in option premium, and the degree of fluctuations that those premiums experience.

In general, two types of volatility are considered in commodity option trading—Historical and implied. Historical volatility is basically the "track record of a given commodity's market price swings". In other words, how stable (or unstable) have market prices been throughout history? There are all kinds of charting tools to measure historical volatility by which regular peaks, valleys, and other trends can be analyzed, especially more seasonal-based commodities like the grains (corns, maize, wheat, soya bean, etc.) and for the most part of the softs (coffee, sugar, cocoa, etc.). Implied, volatility, on the other hand is the kicker. It is basically the market's guess about the stability of the prices in the future. It is also called expected volatility of the underlying commodity. Historical volatility plays a significant role in estimating the implied volatility. If you expect volatility to increase, then it is not to go for writing an option. Conversely, if the volatility is to decrease, then buying option will not be good. Thus, while trading in commodities, volatility factor must be taken into consideration.

## 24.9  OTHER CONSIDERATIONS IN COMMODITY DERIVATIVES TRADING

The basic trading norms in the commodity derivatives are almost same among the various commodity exchanges except for minor changes, however, the norms relating to contract size, tick size, quantity and quality of the products delivery mechanism, clearing arrangement, settlement, procedure, etc., vary according to the category of the commodity. The contract specification of the food grains, metals, chemicals, energy, polymer products are different from each other. When more than hundreds of the products are listed on various exchanges, it is difficult to mention each one of them. Moreover, the exchanges are also updating the norms from time to time as per the market needs. The traders are advised to go through these norms thoroughly of each exchange relating to the commodities before entering into the transactions.

The trading in commodities are subject to sales tax. It is applicable in the case of trade resulting into delivery. Those transactions are squared off, no sale tax would be levied on them. Normally the sale tax is collected by the sellers and deposited in the Government Treasury. Sale tax is applicable at the place of delivery. Further, sales tax registration number is required in case physical delivery of the commodity is desired by the parties. There is no stamp duty applicable in general on the futures contracts which have been generated in an electronic form. However, in case of physical delivery, the stamp duty will be levied as per the prescribed laws of the State the investors' trade in.

Besides the levied of sale tax, stamp duty, margin, etc. the traders also have to pay commission, fees and other charges applicable on the derivatives trade in commodities. Brokerage is a fee charged by the broker for the execution of the transactions. In India, brokerage on commodity futures varies according to the types of commodities. It is also different on the basis of the contract specifications. The maximum limits of the charges have also been specified by the Regulatory Authority in this respect.

## 24.10  OPPORTUNITIES IN THE COMMODITY DERIVATIVES

Commodity derivatives, which were earlier initiated for risk management purposes are now growing in popularity as an investment tool. It is observed that most of the trading in the commodity derivatives market is being alone by the people who have no need for the commodity itself. This is a healthy trend which will lead to develop this sector in future. The commodity derivatives markets provide various opportunities to the traders, investors and other participants in this sector. They facilitate the activities of hedging, speculation, arbitraging, investing, etc. to all types of investors.

### 24.10.1  Hedging of Commodity Risk

Commodity derivatives facilitate to hedge the risk of commodity. Risk, in simple terms, may be defined as the probability or likelihood of the occurrence of an unexpected event. It is deviation between estimates and actuals. If an event actual takes place as expected, then there is no risk. Commodity risk is the uncertainly associated with the fluctuations or volatilities in commodity prices. Besides, price fluctuations in commodity prices, another risk is related to currency risk. Commodity prices often are quoted in foreign currency in international trade specifically. In such case the party is exposed to currency market risk if the transactions are to be executed in the foreign currency. Foreign exchange rates are subject to change regularly. So, this risk should be also taken into consideration. Further commodity futures are less liquid than to financial futures. So liquidity risk should also be incorporated in estimating the risk on commodity futures. Further, the spread between the bids and ask prices in commodity contracts may be relatively wide, which ultimately influence the liquidity.

The producers whether they are farmers, industrial producers, and other manufactures are always at the risk owing to the uncertainly in commodity prices in future. In the developing economies, the producers traditionally diversify their farm crops and income sources to manage price risk. Instead of depending on a single crop, they usually choose various low risk crops. Even the Governments in these countries try to protect the farmers through various measures from price fluctuations of the commodities. However, the said protection experiences are now shifting to market forces. As a result, necessity of the market-based instruments for hedging commodity price fluctuations was felt. Such market-based instruments are commodity derivatives are forwards, futures, swaps and options.

The basic objective of hedging is to minimize the price risk associated with position in cash market by taking opposite position in future market with the said instruments. Let us explain the hedging through commodity futures.

**Short Hedge vs Long Hedge:**   Commodity futures are standard contracts between the two parties to buy or sell an asset at a certain price in future and traded on the organized exchanges. The exchanges specify the norms of trading in futures. These commodity futures usually fulfil two major functions, managing price risk and price discovery. The futures markets provide facilities of setting the positions without even requiring the physical delivery of the goods. This facility attracts hedgers to go for futures in managing their risk in prices of commodities. Further, the presence of various players like hedgers, speculators and arbitrageurs also play a crucial role in the futures price. Such futures prices help the producers, farmers, traders, importers, exporters, processors for taking appropriate decisions in price risk management.

As discussed above, futures contracts are done on the organized exchanges. Hedging through futures means minimizing the price risk by taking opposite position on futures market against the cash position. It means if a person owns an asset or is expected to own in future, then he can take opposite position in futures market by selling the same quantity of commodities and vice versa. To hedge from the rise in prices, he buys (long position) futures contract now. For example, an oil-seed farmer may go short in oil-seed futures, thus, "locking" his sale price and in the process hedging against any adverse price movements, Similarly, on the other hand, a processor of oil-seed may buy oil-seed futures, and thus, assure him a supply of oil-seeds at a pre-determined price. Further, the oil seeds processor may go short in oil futures, which may be bought by a wholesaler of oil.

It should be remembered that the futures are generally used to avoid the uncertainly and to lock in the price but not to make profit. Assume the prices move as against the expectations, then the futures may be result in losses. In such situation, the unhedged position may provide better results. In brief, by using futures, the hedgers can take appropriate position in futures markets and can plan production schedule and allocation of resources efficiently.

*Example of Short Hedge and Long Hedge*

**EXAMPLE:**   A cotton ginner needs to procure 10000 MT of raw cotton sometime in the end of December, as per the production schedule. He intends to produce lint and further sells it to the textile mills with whom he has a control at a pre-agreed price. Now if the prices of raw cotton rise in the month of December, his profit margin might shrink even he may run into losses. He can reduce the price risk by means of hedging his raw material requirement at say, NCDEX exchange.

*Let us assume that on current date the ginner finds that:*

| | | |
|---|---|---|
| Shankar Kapas | : | ₹1,300/20 kg |
| December Futures contract on NCDEX | : | ₹1,400/20 kg |

He buys the Dec expiry contract at NCDEX on current date. On 30th December ( i.e., on the day of expiry of contract) two situations may arise:

**Situation 1:**   Spot price increases to ₹1,440/20 kg so final MTM profit will be ₹40, i.e. (₹1,440 – ₹1,400). On settlement, effective price on December 30, will be ₹1,440 – ₹40 = 1,400

**Situation 2:**   Spot price decreases to ₹1,370. On final settlement, MTM loss will be ₹30, i.e. (₹1,370 – ₹1,400)

Effective price will be ₹1,370 + ₹30 = ₹1,400.

Therefore, irrespective of the spot price movement, his effective purchase price, and hence, his profit margin remains locked in this is called hedging with futures contract.

**The cross hedging in commodity futures:**   The concept of cross hedging is related with the liquidity aspect of underlying commodity. When commodity futures do not have the desired liquidity, which means easily squaring off the futures positions taken in the commodity, then it is quite possible that hedging against market risk might not be possible for the trader. In such cases, cross hedging can be much useful. In the cross hedging, a highly correlated commodity is selected to hedge the underlying commodity. The trader can reduce the risk market by selecting a hedge in closely-related products, for example, silver against gold, *gur* and sugar, diesel and petrol oil and so on.

While selecting the commodity in cross hedging, it is important to check their correlation in the historical price movements and liquidity aspect. Further, the contract size of the commodity futures should be matched with the underlying commodity, so that adequate inherent risk could be covered. The concept of cross hedging has been discussed in detail in Chapter 7.

## 24.10.2   Speculating through Commodity Derivatives

Another important opportunity available from commodity derivatives is speculating facility to the people who are either interested in trading or investing in this market. The speculative position is taken with a small margin amount that is paid to the exchange, and the contract can be square off anytime during the trading hours. The person willingly accepting a risk does so because of the profit from price movements, this is called *speculating*. In speculation, the person is not interested to take delivery of the goods rather plays with the fluctuations of prices. It enhanced liquidity in the market. However, speculating activities, sometimes, create undesired situation in the market. They influence the prices of the assets in the market at extreme levels on both sides: ups and down and thus, creating high volatility in the market.

Speculative activities in the commodity markets are subject to control as per the respective regulatory authority. Speculative activities, in top priority products, namely oil and gas, at the international level, had been recording market volatility at a very high rate. Similarly, the Commodity

Futures Trading Commission (CFTC) has fixed limits for energy markets to prevent single and large investors to influence the price in the market. It has been further authorized to set the limits for certain essential agricultural commodities to control the speculative activities in this respect. Thus, the speculative activities, no doubt, create good turnover and liquidity in the commodity markets, but these should be regulated through appropriate measures as per the needs of the economy.

### 24.10.3    Arbitrage Opportunity

Traders in the commodity markets may exploit arbitrage opportunities which arise on account of different prices between the two exchanges or between different maturities in the underlying commodity. It means through arbitrage process, the market prices will be in equilibrium and no trader can earn super profit in the market. For example, assume the price of wheat in Delhi market is trading at ₹1,500 per quintal and ₹2,000 per quintal in Mumbai market, then the traders will start buying from Delhi food grains market and sell the same in Mumbai market till prices in both the markets becomes equal. The arbitrage opportunity creates healthy competitive environment in the markets, and thus, prices remain stable and reasonable.

### 24.10.4    Investing in Commodity Derivatives

Commodity derivatives, traditionally developed for risk management purposes are now growing as an investment tool. It has been observed recently in the commodity trading volumes that most of the trading is being done by the general investors who have no requirement for the commodity itself. They just speculate on the direction of the prices of these commodities, hoping to earn in future if the prices move in their favour. All over the world, it is noted that the total turnover in commodity markets has increased to almost five times of the financial markets.

The commodity derivative market is a direct way to invest in commodities, rather than investing in the companies which trade in those commodities. For example, investors can invest directly in a steel derivative rather than investing in the shares of Tata Steel Company. Let us assume that an investor buys a ton of steel for ₹35,000 in June anticipation that the price will rise to ₹40,000 by September. He will be able to make profit of ₹5,000 on his investment. Compare this to the scenario if the investor had decided to by steel futures instead. Consider if the steel futures is available at ₹35,000 exercise price at 10% margin maturing in September. Here, he is to pay a margin money ₹3,500 to enter into contract. If the price of steel rises to ₹40,000, then he will make a profit of ₹5,000. On comparing the profits of spot market, i.e., 14.3 percent (₹5,000/35,000) and futures market 142.9 percent (5,000/3,500), it is observed that profits is almost ten times in futures as compared to spot market. However, it can be on reverse side too. Similarly, the same opportunities are available in option contracts too.

In brief, the above example shows that with very little investment, the commodity futures and options offer scope to make big bucks. However, trading in derivatives is highly risky because just as there are huge returns to be earned if prices move in favour of the investors, an unfavorable move results in huge losses.

## 24.11    STRUCTURE OF COMMODITY DERIVATIVES MARKET IN INDIA

Commodity markets play a significant role in the growth and development of an economy. Commodity trading helps the investors to diversify their investment in commodities from the traditional option like financial instruments. Further, trading of commodity futures execute economic functions such as price risk management, price discovery and improved resource allocation in the economy. The commodity market establishes a link between the present and future production and consumption cycles, thereby facilitating the inter-temporal smoothing of prices. In this section we will discuss a brief description of structure of commodity derivatives market in terms of operations and regulatory mechanism in India.

### Regulatory framework

With the establishment of Forward Market Commission in April, 2013, the commodity derivatives market in India took a new turn. The regulatory structure of commodity markets in India can be traced into three tiers, i.e. Government of India, Forward Market Commission (now merged with Securities Exchange Board of India) and Commodity Exchanges. This structure is shown in Figure 24.4.

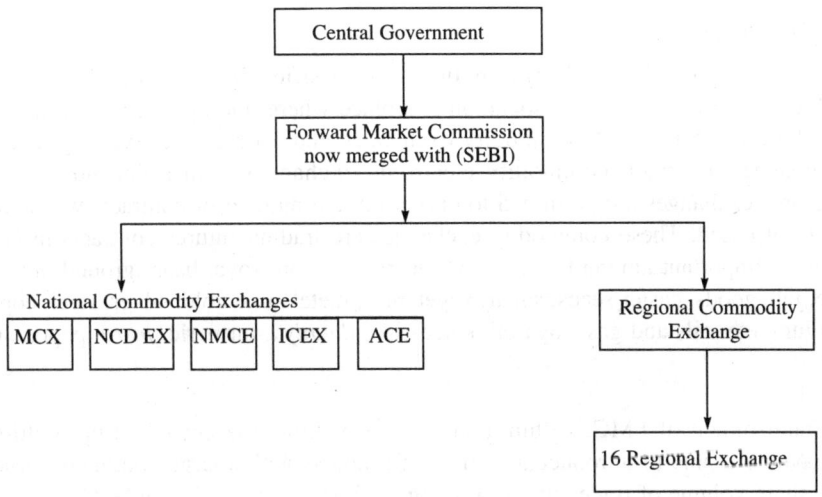

**FIGURE 24.4** Regulatory framework of commodity markets.

### First-tier

The commodity derivatives markets are regulated by the Government of India. The Central Government makes all the policies relating to the future trading in terms of forward and futures for all commodities in India. At present, the Ministry of Consumer Affairs, Food and Public Distribution Department of Central Government is regulating this market.

### Second-tier

The Central Government has established the statutory body named as Forward Market Commission (FMC) under the provision of Forward Contract (Regulation) Act, 1952. It functions under the administrative control of the Ministry of Consumer Affair. As per Section 4 of the FC(R) Act, 1952, the Commission performs the following roles:

(i) To advise the Central Government to assign or withdraw the recognition of commodity exchanges.

(ii) To regulate the forward market trading activities of the commodity exchanges.

(iii) To collect and publish obligatory information related to future trading in commodities.

(iv) To give recommendations to the Central Government for the improvement of derivatives trading in commodities.

(v) To examine the accounts and other documents of recognized commodity exchanges.

(vi) To execute the functions assigned by the Central Government as per the FC(R) Act, 1952, from time to time.

Now the regulation of commodity derivatives market has been assigned to the Securities Exchange Board of India (SEBI) as per Central Government notification dated August 28, 2015 as presented in Annexure-II. Under part-I of the Finance Act, 2015 it provides that all rules, directions, guidelines, instructions, circulars or any like instruments made by the FMC or the Central Government applicable to recognized associations under Forward Contract Act shall continue to remain in force for a period of one year from the date on which the Act is repealed, or till such time as notified by the Security Board, whichever is earlier, as if the Forward Contract Act had not been repealed.

### Commodity exchanges

The structure of commodity exchange in India is classified in two categories—National and Regional. Recognized exchange or association is a place where trading of commodities takes place. At present, there are 5 national commodity exchanges and 16 regional exchanges. Countrywide national exchanges are multi-commodity electronic exchanges with a decentralized ownership pattern. Regional exchanges are permitted to only a limited number of contracts whose membership are usually local based. These commodity exchanges are trading futures contracts in large number of commodities. Important among them are wheat, rice, cotton, soya, bean, ground nuts, groundnut, oil, raw jute, jute goods, caster seeds, sugar, vegetables, metals like gold, silver, steel, copper, nickel, zinc, aluminium, etc. oils and gas, soya oil, spices like *dhaniya*, turmeric, *jeera*, pepper, etc.

### Third-tier

After the establishment of FMC, within a short span of time, the newly set-up multi-commodity exchanges have been able to introduce a number of products with a large volume of turnover in this market. The share volume of trades of various commodities is shown in Table 24.1.

**TABLE 24.1**   Share of Major Commodities Trades (2012–13)

| Sr. No. | Commodities | Volume of Trading ₹ in Lakh (Crores) | % Share (App.) |
|---------|-------------|--------------------------------------|----------------|
| 1 | Bullians | 78.63 | 46% |
| 2 | Energy Products | 37.68 | 22% |
| 3 | Base Metals | 32.60 | 19% |
| 4 | Agricultural Products | 21.56 | 13% |

*Source:* Annual Reports (Forward Market Commission) 2012–2013.

On the analyses of sector-wise development of this market, it is observed that during the 2012–2013, the bullion is the highest traded commodity with 46 percent share value of ₹78.63 lakh crores, follow by energy sector having 22% with ₹37.68 lakh crores. After that metals sector trading share is 19% with a value of ₹32.60 lakh crores, and after that agricultural products trading volume has 13% share with a value ₹21.56 lakh crores.

Among all the commodity exchanges, five exchanges contributes to almost –99.7% of the total values of the commodities traded during the year 2012–2013. There are Multi-Commodity Exchange of India Ltd. (NCX), National Commodity and Derivatives Exchange Ltd. (NCDEX), National Multi-Commodity Exchange of India Ltd. (NMCE), Indian Commodity Exchange Ltd. (ICEX) and ACE Derivatives and Commodities Exchange Ltd. The total volume of trade of these exchanges is shown in Table 24.2

**TABLE 24.2**   Volume Traded of Commodity Exchanges, 2012–13

| Sr. No. | Exchange | Value of Trade (₹ In Crores) | % Share |
|---------|----------|------------------------------|---------|
| 1 | MCX, Mumbai | 1,48,81,057.12 | 87.31 |
| 2 | NCDEX, Mumbai | 15,98425.87 | 09.38 |
| 3 | NMCX, Ahmadabad | 1,76,570,86 | 01.04 |
| 4 | ICEX, Mumbai | 1,69,897.14 | 00.09 |
| 5 | ACE, Ahmadabad | 1,72,010.18 | 01.00 |
|   | Others(app.) | 45,600.00 | 00.26 |

*Source:* Annual Report (Forward Market Commission), 2012–13

It is observed from Table 24.2 that MCX exchange is leading exchange among all the exchanges having 87.3% share of total volume of the traded commodities, followed by NCDEX keeping 9.38% share. About 97% of the total operation is done by these two exchanges, and rest by other. There has been tremendous growth in commodities derivatives market in India in term of volume of trade, number of products offered and technology used in trading.

## SUMMARY

A swap is a bilateral agreement to exchange a series of cash flows between the counterparties at the specified future dates. A commodity swap is an agreement involving the exchange of commodity price payments (fixed amount) against variable price payments (market price), resulting exclusively in cash settlement. Two types of swaps, namely fixed-for-floating and commodity-for-interest are popular in the market. In first case, one party pays the fixed amount and receives the floating amount based upon usually on market price at the settlement date. The counterparty pays the floating amount against the fixed. However, settlement is made on the difference of these payment amounts. In second category of swap, also known as floating-to-floating, one party pays an amount based on a commodity price and receives amount equal to short-term interest rate, plus or minus a fixed spread. The counterparty forks the adjusted jute short-term rate and receives the commodity price.

Commodity options are such contracts which are entered on a specified commodity. Where one party gets the right but no obligation to buy or sell specific quantity of a commodity at an agreed price on or before a particular date. The party which has taken obligation in the option contract will receive a premium from the other party. Trading norms are almost similar in commodity and financial options. Commodity derivatives markets are providing a lot of the opportunities to the concerned participants like producers, wholesalers, retailers as well as to a large number of general investors who are taking the same, as in investment opportunity. Various opportunities like hedging, speculating, arbitraging, etc. are facilitated by the commodities derivatives markets to industrial producers and traders all over the world.

The chapter concentrates on the introductory aspects of commodity derivative markets in order to give a brief view to the investors and traders about the functioning of this market. Commodity derivatives market is a market of future instruments like forwards, futures, swaps, options, etc. traded in the commodities. This is the market where buyers and sellers are contracting for the purchase and sale of the specified commodities at the agreed prices for a delivery at the specified future dates. Four major instruments of derivatives have been briefly described specifically in Indian context.

Commodities market exist in two distinct forms namely the over-the-counter (OTC) market and Exchange Trade Market (ETC). There also exists spot and derivative segment. The spot markets are essentially OTC markets and the participation is restricted to people who are involved with that commodity, say, the farmer processor, wholesaler, producer, etc. Majority of the derivatives trading takes place through exchanges based with the standardized norms.

Futures contracts in commodity are such standard contracts which are initiated on a recognized exchange, in which the parties buy and sell the specified quantity of a specified commodity at specified future date at the agreed price. At present, in India about 113 commodities are listed on various exchanges for future trading purposes. The contract specifications of all these commodities vary in terms of their trading lot size, tick size, quality specification, delivery mechanism, price limits, margin limits, clearing arrangement, settlement procedure, etc. Such norms also vary among exchanges.

A commodity forward contracts is a bilateral OTC contract in which one party buys or sells a commodity at an agreed price at specified future date. The terms of the contract are decided by the parties themselves. These are self-regulatory contracts. In India, Forward Contracts (Regulation) Act, 1952 regulates these forward trading in commodities. It has enacted certain specific norms in this respect. As such, forward contracts have been categorized into transferable specific delivery (TSD), Non-Transferable Specified Delivery (NTSD) and other than specific delivery contracts.

A swap is bilateral agreement to exchange a series of cash flows between the counterparties at the specified future dates. A commodity swap is an agreement involving the exchange of a commodity price payments (fixed amount) against variable price payments (market price) resulting exclusively in cash settlement. Two types of swaps, namely fixed-for-floating and commodity-for-interest are popular in the market. In the first case, one party pays the fixed amount and receives the floating amount based usually on market price at the settlement date. In the second case, the counter pays the floating amount against the fixed. However, settlement is made on the difference of these payments amounts. In second category of swap, also known as floating-to-floating, one party shells an amount based on a commodity's price and receives an amount equal to short-term interest rate plus or minus a fixed spread. The counterparty forks over the adjusted short-term rate and receives the commodity price.

Commodity options are such contracts which are entered on a specified commodity where one party get the right, but no obligation, to buy or sell a specific quantity of a commodity at an agreed price on or before a particular date. The part which has taken obligation in option contract will receive a premium from the other party. Trading norms are almost similar in commodity as well as financial standard options.

Commodity derivatives markets are providing a lot of opportunities to the concerned participants like producers, wholesalers, retailers, as well as to large number of general investors who are taking the same as an investment opportunity. Various opportunities like hedging, speculating, arbitraging are facilitated by the commodities derivative markets to industrial producers and traders all over the world.

## SUGGESTED READINGS

1. Naik, Gopal, and Sudhir Kumar (2001), "Efficiency and Unbiasedness of Indian Commodity Futures Markets", *Indian Journal of Agricultural Economics*, Vol. 56, No. 2, pp. 185–197.
2. Naik, Gopal and Jain Sudhir Kumar (2002), "Indian Agricultural Commodity Futures Market: A Performance Survey", *Economics and Political Weekly*, Vol. 37, No. 30, pp. 3167–3173.
3. Singh, Jatinder Bir (2004), " Futures Market in Management of Price Risks in Indian Agriculture", *Finance India*, Vol. 18, No. 2, pp. 947–952.
4. Ahuja, Narender L. (2006), "Commodity Derivatives markets in India: Development, Regulation and Future Prospective", *International Research Journal of Finance and Economics*, Vol. 1, No. 2, pp. 153–162.
5. Bhattacharaya, Himdari (2007), "Commodity Derivatives Market in India", Economics and Political Weekly, *Money Banking and Finance* vol. 42, No. 13, pp. 1151–1162.
6. Kabra, Kamal Nayan (2007), "Commodity Futures in India", Economics and Political Weekly, *Money, Banking and Finance*, Vol. 42, No. 13, pp. 1163–1170.
7. Dummu, Tata Rao (2009), "Commodity Futures Markets in India: Its Impact on Production and Prices", *Indian Journal of Agricultural Economics*, Vol. 64, No. 3, pp. 333–356.
8. Srivastava, Swami Prakash and Saini, Bhawana (2009), "Commodity Futures Markets and its Role in Indian Economy", *Indian Journal of Agricultural Economics*, Vol. 64, No. 3, pp. 398.
9. Iyer, Vishwanathan and Pillai Archana (2010), " Price Discovery and Convergence in the Indian Commodities Market." Indian Growth and Development Review, Vol. 3, No. 1, pp. 53–61.
10. Kulkarni, B. (2011), "Commodity Markets and Derivatives", Excel Books, New Delhi.
11. Chatnani, N.N. (2012), "Commodity Markets: Operation, Instruments, and Application", Tata McGraw Hill, New Delhi.
12. Annual report, 2012–2013, Forward Markets Commission, Food and Public Distribution, Department of Consumer Affairs, Ministry of Consumer Affairs.

## REVIEW QUESTIONS

1. Explain the term commodity derivatives. Write their features. Explain with examples along with recent developments in this regards.
2. Explain the concept of commodity derivatives. Explain its different types.
3. Distinguish between financial derivatives and commodity derivatives. What are the important applications of commodity derivatives? Explain with examples.
4. Differentiate between OTC derivatives and ETC derivatives with examples.
5. Explain the commodity futures contracts. Explain their common features of trading in Indian context.
6. Explain the trading mechanism of commodity forward contracts with suitable examples in Indian context.
7. Explain the difference between commodity futures and forward contract.
8. Explain the regulatory structure of commodity derivatives market. Also explain its mechanism in India with examples.
9. Explain the term commodity swap. Explain their different types and features with examples.
10. What do you mean by commodity derivatives market? Also explain its historical background along with recent development in this respect.

11. Explain the trading mechanism of commodity swap with suitable illustrations.
12. What do you mean by commodity option contract? Explain its features.
13. Distinguish between options and swap contracts in context to commodity markets. Explain with examples.
14. Explain the various applications of commodity derivatives with illustrations.
15. Explain the hedging strategies in context to commodity derivatives.
16. Explain the investing and speculating opportunities in context to commodity derivatives.

# Annexure-I

## COMMODITIES EXCHANGES ACROSS THE WORLD

### Africa

| Exchange | Abbreviation | Location | Product Types |
|---|---|---|---|
| Africa Mercantile Exchange | AfMX | Nairobi, Kenya | Agricultural, Energy |
| Egyptian Commodities Exchange | EGYCOMEX | Cairo, Egypt | Agricultural, Energy |
| Nairobi Coffee Exchange | NCE | Nairobi, Kenya | Coffee |
| Ethiopia Commodity Exchange | ECX | Addis Ababa, Ethiopia | Agricultural |
| EAST Africa Exchange Rwanda | EAX | Kigali, Rwanda | Agricultural |
| Agricultural Commodity Exchange for Africa | ACE | Lilongwe, Malawi | |
| Auction Holding Commodity Exchange | AHCX | Lilongwe, Malawi | Agricultural |
| Mercantile Exchange of Madagascar | MEX | Antananarivo, Madagascar | Agricultural, Metals, Energy |
| Bourse Africa (previously GBOT) | | Ebene City, Mauritius | Metals, Forex |
| South African Futures Exchange (part of JSE Limited) | JSE | Sandton, South Africa | Agricultural |
| Abuja Securities and Commodity Exchange | ASCE | Abuja, Nigeria | Agricultural products |

### Americas

| Exchange | Abbreviation | Location | Product Types |
|---|---|---|---|
| Brazilian Mercantile and Futures Exchange | BMF | São Paulo, Brazil | Agricultural, Biofuels, Precious Metals |
| Chicago Board of Trade (CME Group) | CBOT | Chicago, United States | Grains, Ethanol, Treasuries, equity index, Metals |
| Chicago Mercantile Exchange (CME Group) | CME | Chicago, United States | Meats, Currencies, Eurodollars, equity index |

| | | | |
|---|---|---|---|
| Chicago Climate Exchange | CCX | Chicago, United States | Emissions |
| Flett Exchange | | Jersey City, United States | Environmental |
| Hedge Street Exchange | | California, United States | Energy, industrial Metals |
| Houston Street Exchange | | New Hampshire, United States | Crude Oil, Distillates |
| Intercontinental Exchange | ICE | Atlanta, United States | Energy, Emissions, Agricultural, Biofuels |
| Kansas City Board of Trade | KCBT | Kansas City, United States | Agricultural |
| Memphis Cotton Exchange | | Memphis, United States | Agricultural |
| Mercado a Término de Buenos Aires | MATba | Buenos Aires, Argentina | Agricultural |
| Mercado a Término de Rosario | ROFEX | Rosario, Argentina | Financial, Agricultural |
| Minneapolis Grain Exchange | MGEX | Minneapolis, United States | Agricultural |
| Nadex Exchange | | Chicago, United States | Energy, industrial Metals |
| New York Mercantile Exchange (CME Group) | NYMEX | New York, United States | Energy, Precious Metals, Industrial Metals |
| U.S. Futures Exchange | USFE | Chicago, United States | Energy |

## Asia

| Exchange | Abbreviation | Location | Product Types |
|---|---|---|---|
| Manila Commodity Exchange | MCX | Manila Philippines | Commodities, Futures Contracts and Options Contracts on various Base Metals, Agriculture Commodities, Energy, and Currencies |
| International Commodity Exchange Kazakhstan | | Almaty Kazakhstan | Industrial and Mineral Products, Oil By-products and Petrochemicals, Agricultural |
| Agricultural Futures Exchange of Thailand | AFET | Bangkok Thailand | Agricultural |
| Bangla Mercantile Exchange | | | |
| Bursa Malaysia | MDEX | Malaysia | Biofuels |
| Cambodian Mercantile Exchange | CMEX | Phnom Penh, Cambodia | Energy, Industrial Metals, Rubber, Precious Metals, Agricultural |
| Central Japan Commodity Exchange | | Nagoya, Japan | Energy, Industrial Metals, Rubber |
| Chittagong Tea Auction | | Chittagong, Bangladesh | Tea |
| Dalian Commodity Exchange | DCE | Dalian, China | Agricultural, Plastics, Energy |

| Dubai Mercantile Exchange | DME | Dubai | Energy |
|---|---|---|---|
| Dubai Gold & Commodities Exchange | DGCX | Dubai | Precious Metals |
| Hong Kong Mercantile Exchange | HKMEx | Hong Kong | Gold, Silver |
| Indonesia Commodity and Derivatives Exchange | ICDX | Indonesia, Jakarta | Agricultural Products, Base Metals, Financial Products |
| Iran Energy Exchange | IRENEX | Tehran, Iran | All energy carriers such as Crude Oil, Petroleum Products, Electricity, Coal... |
| Iran Mercantile Exchange | IME | Tehran, Iran | Industrial and Mineral Products, Oil By-products and Petrochemicals, Agricultural |
| Jakarta Futures Exchange | JFX | Jakarta, Indonesia | Cocoa, Arabica and Robusta Coffee, Precious Metals, Olein, CPO, Coal, Tea, and Rubber |
| Kansai Commodities Exchange | KANEX | Osaka, Japan | Agricultural |
| Commodities & Metal Exchange Nepal Ltd. | COMEN | Nepal | Gold, Silver |
| National Spot Exchange Limited | [NSEL] | Mumbai, India | |
| Nepal Derivative Exchange Limited | [NDEX] | Kathmandu, Nepal | Agricultural, Precious Metals, Base Metals, Energy |
| Mercantile Exchange Nepal Limited | MEX | Kathmandu, Nepal | Agricultural, Bullion, Base Metals, Energy |
| Derivative and Commodity Exchange Nepal Ltd. | DCX | Kathmandu, Nepal | Agricultural, Bullion, Base Metals, Energy |
| Nepal Spot Exchange Limited | NSE | Kathmandu, Nepal | Agricultural, Bullion |
| Indian Commodity Exchange Limited | ICEX | India | Energy, Precious Metals, Base Metals, Agricultural |
| Multi-Commodity Exchange | MCX | India | Precious Metals, Base Metals, Energy, Agricultural |
| National Commodity and Derivatives Exchange | NCDEX | India | Precious Metals, Base Metals, Energy, Agricultural |
| National Multi-Commodity Exchange of India Ltd. | NMCE | India | Precious Metals, Base Metals, Agricultural |
| Chamber of Commerce, Hapur | COC | India | Agricultural |
| Ace Derivatives & Commodity Exchange Ltd. | ACE | India | Agricultural |
| Bhatinda Om & Oil Exchange Ltd. | BOOE | India | Agricultural |

| Universal Commodity Exchange | UCX | India | Agricultural, Energy, Precious Metals |
|---|---|---|---|
| Pakistan Mercantile Exchange | PMEX | Pakistan | Precious Metals, Agricultural Products, Crude Oil, Interest Rate Future |
| Shanghai Futures Exchange | | Shanghai, China | Industrial metals, Gold, Petrochemicals, Rubber |
| Shanghai Gold Exchange | | Shanghai, China | Precious Metals |
| Singapore Commodity Exchange | SICOM | Singapore | Agricultural, Rubber |
| Singapore Mercantile Exchange | SMX | Singapore | Precious Metals, Base Metals, Agricultural, Energy |
| Uzbek Commodity Exchange | UZEX | Tashkent, Uzbekistan | Metals, Crude Oil Products, Chemicals, Base Oils, LPG and Polyethylene, Sugar, Agricultural, etc. |
| Tokyo Commodity Exchange | TOCOM | Tokyo, Japan | Energy, Precious Metals, Industrial Metals, Agricultural |
| Tokyo Grain Exchange | TGE | Tokyo, Japan | Agricultural |
| Zhengzhou Commodity Exchange | CZCE | Zhengzhou, China | Agricultural, PTA |
| Vietnam Commodity Exchange | VNX | Ho Chi Minh city, Vietnam | Coffee, Rubber, Steel |
| Buon Ma Thuot Coffee Exchange Center | BCEC | Buon Ma Thuot, Vietnam | Coffee |
| Mongolian Agricultural Commodity Exchange | MCE | Ulaanbaatar city, Mongolia | Agricultural |

## Europe

| Exchange | Abbreviation | Location | Product Types |
|---|---|---|---|
| APX-ENDEX | APX-ENDEX | Amsterdam, Netherlands | Energy |
| Trieste Commodity Exchange | BMTS | Trieste, Italy | Agricultural |
| Commodity Exchange Bratislava, JSC | CEB | Bratislava, Slovakia | Emissions, Agricultural, Diamonds |
| Climex | CLIMEX | Amsterdam, Netherlands | Emissions |
| Deutsche Börse/Eurex | DBAG/EUREX | Frankfurt, Deutschland | Agricultural, Metals, ETCs, Commodities Index |
| European Climate Exchange | ECX | London, UK | Emissions |
| European Energy Exchange | EEX | Leipzig, Deutschland | Power, Natural Gas, Emissions, Coal |
| Energy Exchange Austria | EXAA | Vienna, Austria | Energy, Emissions |

| Commodities Investment Exchange | COINVEX | London, England | Oil & Gas, Mining, Renewable Energy |
| Integrated Nanoscience & Commodity Exchange | INSCX | United Kingdom | Nanomaterial |
| London Commodity Exchange | LCE | London, UK | Agricultural |
| Nasdaq Commodities | | Oslo, Norway | Power, Natural Gas, Emissions, Freight, Iron Ore |
| Nord Pool Spot | | Oslo, Norway | Power, Energy |
| NYSE Liffe | LIFFE | Europe | Agricultural |
| London Metal Exchange | LME | London, UK | Industrial Metals, Plastics (Delisted in 2011) |
| Power Exchange Central Europe | PXE | Prague, Czech Republic | Power |

## Oceania

| Exchange | Abbreviation | Location | Product Types |
|---|---|---|---|
| Australian Securities Exchange | ASX | Sydney, Australia | Agricultural, Energy, Interest Rate Future |
| ABX Global | ABX | Brisbane, Australia | Precious Metals |

# Annexure-II

## REGULATION OF COMMODITY DERIVATIVES MARKET

The provisions of Part I (excluding Section 132) and Part II of Chapter VIII of the Finance Act, 2015 came into force w.e.f. September 28, 2015 and the provisions of Section 132 of the Act came into force w.e.f. September 29, 2015 in terms of Central Government Notifications F. No. 1/9/SM/2015 S.O. 2362 (E) and F. No. 1/9/SM/2015 S.O. 2363 (E) dated August 28, 2015.

As a result, Securities and Exchange Board of India (SEBI) commenced regulating the commodity derivatives market under Securities Contracts Regulation Act (SCRA), 1956 with effect from September 28, 2015 and the Forward Contracts Regulation Act (FCRA), 1952 got repealed with effect from September 29, 2015.

To fulfil this additional responsibility of regulating the commodity derivatives market, SEBI has created the following additional departments/divisions:

| S.No. | Department | | Division |
|-------|-----------|------|----------|
| 1 | Commodity Derivatives Market Regulation Department (CDMRD) | (i) | Exchange Administration |
| | | (ii) | Market Policy |
| | | (iii) | Risk Management and Products |
| | | (iv) | Exchange Inspection and Complaints against Exchanges |
| 2 | Market Intermediaries Regulation & Supervision Department (MIRSD) | (i) | Commodity Derivatives Division – 1 |
| | | (ii) | Commodity Derivatives Division – 2 |
| 3 | Integrated Surveillance Department (ISD) | (i) | Commodity Derivatives Division – 1 |
| | | (ii) | Commodity Derivatives Division – 2 |
| 4 | Investigations Department (IVD) | (i) | Commodity Derivatives Division |
| 5 | Department of Economic Policy and Analysis (DEPA) | (i) | Commodity Research (Agriculture) |
| | | (ii) | Commodity Research (Non Agriculture) |
| 6 | Legal Affairs Department (LAD) | (i) | Division of Policy and Regulatory Affairs for Commodity Derivatives |
| | | (ii) | Division of Regulatory Assistance for Commodity Derivatives |
| 7 | Enforcement Department (EFD) | (i) | Enforcement Division for Commodity Derivatives – 1 |
| | | (ii) | Enforcement Division for Commodity Derivatives – 2 |

The organizational structure of SEBI and the functions of departments/divisions is available on SEBI website.

Part I of the Finance Act, 2015 provides that "All rules, directions, guidelines, instructions, circulars, or any like instruments, made by the Commission or the Central Government applicable to recognized associations under the Forward Contracts Act shall continue to remain in force for a period of one year from the date on which that Act is repealed, or till such time as notified by the Security Board, whichever is earlier, as if the Forward Contracts Act had not been repealed."

The Act also provides that all recognized associations under FCRA shall be deemed to be recognized stock exchanges under the SCRA. Accordingly, the following recognized associations shall be deemed to be recognized stock exchanges under SCRA, w.e.f. September 28, 2015:

| S.No. | Name of the Exchange |
|-------|----------------------|
| 1 | Ace Derivatives and Commodity Exchange Limited, Mumbai |
| 2 | Bombay Commodity Exchange Ltd., Vashi |
| 3 | Chamber Of Commerce, Hapur |
| 4 | Cotton Association of India, Mumbai |
| 5 | India Pepper & Spice Trade Association, Kochi |
| 6 | Indian Commodity Exchange Limited, New Delhi |
| 7 | Multi-Commodity Exchange of India Ltd., Mumbai |
| 8 | National Commodity & Derivatives Exchange Ltd., Mumbai |
| 9 | National Multi-Commodity Exchange of India Ltd., Ahmedabad |
| 10 | Rajkot Commodity Exchange Ltd., Rajkot |
| 11 | Spices and Oilseeds Exchange Ltd., Sangli |
| 12 | Universal Commodity Exchange Ltd., Navi Mumbai |

# SECTION VII

# Financial Derivatives— Miscellaneous Issues

# Chapter 25

# Accounting and Taxation of Derivatives

## LEARNING OBJECTIVES

*After reading this chapter, students will be able to*

➤ Understand the concept of accounting treatment of derivative transactions.
➤ Be aware of the problems involved in accounting treatment.
➤ Know the methods involved in accounting treatment.
➤ Be aware of the problems of conventional accounting.
➤ Know the hedge accounting and CFTC concept of hedging.
➤ Understand the derivative transactions for accounting purposes.
➤ Know the accounting practice of derivative transaction which can be classified into three categories: (a) specific hedge transaction, (b) general hedge transaction and (c) trading transaction.
➤ Understand the FASB accounting standard on derivatives and in this respect salient features of FAS-133.
➤ Be aware of the Guidance Note of ICAI on derivatives issued in 2015.
➤ Understand the tax treatment of derivatives in India.
➤ Be aware of the tax treatment of specific instruments like forwards, futures contracts, options, warrants, caps, collars, floors, swaps, etc.
➤ Know the general accounting issues relating to financial derivative instruments like IAS 39,32 and Statement of Financial Accounting Standard (SFAS) 133—Accounting for derivative instruments and hedging activities.

## 25.1 INTRODUCTION

Over the last three decades, the trading in derivatives instruments has grown in multifold, however, the accounting framework for these instruments has not kept pace with the rising complexities in the financial markets. It is still relatively new and in a constant process of evolution. Though, some accounting standards have been framed by various institutions but still there is no uniform standard accounting practice for derivative instruments as a whole. Due to the disparity in the level of capital market developments across the world, there is no unanimity on precise accounting treatment of different derivative transactions. Even undeveloped countries like USA, UK and Japan, there are standards for some of the simpler and older derivatives but these are still inadequate for the huge array of existed instruments now.

In this section two aspects on derivative transaction will be examined. The first aspect will concentrate on the methods used and problems involved in accounting treatment. The second aspect will look at the tax treatment of the said instrument transactions under the Income Tax Law in India.

## 25.2 ACCOUNTING TREATMENT OF DERIVATIVE TRANSACTIONS

Accounting for foreign exchange derivatives is guided by AS-11 on 'Accounting for the effect of changes in foreign exchange rates'. The Institute of Chartered Accountants of India has recently issued a Guidance Note on Accounting for Equity Index Futures.

According to International Accounting Standard (IAS) 39 para 10, "a derivative is a financial instrument:

(a) whose value changes in response to the change in a specified interest rate, security price, commodity price, foreign exchange rate, index of prices or rates, a credit rating or credit index or similar variable (sometimes called the underlying);

(b) that requires no initial net investment or little initial net investment relative to other types of contracts that have a similar response to changes in market conditions; and

(c) that is settled at a future date."

The definition of derivative as per FASB 133 and IAS 39 is more or less same. Typical examples of derivatives are futures and forward, swap and option contracts. One of the definition of a derivative is that it requires little initial net investment relative to other contracts that have a similar response to market conditions. An option contract meets that definition because the premium is significantly less than the investment that would be required to obtain the underlying financial instrument to which the option is linked.

Forward contracts in India are in operation for last number of years, mainly to control or to manage the foreign exchange rate risk. That from 1996, cross currency options are also allowed. After that from August 1996, interest rate swaps, currency swaps, purchase of interest rate swap and collars and forward rate agreements have also been allowed. Rupee-based derivatives are also allowed since August 1997, resulting into 5-year forward contract, which were originally available for only six months. Further since June 2000, options and futures trading in equities and stock index have also been commenced at National Stock Exchange and Bombay Stock Exchange.

Following are some important guiding standards on which accounting treatment of derivative transactions are followed:

## 25.2.1  International

- IAS 39: Financial Instruments: Recognition and Measurement (1998)
- IAS 32: Financial Instruments: Disclosure and Presentations (1996)

## 25.2.2  USA

- Statement of Financial Accounting Standards (SFAS) 33
- Accounting for Derivative Instruments and Hedging Activities (1998)
- Some other standards which deal with the other aspects of the Financial Instruments, such as the following:

  (a) SFAS 52: Foreign currency translation lays down the rules for hedging through the interbank forward market but it is used for all currency related derivatives by a process of analogy.

  (b) SFAS 80: Accounting for Futures Contracts, is used for guidance for many other derivatives which are not futures contracts.

  (c) SFAS 105: Disclosure of information about financial instruments with off-balance sheet risk and financial instruments with concentrations of credit risk.

  (d) SFAS 107: Disclosure about Fair Value of Financial Instruments

  (e) SFAS 119: Disclosure about Derivative Financial Instruments and Fair Value of Financial Instruments

  (f) Exposure draft: Reporting financial instruments and certain related assets and liabilities at fair value.

## 25.2.3  UK

Financial Reporting Standard 13 (FRS): Derivatives and other Financial Instruments Disclosures.

The discussion on accounting treatment in this section is based Primarily upon the International Accounting Standard No. 32 and the Statement of Recommended Practice of the British Bankers Association which reflect prevailing generally accepted practice and was also cited by the Sodhani Working Group. The detailed description of all the accounting standards mentioned above are beyond the scope of this chapter. Only important relevant aspects of accounting concerning financial derivatives will be discussed in this chapter. As discussed above, still the accounting treatment of derivative transactions is in its infancy and no unanimity all over the world. At one end of the spectrum are countries, which have established authoritative guidance on accounting standards, on the other hand, countries that have yet to develop accounting standards for derivative financial instruments beyond equity and bond instruments. Some underdeveloped countries have given reference to international accounting standards (IAS) or those standards originating from the advanced capital markets, such as US and UK for guidance to limit the divergence of accounting practices.

## 25.3  PROBLEMS WITH CONVENTIONAL ACCOUNTING

Conventional accounting principles do not specifically describe the accounting treatment of derivative financial instruments (Derivatives Financial Instruments DFI) and their risk reducing effects of a hedge. For example, as per accounting convention of conservatism or prudence, stocks are to be valued at the lower of cost or market value (net realizable value). A firm may hold stocks of a particular material (say particular specification of steel strips) and the price of the steel might have fallen in the market. Assume that the firm has simultaneously have hedged against the fall in price by selling steel strips at the particular exchange. In conventional accounting the unrealized loss on such steel stock will have to be reflected in terms of lower stock valuation in both profit and loss account as well as in balance sheet of the firm. As a result, the profit figure of the company will be reduced. On the other hand, the gain (unrealized) on futures transaction on such material will not be shown, because as per above accounting convention, the unrealized gain cannot be shown. Hence, in these circumstances, the conventional accounting may not show the exact position of the firm.

Three important problems are prevailing in the conventional accounting like mixed attribute method, selective recognition method and existence method. As per mixed attribute method, it uses a variety of measurement attributes for assets and liabilities. For examples, when a firm has two exposures to a change in prices that perfectly offset each other but are measured using different attributes; one at the cost and the other at fair value. Hence, the position presented by the balance sheet and the income statement will not portray the net economic impact of the change in price as nil.

The recognition differences arise from the selective recognition inherent in the current accounting. As observed, in the above example of two exposures, one is recognized in the financial statement whereas second one is not recognized. In case of existence difference, it arises when a firm enters into a derivative transaction because the firm anticipates that an offsetting exposure will arise in the future. In brief, all the three difficulties arise due to current accounting model.

## 25.4    HEDGE ACCOUNTING

In order to meet the growing challenges caused due to growing financial instruments in accounting, the International Accounting Standard Committee has come out with an Accounting Standard IAS-32 exclusive for disclosure and presentation of financial instruments, which has been implemented on January 1, 1996. The objective of the standard is to enhance understanding of the significance of on-balance sheet and off-balance financial instruments of a firm's financial position, performance and cash flows.

Hedge accounting can be defined as a method of accounting, for hedge instruments and other underlying hedged items, which reflects the reduction in exposure to risk. In other words, it refers to a special accounting treatment of a hedge, in which the counter balancing nature of changes in the values of the hedge instrument and the underlying hedged items is taken into account. So it differs from conventional accounting system. Under the hedge accounting system, the unrealized gain or loss on futures offset transactions will be recognized. Now, the question arises when is it appropriate to use hedge accounting? In other words, on which dates and time, transaction is qualified for hedge accounting. Before discussing the issue, let us see a rigorous formal definition of hedging as given by CFTC of USA.

## 25.4.1    CFTC Definition of Hedging

An exhaustive and detailed definition of hedging is provided by the Commodity Futures Trading Commission of the USA. This definition is reproduced in full:

**(1) General definition:**   Bonafide hedging transactions and positions shall mean transactions or positions in a contract for future delivery on any contract market, where such transactions or positions normally represent a substitute for transactions to be made or positions to be taken at a later time in a physical marketing channel, and where they are economically appropriate to the reduction of risks in the conduct and management of a commercial enterprise, and where they arise from:

(i) The potential change in the value of asset which a person owns, produces, manufactures, processes, or merchandises or anticipates owning producing, manufactures, processes, or merchandising.

(ii) The potential change in the value of services, which a person provides, purchases or anticipates providing or purchasing.

Notwithstanding the foregoing, no transactions or positions shall be classified as bonafide hedging unless their purpose is to offset price risks incidental to commercial cash or spot operations and such positions are established and liquidated in an orderly manner in accordance with sound commercial practices and unless the provisions of paragraphs (2) and (3) given below have been satisfied.

**(2) Enumerated hedging transactions:** The definition of bonafide hedging transactions and positions in paragraph (1) of this section includes, but is not limited to, the following specific transactions and positions:

(i) Sales of any commodity for future delivery on a contract market which do not exceed in quantity: (a) Ownership or fixed price purchase of the same cash commodity by the same person and (b) Twelve months' unsold anticipated production of the same by the same person provided that no such position is maintained in any future during the five last trading days of that future.

(ii) Purchases of any commodity for future delivery on a contract market which do not exceed in quantity: (a) The fixed price sale of the same cash commodity by the same person, (b) The quantity equivalent of fixed piece sales of the cash products and by-product of such commodity by the same person and (c) Twelve months unfilled anticipated requirements of the same cash commodity for processing, manufacturing or feeding by the same person, provided that such transactions and positions in the five last trading days of any one future do not exceed the person's unfilled anticipated requirements of the same cash commodity for that month and for the next succeeding month.

(iii) Sales and purchases for future delivery described in paragraphs (2) (i) and 2 (ii) of [this section] may also be offset other than by 1 the same quantity of the same cash commodity, provided that the fluctuations in value of the position for future delivery are substantially related to the fluctuations in value of the actual or anticipated cash position, and provided that the position in any one future shall not be maintained during the five last trading days of that future.

**(3) Non-enumerated cases:** Upon specific request made, the Commission may recognize transactions and positions other than those enumerated in paragraph (2) of this section as bonafide hedging in such amounts and under such terms and conditions as it may specify. Such transactions and positions may include, but are not limited to, purchases or sales for future delivery on any contract market by an agent who does not own or who has not contracted to sell or purchase the offsetting cash commodity at a fixed price, provided that the person is responsible for the merchandising of the cash position which is being offset.

It is observed from the CFTC definition of hedging, it emphasizes more on regulatory aspect rather than accounting context. It is focused as illustration and guide, rather as an authority for accounting purposes.

## 25.5   DERIVATIVE TRANSACTIONS FOR ACCOUNTING PURPOSES

For the purpose of accounting the financial instruments can be classified into two categories:

1. On-balance sheet financial instruments
2. Off-balance sheet financial instruments

The definition of a financial instrument as per IAS 32, "A financial instrument is any contract that gives rise to both a financial asset of one enterprise and a financial liability or equity instrument of another enterprise."

A **financial asset** is any asset that is:

(a) cash

(b) a contractual right to receive cash or another financial asset from another enterprise

(c) a contractual right to exchange financial instruments with another enterprise under conditions that are potentially favourable

(d) an equity instrument of another enterprise

A **financial liability** that is a contractual obligation:

(a) to deliver cash or another financial asset to another enterprise

(b) to exchange financial instruments with another enterprise under conditions that are potentially unfavourable

An equity instrument is any contract that evidences a residual interest in the assets of an enterprise after deducting all of its liabilities.

Monetary financial assets and liabilities (also referred to as monetary financial instruments) are financial assets and financial liabilities to be received or paid in fixed or determinable amounts of money.

*Fair value* is the amount for which an asset could be exchanged or a liability settled between knowledgeable, willing parties in arms length transaction.

*Market value* is the amount obtainable from the sale or payable on the acquisition, of a financial instrument in an active market.

Financial instruments give rise to a number of accounting and reporting issues. These issues relate to recognition, measurement and disclosure. Financial instruments include both primary (basic) as well as derivative instruments. The financial instruments which are shown on balance sheet are called on the balance sheet or basic financial instrument such as receivables, bonds, capital stock, etc. They meet the conventional accounting definitions of assets, liabilities and owner's equity.

Off-the-balance sheet instruments also called as financial derivative instruments like futures contracts, forward contracts, option contracts, swap arrangements, etc. These instruments, whether recognized or unrecognized, meet the definition of a financial instruments, and accordingly, are subject to this standard IAS 32. The derivative financial instruments create rights and obligations that have the effect of transferring between the parties to the instrument one or more of the financial risk inherent in an underlying primary financial instruments. Further, derivative instruments do not result in a transfer of the underlying primary instruments on inception of the contract and such a transfer does not necessarily take place on maturity of the contract.

## 25.6   ACCOUNTING PRACTICE OF DERIVATIVE TRANSACTIONS

The accounting practice depends upon the nature of derivative transactions, for this purpose, the transaction can be classified into following three categories:

**Specific hedge transaction:** Specific hedge transaction refers to that which can be identified with a specific asset, liability or commitment at the time of execution of the hedge transaction. For example, a company is due to make one million dollar to a foreign company in six months time as payment for goods supplied. It is worried that the dollar may appreciate against the rupee in the Interim. For this, the company may enter into a forward exchange transaction for one million dollar. This transaction will be called as a specific hedge.

**General hedge transaction:** A general hedge transaction may refer to such transaction, which does not identify particular asset or liability or commitment, rather it used to cover broad risks for the entity as a whole. For example, assume that a company is an importer of various raw materials from different countries. As a result, the company may have to make payment in one or more than one currencies. In such case, the company may guard itself against rupee currency depreciation against other currencies. As a general protective strategy not backed by specific import purchases, it enters into a forward transaction for one million dollar. This is called a *general hedge*.

It should be further noted that some transactions might fall in a grey area between specific and general hedges. In such case, unless there is a specific anticipated transaction, of known volume and timing, prudence would indicate classification as a general hedge.

**Trading transaction:** The trading transactions refer to such transactions which are of speculative or arbitrage nature or transactions undertaken by financial market intermediaries (like banks, brokers) for whom derivatives are regular business. In other words, hedging transactions done by bankers, brokers, speculators, arbitrageurs, etc. are general trading transactions. For example, assume that a company is not a regular exporter but a manufacturing company with predominantly domestic business may think that it can earn good profits by sale and purchase of particular currencies like dollars and pounds. It enters into a forward transaction for this purpose. This is a trading transaction.

## 25.7 SYNTHETIC ALTERATIONS

Sometimes, it is difficult to say that a particular transaction is of hedging nature or somewhat else. Instead the purpose may be synthetically alternator of the asset or liability. This is generally in case of swap transactions. For example, a currency swap entered into for the purpose of exploiting interest differentials cannot be exactly called a hedge since it is not intended as a reduction of risk. As such, it is the synthetic alteration of an asset or a liability in one currency into liability or asset in another currency.

Further as per the accounting concept of 'substance over form', the substance of the asset or liability is more important than its form. Therefore, any synthetic alteration should be accounted and reflected in the accounts. For all practical purposes, synthetic alterations should be considered as if they were specific hedges.

## 25.8 CRITERIA FOR QUALIFYING SPECIFIC HEDGE

It is observed that the hedge accounting can be used for specific hedges. So, it is essential that a particular transaction must be qualified as specific hedge transaction. For this, certain further conditions must be met which are asunder:

1. The transaction should have been designated as a hedge at the time it was entered into.
2. The transaction should reduce exposure to the identified.
3. The transaction should have a high level of price correlation with the hedged item.

It should be further noted that if the criterion of advance identification is not insisted upon, companies may be able to disguise speculative transaction as hedges on an ex-post facto basis. In brief, whether a particular transaction is a hedge or not, there must be clear written evidence that the transaction was into as a hedge which aims at to reduce the firm's risk or exposure to adverse changes against its assets, liabilities or position. If the transaction does not meet the above criteria then it should be treated as trading transaction.

## 25.9   ACCOUNTING PRACTICE

After the above observations, the appropriate accounting treatment of various transactions are as follows:

### 25.9.1   Specific Hedges

The treatment of specific hedge transaction in accounting records should be the same as the treatment used for the underlying exposure. For example, if the underlying exposure is valued at cost then the hedge too will be at the cost. Further, if the underlying exposure will affect profit or loss for more than one year, the effect of the hedge should be spread over a matching number of accounting years. If the underlying exposure is marked-to-market, the same treatment should be with the hedge.

If the underlying asset in a specific hedge transaction is carried at lower of cost or market value. The market value should include the market value (i.e. net open or loss) on the hedge instrument. The market value of the asset and the hedge are aggregated and treated as one composite market value. Then this composite market value is compared with the cost (book value) and the lower of the two is adopted. This valuation process has explained by an example as follows:

**EXAMPLE:**   A company holds stock of one quintal of silver with a book value of ₹7.5 lakhs (cost) at the rate of ₹7,500 per kg. Its accounting year ends on December 31. It hedges the same by selling January silver futures. It wants to know the correct stock valuation for balance sheet purposes in each of the following scenarios:

1. Sale of futures at ₹7,300 per kg, market price on balance sheet date is ₹7,200 per kg.
2. Sale of futures at ₹7,700 per kg, market price on balance sheet date is ₹7,200 per kg.
3. Sale of futures at ₹7,700 per kg, market price on balance sheet date is ₹8,000 per kg.

**Scenario 1**

| I | Market value of stock | ₹ 7,20,000 |
|---|---|---|
| | Open gain on future (7,300 – 7,200) | ₹ 100 per kg |
| | Composite market value | ₹ 7,30,000 |
| | Cost | ₹ 7,50,000 |
| | So, balance sheet value | ₹ 7,30,000 (lower of the cost or market) |
| II | Market value of stock | ₹ 7,20,000 |
| | Open gain on futures (7,700 – 7,200) | ₹ 500 per kg |
| | Composite market value | ₹ 7,70,000 |
| | Cost | ₹ 7,50,000 |
| | So, the balance sheet value | ₹ 7,50,000 (lower of the two) |

*(Contd.)*

(Contd.)

| III | Market value of stock | ₹ 8,00,000 |
|-----|------------------------|------------|
| | Open loss on futures (8,000 – 7,700) | ₹ 300 per kg |
| | Composite market value | ₹ 7,70,000 |
| | Cost | ₹ 7,50,000 |
| | Hence, balance sheet value | ₹ 7,50,000 (lower of the two) |

*Note:* Composite market value is the same as the sale price of the futures.

In hedge accounting, there will be deferred gain or deferred loss on the hedge instrument, depending upon the market value on the balance sheet date. These deferred amount will be taken to the profit and loss account as and when the asset or liability is sold or liquidated, till then these would be shown in the balance sheet as notional assets (for a deferred loss) or notional liabilities (for a deferred gain). Further, if the hedged asset or liability is carried even after the hedge position is closed out then the realized gain or loss should be used to adjust the cost of the asset.

## 25.9.2 Swap Transactions (Synthetic Alterations)

Swap may be used for hedging purposes. So swap may be entered into as hedges or as synthetic alterations of the nature of the asset or liability. So the net result due to swap contract may result as hedge accounting which can also be attained by simply treating the asset/liability as if it were actually a different asset/liability in the altered form ignoring the pre-swap position. They should be valued at the swap rate. So a rupee loan taken and then swapped for a pound loan would be accounted for as if it were a pound loan.

For example, if a firm has taken floating rate loan and has swapped for fixed rate then for the accounting purposes, the instrument would be treated as being a fixed rate liability and the fixed rate (swap rate) be used. Further the cost of this arrangement and other costs incurred on swap deal should be recognized over the life of the swap.

## 25.9.3 General Hedge Transactions

General hedge transactions for all accounting purposes should be treated as trading transactions. Their accounting treatment is stated as follows:

**Trading transactions:** Any derivative instrument used as a trading transaction should be recorded in accounting records on marked-to-market basis. It means that it has to be valued at market value, and resultant capital gains or losses must be taken into the profit and loss account for the current period as part of earnings. In other words, not only realized gains and losses but also unrealized gains and losses will be accounted for at the end of each accounting period. As mentioned earlier, general hedge transactions and swap transactions not meeting the criteria of specific hedge will also be accounted for marked-to-market basis. Further an entry acting as an intermediary may buy or sell a derivative and soon after re-sell/buy at a profit, such intermediary transactions have to be marked-to-market, as in the case of trading transactions.

## 25.10 ACCOUNTING ENTRIES

Tables 25.1 and 25.2 give a set of illustrative accounting entries for futures and options transactions. The entries are based on the Statement of Recommended Practice (SORP) of the British Bankers' Association (BBA) as general guidelines.

**TABLE 25.1** Accounting Entries for Futures Transactions

| Note ref. | Issue | Methodology | |
|---|---|---|---|
| | | **Hedge accounting**[*] | **Trading transaction** |
| 1. | Treatment of original margin payment | Dr. Original margin | Dr. Original Margin |
| | | Cr. Cash | Cr. Cash |
| 2 (a). | Variation margins payment | Dr. Variation margin | Dr. Losses on trading |
| | | | (P and L A/c) |
| | | Cr. Cash | Cr. Cash |
| 2 (b). | Variation margins receipts | Dr. Cash | Dr. Cash |
| | | Cr. Variation margin | Cr. Gains on trading |
| | | | (P and L A/c) |
| 3. | Refund of original margin | Dr. Cash | Dr. Cash |
| | | Cr. Original margin | Cr. Original margin |
| 4. | Open loss at end of period | Dr. Deferred loss on hedge | — |
| | | Cr. Variation margin | |
| 5. | Open gain at end of period | Dr. Variation margin | — |
| | | Cr. Deferred gain on hedge | |
| 6. | Amortization of deferred gains | Dr. Deferred gains on hedge | — |
| | | Cr. Concerned A/c | |
| | | (P and L A/c) | |
| 7. | Amortization of deferred losses | Dr. Concerned A/c | — |
| | | (P and L A/c) | |
| | | Cr. Deferred losses on hedge | |

*Notes:*

1. This is treated as a deposit.
2. These are margins payable/receivable when the futures contract losses/gains in market value, from the initial level. For trading transactions these are straightaway debited/credited to profit and loss on the 'mark-to-market' principal. For hedge accounting transactions, the margin is treated as deposit/reversal of deposit.
3. Reversal of 1 above.
4. This entry will record the open loss to the extent required under hedge accounting norms.
5. Same as 4 above.
6. The amount deferred under 5 above will be credited to profit and loss in various accounting periods in proportion to the underlying exposure, e.g., if the underlying is a stock, then in proportion to disposal thereof, if it is an interest bearing instrument, in proportion to interest received, etc.
7. The amount deferred under 6, is debited to profit and loss (in proportion to the underlying exposure) in various accounting periods.

---

[*] If the underlying exposure is 'marked-to-market' then the accounting for the hedge will be identical to a trading transaction.

**TABLE 25.2** Accounting Entries for Options Transactions

| Note ref. | Issue | Methodology | |
|---|---|---|---|
| | | **Hedge accounting**[**] | **Trading** |
| (a) | Options bought | | |
| 1. | Option premium payment | Dr. Option premium | Dr. Option expenses |
| | | (P and L A/c) Cr. Cash | Cr. Cash |
| 2. | Recognition of premium (for amount attributable to each period during life of option) | Dr. Option expenses (P and L A/c) Cr. Option premium | — |
| 3. | Realized gain on expiry/disposal | Dr. Cash | Dr. Cash |
| | | Cr. Deferred gain on hedge | Cr. Option gains (P&L A/c) |
| (b) | Option written | Option written | Dr. Cash |
| 4. | Option premium receipt | Cr. Option premium recd. | Cr. Option gains (P&L A/c) |
| 5. | Recognition of premium income | Dr. Option premium received | — |
| | | (on maturity of the option) | Cr. Deferred gain on hedge |
| 6. | Original margin (Payment) | Dr. Original margin | Dr. Original margin |
| | | Cr. Cash | Cr. Cash |
| 7 (i) | Variation margin (Payment) | Dr. Variation margin | Dr. Option expenses |
| | | Cr. Cash | (P and L A/c) |
| (ii) | Variation margin (Receipt) | Dr. Cash | Dr. Cash |
| | Cr. Variation margin | Cr. Option gains | (P&L A/c) |
| 8. | Realized loss on option written | Dr. Deferred loss on hedge | — |
| | | Cr. Variation margin | |
| 9. | Original margin refund | Dr. Cash | Dr. Cash |
| | | Cr. Original margin | Cr. Original margin |
| 10. | Amortization of deferred loss | Dr. Concerned A/c (P&L) | — |
| | | Cr. Deferred loss on hedge | |
| (c) | Common for options bought and written | | |
| 11. | Amortization of deferred gain | Dr. Deferred gain on hedge | — |
| | | Cr. Concerned A/c (P&L) | |

*Notes:*

1. For hedges, this is treated as a prepaid expenses, to be recognized over the life of option. For trading transactions, it is expensed out immediately.

2. See 1 above. The unrecognized balance as a prepaid expenses carried forward to the next period.

3. The gain is deferred, to be recognized (amortized) in proportion to recognition of the underlying exposure—see note 9 below.

4. Treated as a liability for hedges, till recognized. For trade transactions, treated as income straightway.

---

** If the underlying exposure is marked-to-market then the accounting for the hedge will be identical to trading transactions.

5. Recognition of premium as an income (only on maturity of option).
6. Treated as deposit/return of deposit.
7. Treated as deposit/return of deposit for hedges, and as expense/income for trade transactions.
8. Loss deferred for subsequent amortization in proportion to underlying exposure.
9. Return of deposit.
10. Recognized in proportion to underlying exposure.
11. As in 10 above.

## 25.11 FASB'S ACCOUNTING STANDARD ON DERIVATIVES

The Financial Accounting Standard Board (FASB) has constructed a standard FAS No. 133 with effect from January, 1999 entitled Accounting for Derivative Instruments and Hedging Activities. The standard deals exclusive with derivatives. The FASB defines the fair value as:

**Fair value:** The amount at which an asset/liability could be bought (incurred) or sold (settled) in a current transactions between willing parties that is other than in a forced or liquidation sale. Quoted market prices in active markets are the best evidence of fair value and should be used as the basis of measurement, if available. If a quoted price is available, the fair value is the product of the number of trading units times that market price. For most practical purposes, the fair value is the same as market value.

### 25.11.1 Summary of the FAS 133 Salient Features

1. All the derivatives must be recognized as assets or liabilities and taken to the balance sheet at fair value. In other words, all the derivatives must be marked-to-market with gains and losses taken into account in each accounting period.
2. Hedge accounting will be allowed for hedges, which fulfills strict criteria, broadly the same as mentioned earlier in this chapter. However, hedge accounting will be in such a way that the accounting for the hedged asset/liability will match that for the derivative.
3. Gains or losses incurred on derivatives and firm commitments will be recognized, in the profit and loss accounts, subject to off-setting the corresponding change in the budgeted asset/liability.
4. Gains/losses on hedges on forecasted futures transactions (anticipated hedges) will be taken initially as other comprehensive income in the profit and loss account.
5. The degree to which the hedge offset the risk must be checked personally.

### 25.11.2 Accounting of Derivatives Instruments in India

As discussed earlier, accounting for derivatives is guided by AS 11 in India. The Institute of Chartered Accountants of India has recently issued a Guidance Note on Accounting for Equity Index futures. In this respect, we will discuss the accounting mechanism for forward contracts, interest rate swaps, currency swaps, currency options and stock index futures.

**Forward contract:** A forward contract is a contractual arrangement in which one party buys and other party sells designated assets at a forward rate mutually agreed upon the date of contract for delivery at designated future date. Forward contracts in India are allowed for long. Para 13 of Accounting Standard 11, Accounting for effects of changes in foreign exchange rates deals with accounting treatment of forward contract. Any enterprise may enter into a forward contract to establish the amount of reporting currency required or available at settlement date of a transition will be considered income or expense over the life of contract except in same cases.

**EXAMPLE:** Suppose CIPLA Ltd. needs $3,00,000 on May 1, 2001 for repayment of loan in settlement and interest. On December 1, 2000, it appears to the company that the dollar may be dearer as compared to the exchange rate prevailing on the date, say $1 = ₹43.50. Accordingly, CIPLA Ltd. may enter into a forward contract with a banker for $3,00,000. The forward rate may be higher or lower than the spot rate prevailing on the date of forward contract. Let us assume forward rate as on December 1, 2000 was $1 = ₹44 spot rate of ₹43.50. As on future date, i.e., May 1, 2001, banker will pay CIPLA Ltd. $3,00,000 at ₹44 irrespective of spot rate on that date. In this example, CIPLA Ltd. gained ₹2,40,000 by entering into a forward contract. Payment to be made as per forward contract is ($3,00,000 × ₹44) = ₹1,32,00,000 and amount payable if forward contract has not been in place ($3,00,000 × ₹44.80) = ₹1,34,40,000. So gain arising out of forward contract is ₹2,40,000. The treatment of AS 11 for the transaction gain or loss to profit and loss account for non-fixed assess interns in the line with FASB 133 Para 18(d). AS 11 further suggests that profit/loss arising on cancellation of renewal of a forward exchange should be recognized as income or loss for the period.

**Interest rate swap:** Interest rate swap is allowed in India. Swap is basically a financial contract. This involves exchange of one set of payment (which is obligation of other party 'B'). The interest rate swap involves the exchange of one interest rate payment with other interest rate payment where the principal amount is denominated in the same currency.

"The IRS can be as outrace between two parties (called counterparties) to exchange on a particular date in the future, one series of cash flows (variable or floating interest) in the same currency on the same principal for an agreed period of time."

Accounting treatment of interest rate swap can be explained with the help of following example:

Suppose ISGEC, a manufacturing firm, which wants to borrow 5-year fixed rate rupee funding to finance its expansion project. Its credit rating is not very high. It is BBB. It finds that it will have to pay interest @ 11 percent if it borrows at fixed rate. In the floating rate market, it can issue floating rate note at margin of 0.75 percent. Over the prime rate which is 10 percent. On the other hand, TISCO a large unit is lacking for floating rate note but finds that it will have to pay prime rate, which is in the fixed rate market. It can raise 5-year funds at 9.5 percent due to AAA rating and BBB rating is 150 bp in fixed rate segment and 75 bp in floating rate segment. This differential is thrown as quality spread differential. The above can be summarized as follows:

| | ISGEC (BBB) | TISCO (AAA) |
|---|---|---|
| Requirements | Fixed rate | Floating rate |
| Cost of fixed loan | 11% | 9.5% |
| Cost of floating rate | Prime rate + 0.75% | Prime rate (10%) |

So, ISGEC though interest in fixed rate loan, it is advised to go for floating rate which will be 0.25 percent lower than fixed rate. Similarly TISCO, even though it is interested in floating rate team, it is advisable for it to go for fixed rate as it is 9.5 percent lower than floating rate. Both the company can raise a loan the way it is cheaper and then they may enter it swap through an intermediary (Swap bank). Suppose bank pays fixed rate to TISCO @ 9.5 percent which TISCO will pass on to a lender and ISGEC will effectively pay a floating rate of prime rate −0.25 percent (9.75) to bank. So effective cost for ISGEC will be 9.75 percent. Simultaneously, swap bank will pay prime rate −0.25 percent to ISGEC Ltd. which they will pass on to floating rate lender by adding it (as the cost is prime rate + 0.75%) and they will charge a fixed rate of 9.75 percent. So affection cost for TISCO will be 10.75 percent, which is again 0.25 percent lower than the field rate loan raised from the market and swap bank will also have net gain of 0.25 percent. The accounting entries in the books of TISCO Ltd. will be

| 1. | At the time of borrowing: | (₹) | |
|---|---|---|---|
| | Cash | 1,00,00,000 | |
| | To loan | | 1,00,00,000 |
| 2. | **Interest liability for six months will be** | | |
| | Interest | 47,50,000 | |
| | To financial institution | | 47,50,000 |
| | Financial institution | 47,50,000 | |
| | To cash | | 47,50,000 |
| | Interest | 48,75,000 | |
| | To swap bank | | 48,75,000 |
| | Swap bank | 48,75,000 | |
| | To cash A/c | | 48,75,000 |
| | Swap bank | 47,50,000 | |
| | To interest | | 47,50,000 |
| | Cash | 47,50,000 | |
| | To swap bank | | 47,50,000 |

According to para 57 of IAS 32, "An enterprise provides information concerning its exposure to the effects of future changes in the prevailing level of interest rates".

**Currency swap:**    In a currency swap, the two payments streams being exchanged are denominated in two different currencies.

Usually, an exchange of principal amount at the beginning and re-exchange at termination are features of currency swap. The principal amounts are equal at the currency market rate. A typical currency swap situation is explained in the following illustration:

| Requirements | Corp. (AUST) FRF funding | Corp. (FREN) AUD funding |
|---|---|---|
| Cost of AUD funding | 15% | 16% |
| Cost of FRF funding | 11% | 10% |

In their home currencies each company has a 1 percent borrowing advantage. Corp. AUST for example can borrow AUD @ 15 percent or 1 percent below Corp. FREN. Similarly Corp. FREN can borrow FRF @ 10 percent which is 1 percent below the cost to Corp. AUST. It is this relative advantage that allows currency swap to materialize. The currency swap process is as follows:

1. Corp. FREN borrows FRF @ 10 percent and Corp. AUST borrow AUD @ 15 percent.
2. The two companies then exchange the debt with each other so that Corp. AUST has FRF debt @ 10 percent and Corp. FREN has AUD debt @ 15 percent.

Each party reduces its borrowing cost by 1 percent. However, it is difficult for most corporations and government borrowers to locate others that want to do an off-setting transaction at the same time and for the same amount. They also face credit risk with each other. Under the circumstances swap deals will be entered into through a bank. In exchange of services to be rendered, bank will take part of the savings involved in the swap. Consequently, the net savings of the swap for Corp. AUST and Corp. FREN will be less than 1 percent.

Let us assume that spot FRF/AUD exchange rate is 5 FRF per 1 AUD. A deal based on 100 million AUD is executed. In order for swap to work, it is essential that the amount be of the same value. In the above case, 500 million FRF issue is needed to work the swap. Let us further assume that both corporations are raising funds in their own currencies, Corp. FREN, after raising the FRF loan, enters into a swap with bank within turn, will allow Corp. AUST to use FRF loan @ 10.20 percent. Simultaneously, the bank will allow Corp. FREN to use AUD debt @ 15.20 percent. Thus, effectively both of them will be saving 0.80 percent. The transactions can be summarized as follows:

| Time | Transaction | Corp. FREN | Bank | Corp. AUST |
|------|-------------|------------|------|------------|
| 0 | Original loan | 500 million | — | — |
| | FREN to bank | (500) million | 500 million | — |
| | Bank to AUST | — | (500) million | 500 million |
| 1 | Interest payments: | | | |
| | AUST to bank | — | 51 million | (51) million |
| | Bank to FREN | (50) million | (50) million | — |
| | FREN to investor | (50) million | — | — |
| | In terms of AUD: | | | |
| 0 | Original loan | — | — | 100 million |
| | AUST to bank | — | 100 million | (100) million |
| | Bank to FREN | 100 million | (100) million | — |
| 1 | Interest payments: | | | |
| | FREN to bank | (15.2) million | 15.2 million | — |
| | AUST to investor/lender | — | (15) million | 15 million |
| | Initial borrowing: | | | |
| | Cash | — | 500 million | — |
| | To FRF loan | — | — | 500 million |
| | FRF loan | — | 500 million | — |
| | To cash (For FRF loan passed to intermediary/swap bank) | — | — | 500 million |
| | Cash | 500 million | — | — |
| | To AUD loan (For AUD loan received from intermediary/swap bank) | — | — | 500 million |
| | Interest on AUD loan | 76 million | — | — |
| | To cash (Interest payment of 15.2 million AUD @ 5 FRF) | — | 76 million | — |
| | Cash | 50 million | — | — |
| | To interest on FRF loan (int. receipt from swap bank) | — | 50 million | — |
| | Interest on FRF loan | 50 million | — | — |
| | To cash (Int. payment to investor) | — | 50 million | |

In addition to the above entries entered for the purpose of transaction, the fair value of the loan is also likely to change. Therefore, to the extent that the fair value of the loan will be affected on account of currency swap, entries should also be passed, which will be on similar lines as for the interest rate swap. Moreover, at the end of the term of the debt, re-exchange of the debt with the swap bank will also be required and this should also be recorded as per the normal principles of accounting.

**Currency options:**   Currency options provide the corporate treasurer another tool for hedging foreign exchange risk arising out of the firm's operations. Unlike forward contract options allowing the hedger to gain from favourable exchange rate movements, currency options are frequently suggested as an appropriate hedging tool because one can remove downside risk without limiting the upside potential. Options can be put option or a call option. A put option is a contract that specifies the currency that the holder has the right to sell. This can better be explained with the help of an illustration.

In late February, an American Importer anticipates a yen payment of JPY 100 million to a Japanese supplier sometime in late May. The current USD/JPY spot rate is 0.007739 (which implies that JPY/USD rate of 129.22). A June yen call option on the Philadelphia Exchange with the strike price of $0.0078 per yen is available for a premium of 0.0108 cents per yen or $0.000108 per yen. A contract is for JPY 6.25 million. Premium per contract is therefore, $0.000108 × 62,50,000 = $675. The firm decides to purchase 16 calls for a total premium of $10,800. In addition, there is a brokerage fee of $20 per contract. Thus, total expenses in buying the options is $11,120. The firm has, in effect, ensured that its buying rate for yen will not exceed – $0.0078 + (11,120/10,00,00,000) = $0.0079112 per yen. The yen depreciates to $0.0075 per yen in late May when the payment becomes due. The firm will not exercise the option. It can sell 16 calls in the market, provided the resale value exceeds the brokerage commission it will have to pay. Therefore, price per yen is $0.075 + $0.0001125. If yen appreciates then the firm will exercise option.

**Stock index futures:**   Stock index futures are instruments where the underlying variable is a stock index future. Both the Bombay Stock Exchange and the National Stock Exchange have introduced index futures in June 2000 and permit trading on the Sensex Futures and the Nifty Futures respectively. Recently, the Institute of Chartered Accountants of India has issued the Guidance Note on Accounting for Equity Index Futures which deals with accounting treatment of equity index futures from the viewpoint of the parties who enter into such futures contracts as buyers or sellers.

## 25.12   GUIDANCE NOTE ON ACCOUNTING FOR DERIVATIVE CONTRACTS GN(A) 33 (ISSUED 2015)

In order to bring uniformity among the accounting practices followed by the entities in India concerned with the accounting for derivative contracts and hedging activities, the Institute of Chartered Accountants of India (ICAI) issued a Guidance Note of accounting derivative contracts on May 12, 2015. It will become applicable for accounting periods on or after April 1, 2016. A few important features of this Note have been presented asunder:

**(A) Introductory Background:**   A brief history of authorizing guidance on derivative accounting in India is stated in brief before the description of this Guidance Note.

   (i) In the year 2007, the ICAI issued Accounting Standard (AS)-30 on Financial Instruments: Recognition and Measurement, and AS-31 on Financial Instruments: Presentation. These were recommendatory in nature from April 1, 2009 for an initial period of 2 years. Further, these were to become mandatory in respect of accounting periods on or after April 1, 2011.

(ii) In March, 2008, the ICAI issued an announcement relating to accounting of derivatives. According to it, if an entity did not follow AS-30, keeping in view the principle of prudence as stated in AS-I, Disclosure of Accounting Policies, the entity was required to provide for losses in respect of all outstanding derivative contracts at the balance sheet date by making them to market.

(iii) In case of forward contracts to which AS-11 the Effects of Changes in Foreign Exchange Rates (revised 2003) applied the entity needs to fully comply with the requirements of AS-11.

(iv) In the year 2008, AS-32 Financial Instruments: Disclosures was issued by the ICAI, which was also recommendatory initially, and was to become mandatory in respect of accounting periods commencing on or after April 1, 2011.

**(B) Scope of the Guidance Note**

1. The said Guidance Note covers all such derivative contracts which are not covered by an existing Accounting Standards. However, it will not apply to (a) foreign exchange forward contracts covered under AS-11, and (b) derivatives which are covered by regulations to sector specific or specified set of entities.

2. Specified entities like banking, non-banking, finance companies, housing finance companies and insurance companies are required to follow the accounting treatment for derivatives contracts, as prescribed by their Regulators.

3. It will provide guidance on accounting of assets covered by Accounting Standard (AS-2), valuation of Inventories (AS-10), Accounting for Fixed Assets (AS-13), Accounting for Investment, etc.

4. This Guidance Note applies to following derivatives contracts whether or not used as hedging product:
   (i) Foreign exchange forward contracts of highly probable forecast transactions.
   (ii) Cross currency interest rate swaps, foreign currency futures, options and swaps if not in the scope of AS-11.
   (iii) Traded equity index futures, traded equity index options, traded stock futures and other option contracts, and
   (iv) Commodity derivative contracts.

**(C) Definition of Derivatives:**   As per this Note, a derivative is a financial instrument or contract with all the three following characteristics:
   (i) Its value changes in response to change in interest rate, price of financial instrument and commodity, foreign exchange rate, index of price or rates, credit rating or credit index, etc.
   (ii) It requires no initial investment or very smaller to others
   (iii) It is settled at a future date.

**(D) Key Accounting Principles:**   The accounting for derivatives covered by this Note, is based on the following key principles:

1. These should be recognized on the balance sheet and measured at fair value.

2. If any entity decides not to use Hedge Accounting, then it should account for its derivatives at fair value, and any changes be recognized in profit and loss statement.

3. If any entity decides to apply hedge accounting, then it should clearly identity its risk management objective, measuring of derivatives and respective documents in this respect.

4. An entity may decide to use hedge accounting for derivatives not included as part of hedge accounting, then it will apply the principles at (1) and (2) as above.

5. Adequate disclosure of accounting policies, risk management objectives and hedging activities should be made in its financial statements.

**(E) Synthetic Accounting not permitted:**   This guidance note does not permit synthetic accounting which means accounting of combining a derivative and the underlying together as a single package. For example, if any entity has foreign currency of borrowing and hedging by cross-currency interest rate swap, it would require to recognize the loan liability separately from the cross-currency swaps, and not treat them as a package (synthetic accounting) as INR loan.

**(F) Recognition of derivatives on the balance sheets at fair value:**

- This note requires that all derivatives are to be recognized at the balance sheets and measured at fair value.

- Fair value represents the 'exit price', i.e., the price that would be paid to transfer a liability, or the price that would be received when transferring an asset to a knowledgeable, willing counterparty. They should be presented as current and non-current form in the balance sheet.

## 25.13   TAX TREATMENT OF DERIVATIVES

Taxation of derivatives is perhaps as complex exercise as the transaction itself. A number of issues arise out of these transactions to which there are no well-defined answers. The legal analysis of derivatives is fundamental to understanding its taxation. Several questions arise about characterization of income, treatment of the derivative and the underlying transaction. The issues get more intricate in the context of cross-border transactions. Characterization of income assumes greater importance as most of the tax treaties exempt 'business income' or 'income' from taxation in the source country unless there is a permanent establishment. The lack of international consensus on taxation could lead to multiple taxation of a derivative transaction.

IFA has published a comparative study of taxation of derivatives in about 29 countries. As per the study, there are three basic approaches to taxation of derivatives:

1. **Decomposition** principle under which every derivative transaction is analyzed into a number of cash flows, each of which can be separately valued and taxed.

2. **Separate transaction** principle under which each derivative contract is looked at in isolation to establish an overall return on investment.

3. **Linked approach** under which the related transactions are clubbed together to analyze the overall profit of the entire transaction.

## 25.13.1   Tax Treatment of Derivatives in USA

The statutory provisions relating to gains or losses incurred on derivative instruments are different from country to country, and further, they differ on as per nature of the instrument. For example, in USA, the definition of a hedge transaction for tax purposes is different from that for accounting purposes. The tax regulations define a hedging transaction as a transaction entered into the normal course of business activity for one of the following reasons:

1. To reduce the risk of price changes or currency fluctuations with respect to property that is hold or to be held by the taxpayers for the purposes of producing ordinary income.

2.  To reduce the risk or interest rate changes or currency fluctuations with respect to borrowings made by the taxpayers.

Under the tax regulations of USA, the gains or losses from the hedging transactions are treated as ordinary income. The timing of the recognition of gains or losses from the hedging transactions usually matches the timing of the recognition of income or deduction from the hedged items.

**TABLE 25.3**    Comparison of Accounting Treatment for Derivative Instruments

| US standard (FAS 133 and 52) | International standards (IAS 39) | Indian standards (AS 11 and guidance notes) |
|---|---|---|
| 1. Cover all the derivatives with widely applicable definitions | Cover all the derivatives with widely applicable definition | AS 11 cover forward exchange contracts; guidance notes cover equity index futures and options and Equity stock option with specific and narrow definition |
| 2. Fair value accounting for derivatives that are not used for hedging | Fair value accounting for that are not used for hedging | |
| 3. Fair value accounting for both the derivatives and hedged item used for a fair value hedge | Fair value accounting for both the derivatives and hedged items used for a fair value hedge | Gain or loss on foreign currency forward to be charged to earnings of the current year, |
| 4. Securities held-to-maturity or available-for-sale also to be disclosed at fair value if hedged through a derivative instrument for a fair hedge | Securities held-to-maturity or available-for-sale also to be disclosed at fair value if hedged through a derivative instrument for a fair hedge | loss on equity index futures: (Cumulative debit in mark-to-market margin) to be charged to earnings of the current year profits (credit balance) to be deferred till maturity of the contract; losses on equity index/stock option (decrease in the value of the premium in the market) to be charged to earnings of the current year-mark-to-market premium and net gains on it to be deferred till maturity of the contract. |
| 5. The portion of the value of a derivative which is effective in hedging a future cash flow to be disclosed in the earnings of the year in which the hedged cash flow takes place [unrecognized firm commitments included in fair value hedge] | The portion of the value of a derivative which is effective in hedging a future cash flow to be disclosed in the earnings of the year in which the hedged cash flow takes place [unrecognized firm commitments included in cash flow hedge] | |
| 6. The portion of the value of a derivative which is ineffective in hedging charged to the earnings of current year | The portion of the value of a derivative which is ineffective in hedging charged to the earnings of current year | No hedge accounting allowed No hedge accounting allowed No hedge accounting allowed No hedge accounting allowed |
| 7. Gain or loss on foreign currency forwards involving a foreign currency hedge allowed to be deferred till the related foreign currency transaction takes place (FAS52) | No special treatment of foreign currency forward contract: gain or losses to be treated as for any other derivative | Premium or discount at the inception of a forward contract for hedging foreign currency commitment to be amortized over the life of the contract. |
| 8. The portion of the gain or loss on a derivative effective in hedging foreign currency exposure of a net investment in foreign operation allowed to be deferred till the sale or liquidation of the investment in the foreign operation | The portion of the gain or loss on a derivative effective in hedging foreign currency exposure of a net investment in foreign operation allowed to be deferred till the sale or liquidation of the investment in the foreign operation | Gain or loss on the forward (with respect to the exchange rate on the date of inception) as well as the hedged item to be charged to earnings of current year like a fair value hedge (AS 11) No hedge accounting allowed |

*Source: The Chartered Accountant,* September 2003 issue.

## 25.14 TAXATION OF DERIVATIVES IN INDIA

Derivative transactions are still in growing stage in India and their tax implications are still to be tested by the Indian revenue authorities. There are no precedents directly on the subject. Margins in a swap transaction are extremely narrow. Therefore, the imposition of taxes by the country of the payer substantially alters the profitability of a swap.

### 25.14.1 General Provision Under the Income Tax Act

Indian residents are subject to tax on their worldwide income. Non-residents, on the other hand, are taxed only on income received by them in India or income that accrues or arises to them in India. Further, under certain conditions, income can be 'deemed to accrue or arise in India' and thereby be subject to tax in India. Generally, the entire tax payable by a non-resident in respect of income earned in India is liable to be withheld at source.

### 25.14.2 Taxation Under the Income Tax Act

Section 9 of the Income Tax Act covers situations under which income which can be 'deemed to accrue or arise in India'. Under Section 9(1)(i) of the I-T Act, all income accruing or arising, through or from any business connection/property/asset or source of income in India, is deemed to accrue or arise in India. Only such part of the income as is reasonably attributable to the operations carried out in India can be deemed to accrue or arise in India. Unlike in the United Kingdom, the Indian tax laws do not specifically distinguish between 'doing business in India' and 'doing business with India'. The term 'business connection' which is crucial to determination of taxable business income in India, is not statutorily defined. Therefore, this term is to be understood based on interpretation provided by courts. In general, it can be interpreted as a continuous relationship between a business carried on by a non-resident entity, which yields profits or gains and some activities (in India) which contribute directly or indirectly to the earning of these profits or gains.

Whether payments under derivative transactions would constitute 'Income deemed to accrue or arise in India' is a question which can be dealt with only facts of a specific transaction. The I-T Act does not specifically deal with the tax incidence of income flows arising out of a derivative transaction. Indian courts have also not analyzed the taxation of such income. Though there are no direct cases on the point, courts have opined on the taxability of profits/losses arising to an assesse merely due to the appreciation or depreciation in the value of foreign currency held by it. The position adopted by courts has been that such profits/losses would ordinarily be trading profit/losses if the foreign currency is held by the assesse in revenue account or as a trading asset or as part of circulating capital. If, on the other hand, the foreign currency is held by the assessee as a capital asset or as fixed capital, such profit or loss would be of capital nature (*Sutlej Cotton Mills* v. *CIT* (1979) 116 ITR 1, *State Bank of Travancore* v. *CIT* (1986) 158 ITR 102).

Section 10(15)(iv) of the I-T Act exempts certain types of interest payments from taxation in India. The Finance Act, 1999 has enlarged the scope of the word 'interest'. Now, interest includes hedging transaction charges on account of currency fluctuation. This would mean that any payment made for hedging against foreign currency rate fluctuations in respect of foreign currency debt obligation may be exempt from taxation in India.

## 25.15  TAX TREATY PROVISIONS

India has tax treaties with a number of countries. Indian tax law is unique as it statutorily offers a tax payer choice between the provisions of the treaty and the domestic tax law under Section 90(2) of the I-T Act. The effect of this section is that, a tax-payer may opt for the treaty or I-T Act, whichever is more beneficial for him.

Most comprehensive treaties give the country of source the right to tax business income only if the recipient has a Permanent Establishment (PE) in the country of source. PE is a much narrower concept than 'business connection'. Therefore, many foreign parties, which may have a 'business connection' in India by virtue of having the counterparty in India and source of income in India, may not have a PE in India. This distinction is so crucial that the entire income, which could be taxable under the first concept, could be tax exempt under the other one. In the absence of a permanent establishment in India, the business income arising out of the derivative transactions made by the Indian payer, will not be subject to tax in India.

Even if a PE is found to exist, only such part of the business income, which is attributable to the permanent establishment, can be taxable in India. Such income is taxable on 'net' basis after deduction of certain expensed. While foreign companies are taxed at the rate of 48 percent, domestic companies are taxed at the rate of 35 percent on such business profits. The Non-discrimination Article in some of the tax treaties may help to reduce the tax incidence from 48 percent to 35 percent.

For giving effect to the treaty provisions, reliance will have to be placed by the Indian counterparty on the payee representations. The payee may have to provide evidence that it qualifies for the relevant exemption from withholding taxes. The Indian counterparty can withhold the tax at the rates in force.

Non-residents are eligible for applying for an advance ruling which is available on an existing or a proposed transition on questions of law or facts. These rulings are binding upon the applicant and the tax authorities. Such a ruling may help the foreign counterparty to determine the relevant tax implications in India.

## 25.16  WITHHOLDING TAX

In a cross-border Derivatives Financial Instruments (DFI) transaction, withholding tax is a crucial question as the traders want their cash flows free of taxes. Most countries have regarded payments under derivative contracts as falling outside 'interest' and 'dividend' articles as they do not reflect the true return on capital. The same principle should apply to payments of differences on futures contracts, swap fees and premiums on options. Most of these payments fall within 'business profits' or 'other income' articles, and therefore, are remitted gross free of withholding taxes. The taxation is determined in the country of residence.

In India, the position is slightly different. Section 195(1) of the I-T Act entrusts the payer with the liability to withhold tax on certain payments being made to a foreign recipient. An issue arises with respect to withholdings under Section 195 that whether the payer has to deduct tax on the gross amount of payments due to the non-resident or on the income or profit element received by the non-resident. The Supreme Court has authoritatively settled this issue in the case of *Transmission Corporation of AP Ltd.* vs. *CIT*. The Apex Court has held that the scheme under Section 195 of the ITA applies not only to the amounts that bear an element of income or profit, but also to gross sums, the whole of which may not be income or profit of the recipient.

In order to obtain an exemption from withholding any tax or for withholding tax at a lower rate, the payer/payee will have to file an application with the Assessing Officer to determine the appropriate portion of the sum that should be chargeable to tax. However, it should be noted that a certificate granted in this regard is only provisional. Final tax liabilities are ascertained upon regular assessment after a tax return is filed (if necessary).

It is pertinent to note that in case of a banking company, exemption from withholding taxes is available only of the payments (not classified as interest in securities or dividend) are received by the branch operating in India, on its own account and are not received on behalf of the head office or any other branch situated outside India.

Thus, the Indian payer making payments to overseas parties under a derivative transaction is generally liable to withhold tax at source. The procedure for obtaining this lower tax withholding certificate has been recently simplified. Now, based on a Chartered Accountant's certificate, the Indian payer can remit the payment after withholding tax at the lesser rate applicable under the treaty or without withholding any tax, as the case may be. However, it has to submit an undertaking that it shall undertake to pay the shortfall in tax, interest or penalty, which are payable in accordance with the provisions of I-T Act.

## 25.17   GROSS-UP OF TAX

Under the terms of the International Swap Dealers Association (ISDA) Master Agreement, the payer has to bear the burden of withholding taxes, where the tax is payable because of a connection with its chosen tax jurisdiction (i.e., India). The burden to bear the taxes falls upon the payee only in limited circumstances where the payee has made a representation which is not true at the time it is made or which becomes untrue as a result of subsequent events or where the payee fails to conform to a provision in the ISDA Master Agreement requiring performance of a tax-related obligation.

In India, however the payer will have to comply with the provisions of Section 195 of the I-T Act read together with Circular number 370 issued by the Central Board of Direct Taxes. These require that when the payer bears the income tax liability, the calculation of tax to be withheld at source should be made with reference to the 'net-of-tax' amount payable to the non-resident payee but should be made with reference to the gross amount. This provision may further affect the profitability of a derivative transaction in India.

## 25.18   TAX TREATMENT OF SPECIFIC DERIVATIVES IN INDIA

### 25.18.1   Forwards

There are no specific rules governing the taxation of Forward Rate Agreements (FRAs) in India. The Derivatives Financial Instruments (DFIs) market in India is in a nascent stage and consequently been fully determined. The comments below regarding the taxation treatment of forwards are based upon the application of general principles to the Derivatives Financial Instruments (DFI).

**Accessibility/Deductibility of forward contracts:**   Settlement payments under FRAs are generally deductible/assessable on a due and payable basis. However, during the period between the commencement and termination of the Derivatives Financial Instruments (DFIs), profits/losses may be recognized on a mark-to-market basis.

**Application of mark-to-market taxation:**   The law is unclear in regard to the application of mark-to-market taxation. However, the application of mark-to-market taxation is increasingly perceived as the most attractive method and as a consequence, gains/losses on commodity forward contracts, and FRAs are likely to be recognized over the period of the Derivatives Financial Instruments (DFIs) on a mark-to-market basis.

**Settlement payments treated as interest:**   Settlement payments under an FRA are not treated as interest.

**Non-resident issues:**   Settlement payments under an FRA may be subject to withholding tax if attributable to a PE (in treaty countries) or if arising or received in India (in non-treaty countries). Recently, Derivatives Financial Instruments (DFI) payments have been exempted from withholding tax in specific circumstances.

**Other taxes:**   Settlement payments under an FRA are not subject to value-added or other taxes.

## 25.18.2   Futures Contracts

There are no specific rules governing the taxation of futures contracts in India. The Derivatives Financial Instruments (DFIs) market in India is in a nascent stage and consequently the accounting, regulatory and taxation situations relating to Derivatives Financial Instruments (DFIs) have not yet been fully determined. The comments below regarding the taxation treatment of futures contracts are based upon the application of general principles to the Derivatives Financial Instruments (DFIs).

**Taxation of profits/losses of futures contracts sold/purchased on trading account:**   Where a corporate enters into a futures contract for the purposes of hedging only (except cases for the purpose of speculating in commodities), gains/losses arising are dictated by the nature of the underlying transaction. If the underlying transaction is on revenue account (for example, loans taken to purchase raw materials), the gains/losses would also be on revenue account. However, in the case of financial institutions, being authorized dealers, futures contracts would be expected to be always on trading account, and accordingly gains/losses would be on revenue account. However, in practice, it is unlikely that financial institutions will have gains/losses in most Derivatives Financial Instruments (DFIs) since they are expected to have back-to-back or mirror transactions with overseas financial institutions in the Derivatives Financial Instruments (DFIs) they offer. In practice, the only income expected to arise to the local authorized dealers out of futures contracts offered by them to the corporates, is a booking fee for making the market.

**Taxation of profits/losses when futures contracts are closed out:**   As mentioned above, if the underlying transaction is on revenue account (for example, loans taken to purchase raw materials), the gains/losses would also be on revenue account. On the other hand, if the underlying transaction is on capital account (for example, loans taken to purchase fixed assets) then the gains/losses would be adjusted against the capital cost. However, in the case of financial institutions, being authorized dealers, futures contracts would be expected to be always on trading account and accordingly gains/losses would be on revenue account. However, in practice, it is unlikely circumstances that financial institutions will have gains/losses in most Derivatives Financial Instruments (DFIs) since they are expected to have back-to-back or mirror transactions with overseas financial institutions in the Derivatives Financial Instruments (DFIs) they offer. In practice, the only income expected to arise to the local authorized dealers out of futures contracts offered by them to the corporates, is a booking fee for making the market. Taxation of refundable deposits or margin payments received or paid margin payments are assessable/deductible if they are not refundable. In the case of corporates entering into futures for the purpose of hedging, the treatment of margin payments is dictated by the nature of the underlying transaction.

**Non-resident issues:** Payments to a non-resident under a futures contract are subject to withholding tax only if the profits are attributable to a PE (in treaty countries) or the payment arises or is received in India (in non-treaty countries). Recently, Derivatives Financial Instruments (DFI) payments have been exempted from withholding tax in specific circumstances. Other taxes payments under futures contracts will not be subject to value-added or other taxes.

## 25.18.3    Options, Warrants, Caps, Collars and Floors

There are no specific rules governing the taxation of these Derivatives Financial Instruments (DFI) contracts in India. The Derivatives Financial Instruments (DFI) market in India is in a nascent stage and consequently the accounting, regulatory and taxation situations relating to Derivatives Financial Instruments (DFIs) have not yet been fully determined. The comments below regarding the taxation treatment of options, warrants, caps, collars and floors are based upon the application of general principles to the Derivatives Financial Instruments (DFIs).

**Accessibility/deductibility of premium payments:** Premiums relating to equity options and equity warrants are generally assessable/deductible on an accrual basis. The premium received/paid up-front may be spread over the life of the Derivatives Financial Instruments (DFI). The only exception is in the case of a corporate entering into an option/warrant to hedge its investment in equity. The payments may not be deductible in the hands of the corporate, since dividends from shares are currently exempt in the hands of shareholders. In that event, arguably, the payments may be added to the cost of the investment and a deduction claimed at the time of disposal of the shares for computing capital gains. Similarly, the receipts may be reduced by the cost of the investment.

Premiums paid/received in relation to commodity option contracts, foreign currency options and interest rate caps, collars and floors, are generally deductible/assessable on an accrual basis. Premiums paid in advance may be spread over the life of the Derivatives Financial Instruments (DFI).

*Timing of payments* (When an option lapses, is exercised or settled). Settlement payments are generally deductible/assessable on a due and payable/receivable basis. However, during the period between the commencement and termination of the Derivatives Financial Instruments (DFIs), profits/losses may be recognized on a mark-to-market basis.

**Application of mark-to-market taxation:** The law is unclear in regard to the application of mark-to-market taxation. However, the application of mark-to-market taxation is increasingly perceived as the most attractive method and as a consequence, gains/losses on options, warrants and interest rate caps, collars and floors are likely to be recognized over the period of the Derivatives Financial Instruments (DFIs) on a mark-to-market basis.

**Treatment of refundable deposits/margins:** Margin payments are assessable/deductible if they are not refundable. In the case of corporates entering into options, warrants or interest rate caps, collars and floors for the purpose of hedging, the treatment of margin payments is dictated by the nature of the underlying transaction. Specific issues for low-exercise price options (LEPOs), the tax treatment afforded to LEPOs does not differ from the treatment afforded to other options.

**Non-resident issues:** Derivatives Financial Instruments (DFI) payments should not generally be regarded as interest but as business profit. Withholding tax will apply only if the profits are attributable to a PE (in treaty countries) or if arising or received in India (in non-treaty countries). Recently, Derivatives Financial Instruments (DFI) payments have been exempted from withholding tax in specific circumstances.

**Other taxes:**   Payments under options, warrants and interest rate caps, collars and floors are not subject to the value-added or other taxes.

## 25.18.4  Swaps

Taxation of swap payments is fairly complicated. The issue involved is one of characterization of the settlement amount. The characterization of the amount could be either business income or interest income. There is a strong case for the swap payment to constitute business income in hands of the non-resident recipient as against interest income or other income.

Under the I-T Act, the term 'Interest' is defined under Section 2(28A) to mean interest payable in any manner in respect of money borrowed or debt incurred (including deposits, claim or other similar right or obligation) and includes any service fee or other charge in respect of the money borrowed or debt incurred or in respect of any credit facility which has not been utilized.

In a swap transaction, there is no money borrowed or debt incurred. The principal of a swap deal is the notional amount and the adjustment takes place between the bank and the counterparty in respect of the amounts payable by them. Only the net amount changes hands. Therefore, such amounts should qualify as trading income. However, in a synthetic transaction, where the deal is structured in a manner where there is a debt incurred and the payment is made in respect of debt incurred, such payment could be regarded as 'interest'. In the Indian context, such situations may be the practical reality faced by the Indian corporate who are forced to enter into synthetic transactions. The consequences may be different in a cross-border transaction, especially where the non-resident counterparty is from a treaty jurisdiction.

Article 11(3) of the Organization for Economic Cooperation and Developments (OECD) Model Convention defines interest as:

"The term interest as used in this Article means **income from debt-claim**" of every kind, whether or not secured by mortgage and whether or not carrying a right to participate in the debtor's profits, and in particular, income from government securities and income from bonds and debentures. Penalty charges for late payment shall not be regarded as interest for this purpose.

Thus, even the definition of OECD Model Convention (**OECD MC**) lays emphasis on the debt-claim. The commentary to OECD MC also supports the above argument.

Thus, it can be concluded that, as long as the underlying 'debt-claim' remains purely hypothetical, the equalization payment is not interest. The fact that the swap was created, to secure the payments on a loan does not change the payment into interest. However, if one party pay a lump sum amount to the other and the same is repaid over the course of the swap (an off-market swap), the return and equalization payments could be seen to contain a loan element.

If these amounts were to be treated as interest, they may attract a withholding tax in India at the rate of 20 percent on the gross amount. This rate could be reduced further depending upon the tax treaty provisions. If a foreign company earns any business income that is deemed to accrue or arise in India, it would be liable to be taxed at the current applicable rate of 48 percent on its net business income.

For this purpose, first of all, let us explain the definition of 'Hedging and Speculation' under the Indian Income Tax Act. Section 43(5) of the Indian Income Tax Act, defines a speculative transaction as:

A transaction in which a contract for the purchase or sale of any commodity, including stocks and shares, is periodically or ultimately settled otherwise than by the actual delivery or transfer of the commodity or scripts.

**Accessibility/deductibility of swap payments:**    Periodic payments/receipts and premiums under equity swaps, swap options, etc. are generally deductible/assessable for tax purposes. However, in the case of corporates entering into such Derivatives Financial Instruments (DFI) for the purpose of hedging their investments in equities, the situation may be slightly different. Dividends from shares are currently exempt from tax in the hands of shareholders. Therefore, payments made for earning the dividend may not be deductible for tax purposes. In this case, arguably, the payments may be able to be added to the cost of investments and the necessary deduction claimed, yet only while computing capital gains on the transfer of such shares. Similarly, receipts under the swap may be reduced by the cost of investment. However, in the event that the shares are held on trading account (that is, as stock in trade), the payments/receipts will be deductible/assessable in the hands of the corporates for tax purposes. Periodic payments/receipts under an interest rate swap agreement are deductible/assessable on an accrual basis provided the transaction was not entered into to hedge a transaction on capital account. Where the purpose of the swap was to hedge a transaction on capital account, the payment/receipt can be added to/deducted from the cost of the asset. Taxation of gains and losses arising from non-periodic payments (for example, principal exchange at maturity). In relation to interest rate swap and FX swaps agreements, gains/losses arising from non-periodical payments are tax neutral, unless the gain/loss arises due to foreign exchange fluctuation. In this case, the gains/losses are assessable. In the case of financial institutions, or as far as corporates are concerned, the tax treatment depends on the nature of the underlying transaction.

**Specific issues for swaps:**    The Derivatives Financial Instruments (DFIs) is viewed as an asset which the counterparty will not actually purchase, and as such the transaction is deemed speculative in nature. It is unlikely however that such Derivatives Financial Instruments (DFIs) would be permitted to be offered to Indian counterparties in India.

**Non-resident issues:**    Swap payments are not generally regarded as interest but as business profit. Withholding tax is only applied if the profits are attributable to a PE (in treaty countries) or if arising or received in India (in non-treaty countries). Recently, Derivatives Financial Instruments (DFIs) payments have been exempted from withholding tax in specific circumstances.

**Other taxes:**    Swap payments will not be subject to value-added or other taxes.

## 25.18.5    Interest Rate Swaptions

There are no specific rules governing the taxation of swaptions contracts in India. The Derivatives Financial Instruments (DFIs) market in India is in a nascent stage and consequently the accounting, regulatory and taxation situations relating to Derivatives Financial Instruments (DFIs) have not yet been fully determined. The comments below regarding the taxation treatment of swaptions are based upon the application of general principles to the Derivatives Financial Instruments (DFI).

**Accessibility/deductibility of premium payments:**    Premiums paid/received are generally recognized on an accrual basis. Premiums received in advance may be spread over the life of the swaption. Settlement payments are generally assessable/deductible on a due and payable basis. For the intervening period (between commencement and termination of the swaption) profits/loss may be recognized on a mark-to-market basis. The law is unclear in regard to the application of mark-to-market taxation.

However, the application of mark-to-market taxation is increasingly perceived as the most attractive method and as a consequence, gains/losses on swaptions are likely to be recognised over the period of the Derivatives Financial Instruments (DFI) on a mark-to-market basis.

**Non-resident issues:** Premiums paid are not interest. They may however be subject to withholding tax if attributable to a PE (in treaty countries) or if arising or received in India (in non-treaty countries). Recently, Derivatives Financial Instruments (DFI) payments have been exempted from withholding tax in specific circumstances.

# SUMMARY

This chapter on accounting and tax treatment of derivative transactions has introduced the basic concepts of accounting and tax treatment of financial derivatives like forwards, futures, swaps, options, warrants, etc. Over the last three decades, the trading in derivatives instruments has grown in multi-fold but the accounting framework for these instruments has not kept pace with the rising complexities. Though some accounting standards have been framed by various institutions but still there is no uniform standard accounting practice for derivatives. Some underdeveloped countries have given reference to International Accounting Standard (IAS) or those standard originating from the advanced capital markets such as US and UK. At international level IAS 39, IAS 32 and in USA SFAS 33, SFAS 52, SFAS 80, SFAS 105, SFAS 107 and SFAS 119 are the important accounting standard for the accounting treatment of financial derivatives instruments.

Chapter in the next section brings out the problems of conventional accounting which does not specifically recognize the risk reducing effects of a hedge. For example, accounting conventions require stocks to be valued at the lower of cost or market value. A firm may hold stocks of a particular material and price of the material might have fallen in the market. Hence, in these circumstances conventional accounting may not show the exact position of the firms. In order to meet these challenges, the International Accounting Standard Committee has come out with an Accounting Standard (IAS 32) exclusive for disclosure and presentation of financial instruments, which has been implemented on January 1, 1996. Hedge accounting can be defined as a method of accounting for hedge instrument and other underlying hedged items which reflect the reduction in exposure to risk.

For the purpose of accounting, the financial instruments can be classified into two categories: (i) on-balance sheet financial instruments and (ii) off-balance sheet financial instrument. A financial asset is an asset that (a) cash, (b) a contractual right to receive cash or another financial asset from another enterprises, (c) a contractual right to exchange financial instruments with another enterprise under condition that are potentially favourable or (d) an equity instrument of another enterprises. The financial instruments which are shown on balance sheet are called on-the balance sheet or basic financial instrument, such as receivables, bonds, capital stock, etc. Off-the balance sheet instruments, also called as financial derivatives instruments like futures contracts, forward, options, swap, etc.

Future derivatives instruments do not result in transfer of the underlying primary instruments on inception of the contract, and such transfer does not necessarily take place on maturity of the contract. For the purpose of accounting practice transactions can be classified in three categories: (i) specific hedge transactions, (ii) general hedge transactions and (iii) trading transactions. In the next section, chapter describes the appropriate accounting treatment of above stated transactions. The Financial Accounting Standard Board (FASB) has constructed Standard FAS No. 133 with effect from January 1999 entitled 'Accounting for derivative instruments and hedging activities'. It defines fair value as the amount at which an asset/liability could be bought (incurred) or sold (settled) in a current transactions between willing parties that is other than in a forced or liquidation sale.

The ICAI has issued a Guidance Note on Accounting for derivative contracts on May 12, 2015 which provides guidance on recognition, measurement, presentation and disclosure for derivatives in India. It does not apply to macro-hedging and accounting for non-derivative financial assets/liabilities which are designated as hedging instruments. This note will become applicable for accounting periods beginning on or after April 1, 2016.

In the last section, the chapter describes the tax treatment of derivatives. The statutory provisions relating to gains or losses incurred on derivative instruments are different from country to country, and further they differ on as per nature of the instrument. Section 43(5) of the Indian Income Tax Act, defines a speculative transaction as: 'a transaction in which a contract for the purpose or sale of' any commodity, including stocks and shares is periodically or ultimately settled otherwise than by the actual delivery or transfer of the commodity or scripts. There are no specific rules governing the taxation of forward rate agreements (FRAs) in India. The Derivatives Financial Instruments (DFIs) market in India is in a nascent stage and consequently regulatory and taxation situation have not yet been fully determined. The law is unclear about the application of mark-to-market taxation, settlement payments treated as interest, and non-resident issues and accessibility/deductibility of forward contracts.

## SUGGESTED READINGS

1. Jorion, Philippe and Khoury, Joseph Sarkis, *Financial Risk Management*, Blackwell Publisher, USA, 1996.
2. Neil, Doherty A., *Corporate Risk Management—A Financial Exposition*, McGraw-Hill, New York, 1998.
3. Miller, M.H., Derivatives Taxes, *Journal of Finance*, Vol. 32, pp. 266–278, 1977.
4. Vipul, *Accounting For Financial Derivatives*: *US, International and Indian Standards*, The Chartered Accountant, September 2003.
5. Draft Standard on Accounting for Derivatives and Similar Financial Instruments for Hedging Activities, Financial Accounting Standards Board, Norwalk, September 1997.
6. IASC leads the Ways on Derivatives, *Management Accounting*, June 1995.
7. Gorddia, Shefali, *Taxation of Financial Derivatives*, Nitish Desai Associates, Mumbai, 2002.
8. *Taxation Treatment of Derivatives*, A Study of Price Water House Cooper Ltd.
9. ICAI Guidance Note on Accounting for Derivative Contracts GN(A) 33, 2015.

## REVIEW QUESTIONS

1. Discuss the concept of derivative for accounting purpose. How derivatives is treated in accounting record? Explain with examples.
2. "Although the trading in derivatives instruments has grown multi-fold but the accounting and tax framework of these instruments has not been developed so much." Discuss the statement in the light of trading derivatives in India.
3. Explain important guiding standards on which accounting treatment of derivatives is done with suitable examples.
4. What do you understand by the term conventional accounting? Discuss the problems associated with suitable illustrations.
5. Define 'hedge accounting'. What are the various transactions under it? Discuss with suitable examples.

6. Write a detailed note on classification of financial instruments for accounting purposes.

7. What are the various accounting practices of derivatives? Also explain the nature of derivatives transactions and their classifications.

8. Write short notes on:
   (a) Financial assets
   (b) Monetary financial assets and liabilities
   (c) Fair value
   (d) Market value

9. With the help of suitable examples, discuss the accounting treatment of various transactions in currency swap.

10. Write a detailed note on accounting entries of futures transactions with examples.

11. Write notes on:
    (a) Accounting entries for options transactions with the help of suitable examples
    (b) FASB's accounting standard on derivatives

12. Write a critical note on accounting of financial derivatives transactions in India. Briefly discuss the role of ICAI in formulation of various standards.

13. Discuss the problems in accounting entries for derivatives transactions? Also suggest some measures to overcome these problems.

14. What are the various issues relating to derivative financial instruments with respect to accounting? Discuss in the light of recent developments in capital market in India.

15. Describe the tax treatment of derivatives in India with suitable illustrations.

16. Write notes on:
    (a) Tax treatment of forward contracts
    (b) Tax treatment of futures contracts

17. Clearly bring out the various aspects of tax treatment of options, swaps and other derivatives in India.

18. "There is no specific accounting and tax frameworks of derivatives transactions in India." Critically evaluate the statement in the light of various provision for accounting and tax treatment of derivatives in India.

19. Explain the important features of Guidance Note of the ICAI relating to derivatives.

# Chapter 26

# Risk Management in Derivatives

*After reading this chapter, students will be able to*

➢ Understand the concept of management of derivative exposures.

➢ Be aware the nature of derivatives trading and the factors that influence the derivatives.

➢ Know how to set a risk vision, and various strategic components in risk vision like setting policies, risk tolerance, commercial objectives, capital efficiency, etc.

➢ Be aware of the various reasons for managing derivatives risks.

➢ Know the types of risks involved in derivatives trading like credit risk, market risk, liquidity risk, operational risk, legal risk, formal risk, etc.

➢ Understand the concept of value-at-risk (VaR), basic applications of VaR and evaluation of VaR.

➢ To understand the various parameters and techniques of VaR.

➢ To understand the stress testing techniques for VaR.

➢ Know the risk management value chain which includes organizational consideration, role of senior level management, analytical choices and suitability of particular methodology which may be suitable for managing a derivative exposure.

➢ Understand the concept of back testing and factor which should be considered while formulating a back testing plan.

## 26.1 INTRODUCTION

The derivatives trading, today, has become a powerful segment of the international financial markets. In the last two decades, trading in various equity derivatives have begun at different centres of global financial markets. Numerous overseas centres have developed their own derivatives markets, and as such the global derivatives market has become a reality of this time. No doubt the derivatives are powerful tools for risk management but they might turn out to be disastrous weapons if not used properly.

This section will include certain issues relating to derivatives like the nature of derivatives trading, types of risks involved in such trading, setting the risk vision and establishing a system of managing the exposure. Further, the concept of value-at-risk, parameters of VaR, techniques of measurement of VaR, stress testing and back testing will be discussed. At the end, the same will be concluded with risk management-value chain.

## 26.2 NATURE OF DERIVATIVES TRADING

It is evident that all the derivative tools like forwards, futures, options, swaps and other complex instruments are risky in the sense that their use should be most judicious and proper. It is not derivatives that are dangerous. The root of their risk lies in how and why they are used, and under what framework of control. In other words, the derivatives, if not properly controlled and managed, may be harmful to the user. The following factors influence the trading derivatives:

1. Firstly, handling of the financial derivatives are just like handling the dangerous chemicals, or any explosive device. No individual can handle these chemicals or devices without proper system of protocols. Therefore, the financial derivatives are also just like these chemicals or devices, which must be handled through proper control measures in order to prevent wide spread disaster. For example, if ₹ 10 million is deployed in a derivative transaction, it is quite possible that one may lose ₹ 100 million.

2. Secondly, the financial derivative markets move at fast speed. Since, some financial derivatives markets like currency futures and options operate on a 24-hour basis, due to the integration of various exchanges across the world, so changes in prices of various financial derivative products move overnight. So this market is highly liquid but too risky at the same time.

3. Derivative transactions are used for different purposes like hedging the risk, speculation, arbitraging, trading, etc. These may be used as risk reducing device or risk enhancing device. So it is necessary to identify the purpose of the use of derivatives.

4. Some derivatives are very complex in nature like caps, collars, floors, exotic derivatives, swaps and forward rate agreements. These should be structured very cautiously. Each instrument will have different levels of risk. Failure to acknowledge the different levels of risk exposure could result in actual losses.

5. After selecting the proper financial derivatives, it is also essential that the same must be implemented as independent management function to identify, monitor, control and report all its aspects. It must be in compliance with all relevant legal and regulatory standards, including standard relating to disclosure.

6. While implementing any such derivative strategy, there must be high level team of competent persons in this field. They must be suitably qualified and undertake in-house training for continuous professional developments. They must be expert in risk analysis and risk management techniques. Further, they must be aware of latest developments in this field and regulatory compliance.

## 26.3   SETTING THE RISK VISION

Prior to implementing any derivatives transaction, the firm's top management should chalk out a clear-cut guidelines comprising policies, procedures, etc. so that there should be no ambiguity regarding taking decisions by the executives. The top management should set out the general framework of authority for accountability and optimal risk control. The management must understand the impact of derivative transactions on overall objectives and profits of the organization. The following is a list of items which a financial institution may wish to consider in setting its strategic vision regarding derivative trading:

### 26.3.1   Strategic Components in Risk Vision

1. Setting policies
2. Commercial objectives
3. Risk tolerance
4. Capital efficiency
5. Financial capability
6. Enhance competence
7. Reviews

In formulating the strategic vision regarding risk management, the following set of strategic queries which the senior management should consider:

1. The main purposes and reasons for which derivatives are to be used.
2. The particular types of derivatives which are useful for the enterprise.
3. The Board of Directors and its role in relation to control of risk in derivative exposure.
4. The process for approving the use of new derivative instruments.
5. The other alternatives, if any, in case the derivative instruments are not used.

After considering the strategic queries, the top management will proceed to set the long-term direction and considerations of the risk policies. It should be noted that each organization is unique, so formulating risk policies and procedures would also be unique. There cannot be one set of guidelines for all. However, following are set of policies and procedures, which should be made explicit by the top management.

*Policies*

1. Authorized person to make derivatives transactions.
2. The persons involved in entering into negotiating, approving, executing and reviewing the transaction.
3. The types of risks to be identified, monitored and controlled.
4. The mechanism for communication of policies and procedures to the staff members.
5. How such communication will be acknowledged and understood?
6. Criteria for identifying suitable counterparties in relation to various types of risks.
7. Criteria for identifying the method of transaction valuation.
8. Risk methodologies to be used for different derivatives.
9. Professional expertise required of third party advisers.

*Procedures*

1. The mechanism of approving and recording of all the derivative transactions.
2. How will the underlying assets and components of risks of derivative instruments be analyzed?
3. Maintenance of records and their updating.
4. Approval of counterparties for derivative transactions.
5. Reliability of counterparties from banks perspective.
6. Impact of risk management on trading or investment activities.
7. Ways of supervision of derivatives exposures.
8. How will the risk managers exercise their control over approved limits?

## 26.4   REASONS FOR MANAGING DERIVATIVES RISKS

As seen in the preceding section that handling derivative instrument is just like a nuclear device which may be exploded at any time if that is not controlled with a proper system of protocols. That is why the derivatives risks management and control require an in-depth knowledge of risks, how they are identified, how they are measured and how they are controlled. So in this section, we will discuss the reason for managing risks and the various risks inherent in derivatives.

**Increase in complexity of financial market:**   Today, a business firm operates in dynamic business environment, which has also increased the complexity of the financial markets. Changes and other developments in any part of the world may affect the firm in different ways. For example, if US interest rate is decreased by 1 percent, then it may have impact on LIBOR and interest rates in other countries. Due to globalization and liberalization, today the domestic financial markets are linked with the international financial markets. So changes in international financial markets tend to be of interest to both central banks and regulatory bodies, as well as to the derivatives users who seek to understand price dynamics and linkages to create new financial products or linkage in trades.

**Optimization of capital:**   Recently, the use of derivative products by the banking companies has become a primary source of revenue which is a significant development. Earning through derivatives is a very risky venture because derivatives are used as powerful risk-management tools. So, sometimes, miscalculation of prices of derivative products has created disaster for the creators. Used prudently, they offer managers efficient and effective access to techniques for reducing particular risks through hedging as well as reducing financing costs and increasing yield on assets. In brief, to make the optimum use of capital and other financial resources, derivatives should be used judiciously and carefully.

**Technology advances:**   Another important reason for using the derivative instruments is that the risk has increased due to advancement in technology. Increased sophistication and new information technology have created complications and insecurity in the business world. As a result, everyone likes to move safer in future. The derivatives in this respect play a significant role by creating new products as per the requirement. Climate and weather derivatives are due to these factors.

**Market events:**   Today the derivative products are available in all the spheres like agricultural products, metals, commodities and financial product. The activities and developments are increasing in different markets at a fast rate all over the world, resulting into rise in market risk. To cope with these changes and increased risk, there are needs of new derivative products so that the corporate world can act efficiently.

**Changes in accounting practices:**    Another major driver for managing risk includes to measure derivative values accurately in a volatile worldwide market. However to measure the value, there is need of sound techniques and other statistical tools. The accounting standard and practice for the derivative transactions are relative new and in a process of evolution. There is no standard accounting practice for derivatives so far, standards do exist for disclosure of derivative transactions.

**Regulatory initiatives:**    Earlier only the developed countries have the derivatives markets but now the significance and need of such markets are felt by other countries. As a result, the regulatory bodies initiated to establish derivative markets in different fields like agricultural products, metals and financial products. As we know that the future trading is an important tool but the same can be used as well as misused. So to prevent misuse, there is need of proper regulation. Most of the countries have framed various regulatory measures in order to smooth functioning of the derivatives trading. Therefore, it is essential to understand the various provisions of regulation in different products of domestic countries as well as of other countries before initiating any transaction in the derivatives markets.

## 26.5  TYPES OF RISKS IN DERIVATIVE TRADING

Before managing the derivative exposures, it is essential to understand the nature and degree of risk involved. There are different types of risks in derivatives trading. A few important among them are as follows:

**Credit risk:**    It is also called default risk. The risk that a counterparty will default on its obligations is called *credit risk*. Most of the derivatives transactions are executed through over-the-counter (OTC) and recognized exchanges. An exchange-traded futures contract is likely to have significantly less counterparty risk in comparison to OTC driver contracts. The major factors influencing the credit risk are such as, rating systems, scope for credit enhancements, sophistication of users, measurement approach, need for diversified client bases, product-characteristics, valuation data, barriers to entry, etc.

The credit analysis includes the techniques, which are used to measure the ongoing credit risk that the firm is bearing. The major techniques include; using risk adjusted return calculations (similar to value at risk); applying options theory to credit default analysis; using efficient portfolio theory, and aggregating risks into a single measurement by the statistical correlation between individual credit risks.

After analyzing the credit risk of the counterparty, next step is to control credit risk. Various methods have been suggested like collateral agreements, netting agreements, credit guarantees, credit triggers, mutual termination options, etc.

**Market risk:**    This risk relates to adverse changes in the market price of a derivative. In other words, market risk exposes a firm to uncertainty due to changes in various market factors like foreign exchange rates, commodity prices, equity prices, volatility related to options positions, market interest rates, etc. In fact, market risk arises due to market factors, which is beyond the control of the counter-party. Such risk is to be estimated and then steps are taken to manage the same.

There are three important aspects relating to market risk: 'tools' necessary to carry out timely and accurate measurement, techniques of risk analysis and monitoring and strong and effective lines of communication to senior management. In order to develop a sound market risk approach, an organization has to consider a number of factors like risk strategy and policy, organization and culture, executives skill, theoretical underpinnings, systems architecture, procedure and controls, portfolio characteristics, management information, etc.

**Liquidity risk:** Liquidity risk refers to the fluctuation of derivative instruments prices for not quickly sold or purchased in the market. Sometimes, due to various factors, a particular derivative may not be easily sold at a fair price. It is observed that usually liquidity risk is higher at the OTC market in comparison to the exchange-traded derivatives. Two elements of liquidity risk arise due to relative ability of an organization to transfer its assets into, and second the mismatch between the bank's cash inflows and outflows arising out of derivative activity.

The transfer ability of a derivative to be converted into cash at fair value depends largely on the existence of the secondary market. This depends upon three factors: (a) transaction costs incurred on liquidation determined largely by the bid-ask spread (b) cost of exposure of the position maintained and (c) the cost of hedging the exposure, where possible. Trade off between the three components would determine the rate of liquidation. It will be discussed further in context to value at risk concept.

Sometimes, large derivatives portfolios can be subject to sudden cash demands, and thus, creating mismatch between a banks cash inflows and outflows. This position may make liquidity management for off-balance sheets products crucial. Sudden liquidity changes can arise out cash flow risk, which the bank should monitor considering the potential price and volatility changes in derivative instrument.

**Legal risk:** The risk relating to change in law or a regulatory rule may cause an adverse financial impact on a derivative transaction. The external risk management area takes into account information supplied by the global database and the legal and regulatory compliance. Any such new regulatory rule or compliance should be immediately incorporated.

It is also important to note that the top management must be informed about the new rules or regulation so that they should also note the same. As yet there is no specific international framework for law regarding derivative instruments. Therefore, it is important to follow major guidelines and legal principles applicable to derivatives instruments in different jurisdictions.

**Operational risk:** This risk relates to that error or fraud which may occur in carrying out operations, placing orders, making payments, taking deliveries, accounting for derivatives transactions. The main reason for this is that operational risk is everywhere within an organization. Since derivative transactions decisions are taken by the senior management in the organization and implemented by the executory functionaries through business line technologies; various sophisticated instruments are used for placing the orders and then for clearing them. Thus, potential exposures commonly associated with operations are diverse. These may relate to technology choices: batch vs real time processing, intra-day settlement exposure, cross-border payment issue, reliance or manual controls, multilateral vs. bilateral payments systems, timing of payment and delivery. Many of these issues even go beyond the organizational level.

Operational risk is relevant to the entire 'value chain' of an organization technology and people. Manual and automated controls throughout the organization all have a part to play in creating a secure operational environment. Thus, the operational risk can be mitigated internally through proper controls and procedures and a detailed understanding of all the stages of the operational process.

**Model risk (formal risk):** It is evident that derivatives instruments are priced or valued through specific complicated mathematical formula which are based on numerous assumptions, specifically in case of options instruments. It has been observed that, sometimes, these models or formula fail to give accurate results regarding price data. This may be due to changes in assumptions or other environmental factors or undetected flaws in the models. The less experienced and qualified trader takes the models as infallible gospel but these must be used with great precautions.

Besides the above said different risks, there are so many other risks, which should also be considered. A few examples of such risks are as financial risk, interest rate risk, aggregation or interconnection risk, basis risk, systematic risk, etc. Though these risks are not specifically concerned to derivatives trading but they must be appraised while chalking out a plan for risk management in the organization.

## 26.6  VALUE AT RISK (VaR) ANALYSIS: RISK AGGREGATION

Recently, there is significant developments in risk management that how to measure the risk and then incorporate the same into a single variable. The notion of risk capital has become the standard of choice among regulators and bankers. Therefore, value at risk (VaR) technique has become a standard method, in the derivatives market assisting the senior management to understand the risk exposure of a particular derivative asset. This section will discuss the concept of VaR, parameters methods of measurement, stress testing, back testing, historical background, etc.

## 26.6.1  Historical Background of VaR

Value  at risk (VaR) has gained rapid acceptance as a valuable approach to risk management.

The modern age of risk management began in 1973 in which Britton Woods System of fixed exchange rate was collapsed and resulting into floating exchange rate system. Rapid transition of this system among major trading countries provided the right push for measurement and management of foreign exchange risk. In the year 1973, by introducing of the Black-Scholes option pricing formula, which provided the conceptual framework and basic tools for risk measurement, it leads to initiation for derivative instruments which can manage the risks of stocks, foreign currencies and interest rates. The idea behind this model provides the foundation for the measurement and management of volatility of market rate and prices by using of probability and statistical tools.

The origin of VaR has its roots since from the introduction of portfolio theory and capital requirements. In 1922, the New York Stock Exchange (NYSE) imposed the condition of minimum capital requirements for its member companies. This anticipated current capital requirements evolved into VaR measures, which firms use even today. In 1952, Markowitz and Roy independently published VaR techniques which were surprisingly similar. Each one was working to develop a means of selecting portfolios which would optimize the return at a given level of risk. Both the techniques suggested VaR measures which incorporated covariance between risk factors. Though both these measures were mathematically similar, but they initiated different VaR metrics.

Markowitz used a variance of simple return metric whereas Roy used a metric of shortfall risk that represents an upper bound of gross return of portfolio being less than some specified catastrophic return.

In 1982, the development of volatility models for measuring the risk initiated with Eagle's work, and later on, a lot of literature published based on this work. They all contributed for this modern risk management. After that in 1994, J.P. Morgan introduced a model of "Risk Metrics" which enables the companies with just a minimum computational power to arrive at a measure of market risk for a given portfolio of assets. This measure is known as value at risk or the maximum likely loss over the next trading day. Further, in 1998. Risk Metrics has been discussed in detail by Dowd. In 2000, Danielsson and de Vries, observed that active portfolios tend to calculate daily VaR as their internal risk control measure because the portfolio composition is changed with the volatility is the market price

The Risk Metrics approach, as founded by J.P. Morgan, later on formed a company called 'Risk Metrics' which provides risk management consult any consultancy based on this approach. Further, it has also created a huge interest among academicians as it offered a benchmark methodology upon which improvement can be made, and further various other alternatives can be formed and tested.

## 26.6.2 Concept of VaR

The VaR is a statistical concept. It is an attempt to answer the question, "the most that can be lost with a given degree of confidence". In other words, what maximum amount one can lose from this particular set of holdings; within the next specified period (a day or week or month or quarter), at a particular pre-determined confidence interval. This confidence interval can be 95 percent, 98 percent, and 99 percent but not exact 100 percent. The estimate is based on historical data of volatilities of individual prices and of the correlation between prices. For example, if the prices of two derivatives are closely related then the risk during the adverse movement is more than if they are poorly correlated.

The VaR calculation is aimed at making a statement of the following form: "We are $X$ percent certain that we will not lose more than $V$ rupees in the next $N$ days" where $V$ is VaR of the portfolio, $X$ is the confidence level and $N$ is the time horizon. For example, if $N = 10$ and $X = 99$ then the losses cover a ten-day period is expected to happen of one percent of the time. Every user of VaR has to specify his horizon of interest and a probability, i.e., $N$ and $X$. For example: A VaR of ₹1 million for one day at probability of 5 percent means that the firm is expecting to lose at least ₹1 million in one day with a probability of 5 percent  Further, if it is a portfolio, then we can interpret that 5 percent indicates that it is expected to occur once in every 20 trading days. The VaR seeks to measure the maximum loss that portfolio might sustain over a period of time for given a set probability level. Typically VaR looks at 95 percent probability range over 1 day. For example, a portfolio manager might report that the portfolio has one day, VaR of ₹10,000, it means that 95 percent the days the portfolio will not decline in value by more than ₹10,000. Usually, VaR is reported either as rupee amount or as a percentage of fund's assets. For example, in early 2000, the medium value at Risk for the 200 largest corporate of pension funds in the USA was estimated 17 percent of the portfolio value over a one year period based on the 95 percent probability level. Further the range of funds VARs was 9.5 percent to 28 percent.

Further, it is important to note that the probability assigned in VaR is not associated with any particular event, rather it could cover any event that could cause such a loss. It means the loss might be caused by changes of prices of fundamental risk factors like changes in foreign exchange rates, interest rates, commodity price fluctuations changes in stock prices, changes in volatility, etc. In brief, the basic idea behind the VaR is to estimate the probability distribution of the underlying source of risk and to identify the worst given percentage of outcomes. In this respect, normal distribution curves are widely used for computing VaR, though not necessarily appropriate in all the cases. The biggest attraction of normality is that if the portfolio return is normal, the VaR is the multiple of portfolio standard deviation and the normal value of the confidence level.

It is concluded that VaR is based on 3 elements:

$$VaR = \text{Market Value} \times \text{Sensitivity} \times \text{Volatility}$$

**EXAMPLE:**

> 10 years Treasury Bond
>
> Market Value          :    ₹10 m
>
> Holding Period        :    1 month
>
> YTM Volatility        :    30 bp (0.30 percent)
>
> Sensitivity            :    $\sigma$
>
> VaR = ₹10 m $\times$ $\sigma$ $\times$ (2 $\times$ 0.3 percent) = 3,60,000

- 10 m = Market Value (Mark-To-Market)
- $\sigma$ = A proxy of the sensitivity of the bond price to changes in its Yield to maturity (for a stock it would be the beta).
- 0.3 percent = An estimate of the future variability of interest rate (for stock it would be the volatility of the equity market)
- 2 = A scaling factor needed to obtain the desired confidence level under the assumption of a normal distribution of market factor's returns

## 26.6.3   Calculation of VaR in Simple Situation

In VaR calculation, we usually ensure time in days and the volatility of an asset per day. In option pricing, we usually measure volatility 'per year'. We can convert the volatility in year to volatility per day. For example, assuming 252 trading days in a year. It follows that

$$\sigma \text{ yr} = \sigma \text{ day } \sqrt{252}$$

or                        $\sigma \text{ day} = \dfrac{\sigma \text{ yr}}{\sqrt{252}}$ about 6 percent

It means that daily volatility is 6 percent of annual volatility. Daily volatility is approximately equal to the standard deviation of the return on the asset per day.

**EXAMPLE:**   Let us consider a portfolio consisting of a position worth ₹10 million in SBI shares. We assume that $N = 10$, $X = 99$ so that we are interested in a 99 percent confidence level for losses over ten days. We assume that the volatility of SBI is 2 percent per day (corresponding to 32 percent about per year).

Size of the position is ₹10 million, daily volatility is 2 percent, being ₹2,00,000 (10 $M \times 2$ percent). Assuming that the changes in successive days are independent, we expect the standard deviation of the change over a ten-day period to be times the change over a one-day period. Therefore, it will be 2,00,000 = ₹6,32,456.

The basic assumption in VaR calculation is that the portfolio returns are normally distribution. Worse losses are observed 2.5 percent time at the 1.96 ($\sigma$) or close to 2.6. Suppose a person owns ₹10,00,000 of NIFTY. The daily ($\sigma$) of NIFTY is 1.3 percent. Then 97.5 percent VaR of the portfolio is ₹26,000, i.e. 10,00,000 $\times$ 1.3 percent $\times$ 2 which means that the one-day loss on the portfolio will be worst than ₹26,000 on 2.5 percent of days (roughly six days per year).

## 26.6.4   Parameters of VaR

Before discussing the various methods used in measuring the VaR, it is important to discuss the various parameters which are considered in it. Following are important parameters which should be considered for measuring the VaR:

**(I) Time Horizon:** Time Horizon is the first parameter which should be decided for calculating the VaR. The shortest feasible holding period is one day, although theoretically, it is possible for keeping even less than a day as time horizon. Normally, the firms can estimate the VaR based on longer holding period, e.g., one week, one month, one quarter, one year, etc.

The liquidity position of the markets is important factor for deciding the time horizon. Time taken to liquidate a position is generally varies from one market to other. For example, a security trader would prefer daily holding period, whereas a banker that trades in less liquid securities prefers a longer holding period, may be a month.

**(II) Confidence Interval:** The confidence interval refers to the percentage of time the firm should not loose than the VaR amount. Normally, VaR is computed at different confidence levels 90 percent, 95 percent and 99 percent. 90 percent confidence level means that approximately 90% of the values are contained within ±1 standard deviation (SD) from the mean. 95 percent confidence level means that 95 percent of the values are contained within 2SD, and 99 percent confidence level means that approximately, 99 percent of the values are contained with in 3 standard deviation from the mean.

However, we should avoid VaR calculation based on high confidence level, because the losses in excess of VaR becomes relatively rare. We can have different VaR confidence level for different purposes. For example, the Bank of International Settlement (BIS) and the Derivative Policy Group have recommended a confidence level of 99 percent, whereas a lot different studies indicate that 95 percent performs best under back testing due to fat tails. The term fat tails refers to the fact the large market moves occur more frequently than what would occur if market return was normally distributed.

**(III) Data Series:** The nature of data requires for estimation of VaR is an important issue. VaR is fairly data intensive. The choice of historical, implied or other types of data to determine various relationships is important. It is argued that implied correlations and volatilities results in a better prediction of risk rather than the correlations and volatilities based on historical data. However, in fact, very little implied data are available, hence, historical data sets have occupied major place in VaR calculations.

The length of the historical data on the other hand, is also important issue in VaR estimation. Both the data; longer or shorter period are frequently used in such estimation. Three to five years of historical data are typically taken. In addition, the role of some extraordinary events occurred, should also be included in the data compilation. Some experts believe that 10 years of historical data be used to calculate VaR on the equity portfolio. Further, in such analysis, exponentially weighted data should be used which are more reliable, and allowing the VaR to react to changing market conditions quickly.

**(IV) Mapping:** Another important parameter to be used for calculating VaR, we have to assume the instruments for this. However, in practice, it is very difficult to have such information for every instrument in our portfolio. The representative approach for such instruments known as "mapping" which selects a set of core instruments that can be regarded as the representative of the broad types of instruments held. Important "mapping" frequently used in VaR estimation is Risk Metrics-maps

It means estimating VaR requires that each individual position gets associated to its relevant market factors. For example, a long position in Indian Treasury bond is equivalent to a long position on the rupee Exchange rate, a short position on the Indian rupee, etc.

## 26.6.5  Approaches of Computing VaR

There is no standard approach which can be exclusively used for measuring the VaR in a firm, funds or portfolio. However, several approaches have been suggested by the experts to measure VaR. It is important to note that VaR is sensitive to the assumptions made and the approach followed. It means that VaR number will differ as per the assumptions and the method used for this calculation. Following are important approaches used for measuring the VaR:

1. The Variance Covariance Approach
2. Historical Simulation Approach
3. Monte Carlo Simulation Approach

**The variance covariance approach:**   This approach is advanced by J.P. Morgan's risk metrics model. This is also known as the 'delta-normal method'. This method uses the volatility of risk factors in the past and correlation between changes in their values, and then an approximation is to be made of the potential prospect losses of group. The major assumption in this approach is that the returns for each of the assets are normally distributed. The formula used here is the same as used in measuring variance of a portfolio. It is stated below as:

$$VaR(\tilde{R}) : \sum_i \sum_j w_i \, w_j \, \sigma_i \, \sigma_j \, \rho_{ij}$$

or

$$VaR(\tilde{R}) : w_i^2 \sigma_i^2 + w_j^2 \sigma_j^2 + 2w_i \, w_j \, \rho_{ij}$$

$W_i$ = Proportion of the total portfolio value consisting of asset $i$.

$W_j$ = Proportion of the total portfolio value consisting of asset $j$

$\rho_{ij}$ = Covariance of asset $i$ 'returns with asset $j$' return

$\sigma_i$ = Standard deviation of asset $i$' returns.

$\sigma_j$ = Standard deviation of asset $j$' returns.

Under this approach, it is already stated that return of the portfolio is assumed to be normally distributed. So, to estimate the VaR,

- The first step is to obtain an estimate of the variance of the portfolio periodic returns.
- These periodic returns could be calculated daily, weekly, monthly or for any other interval as, desired.
- After that this estimate can be calculated with any desired probability. For example, the value at risk (VaR) will equal 1.645 times the portfolio's standard deviation with a probability of 5 percent. The maximum loss with a 1 percent probability will equal 2.327 time the portfolio's standard deviation.

The variance of each asset's returns, each pair-wise covariance's are estimated from historical data, implied volatilities generated from the risk manager's subjective beliefs, etc. After calculating the portfolio's mean return, variance of returns, desired probability, it is simple to estimate 'What the loss in value of the portfolio, will be during the particular period.

Let us explain this risk with an example:

Assume that a portfolio consisting of two assets has following information:

|  | Asset 'X' | Asset 'Y' |
|---|---|---|
| Current Market Price (Per Unit) | ₹100 | ₹200 |
| Number of units held | 100 | 100 |
| Total Market Value | ₹10,000 | ₹20,000 |
| Historical Volatility (one day) | 2 percent | 3 percent |

Further assume that market risk is calculated by using Basle Committee's Quantitative Criteria, i.e., 99 percent confidence level (or 2.33 standard deviation for one day) and a 10-day holding period. Computation of VaR of these assets as per this formula.

VaR = Market Value × Sensitivity × Volatility

Asset $X$: = $10,000 × 2.33 × 2\% × \sqrt{10}$ = 1473.62

Asset $Y$: = $20,000 × 2.33 × 3\% × \sqrt{10}$ = 4420.86

*Note:* If the holding period is one year, the multiplication factor is square root of 252, because we assume 252 trading days in one year.

After that we have to consider the correlation between these two assets. For that we have to analyze the data, which depends upon the time period. As per Basle Committee's requirements the data of at least one year is required. The popular formula for calculating this is as follows:

$$\text{Risk } (X + Y) = \sqrt{Rx^2 + Ry^2 + 2CRxRy}$$

Where $Rx$ and $Ry$ are the value at Risk and 'C' is correlation coefficient between $X$ and $Y$, which lies between $(-1)$ and $(+1)$ If the prices of these two assets move perfectly in one direction, we can say the correlation is +1, move perfectly in opposite direction, then correlation is –1, if the correlation is 0, it means that these two assets are completely independent of each other.

As per above formula the portfolio value at risk is:
If correlation is +1, then VaR will be:

$$\sqrt{(1473.62)^2 + (4420.86)^2 + 2 × (+1) × 1473.62 × 4420.86} = 5894.48$$

If correlation is –1 then VaR will be: ₹3047.24

If correlation is 0, then VaR will be: ₹4660.00

**Historical simulation approach:**  This approach is based on the assumption that history will repeat itself. It simply reorganizes actual historical returns, putting them in order from worst to best. In this risk manager determines how each relevant price has changed during each of the past 'N' time periods. It is possible to use a historical data base to find the price changes from a specified period. From this, it is estimated how much of the past changes would affect the value of current portfolio. In this method, it is going back in time, say, over the last 05 years, and then applying current weight to a time series of historical assets returns. Thus, it reconstructs the history of a hypothetical portfolio using the current position:

  (i)  For each risk factor, a time-series of actual movements, and

  (ii)  Positions on risk factors.

After putting the data from worst to best, or ranking the estimated value changes from most positive to most negative, then the losses are estimated at the derived confidence level, say, at 95 percent, 99 percent, etc.

**Let us explain this method with an example:**  Consider that we have a portfolio of two assets and assume that their current values are ₹100 and ₹200, respectively. As per this approach, we have to 're-value', and come up with some "Alternatives" normally based on their historically price movements. We further assume that past historical data needed of 100 sets for estimating alternative values (means for past 100 trading days market prices of their assets) to make the result meaningful. These are shown as follows:

**TABLE 26.1**   Historical Simulation Approach

| Historical Period | Observed Market Values of Asset 'A' | Observed Market Values of Asset 'B' | Observed Portfolio Value(P) | Δ in Observed Market Value (ΔP) | Alternative Value (AV) =(Po+(ΔP) | Ranking from Worst to Best |
|---|---|---|---|---|---|---|
| 0 | 100 | 200 | 300 | | | |
| 1 | 102 | 205 | 307 | +7 | 307 | 3 |
| 2 | 98 | 190 | 288 | −19 | 281 | 2 |
| 3 | 104 | 215 | 319 | +31 | 331 | 6 |
| 4 | 95 | 185 | 280 | −39 | 269 | 1 |
| 99 | 102 | 195 | 297 | +17 | 317 | 5 |
| 100 | 103 | 202 | 305 | +08 | 308 | 4 |

Ranking is shown only of the values given in Table. 26.1

In this approach it is assumed that the alternative values are normally distributed. Portfolio (Asset A and Asset B) average return and standard deviation are 0 percent and 5 percent, respectively. Figure 26.1 explains this approach.

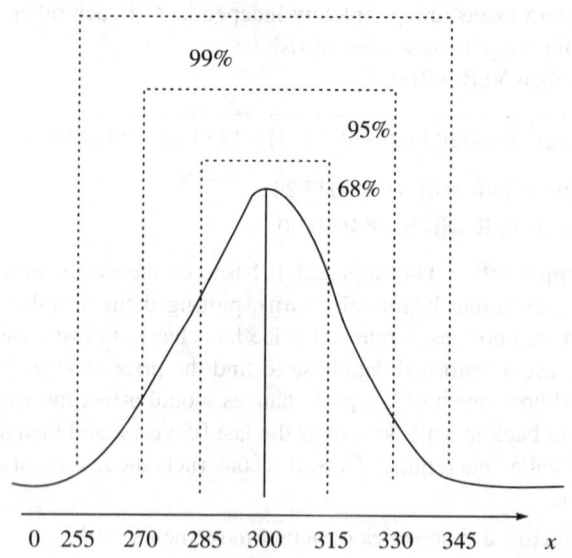

**FIGURE 26.1**   Normal distribution curve of the alternate values.

It is evident from Figure 26.1 that considering the above normal distribution of the alternative values, approximately 68 percent of them fall in the range between 255 and 315. Further, if we expand the range a little wide say between 270 and 330, then approximately 95 percent of the prices fall in this range and so on. For value at risk, we are concerned with the adverse price movement. Since we want to know the maximum loss possibility, in our example, the portfolio's value has decreased to 269, so we can rank the adverse situation. The ranking of these positions from most adverse to most best be chalked on 100 sets of prices. In the historical simulation, there is no need to care about the correlation, since all the data is already available and embedded in the historical data. To make the calculation more meaningful, a significant number of observations points (or historical data) are required. The Basle Committee has pointed out a minimum data of one year for the calculation of market risk. So, normally, longer period (from three to five years) of historical data be used for such calculation.

### Advantages of this approach

- This method is simple to calculate since it is based on the historical data.
- It is accurate in general for all type of instruments.
- It provides a full distribution of potential portfolio values.
- Assumptions relating to distribution need not to be made.
- It is faster than other techniques since less scenarios are used.
- It carefully capture non-linear risks.

### Disadvantages of this approach

- There is no assurance that any given amount of historical data is correct. Whether the distant past or the recent past more accurately predicts what tomorrow will bring.
- Sensitivity analysis becomes difficult.
- Volatility changes overtime, thus cannot use volatility updating schemes.
- It is difficult to scale into future.
- It requires a significant amount of daily rate history.
- It is time consuming and computationally intensive.
- It is not appropriate at high confidence level.
- It incorporates tail risk only if historical data set includes tail events.
- It may not be appropriate for most frequently traded portfolios.

**Monte Carlo simulation approach:**   Generally in forecasting the future, two distinct approaches are followed—deterministic and stochastic model. The model which assumes a fixed relationship between the inputs, and that inputs lead to an unambiguous result is called *deterministic*. On the other hand, the model which depends on random or uncertain inputs which provides a distribution of probable results are called *stochastic*. For example, a model that predicts an eclipse is deterministic because it relies on known fixed laws governing of the motions of the earth, the moon, and the sun. A model that predicts tomorrow's whether, however, is stochastic because many uncertain elements can influence the weather. If the prediction made by the observatory does not come to true, it does not mean that the observatory done poor job, because many uncertain elements, which the observatory could not forecast, might have dominated the result of the forecast.

Monte Carlo Simulation approach involves a stochastic process, to calculate VAR. In this approach, there is need to obtain a series of values from changes in market factors. These are then added to the current market value, and thus, a series of alternative values is derived just like the historical simulation method. Although this approach does not rely on past price experience to predict future, however, it does require the researcher to define certain parameters based on past experience, such as volatility correlations, etc. between market factors.

In this approach the researcher has to derive a value through the use of a sequence of random paths which are selected from each market factor's normal. A different probability distribution can be assumed for each pricing determinant. For example, changes in interest rate might be normally distributed whereas changes in the oil prices might be skewed right or left.

After the distribution or processes are identified, then random realizations of outcomes can be simulated. Each randomly chosen outcome is a set of prices. The change in value of each asset in the portfolio are estimated for each randomly selected set of prices, thereby, producing a probability distribution of future value changes of the portfolio. After that the researcher can then determine what the worst outcome (maximum losses) will be with a desired confidence level.

In this method, the simulation can be done many times and the results of each of the simulation process would be unrelated to each other, because they follow the independent condition. The process actually goes through certain precise mathematical processes. How many times the simulation process is repeated, it depends upon the degree of accuracy desired. Researcher usually uses at least one thousand paths in this approach.

We can summarise the Monte Carlo Simulation approach as such:

### One Day VaR Calculation

1. Value the portfolio today by using the current values of market variables.
2. Sample once from the multivariate normal probability distribution of the $\Delta Xi$
3. Calculate the values of the $\Delta Xi$ which are sampled to determine the value of each market variable at the end of one day.
4. Revalue the portfolio at the end of the day in the usual way.
5. Subtract the values calculated in step (1) from the value in step (4) to determine a sample $\Delta P$.
6. Repeat steps from (2 to 5) many times to build up a probability distribution so obtained.
7. VaR is then calculated at the appropriate percentile of the probability distribution so obtained.

### Advantages of this Approach

- It is able to use pricing models to revalue non-linear securities for each trial.
- It is accurate for all instruments.
- It provides a full distribution of potential values.
- Extensive data as required in historical method is not required.
- It permits use of various distributional assumptions and potential to address the issue of fat tails.

### Disadvantages

- It is time consuming and computationally intensive model.
- It has roots in random number generation which is exposed to sampling error.
- There is risk of running too few simulations to adequately capture the distribution and this could result in an inferior answer.
- It quantifies fat-tailed risk only if market scenarios are generated from the appropriate distributions.

## 26.7  STRESS TESTING

After calculating the VaR of any portfolio, it is important for the researcher or risk manager to go for stress testing. The basic objective of stress testing is to assess the impact of valuation on the performance of the portfolio in worst case scenario. In other words, estimating how the portfolio would have performed under the most extreme market conditions, regardless of whether these outcomes were realized in the past or not. For example, five standard deviation move in any market variable in one day is treated as next to impossible under the assumption of normal distribution, probably which may happen once in 7000 years. However, in reality, it happens about once every 10 years. It means that it is essential to go for stress testing to bring out the estimates of potential economic losses which may occur in abnormal risky markets.

Sometimes, a VaR estimate can be wrong for many reasons which may be due to wrong assumptions, unwise shortcut, computational mistake, etc. Even if we do everything right, still VaR can fail to tell us about reality. Risk managers call them as black holes. In black holes, the portfolio's exposure to one risk factor or several risk factors is extra ordinarily large which may cause to heavy losses. Under stress testing, the economic variables are ranked in order of their effect on portfolio value. For example, if the researcher discovered that his portfolio's value is most sensitive to a rise in short-term or long-term interest rates, then he can take precautions to hedge that price risk specifically. Further, stress tests show historical analysis of market returns which have "fat tails" where extreme market moves far away than a normal distribution would suggest.

The management should eliminate risks and therefore, seek out and eliminate black holes. VaR is not enough to do this. Stress tests are routine in risk management. Stress tests are computations of the value of proportions for specific values of risk factors. Stress testing is an ideal complement to VaR technique. While VAR approaches tell what the firm might lose with a certain maximum probability. Thus, both the techniques VaR and stress testing are ideal compliments to each other. Accordingly, stress testing combined with VAR gives a more comprehensive picture of risk.

**Stress testing techniques:**    It is a simulation technique used on asset and liability portfolios to determine their reactions to different financial situations/events. Normally, stress testing techniques fall into two general categories: **sensitivity tests** and **scenario tests.** Sensitivity tests evaluate the impact of large movements in financial variables on portfolio values without specifying the reasons for such movements, whereas the scenario tests are related with economic scenarios.

## 26.7.1  Sensitivity Tests

The sensitivity tests require considering variations in key assumptions, taking into the purpose/use of the analysis and test to see whether results reflect a reasonable range of variation in the key assumptions, consistent with intended purpose and use. A simple sensitivity test explains the changes in portfolio value for one or more shocks to a single risk factor. For example, in case of insurance risk testing, sensitivity testing should recognize benefits such as distribution of business by benefits period, greater exposure to asset related risk, lower interest rates, inflation benefits, lower termination rates (mortality), asset related risk, lower yield curves, lower margin over treasuries, lower default risk, etc.

*Examples of sensitivity test analysis*

- Changes in yield curve.
- Volatility changes
- Prepayment level changing
- Credit spread squeezing or widening
- Currency revaluations and devaluations

*Sensitivity analysis is concerned with*

- It calculates the impact of a large predefined stock in a specified risk factor (S).
- It is mostly done using the deltas and gammas.
- It is critical that the amount of stress shock used for each factor is extreme but plausible
- It states that largest change may not always be the best.

**Merits:**   It is relatively simple and easy to implement

- This is useful tool for identifying major risk in the books.
- It can be easily used by both traders and managers.

**Demerits:**   In this technique each factor is considered in isolation which may not give reliable estimate of the worst case loss.

- The likelihood of the risk factor going through a large change is not clear, which that no probability assigned to the outcome.

## 26.7.2   Scenario Tests

These are constructed either within the context of a specific portfolio or in light of historical events come across portfolios. A set of economic scenarios is generated in which these drivers are stressed beyond standard risks. Stress scenarios are based on plausible, but unlikely events such as US stock market crash in October 1987, Asian financial crisis of 1997, financial market developed September 2001, Hurricane Katrina in 2005, ERM crisis of 1992–1993, bond market crash of 1994, etc. might also occur historical scenarios are developed more easily since they reflect on actual stressed market environment that can be studied in great detail.

The choice of scenario based stress test depends on several factors, including the relevance of historical events of the portfolio, firm's resources available on conducting the stress testing, etc. The Monte Carlo simulation is one of the important widely used methods of stress testing.

In brief, sensitivity test focuses on the key assumptions and projected over a time horizon, whereas scenarios tests takes portfolio related event driven approach. In practice, the stress testing more often involves the combinations of Monte Carlo technique alongwith historical stress scenarios, sensitivity shocks, historical replays, etc.

*Scenario generated by management*

There is well known fact that history may not repeat itself exactly. It may be partly due to that the management is aware of past performance and thus tries to avoid making mistakes and other weaknesses occur in past. For example, credit crisis of the 2007 occurred due to relaxed mortgage lending criteria which checked later on. However, it is quite possible that there may be credit crisis in future, which may be due to other reasons like rising NPAs in banks.

In stress testing, the scenarios which are generated by the senior managements are most useful because they are in better positions to use their understanding of markets, national and global politics, economic environment, recent uncertainties, etc. Sometimes, the scenarios are generated based on the part, but are adjusted to include key features of the current financial and economic environment. In order to generate the scenarios, a committee of senior managements should be constituted which should meet periodically. The committee should have a three to five members of different backgrounds and there should be healthy dialogue between the members. Not only this, they should understand and recognize the importance of stress testing and have the responsibility for taking strategic decisions based on the stress testing results. Further, the scenario generated by the senior management would be easily implemented, whereas the scenarios created by the middle management positions might not be taken seriously.

### *Involving variables in generating scenario*

While generating scenarios, it is essential that only relevant variables should be chosen. Generally, it is observed that when one market variable shows a big change, others do as well. It has led the firms to develop scenarios where several variables change at same time. In this respect, there is common practice to use extreme movements in market variables change that have occurred in the past. To generate extreme scenarios, a period of time when these were moderately adverse market movements be chosen. Various examples of such time period are stated in historical scenarios. Further, the degree of correlation among the selected variables be measured in order to generate appropriate scenario. The problem in this approach is that correlations increase in stressed market conditions, whereas increasing movements in all market variables by a particular multiple does not increase correlation.

Another important issue in this respect is to identify case and peripheral variables when individual variables are stressed by management, the scenarios likely to be incomplete in that movements of only a few core market variables are specified. One approach is set changes in all other peripheral variables to zero, but this is likely to be unsatisfactory. Another approach is to regress the peripheral variable on the core variables which stressed to obtain forecasts for them conditional on the changed being made core variables. This is also known as conditional stress testing.

In brief, scenarios should be carefully examined and to make sure that all the adverse consequences have been considered. In this respect, the scenarios should include not only the immediate effect of shocks on the portfolio of market variables but also any "knock on" effect which caused due to other competitive firms in the market.

**Types of Scenarios:** Experts have suggested two types of scenarios analysis

    (i) Historical scenario analysis

    (ii) Hypothetical scenario analysis

### *(i) Historical scenario analysis*

#### Concept

- It is based on actual historical events to identify changes in risk factors.
- It informs how the books would have performed under extreme moves in risk factors which actually did occur in the past.
- Current risk factors may be scaled to reflect relative price changes experienced during the historical event.

#### Examples of historical scenarios

- Stock market crash from October 13 to October 19, 1987, Down falls 31 percent, total market value lost app $ 1 trillion
- Bond market crash 1994, FED raises rates by approx. 250 basis points against market expectation.

- Asian crisis July 2, 1987: Bank of Thailand abandons Bahl's peg to the dollar and currency falls 18 percent. At the end of the year, South Korean Won falls 47.5 percent and Indonesian Rupiah falls 56 percent.
- FED or hesitates a $ 3.5 billion bailout for LCTM, the hedge fund. All major banks lose significant amount of money.

**Challenges: which scenario to use?**

- What is the most relevant period to use?
- Start and end of the dates of the period.
- Whether to use absolute or relative changes in risk factors.
- Relationship between market risk factors and regime changes (i.e. liquidity or correlations).

**Hypothetical scenario analysis:** These are based on the expected changes considering recent environment and tailored to particular risk charters tics.

**Examples**

- Economy's condition, e.g., recession, inflationary
- Oil prices, e.g., very high, very low
- War
- Political events
- Bird flu pandemic

**Challenges**

- Selection of scenarios is critical.
- Shocks used should be extreme yet plausible.
- Consider the impact of possibility of changes of regimes.
- Assumed period of the duration.
- The changes in risk factors should be consistent and reasonable.

**Merits**

- It is useful to understand the impact unexpected changes in market on the financials.
- Designed to include future extreme market moves considering recent environment.
- Scenarios used are not constrained by history and can be tailored to portfolio risk characteristics.

**Demerits**

- Subjective in nature.
- Limitations of management capability.
- No probability assigned in selection of scenario.

## 26.7.3  Developing an Effective Stress Testing Program

Stress testing is an effective risk management tool since it provides with additional information on possible portfolio losses arising from extreme although plausible scenarios. In addition, it can be an effective communication tool with the firm and outside parties like investors. Further, a good set of stress tests enables the risks managers to proactively reduce unacceptable risk levels by indicating how to structure hedges for unacceptable risks exposure. Once implemented in the corporate decision making, it can effectively increase enterprise economic profit.

While implementing a stress test program in a firm, the risk manager must consider the following issues:

### Issues to be considered

- The number of the risk factors to stress, and how risk factors are combined.
- Range of shocks and choice of time frame.
- Choosing the right scenarios on the basis of estimated stress events.
- Use relevant scenarios which compass the reality check.
- Assumptions and weaknesses should be transparent.
- In designing and implementation of stress test, involve the right kind of people.
- Success of stress test is based on skills, intuition and experience of developers/risk managers.
- Ensure that system should be flexible enough to support both current and future scenarios.
- Cost factor in developing tests should be considered.

### Technical factors to be considered

- Holding period's assumptions—one day, one week one month, etc.
- Pricing models- full revaluation, grid based, Taylor series, etc.
- Frequency of stress testing—daily, monthly, weekly, etc.
- Breadth of risk factors and proxies used.
- Asset liquidity/correlation assumptions
- Risk limits and responsibilities.

## 26.8  BACK TESTING

It is necessary that the risk managers must evaluate the VaR techniques used by them to know the reliability of the estimation. So, in back testing, VaR estimates of extreme losses are compared with the realized losses so that the risk manager can reassess the accuracy of the existing VaR model used as well as to evaluate the efficiency of new model. In other words, back testing is a technique to determine whether the VaR methods employed by the risk managers in these firms are adequate or not. If this is not done, then it is quite possible that the firm may continue to run the model which is caused to the risk of faulty decisions in future too.

While performing the back testing, the risk manager ensures the days when actual losses exceed the VaR estimations. For example, statistically speaking, if actual losses exceed 5 percent VaR, i.e., 5 percent of the time. It means, over a 250 day trading year, the losses will occur on about 12 days, i.e., $0.05 \times 250 = 12.50$ days. After that a deep analysis relating to various aspects, such as, reasons of gap, reliability of model, reliability of checking days, nature of economic events, etc. should be done. Further, the risk manager must ensure whether the extreme events merely represent an extreme, or whether they indicate that the return distribution assumptions be modified or updated.

Sometimes, past actual losses is just a shade lower than 5 percent VaR, but something quite different to find that actual losses are more than 5 percent of VaR. Further, the composition of the portfolio can also drive actual losses more or lesser than the VaR. For example, tremendous increase in sales on a particular day may be due to heavy discounts offered. Such type of special incentives must be adjusted in VaR before making actual analysis. In brief, back testing is essential for the risk managers to review the VaR models for taking appropriate future prediction.

*Advantages*

- It is easy to calculate and fast method.
- Extensive historical data is not required.
- It is least computationally intensive.

*Disadvantages*

- It may mistake non-linear risks
- Fat tail problems.
- It may not appropriately depict market risk arising from extraordinary events.

*Duration and VaR*

Value at Risk (VaR) is directly linked to the concept of duration in situations where a portfolio is exposed to one risk factor only, and that is, interest rate. Duration, as defined, is the average maturity of all bond's payments. It measures how the cash flows of a bond are spread over time. It is the weighted average time to receipt of cash flows. It measures the sensitivity of the bond price to changes in yield:

$$\text{Bond Return} = -\text{Duration} \times 1/(1 + Y) \times (\Delta Y)$$

So, if the duration increases, then the interest risk will be higher. Let us explain this with an example:

Assume that at the 95 percent confidence interval, the lowest monthly return is –1.7 percent. It means that there is a 5 percent chance that the monthly medium bond return is lower than –1.7 percent. VaR = $100^m \times 1.7$ percent = < ₹1.7 million. In other words, a bond portfolio of ₹100 million, 95 percent of the time, the portfolio's loss will be not more than ₹1.7 million. Further, assume that the typical duration for a 5-year bond is 4.5 years and now of the current yield ($Y$) is 5 percent. From historical data of this bond we find that the worst increase in yields over a month at 95 percent is 40 percent, the most loss, or (VaR) is then calculated as:

$$\text{VaR} = \text{Duration} \times 1/(1 + Y) \times \text{portfolio value} \times \text{Worst Yield Increase}$$

$$\text{VaR} = 4.5 \times \frac{1}{1.05} \times ₹100 \text{ million} \times 0.4 = ₹1.7 \text{ million}$$

## 26.9 BASIC APPLICATIONS OF VaR

1. The VaR summarizes the risk of a portfolio in an easily comprehensive way. In a year with 250 trading days, the 99 percent VaR is the loss will be exceeded on only two to three days. For example, if two alternative portfolios are compared, then the portfolio with the higher VaR is riskier and needs to produce a higher return for it to be justifiable.

2. Once VaR is measured, it is the starting point for understanding risk and for initiating hedging strategies designed at reducing risk. The success of a hedging technique should be immediately seen in reduced VaR.

3. The uses of VaR fall broadly into three categories—determination of capital adequacy, performance measurement and supporting to the risk managers. The notion of risk capital is the relevant measure for determining the capital requirements which has become increasingly important.

4. The VaR technique communicates the true risk of the company to the top management, and assists in reducing the difficulties faced doing the speculative trading using derivatives. Top management can also impose limits on VaR, which can be used to cap the risks taken in the dealing room.

5. The VaR technique also assists in the fixed income market by quantifying the risk that the duration mismatch implies. So the danger of borrowing short and lending long will be frequently checked with this methodology.

## 26.10   VaR—AN EVALUATION

VaR is often criticized as being over-hyped, based on forty-year-old ideas of risk management. As said, there is nothing new about VaR as a way of measuring risk. The weaknesses of the system are two-old. First, on practical side, there are high costs of maintaining and operating a VaR based system—computer hardware and software, obtaining price data, employing expertise analysts, etc. Besides all these, it is quite possible that the results may not be good. Second aspect is more important because VaR is based on the  probabilistic estimate, which is subject to certain assumptions. Sometimes, in real life even one percent risk may create disaster for the institution.

Generally, historical data on volatility and correlation is taken to represent future volatility and correlation, which sometimes, may not be justified. Further, the concept of normal distribution, as used in the VaR method, may not hold in practice. It is observed that the tails of price distributions for financial markets are generally fatter than those of the normal distribution. It means that the probability of extreme value is greater than the implied normal distribution. In brief, these assumptions, sometimes, do not hold true in practice, thus, resulting in adverse situation for the institution.

Despite the weaknesses of the VaR system, it is probably the best available technique for measuring the risk for a large and complicated portfolio. VaR has proved to be vehicle through which modern financial experts and economists rely. Users of VaR are better off in deciding the level of return at the particular degree of risk. However, it must be used with utmost caution and in conjunction with stress tests because it is highly mathematical methodology with a plethora of grade symbols, equations and derivatives. VaR is not like a black box. More than one approach to calculate value at risk should be followed like Monte-Carlo simulation techniques in conjunction with a parametric based approach. Further the outputs from these systems should then be adjusted. There are many situations when portfolio returns are not normally distributed, on such there is no simple link between VaR and $\sigma$. Yet as long as adequate precautions are taken in correctly calculating VaR, the interpretation of VaR remains unchanged. Let us see another example. A company holds a long position worth ₹10 crores which has a daily volatility of 1 percent (based on historical data). What is the value at risk (VaR) over a one-day horizon, using a 98 percent confidence interval?

It is found from the standard normal distribution tables, that 98 percent of the distribution falls within 2.05 standard deviations of the mean (learning only 2 percent in left hand 'tail' of the distribution). The mean in this case is the volatility of 1 percent. The VaR is ₹10 crores × 1 percent × 2.05 = ₹20.50 lakhs. It means that one can be 98 percent sure that the loss from the futures position over the next day will not exceed ₹20.50 lakhs.

## 26.11    RISK MANAGEMENT VALUE CHAIN (RMVC)

After analyzing the different risks and the value at risk in derivative instruments, in this section, it will be discussed how a system of risk control in an organization is established. This process, termed as risk management value chain, will include the organizational considerations, role of senior management, information requirements and finally choosing a model for exposure management.

### 26.11.1    Organizational Consideration

First important aspect of creating a risk management value chain in an institution is to assess whether the present organizational structure is suitable for risk control strategy. Two main factors that impact any assessment are:

**Size and geographical structure:**    In this, two types of structures can be assessed—fully centralized and regional structure. A fully centralized risk control structure provides information on a detailed and consolidated basis to all those involved in derivative activities. This is usually best suited for regional or small commercial banks where there is degree of homogeneity in business operations across the different locations. All the important issues like limit management model calculations would be fully controlled at the centre.

In case of regional structure, regional risk function coexists with a centralized function at the centre of the organization. This type of structure would be suited to large organizations with a wide geographical span of activities. The regional control area would look after and coordinate risk control activities of a routine nature on day-to-day level with the responsibility of limit reporting and control. Central office would control over all risk strategy like limit formulation, consolidation of risk profiles, performance analysis, reviewing risk strategy and assisting in goal formulation.

**Existing functional involvement:**    The existing functional structure of an organization should be reviewed in the light of new changing orientation of the risk management area. Some rationalization of the existing function is inevitable. The review should be conducted over a reasonable period so that the potential barriers be removed.

### 26.11.2    Role of Senior Level Management

Another important consideration in establishing a risk management value chain is the role played by the senior management in this respect. The top management is primarily responsible for developing the notion of an integrated risk culture. Since derivative exposures are unique in nature and different from other risks, it is essential to create appropriate environment and culture in the organization. For this, the top management should sponsor the risk culture, assume responsibility for risk factor and establish objectives.

### 26.11.3    Information Requirements

Information requirements of the participants in the risk management process is an essential characteristics of an integrated risk area. Different levels of information are required to the participants for making decisions. Two inter-related aspects are considered, such as tactical vs strategic user level and timeliness of information. Srategic level information relates to senior level management, which need information for taking strategic decisions. The information moves from top to bottom.

All such matters regarding firms profits, level of expense, risk budget, trading limits and derivative performance are provided at the strategic level.

Tactical level information relates to exposure supervision. The focus would be on detailed information, which includes product, pricing analysis, incremental risk calculations, portfolio exposure breakdowns, mark to model risk calculations and so on. Both level of information is essential for integrated risk management.

The most important point in the derivative exposure management is that information must be provided as quickly as possible to the right person because risk information can be critical to making derivative decision. In this respect, it is essential to develop real time systems. This system provides up to the minute market information for tactical information requirements. Thus, the provision of risk management information is a cost/benefit trade off, which requires careful analysis to ascertain the level and intensity of information required for each derivative product decision.

## 26.11.4 Analytical Choices

After establishing a sound organizational structure and appropriate information network, another aspect which need to be considered in creating a risk control analytical function, are as follows:

**Constructing building block approach:** The management of derivative exposures is a complicated task which needs expertise, adequate sources and appropriate information requirement on various aspects like credit, market, liquidity, etc. Various methodologies and tools are used for risk analysis. Hence, in order to avoid duplication of efforts in constructing risk measurement approaches, a small number of analytical approaches should be followed to form the building blocks upon which further analytical method can be constructed. The intention of each building block is that it should be flexible enough to be utilized across more than one derivatives risk type.

**The risk continuum:** The basic objective of the risk continuum relates to compatibility with two main components of integrated risk system: a centralized risk management function and a performance measurement system, which computes return unit of risk using various methodologies. Key element in risk continuum approach is an awareness of creating efficiencies which can be measured in both time and cost.

**Choosing the models (Methodology):** This relates to the selection of particular suitable methodology or set of methodologies for risk management. In this process various aspects like suitability to portfolio composition, flexibility in relation to different risk types, speed versus accuracy trade off and essential back-testing are taken into consideration.

*Suitability.* Which particular methodology will be suitable for managing a derivative position/exposure depend upon nature of the position and market. The general rule is that a complex portfolio needs a complex solution, as observed:

1. If the portfolio position tends towards linearity (delta at constant rate) and normality (prices move in random manner) then risk estimates can be made by using statistical or parametric model like J.P. Morgan's Risk Metrics Approach.
2. In case of linear position with non-normal markets, one can use historical simulation techniques.
3. In case of non-linear with normal markets, Monte Carlo simulation technique including valuation calculations can be used.

4. When neither the market is normal nor the linear then the hybrid models should be used like combining the option pricing model with scenario analysis. In fact, while choosing between the various standard models, the risk manager should make trade off between computational efficiency, information requirements and theoretical correctness along with financial cost to be incurred on implementing these models.

*Flexibility.* After considering the suitability of the various methodologies to be used for the risk control, they should be assessed for their flexibility in terms of derivative products and risk types. In other words, whether the methodology is subject to desired/required adjustments or not, because some models may not be so flexible.

*Speed versus accuracy.* Another important consideration in selecting a methodology is their accuracy and speed of calculation. Some methodologies tend to be accurate but at the same time more computationally intensive and time consuming. For example, Monte Carlo simulation may be accurate but have to calculate thousands of simulated risk values, whereas parametric models can be run at a much greater speed but may not be so accurate in certain positions and situations. In brief, both speed and accuracy should be considered in selecting a model in the light of nature of derivative exposures and market situations.

*Back-testing.* While selecting a particular model or methodology, its back-testing is essential. If no back-testing plan is formulated, it is quite possible that misleading information be communicated not only to decision-makers but also to the regulators of the organization. Back-testing is concerned to evaluating the performance and its actual experience in the market of the risk model. There is no point in opting for a complex solution which does not lend itself to be benchmarked against actual results. For a back-testing plan, two factors should be considered: choosing the time frequency for back-testing the output and establishing what the accepted margin for model error is. Apart from all the above considerations, constructing a suitable derivative strategy is complicated and delicate task in the sense that it can be disaster for the institution, so the final decision should not be just on the basis of models and methodologies but also on the basis of sound common sense.

# SUMMARY

This chapter briefly describes the management of derivatives exposures. All derivatives tools like forwards, futures, options, swaps and other complex instruments are risky in the sense that their use should be most judicious and proper. It is not derivatives that are dangerous. The root of their risk lies in how and why they are used and what fragment of control. Handling of financial derivatives are just like handling the dangerous chemical or any explosive device. Financial derivatives markets move at fast speed, some derivatives are very competitive in nature like caps, callars, floor, exotic, forward rate agreements, etc., so, these should be structured very cautiously.

There are various reasons for managing derivatives risks. Important among these are: (a) increase in complexity of financial markets, (b) optimization of capital, (c) technology advancements, (d) market events and changes in accounting practices. Before managing the derivative exposure, it is essential to understand the nature and degree of risk involved, the various types of risk in derivatives like credit risk, market liquidity risk, legal risk and operational risk. Model risk or formal risk is another important risk involved in derivatives. It has been observed that, sometimes, various models or formula fail to give accurate results regarding price data.

Recently, there is significant development in risk management that how to measure the risk and then incorporate the same into a single variable. The notion of risk capital become the standard of choice among regulators and bankers. Therefore, Value at Risk (VaR) technique has become a standard method in the derivatives market assisting the senior management to understand the risk exposure of a particular derivative asset. VaR is a statistical concept which indicates towards the most that can be lost with a degree of confidence within the next specified period.

The basic parameters to measure the VaR are time horizon, data series, confidence interval and mapping. The experts have various approaches to measure the VaR, important among these are; the variance–covariance approach, historical simulation approach and Monte-Carlo simulation approach. First approach uses the volatility of risk factors in the past and correlations between changes in their values, and then an approximation is made of potential losses. Second approach is based on changes in actual historical returns, ranking them in order from worst to best and then losses are estimated at particular confidence level. Third approach is a stochastic model based on change in values of market factors and then uses a sequence of random paths for each factors normal distribution. After that worst outcome is determined at a desired confidence level. After calculating the VaR, the stress testing is followed to assess the impact of valuation on the performance of the portfolio in worst case scenario. Two techniques are used for stress testing: sensitivity test and scenario test. Sensitivity test requires considering variations in assumptions taking into the purpose of analysis and test to see whether results reflect a reasonable consistency with the purpose. It explains the changes in portfolio value for one or more shocks to a single risk factor. Scenario tests are constructed either within the context of a specific portfolio or in light of historical events. Choice of scenario between historical or hypothetical depends on several factors. After stress testing, back testing is followed. In back testing, VaR estimates of extreme losses are compared with the realized losses, so that the risk manager can re-assess the accuracy of the existing VaR model.

Prior to implementing the derivatives strategy, the firm's top management should chalkout a clear cut guidelines comprising policies, procedures, etc. In this respect, a risk vision and its various components like setting policies, commercial objectives, risk tolerance, financial capability, enhance competence and reviews should be taken into consideration. The weakness of the system are two-fold. First, on practical side, there are high cost of maintaining and operating a VaR based system—computer hardware and software, obtaining price data, employing expertise analysis, etc. Despite the weaknesses of VaR system, it is probably the best available technique for measuring the risk for a large and complicated portfolio. VaR has provided to be vehicle through which modern financial experts and economists rely. After analyzing the different risks and value at risk, next consideration is to develop a system to manage this risk. First important aspect is to create a risk management value chain in an institution to assess whether the present organizational structure is suitable for risk control strategy. Two main factors that impact any assessment of this are: (a) Size and geographical structure of the organization (b) Existing functional involvement in risk control.

Which particular methodology will be suitable for managing a derivative position/exposure depends upon the position of the market. Back-testing plan is formulated. It is quite possible that misleading information be communicated not only to decision maker but also to the regulators of the organization. Back-testing is concerned to evaluate the performance and its actual experience in the market of the risk model. There is no point in opting for a complex solution which does not lend to be benchmarked against actual results. Choosing the time frequency for back-testing the output and establishing what the accepted margin for model error is apart from all the above considerations. Constructing a suitable derivative strategy is complicated and delicate task in the sense that it can be disaster for the corporate unit.

## SOLVED PROBLEMS

**P1.** Calculate the VaR from the following information:

Probability (2 million in SENSEX index will decrease by more than 20% within a year) < 10%.

*Solution:*

| | |
|---|---|
| Amount of time ($t$) | = One year |
| Probability level ($X$) | = 0.10 |
| VaR = 20% of ₹2 million with 10% probability | = 4,00,000 |
| = (₹2 million × 20 × 10) | = ₹4,00,000 |

**P2.** Consider a portfolio consisting ₹20,00,000 investment in security 'A' and security 'B' each. Assume that the daily volatilities of both the securities are 0.1% and that correlation coefficient between their returns is 0.20. Calculate the 5 day, 95% value-at-risk (VaR) of the portfolio, assuming a parametric model with zero expected return, considering the 95th percentile of the standard normal distribution is 1.645.

*Solution:* The standard deviation of the daily rupee change is the value of each security is ₹2,000. The standard deviation of the portfolio's daily change is:

$$\sigma(A + B) = \sqrt{\sigma^2 A + \sigma^2 B + 2P\sigma A\sigma B}$$

$$\sqrt{(2,000)^2 + (2,000)^2 + 2 \times 0.2 \times 2,000 \times 2,000} = \sqrt{40,00,000 + 40,00,000 + 1,60,00,000}$$

$$\sqrt{96,00,000} = ₹3,098.39$$

The standard deviation of the 5-day change is the portfolio value is

$$₹3,098.39 \times \sqrt{5} = ₹6,928.21$$

The 95th percentile of the standard normal distribution is 1.645. Therefore (assuming zero mean), the 5 day 95% Value at Risk is:

$$1.645 \times ₹6,928.21 = ₹11,396.91$$

**P3.** A foreign commercial bank owns a portfolio of options on the US dollar–pound sterling exchange rate. The delta of the portfolio is given 36. Current exchange rate is $1.30 per pound sterling. Daily volatility of the exchange rate is 0.50%. Determine the approximate linear relationship between the change in the portfolio value and proportional exchange in the exchange rate? Also estimate to 10 day, 99% Value at Risk.

*Solution:* In the above example, value of delta, i.e., approximate relationship between the daily change in the portfolio value ($\Delta P$) and the daily change in the exchange rate ($\Delta S$) is ($\Delta P$) = $36\Delta s - S$ (Assume $\Delta X$ be the proportional daily change in the exchange rate. The $\Delta X = \dfrac{\Delta s - S}{1.3}$. Therefore, $\Delta P = 56 \times 1.3\Delta X = 72.8 \, \Delta s$. The standard deviation of $\Delta X$ equal the daily volatility of the exchange rate, i.e., 0.50%. The standard deviation of $\Delta P$, therefore, is 72.8 × (0.50%) = 0.364. The 10 day, 99%, Value at Risk (VaR) is thus estimated as $0.364 \times 2.33 \times \sqrt{10} = 2.68$.

**P4.** Consider that daily change in the value of a portfolio is combination of two factors calculated from a principal components analysis. The delta of the portfolio with respect to the first factor is 5 and delta of the portfolio with respect to the second factor is –6. The standard deviations of the two factors are 15 and 10 respectively. Calculate the 5 day, 90% value at risk?

*Solution:* It is assumed that the factors used in a principal components analysis are uncorrelated. So the daily variance of the portfolio is:

$5^2 \times 15^2 + (-6)^2 \times 10^2 = 9225$ and standard deviation is ₹96.05. Since the 90th percentile of the standard normal distribution is 1.282, the 5 day 90% VaR is estimated as:

$$₹96.05 \times \sqrt{5} \times 1.282 = ₹275.33$$

**P5.** A finance company has a position in bond worth ₹10 million. The effective duration of the portfolio is 4.7 years. Assume that the yield curve change only in parallel shifts and that the volatility of the yield is 0.08%. Use the duration model for estimating volatility of the portfolio. Estimate the 20 day VaR of the portfolio. The 90th percentile of the standard normal distribution is 1.282 through the parametric VaR model.

*Solution:* According to duration model: $\Delta B = -D \times B \times \Delta Y$ where $B$ is the value of the bond portfolio, '$D$' is the effective duration, and '$Y$' is the yield on bond. In the said example; $D = 4.70$, $\Delta Y$ is 0.08%, then the standard deviation of the portfolio return: $\dfrac{\Delta B}{B} = -D \times AY = (0.08\%)$ $(4.70) = 0.376\%$. Portfolio is 10 million. The standard deviation of its change in value is ₹10,000,000 $\times 0.376\% = ₹37600$. The 90th percentile of the standard normal distribution is 1.282, then VaR of the 20 day, 90% is: $37{,}600 \times \sqrt{20} \times 1.282 = ₹2{,}15{,}571.26$.

## SUGGESTED READINGS

1. Morgan, J.P. (Morgan Guaranty Trust Company), *Introduction to Risk Metrics*, New York, March 1995.
2. Sheridan, T., The Barings Debacle, *Management Accounting*, May 1995.
3. Varma, J.R., Robust Risk Containment Model for Interest Rate Derivatives in India, Report of SEBI group on *Secondary Market Risk Management*, Mumbai, 2002.
4. Bhalla, V.K., *Financial Derivatives—Risk Management*, Sultan Chand and Company Ltd., New Delhi, 2001.
5. Jorion, P., How Long Term Lost its Capital, *RISK*, September 1999.
6. Zhang, P.G., Baring Bankruptcy and Financial Derivatives, *World Scientific*, Singapore, 1995.
7. Thomson, R., Apocalypse Roulette, *The Lethal World of Derivatives*, Macmillan, London, 1999.
8. Barone-Adesi, G.K. Giannopoulos and L. Vosper (1990), "VaR without Correlations for Portfolios of Derivative Securities," *Journal of Futures Markets*, 19, 583–602.
9. Basak, S. and Shapiro, A. (2000), "Value-at-Risk Based Risk Management: Optimal Policies and Assets Prices," forthcoming, Review of Financial Studies.
10. Christoffersen, P. and F.X. Diebold (2000), "How Relevant is Volatility Forecasting for Financial Risk Management," Review of Economics and Statistics, 82, 12–22.
11. Duffie, D. and J. Pan (1997), "An Overview of Value at Risk", *Journal of Derivatives*, Spring 1997, 4,7–49.

12. Hendricks, D. (1996), "Evaluation of Value-at-Risk Models Using Historical Data", *Economics Policy Review*, Federal Reserve Bank of New York, April, 39–69.

13. Jorion, P. (2000), "How Informative are Value-at-Risk Disclosures", manuscript, University of California, Irvine.

14. Jorion, P. (2001), *Value-at-Risk: The New Benchmark for Controlling Market Risk*, Chicago: McGraw-Hill.

15. Morgan, J.P. (1996), Risk Metrics, Technical Document 4th Edition, New York.

16. Kupiec, P. (1995). "Techniques for Verifying the Accuracy of Risk Measurement Models," Journal of Derivatives, 1, 91–111.

17. Marshall, C. and M. Siegel (1997), "Value-at-Risk: Implementing a Risk Measurement Standard," *Journal of Derivatives*, 1, 91–111.

18. Pritsker, M. (1997), "Evaluating Value at Risk Methodologies: Accuracy versus Computational Time," *Journal of Financial Services Research*, 12, 201–242.

19. Zangrari, P., (1997), "Streamlining the Market Risk Measurement Process," Risk Metrics Monitor, 1, 29–35.

20. Kupiec, P.H, (1998), "Stress Testing in a Value at Risk Framework", *Journal of Derivatives*, 6(1): 7–24.

21. Longin, F, (2000), "From Value at Risk to Stress Testing: The Extreme Value Approach." *Journal of Banking and Finance* 24(7): 1097–1130.

22. Peura, S. and Jokivuolle, E. (2004), "Simulation-Based Stress Tests of Banks Regulatory Capital Adequacy", *Journal of Banking and Finance*, 28 (8): 1801–1824.

23. Tan, K. and Chan, I. (2003), "Stress Testing Using VaR Approach—A Case for Asian Currencies", *Journal of International Financial Markets, Institutions and Money*, 13 (1): 39-55.

## REVIEW QUESTIONS

1. Explain the concept and nature of derivatives trading. What are different features of this trading? Explain with examples.

2. What are main purposes and reasons for which derivatives are to be used? Which risks are involved in this respect?

3. "Handling of derivatives instruments should be linked to landing dangerous chemicals, or say, nuclear devices." Critically evaluate the statement in the light of nature of derivatives trading.

4. What is the process for approving the use of new derivatives instruments? Explain with suitable examples.

5. Are derivatives the best things that have never happened to the corporate-treasurer, investment manager and speculator? Discuss the spot event with suitable examples.

6. Describe the various strategic components of risk vision.

7. Explain the concept of Value At Risk (VaR). Also discuss the basic applications of VaR.

8. Explain the various techniques of measuring VaR along with their merits and demerits.

9. Explain the various parameters of determining VaR with suitable examples.

10. Explain the term stress testing. What is its objective?

11. How will you design stress testing framework for a portfolio? Explain in detail with examples.

12. Critically evaluate the weaknesses of the Value at Risk (VaR).

13. Write notes on
    (a) Risk Management Value Chain (RMVC)
    (b) Organizational consideration in RMVC
    (c) Role of senior management in risk management
14. Write detailed note on using and managing derivatives with suitable illustrations?
15. Write notes on
    (a) Operational risk and its management
    (b) Integrated risk framework
16. Discuss the major factors influencing the risk management in a globalized financial derivatives market.
17. "Most of the losses from derivatives transactions have come from defective implementation of risk-vision approach in risk management." Discuss the policies and procedure for risk management in the light of above statement. Also discuss the various examples to justify your answer.
18. Evaluate the key stages of technology strategy for integrated financial derivatives risk management.
19. Examine the factors used to be considered in creating a 'holistic' derivatives risk control analytic functions.
20. Explain the term scenarios generating in context of stress testing. What are different types of scenarios? Explain with suitable examples.
21. Explain the role of duration in VaR measurement with examples.
22. Write a note on back testing in risk management of a firm.

# Answers to Unsolved Problems

## CHAPTER 2

1. Margin call to investor when ₹1,000 will be lost from margin account. Margin call will occur when price of cotton increases by 1,000/5,000 = ₹0.20. So price of cotton must rise to ₹50.20 per bundle for margin call. And in case investor does not make a payment of margin call, broker will close out investor's position.

2. Margins and marking-to-market for XYZ Ltd. at BSE:

   Initial margin = ₹2,000

   Maintenance  = ₹1,500

   w = Withdrawn

   d = Deposit

| Date | Futures price (₹) | Daily losses/ gains (₹) | Starting margin (₹) | Money or margin withdrawn/deposit (₹) | Balance at end (₹) |
|------|------|------|------|------|------|
| January 14 | 450 | — | 2,000 | — | 2,000 |
| January 15 | 449 | −100 | 1,900 | 0 | 1,900 |
| January 16 | 455 | +600 | 2,500 | −500(w) | 2,000 |
| January 17 | 450 | −500 | 1,500 | +500(d) | 2,000 |
| January 18 | 452 | +200 | 2,200 | −200(w) | 2,000 |
| January 19 | 445 | −700 | 1,300 | +700(d) | 2,000 |
| January 21 | 450 | +500 | 2,500 | −500(w) | 2,000 |
| January 22 | 455 | +500 | 2,500 | −500(w) | 2,000 |
| January 23 | 460 | +500 | 2,500 | −500(w) | 2,000 |
| January 24 | 465 | +500 | 2,500 | −500(w) | 2,000 |
| January 25 | 470 | +500 | 2,500 | −500(w) | 2,000 |
| January 27 | 475 | +500 | 2,500 | −500(w) | 2,000 |
| January 31 | 480 | +500 | 2,500 | −500(w) | 2,000 |
| February 1 | 490 | +500 | 2,500 | −500(w) | 2,000 |

3.  (a) ₹4,000 as a margin money

    (b) Value of contract stands at ₹150 × 600 = ₹90,000

    (c) Total loss to Amit if index stands at 155 = (150 – 155) × 600

    $$= 5 \times 600 = ₹3,000$$

    (d) If index decline to 1% means (148.5) then profit % to Amit

    $$= (150 - 148.5) \times 600 = ₹900$$

    $$\text{In percentage form} = \frac{900 \times 100}{4,000} = 22.5\%$$

    (e) Margin money of ₹4,000 as in case of selling the contract

4.  Table showing reverse trading

| Futures market | |
|---|---|
| May 1 | Buy 1st September contract for cotton at ₹170 per Bushel |
| May 25 | Sell 1st September contract for cotton at ₹175 per Bushel |

In this way A can close out his position from futures market.

5.  (a) At the futures prices, exporter will receive ₹13,80,00,000.

    (b) At the current prices, level payment will be ₹1,44,00,000.

    (c) In terms of dollar, the loss to exporter, if dollar worth ₹40 after one year = $50,000.

6.  Table showing daily settlement with futures contract

| Day | Action | Cash flow |
|---|---|---|
| Monday morning | Investor buys pound £ futures contract that matures in two days. Price is $1.70 and price rise to $1.71 at the end. | ($1.71 – $1.70) × 6,250 = 625$. Investor will receive $625 on day Ist. |
| Tuesday close | Futures price rise to $1.72 position is marked-to-market | Investor received 62,500 × ($1.72 – $1.71) = $625. |
| Wednesday close | Futures price rise to $1.702<br>1. Contract is marked-to-market.<br>2. Investor takes delivery of $62,500. | 1. Investor pays 62,500 × ($1.72 – $1.702) = $1125<br>2. Investor pays ($62,500 × $1.702) = $1,06,375. |

7.  Following actions can be taken by the arbitrageur:

    (i) Borrow ₹10,000 at 15% per annum for one year

    (ii) Buy one kg of silver

    (iii) Enter into short forward contract to sell silver for ₹12,000 per kg in one year. Interest on ₹10,000 which is borrowed will be ₹1,500. Trader can, therefore, use ₹11,500 (₹10,000 + ₹1,500) of the ₹12,000 that is obtained for the silver in one year to repay the borrowing. So in this way the arbitrageur can earn ₹500 as a profit.

**8.** Sachin's position on July 15

| Transaction | Mr. X's position | | | |
|---|---|---|---|---|
| | Spot market | | Futures market | |
| | Date | Price (₹) | Date | Price (₹) |
| Sell | June 1 | 9,600 | July 15 | 9,100 |
| Buy | July 10 | 9,100 | June 1 | 9,750 |
| Gain/loss | | +650 | | (–)(650) |
| | | 650 Profit | | –650 loss |
| **Net return (₹) = NIL** | | | | |

# CHAPTER 4

**1.** $A = ₹500$, $R = 12\%$ and $T = 1$ year
Terminal value of investment is:

$$= 500 (1 + 0.12)$$
$$= 500 (1.12) = ₹560$$

**2.** $A = ₹500$, $m = 2$ and $r = 12\%$
Value of investment $= A (1 + r/m)^{mn}$

$$= 500 (1 + 0.12/ 2)^{2×1}$$
$$= 500 (1 + 0.06)^2$$
$$= 500 × 1.06 × 1.06$$
$$= ₹561.80$$

**3.** Because current price of stock (Infosys) is ₹1000 and 10% risk-free interest rate, so amount to be paid after two years will be ₹$(1,000e^{0.10×2}) = ₹1,220.50$ for taking a loan of ₹1,000. Two-year price of stock is ₹1500. So there exhibits an arbitrage opportunity:

1. Borrow ₹1,000 at an interest rate of 10% per annum for two years
2. Buy one share of the stock
3. Enter in futures contract to sell one share for ₹1,500 in two years

So, gain to trader is

$$₹1,500 - ₹1,220.5 = ₹279.5$$

**4.** The futures price of the index:

Current price $= ₹350$
Interest rate $= 8\%$
Dividend $= 4\%$
Therefore,

$$\text{Futures price} = 350e^{(0.08-0.04)(0.3333)} = \$354.7$$

**5.**

| Transaction | Cash flow (₹) |
|---|---|
| *T* = 0 Borrow ₹15,000 for six months | +15,000 |
| @ 10% per annum | −15,000 |
| Buy 100 shares of IDFC at the spot rate | 0 |
| Sell a futures contract for ₹18,000 | |
| For delivery after six months | |
| Total cash flow | 0 |
| *T* = 1 | |
| (a) Delivery taken of 100 shares of IDFC | 0 |
| (b) Deliver the IDFC shares against futures contract | +18,000 |
| Repay loan including interest for | |
| Six months ₹900 + ₹15,000 | −15,900 |
| Total cash flow | +₹2,100 |

**6.** Market participant will take following transactions:
1. Buy spot and store the pepper
2. Sell futures and deliver in December at ₹9,500

Profit/loss to trader: ₹9,500 − ₹7,950 − ₹1,000
$$= ₹9,500 − ₹8,950 = ₹550$$

**7.** Calculation of carrying cost:

$$C_{ct}, T = 4,800 \times 0.12 \times \frac{240}{365} + ₹1 \times 8$$

$$= 576 \times \frac{240}{365} + ₹8$$

$$= ₹387$$

Implicit convenience yield:

$$= \frac{4,800 + ₹387 - 4,600}{4,800} \times \frac{365}{240}$$

$$= \frac{5,187 - 4,600}{4,800} \times \frac{365}{240}$$

$$= 0.001860 \times 100 = 18.60\%$$

**8.** Basis = Current cash price − Futures price

| Contract | Price (₹ per share) | Basis |
|---|---|---|
| Cash | 200 | — |
| July 2015 | 210 | −10 |
| August 2015 | 230 | −30 |
| October 2015 | 240 | −40 |
| November 2015 | 290 | −90 |
| December 2015 | 305 | −105 |
| January 2016 | 310 | −110 |

9. Forward price $F = 30e^{0.06 \times 0.5} = 30.90$

Then

Value of forward contract $f = (F - K)^{-rT}$

$$= (30.90 - 0.28)e^{-0.06 \times 0.5}$$

$$= 3.90 - 0.09 = 2.81 \text{ Approx.}$$

*Alternatively:*

$$f = 30 - 28^{-0.06-0.5}$$

$$= 30 - 27.16 = 2.84 \text{ Approx.}$$

# CHAPTER 7

1. Basis = Cash price – Futures price

So Basis = ₹400 – ₹440 = ₹–40

Futures price is said to be quoted at a premium because futures price is greater than the cash price of XYZ stock at Delhi Stock Exchange. The basis is negative.

2. Hedge ratio

$$= \frac{0.30}{0.50} = 0.6$$

Therefore, $\text{NFC} = \dfrac{5,00,000 \text{ gallons}}{50,000 \text{ gallons}} \times 0.60 = 6$

where 50,000 gallons $= Q_{FC} =$ quantity of the commodity represented by each futures contract.

Thus, the minimum-variance hedge requires selling 6 contractors of heating oil futures.

3. The optimal hedge ratio is:

$$= \frac{0.8 \times 0.65}{0.81} = 0.642$$

This means that the size of the futures position should be 64.2% of the size of the company's exposure in a three-month hedge.

4. Number of contract company should be shorted:

$$= \frac{\text{Beta} \times \text{Value of portfolio}}{\text{Index value}}$$

$$= \frac{1.2 \times 10,00,000}{250 \times 500} = 9.6$$

Rounding the nearest whole number, 10 contracts should be shorted. To reduce the beta to 0.6, half of the above position or a short position in 5 contractors is required.

5. Investor should sell the stock:

Number of contract that investor should shorted gives:

$$\frac{1.3 \times 1,00,00,000}{150 \times 500} = \frac{13,00,00,000}{75,000} = 1,733.33$$

Rounding the nearest whole number, 1733 contracts should be shorted, to hedge against adverse movement in portfolio.

**6.** Long Hedge for Textile

| Cash market | Futures market |
|---|---|
| Anticipate the need of 20,000 metres of textile in three months and expected to pay 2,500 × 200 = ₹5,00,000 | Buy 20, 1,000 metres textile futures contract at ₹2,500 for 100 metres. |
| After 3 months | After 3 months |
| The spot price of textile is ₹2800 per 100 metres. A buys paying ₹5,60,000 | Since the futures contract is at maturity, the futures and spot price are equal and the 20 contracts are sold at ₹2,800 per 100 metres. |
| Cash/opportunity loss = ₹60,000 | Futures profits = ₹60,000 |

**Net wealth change = 0**

**7.** Gain on futures contracts is $19.10 - $18.00 = $1.10 per barrel. The basis when contract is closed out is 20.00 - 19.10 = $0.90 per barrel. The effective price paid is the final spot price on November 20, less the gain on futures 1 - 20.00 - 1.10 = 18.90

$$\text{Total price paid by company} = \$18.90 \times 10,000 = \$1,89,000$$

**8.** Profit/Loss Profile of Treasurer

| Spot market | Futures market |
|---|---|
| **March** | **March** |
| The treasurer intends to borrow £5,00,000 on May 15. The current interest rate is 6.5% p.a. | The treasurer sells a futures contract at a price of (100 - 6.5) = 93.5 |
| **May 15** | **May 15** |
| Interest rate increased to 8%, so increase in borrowing cost of 1.5% p.a. for 3 months on £500,000 amount to £1,875. | Index has fallen to 92 (100 - 8), close out position by buy at 92 and fetching a profit of 93.5 - 92 = 1.5 index point |
| Loss = £1,875 | Profit = £5,00,000 |
| | @ 1.5% p.a. for 3 months, amount to $1,875 |

**Net position – Nil change**

# CHAPTER 8

**1.** A will find out beta of Reliance that is 0.8. Size of NIFTY position that A needs on the index futures market is:

$$0.8 \times 3,85,000 = ₹3,08,000$$

Suppose spot value of NIFTY is 1,540 on that date and multiplier is 200. So value of NIFTY each contract = 200 × 1,540 = ₹3,08,000.

Here A would need to sell one contract of the NIFTY to achieve hedge and his final position will be long Reliance ₹3,85,000 and Short NIFTY ₹3,08,000.

**2.** Short position will be appropriate for the fund manager and he will sell today and hedge his risk of declining the market value of portfolio.

Profit/Loss of Short Position

| Spot market | Futures market |
|---|---|
| Long portfolio 1 crore and beta is 1.25, exposure value of portfolio is 1.25 crore. Current NIFTY is 1,250 and value of NIFTY contract is 1,250 × 200 = ₹2,50,000 | Sell 50 $\left(\dfrac{1.25 \text{ crore}}{2,50,000}\right)$ contract at 1250 and he thereby notionally commit himself to deliver shares worth 1.25 crore (50 × 2,50,000) or (50 × 1250 × 200) |
| Two months later, current index is at 1300 so there is profit on cash position 50 on total portfolio | Close out position buying at 1,300, thereby futures loss = (1,300 – 1,250) |
| 1300 × 200 = ₹3,60,000 | 50 × 1,250 × 200 = ₹5,00,000 |
| (50 × 10,000) = ₹5,00,000 on the whole contract | |

**Net position = 0**

**3.** Hedge ratio = $\left(\dfrac{V_P}{V_F}\right)\beta_P$

$V_P$ = Values of portfolio

$\beta_P$ = Beta of portfolio

$V_F$ = Valued futures contract

$$= \left[\frac{4,00,00,000}{\$212 \times 500}\right] 1.22 = 460 \text{ contracts}$$

| Stock market | Futures market |
|---|---|
| **May 15** | **May 15** |
| Hold $4,00,00,000 in a stock portfolio | Sell 460 S & P futures contract For December delivery at 212 |
| **June 18** | **June 18** |
| Stock portfolio falls by 5% to $3,80,00,000 | Standard and Poor futures contract fall by 4.43% |
| Loss $20,00,000 | Gain = $20,70,000 |

**Net gain on futures contract = $70,000**

**4.**
$$HR = \left(\frac{V_P}{V_F}\right)\beta_P$$

$$= \left(\frac{₹\,10,00,000}{354.75 \times ₹\,500}\right) 0.8801$$

$$= 49.618$$

So estimated risk minimizing futures position is 49.62 contract. So portfolio manager decides to sell 50 contract of S & P 500 index.

**5.** No. of contracts to be shorted:

$$1.2 \times \left( \frac{20,00,000}{1,200 \times 200} \right) = 1.2 \times 8.33 = 9.90$$

No. of contract to minimize risk = 10

If company wants to reduce beta to 0.5 then

$$= 0.5 \times \left( \frac{20,00,000}{11200 \times 200} \right) = \left( \frac{20,00,000}{2,40,000} \right) \times 0.5 = 4$$

4 contracts should be sold in futures market to reduce the portfolio at beta to 0.5.

**6.** Alternative investment strategies:

1. A portfolio of stocks worth = 20 lakhs
2. A portfolio of stock index and T-bills futures = Long ₹20 lakhs T-bill and Long 10 NIFTY futures

$$= \left( \frac{20,00,000}{1,020 \times 200} \right) = \left( \frac{20,00,000}{2,04,000} \right) = 9.80$$

Evaluation of two investment strategies:

1. Value of portfolio using strategy 1

| Value of portfolio using strategy 1 | 10% Increase | No change | 10% Decrease |
|---|---|---|---|
| Initial investment capital appreciation | 20,00,000 | 20,00,000 | 20,00,000 |
| 20,00,000 × (10%) or (–10%) | 2,00,000 | 0 | (2,00,000) |
| Dividend 20,00,000 × 4% × $\frac{3}{12}$ | 20,000 | 20,000 | 20,000 |
| Total | 22,20,000 | 20,20,000 | 18,20,000 |

2. Value of portfolio using strategy 2

| Value of portfolio using strategy 2 | 10% Increase | No change | 10% Decrease |
|---|---|---|---|
| Investment in T-bill | 20,00,000 | 20,00,000 | 20,00,000 |
| Interest on T-bill $\left( 20,00,000 \times 8\% \times \frac{3}{12} \right)$ | 40,000 | 40,000 | 40,000 |

*Gain or loss on NIFTY futures:*

| | | | |
|---|---|---|---|
| (i) NIFTY = (1100 – 1020) × 10 × 200 | 1,60,000 | | |
| (ii) No change = (1000 – 1020) × 10 × 200 | | – 40,000 | |
| (iii) 10% decrease = (900 – 1020) × 10 × 200 | | | (2,40,000) |
| Total | 22,00,000 | 20,00,000 | 18,00,000 |

**7.**

| Spot market | Futures market |
|---|---|
| **April 15** | **April 15** |
| Treasurer intends to borrow ₹50,00,000 on June 15. | Treasurer sells a futures contract at a price |
| The current interest rate is 8% p.a. | (100 – 8%) = 92 |
| If by June 15 the interest rate had risen to 10% p.a., the treasurer would have to pay an extra cost of ₹25,000. | Close out position by booking at ₹90 and profit of ₹25,000 will be earned. |
| However, due to increase, futures price decrease have fallen to 90 so that the futures contract would be bought | |
| Loss of ₹25,000 | Profit of ₹25,000 |

**8.** Calculation of market exposure of the portfolio:

Market Exposure = (No. of shares × Share price and beta)

|   |   |   |
|---|---|---|
| (i) | $1000 \times 140 \times 0.9$ | = ₹ 1,26,000 |
| (ii) | $3000 \times 120 \times 0.5$ | = ₹ 1,80,000 |
| (iii) | $5000 \times 50 \times 1.3$ | = ₹ 3,25,000 |
| (iv) | $10000 \times 140 \times 0.8$ | = ₹ 11,20,000 |
| (v) | $12000 \times 470 \times 0.8$ | = ₹ 45,12,000 |
| | Total market exposure | = ₹ 63,71,000 |

**9.** Current NSE S & P CNX NIFTY futures = 1500

$$\text{Contract volume of NIFTY futures} = 1500 \times 200$$
$$= 3,00,000$$
$$\text{No. of contracts investor should buy} = 3$$

Profit/Loss profile at expiry in December

| Cash market | Futures market |
|---|---|
| Investor wanted to invest ₹10,00,000 in December. Current index is at 1500 | Buy 3 contracts valued at ₹3,00,000 each amounting to ₹9,00,000 |
| **December** | **December** |
| Current Index is at 1600. Investor have to put additional money to buy the share = 100 × 200 × 3 = ₹60,000 Future loss = ₹60,000 | Since futures contract is at expiry. Close out position by selling at 1600 and enjoying a profit of 100 per index point = 100 × 200 × 3 = ₹60,000 Futures profit = ₹60,000 |

Net change in position = 0

**10. Strategy:** Since you believe that price will go down in futures and whereby value of portfolio will also fall. So index futures is a better option to hedge a portfolio of blue chip stocks against a market decline.

Sell three February NSE S&P CNX NIFTY futures contract at ₹1,450 or a contract value of 1450 × 200 = 2,90,000. Suppose in February futures contract settles at 1250 so there is stock loss of 8,00,000 × 14% (decline% in market) = 1,10,000 = 6,90,000, net value of stocks. But in futures market, there is a profit of (1450 – 1250) = 200 points × 200 × 3 = 1,20,000. So net value of portfolio will be ₹6,90,000 + ₹1,20,000 = ₹8,10,000.

**11.** XYZ selling price works out to 2,69,000/200 = 1345 per NIFTY matures Future contract. On the futures expiration day, the futures price converges to the spot price. If index closed at 1260, so there must be a profit to XYZ on futures position = (1345 – 1260) × 200 = ₹17,000.

**12.** Cost of purchase = 3,00,000

$$\text{Index multiplier} = 200$$

$$\text{Per contract cost} = \frac{3,00,000}{200} = 1500$$

On expiration day, the futures price converges to the spot price. Index closed at 1530, futures price will also be 1530 on that day. Hence he will have made profit of (1530 – 1500) × 200 = ₹6,000.

**13.** Total value of 20 market lots:

$$20 \times 200 \times 1,000 = ₹40,00,000$$

At a price of ₹1,025 per NIFTY, profit will be ₹25 per NIFTY contract.

$$\text{Profit} = 20 \times 25 \times 200 = ₹1,00,000$$

OR

$$\text{Value} = 1,025 \times 20 \times 200 = 41,00,000$$

$$\text{Profit} = 41,00,000 - 40,00,000 = ₹1,00,000$$

# CHAPTER 10

**1.**

| Cash market | Futures market |
|---|---|
| **February 10** | **February 10** |
| Company plans to deposit $10 million on April 10. Current rate of interest is 10% p.a. | Buys June 10 three-month eurodollar interest futures contract at a price of $90.5. |
| **April 10** | **April 10** |
| Company deposits $10 million at an interest rate of 9% p.a. | Sells June 10 three-month eurodollar interest rate futures contract at a price of $90.5. |
| Loss equal to 1% $10 million for three months— $25,000 × (0.01 × 10 million × 0.25) | There is no gain since the price is unchanged at $90.5. |

Net loss = $25,000

**2.**

| Cash market | Futures market |
|---|---|
| Intends to borrow £20 million on February 1, fear that interest rate will rise above 10% p.a. | Sells March 20, futures contract, thereby notionally guaranteeing that £20 million will be borrowed at 10% on the March maturity data. |
| **February 1** | **February 1** |
| Borrow £20 million at an interest rate of 12% p.a. | Buys March 20, futures contracts, thereby entering a notional commitment to lend £20 million at 12% p.a. on March maturity date. |

Net change position = Nil

3.                    Cash price = Quoted price + Accrued interest since last coupon date

$$\text{Accrued interest} = \frac{54}{181} \times \$55 \ (11\% \text{ annually})$$

$$= \$1.64$$

The price per $100 face value of bond is:

$$\$95.50 + \$1.64 = \$97.14$$

The cost price of a $1,00,000 bond is $97,140

4.    Forward rate (percent per annum with continuous compounding) are:
Year 2 = 7%
Year 3 = 6.6%
Year 4 = 6.4%
Year 5 = 6.5%

5.    Cash price of treasury bill:

$$= 100 - \frac{1}{4} \times 10 = 97.5$$

The annualized continuously compounded return is:

$$\frac{365}{90} \text{ In } \frac{100}{97.5} = 12.5\%$$

Return on 90-day T-bill = 12.5% p.a.

6.    Speculating with eurodollar futures

| Date | Futures market |
| --- | --- |
| September 20 | Sell December 1, 90 eurodollar futures at 90.30. |
| September 25 | Buy December 1, 90 eurodollar futures at 90.12. |

Profit = 90.30 – 90.12 = 0.18

Total gain = 18 basis point × ₹25 = ₹450

# CHAPTER 11

1.    No. of days between May 5 and July 27 = 83
Cash price of bond on July 27, 1994

$$= 110.17 + \frac{83}{182} \times 6$$

$$= 110.17 + 2.74 = ₹112.91$$

**2.** Calculation of duration

| No. of periods to maturity | Cash flow per ₹100 face value | PV of cash flow | Duration weights | Percentage weights |
|:---:|:---:|:---:|:---:|:---:|
| 1 | 3 | 2.871 | 0.0303 | 0.0303 |
| 2 | 3 | 2.747 | 0.0290 | 0.0580 |
| 3 | 3 | 2.629 | 0.0278 | 0.0834 |
| 4 | 3 | 2.516 | 0.0266 | 0.1064 |
| 5 | 100 | 83.756 | 0.8862 | 3.5448 |
| | | | Duration | 3.8229 |

Annual basis duration $= \dfrac{3.82}{2} = 1.91$ years

**3.**

| Cash market | Futures market |
|---|---|
| **January 2** | **January 2** |
| Corporate intends to raise DM 2 million on February 15 by sale of bonds. Interest rate on undated bonds is 6% p.a. | Sell March 8, German government bonds futures contracts. |
| Treasurer wants to ensure that cost of servicing debt will be limited to DM 1,20,000 p.a. | Futures price is 100, Reflecting a 6% p.a. interest. |
| **February 15** | **February 15** |
| Interest rate on stock has risen to 7½ p.a. | Close out by buying March 8, German government futures contracts, futures price is 82.22, 7½% futures interest rate. |
| The cost of servicing a DM 2 million debt will now be DM 1,50,00 p.a. (20,00,000 @ 7½ percent) | Profit on futures position DM (100 – 82.22) × 20,00,000 = DM 3,57,600 |

So treasurer has hedged his position by selling in futures market at a higher rate and close out position by buying at a lower rate.

**4.** No. of contract $= \dfrac{\text{Normal value} \times \text{Equivalency ratio}}{\text{Futures contract size (market lot)}}$

$= \dfrac{3,75,000 \times 1.3}{50,000} = 9.75$

Since partial contracts cannot be traded, hedger should trade 10 contracts in this case.

**5.** Cost of delivery for each bonds are:

$$\text{Bond 1} = 99.50 - (93.25 \times 1.0382) = 2.69$$
$$\text{Bond 2} = 143.50 - (93.25 \times 1.5188) = 1.87$$
$$\text{Bond 3} = 119.75 - (93.25 \times 1.2615) = 2.12$$

So the cheapest-to-deliver bond is Bond 2.

**6.** Cash price of the treasury bill is $= 100 - \dfrac{1}{4} \times 10 = 97.5$

Annualized continuous compounded return is $= \dfrac{365}{90} \ln \dfrac{100}{97.5} = 10.27\%$

**7.** Value of contract is $100 \times 100 = 1,00,000$
Average duration = 8.4 years
Cheapest-to-deliver duration = 6.2 years
Total value of funds = 50 lakhs

So          No. of contracts $= \dfrac{50,00,000}{1,00,000} \times \dfrac{8.4}{6.2}$

$$= 67.74$$

Number of contracts needed to hedge the position = 68

**8.** The bond price is ₹110 and accrued interest would be 8% p.a. Bond will be delivered at the end of July. Since coupon yield exceeds the financing cost (rate of interest), so the total cost will be

$$114 + 114\,(0.04) = 114 + 4.56 = 118.56$$

Net carry cost must take account coupon receipts plus interest

$$= ₹6 + 0.16 = 6.16$$

Net carry cost $= ₹118.56 - ₹6.16 = ₹112.40$

So          Futures price $= F \times$ (Price factor of cheapest-to-delivery) + Accrued interest

$$= 112.40$$

$$F = 108.4/1.5 = ₹72.27$$

where    Accrued interest $= \dfrac{4}{6} \times ₹6 = ₹4$

$$= (F \times 1.5) + ₹4 = 112.40$$

$$F \times 1.5 = 112.40 - 4$$

$$F = 108.40/1.5 = ₹72.27$$

# CHAPTER 12

**1.** The dealer would simultaneously buy the January sterling futures for \$80,718.75 (62,500 × 1.2915) and sell an equivalent amount of sterling forward, worth \$80,793.75 (62,500 × 1.2915), for June delivery. On settlement, the dealer would earn profit of \$75.

**2.** Daily settlement with a futures contract

| Time | Action | Cash flow |
|---|---|---|
| Day 1st | Trader buys dollar futures contract that matures in two days. Price is ₹48 | None |
| Day 1st closing | Futures price risk to ₹49. Position is marked-to-market | Trader receives 1,00,000 × (49 – 48) = ₹1,00,000 |
| Day 2nd closing | Futures price drops to ₹47.50. Position is marked-to-market | Trader pays 1,00,000 (49 – 47.50) = (2.50) × 1,00,000 = ₹2,50,000 |
| Day 3rd closing | Futures price drops to ₹46<br>1. Contract is marked-to-market<br>2. Trader takes delivery of \$1,00,000 | 1. Trader pays 1,00,000 (47.50 – 46) = 1,00,000 (1.50) = ₹1,50,000<br>2. Trader pays (1,00,000 × 46.00) = ₹46,00,000 |

**3.**

| Day | Action | Cash flow |
|-----|--------|-----------|
| Monday | Trader buys a DEM futures contract, futures price is $0.6246 per DEM | None |
| Tuesday | Futures price decreases to $0.6240, position is marked-to-market. | Cash flow ($0.6240 – $0.6246) × 1,25,000 = –$75.00 |
| Wednesday | Futures prices rises $0.6247, position is marked-to-market | Cash flow ($0.6247 – $0.6240) × 1,25,000 = $87.50 |
| Thursday | Futures price further rises to $0.6251, position is marked-to-market | ($0.6251 – $0.6247) × 1,25,000 = $50.00 |
| Friday | Futures price declines to $0.6249, position is maked-to-market | ($0.6249 – $0.6251) × 1,25,000 = –$25.00 |
| Monday | Futures price declines to $0.6248, position is settled because of last trading day | ($0.6248 – $0.6249) × 1,25,000 = –$12.50 |

Net cash flow during the week

$$= -75.00 + 87.50 + 50.00 - 25.00 - 12.50 = \$25.00$$

**4.** The above case is simply a case of cross hedging, which means hedging one position in other contract, available of same nature. If the firm is long in BEF (it will receive BEF) it must sell DEM contracts. The basis is negative so convergence is in its favour. The number of contracts should be 12 or 13 and in this way company can reduce his risk by selling currency futures in futures market.

**5.** Speculator will sell a September DEM contract 0.6005 and close his position by buying a September contract. The profit is: ($0.6005 – 0.5948) = $0.0057 per DEM or ($1,25,000 × 0.0057) = $712.5, per contract excluding the commissions and transactions costs.

**6.** Initial margin = $1,500, Maintenance margin = $1,200

| Day/Date | Action | Cash flow | Margin balance |
|----------|--------|-----------|----------------|
| April 12 | Buy one May IMM Sfr at price of $0.6350 | — | + $1,500 |
| April 12 closing | Futures price = $0.6250 | Loss = (0.6280 – 0.6350) × 1,25,000 = –$875 | + $625 |
| April 13 | Futures closing price = $0.6355 | Profit = (0.6355 – 0.6280) = (0.0075) × 1,25,000 = $937.50 | $1,562.50 |
| April 14 | Futures closing price position settled at $0.6365 | Profit = (0.6365 – 0.6355) × 1,25,000 = $125 | $1,687.50 |

**7.** Hedging with currency futures

| Cash market | Futures market |
|-------------|----------------|
| **March 3** | |
| Exporter anticipates receipt of $1/2 million on June 1. The spot exchange is £ = $1.50(1/2 million = £3,33,333) | Buys June 5, sterling futures contracts at an exchange rate of £1 = $1.50. Nationally $4,68,750 is to be paid for £3,12,500. |

*(Contd.)*

*(Contd.)*

| June 1 | June |
|---|---|
| The dollar has fallen so that exchange rate stands at £1 = $1.60. The sterling value of the $1/2 million is now £3,12,500 | Sells June 5, sterling futures contract at £ = $1.58. This will fetch $4,93,750 (3,12,500 × 1.58) in exchange for £3,12,500 |
| Loss = (3,33,333 – 3,12,500) = £20,833 | Profit = ($4,93,750 – $4,68,750) = $25,000 |

**8.** No. of contracts needed by the investor:

$$= \frac{\$3,75,000}{(\$0.15/FF)(2,50,000\,FF)} = 10$$

So the investor needs to go short in 10 FF futures contract expiring in three months.

**9.** The UK equity exposure is reduced by selling FTSE. 100 futures and US exposure is increased by buying S&P 500 futures. The US dollar currency exposure implicit in a US stock holding is obtained by selling pound currency futures. Futures positions are progressively closed out as the cash market transactions take place.

$$\text{No. of futures contracts} = \frac{1,00,000}{25 \times 2,500} = 16 \text{ FTSE 100 contracts}$$

$$= \frac{1,00,000}{62,500} = 16 \text{ sterling currency futures contracts}$$

$$= \frac{2,00,000}{500 \times 200} = \text{S\&P 500 futures contracts}$$

**10.** Indian importer enters into a futures contract which calls for delivery of US$25,000 at the price of (₹/$)45.5600. This allows him to fix the purchase cost of the machinery at Indian rupees: 11,39,000 ($25,000 × 45.56) on December 25, 2002 irrespective of the market conditions that prevail on December 25.

*Outcome of the hedging strategy*

*Case 1.* US$ appreciates

| | |
|---|---|
| Spot rate on December 28, 2002 | = ₹45.8900 |
| Purchasing cost = (US$25,000 × 45.89) | = ₹11,47,250 |
| Less gain on futures contract = (45.89 – 45.56) × 25,000 | = ₹8,250 |
| Net purchase cost | = ₹11,39,000 |

*Case 2.* US$ depreciates to 45.23 on December 28.

| | |
|---|---|
| Purchase cost = (US$25,000 × 45.23) | = ₹11,30,750 |
| Add futures contract loss (45.56 – 45.23) × 25,000 | = ₹8,250 |
| Net purchase cost | = ₹11,39,000 |

**11.**

*Case 1.* When US$ appreciates to 39.8900 on November 25, 2001.

| | |
|---|---|
| Sales revenue = US$ (1,00,000 × 39.8600) | = ₹ 39,86,000 |
| Less futures loss = (39.89 – 39.86) × 1,00,000 | = ₹ 3,000 |
| Net sales revenue | = ₹ 39,83,000 |

*Case 2.* When US$ depreciates to 39.2500 on November 25, 2001.

| | |
|---|---|
| Sales revenue = US$ (39.25 × 1,00,000) | = ₹ 39,25,000 |
| Add futures profit = (39.86 – 39.25 × 1,00,000) | = ₹ 61,000 |
| Net sales revenue | = ₹ 39,86,000 |

In both the cases, the net revenue remains the same despite the adverse movement in exchange rate.

# CHAPTER 14

**1.** Interest rate swap arrangement (Firm A and Firm B)

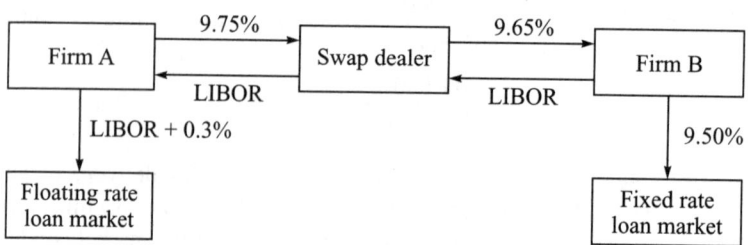

Cost of borrowing

| Firm A | | Firm B | |
|---|---|---|---|
| Cost of floating rate loan | = LIBOR + 0.3% | Cost of fixed rate borrowing | = 9.50% |
| Less floating interest rate received | = LIBOR | Less fixed rate received | = 9.65% |
| Net cost difference | = 0.3% | Net cost differential | = 0.015% |

**2.** Swap arrangement

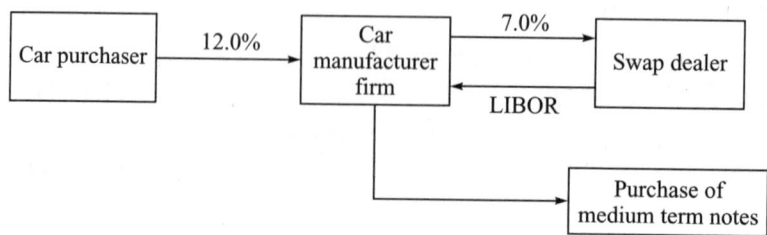

After the swap, the interest margin of the firm will be equal to the difference between the interest received from the customers as well as from swap dealer. If LIBOR is 7%, this margin, assuming the cost involved to be zero, is:

$$(12 + 7) - [7 + \text{LIBOR} + 0.25] = 4.75\%$$

If LIBOR rises to 8%, the interest margin is:

$$(12 + 8) - [7 + 8 + 0.25] = 4.75\%$$

So by using swap, car manufacturer reduces the risk to zero and leading to no change in margin of the firm.

3. (a) Swap contract:

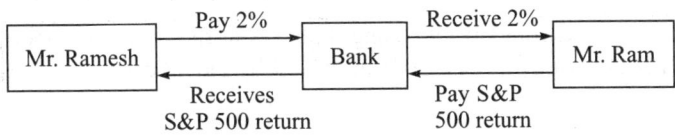

(b) The cash flow (accounts in millions) for Mr. Ramesh

| Quarter | S & P 500 return(%) | Payment from Ram(%) | Payment to Ram(%) | Net(%) | Payment from Ramesh(%) | Payment to Ramesh(%) | Net(%) |
|---|---|---|---|---|---|---|---|
| I | 3 | 3 | 2 | 1 | 2 | 3 | 1 |
| II | −4 | −4 | 2 | −2 | 2 | −4 | −6 |
| III | 1 | 1 | 2 | −1 | 2 | 1 | −1 |
| IV | 5 | 5 | 2 | 3 | 2 | 5 | 3 |

4. Following can be sequence of swap transaction:
   Company X borrows dollars at 8% p.a.
   Company Y borrows sterling at 12% p.a.
   Swap arrangement:

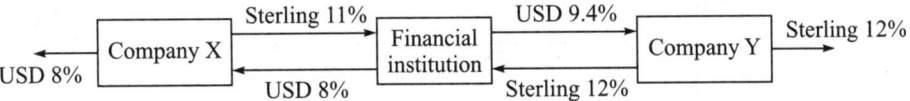

Company X ends up borrowing sterling at 11% per annum. The financial institution makes a gain of 1.4% per annum because Y ends up borrowing dollar at 9.4% and loses 1% per annum in sterling. The financial institution can hedge its sterling outflows to lock profits in dollars.

5. (a) By directly borrowing on the required basis, the total interest paid by the ICICI and IDBI is: ₹50 crores (10% + LIBOR + 0.5%)
   (b) By borrowing according to comparative advantage, total interest paid ₹50 crores × (9% + LIBOR + 1%). Borrowing according to comparative advantage, total savings of 50 crore × ½% to be shared between ICICI and IDBI Ltd. Both have a ¼% reduction in interest charge.
   Swap arrangement:

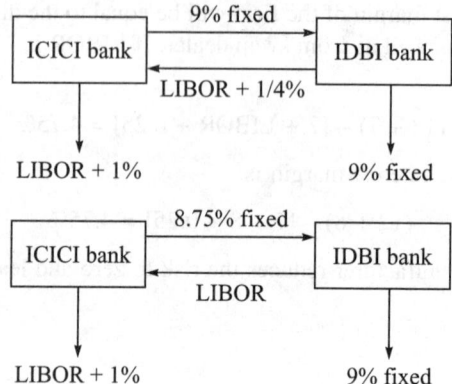

(c) IDBI Ltd. is at risk from LIBOR rising. ICICI is at risk from an opportunity loss in event of fall in LIBOR. Both are at risk from default by the other.

# CHAPTER 16

**1.** Manoj should pay 25 put option contracts each lot size of 200 shares with a strike price of ₹50 and an expiration date in four months. If at the end of four months the stock price proves to be worth less than ₹50, Manoj can exercise the option and sell the shares for ₹50 each.

**2.** Investor has a right to sell IBM shares at $55 per share by paying $4 per share as a premium. So on the day of expiry if price of the IBM declines to 50 then investor can exercise the option and earn to profit of ($55 – $4 – $50) = $1 per share or $1,000 on the total shares.

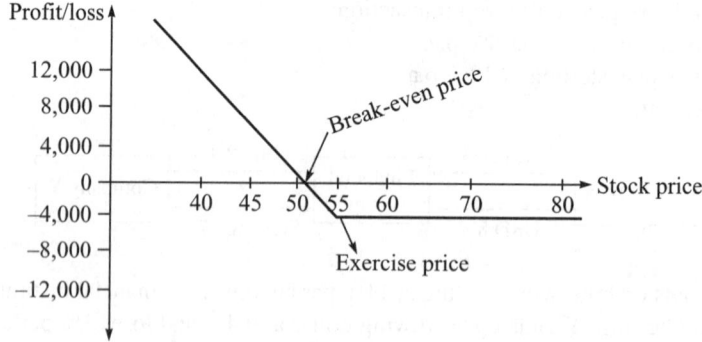

**3.** Table summarizing Romesh's Position:

| | |
|---|---|
| Current price of Reliance | ₹ 400 per share |
| Call option on Reliance | ₹ 450 per share |
| Premium | ₹ 10 per share |

Buys to call option by paying ₹10 of premium of a strike price of ₹450 per share.

*Outcomes*

(a) One month spot rate of Reliance is 500. Romesh will exercise the option by buying Reliance at 450, which worth to ₹50 per share.

(b) Profit from position = 1000(500 − 450 − 10) = ₹40,000

4. The total cost of 200 shares = $63 × 200 = $12,600
   Borrow from Margin account (50%) = 50% $12,2,600 = $6,300
   Price of option can be used by the investor = $7 × 200 = $1400
   Initial cash required = $12,600 − $6,300 − $1,400 = $4,900

5. Call option strike price = ₹4,500
   Premium = ₹200
   (a) At-the-money = Strike price + Premium
       = ₹4,500 + ₹200 = ₹4,700
   (b) In-the-money = If spot price is greater than ₹4,700
   (c) Out-of-money = If spot price is less than ₹4,700

6. Payoff to investor:
   (a) Buying a put option = Max $(X − S_t, 0)$
   (b) In writing a call option = Max $(S_t − X, 0)$
       So payoff = Max $(X − S_t, 0)$ − Max $(S_t − X, 0)$

7. Put option strike price = $70
   Option premium = $7
   Current price = $65

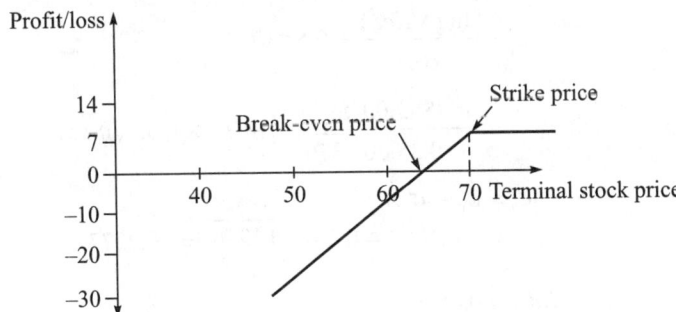

8. Strike price = ₹2,500
   Option price (Premium) = ₹125

The investor makes a profit if the price of the stock on expiration date is greater than ₹2,625. This is because the gain from exercising the option in these circumstances greater than ₹125. The option will be exercised if the stock price is greater than ₹2,500 at the maturity of the option. The variation of the investors profit with the stock price is shown in the following diagram.

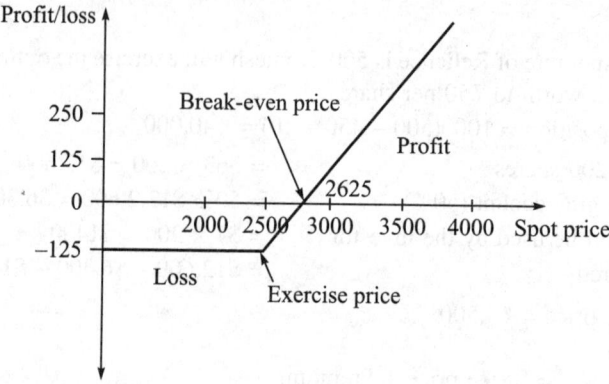

**9.** Investor makes a profit if the price of the stock on expiration date is less than ₹4,800. This is because gain from exercising the option in these circumstances is greater than ₹200. The option will be exercised if the stock price is greater than ₹5,000.

# CHAPTER 17

**1.** Compute the present value of the strike price.

$$Ke^{-rt} = \$95e^{(0.0712)(0.1370)} = \$94.08$$

Compute $d_1$ and $d_2$.

$$d_1 = \frac{\ln(S/Ke^{rt})}{\sigma\sqrt{t}} + 0.5\sigma\sqrt{t}$$

$$= \frac{\ln(\$92.00/\$94.08)}{0.35\sqrt{0.1370}} + 0.5 \times 0.35\sqrt{0.1370} = -0.1082$$

$$d_2 = d_1 - \sigma\sqrt{t}$$
$$= -0.1082 - 0.35\sqrt{0.1370} = -0.2377$$

Thus,

$$N(d_1) = 0.4570$$
$$N(d_2) = 0.4061$$

Fair value of the call option

$$C = (\$92.00)(0.4570) - (\$94.08)(0.4061)$$
$$= \$3.46$$

**2.** The Black-Scholes model for option pricing is expressed as

$$C = S.N(d_1) - Ke^{-rt}N(d_2)$$

$$d_1 = \frac{\ln(S/Ke^{rt})}{\sigma\sqrt{t}} + 0.5\sigma\sqrt{t}$$

$$d_2 = \frac{\ln(S/Ke^{rt})}{\sigma\sqrt{t}} - 0.5\sigma\sqrt{t}$$

Putting values we can calculate the value of $d_1$ as follows:

$$d_1 = [(0.06 \times 0.167)/0.1 \times 0.405] + 0.5 \times 0.1\sqrt{0.167} = 0.2655$$
$$d_2 = 0.2247$$

Then

$$C = S.N(d_1) - Ke^{-rt}N(d_2)$$
$$= 100 \, N(0.2655) - Ke^{(-0.06)(0.167)}N(0.229)$$
$$= 100 \times 0.6046 - 99 \times 0.5888 = ₹60.46 - 58.29$$
$$= ₹2.17$$

Fair price of an option = ₹2.17 per share.

**3.** Here $\quad S = 42, X = 40, r = 0\%, \sigma = 0.2, T = 0.5$

Then
$$d_1 = \frac{\ln 1.05 + 0.12 \times 0.5}{0.2\sqrt{0.5}} = 0.7693$$

$$d_2 = \frac{\ln 1.05 + 0.08 \times 0.5}{0.2\sqrt{0.5}} = 0.6278$$

$$X_e^{-rt} = 40_e^{-0.05} = 38.049$$

European call option $C = 42N(0.76395) - 38.049 \, N(0.6278)$
$$= N(0.7639) = 0.7791$$
$$= N(0.6278) = 0.7349$$
$$C = 42(0.76395) - 38.049(0.7349)$$
$$C = ₹32.0838 - ₹27.96$$
$$C = ₹4.76$$

**4.** In this case, $\quad S = 50, X = 50, r = 0.1, \sigma = 0.3, T = 0.25$

Then
$$d_1 = \frac{\ln(50/50) + 4(0.1 + 0.09/2)0.25}{0.3\sqrt{0.25}} = 0.2417$$

$$d_2 = d_1 - 0.3\sqrt{0.25} = 0.2417 - 0.15 = 0.0917$$

The European price is

$$P = 50N(-0.0917)e^{-0.1\times0.25} - 50N(-0.2417)$$
$$= 50 \times 0.4634e^{-0.1\times0.25} - 50 \times 0.4045 = 2.37$$
$$P = ₹2.37$$

**5.** We must subtract the present value of the dividend from the stock price before using Black-Scholes model.

$$S = 50 - 1.50e^{-0.1667\times0.1} = 48.52$$

As before $\quad X = 50, r = 0.1, \sigma = 0.3, T = 0.25$

Then
$$d_1 = \frac{\ln(48.52/50) + (0.1 + 0.09/2)0.25}{0.3\sqrt{0.25}} = 0.0414$$

$$d_2 = d_1 - 0.3\sqrt{0.25} = -0.1086$$

The European put price is:

$$= 50N(0.1086)e^{-0.1\times0.25} - 48.52N(-0.0414)$$

$$= 50 \times 0.5432e^{-0.1\times0.25} - 48.52 \times 0.4835 = ₹3.03$$

6. First of all we need to calculate the present value of dividend:

$$0.5e^{-0.1667\times0.09} + 0.5e^{-0.4167\times0.09} = 0.9741$$

The option price, therefore, be calculated from the Black-Scholes formula with

$$S = (40 - 0.9741) = 39.0259, X = 40, r = 0.09, \sigma = 0.3 \text{ and } T = 0.5$$

Then
$$d_1 = \frac{\ln 0.9756 + 0.135 \times 0.5}{0.3\sqrt{0.5}} = 0.2017$$

$$d_2 = \frac{\ln 0.9756 + 0.045 \times 0.5}{0.3\sqrt{0.5}} = -0.0104$$

Thus
$$N(d_1) = 0.5800$$

$$N(d_2) = 0.4909$$

$$C = 39.0259 \times 0.5800 - 40e^{-0.09\times0.5} \times 0.4959 = 3.67$$

$$= \$3.67$$

# CHAPTER 18

1. Investor can create butterfly spread by buying call option with a low and high strike prices, i.e., ₹100 and ₹125 and selling two call options with strike prices of ₹120. Total initial investment is $20 + 5 - 2 \times 12 = ₹1$.

*Variation of profit with final stock price:*

| Stock price | Profit |
|---|---|
| $S_t < 100$ | $-1$ |
| $100 < S_t < 120$ | $(S_t - 100) - 1$ |
| $120 < S_t < 125$ | $(125 - S_t) - 1$ |
| $S_t > 125$ | $-1$ |

2. If the stock price is between ₹1,500 and ₹1,750, the payoff is the amount by which the stock price exceeds ₹1,500. The cost of strategy is ₹150 – ₹50 = ₹100. Profit is, therefore,

| Stock price (₹) | Profit (₹) |
|---|---|
| $S_t \times 1,500$ | $-100$ |
| $1,500 < S_t < 1,750$ | $S_t - 1,600$ |
| $S_t \geq 1,750$ | $150$ |

3. Trader could create a straddle by buying both call and a put options with a strike price of ₹70 and an expiration date in three months. If the stock price moves up ₹70, trader will have to bear loss of ₹7. Assume ₹4 and ₹3 are the costs of put and call options.

Payoff from a straddle

| Range of stock price | Payoff from call | Payoff from put | Total payoff |
|---|---|---|---|
| $S_t \times X$ | 0 | $X - S_t$ | $X - S_t$ |
| $S_t > X$ | $S_t - X$ | 0 | $S_t - X$ |

Suppose if the stock price jumps to ₹90, a profit of ₹13 is made; if the stock price moves down to ₹55, a profit of ₹8 is made and so on.

**4.** Total cost or investment in straddle is ₹10 + 8 = ₹18. If the stock moves below ₹200 and above ₹200, payoff profile will be

| Stock price | Profit |
|---|---|
| $S_t < 150$ | $(200 - S_t) - 18$ |
| $150 < S_t < 200$ | $-18$ |
| $S_t > 200$ | $(S_t - 200) - 18$ |

**5.**

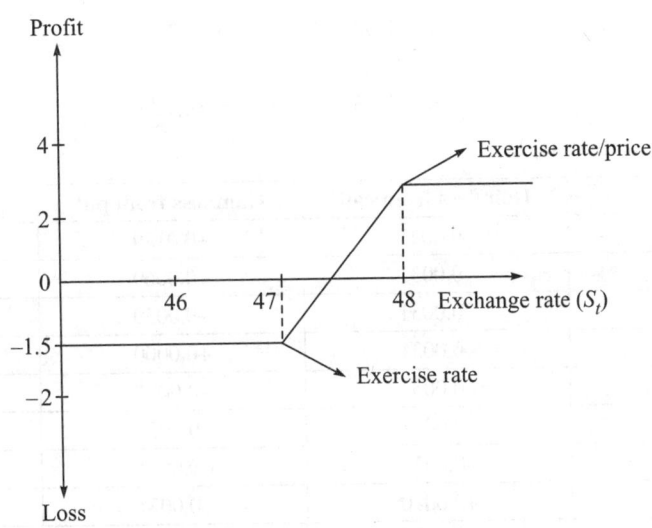

Profit and loss profile of a bull call spread at expiry.

**6.** 
Premium received on call     = 1 cent/£  
Premium paid on call        = 4 cent/£  
Net premium              = 3 cent/£  
Below \$1.85 neither option is exercised: the loss of net premium of 3 cent/£  
Maximum profit will occur above \$1.85  
Profit from exercising \$1.85 option  
Less loss from exercise of \$1.95 option  
Less initial net premium equals to 7 cent/£  
Above \$1.95 the additional profit from long \$1.85 calls are offset by losses from the short \$1.95 call.

# CHAPTER 20

1. Buy call option on February 1 $= -\$0.0110$

   Exercise the option on May 1 $= -\$1.6000$ per pound

   Sell the pound on May 1 $= +\$1.7000$ per pound

   Net profit as of May 1 $= \$0.0890$ per pound

   Net profit per contract $= 31,250 \times \$0.890$

   $= \$2,781.25$

2. Buy options $= +\$1.90$

   Premium loss $= -\$0.05$

   Strike price $= \$1.90$

   Spot price on October 25 $= \$1.72$

   Profit $= (\$1.90 - \$0.05) - \$1.72$

   $= \$1.13$

   Net profit $= (\$1.13 \times 62,500) = \$8,125$

3. Profit profile with strangle

| $S_t$ | Gain/loss from call | Gain/loss from put | Net gain/loss |
|---|---|---|---|
| 1.7145 | −0.0031 | +0.0189 | +0.0158 |
| 1.7265 | −0.0031 | +0.0069 | +0.0038 |
| 1.7295 | −0.0031 | +0.0039 | +0.0008 |
| 1.7334 | −0.0031 | +0.0000 | −0.0031 |
| 1.7425 | −0.0031 | −0.0031 | −0.0062 |
| 1.7455 | −0.0031 | −0.0031 | −0.0062 |
| 1.7475 | −0.0031 | −0.0031 | −0.0062 |
| 1.7536 | +0.0010 | −0.0031 | −0.0021 |
| 1.7585 | +0.0059 | −0.0031 | +0.0028 |
| 1.7895 | +0.0369 | −0.0031 | +0.0338 |

4. Premium paid $P$ $= \$0.04/£$

   Profit per unit pound sterling $= X - S_t$

   $= \$1.65 - \$1.50$

   $= \$0.15$

   Net profit $= \$0.15 - \$0.04 = \$0.11$

   Total profit on the option $= \$0.11 \times \$31,250$

   $= \$3,437.50$

5. Premium amount $= 0.03 \times 0.9920$

   Euro $= 0.02976$

   So on maturity date, there will be neither profit nor loss if the spot rate happens to be 0.99 − 0.02976 or Euro 0.96024/\$ of the dollar rate on maturity is less than Euro 0.86284/\$, the buyer of the put option will make a net profit. If rate is higher than Euro 0.86234/\$, he incurs a net loss.

**6.** (a) Intrinsic value from a call option = Spot price – Strike price

= 48.00 – 46.00

Intrinsic value = ₹2.00

(b) Time value of option = Premium – Intrinsic value

= 2.60 – 2.00

Time value = ₹0.60 per dollar

**7.** The exporter pays the premium immediately, that is a sum of 0.025 × $5,00,000 × 43.00 = ₹5,37,500. Now there can be three different possibilities that can occur.

(a) The rate becomes ₹42/$ means US$ depreciated. In this situation, the exporter will sell the dollar, exercise the option at ₹43.00 per dollar and net receipts would be

= ₹43 × $5,00,000 – (43.00 × 0.025 × 5,00,000)

= ₹2,15,00,000 – ₹5,37,500 = ₹2,09,62,500

If he had not covered with option, the net loss he has to incur ₹21,00,000 but would not be certain about actual amount to be received.

(b) If the dollar rate becomes ₹43.50. This means dollar appreciates. He sells his dollar directly in the market at the rate of ₹43.50 and the net amount to be received

= ₹43.50 × $5,00,000 – 43.00 × 0.025 × $5,00,000

(₹42.425 × $5,00,000 = ₹2,12,12,500)

If he had not covered, he would have got

₹43.50 × $5,00,000 = ₹2,17,50,000

(c) Dollar rate on settlement become equals to strike price. Net amount received by the exporter = ₹(43 × 5,00,000 – 43.00 × 0.025 × 5,00,000)

= ₹(43 – 43 × 0.025) × 5,00,000

= ₹2,09,62,500

**8.** Importer pays premium amount mendatory, that is sum of ₹45 × 0.03 × 20,00,000 or ₹2,70,000. Let us examine the following possibilities:

(a) Spot rate on date of settlement becomes ₹42.50 slight depreciation in US$. The net amount to be paid is:

₹44.50 × $20,00,000 – ₹45 × 0.03 × $20,00,000

= 8,90,00,000 + 1,29,000 = 8,91,29,000

(b) Spot rate on settlement date is ₹45.75 per US dollar. The net sum pays is:

= ₹45.75 × $20,00,000 + 45 × 0.03 × 1,00,000

= ₹45 × 1.03 × $20,00,000 = 92,70,00,000

Spot rate, on the settlement, is same as the strike price. In such situation, importer will not exercise option or rather he is indifferent between exercise and non-exercise of the option. The net payment:

= ₹45 × 1.03 × $20,00,000 = ₹9,27,00,000

# Appendix A

## Tables for N(x) when x ≤ 0 and x ≥ 0

This table shows values of $N(x)$ for $x \le 0$. The table should be used with interpolation. For example,

$$N(-0.1234) = N(-0.12) - 0.34[N(-0.12) - N(0.13)]$$
$$= 0.4522 - 0.34 \times (0.4522 - 0.4483)$$
$$= 0.4509$$

| x | 0.0 | 0.1 | 0.2 | 0.3 | 0.4 | 0.5 | 0.6 | 0.7 | 0.8 | 0.9 |
|---|---|---|---|---|---|---|---|---|---|---|
| -0.0 | 0.5000 | 0.4960 | 0.4920 | 0.4880 | 0.4840 | 0.4801 | 0.4761 | 0.4325 | 0.4681 | 0.4641 |
| -0.1 | 0.4602 | 0.4562 | 0.4522 | 0.4483 | 0.4443 | 0.4404 | 0.4364 | 0.4325 | 0.4286 | 0.4247 |
| -0.2 | 0.4207 | 0.4168 | 0.4129 | 0.4090 | 0.4052 | 0.4013 | 0.3974 | 0.3936 | 0.3897 | 0.3859 |
| -0.3 | 0.3821 | 0.3783 | 0.3745 | 0.3707 | 0.3669 | 0.3632 | 0.3594 | 0.3557 | 0.3520 | 0.3483 |
| -0.4 | 0.3446 | 0.3409 | 0.3372 | 0.3336 | 0.3300 | 0.3264 | 0.3228 | 0.3192 | 0.3156 | 0.3121 |
| -0.5 | 0.3085 | 0.3050 | 0.3015 | 0.2981 | 0.2946 | 0.2912 | 0.2877 | 0.2843 | 0.2810 | 0.2776 |
| -0.6 | 0.2743 | 0.2709 | 0.2676 | 0.2643 | 0.2611 | 0.2578 | 0.2546 | 0.2514 | 0.2483 | 0.2451 |
| 0.7 | 0.2420 | 0.2389 | 0.2358 | 0.2327 | 0.2296 | 0.2266 | 0.2236 | 0.2206 | 0.2177 | 0.2148 |
| -0.8 | 0.2119 | 0.2090 | 0.2061 | 0.2033 | 0.2005 | 0.1977 | 0.1949 | 0.1922 | 0.1894 | 0.1867 |
| -0.9 | 0.1841 | 0.1814 | 0.1788 | 0.1762 | 0.1736 | 0.1711 | 0.1685 | 0.1660 | 0.1635 | 0.1611 |
| -1.0 | 0.1587 | 0.1562 | 0.1539 | 0.1515 | 0.1492 | 0.1469 | 0.1446 | 0.1423 | 0.1401 | 0.1379 |
| -1.1 | 0.1357 | 0.1335 | 0.1314 | 0.1292 | 0.1271 | 0.1251 | 0.1230 | 0.1210 | 0.1190 | 0.1170 |
| -1.2 | 0.1151 | 0.1131 | 0.1112 | 0.1093 | 0.1075 | 0.1056 | 0.1038 | 0.1020 | 0.1003 | 0.0985 |
| -1.3 | 0.0968 | 0.0951 | 0.0934 | 0.0918 | 0.0901 | 0.0885 | 0.0869 | 0.0853 | 0.0838 | 0.0823 |
| -1.4 | 0.0808 | 0.0793 | 0.0778 | 0.0764 | 0.0749 | 0.0735 | 0.0721 | 0.0708 | 0.0694 | 0.0681 |
| -1.5 | 0.0668 | 0.0655 | 0.0643 | 0.0630 | 0.0618 | 0.0606 | 0.0594 | 0.0582 | 0.0571 | 0.0559 |
| -1.6 | 0.0548 | 0.0537 | 0.0526 | 0.0516 | 0.0505 | 0.0495 | 0.0485 | 0.0475 | 0.0465 | 0.0455 |
| -1.7 | 0.0446 | 0.0436 | 0.0427 | 0.0418 | 0.0409 | 0.0401 | 0.0392 | 0.0384 | 0.0375 | 0.0367 |
| -1.8 | 0.0359 | 0.0351 | 0.0344 | 0.0336 | 0.0329 | 0.0322 | 0.0314 | 0.0307 | 0.0301 | 0.0294 |
| -1.9 | 0.0287 | 0.0281 | 0.0274 | 0.0268 | 0.0262 | 0.0256 | 0.0250 | 0.0244 | 0.0239 | 0.0233 |
| -2.0 | 0.0228 | 0.0222 | 0.0217 | 0.0212 | 0.0207 | 0.0202 | 0.0197 | 0.0192 | 0.0188 | 0.0183 |
| -2.1 | 0.0179 | 0.0174 | 0.0170 | 0.0166 | 0.0162 | 0.0158 | 0.0154 | 0.0150 | 0.0146 | 0.0143 |

*Contd.*

| x | 0.0 | 0.1 | 0.2 | 0.3 | 0.4 | 0.5 | 0.6 | 0.7 | 0.8 | 0.9 |
|---|------|------|------|------|------|------|------|------|------|------|
| -2.2 | 0.0139 | 0.0136 | 0.0132 | 0.0129 | 0.0125 | 0.0122 | 0.0119 | 0.0116 | 0.0113 | 0.0110 |
| -2.3 | 0.0107 | 0.0104 | 0.0102 | 0.0099 | 0.0096 | 0.0094 | 0.0091 | 0.0089 | 0.0087 | 0.0084 |
| -2.4 | 0.0082 | 0.0080 | 0.0078 | 0.0075 | 0.0073 | 0.0071 | 0.0069 | 0.0068 | 0.0066 | 0.0064 |
| -2.5 | 0.0062 | 0.0060 | 0.0059 | 0.0057 | 0.0055 | 0.0054 | 0.0052 | 0.0051 | 0.0049 | 0.0048 |
| -2.6 | 0.0047 | 0.0045 | 0.0044 | 0.0043 | 0.0041 | 0.0040 | 0.0039 | 0.0038 | 0.0037 | 0.0036 |
| -2.7 | 0.0035 | 0.0034 | 0.0033 | 0.0032 | 0.0031 | 0.0030 | 0.0029 | 0.0028 | 0.0027 | 0.0026 |
| -2.8 | 0.0026 | 0.0025 | 0.0024 | 0.0023 | 0.0023 | 0.0022 | 0.0021 | 0.0021 | 0.0020 | 0.0019 |
| -2.9 | 0.0019 | 0.0018 | 0.0018 | 0.0017 | 0.0016 | 0.0016 | 0.0015 | 0.0015 | 0.014 | 0.0014 |
| -3.0 | 0.0014 | 0.0013 | 0.0013 | 0.0012 | 0.0012 | 0.0011 | 0.0011 | 0.0011 | 0.0010 | 0.0010 |
| -3.1 | 0.0010 | 0.0009 | 0.0009 | 0.0009 | 0.0008 | 0.0008 | 0.0008 | 0.0008 | 0.0007 | 0.0007 |
| -3.2 | 0.0007 | 0.0007 | 0.0006 | 0.0006 | 0.0006 | 0.0006 | 0.0006 | 0.0005 | 0.0005 | 0.0005 |
| -3.3 | 0.0005 | 0.0005 | 0.0005 | 0.0004 | 0.0004 | 0.0004 | 0.0004 | 0.0004 | 0.0004 | 0.0003 |
| -3.4 | 0.0003 | 0.0003 | 0.0003 | 0.0003 | 0.0003 | 0.0003 | 0.0003 | 0.0003 | 0.0003 | 0.0002 |
| -3.5 | 0.0002 | 0.0002 | 0.0002 | 0.0002 | 0.0002 | 0.0002 | 0.0002 | 0.0002 | 0.0002 | 0.0002 |
| -3.6 | 0.0002 | 0.0002 | 0.0001 | 0.0001 | 0.0001 | 0.0001 | 0.0001 | 0.0001 | 0.0001 | 0.0001 |
| -3.7 | 0.0001 | 0.0001 | 0.0001 | 0.0001 | 0.0001 | 0.0001 | 0.0001 | 0.0001 | 0.0001 | 0.0001 |
| -3.8 | 0.0001 | 0.0001 | 0.0001 | 0.0001 | 0.0001 | 0.0001 | 0.0001 | 0.0001 | 0.0001 | 0.0001 |
| -3.9 | 0.0000 | 0.0000 | 0.0000 | 0.0000 | 0.0000 | 0.0000 | 0.0000 | 0.0000 | 0.0000 | 0.0000 |
| -4.0 | 0.0000 | 0.0000 | 0.0000 | 0.0000 | 0.0000 | 0.0000 | 0.0000 | 0.0000 | 0.0000 | 0.0000 |

This table shows values of $N(x)$ for $x \geq 0$. The table should be used with interpolation. For example,

$$N(0.6278) = N(0.62) + 0.78\,[N(0.63) - N(0.62)]$$
$$= 0.7324 + 0.78 \times (0.7357 - 0.7324)$$
$$= 0.7350$$

| x | 0.0 | 0.1 | 0.2 | 0.3 | 0.4 | 0.5 | 0.6 | 0.7 | 0.8 | 0.9 |
|---|------|------|------|------|------|------|------|------|------|------|
| 0.0 | 0.5000 | 0.5040 | 0.5080 | 0.5120 | 0.5160 | 0.5199 | 0.5239 | 0.5279 | 0.5319 | 0.5359 |
| 0.1 | 0.5398 | 0.5438 | 0.5478 | 0.5517 | 0.5557 | 0.5596 | 0.5636 | 0.5675 | 0.5714 | 0.5753 |
| 0.2 | 0.5793 | 0.5832 | 0.5871 | 0.5910 | 0.5948 | 0.5987 | 0.6026 | 0.6064 | 0.6103 | 0.6141 |
| 0.3 | 0.6179 | 0.6217 | 0.6255 | 0.6293 | 0.6331 | 0.6368 | 0.6406 | 0.6443 | 0.6480 | 0.6517 |
| 0.4 | 0.6554 | 0.6591 | 0.6628 | 0.6664 | 0.6700 | 0.6736 | 0.6772 | 0.6808 | 0.6844 | 0.6879 |
| 0.5 | 0.6915 | 0.6950 | 0.6985 | 0.7019 | 0.7054 | 0.7088 | 0.7123 | 0.7157 | 0.7190 | 0.7224 |
| 0.6 | 0.7257 | 0.7291 | 0.7324 | 0.7357 | 0.7389 | 0.7422 | 0.7454 | 0.7486 | 0.7517 | 0.7549 |
| 0.7 | 0.7580 | 0.7611 | v 7642 | 0.7673 | 0.7704 | 0.7734 | 0.7764 | 0.7794 | 0.7823 | 0.7852 |
| 0.8 | 0.7881 | 0.7910 | 0.7939 | 0.7967 | 0.7995 | 0.8023 | 0.8051 | 0.8078 | 0.8106 | 0.8133 |
| 0.9 | 0.8159 | 0.8186 | 0.8212 | 0.8238 | 0.8264 | 0.8289 | 0.8315 | 0.8340 | 0.8365 | 0.8389 |
| 1.0 | 0.8413 | 0.8438 | 0.8461 | 0.8485 | 0.8508 | 0.8531 | 0.8554 | 0.8577 | 0.8599 | 0.8621 |
| 1.1 | 0.8643 | 0.8665 | 0.8686 | 0.8708 | 0.8729 | 0.8749 | 0.8770 | 0.8790 | 0.8810 | 0.8830 |
| 1.2 | 0.8849 | 0.8869 | 0.8888 | 0.8907 | 0.8925 | 0.8944 | 0.8962 | 0.8980 | 0.8997 | 0.9015 |
| 1.3 | 0.9032 | 0.9049 | 0.9066 | 0.9082 | 0.9099 | 0.9115 | 0.9131 | 0.9147 | 0.9162 | 0.9177 |

*Contd.*

| x | 0.0 | 0.1 | 0.2 | 0.3 | 0.4 | 0.5 | 0.6 | 0.7 | 0.8 | 0.9 |
|---|------|------|------|------|------|------|------|------|------|------|
| 1.4 | 0.9192 | 0.9207 | 0.9222 | 0.9236 | 0.9251 | 0.9265 | 0.9279 | 0.9292 | 0.9306 | 0.9319 |
| 1.5 | 0.9332 | 0.9345 | 0.9357 | 0.9370 | 0.9382 | 0.9394 | 0.9406 | 0.9418 | 0.9429 | 0.9441 |
| 1.6 | 0.9452 | 0.9463 | 0.9474 | 0.9484 | 0.9495 | 0.9505 | 0.9515 | 0.9525 | 0.9535 | 0.9545 |
| 1.7 | 0.9554 | 0.9564 | 0.9573 | 0.9582 | 0.9591 | 0.9599 | 0.9608 | 0.9616 | 0.9625 | 0.9633 |
| 1.8 | 0.9641 | 0.9649 | 0.9656 | 0.9664 | 0.9671 | 0.9678 | 0.9686 | 0.9693 | 0.9699 | 0.9706 |
| 1.9 | 0.9713 | 0.9719 | 0.9726 | 0.9732 | 0.9738 | 0.9744 | 0.9750 | 0.9756 | 0.9761 | 0.9767 |
| 2.0 | 0.9772 | 0.9778 | 0.9783 | 0.9788 | 0.9793 | 0.9798 | 0.9803 | 0.9808 | 0.9812 | 0.9817 |
| 2.1 | 0.9821 | 0.9826 | 0.9830 | 0.9834 | 0.9838 | 0.9842 | 0.9846 | 0.9850 | 0.9854 | 0.9857 |
| 2.2 | 0.9861 | 0.9864 | 0.9868 | 0.9871 | 0.9875 | 0.9878 | 0.9881 | 0.9884 | 0.9887 | 0.9890 |
| 2.3 | 0.9893 | 0.9896 | 0.9898 | 0.9901 | 0.9904 | 0.9906 | 0.9909 | 0.9911 | 0.9913 | 0.9916 |
| 2.4 | 0.9918 | 0.9920 | 0.9922 | 0.9925 | 0.9927 | 0.9929 | 0.9931 | 0.9932 | 0.9934 | 0.9936 |
| 2.5 | 0.9938 | 0.9940 | 0.9941 | 0.9943 | 0.9945 | 0.9946 | 0.9948 | 0.9949 | 0.9951 | 0.9952 |
| 2.6 | 0.9953 | 0.9955 | 0.9956 | 0.9957 | 0.9959 | 0.9960 | 0.9961 | 0.9962 | 0.9963 | 0.9964 |
| 2.7 | 0.9965 | 0.9966 | 0.9967 | 0.9968 | 0.9969 | 0.9970 | 0.9971 | 0.9972 | 0.9973 | 0.9974 |
| 2.8 | 0.9974 | 0.9975 | 0.9976 | 0.9977 | 0.9977 | 0.9978 | 0.9979 | 0.9979 | 0.9980 | 0.9981 |
| 2.9 | 0.9981 | 0.9982 | 0.9982 | 0.9983 | 0.9984 | 0.9984 | 0.9985 | 0.9985 | 0.9986 | 0.9986 |
| 3.0 | 0.9986 | 0.9987 | 0.9987 | 0.9988 | 0.9988 | 0.9989 | 0.9989 | 0.9989 | 0.9990 | 0.9990 |
| 3.1 | 0.9990 | 0.9991 | 0.9991 | 0.9991 | 0.9992 | 0.9992 | 0.9992 | 0.9992 | 0.9993 | 0.9993 |
| 3.2 | 0.9993 | 0.9993 | 0.9994 | 0.9994 | 0.9994 | 0.9994 | 0.9994 | 0.9995 | 0.9995 | 0.9995 |
| 3.3 | 0.9995 | 0.9995 | 0.9995 | 0.9996 | 0.9996 | 0.9996 | 0.9996 | 0.9996 | 0.9996 | 0.9997 |
| 3.4 | 0.9997 | 0.9997 | 0.9997 | 0.9997 | 0.9997 | 0.9997 | 0.9997 | 0.9997 | 0.9997 | 0.9998 |
| 3.5 | 0.9998 | 0.9998 | 0.9998 | 0.9998 | 0.9998 | 0.9998 | 0.9998 | 0.9998 | 0.9998 | 0.9998 |
| 3.6 | 0.9998 | 0.9998 | 0.9999 | 0.9999 | 0.9999 | 0.9999 | 0.9999 | 0.9999 | 0.9999 | 0.9999 |
| 3.7 | 0.9999 | 0.9999 | 0.9999 | 0.9999 | 0.9999 | 0.9999 | 0.9999 | 0.9999 | 0.9999 | 0.9999 |
| 3.8 | 0.9999 | 0.9999 | 0.9999 | 0.9999 | 0.9999 | 0.9999 | 0.9999 | 0.9999 | 0.9999 | 0.9999 |
| 3.9 | 1.0000 | 1.0000 | 1.0000 | 1.0000 | 1.0000 | 1.0000 | 1.0000 | 1.0000 | 1.0000 | 1.0000 |
| 4.0 | 1.0000 | 1.0000 | 1.0000 | 1.0000 | 1.0000 | 1.0000 | 1.0000 | 1.0000 | 1.0000 | 1.0000 |

# Appendix B

## LIST OF IMPORTANT STOCK EXCHANGES IN WORLD

Abidjan Stock Exchange
African Stock Exchange Guide
Alberta Stock Exchange
Alternative Investment Market (*see* also: London Stock Exchange)
American Stock Exchange (AMEX)
Amman Financial Market
Amsterdam Exchanges
Arizona Stock Exchange
Athens Stock Exchange
Australian Stock Exchange
Austrian Futures and Options Exchange
Bangalore Stock Exchange
Barcelona Stock Exchange
Beirut Stock Exchange
Belgian Futures and Options Exchange
Berlin Stock Exchange
Bermuda Stock Exchange
Bilbao Stock Exchange
Bogotá Stock Exchange
Botswana Stock Exchange
Bratislava Stock Exchange
Brussels Stock Exchange
Bucharest Stock Exchange
Budapest Stock Exchange
Buenos Aires Stock Exchange
Bulgarian Stock Exchange
Cairo Stock Exchange
Caracas Stock Exchange
Casablanca Stock Exchange

Chicago Board of Trade (CBOT)
Chicago Board Options Exchange (CBOE)
Chicago Mercantile Exchange (CME)
Chicago Stock Exchange
Chile Electronic Stock Exchange
Coffee, Sugar and Cocoa Exchange (CSCE)
Colombo Stock Exchange
Copenhagen Stock Exchange
Costa Rica National Stock Exchange
Cyprus Stock Exchange
Dublin Stock Exchange (*see:* Irish Stock Exchange)
EASDAQ
EURO.NM
European Exchange (EUREX)
Frankfurt Stock Exchange (*see also:* German Stock Exchange)
Geneva Stock Exchange (*see:* Swiss Exchange)
German Stock Exchange
German Derivatives Exchange (Deutsche Terminbörse DTB)
German Munich Stock Exchange
Ghana Stock Exchange
Guayaquil Stock Exchange
Helsinki Stock Exchange
Hiroshima Stock Exchange
Hong Kong Futures Exchange
Hong Kong Stock Exchange
Indian Stock Exchange (NSE)
Irish Stock Exchange (NSE)
International Federation of Stock Exchanges (FIBV)
Istanbul Stock Exchange
Italian Stock Exchange
Jakarta Stock Exchange
Jamaica Stock Exchange
Johannesburg Stock Exchange
Kansas City Board of Trade
Karachi Stock Exchange
Korea Stock Exchange
Lahore Stock Exchange
Lima Stock Exchange
Lisbon Stock Exchange
Ljubljana Stock Exchange
London International Financial Futures and Options Exchange (LIFFE)
London Stock Exchange

Lusaka Stock Exchange
Luxembourg Stock Exchange
Macedonian Stock Exchange
Madrid Stock Exchange
Mangalore Stock Exchange
MATIF Marche a Terme International de France
Mauritius Stock Exchange (MSE)
Medellin Stock Exchange
Mexican Stock Exchange
Mid America Commodity Exchange
Milan Stock Exchange (*see:* Italian Stock Exchange)
Minneapolis Grain Exchange
Montreal Stock Exchange
Moscow Central Stock Exchange
Munich Stock Exchange (*see:* German Stock Exchange)
Nagoya Stock Exchange
Nairobi Stock Exchange
Namibian Stock Exchange
NASDAQ
New York Coffee, Sugar and Cocoa Exchange
New York Cotton Exchange
New York Mercantile Exchange
New York Stock Exchange
New Zealand Stock Exchange
Nicaragua Stock Exchange
Nigerian Stock Exchange
Nijny Novgorod Stock and Currency Exchange (in Russian)
Nouveau Marché Paris
Occident Stock Exchange (Cali)
Oporto Derivatives Exchange
Options Market Stockholm
Oslo Stock Exchange
Pacific Exchange (Los Angeles and San Francisco)
Panama Stock Exchange
Parana Mercantile Exchange
Paris Stock Exchange
Philadelphia Stock Exchange
Prague Stock Exchange
RASDAQ
Rhenish-Westphalian Stock Exchange (Dusseldorf)
Russian Exchange
Russian Trading System

Santiago Stock Exchange
Sao Paulo Mercantile and Futures Exchange
Sao Paulo Stock Exchange
Shanghai Metal Exchange
Shanghai Stock Exchange
Shenzhen Stock Exchange
Singapore International Monetary Exchange (SIMEX)
Singapore Stock Exchange
South African Futures Exchange (SAFEX)
Spanish Financial Futures and Options Exchange (MEFF)
St. Petersburg Futures Exchange
St. Petersburg Stock Exchange
Stockholm Stock Exchange
Swaziland Stock Market
Swiss Options and Financial Futures Exchange (SOFFEX)
Swiss Exchange
Sydney Futures Exchange
Taiwan Stock Exchange
Tallinn Stock Exchange
Tanzanian Stock Exchange
Tehran Stock Exchange
Tel Aviv Stock Exchange
Thailand Stock Exchange
Tokyo Grain Exchange
Tokyo Stock Exchange
Toronto Stock Exchange
Tunis Stock Exchange
Ural Stock Exchange
Vancouver Stock Exchange
Venezuelan Electronic Stock Exchange
Vienna Stock Exchange
Warsaw Stock Exchange
Winnipeg Commodity Exchange
Zagreb Stock Exchange
Zimbabwe Stock Exchange
Zurich Stock Exchange (*see:* Swiss Exchange)

# Appendix C

## LIST OF IMPORTANT WEBSITES ON FINANCIAL DERIVATIVES

1. www.atimes.com
2. www.amfiindia.com
3. www.authentic money.com
4. www.bai.org
5. www.bankerme.com
6. www.bis.org
7. www.bobsguide.com
8. www.businessstandard.com
9. www.cfo.com
10. www.cfoweb.com.all
11. www.cls-group.com
12. www.creditguru.com
13. www.crisic.com
14. www.dailyfx.com
15. www.derivativesreviw.com
16. www.economictimes.com
17. www.economist.com
18. www.financeasia.com
19. www.financegates.com
20. www.financialexpress.com
21. www.fmc.gov.in
22. www.forexblog.org
23. www.forexnews.com
24. www.foreynews.com
25. www.fpanet.org
26. www.ftmandate.com
27. www.futuresindustry.org
28. www.Ganda.com
29. www.garp.com
30. www.gtnews.com
31. www.hedgeweek.com
32. www.icfmindia.com

33. www.icicidirect.com
34. www.icraratings.com
35. www.iht.com
36. www.indiamarkets.com
37. www.indianivesh.in
38. www.indiantradingleague.com
39. www.investopedia.com
40. www.itreasurer.com
41. www.mises.org
42. www.moneycentral.msn.com
43. www.msnbe.com
44. www.nseindia.com
45. www.phdcci.in
46. www.rbi.org.in
47. www.rediff.com
48. www.reuters.com
49. www.riskcentre.com
50. www.riskglossary.com
51. www.risk.net
52. www.rmubg.org
53. www.ruf.org
54. www.sec.gov
55. www.smcindiaonline.com
56. www.stockhouse.com
57. www.swift.com
58. www.theage.com.ue
59. www.thebanker.com
60. www.thedailystar.com
61. www.treasurer.com
62. www.vectorvest.co.in/ET
63. www.zeenews.com

## Case studies journal sites

64. www.businessweek.com
65. www.detnews.com
66. www.ecch.creanfield.ac
67. www.findarticles.com
68. www.forbes.com
69. www.icmrindia.org
70. www.knowledgebusiness.com
71. www.marketgurukul.com
72. www.money.cnn.com
73. www.stockdunia.com
74. www.uber.org
75. www.washingtonpost.com

# Glossary

**Accrual Accounting:**   When swaps are used to hedge specific on-balance sheet exposures, they are often accounted on an accrual basis. Under the accrual method, the net payment or receipt in each period is accrued and recorded as an adjustment income or expense.

**Accrual Swap:**   An interest rate swap where interest on one side accrues only when a certain condition is met.

**Accrued Interest:**   The interest earned on a bond since the last coupon payment date.

**Actual Hedging:**   Is the risk management of a position when a hedger has a bonafide long or short actual position and is involved in an offsetting transaction. This offset is usually in the derivatives market.

**Actuals:**   Financial instruments that exist in one of the four main asset classes: interest rates, foreign exchange, equities or commodities. Typically, derivatives are used to hedge actual exposure or to take positions in actual markets.

**Add-lot:**   A quantity of stock that is not evenly divisible by 100 shares.

**Add-on yield:**   The yield convention with Eurodollars, equal to the ratio of the discount to the price, multiplied by the ratio of 360 to the number of days until maturity.

**After Hours Dealing:**   Trading outside the trading hours of the futures markets, e.g. trading a futures month in Brent crude outside the IPE and Singapore International Monetary Exchange trading periods.

**All or Nothing:**   An option whose payout is fixed at the inception of the option contract and for which the payout is only made if the strike price is in-the-money at expiry. If the strike price is out-of-the-money at expiry, there is no payout made to the option holder.

**Alternative Investments:**   Are usually investments other than mutual funds, certificates of deposit or direct investments in equities and bonds. Some of these alternatives are: art, collectibles, commodities, commodity funds, commodity pools and derivatives.

**American Depository Receipt:**   Receipt indicating a claim on some number (less than one, one or more than one) of shares in a foreign corporation that a Depository Bank holds for US investors.

**American Style Option:**   An option that can be exercised at any time from inception as opposed to a European style option which can only be exercised at expiry. Early exercise of American options may be warranted by arbitrage. European style option contracts can be closed out early, mimicking the early exercise property of American style options in most cases.

**Amortizing Swap:**   A swap where the notional principal decreases in a predetermined way as time passes.

**Arbitrage:** The act of taking advantage of differences in price between markets. For example, if a stock is quoted on two different equity markets, there is the possibility of arbitrage if the quoted price (adjusted for institutional idiosyncrasies) in one market differs from the quoted price in the other. The term has been extended to refer to speculators who take positions on the correlation between two different types of instrument, assuming stability to the correlation patterns. Many funds have discovered that correlation is not as stable as it is assumed to be.

**Arbitrage pricing:** Pricing an asset by relying on the condition that there is no arbitrage opportunity, i.e. no opportunity to make riskless profits.

**Arbitrage profits:** Riskless profits that can be obtained without investing any of one's own money.

**Arbitrageur:** A person who actively seeks arbitrage situation, add by exploiting them helps keep the marketplace efficient.

**Asian Option:** An option that is exercised against an average over a period.

**Ask price:** The lowest price at which anyone has expressed willingness to sell a security.

**Asset and Liability Management:** Is the process for financial institutions and corporations to adjust their funding and usage of funds. Some approaches are the Bucket, GAP, Hedging, Matched book, Matched finding, Financial swaps and Structured products.

**Asset Swap:** A swap that converts a fixed- (floating-) coupon asset into a floating- (fixed-) coupon asset. This is in contrast to the more familiar (liability) swap that converts a fixed- (floating-) coupon liability into a floating- (fixed-) coupon liability.

**At-the-Money Option (ATM):** An option with an exercise price at the current market level of the underlying.

**Back Month:** Back month contracts are any exchange-traded derivatives contracts apart from the nearest or front contract month.

**Back-testing:** Testing a value-at-risk or other model using historical data.

**Backwardation:** A term often used in commodities or futures markets to refer to markets where shorter-dated contracts trade at a higher price than longer-dated contracts. Plotting the prices of contracts against time, with time on the $x$-axis, shows the commodity price curve as sloping downwards as time increases.

**Barrier Option:** An option whose payoff depends on whether the path of the underlying asset has reached a barrier (i.e., a certain predetermined level).

**Barrier option:** An exotic derivative that can be exercised only if the price of the underlying, during the life of the option, satisfies some condition defined by a barrier.

**Barrier Options:** An option contract for which the maturity, strike price and underlying are specified at inception in addition to a trigger price. The trigger price determines whether or not the option actually exists. In the case of a knock-in option, the barrier option does not exist until the trigger is touched. For a knock-out option, the option exists until the trigger is touched.

**Basic:** The gap between the active futures price and the implied forward price of the underlying commodity.

**Basis:** The difference between the spot price and the futures price of a commodity.

**Basis:** The difference in price or yield between two different indices.

**Basis point:** One one-hundredth of one percent.

**Basis Risk:** The risk to a hedger arising from uncertainty about the basis at a future time.

**Basket Option:** An option that provides a payoff dependent on the value of a portfolio of assets.

**Basket option:** An option to buy a basket or portfolio of foreign currencies at a given exercise price.

**Basket rainbow option:** Pre-determined basket of assets such as interest rate, foreign exchange rate, equity or commodities whose average performance is the basis for payout on an option contract.

**Bear Spread:** A short position in a put option with strike price $K(1)$ combined with a long position in a put option with strike price $K(2)$, where $K(2) > K(1)$ (can also be created with call options.)

**Benchmarking:** A benchmark is a reference point. Benchmarking in financial risk management refers to the practice of comparing the performance of an individual instrument, a portfolio or an approach to risk management to a predetermined alternative approach.

**Beta:** A measure of the systematic risk of an asset.

**Bid:** The price at which a dealer (market maker) stands ready to buy. Ordinarily the bid is less than the ask, and the bid-ask spread is what the dealer stands to make by quickly turning around one unit of product.

**Bid-ask-spread:** The difference between the exchange rate of currency for its buying and selling quotes.

**Binary options:** An option contract where option seller pays a fixed pre-determined amount if the option is in-the-money at the time of expiry. These are also known as all or nothing.

**Binomial distribution:** The probability distribution of a random variable that can take only one of two values for each realization.

**Binomial model:** Option pricing model based on the assumption that the price of the underlying asset can reach only one of two values after one period has elapsed.

**Binomial pricing:** A method of option pricing based on arbitrage arguments in which the underlying asset moves to one of only two prices during each period.

**Black-Scholes:** A closed-form solution (i.e., an equation) for valuing plain vanilla options developed by Fischer Black and Myron Scholes in 1973 for which they shared the Nobel Prize in Economics.

**Bootstrapping:** A recursive technique for extracting implied forward interest rates or spot rates from other interest rate data.

**Break forward:** A forward contract where one party has the right to terminate the contract at one or more predetermined times during the contract period. This is also known as cancelable forward contracts.

**Butterfly option:** This strategy involves buying or selling three calls or three puts on at a lower price and the other two at a higher and highest price.

**Calendar Spread:** A position that is created by taking a long position in a call and a short position in a call that matures at a different time (can also be created with put options).

**Call Option:** The right but not the obligation to buy the underlying asset at the previously agreed-upon price on (European) or anytime through (American) the expiration date.

**Callable Bond:** A (non-callable) bullet bond minus (i.e., short) a call option on the bond. The call price as a function of calendar time is the call schedule.

**Cancellable Swap:** Swap that can be cancelled by one side on prespecified dates.

**Cap:** A cap is a financial contract giving the owner the right but not the obligation to borrow a preset amount of money at a pre-set interest rate with a pre-set maturity date.

**Capital Asset Pricing Model:** A model relating the expected return on an asset to its beta.

**Caplet:** An interest rate option to pay fixed in an FRA. Its pay off is proportional to that of a call option on a floating rate of interest.

**Car:** The size of one futures contract, based on the idea that some commodity futures contracts historically called for the delivery of one railroad car of the underlying commodity.

**Carry Trade:** Trade that consists of borrowing and paying interest in order to finance the purchase of an investment that pays a greater interest or a dividend stream.

**Carrying cost:** The cost of actually holding a commodity, including insurance costs, storage costs, interest charges, and so forth.

**Cash flow at risk (CaR):** When CaR is estimated at the probability level $p$, it is the cash flow shortfall that has probability $p$ of being exceeded.

**Cash price:** The current price of an asset, particularly as asset on which futures contracts trade. It is also called the spot price.

**Cash Settlement:** Some derivatives contracts are settled at maturity (or before maturity at closeout) by an exchange of cash from the party who is out-of-the-money to the party who is in-the-money.

**Cash settlement:** The settlement procedure used with stock index futures and options. No delivery of the underlying asset occurs with these securities.

**Cheapest to deliver bonds:** Treasury futures if held till expiration creates an obligation to deliver the Treasury security. The holder has a wide choice of Treasury securities with similar features. The holder hence can choose the cheapest to deliver Treasury security based on the conversion rates quoted by the exchange.

**Chooser option:** An option contract in which the holder has a right to choose whether the option is a call or put at a specific time during the life of the option.

**Circuit Breakers:** These are price bands fixed by regulators that help traders to identify undue price volatility through a sudden price increase or decrease.

**Clearing House:** A firm that guarantees the performance of the parties in an exchange-traded derivatives transaction.

**Clearing:** It is the clearing facility by a derivative exchange.

**Clearing Margin:** A margin posted by a member of a clearing house.

**Clearing member:** A person recognized to trade and settle their own trades as well as other member's trades though the clearing house.

**Collar:** A combination of options in which the holder of the contract has bought one out-of-the-money option call (or put) and sold one (or more) out-of-the-money puts (or calls). Doing this locks in the minimum and maximum rates that the collar owner will use to transact in the underlying at expiry.

**Combination:** A position involving both calls and puts on the same underlying asset.

**Commodity derivative:** It is financial instrument created in the derivative market to cover hedge risk on account of price change of a commodity in commodity markets.

**Commodity derivatives:** These are hedge instruments used for protecting a firm or trader from the fluctuating prices of underlying commodities.

**Commodity Futures Trading Commission:** A body that regulates trading in futures contracts in the United States.

**Commodity Swap:** A contract in which counterparties agree to exchange payments related to indices, at least one of which (and possibly both of which) is a commodity index.

**Commodity swap:** It is a commodity derivative product that trades in physical commodity market and is used to lock in a known price in advance in exchange of another market index return thus reducing exposure to price in advance in exchange of another market index return thus reducing exposure to price.

**Component VaR:** Contribution of a portfolio's component to portfolio VaR is called component VaR.

**Compound option:** An option on an option.

**Compound option:** These are options on option contracts in the form of call on call or put on put or put on call or call on put or put on put or put on call options.

**Conditional VaR:** It states the expected loss on the condition the loss being greater than or equal to VaR.

**Condor:** A condor strategy is built with four derivative positions using all call or put options wherein one has a lowest price. One has highest price and two intermediary prices.

**Contango:** A term often used in commodities or futures markets to refer to markets where shorter-dated contracts trade at a lower price than longer-dated contracts. Plotting the prices of contracts against time, with time on the x-axis, shows the commodity price curve as sloping upwards as time increases.

**Contingent Cap:** Contingent option contract on cap positions that enhances profit position or limits losses to the holder. It is created using a long position in a standard cap and a short position in a binary call option.

**Contingent Premium Cap:** An instrument that enables holder to defer the initial premium payment for a hedge requirement.

**Continuous Compounding:** A way of quoting interest rates. It is the limit as the assumed compounding interval is made smaller and smaller.

**Convenience Yield:** A measure of the benefits from ownership of an asset that are not obtained by the holder of a long futures contract on the asset.

**Convergence:** The movement of the cash asset price towards the futures price as the expiration date of the futures contract approaches.

**Conversion Factor:** A pricing factor used to determine the price of T-bonds or T-notes eligible for delivery on futures contracts. These factors are provided by the exchanges.

**Convertible Bond:** A bond that the owner can convert into common shares under specific terms. A convertible bond is an ordinary bond plus the option to exchange the bond for the shares.

**Convertibles:** Convertible bonds are securities with a right to the holders to exercise conversion of bonds into shares at a predetermined date at the option of the holder/owner.

**Convexity:** A financial instrument is said to be convex (or to possess convexity) if the financial instrument's price increases (decreases) faster (slower) than corresponding changes in the underlying price.

**Correlation:** Correlation is a statistical measure describing the extent to which prices on different instruments move together over time. Correlation can be positive or negative. Instruments that move together in the same direction to the same extent have highly positive correlations. Instruments that move together in opposite direction to the same extent have highly negative correlations. Correlation between instruments is not stable.

**Cost of carry model:** This theory postulates that an underlying asset could be bought in the spot market and stored for later consumption and hence the future price ought to reflect the cost of storing and financing the underlying asset till the expiry date.

**Costless Collar:** A collar in which the proceeds of the sale of the short call option exactly finance the purchase of the long put option.

**Covariance:** The expected value of the product of the deviations of two random variables from their mean.

**Covered Call Option Writing:** A technique used by investors to help fund their underlying positions, typically used in the equity markets. An individual who sells a call is said to "write" the call. If this individual sells a call on a notional amount of the underlying that he has in his inventory then the written call is said to be "covered" (by his inventory of the underlying). If the investor does not have the underlying in inventory, the investor has sold the call "naked".

**Covered position:** Hedging an underlying asset along with a derivative contract is called a covered position.

**Credit Default Swap:** A swap in which A pays B the periodic fee, and B pays A the floating payment that depends on whether a predefined credit even has occurred or not. The fee might be quarterly, semi-annual or annual.

**Credit Derivatives:** Derivative product with payoff that depends on risk factors related to credit quality such as yield spread over treasuries, price discount from par or a credit event.

**Credit Linked Note:** A note that pays interest and repays principal that depends on a credit event such as bankruptcy and default.

**Credit Metrics™:** A risk model that provides the distribution of the value of a portfolio of debt claims, which leads to a VaR measure for the portfolio.

**Credit Option:** An option with a payoff that depends on credit quality, without bearing ordinary interest-rate risk.

**Credit Risk:** Credit risk is the risk of loss from a counterparty in default or from a pejorative change in the credit status of a counterparty that causes the value of their obligations to decrease.

**Credit spread:** The difference between the yield on risky debt and the yield on risk-free debt of same maturity.

**Credit spread risk:** It is the risk that difference over a reference rate will increase in the financial market for the debt obligation of a firm.

**Credit Swap:** A swap whose value depends on underlying credit quality, preferably without bearing ordinary interest-rate risk.

**Credit Value-at-Risk:** The credit loss that will not be exceeded at some specified confidence level.

**Cross Currency Option:** An option to exchange units of one currency for units of another, as seen from the point of view of a third currency.

**Cross rate:** Currency exchange rate between two countries in terms of a third country's currency.

**Cross-hedge:** Using a futures contract to hedge a cash position on a good that would not be deliverable with the futures contract.

**Cumulative distribution function:** Specifies the probability that the realization of the random variable will be no greater than a certain value.

**Currency Derivative:** A financial instrument used for hedging currency risk and to provide value protection to international financial transactions.

**Currency derivative:** An agreement between buyer and seller of currency at present to settle the transaction at a future time.

**Currency forward contract:** A contract in which counter parties agree to exchange a quantity of one currency for a quantity of another currency at a fixed rate on a future settlement date.

**Currency futures:** A contract where hedger agrees to buy/sell a currency at a specified rate on a future settlement date. This is similar to a forward contract but more flexible, liquid and less risky since the trades are standardized.

**Currency option:** Option contract gives the hedger a right to buy/sell a currency at a specified strike rate for specified time duration.

**Currency Swap:** An exchange of interest rate payments in different currencies on a preset notional amount and in reference to predetermined interest rate indices in which the notional amounts are exchanged at inception of the contract and then re-exchanged at the termination of the contract at preset exchange rates.

**Daily price limit:** An exchange-imposed restriction on how much the price of a particular futures contract is allowed to move in a single trading day. Contracts are said to be "limit up" or "limit down" when the daily price limit is reached.

**DAX:** A stock performance index (dividends added in) composed of the 30 most actively traded German blue chip stocks on the Frankfurt Stock Exchange.

**Day Count:** A convention for quoting Interest rates.

**Day Trade:** A trade that is entered into and closed out on the same day.

**Default Risk:** A measure of the likelihood that a borrower will be unable to repay principal and interest as agreed. It is also called credit risk.

**Default risk:** The risk that a borrower will not repay outstanding obligations partly or fully.

**Deferred Payment Option:** An option where the price paid is deferred until the end of the option's life.

**Deferred Swap:** An agreement to enter into a swap at some time in the future.

**Deliverable Bond:** A bond that satisfies the delivery requirements of the Treasury bond futures contract. A deliverable bond has at least 15 years until maturity, and if callable, at least 15 years of call protection.

**Delivery day:** The day that a commodity of financial instrument is actually delivered against a futures contract.

**Delivery month:** The month during which a commodity is due to be delivered in a futures contract.

**Delivery Notice:** The Written notice that a futures seller gives, indicating a desire to make delivery of the commodity underlying the futures contract.

**Delivery Price:** Price agreed to in a forward contract.

**Delta exposure:** The sum of deltas in a portfolio.

**Delta Gamma hedging:** Hedging a portfolio through option instruments to minimize delta, gamma, values to zero.

**Delta Management:** A method of risk management in which the manager seeks to maintain position delta within a certain range.

**Delta neutrality:** Holding delta times the underlying asset for each contract in the derivative creates delta neutral position.

**Delta:** The sensitivity of the change in the financial instrument's price to changes in the price of the underlying cash index.

**Derivative:** An instrument whose price depends on or is derived from the price of another asset.

**Derivative Greeks:** Risk means associated with derivative instruments which are indicated through Greek letters/symbols.

**Derivative market:** This is an exchange that facilitates trading in specified products (derivatives) whose values are linked to specific assets available in regular markets thereby allowing distribution of risks among participants.

**Derivative strategy:** It is an action plan of hedging risk aimed at minimizing specific financial risk using derivative instruments.

**Designated hedge:** A hedge transaction identified and classified as hedge at the inception of hedge.

**Diagonal Spread:** A spread in which the options are selected from different expiration months and in which the options have different striking prices.

**Discount Rate:** The annualized dollar return on a Treasury bill or similar instrument expressed as a percentage of the final face value.

**Documentation Risk:** The risk of loss due to an inadequacy or other unforeseen aspect of the legal documentation behind the financial contract.

**Downgrade risk:** It is the risk associated with the credit rating of a firm due to lowering of rating by the credit rating agency.

**Duration:** A measure of the average life of a bond. It is also an approximation to the ratio of the proportional change in the bond price to the absolute change in its yield.

**Dynamic Hedging:** A procedure for hedging an option position by periodically changing the position held in the underlying assets.

**Early Exercise:** Exercise prior to the maturity date.

**Effective exchange rate:** These are trade weighted exchange rates against other currencies.

**Efficient frontier-upward:** Sloping part of the curve graphing for each expected return the lowest volatility portfolio that produces that expected return.

**Embedded Option:** An option that is an inseparable part of another instrument.

**Equity derivative:** It is a financial instrument traded in derivative exchange with a view to hedge risk of price fluctuations of equity securities traded in stock exchanges.

**Equity Swap:** A swap in which one of the payment streams derives from an equity instrument.

**Eurodollar:** A dollar held in a bank outside the United States.

**European Style Option:**   An option that can be exercised only at expiry as opposed to an American style option that can be exercised at any time from inception of the contract. European style option contracts can be closed out early, mimicking the early exercise property of American style options in most cases.

**Even risk:**   Risk of changes in business prospectus or return. An example would be risk due to policy changes announced by Government.

**Exchange Option:**   An option to exchange one asset for another.

**Exchange-traded Contracts:**   Financial instruments listed on exchanges such as the Chicago Board of Trade, Bombay Stock Exchange, National Stock Exchange, etc.

**Exercise Price:**   The exercise price is the price at which a call's (put's) buyer can buy (or sell) the underlying instrument.

**Exercise Price:**   The price at which the underlying asset may be bought or sold in an option contract.

**Exotic derivatives:**   Nonstandard derivatives whose payoffs cannot be created through a portfolio of plain vanilla derivatives.

**Exotic Option:**   Any option that is well out of the ordinary, hence not a plain vanilla option.

**Expectation hypothesis:**   A theory that bond holder's expectations determine interest rates. It states that current forward rates are unbiased estimates of futures spot interest rates.

**Expected return:**   Probability weighted average of all possible returns.

**Expiry date:**   The date on which the contract is to be settled.

**Exposure:**   The maximum loss from default by a counterparty.

**Fair value model of hedge accounting:**   Accounting for change in the fair value of hedged asset in the income statement.

**Financial risk:**   Risk of delay or default in financial obligations.

**Fixed rate:**   A predetermined constant rate of exchange that remains fixed for a specified duration.

**Fixed return options:**   These are binary options traded in American Stock Exchanges.

**Flex Option:**   An option traded on an exchange with terms that are different from the standard options traded by the exchange.

**Floating rate:**   A fluctuating exchange rate which moves according to the supply and demand for the currency.

**Floor Rate:**   The rate in an interest rate floor agreement.

**Floor:**   A strip of floorlets.

**Floor:**   A floor is a financial contract giving the owner the right but not the obligation to lend a preset amount of money at a preset interest rate with a preset maturity date.

**Floorlet:**   An interest rate option to receive fixed in an FRA (q.v.). Its payoff is proportional to that of a put option on a floating rate of interest.

**Foreign Currency Option:**   An option on a foreign exchange rate.

**Forward Contracts:**   An over-the-counter obligation to buy or sell a financial instrument or to make a payment at some point in the future, the details of which were settled privately between the two counterparties. Forward contracts generally are arranged to have zero mark-to-market value at inception, although they may be off-market. Examples include forward foreign exchange contracts in which one party is obligated to buy foreign exchange from another party at a fixed rate for delivery on a preset date. Off-market forward contracts are used often in structured combinations, with the value on the forward contract off setting the value of the other instrument(s).

**Forward Interest Rate:**   The interest rate for a future period of time implied by the rates prevailing in the market today.

**Forward or Delayed Start Swap (see also Interest Rate Swap):**   Any swap contract with a start that is later than the standard terms. This means that calculation of the cash flows does not begin straightaway but at some predetermined start date.

**Forward Price:**   The delivery price in a forward contract that causes the contract to be worth zero.

**Forward Rate Agreements (FRAs) (see also Interest Rate Swap):**   A forward rate agreement is a cash-settled obligation on interest rates for a preset period on a preset interest rate index with a forward start date. A $3 \times 6$ FRX on US dollar LIBOR (the London Interbank Offered Rate) is a contract between two parties obliging one to pay the other the difference between the FRA rate and the actual LIBOR rate observed for that period. An interest rate swap is a strip of FRAs.

**Forward rate:**   The rate at which counter parties agree to exchange one currency with another currency at a specified future date.

**Forward Swap:**   An agreement to enter into a swap at some time in the future.

**Full-valuation Monte Carlo VaR:**   VaR-computation where the financial instruments in the portfolio are valued for each set of values of the risk factors generated by the simulation.

**Future options:**   It is an option contract with the underlying asset as a future contract.

**Futures Contract:**   An exchange-traded contract that on its last trading day settles into a forward contract.

**Futures Contracts:**   An exchange-traded obligation to buy or sell a financial instrument or to make a payment at one of the exchange's fixed delivery dates, the details of which are transparent publicly on the trading floor and for which contract settlement takes place through the exchange's clearing house.

**Futures Price:**   The delivery price currently applicable to a future contract.

**Gamma (see also Delta):**   Gamma (or convexity) is the degree of curvature in the financial contract's price curve with respect to its underlying price. It is the rate of change of the delta with respect to changes in the underlying price. Positive gamma is favourable. Negative gamma is damaging in a sufficiently volatile market. The price of having positive gamma (or owning gamma) is time decay. Only instruments with time value have gamma.

**Gamma-neutral Portfolio:**   A portfolio with a gamma zero.

**Hedge accounting:**   Accounting for gain or loss on hedging through derivative instruments.

**Hedge:**   A transaction that offsets an exposure to fluctuations in financial prices of some other contract or business risk. It may consist of cash instruments or derivatives.

**Hedge effectiveness:**   Ability of the hedge to protect against risk which is measured by comparing cumulative value offset over a time period.

**Hedge Ratio:**   The ratio of the size of a position in a hedging instrument to the size of the position being hedged.

**Hedging:**   It is an agreement between buyer and seller at the present time for locking the future price of an asset in order to protect a risk exposure.

**Hedging costs:** Costs of putting on a hedge; examples include transactions costs, monitoring costs and design costs.

**Historical Volatility:** A measure of the actual volatility (a statistical measure of dispersion) observed in the marketplace.

**Hybrid Security:** Any security that includes more than one component. For example, a hybrid security might be a fixed income note that includes a foreign exchange option or a commodity price option.

**Immunization:** The process of removing interest rate risk by adjusting the duration of assets and liabilities via the futures market or with portfolio rebalancing.

**Implied Volatility:** Option pricing models rely upon an assumption of future volatility as well as the spot price, interest rates, the expiry date, the delivery date, the strike, etc. If we are given simultaneously all of the parameters necessary for determining the option price except for volatility and the option price in the marketplace, we can back out mathematically the volatility corresponding to that price and those parameters. This is the implied volatility.

**Implies forward rate:** The forward interest rate expected to prevail in the future given the current yield curve.

**Incremental VaR:** It is the difference in VaR before and after a change in portfolio position.

**Index Amortizing Swap:** A swap where the principal declines over time. The reduction in the principal on a payment date depends on the level of interest rates (also called indexed principal swap).

**Index Arbitrage:** An arbitrage involving a position in the stocks comprising a stock index and a position in a futures contract on the stock index.

**Index Futures:** A futures contract on a stock index or other index.

**Index options:** An option contract linked to the underlying index values.

**Initial Margin:** The cash required from a futures trader at the time of the trade.

**Inter-commodity spread:** This type of spread involves a long and short position in two related commodities.

**Interest Rate Cap:** An option that provides a payoff when a specified interest rate is above a certain level. The interest rate is a floating rate that is reset periodically.

**Interest Rate Collar:** A combination of an interest rate cap and an interest rate floor.

**Interest rate derivative:** A financial instrument credited to protect against interest rate fluctuations.

**Interest rate derivatives:** An agreement between buyer and seller at present to settle a interest rate obligation at a future time.

**Interest Rate Floor:** An option that provides a payoff when an interest rate is below a certain level. The interest rate is a floating rate that is reset periodically.

**Interest Rate Option:** An option where the payoff is dependent on the level of interest rates.

**Interest rate parity:** The fact that differences in national interest rates are reflected in the currency forward market.

**Interest rate risk:** The probability of loss on account of fluctuation in interest rate.

**Interest rate sensitive:** An asset whose price may change if the level of interest rate changes.

**Interest Rate Swap:** An exchange of a fixed rate of interest on a certain notional principal for a floating rate of interest on the same notional principal.

**Interest Rate Swap:** An exchange of cash flows based upon different interest rate indices denominated in the same currency on a preset notional amount with a predetermined schedule of payments and calculations. Usually, one counterparty will receive fixed flows in exchange for making floating payments.

**Internal rate of return:** The discount rate that will cause a series of future cash flows to have a present value equal to the cost of acquiring the future cash flows.

**International Swaps Dealers' Association:** In order to minimize the legal risks of transacting with one another, counterparties will establish master legal agreements and sidebar product schedules to govern formally all derivatives transactions into which they may enter with one another.

**In-the-money contract:** When the strike price is less than the price quoted on the trading date for a call option when the strike price is more than the quoted price for a put option, it is called in-the-money contract.

**In-The-Money Spot:** An option with positive intrinsic value with respect to the prevailing market spot rate. If the option were to mature immediately, the option holder would exercise it in order to capture its economic value. For a call price to have intrinsic value, the strike must be less than the spot price. For a put price to have intrinsic value, the strike must be greater than the spot price.

**Intrinsic Value:** The economic value of a financial contract, as distinct from the contract's time value. One way to think of the intrinsic value of the financial contract is to calculate its value if it were a forward contract with the same delivery date. If the contract is an option, its intrinsic value cannot be less than zero.

**Invoice price:** The amount that the buyer of an interest rate future contract must pay when the securities of futures contract are delivered.

**IO:** Interest Only. A mortgage-backed security where the holder receives only interest cash flows on the underlying mortgage pool.

**Jamming:** Executing a large sell (buy) order in stages by asking for a market on a small size, hitting the bid (offer) then repeating the process with a different market maker, ultimately driving the price considerably lower (higher).

**Junk Bond:** Historically, a junk bond is any bond rated below BBB by Standard and Poor's rating agency.

**Kappa:** The rate of change in the price of an option or other derivative with volatility.

**Knock-in Option:** An option the existence of which is conditional upon a preset trigger price trading before the option's designated maturity. If the trigger is not touched before maturity then the option is deemed not to exist.

**Knock-out Option:** An option the existence of which is conditional upon a preset trigger price trading before the option's designated maturity. The option is deemed to exist unless the trigger price is touched before maturity.

**Kurtosis:** A measure of the fatness of the tails of a distribution.

**Lambda:** The rate of change in the price of an option or other derivative with volatility.

**Law of one price:** The fundamental economic principle that requires equivalent assets to sell for the same price.

**LEAPS:** Long-term equity anticipation securities. These are relatively long-term options on individual stocks or stock indices.

**LED Spread:** An interest rate spread involving the LIBOR and Eurodollar futures contract.

**Legal Risk:** The general potential for loss due to the legal and regulatory interpretation of contracts relating to financial market transactions.

**Levered swap:** Swap in which the cash flows are those of a plain vanilla swap with additional borrowing.

**LIBID:** Long interbank bid rate. The rate bid by banks on Eurocurrency deposits (i.e., the rate at which a bank is willing to borrow from other banks).

**LIBOR:** London interbank offer rate. The rate offered by banks on Eurocurrency deposits (i.e., the rate at which a bank is willing to lend to other banks).

**Limit Order:** An order to buy or sell securities or other assets in which the client has specified the time for which the order is to be kept open and the minimum price acceptable for the trade.

**Liquidity preference theory:** A theory that postulates that long-term interest rate will be higher than short-term interest rate since investors prefer cash.

**Liquidity Risk:** The risk that a financial market entity will not be able to find a price (or a price within a reasonable tolerance in terms of the deviation from prevailing or expected prices) for one or more of its financial contracts in the secondary market. Consider the case of a counterparty who buys a complex option on European interest rates. He is exposed to liquidity risk because of the possibility that he cannot find anyone to make him a price in the secondary market and because of the possibility that the price he obtains is very much against him and the theoretical price for the product.

**Locals:** Members of an exchange who trade for their own account. They are not employees of another firm.

**Lognormal distribution:** A distribution where the log of a random variable is normally distributed.

**Long Hedge:** A hedge involving a long futures.

**Long position:** An obligation to purchase at a future date at an agreed price at the time when the contract was entered into.

**Long Position:** The common investment position in which an asset is held as opposed to borrowed or written.

**Long Term Equity Anticipation Security (LEAP):** An exchange traded long-term option.

**Look-back option:** An option with a payout equal to the highest intrinsic value of the option at any time over its life.

**Look-back Options:** An option which gives the owner the right to buy (sell) at the lowest (highest) price that traded in the underlying from the inception of the contract to its maturity, i.e., the most favourable price that traded over the lifetime of the contract.

**Lot size:** The fixed quantity in terms of which trade is permitted.

**Maintenance Margin:** When the balance in a trader's margin account falls below the maintenance margin level, the trader receives a margin call requiring the account to be topped up to the initial margin level.

**Margin:** The cash balance (or security deposit) required from a futures or options trader.

**Margin:** A credit-enhancement provision to master agreements and individual transactions in which one counterparty agrees to post a deposit of cash or other liquid financial instruments with the entity selling it a financial instrument that places some obligation on the entity posting the margin.

**Margin Call:**  A request for extra margin when the balance in the margin account falls below the maintenance margin level.

**Margin Payment**:  Payment made by the trader to the exchange on the value of the contract. This is adjusted on a daily basis for the profit or loss from market price fluctuations. Margin payments are adjusted towards contract settlement dues of the trader.

**Margin system:**  Amount to be kept in clearing account by trading member to cover price uncertainly over contract period.

**Marginal VaR:**  It is first derivative that signifies the change in portfolio VaR given a change in the component weight in a portfolio.

**Margrabe Option:**  The option to exchange one asset for another. Margrabe (1978) showed several applications for this sort of option (margin account, corporate exchange offer and standby commitment) and derived a model for pricing this option.

**Market order:**  The simplest type of order. It instructs a broker to execute a clients order at the best possible price at the earliest opportunity.

**Market Risk:**  The exposure to potential loss from fluctuations in market prices (as opposed to changes in credit status).

**Market-maker:**  A participant in the financial markets who guarantees to make simultaneously a bid and an offer for a financial contract with a preset bid/offer spread (or a schedule of spreads corresponding to different market conditions) up to a predetermined maximum contract amount.

**Markovian stochastic process:**  It is a process of value movement, where current prices of assets are assumed to be the basis for predicting future values and past prices are not relevant.

**Mark-to-Market Accounting:**  A method of accounting most suited for financial instruments in which contracts are revalued at regular intervals using prevailing market prices. This is known as taking a "snapshot" of the market.

**Master agreement:**  A legal document issued by the International Swaps and Derivatives Association outlining the terms of a swap or interest rate options contract.

**Matching trades:**  The act of processing one's deck through a clearing corporation.

**Maturity Date:**  The end of the life of a contract.

**Mean Reversion:**  The tendency of a market variable (interest rate) to revert back to some long-run average level.

**MIBID:**  Mumbai Inter-Bank-Bid Rate.

**MIBOR:**  Mumbai Inter-Bank-Offer Rate.

**Modified duration:**  Duration with present values computed using the yield of the bond and divided by one plus the yield.

**Monte Carlo Simulation:**  A technique for approximating a probability distribution by generating uniformly distributed pseudo random numbers and transforming them into the required sort of random numbers.

**Mortgage Backed Securities:**  A security such as a bond, pass-through, CMO or REMIC that derives its cash flows and market value from underlying mortgage backed securities and/or mortgage bonds, Loans, and/or notes.

**Multilateral netting**:  Netting that offsets open derivative contracts of each trading party across all other trading parties.

**Naked Call:** A short call option in which the writer does not own or have claim to the underlying security or asset.

**Naked Option Writing:** The act of selling options without having any offsetting exposure in the underlying cash instrument.

**Naked option:** This term properly is given only to the writing of an uncovered call option. To the writer of an uncovered call, potential losses are theoretically unlimited.

**Near-the-money:** An option in which the striking price and the price of the underlying asset are approximately equal.

**Netting:** When there are cash flows in two directions between two counterparties, they can be consolidated into one net payment from one counterparty to the other thereby reducing the settlement risk involved.

**Nominal interest rate:** Stated interest rate.

**Non-systematic Risk:** Risk that can be diversified away.

**Normal Backwardation:** The theory of futures pricing that predicts the future price is downward based in order to provide a risk premium to the speculator, who normally have a net long position.

**Normal distribution:** The distribution that produces the familiar bell-shaped curve; the values that a random variable can take are symmetrically spread around its mean, so that we only need information about mean and variance to determine the characteristics of the distribution.

**Notional Principal:** The principal used to calculate payments in an interest rate swap. The principal is notional because it is neither paid nor received.

**Obligors:** Those who have legal financial obligations to a firm.

**Offer Price:** The price that a dealer is offering to sell an asset.

**Offer price:** See asked price.

**Open contracts:** Contracts that are not settled and are permitted to be traded again and again during a specified period (maturity duration).

**Open Interest:** The total number of long positions outstanding in a futures contract (equals the total number of short positions).

**Open Outcry:** System of trading where traders meet on the floor of the exchange.

**Operational Risk:** The potential for loss attributable to procedural errors or failures in internal control.

**Option:** The right but not the obligation to buy (sell) some underlying cash instrument at a predetermined rate on a predetermined expiration date in a preset notional amount.

**Option Class:** All options of the same type (call or put) on a particular stock.

**Option premium:** The upfront payment made by the buyer of the contract to the seller for acquiring the option right is called option premium.

**Option Series:** All options of a certain class with the same strike price and expiration date.

**Option writer:** Whoever sells an option at inception of the contract.

**Option-Adjusted Spread:** The spread over the treasury curve that makes that theoretical price of an interest derivative equal to the market price.

**OTC derivative:** These are derivative products whose trading terms are not standardized but are negotiated between parties in OTC.

**Out trade:** When a clearing corporation's computer is not able to exactly match all trades, the mismatches are called "out trades".

**Out-of-The-Money Spot:** An option with no intrinsic value with respect to the prevailing market spot rate. If the option were to mature immediately, the option holder would let it expire. For a call price to have intrinsic value, the strike must be less than the spot price. For a put price to have intrinsic value, the strike must be greater than the spot price.

**Out-of-The-Money-Forward:** An option with no intrinsic value with respect to the prevailing market forward rate. If the option were to mature immediately, the option holder would let it expire. For a call price to have intrinsic value, the strike must be less than the spot price. For a put price to have intrinsic value, the strike must be greater than the spot price.

**Over-the-Counter:** Any transaction that takes place between two counterparties and does not involve an exchange is said to be an over-the-counter transaction.

**Overwriting:** The practice of writing options against an existing portfolio.

**Package:** A derivative that is a portfolio of standard calls and puts, possibly combined with a position in forward contracts and the asset itself.

**Par Value:** The principal amount of a bond.

**Par Yield:** The coupon on a bond that makes its price equal the principal.

**Participative forward:** A forward contract where the hedger has complete protection against an unfavorable currency fluctuation while allowing unlimited participation in favorable currency rate market movement.

**Path-dependent Option:** An option whose payoff depends on the whole path followed by the underlying variable—not just its final value.

**Perfect hedge:** It eliminates all risk so that the hedged position, defined as the cash position plus the hedge, has no exposure to the risk factor.

**Plain vanilla derivatives:** Conventional calls, puts, forwards, and futures contracts generally traded on exchanges or on liquid over-the-counter markets.

**Plain Vanilla:** A term used to describe a standard deal.

**Portfolio Immunization:** Making a portfolio relatively insensitive to interest rates.

**Portfolio Insurance:** Entering into trades to ensure that the value of a portfolio will not fall below a certain level.

**Potential Exposure:** An assessment of the future positive intrinsic value in all of the contracts outstanding with an individual counterparty who may choose (or may be unable) to make their obligated payments.

**Premium:** The cost associated with a derivative contract, referring to the combination of intrinsic value and time value. It usually applies to options contracts. However, it also applies to off-market forward contracts.

**Price discovery:** The function of the futures markets that produces a "best estimate" of the future spot price of a commodity; a function of the futures market which helps indicate the market's consensus about likely future prices for a commodity security.

**Price risk:** Probability of loss due to value increase or decrease of the financial instrument.

**Probability of default:** The likelihood of default of a credit instrument.

**Professional clearing member:**   A member who performs a clearing and settlement function for trading members but do not trade themselves.

**Program trading:**   A generic term used for any activity that involves the trading of portfolios via computer, in which the decision to make a trade is also computer generated.

**Protective Put:**   A put option combined with a long position in the underlying asset.

**Put Option:**   A put option is a financial contract giving the owner the right but not the obligation to sell a preset amount of the underlying financial instrument at a preset price with a preset maturity date.

**Putable Bond:**   A bullet bond that the bondholder can force the issuer to buy back at a scheduled price. The put price as a function of calendar time is the put schedule. A bullet bond plus a put option on the bond.

**Put-call parity theorem:**   The price of a European put is equal to the value of a portfolio long the call, long an investment in discount bonds for the present value of the exercise price of the call and the same maturity as the call, and short the underlying asset.

**Put-Call Parity Theorem:**   A long position in a put combined with a long position in the underlying forward instrument, both of which have the same delivery date has the same behavioural properties as a long position in a call for the same delivery date. This can be varied for short positions.

**Puttable Bond:**   A bond where the holder has the right to sell it back to the issuer at certain predetermined times for a predetermined price.

**Puttable Swap:**   A swap where one side has the right to terminate early.

**Qualified hedge:**   IAS 39 requires hedge transaction to meet certain criteria in order to qualify for hedge accounting.

**Quality option:**   The right of the holder of a short position in Treasury bond futures contracts to deliver any eligible bond against the contract.

**Quality Spread:**   The difference in interest rates on loans of differing levels of credit risk.

**Quantity out:**   An out trade in which the number of contracts in a particular trade is in dispute.

**Quanto:**   A derivative where the payoff is defined by variables associated with one currency but is paid in another currency.

**Rainbow Option:**   An option that has several risk factors of the same type, e.g., two stock prices or three exchange rates.

**Range-Forward Contract:**   The combination of a long call and short put or the combination of a short call and long put.

**Ratio spread:**   A spread with an unequal number of long and short options.

**Rational boundaries:**   These are upper and lower limits within which the fair theoretical price of an option contract will occur.

**Real Asset**:   An asset for which there is no corresponding liability.

**Real option:**   Any of various types of options that are embedded in other assets, such as the right to abandon a project, the right to expand, the right to choose, and the right to postpone.

**Real option:**   These are derivative instruments that help investor to hedge the risk of investments in real assets such as business projects or property.

**Recovery Rate:**   Amount recovered in the event of a default as a percent of the claim.

**Regulatory Risk:**   The potential for loss stemming from changes in the regulatory environment pertaining to derivatives and financial contracts, the utility of these instruments for different counter-parties, etc.

**Reinvestment rate risk:**   The chance of loss associated with reinvesting cash flows at a lower rate than previously available.

**Reinvestment risk:**   Probability of reduced returns on the reinvestment of cash flows (dividends or interest) from the financial instrument.

**Repo:**   A transaction that involves a spot market sale of a security and the promise to repurchase the security at a later day at a given price.

**Reset Date:**   The date in a swap or cap or floor when the floating rate for the next period is set.

**Retrospective effectiveness test:**   Examining effectiveness of a hedge in a past period on the retrospective date based on actual results of hedge.

**Reverse knock in barrier options:**   Reverse knock is an up and in barrier option where the underlying asset price touches upper barrier from down and is in the money.

**Reverse repo:**   A repo transaction viewed from the perspective of the dealer who receives the securities.

**Reversion Level:**   The level to which the value of a market variable (e.g., an interest rate) tends to revert.

**Rho:**   Rate of change of the price of a derivative with the interest rate.

**Risk factor:**   A variable, price, or quantity that impacts cash flow or return and can change unexpectedly for reasons beyond one's control; an identifiable source of risk.

**Risk Metrics:**   A parametric methodology for calculating value-at-risk using data conditioned by JP Morgan's spinoff company Risk Metrics that is most useful for assessing portfolios with linear risks.

**Risk premium:**   The expected return of a security or portfolio in excess of the risk-free rate.

**Risk-free Rate:**   The rate of interest that can be earned without assuming any risks.

**Riskless rate of interest:**   A theoretical value representing the price of deferring consumption from one period to the next. The riskless interest rate is usually peroxide by the rate on a 30 day U.S. Treasury bill.

**Risk-neutral probabilities:**   The probabilities that, given the financial asset's payoffs, make its expected return equal to the risk-free rate, which is the expected return the asset would have if investors were risk neutral.

**Scalper:**   See local.

**Scenario Analysis:**   An analysis of the effects of possible alternative future movements in market variables on the value of a portfolio.

**Sequential real options:**   Application to a real option phased property development with an option of abandonment or delay at each future phase of development.

**Settlement Price:**   The average of the prices that a futures contract trades for immediately before the bell signaling the close of trading for a day. It is used in market-to-market calculations.

**Settlement Risk:**   The risk of non-payment of an obligation by a counterparty to a transaction, exacerbated by mismatches in payment timings.

**Short Call:**   A written call.

**Short Hedge:** A hedge using futures contracts in which the hedger promises to deliver the underlying commodity.

**Short Position:** A position assumed when traders sell shares they do not own.

**Short Rate:** The interest rate applying for a very short period of time.

**Short Selling:** Selling in the market shares that have been borrowed from another investor.

**Shout Option:** An option where the holder has the right to lock in a minimum value for the pay off at one time during its life.

**Sigma:** The rate of change in the price of an option or other derivative with volatility.

**SPAN:** Standard Portfolio Analysis of Risk System used by NSCCL for monitoring online position and margins on an intraday basis.

**Special Purpose Vehicle (SPV):** A merger of a bond and a derivative trade into a single contract.

**Speculation:** Taking positions in financial instruments without having an underlying exposure that offsets the positions taken.

**Speculator:** In the futures market a speculator is a person who, for a price, is willing to bear the risk that the hedger does not want.

**Spot:** The price in the cash market for delivery using the standard market convention. In the foreign exchange market, spot is delivered for value two days from the transaction date or for the next day in the case of the Canadian dollar exchanged against the US dollar.

**Spot rate:** Market rate for exchange of a currency into another currency that requires immediate settlement.

**Spread:** The difference in price or yield between two assets that differ by type of financial instrument, maturity, strike or some other factor. A credit spread is the difference in yield between a corporate bond and the corresponding government bond. A yield curve spread is the spread between two government bonds of differing maturity.

**Spread Option:** An option where the pay off is dependent on the difference between two market variables.

**Stack hedge:** A Eurodollar futures hedge in which the required quantity of futures contracts all have the same delivery month.

**Standard Deviation:** In finance, a statistical measure of dispersion of a time series around its mean; the expected value of the difference between the time series and its mean; the square root of the variance of the time series.

**Static Hedge:** A hedge that does not have to be changed once it is initiated.

**Stock Index:** A measure of the general level of stock market prices.

**Stop loss order:** A special type of limit order that becomes a market order if the stop price is touched.

**Stop order:** *See* stop loss order.

**Stop Price:** The "trigger" price with a stop order, causing the order to be executed.

**Straddle:** Buying or selling a call and a put option at the same strike price creates a straddle strategy.

**Straddle:** Holding a put and a call with the same striking price, expiration date, and on the same underlying security, is being long a straddle. If one is short these options, they have written a straddle.

**Straddle:** An option portfolio consisting of one call option and one put option, both with the same underlying, direction (long or short), strike and expiration date.

**Strangle:** Similar to a straddle, except that the puts and calls have different striking prices.

**Strangle:** Using a combination of a call and a put at two different strike prices (One at a lower and the other at a higher price) is called a strangle strategy.

**Strap:** Strap strategies are created using one call and two put options at the same strike price and maturity.

**Stress Testing:** The act of simulating different financial market conditions for their potential effects on a portfolio of financial instruments.

**Strike Price:** The price at which the holder of a derivative contract exercises his right if it is economic to do so at the appropriate point in time as delineated in the financial product's contract.

**Strip:** A straddle plus another one of the put options.

**Strip hedge:** A Eurodollar futures hedge in which the required quantity of futures contracts are distributed throughout a time period rather than concentrated at one point.

**Structured credit derivative:** A derivative instrument with the backup of cash flows of a loan/asset/mortgage that facilitates risk transfer across investors in the market.

**Structured Product:** Essentially a portfolio of securities and other (often, Vanilla) derivative products. Although the dealer that creates it, hopes the customer doesn't realize this.

**Swap:** The exchange of a sequence of cash flows that derive from two different financial instruments.

**Swap clear system:** OTC clearing service for interest rate swaps.

**Swap facilitator:** An institution that funds and arranges for two parties to engage in a swap transaction.

**Swap price:** The fixed interest rate on a swap that causes the present value of the floating rate payments to equal the present value of the fixed rate payments.

**Swap rate:** It is the rate pre-determined at the same time of entering into an agreement at which exchange of contracts will take in future.

**Swap Spread:** An increment added to the swap price to compensate the swap dealer for providing the service.

**Swap value:** The difference between the present value of the payments one party to a swap agrees to make and the present value of the payments to be received.

**Swaption:** An option enter into an interest rate swap where a specified fixed rate is exchanged for floating.

**Synthetic derivatives:** When a hedge product is not available in the market, the investor can create a position mimicking the product profile with other available instruments. This would imitate the instrument profit or loss that is expected from the hedge position.

**Synthetic forward agreement:** It is an agreement for the exchange of a notional amount of principal in two currencies through two individual contracts that are linked together to create the same economic result as that of one forward instrument.

**Synthetic Option:** An option created by trading the underlying asset.

**Synthetic swap:** Forming a portfolio of swap and Treasury future contracts and gaining by the differential yield between underlying swap yield and Treasury yield.

**Systematic risk:** Probability of loss due to sudden collapse of the market on account of the technology and process that is integrating the derivative market functions.

**Systematic risk:**   The risk associated with owning equity securities due to their tendency to move intandem.

**Tailing the hedge:**   The futures and underlying asset price difference requires that an investor to use a hedge ratio as a hedge tool. This ratio implies that the hedging needs for the change in underlying asset price is adjusted through change in futures price. The hedge ratio needs to be changed whenever future prices changes. This is called tailing the hedge.

**Ted spreads:**   These are constructed by combining Treasury bill futures and Eurodollar futures considering a 3-month LIBOR and a 3-month US Treasury bill.

**Term structure:**   Yield to maturity rates for various maturities on a date is known as term structure of interest rates.

**Terminal Value:**   The value at maturity.

**Theta:**   The rate of change of the price of an option or other derivative with the passage of time.

**Tick:**   The minimum allowable price change in a futures or options position.

**Time Value:**   For a derivative contract with a non-linear value structure, time value is the difference between the intrinsic value and the premium.

**Total return swap:**   It is a financial contract to transfer credit risk between parties. The total return payer exchange total return of an underlying asset for another cash flow from total return receiver.

**Trading member:**   A person recognized to operate/trade on their client's account in a derivative market.

**Transaction Costs:**   The cost of carrying out a trade.

**Treasury Bill:**   A short-term non-coupon-bearing instrument issued by the government to finance its debt.

**Treasury Bond:**   A long-term coupon-bearing instrument issued by the government to finance its debt.

**Treasury Note:**   A long-term coupon-bearing instrument issued by the government to finance its debt. Treasury notes have maturities less than 10 years.

**Tree:**   A representation of the evolution of the value of a market variable for the purposes of valuing an option or other derivative.

**Two branch binomial model:**   This model of pricing an option assumes that rates of return on an asset will have two possible outcomes, an increase 'u' and a decrease of 'd' percentage.

**Underlying Variable:**   A variable that price of an option or other derivative depends on.

**Up-and-In Option:**   An option that comes into existence when the price of the underlying asset increases to a prespecified level.

**Up-and-Out Option:**   An option that ceases to exist when the price of the underlying asset increases to a prespecified level.

**Value at risk margin:**   When margin is linked to probable loss of value of asset estimated based on price trends, it is called VaR margin.

**Value of a Basis Point:**   The change in the value of a financial instrument attributable to a change in the relevant interest rate by 1 basis point (i.e., 1/100 of 1%).

**Value-at-Risk or VaR:**   The calculated value of the maximum expected loss for a given portfolio over a defined time horizon (typically one day) and for a preset statistical confidence interval, under normal market conditions.

**Variance Rate:**   The square of volatility.

**Variance Swap:**   A contract that pays off an amount proportional to the difference between the realized variance over a specific period of time and the contractual variance.

**Variation Margin:**   An extra margin required to bring the balance in a margin account up to the initial margin when there is a margin call.

**Vega:**   The rate of change in the price of an option or other derivative with volatility.

**Vega-neutral Portfolio:**   A portfolio with a vega of zero.

**Vertical spread:**   A spread in which the options have the same expiration but different striking prices.

**Volatility:**   In finance, a statistical measure of dispersion of a time series around its mean; the expected value of the difference between the time series and its mean; the square root of the variance of the time series.

**Volatility Smile:**   The variation of implied volatility with the strike price.

**Volatility Term Structure:**   The variation of implied volatilities with strike price and time to maturity.

**Volume:**   The quantity of futures or options contracts traded during a given period of time.

**Warehouse receipt:**   A document representing the ownership of a specific quantity and quality of a commodity. Warehouse receipts are sometimes called depository receipts, especially with gold.

**Warrant:**   An option that a corporation issues, with its own shares as the underlying asset. The crucial implication is that exercise of the option changes the number of claims against the corporation's assets.

**Wasting asset:**   A property of an option that, when everything else remains equal (i.e., the stock price does not change), the value of the option will decline over time.

**Weather derivative:**   Derivative where the payoff depends on the weather.

**Wild card option:**   The right of someone with a short position in T-bond futures to choose to deliver based upon a settlement price determined earlier in the day.

**Xerxes:**   The convexity of modified duration.

**Yard:**   One billion units of a currency.

**Yield Curve:**   For a particular series of fixed income instruments such as government bonds, the graph of the yields to maturity of the series plotted by maturity.

**Yield curve:**   Yield from bonds from the same credit class with similar liquidity over varying maturities are plotted to get yield curve for specific time duration.

**Zero Coupon Instruments:**   Fixed income instruments that do not pay a coupon but only pay principal at maturity; trade at a discount to 100 percent of principal before maturity with the difference being the interest accrued.

**Zero Exercise Price Option:**   A European call option with strike price of zero. The owner will certainly exercise it, so it is equivalent to owning the underlying asset without receiving the cash flow (dividends or interest) through expiration.

**Zero-coupon Yield Curve:**   A plot of the zero-coupon interest rate against time to maturity.

**Zeta:**   The market value of an option less its model value, using the ATM implied volatility for the same expiration.

# Bibliography

A New Nightmare in the boardroom, *The Economist*, pp. 3–5, February 10, 1996.

Abken, Peter A., Over-the-counter derivatives: Risky business?, *Federal Reserve Bank of Atlanta Economic Review*, pp. 1–20, March/April 1994.

Apostolou, Nicholas and Thomas Wilson, The futures market: What the internal auditor needs to know, *Internal Auditing*, pp. 40–49, Spring 1992.

Applegate, John S., The Perils of unreasonable risk: Information, regulatory policy, and toxic substances control, *Columbia Law Review*, Vol. 91, No. 261, pp. 278–99, 1991.

Bahr, R., Interest rate futures options: An empirical test of the Ho and Lee model in the Australian context, *Review of Futures Markets*, Vol. 12, No. 3, pp. 661–684, 1993, "Discussion," by Malick Sy, pp. 685–686.

Barnhil, Theodore and William Seale, Financing with hybrid securities having commodity option and forward-contract characteristics, *Advances in Futures and Options Research*, Vol. 4, pp. 137–151, 1990.

Bates, David, The crash of '87: Was it expected? The evidence from options markets, *Journal of Finance*, pp. 1009–1044, July 1991.

Betsey, Dotson, Financial derivatives: Governments as end users, *Government Finance Review*, pp. 13–17, August 1994.

Bobin, Christopher, *Agricultural Options: Trading, Risk Management, and Hedging*, John Wiley and Sons, New York, pp. 253, 1990.

Bradbury, Michael et al., Accounting for interest rate swaps regarded as a specific hedge, *Accountants' Journal*, pp. 50–54, December 1992.

Bradbury, Michael et al., Accounting for interest rate swaps regarded as a general hedge or trade, *Accountants' Journal*, pp. 61–64, March 1993.

Brenner, Menachem, Georges Coutadon, and Marti Subrahmanyam, Options on stock indices and options on futures, *Journal of Banking and Finance*, pp. 773–782, September 1989.

Brief history of derivatives, *The Economist*, pp. 6–10, February 10, 1996.

Bullock, David and Dermot Hayes, Speculation and hedging in commodity options: A modification of Wolf's portfolio model, *Journal of Economics and Business*, pp. 201–222, August 1992.

Cakici, Nusret, Sris Chatterjee, and Avner Wolf, Empirical tests of valuation models for options on T-note and T-bond futures, *The Journal of Futures Markets*, pp. 1–14, February 1993.

Chaudhury, M.M., Some easy-to-implement methods of calculating American futures option prices, *The Journal of Futures Markets*, pp. 303–344, May 1995.

Chaudhury, Mohammed and Jason Wei, Upper bounds for American futures options: A note, *The Journal of Futures Markets*, pp. 111–116, February 1994.

Chen, Ren-Raw, Exact solutions for futures and european futures options on pure discount bonds, *Journal of Financial and Quantitative Analysis*, pp. 97–108, March 1992.

Chiang, Raymond and Hohn Okunev, An alternative formation on the pricing of foreign currency options, *The Journal of Futures Markets*, pp. 903–908, December 1993.

Chorafas, Dimitris N., *Managing Derivatives Risk*, Chicago, Irwin Press, 1995.

Claire, Makin, Doesn't anybody remember risk? *Institutional Investor*, pp. 41–46, April 1994.

Coffee, John C., Jr., Shareholders versus managers: The strain in the corporate web, *Michigan Law Review*, Vol. 85, No. 1, pp. 61–63, 1986.

Craig, Alastair, Ajay Dravid, and Matthew Richardson, Market efficiency around the clock: Some supporting evidence using foreign-based derivatives, *Journal of Financial Economics*, Vol. 39, pp. 161–180, 1995.

Culp, Christopher L. and Robert J. Mackay, Regulating derivatives: The current system and proposed changes, *Regulation*, No. 4, 1994.

D. Regulation, Legal Issues, and Other Topics.

Darby, Michael R., Over-the-counter derivatives and systemic risk to the global financial system, *Working Paper Series*, National Bureau of Economic Research, July 1994.

Davis, Kevin, The pricing of options on Australian bank bill futures: A test of the black model using transactions data, *Review of Futures Markets*, Vol. 10, No. 3, pp. 460–476, 1991, Discussion, by K.R. Sawyer, pp. 477–479.

Doering, James, The Impact of Hedging Transactions on Real Estate Investment Trusts, *Journal of Real Estate Taxation*, pp. 133–152, Winter 1994.

Feeney, Francis D., *A Guide to International Financial Derivatives*, Quorum Books, New York, 1991.

Feldman, David, European options on bond futures: A closed form solution, *The Journal of Futures Markets*, pp. 325–334, May 1993.

Filling the gaps in hedge accounting, *Futures*, p. 41, March 1993.

Financial Accounting Standards Boards, Report on Deliberations, Including Tentative Conclusions on Certain Issues, Relating to Accounting for Hedging and Other Risk-Adjusting Activities, pp. 1–99, 1993.

Financial innovation: The last twenty years and the next, *Journal of Financial and Quantitative Analysis*, Vol. 21, pp. 459–71, 1986.

Franke, Gunter, Uncertain perception of economic exchange risk and financial hedging, *Managerial Finance*, Vol. 18, No. 3–4, pp. 53–70, 1992.

Franklin, Allen, and Douglas Gale, *Financial Innovation and Risk Sharing*, The MIT Press, Cambridge, 1994.

Gary, Herrman and Steven Malvey, New rules for business hedges resolve many uncertainties of Arkansas best, *Journal of Taxation*, pp. 132–138, March 1994.

Gastineau, Gary, Option position and exercise limits: Time for a radical change, *Journal of Portfolio Management*, pp. 92–96, Fall 1992.

Ghalbouni, Joseph, Lawrence Kryzanowski, and Minh Chau To, Transaction costs and option-pricing biases: Some evidence for options on foreign exchange futures, *Review of Futures Markets*, Vol. 9, No. 1, pp. 26–48, 1990, Discussion, by Margaret Monroe and Francis Russell, pp. 49–53.

Global Derivatives Study Group of the Group of Thirty, Derivatives: Practices and Principles, A Report by the Global Derivatives Study Group of the Group of Thirty, Washington, Group of Thirty, 1993.

Goldman, Geoffrey B., Note: Crafting a suitability requirement for the sale of over-the-counter derivatives: Should regulators 'Punish the wall street hounds of greed'?, 95, *Columbia Law Review* 1112, June 1995.

Greene, Edward F., Raplh C. Ferrara, and A. Patricia, Vlahakis, Twenty-Seventh Annual Institute on Securities Regulation, New York, Practicing Law Institute, 1995.

Harrision, Mark, Toan Pham, and Ah Boon Sim, The market for options on ten-year treasury bond futures in Australia: Some empirical evidence using the black model, *Review of Futures Markets*, Vol. 11, No. 3, pp. 369–410, 1992, Discussion, by Jayaram Muthuswamy, pp. 411–413.

Hearing Before the Committee on Banking, Finance and Urban Affairs, House of Representatives, Recent Derivatives Losses, 103rd Congress, Second Session, Washington, US Government Printing Office, October 4, 1994.

Hearing Before the Committee on Banking, Finance, and Urban Affairs, The Risks and Regulation of Financial Derivatives, 103rd Congress, Second Session, May 19, 1994.

Hearing Before the Committee on Banking, Finance, and Urban Affairs, H.R. 4503; The Derivatives Safety and Soundness Supervision Act of 1994, 103rd Congress, Second Session, Washington, US Government Printing Office, June 23, 1994.

Hearing Before the Committee on Banking, Finance, and Urban Affairs, Subcommittee on Financial Institutions Supervision, Regulation and Deposit Insurance, H.R. 4503; The Derivatives Safety and Soundness Supervision Act of 1994, 103rd Congress, Second Session, Washington, US Government Printing Office, July 12, 1994.

Hedge accounting: An exploratory study of underlying issues, (FASB Research Report) *Cooperative Accountant*, pp. 62–63, Spring 1992.

Hedges, mark-to-market rules, *Taxation of Accountants*, p. 321, December 1993.

Hedging in the theory of corporate finance: A reply to our critics, *Journal of Applied Corporate Finance*, Spring 1995.

Herrera, Paul and Jeffrey Callender, Financial products and services: Arkansas best and financial products, *International Tax Journal*, pp. 75–81, Spring 1992.

Herz, Robert, Hedge accounting, derivatives, and synthetics: The FASB starts rethinking the rules, *Journal of Corporate Accounting and Finance*, pp. 323–335, Spring 1994.

Hewitt, Michael E., Systemic Risk in International Securities Markets, in Patrick and Edwards.

Ho, Thomas and Sang Bin Lee, Interest rate futures options and interest rate options, *Financial Review*, pp. 345–370, August 1990.

Hooks, Linda M., Capital, Asset Risk and Bank Failure, Occasional Paper of the Group of Thirty, Washington, Group of Thirty, 1994.

Hutchinson, James M., Andrew W. Lo, and Tomaso Poggio, A non-parametric approach to pricing and hedging derivative securities via learning networks, *Working Paper Series*, National Bureau of Economic Research, April 1994.

Hutchinson, James, Andrew Lo, and Tomaso Poggio, A non-parametric approach to pricing and hedging derivative securities via learning networks, *Journal of Finance*, pp. 851–890, July 1994.

Jamshidian, Farshid, Commodity option evaluation in the gaussian futures term structure model, *Review of Futures Markets*, Vol. 10, No. 2, pp. 324–346, 1991, Discussion, by Andrew Morton and Alfred Kanzler, pp. 347–349.

Jarrow, Robert A. and Stuart Turnbull, Pricing derivatives on financial securities subject to credit risk, *Journal of Finance*, Vol. L, No. 1, March 1995.

Jennings, Dennis, Current developments in Financial accounting and reporting, *Petroleum Accounting and Financial Management Journal*, pp. 1–11, Summer 1992.

Kanda, Hideki, ™D2 "Systemic Risk and International Financial Markets," in Patrick and Edwards.

Kawaller, Ira, A novel approach to transactions-based currency exposure management, *Financial Analyst's Journal*, pp. 79–80, November–December 1992.

Kawaller, Ira, Paul Koch, and Hohm Peterson, Assessing the intraday relationship between implied and historical volatility, *The Journal of Futures Markets*, pp. 323–346, May 1994.

Kim, In Joon, Analytic approximation of the optimal exercise boundaries for American futures options, *The Journal of Futures Markets*, pp. 1–24, February 1994.

Kim, Joon, The analytic valuation of American options, *Review of Financial Studies*, Vol. 3, No. 4, pp. 547–572, 1990.

Kuo, Cheng-kun, The valuation of futures-style options, *Review of Futures Markets*, Vol. 10, No. 3, pp. 480–487, 1991, Discussion, by Malick Sy, pp. 488–489.

Kuprianov, Over-the-counter interest rate derivatives, *Federal Reserve Bank of Richmond Economic Quarterly*, Vol. 79, No. 3, pp. 65–93, 1993.

Ladd, George and Steven Hanson, Price-risk management with options: Optimal market positions and institutional value, *The Journal of Futures Markets*, pp. 737–750, December 1991.

Leach, James A. et al., Global Derivatives: Public Sector Responses, Occassional Paper of the Group of Thirty, Washington, Group of Thirty, 1993.

Lei, Li-Fen, Donald Liu, and Arne Hallam, Solving for optimal futures and options positions using a simulation-optimization technique, *The Journal of Futures Markets*, August 1995.

Levonian, Mark E., Bank capital standards for foreign exchange and other market risks, *Federal Reserve Bank of San Francisco Economic Review*, No. 1, pp. 3–18, 1994.

Love, Bruce and Milton Boyd, The effectiveness of commodity options for stabilizing grain revenues, *Review of Futures Markets*, Vol. 13, No. 1, pp. 155–180, 1994, Discussion, by Mario Miranda and Christopher Bobin, pp. 181–186.

Malindretos, John et al., Hedging considerations under FASR, *Mid-Atlantic Journal of Business*, pp. 199–211, June 1993.

Marchand, Patrick, James Lindley, and Richard Followill, Further evidence on parity relationships in options on S&P 500 index futures, *The Journal of Futures Markets*, pp. 757–772, September 1994.

Marchand, Patrick, Relative futures-option pricing and options on S&P 500 index futures: A test of market efficiency, dissertation, The University of Alabama, p. 171, 1990.

McCarthy, Elizabeth, FASB: Stock compensation, hedging, and other matters, *Journal of Corporate Accounting and Finance*, pp. 497–503, Summer 1992.

Merton, Robert C., Financial innovation and economic performance, *Journal of Applied Corporate Finance*, pp. 12–22, Winter 1992.

Michael, Roth, 'Too-Big-To Fail' and the stability of the banking system: Some insights from foreign countries, *Business Economics*, pp. 43–49, October 1994.

Mike, Girou A., Scott McIllwain, and Dix Pettey, Options market implied consensus views, *Review of Futures Markets*, Vol. 13, No. 3, pp. 943–978, 1994, Discussion, by Paul Fackler and Scheldon Natenberg, pp. 979–996.

Miller, Merton, H., Financial innovation: Achievements and prospects, *Journal of Applied Corporate Finance*, pp. 4–11, Winter 1992.

Miranda, Mario and Joseph Glauber, The effects of price supports on the valuation of options on agricultural futures contracts, *Review of Futures Markets*, Vol. 9, No. 1, pp. 108–125, 1990, Discussion, by Paul Fackler and David Parker, pp. 126–133.

Molvar, Roger H.D. and James F. Green, The question of derivatives, *Journal of Accountancy*, pp. 55–61, March 1995.

Monroe, Margaret, The profitability of volatility spreads around information releases, *The Journal of Futures Markets*, pp. 1–10, February 1992.

Moore, N. and S. Pruitt, Arbitrage opportunities and the design of call and put price schedules of a bond, *Advances in Futures and Options Research*, Vol. 5, pp. 289–295, 1991.

Morris, Charles S., Managing interest rate risk with interest rate futures, *Federal Reserve Bank of Kansas City Economic Review*, pp. 3–20, March 1989.

Morris, Charles S., Managing stock risk with stock futures, *Economic Review*, pp. 3–20, March 1989.

Morris, David, Practical problems in hedge accounting: Case histories, *Bank Accounting and Finance*, pp. 3–12, Summer 1992.

Munter, Paul, What constitutes a hedge is still debatable, *Journal of Corporate Accounting and Finance*, pp. 483–490, Summer 1993.

Natenberg, Sheldon et al., Panel: Research directions in commodity option—Academic and Practitioner Views, *Review of Futures Markets*, Vol. 9, No. 1, pp. 134–155, 1990, Discussion, pp. 156–157.

Nusbaum, David, Surviving an NFA Audit, *Futures*, pp. 50–52, January 1993.

Ogden, Joseph, Alan Tucker, and Timothy Vines, Arbitraging American gold spot and futures options, *Financial Review*, pp. 577–592, November 1990.

O'Sullivan, Jon, How to avoid pitfalls in financial restructure, *Oil and Gas Journal*, pp. 21–23, June 15, 1992.

Overdahl, J. and J. Choi, Option exercises: Evidence from the treasury bond futures option market, *Advances in Futures and Options Research*, Vol. 5, pp. 217–240, 1991.

Overdahl, James and Andrew Chen, The exercise of options on agricultural commodity futures, *Review of Future Markets*, Vol. 10, No. 2, pp. 296–317, 1991, Discussion, by Bruce Sherrick and James Bittman, pp. 318–323.

Patrick, Hugh T. and Franklin Edwards, *Regulating International Financial Markets: Issues and Policies*, Kluwer Academic Publishers, Boston, 1992.

Rane, David, Hedge or not a hedge? EITF 91-4 tried to answer the question, *Journal of Corporate Accounting and Finance*, pp. 279–284, Spring 1992.

Rawansley, Judith H., *Total Risk: The Fall of Barings Bank*, Harper Collins Publishers, New York, 1995.

Remolona, Eli M., The recent growth of financial derivative markets, *Federal Research Bank of New York Quarterly Review*, pp. 28–43, Winter 1992.

Robert, Shiller, *Macromarkets*, Oxford University Press, London, 1993.

Ronn, Ehud and Robert Bliss, Jr., A non-stationary trinomial model for the valuation of options on treasury bond futures contracts, *The Journal of Futures Markets*, pp. 597–618, August 1994.

Ross, Derek, Hedge Accounting: The treasurer's view, *Certified Accountant*, pp. 38–39, June 1992.

Schap, Keith, Enhancing cash yield with treasury bond options, *Futures*, pp. 40–42, September 1990.

Shimko, David, Options on futures spreads: Hedging, speculation, and valuation, *The Journal of Futures Markets*, pp. 183–214, April 1994.

Silva, Elvira Maria de Sousa and Kandice Kahl, Reliability of soyabean and corn option-based probability assessments, *The Journal of Futures Markets*, pp. 765–780, October 1993.

Smith, Stephen D. and Larry Wall, Financial panics, bank failures, and the role of regulatory policy, *Federal Reserve Bank of Atlanta Economic Review*, pp. 1–11, January/February 1992.

Sternberg, Joel, A reexamination of put-call parity on index futures, *The Journal of Futures Markets*, pp. 79–102, February 1994.

Stewart, John, Challenges of hedge accounting, *Journal of Accountancy*, pp. 48–50, 52, November 1989.

Swidler, Steve and J. David Diltz, Implied volatilities and transaction costs, *Journal of Financial and Quantitative Analysis*, pp. 437–448, September 1992.

Sy, Malick, Pricing of options on futures in thin markets: Empirical evidence from the Singapore international monetary exchange, *Review of Futures Markets*, Vol. 9, Supplement, pp. 228–250, Discussion, by W.K.H. Fung, 251–257.

Taming the derivatives beast, *The Economist*, pp. 81–82, May 23, 1992.

The art of risk spreading, *The Economist*, pp. 16–18, February 10, 1996.

The fall of barings, *The Economist*, p. 78, March 4, 1995.

The hedge or not to hedge, *The Economist*, pp. 10–16, February 10, 1996.

The over-the-counter derivatives market and its regulation, report by the Commodities and Futures Trading Commission, 1993.

Those damned dominoes, *The Economist*, p. 12, March 4, 1995.

Todd Johnson, L. and Victoria Wall, Might synthetic instrument accounting be substituted for hedge accounting for some hedging relationships? *Financial Accounting Standards Board Status Report,* No. 235, pp. 4–9, September 30, 1992.

Todd Johnson, L. et al., Hedge accounting: Is deferral the only option?, *Journal of Accountancy*, pp. 53–58, January 1994.

Tribe, Lawrence H., Trial by mathematics: Precision and ritual in the legal process, *Harvard Law Review*, Vol. 84, No. 1329, pp. 1361–1372, 1971.

Turnbull, Stuart and Frank Milne, A simple approach to interest-rate option pricing, *Review of Financial Studies*, Vol. 4, No. 1, pp. 87–120, 1991.

United States General Accounting Office, Financial System, Report GAO/GGD-94-133, Washington: General Accounting Office, 1994.

Volkert, Linda, EITF update: Financial accounting—Hedging foreign currency risks, *Journal of Accountancy*, pp. 115–116, July 1992.

Weinberger, David B. et al., Using derivatives: What senior managers must know, *Harvard Business Review*, pp. 33–41, January–February 1995.

William, Wilson W. and Hung-Gay Fung, Put-call parity and arbitrage bounds for options on grain futures, *American Journal of Agricultural Economics*, pp. 55–65, February 1991.

Wolf, Avner and Jack Clark Francis, Optimal portfolio choices of commodity options in incomplete markets: A simulation analysis, *Advances in Quantitative Analysis of Finance and Accounting*, Vol. 1, Part A, pp. 165–196, 1991.

Wu, Henry T.C., Misunderstood derivatives: The causes of informational failure and the promise of regulatory incrementalism, *Yale Law Journal*, Vol. 102, No. 6, pp. 1457–1513, April 1993.

Wu, Henry T.C., Swaps, the modern process of financial innovation and the vulnerability of a regulatory paradigm, *University of Pennsylvania Law Review*, Vol. 138, No. 333, pp. 347–353.

# Index